Garrick

BY THE SAME AUTHOR

The Proud Doers: Israel after Twenty Years

Words: Reflections on the Use of Language
(editor and contributor)

Dogfight: The Transatlantic Battle over Airbus

The Expense of Glory: A Life of John Reith

Dirt and Deity: A Life of Robert Burns

The Drury Lane audience first saw Garrick's Lethe in 1740, a year before his début as an actor. It was frequently revived and reworked, and in 1756 he added the part of Chalkstone, which became one of his most celebrated characterizations. Slight as it was, the farce achieved 263 performances in 26 seasons. (By permission of the Folger Shakespeare Library)

IAN McINTYRE

Garrick

ALLEN LANE
THE PENGUIN PRESS

ALLEN LANE
THE PENGUIN PRESS

Published by the Penguin Group
Penguin Books Ltd, 27 Wrights Lane, London w8 5tz, England
Penguin Putnam Inc., 375 Hudson Street, New York, New York 10014, USA
Penguin Books Australia Ltd, Ringwood, Victoria, Australia
Penguin Books Canada Ltd, 10 Alcorn Avenue, Toronto, Ontario, Canada m4v 3b2
Penguin Books (NZ) Ltd, Private Bag 102902, NSMC, Auckland, New Zealand

Penguin Books Ltd, Registered Offices: Harmondsworth, Middlesex, England

First published by Allen Lane The Penguin Press 1999
1 3 5 7 9 10 8 6 4 2

Set in 9.5/12 pt PostScript Monotype Sabon
Typeset by Rowland Phototypesetting Ltd, Bury St Edmunds, Suffolk
Printed in England by Clays Ltd, St Ives plc

A CIP catalogue record for this book is available from the British Library

ISBN 0-713-99328-6

For Leik
with love always

Oh what a pity it is that the strong and beautiful strokes of a great actor should not be as lasting as the strokes of the pencil or the chisel of inferior artists.

An Apology for the Life of Colley Cibber, 1740

Contents

List of Illustrations   xi
List of Plates   xii

Prologue   1
1 Fat Central England   9
2 'To Save You from the Gallows'   17
3 The Stage-Struck Wine Merchant   28
4 Garrick Fever   52
5 Pig in the Middle   73
6 Vaulting Ambition   82
7 Dear Charmers   94
8 Violette   112
9 Enter the Manager   123
10 Rescued Nature and Reviving Sense   139
11 Fixing the Weathercock   153
12 Britannia and the French Vagrants   164
13 The Battle of the Romeos   174
14 A Most Agreeable Jaunt   186
15 Wire Dancers, the Jew Bill and a Place
   in the Country   204
16 Signor Shakespearelli   222
17 The Chinese Festival   235
18 Memento Mori   257
19 Slings and Arrows   272
20 Heart of Oak   287
21 A Pleasant and Reasonable Retaliation   298
22 Scratching Fanny and the Riotous Fribbles   312
23 Away from It All   334
24 The Sick Monkey Restored   361
25 Assorted Theatrical Trash   384
26 All Hurry and Bustle   393

27 Rain Stops Play   412
28 A Devilish Lucky Hit   433
29 'Nothing Till Lately Could Subdue
     My Spirits'   446
30 The House Shows the Owner   462
31 Clipping the Wings of Calumny   475
32 Doing Away with the Gravediggers   483
33 Lawful Game in the Winter   497
34 The Monstrous Regiment of Actresses   518
35 A Face-Lift for the Old Lady   537
36 Enter Garrick's Venus   545
37 To Strut and Fret No More   553
38 Frail Tenement   566
39 Retired Leisure   580
40 'Farewell! Remember Me!'   596
     Epilogue   607

     Bibliography   624
     Notes   633
     Acknowledgements   649
     Index   651

'When we see a natural style,' wrote Pascal, *'we are astonished and delighted; for we expected to see an author, and we find a man.'*

With that in mind, no attempt has been made to tidy up any of Garrick's idiosyncracies of spelling or punctuation. What you see is what he wrote.

List of Illustrations

Frontispiece   Garrick as Lord Chalkstone

1. John Rich as Harlequin	54
2. Garrick as Abel Drugger in *The Alchymist*	68
3. James Lacy	134
4. 'The Theatrical Steel-Yards of 1750'	180
5. Woodward as Bobadil	197
6. 'Enchanting Bellamy'	208
7. A Drury Lane playbill for *Hamlet*	213
8. Garrick's place on the Thames at Hampton	221
9. 'The Boxes in an Uproar'	240
10. Arthur Murphy, one of Garrick's early biographers	255
11. Garrick and Mrs Yates in *Zara*	368
12. The Barrys in *Venice Preserved*	394
13. The Pit Door	407
14. Boswell in his Corsican finery	423
15. Garrick delivering his *Ode to Shakespeare*	435
16. The Adelphi under construction	470
17. Fanny Abington	528
18. A face-lift for Old Drury	534
19. Garrick as Sir John Brute	549
20. A sketch of Garrick by de Loutherbourg	571
21. Samuel Foote as Fondlewife	589
22. Invitation to Garrick's funeral	610
23. James Burnett, Lord Monboddo	618
24. Mrs Garrick in old age	622

List of Plates

(*Between page 210–211*)

1. *David Garrick as Richard III*, c. 1771, painting by Henry Morland after Nathaniel Dance, in the Garrick Club, London (photo: E T Archive).

2. Margaret Woffington, c. 1735–6, portrait by Philip Mercier in the Garrick Club (photo: E T Archive).

3. James Quin, c. 1740–45, portrait by William Hogarth, in the Tate Gallery, London

4. *Charles Macklin as Shylock and ?Michael Stoppelaer as Tubal in* The Merchant of Venice, c. 1767–9, painting by Herbert Stoppelaer in the Yale Center for British Art, Paul Mellon Collection, New Haven, Connecticut.

5. Kitty Clive, 1740, portrait by Willem Verelst in the Garrick Club, (photo: E T Archive).

6. *Colley Cibber as Lord Foppington in* The Relapse or Virtue in Danger, c. 1715–20, portrait by Giuseppe Grisoni in the Garrick Club (photo: E T Archive).

7. Eva-Maria Garrick c. 1750–55, pastel by Jean-Etienne Liotard in the Devonshire Collection, Chatsworth, reproduced by permission of the Duke of Devonshire and the Chatsworth Settlement Trustees.

8. *David Garrick as Macbeth and Mrs Pritchard as Lady Macbeth*, c. 1765–8, painting by Johann Zoffany in the Garrick Club (photo: E T Archive).

9. *David Garrick as Jaffier and Mrs Cibber as Belvidera in a scene from* Venice Preserved, 1762, painting by Johann Zoffany in the Garrick Club (photo: E T Archive).

10. *David Garrick as Sir John Brute in* The Provok'd Wife, c. 1763–5, painting by Johann Zoffany in Wolverhampton Art Gallery, West Midlands, reproduced by courtesy.

11. Samuel Foote, c. 1767, portrait by studio of Joshua Reynolds in the Garrick Club (photo: E T Archive).

12. David Garrick, 1771, pencil drawing by Nathaniel Dance, in the National Portrait Gallery, London, reproduced by courtesy.

(*Between pages 466–467*)

13. David Garrick, *c.* 1769, mezzotint by Valentine Green (after a lost portrait by Thomas Gainsborough) in the Lennox-Boyd Collection, Burford.

14. 'A Stage Box in London: George III and Queen Charlotte', pen-and-ink drawing with watercolour, by John Nixon in the Garrick Club (photo: E T Archive).

15. *Henry Woodward as Razor in* The Upholsterer, 1811, painting by Samuel De Wilde after Johann Zoffany in the Garrick Club (photo: E T Archive).

16. George Colman, *c.* 1778, portrait by Thomas Gainsborough in the National Portrait Gallery, London, reproduced by courtesy.

17. *David Garrick in the Character of King Lear, Act III, scene v, c.* 1760, mezzotint by Charles Spooner (from a drawing by Richard Houston after Benjamin Wilson's original) in the Lennox-Boyd Collection, Burford.

18. Samuel Johnson, 1769, portrait by Joshua Reynolds in the National Gallery of Ireland, Dublin.

19. Oliver Goldsmith, 1772, portrait by Joshua Reynolds in a private collection.

20. *David Garrick and his wife by his Temple to Shakespeare, Hampton, c.* 1762, painting by Johann Zoffany in the Yale Center for British Art, Paul Mellon Collection, New Haven, Connecticut.

21. *David Garrick as the Steward of the Shakespeare Festival, Stratford-on-Avon, 1769,* portrait by Benjamin Van der Gucht in the collection of Parham Park, West Sussex.

22. David Garrick, *c.* 1765, unfinished portrait by Johann Zoffany in the Garrick Club (photo: E T Archive).

23. Hannah More, 1780, portrait by Frances Reynolds in Bristol Museums and Art Gallery.

24. *Mrs Abington as Miss Prue in Congreve's* Love for Love, 1771, portrait by Joshua Reynolds in the Yale Center for British Art, Paul Mellon Collection, New Haven, Connecticut.

25. Richard Brinsley Sheridan, portrait by an anonymous engraver after a portrait by Joshua Reynolds (photo: The Fotomas Index).

26. *Thomas King as Touchstone in* As You Like It, 1767, by Johann Zoffany in the Garrick Club (photo: E T Archive).

Prologue

An actress is standing in the wings of the Theatre Royal, Drury Lane. Her attention is fixed on the man who holds the centre of the stage. He is below middle height (he sometimes builds up his shoes with cork heels to conceal this) and he moves with notable grace and assurance. His face is strikingly mobile, the large eyes dark and expressive. He has a big nose.

The actress's name is Kitty Clive. As a comedienne and comic singer on the London stage she has no equal. 'Damn him!' she bursts out suddenly to no one in particular, admiration and exasperation wrestling for the upper hand, 'he could act a gridiron!'

Very possibly. Certainly he could draw shrieks of delight from the children of his friends by pretending to be a turkey or a peacock or a water-wagtail, and in his youth he had given recklessly free rein, as young men do, to a devastating gift for mimicry. But no eighteenth-century playwright had come up with any good lines for gridirons, and David Garrick was obliged to confine himself to the conventional repertoire. He did so to electrifying effect for more than thirty years.

The London stage was the last place one would expect to find someone brought up in a provincial cathedral Close. Puritan hostility to the theatre was not dead. 'Play-actors are the most profligate wretches, and the vilest vermine, that hell ever vomited out,' shrilled the anonymous author of *Players' Scourge* in 1757. 'They are the filth and garbage of the earth, the scum and stain of human nature, the excrements and refuse of all mankind, the pests and plagues of human society, the debauchees of men's minds and morals.'

Actors were seen as dissolute, and sometimes as quarrelsome and violent into the bargain—James Quin and Charles Macklin, two of the best-known players of the day, had both stood trial for murder—while actresses were generally viewed as little better than whores. Theatreland was the happy hunting ground not only of pickpockets and sharpers but of ladies of the town. The 'nuns' who worked for a 'Covent Garden abbess' did not devote their lives exclusively to prayer and contemplation; a person suffering from 'Drury Lane ague' required treatment not for some form of malarial fever but for syphilis. And it was possible to become infected without setting foot in one of the many brothels or bagnios with which the neighbourhood was so generously supplied. A writer in *The*

Connoisseur in November 1754 described the so-called 'green boxes' at Covent Garden as 'that division of the upper boxes properly distinguished by the name of the flesh market'. Visiting provincials who felt the need of guidance in such matters could consult *Harris' List of Covent Garden Ladies*, a Georgian cross between *Which?* and the *Yellow Pages*.

Garrick said later in life that he had held back from going on the stage so long as his mother was alive out of regard for her happiness and peace of mind. There were still uncles and aunts and brothers and sisters to be mollified, however, and the 24-year-old Garrick knew well enough that they would be appalled at his decision: 'I hope when You shall find that I may have ye genius of an Actor without ye Vices, You will think less Severe of Me & not be asham'd to own me for a Brother.'

They were soon won over. The meteoric brilliance of his first season was the guarantee of that. He made his début in the role of the usurper Richard III, and he himself would quickly usurp the place of James Quin, unchallenged on the London stage since the death of Barton Booth in 1733. Not that Quin's declamatory, neo-classical style—elevated, orotund, stentorian, monotonous— would disappear overnight, any more than the 'tragic strut' which went with it. The acclaimed naturalism which was at the heart of Garrick's style did not constitute a theatrical revolution; Garrick had his shoulder to a door which had already been pushed ajar, notably by Charles Macklin with his interpretation of Shylock. Years later, long after they had ceased to be friends, Macklin would give characteristically extravagant expression to the view that his former protégé had gone too far:

> Garrick huddled all passions into strut and quickness—bustle was his favourite. In the performance of a Lord Townly he was all bustle. In Archer, Ranger, Don John, Hamlet, Macbeth, Brute—all bustle! bustle! bustle! The whole art of acting, according to the modern practice, is compriz'd in—bustle! 'Give me a Horse!'—'Bind up my Wounds!'—'Have mercy Jesu!'—all bustle!—everything is turned into bustle![1]

Garrick may well, in his early efforts to distance himself from the static grandeur of the Quin style, have been over-exuberant, but what the theatre-going public quickly came to marvel at and applaud was his unparalleled vitality and versatility. He was not only Richard, he was also the wily Sharp in his own *The Lying Valet*; he was not only Fondlewife, the jealous old Puritan banker in Congreve's *The Old Bachelor*, but also Bayes, the conceited author in Buckingham's *The Rehearsal*. After a draining performance as Lear, he could bounce back on stage for the afterpiece and play the loutish Master Johnny in *The School Boy* by Colley Cibber.

Garrick never needed much coaxing to sing for his supper on social occasions. Among those who witnessed his *salon* performances during the time he spent in Paris in the early 1760s was the baron de Grimm, who wrote about it in his *Correspondance littéraire*:

We saw him play the dagger-scene from the tragedy of *Macbeth*—in a room, in his ordinary clothes, and without benefit of theatrical illusion. His eyes followed the dagger, moving suspended through the air, and it was so beautifully done that he drew a cry of admiration from everyone present. Who could believe that the next moment, the same man could give just as perfect an imitation of a pastrycook's boy, carrying a tray of pies on his head, gaping around him as he walks, dropping the tray in the gutter, standing at first stupefied at what has happened, and finally bursting into tears?[2]

Another of the *encyclopédistes* who witnessed Garrick's party pieces in Paris was Diderot. On one occasion he saw him put his head through a folding door and in the course of a few seconds alter his expression 'successively from wild delight to temperate pleasure, from this to tranquillity, from tranquillity to surprise, from surprise to blank astonishment, from that to sorrow, from sorrow to the air of one overwhelmed, from that to fright, from fright to horror . . .' Here was an actor who did not simply rely on his voice and a few conventional gestures, but who put his face, his body, his whole being to work.

Including his mind. The performance was always calculated and controlled. Someone once remarked to the actor Tom King that nobody roused feelings in a spectator in the way that Garrick did, and 'none suffered more than he from these exertions'.

'Pooh,' King retorted, 'he suffer those feelings! Why, Sir, I was playing with him one night in *Lear*, when in the middle of the most passionate and affecting part, and when the whole house was drown'd in tears, he turned his head around to me and whisper'd 'D—mn me, Tom, it'll do.'[3]

Garrick's reputation would extend through France, Germany and Italy—even to Russia, then on the fringe of the civilized world. But his importance in the history of the English theatre does not rest solely on his position as the most celebrated actor of the day. He was also, for almost thirty years, an outstandingly successful manager. 'The theatre engrossed the minds of men to such a degree,' wrote an early biographer, 'that there existed in England a *fourth estate*, King, Lords, and Commons, and *Drury-Lane play-house*.'

The terms 'director' and 'producer' would not become current until the generation of Gordon Craig and Reinhardt and Stanislavski, but Garrick was in effect the first of the breed. Only Henry Irving, a century later, has any serious claim to equality with him. He was an incomparable judge of theatrical effect. During his time at Drury Lane there were significant advances in scenery, lighting and staging techniques. He insisted on thorough rehearsal and orderly ensemble playing. The discipline he brought to the financial management of the house was fully appreciated only after he retired and things began to fall apart under Richard Brinsley Sheridan.

As manager of one of the two patent companies he was technically a servant of the crown. He was assiduous in his attendance at court, but during the early years of his tenure at Drury Lane Garrick could look for little in the way of royal patronage. George II hated 'blays, boetry, and bainting'. He quite often nodded off in the royal box, and even when awake his attention was likely to fasten on an actor or incident of no particular significance. He was present once at a performance of *Richard III*. Totally oblivious of the performance of Garrick in the title role, he had eyes only for the buffooneries of Taswell, the actor cast as the Lord Mayor. 'Duke of Grafton, I like dat Lord Mayor,' he announced to the Lord Chamberlain, whose duties obliged him to be in attendance. 'Duke of Grafton, dat is good Lord Mayor.' And a third time, while Garrick was at his superlative best in the last act, 'Duke of Grafton, will dat Lord Mayor not come again?'

Garrick was also a major artificer of the remarkable change that came about in the course of the eighteenth century in the status of Shakespeare. By the time of the Civil Wars, no more than a handful of his plays retained their place in the repertory: *Othello, Hamlet, The Merry Wives of Windsor, Julius Caesar,* the first part of *Henry IV*. By the time Garrick mounted his famously disastrous Stratford Jubilee in 1769, the situation was transformed. Such illustrious names as Pope and Johnson had brought out collected editions of the works, and it would have been a foolish player at either of the Theatres Royal who did not have a nodding acquaintance with at least two dozen of Shakespeare's plays— by that time more than one in six of all London performances were accounted for by revivals of the work of the Bard.

Which was just as well, because the eighteenth century was not distinguished by the quality of what was being written by contemporary dramatists. Garrick was not in the happy position of Richard Burbage, who could look to Ben Jonson or Shakespeare or Beaumont and Fletcher, or of Betterton, at the turn of his own century, who could command the pen of Otway or Congreve. Leave aside a couple of Sheridan's plays and Goldsmith's *She Stoops to Conquer* and there is next to nothing from the Garrick era that survives in the modern repertory. England's greatest actor-manager flourished in an age of eminently forgettable drama—turgid tragedies, many of them adapted from the classics by stage-struck clergymen or the work of a formidably determined regiment of lady dramatists.

Somehow, in the intervals of managing the company, dealing with recalcitrant players, adapting Shakespeare and devoting long hours to rehearsal, Garrick found time to write nearly a hunded prologues and more than twenty dramatic pieces of his own. Some of them were pure hack work, often Christmas shows churned out under pressure to meet the needs of the moment, but some of his more substantial efforts make plain his admiration for Ben Jonson and for the dramatists of the Restoration. Goldsmith and Sheridan were more polished writers, but Garrick at his best is not far behind them as a social satirist. *The Clandestine Marriage*, which he wrote with George Colman, is still sometimes performed today, and lives on in the opera house as Cimarosa's *Il Matrimonio Segreto*.

Garrick was intensely gregarious, and his work in the theatre was intertwined with a hectic social life. Dukes and duchesses, men of letters, portrait painters and prime ministers, bishops and bluestockings—he knew everybody who was anybody.

Mrs Thrale once amused herself by drawing up a sort of league table in which she classified the social accomplishments of her friends and acquaintances. Nobody scores higher than Garrick under 'Wit and Humour', where she gives him 19 out of 20 (although under 'Good Humour', by which she explains 'is meant only the Good humour ne[ce]ssary to conversation', he scores a duck, while Boswell and Dr Burney both get 19). Under 'General Knowledge' Burke scores 19 and Garrick 16, whereas under 'Scholarship' Burke gets 14, Boswell 5 and Garrick only 3. Johnson's name does not appear in the table—presumably he was deemed to be *hors concours* in all categories.

Happily for posterity, Garrick was a compulsive letter-writer, even though one of the American scholars who edited his correspondence ventured a guess that the fifteen hundred or so letters which survive may represent no more than a tenth of all that he wrote. They are shot through with the naturalness and vitality which were the hallmarks of his acting. He wrote at all hours of the day—sometimes from his sickbed, often as he waited to go on at Drury Lane. In his prologue to *The Clandestine Marriage*, he lamented the fleeting and transitory nature of an actor's fame:

> No pen nor pencil can the Actor save,
> The art, and artist, share one common grave.

Thanks to his own pen, much of the humour and spontaneity which made his acquaintance so sought after by his contemporaries can still be summoned up today.

Like many actors, Garrick had in his make-up a generous streak of vanity and jealousy. Much given to self-advertisement, he had a correspondingly gargantuan appetite for praise. When he sat to the sculptor Nollekens during his visit to Rome in 1763 he was eager to know what was said of him by his compatriots at the city's English coffee-house.

'Indeed, I heard somebody there speaking very highly in your praise, as high as possible,' Nollekens told him gravely.

'Ah! Ah!' said Garrick. 'Pray who was it—who was it spoke so highly in my praise?'

'Why,' came the answer, 'it was yourself.'

Tom Davies, his first biographer, asserted that he never heard Garrick speak warmly of any other actor, living or dead, but with Davies it is sometimes necessary to aim off for the fact that he himself had been an unsuccessful and disappointed member of the Drury Lane company. Garrick pronounced Quin's Falstaff to be perfect, and when he saw his great rival Barry as Romeo he conceded, 'He makes love better than I do.'

The stories that circulated in his lifetime about his meanness in money matters were largely malicious inventions, many of them originating with Samuel Foote. When Burke asked for the loan of £1,000—£70,000 or so today—he was given it without hesitation. When the French actress Clairon found herself in prison for attempting to organize a strike at the Comédie-Française, Garrick offered her five hundred *louis*: Voltaire asked whether any duke or marshal in France would have done as much.

The time that Garrick spent in France in 1763 and 1764 (he had been there briefly twelve years previously) was an important chapter in his life. It also marked a caesura in his professional career. He would take up the reins of management again for twelve more seasons, but from that time on his thoughts turned increasingly to private leisure; his appearances on the stage became much less frequent, and he never, after his return from the continent, created a new role.

Sixteen years of running Drury Lane and acting at full stretch had taken their toll. There had been serious disturbances at both Drury Lane and Covent Garden during the preceding season, and it was the instigators of the 'half-price riots', as they were called, who had carried the day. It was high time for a sabbatical. The Seven Years War was over, and Paris was in the grip of one of its periodic bouts of Anglomania. Shakespeare and Swift were all the rage, and David Hume, Sterne, Wilkes and Horace Walpole had all been lionized in the salons.

So was Garrick. 'I am so plagu'd here,' he wrote to his brother George, 'that I must desire you to send me by the first opportunity six prints from Reynolds' picture.' (Joshua Reynolds's well-known portrait of Garrick being tugged in opposite directions by Tragedy and Comedy had been shown at the exhibition of the Society of Artists the previous year.)

Garrick was also in some ways taken more seriously by the French than he was at home—rather as Peter Brook would be two centuries later. The *beau monde* and the literati he met in Paris saw acting not just as a form of entertainment but as one of the fine arts. Concerned to establish a philosophical basis for their view of the theatre, they deferred to Garrick as an authority on the literary qualities of a play. It was noted on his return to England that his acting had acquired a new dimension of ease and authority.

So convinced was he that he would be back among his French friends the following spring that when he returned to London he left a trunk of clothes with his friend Monnet, the former Director of the Opéra-Comique. '*Ce Monsieur Garrick étoit fait pour vivre parmi nous,*' enthused one of his Parisian admirers. '*Sans la révocation de l'édit de Nantes,*' lamented another, '*ce trésor n'eût jamais enrichi la Grande Bretagne.*'

Quite possibly not. Louis XIV's revocation of the Edict, in 1685, withdrew the privileges that his Protestant subjects had enjoyed for almost a century. Promulgated in 1598 by Henry IV, it had guaranteed a broad measure of religious freedom. The Huguenots, as they had been pejoratively known since the sixteenth century,* were granted liberty of conscience throughout the realm and, with

---

* The origin of the word is disputed. The sixteenth-century French writer Henri Estienne, in his *Apologie pour Hérodote* (1566), ascribes it to the practice of the Protestants at Tours of assembling by night near the gate of King Hugo. Philologists tend to the view that it was a nickname imported from Geneva, where *Eidgenossen*, meaning confederates, was the name given to those who were opposed to the Duke of Savoy and favoured confederation.

some restrictions, the right to engage in public worship. (They were still, for instance, forbidden to hold services in Paris—although they might now do so at a distance of five leagues from the capital, instead of ten as formerly.) They also secured extensive civil rights, allowing them to inherit property, to enter the universities and to engage freely in trade.

The measure was anathema to the Roman Catholic clergy, and in the early years of the seventeenth century, during the minority of Louis XIII, the political strength of the Huguenots came to be perceived as a danger to the state. Richelieu crushed their civil power, and from the time that Louis XIV emerged from the shadow of Mazarin in 1661 the Protestants of France were subjected to a rolling barrage of persecution. Twenty years of judicial warfare culminated in the *dragonnades* of the 1680s, when mounted troops were employed to effect forcible conversions; it was said that, in Languedoc alone, as many as 60,000 took place in three days.

Louis had been secretly married in 1683 to Madame de Maintenon. Under her influence he had become increasingly devout. Ever eager for uniformity, he was now also anxious to mend fences with the Papacy. When sufficient numbers of his Protestant subjects had been tortured or otherwise coerced into embracing the 'king's religion', it seemed logical to the ageing Roi Soleil to declare that the Edict of Nantes had become unnecessary.

From 1682 onwards, even though it was forbidden on pain of the galleys, there had been a steady stream of emigration. Now it swelled to a flood. The skills and thrift of the Huguenots had done much to make the French the wealthiest nation in Europe. Now they took their industry to France's enemies. Many found refuge in the Netherlands, traditionally less intolerant in matters of religion; others took advantage of an imperial *ukaz* that offered liberty and employment in Russia; twenty thousand Frenchmen were attracted to Brandenburg, where they helped to lay the foundations of its industrial prosperity.

Above all, just as they had done after the massacre of St Bartholomew's Day in 1572, they sought asylum in England. Shipwrights from Dieppe and Le Havre, glass-makers from Paris; lacemakers from Valenciennes, paper manufacturers from Bordeaux and the Auvergne and weavers from Meaux; Spitalfields came to be almost entirely inhabited by manufacturers of silk, who came in great numbers from Lyons and Tours. By the early eighteenth century, when London had some 600,000 inhabitants, it numbered among its places of worship no fewer than thirty-five French Protestant churches.

One of those who decided to try his luck in the England of James II was a Bordeaux merchant called David Garric.* Leaving behind his wife and four-month-old son, he made his way to St Malo and, after kicking his heels for a time in Guernsey, reached London early in October. Some weeks later his wife followed him, spending a month at sea in a fourteen-ton bark. She was 'hid in

---

* Garric is described on his marriage certificate as *bourgeois et marchand*. He had been married three years previously to Jeanne Sarrazin, the daughter of a merchant from Pons, a small town sixty miles north of Bordeaux in the ancient province of Saintonge.

a hole,' Garric wrote in his journal, 'with strong tempests, and at great peril of being lost, and taken by our persecutors, who were very inveterate. Pray God convert them!'

A more urgent and personal petition was that their child might be smuggled out to rejoin them, but it was eighteen months before he could record the answer to that prayer: 'Little Peter arrived in London, by the grace of God, in the ship of John White, with a servant, Mary Mongorier, and paid for their passage twenty-two guineas.'*

They settled in London, and the following year were naturalized. The family, the name anglicized by the addition of a *k*, grew rapidly. By the time of her death in 1694 Jeanne Sarrazin had borne her husband six more children, three of whom survived infancy. A younger son, David, was sent off to Portugal to try his luck in the wine trade. For Peter, his father purchased a commission in the army and, in 1706, at the age of twenty, he became an ensign in Colonel James Tyrrel's Regiment of Foot.† Posted to the garrison at Lichfield, he fell in love with the daughter of one of the vicars-choral at the cathedral there. They were married in November 1707.

Arabella Clough was to bear Peter Garrick ten children, of whom the three youngest died in infancy ('happily for his slender resources,' a nineteenth-century biographer wrote unfeelingly). Their third child and second son was born on 19 February 1717, in the fourth year of the reign of George I, and christened David after his Huguenot grandfather.

Purely French on his father's side and partly Irish on his mother's, the child who was to become England's greatest man of the theatre had precious little English blood in his veins.

---

* Garric's journal now belongs to the College of Arms. It comprises one manuscript sheet, closely written on both sides, and was translated into English by his great-nephew, Peter Fermignac. The text is printed in *Protestant exiles from France in the reign of Louis XIV; or the Huguenot refugees and their descendants in Great Britain and Ireland*, by the Reverend David Agnew, London, 1871, pp. 284–5.

† There was a strong military tradition among French Protestants, and the revocation of the Edict of Nantes had deprived France of a number of outstanding soldiers. One of the most notable was Schomberg, the last Huguenot to be awarded the coveted marshal's truncheon. He served briefly as general-in-chief of the army of Brandenburg and in 1688 came to England with the Prince of Orange. He was made a Knight of the Garter and created successively baron, marquis and duke; to compensate him for his losses in France, Parliament voted him the sum of £100,000. He was killed at the Battle of the Boyne in 1690.

I

Fat Central England

David Garrick was brought up in Lichfield, but he was born at the Angel Inn in Hereford, where his father was temporarily quartered as a recruiting officer. For anyone eager for military glory the times were not auspicious. The Peace of Utrecht, concluded four years previously, had determined the disposition of power in Europe for many years to come. Britain had secured French recognition of the Protestant succession of 1689, the expulsion of the Pretender from the French dominions and the destruction of the harbour and fortifications at Dunkirk. She had also acquired the monopoly of the slave trade to the Spanish colonies and the cession of Gibraltar, Minorca, Hudson's Bay, Newfoundland and Nova Scotia.

The notion that a standing army in time of peace constituted a threat to civil liberties, planted in the English mind by the military despotism of Cromwell, remained stubbornly rooted. Peter Garrick's regiment was one of those that were disbanded, and for two years he found himself on half-pay. His fortunes revived briefly in 1715 when twenty-one new regiments were hastily raised to counter the Jacobite invasion. One was a regiment of dragoons raised by Tyrrel, and Garrick was advanced to the rank of captain-lieutenant. By the spring of the following year, however, the rising had been suppressed in both Scotland and England, and it was not long before Colonel Tyrrel's men were once more deemed surplus to requirements.

Lichfield—it was spelt 'Litchfield' in Garrick's day—lies between the high ground of Cannock Chase on the west and the valley of the Trent on the east, a hundred and eighteen miles north-west of London. At the turn of the eighteenth century, with a population of some three thousand, it was one of the largest and wealthiest towns in Staffordshire. It was also an important garrison town, and this, together with its cathedral and its position on important main roads, made it the social hub of the county, even if there was more than one view of its salubrity. Celia Fiennes, visiting the city in 1697, considered it 'low and waterish',*

---

* Morris, C. (ed.), *Journeys of Celia Fiennes*, London, 1947, 111, 114. Celia Fiennes (1662–1741) travelled through every county in England between 1685 and 1703. Her somewhat breathless Journal first appeared in 1888 as *Through England on a Side Saddle in the Time of William and Mary*.

and Horace Walpole wrote to a friend that 'the bog in which the cathedral . . . stands stagnates, I believe, midst beds of poppy and makes all its inhabitants as sleepy as its Bishop and canons.'[1]

The cathedral church of St Mary and St Chad, built of dark red sandstone, stands near the Minster Pool. Daniel Defoe, passing through in the 1720s, thought it one of the finest and most beautiful in England, and for the Staffordshire poet Francis Mundy its three beautiful spires were 'the triumphant ladies of the vale'.

Lichfield had been important in church affairs since the seventh century. When Chad (Ceadda) was sent to be Bishop of the Mercians in 669 it was at Lichfield that he fixed the see, building a small church and monastery there. The reverence in which Chad was held as an English saint made the town a place of pilgrimage. A lunatic who had evaded his keepers was said to have rested for the night on Chad's tomb and to have been restored in the morning to his right mind: 'The very dust taken from his grave was a certain remedy for all disorders incident to man or beast.'[2]

A magnificent shrine was built to accommodate the saint's relics. By 1335 Chad's head was being kept in a painted box, and by 1445, the law of supply and demand being what it is, the faithful might also gaze on a reliquary containing his right arm. The lucrative trade which this brought to the town came to an end with the destruction of the shrine in 1538, an event calculated to make the shopkeepers of Lichfield regard the English Reformation with less than total enthusiasm.

Over the centuries, the town had enjoyed a generous measure of royal patronage. King John favoured Staffordshire with several visits, partly because the county was particularly loyal to him, but also because he was fond of the hunting offered by its forests. Richard II 'kept his Christmas' at the Close in 1397, and in the course of the festive season the company consumed two thousand oxen and two hundred tuns of wine. The town was also the setting for one of the splendid tournaments held by Edward III after his victories at Crécy and Calais.

When Queen Elizabeth I came on a visit in 1575, the bailiffs had the market cross and the Guildhall painted; they also paid 5 shillings to one William Holcroft 'for keeping Mad Richard when Her Majesty was here'.* Charles I spent the night in Lichfield after the battle of Naseby in 1645, lodging in the Bishop's palace, and in the cathedral, on an August morning in 1687, James II 'touched divers persons that had the evil'.†

Lichfield's importance as a centre of communications brought it much misery during the Civil Wars. The cathedral authorities were for the King, the towns-

---

* A less welcome visitor, in 1564, had been the plague. It returned in 1593 and 1594, carrying off upwards of 1,100 of the town's inhabitants.
† The King's Evil was the popular name for scrofula, a tubercular infection of the lymph nodes of the neck. In England the belief that it could be cured by the King's touch originated in the supposed sanctity of Edward the Confessor, and a special Office for the ceremony continued to be printed in the Book of Common Prayer until 1719. In France, the practice dated from the days of Clovis the Frank in the fifth century. The French kings touched regularly until 1775, and the practice was briefly revived by Charles X in 1824.

people sided with the parliament. The cathedral Close was fortified and came under siege three times, passing from royalist to parliamentary control and then back again. The Royalists used the cathedral's central spire as a look-out post, and also flaunted regimental colours and officers' sashes from it on May Day. Brereton, the commander of the Parliamentary forces, believed that it not only contained the powder magazine, but also housed 'their ladies and grandees'. After a five-day bombardment it collapsed, causing extensive damage to the nave and choir.

The cathedral had already been desecrated by the parliamentarians two years previously. The historian William Dugdale described how the New Model Army had disported itself in off-duty moments:

> They kept courts of guard in the cross isles; broke up the pavement; every day hunted a cat with hounds throughout the church, delighting themselves in the echo from the goodly vaulted roof; and to add to their wickedness, brought a calf into it, wrapt in linen; carried it to the font; sprinkled it with water; and gave it a name in scorn and derision of that holy sacrament of baptism.*

The final siege left the cathedral in ruins, and the devastation spilled over from the Close into nearby Bacon Street, which was put to the torch by the Royalists to deprive the attackers of cover. Subsequently the fabric fell prey to looters. Lead and other materials were stripped away, and by 1649 much of the roof was open to the sky. Many of the statues on the west front, which had somehow escaped the attentions of the Reformers in the previous century, were now badly knocked about.

The abolition of the cathedral chapter meant that there were no clergy to concern themselves with repairs. Many of the fine houses in the Close were quarried for building materials or commandeered by squatters. A number of alehouses were established, and pigs rooted in the graveyard. It took more than twenty years to repair the ravages of war. Not until Christmas Eve 1669 was the cathedral rededicated.

There was a flourishing wool trade in Lichfield as early as the fourteenth century, but there had been no great development of manufacturing, which was confined in the main to cloth and leather working and some coach building. When James Boswell remarked on the relative absence of industry, his guide and travelling companion, the town's most famous son, was ready with an explanation: 'We are a city of philosophers,' Johnson told him loftily. 'We work with our heads and make the boobies of Birmingham work for us with their hands.'

Johnson was right. The town could point to a distinguished list of native sons who had made good in the world—clerics, lawyers, scholars, men of science— and many of them had gone through the mill of the local grammar school.

---

* Dugdale, William, *A Short View of the Late Troubles in England*, published anonymously, London, 1681, p. 560.

William de Lichfield, fifteenth-century poet and divine, was a celebrated preacher. After his death, his study was found to contain 3,083 sermons, all written in English in his own hand. The town also produced the versatile Gregory King (1648–1712). King was a gifted engraver, served the College of Arms as Rouge Dragon Pursuivant and Registrar, laid out the streets and squares of Soho Fields and was a notable statistician—Macaulay called him 'a political arithmetician of great acuteness and judgement'.*

One of the best remembered of those who had progressed from Lichfield to a wider stage was Elias Ashmole: antiquarian and astrologer, Rosicrucian and freemason, Windsor Herald, commissioner for Surinam and much else besides. Thrice married, intensely curious and relentlessly acquisitive, Ashmole had been born in 1617, the son of a saddler. The Ashmolean was the first public museum of curiosities in the kingdom. When he presented his collection to the University of Oxford it filled twelve wagons. 'The last load of my rarities was sent to the barge,' he noted in his diary, 'and this afternoon I relapsed into the gout.'†

Cathedral clergy apart, the main group of professional men in the city since the sixteenth century had been lawyers. There was always plenty of work to be had in the ecclesiastical courts, and the growth of polite society in Lichfield meant that there was no shortage of private clients seeking legal advice. A number of Lichfield men attained national prominence in the law. In Garrick's time, no fewer than five judges who were natives of the town sat on the bench at the same time.

Sir John Willes (1685–1761), a clever but indolent man, was the son of a canon at the cathedral. He often seemed more interested in politics than in the law and intrigued ceaselessly for preferment, which as often as not eluded him. He eventually became Chief Justice of Common Pleas, but was disappointed more than once in his hopes of the Chancellorship.‡ Sir John Eardley-Wilmot, fourteen years his junior, succeeded to the same office. Unlike Willes, however, he held aloof from politics, and declined the Lord Chancellorship on no fewer than three occasions. Towards the end of his career he was to have a prominent role in the cases arising from John Wilkes's publication of the *North Briton*, No. 45.

One of Lichfield's more singular distinctions was that it had been the scene of the last burning in England for heresy. That was in 1611. When David Garrick was a boy, the town gallows still stood on the west side of the London Road. It had collapsed at the turn of the century, the foundations undermined by people

---

* He was referring to King's *National and Political Observations and Conclusions upon the State and Condition of England, 1696.*
† Ashmole inherited the greater part of his collection from his friend John Tradescant, the keeper of the botanic garden at Chelsea.
‡ This was partly because George II disapproved of his morals ('Chief Justice loved a wench,' Johnson told Boswell). When the great seal was finally offered in the administration of Pitt and Newcastle, he overplayed his hand by asking for a peerage as a condition of his acceptance and the prize went elsewhere.

digging for sand, but it had been rebuilt, and was to remain in use for another hundred years.*

For dealing with non-capital offences, the town authorities had an eclectic range of punitive instruments at their disposal. Harlots, fraudulent tradesmen and the like could be fastened into the cucking-stool and exposed to the jeers of the bystanders or conveyed to Minster Pool to be ducked. For women who disturbed the peace of the neighbourhood with ribald or abusive language there was the branks, or scold's bridle—the offender's head was enclosed in a sort of iron framework, and a sharp metal bit entered the mouth and restrained the tongue. There were stocks in the cathedral Close, and in the market square, where they formed part of the pillory. The town also boasted a whipping post and a branding iron.

Lichfield was without a theatre in the early 1700s—no record exists of visits by professional companies before the middle years of the century—but the townspeople were not starved of entertainment.† There were four annual fairs. The liveliest of them was held on Whit Monday, when country folk from miles around flocked into the town for the 'Greenhill Bower'. The festival dated back to pagan times, and people enjoyed themselves in those traditional English ways which had caused so much pursing of lips among the Puritans. Then, in early September, Lichfield turned out in force for the ancient ceremony of the Riding, when the sheriff rode out at the head of a large company to beat the city bounds. Since the 1680s there had also been a race meeting that month. This was the occasion for dinners and concerts and was usually accompanied by a ball.

Periodically, diversions of a coarser kind were to be had, notably from politics. Violence flared at a by-election in 1718 when the sitting Whig member, Walter Chetwynd, was unseated by a Tory. Chetwynd's supporters cried foul, claiming that they had been 'barbarously beaten and abused and their lives endangered by a very great mob with papers in their hats resembling white roses'.[3] (The white rose was the emblem of the Pretender.) Thirty years later, when the Whigs captured both Parliamentary seats, there was rioting at the September race meeting, and the Duke of Bedford, the Whigs' leader, was assaulted on the racecourse. One account says that he 'received a horse-whipping from a country farmer'; another has it that he was struck by 'one Joul, a dancing master'.

Expenditure on bribery at elections was prodigious; the Whigs were reckoned to have bought their victory at a cost of £20,000, a figure which prompted Lady Anson, the sister-in-law of one of the successful candidates, to describe Lichfield as 'the borough of Guzzledown'.‡ For a by-election in 1755 a degree of scientific method would be brought to bear. The refreshment of voters was centralized at the house of the Whig agent, John Cobb, and the keeper of each alehouse was

---

* It seems to have been used for the last time in 1810, for the execution of three forgers (*Staffs Advertiser*, 2 June 1810).

† The town was certainly visited by strolling players. The first theatre was built in Bore Street on the site of the White Hart Inn in 1790.

‡ She was the wife of Admiral Sir George Anson, celebrated for his voyage round Cape Horn and newly raised to the peerage for his victory over the French off Cape Finisterre.

invited to send a hogshead of ale: 'We think a hogshead from every house will be as much as can be drank by all our friends that are voters from this time to the end of the election if the tap is kept open every day.'[4]

Between elections there was cock-fighting and bear-baiting, spectator sports popular with all ranks of society. The heavy iron ring to which the wretched bear was chained was secured to a large stone slab in the centre of the market-place, and was still in place late in the nineteenth century. There was a society of gentleman archers and another of bellringers, who called themselves the Loyal Youths. By 1735 a gentlemen's drinking club known as the Court of Truth was meeting weekly at the George. At this time there were some eighty inns in the town.

The old craft guilds or trade companies were also a focus of conviviality. The Smiths' Company laid out £20 1s on a ceremonial cup in 1708–9, and the records show that both they and the Tailors' Company made regular payments to musicians, including drummers, trumpeters and boy choristers.[5] The income of the companies was not spent solely on roistering, however. A portion of it was assigned to poor relief; in the early eighteenth century, for instance, the Smiths were still making regular payments of up to 5s a year to poor travellers.[6]

Some of the guilds were of great antiquity—there had been a flourishing leather industry in the town in the sixteenth and seventeenth centuries and the Saddlers' Company claimed that their incorporation dated from the reign of Edward I.* The laws of the Company of 'Smythes, Goldsmythes, Ironmongers, Card-Makers, Pewterers, Plumbers, Cutlers and Spurryers' were drawn up in 1601; many other trades—mercers and apothecaries, tailors and cappers—could point to pedigrees almost as venerable. The ordinances of the companies laid down rules for the manufacture and sale of goods and the records offer evidence that the history of restrictive practices is also a venerable one. In 1659 the Tailors of Lichfield investigated 'foreigners' working in the city, and in 1701–2 the Smiths took action against a man selling scythes and another selling candlesticks.[7]

Many Lichfield householders still owned pigs or cattle in those early years of the eighteenth century, and enjoyed grazing rights on the town's common lands. These were extensive; when the sheriff and his retinue beat the bounds they had to ride a distance of some sixteen miles. The town accordingly employed a 'pinner', whose job it was to impound stray animals—a strenuous and stressful occupation, because his two pounds were not notably secure, and the citizenry were not above forcing an entry after dark to retrieve their stock.

Public services were generally sketchy. Anyone going about the streets after dark was expected to light their own way; those who failed to do so risked incurring the suspicion of the watch. Except when there was a moon, the city fathers encouraged householders to show a lamp in the window; it was not until the late 1730s that a system of street lighting was introduced.

The town did, however, boast its own water supply—had done so, indeed,

---

* The Saddlers' Company included glovers, bridle-makers and whittawers—fine-leather workers who dressed skins with alum and salt to make them pliant and light in colour.

since the Middle Ages. There was an aqueduct in the 'high street' as early as 1270, and over the next four centuries distribution was gradually extended by a system of watercourses and public cisterns. The first private connections were made in 1707, and one of the three beneficiaries was the master of the grammar school.

There were also several bathing pools on the outskirts of the town. Lichfield was indebted for these to the distinguished physician Sir John Floyer, who was still in practice in the town when Garrick was a boy.* Floyer was the first to make regular observations on the rate of the pulse, and had published an important treatise on asthma. An advocate of cold water bathing (and of infant baptism by immersion), his *Enquiry into the Right Use of Baths* was translated into German, French and Latin. Floyer was instrumental in having a bathing site developed on the east side of the town, near St Chad's Well, and for many years the medicinal properties of the chalybeate waters there attracted visitors from far afield.

Since medieval times, the recognized way of getting rid of rubbish had been by dumping it in the great ditch that had been dug round the old city in the twelfth century. The catalogue of fines entered in the records of the manorial courts shows that the people of Lichfield were just as lazy as those of Edinburgh or London, and threw their 'muck' into the open channels in the roadway— with luck the next rain might carry some of it away.

Those who failed to keep the street in front of their houses clean were liable to prosecution. Anyone shovelling 'muck' into the street—the term covered animal dung as well as domestic waste—had to move it within two days. Leaving it over Sunday attracted a fine: up to two shillings for an ordinary infraction, and as much as three shillings and fourpence if the muck-hill occasioned 'annoyance or hindrance of any persons whatsoever passing that way'.

So long as buildings were of timber and thatch, fire was a constant hazard. The citizens of each ward were enjoined to have a ladder in readiness—it was specified that it should be of twenty-four rungs—along with poles and leather buckets. The poles were fitted with iron hooks, and if fire broke out, the normal method of tackling it was simply to pull the roof down.

The town also owned several fire-engines, however. To have one filled with water and trundled to the scene of the blaze cost roughly a shilling; payment was usually in kind, which meant ale or beer for the volunteer firemen. The town was very proud of these contraptions, variously described in the local parlance as 'engons', 'ingens', 'engins' and 'Indians'. They were carefully maintained and regularly repainted, and many of them had pet names—there was the 'squirt ingen' and the 'traddle engin' and, more mysteriously, the 'virgin's' and the

---

* Floyer was born in 1649 and lived until 1734. He was educated at Oxford, and knighted while still in his thirties, before the publication of any of the works on which his medical reputation rested. He is thought to have had some involvement in the intrigues of James II in 1686 to gain control over the corporation of Lichfield. His knighthood may therefore have been a reward for political services rather than a recognition of professional eminence.

'bachelor's' engines. Three times a year—on Holy Thursday, Whit Monday and Guy Fawkes Day—they were put on public display, and their crews showed off their capabilities.

From the late 1600s, brick began to be preferred to timber for housebuilding, and by early in the eighteenth century, decorative features in the baroque style began to appear on the façades of some houses, although a visitor to the town in 1732 considered the brick buildings 'not very handsome'.[8] Although a new Bishop's palace had been completed on the site of the old in 1687, the bishops declined to live there, preferring to occupy Eccleshall Castle, more than twenty miles away. This was a blow to the *bon ton*, because the Close was important to the social life of the town, but Defoe still rated it the best town in Staffordshire and the neighbouring counties for 'good conversation and good company'. For his part, the minor poet Isaac Hawkins Browne was so carried away with the beauty of Lichfield's womenfolk that he called it 'the Paphos of England'.[9]

Such was the community of which Peter Garrick found himself a part in the early years of the eighteenth century—in the heart of what George Eliot, a hundred years later, would call 'fat central England'. Sleepy canons in the Close and muck-hills in the streets notwithstanding, there were many worse places for a half-pay officer in straitened circumstances to bring up a family.

2

'To Save You from the Gallows'

David Garrick grew up in the small, close-knit community that lived in and around the cathedral Close. His maternal grandfather (and several uncles and grand-uncles) were vicars-choral—junior clergy who assisted in certain parts of the liturgy. There were twelve of them at Lichfield, and although not high in the pecking order of the Close, their position and privileges were well established. They had been given land at the west end of the Close as early as 1315; originally they had built their houses college-style around two courtyards.

Garrick's boyhood home was in what was then called Bacon Street, almost opposite the west gate of the cathedral.* Rebuilt after the Civil War, it stood in an acre or so of ground that fell away to the old marshes to the south and west. It was a substantial house, and it needed to be. The eldest child in the family, Peter, was seven years older than Garrick, and his sister Magdalene was two years his senior. There were two younger sisters, Jane and Merrial, and two younger brothers, William and George. Cathedral folk tended to marry their own kind, and on their mother's side there were numbers of uncles and aunts and cousins living close by—Bailyes, Kynastons and Morgans.

Happily for the family finances, Garrick was able to attend the grammar school free of charge—in 1697 the Corporation had forbidden the charging of fees for local children. The school, founded in 1495, was an unremarkable brick building with four gables almost opposite the old Hospital of St John. There was a single oak-panelled room, and a small enclosed playground; the boys were also allowed to amuse themselves in a nearby field that belonged to the town clerk, Theophilus Levett.

The education provided was narrow, but thorough. There was nothing remotely fancy about the curriculum, or particularly strange in the fact that the school day was largely given over to learning Latin—only in 1730, after all, would the practice of drawing up the written pleadings in the law courts in that language be abolished.† And so for six days in the week, young Davy sat at his

---

* Bacon Street did not become Beacon Street until well into the nineteenth century. The old name still appears on a map by J. Dewhirst published in 1836.
† And that in the face of strenuous opposition from the Lord Chief Justice of the day, Sir Robert Raymond.

oak desk, memorizing the rules of grammar, construing and parsing, reading the simpler authors. Moods and tenses, nouns and participles, *oratio obliqua* and the ablative absolute—it had been good enough for John Milton at St Paul's a century earlier and it was good enough for the pupils of Prebendary John Hunter at Lichfield. An educated man must be able to read and write Latin and get by in Greek. A boy who had difficulty in understanding that must be stretched over the flogging-horse and birched until he did.

Many years later, Sir John Eardley-Wilmot recalled 'a long, lank, lounging boy' who had left the school two years before Garrick's arrival and whom he 'distinctly remembered to have been punished by Hunter for idleness'. The lounging boy was Samuel Johnson, the son of a local bookseller, and half a lifetime on he had not forgotten it either. When someone remarked on Hunter's severity, Johnson retorted, 'He was not severe, Sir. A master ought to be severe. Sir, he was cruel.'

What Johnson mainly held against Hunter was his failure to distinguish between ignorance and negligence:

> He would ask a boy a question; and if he did not answer it, he would beat him, without considering whether he had an opportunity of knowing how to anwer it. For instance, he would call up a boy and ask him Latin for a candlestick, which the boy could not expect to be asked. Now, Sir, if a boy could answer every question, there would be no need of a master to teach him.[1]

When a friend asked how he had acquired so accurate a knowledge of Latin, however, he replied: 'My master whipped me very well. Without that, Sir, I should have done nothing.'* In an age of floggers, Dr Hunter was unusual only in that as he flourished the rod, he would intone, 'And this I do to save you from the gallows.' But then there were still more than two hundred offences on the statute book punishable by hanging, substantially more, as a scholarly correspondent of the *Gentleman's Magazine* pointed out, than are mentioned in the Bible.[2]

Garrick and his schoolfellows were pupils at the grammar school in something of a golden age. Hunter's reputation attracted gentlemen's sons not only from Staffordshire but from Leicestershire and Derbyshire, and he sometimes had almost a hundred boarders. A cultivated man of High Church inclinations, he took pleasure, in the intervals of beating Latin into his charges, in playing the bass viol. He was also a keen sportsman—'a great setter of game', as Tom Davies put it: 'Happy was the boy who could slyly inform his offended master where a covey of partridges was to be found: this notice was a certain pledge of his pardon.'[3]

Garrick was small for his age, a quick and lively boy with a lot of charm and, one suspects, a tendency to be cheeky. He was not a natural or particularly diligent scholar. Arthur Murphy, another early biographer, put the matter succinctly: 'His

---

* The friend was Bennett Langton, Professor of Ancient Literature at the Royal Academy and famous for his Greek scholarship.

vivacity was superior to serious application.'⁴ That seems also to have been the view of Garrick's uncle David, comfortably settled in Lisbon in the wine trade. When Garrick was about eleven he was packed off there—possibly, as his uncle was childless, with a view to his being taken into the firm. Within a year, however, he was back in Lichfield. Socially, he had been quite a success in Portugal—his after-dinner recitations went down well with the British business community, it seems, and he made numbers of Portuguese friends of his own age—but his uncle chose not to continue the apprenticeship. 'It is imagined,' writes Davies, 'that the gay disposition of the young gentleman was not very suitable to the old man's temper, which was, perhaps, too grave and austere to relish the vivacities of his nephew.'⁵

Of Garrick's father we read that he was 'a man of amiable disposition, much respected for his affable demeanour and agreeable conversation'. Davies had no first-hand knowledge of Garrick's parents, but when his biography appeared in 1781 he acknowledged his indebtedness for the details of Garrick's early life to someone 'who has long honoured me with his friendship and patronage'. The friend and patron in question was Samuel Johnson, and it may well be that his descriptions of the Captain and his wife are couched in Johnson's actual words: 'Mrs. Garrick,' we are told, 'though not beautiful in her person, was very attractive in her manner; her address was polite, and her conversation sprightly and engaging: she had the peculiar happiness, wherever she went, to please and to entertain.'*

Genteel poverty was no obstacle to an agreeable social life: 'Though restrained in their circumstances, Captain Garrick and his wife were welcome to the best families in Lichfield.'† They were on friendly terms with Gilbert Walmesley, the registrar of the Ecclesiastical Court. As the bishops still preferred to live at Eccleshall, the Bishop's palace, the finest house in Lichfield, was leased out. Walmesley, a wealthy bachelor whose father had been chancellor of the diocese, lived there in some style, an open-handed host and a generous patron of the younger generation. Years later Samuel Johnson remembered him with gratitude as 'one of the first friends that literature procured me', and although they were poles apart politically, eulogized him memorably in *Lives of the Poets*:

> He was a Whig, with all the virulence and malevolence of his party; yet difference of opinion did not keep us apart. I honoured him, and he endured me. . . . . Such was his amplitude of learning, and such his copiousness of communication, that it may be doubted whether a day now passes, in which I have not some advantage from his friendship.‡

---

* *Davies*, i, 3. Davies (*c*.1712–85) attended Edinburgh University briefly in the late 1720s and then drifted into acting. Later he became a bookseller. It was in his shop in Russell Street in 1763 that Boswell was introduced to Johnson.
† *Ibid*. The wording here again suggests that Davies's pen was guided by Johnson—whose family circumstances were narrow in a different way.
‡ The passage occurs in the Life of the poet Edmund Smith, 'the handsome sloven' or 'Captain Rag' as he was called, who in 1705 was expelled from Christ Church, Oxford, for riotous behaviour and lampooning the Dean. In the early years of the century, Walmesley and he had

David Garrick might have said the same. Walmesley, Davies wrote, 'took early notice of him; he would often unbend himself by listening to his odd questions, and divert himself with his smart repartees and frolicsome actions.'[6] One of those 'frolicsome actions'—Garrick was ten or eleven at the time—was to get up a play. He chose *The Recruiting Officer* by George Farquhar—possibly he had seen it performed by a troupe of strolling players. The plot is slender, and the characters for the most part straight out of the property box—the name-dropping Captain Brazen, an officer but not quite a gentleman, his rival Captain Plume and the archetypal old soldier, the resourceful Sergeant Kite. Garrick cast his elder sister Magdalene—'Lennie'—as Lucy the chambermaid, and he himself played Kite; possibly the attraction was the scene in which he holds the stage disguised as an astrologer.

Walmesley made a room available in the palace for the performance. The plot requires Kite to appear roaring drunk, but that seems to have bothered the spectators as little as the coarseness of some of Farquhar's language. Davies records that the play 'was acted in a manner so far above the expectation of the audience, that it gave general satisfaction, and was much applauded. The ease, vivacity, and humour of Kite are still remembered with pleasure at Lichfield.'[7]

In 1732 there was a change in the family circumstances. Some years previously Captain Garrick had transferred to Kirke's Second Regiment of Foot.* He now accepted the offer of a brother officer to take his place in Gibraltar. Spain had not been reconciled to Britain's conquest of the Rock—Philip V likened it to a thorn in his foot. George I complicated matters in 1721 by sending the Spanish king an imprudent letter which appeared to recognize his claim; after an unsuccessful Spanish siege in 1727, the British garrison had been reinforced. To Captain Garrick, with his debts to the tradesmen of Lichfield growing as steadily as the six children who remained at home,† the prospect of a return to active service on full pay was irresistible.

With his elder brother away at sea, the fifteen-year-old David became in effect the head of the family. Some of the letters he wrote to his father survive, and it is plain from them that Mrs Garrick did not bear up well in his absence. 'My poor Mamma was in very good Spirits two or three Days after she receiv'd your Letter,' he wrote in the first winter of their separation, 'but now begins to grow maloncolly again, and has little ugly fainting fits.'

The state of the family finances is a constant theme:

---

been members of the same London set—'as violent in their antipathies towards the Tories,' wrote James L. Clifford, 'as they were towards sobriety.' (*Young Samuel Johnson*, London, 1955, p. 94.)

* Originally raised for service in Tangier, the regiment, because of its badge, was known as 'Kirke's Lambs': Macaulay speculated that a Paschal Lamb was thought a fitting device for Christian soldiers going to fight the infidel.

† Peter was now a midshipman serving in the West Indies under Sir Chaloner Ogle.

My Mamma rec'd ye thirty Pounds you was so good to send her, she has
Paid ten Pounds to Mr Rider for one Year's Rent, and ten Pounds to the
Baker, and if you can spare her a little more as you tell her you will, she
is in hopes of paying all ye Debts, that you may have nothing to fret you
when you come home. . . . My Mamma paid for your Stockings & Holland
as soon as you left her, and as soon as She came down to us, not to her
great Joy, she found us very shabby in Cloaths, & in all our accoutrements,
that we was rather like so many beggars than Gentlemen Soldiers, but
with much ado at last she equipt us out a little better, & now with a great
Deal of Mending & Patching we are in Statu quo.

He had been taken on a visit to a family called Offley who lived at Wichnor
Park, near Lichfield, and the good-hearted Walmesley had found a delicate way
of sparing him embarrassment: 'Mr Walmisley gave me slyly, half a Crown for
ye Butler & another for ye Groom, for my self, which made me look very grand.'
Garrick signs himself 'Y^r ever Dutifull Son' and then adds a postscript: 'Dr Sir
if you could possibly send Mr Walmisley a little Wine, I am sure he would take
it as a Particular Favour.'[8]

The mails between Lichfield and Gibraltar were erratic, and there was no
means of knowing which items of family news had reached their destination. 'I
write to you the Beginning of May last in which Letter I gave you an account of
my Sister Jenney's Illness,' Garrick wrote in the summer of 1733, 'but I suppose
you have not receiv'd, by y^r not mentioning any thing of it in Y^r Letters.' Garrick
also passed on snippets of local news: 'Mr Perkins is cited into ye Court for
Drunkenness & swearing by Mr Rider. Mr Sharpless has lost a Tankard of twelve
Pounds which was stole from him, and there is a Dragoon in Gaol upon
Suspicion.'[9]

His father's health did not hold up well in Gibraltar: 'We All have been very
uneasy to hear you have not been well,' Garrick wrote in September, 'and hope
that at the receiving of this you'll have got y^r Stomach up again. All the Family
is pretty well except my Grandmother who is often out of order.' (Mrs Clough,
Mrs Garrick's mother, lived with them in Bacon Street.) The family was exerting
itself to get the Captain some home leave; Mrs Garrick had spoken to Gilbert
Walmesley, and he had sounded out the local MP, Richard Plummer, 'who has
promis'd to use his interest'. The scheme was simple, and there was something
in it for everybody:

Mr Walmisley has set you in ye list among the Voters, and has made over
a Burgess to you to qualify you for voting, without taking any Oath, So
we are in great hopes we shall see You in ye Spring, or else my Mamma is
determin'd to come to you.

Captain Garrick had apparently enquired when David would be ready to go to
university: 'I fancy in about two Years, I should have been ready by now, only
my going to Lisbon backened me a great deal, but every body thinks at 18 or 19
Years of Age is time enough.'[10]

Walmesley's scheme for getting Captain Garrick and his vote home ran into difficulties. There was much talk of war in the winter of 1733–4, and the word from the influential Mr Plummer was that it was impossible to obtain leave until it was certain whether there would be peace or war.*

By the early spring of 1734, Garrick was able to report that the family's finances were almost in order: 'My Mamma sends her dearest Love & affection to You, and desires me to tell You that she has almost clear'd all the Debts, except a little to yᵉ Butcher, which she hopes to clear in a Month or two.' There was also a royal wedding to describe:

> We have had great rejoicings all over England, on account of the Nuptials of yᵉ Prince of Orange with yᵉ Princess Royall, every Body almost wears Orange Cockades & favours, houses are illuminated, Burnfires, Drinking yᵉ healths of yᵉ Royal couple, togeather with all yᵉ Royal Family. Mʳ Walmisley treated the Ladies & Gentᵐ at yᵉ Assembly with Rack Punch, and presented yᵉ Gentᵐ with Cockades & yᵉ Ladies with Favours, His House was illuminated from top to bottom, all yᵉ Town came up to see it.†

Dr Hunter would have marked his pupil's handwriting more highly than his spelling, but the letters are full of graphic and racy detail: 'Poor Mʳˢ Lowndes'— [a servant, or perhaps a family dependent]—'is almost constantly rowling about yᵉ flower with yᵉ Cholick or has her Head tide about with a Napkin with yᵉ head Ach, like one that is a Victim for a Sacrifice.'

About his mother's health, he writes more soberly; in a letter written at Christmas, 1734, he says that she had been confined to her room for four months, and has had several severe relapses:

> My Mama's Disorder is a violent pain in her Hip & Thigh attended with a Fever on her Spirits, that Nothing gives her ease but opium, and she has been easy these three Weeks. We were in Hopes of seeing You this Xmas, and expect every Post News from London; My Mama says she believes your presence would do more good than all the Physicians in Europe.‡

---

* The death of Augustus II of Poland had led to the outbreak of hostilities on the continent, although what became known as the War of the Polish Succession was essentially about the desire of France, allied with Spain and Savoy, to tilt the balance of power in Europe by weakening the Empire. George II, a German prince with ambitions to distinguish himself in the field, was violently anti-French; Queen Caroline and their Hanoverian advisers also favoured intervention; Walpole, on the eve of a general election, remained ingloriously resolute for peace, even though it meant reneging on treaty obligations to the Austrians. 'Madam,' he told the Queen, 'there are fifty thousand men slain this year in Europe and not one Englishman.'

† *Letters*, 5. The marriage had been solemnized in the French chapel adjoining St James's Palace. The Princess was short, fat and disfigured by the smallpox. The Prince was deformed. Told that she might refuse him if she wished, she replied that she would marry him if he were a baboon. 'Well, then,' said the King, 'there is baboon enough for you.'

‡ *Ibid.*, 7. Written on the same sheet as this letter there is a note to Captain Garrick from Robert James, then a young doctor in practice in Lichfield, asking if he could help him to get hold of some genuine Peruvian bark for quinine.

But that was denied her, and she continued up and down. Two months later Garrick reports that her lowness of spirits now compels her to drink wine, 'which gives a great deal of uneasiness upon two accounts, as it goes against her inclination, and Pockett'. The state of Mrs Garrick's pocket also meant that sisters Lennie and Jenny could not be provided with lace:

They with ye greatest Duty & Obedience request a small Matter to purchase their Head ornaments, great Necessity compells them to give you this Trouble, for they have never wore any thing else but plain head Cloaths which hardly distinguishes them from ye Vulgar Madams.[11]

There had been a great many recruiting officers from Ireland in the town, and early in 1735 Garrick's own thoughts had turned briefly to a military career: 'I was in great hopes I should have Recruited my Self this Spring,' he wrote excitedly.[12] Henry Hervey, fourth son of the Earl of Bristol, and brother of the Lord Hervey whom Pope would pillory as 'Sporus', was a Cornet in the King's Own Regiment of Horse (Kerr's Dragoons) and had been quartered in Lichfield. Because of the illness of a brother-in-law, it had looked for a time as if this wild young man's wife might succeed to a large estate, and in that event Hervey had apparently promised Garrick his commission. The brother-in-law shook off his 'dead Palsie', however, and made a complete recovery.*

Garrick concludes this particular letter with a piece of agreeable nonsense: 'I have sent you Dear Sir the following Piece of Wit, hoping it may prove some Diversion to you Gibralterians, it was Deliver'd by ye Hands of a Halequin at a late Masquerade, to all the People he Met, and delivred one also to the King upon his Knees.' What he then transcribes is a political squib, in the form of a playbill, aimed at Sir Robert Walpole and his brother Horace:

G: R. by permission
. . . On Thursday next, by ye Norfolk Company of Artificial Comedians, at Robin's great Theatrical Booth in Palace Yard, will be presented a Comical & Diverting Play of Seven Acts, call'd Court & Country, in which will be reviv'd the entertaining Scene of ye two Blundering Brothers, with the Cheats of Rabbi Robin, Prime Minister to King Solomon: the whole concluding with a great Masque call'd the Downfall of Sejanus, or the Statesman's Overthrow: With Axes, Gibbetts, & other Decorations proper to ye Play, to begin exactly at twelve a'Clock. . . . .
    Vivant Rex et Regina.†

'If this impudent thing affords any Pleasure I have my Aim,' Garrick wrote. A copy of this 'impudent thing' is preserved in the British Library. It is dated 18 January 1735—it had been published, therefore, only a month before Garrick

---

* The brother-in-law was Sir Thomas Aston, of Aston Hall in Cheshire.
† *Letters*, 8. Horatio or Horace, later first Baron Walpole of Wolterton, was Sir Robert's younger brother. He had been ambassador at Paris from 1723–30, where he had gained the confidence of Cardinal Fleury; he was currently ambassador at The Hague.

copied it out for his father's amusement. It is possible that he picked it up himself on a visit to the capital. 'Several of his father's acquaintance,' writes Davies, 'who knew the delight which he felt in the entertainments of the stage, often treated him with a journey to London, that he might feast his appetite at the playhouse.'[13] However he came by it, it offers an insight into the direction in which the interests of this provincial eighteen-year-old were beginning to turn.

It is clear from his next letter that his mother was still struggling to make ends meet. 'I must tell my Dear Papa that I am quite turn'd Philosopher,' he wrote:

> you perhaps may think me vain, but to shew you I am not, I would gladly get shut of my Characteristick of a Philosopher, viz. a ragged p^r of Breeches, now the only way you have to cure y^r Son of his Philosophick qualification is to send some hansome thing for a wastecoat & p^r of Breeches to hide his Nakedness; they tell me Velvet is very cheap at Gibralter, Amen, & so be it.[14]

Garrick had not altogether abandoned the idea of a military career. 'I can tell my Papa I stand a good chance to get into ye Army,' he writes in April 1735. 'I have the promise of three Lieutenant Colonells to provide for me.' And there is a line which suggests that there may have been talk of his going into the church; one of the colonels he mentions, Pyot by name, 'has swore to make [me] Chaplain to his Reg^t if I should be in orders'.[15]

A month later, Garrick was able to tell his father that the efforts of his family and friends in Lichfield had finally paid off:

> 'Mr Rider who is made Chancellour has been up to Town & has got Brigadeer Kirk's Leave & Interest for y^r coming over to England; but you must not mention it to any Body till y^r Orders come which will be very Soon.'*

In the excitement of the homecoming, Garrick's over-eagerness to amuse carried him beyond the bounds of taste. He told the story many years later to the parson-poet Percival Stockdale:

> 'I suppose, sir,' (said he to his father) 'I have a good many brothers and sisters at GIBRALTAR?' Tears came into the eyes of poor Mrs. GARRICK.—'Hold your tongue, DAVY;' (said the captain) 'Don't talk in that manner; you see how it affects your mother.'[16]

Garrick was by this time no longer in the tender care of Dr Hunter. For a short period he passed instead under the tutelage of Samuel Johnson. It was the beginning of a complex and sometimes uneasy relationship between Lichfield's two most famous sons that would end only with Garrick's death.

---

* *Ibid.*, 11. In fact almost a year was to pass before the Captain was reunited with his family. His grant of leave, signed at Lichfield, is dated 31 May 1736.

Johnson was now in his middle twenties. In 1728 he had gone up to Pembroke College, Oxford. Thirteen months later, his toes showing through his shoes and hopelessly behind in the payment of his fees, he had returned home and lapsed into indolence and melancholy; it was then that began to appear the nervous tics and other convulsive mannerisms which remained with him for the rest of his life. He had tried his hand at schoolmastering in Leicestershire and during some months in Birmingham he dabbled in journalism and picked up £5 for a translation from the French.* He had also met and married Elizabeth Porter, a widow twenty years his senior. She brought with her a fortune of £600—a sum which in those days was equivalent to perhaps fifteen times a modest annual income. With his wife's money, and the advice and help of Gilbert Walmesley, he set up a boarding school for young gentlemen—'whom I shall endeavour to instruct,' he told a friend, 'in a method somewhat more rational than those commonly practiced.'

Johnson established his school in a village two and a half miles west of Lichfield. Edial Hall—a large brick box of a building with a roof in the shape of a sawn-off pyramid and a chimney resembling an Egyptian obelisk—had been put up seventy years previously by a local worthy of unusual architectural taste called Hammond. Garrick and his younger brother George were the first pupils when the school opened in the autumn of 1735, and they were joined by one of the Offley boys from Winchnor Park, a lad of sixteen who was a cousin of Harry Hervey's wife.

An academy with a roll of three was hardly an economic proposition, and an advertisement placed in the *Gentleman's Magazine* the following summer did nothing to help matters. With the grammar school so close, there was no good reason for parents to place their sons in Johnson's care; he had no university degree, and his odd appearance and uncouth manner counted against him. What sort of a fist George Garrick or young Offley made of the curriculum at Edial is not known, but David Garrick's interest in the glories of Greece and Rome was limited. 'Notwithstanding the brilliance of his parts, the classic authors had as yet no charms for Mr Garrick,' wrote Davies:

> His thoughts were constantly employed on the stage; for even at that time he was very busy in composing plays. When his master expected from him some exercise or composition upon a theme, he showed him several scenes of a new comedy, which had engrossed his time; and these, he told him, were the produce of his third attempt in dramatic poetry.†

The 'brilliance of his parts' also found expression in what was already a highly developed talent for mimicry and ridicule, directed as often as not, by Boswell's account, against Johnson:

* The French book was itself a translation from the Portuguese—an account by a seventeenth-century Jesuit, Father Jerome Lobo, of his travels in Abyssinia and of Jesuit missionary efforts there. Johnson's abridgement—his first published work—appeared at the beginning of 1735. Then £5 would be worth perhaps £375 today.

† *Davies*, i, 8. Many years later Johnson said of his old pupil, 'He has not Latin enough. He finds out the Latin by the meaning, rather than the meaning by the Latin.' (*Life*, ii, 377.)

His oddities of manner, and uncouth gesticulations, could not but be the subject of merriment to them; and, in particular, the young rogues used to listen at the door of his bed-chamber, and peep through the key-hole, that they might turn into ridicule his tumultuous and awkward fondness for Mrs Johnson, whom he used to name by the familiar appellation of Tetty or Tetsy.[17]

'Very fat, with a bosom of more than ordinary protuberance, with swelled cheeks of a florid red, produced by thick painting, and increased by the use of cordials'—Garrick's unsparing descriptions of Tetty are well known: on another occasion he called her 'a little painted poppet; full of affectation and rural airs of elegance'. Years later, at the height of his fame, he did not need to be asked twice to perform what had become very much the *pièce de résistance* in his repertoire of party turns. In its broader versions, it was reserved for occasions when only men were present. Garrick would give grotesque impersonations of the fond pair, 'the lady thinking he delayed too long to come to bed', her shambling lover puffing and blowing and uttering cries of 'I'm coming, my Tetsie, I'm coming, my Tetsie.' In an alternative routine, Johnson, deaf to Tetty's urgings that he should come to bed, sits at work on a tragedy, pausing occasionally to regale her with some of the best lines. Totally absorbed in composition, and short-sighted into the bargain, he mistakes the bedclothes for his own shirt-tails and begins to stuff them into his breeches, exposing the increasingly frantic Tetty to the night air.

Johnson was, as it happens, at work on a tragedy during his time at Edial. A success in the theatre would make his name; more importantly, it would make him some money. He had borrowed from Garrick's brother Peter a copy of Richard Knolles's *Generall Historie of the Turkes*, first published in 1604. There he found the story of the Sultan Mahomet II and the Greek Christian slave Irene, captured at the fall of Constantinople and given to the Sultan as a mistress. Gilbert Walmesley, to whom Johnson read extracts of his manuscript, was complimentary, but objected that he was inflicting so much suffering on Irene in the early scenes that there was little possibility 'of heightening the catastrophe in the concluding part of the play'. Johnson was not at a loss for an answer. Recalling that the conduct of Walmesley's ecclesiastical court had been the subject of a petition for redress to Parliament a few years previously, he slyly assured him that there was 'enough in reserve for my purpose'. In the final act, he said, he intended to put his heroine into the ecclesiastical court of Lichfield, 'which will fill up the utmost measure of human calamity'.

A half-written tragedy was of little use in keeping a foundering academy afloat, however. In November 1736 Lawrence Offley was admitted to Clare College, Cambridge, and three months later George Garrick went off to the Appleby Latin School. What was to be done with David? Once again, it was Gilbert Walmesley who extended a helping hand, and in February 1737 he wrote to an old friend to ask a favour:

My neighbour, Capt. Garrick, (who is an honest, valuable man,) has a son, who is a very sensible young fellow, and a good scholar, and whom the Captain hopes, in some two or three years, he shall send to the Temple, and breed to the Bar. But, at present, his pocket will not hold out for sending him to the University. I have proposed your taking him, if you like well of it, and your boarding him, and instructing him in mathematics, philosophy, and humane learning. He is now nineteen, of sober and good disposition, and is as ingenious and promising a young man as ever I knew in my life ... I have taken a pleasure often in instructing him, and have a great affection and esteem for him; and I doubt not but you will soon have the like, if it suit with your convenience to take him into your family. . . . . .[18]

The 'dear old Friend' to whom Walmesley addressed this appeal was the Reverend John Colson, the son of a Lichfield vicar-choral and a well-known mathematician. A Fellow of the Royal Society, and the master of a mathematical school at Rochester, in Kent, he was also the vicar of the parish of Chalk, near Gravesend. He did 'like well' of the proposition, and Walmesley wrote to express his appreciation. 'Had I a son of my own, it would be my ambition, instead of sending him to the university, to dispose of him as this young gentleman is,' he wrote:

He and another young neighbour of mine, one Mr. S. Johnson, set out this morning for London together. Davy Garrick is to be with you early next week; and Mr. Johnson, to try his fate with a tragedy, and to see to get himself employed in some translation . . . . .*

The oddly assorted pair set out on 2 March 1737. Garrick, when describing the journey, used to say that they 'rode and tied'—that they shared one horse, that's to say, and took it in turn to ride and go forward on foot. This was an account which Boswell was inclined to take with a pinch of salt; nor is it likely that Johnson, taking his ease in good company many years later, regarded himself as being on oath when he tossed out a remark that portrayed them as a couple of Dick Whittingtons: 'Why yes; when I came with two-pence half-penny in *my* pocket, and thou, Davy, with three half-pence in thine.'[19]

However they covered the distance, they were in London within the week. On 9 March Garrick, the budding lawyer, paid out £3 3s 4d for the privilege of being enrolled at Lincoln's Inn. Johnson, meanwhile, the budding man of the theatre, had found lodgings in Exeter Street with one Norris, a staymaker.

---

* *Boaden*, i, 2. According to Davies, Garrick's friends entertained some hopes that if Walmesley had remained single, 'young Garrick would have gained, by his means, a settlement for life'. The previous year, however, at the age of fifty-six, Walmesley had married one of Sir Thomas Aston's eight sisters—which also made him the brother-in-law of Harry Hervey.

3

The Stage-Struck Wine Merchant

Almost at once, for both men, there came distressing family news—the deaths of Johnson's brother and Garrick's father. Nathaniel was three years younger than Johnson. He had worked briefly in their father's shop and later had opened a small book business in Stourbridge. He got into some sort of financial trouble, drank more than was good for him, contemplated emigration to the recently founded colony of Georgia. In the event he drifted no further than Somerset, working as a bookbinder and stationer in Frome. A letter from Nathaniel to his mother makes it clear that relations between the brothers were not good: 'As to my Brothers assisting me I had but little Reason to expect it when He would scarce ever use me with common civility.'* Any remorse which Johnson felt in later years was bottled up inside him. He never spoke of Nathaniel, although in old age he made enquiries about him; and on the day their mother was buried, in 1759, he ended the long prayer which he wrote in his journal with the poignant and haunting words, 'The dream of my Brother I shall remember.'

Captain Garrick had been in poor health since his return from Gibraltar. In his will he left £500 apiece to Peter, Magdalene and Jane, £400 to William and £300 to George and Merrial. His final bequest—'To my son David, One Shilling'—was less startling than it sounds. It was not the proverbial token of disinheritance. The Captain's brother, the Lisbon wine merchant, had died a few months previously, and in his will he had made generous provision for his namesake, 'son of my Brother'. The bequest, however, was hedged about by conditions. The £1,000 legacy was 'to be put out at interest by the Executors, jointly with my brother, until he is of age'. And there was an intriguing proviso: 'If [he] should be disobedient to his father and mother before [he] comes of age the money must be given to the father to doe as he thinks most convenient.' This may have been nothing more than an expression of traditional Huguenot prudence. It is just possible, on the other hand, that he was not entirely persuaded of his nephew's steadiness and was signalling that any flightiness in the matter of choosing a career could have painful consequences.

Garrick made his way to Rochester and took up residence with Colson. Cole the antiquary called him 'a plain, honest man, of great industry and assiduity',

---

* The letter is preserved in the Birthplace Museum.

although he added that he was also 'an humourist and peevish'. Garrick did not stay long under his roof. He apparently found time to get up some amateur theatricals in the town, and Davies, in one of his flabbier passages, says that 'in the company of so rational a philosopher, he was imperceptibly and gradually improved in the talent of thinking and reasoning'. After some months, however, he packed his bags. 'Sublime geometry,' wrote Murphy, 'had no attraction for him whose ruling passion was the dramatic art.' The law also appeared to have lost whatever small appeal it originally had; Garrick thought no more of Lincoln's Inn and returned briefly to Lichfield.*

His brother Peter had now left the Navy. Each had a capital sum of £1,000 or so at his disposal, and they resolved to set up in business together. In a hard-drinking age, they sensibly concluded that they could do worse than put their money to work for them in the wine trade, Peter operating in Lichfield, David in London.† They acquired premises in Durham Yard, between the Strand and the Thames, and Garrick set about drumming up business. Much of their wine came from Portugal. The Treaty of Methuen, signed with the Portuguese in 1703, had been designed to injure one of the most prosperous branches of French trade; duty on French wines was set at £55 per tun, compared with a paltry £7 levied on the generally rougher wines of Portugal. Garrick Brothers were able to sell red port (what the Portuguese called *consumo*) at eighteen shillings a dozen—a *vin du pays* that was brandied for export and darkened with elderberries.‡ Light sweet wines like Canary were also popular, and so was Mountain, a variety of Malaga.§

Garrick's brief foray into commerce is thinly documented. We know from one of his letters to Peter that he secured the custom of the Bedford ('one of yᵉ best in London'),¶ but the brothers were not cut out to be business partners:

> Peter was calm, sedate, and methodical; David was gay, volatile, impetuous, and, perhaps, not so confined to regularity as his partner could have

---

* Colson was also shortly to move on. In May 1739 he was appointed to the Lucasian Chair of Mathematics at Cambridge.

† Peter, in addition to the £500 from his father, had been left the same amount by his uncle.

‡ Demand for French wine was only seriously revived by Pitt's Commercial Treaty of 1786.

§ When Garrick was rich and famous, the insufferable Samuel Foote used to tell anyone who would listen that he could remember him living in Durham Yard 'with three quarts of vinegar in the cellar, calling himself a wine-merchant'. For someone who for a time went into partnership with a notorious swindler called Charles Price to brew and sell small beer, that was the height of impertinence. It was a characteristic piece of malice, but the dates don't quite fit. Foote, who was born in Truro and went to the grammar school there, did not matriculate at Worcester College, Oxford, until July 1737, and in spite of his frequent gambling sprees unaccountably avoided being sent down until February 1740. By the time he set about trying to establish himself as a wit and a man of fashion at the Grecian and Bedford Coffee Houses, Garrick's days in the wine trade were over.

¶ *Letters*, 12. Another letter, written in September 1740, indicates that Garrick was having cash-flow problems: 'I must desire you to Send Me up a Bill asoon as possible, For Cash is rather Low & Brounker wants his Money, pray let me have It asoon as possible.' (*Ibid.*, 13.)

wished. To prevent the continuance of fruitless and daily altercation, by the interposition of friends, the partnership was dissolved amicably.*

The London in which David Garrick found himself as a young man in the late 1730s was a sprawling, disorderly metropolis of half a million people. The portraits of Gainsborough, the satires of Pope, Wedgwood's china, Chippendale's furniture, the oratorios of Handel, the architecture of the Adam brothers—the received impression of Georgian England as the acme of elegance and urbanity and proportion is not a false picture, but it is an incomplete one. It was also coarse and brutal and earthy and drunken—Hogarth and Rowlandson are not less faithful chroniclers of the age than Reynolds and Zoffany. The popular sights of the town included the antics of the lunatics in Bedlam or the whipping of half-naked women at the Bridewell. The painted signs outside gin-shops advertised cheap passports to oblivion—drunk for a penny, dead drunk for twopence, no charge for the straw on which you sprawled until you regained your senses.

Although his fall was not imminent, the immense power exercised for fifteen years past by Sir Robert Walpole was beginning to crumble, even though he continued to marshal his army of placemen with superb skill and to work wonders with what passed in the eighteenth century for the machinery of government.† Was it true that he opened letters from his huntsman and his gamekeeper before those from the King? At Richmond he hunted the stag in the Park and lived in open adultery with the amiable Molly Skerret, the daughter of a prosperous Irish merchant. (The Queen, keenly interested in sexual matters, expressed astonishment that such an agreeable girl could lie with anyone so grossly fat.)‡

To the casual eye, the impress of Eton and King's College, Cambridge, on the First Minister of the Crown had been slight. Squat, blunt, coarse-featured, Walpole looked and sounded like a Norfolk squire, although at Houghton, boisterous in his hospitality, confident in his taste, surrounded by his Rembrandts and his Poussins, he lived more in the style of a Duke. He was now in his early sixties. His majorities in the Commons were in decline, and his influence had

---

* *Davies*, i, 16. It took Garrick some time to run down his end of the business and to square accounts with his brother. 'I don't design to bottle any more wine, but Sell yᵉ rest in Cask,' he wrote at the end of December 1741, and again, a month later, 'Yᵉ Two Pipes of Testace Port will be wᵗʰ You on Saturday—I shall pay Farnells Bill immediatly.' (*Letters*, 20 and 21.)

† To the impotent rage of his opponents—who would themselves have done exactly the same— and of their friends in the press. One opposition newspaper catalogued the offices he had garnered for himself and his relatives: 'First Lord of the Treasury, Mr Walpole. Chancellor of the Exchequer, Mr Walpole. Clerk of the Pells, Mr Walpole's son. Customs of London, second son of Mr Walpole, in Reversion. Secretary of the Treasury, Mr Walpole's brother. Postmaster-General, Mr Walpole's brother. Secretary to Ireland, Mr Walpole's brother. Secretary to the Postmaster-General, Mr Walpole's brother-in-law.' (*The Craftsman*, Collected Edition (1737), XI, 16.)

‡ After the death of his wife in 1737 he married her, but she died the following year of a miscarriage, plunging him into what his brother described as 'a deplorable and comfortless condition'. She had previously borne him two daughters.

been seriously undermined by conflicts in the royal family. George II and his Queen had both grown to detest the Prince of Wales—'a monster and the greatest villain that ever was born', his father said of him.[1] In 1737 the breach had become irreparable: Frederick was turned out of St James's Palace and set up what was in effect an alternative court at Leicester House.*

Walpole dismissed the opposition politicians who gathered there—they included the young William Pitt—as the 'Patriot Boys'. He also underestimated the importance to the Prince's party of the wits and writers he drew into his orbit; men of the calibre of Gay and Pope and Fielding were infinitely more effective as pamphleteers than the hacks that Walpole was able to recruit by the expenditure of large sums of secret service money.

The Queen, with whom he had joked coarsely about her husband's infidelities, had been his most loyal supporter. In 1737 the ruptured womb which she had tried so long to conceal turned malignant. Her death that November was a severe blow.

Walpole also found himself increasingly unable to ignore the virulence of popular feeling against Spain. Had the gallant Captain Jenkins really had one of his ears cut off by Spanish *guarda-costas* in 1731 when they boarded his ship on the high seas to search for contraband? Paraded before the House of Commons seven years later, that was certainly his story, and he was sticking to it. When asked how he had responded to such treatment, he had his answer pat: 'He had recommended his soul to God and his cause to his country.'† This early example of what a later age would call a sound-bite had the war-party growling their approval. A year later, when he finally yielded to their clamour, Walpole capped it bitterly with one of his own: 'They now ring the bells, but they will soon wring their hands.'

He hated cant. 'Patriots spring up like mushrooms,' he growled to the Commons. 'I could raise 50 of them within the four and twenty hours.' 'Saint' and 'Spartan' were also favoured terms of abuse. For so cynical a man, he was curiously sensitive to criticism—not a helpful attribute for a politician. The baiting of Walpole and his ministry was conducted not only in the press and in pamphlets and ballads but also in the theatres; indeed, some of his supporters believed in the existence of a Jacobite conspiracy to manipulate the London stage to create generalized disaffection.

The Beggar's Opera, when it appeared in 1728, had combined burlesque of Italian opera with satire of the ministry. The song 'How happy could I be with either/ Were t'other dear charmer away' was widely understood to refer to Walpole's irregular domestic arrangements, and the quarrel between Peachum and Lockit to his disagreements with Townshend, his brother-in-law and

---

* The occasion was the pregnancy of the Princess of Wales. The King had decreed that her lying-in should take place at Hampton Court; when she went into labour the Prince, at some danger to her life, hurried her off to St James's Palace so that the child should not be born under his parents' roof.

† Horace Walpole asserted that when Jenkins died both ears were found to be intact. Burke, in his *Letters of a Regicide Peace*, writes of 'the fable of Jenkins' ears'.

ministerial colleague.* When Gay wrote a sequel called *Polly*, in which Macheath has been transported to the West Indies, it was promptly banned. The Lord Chamberlain acted at the behest of the King, but his intervention was believed to be prompted by Walpole's resentment.†

By the early 1730s, however, the powers which the government had traditionally relied on to regulate the theatres had been eroded—even the laws against profanity were no longer actively enforced. Walpole's differences with the King—over foreign policy, over the Prince of Wales's allowance—were serious enough; the steady stream of ridicule to which both his administration and the royal family were exposed in the theatre exacerbated relations still further.

There had also been a disturbing increase in civil disorder—'a licentious, riotous, seditious, and almost ungovernable spirit in the people showed itself in many tumults and disorders, in different shapes, and in several parts of the kingdom,' wrote Hervey.[2] There was an explosion in Westminster Hall while the courts were sitting in July 1736, disturbances later that month in the East End over immigrant Irish labour, the Porteous Riots in Edinburgh.‡

Walpole had inherited from former governments an effective system for dealing with printed libels on the King and his ministers. But criticisms of the government or of the monarch which had to be disguised when they appeared in print could be presented with impunity on the stage. A particular thorn in the ministerial side was Henry Fielding, whose satirical broadsides from the stage of the New Haymarket regularly found their target. In the mind of the ministry, dislike of sitting in the pillory was now transmuted into fears of sedition, and Walpole's thoughts turned towards legislation to regulate the theatres. He knew that he was not without allies, in and out of Parliament. Religious opposition to dramatic entertainments, of the sort which had closed the theatres between 1642 and 1660, had by no means been extinguished. Many merchants and tradespeople also tended to disapprove of playhouses as places which lowered the tone of a neighbourhood and where their apprentices could all too easily fall into bad company.

The bill which was introduced in the Commons in May 1737 was not a new measure but an amendment to a vagrancy statute from the reign of Queen Anne. Walpole announced that he intended to move an additional clause empowering

---

* Charles Townshend, the second Viscount, had become Secretary for the Northern Department for the second time in 1721. His instincts were more bellicose than Walpole's; he ultimately resigned in 1730 and devoted the remaining eight years of his life to agriculture.

† *Polly* earned Gay more than £1,100 in subscriptions when it was published in 1729, which was considerably more than he would have got from a stage presentation. It was not performed in the theatre until the 1770s.

‡ The execution of a smuggler called Andrew Wilson for robbing a customs officer occasioned public disorder and when John Porteous, Captain of the Edinburgh Town Guard, ordered his troops to fire into the crowd eight people were killed. Porteous was subsequently convicted of wilful murder. When it became known that the death sentence had been postponed, a mob stormed the Tolbooth and hanged Porteous from a dyer's pole in the Grassmarket.

the government to censor dramatic performances. He read to the House, with a great show of indignation, some extracts from a play which he said he had recently received. It was called *The Golden Rump*, and it contained not only obscene allusions to Walpole himself, but 'the most barefaced and scurrilous abuse on the persons and characters of the King and Queen and the whole Court'.[3]

It was not long before there were suggestions that this was a ploy by Walpole to secure the passage of his censorship clause: 'Suppose Sir,' wrote the author of a mock autobiography of Theophilus Cibber, 'that the *Golden Rump* Farce was wrote by a certain great Man's own Direction, and as much Scurrility and Treason larded in it as possible . . .'* It was also alleged that the play had been carried to Walpole by Henry Giffard, who was then managing the Lincoln's Inn Fields Theatre, in the expectation that he would in some way be rewarded by the government—possibly by the granting of a separate licence.

The bill met little opposition in the Commons. It had its third reading on 1 June and went to the Lords, and it was there that the most celebrated objection to the measure was heard—the speech made by Lord Chesterfield is still regarded as a classic statement of the case against censorship.

Chesterfield's argument was essentially libertarian. He said little in direct defence of the stage. He conceded that many recent plays—he instanced Fielding's *Pasquin* and Havard's *King Charles I*—should have been prosecuted: 'How these Pieces came to pass unpunished, I do not know: If I am rightly informed, it was not for Want of Law, but for Want of Prosecution.' It would, he contended, be impossible to enforce the proposed measure. It would tend, moreover, 'towards a Restraint on the Liberty of the Press, which will be a long Stride towards the Destruction of Liberty itself'.

He foresaw that plays would be written 'on Purpose to have a Refusal'. Once banned, a play would be printed and published 'with the Refusal in capital Letters on the Title Page', which would certainly 'procure a good Sale'. Parliament, he argued, would then be asked for a bill to prevent such plays from being published; the way round that would be for satires to be written 'by way of Novels, secret Histories, Dialogues, or under some such Title'; finally, there would be pressure for a bill that would put the press under a general licence— 'and then we may bid adieu to the Liberties of *Great Britain*.'

This was good rousing stuff, but while many admired the elegance of Chesterfield's prose and the ease of his delivery (he was said to have written his speech out and committed it to memory), his eloquence did little to move their Lordships. Indeed, by the time the House divided, their number had dwindled to forty-two and, of those, only four joined him in voting against the bill.

---

* *An Apology for the Life of Mr T . . . C . . . , Comedian*, London, 1740, p. 94. This 'autobiography' has often been attributed to Fielding. Fielding denied it. Theophilus Cibber (1703–58) was the fourth child and first son of Colley Cibber. He was sent to Winchester, and there seems to have been a hope that he might become a doctor or lawyer. At the age of sixteen, however, he left school and joined the company at Drury Lane, where his father was then co-manager.

The parliamentary session ended on 21 June. The King, in the presence of both Houses and the Prince of Wales, gave his assent to the bill. He expressed his gratitude to Parliament for its loyalty during the past five months: 'You cannot be insensible,' he told them, 'what just Scandal and Offence the Licentiousness of the present Times, under the Colour and Disguise of Liberty, gives to all honest and sober Men.'[4]

The court then retired to Richmond. It had been expected that the King would return to Hanover and the embrace of Madame Wallmoden,* but he seemed content to stay in England and enjoy the company of his new mistress, Lady Deloraine. Hervey remarked to him that he must be very glad, after so long a session, to get a little fresh country air:

> His Majesty very naturally, but very impoliticly, replied: 'Yes, my Lord, I am very glad to be got away, for I have seen of late, in London, so many hungry faces every day, that I was afraid they would have eat me at last.'[5]

Garrick's arrival in London thus coincided with a sharp check to the expansion of theatrical activity. Until the passage of the Licensing Act, there had been flourishing companies in as many as five theatres and performances at numerous booths during the seasons of the Mayfair and Bartholomew Fair. Now, entertainment was legally restricted to the two theatres which operated under royal patent in Drury Lane and Covent Garden, although opera was sanctioned at the Haymarket. The Lord Chamberlain might prohibit any theatrical performance, and a licence must be sought from his office for all new plays, additions to old plays, prologues and epilogues. The penalty for non-compliance was a fine of £50 for 'every person so offending, and for each offence'.

'There is a common saying,' a pamphleteer wrote the following year, 'that all Acts of Parliament have a Hole to creep out of.'[6] That is especially so of legislation introduced in haste by harassed administrations, and even though its main provisions would remain in force for more than two centuries, the Stage Licensing Act of 1737 operated only imperfectly. For a good fifteen years or so, a succession of crafty actors and managers would find ways of keeping minor theatres open.

There were fewer loopholes in the clauses of the Act relating to censorship, but there was a certain amount of nodding and winking between the Lord Chamberlain and the theatre managers, and they rubbed along well enough together. The requirement to submit new plays 'fourteen days at least before the acting, representing, or performing thereof' was fairly strictly observed for some months after the passing of the Act, but in time—for purely practical reasons relating to rehearsal, for instance—the interval often dropped to a few days. Again, a new play was often revised to meet objections voiced by the audience on the first night; the Lord Chamberlain's office frequently turned a blind eye to

---

* Amalie Sophie Marianne Wallmoden had become George II's mistress in 1735. Three years later, after the death of Queen Caroline, she was installed in St James's Palace. She was created Countess of Yarmouth in 1740.

such unexamined material. There was also a fair degree of tolerance to the practice of ad libbing, which between 1737 and 1968 was technically illegal on the British stage.

Something that had not occurred to those who drafted the Act was the ease with which speeches and characters in *old* plays might be construed to have contemporary significance. There was a good example when *Richard II* was performed at Covent Garden in February 1738. When Northumberland spoke the words 'The king is not himself, but basely led/ By flatterers', it was recorded that 'the noise from the clapping of hands and clattering of sticks was loud and boisterous'. Ross's line, 'The Earl of Wiltshire hath the state in farm' was immediately taken to apply to Walpole, and was received 'with the loudest shouts and huzzas I ever heard'.[7]

The Lord Chamberlain's office also sometimes missed political allusions in new plays. James Thomson's *Agamemnon* offered a case in point. Thomson was well known to be associated with the opposition and with the cause of the Prince of Wales, and a number of lines which he put in the mouth of Agamemnon were unmistakably directed at Walpole:

> . . . those dust-licking, reptile, close,
> Insinuating, speckled, smooth Court-Serpents,
> That make it so unsafe, chiefly for Kings,
> To walk this weedy World.

The following year, Thomson's friend David Mallet, another prominent member of the Prince's camp, had his tragedy *Mustapha* produced at Drury Lane. The Lord Chamberlain's office had failed to register that the characters of Solyman the Magnificent and his vizier, Rustan, were intended to represent the King and Walpole (Rustan is described as 'meanly cunning, cooly cruel,/ Grown old in arts of treachery and ruin.'). Nor did his examiner pick up the many allusions in the text to Walpole's closeness to Queen Caroline, the influence they exercised together over the King, or the Prince of Wales's estrangement from his parents.

Gradually, the Lord Chamberlain's grip tightened, and over the next few years several new plays were banned. Walpole's resignation in 1742 removed the opposition playwrights' main target, however, and the landing of the Young Pretender in Scotland in 1745 profoundly affected the public mood. Very little criticism of the government of the day would be heard on the London stage for the rest of the century, and there would be little occasion for the Lord Chamberlain to exercise his role of dramatic censor until the outbreak of the French Revolution.

To David Garrick, fresh from the provinces, such weighty matters were of little moment. If the Licensing Act shut off opportunities to many established players, it was not of great concern to a resilient, stage-struck young wine-merchant. His interest in everything that related to the theatre had quickly become all consuming. One of those he got to know was Giffard. It was through him that he had secured the business at the Bedford, a regular haunt of literary and theatre people; there, and in the other taverns and coffee-houses around the piazza in Covent Garden he sought the company of actors and writers and the opinionated young lawyers from the Inns of Court who were such vocal *habitués* of the pit. He worked at his gift for mimicry; he had some notices accepted by the newspapers; at St John's Gate, in Clerkenwell, where Johnson was now busy with hack work for Cave's *Gentleman's Magazine*, he mounted a performance of Fielding's *The Mock Doctor*.* The title role, naturally, he assumed himself and some of Cave's printers and journeymen were pressed into service to read supporting parts.

Garrick also tried his hand at writing for the stage, and on 15 April 1740 he had his first play produced at Drury Lane. *Lethe; or, Esop in the Shades* was described as 'a new Dramatic Satire'. The characters in Garrick's first farce are ferried across the Styx to Elysium by Charon; there Aesop is to be the judge of whether they may drink from the waters of Lethe and forget their troubles. This can hardly be said to add up to a plot. The piece—the French would call it a *pièce à tiroirs*—is essentially a sequence of satirical portraits; Mr and Mrs Tatoo, eager for a divorce only three months after their elopement; a bogus French marquis (in reality a hairdresser from Provence) anxious to shake off his creditors and marry English money; Mrs Riot, who fancies herself a lady of fashion, and finds her husband insufferable: 'The man talks of nothing but his money and my extravagance.'

Some of the best lines are given to the foppish Fine Gentleman, who tells Aesop how he has benefited from the three years he spent on the Grand Tour:

> . . . Sir, I learnt drinking in Germany, music and painting in Italy, dancing, gaming, and some other amusements at Paris, and in Holland—faith nothing at all. I brought over with me the best collection of Venetian ballads, two eunuchs, a French dancer, and a monkey, with toothpicks, pictures and burlettas. In short, I have skimmed the cream of every nation, and have the consolation to declare I never was in any country in my life but I had taste enough thoroughly to despise my own.[8]

The Fine Gentleman's days are passed lying in bed. Garrick's waggish account of how he spends his evenings casts doubt on the sanity of anyone who in the mid-eighteenth century chose to earn a living in the theatre:

> . . . I dress in the evening and go generally behind the scenes of both playhouses; not, you may imagine, to be diverted with the play, but to intrigue and show myself. I stand upon the stage, talk loud and stare about, which confounds the actors and disturbs the audience. Upon which the galleries, who hate the appearance of one of us, begin to hiss and cry 'Off, off!' while I undaunted stamp my foot so, loll with my shoulder thus, take snuff with my right hand and smile scornfully, thus. This exasperates the savages, and they attack us with vollies of sucked oranges and half-eaten pippins—
>
> AESOP And you retire.

* First staged in 1732, this was an adaptation of Molière's *Le Médecin malgré lui*.

FINE GENTLEMAN Without doubt, if I am sober; for orange will stain silk and an apple may disfigure a feature.[9]

After a slow start the piece established itself in the repertoire. Garrick would tinker endlessly with it over the years, and it served as a vehicle for numbers of new characterizations, notably Lord Chalkstone, which became one of his most celebrated parts. Mrs Riot, with her idiosyncratic way with words ('Oh, you *Goats* and *Vandils!*'), is a forerunner both of Mrs Heidelberg in *The Clandestine Marriage*, which Garrick later wrote with George Colman the Elder, and of Sheridan's Mrs Malaprop in *The Rivals*.

The modest role of the Drunken Man in *Lethe* had been played by the cantankerous Irish actor Charles Macklin. Although he was almost twenty years older than Garrick, a warm friendship sprang up beween the two men. Macklin had come up the hard way, and had spent many years as a stroller in the provinces before gaining a foothold in London. His appealing habit of ad libbing bits of naturalistic business was a source of friction with some of his more venerable colleagues, detracting as it did from the gravity of their high-flown declamation and stately progress about the stage.

Relations with James Quin were particularly rancorous. 'Mr Macklin,' Quin is supposed to have said, 'by the *lines*—I beg your pardon, Sir—the *cordage* of your face, you should be hanged.' In 1735 he very nearly had been. During an argument over a wig in the green room, he had lunged at a fellow-actor with his stick. The point entered the man's eye and penetrated his brain; Macklin stood trial for murder, but got off with manslaughter and was sentenced to be burned in the hand.*

Then, during the winter of 1740–41, this rough, brawling, hard-drinking son of Donegal enjoyed a sensational success. Shylock, in *The Merchant of Venice*, was traditionally portrayed as a minor character, and the part was normally played by a low comedian. Macklin, having immersed himself in Josephus and the Old Testament, produced an interpretation that was startlingly different— bold, fierce, unforgiving. The town flocked to see him. The Prince and Princess of Wales honoured him with command performances on the fourth and again on the sixteenth night. Later, when George II saw the performance, it was reported to have given him nightmares; when Walpole sighed despairingly over the difficulty of frightening the Commons into swallowing some measure or other, the monarch offered a sly suggestion: 'Vat you tink of sending dem to see dat Irishman play Shylock?' Macklin's long years in country companies had made of him a formidable jack-of-all-trades. For several years he and Garrick were very close; the younger man turned eagerly to him for advice and profited greatly from it.

A letter which Garrick wrote to Peter early in September 1740 expresses concern about the health of their mother: 'I hear by Severall hands she is in great Danger,

---

* The sentence was carried out with a cold iron.

pray my Duty, & I desire nothing may be concealed from Me.'[10] Mrs Garrick had never really got over the death of her husband three years earlier. Her condition worsened rapidly, and she was dead before the month was out.*

Garrick was later to declare that so long as his mother lived, his regard for her 'peace and happiness' would never have allowed him to appear on the stage.[11] Even after her death, however, he knew that anything so disreputable would meet with strong disapproval from the rest of the family, although Peter must have been pretty obtuse if he did not see which way the wind was blowing. 'At present very busy with Jack Arthur upon our Catapult-project', Garrick wrote in the summer of 1741. 'We have laid out above Six pounds already in Timber & ye Carpenter has almost finished ye Catapulta, I don't doubt but it will tu[rn to] good Account.' John Arthur was an actor with a talent for devising stage machinery and other theatrical devices used in pantomime. 'Jack has finish'd his Shop,' Garrick told Peter, 'and begs of You to let him know ye price of a Set of Tools you talk'd about & what tools they are, for he wants to be Set up with those materials.'†

What Garrick did not tell his brother was that in the previous month he had gone down to Ipswich with a touring company directed by Henry Giffard. There, in a short summer season, he had appeared in a range of parts that included Orestes in *Iphigenia*, Lord Foppington in *The Careless Husband* and Sir Harry Wildair in *The Constant Couple*. Suitably blacked up, he had also appeared as Aboan, a character in Thomas Southerne's old play *Oroonoko*. In this he was doubly disguised, because he masqueraded on the bills as Mr Lydall (Mrs Giffard had been a Lydall before her marriage). These performances are usually held to constitute Garrick's stage début, although he subsequently admitted to his brother that he had made a brief—and anonymous—appearance the previous winter at Goodman's Fields in the part of Harlequin.‡

Encouraged by his reception at Ipswich, Garrick now knocked at the door of both Drury Lane and Covent Garden, but neither was willing to take him on. Giffard, meanwhile, had returned to his London home at the theatre in Goodman's Fields. On 19 October, between the two parts of 'A Concert of Vocal and Instrumental Music', he offered to a thin house Colley Cibber's version of *Richard III*—'The Part of King Richard by a GENTLEMAN (*who never appear'd on any Stage*).'

The writers of theatre bills are not on oath. The form of words was common enough; there was no loss of face if the anonymous novice flopped, and if he did reasonably well he could be hailed as a prodigy. Garrick no doubt had friends in the house, but the first-night audience had no reason to entertain any particular

---

* The Lichfield Cathedral Registers record that she was buried on 28 September.

† *Letters*, 14. Some of the commissions Arthur accepted were distinctly bizarre: 'When Paul Whitehead, and Carey the surgeon, from some ridiculous pique, were determined to affront the Free Masons, by a mock procession of strange figures in a dung-cart, they applied to Arthur to furnish them with an ass's head, which he executed to their satisfaction.' (*Davies*, i, 36.)

‡ 'Yates last Season was taken very ill & was not able to begin ye Entertainment so I put on ye Dress & did 2 or three Scenes for him, but Nobody knew it but him & Giffard.'

expectations of what they were about to see. 'They had long been accustomed to an elevation of the voice,' writes Davies, 'with a sudden mechanical depression of its tones, calculated to excite admiration, and to intrap applause. To the just modulation of the words, and concurring expression of the features from the genuine workings of nature, they had been strangers, at least for some time.'[12]

There are generally, long after the event, mysteriously large numbers of people who remember being present at the birth of a star. So far as that particular Monday evening in 1741 is concerned, next to nothing has come down to us, although two particular circumstances were observed:

> One, that, on his entrance on the stage, he was under so much embarrass-ment, that for some time he was unable to speak: the other, that, having exerted himself with much vehemence on the first two acts, he became so hoarse as to be almost incapable of finishing the character. This difficulty was obviated by a person behind the scenes recommending him to take the juice of a Seville orange, which he fortunately had in his pocket.*

A short paragraph in the next day's *Daily Post and General Advertiser* said that the reception accorded to the anonymous gentleman 'was the most extra-ordinary and great that was ever known upon such an Occasion'. That may have been a piece of honest journalism or it may have been a puff. There is one other first-hand account of the events of that evening, written the following morning by a man called John Swinfen and sent to Garrick's brother Peter. Swinfen was a Lichfield man—the son of Dr Samuel Swinfen who had stood godfather to Samuel Johnson. 'For fear you should hear any false or malicious Account that may be disagreeable to you, I will give you the truth which much pleased me,' he wrote:

> I believe there was not one in the House that was not in raptures. I heard several men of judgment declare it their opinion that nobody ever excelled him in the part, and that they were surprised, with so peculiar a genius, how it was possible for him to keep off the stage so long.

Did Swinfen write entirely off his own bat? Did Garrick possibly sit at his elbow and suggest one or two helpful lines of argument? The letter certainly shows a shrewd awareness of how matters were likely to be viewed in and around the cathedral Close in Lichfield. Many of Garrick's country friends, Swinfen continued, might think there was nothing more to the theatre than the sort of performances put on in the local town hall by strolling players:

> And there are many others who, because their fathers were called Gentlemen, or perhaps themselves the first, will think it a disgrace and a scandal that the

---

* The story appears in the short account of Garrick's life which prefaced the collection of his poetical works published six years after his death (*The Poetical Works of David Garrick, Esq. now first collected into Two Volumes. With Explanatory Notes*, London, 1785). The man with the orange in his pocket was a printer called Dryden Leach, who frequently reminded his friends of the signal service he had performed to the English stage.

child of an old friend should endeavour to get an honest Livelihood, and not live all his life in a scanty manner because his father was a gentleman.

Is there a veiled allusion there to recent Garrick family history? It is quite strong stuff, and perhaps not guaranteed to have the intended effect. No matter. Swinfen takes the chance and sweeps on to his distinctly rhetorical conclusion:

> I think I know you well enough to be convinced that you have not the same sentiments, and I believe there are some other of his friends who will not alter their opinion or regard for him, till they find the stage corrupts his Morals and makes him less deserving, which I do not take to be a necessary consequence nor likely to happen to my honest friend, David.

Whether or not he was party to Swinfen's letter, Garrick knew well enough that he could no longer prevaricate about his intentions and that he must be his own leading counsel. He too now put pen to paper:

> Dear Peter
> I rec'd my Shirt safe & am now to tell You what I suppose You may have heard of before this, but before I let you into ye Affair tis proper to premise Some things that I may appear less culpable in y^r Opinion than I might Otherwise do. I have made an Exact Estimate of my Stock of wine & What Money I have out at Interest & find that Since I have been a Wine Merchant I have run out near four hundred pounds & trade not encreasing I was very Sensible some way must be thought of to redeem it. My Mind (as You must know) has been always inclin'd to ye Stage, nay so strongly so that all my Illness & lowness of Spirits was owing to my want of resolution to tell You my thoughts when here, finding at last both my Inclination & Interest requir'd some New way of Life I have chose ye most agreeable to my Self & tho I know You will bee much displeas'd at Me yet I hope when You shall find that I may have ye genius of an Actor without ye Vices, you will think Less Severe of Me & not be asham'd to own me for a Brother— I am willing to agree to any thing You shall propose about ye Wine, I will take a thorough Survey of ye Vaults & making what You have at Lich^d part of ye Stock will either Send You Y^r Share or any other way You shall propose—

Now for it:

> Last Night I play'd Richard ye Third to ye Surprize of Every Body & as I shall make very near £300 p Annum by It & as it is really what I doat upon I am resolv'd to pursue it—I believe I shall have Bowers Money wch when I have, it shall go towards my part of ye Wine You have at Lichf^d pray writ[e] me an Answer immediatly. I am D^r bro[ther]
>
> Y^{rs} Sincerely
> D Garrick
>
> I have a farce (Y^e Lying Valet) coming out at Drury Lane

Family reaction was even worse than he had expected. What precisely Peter said we no longer know, but it is plain from Garrick's reply a week later that his brother must have expressed himself forcefully. Their uncle, Louis La Condé, a well-to-do merchant in Carshalton, also appears to have weighed in with some disobliging comments about the brothers' conduct of their business.* Garrick conceded that the reputation of the stage was not all it might be ('I know in ye General it deserves Y^r Censure'), but he claimed that it was possible for actors to live 'hansomely and reputably', and cited the names of Booth and Mills and Wilks and Cibber by way of example. 'As to Company,' he continued a shade defiantly, 'ye Best in Town are desirous of Mine, & I have rec'd more Civilities & favours from Such Since my playing than I ever did in all my Life before.' But that Garrick was badly shaken is clear from the extraordinarily conciliatory note on which he ended: 'however Dear Peter so willing am I to be continu'd in y^r Affections, that were I certain of a less Income with more reputation I would gladly take to It—I have not yet had my Name in ye Bills & have play'd only ye Part of Richard ye 3^d.'[13]

It is difficult now to believe that Garrick would seriously have considered drawing back. He repeated his sensational performance on seven of the next eight nights, and news of it travelled quickly. 'His fame ran through the metropolis,' wrote Murphy:

> The public went in crowds to see a young performer, who came forth at once a complete master of his art. From the polite ends of Westminster the most elegant company flocked to Goodman's Fields, insomuch that from Temple Bar the whole way was covered with a string of coaches.[14]

One of those coaches did not come from 'the polite ends of Westminster' but had made the rather longer journey from Twickenham. 'When I was told that POPE was in the house, I instantaneously felt a palpitation at my heart,' Garrick told his friend Percival Stockdale many years later:

> As I opened the part, I saw our little poetical hero, dressed in black, seated in a sidebox near the stage; and viewing me with a serious, and earnest attention. His look shot, and thrilled, like lightning through my frame; and I had some hesitation in proceeding, from anxiety, and from joy.

To his friend Lord Orrery, who sat with him in the box, Pope is supposed to have said, 'I am afraid the young man will be spoiled, for he will have no competitor.'[15]

Garrick was still clutching the cloak of anonymity about him on 28 October when Clodio in Cibber's *Love Makes a Man* was played 'By the Gentleman who

---

* Garrick had written to his cousin, Peter Fermignac, a lawyer who lived at Clay Hill, Middlesex, saying much what he had said to Peter, and asking him to break the news to their aunt and uncle. Fermignac sent them a copy of Garrick's letter, with a covering note saying that he was 'very Sorry for the Contents'. (*Letters*, 16.)

perform'd King Richard'; indeed the designation was by now a formidable crowd-puller. They flocked to see him as Chamont in Otway's *The Orphan* on 6 November and as Jack Smatter in a stage adaptation of Richardson's *Pamela*. Peter and his sisters remained hostile to what he was doing but, by the middle of November, Garrick was taking a harder and more confident line:

> Dear Brother.
> I am very Sorry You still Seem so utterly Averse to What I am so greatly Inclin'd & to What ye best Judges think I have ye Greatest Genius for— The Great nay incredible Success & approbation I have met with from ye Greatest Persons in England have almost made Me resolve (tho Im sorry to Say it against Y^r Entreaties) to pursue it as I certainly shall make a fortune by it, if Health continues—Mr Littleton Mr Pit & Several Other Members of Parliament were to See Me play Chamont in ye Orphan & Mr Pit, who is reckon'd ye Greatest Orator in the house of Commons, said I was ye best Actor ye English Stage had produc'd, & he Sent a Gentleman to Me to let Me know he and ye Other Gentlemen would be glad to See Me—the Prince has heard so great a Character of Me that we are in daily Expectations of his comming to See Me . . . . .*

He was playing old men, young men, men who were neither one nor the other; he was appearing in comedy and in tragedy and in farce. 'I have ye Judgment of ye best Judges,' he wrote to Peter towards the end of November, 'that I shall turn out (nay they Say I am) not only ye Best Trajedian but Comedian in England. I would not say so much to any body else, but as this may Somewhat palliate My Folly you must Excuse me.'

This flurry of letters to his brother in the closing weeks of 1741 tell us a great deal about Garrick—his deep sense of family obligation, his native Huguenot caution, his instinct to avoid confrontation. 'We have greater Business than Either Drury Lane or Covent Garden,' he told Peter excitedly; he had 'great Offers' from Fleetwood, the manager of Drury Lane; and yet even now, with London at his feet, he still chose to present his decision in terms suggesting that he could just conceivably change his mind—'I may now venture to tell You I am very near quite resolv'd to be a player.' And he was still at great pains not merely to mollify Peter but to reassure him about the prospects for their business:

> As to hurting you in Y^r affairs it shall be my constant Endeavours to promote Y^r Welfare with my all; If you should want Money & I have it You shall command my whole & I know I shall soon be more able by playing & writing to do You Service than any other Way.[16]

* *Letters*, 18. George Lyttelton, later the first Baron Lyttelton, had been the MP for Okehampton since 1735. A strenuous opponent of Walpole's, he composed, together with Pitt and the Grenvilles, the 'Cobhamite' party. A poet as well as a politician, he was the friend of Pope, Shenstone and Fielding and a liberal patron of literature. He was caricatured as Scragg by Smollett in *Peregrine Pickle* and gored by Johnson in *The Lives of the Poets*.

He wrote these words on a Tuesday night. Four days later the fiction of anonymity was abandoned. On Saturday 28 November he played Chamont again, and his name was on the playbills. He had crossed his professional Rubicon. He appeared in the same part again two days later, and also played the lead in his own new farce *The Lying Valet*, originally destined for Drury Lane*—the first of many occasions during the season when he played in both the main piece and the after piece.

He sent the text of his play to Peter. 'The Valet takes prodigiously,' he wrote jubilantly, '& is approv'd of by Men of genius & thought yᵉ Most diverting Farce that ever was perform'd; I believe You'll find it read pretty well, & in performance tis a general Roar from beginning to End.'[17]

The farce still reads well today. Garrick based it on a translation of a French verse comedy called *Le Souper mal apprêté*, written in the previous century by Noël-Jacques le Breton, sieur de Hauteroche. A prodigal youth, Charles Gayless, seeks escape from his creditors in marriage. Sentimental in tone—it is the only one of Garrick's plays in which the hero ends up as a reformed character—the piece is fast moving and the dialogue amusing. Sharp, the scheming valet, stands in a clear line of descent from Molière's Scapin and Mascarille. Over the next thirty-five years the piece would have almost 400 London performances, and Garrick's appearance as Sharp never failed to raise that 'general Roar' of which he boasted to Peter.

He was frantically busy, not just on the stage but in trying to wind up his business affairs. 'I am making out yᵉ Bills & will get in yᵉ Money as fast as I can,' he told Peter. 'I don't design to bottle any more wine, but Sell yᵉ rest in Cask.' His next letter, before going on to detail his latest triumphs at Goodman's Fields, was also about Durham Yard: 'Ye Two Pipes of Testace's Port will be wᵗʰ You on Saturday—I shall pay Farnell's Bill immediatly.'[18]

Garrick also passed on the latest political news from the capital: 'Sʳ Robᵗ is in a very bad hole & I believe He Cant find a Rope strong enough not even in yᵉ Treasury to draw him out of It.' Garrick was right. Walpole, his majority paper-thin, had been defeated on 28 January by one vote after eight weeks of ferocious wrangling—not on some great issue of state, but on a question relating to an election petition in the constituency of Chippenham. The Orders of the Bath and the Garter were already his. He now retired with a pension of £4,000 and an earldom, procuring in the process the rank and precedence of an earl's daughter for one of his illegitimate daughters. When he encountered his old rival Pulteney for the first time in the House of Lords, his greeting reflected ironically on the eminence to which he had raised the House of Commons: 'You and I, my lord, are now two as insignificant men as any in England.'

Political drama at Westminster did nothing to detract from the exciting theatrical fare offered on the smaller stage at Goodman's Fields, and the coaches of the beau monde continued to jam the road to Whitechapel. Garrick had acted

---

* The presumption is that Giffard made him a better offer.

Lothario in Nicholas Rowe's *The Fair Penitent* on 2 December (it was his benefit night), the Ghost in *Hamlet* a week later, Fondlewife in Congreve's *The Old Bachelor* on 5 January and Costar Pearmain in *The Recruiting Officer* on 14 January. He had played Aboan again on 23 January and Witwoud in Congreve's *The Way of the World* four nights later.

There was living at the time in London a man of the cloth from Lichfield who took a close and, on the whole, sympathetic interest in the success of his fellow-townsman. This was the Reverend Thomas Newton, the son of a brandy and cider merchant, who had gone on from the grammar school to Westminster and Trinity College, Cambridge. Now a fashionable and ambitious young clergyman in his thirties, Newton was currently tutor to the family of Lord Carpenter, reader and afternoon preacher at the Grosvenor Chapel in South Audley Street and also an assistant preacher at St George's, Hanover Square. He took to writing Garrick inordinately long letters in which he offered him the benefit of his advice on his various performances:

> . . . . . Richard says to Buckingham, comparing the young Princes to spiders,
> 'I would have some friend *to tread upon them.*'
> Your action there was only with your hand, but surely it should rather have been with a little stamp of your foot *to tread upon them.* These I cannot call faults, they are omissions which might be occasioned by absence of thought at the instant; but though it is easy to reckon up these little oversights, for these are all I could observe, it is not easy to count your beauties and excellencies, which are indeed innumerable. All that we wanted was to see more of your face and the expression of your countenance; and therefore beg you will remember to secure for us that stage-box where we may see your looks in the scene with Lady Ann, and as you lie upon the couch, that is, that we may sit with the stage on our right hand, and the pit on our left . . . . .[19]

Newton became distinctly importunate in the matter of asking for seats. A few weeks later he solicited a front box, telling Garrick that Mr Pulteney would be of the party. Garrick, it seems, was unable to oblige, and this earned him a note that began by being stuffy but quickly became censorious:

> It would certainly have been a very great honour to you, if of no other advantage, for such a person as Mr. Pulteney to come so far to be one of your audience; and, if I had been in your capacity, I should have thought it worth while to have strained a point, or done almost any thing, rather than have disappointed him . . . . . I am sorry for these disappointments, but I was almost angry with you, to see your name last week in the bills for Costar Pearmain. I am not fond of your acting such parts as Fondlewife, or even Clodio, nor should be of the Lying Valet, if it was not of your own writing. You who are equal to the greatest parts, strangely demean yourself in acting any thing that is low and little; and not only I, but really all who admire you and wish you well, that is all who know you, are

grieved and wonder at it. There are abundance of people who hit off low humour, and succeed in the coxcomb and the buffoon very well; but there is scarce one in an age who is capable of acting the hero in Tragedy, and the fine gentleman in comedy. . . . .[20]

Criticism privately expressed was one thing. Garrick would soon have his first taste of something less agreeable—malicious gossip in the public prints. On 3 February 1742 he appeared for the first time as Bayes in *The Rehearsal* by George Villiers, second Duke of Buckingham, son of the favourite of Charles I.* This celebrated comedy had originally satirized the heroic dramas of such writers as Davenant, Killigrew and Dryden—scholars have identified some seventeen plays parodied in it.† It had been in the repertory since 1671, and was constantly revived with the insertion of new topical allusions, much as the Savoy operas of Gilbert and Sullivan would be in a later age.

Bayes, a playwright, takes two friends to a rehearsal of his new tragedy. He fails totally in his attempts to explain the absurdities of the plot, and is even less successful in his efforts to coach the bewildered players as they blunder about the stage. To someone like Garrick, with his talent for mimicry, it offered enormous scope, and the temptation to take off some of the older-established members of his new profession was irresistible.

Lacy Ryan, now well into his forties, and long established at Covent Garden, was one obvious target. Brought up in the tradition of Betterton and Booth, he was a spirited and impassioned Orestes and celebrated for his Iago, but he moved his head awkwardly and some thought his voice harsh and dissonant. Roger Bridgwater, a dancer as well as an actor, had also been around a long time, specializing in the weightier dramatic roles—'in Tamerlane,' Davies writes, 'he was solemnly drowsy in speaking, and struttingly insignificant in action.' Then there was Dennis Delane, an Irishman like so many actors in the eighteenth century.‡ Originally intended for the bar, he had developed a substantial repertoire, mainly of tragic roles. Admired as Alexander the Great in Nathaniel Lee's *The Rival Queens*, he had enjoyed considerable success at both Goodman's Fields and Covent Garden, and in September 1741 he had made his début at Drury Lane as Othello.

'To the Duke of Buckingham's admirable satire, Garrick was able to make a considerable, and, indeed, requisite addition,' wrote Murphy:

* Buckingham had a number of collaborators, variously held to include Samuel Butler, the author of *Hudibras*, Thomas Sprat, later Bishop of Rochester, Martin Clifford, subsequently Master of Charterhouse and the poets Abraham Cowley and Edmund Waller.
† Dryden retaliated ten years later by depicting Buckingham as Zimri in his satirical poem *Absalom and Achitophel*.
‡ Eighteenth-century Dublin is sometimes described as the nursery for the English stage. Wilks, Doggett, Delane, Quin and Macklin were all Irish, as were Mrs Clive and Miss Bellamy. Later in the century came Miss Farren, Mrs Fitzhenry and Mrs Jordan. The roll of Irish dramatists— Farquhar, Southerne, Goldsmith, Sheridan—was also an impressive one, while Steele and Congreve, each with one Irish parent, might be allowed dual nationality.

The actors had lost all judgement; the vicious taste of the poets introduced a total departure from nature; and, to vie with their authors, the best performers of the day had recourse to strutting, mouthing, and bellowing. . . . . Delane was at the head of his profession. He was tall and comely; had a clear and strong voice, but was a mere declaimer. Garrick began with him: he retired to the upper part of the stage, and drawing his left arm across his breast, rested his right elbow on it, raising a finger to his nose, and then came forward in a stately gait, nodding his head, as he advanced, and, in the exact tone of Delane, spoke the following lines:

> So boar and sow, when any storm is nigh,
> Snuff up, and smell it gath'ring in the sky.
> Boar beckons to the sow in chesnut groves,
> And there consummate their unfinished loves,
> Pensive in mud they wallow all alone,
> And snort, and gruntle to each other's moan.*

Davies notes that Garrick's interpretation of Bayes differed conspicuously from that of his immediate predecessors:

> They, by their action, told the spectators that they felt all the ridicule of the part; he appeared quite ignorant of the joke that made against him. They seemed to sneer, at the folly of Bayes *with* the audience; the audience laughed loudly *at* him.[21]

Garrick got himself up for the part in a shabby old-fashioned coat, cut-fingered gloves, red-heeled shoes and a small hat perched on a flowing brown wig. It was a triumph. 'Instead of clapping Me they huzza wch is very uncommon approbation,' he told Peter—'& tho The Town has been quite tir'd out with ye Play at ye Other End of ye Town Yet I have ye Great Satisfaction to See crowded Audiences to It Every Night.' Physically, his success acted like a tonic:

> I never was better in health in my Life & can undergo fatigue like a little Hercules, wch makes me of Opinion that Sobriety & regularity will at any time put an Indifferent Constitution upon an equality with a Good one without those Advantages—[22]

The little Hercules spoke too soon. After seven consecutive performances of *The Rehearsal* he developed a fever and was unable to appear. His Bayes may have earned him 'uncommon approbation' but it had also, inevitably, made him enemies, and there were malicious tongues in the coffee-houses who put it about that the new prodigy was not ill at all—had, indeed, been seen at the ridottos. An older and less thin-skinned man would have ignored such nonsense, but

---

* *Murphy*, i, 53–4. Tate Wilkinson and others put it about that Garrick's mimicry drove Delane to drink and an early grave, but this is nonsense. His attachment to the bottle was of long standing. He continued to act at both Drury Lane and Covent Garden for several more seasons, and did not die until 1750.

Garrick's temper flared and he dashed off an unwisely worded card for insertion in the *Daily Post and General Advertiser*:

> Whereas it has been industriously reported to my prejudice, that I was at the Masquerade in the Habit of a Madman; this is to assure the Gentlemen or Ladies, who are offended at me, without Cause, I was not at either of the Masquerades this Season, as can be testify'd by several Gentlemen in whose Company I was. If any Person has a Mind to be further satisfy'd, I will fully convince them of the Truth of this Advertisement. David Garrick.

Garrick's detractors no doubt sniggered behind their hands, but none stepped forward to pick up the gauntlet. There is, however, a story that went round the green rooms at the time which offers a different explanation of his absence from the stage. This suggests that Garrick was initially nervous about taking off his fellow actors, and proposed to Giffard that it would make matters easier if he included him in his gallery of impressions. Giffard gave his agreement to this, assuming that Garrick would let him off lightly—the phrase used was that he would 'just glance at him'. When he saw what Garrick made of him at rehearsal, however, he felt that he had been made to look ridiculous, and sent him a challenge; they met the following morning, and Garrick sustained a slight wound in his sword arm. The first night was put off, and it was announced that this was 'on account of the sudden indisposition of a principal performer'. When the play was finally performed, the imitation of Giffard was omitted.* His feathers may have been momentarily ruffled by Garrick's exuberance as a mimic, but Giffard could be in no doubt that his young friend was now a very hot theatrical property, and he prudently recognized this by allowing him half of the profits (Garrick had until now been paid six guineas a week).

In the spring of 1742 Garrick attempted something which today, for a young man in his first season as a professional actor, would be not only impossible but also inconceivable. On 11 March he appeared at Goodman's Fields in *The True and Ancient History of King Lear and His Three Daughters*. He had taken advice on the interpretation of the role from Macklin and from a convivial acquaintance of theirs called Barrowby, who was a physician.† On the first night they were disappointed. He had not, they said, 'caught the spirit of old age'—not, perhaps, an altogether surprising deficiency in one who had just passed his twenty-fifth birthday. By the middle of April, however, after seven more appearances in the role, his performance was being widely praised and earned him an effusive letter from Thomas Newton:

---

* The difficulty about this version is that during the fortnight of the play's postponement, Garrick's name appears regularly in the bills as playing other parts. The authority for the story, on the other hand, was Cooke, the biographer of Macklin, an experienced theatre critic whose ear was normally fairly close to the ground.

† William Barrowby (1682–1751) had been a Fellow of the College of Physicians since 1718 and of the Royal Society since 1721. The Rawlinson MSS in the Bodleian describe him as 'a monster of lewdness and profaneness'.

It is not only my opinion, but several good judges I know, and particularly one of the Masters of Westminster School, and one of the Chief Clerks in the Treasury, say that you far exceed Booth in that character, and even equal Betterton. The thing that strikes me above all others, is that variety in your acting, and your being so totally a different man in Lear from what you are in Richard. There is a sameness in every other actor, Cibber is something of a coxcomb in every thing; and Wolsey, and Syphax, and Iago, all smell strong of the essence of Lord Foppington. Booth was a philosopher in Cato, and was a philosopher in every thing else. His passion in Hotspur and Lear was much of the same nature, whereas yours was an old man's passion, and an old man's voice and action; and in the four parts wherein I have seen you, Richard, Chamont, Bayes, and Lear, I never saw four actors more different from one another than you are from yourself.*

Shakespeare would have admired some parts of the performance more than others. The *Lear* in which Garrick first appeared in 1742 was the 'improved' version written sixty-one years previously by the Restoration poetaster Nahum Tate.† Shakespeare's text offended against the canons of neo-classical taste in a number of ways. It had two plots, and therefore violated one of the three unities; it was also guilty, by introducing the comic figure of the Fool into a tragedy, of mixing the genres—if anything, an even more heinous breach of dramatic decorum.

Tate attended to these deficiencies by eliminating the Fool, introducing a love interest (Cordelia is enamoured of Edgar) and subscribing to the law of poetic justice by contriving a happy ending—at the end of Act V Albany restores to Lear that part of his kingdom which was not included in his marriage contract and Lear makes it over to Cordelia and Edgar. This all accorded very well with the sentimental proclivities of the eighteenth-century theatregoer. The love of Edgar and Cordelia, wrote Arthur Murphy, and the restoration of the crown to Lear, 'can never fail to produce those gushing tears, which are swelled and ennobled by a virtuous joy'.[23]

Apart from cutting the text by about a third, Tate also believed that he could improve on Shakespeare's way with words. If the effect of his changes to the plot is to make *Lear* an altogether blander affair, however, some of his liberties

---

* *Boaden*, i, 7. Letter dated 19 April 1742. Before the end of the season in May Macklin too thought much more highly of his protégé's performance. The curse scene, he said, 'seemed to electrify the audience with horror. The words "kill—kill—kill" echoed all the revenge of a frantic king, whilst he exhibited such a scene of the pathetic discovering his daughter Cordelia as drew tears of commiseration from the whole house.' (Cooke, William, *Memoirs of Charles Macklin*, London, 1804, p. 107. Cited hereafter as *Cooke*.)

† Tate (1652–1715), with Dryden, was the author of the second part of *Absalom and Achitophel*. He also wrote the libretto of Purcell's *Dido and Aeneas*, and is credited with the words of 'While shepherds watched their flocks by night'. He was appointed Poet Laureate in 1692 and Historiographer Royal ten years later. Pilloried by Pope in *The Dunciad*, his chief original poem is 'Panacea—a poem on Tea'.

with the text are distinctly bloodthirsty. In Act II, for example, where Regan questions her father's need for retainers, Tate clearly felt that Shakespeare's 'O reason not the need' was inadequate, and provides Lear with a more spirited response:

> Blood! Fire! here—Leprosies and bluest Plagues!
> Room, room for Hell to belch her Horrors up
> And drench the *Circes* in a stream of Fire;
> Hark how th'Infernals eccho to my Rage
> Their Whips and Snakes—*

Garrick had agreed with Giffard that he should have two benefits, and for the second of them he had chosen to play not only Lear (it was his third appearance in the role), but also the lumpish, fifteen-year-old Master Johnny in Cibber's *The School Boy*, which was presented as the afterpiece. It was a remarkable display of versatility—and of stamina.† Tickets were to be had at Tom's Coffee-House, Cornhill and at Garrick's lodgings, which were then in Mansfield Street, Goodman's Fields. A well-known passage in Murphy describes how Garrick's study of Lear's madness was informed by a domestic tragedy which befell a neighbour of his there:

> He was acquainted with a worthy man, who lived in Leman-street, Goodman's Fields; this friend had an only daughter, about two years old; he stood at his dining room window, fondling the child, and dangling it in his arms, when it was his misfortune to drop the infant into a flagged area, and killed it on the spot. . . . . . He lost his senses, and from that moment never recovered his understanding. . . . . . Garrick frequently went to see his distracted friend, who passed the remainder of his life in going to the window, and there playing in fancy with his child. After some dalliance, he dropped it, and, bursting into a flood of tears, filled the house with shrieks of grief and bitter anguish. He then sat down, in a pensive mood, his eyes fixed on one object, at times looking slowly round him, as if to implore compassion. . . . . . There it was, said Garrick, *that I learned to imitate madness*; I copied nature, and to that owed my success in *King Lear*.[24]

Immediately after his début as Lear Garrick added to his repertoire the part of Lord Foppington in Colley Cibber's *The Careless Husband*, and at the beginning of April he made his début as Pierre in Otway's *Venice Preserv'd*.‡ The egregious Thomas Newton was still regularly shepherding his aristocratic patrons down to Goodman's Fields, all of them now apparently in a state of more or less

---

* On the other hand, Tate clearly considered that Shakespeare was too free with his figures of speech: 'lilly-liver'd' becomes 'white-liver'd'.
† The audience needed stamina, too. That night's programme also included *The Leek,* billed as 'a new Comic Dance by David and Winifred ApShenkin'.
‡ He appeared the same evening in the afterpiece, which was his own *The Lying Valet*.

continuous rapture. But he was also able to report an altogether more important expression of approval:

> Mrs. Porter is no less in raptures than the rest; she returned to town on purpose to see you, and declares she would not but have come for the world. You are born an actor, she says, and do more at your first appearing, than ever any body did with twenty years' practice; and, Good God, says she, what will he be in time! And when somebody in company mentioned your not doing Lord Foppington so well, she made answer, that she was sure it was impossible for you to do any thing ill; you might perhaps excel less in that, but you must excel in every thing.[25]

The redoubtable Molly Porter was now close to the end of her long career, but she had had no rival as a tragedienne since the 1720s.* Praise from her was worth a great deal.

Garrick was assiduous in keeping his brother and sisters in Lichfield posted about his growing reputation. 'The favour I meet with from yᵉ Greatest Men has made me far from Repenting of my Choice,' he wrote to Peter as the season drew to a close:

> I have sup'd twice wᵗʰ yᵉ Great Mr Murray Councellʳ & Shall with Mʳ Pope by his Introduction—I sup'd wᵗʰ yᵉ Mr Littleton yᵉ Prince's Favourite last Thursday night & Met with yᵉ highest Civility & complaisance, He told me he never knew wᵗ Acting was till I appear'd & Said I was only born to act wᵗ Shakespear writ, these Things daily occurring give me great Pleasure I din'd with Lᵈ Hallifax & Lᵈ Sandwich Two very ingenious Noblemen Yesterday & am to dine at Lᵈ Hallifax's next Sunday with Lᵈ Chesterfield.†

Some accounts of Garrick's meteoric first season suggest that his success at Goodman's Fields emptied the pit and boxes at Covent Garden and Drury Lane and threw their managers into a panic. It was not, in fact, quite like that. The patent houses maintained large and talented companies—88 strong at Drury Lane, 98 at Covent Garden. Accounts for Covent Garden do not survive, but receipts for that season at Drury Lane were extremely healthy and amounted to a gross figure of more than £18,000.‡

---

* Samuel Johnson told Mrs Siddons that 'in the vehemence of tragic rage' he had never seen Mrs Porter equalled (*Life*, iv, 243). Off stage she was celebrated for having levelled a brace of pistols at a highwayman who unwisely stopped her one night as she drove home alone to Hendon.

† *Letters*, 23. William Murray (1705–93), later first Earl of Mansfield and Lord Chief Justice, was a brilliant young lawyer who in 1742 was made Solicitor-General. In parliamentary debate, he would be outshone only by Chatham; Macaulay described him as 'the father of modern toryism'. Halifax and Sandwich, fashionable young noblemen, were closer to Garrick in age; both were on the threshold of long political careers.

‡ The figures are preserved in the John Rylands Library in Manchester.

Both managements, however, were quick to realize that they had made an expensive mistake in failing to take Garrick on. Rich, the manager at Covent Garden, seems to have been the first to put out feelers. 'My Lord Essex has sent word Just now he would be glad to See me to Morrow,' Garrick wrote to Peter at the end of January 1742. 'I guess it must be t[o] Engage me next Season for Rich but I have fixt my Mind upon Drury Lane, tho 'tis quite a Secret—'[26] By the middle of April, five or six weeks before the end of the season, nothing had been decided although Garrick told Peter that he would certainly be 'at ye Other End of ye Town'. The inducement held out by Fleetwood at Drury Lane was a substantial one—'I am offer'd £500 Guinea & a Clear Benefit or Part of ye Management; I can't be resolv'd w^t I shall do till ye Season is finish'd.'[27]

In the event he made his mind up rather more quickly. He played at Goodman's Fields for the last time on 24 May, taking the part of Lothario in *The Fair Penitent* and Sharp in his own *Lying Valet*. Two days later he made his début at Drury Lane in *The Rehearsal*, replacing Theophilus Cibber as Bayes. The next night he played Lear and on 31 May he closed the season, as he had begun it, by playing Richard III. The circumstances, however, were rather different. There was nothing anonymous about his last appearance of the season. The bills, what is more, announced that the performance was 'By Command of their Royal Highnesses the Duke, and the Princesses Amelia, Caroline, and Louisa'. Horace Walpole, in his sniffy way, had described him as 'the young wine merchant turned player at Goodman's Fields'. As the crow flies, Drury Lane was only a few miles to the west, but the distance travelled by the young wine merchant in those seven short months was immeasurably greater than that.

Now, as summer came on, he set off on another journey. An invitation had come from Dublin to play at the Smock Alley Theatre, and in the first week in June Garrick posted down to Park Gate, near Chester, to make the tedious and sometimes dangerous crossing of the Irish Sea. He did not travel alone. 'There is much in vogue a Mrs Woffington,' Horace Walpole had written to his cousin Horace Mann a few months previously. 'A bad actress, but she has life.' She had played Cordelia to Garrick's Lear at Drury Lane, and the whole town knew that he had been in love with her for some time. ('You may have heard too that I am Married, but I will assure You 'tis false,' he had written to his brother during the winter, though he had added, 'You may be Sure of ye first intelligence.')*

---

* *Letters*, 21. Garrick and Woffington were accompanied to Dublin by Barbarina Campanini, a brilliant young Italian ballet dancer who had made her début in Paris three years previously in Rameau's *Les Fêtes d'Hébé* and distributed her favours widely among the French nobility. 'La Barbarina' later enjoyed great success at the Court of Frederick the Great, and was married for a time to the son of the emperor's Grand Chancellor.

4

Garrick Fever

Almost everything about Peg Woffington's parentage and early life is obscure. In the parish church at Teddington where she lies buried a memorial inscription records her date of birth as 1720; Joseph Knight, in the *Dictionary of National Biography*, favoured 1714. Was she the daughter of 'reputable Parents, who gave her a genteel education'[1] or of a poor bricklayer who died young, leaving his family in poverty? Long after she was dead, the actor Charles Lee Lewes waxed maudlin in his *Memoirs* about her childhood:

> I have met with more than one in Dublin, who assured me, that they remember to have seen the lovely Peggy, with a little dish upon her hand, and without shoes to cover her delicate feet, crying through College-green, Dame-street, and other parts of that end of town—'All this fine young salad for a halfpenny—all for a halfpenny . . . .'*

What is certain is that as a young girl she was taken up by the Italian rope dancer and tumbler Signora Violante, whose feats included dancing on the rope with pails of water on her legs or with a man tied to each foot.† In the early 1730s she had a booth at Fownes's Court in Dublin. One of the entertainments she presented there was a pirated Lilliputian version of *The Beggar's Opera*, and in this Peg Woffington played Macheath. In 1732 Signora Violante took this production to London, and there, at the Haymarket Theatre, the part of Polly was sung by 'the celebrated Miss Woffington'.

By 1735 she was employed at the Aungier Street Theatre in Dublin, dancing and acting as well as singing. Early in 1738 she went off to join a troupe in Paris. Back in Ireland at the end of the following year, she began to win important parts—the title role in Charles Shadwell's *The Fair Quaker of Deal*, and two

---

* *The Memoirs of Charles Lee Lewes, containing anecdotes, historical and biographical, of the English and Scottish stages, during a period of forty years*, was edited by Lewes's son, John Lee Lewes and published in four volumes in 1805. 'Among theatrical compilations,' Joseph Knight wrote severely in the *Dictionary of National Biography*, 'it has an unenviable precedency of worthlessness.'

† Her husband, whose name was Larini, was an accomplished rope slider. On a visit to Bristol in 1728 he descended from the top of St Vincent's Rocks to the other side of the river. Later, in a less successful performance, he accidentally hanged himself.

so-called 'breeches roles' in plays by Farquhar—Silvia in *The Recruiting Officer*, and Sir Harry Wildair in *The Constant Couple*. These allowed her to show off her legs, which were shapely, and she scored an enormous success with the Dublin audience. She also caught the eye of Theobald Taaffe, the dissolute son of an Irish peer, who is said to have enticed her to his country mansion, proposed marriage, seduced her, and then decided to marry money instead.

She went to London and called on John Rich, the manager of Covent Garden, famous as Harlequin and for his eccentricities. Fitzgerald, rather quaintly, writes of his 'odd, blunt, "Abernethy" manner' and says that he had 'a kind of provincial dialect',[2] which, if it was the case, sounds like an affectation, because he was born in London, the son of the lawyer and theatre manager Christopher Rich, and spent all his life there. One of his attested oddities was to address everybody as 'Muster' and to mangle their names. It seems likely that this too was intentional—Garrick was Griskin, Foote Footseye, Barry Barleymore, Sparks Sparkish.*

The story goes that when Woffington was admitted to his house in Bloomsbury Square, she found Rich lolling on a couch, a play-book in one hand, a china tea cup in the other:

> Round him, *upon* him, and *about* him, were seven-and-twenty Cats of different Sizes, Ages, and Complexions. Some were staring him in the Face, some eating the Toast and Butter out of his Mouth, some licking the Cream out of a Cup, some frisking about, some lying down, some perched upon his Knee, some upon his Head.†

Sir Joshua Reynolds wrote later that Rich told him it was fortunate for his wife that he was not of a susceptible temperament: 'Had it been otherwise, I should have found it difficult to retain my equanimity enough to arrange business negotiations with the amalgamated Calypso, Circe and Armida who dazzled my eyes.'‡

The 'dazzling amalgamation' made her début at Covent Garden in November 1740 in a performance commanded by the Prince of Wales. She appeared as Silvia in *The Recruiting Officer*, in which the heroine first appears demurely in skirts

---

* The theatre manager Tate Wilkinson said that when he suggested Ned Shuter for the part of the Gardener in *The Spirit of Contradiction*, Rich 'took his snuff, stroked his cat, and said, "If I give it to *Muster Shuttleworth* he will not let me teach him, and he is so idle: I want it perfect *Muster Williamskin*; but I will *larn* you *Muster*, if you will play the part from my tuition." '

† The Woffington has not been lucky in her biographers. This anecdote appears in *Memoirs of the celebrated Mrs. W*ff**gt*n. Interspersed with several theatrical anecdotes; the amours of many persons of the first rank . . . drawn from real life*, which appeared after her death in 1760. The encounter is the subject of an amusing engraving by Finden, after Smallfield, in the Harvard Theater Collection.

‡ Rich, who had spent a lot of the fortune he had made out of *The Beggar's Opera* on horses and women, was romancing. In 1740 his second wife had been dead for three years, and he did not marry his third until 1744. She was a Methodist, and apparently took him in hand. Smollett, in *Roderick Random*, portrayed her as greedy and tyrannical and Rich as having a head 'disordered with superstition'.

*John Rich as Harlequin. 'They may say what they will of the Hero of Drury Lane,' wrote Arthur Murphy: 'he only imitates Men, whereas the Covent-garden chief converts himself into a wild Beast, a Bird, or a Serpent with a long Tail, and what not . . .' (*The London Stage, *part IV, Volume ii)*

and later dressed as a boy. London was as enthusiastic as Dublin had been. A correspondent in the *Daily Post and General Advertiser* was moved to rhyme:

> *When first in petticoats you trod the stage,*
> *Our sex with love you fired, your own with rage:*
> *In breeches next, so well you played the cheat—*
> *The pretty fellow and the rake complete—*
> *Each sex was then with different passions moved:*
> *The men grew envious and the women loved!*

Later in the month she appeared as Sir Harry Wildair in *The Constant Couple*. She played the part in ten successive performances, two of them by royal command; the Prince of Wales was present on 25 November, and two nights later, not to be outdone, the King made an appearance. This run gave rise to the best known of all Woffington anecdotes, though whether it originated in the playhouse or in the imagination of some coffee-house wit cannot now be determined:

> This agreeable Actress, in the Part of Sir *Harry*, coming into the Green-Room, said, pleasantly, *In my Conscience! I believe Half the Men in the House take me for one of their own Sex.* Another Actress reply'd, *It may be so; but, in my Conscience! the other Half can convince them to the contrary.**

Woffington's agreement with Rich stipulated that she should be paid five guineas a week. The Covent Garden account book for that season[3] also shows that £12 was laid out on an embroidered waistcoat for her, presumably part of her costume as Wildair. She was not entirely dependent on her theatrical earnings, however. She was besieged by admirers from the moment she appeared in London, and quickly became the mistress of the Earl of Darnley. Horace Walpole, in a letter to Horace Mann in Rome, passed on a coarse tale that was going the rounds about them:

> One night that she played Sir Harry Wildair, he told her, she had pleased him so well, that he should play five acts that night as well as she: she offered to bet him ten guineas, that he did not—but he did—and then asked her to pay him—'No, my Lord,' said she, 'double or quit!'†

Before the season was out Woffington quarrelled with Rich over money and she did not appear at Covent Garden after 20 April. She went off with Darnley to Tunbridge Wells and Bath during the summer recess, made a fleeting appearance at Goodman's Fields in September and was then snapped up by Drury Lane. Her

---

* The story first appears in Chetwood. Others attribute the retort to James Quin or to Kitty Clive, but they were both at Drury Lane that season.

† *Walpole*, xxi, 157, letter dated 21 October 1741 OS. Walpole, like many gossips, was sometimes careless of detail. Ten years later he told Mann the same story again, but on this occasion he made Taaffe its hero. (*Ibid.*, xx, 87. Letter dated 22 November 1751, OS.)

first appearance there was in September 1741 as Mrs Sullen in Farquhar's *The Beaux' Stratagem*, with Kitty Clive in the part of Cherry.

Mrs Clive, forthright and abrasive, had been established at Drury Lane for the past dozen seasons, and was now, at thirty, recognized as the outstanding comedy actress and singer on the London stage. It did not take long for hostilities to break out. Lady Hertford, writing to her son in January 1742, described one of the early skirmishes:

> About ten days ago Mrs Woffington and Mrs Clive met in the Green room. Mrs Woffington came up to Mrs Clive and told her she had long looked for the favour of a visit from her and begged she would let her know when she designed her that pleasure, for she was often engag'd in an afternoon. Mrs Clive paused a little and then answered, Madam, I have a reputation to lose. Madam, said Mrs Woffington, so should I have too if I had your face.*

Exchanges like these did not make it likelier that Clive would cede any of the roles Woffington coveted. Clive, after all, had been round that course before. A few years previously she had seen off the shifty Fleetwood when he had tried to take the part of Polly in *The Beggar's Opera* from her and give it to Mrs Cibber. Clive carried the battle vigorously into the public prints with a spirited letter to the *London Daily Post and General Advertiser*. It was, she wrote, 'a receiv'd Maxim in the Theatre, That no Actor or Actress shall be depriv'd of a Part in which they have been well receiv'd, until they are render'd incapable of performing it either by Age or Sickness'.[4] It took her three months, but she carried the day.

Woffington managed to add a number of substantial new roles to her repertoire in the course of the 1741–2 London season, for all that—Rosalind in *As You Like It*, Lady Brute in Vanbrugh's *The Provok'd Wife*, Clarinda in *The Double Gallant* and Lady Betty in *The Careless Husband*, both by Colley Cibber. Now, in the summer of 1742, she was topping the bill in Dublin with Garrick.

Percy Fitzgerald, Garrick's nineteenth-century biographer, compared eighteenth-century Dublin with one of those small German courts where an Elector or a Grand Duke reigned. The blessings secured to England by the 'Glorious Revolution' of 1689 had not been extended to John Bull's Other Island. The Protestant ascendancy went unchallenged in church and law and there was little semblance of constitutional or responsible government.

The Irish House of Commons was even more packed with members from pocket or rotten boroughs than the mother of Parliaments. Elections were practically unknown—in the reign of George II the same Parliament sat for

---

* Quoted in *Biographical Dictionary of Actors, Actresses, &c.*, A, Highfill, Philip H., Jr, Burnim, Kalman A. and Langhans, Edward A., 16 vols., Carbondale, Ill., 1973–93, 3, 348. Cited henceforth as *Highfill*. After they had acquired a certain seniority (or celebrity)—and regardless of their marital status—actresses, like French *concièrges*, were generally addressed as if they were married women.

thirty-three years. The country was effectively ruled by two or three Lords Justice, expert in the art of political management. Hugh Boulter, Archbishop of Armagh from 1724 to 1742, served in that capacity on thirteen occasions. This 'Irish Walpole' (he was in fact a pure-bred Englishman), intent always on securing what he termed 'a good footing' for the English interest, saw to it that the great offices of church and state went to reliable compatriots and maintained his parliamentary majorities by the judicious distribution of bribes and pensions.

The powers of Parliament were nugatory. The Declaratory Act of 1719 had abolished the appellate jurisdiction of the Irish House of Lords and affirmed the right of the Westminster Parliament to bind Ireland by its acts. The Dublin Parliament met every second year to deal with domestic matters and vote the necessary supplies; the Lord Lieutenant came over for the session and installed himself in great state in the castle, which stood on a ridge overlooking the Liffey and the low ground to the east.

Dublin in 1742 was not yet the elegant city it was to become later in the century; the Palladian façade of Trinity College, for instance, would not be built until the end of the following decade. The poverty of the Irish countryside, where famine was endemic,* was matched by the squalor of some quarters of the capital—Samuel Foote, after a visit there, said that he never knew before what the beggars in England did with their cast-off clothes. The nobility and gentry of the Anglo-Irish establishment lived in some style, however, and they did not lack for entertainments.

It was at the city's Fishamble Hall in Holy Week, two months before Garrick's arrival, that *Messiah* had had its first performance, with Handel himself at the organ and Susannah Cibber, the serious-minded and devout sister of the composer Thomas Arne, singing the contralto arias.† The hall was designed to hold six hundred, but as the performance was in aid of three charities, the stewards were eager to pack in as many as they could. A notice was placed in the press requesting 'the favour of the ladies not to come with hoops this day'; gentlemen were asked to come without their swords.[5] One of the gentlemen present was Dr Delany, the chancellor of St Patrick's Cathedral. Recently widowed, he sat with a family friend, a young, seriously stage-struck Trinity College graduate called Tom Sheridan. As Mrs Cibber's small voice fell silent Delany rose to his feet, stretched out his hands towards the stage and cried, 'Woman, for this all thy sins be forgiven thee!'

An eccentric expression of approbation, one might think, but nobody in the audience would have been puzzled by it. All the world knew that Mrs Cibber was trapped in a nightmarish marriage to Colley Cibber's unspeakable son

---

* The famines of 1730 and 1741 had been particularly severe.
† Handel had written 'He Was Despised' with Mrs Cibber's voice in mind. After he began rehearsing with her in Dublin he reset several other arias, originally for soprano, for her. 'If God be for Us' was dropped from G minor to C minor and 'He Shall Feed His Flock' was transposed '*una quarta bassa*' from B-flat major to F major. Not everyone shared his admiration for her. There were those who said that she sang when she spoke tragedy and spoke tragedy when she sang.

Theophilus, who had coerced her into becoming the mistress of a rich and earnest young country gentleman called Sloper. Cibber, who had borrowed large sums of money from Sloper (he sometimes referred to him as 'Mr Benefit'), subsequently pursued him in the courts, charging him with 'assaulting, ravishing and carnally knowing Susannah Maria Cibber, the Plaintiff's Wife . . . . . whereby the Plaintiff lost the Company, Comfort, Society and Assistance of his Wife to his Damage of £5000'. The jury took only half an hour to find in his favour, but indicated what they thought of someone who had in effect sold his wife by awarding damages of £10.* When he returned to Drury Lane a month later as Lord Foppington in *The Relapse*, the Templars, who were keen theatre-goers, were ready for him, and he was pelted with volleys of rotten apples and potatoes.† 'Young Cibber was vastly hiss'd a Thursday,' Lord Wentworth wrote to his father in the country, 'but his old friend Impudence kept him from being either out of countenance or in the least disturb'd at the noise.'[6]

For his wife things were very different. Susannah Cibber would never again be received in polite society, although she had contrived to begin slowly to pick up the pieces of her professional career. She had been in Dublin since the previous November, and had been performing at the Theatre Royal in Aungier Street with James Quin.‡ Her first appearance, in *The Conscious Lovers*, had been a disaster—takings for the night amounted to less than £10—but the Duke of Devonshire, the Lord Lieutenant of the day, came to the rescue with a command performance of *Venice Preserv'd*, and for the rest of her stay Mrs Cibber played to full houses.

Elsewhere in Dublin that summer there was unfolding a drama more pitiful and more grotesque than anything the theatre could offer. At St Patrick's Deanery the mind of Jonathan Swift was rapidly collapsing into darkness. Soon a Commission of Lunacy would find that he was 'of such unsound mind and memory that he is incapable of transacting any business, or managing, conducting, or taking care either of his estate or person'.[7] His sardonic genius had compelled the English for once to take the Irish seriously; now the creator of Gulliver had come to resemble one of his own Struldbrugs.§

No such shadows fell on Garrick's and Woffington's short season at Smock Alley. The theatre was badly placed, in a miserable lane close to the quayside, wide enough only for one carriage. But it was better built and larger than

---

* *Tryal of a Cause for Criminal Conversation*, London, 1739, p. 3. This account of the trial, based on a surreptitious shorthand note, sold like hot cakes. A century later it was much sought after by Victorian connoisseurs of 'naughty' literature. A junior counsel for the defence was Garrick's friend William Murray, and his performance on this steamily sensational occasion was the making of him.

† Templars were strictly barristers or others who had chambers in the Inner or Middle Temple, but the word was applied to lawyers generally.

‡ Quin had been in Ireland since June of the previous year and had been joined for the summer season at Aungier Street by Kitty Clive.

§ He lived on until 1745. 'Swift expires, a driv'ler and a show,' wrote Johnson in *The Vanity of Human Wishes*. He is now thought not to have been insane, but to have suffered from Ménière's disease.

Aungier Street, where the acoustics were poor and there were bad lines of vision. Woffington opened on 16 June as Sir Harry Wildair, and Garrick followed two days later as Richard, with Woffington as Lady Anne. On 23 June, from his lodgings in Aungier Street, he wrote an excited note to his brother Peter:

> I am got safe to Ireland & have had Success Equal to that in England. My Lord Orrery who is a Demi-God has wrote Such affectionate Letters to all ye Noblemen & Gentlemen of his acquaintance that I am more caress'd here than I was at London.*

The letter also indicates that he had seen off the competition: 'Delane has play'd against Me, but wanting allies has quitted ye field.'†

The change of air, he told Peter, 'has agreed vastly with Me'. He was lucky. The weather was unusually hot during his stay, and an epidemic of some sort broke out, which Dubliners, in their cheerful way, dubbed 'Garrick fever'. In everything he played he was enthusiastically received—Bayes, Fondlewife, Foppington, Master Johnny, Clodio. On 12 August, the night of his second benefit, he appeared for the first time as Hamlet, with Woffington as Ophelia. This earned him a long unsigned letter from a playgoer who had detected some errors of pronunciation 'which I insist upon that you reform'. His sharp-eared correspondent offered chapter and verse: '*Matron, Israel, villain, appal, Horatio, wind*; which you pronounced *metron, Iserel, villin, appeal, Horetio* . . . . .'[8]

If Irish playgoers were no less attentive than those in London, Garrick quickly discovered that they could be every bit as disorderly. His friend William Windham had the story many years later from Thomas Sheridan:

> He told that when Garrick was acting Lear, and reclining his head on Mrs Woffington's lap as Cordelia, one of the Audience on the stage came and thrust his hand into her bosom: He afterwards searched G. through the house with intent to chastise or perhaps to kill Him, because he heard He had looked displeased at it.[9]

Garrick escaped the attentions of this Dublin dandiprat. He concluded his Smock Alley engagement on 19 August by playing Captain Plume in *The Recruiting Officer* to Woffington's Sylvia. 'My Affairs are quite finish'd here,' he wrote to Peter three days later, '& with great Success, applause & w^t Not.' Part of the success had been social. 'I have an Invitation from Ld Tyrawley to come with him,' he told his brother, '& believe shall Stay for ye Hon^r of his Lordship's Company.'[10]

James O'Hara, second Baron Tyrawley, had had a colourful career as a soldier and diplomat. Now in his early fifties, he had been wounded at Almanza and

---

* *Letters*, 24. Orrery, it will be remembered, had accompanied Pope to see Garrick during his first season at Goodman's Fields.
† Poor Delane had been returning regularly to Dublin since his début there in 1729. On this occasion he had arrived two days after Garrick and had unwisely attempted Richard at Aungier Street; the house was thin and hostile.

Malplaquet and was a former ambassador to Portugal; Horace Walpole asserted that he had once returned from an extended diplomatic mission with three wives and fourteen children. He was certainly the father of George Anne Bellamy, then a child of ten or eleven, who had made her first appearance the previous year in pantomime at Covent Garden where her mother was a member of the company.

Garrick had four other companions when the packet *Lovely Jane* weighed anchor in Dun Laoghaire harbour on 23 August—Delane, Mrs Cibber, her brother Tom Arne and his wife Cecilia. Arne, now aged thirty-two, had written the music for an adaptation of Milton's *Comus*, and his setting for the masque *Alfred* included 'Rule Britannia'; he had also written some lovely songs for productions of Shakespeare at Drury Lane, where he was effectively composer in residence.* Cecilia Arne (née Young) had been a pupil of Geminiani's. Between 1735 and 1750 she was one of the most popular singers of the day.†

Peg Woffington stayed behind to see something of her mother—'a respectable looking old lady in a black velvet cloak,' Keeffe wrote in his *Recollections*, 'with a deep silk fringe, a diamond on her finger, and an agate snuff-box'.[11] Her loyal and generous daughter made her an allowance of £40 or £50 a year.‡ Woffington also watched carefully over her much younger sister, Polly, whom she sent to be educated in a convent in Paris. William Windham, in the diary he kept of a visit to Dublin many years later, recorded a story he had from Tom Sheridan:

> He remembers, when she acted in his company, her bringing her sister into the green room; and upon his inquiring what she intended to do with her, her answering, 'There were two things she should never become, by her advice—a whore, & an actress, for that she had sufficiently experienced the inconveniences of those ways of life herself.'[12]

It was, however, to such inconveniences that she herself now returned. The Drury Lane company of which she and Garrick were to form part in the 1742–3 season was a strong one—Kitty Clive, Mrs Pritchard, Macklin and Delane had all been retained and the manager, Fleetwood, had recruited two new dance teams and advertised twenty-one new dances.

At Covent Garden, Rich had hired even more dancers, and would rely heavily

---

* These included 'Blow, blow, thou winter wind' and 'Under the greenwood tree' for a revival of *As You Like It* in 1740. Six years later he would compose 'Where the Bee sucks' for a revival of *The Tempest*.

† The Arnes had been given a benefit concert in Fishamble Street in July, and Cecilia and her sister-in-law had sung songs by Arne and Handel. According to Charles Burney, Mrs Arne had 'a good natural voice and a fine shake'. She later became over-fond of gin. Francesco Geminiani (1687–1762) was a native of Lucca and had studied in Rome under Scarlatti and Corelli. He had come to London in 1714, where he quickly established himself as a teacher, composer and virtuoso violinist.

‡ Her daughter might be famous, but Hannah Woffington's feet remained firmly planted on the ground. Woffington told Tom Sheridan that when her mother came to England and was taken to Hampton Court, she remarked only that 'the floors were mighty neat'. *Ketton-Cremer, op. cit.*, p. 80.

for afterpieces on such elaborate pantomimes as *The Royal Chase* and *The Necromancer*. He opened on 22 September, eleven days later than Drury Lane, with Quin as Othello and Mrs Cibber as Desdemona: 'Play written by Shakespear', said the bills. 'The Principal Characters new dress'd, and the Theatre New Decorated'. Susannah was cheered for her performance, but the Covent Garden company was hard put to it to compete with talent assembled by the rival house—Macklin had opened the Drury Lane season as Shylock (Portia was played by Mrs Clive), and this was followed by *As You Like It* with Macklin as Touchstone and Woffington as Rosalind.

Fleetwood, for whatever reason, did not let the town see his new star for several weeks—Garrick made his first appearance on 5 October as Chamont in *The Orphan*. Two nights later he appeared as Bayes in *The Rehearsal* ('Perform'd to a very numerous and crowded Audience', reported the *Daily Advertiser*). The following week both patent theatres offered *Richard III*, and anyone prepared to run between the two houses might have savoured the first confrontation between Garrick and Quin in the same role. Garrick and Woffington played together for the first time in the middle of October in *The Recruiting Officer*, and again a week later in *Lear*. Towards the end of the month there was a command performance of *Richard*, and Garrick acted for the first time before George II.

In the middle of November, three months after he had tried it out in Dublin, he gave his first London interpretation of *Hamlet*. The tragic role he was to play more frequently than any other seems initially to have been received with respect rather than enthusiasm. When, after a dozen more performances, he gave it for his first benefit on 13 January, it had still not set the town on fire.

It was less than a year since Garrick had played the Ghost to Henry Giffard's Hamlet, but the sensational success Giffard had enjoyed at Goodman's Fields in the previous season had been his undoing. His challenge to the Licensing Act there did not survive Garrick's departure; the theatre in Aycliffe Street was closed, and he decided to try his luck (still without a licence) at the old house in Lincoln's Inn Fields. He opened there in late November with *The Careless Husband*. Foppington was played by Theophilus Cibber, who had found the door closed to him at both the patent theatres. Giffard tried everything he knew to attract an audience ('Particular Care has been taken to have the whole House exceedingly well Air'd', his bills announced on 1 December), but the cards were stacked against him. Allowing Theophilus to go on as Richard was not one of his better ideas; in the spring of 1743 he bowed to the inevitable and disbanded the company.

Garrick was no longer a big fish in a small pool as he had been at Goodman's Fields. It had been very agreeable to be 'caressed' by the Dublin audience during the summer, but he knew well enough that it was only now, in this first season at Drury Lane, that his metal would be properly tested. Not that there was much to complain about in a piece which appeared at the beginning of the new season in the *Gentleman's Magazine*:

Mr. Garrick is but of middling stature, yet, being well-proportioned and having a peculiar happiness in his address and action is a living instance that it is not essential to a theatrical hero to be six feet high. His voice is clear and piercing, perfectly sweet and harmonious, without monotony, drawling, or affectation; it is capable of all the various passions, which the heart of man is agitated with, and the Genius of Shakespeare can describe; it is neither whining, bellowing, or grumbling, but in whatever character he assimilates, perfectly easy in its transitions, natural in its cadence, and beautiful in elocution. He is not less happy in his mien and gait, in which he is neither strutting or mincing, neither stiff nor slouching.

It emerges, however, that much as he admired Garrick, the writer was not measuring him against a particularly exacting standard:

When three or four are on stage with him, he is attentive to whatever is spoke, and never drops his character when he has finished a speech, by either looking contemptibly on an inferior performer, unnecessary spitting, or suffering his eyes to wander through the whole circle of spectators . . . . .*

The views of anonymous scribblers might not matter all that much, but it had been quickly borne in on Garrick that his success was deeply unsettling to the older generation in the theatre. 'If this young fellow be right,' growled Quin, 'then we have all been wrong.' Shrewder—and wittier—than most of his fellow-actors, he compared his new rival with the Methodists. Garrick, he said, was a new religion: 'Whitefield was followed for a time; but they will all come to church again.' Garrick, confidently and good-naturedly, hit back in verse:

> Pope *Quin*, who damns all churches but his own,
> Complains that heresy corrupts the town:
> 'That Whitefield Garrick has misled the age,
> 'And taints the sound religion of the stage;
> 'Schism, he cries, has turn'd the nation's brain;
> 'But eyes will open, and to church again!'
> Thou great infallible, forbear to roar,
> Thy bulls and errors are rever'd no more;
> When doctrines meet with gen'ral approbation,
> It is not heresy, but reformation.[13]

James Quin, son of a lawyer, grandson of a former Lord Mayor of Dublin, was now approaching fifty. He had appeared at Drury Lane as early as 1715. 'At that

---

* *Gentleman's Magazine*, October 1742. Charges of inattention to the stage ensemble—and of flirtation—were more often directed at actresses, and even Woffington, generally admired for her professionalism, did not escape. John Hill, for instance, took her severely to task for her performance as Andromache in *The Distressed Mother*: 'Who could bear to behold the simpering widow casting her eyes into the boxes to see who most admired her?' (*The Actor: a Treatise on the Art of Playing*, 1750.)

time, seniority of date was considered with as much jealousy in the green-room as in the army or navy,' noted an early biographer:

> An actor that should at once have rushed upon the town, with all the powers of a Betterton or a Booth, in a capital character, would have been looked upon by his competitors for fame as little better than a usurper of talents and applause.[14]

Since the departure of Booth and Wilks, Quin had had no serious rival on the London stage.* He was coarse, generous, witty, hot-tempered. In his earlier days he had killed two men in drunken brawls; he had issued a challenge to Macklin on one occasion and in 1740 (although they were members of the same Masonic lodge) he had fought a duel with Theophilus Cibber.† He was on friendly terms with Pope and Swift, was a frequent guest at Lord Chesterfield's table and was patronized by Frederick, Prince of Wales, who appointed him 'to instruct his children in the true pronunciation of their mother tongue'.‡

His most famous role was Falstaff (as he tipped the scale at 20 stone he had the figure for it), though he was also admired for his King John and his Comus and as Pierre in *Venice Preserved*. He was ridiculed not only for his delivery but also for his deportment—'he might be said to walk in blank verse as well as talk', wrote one critic, and Smollett captured him memorably in *Peregrine Pickle*: 'His utterance is a continual sing-song, like the chanting of vespers; and his action resembles that of heaving ballast in the hold of a ship.'

He was roughly handled in Charles Churchill's *The Rosciad*, although Churchill, a young man of thirty in the 1760s, could not have seen Quin in his prime:

> In whate'er cast his character was laid,
> Self still, like oil, upon the surface play'd.
> Nature, in spite of all his skill, crept in,
> Horatio, Dorax, Falstaff—still was Quin.

'He seems clearly to have been one of the worst, but most lauded, actors of his day,' writes a modern American historian of the eighteenth-century theatre:

> The evidence would suggest, indeed, that he was not really an actor at all, but, like so many film stars of the twentieth century, a magnetic personality who tailored characters to his own personality and won a following so great that the criticisms of the judicious could not topple him from his

---

* Booth did not act after 1727, though he lived another six years; Wilks was last seen a few months before his death in September 1732.
† The animosity that existed between the two men was well known. In the anonymous *Apology for T. . . C. . .* , attributed to Fielding, Quin is made to say of him, 'Quarrelling with such a Fellow is like sh——t——g on a T——d.'
‡ Quin was suitably gratified in 1760 when he heard that the 22-year-old George III had made a good job of his first speech from the throne. 'Ay,' he said, 'I taught the boy to speak!' Soon after his accession, the King ordered that Quin should be paid 'a genteel pension' during his life.

position at the top of his profession. . . . . . With the exception of his Falstaff, which seems clearly to have been splendid, Quin may have been the best-worst really prominent actor of the first half of the eighteenth century.[15]

Colley Cibber observed Garrick's assault on the theatrical ramparts from a different vantage point. He was son of the distinguished Danish-born sculptor Caius Gabriel Cibber,* and as a young man had served briefly in the Earl of Devonshire's levy for the Prince of Orange. At the age of nineteen he drifted into the theatre. He failed to impress in tragedy, although he made a good impression in some minor comic parts. His first real success came in 1696 when he created the role of the foppish Sir Novelty Fashion in his own first play. *Love's Last Shift* was the first sentimental comedy, and the Lord Chamberlain of the day gave it as his opinion 'that for a young Fellow to shew himself such an Actor and such a Writer in one Day, was something extraordinary'.

He was to bring out some thirty dramatic pieces in all, including *The Careless Husband*, in which he wrote the part of Lord Foppington for himself, and he subsequently acquired a profitable share in the management of Drury Lane. He made an enemy of Pope, and was rewarded by being made the hero of *The New Dunciad*.† He also wrote a play called *The Non-Juror*, based on Molière's *Tartuffe*, a blatant piece of anti-Jacobite propaganda which branded all non-jurors as dupes or hypocrites; his reward for this came in 1730 when his friend the Duke of Grafton, the Lord Chamberlain, appointed him Poet Laureate in succession to the drunken parson Laurence Eusden. By far his greatest contribution to arts and letters was his autobiography, *An Apology for the Life of Mr Colley Cibber, Comedian*, which appeared in 1740 and which remains one of the liveliest and most perceptive books about the theatre ever written.

Cibber was not initially critical of Garrick. He had seen him during his season at Goodman's Fields, and Garrick, in a letter to Peter in December 1741, reported that 'Old Cibber has spoken with y[e] Greatest Commendation of my Acting'.[16] Things were soon to change, however. Cibber had little enough time for Theophilus, but he realized that the new star posed a threat to many of the roles his son

---

* Cibber was employed by the first Duke of Devonshire at Chatsworth, where he executed two sphinxes on large bases, several doorcases of alabaster, and two statues in the chapel representing Faith and Hope. Sir Christopher Wren commissioned him to carve the phoenix, in bas-relief, which is placed above the southern door of St Paul's Cathedral.

† Cibber responded with a sixty-odd-page *Letter* in which he gave a brilliantly malicious account of how a young nobleman had carried Pope and himself off one evening to 'a certain House of Carnal Recreation near the Haymarket, where his Lordship's Frolick propos'd was to slip his little Homer, as he call'd him, at a Girl of the Game . . . .' Cibber recounts how after a time, growing anxious for 'the Honour of our Nation', he threw open the door, 'where I found this little hasty Hero, like a terrible *Tom Tit*, pertly perching upon the Mount of Love! But such was my Surprize, that I fairly laid hold of his Heels, and actually drew him down safe and sound from his Danger . . . . .' The ridicule was devastating. The engravers of the town were quick to see the possibilities of the anecdote, and prints appeared with such titles as 'An Essay on Woman, by the Author of the Essay on Man: Being Homer Preserv'd, or the Twickenham Squire Caught by the Heels'.

had made his own: 'Garrick was well enough,' he said grudgingly after he had seen him as Bayes, 'but not superior to my son Theophilus.'

He was reproved for his lack of generosity by someone who could claim a longer theatrical memory than his. By the time Garrick first appeared at Drury Lane, Anne Bracegirdle, now almost eighty, had already been in retirement for thirty-five years. She had been with Betterton's company at the old converted tennis court at Lincoln's Inn Fields in the 1690s and it was for her that Congreve, who was long infatuated with her, had written the roles of Angelica in *Love for Love* and, most famously, Millamant in *The Way of the World*.*

When Cibber visited her at her house in Howard Street in 1742 and spoke disparagingly of Garrick, she tapped him with her fan and said, 'Come, come, Cibber, tell me if there is not something like envy in your character of this young gentleman. The actor who pleases everybody must be a man of merit.' Cibber took a pinch of snuff and replied, 'Why, 'faith, Bracey, I believe you are right; the young fellow is clever.'[17]

That was certainly the opinion of the town throughout Garrick's first full season as one of His Majesty's Servants of the Theatre Royal, even if his growing volume of fan mail contained the occasional brickbat: 'I saw you last night act Fondlewife,' wrote an anonymous correspondent on 4 December, 'and could not help thinking it a good deal overacted, especially in that sort of feeble trot you seemed to affect so much. A part overacted makes the actor look foolish.'[18]

More often, however, he was praised because there seemed to be so little of the actor in him:

> I have an Actor in my Eye whose greatest Merit is, that he is none; whose Look, whose Voice, whose Action have nothing of the Player, but so much of the Person he represents.[19]

Fielding made the same point some years later in *Tom Jones* when he sends Partridge to Drury Lane with Tom and Mrs Miller to see *Hamlet*. When the curtain falls Tom asks him which of the players he liked best:

> To this he answered, with some appearance of indignation at the question, "The king, without doubt."— "Indeed, Mr. Partridge" says Mrs. Miller, "you are not of the same opinion with the town; for they are all agreed, that Hamlet is acted by the best player who was ever on the stage."— "He the best player!" cries Partridge with a contemptuous sneer. "Why, I could act as well as he myself. I am sure if I had seen a ghost, I should have looked in the very same manner, and done just as he did. And then, to be sure, in that scene, as you called it, between him and his mother, where you told me he acted so fine, why, Lord help me! any man, that is, any good man, that hath such a mother, would have done exactly the same. I know you are only joking with me; but, indeed, madam, though I

---

* Her train of admirers also included the Earl of Scarsdale (who left her £1,000 in his will), Lord Lovelace, Lord Burlington and Lord Halifax, the Dukes of Dorset and Devonshire and the dramatist Nicholas Rowe, who was Eusden's immediate predecessor as Poet Laureate.

was never at a play in London, yet I have seen acting before in the country; and the king for my money: he speaks all his words distinctly, half as loud again as the other. Anybody may see he is an actor.[20]

It was a play of Fielding's, as it happens, which was the one flop of Garrick's first Drury Lane season. *The Wedding Day* was the only new play presented at either patent house that year, although Fielding had written it some years previously. The piece ran into trouble even before it had gone into rehearsal: 'Mr Fielding has wrote a comedy which has been refused by the Licenser,' Lady Hertford wrote in a letter to her son on 25 January, 'not as a reflecting one, but on account of its immorality.' She wrote again three weeks later:

> Mr Fielding, by suffering the bawd to be carted, tho she is his favourite character in the new play, has obtained a licence to have it acted, and it was perform'd on thursday for the first time, but so much dislik'd that it is believ'd that it will be impossible to prevail with a second audience to hear it through.*

To old troupers like Macklin and Mrs Pritchard, the occasional hiss and catcall were all in the day's work, but Garrick had no experience of a play being damned, and he was rattled. He had asked Fielding to rewrite some of his lines, but Fielding had refused: 'No, damn them! If the scene is not a good one, let them find that out.' They found it out rather quickly, and their displeasure was audible in the green room, where Fielding sat drinking champagne and chewing tobacco. 'What's the matter, Garrick? What are they hissing now?'

'Why, the scene that I begged you to retrench,' replied the exasperated Millamour.

Fielding, a large man of great constitutional vigour, was philosophical. 'Oh! damn them. They *have* found it out, have they?'†

The only other occasion that year when Garrick was greeted with less-than-rapturous applause was on Woffington's benefit night in March. The town's favourite Sir Harry Wildair unwisely ceded the part on that night to her lover, appearing herself as Lady Lurewell. The house felt cheated. A breeches part was a breeches part, and they had been robbed of the chance to fantasize at the sight of Woffington's legs. Garrick had good antennae and quickly got the message; he appeared three more times in the role and then never again.

His own benefit, a fortnight earlier, a command performance by the Prince and Princess of Wales, had been a triumph. He had appeared for the first time

---

* Hughes, Helen Sard, *The Gentle Hertford: Her Life and Letters*, New York, 1940, p. 233. Public exposure by carting through the streets was a common punishment, especially for bawds, that dated from Shakespeare's day and earlier.

† In the Winston MS in the Folger Library in Washington a note against the third performance of *The Wedding Day* on 21 February reads, 'Benefit the author of this bad new play, which would have sunk the 1st night but for Garrick's acting.' Fielding received one more benefit, but the play came off after six nights, and his earnings from the run did not amount to more than £60.

as Hastings in Nicholas Rowe's tragedy *Jane Shore* and also played Sharp in his own *The Lying Valet*. Seven rows of the pit were railed into the boxes for the occasion, and side boxes were formed on the stage where it was announced that servants might keep places.* It was to become one of his best-known tragic roles.

Although Drury Lane and Covent Garden now enjoyed a near-duopoly in theatrical performance, they had to keep a sharp eye on competition in the form of musical entertainment. 'Handel has set up an oratorio against the operas; and succeeds,' Horace Walpole wrote to Horace Mann in February 1743:

> He has hired all the goddesses from farces and the singers of *Roast Beef* from between the acts at both theatres, and with a man with one Note in his voice, and a girl without ever a one; and so they sing, and make brave hallelujahs; and the good company encore the recitative, if it happens to have any cadence like what they call a tune.[21]

There were no hallelujahs, as it happens—London would not hear *Messiah* for a month yet. The oratorio was *Samson*, adapted from Milton's *Samson Agonistes*, and it was a resounding success. Handel had indeed assembled his cast with a catholic ear. His 'goddess from farce' was Kitty Clive, who sang Dalila in her high, some thought slightly vulgar, soprano. The 'man with one note' was John Beard, who was Samson. He was one of the most celebrated English singers of the mid century; Handel had written many of his greatest tenor parts with him in mind, often in roles previously reserved for the *castrati*—a development not to the taste of those, like Walpole, who could not see beyond things Italian. And of course the 'girl without ever a one' was Susannah Cibber, for whom Handel had expressly composed the role of Micah—the second longest in the oratorio, even though no such character existed either in Milton or in the Bible.

Garrick scored his greatest success in this first season at Drury Lane in the minor role of Abel Drugger. Ben Jonson's comedy *The Alchymist*, a satire on cupidity, had first been acted in 1610. It was performed repeatedly until the closing of the theatres, and given some of the credit for ridding London of alchemists. Pepys saw it in 1661, and thought it 'a most incomparable play';[22] Coleridge was later to assert that it has one of the three most perfect plots in all literature.

Love-wit, during an outbreak of plague, leaves his house in Blackfriars in the care of his servant Face. Face, with his crony Subtle, a bogus alchemist and astrologer, and Doll Common, a prostitute, gull a succession of credulous dupes by promises of what the philosopher's stone will do for them—Sir Epicure Mammon, Tribulation and Ananias, two Puritans from Amsterdam, Abel Drugger a tobacconist.

---

* Rowe called *Jane Shore* one of his 'She-Tragedies'—highly moral in tone, their emphasis was on the suffering and penitence of victimized women. Later in the century Jane, and Calista in his *The Fair Penitent*, became two of Mrs Siddons's most famous roles.

One of Garrick's earliest and most enduring comic triumphs. 'Abel Drugger is certainly the standard of low comedy, and Mr Garrick's playing it the standard of acting in this species.' (Thomas Wilkes, A General View of the Stage, 1759) (Bell's British Theatre, vol. 17, 1780)

Garrick owed his success in the part to the way in which he cleverly underplayed it. Theophilus Cibber had for some years regarded the role as very much his property, but Cibber 'was never commended for strictly adhering to nature in the drawing of his characters':

Whether he had acquired a sort of extravagant manner, from his frequently playing Ancient Pistol with applause; or, whether he imagined that every imposition upon the understanding of an audience, which happened to be applauded, was justifiable, I know not; but he mixed so much absurd grimace and ridiculous tricks in playing this part, that although the galleries laughed and clapped their hands, the judicious part of the audience was displeased.

Not so, it seems, with Garrick:

The moment he came upon the stage, he discovered such awkward sim- plicity, and his looks so happily bespoke the ignorant, selfish, and absurd tobacco-merchant, that it was a contest not easily to be decided, whether the burst of laughter or applause were loudest. Through the whole part he strictly preserved the modesty of nature.[23]

A Lichfield grocer had occasion to go up to London on business, and went armed with a letter of recommendation to Garrick from Peter. He got to town late, and seeing Garrick's name on the bills for *The Alchymist*, went up into the two-shilling gallery. When he returned home, Peter Garrick was eager to know how he had been received by his brother, and how he had liked him:

The man at first wished to parry the question, but at length owned that he never delivered the letter. 'Not deliver my letter!' says Peter; 'how came that about?'—'Why, the fact is, my dear friend,' said the other, 'I saw enough of him on the stage to make that unnecessary. He may be rich, as I dare say any man who lives like him must be; but by G—d' (and here, said the Doctor, the man vociferated an oath), 'though he is your brother, Mr. Garrick, he is one of the shabbiest, meanest, most pitiful hounds I ever saw in the whole course of my life.'[24]

Garrick would go on playing Drugger for the rest of his career—it became one of his dozen most frequent roles.* *The Alchymist* is an enormously long play, and over the years he cut almost a thousand of Jonson's original three thousand lines, paring the complications of the plot and reducing the playing time to just over two hours (malicious tongues suggested that other parts were much more heavily pruned than Drugger's, and he was sometimes criticized for the amount of stage business he inserted). Many of the lines omitted referred to alchemy or to religion, but Garrick also took his blue pencil to some of Jonson's more sexual and scatological passages, judging the taste of his own day to be less robust.

---

* And one that did excellent business for the theatre. The Treasurer's Account Books in the Folger Library show that one single performance in March 1753 brought in a record £330.

Subtle, in his very first speech, is made to say 'I dare thee' instead of 'I fart on thee', and Surly later refers to catching 'a certain ruin' instead of 'a certain clap'; 'Heaven' is substituted more than once for 'God' and at one point 'God's will' becomes 'Adzooks!'

A year after he first appeared as Drugger, Garrick would publish—anonymously—his short *Essay on Acting*. He describes a piece of stage business which was apparently first introduced by Colley Cibber—Drugger, fiddling about with Subtle's equipment while other characters are speaking, accidentally drops a glass urinal, and Garrick speculates that two different ideas chase each other through the tobacconist's mind—that he has broken something of great value, and that the curiosity which led him to do so is likely to be punished:

> Now, if this, as it certain *is*, the Situation of his Mind, How are the different Members of the Body to be agitated? Why Thus,—His *Eyes* must be revers'd from the Object he is most intimidated with, and by dropping his *Lip* at the some Time to the Object, it throws a trembling *Languor* upon every *Muscle*, and by declining the right Part of the Head *towards* the *Urinal*, it casts the most *comic Terror* and *Shame* over all the *upper* Part of the Body, that can be imagin'd; and to make the *lower* Part equally ridiculous, his *Toes* must be *inverted* from the Heel, and by *holding* his *Breath*, he will unavoidably give himself a *Tremor* in the *Knees*, and if his *Fingers*, at the same Time, seem *convuls'd*, it finishes the compleatest low Picture of *Grotesque Terror* that can be imagin'd by a *Dutch* Painter.[25]

It is an intriguing insight into the minute attention he gave to the physical detail of his characterizations.

Of Garrick's domestic arrangements at this time, only purveyors of romantic fiction may write with assurance. When he played Hamlet for his first benefit in the middle of January 1743, he was living in the Great Piazza, Covent Garden—that much we know because those seeking tickets were directed to his lodgings there. Similarly, we know that by the first week in March, when he made his début in *Jane Shore*, he had moved to Bow Street: a note in the Winston MS confirms this, but tells us something else as well: 'In 1743 Macklin, Mrs Woffington, and Garrick took house No. 6 Bow Street—a joint establishment.'

Cooke and some of Macklin's other biographers have made of this that they set up some sort of academy of dramatic art together. There is no evidence for the story, and it seems inherently unlikely; while the related idea that they established some sort of *ménage à trois* is not just improbable but quite simply absurd. Macklin had been living for many years with Ann Grace, like himself a former strolling player, and would go on doing so until her death in 1758; she had been appearing in the bills as 'Mrs Macklin' since late 1740. Their daughter, Maria, born about 1733, had made her stage début in 1742 as the little Duke of York in *Richard III* (a traditional introductory role for child actors); mother and daughter, what's more, were both currently members of the Drury Lane company. The most likely sequence of events is that Woffington, on her return from Dublin, took lodgings in the same house in Bow Street as Macklin and his family and that after a time Garrick moved in with her.

They were not a well-assorted pair. Apart from their ability to entrance an audience they had little in common. Garrick, for all his bustle and liveliness, was essentially serious-minded—his Huguenot chromosomes had attended to that. Woffington's genetic material was organized very differently. 'Forgive her one female error,' Murphy wrote gallantly, 'and it might fairly be said of her, that she was adorned with every virtue;'[26] but William Windham, gossiping to Tom Sheridan in Dublin one morning in the 1770s, heard the emphasis placed less charitably:

> Mrs W., by his account was a most willing bitch, artfull, dissembling, lewd and malicious, a very captivating woman, and never failed to get a great influence over all men that lived with her.[27]

Small wonder. 'She was so happily made, and there was such symmetry and proportion in her frame, that she would have borne the most critical examination of the nicest sculptor,' wrote James Quin's anonymous biographer. Her voice was against her (Tate Wilkinson, in his *Memoirs*, remembered it as 'a most unpleasant squeaking pipe,—an *Orange Woman to the Playhouse*') but she knew it and, possessing the rare and happy gift of not taking herself over-seriously, could join in jokes about it. She was witty; she preferred the company of men to that of women; she was intelligent—something not the general rule with either sex in her profession. She was also generous and open-hearted, though many years later Johnson told Boswell that in matters of household economy, Garrick thought her extravagant:

> I remember drinking tea with him long ago, when Peg Woffington made it, and he grumbled at her for making it too strong. He had then begun to feel money in his purse, and did not know when he should have enough of it.*

As the season of 1742–3 drew to a close, however, Garrick had considerably less money in his purse than he had counted on having—his salary from Drury Lane was more than £600 in arrears. Behind the scenes, in spite of good houses, the affairs of the theatre were in a critical state, and there had already been more than one visit from the bailiffs.†

Matters had been degenerating for some time. Charles Fleetwood, an amiable man of good family, had bought the patent in 1734 with the remains of a large

---

* *Life*, iii, 264–5. Boswell added a footnote: 'When Johnson told this little anecdote to Sir Joshua Reynolds, he mentioned a circumstance which he omitted today:—'Why,' said Garrick, 'it is as red as blood.'

† On one occasion, sifting through clothes and properties, they had been about to seize the hat worn by Garrick as Richard III, a splendid affair adorned with feathers and paste jewels. 'Look you,' Garrick's crafty Welsh servant, Davy, told them, 'that hat belongs to the king.' The sheriff's officers, persuaded that they had been about to commit an act of *lèse-majesté* against the person of George II, turned their attention to less dangerous items.

private fortune.* He had no experience of the theatre, but initially he had done quite well. He had been well served by advice from Macklin, although as time went by the pair of them were seen rather too frequently at the gaming tables at White's Chocolate House. Gambling was not Fleetwood's sole interest. 'He was seized with an unaccountable passion for low diversions, and took a strange delight in the company of the meanest of the human species,' writes Davies:

> This man of genteel address and polite manners conceived a peculiar fondness for the professors of the art of boxing; his company was divided between sturdy athletics and ridiculous buffoons; between Broughton, James, and Taylor, the most eminent of our boxers, and the tumblers of Sadler's Wells: the heroic combatants of Hockley in the Hole and the Bear Garden graced the patentee's levy almost every morning.[28]

Fleetwood increasingly appropriated the profits from the theatre to these private amusements. He also began to borrow large sums from the theatre's treasurer, a man called Pierson. Matters came to a head early in April when Pierson was due for a benefit; his manner to the actors was generally so offensive that Garrick refused to act for him.

It was the opening shot in a battle that was to drag on for more than eighteen months, and it rang out at a time of wars and rumours of wars on a larger stage. For the past three years the continental armies had been marching and counter-marching in what is now known as the War of the Austrian Succession, with France and Prussia disputing the right of Maria Theresa to the Austrian crown. George II, always eager to cut a figure on the European stage, and free now of Walpole's restraining influence, had taken nominal command of his British and Hanoverian troops. Britain had not yet formally declared war on France, but in late June, with his Austrian allies, George found himself facing a formidable French force at Dettingen in Bavaria.

The King's horse bolted early in the action, but he placed himself, sword in hand, at the head of his troops. 'Now boys,' he cried, if the *Gentleman's Magazine* is to be believed, 'now for the honour of England. Fire, and behave bravely, and the French will soon run.' Rather an extended word of command, one might think, in German or in English, but the French at all events obligingly withdrew across the Main. George became something of a popular hero, and Handel celebrated the occasion by composing a *Te Deum*, which was performed at St James's Chapel on the King's return home in November.

The campaign on which Garrick and his fellow-actors at Drury Lane embarked in that summer of 1743 turned out to be rather more extended and its outcome was less clear-cut. It was to have consequences that none of the warring parties could have foreseen. It would teach Garrick many things about the theatre, and even more about human nature. And it would destroy for all time his friendship with Charles Macklin.

---

* At the age of twenty-one he had inherited an estate said to have been worth £6,000 a year.

5

Pig in the Middle

Fleetwood was extremely charming and hugely plausible. Joseph Knight, in his life of Garrick, compares him with a later and more celebrated manager, Richard Brinsley Sheridan—'wont to beguile into further loans those who had come with the sternest resolution of recovering their debts'. He listened courteously to the actors' grievances, acknowledged the justice of their complaints, expressed his sincere regrets and made them the most solemn undertakings that everything would be attended to.

Promises did nothing to pay the rent, however. Indeed, it came to the ears of the actors that Fleetwood, as a further measure of retrenchment, was intent on cutting salaries, and that he had offered Macklin an extra £200 if he would exert himself to frustrate opposition to such a move. By the end of the summer, nerves were jangling and tempers were frayed, and ten or twelve of the more senior members of the company agreed on a plan of action.* There is a conflict of evidence on who was the prime mover. Murphy says that it was Macklin who 'invited them to enter into a general confederacy'; Fitzgerald believes that it was Garrick who 'submitted a plan of combination for their adoption'. That was certainly always Macklin's contention: 'I do solemnly aver,' he later wrote, 'that I was not the ring-leader in this secession from Mr Fleetwood, but concurred in it merely by the influence of Mr Garrick.' That has the ring of truth to it, and seems most in keeping with the sharp contrast in character and temperament between the two men.

What was proposed was that they should draw up a petition stating their grievances to the Lord Chamberlain and apply to him for a licence or patent to perform at the Opera House in the Haymarket or elsewhere.† This was done, and twenty members of the company put their signatures to the document. The rebels were confident that Garrick's weight with his aristocratic admirers would

---

* There were some sixty actors and actresses on the strength that season, and seventeen dancers.
† There was a useful precedent for such a move. In 1694, when Christopher Rich had cut salaries and redistributed some of the roles in the old United Company, Betterton and several of the younger players (they included Anne Bracegirdle) decided to try and form a company of their own: they succeeded in negotiating directly with King William, and were granted a licence to convert the old tennis court at Lincoln's Inn Fields into a playhouse. But it was naïve not to take account of the Licensing Act.

count heavily in their favour. But they also—this at the urging of Macklin—signed a formal agreement by which they bound themselves not to accede individually to any terms which Fleetwood might subsequently offer. 'An embodied phalanx was thus drawn up against the manager,' writes Murphy, 'who had notice early in September, that none of the junto would act under him, if he did not accede to their terms.'[1] As things turned out, what was intended as a safeguard against any attempt by Fleetwood to pick them off one at a time subsequently became the source of much grief.

Fleetwood, meanwhile, coolly exploited the advantages offered by the duopoly. By no means all his principals had jumped ship. Those who remained on board included Delane, Giffard and Yates—and, perhaps more surprisingly, Woffington. He had little difficulty in making up numbers by recruiting strolling players and drawing on those thrown out of work by the disbandment of Giffard's company. What had begun as a walk-out had now in effect become a lock-out. Fleetwood opened his season on 13 September, a week ahead of Covent Garden, with a performance of Steele's *The Conscious Lovers*.

The town was awash with rumour. 'We are informed, General Theophilus Cibber arriv'd in Town on Saturday Morning,' announced the *Daily Advertiser* on 4 October, in what sounds suspiciously like a puff placed by Cibber himself:

> He made a Campaign this last summer in Dublin, where he maintained the Field, with great reputation against the illustrious Count Sheridan.* We further hear the young Gentleman has taken up his Winter Quarters in the Territories of Covent Garden; but his Scene of Action, 'tis said, will be Drury Lane. 'Tis rumored he will soon be join'd by some Auxiliaries, draughted from the Forces on the Irish Establishment, who are to supply vacant commissions of the present Theatrical Mutineers and Deserters.

Sure enough, he was billed to appear as Foppington a fortnight later, although on the day *The Relapse* had to be deferred owing to his sudden indisposition. He bobbed up as Clodio in *Love Makes a Man* a few weeks later, however, and as Brazen in *The Recruiting Officer*. Delane was another who had no reason to regret Garrick's absence from the boards; Lear fell into his lap once more, and so did Jaffier in *Venice Preserv'd* and Hastings in *Jane Shore*. Woffington, for whatever reason, got off to a slow start, making her first appearance of the season as Sir Harry Wildair on 1 November.

Throughout the autumn there was a spate of pamphlets and cartoons and articles in the press. A piece that appeared in mid-October, clearly planted by Fleetwood, compared actors' salaries with those in the days of Wilkes and Betterton, suggesting that the likes of Garrick and Macklin were grossly overpaid. William Chetwood, the former prompter at Drury Lane, weighed in with *The*

---

* At Smock Alley, during the summer, Sheridan had accused Theophilus of trying to undermine him by spiriting away the robe he wore in *Cato*. A week later a noisy group of Sheridan's student supporters had broken up a performance of Cibber's, and he had to make his escape through a window.

Dramatic Congress. A Short State of the Stage under the Present Management,
an attack on Fleetwood and Rich as the operators of a cartel. Fleetwood came
under even heavier fire in *Queries to be Answer'd by the Manager of Drury-Lane
Theatre*, a comprehensive and devastating indictment of his record as manager
presented in the form of thirty-four rhetorical questions:

> ... Have not the dressers and others at 1 shilling or 18 pence per night
> been unpaid fifteen or sixteen weeks together? Have not collections been
> made among the actors to prevent some from starving, and to bury others?
> Has not his treasurer insolently refused to pay them their due, and laughed
> at their distresses? Have not the doors of the theatre been kept shut at
> Benefit Nights till near five o'clock, in order to get money for coals, candles,
> etc., from the persons concerned, tho' large arrears were due to 'em? Was
> not word sent to Mr. Berry at a time when nobody expected his life, that
> the doors shou'd not be open'd, unless the whole charge of his benefit was
> paid, a thing most unprecedented? Are not Mr Mills and Mrs Butler in a
> most melancholy situation upon his account? Was not one arrested for
> £500, and the other forc'd to keep her chamber four months, for fear of
> being arrested too? . . . . . Has he not drove some of the poorer people to
> beg their bread for want of the smallest part of their just debts, and does
> he think upon publishing the many calamitous cases of particular persons,
> that the publick will be surpriz'd at the present struggle of the actors
> against such a manager?

Fleetwood's defence, in *Queries upon Queries*, was generally held to be weak,
but successes in a paper war count for little, and predictably enough the solidarity
of the rebels began to come under strain. One valuable member of the company
who decided to make alternative arrangements was the actor and singer Thomas
Lowe. He inserted a note in the *London Daily Post* on 8 October thanking the
town for the many favours he had received from them and announcing that 'by
an Invitation of Several Persons of Distinction in Ireland' he had engaged to
perform that winter in Dublin.* Lowe's sense of timing was good—the same
day's press carried the news that the dissidents had failed in their bid: 'We hear
that the Lord Chamberlain has refus'd granting a License to the seceding
players to act in the Theatre in the Haymarket,' the *Daily Advertiser* told its
readers.

Garrick spent most of the next two months trying to put Humpty-Dumpty
together again. The general view among the would-be seceders was that their
failure to secure a licence had dissolved the agreement between them and set
them at liberty to shift for themselves. There was nothing for it but to tuck their
tails between their legs and make the best terms with Fleetwood that they
could.

Fleetwood shrewdly concentrated on securing Garrick's return, and offered

---

* Lowe, then in his middle twenties, had first come to attention in 1740 when at a performance
at Cliveden of the masque *Alfred* he had been the first to sing 'Rule Britannia'.

strong inducements, but Garrick refused to settle unless provision was made for the others. The fly in the ointment was Macklin. Fleetwood refused to have him back on any terms. They had gambled away long nights together at White's; he had stood by Macklin during his trial for murder eight years previously; now he felt that he had been betrayed, and he was adamant that Macklin would never appear in his theatre again. The craggy Irishman, for his part, was equally adamant that he and Garrick and the others must swim or sink together—and had a piece of paper to prove it.

Garrick then proposed that he would in effect stand surety for Macklin's behaviour, but Fleetwood would have none of it. This was followed by an attempt at arbitration, by two nominees of Macklin's and two of Garrick's; the latter suggested that if Macklin went off to Ireland for the winter, he and the others would provide for Mrs Macklin during his absence. Macklin rejected this, as he did a further offer from Garrick to make up his Irish earnings to an agreed sum—he was interested only in a return to Drury Lane.

It was now early November. The other rebels were seriously alarmed at the continuing deadlock. Their alarm turned to anxiety when it was reported that Garrick had decided to accompany Macklin to Ireland. They wrote to both men, appealing to Macklin not to drag them all down to ruin and imploring Garrick not to desert them:

> . . . . . You very well know, that, if you go, we must be made a sacrifice, nor can we see how it will benefit him in the least. We likewise think, that, if any tie or obligation be subsisting, we have an equal title to it with Mr. Macklin.*

The eight signatures on these letters did not include that of Kitty Clive, who until then had taken an enthusiastic part in the paper war; Macklin later asserted that when approached to sign 'she had the honour and spirit to refuse to be made so ridiculous a fool to so base a purpose'.† Her reasons may have been more complicated than that, but Clive certainly did now lose patience with the whole affair; within days she had accepted an offer from Rich to go over to Covent Garden, and she appeared there on 17 November as Lappett in Fielding's *The Miser*—one of her favourite roles.‡

Garrick was running out of bright ideas. He offered to play for a hundred guineas less if Macklin were taken back—Fleetwood was not interested. He got Rich to agree to take on Mrs Macklin for £3 a week and to give her a benefit, and he offered to pay Macklin £6 a week out of his own pocket—more, if his friends thought that not enough. Both offers were contemptuously refused.

---

* It is interesting to note from their letter to Macklin how unquestioningly Garrick's ascendancy was already accepted: 'By insisting upon this punctilio of honour,' they wrote, 'you prevent Mr Garrick from receiving an handsome income for his performance this season.'

† The signatories were Mr and Mrs Mills, Mr and Mrs Pritchard, Leigh, Havard, Berry and Woodburn.

‡ She soon regretted the move. The terms she got from Rich were little better than those she had just refused. She returned to Drury Lane in November 1745.

Macklin had learned the part of Shylock all too well; he was unshakeable in the belief that there existed a particular pound of theatrical flesh and that his title to it was inalienable.

Towards the end of November Garrick placed a notice in the press:

> As there have been many reports to my prejudice, I desire you will publish the *true* and *only* Reason why I have not yet appear'd upon the stage this winter. Many of the Persons concerned in the late struggle with the Manager might have been left destitute had I deserted them: therefore, I thought it incumbent on me to endeavour at their reconciliation with my own, upon reasonable terms; this I have almost accomplish'd, and hope I am excusable for not playing till it is determin'd.[2]

Garrick and Fleetwood came to terms—a figure was agreed of between £600 and £700. Others were less fortunate. Macklin later alleged that some of them had settled for two-thirds or even half of what they had formerly been paid. Mrs Pritchard found it impossible to agree articles, and followed Mrs Clive to Covent Garden.

Garrick's return was announced in the playbills and newspapers for 6 December. He was to play Bayes in *The Rehearsal*—Mills and Havard, two of his fellow-rebels, were also billed to appear. That morning, a pamphlet called *The Case of Charles Macklin, Comedian*, made its appearance. It was a well-presented piece—Macklin was thought by some to have had the assistance of an experienced polemicist called Corbyn Morris.* He still refused to accept that circumstances alter cases. He and Garrick, he maintained, had 'entered into a strict friendship together', mutually engaging 'to adhere to each other, and not to act upon separate stages'. It was only out of a strict regard for that agreement that he had turned down Fleetwood's attractive offer to re-engage (there was no mention of what Fleetwood expected by way of a *quid pro quo*). Garrick, he insisted, had sworn never to desert him, promised that they would 'share their theatrical fortunes' and assured him that if the worst came to the worst, they would go off together to Ireland.

He was clearly sensitive to the charge of ingratitude towards Fleetwood, and defended himself from it with some dignity: 'I have not apprehended, because a gentleman has acted towards me with humanity in my distress, that, therefore, he has an absolute right over me, and to load me with oppression as long as I live.' But it was plain from a short, almost throwaway paragraph at the end, that his resolution was beginning to falter:

> That my desire of accepting any reasonable terms may clearly appear, I beg leave to declare, that I shall thankfully receive from Mr. Fleetwood

---

* Corbyn Morris (1710–79), a friend of Hume's, would make proposals to the government after the '45 for the pacification of the Highlands. Horace Walpole thought his *Essay towards fixing the True Standards of Wit, Humour, Raillery, Satire, and Ridicule, &c* 'one of the only new books at all worth reading', but that may have been because it was dedicated to his father. Morris was later appointed Commissioner of the Customs.

three-fourths of the same weekly salary for myself and my wife for the remainder of this season, with our benefits, which we had last season, or whatever other terms shall be judged to be reasonable, by any three impartial gentlemen.

Any chance that Fleetwood would respond to that overture was almost immediately blown away. That same evening Macklin's crony Dr Barrowby led a large party from the Horn Tavern in Fleet Street to the playhouse, intent on causing a riot. They occupied much of the pit, and broke into some of the boxes, knocking down the doorkeepers and turning out large numbers of servants who were keeping places for 'persons of Quality and Distinction'.

Bayes makes his entry early in the first scene, and is supposed to say, 'Your most obsequious and most observant very servant, sir.' Garrick made a number of submissive bows and asked to be heard. He was greeted with loud hisses, and a continual chant of 'Off! Off! Off!' 'The playhouse,' writes Davies, 'showed more like a bear-garden than a theatre-royal. The sea, in a storm, was not more terrible and boisterous than the loud and various noises which issued from the pit, galleries, and boxes.'[3] Garrick stood aloof, well upstage, trying as best he might to avoid the barrage of rotten eggs and apples (and peas—the approved eighteenth-century method of doing to actors what marbles did to police horses in the twentieth).

Two days later, Garrick published his answer to Macklin's 'False and scandalous Libel'. It was a prosy and somewhat repetitious effort; Garrick is thought to have had the assistance of William Guthrie, who, as a parliamentary reporter for Cave's *Gentleman's Magazine*, was a colleague of Johnson's.* Guthrie was the son of a Scottish episcopal clergyman and a graduate of the University of Aberdeen, and it could be that some of the more turgid passages are his—'Our particular engagement every man of common sense must understand to be engrafted into that posterior and more general one' doesn't sound at all like Garrick, even at his most formal.

It didn't much matter. The violence of Tuesday evening had given Garrick a useful stick to beat Macklin with, and he was able to work in a smug reference to 'the unjust and dishonest methods he took to disturb the audience, and prejudice my performance, without giving me time to answer him'. For the rest, he was content to rehearse arguments with which the town was becoming wearisomely familiar, emphasizing the distress of the other players, and his own embarrassment at finding himself caught 'betwixt their pressing real necessities and Mr. Macklin's untractable and unreasonable obstinacy'.

That evening he was once more billed to appear as Bayes. It was known that Dr Barrowby and his friends again intended to grace the occasion with their

---

* Guthrie later collaborated in the 12-volume *General History of the World, from the Creation to the Present Time*; this was favourably noticed in the 'Critical Review', allegedly by Guthrie himself. He also wrote a notably inaccurate *General History of Scotland* in 10 volumes. 'Sir, he is a man of parts,' Johnson told Boswell. 'He has no great regular fund of knowledge; but by reading so long, and writing so long, he no doubt has picked up a good deal.' (*Life*, ii, 52.)

presence, but by now the Garrick faction had got itself organized. Garrick had formed a close friendship with a young man of his own age called William Windham, whose family had been prominent for many generations in the affairs of Norfolk. Windham was extremely talented. As much at home in Spanish and French as in Latin and Greek, he could also get by in Dutch and German; he was a gifted mathematician and draughtsman; he had spent several years abroad with a tutor, returning to England only in 1742, and his unconventional education had nurtured a catholic range of interests—botany and fencing, military history and fiddling, mountaineering and philosophy. Tall, thin and narrow-chested, Windham also excelled in every feat of strength and agility. He was devoted, in particular, to what was then sometimes called 'the athletic art', and since his return to London had made the acquaintance of the famous John Broughton*— hence the nickname 'Boxing Windham'. That evening, with the connivance of Fleetwood, he smuggled thirty pugilists into the theatre before the doors were open:

> The bruizers took possession of the middle of the pit. When the last music was playing, one of them stood up, and stopping the band in the orchestra, said, in a loud voice, "Gentlemen, I am told that some persons here are come with an intention not to hear the play; I came to hear it; I paid my money for it, and I desire that they who come to interrupt, may all withdraw, and not stay to hinder my diversion." This occasioned a general uproar; but the Broughtonians knew how to deal their blows with irresist-ible vigour. They fell upon Macklin's party, and drove them out of the pit.[4]

Enter Garrick—who bowed respectfully to the audience, and was allowed to play through without interruption. Macklin, like a brain-damaged boxer unaware that he has been counted out, attempted a further flurry of punches some days later, several of them of them aimed well below the belt. His *Reply to Mr Garrick's Answer to the Case of Charles Macklin, Comedian*, is a rehash of his earlier arguments, but the tone is more sourly *ad hominem*—'your usual propensity to falsehood'; 'a treacherous, but also an avaricious disposition'; 'the vanity and dirtiness of your temper'. There is also a first taste of the glancing francophobia which would be directed against Garrick more than once in the course of his career—Macklin, referring to his own suggestion that Fleetwood should take him back at three-quarters of his former salary, qualifies it sneeringly as 'a proper punishment of my folly in relying upon your faith, which is nearly allied in every respect to Gallic fidelity'.

The town was inclined to think he had got what was coming to him. The

---

* John Broughton (1705–89), 'the father of British pugilism', began life as a waterman. In 1743 he was running a boxing theatre which he had built for himself in Hanway Street, off the Tottenham Court Road. One of his patrons was the Duke of Cumberland, who had him made a yeoman of the guard. His career came to an end in 1750 after a bout in which he had been heavily backed by the Duke. Broughton was blinded by his opponent, and Cumberland, suddenly poorer by £10,000, withdrew his patronage.

Daily Advertiser mockingly dedicated 'The Fable of the Iron and the Earthen Pot' to him:

> Vers'd thou art in every Wile
> Thy conduct who can Reconcile?
> Who'll think thee knowing in Intrigue
> With Garrick e'er to join in League?
> Was not the Maxim to thee known
> That Leaguers 'Twixt Equals suit alone?
> We grant thee Merit; yet how far
> Does Sol outshine the brightest Star?
> Thy strength hads't thou but duly weigh'd
> No Feuds had then to ills betray'd.
> Still if thou well or ill deserve
> Pity, methinks, to let thee starve
> Pity that thou shoulds't find too late
> Sage Aesop's Earthen Pot thy fate.

It is well-nigh impossible, at a distance of two-and-a-half centuries, to assess the rights and wrongs of this messy and unhappy quarrel. It is difficult not to feel some sympathy with Macklin: the snarling anger is unattractive, but there is real pain there, too:

> You know very well, that I have often advised you, upon many circumstances of your acting, which you have allowed to be right, and accordingly adopted my advice; and I am not conscious that I had ever more benefit from you, than you constantly received from my friendship. But as your merit upon the stage is vastly superior to mine, this gives me the greater right to complain of your breach of engagements. It was upon the strength of your power, that I ventured to secede from the manager; and when we had united our force together, it was the more ungenerous in you, who was the strongest, to be guilty of desertion.

Not easy words for a man well into middle life to write to someone almost twenty years his junior.

Garrick's role in the affair is less easy to judge. To write, as Kirkman does, of the 'infamy of Garrick's apostasy'[5] is obviously excessive, even by the standards of theatrical biography, although he clearly did renege on his initial agreement with Macklin. Equally, however, it is plain that he subsequently exerted himself in his efforts to salvage something for everybody from the wreck of their venture. Tom Davies knew both men, and was an informed observer of their quarrel. Reflecting on it more than thirty years later, his conclusion was that Garrick had been the victim of his own impetuosity:

> The trouble and anxiety which Garrick brought upon himself, during this disagreeable contest, proceeded from a conduct, which, in a greater or less degree, pursued him through life; the precipitancy of his temper often

hurried him into engagements, which he either could or would not, and, indeed, sometimes, ought not, to fulfil.[6]

The breach between Macklin and Garrick was never mended. From that time on, the older man lost no opportunity to belittle Garrick or spread stories about his alleged meanness. This did not inhibit him from soliciting favours or prevent him from returning to act at Drury Lane from time to time after Garrick became the manager there, but until the end of his very long life he drew on a deep well of animosity.

He left the stage for a time, and one of his schemes was for a series of lectures, on topics ranging from the plays of Shakespeare to the argument for Protestantism. After his death, Kirkman found in his papers notes for one he intended to call 'Garrick-bane':

> The *Garrick-bane* was invented by a *Quack*, somewhere about Wapping; one Doctor *Guichard*, or *Giffard*, was the purchaser of it: he bought it, according to report, from a *little Smouse*, a damned fly little fellow, who was quacking about town, in clubs, at Ale-houses, Coffee-houses, and Punch-houses, at that time of the day; and the *Smouse*, perceiving that the *nostrum* took, sold it to the Doctor six several times. . . . . . This little *Smouse* was a daily canker to men's fame; nothing plagued him so much as the merit of his contemporaries; and every device that envy, policy, mimickry, and tyranny could invent, he constantly practised, to obscure and blast the worth of every Actor of reputation.[7]

'Smouse' was a pejorative eighteenth-century word for a Jew. In Macklin's xenophobic book, it seems, that was an even lower form of animal life than a Frenchman.

6

Vaulting Ambition

Fleetwood, having busked his way through the first three months of the season without his star performer, was understandably eager to make up for lost time. So was Garrick. In the few weeks of 1743 that remained he appeared as Lear, Hamlet and Richard, and he was also seen as Lothario in *The Fair Penitent* and Archer in *The Stratagem*.

With these all now established in his repertoire, Garrick struck out on his fourth great Shakespearean role. In the first week of 1744 he was announced to appear in *Macbeth*—'Tragedy reviv'd,' said the bills. 'As written by Shakespeare.' Quin was taken aback, and not a little indignant. 'What does he mean?' he enquired. 'Don't I play *Macbeth* as written by Shakespeare?' To which the answer was 'no'. *Macbeth* had first been performed at Lincoln's Inn Fields in 1664 in a version by Sir William Davenant, Poet Laureate to Charles I. That altered text had held the stage ever since. Although it had more than two hundred performances in that time, it was not a vehicle that held a strong appeal for the actors of the day:

> Macbeth, they constantly exclaimed, was not a character of the first rate; all the pith of it was exhausted, they said, in the first and second acts of the play. They formed their judgment from the drowsy and ineffectual manner of Garrick's predecessors, who could not force attention or applause from the audience during the last three acts.[1]

Garrick resolved to change all that, and had set about the task with characteristic thoroughness. He certainly consulted Johnson—that much is plain from a comparison of his text with the latter's *Miscellaneous Observations on the Tragedy of Macbeth* which appeared the following year. He also took the advice of the scholar and theologian William Warburton, who was then at work on a new edition of Shakespeare.*

Garrick did not restore the Porter's scene in Act II—his discourse on the effects of drink would have gone down well enough in the footman's gallery, but not elsewhere in the house. He also stopped short of doing away with the

---

* William Warburton (1698–1779), formidable and cantankerous, was a close friend of Pope's, and later became Bishop of Gloucester. He and Garrick were to develop a lifelong friendship.

songs and dances Davenant had devised for the witches although, except for Hecate, they no longer flew about the stage.* The temptation to write a dying speech for himself was altogether too strong to resist (he has Macbeth expire on stage):

'Tis done! the scene of life will quickly close.
Ambition's vain, delusive dreams are fled,
And now I wake to darkness, guilt and horror
I cannot bear it! Let me shake it off.—
'Twa' not be; my soul is clogged with blood.
I cannot rise! I dare not ask for mercy.
It is too late, hell drags me down. I sink,
I sink—Oh!—my soul is lost forever!
Oh! (Dies.)

This rather embarrassing piece of fustian almost certainly sounded better on the boards than it reads on the page. Its purpose was to allow Garrick to go into what became one of his most celebrated routines, vividly described some years later by the French ballet master Jean Georges Noverre:

..... The approach of death showed each instant on his face; his eyes became dim, his voice could not support the efforts he made to speak his thoughts. His gestures, without losing their expression, revealed the approach of the last moment; his legs gave way under him, his face lengthened, his pale and livid features bore the signs of suffering and repentance. At last, he fell; at that moment his crimes peopled his thoughts with the most horrible forms; terrified at the hideous picture which his past acts revealed to him, he struggled against death; nature seemed to make one supreme effort. His plight made the audience shudder, he clawed the ground and seemed to be digging his own grave, but the dread moment was nigh, one saw death in reality, everything expressed that instant which makes all equal ... The death rattle and the convulsive movements of the features, arms and breast, gave the final touch to this terrible picture.†

One can see what Colley Cibber meant when he said that, as Macbeth, Garrick

---

* The witches were traditionally played by men, and presented in what Horace Walpole termed 'a buffoon light'. Garrick's witches usually wore blue-checked aprons, torn mob-caps and high-crowned black hats. Interestingly enough, when his friend William Windham was on the Grand Tour he and some friends put on a performance of *Macbeth* in Geneva and for the witches and their broomsticks substituted magicians with long beards and black gowns. 'This alteration,' one of the friends later wrote, 'instead of ridicule, produced additional awe and horror. Garrick has since approved the idea; but owned he durst not carry it into execution himself for fear of offending the Gallery.' (*Ketton-Cremer, op. cit.*, p. 30.)

† *Lettres sur la Danse et sur les Ballets*, Lyons, 1760, translated as *Letters on Dancing and Ballet* by Cyril Beaumont, London, 1930, pp. 84–5. The Folger Library owns a prompt-book for *Macbeth* dating from Garrick's day. At the beginning of Act V the direction 'Stage Cloth on' appears. In order to protect the actors' clothes from the bare boards, it was the custom before all death scenes to lay out on the stage a six-foot square of green baize.

'out-did his usual out-doings'. The powerful realism of his performance was known to affect even those who appeared on the stage with him. On one occasion, in the banquet scene in Act III, he hissed the line, 'There's blood upon thy face', with such intensity that the actor playing the first murderer was completely thrown. Instead of growling ''Tis Banquo's then', his hand flew involuntarily to his face and the words that came out were 'Is there, by God?'

Murphy, in his account of Garrick's performance, writes that when he re-appeared after the murder, with the dagger in his hand, 'he looked like a ghastly spectacle, and his complexion grew whiter every moment'—a tricky feat, even for someone of Garrick's virtuosity. A writer in the *Connoisseur* later came to the commonsense conclusion that he simply wiped the make-up from his face before making his entrance. The *Connnoisseur*'s critic also noted that Garrick came on at this point with his wig awry and one of its ties undone, a piece of business which left him unimpressed: 'The player would have us imagine that the same deed, which has thrown all that horror and confusion into his counten-ance, has also untwisted one of the tails of his periwig.'[2]

The critic John Hill, writing in 1750, said that when Garrick first appeared as Macbeth, he 'took occasion in one of his scenes of greatest confusion to enter upon the stage with his coat and waistcoat both unbuttoned'.[3] That is indeed how he appears in Zoffany's famous painting of him with Mrs Pritchard as Lady Macbeth, although Hill says that after the first night he was dissuaded by friends from repeating that particular piece of business. He appears on the Zoffany canvas in black shoes and white stockings, red breeches, a blue-green collarless coat edged with gold braid and buttons, and a red waistcoat also trimmed with gold braid.* Only much later in the century would there be an attempt to achieve any sort of historical accuracy in the matter of stage dress.†

Just before Garrick's début as Macbeth there had appeared a short sixpenny pamphlet with a very long title: *An Essay on Acting: In which will be considered The Mimical behaviour of a Certain fashonable faulty Actor, and the Laud-ableness of such unmannerly, as well as inhumane Proceedings. To which will be added, A short Criticism on his acting Macbeth.*‡ The anonymous author ridicules Garrick's pretensions to be seen in a role for which he is manifestly unsuited:

> *Valour* and *Ambition*, the two Grand *Characteristicks* of *Macbeth*, form
> in the *Mind's Eye* a Person of *near six Feet High, corpulently Graceful,* a
> *round Visage,* a *Large hazel Eye, acquiline Nose, prominent Chest,* and a
> *well-calv'd Leg,* rather inclin'd to that which is call'd an *Irish Leg*; this, I

---

* Joseph Knight wrote rather unkindly that the Zoffany portrait showed Garrick 'like a little man disguised as a footman'. (*Knight*, 329.)

† The way in which Macklin had got himself up to play Shylock in 1741 must perhaps be allowed as a proving exception to this. And it was Macklin, in 1773, who would first act Macbeth 'in the old Caledonian habit'. A contemporary engraving depicted him in tartan stockings and a Balmoral bonnet, and tradition has it that in some scenes he wore the kilt.

‡ London, 1744.

say, would be the *Painter's* Choice, was he to give us the *Macbeth* of *his Imagination*; I mention this only to prove that Mr *G - - - - - k* is not form'd in the least, *externally*, no more than *internally*, for that Character . . . . . Mr. *G - - - - - k*, could he *Speak* the *Part*, is well form'd for *Fleance*, or one of the *Infant Shadows* in the Cauldron Scene, but for the Manager to impose *him* upon the Town for a *Macbeth*, and to refuse taking *another Comedian* into his House, is such an Example of *Ignorance* and *Impudence*, that it is not to be *parallel'd* but by his own *unparallel'd* Behaviour.

The mockery is not all directed at Garrick, however—the manner in which it had become customary to treat Banquo's ghost in the banquet scene also comes under attack, for example, as does the way in which Quin, until then a leading exponent of the role, clutched at the air-drawn dagger. Gradually it dawns on the reader that this pamphlet is not entirely what it seems. And no more it is— because it was written by Garrick himself. His most straightforward aim was to attract attention to himself, but the pamphlet was also intended to blunt any possible criticism by anticipating it, and to signal some of the ways in which his interpretation and performance would be distinctive. He concludes with a rapturous hymn of praise to the author to whose text he claims to be returning:

> Shakespear was a Writer not to be confin'd by *Rule*; he had a *despotick Power* over all Nature; *Laws* would be an *Infringement* of his *Prerogative*; his *scepter'd Pen* wav'd Controul over every *Passion* and *Humour*; his *Royal Word* was not only *Absolute*, but *Creative*; *Ideas, Language*, and *Sentiment* were his *Slaves*, they were *chain'd* to the *Triumphal Car* of his *Genius*; and when he made his *Entry* into the *Temple* of *Fame*, all *Parnassus* rung with *Acclamations*; the *Muses* sung his *Conquests*, crown'd him with never-fading *Laurels*, and pronounc'd him *Immortal*. AMEN.*

It was the first time Garrick had resorted to this curiously tortuous self-puffing routine, but it would not be the last.

Early in March, France declared war on Britain. Rich, at Covent Garden, was quick to show that he knew where his duty lay:

> Last Night their Royal Highnesses the Prince and Princess of Wales were at the Theatre Royal in Covent Garden to see the Merchant of Venice; when the song of *Britons strike home* was commanded to be sung, which was accordingly done, with the Chorus's, accompanied by Trumpets, Kettle-Drums, etc. and met with the Greatest Applause.[4]

There were frequent repeat performances in the weeks that followed, together with a piece called *To Arms,* and by the middle of April Rich was also ready

---

* Garrick also included a passage aimed at conciliating Macklin: 'I shall not enter into the reasons why he is excluded at present, but shall only say as an advocate for the public, that I wish for their sake there were many more such actors as him upon both theatres.'

with a production of *Henry V*—'Reviv'd by particular desire,' announced the
bills. 'Containing the memorable battle of Agincourt, with the total overthrow
of the French Army.'

The management at Drury Lane was slower off the mark—the audience there
was not offered *Britons Strike Home* until the second week in April. Nor, later
in the month, did Fleetwood feel inhibited by the public mood from presenting
a play recently translated from the French—but then it was a piece that offered
just as big a stick to beat France with as *Henry V*, even if it did so rather more
subtly. A correspondent in the *General Advertiser* had obviously been well briefed
to spell it out:

> It is with great Pleasure I find by the Publick Papers that a tragedy founded
> on Voltaire's *Mahomet* is now in rehearsal at Drury Lane Theatre. The
> Original was by Authority forbid to be played in France on account of the
> free and noble Sentiments with regard to Bigotry and Enthusiasm, which
> shine through it; and which that Nation found as applicable to itself, as
> to the bloody propagators of Mahomet's religion. . . . . . It is not doubted
> but these very Sentiments, which in France, prevented the Representation
> of this piece, will, in England speak loudly in its favor (provided our
> English poet is not unequal to his subject) especially since so audacious an
> attempt has been lately made by the Common Enemy of Europe to establish
> at once a Civil and Spiritual Tyranny over those injur'd Nations, by the
> old Mahometan and Roman Arguments of Fire and Sword.[5]

Le Fanatisme, ou Mahomet le Prophète had been acted two years previously in
Paris, but had come off after three nights. Voltaire, in his dedication to Frederick
the Great, wrote that his pen was guided by the twin principles of love of mankind
and hatred of fanaticism, but it reads like a thoroughgoing assault on religion
in general and revealed religion in particular.*

Madness—poison—incest—parricide—suicide—there is something for
everybody in *Mahomet the Impostor* and plenty of work for the stage-hands
charged with laying out the stage cloth. The English version was the work of
James Miller, a member of that large army of stage-struck clergymen who figure
so prominently in the eighteenth-century theatre.† His text, high-flown and
rhetorical, reads like a parody of a Hollywood epic starring Charlton Heston.
Garrick played the Christian captive Zaphna, and had to grapple with lines like

> Down, down, good Pharon. Thou, poor injured corse,
> May I embrace thee? Won't thy pallid wound

---

* He later, with characteristic impudence, re-dedicated it to Pope Benedict XIV.
† Miller, who had previously written only sentimental comedies (and who died on his benefit
night), seems to have had difficulties in completing *Mahomet*, and Garrick's friend John Hoadly
— also a parson — had been called in to lend a hand. Hoadly was the son of the Bishop of
Winchester. His father's extensive patronage allowed him to indulge his passion for the theatre
to the exclusion of almost all else. He and Garrick were lifelong friends and Garrick leaned
heavily on his advice.

Purple anew at the unnatural touch
And ooze fresh calls for vengeance?

It was his thirtieth theatrical role, and not his most distinguished, although twenty years later he would revise the play successfully enough for it to play twelve times in a single season.

Garrick's greatest success of 1743–4 came when he appeared for the first time in *The Provok'd Husband*. Left unfinished by Vanbrugh as *A Journey to London*, it had been completed by Colley Cibber and first produced in 1728. The husband in question is Lord Townly, and the provocation is afforded by the dissipation and extravagance of his wife. Garrick made his début on Woffington's benefit night, and she played opposite him as Lady Townly. It was common knowledge by now that their private relationship had become turbulent; to the pit and the boxes some of their stage exchanges as man and wife had a delicious piquancy:

LADY TOWNLY: My lord, my lord—you would make a woman mad!

LORD TOWNLY: Madam, madam, you would make a man a fool.

LADY TOWNLY: If Heaven has made you otherwise, that won't be in my power.

LORD TOWNLY: Whatever may be in your inclination, madam, I'll prevent your making me a beggar at least.

LADY TOWNLY: A beggar! Croesus! I am out of patience!—I won't come home till four tomorrow morning

LORD TOWNLY: That may be, madam; but I'll order the doors to be locked at twelve.

LADY TOWNLY: Then I won't come home till tomorrow night.

LORD TOWNLY: Then, madam, you shall never come home again.
       (*Exit.*)

Blood-red tea notwithstanding, it was not extravagance which lay at the root of the trouble. That she should be pursued around town and at the spas by the likes of Colley Cibber and his friend Owen Mac Swiney was merely a comic subplot.* Cibber, it is true, was exceptionally well-preserved, but he was now in his seventies, and Swiney was only a few years younger.† The sight of these two elderly swains proffering their nosegays and panting to hand her into her coach was the cause of much merriment and allowed a wag who knew his Apocrypha to pass into circulation a good joke about Susannah and the elders.‡

---

* Swiney (1680–1754) was born near Enniscorthy, County Wexford. After a chequered career in theatre management, he was made bankrupt and lived abroad for some years, commissioning portraits as an agent and recruiting opera singers for Handel. He had returned to England in 1735.
† In *Common Sense* in 1739, Thomas Earl wrote that Colley was 'return'd from Tunbridge, where he went to drink the Waters — for a little Immortality, I suppose: — Health and Spirits I am sure he does not want (for he looks but Forty, 'tho he is, I believe, Sixty-nine).'
‡ The translators of the Authorized Version of 1611 rehearsed the story-line of *The historie of Susanna* with delightful economy: 'Two Iudges hide themselues in the garden of Susanna to haue their pleasure of her: which when they could not obteine, they accuse and cause her to be condemned for adulterie; but Daniel examineth the matter againe, and findeth the two iudges false.'

Garrick had younger and more serious rivals, although to establish any but the sketchiest of chronologies for the numerous liaisons into which Woffington was drawn by her cheerful promiscuity is impossible. There was Sir Charles Hanbury Williams, who had been the MP for Monmouthshire for some years and held office under Walpole as Paymaster of the Marine Forces. He seems to have fallen under her spell as early as 1740 but, finding Darnley in possession at the time, had to content himself with penning a number of amorous songs to her, which were privately circulated.

Williams had been the contemporary at Eton of Pitt and Fielding and Henry Fox, and was known as a witty conversationalist and a writer of light, satirical verse, some of it rather coarse. One piece of his which went the rounds was called 'Old England's *Te Deum*', a ribald parody addressed to the King: 'The Holy Bench of Bishops throughout the land: doth acknowledge thee; Thine honourable true: and steady son; Also my Lady Yarmouth: the Comforter . .'

Williams's efforts to persuade Woffington to be his Comforter do not seem to have succeeded until 1743—that, at least, was the year in which he commissioned a portrait of her from the French painter Jean-Baptiste Van Loo.* It was also the year in which she was satirized, in a squib entitled *Theatrical Correspondence in Death*, as being like 'Madam Nell Gwin herself . . . (excepting a Royal Cully)'.†
Williams did not remain long in favour, however. Soon after he left town for his Welsh estates in the summer of 1744, he had a letter from his friend Horace Walpole: 'Rigby will have told you that Lord Darnley is on the *tapis* again.'
Williams responded with six stanzas of abuse:

> . . . Venus, whose charms rule all above,
> Is famed for fickleness in love,
> And for her beauty's pow'r;
> You are her copy drawn with care,
> Like her, are exquisitely fair,
> Like her a thorough whore.

He had, of course, treated her like one—his correspondence indicates that he had arranged for his (and Garrick's) friend Rigby to keep his place warm for him during his absence. By August he was able to be more philosophical. 'I am glad the man has got his mare again,' he wrote in a letter to another old friend, Stephen Fox. 'She is so handsome that anybody must like her; and he is so rich that any woman must like him. I am forced to be content with her picture, which I have hung up in my room in the wood.'‡

---

* Van Loo (1684–1745), a native of Aix-en-Provence, was one of many European painters — Watteau, Canaletto, Cipriani — who crossed the Channel in the eighteenth century to compete for commissions from rich English connoisseurs. His younger brother, Carle, also a portraitist, became principal painter to the French king.
† Cully is an old slang word meaning dupe or gull. This was Woffington's good luck. On the whole the House of Hanover looked after its kept women less well than the House of Stuart.
‡ In 1746 Williams turned to diplomacy, serving in Dresden, Berlin and St Petersburg. Caught in a diplomatic crossfire, and instructed to reverse the successful policies he had been pursuing

How Garrick took all this can only be guessed at. After the rupture between them, Macklin used to put it about that his former friend took a complaisant view of the way Woffington distributed her favours, but that does not seem in character. Actresses might well be regarded as a sexual commodity—there is some evidence that that is how Woffington regarded herself—but it is difficult to envisage Garrick contemplating marriage with a good-hearted whore.

He now had lodgings in St James's Street, adjoining the Great Piazza in Covent Garden, and Woffington had taken—or perhaps been installed—in a house thirteen miles or so up the Thames from St Paul's at Teddington. Her sister Polly, now aged fifteen, had returned from her French convent. Woffington's ambitions for her were purely social and highly conventional, but Polly, who had danced briefly at Covent Garden three years previously, was showing an interest in the stage. A play was got up privately, perhaps to assess what her talents amounted to, and Garrick was prevailed upon to take part.

The only account we have of the occasion is that of the actress George Anne Bellamy, the illegitimate daughter of Garrick's Irish admirer, Lord Tyrawley, who maintained that Garrick was there because he 'languished to be reconciled to Mrs Woffington'. That may or may not be the case. Bellamy was a girl in her early teens at the time, and her six-volume 'autobiography' is not a model of accuracy.* The play chosen was *The Distressed Mother*, by Ambrose Philips,† an adaptation of Racine's *Andromaque*. 'My mother and Mrs Woffington played the attendants,' wrote Bellamy, 'Mr Garrick, Orestes; Mr Sullivan, a Fellow of Trinity College, Dublin, Pyrrhus; Miss Woffington, Hermione, and Andromache fell to my lot. . . . . . All the people of fashion in the neighbourhood honoured our barn with their presence.'‡

Garrick's circle of friends and acquaintances was becoming increasingly grand. He spent some days visiting his friend Richard Rigby at his estate in Essex. Rigby's father had amassed a fortune as a factor to the South Sea Company and had built a mansion at Mistley, on the Stour, which the son had inherited as a child. After the grand tour, he had attached himself to Frederick, Prince of Wales, to whom, as the *Dictionary of National Biography* puts it, 'he politely lost money at the gaming table'. Although he would remain a bachelor, he was a considerable ladies' man; still only twenty-two, he would shortly enter Parliament as the Member

---

at the Russian court, he eventually went out of his mind and committed suicide in 1759 at the age of fifty-one. He is buried in Westminster Abbey.

* *An Apology for the Life of George Anne Bellamy, late of Covent Garden Theatre, written by herself*, London, 1785. In fact it was written by Alexander Bicknell, a busy hack who had written lives of the Black Prince and Alfred the Great. When publication was announced, Kitty Clive wrote to a friend, 'It can have no other subject than how many different men she has been strumpet to.'

† Philips (1674–1748), a friend of Addison's, had quarrelled violently with Pope over the respective merits of their pastorals. Lines like 'Dimply damsel, sweetly smiling', in one of his poems to children, earned him the nickname of 'Namby-Pamby'.

‡ Mr Sullivan of Trinity College was there because he was a friend of Tom Sheridan's. Sheridan had come over to play at Covent Garden in the spring and was now living in some style in a villa at nearby Kingston-on-Thames.

for Castle Rising, the beginning of a lucrative political career—at the time of his death in 1788 it was said that he left 'near half a million of public money'.

Garrick subsequently stayed with William Windham at his hunting box near Capel St Mary in Suffolk, and Windham accompanied him when he moved on to Easton Hall, in the same county, as the guest of the Earl and Countess of Rochford.* Rochford was exactly the same age as Garrick, and had been appointed a Lord of the Bedchamber at the age of twenty-one. Lady Rochford was said to have refused the Duke of Cumberland and various other royals. Horace Walpole described her as 'one of our court-beauties—large, but very handsome, with great delicacy and address'.

She was delighted to hear that Garrick would arrive on her husband's birthday, she wrote. And it is clear from her letter that Garrick still had his problems with Fleetwood, and had been daydreaming about giving it all up and retiring to a life of rural ease: 'I wish it was as much in my power to hinder your attendance on Mr Fleetwood and settle you in a pretty farm, agreeable to your wishes, in Suffolk at £200 a year.'

That the affairs of Drury Lane were much on his mind during his stay at Easton emerges from a letter he sent from there to another friend, Somerset Draper. 'Though I have little to say to you of consequence,' he began, 'I must write to you because I love you; we are generally most troublesome to our best friends.' But it quickly emerges that he has something of considerable consequence to communicate:

> Mr. Fleetwood, before I went out of town, had a conference with me. I proposed you to be present; but he refused it. He put on an air of importance, charging me with breach of faith in telling every body I would not play without my arrears; you may imagine I gave him as good as he brought; in short, after many warm words, expostulations, and invectives on both sides, he took me by the hand, and finding I was resolute, he agreed to pay me the last year's arrears immediately, and to give me such security for the bond and judgment, as Mr. Whitehorse should approve of. I told him, when he had done that, I was ready to agree with him; he invited me several times to dinner; but I would not go. He desired I would not say any more about my debt, and he would convince me how willing he was to live in harmony and friendship.[6]

Draper, twenty years Garrick's senior, was a brewer—they could well have met during Garrick's days as a vintner in Durham Yard. He had also recently become a partner of the publishers Jacob and Richard Tonson. He was to make himself useful to Garrick in all sorts of ways over the years: acting for him in his negotiations with managers and actors, looking after his investments, keeping an eye on his house when he was away.†

---

* Rochford had inherited Easton from an uncle two years previously; the main family seat was St Osyth Priory in Essex.

† 'I'll tell you a fact,' Garrick wrote to a correspondent years after his death in 1756. 'The Man of all Men I lov'd the best, one *Draper* by name, & now an arch angel in Heav'n, was for many years Every Morning with Me at breakfast time.' *Letters*, 1299.

A short aside in his letter to Draper indicates that at that stage his relations with Woffington were still close. 'Mrs Woffington is engaged to her satisfaction,' he wrote. 'As the particulars are a secret, and I am intrusted with them, I can tell you no more upon that head.' Garrick was writing the day after the start of the Drury Lane season, and the bills show that Woffington was Mrs Frail in *Love for Love* on the opening night and made frequent appearances in the ensuing weeks; Garrick himself did not appear until 19 October, however, an indication, possibly, that Fleetwood had found it difficult to honour his undertakings to him.

Fleetwood's affairs were now, in fact, spinning disastrously out of control. On the night of Garrick's belated first appearance as Bayes, the afterpiece was an extravagant pantomime called *The Amorous Goddess*, and the manager, in a last effort to avert bankruptcy, announced an increase in the price of tickets—boxes were to be 5s instead of 4s, the pit 3s instead of 2s 6d, the first gallery 2s instead of eighteen-pence.

This lit a not particularly slow fuse. 'I remember in *Cibber's* Time, the Prices to have been raised when a *new* Play has been thoroughly new dressed,' wrote Benjamin Victor:

> That carried the Appearance of Reason; because, after the Run of that Play was over, the Prices fell again to their old Standard: the Prices were also raised at the Introduction of a Pantomime, when it was supposed a Thousand Pounds, or upwards, were generally expended in the Decoration of those Raree-shews; but in the Case before us, full Prices were demanded, and taken, for an old Pantomime of no Manner of Merit.[7]

Over the next four weeks Fleetwood compounded his offence by continuing to charge the new prices for a whole raft of other pantomimes—*Columbine Courtezan*, *Harlequin Shipwrecked*, *The Fortune Tellers*, *Robin Goodfellow*—all of which had been in the repertory for a number of years.

On 17 November, a performance of *The Conscious Lovers*, with Delane and Woffington in the cast, was brought to a halt by noisy calls for the manager. Fleetwood, who did not lack spirit, responded loftily that as he was not an actor he was not required to appear on the stage—perhaps it was this which provoked Horace Walpole to rise from his seat in a box and denounce the manager as 'an impudent rascal.' Fleetwood may well have been tipped off that there was trouble brewing; it was later alleged that he had positioned a number of bruisers in the pit 'to insult Gentlemen'. One would not expect him to confirm that he had taken such a sensible precaution—'there was none but Peace Officers, Carpenters and Scene-men,' he maintained, and they had only appeared when the rioters started tearing up benches and threatening to go on to the stage and demolish the scenery. 'Nor,' he added, 'could the Manager apprehend this legal precaution to *prevent mischief* and *defend* his property would ever be construed as an infringement on the liberty of an audience.'*

---

* Fleetwood gave his version of events in an *Address to the Public* published in the *General Advertiser* on 22 November.

Fleetwood did eventually agree to see a deputation on that Saturday night, and to them he made a concession—the 'advanced prices' would be returned to those who, as the *General Advertiser* put it, 'did not choose to be tortured with entertainments'. He might have saved himself the trouble. The following Monday, Garrick was billed to make his second appearance as Sir John Brute in *The Provok'd Wife*. The moment the house opened, the rioters swept in, drove the door-keepers from their posts and gave renewed expression to their traditional liberties. More benches were ripped out and candle sconces were torn from the walls and flung on to the stage; it seemed for a time as if the building might go up in flames.

Remarkably enough, it took the carpenters, plasterers and glaziers only two days to repair the worst of the damage. The theatre reopened on Thursday, 20 November, with a performance of *Tamerlane*. The evening was not without incident, however:

> To Those who remained in the Pit in Drury Lane Playhouse on Thursday Evening, and were refus'd their money: GENTLEMEN: If you are sensible of the Insults that we receiv'd from the servants of the Manager (after we had remain'd orderly in the House expecting our money for the best part of an hour) being expos'd to the danger of our lives from several sticks, &c being thrown at us from the stage, and from the attack of Soldiers jumping into the Pit with their bayonets fix'd, you'll meet tomorrow several Gentlemen equally injur'd, at the *Fountain Tavern* in Catherine Street in the Strand, at two o'clock.[8]

Fleetwood, 'whose Body was as much impaired by an excessive Gout, as his Fortune by his Misconduct',[9] had had enough, although for several weeks he succeeded in keeping his cards close to his chest. On 29 December, Garrick wrote an excited letter to John Hoadly. 'The Reason of my Silence was the Hope of Seeing our Theatrical Revolutions quite Settled,' he told him:

> I thought ye first Lett^r I had wrote to you should have been sign'd *Manager of Drury Lane* for I have been very near buying ye Patent, Lease of ye House, Cloaths Scenes &—No more of that—Mr Fleetwood has sold all his Right & Title to Mr Orator Lacy (that was) who has furnish'd ye Money, is yet a Secret, However I hope things will turn out well in ye End, for I am invited Strongly to take a Share of it; what I shall do I have not yet resolv'd, when I have You shall immediatly be acquainted with it . . . . .[10]

It soon became known that the money had been put up by two bankers called Norton Amber and Richard Green. James Lacy, the Irishman to whom they advanced it, had at one time been an actor, but he had been many other things too. 'A man of good understanding, uncultivated by education,' wrote the discerning Davies:

> his notions of business were clear, and his observations on men and manners judicious; he was liberal in his sentiments, though rough, and sometimes

boisterous, in his language: he was one whom no repulses of fortune, or checks of disappointment, could intimidate or divert from his purpose.[11]

He was known as 'Orator' Lacy because of the ingenious way in which in 1737 he had attempted to get round the terms of the Licensing Act. The *Oratory* which he tried to present in York Buildings, Villiers Street, was announced as a 'lecture', but 'Mr Professor Lacy' begged leave to inform the public that 'to avoid the tediousness of one sole speaker the Lecture is artificially divided among his Assistants, and cannot fail of being greatly to the Edification of his auditory . . . . .' The authorities were neither deceived nor amused, and for the next few months Lacy found himself cooling his heels in Bridewell.

He quickly bounced back, however, and is next heard of developing a scheme for an outdoor place of entertainment. In no time at all people of quality were deserting the pleasure gardens at Vauxhall and flocking to Lacy's Ranelagh, close to the river beside the Royal Hospital in Chelsea (the famous Rotunda was his own design); by 1742 he had disposed of the lease and was the richer by £4,000.

No financial transaction involving Fleetwood—'strange, profligate, unprincipled, swindling, gay, winning fascinating Charles Fleetwood'[12]—could be in the least straightforward. Some time previously he had already mortgaged the patent for £3,000 to Sir John de Lorme and a man called Masters. He had then persuaded a man called Hutchinson Mure that £7,000 would clear the mortgage and meet all other demands on the theatre. Mure, a prosperous upholsterer and cabinet-maker, foolishly advanced this amount, accepting as security the theatre's stock of costumes and scenery and a title to the receipts; Fleetwood's chicanery was revealed only when it was advertised that the patent was to be sold before a Master in Chancery.

Lacy had originally been approached by the Clerk of the Vintner's Company, who was acting as an intermediary for two men in the City. Amber and Green were their bankers, and when one of the principals fell ill and had to withdraw, they decided to act on their own account. They offered Lacy a partnership: if he would undertake the management of the theatre, they would find the whole of the purchase money, holding his third in mortgage until he could pay it out of his share of the profits. Mure was squared by the addition of the patent to his security; Green and Amber paid out £3,200 for the patent, guaranteed Fleetwood £600 a year for life and the deal was done.

Fleetwood prudently decided that his annuity would be safer if he put some distance between himself and his many creditors. Before slipping across the Channel to France he charmed the satirical poet Paul Whitehead into backing a bill for £3,000, a last, characteristic gesture of friendship which obliged Whitehead to take up residence in the Fleet prison for a number of years. Fleetwood and his wife ended up in Chalon-sur-Saône in Burgundy. He died there three years later.

7

Dear Charmers

One of Lacy's first acts was to reinstate Macklin.

Excluded by the cartel of the patent houses, he had formed a small company of mainly young actors and hired the Haymarket Theatre, getting round the Licensing Act by employing the 'Concert of Musick' formula. They had given little more than a dozen performances over a period of five months; when they played *Othello* early in February, Macklin had been Iago and Samuel Foote made his stage début in the title role. Macklin and his wife went off and acted on the Kentish circuit during the summer, but they were clearly having a thin time of it and early in November, just before Fleetwood's final exit, Macklin swallowed his pride and wrote begging to be reinstated: 'You must imagine, Sir, that by this time I am in no small distress, and distress, they say, even in an Enemie, will excite Humanity.'

Before the year was out he was back. On 19 December he appeared as Shylock. He had written a prologue for the occasion, and had clearly decided that if it seemed politic to grovel, one should grovel in style:

> From scheming, pelting, famine, and despair,
> Behold to grace restored an exil'd Play'r:
> Your Sanction yet his fortune must compleat,
> And give him privilege to laugh and eat.
>
> No revolution plots are mine again;
> You see, thank Heaven, the quietest of men.
> I pray that all domestic feuds might cease;
> And beggar'd by the war, solicit peace;
> When urg'd by wrongs, and prompted to rebel;
> I sought for freedom, and for freedom fell;
> What could support me in the sevenfold dame?
> I was no *Shadrak* and no angel came.
>
> Once warn'd, I meddle not with state affairs;
> But play my part, retire, and say my pray'rs.
> Let nobler spirits plan the vast design,
> Our green-room swarms with longer heads than mine. . . . .[1]

As it happened, the longest head in the green-room was not having an easy time under the new management. Lacy refused to pay Garrick the £250 in arrears which was still due to him from the bad old days under Fleetwood. There was also friction over the frequency of Garrick's appearances, Lacy insisting that this was something which it was his prerogative to decide, Garrick maintaining that his health must be a consideration; nor did he take kindly to Lacy's assertion that he had added too few new parts in the previous season.

He did add several major new roles to his repertoire during the season, nevertheless. He had played Sir John Brute in *The Provok'd Wife* only once before the riots had erupted in November, but he gave seven more performances before the season ended. It was a role in which it was of particular importance that he should succeed. This was the play that had established Vanbrugh's reputation. The first Brute had been Betterton in 1697—it is possible that the part was written for him. Quin had first played it in 1719 and Cibber had taken it on in the 1725–6 season opposite Mrs Oldfield.

Vanbrugh had quickly come under fire for the play, which was much coarser than anything he had previously produced. The tone of the piece—a savage portrait of a marriage of convenience—is set by Sir John's opening speech and his first encounter with his wife:

SIR JOHN. What cloying meat is love, when matrimony's the sauce to it! Two year's marriage has debauched my five senses. Everything I see, everything I hear, everything I feel, everything I smell, and everything I taste— methinks has wife in it. No boy was ever so weary of his tutor, no girl of her bib, no nun of doing penance or old maid of being chaste, as I am of being married . . . . . . But here she comes.
    Enter Lady Brute
LADY BRUTE. Do you dine at home today, Sir John?
SIR JOHN. Why, do you expect I should tell you what I don't know myself?
LADY BRUTE. I thought there was no harm in asking you.
SIR JOHN. If thinking wrong were an excuse for impertinence, women might be justified in most things they say or do.
LADY BRUTE. I'm sorry I have said anything to displease you.
SIR JOHN. Sorry for things past is as of little importance to me as my dining home or abroad ought to be to you.
LADY BRUTE. My enquiry was only that I might have provided what you liked.
SIR JOHN. Six to four you had been in the wrong there again; for what I liked yesterday I don't like today, and what I like today 'tis odds I mayn't like tomorrow.
LADY BRUTE. But if I had asked you what you liked?
SIR JOHN. Why, then there would be more asking about it than the thing is worth.
LADY BRUTE. I wish I did but know how I might please you.
SIR JOHN. Aye, but that sort of knowledge is not a wife's talent.

Vanbrugh came under attack from Jeremy Collier in his *A Short View of the Immorality and Profaneness of the English Stage* (1698), and a number of actors, including Betterton and Mrs Bracegirdle, had faced prosecution 'for using indecent expressions in some late plays, particularly *The Provok'd Wife*'. Vanbrugh had made some slight alterations in response to this, but in the course of half a century taste had changed enormously, and the revisions which Garrick felt obliged to make (and went on making over some thirty years) went much further.*

Most of the cuts were of sexual references regarded as unacceptable in Garrick's day. He omitted, for instance, most of Lady Brute's reverie on the pleasure she would find in making a cuckold of her husband, and cut numbers of words and phrases like 'clap', 'pox' and 'kiss her *Tetons*'. 'Commit Fornication' was changed to 'have me do I don't know what'. Curiously enough, one line to which Jeremy Collier had taken particular exception was retained—Rasor's remark that for punishment Lady Fanciful 'shou'd lie upon her face all the days of her life'.†

Garrick was also alert to the religious sensibilities of his audience. He removed a number of slighting references to saints and martyrs and to the gospel and several lines about divorce and sexual thoughts while at prayer. He also cut a satiric comment on the probity of the Bank of England: where Vanbrugh wrote 'and the Bank of England's grown honest', Garrick's prompt copy reads 'and the Pope's turned Protestant'. Many of his changes, however, are purely technical, and are shrewdly aimed either at shortening the play or increasing its dramatic impact.

Sir John became one of Garrick's most popular comic roles, and the finer points of his interpretation were eagerly debated and compared with those of Cibber and Quin. Quin, still at fifty-one a stubborn defender of his patch, affected patronizing unconcern when he heard that his young rival was about to attempt the role: 'He may possibly act Master Jacky Brute, but he cannot possibly be Sir John Brute.' Some years later, when Charles Churchill came to finger Quin in *The Rosciad*, he delivered a verdict that was neatly double-edged:

> In Brute he shone unequalled; all agree
> Garrick's not half so great a Brute as he.

Quin's performance was coarse and drink-sodden; Garrick's altogether more subtle and rakish. His impersonation of Lady Brute was particularly admired:

> You would swear he had often attended the Toilet, and there gleaned up the many various Airs of the Fair Sex: He is perfectly versed in the Exercise

---

* Garrick used a copy of the 1743 Dublin edition when he was preparing himself for the play, and this became the Drury Lane prompter's copy during his subsequent management. It is now in the Folger Library in Washington.

† Collier had been so shocked by this that he could not bring himself to quote it, but Vanbrugh understood what he was referring to and commented, 'All I shall say to this, is, That an Obscene Thought must be buried deep indeed, if he don't smell it out.'

of the Fan, the Lips, the Adjustment of the Tucker, and even the minutest Conduct of the Finger.[2]

He went on playing the role throughout his career,* and could always be assured of a full house and a lively response from all sections of the audience. One November night in 1753, when he played opposite Mrs Pritchard, Cross, the Drury Lane prompter, made one of his occasional laconic diary entries: 'A whore taken out for Noise in Green Box.'

In February 1745 Garrick made his first appearance in Shakespeare's *King John*, a production owing something both to affairs of state and theatrical rivalry.

Open hostilities with the French always revived fears of what the adherents of the House of Stuart might get up to. The ministry's intelligence services were good. It was known that even before the declaration of war the previous spring, Marshal Saxe had been making secret preparations at Dunkirk for a Jacobite invasion which was to be covered by Roquefeuil's fleet; on that occasion easterly gales had driven the French out of the Channel and largely destroyed the flotilla of transports that was being assembled at Dunkirk.

Colley Cibber's literary output in the 1730s had largely been confined to birthday odes and other such ephemera expected of him as Poet Laureate:

> Behold in ev'ry Face, imperial Graces shine,
> All native to the Race of George and Caroline

he trilled in the year of his appointment. Maynard Mack's description of him as 'Literary Toad Eater Extraordinary to the Hanoverian regime' is a good one,[3] and in that capacity he had also tried his hand at a re-working of *King John*. It had occurred to him that at a time when the Protestant succession in Britain was threatened by the claims of a Roman Catholic Pretender, the story of King John, famous as an opponent of papal tyranny, had some contemporary relevance.

Shakespeare had based his play on the anonymous *The Troublesome Reign of John, King of England*, published in 1591, only three years after Drake had seen off the Armada, but he had toned down its violent anti-Catholicism. Cibber thought this a mistake, and attempted a reconstruction of the tragedy from the same source. He offered this to Fleetwood in 1736. It was put into rehearsal, but then hastily withdrawn; 'King John in silence modestly expires,' Pope wrote in *The Dunciad*. But now that old enemy was dead, and Cibber was emboldened to offer his *Papal Tyranny in the Reign of King John* once more, this time to Rich at Covent Garden.

Garrick, already showing some tendency to regard himself as Shakespeare's vicar on earth, persuaded Lacy that Drury Lane should make a pre-emptive strike by reviving the genuine article. (He was also still smarting under Cibber's criticism of his performance as Brute.) Cibber cried foul, claiming that this was a ploy by

---

* Garrick played Brute on 105 occasions, appearing more frequently only as Ranger in *The Suspicious Husband* and Benedick in *Much Ado*.

the Drury Lane department of dirty tricks to sabotage his author's benefit. Lacy felt confident enough to be gracious, and allowed Covent Garden a free run for four nights. Then, for six nights in succession, the town was given the opportunity to compare and contrast for itself.

It was a particularly even contest. Cibber himself, emerging yet again from retirement, played Pandulph, the papal legate. Davies thought it a mannered performance, more like Lord Foppington than a man of the cloth: 'He affected a stately magnificent tread, a supercilious aspect with lofty and extravagant action, which he displayed by waving up and down a roll of parchment in his hand.' He also mumbled, because he was now in his mid-seventies and had recently lost his teeth.

Macklin took the part at Drury Lane, and he too did not escape criticism; Quin said he looked like a cardinal who had very recently been the parish clerk. But then Quin, on this occasion, was an interested party, because he was Cibber's King John, a part in which he was judged to be wooden. Although it did not become one of Garrick's major roles, Davies noted the care and intelligence that he brought to it. 'It was the great excellence of Garrick to hold in remembrance the character he played through all its various stages,' he wrote: 'Garrick's look, walk, and speech confessed the man broken with incessant anxiety, and defeated both in body and mind. Despair and death seemed to hover round him.'[4]

Professionally, the most important thing about this production for Garrick was that he played for the first time opposite Susannah Cibber. She had been at Drury Lane since the beginning of the season, but he had hitherto fought shy of her. Her slender figure, the low-pitched voice, the sad cast of her features, all contributed to an effective performance in certain tragic roles, but she retained from the coaching of her father-in-law something of 'the good old manner of singing and quavering out their tragic notes' so characteristic of the old school. That was something Garrick could not bring himself to admire, and when the casting of *King John* came to be discussed he found it difficult to see her in the virago role of Lady Constance.

It seems that he was persuaded otherwise by Quin. They ran into each other one day at the Bedford Coffee House and Quin, who had long been her champion, was vehement in her defence: 'Don't tell *me*, Mr Garrick! That woman has a heart, and can do anything where passion is required!'[5] So it proved. On the first night, at the point where Constance learns of the capture of her son by his wicked uncle, the other players were so transfixed by her 'piercing notes of wild, maternal agony' that they forgot their lines and had to be prompted. Her short speech which brings Act II to a close is said to have created such a powerful impression that each night during the play's run there was an influx of people eager to hear it a second time:

> I will instruct my sorrows to be proud,
> For grief is proud and makes his owner stoop.
> [*She sits upon the ground*]
> To me and to the state of my great grief

Let kings assemble, for my grief's so great
That no supporter but the huge firm earth
Can hold it up. Here I and sorrows sit;
Here is my throne; bid kings come bow to it.

The pit and the gallery did just that, and so too, his reservations swept away, did Garrick. When he made his début as Othello early in March, she was his Desdemona.

Garrick had been preparing himself for the part over several months. 'I rise or fall by Othello very soon,' he had written to John Hoadly three months previously. 'Man or Mouse You shall have as Impartial an Account (as my Vanity will permitt me) of my Success in yᵉ Character.'[6] That impartial account, if it was ever written, has not survived, but several others have, and they all tell much the same story.

Betterton had been a great Othello, and so had Booth—that, at least, was Colley Cibber's view, who had seen them both and indeed attempted the role himself. For Garrick, and for the audience of his day, the standard was Quin, and most competent judges for once gave best to the older man. 'He endeavoured throughout to play everything different from Quin,' wrote Garrick's friend Richard Rigby, 'and failed, I think, in most of his alterations.'

One of his alterations—he had, as always, paid close attention to the text—was to restore the 'trance' scene at the beginning of Act IV. This won applause on the night, and Benjamin Victor, who sent Garrick an extended critique of his performance, thought it highly effective—'your manner of falling into it and recovering from it was amazingly beautiful.'* But there was someone present who was in a position to observe Garrick's performance even more closely than Victor, and he thought differently:

> Garrick himself was a diminutive mean figure for the Moor; therefore he knew that Quin could not fall suddenly on the ground, as it were in a fit, without greatly hurting himself, and perhaps raising laughter in the audience; but that he might with his insignificant person do it without risk of either; and therefore introduced that shameful scene of epilepsy in the fourth act, which instead of being applauded, ought to have been exploded with indignation and contempt for his impudence in the first place. . . . .[7]

Macklin, of course—marvellously well cast that night as Iago.

Quin, naturally, was in the audience, in the company of John Hoadly. He himself normally wore a large powdered bag wig in the part, and made a great business of peeling off a pair of white gloves to show that his hands were as black as his face. Garrick made his entrance in the scarlet tunic of an army

---

* Genest, John, *Some Account of the English Stage from the Restoration in 1660 to 1830*, 10 vols., Bath, 1832, iv, 147–8. Victor urged Garrick to be more restrained in his gestures, however: 'As you have the happiness of a most expressive countenance, you may safely trust to that, which with your proper and pathetic manner of speaking would charm more succesfully if those violent and seeming artful emotions of body were a little abated.'

officer; possibly with the idea of adding an inch or two to his height he also wore some sort of plumed turban. Everybody within earshot of Quin in the pit would have been familiar with the eloquent dumb show of Hogarth's 'A Harlot's Progress', which had been published thirteen years previously—the prints had sold like hot cakes, the story had been turned into a pantomime by Theophilus Cibber, it had been painted on fan-mounts and transferred on to cups and saucers. In one of the scenes, the heroine upsets her breakfast table just as her Pompey— a generic name in the eighteenth century for a black page or footman—is bringing in the tea kettle. Quin had a famously quick tongue. 'Why, here's Pompey,' he boomed—'but why does he not bring the tea kettle and lamp?' Garrick appeared once more as Othello that season, and one last time in 1746. But long years later, turning over his own precious folio of Hogarth, he paused when he came to Pompey, and had the grace to laugh: 'Faith,' he said, 'it is devilish like.'*

Garrick played opposite Mrs Cibber a second time almost immediately. 'The Town flocks to a new play of Thomson's call'd *Tancred and Sigismunda*: it is very dull,' Horace Walpole wrote to Sir Horace Mann at the end of March. 'I cannot bear modern poetry; these refiners of the purity of the stage, and of the incorrectness of English verse, are most woefully insipid.'[8] Thomson had based his tragedy on one of the stories inserted in Lesage's picaresque novel *Gil Blas*. A letter published in the *Daily Post* — the writer signed himself 'Bellario'— suggests that it did not force its way into the Drury Lane schedule purely on merit:

> A very remarkable new Lord of the Treasury was proud of appearing its Foster Father, and attended at the public rehearsals; the first night of the performance this celebrated person and his friends in the Box with him (all very lately most flaming Patriots) were seen clapping their hands at the following remarkable speech . . . . .[9]

The new Lord of the Treasury was Thomson's friend and patron Lyttelton, and it was not the first favour he had bestowed on the poet—when he went to the Treasury the previous year he appointed Thomson to the Surveyor-Generalship of the Leeward Islands, a delightful sinecure involving no foreign travel and worth £300 a year. One of the friends seen clapping in the box with him was Pitt. The pair of them had indeed attended rehearsals—'with great assiduity', according to Davies: 'Their instructions were heard by the players with great respect, and embraced with implicit confidence.'

After the first night, three hundred lines were cut; Bellario, the *Post*'s well-informed correspondent, gave it as his opinion that double that amount would have been beneficial. And yet Garrick and Mrs Cibber pulled it off. They were 'formed by nature for the illustration of each other's talents,' writes Davies:

---

* Quoted in Parsons, Mrs Clement, *Garrick and his Circle*, London, 1906, 76. There may be something in a comment of Murphy's: 'Othello could not be a well-chosen part for a man, who performed wonders with that expressive face. The black complexion disguised his features, and the expression of the mind was wholly lost.' (*Murphy*, i, 106.)

In their person they were both somewhat below the middle size: he was, though short, well made; she, though in her form not graceful, and scarcely genteel, was, by the elegance of her manner and symmetry of her features, rendered very attractive. From similarity of complexion, size, and countenance, they could have been easily supposed to be brother and sister; but in the powerful expression of the passions, they still approached to a near resemblance. He was master of all the passions, but more particularly happy in the exhibition of parts where anger, resentment, disdain, horror, despair, and madness, predominated. In love, grief, and tenderness, she greatly excelled all competitors; and was also unrivalled in the more ardent emotions of jealous love and frantic rage, which she expressed with a degree of sensibility in voice, look, and action, that never failed to draw tears from the most unfeeling.[10]

The celebrated French nineteenth-century actor Coquelin maintained that his first stage part consisted of the three words *'Il est mort.'* When he grumbled about having so little to say, he was rebuked by his old master, Régnier, who told him he should be proud to have been entrusted with a sentence that might be spoken in so many different ways.* Garrick would have approved. His professional sense told him that no part was too small to be well played, and he would sometimes take a subordinate role to emphasize the point. When *The Beaux' Stratagem* was announced for Woffington's benefit night at the end of March in 1745, the role of Cherry, the pert little servant girl, was played by her sister Polly ('First Appearance on any Stage' said the bills, not entirely truthfully). Garrick took the part of Lady Bountiful's servant Scrub, and scored as great a success as he had previously done with Archer.

Polly Woffington's first appearance was also her last. By the summer of 1746 she had won the heart of Robert, younger son of the Earl of Cholmondeley. It was not exactly the 'marriage and a coach' scenario envisaged by her sister, because the Earl, though related to the Walpoles (his wife was Horace's sister), was impoverished. The Honourable Robert, what is more, an ensign in the guards at the time, had not exactly distinguished himself at the Battle of Fontenoy in May 1745. If Boswell is to be believed, he 'fairly hid himself, for which he was disgracefully broke at the head of the army'. He gave up soldiering and became a curate; he and Polly were married towards the end of 1746 without the blessing of either family.

The Earl, it seems, subsequently conceived the dangerous notion of remonstrating with Peg Woffington, and was sent away with an outsize flea in his ear. 'My lord,' she told him, 'I have much more reason to be offended at it than your lordship, for I had before but one beggar to maintain, and now I have two.'[11] She maintained them generously, as it happens, and the Cholmondeley family

* Like so many theatrical stories, French or English, it is apocryphal. Coquelin (1841–1909) entered Régnier's class at the Conservatoire in 1859 and within a year won the first prize for comedy. He made his début at the Comédie-Française at the age of nineteen in the substantial part of Gros-René in Molière's *Le Dépit Amoureux*.

made its contribution in the shape of two livings that were in their gift in Hertfordshire. Polly—'gay, flighty, entertaining and frisky' according to her friend Fanny Burney—lived on into the next century. She bore her husband ten children and charmed Samuel Johnson with her wit and beauty. Even snobbish old Uncle Horace came round in the end, squiring her to Paris to meet French bluestockings like Mme du Deffand and making provision for her and her family in his will.

Early in April, it was announced that Garrick's place as Lothario in *The Fair Penitent* would be taken at short notice by Mills. It proved to be more than a passing indisposition. 'Mr Garrick lies very ill of a fever at his Lodgings in Covent Garden,' the *Daily Advertiser* reported five days later. He was not well enough to perform for the rest of the season, but some weeks later, as he was slowly beginning to mend, an invitation was delivered to his rooms over the Great Piazza:

> Sir,
>   I am very glad to hear you are better, and if you dare venture out, shall be glad of your company at dinner. As you are an invalid, pray send me word what you can eat, and at what hour you'll dine. I shall send to Tom to meet you, and am
>   Sir David,
>   Yr most humble friend
>   & Servant
>   to Command
>   till Death
>   Margery—Pinchwife.

Margery Pinchwife is the heroine of Wycherley's bawdy comedy *The Country Wife*. The demure Susannah Cibber—whose letter it was—does not only appropriate her name. She also signs off with the precise form of words—'Your most humble friend & servant to command till death'—used by the uninhibited Margery to propose an assignation to Horner, a witty lecher who has made himself irresistible by putting it about that an operation for the pox has rendered him impotent.

A joke, of course. But an interesting one. Mrs Cibber's Sunday evenings were decorous affairs, where Garrick might have expected to encounter Quin, or Pitt, or Lyttelton, with Handel at the harpsichord, perhaps, or Tom, her brother, directing a string ensemble. Whether he accepted that particular invitation we do not know, but he certainly accepted one from another quarter later in the month; the end of May found him convalescent at Teddington, presumably at Woffington's house. 'I have been very near making my Exit from this World,' he wrote to John Hoadly. 'I am now (thank God) recovering Daily, & my Physicians tell me I shall be a much better Man (bodily I mean) than I was before.'

He had not been idle during his enforced absence from the stage:

> You must know that since my Illness I have found my head as Keen as a Razor, & you must Know too, that finding I was overcharg'd with Wit

and Humour, I have let fly at a Comedy, in Short, tis quite plan'd, & Some
Scenes wrote, but more of this when I have ye pleasure of seeing You—*

It was almost certainly during this visit to Teddington that the final rupture
between Garrick and Woffington came about. That he had hoped to marry her
is not in doubt. Murphy, who knew her well in the last five years of her life, is
firm on the point: 'This writer has heard her declare at different times, that he
went so far as to try the wedding-ring on her finger.'[12] The story of the ring was
very widely believed, and is borne out by the account which Garrick's friend
Windham had many years later from Sheridan during a visit to Dublin, and
which he dashed down in his diary on the day it was given to him without too
much regard for punctuation. Lord Darnley's interest in her was far from
extinguished, and it seems that it is he who acted as a catalyst in the affair:

> This Nobleman was so passionately fond of her, that He sent one Swiney,
> with a proposal, that if she would give her word of honour, never to have
> any more connexion with Garrick, with whom she then, almost exclusively
> lived, He would settle upon her, £500 a year. He gave her a certain time
> to consider of his offer, declaring that if no answer was returned by the
> expiration of that, His resolution was fixt for abandoning her for ever. this
> proposal was made immediately known to G., and He asked by Her, whether
> he would consent to part with her, or marry her. the last day of the time fixt
> for receiving her answer was arrived, before He would give any determi-
> nation. He then, according to Sher[ns] account, made her a promise of mar-
> riage; Swiney was employed to get the ring and the licence; and He slept with
> her that night as usual: but after some time being in bed, He began to groan
> most piteously, declaring He was ruined and undone if He married her,
> and, in short, signifying that He could not bring Himself to consent. in this
> situation they were found by Swiney the next morning. It was then too late
> to alter her determination; the answer had been given to Lord Darnley; who
> either had already gone, or went soon after abroad, and, it was supposed,
> died partly of grief for her loss.—this account Sherid. said He had from
> Swiney; and was the story told by M[rs] Woff.[13]

Macklin's biographer, Cooke, gives a rather more operatic account of the end
of the affair, and has Garrick telling Woffington that during a sleepless night he
had 'worn the shirt of Dejanira'. Woffington, in equally histrionic mode, replies,
'Then Sir, get up, and throw it off! For from this hour I separate myself from
you, except in the course of professional business, or in the presence of a third
person.'[14]

This is pretty high-flown pillow talk, even between theatre folk. The mythology
of Hercules, most famous of Greek heroes, is enormously complicated. Dejanira,
daughter of the king of Calydon, was his second wife, and the unwitting cause

---

* *Letters*, 30. The play was *Miss in Her Teens*, Garrick's third play for the professional theatre.
It was an adaptation of a French piece called *La Parisienne*, written by Carton sieur Dancourt
in 1691. It was first seen at Covent Garden in January 1747.

of his death. The villain of the piece was the centaur Nessus, who tried to molest her, whereupon Hercules, understandably enough, let fly at him with an arrow dipped in the venom of the Hydra. The dying centaur devised a poetic revenge. He told Dejanira (who cannot have been particularly bright) that she should take his blood-stained tunic and keep it safe; anyone who subsequently put it on would love her for ever. Years later, when her husband transferred his affections to Iole, daughter of another kinglet, Dejanira sent the garment to him; Hercules, seized with agonies from the powerful poison, had himself carried up on to a mountain top and immolated himself on a huge funeral pyre.

The Shirt of Nessus—a fatal present, then, a source of misfortune from which there is no escape. The idea of Garrick and Woffington lying in bed at Teddington and conducting a lovers' quarrel by bandying abstruse classical allusions is distinctly the stuff of comedy. But before dismissing it as totally improbable, it is worth pausing over one intriguing detail.

There seems to have been no play in the eighteenth-century repertory that would have given Garrick or Woffington any help in improvising their lines as they played out their last intimate scene together. A scrutiny of the theatrical calendar so painstakingly assembled by the editors of *The London Stage*,[15] however, discloses that a few months previously, on two successive Saturdays in January 1745, the King's Theatre had presented 'a new Musical Drama, composed by Mr Handel'—*Hercules*. Garrick and Woffington were both on stage at Drury Lane on each of the evenings in question, as it happens, but that does not completely rule out familiarity with the piece—particularly as at the second performance one of the parts had been sung by Mrs Cibber. Perhaps the Cooke version—like so much of his material, it almost certainly came from Macklin—should not after all be consigned to that outsize biographical waste-bin marked 'anecdotal'.

From Teddington, Garrick went to visit his uncle Louis la Condé at Carshalton, in Surrey, and from there he travelled north to visit his family in Lichfield and to take the waters at Buxton in Derbyshire. If he was cast down by the break with Woffington, there is no evidence of it in his correspondence: 'The Buxton waters, or at least the company there, agreed mighty well with me,' he wrote to Somerset Draper. 'I staid but five days, and never was more merry or in higher spirits in my life.'[16] He lingered at Lichfield until the early autumn, cosseted by his sisters, soothed by the dull, uncomplicated routines of family life; 'I write to You without connection or Correction,' he wrote to his friend Francis Hayman:

> I am now in a Room full of Brothers & Sisters, the greater part is female & consequently more noisy & confounding; however if Your Taste is like Mine, You'll chuse a plain Simple Meal with a Hearty Wellcome, before the most regular, ceremonious entertainments.*

---

* *Letters*, 33. Hayman (1708–76), had started as a scene-painter at Drury Lane. He was best known for the pictures of contemporary life and fashion which ornamented the alcoves at Vauxhall. Gainsborough was his pupil for a time, and he was later one of the founders of the Royal Academy. After Fleetwood's death, Hayman married his widow.

Mrs Cibber had been in determined pursuit of him by letter throughout the summer, pressing him to visit her at Sloper's house at West Woodhay in Berkshire, filling him in on theatre gossip: 'I must tell you that I hear we are both to be turned out of Drury Lane Playhouse, to breathe our faithful souls out where we please,' she had written in July:

> But as Mr Lacy suspects you are so great a favourite with the ladies that they will resent it, he has enlisted two swinging Irishmen of six feet high to silence that battery. As to me, I am to be brought to capitulate another way, and he is to send a certain hussar of our acquaintance to plunder me.
>
> In this melancholy situation, what think you of setting up a strolling company? Had you given me timely notice of your going to Buxton, I am sure the landlord of the Hall Place would have lent us a barn, and with the advantage of your little wife's first appearance in the character of Lady Townley, I don't doubt but we could have pick'd up some odd pence: this might have given a great turn to affairs, and, when Lacy found we could get our bread without him, it might possibly have altered these terrifying resolutions.
>
> But joking apart, I long till you come that we may consult together: don't let the charms of Buxton make you break your word; and since I am to be plundered, you need not grudge the expense you put me to in victuals and drink.[17]

The 'swinging Irishmen' were Sheridan and Spranger Barry, with whom Lacy was indeed in negotiation. Barry, the son of a wealthy silversmith, had been making quite a name for himself at both Dublin theatres; six feet was a good height in the eighteenth century, and Mrs Cibber, well aware that Garrick was sensitive about his lack of inches, was putting a subtle feminine finger on a tender spot. The light and flirtatious tone of the letter belies the gravity of her news about herself: the 'certain hussar of our acquaintance' was of course her husband, the appalling Theophilus, and plunder her was something he was well able to do within the limits of the law.

What she wanted to discuss with Garrick was some sort of joint enterprise, but that was something he shied away from: 'She still presses me to *visit her*,' he wrote to Somerset Draper early in October, 'that we may *settle something*; but my head runs on the *buck basket*, and no more intrigues for me.' His relations with Mrs Cibber and Woffington only vaguely resembled those of Falstaff with Mistress Ford and Mistress Page, but the allusion to the fat knight's humiliation in the laundry-basket in *The Merry Wives of Windsor* is a revealing one. All his instincts told him to be wary and to avoid the sort of entanglement from which he had so recently extricated himself. There is an echo of the same concern in a further letter to Draper a fortnight later:

> *Woffington*, I am told, shews my letters about; pray have you heard any thing of that kind? What she does now, so little affects me, that, excepting her shewing my letters of nonsense and *love* to make me ridiculous, she

can do nothing to give me a moment's unease—*the scene is changed—
I'm alter'd quite.*[18]

Well, perhaps, although the show of indifference is not entirely convincing. He
acted less well on paper than on the stage.

There were, however, more important things than play-acting to occupy
people's minds in those late summer months of 1745. In June, losing patience
with the equivocation of his French allies, Prince Charles Edward, the Young
Pretender, had chartered two vessels and sailed out of Nantes, accompanied
mainly by Irish exiles. The *Elizabeth*, a well-armed privateer with 700 troops
and supplies on board, was intercepted off the Lizard by a British warship and
forced back into Brest; Charles, on the *Du Teillay*, pressed on, and on 23 July
landed on the Isle of Eriskay in the Outer Hebrides. In mid-August, he raised
the standard of his house at Glenfinnan, in mainland Inverness-shire. Edinburgh
fell to the rebels without resistance on 17 September; four days later, a few miles
to the east at Prestonpans, the Jacobites surprised and routed the Hanoverian
army of Sir John Cope, an inglorious encounter which lasted every bit of five
minutes, but which lives on in the mocking refrain of that born-again Jacobite
Robert Burns:

> Hey Johnie Cope are ye wauking yet   *awake*
> Or are ye sleeping I would wit
> O haste ye get up for the drums do beat
> O fye Cope rise in the morning.

News of the Jacobite uprising travelled slowly. The Young Pretender's landing
on Eriskay became known in London only in the second week in August.* The
newspapers began to demonstrate their loyalty to the House of Hanover by
printing appropriate slogans vertically in the margins in bold type—*No Pretender.
No Popery. No Slavery.* In the bottom margin, the message was sharpened up
with exclamation marks—*No Wooden Shoes! No Arbitrary Power!*†

The theatre managers were soon bobbing equally vigorously to demonstrate
their patriotism:

> We hear that Mr Lacy, Master of his Majesty's company of Comedians at
> Drury Lane has applied for leave to raise 200 men in defence of his Majesty's
> person and government, in which the whole company of players are willing
> to engage.[19]

While he awaited his sovereign's call to arms, Lacy got Thomas Arne to work
up a suitable anthem. It was billed as 'God Save Our Noble King' and it was
performed before the curtain at Drury Lane by Mrs Cibber, Beard and Reinhold,

---

* The unwelcome news reached the ears of George II even later, because he was in Hanover.
† 'Wooden shoes' was a multi-purpose phrase used to express the traditional English mistrust
of foreigners — here obviously *sabot*-wearing Frenchmen who were the power behind the
Pretenders. A few years later, however, when the 'Jew Bill' was before Parliament, the words
'No Jews.—No Wooden Shoes' appeared on walls — an early example of rhyming slang.

backed by the whole company and accompanied by horns and violins. The *General Advertiser* recorded scenes of enthusiasm:

> The Universal Applause it met with being encored with repeated Huzzas sufficiently denoted in how just an abhorrence they hold the arbitrary schemes of our invidious enemies and detest the despotic attempts of Papal Power.

Arne, a lukewarm Catholic in bad times, a lapsed one in good, had first heard the tune when he had been taken to Mass as a child in one of the embassy chapels. It would not have done to tell Lacy, but an earlier set of words besought the Almighty to save 'Great James, our King', the James in question being the Young Pretender's Papist grandfather. Covent Garden quickly jumped on the bandwagon with an alternative arrangement by Arne's pupil Charles Burney, and from then on the anthem was sung each night at both houses. It was the beginning of a custom which would survive in British theatres and other places of entertainment for more than two hundred years.*

As the season got under way, the playbills bore witness to the managers' awareness that patriotic and commercial interest could march hand in hand. Drury Lane capitalized neatly on anti-French, anti-Catholic sentiment by putting on as an afterpiece Fielding's bawdy farce *The Debauchees, or The Jesuit Caught*; in the course of the season it had twenty-five performances. Both houses revived Cibber's *The Non-juror*, written a quarter of a century earlier against non-juring supporters of the Stuarts and in favour of the House of Hanover. Goodman's Fields also found a way of getting in on the act by offering 'A Concert of Vocal and Instrumental Musick' with a performance in the interval of *Massacre at Paris*, an historical play 'not acted these 50 years and founded on Facts which happened in France in the Reign of Queen Elizabeth':

> Shewing the unparalleled Dissimulations, Imprecations, and Perjuries of Charles the 9th of France, the Queen Mother, and Cardinal Lorrain, to draw the Hugonot Party into their snares, by which means the death of the Queen Navarre was effected by Poison, and most of the Protestant Princes of the Blood destroyed. Chastillon, the famous Admiral of France, with his Wife, Children, Commanders, and Followers, all put to Death, with the King's Consent, by the cruel and Revengeful Duke of Guise, and his Adherents. After which the Massacre becoming general over the Kingdom, near 100,000 Protestants were destroyed in the most barbarous and inhuman manner.†

---

* The tune has been borrowed at one time or another by some twenty countries as their anthem. It became extremely popular in colonial America, where it was sung to many different sets of words, including *God Save George Washington* and *God Save the Thirteen States*. The present words, *My country, 'tis of Thee*, date from 1831.

† *Massacre at Paris* was the work of Nathaniel Lee (?1649–92), a failed actor turned playwright, whose extravagant and passionate tragedies had been highly popular in the last quarter of the seventeenth century. He eventually lost his reason, was committed to Bedlam and died after a drinking bout.

This seems to have gone down so well that Covent Garden mounted a production of the same piece three days later, and for a couple of nights the two theatres played against each other. Nicholas Rowe's *Lady Jane Grey* was another Drury Lane revival ('Containing a Relation of the Death of Edward VI, Founder of the Reformation'). A song called *Stand around, my brave boys*, also went down well ('set by Handel, for the Gentlemen Volunteers of the City of London').

A hundred and more miles closer to the action, in Lichfield, thoughts of volunteering were running in Garrick's mind. 'The Country is much allarm'd by the Rebels,' he wrote to Hayman in mid-October:

> For my own part I have little fear of 'em & intend offering my Service as a Volunteer as I have no other Engagements upon me & cannot be better employ'd. I suppose the Playhouses will find little Encouragement till these Clouds are blown over; for my own Part, till these Gentlemen have done playing the Knave in ye North, I can't think of playing the Fool—[20]

To Draper he was more specific: 'I hear *my Lord Rochford* is raising a sort of *gens d'armes. I should be glad to make one*, and if you think it not improper, will offer my services in a strong manner.'[21] The offer was made, but politely declined:

> I must commend your laudable zeal in offering your services for the suppression of the Rebels, and thank you more particularly for shewing your inclination to fight under my command. Had I a design to raise a regiment, or to raise a troop, on this occasion, I know nobody I would be so proud of commanding as yourself. But, thank God! we have now old regiments 'enow at home to quell the sad remains of those rash traitors, without raising any new ones . . . . .[22]

Those old regiments still had to demonstrate what they were capable of. Rochford wrote his letter on 31 October; two weeks later Carlisle surrendered to the rebels and Charles Edward, bent on reaching London, ordered his troops to march on through Cumberland and Lancashire.

Six weeks into the new season, Garrick's plans were still up in the air. None of the offers that had come from Ireland had been sufficiently tempting, and he was still at odds with the Drury Lane management over a whole cluster of issues—the arrears due to him under his articles with Fleetwood, the question of whether he was contractually free to go to Ireland and the terms on which he might re-engage. He was scathing to Hayman about 'a most surprizing Epistle' he had received from Lacy—'full of false Accusations, many of 'em contradictory & interspers'd with low, weak Calumny & defamation the usual Resources of a Bad Cause & Malevolent Disposition.' In another 'most impudent' letter from Lacy he thought he detected the hand of Macklin. 'I shall very fully answer each paragraph,' he told Draper, 'and send it to you for your advice; it is a most weak, scurrilous performance, and writ *in terrorem*; I should not care to have any more controversy, but if villains will attack me, I must defend myself.'

Lacy was not negotiating from strength. The *Daily Gazetteer* had carried a report on 5 September that the minor players were scurrying like rats between the two Theatres Royal, reluctant to sign articles until it was clear which way the star performers were going to jump. Garrick apart, and for a variety of reasons, numbers of those stars had still not shown their hand: 'Temperate Jack is swilling Hogsheads of Claret in Boeotia, Poor Pistol is in Durance Vile, and penitent Calista is solacing at her villa and sliding down the Slope of Pleasure.'* Lacy's position was also weakened by the rebellion. The news of Cope's defeat at Prestonpans had caused a run on the Bank of England, and when the Bank sneezed, more modest concerns like Green and Amber, Lacy's backers, could very easily catch a cold.

William Windham spent some time with Garrick in Lichfield in the early autumn, and carried back with him to London the draft of a letter to Lacy. It was Garrick's good fortune that he had friends like Draper and Windham on whom he could rely for guidance in such matters. Quick to take offence and inclined to be hot-tempered, he was not always a good judge of how best to present his case.† He was not unaware of this. 'I had a design to engage *Johnson* to help me in my answer,' he told Draper:

> I have written to him on that account, but if you conclude it unnecessary, pray desire Mr Wyndham to tell him so when he shall see him for that purpose . . . If you, Mr. Wyndham, and Clutterbuck, shall think it necessary to offer myself, upon the terms of my last articles, to Drury Lane, I will; but I imagine, to lie quiet a while, will be the best thing I can do.[23]

He leaned heavily on Somerset Draper for advice on all his affairs. 'Pray what do you think of the stocks?' he asked him at the height of the Jacobite scare. 'I should chuse to sell out, if I could conveniently. Pray, if Clutterbuck is in town, consult with him about it.'‡

Mrs Cibber did not give up easily. 'I am sorry to find you do not propose coming to town,' she wrote at the end of October, 'because nothing farther can be done in the affair I mentioned to you without your being here.' The Rebellion, she told him, far from being a disadvantage to the playhouses, was bringing them very good houses, and this had prompted second and better thoughts:

> There will be no Operas this year; so if you, Mr. Quin, and I, agree to play without any salary, and pick up some of the best actors and actresses that are disengaged, at what salary you both think proper, I make no doubt we shall get a licence to play there for fifty, sixty, or any number of nights

---

* Seven years on, any reference to Mrs Cibber and Sloper was still good for a snigger. Temperate Jack was Quin, who was abroad; Pistol was one of Theo Cibber's best-known roles, and he was back inside the Fleet prison once more for debt.

† There is a good illustration of this in a manuscript preserved in the Yale University Library — an interminable draft letter to Lacy full of rhetorical flourishes and convoluted rebuttals. The text is reproduced in *Letters*, 36.

‡ James Clutterbuck (?1704–76) had substantial business interests, and was in partnership with Gastrell, a mercer, who often supplied Drury Lane with stage materials. He was also Draper's brother-in-law. Garrick saw both men frequently at the Queen's Arms in St Paul's Churchyard, where they formed a club — 'my brethren at the Queen's-Arms'.

you agree upon. Mr. Heidegger shall pay scenes, &c. and pay those that receive wages; and deliver the overplus to some proper person to enlist men to serve in any of the regiments of Guards, at five pounds per man;— this is the service St. Martin's Parish puts the money to that they collect,— and I mention it, because it is thought the most serviceable to the Government, of any scheme yet proposed. . . .

This put Garrick on the spot. He had by now all but made up his mind to go to Ireland, and had asked Draper to start making certain financial and other arrangements for him.* Mrs Cibber's letter threw him into uncertainty, and he once again wrote urgently to Draper to enlist his help:

Now, although I imagine this proposal merely chimerical and womanish; yet, as I would not give my opinion too hastily upon such an affair, I must desire you to wait upon her; and to be sure if I can, in any way, contribute to the general good, I shall be ready, upon the first notice, to come and give my assistance.[24]

Before Draper had time to form a view of the merits of this 'chimerical and womanish' plan, Garrick finally stopped shilly-shallying and accepted Sheridan's offer to engage for the season at Smock Alley. His decision to go there straight from Lichfield earned him a letter of subtle reproach from Mrs Cibber:

Sir,
    I had a thousand pretty things to say to you, but you go to Ireland without seeing me, and to stop my mouth from complaining, you artfully tell me I am one of the number you don't care to take leave of. And I tell you I am not to be flammed in that manner.
    You assure me also you want sadly to make love to me; and I assure you, very seriously, I will never engage upon the same theatre again with you, without you make more love to me than you did last year. I am ashamed that the audience should see me break the least rule of decency (even upon the stage) for the wretched lovers I had last winter. I desire you always to be my lover upon the stage, and my friend off of it.[25]

In time she would have both the things she desired.

    The tone and language of these letters of Mrs Cibber's have prompted much speculation about the nature of her relationship with Garrick. She was clearly powerfully drawn to him, although it is not always easy to distinguish between the personal and professional elements in that attraction. It certainly transmitted itself strongly across the footlights. Some years later, a writer in the *Morning Chronicle* noted that 'they seemed to warm and animate each other to such a Degree, that they were both carried beyond themselves'.†

* 'If I resolve for Dublin, I shall send for my wigs, and some jewels in the book-case-drawers, and I think, for a suit of cloaths, which Ned will pack up by your direction.' Letter dated 23 October 1745. (*Letters*, 37.)
† 8–10 March 1757. They were appearing together in *The Fair Penitent*.

Behind the scenes, inevitably, there was talk. They were very alike in colouring and build, and there were those who whispered that Garrick was the father of her child Molly. Mary Nash, in her biography of Mrs Cibber, knocks such gossip convincingly on the head. She points out that after his retirement, Garrick reviewed his vast correspondence closely and weeded it of anything that he regarded as remotely compromising. The very survival of many of Mrs Cibber's letters, therefore, offers convincing proof of the chasteness of their relationship. Phrases like 'your little wife' or 'your affectionate mother' Nash categorizes as 'little flourishes of nonsensical stage consanguinity'.[26]

Susannah Cibber could certainly be coquettish and flirtatious in her dealings with Garrick. There was undoubtedly at times a degree of erotic tension between them. But the attraction she felt towards him plainly co-existed with absolute fidelity to Sloper.

8

Violette

'Sheridan is a —.'

Thus Garrick to Draper a few days after his arrival in Dublin. The letter does not survive, but the editor of the *London Morning Post*, who published it some years after Garrick's death, was clearly a man of delicacy, because at this point he inserted an asterisk and a note: 'There is not any hiatus in the Manuscript; but out of respect to the living, we have created one.'

The two men had quarrelled about terms. Garrick wished to have an agreed sum, Sheridan favoured a sharing of the profits. 'After some little dispute,' writes Davies, 'which Sheridan decided by taking out his watch and insisting upon an answer in a few minutes, Mr Garrick submitted.'[1] What was agreed was that they should be joint managers, that they should each have a third of the profits (the remaining third going to the proprietors) and that Garrick should act twice a week until the first week in March, with a guarantee of two benefits. 'My brother Manager and I at present are civil, so I would not have you say anything about him,' Garrick wrote to Draper on 1 December:

> I intend to behave in such a manner, that no blame shall light upon me, but (*entre nous*) he is as shifting as Lacy, and has got an indifferent character among the people here: He has played Sir Harry Wildair lately, and hurt himself as an actor among his friends.[2]

In mid-December news came from Lichfield of the death of a sister. Jane Garrick's health had never been good. 'She was the handsomest of the family, and a very good girl,' Garrick wrote to Draper:

> I am sure she is happy, and am not sorry she is released from the pain and anxieties of this world: I believe the terrors and alarms of the country was under on account of the rebels, hastened her death—but let her rest.[3]

The reports reaching Ireland about the rebellion were inaccurate. The Lord Lieutenant's secretary had told someone that the London theatres had been closed, but it was not so. The Highland army had reached Derby on 4 December, but with no sign of support from English Jacobites Charles Edward's officers refused to follow him further. Two days later—'Black Friday' both for the Scots

and for the citizens of London stricken with panic at news of their proximity—
the Prince sullenly agreed to a retreat.

It was too late for Green and Amber. Official notice of their bankruptcy
was posted in the *London Gazette* just before Christmas, and Lacy, hardened
entrepreneur that he was, teetered for some time on the brink of insolvency.[4] All
of which was grist to Mrs Cibber's mill, and she continued, with shrewd good
humour, to goad Garrick on the question of the Drury Lane patent, urging him
to consider joining with her in the purchase:

> I know you reckon yourself a very politic prince with your journey to
> Ireland; and I think the great Garrick never acted so simply since I had the
> honour of knowing him. You are out of the way at the very time that the
> fate of the stage is depending . . . . .[5]

Garrick was torn. 'What can I say to her?' he wrote to Draper:

> *Mure*, you know, is the person I have hopes of joining with; and yet, if she
> can procure it (as I believe he is very slow in his motions), why should not I
> (upon a good agreement and easy terms) be concerned with her? We ought
> always to play together; and I could wish we were both settled at the same
> house. Pray think of this affair; and as I know you are so much more cool
> and judicious than myself, I shall follow your advice in every thing.[6]

He returned to the subject in his next letter: 'Sure some thing must happen in
the theatrical state, that may turn to my advantage,' he wrote, 'therefore my
dear Draper, look about a little, and *if you can conveniently wriggle your little
friend into the patent upon good terms, you make me for ever.*' His thinking
about Mrs Cibber had swung about, however:

> I should be glad of your visiting *Mrs Cibber*, she certainly has had proposals
> made to her; but how can she be a joint patentee? Her husband will interfere,
> or somebody must act for her, which would be equally disagreeable:
> but I am talking without book, and shall desire you to send me better
> intelligence.

This letter, written towards the end of December 1745, also demonstrates how
wide of the mark were the stories spread by Macklin and others of Garrick's
tight-fistedness. He was undoubtedly careful with his money—people who have
grown up in straitened circumstances often are—but there are numerous instances
of his generosity to friends in trouble. He had heard that a friend called Henry
Harnage had suffered greatly from the bankruptcy of a banking firm called
Robinson Knight and William Hanson. In his letter to Draper, he enclosed a bill
of exchange and asked him to enquire into Harnage's circumstances:

> If this Bill of Exchange will be of the least service to him, pray let him
> have it immediately; I shall leave that business to your management; *if the
> sum were twenty times as much, and the whole of my fortune, he should
> have it,* for I know his worth and honour.[7]

Garrick's second Dublin season was going well. He and Sheridan had reached a *modus vivendi* and agreed to play in Shakespeare alternately. A good supporting company had been assembled. It included troublesome little George Anne Bellamy and the silver-tongued Spranger Barry, playing his second season in Dublin. Garrick thought highly of him—'a man of merit, worth and integrity,' he told Draper. 'He is a fine figure, and is ready to go to the Indies if I desire him.'*

The new Lord Lieutenant was Lord Chesterfield. George II had needed a lot of persuading before agreeing to his appointment. Chesterfield had not only been an outspoken critic of successive administrations, but had frequently directed his acerbic wit against the person of the monarch. He had once mocked the King and Queen for their determined admiration of Handel; leaving a thinly attended performance of an oratorio, he offered as his barbed reason that he did not wish to intrude on the privacy of his sovereign. He had also consistently opposed proposals to take Hanoverian troops into British pay: 'The crown of three kingdoms,' he told the Lords in January 1744, 'was shrivelled beneath an electoral cap.'†

Chesterfield knew well enough that Ireland was often regarded as a dumping ground for ministers who had fallen from favour, but whom it would be dangerous to dismiss.‡ That did not prevent him, during his short tenure—he was in residence for only eight months—from applying himself to the task in hand with diligence and flair. He entertained lavishly at the Castle, and managed the potentially explosive situation created by the Jacobite rebellion across the water not only with great political skill, but with wit and charm. He rejected the precedent of 1715, when all the Catholic chapels had been closed, and declared that the only dangerous Papist of his acquaintance was Miss Eleanor Ambrose, the daughter of a wealthy brewer and a reigning beauty in Dublin society, to whom he improvised some gallant verses.§

Although Chesterfield was a frequent theatre-goer, a story went the rounds that Garrick was offended because he felt excluded from all the flattering attentions bestowed so lavishly on the natives. Sheridan was received with great affability at the Castle, but he was not. On Garrick's benefit night Sheridan and he, as

---

* *Letters*, 42. Lord Chesterfield, the Lord Lieutenant, also admired his figure, but predicted his sudden withdrawal from the stage, carried off by some rich predatory widow.
† There were more personal reasons for the royal family's hostility to Chesterfield. The Queen had not taken kindly to his cultivation of Henrietta Howard, later Countess of Suffolk, her husband's mistress; the King, for his part, was not best pleased that Chesterfield had made a lucrative marriage of convenience with the Countess of Walsingham — the natural daughter of George I's 'Maypole' mistress, the Duchess of Kendal.
‡ Two of his predecessors, Sunderland and Townshend, had not even bothered to visit the country during their term.
§ The occasion was a ball at the Castle on the anniversary of the Battle of the Boyne, when she appeared with an orange lily at her breast:

> Say, lovely Tory, where's the jest
> Of wearing orange in thy breast,
> When that same breast uncovered shows
> The whiteness of the rebel rose?

was the agreeable custom in Dublin, ceremoniously lit the Lord Lieutenant to his box with candles: Chesterfield spoke graciously to Sheridan but largely ignored his English counterpart, although they had previously met in London. Garrick's sensitivity to slights, real or imagined, was already well developed.*

Garrick's letters to friends in England exude nothing but satisfaction—at his success on the stage, but also as a tuft-hunter. 'We still sail before the Wind here,' he told Windham:

I have had another large Benefit & the Business continues as good as ever. I have done Myself great Service with yᵉ Learned & the choice few by the Characters of Macbeth & Lear, & never play'd 'em so well in my Life; & by the Strength of 'em I have got myself introduc'd to yᵉ Lord Chancellour, Lord Chief Baron Bowes & Mr Baron Mounteney &c.†

Neglect by the Castle apart, Garrick found the social life of the Irish capital highly congenial. 'I am rather idle, see much company, and drink cheerfully; I assure you I am grown a very *bon compagnion*,' he told Draper. He had also got Woffington out of his system:

Pray tell *Mr Mendez*—when you see him, that he is much mistaken about the situation of my heart; I assure him I have transplanted it long ago, and change of climate agrees with it wonderfully; it flourishes, and I do not doubt but that it will bring forth fruit, for it is fixed in a very *rich soil*.⁸

Possibly it was this new affair of the heart that caused Garrick to linger in Dublin beyond the end of the season. He returned to London early in May, and almost at once fell ill:

Tho I got well to London & was congratulated by all my Friends for my healthy Looks & sleek Countenance, Yet trusting too much to my Spirits & Constitution, I have got a most Severe Cold & Sore Throat attended with a Small Feaver; I rambl'd with Some choice Spirits to Renelaugh Gardens last wednesday Night, & being too thinly clad, & some rain falling, I have suffer'd ever since for my Imprudence: I have purg'd, bled & kept my Room & am now scarce able to keep my head up to write to You.⁹

The capital had been *en fête*. The hero of the hour was the Duke of Cumberland— 'martial boy' or 'butcher' depending on the where you stood. Thomas Carlyle's

---

* Chesterfield, as Johnson would later discover in the matter of his *Dictionary*, was not the most constant of patrons. Sheridan would discover it too. While in Dublin, Chesterfield encouraged him to think that he could look to him for patronage in establishing an academy for oratory; when he called on him in London some years later with hopes of advancing the scheme, he went away with a contribution of a guinea.
† Undated half-page letter preserved at Felbrigg. John Bowes (1690–1767) had been Chief Baron of the Exchequer in Ireland since 1741. An opponent of the relaxation of penal laws against Irish Catholics, he was later promoted to the Lord Chancellorship. Richard Mountney (1707–68) had been Baron of the Exchequer since 1737. A fellow of King's College, Cambridge, he was a classical scholar as well as a lawyer, and had edited Demosthenes.

view was that he 'was beaten by everybody that tried, and never beat anything, except some starved highland peasants'. The Culloden Medal, one of the earliest to be struck for the British Army, presented the matter less sardonically. On the face, a Roman bust of the Duke; on the reverse, Apollo transfixing the neck of a dragon. *Actum est ilicet periit*, ran the legend—'The deed is done, it is all over.'

London had celebrated with gun salutes at the Tower and in Green Park and the ringing of church bells, and the night sky had been ablaze with fireworks and illuminations. Likenesses of Duke Billy were on sale in the streets within hours, the features perhaps slightly more classical than those of the pop-eyed, pudgy-faced original. Scots were jostled or stoned in the streets, and a Catholic chapel was set on fire. Handel would soon be at work on *Judas Maccabeus*, commissioned by Frederick, Prince of Wales, to celebrate his brother's victory; later in the year, when the conquering hero returned to the capital, there would be a service of solemn thanksgiving in St Paul's.

The theatre managers had risen nobly to the occasion. Drury Lane dredged up a piece called *The Humours of the Army, or The Female Officer*, originally written to celebrate victory in the War of the Spanish Succession in 1713. This was pretty smart work on Lacy's part—its first performance was on 23 April, which was the day before that rakish young dandy Lord Bury, Lord Albemarle's son and heir and the Duke's aide-de-camp, galloped into town with the Culloden dispatches. Covent Garden countered with *Liberty Asserted, or French Perfidy Displayed*, an even older piece, by John Dennis, which had not had an outing for forty years. Four nights later the manager of the New Wells in Goodman's Fields showed himself a sharper impresario than either of his confrères at the patent theatres by mounting a production of *Harlequin, A Captive in France, or the Frenchman trapt at last*:

> . . . . . The whole to conclude with an exact view of our Gallant Army under the Command of their Glorious hero passing the River Spey, giving the Rebels battle, and gaining a complete Victory near Culloden House, with the horse in pursuit of the Pretender.

Garrick's absence from London had been well-timed. 'It is surprising that Drury Lane goes on acting,' Mrs Cibber had written in one of her letters during the winter: 'one night with another, to be sure, they have not received above forty pounds; the actors are paid only three nights a week; though they play every night.'* Garrick, by contrast, had returned from Dublin £600 the richer. He now added half as much again to that sum by accepting an invitation from Rich to give a number of performances at Covent Garden during June in return for an

---

* *Boaden*, i, 49. Mrs Cibber expected some return for the flow of theatrical intelligence and gossip with which she kept Garrick supplied. 'You will by this post receive a glove,' she wrote to him in February, 'and if you will get me ten dozen made exactly of the same size, and bring them over with you, I shall take it as a particular favour . . . .' (*Boaden*, i, 40.)

equal share of the profits; he also signed formal articles to appear there for the winter season of 1746–7.*

Drury Lane also stayed open later than usual. A notice in the newspapers said that this was 'for the Entertainment of his Serene Highness the Prince of Hesse', which was only fair, given that his Serene Highness had been on the staff of his brother-in-law Cumberland during the Scottish campaign and had made available—at a price—6,000 of his troops. He dined with the King, who presented him with a sword set with diamonds, and he was taken to sup at Ranelagh, where he exchanged some words with Garrick. ('Don't forget what the Prince of Hesse said to you at Ranelagh,' wrote Mrs Cibber, who was pressing him to visit her in the country, 'for I shall expect every word from you.')

The Prince also went to the opera at the King's Theatre, where it was remarked that to get a better view of the last dance, he moved from his own box into that of the Prince of Wales. The attraction was a 22-year-old dancer from Vienna who had been with the Italian company in the Haymarket since the spring. Her professional name was Violette, and her début had caused something of a stir: 'At her beginning to caper,' wrote Lord Strafford, 'she shewed a neat pair of black velvet breeches, with roll'd stockings; but finding they were unusual in England, she changed them the next time for a pair of white drawers.'† She quickly became the talk of the town. 'The fame of the Violetta increases daily,' Horace Walpole wrote on 6 June.[10]

She had certainly caught the attention of the Prince of Wales, but that was scarcely surprising, as his friend Lord Middlesex was the impresario at the opera house. The Prince proposed that she should come to Carlton House to take private lessons from his French dancing master Denoyer. The fact that she declined the invitation suggests either that she was a young woman of great good sense or that she had the benefit of wise advice, perhaps from those to whom she had brought letters of introduction. In Vienna, where she had danced with the Imperial Ballet from the age of ten, she had been patronized by the nobility and taken up by the Court. The idea that she should go abroad had been Maria Theresa's, who was not blind to the Emperor's quickening interest in the young dancer.

She had made the crossing to Harwich from the small port of Helvoetsluis in Holland, accompanied by her father and by her brother, Ferdinand Charles, who was also a dancer. One of their fellow-passengers was a young Scottish son of the manse called Alexander Carlyle, returning home from the University of Leyden.‡ It was a very rough crossing, and many years later Carlyle described it in his memoirs:

---

* Garrick's first summer appearance was in *Lear* on 11 June, and this was followed by performances of *Hamlet*, *Richard III*, *Othello*, *The Beaux' Stratagem* and *Macbeth*.
† Quoted in *Highfill*, vi, 104–5. The piece in which Violette made her début was *Artamene*, the second London composition of Gluck, who had arrived in England the previous autumn in the company of his patron Prince Lobkowitz. A *pasticcio* taken from three of his earlier works, it had been written in extreme haste and was not well received.
‡ Carlyle (1722–1805) became known as 'Jupiter' Carlyle because of his noble profile and bearing: 'The grandest demi-god I ever saw was Dr Carlyle,' wrote Walter Scott. He became a

When we were on the Quarterdeck in the Morning, we observ'd 3 For-
reigners of Different Ages who had under their care a Young Person of
about 16 very Handsome indeed, whom we took for a Hanoverian Baron
Coming to Brittain to pay his Court at St James's.

The freshening gale drove them below to the cabin, where they found that the
'Young Person' was the only one of the party of foreigners who had a berth:

> My Bed was Directly opposite to that of the Stranger. But we were so Sick
> that there was no Conversation among us, till the Young Forreigner became
> very frightened, in Spite of the Sickness, and call'd out to me in French, if
> we were not in Danger—Her voice betraid her Sex at once, no less than
> her Fears; I consold her as well as I could, and soon brought her above
> the Fear of Danger.[11]

Why it had been decided that Violette should travel disguised as a man is obscure.
It was the cause of some unpleasantness at Colchester; the servants at an inn
there were not taken in by her disguise and took exception to the party's request
to be put up in one room; Carlyle and his companions intervened and 'prevented
their being insulted'. In London, after a night spent at the same inn off Cheapside,
they went their separate ways, swearing, as ships that pass in the night so often
do, eternal friendship. Carlyle went twice to the Haymarket to admire Violette's
dancing, but he did not linger long in the capital—'The theatres were not very
attractive this season, as Garrick had gone over to Dublin.'

Whether Garrick met Violette socially after his return from Ireland in that
summer of 1746 is not known. When his Covent Garden engagement ended he
set off on a social round. He had accepted an invitation to visit John Hoadly at
his vicarage at Old Alresford in Hampshire. Hoadly's brother Benjamin, physician
to the King's household and to that of the Prince of Wales, was to be there,
and so was snuff-covered, free-thinking Messenger Monsey, the rough-spoken
physician to Chelsea Hospital and unofficial medical adviser to half the Whig
grandees of the day—he was said to be the only man who dared to beat Walpole
at billiards. Garrick travelled down with Hogarth. The two had been acquainted
for some years, but had got to know each other much better the previous summer
when Hogarth, intensely interested in everything to do with the theatre, was at
work on his huge canvas of Garrick as Richard III. The engraving of that portrait,
which Hogarth had worked on with Charles Grignion, had just appeared.*

John Hoadly had helped Hogarth with the verses for the engravings of 'The
Rake's Progress' a dozen years previously, and more recently Hogarth had painted
both brothers and their father, the Bishop of Winchester. The prospect of taking

---

prominent figure in the Scottish Enlightenment and a leader of the Moderate party in the
established church. In 1770 he was elected Moderator of the General Assembly.
* Garrick's constant mobility of feature made him a difficult subject. Hogarth attempted the
face several times. He finally gave up and resorted to trying out faces on another canvas until
he had a likeness that satisfied him. He then cut this out and sewed it into place. (See Paulson,
Ronald, *Hogarth, Volume 2, High Art and Low, 1732–1750*, Cambridge, 1992, p. 250.)

his ease in such congenial company put Garrick in high good humour and he left London determined, he told his host, 'to be as Merry, facetious Mad & Nonsensical, as Liberty, Property & Old October can make Em!'*

Hoadly entertained his guests in some style in a house at Old Alresford, 'as spacious and elegant a parsonage as any in the kingdom'.† The Hoadlys were devoted to amateur theatricals. One of the pieces they performed that summer was called *Ragandjaw*, and it was written by Garrick. It does not appear in his collected works, but it survives in manuscript—a bawdy parody of the quarrel scene between Brutus and Cassius in *Julius Caesar*. The fact that they were in a parsonage does not seem to have inhibited him—the Roman generals are transformed into an English sergeant and corporal, lamenting the loss not of Brutus's noble wife but of her mastiff bitch Brindle, who had been after sheep. Brutus becomes Brutarse, and was played by John Hoadly. Cassius becomes Cassiarse, played by Garrick. The servant Lucius becomes Loosearse and Caesar's ghost was replaced by the Devil's Cook—this part was taken by Hogarth.

Scene: A Tent; a Table, Pot of Beer, Pipes & Tobacco &c.

Thunder and Lightning. Enter Grilliardo the Devil's Cook

BRUTARSE.   How ill this farthing Candle burns, and blue!
I'll top the Glim—(*snuffs it with his Fingers*)—
What's here?—Zounds who are you?

GRILLIARDO.   I am Old Nick's Cook—& hither am I come
To slice some Steaks from off thy Brawny Bum,
Make Sausage of thy Guts, & Candles of thy Fat,
And cut thy Cock off, to regale his Cat.

BRUTARSE.   Art thou, in Hell, a Ruler of the Roast?
I would not care a—(*snaps his Fingers*)—for such a Ghost

GRILLIARDO.   And dost thou think to hide thy Crimes from me?
Tho' thou blind'st Cassiarse, yet thou can'st not *We*.
Your Wife you Murther'd—Shall I say for What?
Because she leak'd beside the Chamber-Pot:
Your Sisters you Debauch'd in Anger sudden
Because they put no Plumbs into your Pudding.
You, Nero like, rip'd up your Mother's Belly,
And boil'd your Father to make Calvesfoot Jelly.
Adieu; to Hell I'm going to prepare

---

* 'October' was a common word for ale in the eighteenth century.
† He could afford to. Thanks to the patronage at the disposal of his father, he was at that time not merely rector of Alresford; he was also chaplain to the Prince of Wales, chancellor of the diocese of Winchester and rector of Mitchelmarsh in Hampshire, Wroughton in Wiltshire and St Mary near Southampton. He occupied, for good measure, a prebendal stall in Winchester Cathedral and would later in the year be instituted to the vicarage of Overton, Hampshire. ('Memoirs of the Life of the Late Dr. John Hoadly', *Annual Register*, 19 (1776), 39–40.)

This redhot Gridiron against you come there:
Pack up your Duds and meet me at Rag-Fair.

BRUTARSE.   My Trull keeps Shop in Porridge Row—I'll meet thee there.

GRILLIARDO.   But first to Westminster I'll take my Way,
And with a Gang of Lawyers load my Dray;
Next to fam'd Warwick Lane away I'll Whiz,
My Master Satan wants a Household Phiz:
Last to where Convocation sits I'll fly,
For I've a fatars'd Chaplain in my Eye.
But ha! I'm called—Hell gapes! I'm on the Brink!
Brutarse, prepare—for now I feel, I sink.
       Walks off.

The set was painted by Hogarth. It represented 'a sutling booth', with—what else in the year of Culloden?—'the *Duck of Cumberland's* head by way of sign'.*

Garrick was briefly back in London early in August and then headed for Cheltenham:

> I came to this Place last Thursday, & a damn'd dull Place it is, notwithstanding We have Balls twice a Week, Assemblies every Night, & the facetious Mr Foote to Crown the Whole: He is full of Spirits, abounds in Pleasantry, Plays at Whist for five pounds a Rubber, wears lac'd Frocks with dirty Shirts, & to the eternal Mortification of the Beaux Esprits he has renounc'd the Stage for Ever . . . . . I have drank the Waters & they agree very well with Me; but I have unfortunately got a Boil under the Wasteband of my Breeches, that greatly discomposes Me, & perhaps my Want of Relish for the Pleasures of Cheltenam may be chiefly owing to that . . . . .

This letter (it was to Francis Hayman) contains a passage that is very revealing of the curious mixture of suspicion and spontaneity that governed Garrick's relations with others:

> I will assure You that my Shyness some time ago proceeded from Yr great Intimacy with some People, who (I imagin'd) would take all Methods (however unjustly) to shew their Aversion; & tho I had no fear of their Malice, yet it was natural to avoid both them & their Intimates: I have no luke-warmness in my Temper, & as I am naturally open & Impetuous, it is a necessary prudence in me to shun Company I am doubtfull of; I cannot confine my Spirits or be upon the Reserve, & therefore till I know my Man, I ought not to trust him . . . . .[12]

He also dashed off a gossipy bread-and-butter letter to Hoadly from Cheltenham—'I never was happier in My Life or so desirous to continue so.' *Ragandjaw*, he announced, had been greeted by his friends with universal applause: 'I have dedicated it to My Friend Windham (the Prince of BlackGuards) ye Dedication

---

* A sutler was one who supplied provisions to soldiers.

is Short & you shall see it at our next Meeting.'* His mind was swarming with stage possibilities. He told Hoadly that he was studying the part of Varanes in Nathaniel Lee's *Theodosius*:

> There is Something very moving in yᵉ Character, but such a Mixture of Madness & Absurdity was never Serv'd up, upon yᵉ Stage before, except by yᵉ Same incomprehensible Nat Lee: I have been looking into Philaster or Love lies a Bleeding; there is good Stuff; but yᵉ Intrigue between Megra and Pharamond, upon wᶜʰ yᵉ whole turns, is very indecent & requires great alterations—†

When he next wrote to Hoadly the best part of a month later he began with an apology—'I am sorry My inadvertency caus'd You so much trouble to find out where I was; But You see I have mended that fault in this & will endeavour for the future to give You the Place where, & Time When.' He was being more than a little disingenuous. He gave his address simply as 'Newberry', but if he had really wanted to inform Hoadly about 'the Place where, & Time When' he could have been a good deal more specific. 'Mr Garrick has been here these three weeks in great good humour,' Mrs Cibber wrote to her brother Tom towards the end of September, 'I am in charming health and spirits and as full of fun as I can hold.'

So was Garrick, for all his reluctance for it to be known that he was visiting this notorious ménage. There was good riding to be had on the Downs; there was an angling pond spanned by a bridge and Sloper had a fine library of books and prints. 'I have been lately allarm'd with some Encroachments of my Belly upon the Line of Grace & Beauty,' he told Hoadly, 'in short I am *grow*ing very fat, & unless Shakespear in yᵉ Winter reduces me to my primitive insignificance, I shall produce as good a title for a place at yᵉ Quarter Sessions as Yʳ Worship or any of yʳ Well-fed Family.'

Hoadly had produced a 'dock'd and alter'd' version of *Cymbeline*, and Garrick was eager to see it: 'What Character have you fix'd for Me in yʳ Mind?'‡ He also felt in need of some advice:

> I have a Play now with Me, sent to me by My Lord Chesterfield, & wrote by One Smollett; it is a Scotch Story, but it won't do, & yet recommended by his Lordship & patroniz'd by Ladies of Quality: what can I say, or do? must I belye my Judgment or run the risque of being thought impertinent, & disobliging yᵉ Great Folks? some advice upon that Head if You please—§

---

* The dedication, which is not, in fact, particularly short, is preserved at Felbrigg. 'I must declare,' it concludes, 'that the Choicest Flowers which I have added to this Poetical Nosegay, were all gathered and cull'd from your private Conversation, Writings & Publick Disputations on the Water, the Road, in the Streets, at Cuper's Gardens and Mr Broughton's Amphitheatre . . . . .'

† *Letters*, 48. Nothing came of either idea. Lee's *Theodosius* was not revived until 1767, when Barry played Varanes; a version of Beaumont and Fletcher's *Philaster* was mounted at Drury Lane in 1763 in Garrick's absence abroad.

‡ Nothing came of it. Garrick eventually brought out his own version fifteen years later.

§ *Letters*, 49. The play in question was *The Regicide*, which Smollett had been hawking about since first coming to London seven years previously. When Rich rejected it in the autumn, Smollett was convinced that it was Garrick's doing, and he embarked on a lengthy feud.

Autumn was coming on, and Garrick returned to town to prepare for the new season. His hostess at West Woodhays knew now that her campaign to acquire the Drury Lane patent jointly with Garrick and Quin would not succeed, and she was reconciled to that. One of her lesser dreams was about to be realized, however. Garrick and Quin would now for the first time be members of the same company. Better still, she would act with them.

9

Enter the Manager

If Mrs Cibber had a vision of Covent Garden in the autumn of 1746 as some sort of thespian holy mountain where the calf and the young lion and the fatling would all lie down together, the expectations of the pit and the gallery were altogether more gladiatorial. What they looked forward to was the clash of the old and the new. They were impatient to witness Quin and Garrick pitted against each other on the same stage. Rich would give them what they wanted—although, characteristically, he would make them wait two months for it.*

The season opened with the companies of the two patent theatres more evenly matched than for many years. In addition to Garrick and Quin and Mrs Cibber, Rich could call on Mrs Pritchard, supreme in tragedy, the veteran Lacy Ryan,† Henry Woodward, formidably talented as both a comedian and a dancer‡ and the versatile John Hippisley, a great favourite with audiences, who would 'clap him heartily, and fall a laughing at him as soon as he appeared upon the Stage, before he had opened his Mouth to speak one Word'.§ It was as strong a team as had been seen since the days of Booth, Wilks and Colley Cibber.

At Drury Lane, Lacy was banking heavily on Spranger Barry (whom Macklin had taken under his wing) and in Clive and Woffington he had at his command the capital's leading comediennes. He had also recruited a strong team of dancers, which included two of the stars from the opera corps at the King's Theatre— Salomon and Mlle Violette.¶ Drury Lane opened on 22 September, a week before

---

* Davies says that Rich used to peep through the curtain at the packed house waiting his great performers, and retreat muttering, 'Ah, you're there, are ye? Much good may it do ye.'
† Tate Wilkinson, in his *Memoirs*, says that Garrick once went to a performance of *Richard III* to be merry at Ryan's ungraceful and raggedly dressed Richard, but stayed to admire the presentation and borrow touches from it.
‡ Woodward had been taught by Rich, and was sometimes billed as 'Lun, Jr' when he danced in pantomime.
§ This was partly because he had a deformed face. 'This great Comedian,' wrote Samuel Foote in his *Roman and English Comedy* (1747), 'was so fortunate as in his Infancy to fall in the Fire, by which means the left Corner of his Mouth, and the Extremity of his Chin, became very near Neighbours.'
¶ Giuseppe Salomoni (1710–77) had danced in Venice and elsewhere on the continent before coming to London in 1745. Violette may well have been driven from the King's by jealousy. She had quickly demonstrated that she was a much better dancer than Mlle Nardi, but Nardi happened to be the mistress of Lord Middlesex, the theatre's director.

Covent Garden, and got off to a strong start with Macklin as Shylock in *The Merchant of Venice* and Peachum in *The Beggar's Opera*, although they took a risk by following this with a production of *The Constant Couple* in which Theo Cibber was preferred to Woffington as Sir Harry Wildair.*

Covent Garden made a somewhat muted start, with Ryan cast first as Hamlet and then as Townly in *The Provok'd Husband* and Woodward playing Foppington in *The Relapse*. Drury Lane was still calling the shots in early October when Barry made his first London appearance as Othello—'before a numerous and polite audience,' according to the *General Advertiser*, 'and met with as great Applause as could be express'd.' One of those who applauded most vigorously was Colley Cibber, and Barry was told that the old man preferred his Othello to that of Booth or Betterton. The poet Thomas Gray was also in the audience, and sent his impressions to Horace Walpole. 'I can say nothing of his face but that it was all black,' he reported, somewhat redundantly, but he had more interesting things to say about the rest of Barry's performance:

> His voice is of a clear and pleasing tone, something like Delane's, but not so deep-mouthed, not so like a passing bell. When high strain'd it is apt to crack a little and be hoarse, but in its common pitch, and when it sinks into any softer passion, particularly expressive and touching. . . . . . He is not perfect to be sure, but I think may make a better player than any now on the stage in a little while.[1]

Covent Garden's relative slowness to respond may have reflected some difficulty in devising the terms of a concordat between Quin and Garrick, although Davies records that both men 'had too much sense and temper to squabble about trifles' and that after one or two friendly meetings they came to an amicable agreement about who was to do what and in which order. Quin appeared as Richard III on 20 October and Garrick on the last day of the month. According to Davies, the contest was a disaster for Quin:

> His Richard the Third could scarce draw together a decent appearance of company in the boxes; and he was, with some difficulty, tolerated in the part, when Garrick acted the same character to crowded houses, and with very great applause.[2]

This account of Davies's has been accepted uncritically by almost all subsequent biographers of Garrick. There is no way of measuring the volume of applause two hundred and fifty years after the event, but it is still possible to consult the treasurer's account books for Covent Garden, and they tell a less dramatic story. The receipts for the evening that Quin played the part were £160 19s; when Garrick appeared in the role eleven nights later they amounted to £188 6s 2d.[3]

When the evening came for the two to appear together in the same play for the first time, the house was in partisan mood, and the atmosphere that of the

* Woffington was cast as Lady Lurewell.

prize-ring. The Prince and Princess of Wales were present, and the play was Rowe's She-tragedy in blank verse, *The Fair Penitent*. Mrs Cibber appeared as the fair Calista, who eventually quits the scene in the high Roman fashion. Quite a few of the lines she had to utter must have come from the heart:

> How hard is the condition of our sex,
> Through ev'ry state of life the slaves of men!
> In all the dear, delightful days of youth
> A rigid father dictates to our will,
> And deals out pleasure with a scanty hand.
> To his, the tyrant husband's reign succeeds;
> Proud with opinion of superior reason
> He holds domestic business and devotion
> All we are capable to know, and shuts us,
> Like cloistered idiots, from the world's acquaintance
> And all the joys of freedom . . . . .*

Garrick played her seducer, the 'haughty, gallant, Gay Lothario'; Quin was her noble avenger, Horatio. The two characters come together on the stage for the first time in Act II, and this was the signal for prolonged shouts of applause from the supporters of both actors. Quin was observed to change colour, and Garrick seemed to be embarrassed: 'Faith, I believe Quin was as much frightened as myself,' he said afterwards. There was a moment of light relief. At one point Lothario challenges Horatio to a duel. Quin, who was supposed to respond with the line 'I'll meet thee there!' paused for such an eternity that a wag in the gallery had time to call out, 'Why don't you tell the gentleman whether you will meet him or not?'

Also in the gallery that night was a boy called Richard Cumberland, later well known as a dramatist, then a pupil at Westminster. 'I have the spectacle even now as it were before my eyes,' he wrote in his memoirs (this was in 1804, when he was in his early seventies):

Quin presented himself upon the rising of the curtain in a green velvet coat embroidered down the seams, an enormous full-bottomed periwig, rolled stockings and high-heeled square-toed shoes; with very little variation of cadence, and in a deep full tone, accompanied by a sawing kind of action, which had more of the senate than of the stage in it, he rolled out his heroics with an air of dignified indifference, that seemed to disdain the plaudits that were bestowed upon him. Mrs. Cibber in a key, high-pitched but sweet withal, sung or rather recitatived Rowe's harmonious strain, something in the manner of the Improvisatories: it was so extremely wanting in contrast, that, though it did not wound the ear, it wearied it; when she had once recited two or three speeches, I could anticipate the manner of every succeeding one; it was like a long old legendary ballad of innumerable stanzas, every one of which is sung to the same tune, eternally

---

* Act III, scene i.

chiming in the ear without variation or relief. Mrs. Pritchard was an actress of a different cast, had more nature, and of course more change of tone, and variety both of action and expression: in my opinion the comparison was decidedly in her favour; but when after long and eager expectation I first beheld little Garrick, then young and light and alive in every muscle and in every feature, come bounding on the stage, and pointing at the wittol Altamont and heavy-paced Horatio—heavens, what a transition!—it seemed as if a whole century had been stept over in the transition of a single scene; old things were done away, and a new order at once brought forward, bright and luminous, and clearly destined to dispel the barbarisms and bigotry of a tasteless age, too long attached to the prejudices of custom, and superstitiously devoted to the illusions of imposing declamation.

Garrick's impact on acting style in the eighteenth century is often depicted as a sort of effortless *blitzkrieg*; indeed, Cumberland's account is frequently quoted as a major piece of evidence for that view. It is important therefore to read on, and see how that account concludes:

This heaven-born actor was then struggling to emancipate his audience from the slavery they were resigned to, and though at times he succeeded in throwing some gleams of new born light upon them, yet in general they seemed to *love darkness better than light*, and in the dialogue of altercation between Horatio and Lothario bestowed far the greater *show of hands* upon the master of the old school than upon the founder of the new.[4]

No question, then, as theatrical legend would have it, of almost a century of tradition being swept away overnight, even if it was the case that 'the master of the old school', Quin, represented the fag-end of that tradition.

Eighty years earlier, the theatre had been essentially an appanage of the court; now, when members of fashionable society went to the play, they rubbed shoulders with increasing numbers of the middle class, whose tastes were not at all the same. There had been an important political dimension to the reopening of the theatres after the Restoration. The court, returning from its French exile, looked to the drama not simply for diversion but for confirmation of the grandeur of majesty that they had witnessed at Versailles. In 1662 Thomas Betterton, then still in his twenties, was sent to France by Charles II to gather ideas about how the English theatre might be revivified—the King was well aware of how much ground had been lost in the eighteen years that had followed the closure of the playhouses in 1642.

The English stage had accordingly been strongly influenced by the French classical tradition, and the London theatre-goer had been offered an essentially static style of acting characterized by lengthy exposition, conventional gestures and extended soliloquies. A player would advance to the footlights and deliver a set speech much as today an operatic diva at La Scala might halt the action with a lyric aria. Gestures were minutely codified—Aaron Hill's *The Prompter*, published between 1734 and 1736, had identified ten basic dramatic passions—

joy, grief, anger, fear, pity, scorn, jealousy, hatred, wonder and love. ('Joy is pride possessed with triumph—forehead raised and open, eye full and sparkling, neck expanded and erect . . .') Performance routinely programmed in this way could easily degenerate into cliché, especially with less talented players.*

Frank Hedgcock has a good phrase about 'the daring pliancy of Garrick's genius', and it was undoubtedly the protean quality of his acting which set him most strikingly apart from the formalism into which the London stage had declined by the 1740s. He was small,† he was not conventionally handsome and his voice was liable to strain, but these disadvantages were neutralized by the impassioned force and variety of his performance. He spoke much more conversationally than had been customary, breaking up speeches with frequent pauses and shifts of tone. (When he encountered the Ghost in his first appearance as Hamlet, he remained silent so long after gasping out the words 'Angels and ministers of grace defend us' that some of the audience thought he had forgotten his lines.)‡

Here then was an actor who, instead of presenting the audience with familiar stereotypes, constantly explored ways of revealing new aspects of a character, and who did so with equal success in tragedy and comedy—this at a time when many saw something almost indecent in a great tragedian playing a comic role. He was powerfully aided by the mobility of his features and by the extraordinary effects he achieved by modifying the expression of his eyes.§

Quin, imperturbably set in his neo-classical ways, must have regarded him much as exponents of Method acting would be viewed by the more staid members of the profession in the 1930s. To twentieth-century eyes Garrick might well— particularly in his death scenes—seem a considerable ham, but he and Macklin, by their insistence that a true interpretation of a part must be based on personal exploration of the character, can now be seen both as precursors of romanticism and the first of the moderns.¶

---

* Reverence for heroic tragedy was not universal. Farquhar, for instance, in *Love and a Bottle*, has one of his characters describe the tragic hero as 'either a whining cringing fool, that's always stabbing himself, or a ranting hectoring bully, that's for Killing everybody else'. (Act IV, scene ii.)

† Probably not much more than 5'3" (1 m 60). Zoffany's painting of the scene in Act II, scene ii, of *Macbeth*, for example, shows him a good head shorter than Mrs Pritchard.

‡ A modern critic has an acute observation about how Garrick achieved his aim of speech charged with feeling and capable of representing fleeting sensations. 'He got it by splintering his syntax into emotional rather than grammatical units . . . . The timing of his lines was determined by psychological factors, not mechanical rules.' Hafter, Ronald, 'Garrick and Tristram Shandy', *Studies in English Literature, 1500–1900*, VII, Summer 1967, p. 484.

§ Sitting to Joshua Reynolds on one occasion, Garrick drove the painter to distraction by constantly changing his expression. Eventually, in a great rage, Reynolds 'threw down his pallet and pencils on the floor, saying he believed he was painting from the devil, and would do no more to the picture'. (Northcote, James, *Memoirs of Sir Joshua Reynolds*, 2 vols., London, 1813–15, i, 58–9.) George Colman Jr wrote that in the part of Sir Anthony Branville, in Frances Sheridan's *The Discovery*, Garrick 'made the twin stars, which nature had stuck in his head, look as dull as two coddled gooseberries'.

¶ Macklin, when he was preparing to play Shylock, 'made daily visits to the centre of business, 'Change and the adjacent Coffee-Houses, that by a frequent intercourse and conversation with

Old and new appeared again together early in December in *Henry IV Part 1*, with Quin triumphant as Falstaff and Garrick cast as Hotspur. He was not a success; when he became ill after five performances, Havard took over the part and Garrick, realistic as always, did not reclaim it. But he and Quin were now getting on famously. Towards the end of the last act of *Henry IV*, after the battle of Shrewsbury, Falstaff makes his exit with the slain Hotspur slung over his shoulder. At the edge of the wings, Quin, always attentive to the needs of the inner man, was heard to address a hoarse whisper to his gory and lifeless burden: 'Well then—where shall we sup tonight?'

Garrick's old friend and patron Gilbert Walmesley still followed his fortunes with a concerned and kindly eye. 'I hope you will take care not to hurt your health, by playing more than you can well bear,' he wrote to him that winter from Bath; 'for that would be the worst husbandry in the world.' He also had some largely flattering gossip to pass on to his 'Dear Davy':

> I must not forget to tell you what Lord Chesterfield says of you. He says you are not only the best tragedian now in the world, but the best, he believes, that ever was in the world; but he does not like your comedy, and particularly objects to your playing Bayes, which he says is a serious, solemn character, &c. and that you mistake it. He spoke much in praise of Barry's handsome figure, but made a joke of his rivalling, or hurting you. When I hoped his Lordship would give you his protection, his answer was, you wanted no protection:what led me to say so, was his expressing himself as if he intended doing all the good offices in his power for Barry. But, in fine, his Lordship concluded, Barry was so very handsome he could not continue long upon the stage, but that some widow or other would take him off soon.[6]

The lively competition between the two patent companies and, in particular, the resurgence of Covent Garden were doing serious injury to the fortunes of opera. 'We have operas but no company at them,' Horace Walpole wrote to Sir Horace Mann on 5 December. 'Plays only are in fashion; at one house the best company that perhaps ever were together, Quin, Garrick, Mrs Pritchard, Mrs Cibber: at the other Barry, a favourite young actor and the Violette, whose dancing our friends don't like: I scold them, but all they answer is "Lord, you are so English." '[7]

Violette, dancing with Salomon, had made her Drury Lane début only two days previously, as it happens—a command performance. The following night they appeared again in two dances called *The German Camp* and *The Vintage*, 'With new Habits, scenes, Machines, and other Decorations for the Dances'. This was followed after Christmas by Salomon's 'New Grand dance call'd *The Turkish Pirate; or a descent on the Grecian Coast*' and an entertainment called

---

the "unforeskinned race" he might habituate himself to their air and deportment'. (*The Connoisseur*, 31 January 1754.)

the *Laundress's Visiting Day*—'a fine piece of low humour,' thought the *London Courant*.

Violette was shortly to discover that her London public was demanding as well as appreciative, however. On 14 January, when she was scheduled to perform in three dances, she appeared in only two. Quite uninhibited by the fact that it was a command performance for the Prince and Princess of Wales, the audience gave noisy expression to their displeasure; Lord Bury and several other young blades who were present clamoured for her to be sent for from Burlington House (she was now living there under the protection of the Earl and Countess of Burlington). A gracious apology appeared in the *General Advertiser* two days later:

> Mademoisele Violette humbly begs leave to acquaint the Publick, that she is very much concern'd to hear that she is charg'd with having been the occasion of the Noise at the Playhouse in Drury Lane on Wednesday night. That she was entirely ignorant that three Dances had been advertised, until it was too late to prepare herself; and as she cannot possibly be guilty of an Intention to disoblige, or give offence to an English Audience (from whom she has receiv'd so much Applause) she presumes to hope they will not impute to her a fault which she is not capable of committing, and especially where she has met with so much indulgence, for which she retains all possible gratitude.[8]

Garrick enjoyed a double success early in 1747 when he appeared as Fribble, a mincing Macaroni, in his own two-act *Miss in Her Teens*. 'This farce has little of *novelty* to recommend it, the subject having often been handled with equal *mastership* and *delicacy*,' wrote a reviewer in *The Anatomist and News Regulator*:

> Some characters are *unnatural*, and others *faulty*; there is very little *plot*, and no *moral*: But these are blemishes which it shares in common with many celebrated comedies: It is merit enough, to entitle it to be made a *skeleton*, that
>
>   Mr. G-rr-ck is the author of it,
>   The best actors have performed in it.
>   And the Town have been hugely diverted
>   with it.[9]

This reads very much like the sort of low-key, self-deprecatory puff that Garrick was so adept at placing in the press himself. There was indeed a strong cast, with Woodward as the bogus and cowardly Captain, Flash and Mrs Pritchard as the comic servant Tag. And the town was certainly hugely diverted. 'Nothing *can be lower*,' wrote Mrs Delany to a friend in the country, 'but the part he acts in it himself he makes so very ridiculous that it is really entertaining. It is said he mimics *eleven* men of fashion.'* The piece had a remarkable first run of

* *The Autobiography and Correspondence of Mary Granville, Mrs Delany*, ed. Lady Llanover, 1st ser., 1861, ii, 453. Mary Delany (1700–88) a niece of Lord Lansdowne, became the second

eighteen nights; it was also played at Goodman's Fields, at the Haymarket and at Bartholomew and Southwark Fairs, and by the end of the season it had had forty-six performances.

'Captain Flash and Fribble are not the mere offspring of the poet's imagination, they were copied from life,' wrote Murphy:

> The coffee-houses were infested by a set of young officers, who entered with a martial air, fierce *Kavenhuller* hats, and long swords. They paraded the room with ferocity, ready to draw without provocation. In direct contrast to this race of braggarts, stood the pretty gentlemen, who chose to unsex themselves, and make a display of delicacy that exceeded female softness.[10]

Miss in Her Teens, for all its success, was only an afterpiece (when it was published later in the year Garrick, in thanking the public for their favourable reception of it, described it, unduly modestly, as a 'Trifle').* His main comic triumph of the season came in February when he appeared as the rake Ranger in *The Suspicious Husband*, written specially for him by Benjamin Hoadly. It was the first new play to be put on at Covent Garden for four seasons. Foote thought it was the first good comedy that had appeared since *The Provok'd Husband* twenty years earlier; when George II went to see it he laughed so much that he sent Hoadly £100 and graciously allowed the piece to be dedicated to him.

It is essentially a comedy of manners, slightly tinged with the blandness which eighteenth-century notions of morality and benevolence imparted to the genre. Hoadly pressed into service an impressive range of traditional comic devices— quick-witted servants, letters that fall into the wrong hands, mistakes of identity. There is even, in Act III, as Ranger ambles home in the moonlight from the piazza, the inevitable rope-ladder, dangling invitingly from a bedroom window:

> Now I am in an admirable mood for a frolic; have wine in my head, and money in my pocket, and so am furnished out for the cannonading of any countess in Christendom. Ha! what have we here? a ladder!—this cannot be placed here for nothing—and a window open! Is it love or mischief, now, that is going on within? I care not which—I am in a right cue for either. Up I go, neck or nothing . . . . .

Quin is said to have declined the part of Strickland, the suspicious husband of the title, and it was entrusted to the lesser talents of Bridgewater.† Woodward

---

wife of Patrick Delany, the Chancellor of St Patrick's, Dublin and the friend of Swift, in 1743. She later became a favourite of the royal family, to whom she introduced Fanny Burney. Famous in old age for her paper mosaic flower work, she left six volumes of autobiography and letters.
* Quin is said to have grumbled that the success of the piece reduced some of his performances to the level of curtain-raisers, and declined to 'hold up the tail of any farce'. He was quite happy to hold it up on his own benefit night on 9 April, however, when he himself played Pierre in *Venice Preserved*.
† Roger Bridgwater had been on the stage since the early 1720s. He was now in his declining years, and playing less than formerly. For some years he had also been carrying on business as a coal-dealer at a wharf near Whitefriars. He died in 1754.

was Jack Meggott and Mrs Pritchard played Clarinda. Garrick wrote a prologue for the piece, which was spoken by Ryan, and an epilogue, spoken by Mrs Pritchard. The prologue was a fairly pedestrian affair: 'Each trite dull Prologue is the bard's petition,' it ran:

> A stale device to calm the critick's fury,
> And bribe at once the judges and the jury.

The epilogue was an altogether bolder and more interesting affair, cleverly cast in the form of an animal fable, and wittily holding up a mirror to the audience:

> An Ass there was, our author bid me say,
> Who needs must write—he did—and wrote a Play.
> The parts were cast to various beasts and fowl:
> Their stage a barn—the Manager an Owl!

('He means me,' whispered Rich, sitting in the orchestra with a friend.)

> The house was cramm'd at six, with friends and foes;
> Rakes, Wits, and Criticks, Citizens, and Beaux.
> These characters appear'd in different shapes
> Of Tigers, Foxes, Horses, Bulls and Apes;
> With others too, of lower rank and station:—
> A perfect abstract of the brute creation!
> Each, as he felt, mark'd out the Author's faults,
> And thus the *Connoisseurs* express'd their thoughts.
> The Critick-curs first snarl'd—the rules are broke!
> Time, Place, and Action, sacrific'd to joke!
> The Goats cry'd out, 'twas formal, dull, and chaste—
> Not writ for beasts of gallantry and taste!
> The Horned-Cattle were in piteous taking,
> At Fornication, Rapes, and Cuckold-making!
> The Tigers swore, he wanted fire and passion.
> The Apes condemn'd—because it was the fashion![11]

In a repertoire that grew over the years to include more than ninety roles, Garrick would play Ranger more often than any other.* In that first season, he did extremely well out of the play. It seems that Benjamin Hoadly generously assigned his author's profits to Garrick—the takings, minus house charges, that is to say, from the third, sixth and ninth nights. By a bargain reached with Rich on 27 December 1746, Garrick was to receive a cash advance of £80 and promised in return to pay nightly charges of £60 and share the profits that remained equally with the manager. Receipts for the three nights totalled £570 11s. Total expenses came to £182 2s (this included a licensing fee of £2 2s paid to the Lord Chamberlain's office). When settlement for the three performances was made on 6 April,

---

* He played it 121 times in all — eight more performances than he was to give of Benedick in *Much Ado*.

Garrick accordingly received a payment of £194 4s 6d. He had a keen eye for the small print of such agreements. On this one he noted, 'N.B. the copy of the play is my own, and the profit arising from the printing of it.'[12]

If Rich derived any pleasure from the succession of good houses which Covent Garden enjoyed during the season, he concealed it with remarkable skill. 'It was imagined, by those who knew his humour best,' writes Davies, 'that he would have been better pleased to see his great comedians show away to empty benches, that he might have had an opportunity to mortify their pride, by bringing out a new pantomime, and drawing the town after his raree-show.'[13] One of his more bizarre party tricks, performed for the benefit of the house musicians and stage-hands, was to go down on his knees and give an impersonation of Garrick as Lear in the scene where he curses Cordelia.

In Rich's ideal world there would have been no five-act tragedies with their improbable plots and high-flown language, no temperamental actors and actresses with their inflated egos and even more inflated salaries; he would have peopled the stage with sword-swallowers, dancing bears and undemanding rope-walkers. For him the theatre existed only so that Harlequin might court Columbine and astonish and delight the audience with the power of his magic wand—'the sudden transformation of palaces and temples to huts and cottages; of men and women into wheel-barrows and joint-stools; of trees turned to houses; colonnades to beds of tulips; and mechanic shops into serpents and ostriches.'[14]

Covent Garden's *annus mirabilis* made Lacy increasingly thoughtful. His patent at Drury Lane had only six more years to run. He believed that the Lord Chamberlain, the Duke of Grafton, would be prepared to renew it—provided he was able to find a substantial partner. (Lacy, it was said, had ingratiated himself with Grafton by riding close to him in the hunting-field and choosing his moment to proffer 'elegant and savoury refreshment'.). Despite their earlier differences, everything pointed to Garrick—the experience of management he had acquired during his association with Giffard at Goodman's Inn Fields, and with Sheridan in Dublin, above all his enormous drawing power at the box office. During the early spring, there was a period of intense negotiation. Garrick, unwell for most of the time, had the guidance of Somerset Draper and James Clutterbuck and of his friend Samuel Sharp, surgeon to Guy's Hospital.* For legal advice he relied on a City solicitor called John Paterson—'ye most Amiable, sensible sweet fellow, that ever the Law produc'd', as he had described him in a letter to his brother Peter the previous year.†

The contract laid the responsibility for securing the new patent on Lacy, who agreed to sell Garrick a half interest in it for £12,000. Garrick was able to raise

---

* Samuel Sharp (?1700–78), was a pupil of William Cheselden, the great surgeon at St Thomas's, and had spent part of his apprenticeship in France, where he knew Voltaire. He had recently given over his course of anatomical lectures to William Hunter. He later became a member of the Paris Royal Society and of the Royal Society of London.

† *Letters*, 44. Garrick had approached Paterson about an opening for his younger brother George, and Paterson had obligingly agreed to shed a clerk to make a place for him in his office. (*Letters*, 46.)

£8,000 immediately and signed for the rest. A statement was drawn up of the encumbrances assumed by Lacy and Garrick at the beginning of their partnership—there was a mortgage of £4,675, arrears in salary to actors, dancers and musicians amounted to £2,447 14s, tradesmen were owed £1,100. When other miscellaneous debts were taken into account, total liabilities were £8,808 14s. It was also agreed to pay Fleetwood £4,000 to relinquish his share in the patent.[15]

The two men were to become 'jointly and equally possessed of & Interested in' the lease, the patent, the scenery and the wardrobe. Each patentee was to receive £500 a year, and Garrick was to have an additional 500 guineas as his salary for acting, together with a clear benefit night each year;* he agreed not to 'act or Perform' except for the joint benefit of himself and Lacy—a clause presumably intended to cover the unlikely possibility of his appearing elsewhere than at Drury Lane. The signatories agreed to 'enter into & execute proper Articles of Copartnership for the carrying on & managing the Business of the s^d Patents for their joint & equal benefit'. Precisely how their responsibilities should be divided was not in the first instance committed to paper, an omission which would later cause some friction—all that was verbally agreed at the time was that 'the business of the Stage should be under the management of Mr Garrick there being sufficient other matters of importance to employ Mr Lacy'.[16]

The agreement was signed on 9 April. That night Garrick played in *Miss in Her Teens* for Quin's benefit. Earlier in the day, a much larger crowd than Covent Garden could accommodate had flocked to Tower Hill to witness an episode of street theatre—the beheading of Lord Lovat, last of the Scottish peers to be executed for complicity in the 'late unpleasantness'.†

The octogenarian chief of clan Fraser made an exit that would have commanded Garrick's professional admiration. 'Why,' he asked, 'should there be such a bustle about taking off an old grey head that cannot get up three steps without two men to support it?' The spectators were unexpectedly drawn into the action by the collapse of a stand holding four hundred people. Twenty were killed, and many more had broken limbs. 'The more mischief the better sport,' observed Lovat. Then, declaiming a line from Horace and another from Ovid, he laid his head on the block.‡

The Covent Garden season ended that year on 29 May. Garrick had enjoyed a lucrative free benefit at the end of April. It was a command performance by the Prince and Princess of Wales. 'Characters All New Dress'd', announced the playbills. 'To prevent mistakes Ladies are desired to send their servants by three o'clock.' Receipts seldom dropped below £200 when royalty were present, and

---

* This was shrewdly qualified: 'or shall have such better terms as shall at any Time during the s'^d Copartnership be given to any actor or actress.'

† He had been found guilty of high treason by the House of Lords on 18 March. The spectators at his trial in Westminster Hall had included Violette, taken there by Lady Burlington.

‡ Lovat had taken the degree of Master of Arts at King's College, Aberdeen, in 1683. The line from Horace was — what else? — *Dulce et decorum est pro patria mori*: 'It is sweet and honourable to die for one's country.' Wilfred Owen, a war poet in a different age, thought differently, and called it 'The old Lie'.

European Magazine

JAMES LACY ESQ.

(Late Patentee of the Theatre Royal Drury Lane.)
From an original Portrait in the Possession of W. Lacy.

Pub. by J. Sewell Cornhill July 7. 1802

James Lacy. 'What yᵉ Devil has he in his maggot-breeding pericranium?' Garrick
was quite often at odds with his co-patentee at Drury Lane. Lacy had had an
undistinguished career as an actor before turning to theatre management, but
his involvement in the development of Ranelagh Gardens had earned him a tidy
profit of £4,000 and the first year of his partnership with Garrick would clear
them more than £6,000. (Mander & Mitchenson)

Garrick's appearance that evening in *The Suspicious Husband* brought him in £274 17s.

The closing weeks of the 1746–7 season were enlivened by Samuel Foote, who decided to test the tolerance of the Lord Chamberlain (and of the managers of the two patent theatres) by advertising an evening 'Concert of Musick' at the Haymarket. In the intervals he offered, free of charge, 'a New Entertainment, call'd 'The Diversions of the Morning; or, A Dish of Chocolate' . . . To which will be added a Farce taken from 'The Old Batchelor,' call'd 'The Credulous Husband.'

It was a characteristically impudent venture on Foote's part. He had assembled a cast of players who were mainly from Goodman's Fields, which had continued to operate outside the licensing laws in competition with the patent houses. He set about publicizing the event by placing an anonymous letter in the *Daily Advertiser* in which he was threatened with a horse-whipping if he dared to carry out his plan of 'taking off' a number of well-known people. One of his intended victims, 'Orator' Henley, rose obligingly to the bait, and inserted a notice in the *General Advertiser* on 21 April: 'Whoever attacks my Reputation, or Livelihood, is a mad Bull to me, and ought to be knocked down, prosecuted , etc. I hear I am to be hung up on Wednesday, at the Haymarket, by one Foote, a Fool.'*

A clever and resourceful fool, however. Although Foote had taken the precaution of not selling tickets at the door, but at a Mr Waller's, a bookseller in Fleet Street, one or other of the patent managers called on the magistrates to intervene. Foote promptly switched to a less provocative time of day:

> This Day at Noon, exactly at Twelve o'Clock . . . Mr Foote begs the favour of his Friends to come and drink a dish of Chocolate with him; and 'tis hoped there will be a great deal of good Company, and some joyous Spirits; he will endeavour to make the Morning as Diverting as possible.

There had been matinées in Jacobean times, but by the 1740s only prize fights and fair shows took place in the middle of the day. But Foote's gamble paid off, and he attracted large crowds—so large that as soon as Drury Lane and Covent Garden closed down at the end of May, he was emboldened to abandon the matinée and revert to evening performances:

> At the request of several Persons who are desirous of spending an Hour with Mr Foote, but find the Time inconvenient, instead of Chocolate in the Morning, Mr Foote's Friends are desir'd to drink a Dish of Tea with him, at half an Hour after Six in the Evening.

What those 'Friends' saw was essentially a revue, in which Foote's formidable

---

* John Henley (1692–1756), an eccentric London preacher, had been employed by Walpole between 1730 and 1739 to counter the arguments of the opposition journal *The Craftsman*. He had been caricatured by Hogarth and his claims to be the 'restorer of eloquence to the church' were ridiculed by Pope in *The Dunciad*. The British Library owns some fifty volumes of his lectures in his own hand.

powers of mimicry were directed against his fellow-players. He entirely understood their concern that this could be the professional ruin of them, he gravely
told his audience (this account occurs in the memoirs of the actor-manager Tate
Wilkinson):

> Since that was the case, it was his duty to provide a situation for each lady
> and gentleman, so circumstanced; and that, instead of murdering blank
> verse, and assuming the characters of Kings and Queens, Lords and Ladies,
> for which their abilities were far from being suitable, he would place them
> where their talents and behaviour could with more propriety be employed:
>
> Mr QUIN,—from his sonorous voice and weighty manner he
> appointed—*a Watchman*:
>
> AS THUS;
> "Past twelve o'clock, and a cloudy morning."
>
> Mr DELANE,—was supposed to have but one eye, therefore he fixed
> him as—*a Beggar Man in St. Paul's Church-yard*:
> "Would you bestow your pity on a poor blind man."
>
> Mr. RYAN,—whose voice for oddity and shrillness was remarkable,—
> *a Razor Grinder*:
> "Razors to grind, scissars to grind, penknives to grind."
>
> Mrs. WOFFINGTON,—though beautiful to a degree had a most
> unpleasant squeaking pipe,—*an Orange Woman to the Playhouse*:
> "Would you have some,—have some orange chips, ladies and gentle-
> men,—would you have some nonpareils,—would you have a bill of the
> play?"
>
> ... He was also very severe on GARRICK, who was apt to hesitate, (in
> his dying scenes in particular) as in the character of Lothario—
>
> "adorns my fall, and che—che—che—che—che—chears my heart in
> dy—dy—dying."[17]

Foote attacked Garrick more directly in a pamphlet, published anonymously,
called *A Treatise on the Passions*.[18] 'It has been proclaimed at Market-Crosses,
and industriously whispered, even in Churches, that Mr G was the Author of a
paltry Farce, lately exhibited, call'd, *Miss in her Teens*,' he wrote slyly. 'How
improbable it is, that so judicious, correct, and lively a Genius would produce
so contemptible and miserable a Work.' It must really have been written, he
suggested, by the 'peasant' poet, Stephen Duck.* He was also critical of Garrick's

---

* Stephen Duck (1705–56) started life as a farm labourer in Wiltshire. His poems were brought
to the attention of Queen Caroline, who gave him a pension and had him made a Yeoman of
the Guard. In 1746 he took holy orders. Ten years later, in a fit of dejection, he drowned himself
in a trout stream.

interpretation of Lear: 'this might be a proper Representation of a mad Taylor, but by no means corresponds with my Idea of King *Lear*.'

In another passage, he put a malicious finger on what he knew to be a particularly sensitive point and dwelt on Garrick's comparative lack of inches: 'Here I am afraid frail Nature has been a little unkind,' he wrote:

> Such is the Folly of the Million, that they expect a more than ordinary Appearance from a Man, who is to perform extraordinary Actions; it is in vain, to tell them, that *Charles* of *Sweden*, was but five feet five, or *Alexander* the Great, a very little Man . . . . . they are dissatisfied, when they see a Bulls-Pizzle, a dried Elves-Skin, in *Falstaff's* language, bullying a congregation of heroes. . . . .

Unflattering though it was to be compared to a bull's penis, Garrick had the good sense not to respond—not directly, at least, although he may have had something to do with a point-by-point rebuttal of Foote's strictures that appeared shortly afterwards.[19] There were much more important things to attend to in those summer months of 1747. These included structural improvements at the theatre; Lacy believed that by altering the seating arrangements they might take in an additional forty pounds a night. 'We are in ye midst of alterations & Mortar,' Garrick wrote in early July.* There were decisions to be made about the repertory for the coming season, bargains to be struck with existing members of the company, inducements to be offered to those he hoped to bring in his train from Covent Garden— 'I shall Engage the best Comp^y in England if I can,' he assured the same correspondent, '& think it ye Interest of the best Actors to be together.'

He allowed himself a break in Lichfield. On the way there he was laid low at Coventry with what he described as 'a very sorry Throat, caught (as I imagine) by lying in damp sheets at Dunstable', but after being bled and purged he was soon, as he put it, 'perfectly recover'd & in Statu quo'.[20] Towards the end of July he went to Tunbridge Wells to take the waters—'I am taking an Ounce of Bark with them & hope they will Strengthen & recruit me,' he reported to his brother George. The company was congenial, and he wrote virtuously about the orderly regime he had devised for himself:

> I go to bed at Eleven, rise at Seven, drink no Malt Liquor, & think of Nothing; which last I am sure has done me more good than any thing Else . . . . . Old Cibber is here, & very merry we are—Mr Littleton & I are Cup & Can: in short Every body is good-humour'd & for ye time I shall Stay, I shan't repine or repent ye Expedition—I have play'd at E:O. & won—I don't dance, but I sleep without my cold Sweats, & Eat like a Ploughman.†

* *Letters*, 51. Garrick was writing to William Pritchard, who was about to become treasurer at Drury Lane.
† *Ibid.*, 52. *Cup and can* was an expression meaning close and constant associates; *E. and O.* was a form of roulette, played at a circular table.

By the second week in September, the alterations to Drury Lane were finished. Garrick had assembled a company of seventy—fifty-three actors and actresses, fifteen dancers and two singers. It was the general practice to open the season with an established favourite calling for a relatively large cast. Garrick opted for *The Merchant of Venice*, shrewdly inviting Macklin to play Shylock.*

He reserved to himself the speaking of a prologue. It was clearly an occasion that called for some sort of verbal fanfare, but he recognized that the writing of it called for a weightier pen than his. As it happenened, he knew the very man. A month previously he had published his *Plan of a Dictionary of the English Language*, with a dedication to the Earl of Chesterfield. Now Samuel Johnson produced for his old pupil a sonorous manifesto for a new theatrical era.

---

* Macklin managed to persuade his biographer, Kirkman, that this was something which redounded to his credit rather than to Garrick's: 'Although Mr Macklin had just cause to remember the cruel treatment he had formerly experienced at the hands of Mr. Garrick, yet the nobleness and generosity of his mind prompted him now to dismiss it totally from his recollection.' (*Kirkman*, op. cit., 410.)

10

Rescued Nature and Reviving Sense

> When Learning's triumph o'er her barb'rous foes
> First rear'd the stage, immortal Shakespeare rose . . . .

Everything that Samuel Johnson wrote had a moral purpose. His prologue reviewed the progress of English drama from the time of Elizabeth—or, as it seemed to him, its decline:

> The wits of Charles found easier ways to fame,
> Nor wish'd for Jonson's art or Shakespeare's flame.
> Themselves they studied; as they felt they writ;
> Intrigue was plot; obscenity was wit.
> Vice always found a sympathetic friend;
> They pleas'd their age, and did not hope to mend.

He deplored equally the decline of tragedy and the ascendancy of 'Pantomime and Song', but then reminded the audience where the ultimate responsibility for this state of affairs rests—'The stage but echoes back the public voice.'* If the public does not like what it hears, the remedy lies with them:

> 'Tis Yours this night to bid the reign commence
> Of rescued Nature, and reviving Sense;
> To chase the charms of Sound, the pomp of Shew,
> For useful Mirth, and salutary Woe;
> Bid scenic Virtue form the rising age,
> And Truth diffuse her radiance from the stage.

Garrick had at his disposal the cream of the capital's acting talent. Mrs Pritchard, Mrs Cibber, Havard and Vaughan all followed him to Drury Lane.† Kitty Clive and Peg Woffington were already there, and so, in addition to Macklin, were Barry and Delane. Only Quin was not to be wooed. Having, in Mary Nash's

---

* Johnson was echoing words of Defoe written more than forty years previously — 'the errors of the stage lie all in the auditory.' (*Review*, 3 May 1705.)
† Woodward had already been lured to Dublin by Thomas Sheridan, although he had undertaken to join Garrick on his return.

nice phrase, 'rolled with majestic indolence' through the previous season, he had taken himself off to Bath, and there he remained for several months.

Over at Covent Garden, the manager seems to have viewed the depletion of his ranks with equanimity: 'Rich said he was glad he had got rid of such turbulent servants, who were better paid than the admirals of his majesty's navy, without being of any advantage either to him or the state.'[1] The fact that he was left without any tragedians of the first rank brought him a lordly hint from the west country: 'Dear Sir, I am at Bath. Yours James Quin.' 'Lun', unmoved, returned an equally laconic reply: 'Dear Sir, Stay there and be damned; Yours John Rich.'

Garrick's new kingdom was both older and smaller than Covent Garden. Designed by Wren in 1674, the Theatre Royal, Drury Lane, stood on an irregular plot of some 13,000 square feet bounded by Bridges Street, Russell Street and Drury Lane.* The lot of land which contained the stage and auditorium measured only 112 feet by 58—in some continental theatres of the day the stage alone was that size. At Drury Lane the stage was 45 feet wide and about 28 feet deep; thirteen feet of this depth projected forward to the footlights, forming a semi-oval apron; the remaining fifteen feet, the scenic area, lay behind the proscenium arch, and into that arch, on each side, were set the proscenium doors, through which the players mainly made their entrances and their exits. The stage was gently raked; an actor standing up against the rear drop would be 15 inches higher than one at the footlights.

Beyond the footlights, and separated from the stage by a line of ornamental spiked railings, were the fixed and backless benches of the pit; the markings on them assumed that nobody had a bottom broader than 21 inches. The pit sloped upwards to meet the first of two galleries of boxes, and these ran round the whole ellipse of the auditorium. A third gallery faced the stage, but did not at this period extend round each side of the house.

Eighteenth-century theatre lighting would strike the modern eye as dim. The stage at Drury Lane was lit by wall sconces and by six girandoles—huge hoop-shaped chandeliers suspended from the ceiling. These were lowered to be lit by house servants at the start of a performance and could be raised into the upper stage-house when an effect of darkness was required. Each girandole had twelve brass sockets which held candles made of wax or spermaceti.† They were an obvious fire hazard; they also tended to drip wax on the players. Even the finest-quality candles tended to smoke and gutter and were therefore unsuitable for the footlights. There oil lamps stood in front of tin reflectors; they too could be lowered into a sort of trough to darken the stage.‡

---

* The land belonged to the Duke of Bedford; Lacy and Garrick paid ground rent to him for ten separate parcels of land.

† The 1737 edition of Chambers's *Cyclopedia* pronounced candles made from the fat of the sperm-whale to be 'superior to the finest wax-candles'. The auditorium and other areas of the theatre were also lit by candles. The Drury Lane Account Book entries for the seasons 1747–8 and 1749–50 record expenditure on lighting of £421 and £414 respectively.

‡ The Drury Lane prompt books at the Folger Library contain several directions such as 'Lamps down' and '*Sink Lamps*'.

The theatre was not contained within a single building. Around the stage and auditorium there was a clutter of nine other structures, and this warren of rooms and passages accommodated such facilities as carpenters' and painters' shops, rehearsal and dressing rooms, the wardrobe, a copying room and libraries of acting copies and scores. There was also the green-room, where the players lounged and gossiped between scenes, where privileged guests were entertained and where the company came together for the casting and reading of a new play.*

When Lacy and Garrick took over, the seating capacity was roughly a thousand; the alterations carried out before the start of their first season added an extra 267 seats—still small enough (if the house was quiet) for the actors to be heard easily and for their facial expressions to be seen.

The house, of course, was not always quiet. Nor was the audience confined to one side of the footlights. Above the proscenium doors there were stage boxes, which, when they were not needed for balcony scenes, were used for spectators. It was also the custom, on benefit nights, to increase the capacity of the house (and thus the profit of the actor) by erecting additional boxes on the stage. During the benefit season, the playbills frequently gave notice that this would be done: 'Pit and Boxes laid together, and Stage, for better accommodation of the Ladies, will be form'd into Front and Side Boxes.'† A large amphitheatre covered much of the stage. This was theatre-in-the-round with a vengeance. It was also death to any degree of theatrical illusion: 'The battle of Bosworth Field,' wrote Davies, 'has been fought in a less space than that which is commonly allotted to a cock-match.'‡

Garrick had before him the example of Thomas Sheridan, who had boldly grasped the nettle during his second season of management in Dublin; now, as joint master of Drury Lane, he determined to begin as he meant to go on. The bills for *The Merchant* on the first night carried a brief announcement: 'As the Admittance of Persons behind the Scenes has occasioned a general complaint on Account of the frequent Interruptions in the Performance, 'tis hoped Gentlemen won't be offended, that no Money will be taken there for the future.'

After the play, he attempted to sugar the pill with an epilogue—this not from Johnson's pen, but from his own:

---

* George II was said to prefer Covent Garden to Drury Lane partly because its green-room was located on the same side of the theatre as the Royal Box, and therefore more accessible. The origin of the name is obscure. One theory is that it was originally painted green to relieve the eyes of the players affected by the glare of the stage lights.

† Playbill announcing Barry's first appearance as Orestes in *The Distressed Mother* for his benefit on 10 March 1748.

‡ *Davies*, i, 376. Davies, noting how often Molière complains of this 'absurd intrusion', believed that things were even worse in France: 'Their young nobility did not only accustom themselves to talk louder than the players, but they were so intermingled with them during the time of action, that you could scarcely discover the real from the represented Marquis.' (*Ibid.*, 375.)

Sweet doings truly! we are finely fobb'd!
And at one stroke of all our pleasures robb'd!
No *beaux behind the scenes!* 'tis innovation!
Under the specious name of reformation!
Public complaint, forsooth, is made a puff,
Sense, order, decency, and such like stuff.
But arguments like these are mere pretence,
The beaux, 'tis known, ne'er give the least offence;
Are men of chastest conduct, and amazing sense!
Each actress now a lock'd-up nun must be,
And priestly managers must keep the key . . . . .

It was a beginning. And the manner of it was highly characteristic. Although he could be hasty and quick-tempered, Garrick's underlying instinct was to seek accommodation, to attempt to disarm opposition with facetious banter, to affect an ironic concession of the other side's case. Of one thing he could be sure. The couplet about locked-up nuns and priestly managers would raise a big laugh—the player he had sent out to deliver the epilogue was Peg Woffington.

The Covent Garden season started very late, and for several weeks Drury Lane had a free run. Garrick came in for some early sniping, for all that. A pamphlet that appeared in the middle of October complained that although the theatre had been open for a month, he himself had appeared only as Archer in *The Stratagem* and to deliver a prologue. (So he had, but it was partly because he had been ill again.) The pamphlet also criticized his judgement in offering to the public plays such as *Albumazar* and *The Scornful Lady*.[2]

The Scornful Lady, a comedy of English domestic life ascribed to Beaumont and Fletcher, had been popular both before and after the Restoration, but tastes had changed; the pamphleteer, identified only as E.F., found it 'irreligious and atheistical' and the Drury Lane audience was unimpressed. 'Play dislik'd,' the prompter Cross noted in his diary. 'Hiss'd much.' Garrick was quick to bow to popular sentiment and the first night was also the last.

Albumazar, which ridiculed the pretensions of astrologers, was also at first sight a curious choice. Adapted from *L'Astrologo*, a Neapolitan comedy, it was the work of Thomas Tomkis, a fellow of Trinity College, Cambridge, and had been performed there before James I in 1615. A contemporary wrote that 'there was no great matter i yt, more than one goode clowns part';[3] that being so, it is not immediately apparent why Garrick thought it a substantial enough vehicle for the talents of Macklin, Yates, Havard and Woffington.

Cross noted in his diary that on the first night it went off 'with toll: success'; on the fourth night, however, it was hissed, and it was given only three further performances during the season. The house grossed £852 on the comedy, an entirely respectable figure. Nor was it consigned for all time to the graveyard of old plays. Garrick at Drury Lane was as careful of what he judged to be serviceable stage material as John Rich was of candle ends and tallow drippings at Covent

Garden.* A quarter of a century later he would substantially revise the text of *Albumazar* and revive it a second time.

At the end of November, Garrick presented *George Dandin*, a new afterpiece— 'Farce never acted before, taken from Molière,' said the bills. It was damned before the end of the first act. Perhaps the moment was not well chosen. Anson and Hawke had won a string of naval victories over the French during the spring and summer of 1747, and there had been a certain amount of theatrical flag-waving over the battle fought on 25 October off Cape Finisterre.

Three months into the season, however, things gave every appearance of running smoothly under the new management. A letter survives from William Windham to Peter Garrick:

> The affairs of the Theatre appear to go on extreamly easy. Everything is done with the greatest order and regularity, and there is a most exact discipline observed by all belonging to the house. Lacy and he agree very well, and every thing is done just as David pleases, so that he seems to have little disagreeable work. He has made a regulation for the boxes which is of great advantage to the managers, as it prevents bilking, and to the audience, as it prevents the continual disturbance there was in the boxes, opening and shutting doors and frisking in and out. For he makes people pay at coming in to the box. No manager but himself would have dared to have attempted such a thing, but he has all the people of fashion strenuously for him, as indeed they are in everything . . . .[4]

Garrick was not going to be allowed to build his uncluttered New Jerusalem overnight, however. On 13 February he mounted Edward Moore's new comedy *The Foundling*. Horace Walpole was in the first-night audience, and he wrote about it enthusiastically to Sir Horace Mann in Italy. A week later, however, on the night of the piece's seventh performance, things began to get a little rough:

> There was a report, that my Lord Hubbard had made a party this night to hiss The Foundling off stage, that yᵉ Reason was it ran too long, & they wanted variety of Entertainments. Mr Garrick was sent for, he met 'em, & so far prevail'd that they promis'd peace 'till after the 9th night. However there was an attempt made by one Catcall, & an apple Thrown at Macklin & some other Efforts made by a few but without effect— Greatly hiss'd wⁿ given out I believe the main cause of this anger, in spite of their Excuses, was their being refus'd admittance behind the Scenes.[5]

Hubbard, or Hobart, was the son and heir of the Earl of Buckinghamshire, and had recently become the MP for Norwich. He made up a party of friends to damn the play again three nights later—'merely for the love of damnation' in

---

* For many years a house servant called Mrs Carne collected the candle ends and tallow drippings at Covent Garden; their re-sale realized an annual sum approaching £120, which was handed over to the treasurer. At Drury Lane, though Garrick was often mocked as a penny-pincher, the dressers were allowed the candle ends as a perk. (*London Stage*, Part 4, i, lii n.)

Walpole's view. But the young beaux had reckoned without the young lawyers in the pit:

> The Templars espoused the play, and went armed with syringes charged with stinking oil and with sticking plasters for *Bubby's* fair hair: but it did not come to action; Garrick was impertinent, and the pretty men gave over their plot the moment they grew to be in the right.[6]

Garrick received a great deal of unsolicited advice, and his correspondence reveals that he paid an impressive amount of attention to it. He replied at length in the spring of 1748 to a letter from the Reverend Peter Whalley, a schoolmaster parson in Northamptonshire: 'The candid Remarks of a true Critick are to me the greatest Favours; my Ears are always open to Conviction; I willingly kiss the Rod, and would shake the Hand that administers such wholesome Correction as yours has done.' He responded in detail to points Whalley had made about his performance in *Hamlet*, and promised amendment; he also conceded that he had not delivered a particular passage in the first act of *Venice Preserv'd* as well as he might:

> I am in hopes the other Slips you speak of in the same Play, were owing to my Illness on Mrs Cibber's Benefit Night; I could scarce bring my Words out, and all the Time did not know whether I stood on my Head or Heels— the part of Jaffier is a most difficult, laborious Character, and will take me up much Time, before I have attain'd what I imagine may be done with it. I must now beg leave to mention a Circumstance, which may in some Measure be my Excuse for those many seeming Errors of Judgment; I am often troubled with Pains in my Breast, arising from Colds; and at such Times I have it not in my Power to speak as I would; my Breath often fails me, and I am oblig'd to stop in wrong Places, to enable me to finish the Sentence—this has the Air of an Excuse for my Failings; suppose it so, it is a very natural one . . . . .*

Woffington took her benefit in the middle of March. She chose to appear in the title role of *Jane Shore*, and Garrick played opposite her as Hastings. A comical episode just as the afterpiece was about to begin demonstrated that his campaign to clear the stage still had some way to go:

> As ye Curtain was rising for ye farce a Gentleman's sword was taken out of ye scabbard & carry'd up with ye Curtain & there Hung to ye terror of those under it (least it shou'd fall) & ye Mirth of ye rest of ye Audience— a Scene man fetch'd it down.[7]

Late in March there was a disastrous fire in an alley close to the Royal Exchange in Cornhill. It raged for ten hours, and 'consumed a great number of houses occupied by persons in middling circumstances and with large families'. A committee of ten bankers was formed to raise and administer a relief fund, and

---

* *Letters*, 54. The night he refers to was only his second appearance as Jaffier.

the theatrical profession responded generously. Quin, who had by now tired of Bath and made up his differences with Rich, appeared as Othello at Covent Garden; all the players and musicians performed without payment that night, and a sum of £218 12s 4d was donated to the fund. Foote, still up to his tricks at the Haymarket, followed suit* and so did Garrick with a performance of *King Lear*.†

It had been a conspicuously successful first season and the managers had made a handsome profit—income for the season totalled £20,563 19s 10d, expenditure £14,229 7s 6d.[8] Candle in hand, Lacy and Garrick had backed and bowed their way to the royal box before royal visitors on seven occasions ('Christmas boxes to the duke's footmen, and Prince and Princess of Wales's chairmen,' says an entry in the accounts for 8 January). Garrick had performed all his established roles, and in Mrs Pritchard, despite what Davies delicately termed 'the fulness of her person', he had found an incomparable Lady Macbeth:

> When she snatched the daggers from the remorseful and irresolute Macbeth, despising the agitations of a mind unaccustomed to guilt and alarmed at the terrors of conscience, she presented to the audience a picture of the most consummate intrepidity in mischief. . . . . . In exhibiting the last scene of Lady Macbeth, in which the terrors of a guilty conscience keep the mind broad awake while the body sleeps, Mrs Pritchard's acting resembled those sudden flashes of lightning which more accurately discover the horrors of surrounding darkness.[9]

Hannah Pritchard was to remain at Drury Lane until her retirement in 1768, but at the beginning of his second season as manager Garrick suffered a number of defections. Delane and Sparks accepted engagements at Covent Garden and so, more seriously, did Peg Woffington. She had found it increasingly difficult to maintain her place in the Drury Lane pecking-order.‡ She was jealous of Mrs Pritchard and Mrs Cibber and at daggers drawn with Kitty Clive. 'No two women of high rank ever hated one another more unreservedly than these great dames of the theatre,' writes Davies. 'But though the passions of each were as lofty as those of a first dutchess, yet they wanted the courtly art of concealing them; and this occasioned, now and then, a very grotesque scene in the green-room.'[10]

One such scene had ended in a brawl between Woffington's old admirer Owen Mac Swiney and Kitty Clive's normally mild-mannered brother James Raftor, who was also a member of the Drury Lane company. The encounter found its way into *The Foundling Hospital for Wit* as a cartoon entitled 'The Green-Room

---

* 'For the Relief of the Sufferers by a late Calamity . . . at his Auction-Room late the Little Theatre in the Hay-Market Mr Foote will exhibit for the satisfaction of the curious a choice Collection of Pictures, all warranted Originals, and entirely new.' In one of his 'pictures' on this occasion he mimicked Fielding as 'Trottplaid'.

† Quin was no doubt gratified to note that Drury Lane's contribution of £208 1s was £10 less than Covent Garden's.

‡ The order of benefits provides a useful pointer to how the players were ranked. In the 1747–8 season it was Garrick, Cibber, Pritchard, Clive, Woffington, Barry, Macklin.

Scuffle: Or, Drury-Lane in an Uproar', Raftor figuring as 'Sad Jemmee' and Swiney as 'Old Limpo'.

When Drury Lane closed for the summer in May 1748, Woffington had travelled to Paris, ostensibly to study the technique of the French tragedienne Marie Dumesnil. 'Old Limpo' went with her, which provided good exercise for idle tongues, but if Woffington had taken him as her lover, he quickly had to move over. The new man in her life was a handsome thirty-two-year-old native of Leghorn called Domenico Angelo Malevolti Tremamondo, an instructor at both the Manège Royal and the Académie d'Armes. At a reception at the house of the duc de Nivernais, Angelo was persuaded by the Duke to take on all comers in a fencing match. Woffington, 'suddenly captivated by his person and superior address', stepped forward and presented him with a small bouquet of roses (we owe this account to the sometimes fanciful memoirs of Angelo's son Henry):

> He placed it on his left breast, and addressing the other knights of the sword, exclaimed, "This will I protect against all opposers." The match commenced, and he fenced with several of the first masters, not one of whom could disturb a single leaf of the *bouquet*.[11]

Woffington and her new lover shortly afterwards set off together for London, he to turn his skills as a rider and swordsman to profitable account,* she to play Lady Brute in her first appearance at Covent Garden for seven years.

At Drury Lane Garrick relied heavily in the early weeks of the season on the versatile comic skills of Woodward, now back from Dublin. Barry was also deployed to good effect early in the season, appearing as both Hamlet and Othello. Garrick played himself in as Ranger in *The Suspicious Husband* towards the end of September, and in November he enlarged his repertory of Shakespearean roles by appearing for the first time as Benedick in *Much Ado About Nothing*. As always, he prepared himself meticulously; he told the actor John Henderson that he had been 'up to two months rehearsing Benedick before he could satisfy himself that he had modelled his action and recital to his own idea of the part'.[12] *Much Ado* had been performed only eight times since the beginning of the century, but Garrick now restored it to a central place in the repertory. He was to play only three comic Shakespearean roles during his career and of these Benedick was far and away his favourite; he would appear in it on 113 occasions.†

Beatrice was played by Mrs Pritchard and, as in *Macbeth*, her performance was crucial to Garrick's success. 'Mrs Pritchard was Garrick's rival in every scene,' wrote Murphy:

---

* George II pronounced him the most elegant horseman of his day. His *école d'escrime* in Soho became a fashionable haunt for young men of rank, and his fencing pupils included the Prince of Wales and the Duke of Devonshire. Garrick, Gainsborough, Reynolds and Wilkes all became close friends. In 1763 he brought out his celebrated treatise on fencing which Diderot subsequently incorporated in the *Encyclopédie*.

† His two other comic Shakespearean roles were Leontes in *The Winter's Tale* and Posthumus in *Cymbeline*, both of which he played on only twenty-three occasions.

Which of them deserved the laurel most was never decided; but their united merit was such that *Much ado about Nothing* continued to be a favourite comedy, as long as that excellent actress chose to perform the part. She resigned it in favour of her daughter, and the play lost half its value.*

One of the few people who seem not to have admired Garrick's performance was Theophilus Cibber, who took sour exception to what he called his 'pantomimical manner of acting every word of a sentence'. He instanced a line of Benedick's in Act I, scene i—'If I do, hang me in a bottle like a cat, and shoot at me.' This short sentence, wrote Cibber, 'requires not such a variety of action as minutely to describe the cat being clapped into the bottle, then being hung up, and the farther painting of the man shooting at it'. From someone best known for his Pistol and notorious for over-acting—Davies writes of his 'effronterie' on stage and his 'ridiculous squinting and vile grimace'—this was a bit rich.

Given the background of personal and family animosity, Cibber's strictures were of little significance, but a work of fiction which appeared in 1748 was calculated to make Garrick squirm a good deal more uncomfortably. Tobias Smollett had taken only eight months to write his first novel, *The Adventures of Roderick Random*. He was still smarting from Garrick's rejection of *The Regicide* two years previously, and now he would have his revenge.

Into his picaresque narrative he spatchcocked the long digressive story of the poet Melopoyn—a tedious account of his own unsuccessful attempts to get his play accepted for the stage. Chesterfield becomes Lord Sheerwit—'this nobleman had the character of a Maecenas in the nation, and could stamp a value upon any work by his sole countenance and approbation.' Garrick is portrayed as Marmozet, 'a celebrated player, who had lately appeared on the stage with astonishing eclat, and bore such sway in the house where he acted, that the managers durst not refuse anything he recommended.'

Rich and Lacy are roughed up in passing, but Melopoyn is in no doubt that Marmozet was the real villain of the piece: 'he had acted from first to last with the most perfidious dissimulation, cajoling me with insinuating civilities, while he underhand employed all his art and influence to prejudice the ignorant manager against my performance.' Random attempts to reason with his indignant friend, arguing that such behaviour on Marmozet's part could only lead his patrons to hold him in contempt and abhorrence, but the poet dismisses this as naïveté:

> He pretended to laugh at my simplicity, and asked if I knew for which of
> his virtues he was so much caressed by the people of fashion. 'It is not,'
> said he, 'for the qualities of his heart, that this little parasite is invited
> to the tables of dukes and lords, who hire extraordinary cooks for his

---

* *Murphy*, i, 155–6. The daughter in question was Hannah Mary, the youngest of Mrs Pritchard's three daughters, who made her Drury Lane début as Juliet in 1756 at the age of seventeen. She later married the Drury Lane comedian John 'Gentleman' Palmer, but withdrew from the stage on his death in 1768. Her second husband was Maurice Lloyd, an importer and stock-jobber, who was a close friend and agent of Lord North.

entertainment. His avarice they see not, his ingratitude they feel not, his hypocrisy accommodates itself to their humours, and is of consequence pleasing; but he is chiefly courted for his buffoonery, and will be admitted into the choicest parties of quality for his talent of mimicking Punch and his wife Joan, when a poet of the most exquisite genius is not able to attract the least regard.[13]

With the author of another novel which came out that year Garrick enjoyed altogether more cordial relations. The first four volumes of Samuel Richardson's interminable *Clarissa* had already been published and now, in the autumn of 1748, three more volumes appeared. Richardson sent these to Garrick—the two men were already acquainted—and received an effusive letter of thanks: 'The honour you have done Me (& I do most sincerely think it a great one) in y[r] last Volume, has flatter'd me extreamly.'[14] It is not certain whether Garrick had done more than dip into the adventures of Miss Harlow—novels of more than a million words tend to be more admired than read*—but he had obviously found his way to a passage in volume 7 about the possibility of reviving *King Lear*:

> And yet, if it were *ever* to be tried, *Now* seems to be the Time, when an *Actor* and a *Manager*, in the *same person*, is in being, who deservedly engages the public favour in all he undertakes, and who owes so much, and is gratefully sensible that he does, to that great Master of the human Passions.

That was much more like it.

Garrick, as it happened, had been hard at work during the autumn on a revival of another Shakespearean tragedy. *Romeo and Juliet* had first been revived during the Restoration. Samuel Pepys saw it on the opening night and was unimpressed— 'a play of itself the worst that ever I heard in my life.' Theophilus Cibber had had some success with a production during a brief season at the Haymarket in 1744 ('The play was tolerable enough, considering Theophilus was the hero,' Garrick had written to a friend)†, but before that nothing remotely resembling Shakespeare's text had been heard for sixty-five years—it had been driven from the stage by an adaptation called *The History and Fall of Caius Marius*, the work of Thomas Otway.

Garrick's new Drury Lane production opened on 29 November with Mrs Cibber as Juliet, Barry as Romeo and Woodward as Mercutio. 'Play Never acted there,' said the bills. 'Characters New Dress'd.' Cross's diary for the first night has the cryptic entry 'toller', short for 'tolerable', presumably, but the town liked what they saw and heard, and it ran for another eighteen performances during the season.

---

* Johnson and his assistants read it thoroughly, however: *Clarissa* provided the *Dictionary* with 97 quotations, almost twice as many as any other single work.

† *Letters*, 28. Garrick was writing to Somerset Draper. Cibber's version was, in fact, something of a rag-bag. Theophilus retained some of Otway's lines and also lifted some passages from *Two Gentlemen of Verona*.

The play was printed, and in a note to the reader Garrick explained his intentions:

> The Alterations in the following Play are few and trifling, except in the last Act; the Design was to clear the Original, as much as possible, from the Jingle and Quibble, which were always thought the great Objections to reviving it.

By 'Jingle' he meant those passages which Shakespeare had written not in blank verse but in rhyme. 'Quibble' referred to puns and other varieties of word-play which held great appeal for an Elizabethan audience but which Garrick's contemporaries appreciated less, even when they understood it. He went on to defend his decision not to follow Otway and Cibber in removing Shakespeare's references in the first act to Rosaline, the 'pale hard-hearted wench' Romeo is in love with before he encounters Juliet:

> Many People have imagin'd that the sudden Change of Romeo's love from Rosaline to Juliet was a blemish in his Character, but an Alteration of that kind was thought too bold to be attempted; Shakespear has dwelt particularly upon it, and so great a Judge of Human Nature, knew that to be young and inconstant was extremely natural . . . . .

The text was substantially cut—Garrick dispensed with almost a quarter of Shakespeare's 3,000 lines. The greatest alterations occur in Act V, where in Garrick's version Juliet awakes in the tomb before the poison begins to work on Romeo. The 75-line death scene which he inserted at this point has been the occasion of much curling of critical lips over the years:

JULIET.	Dost thou avoid me, Romeo? Let me touch
	Thy hand, and taste the cordial of thy lips.
	You fright me—speak! O let me hear some voice
	Besides my own in this drear vault of death
	Or I shall faint. Support me!
ROMEO.	O! I cannot;
	I have no strength, but want thy feeble aid,
	Cruel poison!
JULIET.	Poison! what means my lord, thy trembling voice?
	Pale lips! and swimming eyes! Death's in thy face!
ROMEO.	It is indeed. I struggle with him now.

The 1748 audience clearly loved it: 'The favorable Reception the new Scene in the fifth Act has met with, induc'd the Writer to print it,' says Garrick's note to the reader, and in the advertisement to a later edition he pointed out that he was doing no more than follow Bandello, from whom Shakespeare borrowed the subject: 'this circumstance Shakespeare has omitted, not perhaps from judgment, but from reading the story in the French or English translation, both which have injudiciously left out this addition to the catastrophe.'

Joseph Knight, writing in the late nineteenth century, was severe, describing

Garrick's version as 'mangled'—'the earliest of those perversions of Shakespeare's texts which are Garrick's crowning disgrace, and cast something more than doubt upon his much vaunted reverence for Shakespeare.'[15] Frank Hedgcock, considering the matter in 1911, ascribed Garrick's remodelling to the vanity of the actor-manager ('plenty of contortions and groans for himself')—an unfair gibe so far as the 1748 production is concerned, because Garrick at that stage had no ambitions to play the role himself.

Hedgcock was on firmer ground when he attacked some of the changes in poetical form. In his view Garrick had 'unpoetized' some of the finest passages. It can certainly be argued that the drive on 'quibble' sometimes robs Shakespeare's text of an important dimension. The comic bawdiness of the servants—and of the Nurse, for that matter—was not intended merely to raise a guffaw among the groundlings. It also threw into relief the rapt and impassioned poetry which Shakespeare wrote for his star-crossed lovers.[16]

None of which should make one forget that Shakespeare did not write texts for scholars to take apart in libraries. First and always he was a man of the theatre, with as sure a grasp of what his age would accept as Garrick had of his. Of what the age would accept, but also of what would actually work best on stage—twin elements of theatrical flair in any generation. Garrick's sense of stagecraft told him that for the audience of his day the action should be faster. Out accordingly went the prologue to Act I and the lines given to the Chorus at the beginning of Act II; the portrayal of the street brawl in the first act came down to sixty lines, and the stage fight in which Mercutio is killed in Act III was similarly speeded up. His arrangement of the play held the London stage until late in the nineteenth century. His tomb scene was played as late as 1875 by Charles Wyndham; only in 1882 did Henry Irving revert to the Shakespearean original.[17]

On the day that Romeo and Juliet was first performed, a brief note appeared in the General Advertiser: 'We hear a new Tragedy called Mahomet and Irene will be acted at the Theatre Royal in Drury Lane after Christmas.' Garrick was preparing to repay a debt of friendship. Twelve years on, Samuel Johnson's tragedy, written back in the Lichfield days when he was twenty-eight, was at last to be performed.

Only now was Johnson emerging from years of anonymous hack work. A few days previously, he had sold, for fifteen guineas, the copyright of his poem The Vanity of Human Wishes, loosely based on the Tenth Satire of Juvenal.* It would be the first of his works to carry his name on the title page, and he was already in his fortieth year. Work on the Dictionary was going forward, but painfully slowly—it would be two years before even the first three letters of the alphabet were set up in print. He was still plagued by financial worries, and increasingly his spirits were depressed by his domestic circumstances. Plump, painted Tetty, whom he had taken as his bride in 1735, was now a difficult

---

* Boswell speaks of the 'fervid rapidity' with which he wrote it. Johnson told him that he composed seventy lines in one day without putting pen to paper until they were finished. Of the Satires, he said that 'he had them all in his head'. (Life, i, 192.)

hypochondriac of sixty-one. She was living most of the time out at Hampstead ('indulging herself in country air' was how Boswell put it), drinking much more than was good for her and now totally disinclined—possibly no longer able—to satisfy Johnson's strong sexual appetite.

Garrick's decision to put *Irene* into rehearsal must therefore have come as a welcome tonic. If there was a case for amending Shakespeare, however, there were even stronger reasons for tweaking Johnson's stiff, pseudo-classical text into shape for the stage. This led to some heated exchanges. Garrick called on Johnson's friend the Reverend Dr Taylor to mediate, and he took the full force of the author's indignation: 'Sir, the fellow wants me to make Mahomet run mad, that he may have an opportunity of tossing his hands and kicking his heels.'*

The play opened on 6 February. On the night, Johnson was to and fro between the coulisses and one of the side boxes. He had discarded his customary old brown suit in favour of a scarlet waistcoat braided with gold and a gold-laced hat. Tetty did not accompany him. There was some initial whistling and catcalling, but the house soon settled down. Garrick had done his old friend proud. 'The dresses were rich and magnificent,' wrote Davies, 'and the scenes splendid and gay, such as were well adapted to the inside of a Turkish seraglio: the view of the gardens belonging to it was in the taste of eastern elegance.'[18]

Cali Bassa, the First Vizier, who was played by Edward Berry, had a speech in the first act which was particularly well-received:

> Such are the woes when arbitrary pow'r,
> And lawless passion, hold the sword of justice.
> If there be any land, as fame reports,
> Where common law restrains the prince and subject,
> A happy land, where circulating pow'r
> Flows through each member of th'embodied state;
> Sure, not unconscious of the mighty blessing,
> Her grateful sons shine bright with every virtue . . . . .

This was taken to be an encomium of the British constitution. As the tragedy is set in the Ottoman Empire in the fifteenth century, Cali was obviously endowed with an unusual degree of prophetic insight.

One of Garrick's brainwaves for geeing up the action misfired rather badly. In the fifth act, the heroine meets her end by strangulation, and it seemed to him that there would be a heightening of dramatic effect if this took place on stage. As the two turbaned mutes who were to do the deed made as if to tighten the bow-string round her neck, however, there was hissing, and cries of 'Murder!' from the gallery. Mrs Pritchard made several attempts to deliver her dying lines but then abandoned the attempt and made her exit still very much alive. The following night she was carried off to meet her end less publicly, but the hissing was repeated.

---

* It is not known whether Garrick originally intended to play the tyrant Mahomet. In the event he cast Barry in the part, appearing himself in the lesser role of Demetrius. Mrs Pritchard was Irene and Mrs Cibber Aspasia. The piece could not have been more strongly cast.

Garrick generously kept the play on the bills for nine performances, which meant that Johnson got his three author's-benefit nights. This brought him £195. He also sold the copyright to Robert Dodsley for £100, so he did rather well— indeed, he earned more in little over a week than he had ever done before in a year.* He never attempted another tragedy. 'When asked how he felt upon the ill success of his tragedy,' wrote Boswell, 'he replied, "Like the Monument;" meaning that he continued firm and unmoved as that column.'[19]

He had taken frequent advantage of his author's privilege to attend rehearsals—rather too frequently for the manager's liking, one suspects—and had formed strong likes and dislikes. 'Pritchard, in common life, was a vulgar ideot,' he informed Mrs Siddons many years later; 'she would talk of her *gownd*.'[20] On another occasion he announced that her playing was 'quite mechanical'. 'It is wonderful how little mind she has,' he told the company:

> Sir, she had never read the tragedy of *Macbeth* all through. She no more thought of the play out of which her part was taken, than a shoemaker thinks of the skin, out of which the piece of leather, of which he is making a pair of shoes, is cut.†

He had as little time for Susannah Cibber. He would rather, he said, 'sit up to the chin in water for an hour than be obliged to listen to the whining, daggle tailed Cibber'.‡ Kitty Clive, on the other hand, he could not praise too highly— 'what Clive did best, she did better than Garrick; she was a better romp than any I ever saw in nature.'[21] He also had a good opinion of her social accomplishments: 'Clive, Sir, is a good thing to sit by; she always understands what you say.'[22]

He enjoyed the buzz and gossip of the green-room, but there came a time when Johnson the moralist resolved that this was a diversion he must deny himself. Boswell heard the reason from David Hume some months before his first meeting with the great man, and recorded it in his diary with greater freedom than he subsequently permitted himself in the *Life*:

> Garrick told Mr. Hume that Johnson past one Evening behind the Scenes, in the Green room. He said he had been well entertained. Mr. Garrick therefore hoped to see him often. No David said he I will never come back. For the white bubbies & the silk stockings of your Actresses excite my Genitals.§

---

* The contract for the *Dictionary*, signed with Dodsley three years previously, provided that he was to be paid £1,575 in instalments. Out of this sum he was to defray all expenses and meet the cost of any help he recruited.

† *Life*, ii, 348–9. Mrs Thrale believed that he held Mrs Pritchard responsible for the failure of his play.

‡ Boswell, James, *Private Papers*, Marshall Waingrow (ed.), 2 vols., New York, 1950, ii, 181. Daggle tailed usually meant untidy or sluttish, but had originally signified splattered with mud or mire. Johnson may have been referring to her private life.

§ In the *Life* (i, 201) this becomes 'I'll come no more behind your scenes David; for the silk-stockings and white bosoms of your actresses excite my amorous propensities.'

11

Fixing the Weathercock

Garrick was in love again—had been, indeed, for quite some time past. Anyone who had not picked that up by the late spring of 1749 must have been living a life of unimaginable seclusion. The May number of the *Gentleman's Magazine* published some skittish verses on the subject under the title 'to Mr G - - - - - K, on the Talk of the Town':

> No, No, the Left-hand Box, in Blue—
> There, don't you see Her? See Her? Who?
>   Nay, hang me if I tell.
> There's G - - - - - k in the Music-Box!
> Watch but his Eyes: See there! O P-x!
>   Your Servant, *Ma'moiselle!*

The Ma'moiselle in blue in the left-hand box was Violette. There is no record of her having danced in public since the season before Garrick took over at Drury Lane. Whether he attempted to engage her once he became manager is not known; in the circles in which they both moved, there was no lack of occasion for their being thrown together socially.

The Burlingtons—Lady Burlington in particular—were obviously eager to see her established in English society; not just marriage and a coach, but a coach with a suitably glossy coat of arms emblazoned on its doors. Horace Walpole could always be relied upon for the latest gossip on such matters. 'They say the old monarch at Hanover has got a new mistress—I fear he ought to have got something else new first,' he tittered to his Etonian school-friend George Montagu in October 1748:

> Now I talk of getting, Mr Fox has got the ten thousand pound prize; and the Violette, as it is said, Coventry for a husband. It is certain that at the fine masquerade, he was following her, as she was under the Countess's arm, who pulling off her glove, moved her wedding ring up and down her finger, with a motion that does not just express matrimony, but it seems was to signify that no other terms would be accepted.*

---

* *Walpole*, ix, 79–80. The masquerade was given at Richmond by the wildly eccentric Duchess of Queensberry.

Violette herself plainly had other ideas: Coventry carries his spear across the stage and is seen no more.

The spring and summer of 1749 were a time of festivity in London. The Peace of Aix-la-Chapelle had brought an end to what the history books label the War of the Austrian Succession and what Thomas Carlyle perceived as 'an unintelligible, huge English-and-Foreign Delirium'. Britain had no great cause to be pleased with the terms of the peace, even though the French once again agreed to repudiate the Pretender. The British were obliged to give up Louisburg in exchange for Madras, and there was some indignation that they had to send two peers to France as hostages for the restoration of Cape Breton.

Public celebration was the order of the day, for all that. The court conceived the idea of a gigantic firework display, to be accompanied by the firing of 101 brass cannon. A huge Doric temple was erected in Green Park, designed by the celebrated Giovanni Niccolò Servandoni, who had been in charge of the scenery at the Paris Opera for eighteen years and had also worked for Rich at Covent Garden. This enormous structure, made of wood and canvas, took five months to build. More than 400 feet long and 114 feet high, it was adorned with statues and allegorical pictures; one bas-relief depicted George II handing Peace to Britannia.

When Handel was asked to write a concerto for this extravaganza, his mind turned first to strings and woodwind. The King, however, who had initially objected to there being any music at all, 'hoped there would be no fidles'—his preference for martial instruments was well known. The *Musick for the Royal Fireworks* was accordingly scored not only for flutes and hautboys but for large numbers of bassoons, horns, trumpets and kettledrums.

Not everyone approved of this ostentatious regal display (although much of the cost seems to have been borne by the Duke of Montagu, the King's Master-General of the Ordnance). The opposition press carried critical articles and letters (one of them by Samuel Johnson). Would not the money be better spent on sailors and soldiers home from the war who would now be thrown on a glutted labour market?

The weather was very hot on 27 April, but by the early evening the sky had become overcast. A light drizzle spoiled many of the fireworks, although there was enough life in one rogue rocket to set fire to a lady's clothes; bystanders saved her from serious injury by stripping her to her petticoat and stays. An hour into the display one wing of the pavilion caught fire and burned to the ground. Servandoni, enraged to see his handiwork destroyed, drew his sword and threatened Charles Frederick, the Comptroller of the Ordnance and Fireworks; he was disarmed and taken into custody, but released the next day on asking pardon before the Duke of Cumberland.

There were competing private festivities. The Duke of Richmond, Master of the Horse, influenced perhaps by the swirling rivalries of the court, decided that he too should have 'a firework, as a codicil to the peace'. He bought up the fireworks that remained from the Green Park fiasco and three weeks later put on a much more successful show at his mansion in the Privy Garden, Whitehall. Montagu had news of it from Walpole:

Then for royalty, Mr Anstis himself would have been glutted; there were all the Fitzes upon earth, the whole court of St Germains, the Duke, the Duke of Modena and the two Anamaboes . . . . . There was another admirable scene; Lady Burlington brought the Violette, and the Richmonds had asked Garrick, who stood ogling and sighing the whole time, while my Lady kept a most fierce lookout.*

Violette, inevitably, had become the subject of a great deal of highly coloured conjecture and gossip. There were those who said that she was Lord Burlington's illegitimate daughter—why else should he go to the extraordinary length of having the tickets for her benefit designed by the celebrated architect and painter William Kent and engraved by George Vertue?† (There was a perfectly straightforward reason, as it happens. The Earl had been Kent's patron since they had met in Rome in 1716 and Kent had been installed since then in apartments of his own at Burlington House.)‡ Burlington, what is more, had already been married for two years at the time of Violette's birth, and the *Journals of the House of Lords* attest to the fact that since that time he had been uninterruptedly in England.

When she was an old lady, Violette read the memoirs of the actor Charles Lee Lewes, in which he repeated the Burlington story. 'He is a great liar,' she said. 'Lord Burlington was not my father, but I am of noble birth.' Her connection with the Austrian nobility was rather more tenuous than that, however—her father, Johan Veigel, a resident burgher of Vienna at the time of her birth, had once been valet to the Graf von Paar. His daughter was born on 29 February 1724 in a house called 'Zum weissen Hasen' (the white hare) on the corner of the Tiefer Graben and Heidenschuss. She was baptized in St Stephen's Cathedral and given the names Eva Maria. The stage name Violette was the French translation of her surname.

So far as the Countess was concerned, the idea of marrying her protégée off to a mere player was preposterous, even if he was the celebrated manager of Drury Lane. It was Garrick's good luck that he was on cordial terms with the young Marquess of Hartington, the son and heir of the Duke of Devonshire. The previous year Hartington had married the Burlingtons' daughter, Charlotte, and this meant that Garrick had a friend at court.

The 'Talk of the Town' verses were attributed to Garrick's friend Edward Moore, author of *The Foundling*—indeed, they appear in his collected works—

* *Walpole*, ix, 81. John Anstis (1669–1744) had been Garter-King-of-Arms. The court of St Germain's were Jacobites, the Fitzes descendants of Charles II. The Anamaboes were two Africans from the Gold Coast who had been sold into slavery, ransomed by the government and put in the care of Lord Halifax.

† Vertue (1684–1756), a pupil of Michael Van der Gucht, was a leading engraver of the day. His many patrons included the Earl of Oxford and Frederick, Prince of Wales, who employed him in cataloguing the royal collections.

‡ Kent (1684–1748) was a fashionable arbiter of all matters of taste. He had been principal painter to the Crown since 1739 and was also master-carpenter, architect and keeper of the pictures. He decorated Kensington Palace, designed the 'Temple of Venus' at Stowe and built the Horse Guards in Whitehall. He was also a noted landscape gardener.

but they have Garrick's fingerprints all over them, slyly pre-empting criticism by appearing to bend to it:

> And pray, what other News d'ye hear?
> Married!—but don't you think, my Dear,
>   He's growing out of Fashion.
> People may fancy what they will,
> But *Q - - n's* the only actor still
>   To touch the tender Passion.
>
> 'Twas prudent tho' to drop his Bays
> And (*entre Nous*) old *C - bb - r* says,
>   He hopes he'll give up *Richard*;
> But then it tickles me to see,
> In *Hastings*, such a Shrimp as He,
>   Attempt to ravish *Pr - - ch - rd*.

The last two stanzas advise Garrick to ignore the *malevoli* and take the plunge:

> But if you find your Spirits right,
> Your Mind at Ease, and Body tight,
>   Take Her, you can't do better.
> A P-x upon the tatling Town!
> The Fops that join to cry you down,
>   Wou'd give their Ears to get her.
>
> Then, if her Heart be good and kind,
> (And sure that Face bespeaks a Mind
>   As soft as Woman's can be)
> You'll grow as constant as a Dove,
> And taste the purer Sweets of Love,
>   Unvisited by *R - - - y*.[*]

By the early summer of 1749, Lady Burlington had conceded defeat. 'I don't know whether or no you knew that Garrick was going to be married to the Violette when you went away,' William Hogarth wrote to his wife on 6 June. 'I supt with him last night and had a deal of talk about her.'[1]

They were married on 22 June—twice, because the bride was a Roman Catholic. They went first, at eight o'clock in the morning, to a chapel near Russell Street in Bloomsbury where the ceremony was conducted by Garrick's friend the Reverend Thomas Francklin.[†] From there they crossed town to South Audley

---

[*] R - - - y alludes to John Ranby (1703–73), principal surgeon-sergeant to George II since 1743. The *DNB* describes him as 'a man of strong passions, harsh voice and inelegant manners.' It was he who had carried out the operation of which Queen Caroline died, but this seems not to have affected the size of his surgical practice.

[†] Francklin (1721–84) was a Fellow of Trinity College, Cambridge at the time and later for some years Professor of Greek. He was a popular preacher, but lived mainly by writing for the

Street, for a Roman Catholic ceremony in the chapel of the Portuguese Embassy.

Garrick settled £10,000 on his wife, together with the sum of £70 a year as pin money. 'The chapter of this history is a little obscure and uncertain as to the consent of the protecting Countess,' Horace Walpole wrote to Mann, 'and whether she gives her a fortune or not.'[2] As always, Walpole's sharp nose was pointed in the right direction; when Lady Burlington died in 1758 her will revealed that she had settled on Eva Maria the interest on £5,000 derived from estates she owned in Lincolnshire.*

The bride kept the cream silk apron edged with guipure which she wore over her dress that day for the rest of her life. Her husband presented her with a service of silver: a tea kettle and lamp, a coffee pot, two ladles for cream, three pairs of candlesticks, and 'a Complete Tea Chest'.†

After Garrick's death, there were found among his papers some lines which he had marked 'Verses sent to me on my marriage':

> What! has that heart, so wild, so roving,
> So prone to changing, sighing, loving,
> Whom widows, maids, attacked in vain,
> At last submitted to the chain?
> Who is the paragon, the marvellous she,
> Has fix'd a weather-cock like thee?

Who the author was is not known, but Garrick also kept a copy of his reply:

> . . . A gaiety with innocence,
> A soft address, with manly sense,
> Ravishing manners, void of art,
> A cheerful, firm, yet feeling heart,
> Beauty, that charms all public gaze,
> And humble, amid pomp and praise . . . . .
>
> These are the charms my heart have bound,
> Charms often sought, so rarely found!
> Nor think the lover's partial voice
> In flatt'ring colours paints his choice . . .

It is not great love poetry, but it tells us a good deal about both partners in the marriage. Garrick's 'partial voice' was echoed by a host of others over the years, writers, lawyers and statesmen all paying her eloquent homage. 'I love Garrick on

---

press and the stage. He and Garrick subsequently fell out; by 1774 the latter was referring to him as 'that strange heap of insincerity & contradiction Dr Franklin.' (*Letters*, 867)

* The marriage contract is reproduced in Baker, George Pierce, *Some Unpublished Correspondence of David Garrick*, Boston, Mass., 1907, pp. 16–22. After Lady Burlington's death, the payments were continued by her son-in-law, Hartington, by then fourth Duke of Devonshire.

† The service was still in Mrs Garrick's possession seventy years later. She itemized it in this way in her will, in which she bequeathed it to one of Garrick's nephews — together with the 'table service of pewter which my dear husband made use of when a Bachelor'.

the stage better than anything in the world,' wrote Laurence Sterne—'except Mrs Garrick off it.' Sir John Eardley-Wilmot, Johnson's contemporary at the grammar school in Lichfield and later Chief Justice of Common Pleas, was an equally fervent admirer. Garrick, threatened with a lawsuit on some occasion, had turned to him for advice. 'I think,' Wilmot told him amiably, 'I had rather you should go to gaol, and then Mrs Garrick (to whom I beg my love) may come and live with me.'

She was as great a jackdaw as her husband. An assembly of her unsorted papers at the Folger Library in Washington contains everything from her marriage certificate to an elderflower and camphor recipe for 'weak Eyes, sore eyes and decay'd eyes'. There is also an undated note from Lord Bath, headed simply 'Saturday mrn 12 o'clock':

> Madam
>   Has Mr Colman told you all the fine things we said of you, when we dined together, and that we drank your health in a Bumper? When I send you the Game, I cannot help accompanying it with a gentle Billet doux, to tell you how much I honour, and admire you, let Mr Keightly be as jealous & as angry as he pleases . . . . .*

William Pulteney, Earl of Bath, was well into his sixties by the time the Garricks married and no longer a force in Whig politics, but in his prime Walpole had said of him that he feared Pulteney's tongue more than another man's sword. A 'gentle Billet doux' from that quarter was certainly a memento to be treasured.

The newlyweds honeymooned first at Chiswick. In the early 1730s Lord Burlington had pulled down old Chiswick House and built in its place a villa built on the general plan of Palladio's Villa Capra near Vicenza.† The waspish Lord Hervey dismissed it as 'too small to live in and too large to hang to a watch', but that was of no concern to the Garricks, who for several weeks had its eight principal reception rooms, its long gallery and its central domed hall entirely to themselves.‡ The grounds were laid out in the Italian style, adorned with temples, obelisks and statues. There were gravel walks between yew hedges and a canal—'Chiz river'—which was spanned by a classical bridge.

The middle of July found them installed in a rented house at Merton, in Surrey. Garrick was ill for a few days; he was plainly not the easiest of patients, and his wife sent a charming account of his indisposition to Lady Burlington:

> His Swell'd Face began to be more troublesome than Ever it was, I thought by telling him a fat face is very becoming, I might perhaps bring him to compose his fancies, but then the nasty Looking-glasses to whom he flew

---

* Kitely, the jealous husband in Jonson's *Every Man in His Humour*, was one of Garrick's most popular comedy roles. The Whig politician Sir William Pulteney (1684–1764) was created Earl of Bath 1742. He is chiefly remembered for his powers of oratory.

† Burlington, who had translated Palladio, had already transformed Burlington House from Restoration Classic to a pure imitation of his style. This was heavily overlaid when the building was turned into a home for learned societies in 1866, but some features survive, notably the *piano nobile*, which imitates Palladio's Palazzo Porto.

‡ The Burlingtons had gone north to visit the Devonshires at Chatsworth.

every minute, destroy'd all my project—the next Day it was wars and wars, the pain was greater than before: I recollected a remedy, which was, Tobacco and a Large Bason of punch, that made him drunk and consequently Easy for half a night, but then began again to complaind how much his Beauty Suffer'd—I try'd another thing which is compos'd of warm flower, wich entirely reduc'd the Swelling of his Cheek. in Short in three days hi was as beautiful as before.[3]

Garrick also wrote to the Countess from Merton: 'how is it possible for Me Madam to say enough to You when I think of ye Numberless Obligations You have heaped upon Me; for exclusive of the favours I have receiv'd before & since My Marriage, 'tis owing to You Madam & You alone, that I am now the Happiest of Men, & in possession of Mrs Garrick.' This somewhat oily passage goes on to shed interesting light on the battle of wills that had been fought before the wedding. Eva Maria, although prepared to defer to a remarkable extent to the wishes of the Countess, was clearly made of redoubtable stuff:

She has more than once confess'd to Me, that tho She lik'd me very well, & was determin'd not to marry any body else, yet she was *as* determin'd not to Marry *Me*, if Your Ladyship had put a Negative upon Me.[4]

The country air agreed with both of them. 'My Tyrant continues extreamly well and in Spirits, I think she grows visibly fat,' he told the Countess in another letter, and he sent a similar report to his brother Peter:

Your old friend Mr Cockram, the apothecary, has favoured us twice with his company, and hopes to have the honor of purging us; but I intend to keep his catharticks out of my guts, for I never had such health and spirits in my life.[5]

They had other news for their friends: 'Mr Garrick has bought the house in Southampton Street for five hundred Guineas, *Dirt* and all,' his wife wrote to Lady Burlington at the end of July; ''tis reckon'd a very good bargain.' She also gave the Countess a blow-by-blow account of their latest domestic drama:

Oh what a misfortune! how Shall I be able to tell it! a new Kitchin Lady was order'd to kill a Chickin for Supper and being possess'd by the Devil, & not knowing a Bathan from a gouse, touk the white good natur'd hen yr Ladyp gave Us, and Cut It's throet without mercy—I found it out by the whiteness & hardness of the flesh, & a Belly fall of Eggs into the Bargain—I behav'd upon the occasion with great Philosophy as usual, but had much to do to hinder my tender Spouse from cutting the mads throat, & after making him reflect upon his Late happy recovery, he Soften'd his mind a Little, hearing that Passion Spoils the Beauty.*

---

* Letter dated 25 July 1749, now in the Folger Library. The same 'Kitchin Lady' found another way of raising Garrick's blood pressure only a few days later: 'the very Same *illstarr'd Wench* has this Morng done a second deed more horrid than ye first! — She absolutely brush'd the Chimney with Our Brush from Vienna!' (*Letters*, 62.)

They found themselves much sought after socially—'We are in great Vogue, & much Civility is paid Us,' Garrick told Lady Burlington in yet another letter. They declined two pressing invitations from Lord and Lady Cobham and wished, when it was too late, that they had been equally firm with another importunate nobleman whose house and gardens adjoined Horace Walpole's at Strawberry Hill:

> My Lord Radnor plagu'd our hearts to dine with him, we at last agreed (for we hate to dine from home) and he had invited the Parson's Wife to meet Mrs Garrick—but such a Dinner, so dress'd & so serv'd up in unscour'd Pewter, we never Saw. The Wine was worse, but made somewhat better, by the dead flies; in Short, we were both sick & unsatisfy'd; & rattled the one horse chair home as fast as we could, where we recruited our Spirits again, with a clean Cloth, two roasted Pigeons, and the best currant Pye in ye Kingdom, the county of York excepted.*

They lingered at Merton until early in September, with occasional visits to London to see how the work at Southampton Street was going forward. Mrs Garrick, anxious not to offend, dashed off a note to the Burlingtons in Yorkshire:

> I Shall be So impertinent, as I don't like to be in his Logings under all them Strange people, to lie at B: House in my Little yeallow bed; if we have not room enough, he mus Lie under it; I hope Lord & Lady won't be angry at us? I promise I Shall not be so free another time.[6]

Lady Burlington had decided to publish two previously unknown works by her grandfather, the first Marquess of Halifax. Garrick had been enlisted to help her, and devoted some time during his honeymoon to assessing the material she had sent him: 'I will make an Assortment of 'em to ye best of My Judgment & shew 'em to Yr Lad^P.'[7] She had also retailed to him snippets of a conversation with Colley Cibber, which appears to have taken place at Chatsworth. Her account does not survive, but Garrick's response to it shows just how prickly and thin-skinned he could be and how difficult he found it to let things pass:

> Your Lady^P must know, that Notwithstanding the great Nonchalance that Cibber boasts of, he has as much Envy, as Vanity, & as little Benevolence, as Judgment: My Success in Life & in his own Profession, has given him visible uneasiness, he can't bear to think of my obtaining that in a few Years, which he & his Brother Patentees were labouring for thirty or forty Years; I have been told by some Gentlemen of the White's Club, that any Praises they bestow'd upon Me, were Death to him, & he always Endeavour'd as much as in him lay, to hurt me in their Opinions, & to criticise Me in my Characters; his Behaviour to Me was always the reverse, which is so certain an indication of a mean contemptible Mind, that I have

---

* *Letters*, 63. The Burlingtons had now moved on to Londesburgh Park, near Market Weighton in the East Riding of Yorkshire, where Burlington, with his passion for building, had designed a new house for himself in the Elizabethan style.

never cultivated his Acquaintance, & I believe have disappointed him, by not offering that incense to his vanity, which he has so often receiv'd, & which He expects from Every Young Actor.*

Towards the end of August, dinner with neighbours at Merton suffered a sudden and alarming interruption:

> Mrs Garrick, from being in perfect health, & high bloom, was taken very ill, extreamly sick, & turn'd pale; We went home immediatly, & by unlacing her Stays, & drink^g a Glass of Water, she was quite recover'd & is now in higher Spirits than ever I knew her.[8]

Eva Maria forbade Garrick to say anything about this to the Burlingtons—an injunction which he ignored. From a letter he wrote to the Countess some days later it is plain he thought his wife might be pregnant—'what was ye Cause of it, I am not yet certain of, but I am in hopes, I had more reason to be rejoyc'd, than shock'd at it, which I was exceedingly, at ye Time it happen'd.'[9] The matter was still in doubt a week later:

> I wish from my soul I could send a Confirmation of what was Suspected; & which at present is my greatest Wish; but be it as it will, I ought to be satisfy'd, for I have really more true happiness than comes to my Share— to ask more would be arrogance & presumption—*She* is well & happy, & *I* cannot be otherwise.[10]

It was a false alarm.

The opening of the new season had been fixed for 16 September. The house in Southampton Street was not going to be ready in time; '*She*,' Garrick reported indulgently, 'is most prodigiously busy in *ranging, settling, furnishing, & changing* her mind twenty Times a Day.'[11] It was agreed that for the time being they should live at Burlington House.

Garrick had worked hard at buttressing his position as a sort of honorary son-in-law to the Burlingtons. He had addressed the matter directly in a bread-and-butter letter to the Earl soon after their arrival at Merton:

> I have lately had ye highest Satisfaction in flattering Myself, that Your Lordship has now some hopes of Mrs Garrick & I being happy togeather; Your former Doubts proceeded from Your Esteem for her, & and from a very just Opinion you had conceiv'd of ye People in my Profession: however if it should be my good fortune to afford Your Lordship One Exception to ye General Rule against Us, I shall then gain the heigth of my Wishes . . . . .[12]

He knew that to establish himself in the good books of the Countess was a more difficult proposition, and he exerted himself very considerably to that end. He was quick, for instance, to carry out small errands for her ('The Moment I

---

* *Letters*, 64. Several of Garrick's friends — Rigby, Hartington, Richard Cox, the founder of Cox's Bank — were members of White's.

receiv'd You Ladyship's Letter, I sent the Porter to enquire after the rich Stuff, he took it to the D: of Newcastle.').[13] The stream of letters he fired off to her during his honeymoon—he wrote twice a week on average—are full of elaborate flattery, and the strategy was successful: 'I am so Embolden'd by Your Praise,' he wrote ingratiatingly from Merton at the end of July, 'that I will venture to say of Myself (once for all) that if I have obtain'd my Wishes, by having a place in Lady Burlington's Esteem, I shall not quickly resign.'

Rather touchingly, the Burlingtons sent regular consignments of food and drink rattling down the Great North Road from the Londesburgh brewhouse and kitchens:

> Your Lad^P will scarcely give Us time to finish one Pye before You Send Another: We do 'Em great Justice I assure You, & Eat 'em to y^e last Inch— that which is mention'd in your Lad$^{P's}$ last, is just now arriv'd, and to morrow, we shall certainly begin the Attack—I am affraid we shall take very little of our Ale to Southampton Street; It is the best was ever drank, & we are convinc'd from *daily* Experience, that it is as Wholesome, as palatable—*

During one of his visits to London to attend to the house and prepare for the new season, his vanity was most agreeably tickled by a small incident in the Strand:

> As I was walking along I saw a number of People got togeather about a Bookseller's Shop; My Curiosity led me to make one & I just came as a Man was getting up a Ladder to hang on a Sign for the Shop, which was New & fitted up very hansomely; I jostled in among the Crowd to See whose head had the honour of being Exalted; when behold, I saw my own; & My Name written about it, in Letters as tall as Myself; You may imagine I was much disconcerted to be thus caught; however I slunk away as fast as I could, & I believe was lucky enough not to be known by any present, or seen by any, who might have given out that I was superintending the work . . . . .[14]

Marriage and the long summer days had relaxed him greatly. It would have been unthinkable only a few months previously, but on the very day the Theatre Royal was due to re-open its doors, the co-manager of Drury Lane and his wife crossed the Thames and drove out of London:

> We are just now going back to Merton: tho the Playhouse opens to Night, I have taken the Liberty (as I am not personally wanted) to Excuse Myself from attending it—We are so happy in ye Country, when we are alone, that I shall take Every opportunity of enjoying it with convenience to my affairs—[15]

---

* *Letters.* An amusing footnote to this letter indicates that Mrs Garrick's relations with the English aristocracy had not affected her native sense of bourgeois thrift: '*She* has put so much Water into ye Ink that I fear my Letter is not legible—'

His affairs suffered not in the slightest from his absence. The house for the first night of the 1749–50 season was the fullest that had been known for twelve years.

12

Britannia and the French Vagrants

'The small wits nibbed their pens upon the occasion of Garrick's marriage,' wrote Murphy, 'and lampoons, epigrams, sonnets, epithalamiums, fluttered in every coffee house. To give them the finishing blow, *Much Ado About Nothing* was revived.'[1]

Garrick's Victorian biographers did not approve the choice. Joseph Knight thought it showed 'characteristic bad taste'[2] and Percy Fitzgerald was equally censorious:

> As he had intended, passages like 'Here you may see Benedick, the married man;' 'I may chance to have some odd quirks and remnants of wit broken on me, because I have railed so long against marriage;'—all excited the heartiest laughter and enjoyment. This restless craving to make the public partners in all his little domestic concerns was one of Garrick's weaknesses to the end.[3]

To Garrick's contemporaries, such prissiness would have been incomprehensible. It had been his last role before his marriage, and it was pretty much a foregone conclusion that it would be his first on his return: 'The Town has it, that I shall open with Benedick *the Married Man*,' he had told Lady Burlington; 'I have so resolv'd, & I find the People are very impatient to laugh with Me & at Me.'[4] Which is just what they did: 'the jests in Benedick were receiv'd with uncommon applause,' Cross noted in his diary. Just as importantly, he recorded that the receipts for the evening were £180. The season was off to a good start.

It was important that it should be. Covent Garden had attracted almost as good a house to see Quin and Woffington as Sir John and Lady Brute the previous week,* and there was an equally full attendance when they appeared as Richard and Lady Anne in *King Richard III*. Garrick had discovered on his return to town that he would not have the services of Mrs Cibber, who had sent word that her health would not permit her to play. Mrs Pritchard and Mrs Clive were in place, but Garrick suddenly found himself with a worrying string of blanks in his cast lists—no Cordelia, no Desdemona, no Ophelia, no Juliet, no Sigismunda, no Belvidera.

---

* Covent Garden's receipts for *The Provok'd Wife* were £167 19s. 6d.

There was no time to go talent-spotting in the provinces or in Dublin. Instead he went sniffing round the Covent Garden hen-coop, and succeeded in poaching Sarah Ward. Mrs Ward, still only in her early twenties, had made her Covent Garden début as Cordelia two years previously to Quin's Lear, and it was as Cordelia that she now first appeared with Garrick. Quin described her as 'a flat-baked pancake' and George Anne Bellamy, although conceding that she had a beautiful face, added that 'by the stoop and magnitude of her shoulders it might be imagined that she had formerly carried milk pails'. (This was unlikely— she was the daughter of a York actor called Achurch and her upbringing was purely urban.) She did not fill the gap left by Mrs Cibber with any great distinction, but Garrick was obliged to make extensive use of her. Her roles included Monimia in *The Orphan* and Lady Easy in *The Careless Husband*. Garrick quickly discovered that she was unresponsive to production and Barry, moody and difficult in the absence of Mrs Cibber, declined to appear with her, which put paid to any idea of a new run of *Romeo and Juliet*.

By the middle of October, the Garricks were installed in their freshly painted new home, an elegant brick-built house on the west side of Southampton Street, just off the Strand and less than ten minutes walk from the theatre. Garrick was in high good humour: 'We are as busy as two Bees,' he wrote to Lady Burlington, who was still in Yorkshire, '& till our hive is well *rang'd*, my Sweet Charmer hums about to some tune. Every thing in All our Affairs goes on as We could wish.'[5] It was not a particularly grand neighbourhood. When George Winchester Stone and George M. Kahrl were at work on their biography of Garrick, they had the idea of studying the Westminster parish registers for the year 1749 and cataloguing the occupations of some 440 residents who were Garrick's neighbours—bakers and haberdashers, shoemakers and staymakers, apoth-ecaries, tailors, jewellers and victuallers.*

The King paid an early visit to Drury Lane that season to see *Twelfth Night*, with Mrs Clive as Olivia, Woodward as Andrew Aguecheek and Mrs Pritchard as Viola. He came a second time a week later, but gave instructions that his name was not to be mentioned in the bills: 'I am not Surpriz'd at it,' Garrick confided to Lady Burlington, 'for it is the London Cuckolds, & a very *unroyal* Entertainment it must be.'[6] Unroyal or not, it was very much to the theatrical taste of the current head of the House of Hanover: 'Among his many kingly virtues,' wrote Davies, 'George the Second could not enumerate the patronage of science and love of the Virtù.' Edward Ravenscroft's farce, dating from 1681, fell into the category which text books usually describe as 'rollicking' and was traditionally presented on Lord Mayor's Day. Its days in the Drury Lane repertoire were numbered. The *Gentleman's Magazine* for November 1752 would note with satisfaction that Garrick had quietly substituted a performance of *The*

---

* Stone, George Winchester Jr and Kahrl, George M., *David Garrick, a Critical Biography*, Carbondale, Ill., 1979, 40–41. Cited henceforth as *Stone and Kahrl*. Twenty-five residents (they included John Rich and Spranger Barry as well as Garrick himself) described themselves as gentlemen — the same number as there were peruke-makers.

Merchant of Venice. The other house continued to give its patrons what they wanted for a little longer, but after 1758 this 'monstrous production of nonsense and obscenity,' as the *London Chronicle* of that year described it, was seen no more.*

During the autumn of 1749 a troup of French players arrived in London. They had been assembled by Jean Louis Monnet, who some years previously had revived the fortunes of the Opéra-Comique in Paris.† Monnet had originally been encouraged to come by Rich, who had agreed to advance salaries and allow two performances a week at Covent Garden. Later, however, when Monnet asked to have this in writing, Rich lost his nerve, pleading that it 'might prejudice him with the public'—less than a year after the signing of the peace there was still a good deal of anti-French feeling in London.

Monnet had then appealed to Garrick, who prudently declined to offer him the hospitality of Drury Lane, but suggested, as did others, that he apply to the Lord Chamberlain for a licence to perform at the Haymarket. This was granted, and when a subscription raised the healthy sum of £294, Monnet felt justified in bringing over his company.

Garrick might have done better to advise him to stay in Paris. Twelve years after the passing of the Licensing Act, there were plenty of unemployed English actors to resent the appearance of a French company in a theatre closed to them, particularly as stories surfaced in the press from time to time about the obstacles put in the way of English players who attempted to perform in France. London's sizeable Huguenot population had even longer memories, and were not disposed to give Monnet's putatively Catholic troupe a friendly reception.

Garrick observed their prospects with a mixture of detachment and calculation. 'The french Players are at present the only Topick of Conversation,' he wrote to Lady Burlington at the end of October:

> There are many Parties forming for & against 'Em—I don't in the least concern Myself in the Matter, for if they are permitted they can't hurt Drury Lane; so I am quite Neuter, & am very well satisfy'd, whether they succeed or Not.[7]

The French season was billed to open on 14 November with a mainpiece called *Les Amans Réunis* and the comic opera *Le Coq du Village*. By six o'clock the gallery was packed with French refugees, and as soon as the orchestra struck up the overture, there was a chant of 'We don't want French comedians.' The first actor and actress to appear were met with a shower of apples and oranges, and

---

* The *Chronicle* took the trouble to give the *Cuckolds* a pedigree of sorts — 'the squeezings from an extravagant novel of Scarron, and two or three ill-chosen fables of La Fontaine; of which ingredients he has contrived to mix up a sort of hog-wash, sweetened with a few luscious expressions and a large portion of the grossest lewdness, to the palates of swine . . . . .'

† Monnet (1703?—85) was born at Condrieux on the Rhône, the son of a poor baker. He had had an eventful life, having been a page to the duchesse de Berry, worked as a printer, considered entering a Trappist monastery and been confined in the Bastille as the '*auteur de mauvais ouvrages, vers et chansons infâmes*'.

the actress was struck in the throat by a candle. A group of Monnet's subscribers—in his memoirs Monnet said that they were led by a Lord 'G' and Duke 'D'[8]—had stationed themselves in the upper boxes, and they now made for the gallery and laid about them with canes and swords. A detachment of soldiers appeared on the stage with drawn swords, and the performance then went ahead without further interruption.

For the following night *Le Coq du Village* was again given out, preceded by Molière's *L'Ecole des Femmes*. Monnet's supporters had been out and about hiring reinforcements and a militia made up of Smithfield butchers and Thames boatmen quickly cleared the gallery, tipping some of their adversaries into the pit in the process. 'After which,' wrote Monnet, 'the performance went on in the midst of a silence so complete that none dared spit nor blow his nose.'

That might have been the end of the matter, but at this juncture the affair acquired a political dimension. The Member of Parliament for Westminster, Lord Trentham, had been appointed to an office of profit under the crown, and was therefore obliged to resign his seat and seek re-election. The by-election had been fixed for 24 November; Trentham had been one of Monnet's subscribers, and had been present at the Haymarket on the first night; his opponents seized on this as a brush to tar him with and procured a damaging deposition before a notary alleging that it was he who had hired the thugs who had kept order at the playhouse on the second night.

The controversy rumbled on for several weeks. A satirical print of the day shows Britannia nursing Rich and Garrick: 'Lunn & Frible are my only Theatrical Children,' reads the caption. 'I will cherish no French vagrants.' New disorders broke out, no longer confined to the playhouse, and the authorities became increasingly nervous. The *General Advertiser* had reported as early as 16 November that the city officers had been instructed not to permit the French company to post any playbills; finally, just before Christmas, the Lord Chamberlain brought the axe down:

> We hear that His Majesty has been graciously pleased to order the Licence to the French Strollers to be withdrawn, in order to prevent any more Disturbances or ill Blood among his Subjects.[9]

Monnet, accompanied by one of his actresses, spent some months in a debtor's prison. The Duke of Grafton made him a gift of money; the following May, at the end of the season, Garrick allowed him a benefit at Drury Lane and Monnet, in a statement that accompanied the advertisement, grovelled comprehensively:

> Mr Monett, the innocent tho' unfortunate cause of disgusting the Public by his attempting to represent French Plays, most humbly implores their assistance, by the means of this Benefit Play, to extricate him out of his present most deplorable situation. Without such relief his Misfortunes must detain him a ruined Man in England . . . . .[10]

Monnet returned to France still up to his ears in debt,* but Garrick had made a friend for life, and one who was to prove immensely useful to him in all sorts of ways.

Towards the end of 1749, three months or so into Garrick's second season as joint patentee, there was some friction between him and Lacy. The agreement which they had signed two and a half years previously did not go into detail about the division of their responsibilities, and now some rather stiff letters passed between them. 'You may remember S^r that an equality of Power was insisted upon, when we first met,' wrote Lacy, 'and ye original articles will sufficiently prove y^t you did agree to it.'[11] Garrick replied rather huffily that he was at a loss to know what Lacy was driving at. 'Nay I will go farther,' he added, 'I defy You to produce one instance, where You have in ye least Suffer'd in Your Credit, Interest or Importance.'[12] Their legal advisers put their heads together, and hammered out an agreement. It was left in the hands of Garrick's lawyer, John Paterson, who undertook to act as the 'common friend' of both parties.

There were seven headings. The first provided that the 'settling or altering the business of the Stage' should be left entirely to Garrick, although he was required to keep Lacy informed of his dispositions through the prompter. If Lacy felt that Garrick was pursuing measures 'injurious to his,'Mr Lacy's property' his objections were to be stated to Paterson, and Garrick agreed to accept his arbitration.

The hiring and firing of players and all other servants of the house and the determination of their salaries was to be a joint responsibility. The accounts and all other business of the co-partnership were similarly to be carried on jointly, although it was agreed that Garrick's brother George might act for him when he was caught up in stage business. Garrick undertook to give his personal attention to any matter which Lacy judged to require it.

Any future differences were to be referred to Paterson—both parties agreed to do this 'without venting any speeches in publick to the disadvantage of the other'—and Paterson's decision would be final. They also agreed a procedure for dissolving the partnership in the event of insurmountable differences between them or on the death of either party: Paterson would conduct an auction, and the successful bidder would be entitled to the whole joint property on payment to the other of one half of the sum last bid. 'This agreement,' they concluded, 'is understood to be honorary and shall not be divulged upon any pretence whatsoever Unless upon a breach of some part thereof.'[13]

The Drury Lane company, eighty-four strong that season, included the largest number of dancers and singers Garrick had yet employed. They had been deployed

---

* The details of Monnet's accounts for this disastrous venture are preserved in the Bibliothèque Nationale in Paris and are reproduced in *The London Stage*, Part IV, i, 200. His total outlay amounted to more than £2,000 and he was able to recoup only £850. He soon bounced back, however. He was reappointed director of the Opéra-Comique at a salary of 6,000 francs, and was able to retire from the theatre in 1757.

to good effect on 2 December in a musical entertainment called *The Chaplet*, the first of the season's five new productions, the words by Moses Mendez and the music by William Boyce. Early in the New Year, Garrick and Barry took the leading parts in Drury Lane's second new offering of the season, *Edward, The Black Prince; or, The Battle of Poictiers*. The author was one William Shirley, who had been engaged in business in Portugal for many years, and was regarded as something of an authority on foreign trade. His talents as a dramatist were less evident—an earlier effort of his, *The Parricide*, had caused a riot at Covent Garden in 1739. Cross recorded that *Edward* was received 'with great Applause— only a little groaning at some of the Love Scenes', but although it ran for nine nights, it did not remain in the repertory. Fitzgerald dismissed it as 'one of the long series of bald, dreary, tedious plays, constructed on the French model':

> There seems to have been but the one strict pattern for these chilling dramas, and we look back wearily to the long procession of Roman generals, sultans, Greek matrons, Persian kings, and mythological heroes, whose costume, feelings, and religion, wrapped in hopeless mists, become removed from all dramatic interest and sympathy.*

A second new musical entertainment, Thomas Arne's *Don Saverio*, had its première in February, but was not liked—'much hiss'd but suffer'd to be given out again,' Cross recorded. It had one more performance and then sank without trace. There was a much more favourable reception, later in the month, for *The Roman Father*, a tragedy by William Whitehead.† Whitehead based his play on Corneille's *Horace*, which in turn was derived from Livy. It was not a piece of any great literary merit, but it proved a theatrical success, even if a paragraph in *The Midwife* suggested that this did not please everybody: 'Those Gentlemen who borrow'd gold laced hats to go to Drury Lane in order to damn the new play are desir'd to return them to the owners, or their names will be publish'd at full length.'[14] Garrick, who always relished old men's parts, cast himself as Horatius‡ and Mrs Pritchard was Horatia. The play passed into the repertory, and also enjoyed the unusual distinction of having a ship plying between London and Dublin named after it.

In the middle of March Garrick appeared as Hamlet for Kitty Clive's benefit night. The tragedy was followed by Clive's first—and last—foray into author-ship, a farce called *Bayes in Petticoats*, in which the characters had names like Miss Daudle, Miss Giggle and Sir Albany Odelove. Enlivened by some of Boyce's

---

* *Fitzgerald*, 131. Shirley, like so many disgruntled playwrights, later fell out with Garrick and attacked him in a pamphlet.

† Whitehead (1715–85), the son of a Cambridge baker, was a former fellow of Clare Hall. He had been employed by Pope to translate into Latin the first epistle of the *Essay on Man*, and was currently tutor to the Earl of Jersey's son. In 1757, on the death of Colley Cibber, and after Grey had turned it down, he would be appointed Poet Laureate.

‡ It never became one of his major roles, but he played it a further eighteen times in the course of his career. Among English versions of French classical tragedy, the play was surpassed in popularity only by *The Distressed Mother*.

music, it went well, although at thirty-nine, Clive no longer had the ideal figure for a breeches part and she came in for some ribbing.

There was a flurry of interest in the work of Milton during 1750. Garrick's old admirer Thomas Newton, now chaplain to Lord Bath and rector of St Mary-le-Bow, had recently published a new edition of *Paradise Lost*, and it had become known that the poet's last surviving granddaughter was still alive. Elizabeth Foster and her husband had kept a small grocer's shop in the Holloway Road; now, aged about sixty, she was weak and infirm. Samuel Johnson had become involved in raising a subscription for her relief, and it seems likely that it was he who persuaded Garrick to put on a performance of Milton's *Comus* for her benefit.* He wrote a prologue for the occasion, which Garrick spoke, and placed a long letter in the *General Advertiser* urging attendance at the performance. The occasion brought Mrs Foster £130. 'She had so little acquaintance with diversion or gaiety,' Johnson later wrote, 'that she did not know what was intended when a benefit was offered her.'[15] A hundred pounds was placed in the stocks. With the remainder the Fosters were enabled to remove to rural Islington.

Garrick's last appearance before the summer was in *The Roman Father* on 11 May. It had been a difficult season, and he was eager to get away, even though all manner of uncertainties loomed for the autumn. Barry's increasingly frequent displays of temperament had become tedious. That there should be a degree of rivalry between the two men was inevitable. Was Garrick jealous of Barry's success as Romeo? Barry was certainly jealous of his manager's Hamlet. Had Barry, 'bewitching to hear, and dangerous to believe', made a pass at Mrs Garrick? He was certainly vain enough to do so, but we shall never know.† Garrick had generously ceded to Barry several of his own parts, but that did not stop Barry complaining that he was required to act 'at improper seasons, and on unlucky days; such as when a great lady had summoned a prodigious company to a concert of music or a rout'.[16] The number of occasions on which he was suddenly 'indisposed' multiplied. When questions were raised about this he had gone so far as to take space in the press to deny that he had 'frequently of late refused to act', indignantly asserting that he would never make use of 'tricks or Evasions of this kind'.[17]

By the end of May the Garricks were launched on a round of visits to some of their grander acquaintances—to the Hartingtons at Hardwick Hall, to the

---

* As part of the hack work he still did for Cave at the *Gentleman's Magazine*, Johnson had also written a brief preface to a work by one William Lauder which purported to demonstrate that *Paradise Lost* had been plagiarized from a group of modern Latin poems. Lauder, a somewhat twisted Scottish Latin scholar, was later exposed as a fraud; Johnson dictated and forced him to sign a retraction, and himself published an apology, but the episode was sometimes used as a stick to beat him with.

† Lee Lewes, in his highly suspect memoirs, has a story about a letter sent to Mrs Garrick shortly after their wedding in which an anonymous admirer told her that she had chosen unwisely — 'a wretch, as incapable of love as generosity—a pitiful little animal, who has no other passion but avarice and no other mistress but a guinea.' *Lee Lewes, op. cit.,* ii, 89–91.

Devonshires at Chatsworth, to the Burlingtons at Londesburgh. They also stayed briefly with Lord Rockingham, at Wentworth Woodhouse in the West Riding.* Garrick revelled in these summer jaunts, but he never relaxed for very long. However much he relished the change of air and scene, the affairs of Drury Lane were seldom far from his mind. 'I shall work this summer like a dragon,' he told Somerset Draper in a letter from Chatsworth. 'I expect to hear from you often, with an account of reports, hints, facts, &c. dashed with your's and Clutterbuck's advice.'

Draper was not only his eyes and ears and man of business; he obviously had the run of Southampton Street, and Garrick seems to have regarded him as general factotum, universal aunt and security guard all rolled into one:

> I have left behind me a box of *Rhubarb Pills*, they are in the closet next to my Study; I wish you would send them, wrapt in paper, with the *Faithful Shepherdess*, you will find among the single plays in the same place . . . . .
> My wife desires her best respects to you and your's, and to Clutterbuck and his; and she begs you will speak to Brother George, to take care the windows of her little India Closet are well barred; for she says, the "*Tieves may sdeal her dings dere*," if they are not taken care of . . . . .[18]

While they were in Yorkshire with the Burlingtons the Garricks celebrated their first wedding anniversary:

> This day, being the *Twenty-second* of June, is wholly devoted, by the whole house here, to mirth and jollity; my Lord and Lady would have it so; the parish bells ring, and the fiddles are ready to strike up . . . . . and although our Noble Friends here make too much of it, much against my consent, yet I never had such reason to rejoice in all my life![19]

July was insufferably hot in 1750. In London, fish died in the Thames—Horace Walpole said that the water in the river was hotter than the springs at Bristol. Garrick, in a gossipy letter to Lord Hartington, told him how obliged Lady Burlington had been to receive a letter from his wife in such weather—'the Hand that wrote it (I hear) melted like a Patt of Butter.' It was hot in the north, too, but that did not protect the wildlife of the Yorkshire wolds from the erratic enthusiasm of Garrick the sportsman:

> I murder a Rabbit now & then, and have been fatal to yᵉ woodpeckers, but from a five Years cessation of Arms, I really cannot distinguish between tame & Wild Pigeons; for unluckily I fir'd among a flock of 'Em Yestrday upon yᵉ Wolds, & incurr'd a penalty of twenty pounds by Act of Parliamᵗ.[20]

The heat did nothing to take the edge off Garrick's appetite, and a good deal of serious eating and drinking went on at Londesburgh:

---

* Thomas Watson-Wentworth, first Marquess of Rockingham. His wife was a cousin of Lady Burlington's. He was succeeded later that year by his son Charles, the future Prime Minister and a close friend of Hartington's.

I have at this present writing such a Mixture of Ale Champaign, florence, claret & Cowslip Wine within Me, that My head may be in my Pocket for any Use I have of it . . . . . My Lord Langdale who had Eaten three plates of Soup, two of Salmon, one of Carp besides ye head, two dozen of Gudgeons, some eels, with Macaroni, Omlett & Raspberry tart, & adding to these, Strawberries & cream, Pineapple, &c &c &c, grew a little sick after ye third Bottle of Burgundy, & I believe had left the Maigre Compound upon ye table he took it from, had not a handsome dram of brandy come to his & Our Relief—[21]

Something which emerges very clearly from Garrick's correspondence is that he did not much like or altogether trust Lacy. He constantly drew Draper and Clutterbuck into discussions of Drury Lane business which might seem purely the concern of himself and his partner. 'If *Bellamy* is disengaged, why are we not to engage her?' he enquired impatiently of Draper. 'We know *Cibber* will not be with us.' Then, sarcastically:

If Lacy's great penetration cannot yet fathom the obscure, inconceivable, and impenetrable designs of our antagonist, by his spies, deep researches, and anonymous letters, why are we not to take things as they *probably* are, and act *justly* for our own preservation? Some folks have a pleasure in raising molehills upon the evenest ground, and strain at gnats, when they swallow camels like poached eggs.

He went on to report that Quin had taken lodgings at Beverly, about seven miles from where he was staying with the Burlingtons, and from there had gone off to Scarborough for a few days: 'By all acounts, he knows nobody there, and was never there before—is not it something odd? Do you understand it?'[22] It was indeed odd. Quin liked his comforts, and generally found them only in London or Bath. But Scarborough was a fashionable spa, and those taking the waters there that summer included Sloper and Mrs Cibber. Could Quin have come north at Rich's behest to inveigle her to Covent Garden for the following season?

By the end of July, Garrick, still at Londesburgh, was pretty clear about how matters stood:

Dear Lacy,

As our season approaches, and we are like to have warm work, you shall have me in council in less than a fortnight.—I have been informed that Barry and Cibber are certainly engaged with Rich, which neither amazes nor intimidates me:—Let them do their worst, we must have the best company, and by a well layed regular plan, we shall be able to make them as uneasy with Rich, as Rich will be with them.—I shall soon be ready in *Romeo*, which we will bring out early; I have altered something in the beginning, and have made him only in love with Juliet.—I believe you'll like it.—If Bellamy agrees with us, she may open with it;—then, if we can get out *King John* before 'em, (as we certainly may) and dress the characters half old English, half modern, as in Edward the Black Prince, we shall cut their combs there too.

His mood was not just confident but downright combative. 'Our company, I think, will pull at the oars with their heads and hearts,' he told Lacy. 'We shall have no false brothers I hope, nor intriguing sisters; and then—*that* for Goliah and the Philistines!'[23]

Bellamy did come on board—Lacy called on her at Richmond and signed her up for three years.* Garrick could still rely on Mrs Clive and Mrs Pritchard, and on the solid support of Woodward and Ned Shuter. At Covent Garden, however, Rich once more commanded a formidable array of talent—Barry and Mrs Cibber, Macklin, Woffington and Quin were all outstanding performers, each with a devoted following in pit and gallery, each, as it happened, motivated by a degree of animus against the 'little tyrant' of Drury Lane.†

Early in August the Garricks bade farewell to their hosts at Londesburgh and boarded a coastal vessel in the Humber for the four-day voyage to London. There, in the two Theatres Royal, the stage was set for what promised to be a contest with few holds barred.

---

* By Bellamy's account, Lacy told her that Mrs Cibber had already been engaged for the forthcoming season at Covent Garden. This clearly meant that Bellamy would be out in the cold there. Would she care to sign up with Drury Lane? It so happened that he had some articles with him . . . Rich arrived some hours later with a rather different account of the state of play, but the deed was done.

† Garrick is thought to have tried to detach Quin from Rich. Quin declined the offer, but used it to extract from the Covent Garden management a salary of £1,000, at that time the largest known to have been paid.

13

The Battle of the Romeos

Garrick opted to open with a bold tug on Macklin's beard and presented his first-night audience with *The Merchant of Venice*.* He also wrote a new prologue for the occasion, in which he glanced good-naturedly at the recent flurry of defections. He acknowledged the strength of the challenge from Covent Garden, but fortifying himself with a line from *Julius Caesar*, he struck a defiant note:

> Strengthen'd by new allies, our foes prepare;
> Cry havock! and let slip the dogs of war.
> To shake our souls, the papers of the day
> Drew forth the adverse pow'r in dread array;
> A pow'r might strike the boldest with dismay.
> Yet fearless still we take the field with spirit,
> Armed *cap-a-pé* in self-sufficient merit . . . . .

Rich was slow to join battle. By the time Macklin appeared in *The Miser* on 24 September, Garrick's ensemble already had seven nights' performances under their belt. Kitty Clive had appeared as Polly in *The Beggar's Opera*, and Garrick and Mrs Pritchard had played together in *The Stratagem*. There had also been two performances of George Lillo's *The London Merchant*.† *Lethe* was played a couple of times as an afterpiece, and engravings of Mrs Clive and Woodward went on sale in the print shops in the characters of the Fine Gentleman and Lady. Garrick was determined not to miss a trick; the Drury Lane public relations machine had moved into top gear.

When it came, Barry's retort to Garrick's prologue was an unconvincing and mean-spirited affair:

---

* Shylock was played by Richard Yates, one of Garrick's work-horses at Drury Lane. Yates, now in his middle forties, was a comic actor of great versatility and wide experience. He was frequently praised as an interpreter of Shakespeare's clowns — Feste, Touchstone, Launce.
† *The London Merchant, or, The History of George Barnwell*, first produced in 1731, was the first tragedy to take everyday commercial life as its theme. Goldsmith mocked it as a 'Tradesman's Tragedy' but it was admired by Pope and Diderot and translated into French, German and Dutch. The story is of an innocent apprentice seduced by a heartless courtesan and encouraged by her to rob his employer and murder his uncle. It was often performed at holidays as a moral warning to apprentices.

> When jealousies and fears possess the throne,
> And kings allow no merit—but their own,
> Can it be strange that men for flight prepare,
> And strive to raise a Colony elsewhere?. . . . .
>
> The Ladies too with every power to charm
> Whose face and fire an anchorite might warm
> Have felt the fury of the Tyrant's arm. . . . . .

Three weeks of phoney war came to an abrupt end on 28 September when both houses unveiled their productions of *Romeo and Juliet*. The 'Battle of the Romeos', the most famous theatrical duel of the century, lasted for twelve successive performances, and by the second week in October, the town was sick and tired of it:

> Well—what tonight, says angry Ned,
> As up from bed he rouses,
> Romeo again! and shakes his head,
> Ah! Pox on both your houses![1]

Garrick, who had directed Barry and Mrs Cibber in the 1748 production of the play, had never previously shown any inclination to play Romeo. He was always very clear about his own limitations, and he must have known that there was an element of risk in testing his drawing power in the role against Barry's; he also had an intensive job of coaching on his hands in equipping the Bellamy for her challenge to Mrs Cibber.

'I shed more tears in seeing Mrs Cibber,' wrote one critic, 'but I am more delighted in seeing Miss Bellamy.' The general view in the coffee-houses was that Mrs Cibber had the edge, even though at thirty-six, she was old enough to be her luscious young rival's mother. Woodward was adjudged a better Mercutio than Macklin, who was thought to be miscast in the role. At Covent Garden Rich, with his penchant for spectacle, had laid out a good deal of money on a funeral procession for Juliet, 'accompanied by a Solemn Dirge, never performed before'. This was set to music by Arne, and Juliet's bier was borne across the stage by servants in Capulet livery carrying live torches, with flower girls strewing blossoms in their path and the clergy got up in medieval garb. Garrick had the weekend to organize his response, and by the third night Drury Lane also had its funeral procession, a less lavish affair than Rich's extravaganza and with music by Boyce.

After six performances, Garrick sent a dispatch from the war-zone to Lady Burlington:

> The Battle between yᵉ Theatres yet remains doubtfull, tho upon my Word I most sincerely & impartially think that we have yᵉ Advantage; Our house to Night was much better than theirs, & I believe 'tis generally thought that our Peformance is best—but this Yʳ Ladᴾ must hear from other People—

He admitted that the strain was beginning to tell: 'My Lady attends Us constantly Every Night & I could wish that I was as little tax'd with Acting, as she with Seeing Us Act.'[2]

For another week the town talked of little else. Playgoers darted from one theatre to the other, sometimes in mid-performance, and the performance of the two principals was hotly debated. The two men were the same age, but the physical advantage undoubtedly lay with Barry: 'The amorous harmony of Mr Barry's features,' wrote Macklin's biographer, Kirkman, 'his melting eyes, and unequalled plaintiveness of voice, and his fine graceful figure gave him a great superiority.'

> So reversed are the notions of Capulet's daughters,
> One loves a whole length, the other three quarters.

The press was awash with squibs and epigrams, many of them about the contrasting stature of the rivals. Some of these were wittier than others, but one of the better ones was widely attributed to Garrick himself—a further interesting example of what might be termed his quasi-homoeopathic approach to criticism or ridicule:

> Fair *Juliet* at one house exclaims with a sigh,
> No *Romeo's* clever that's not six feet high.
> Less ambitiously t'other does *Romeo* adore,
> Though in size he scarce reaches to five feet (and) four.*

Garrick might be a head shorter, but he was a more intelligent man than Barry, and completely the master of the text. 'Though he had imparted his ideas to his antagonists,' wrote Murphy, 'yet such a genius was not exhausted. To strike out new beauties in passages, where the most penetrating critic could not expect them, was his peculiar talent.'[3]

Tate Wilkinson gave it as his opinion that Barry 'was as much superior to Garrick in Romeo, as York Minster is to a Methodist Chapel', but as he was a boy of eleven at the time his opinion does not carry great weight. A more perceptive judgement is that of Francis Gentleman, writing twenty years later in his *Dramatic Censor*. He believed that 'Garrick drew the most applause while Barry drew the most tears'. In his view, Barry had been superior in the balcony scene, in the lovers' early morning parting and in the first part of the tomb scene; Garrick was unsurpassed in Friar Lawrence's cell and in the tomb scene from the point at which the poison begins to operate.[4]

The judgement of the ladies in the audience was much more matter of fact, as the judgement of ladies often is. 'Had I been Juliet to Garrick's Romeo,' said one, 'so ardent and impassioned was he, I should have expected he would have

---

* S.C.F. Hahnemann's system of therapeutics, based on the maxim *similia similibus curentur* ('like should be cured by like') was not introduced until 1796, although some elements of it had been anticipated by Hippocrates and, more especially, by Paracelsus.

come up to me in the balcony; but had I been Juliet to Barry's Romeo,—so tender, so eloquent, and so seductive was he, I should certainly have *gone down* to him.'[5] We also know what Mrs Garrick thought:

> I was at the Play Last Saturday at Coven-Garden, all what I can Say of it is, that M[r] Barry is to jung (in his ha'd) for Romeo, & M[rs] Cibber to old for a girle of 18 . . . . . I wish thie woold finish both, for it is to much for My Little Dear Spouse to Play Every Day.[6]

It was too much for Mrs Cibber, too, and on 11 October she declared that she would play no longer. Mrs Garrick's Little Dear Spouse dashed off an exultant communiqué to Yorkshire:

> I can give Y[r] Lad[p] the Satisfaction, & I flatter myself that it will be so to You, of assuring You that ye battle is at last Ended, & in our favour— our antagonists yielded last thursday Night & we play'd ye Same Play (Romeo & Juliet) on ye Fryday to a very full house to very great applause; Mr Barry & Mrs Cibber came incog to see Us, & I am very well assur'd they receiv'd no little Mortification—Miss Bellamy has surpriz'd Every body, & I hope before Y[r] Lad[p] returns, that she will almost be a Match [for] Madam Cibber, who I believe now begins to repent of leaving Drury Lane—I have written an Epilogue for Clive, which is an Answer to Barry's almost universally Exploded prologue—We have got y[e] Laugh on our Side, & by turning the whole to Joke, We are at present in y[e] highest Spirits—I have receiv'd great favour indeed from y[e] Town in y[e] Character of Romeo; & I am so extreamly well, that no fatigue hurts Me, & I have not once lost my Voice or Powers for thirteen Nights togeather, which is amazing; I need not tell Y[r] Lad[p] that this is all owing to my happiness at Home—[7]

The epilogue he wrote for Kitty Clive was a clever piece of work, ostensibly aimed at bringing the temperature down. She tells of a schoolmaster who has to deal with two boys who have been throwing dirt at each other and to whom he administers a whipping:

> In the same master's place, lo! here I stand,
> And for each culprit hold the lash in hand.
> First for our own—oh, 'tis a pretty youth!
> But out of fifty lies I'll sift some truth.
> 'Tis true, he's of a choleric disposition,
> And fiery parts make up his composition.
> How have I seen him rave when things miscarried!
> Indeed he's grown much tamer since he married. . . . .
> Faults he has many—but I know no crimes;
> Yes, he has one—he contradicts sometimes:
> And when he falls into his frantick fit,
> He blusters so, he makes e'en ME submit.

All very disarming, if a shade narcissistic. Barry, the renegade, comes in for much rougher treatment. The suggestion in his prologue at Covent Garden that Garrick treated his actresses badly had clearly rankled:

> —The other youth comes next,
> Who shews by what he says, poor soul, he's vext.
> He tells you tales how cruelly THIS treats us,
> To make you think the little monster beats us. . . . .
> Should any Manager lift arm at me,
> I have a tyrant arm as well as he!—
> In fact, there has some little bouncing been,
> But who the bouncer was, enquire within. . . . . .

Garrick was determined to rub Barry's nose in it. Mrs Clive delivered the epilogue on no fewer than five occasions, and it was then, for good measure, published in the *General Advertiser*.

Competition between the two patent houses now resumed in a less frenzied key. Garrick appeared as Ranger and Archer and also, for the first time in two years, as Hastings in *Jane Shore*. The part of Alicia in this was attempted by Jane Cibber, a daughter of Theophilus by his first wife, whom Garrick had taken into the company at the beginning of the season. Now a young woman of twenty, she had been absent from the stage for some years, but recently had apparently been receiving some instruction from her grandfather, old Colley. Garrick, writing to Lady Burlington the night before the performance, clearly did not have high hopes of her:

> The Young lady may have Genius for ought I know, but if she has, it is so eclips'd by the Manner of Speaking ye Laureat has taught her, that I am affraid it will not do—We differ greatly in our Notions of Acting (in Tragedy I mean) & If he is right I am, & ever shall be in ye wrong road—[8]

Garrick's hunch was right. On the night, Cross noted in his diary that Miss Cibber had played her part 'quite in the old style, not lik'd at all, tho' not hiss'd— given out again and great hiss'd & so not done'.[9]

Garrick added a new role to his repertoire early in December when he appeared as Osmyn, the hero of Congreve's only tragedy, *The Mourning Bride*, with Mrs Pritchard in the part of the Moorish queen, Zara, and Miss Bellamy as Almeria, the king of Granada's daughter. True love triumphs in the end, although not before the bride's father is decapitated as a result of trying to be too clever and Zara, disappointed in love, ends it all by taking poison. Johnson, in the *Lives of the Poets*, judged the piece to have 'more bustle than sentiment', but singled out one passage for the highest praise: 'If I were required to select from the whole mass of English poetry the most poetical paragraph, I know not what I could prefer to an exclamation in *The Mourning Bride*':

How rev'rend is the face of this tall Pile,
Whose antient Pillars rear their Marble Heads,
To bear aloft its arch'd and pond'rous Roof,
By its own Weight, made stedfast and immoveable,
Looking Tranquillity. It strikes an Awe
And Terror on my aking Sight; the Tombs
And Monumental Caves of Death look cold,
And shoot a Chilness to my trembling Heart. . . . . .*

Almeria's description of the temple is now forgotten. The play is remembered today only because it opens with the line 'Music hath charms to soothe a savage breast',† and for a couplet of Zara's in Act III that is even better known:

Heaven has no rage, like love to hatred turned,
Nor Hell a fury, like a woman scorned.

At Christmas Garrick once again carried the war into the enemy camp. On Boxing Day, as the afterpiece to a production of *The Beggar's Opera*, he presented *Queen Mab*, a new pantomime by Woodward. 'New Music, Dresses, Habits and Decorations,' announced the bills. Garrick never allowed dogma to blind him to the need to pull in an audience. There was no point in having a shrine 'sacred to Shakespeare' unless it attracted appropriately large numbers of worshippers, and the 1750–51 season marked the beginning of a decade of competition with Rich in both dance and pantomime. More dancers were employed (Garrick had twenty-three in his company this season, which was two more than Rich at Covent Garden) and the quality of entr'acte dances was improved.

Queen Mab, with Woodward himself as Harlequin, had a great success, and was played thirty times before the end of January. A cartoon of the day, *The Theatrical Steel-Yards of 1750*, shows Quin, Barry, Cibber and Woffington suspended from hooks on a giant scale. Cibber holds her arms out imploringly to her former stage lover, but he, waving a plumed hat, ignores her, his small figure alone decisively weighing down the heavy end of the scale. On the ground, beneath his dangling principals, lies a dejected Rich, hand on heart and eyes turned heavenwards; under the point of balance, Woodward, dressed as Harlequin, triumphantly holds aloft the doll-like figure of Queen Mab. According to Murphy, Garrick was fond of saying that a good play was the roast beef of Old England, and that 'song and gawdy decorations were the horse-redish round the dish'.

---

* Boswell and Murphy both describe a dinner party at which Garrick, 'all alarmed for "the god of his idolatry"', challenged this view of Johnson's, saying, 'Shakespeare must not suffer from the badness of our memories' and beginning to recite the description of Dover cliff from *Lear*. Johnson was unmoved. (*Murphy*, i, 196–7; *Life*, ii, 82. The dinner, at Boswell's lodgings in Old Bond Street, took place in October 1769. The other guests were Reynolds, Goldsmith, Bickerstaffe and Davies.)

† Or perhaps misremembered. Many people think it is from Shakespeare. In Act V, rather less memorably, poor Almeria has to say, 'Is he then dead?/ What, dead at last, quite, quite for ever dead!'

The Theatrical Steel-Yards of 1750.

Patrick O'Brian Sculp.   Publish'd 27 April 1751.

'The Theatrical Steel-Yards of 1750.' At Christmas that year Garrick challenged
Covent Garden's ascendancy in pantomime with his production of Queen Mab.
This contemporary cartoon shows him effortlessly outweighing the formidable
array of individual talent Rich had at his disposal at the other house. (By
permission of the Folger Shakespeare Library)

With *Queen Mab* he showed that he could serve up condiments every bit as skilfully as Rich.

The first of the season's two new main dishes, *Gil Blas*, was much less well received. Edward Moore, linen draper turned dramatist, found the plot for his comedy of intrigue in Lesage's *Gil Blas de Santillane*—a lady masquerades as a student in order to become acquainted with a young man who has caught her fancy. Garrick had to work hard to keep his friend's piece going for the requisite nine nights. Woodward contributed an ironic and coat-trailing prologue, which he spoke in the character of a critic—possibly the pit found that provocative:

> . . . . . Besides, what men of spirit, now a-days,
> Come to give sober judgements of new plays?
> It argues some good nature to be quiet—
> Good nature!—ay—but then we lose a riot.

It didn't quite come to that, but vociferous parties were formed for and against the piece. By the fourth night there was a good deal of hissing from the pit, and Mrs Pritchard was struck by an apple.

Garrick's second new mainpiece of the season, the masque *Alfred*, was more warmly received. Davies, in describing it, reached for superlatives: 'In decorations of magnificent triumphal arches, dances of furies, various harmony of music and incantations, fine scenes and dresses, this masque exceeded every thing which had before made its appearance on the English stage.'[10] Cross, however, records that on the first night 'some of the Dances, being too long were dislik'd, & some of the Songs had ye same reception',[11] and this is confirmed by a report in the *General Advertiser*:

> The Piece itself, as it justly deserved met with great and universal applause: However, the spectators rightly found fault with some improprieties in the performance of the inferior dancers and actors, which we hear will all be corrected in this night's representation.[12]

The words were by James Thomson and David Mallett, written for their patron the Prince of Wales in 1740 to celebrate the birthday of his daughter Augusta. It had been set to music by Arne, and performed in the gardens of Cliveden.* After Thomson's death in 1748, Mallett revised the masque, and it was this version in which Garrick now appeared.

The run of *Alfred* was interrupted after seven nights for what now seems a rather curious reason. Cross recorded in his diary that at the end of the performance on 5 March, Garrick stepped forward and announced that on the following Thursday, the theatre had been made available to some ladies and gentlemen who were to put on a private play 'for ye Entertainment of some of ye Royal family, & principal people of Distinction'.

---

* 'The players,' writes Davies, 'were not treated as persons ought to be who are employed by a prince,' but he notes two exceptions: 'Quin, I believe, was admitted among those of the higher order; and Mrs Clive might be safely trusted to take care of herself any where.' (*Davies*, ii, 36.)

The play was *Othello*. This elaborate venture in amateur theatricals had been organized by Francis Delaval, a young man of twenty-four who was a close friend of Samuel Foote's.* The Delavals were an old Northumberland family, a wild, spendthrift lot whose estates, ten miles or so from Newcastle, sat profitably on top of extensive coal-workings; earlier in the century Seaton Delaval Hall had been demolished to make way for a mansion designed by Vanbrugh. Francis Delaval, handsome, raffish and severely stage-struck, had hired Drury Lane for the night for £150 and laid out ten times as much again on costumes and sets.

The occasion excited enormous interest. The House of Commons adjourned at three o'clock: 'the streets and avenues were so filled with coaches and chairs,' reported the *Daily Advertiser*, 'that the greatest company of the ladies and gentlemen were obliged to wade through dirt and filth to get to the house which afforded good diversion and benefit for the pickpockets and other gentlemen of that trade.' The Prince and Princess of Wales were present, and so were the Duke of Cumberland, Prince George and the Princesses Amelia and Augusta; even the footmen's gallery glittered with stars and jewels. Cross thought the performance 'very decent'. So did Horace Walpole. 'They really acted so well,' he wrote to Sir Horace Mann, 'that it is astonishing they should not have had sense enough not to act at all.'[13]

It was one of the Prince of Wales's last public appearances. He was at Covent Garden the following week for Mrs Cibber's benefit; two days later he was dead, and all theatrical activity was brought to an abrupt halt. 'My dear first-born,' his mother the Queen had once said, 'is the greatest ass, and the greatest liar, and the greatest *canaille*, and the greatest beast in the whole world, and I heartily wish he was out of it.' He was none of those things, but now, if posthumously, his mother had her wish, and George II's estrangement from his son and heir, the most enduring scandal of his reign, was at an end. The Lord Chamberlain immediately instructed the playhouses 'to forbear acting till further Orders', but the patentees of the Theatre Royal were familiar with the drill—Cross records that the bills had been torn down and the house shut up before the order arrived.

There were areas where the Lord Chamberlain's writ did not run; he had no control over the writers of street ballads:

> Here lies Fred
> Who was alive and is dead.
> Had it been his father,
> I had much rather.
> Had it been his brother,
> Still better than another.

* The friendship had cooled for a time after Foote botched an attempt at marriage broking. The scheme aimed at gaining for Delaval the fortune of a widow twice his age called Lady Isabella Pawlett. The couple were married in March 1750, but it transpired that most of the bride's money was tied up in trusts; Foote had to settle for considerably less than the broker's fee of £12,000 which had been agreed.

> Had it been his sister,
> No one would have missed her.
> Had it been the whole generation
> Still better for the nation.
> But since 'tis only Fred
> Who was alive and is dead,
> There's no more to be said.

Garrick decided that it was a good moment to take his wife off for a short visit to Bath. 'The Moment you have yᵉ least intelligence when we open at yᵉ Playhouse let me know,' he wrote to brother George. 'If we don't begin Easter Monday, I will drink yᵉ waters, for my Stomach is not in yᵉ best Order.'[14]

They stayed in Bath for a week, and Garrick devoted some of his leisure to family matters. George's thoughts (he was now twenty-eight) were turning to matrimony. Unfortunately he had not yet succeeded in being introduced to the young woman who had taken his fancy, and Garrick was concerned lest he should be going before his horse to market:

> I must beseech You to look narrowly into things & be sure of Matters before you Engage—Your Whole depends upon it, & should You be deceiv'd (I only say should you) You will be certainly worse than You are, & Miserable, therefore I say, take Heed . . . . .

He sent George a somewhat flowery draft, aimed at moving matters forward:

> Madam.
>   Tho I have not yᵉ Pleasure of knowing You but by sight, yet from that little Knowledge of You, I have often wish'd for more; I could not help making this Declaration to Mr —— who has most kindly offer'd me his assistance to introduce me to yʳ acquaintance; I am most Sincerely oblig'd to him, but how I can make my Excuses to You, for desiring him to use his Interest for Me, gives me great Perplexity. . . . .[15]

Whether George adopted this less-than-dynamic form of words is not known. At all events his suit prospered; sometime within the next year he was married in the Savoy Chapel to Catherine, the daughter of Nathan Carrington, a King's Messenger. Carrington procured for him the minor sinecure of stable-keeper in the Royal Household, and George and his wife moved into Somerset House, where his father-in-law already had an apartment.

The Lord Chamberlain gave the theatres leave to reopen on 8 April, although they had to close for the Prince's funeral five days later. He was buried in Henry VII's Chapel in Westminster Abbey, 'without either anthem or organ'. His titles of Prince Elector of Brunswick-Lüneberg and Duke of Edinburgh passed to his son George William Frederick; five days after his father's funeral, the future George III, not yet thirteen years old, was also created Prince of Wales and Earl of Chester.

The season was almost over. Garrick had performed major roles on 97 occasions, spoken 15 prologues and appeared in three afterpieces. Staleness and fatigue apart, the closing months were always much less enjoyable for him—for any manager—than the earlier part of the theatrical year. From September to late November the emphasis was generally on established successes with large casts. In December, the audience might expect to see a new play or two or an interesting revival. The first two months of the new year were regarded as the height of the season, usually marked by further innovation and the reprise of the best stock productions the house had in its locker. But March saw the beginning of the benefits, and then, as Garrick once wrote to his brother, 'adieu to all Pleasures of the Theatre'.

The highest paid players naturally got first pick of date and production. By April both companies were well down the benefit pecking order (multiple benefits for several players or house servants were not unusual); choices were narrowing, egos were becoming bruised and displays of temperament were more frequent by the day.

At the end of his fourth season as manager, Garrick could look across at Covent Garden and observe that it was a much less disciplined and much less happy crew than his own. His prediction after Barry and Cibber had jumped ship that they would soon be as uneasy with Rich as he with them had come true. Macklin's nose was out of joint because Rich had effectively handed over responsibility for anything other than pantomime to Quin. Quin was a good task-master, but he no longer wielded the authority that had been his ten years previously, and his lordly manner did not go down well, especially with Barry. The two men were barely civil to each other, and declined to rehearse together; this unsettled and confused more junior players and members of the stage staff, who constantly found one man's decisions about stage business and cues overturned by the other. The clubs and the coffee houses buzzed with accounts of the hostility between them: 'I will tell you one or two bon mots of Quin the actor,' wrote Horace Walpole, prattling on from Arlington Street to Mann in Florence:

> Barry would have had him play the Ghost in Hamlet, a part much beneath the dignity of Quin, who would give no other answer, but, 'I won't catch cold in my z—.' I don't know whether you remember that the Ghost is always ridiculously dressed with a morsel of armour before, and only a black waistcoat and breach behind.[16]

Cibber and Woffington were also at daggers drawn. Cibber was quite often genuinely ill, but Woffington, who had never in her life disappointed her public, didn't believe it for a moment. The bad blood between his two leading ladies appeared to give particular pleasure to Rich, who took to referring to them as his Catherine Hayes and his Sarah Malcolm. (Hayes had been convicted of murdering and dismembering her husband in 1726 and had been burned alive at Tyburn; Malcolm, a charwoman in the Temple, had been hanged for the murder of her employer, an aged widow, and two other servants, and had been painted by Hogarth in the death cell.)

Early in May Mrs Garrick was unwell, and Garrick called in his friend Messenger Monsey. The treatment he prescribed seems to have been highly effective, and from Chiswick, Garrick wrote Monsey a cheerfully earthy note with details of her recovery:

> On Wednesday she intends taking the three pills, as directed, and four of the others, as before, in the morning. They were sufficiently strong for her; and, unless you would have her manure the whole parish, she shall leave the other two for another opportunity. . . . . .
>
> Madam and I are invited to dine with our friends at Windsor, at Mr Naylor's, to-morrow; but we cannot stir from this place till she has done ********; and then we shan't hang an a—e at any invitation whatever. . . . . .
>
> P.S. As this is the day after operation, and Madam can trust her **** with a ****, she sends you one, with her best respects.*

By the middle of the month, Mrs Garrick was quite restored and able to venture further afield. On 20 May, three days before Drury Lane closed for the summer, she and Garrick set out from Southampton Street to visit Paris.

---

* *Letters*, 102. This letter was first published in volume 6 of *The British Stage, and Literary Cabinet* in 1822. 'The place of one or two gross passages, I have been compelled to supply with asterisks,' wrote the editor, Thomas Kenrick. The words in question are presumably 'shitting', 'arse' and 'fart'. To 'hang an arse' is an old slang expression meaning to hold back or hesitate.

14

A Most Agreeable Jaunt

The crossing from Dover took only three and a half hours. Garrick dashed off a note to Somerset Draper to say that they had arrived 'safe, sound, and in spirits'. Mrs Garrick had been slightly seasick, but he himself was 'as hearty as the most stinking tar-barrel of them all'.[1] His good spirits were quickly dissipated by the welcome that awaited them at Boulogne, however, and he made a tetchy entry in the quarto volume he had brought with him as a journal:

> I never saw so much Dirt, Beggary, imposition & Impertinence as I did at Boul^e. The Custom house Oficers (notwithstanding ye freedom of ye Port) were very uncivil & strict; & ye Collector, whom we went before, had our things (tho my wife was wth us) open'd in ye Passage of his House & shew'd not ye least politeness to her or us—[2]

They had with them as a travelling companion Charles Denis, who had studied surgery in Paris for eight or nine years before turning to writing and was, like Garrick, of Huguenot stock.* After some difficulty in finding post horses, they headed for Paris. The roads were good for the most part, the inns very bad—except at Abbeville, where he found 'the People very civil and ye wine very good'. Garrick was struck by how few buildings there were at the roadside, apart from churches and convents—'no Country Seats till we got nearer Paris'. He also noticed that as they got closer to the capital, the behaviour of the post boys deteriorated:

> I made an Observation, that ye nearer we approach'd to Paris, the Post Boys were less religious—all through Picardy, & farther, ye Boys pull'd off their hats to ye crucifixes which are set up at ye ends of all ye Towns & Villages but within forty miles of Paris, they shew'd not ye least regard to 'em, but cock'd up their hats & whistl'd on.

They got to Paris between six and seven in the evening—'did nothing that night but clean ourselves and stare out of ye window of our Hotel d'Estrangers, which

---

* He was the son of a pastor, the Reverend Jacob Denis. His brother Peter, later a vice-admiral, was married to the illegitimate daughter of John James Heidegger, the Swiss impresario who had managed Italian opera at the Haymarket in partnership with Handel for many years.

looks on ye Palais Luxemburgh.' The next night, however, they went to the Comédie-Française to see Molière's *L'Ecole des Maris*. Garrick was unimpressed—'very ill acted'—although it was explained that as there had been the first night of a new tragedy the previous evening they were seeing only players of the second rank:

> The Appearance of ye house was not so bad as I expected from ye report of others, ye glass branches give it a rich look, but ye candles instead of lamps at ye front of ye stage are very mean & ye building on ye stage wholly destroys all *vraysemblance* (as ye french call it).

The next night they were at the Comédie-Italienne and saw a piece by Marivaux—much better acted than the Molière, Garrick thought, although he believed a London audience would have hissed the dancing which accompanied it off the stage.

He was quick to form a view about what he saw as he went about the streets of the French capital:

> The women in general tho very ugly & most disagreeably painted are in general very easy, well shap'd & genteel—they tread much better than our Ladies & their Legs (from their shape & neatness) are more worth seeing than anything else about them—

On the Feast of Corpus Christi they stayed in their hotel all morning to have a view of the procession; Garrick thought it 'regularly conducted' but not so magnificent as the one he had seen as a boy in Lisbon. The English Benedictine Church was not worth seeing, 'tho they shew you King James's head in wax'. They made a very pleasant excursion, on the other hand, to L'Etoile, 'a very pleasant Hill out of Paris & from which are seen many country houses and fine prospect—'

Thirty years or so before the word entered the language, Garrick was an immensely energetic tourist. Notre Dame was the most splendid church he had ever seen, and he was swept off his feet by Nicolas Coustou's Pietà behind the high altar. He admired Saint Sulpice, the tapestries at the Gobelins factory and the King's pictures at the Louvre. From certain expeditions it seemed sensible that Mrs Garrick should be excluded. One morning, for instance, Garrick and Denis set out on foot together to inspect the Hôtel Dieu, the city's oldest hospital: 'only worth seeing for ye numbers of sick & the manner of disposing of 'em,' Garrick noted in his journal; 'otherwise 'tis a most stinking place & very disagreeable.' Later that morning they took in the Bastille, which 'has a horrid appearance, & looks ye thing it is'. Then they moved on to the open charnel house of the Churchyard of the Innocents:

> They make great Holes in the Churchyard of *les Innocens* & don't fill it up, till it is full of Coffins & Bodies—I look'd into one, & there was a man sew'd up in a coarse sacking, but one of his feet was out; when ye hole is full, they throw lime upon 'em wch consumes ye flesh soon, & when

they open that again, they take out yᵉ Bones & Pile 'em up, on one side
of yᵉ Church Yard.

One evening they drove out to Versailles. Garrick was impressed by the view
from the terrace down to the lake, but found the palace itself inelegant: 'The
Waterworks to be sure are in general better than any where, but there is no
Cascade so large as that at Chatsworth, nor any Jet d'Eau that equals that I have
seen there.' In the evening they caught a glimpse of the King, returning from
hunting at Crécy—'we saw him enter his palace, with great haste & a very dirty
dusty retinue.'

They returned to Paris for a further round of theatre-going. In a performance
of Thomas Corneille's *Ariane*, Garrick had his first sight of La Clairon, then in
her late twenties.* He admired what he saw, but not unreservedly: 'Claron has
powers but outrée in the Parts of her Character where she might be less violent
& tame in yᵉ places of yᵉ highest & finest passages.' He strongly disapproved of
the manners of the audience, however:

> Notwithstanding all yᵉ Reports we have had of yᵉ great decency
> and politeness of a French Audience yet in yᵉ middle of yᵉ strongest
> and best scenes of Arianne, they laugh'd at a messenger who brought
> news of Theseus, because he happened to be one who acted in comedy—
> this was repeated at 3 diferent times in yᵉ same play for nothing at
> all—

Marie Dumesnil, whose reputation had drawn Peg Woffington to Paris, also
came under critical scrutiny, and was rated less highly: 'Dumisnil has a face that
expresses terror & Despair but she has many faults, too violent at times, very
unequal & in yᵉ whole does not seem to me so good as actress as Clarron.'
Dumesnil, born Marie-Françoise Marchand, had been established at the Comédie-
Française since 1737; before the inevitable rivalry sprang up between them, she
had extended generous protection to Clairon, who was ten or twelve years her
junior. As Cleopatra in Corneille's *Rodogune*, she is said to have roused such
feelings of terror that those in the pit recoiled before her.† Voltaire said that
when she created the title role in his *Mérope* in 1743, she kept the audience in
tears for three successive acts. It was also in *Mérope* that she created a sensation
by daring to *run* across the stage.

Garrick sat to the Swiss painter Jean-Etienne Liotard while he was in Paris.
Liotard had been court painter to the Emperor Francis I at Vienna and had
painted portraits of the Pope and many cardinals. He was known as 'le peintre
turc' because during a stay in Constantinople he had let his beard grow and

---

* Clairon's full name was Claire-Hippolyte-Josephe Legris de Latude. She was born at Condé-
sur-l'Escaut, near Valenciennes, in 1723, the illegitimate daughter of an army sergeant. She
made her first stage appearance at the Comédie-Italienne at the age of thirteen. For her début
at the Comédie-Française at the age of twenty she had boldly chosen the title role in Racine's
Phèdre.
† There were no seats in the pit at that time in the French theatre.

taken to wearing Turkish dress.* Garrick also spent some time looking at pictures. He admired the Rubens gallery in the Palais Luxembourg, 'notwithstanding most of yᵉ Pictures are very much damag'd'. In general, however, he felt there were better things to see at home: 'No hotel has so good a Collection of Pictures as there is at Chiswick, in general Rubbish to 'em.'

Garrick was already by this time an eager book collector, and during his stay he bought Voltaire's works in eleven volumes and Rousseau's *Letters* in five. He also found time to polish up his dancing, enrolling with a Signor Frederick for a course of twelve lessons at a cost of two guineas.

There are no entries in Garrick's diary after 2 July, but the journal of the dramatist and song-writer Charles Collé indicates that he was still there ten days later—and airing his opinions of the French theatre with some freedom:

> He gave us a sketch of that scene where Macbeth thinks he sees a dagger in the air, leading him to the room where he is to murder the king. He filled us with terror . . . . . His face expresses all the passions one after the other, and that without any grimace, although that scene is full of terrible and tumultuous movements. What he played before us was a kind of tragic pantomime, and from that one piece I would not fear to assert that that actor is excellent in his art. As to ours, he considers them all bad, from the highest to the lowest, and on that point we fully agreed with him.†

By the end of July Garrick was back in London. 'I am return'd with my better half, safe & sound from Paris & as true an Englishman as Ever,' he wrote in a cheerful letter to John Hoadly:

> I am much, very much pleas'd with my Jaunt, & am ready & willing to take yᵉ Same & for a Month longer, whenever Business will permit & I am call'd upon—I am sorry that son of a Bitch yᵉ Gout, likes the tenement so well, that there's no routing him from thy Plump Body; the Bugs in France would be glad to see thee there, & many a delicious Meal they would make of thee . . . !³

To Peter, too, he enthused about France. 'It is the best place in the world to make a Visit to,' he wrote:

> I had much honour done Me both by French & English, & every body & thing contributed to make me happy—The great fault of our Countrymen is, yᵗ when they go to Paris, they keep too much among themselves; but if they would mix wᵗʰ yᵉ French as I did, it is a most agreeable Jaunt—

---

* The present whereabouts of this painting are unknown, although there is a copy at Drury Lane. A pastel by Liotard done at the same time is in the collection of the Duke of Devonshire at Chatsworth.
† Charles Collé (1709–83) was the son of a Paris notary. Many of his bright, usually licentious, comedies were originally written for the private theatre of the duc d'Orléans, who was an enthusiastic amateur actor, especially of low-life parts.

Intriguing evidence exists in the French archives to suggest that during his stay in Paris Garrick may in fact have mixed with the French rather more than was prudent—that he may, indeed, wittingly or unwittingly, have committed a criminal offence and left the country in some haste to avoid arrest.

Apart from the keen interest he took in all aspects of theatrical performance, there is no indication in his Paris journal that he had gone there with the intention of combining pleasure with business. It seems, however, although there is no mention of him in the diary, that Garrick's Drury Lane ballet-master, the French dancer Charles Leviez, was in Paris at the same time, and on 4 June Garrick made the briefest of references in his diary to another French dancer who was well known to him—'Saw Dévisse.' Dévisse, a leading dancer at the Paris Opera, had made his début at Drury Lane in November 1750, and was received 'with general Applause'. He danced in the masque *Alfred*, and made numerous appearances during the season before returning to Paris some time after his benefit the following April.

In the early years of this century, an English scholar called Frank Hedgcock decided that Garrick's relations with France and the French had not been adequately treated by his English biographers, and that this would make a suitable subject for the Doctorat-ès-Lettres thesis which he proposed to present to the University of Paris. As he burrowed away in the French archives, he came upon a letter dated 1 July 1751 and addressed to the Lieutenant-General of Police, Nicolas-René Berryer:*

> On what you were good enough to acquaint me with, as to the design which brought to this place Messrs. Garrick and Lévié, I have had them sought for but have not succeeded in discovering them.

The writer of the letter was Louis-Basile de Bernage, the *prévôt des marchands de Paris*. The provost of the Paris merchants was the chief magistrate of the municipality and entitled to stick his nose into matters concerning dancers because from 1749 to 1780, the Opera was a municipal responsibility. 'I know without any doubt that one of our dancers named Devisse, who left furtively in the month of August last year and passed into England, is at present in Paris,' he continued:

> I have reason to believe that the object of his voyage, about which he addressed certain entreaties to me, alleging business affairs, is to help forward, by his special knowledge, the steps that Messrs. Garrick and Levié may take to entice some of our actors and actresses and to carry them off with them . . . . .

Bernage expressed the hope that Berryer would respond to this 'infringement of the regulations and orders of the king' by having Dévisse arrested and sent to Fort l'Evêque.†

---

* Nicolas-René Berryer de Ravenoville (1703–62) had held his police post since 1748. He was later Minister of Marine.

† This was a prison for lesser crimes and misdemeanours such as debt, poaching and military indiscipline: French theatre folk, whose status was much worse than that of their English confrères, quite often found themselves doing time there for 'inobservance of the king's regulations' or for 'want of respect to the public'.

'After the peace,' the Duke de Choiseul would write in his Memoirs—he meant the Peace of Aix-la-Chapelle—'the only concern in France was with court intrigues. That is natural enough in every court wherein a weak king has a mistress and ambitious ministers.'[4] Bernage knew that Berryer was a protégé of the King's mistress, Madame de Pompadour; what more natural then, than that he should casually drop into his letter a reminder that he too had friends in high places:

The duc de Gesvres, to whom I have reported this, is of my opinion; and M. d'Argenson will approve your action. The example is absolutely necessary; first to keep our actors and actresses within bounds and to assure that the public service be properly carried out; secondly, to forestall M. Devisse's evil intentions and the operations of these foreigners.[5]

The decadent duc de Gesvres* was the Governor of Paris; the comte d'Argenson,† although still Minister of War, had also for the past two years had ministerial responsibility for the administration of the capital. Berryer saw no reason to disagree with de Bernage's suggestion and a warrant was issued for Dévisse's arrest, although he was not apprehended until the end of September.

Little more is known of this obscure episode. The Garricks took four and a half days to reach London,‡ which was no shorter than the outward journey— no evidence there of anxious glances over the shoulder and post horses being whipped into a lather. If Dévisse was committed to Fort l'Evêque he did not stay there long, because by the autumn of the following year he was once more in London (he danced at Drury Lane for the following two seasons). It is entirely possible that Garrick had been contemplating employing more dancers as a means of countering the brilliant spectacles he knew Rich was capable of mounting at Covent Garden; whether he had been using Leviez as a discreet recruiting sergeant in Paris during that summer of 1751 cannot now be established. What de Bernage described as 'les mauvaises intentions du Sr Devisse et les manoevres de ces étrangers' may in reality have owed more to conspiracy theory and xenophobia than to anything else.

Garrick's original plan for the rest of the summer had been to visit Lichfield before joining the Burlingtons in Yorkshire, but he was obliged to tell Peter that this had not been well received:

When we came to hint it to ye Family here, We had grave faces & cool

---

* François-Joachim-Bernard Potier (1692–1757); the Duke did not allow his civic duties to get in the way of the profits he made from a gambling saloon.
† Marc-Pierre de Voyer de Paulmy (1696–1764), comte d'Argenson. His elder brother, the marquis d'Argenson, had been Foreign Minister from 1744 to 1747; their father was for twenty-one years Louis XIV's Lieutenant-General of Police. The superintendence of Paris had previously been part of the multiple portfolio of the comte de Maurepas, disgraced in 1749 for being witty at the expense of Madame de Pompadour. D'Argenson played a prominent part in the intrigue which brought him down.
‡ We know this from a letter Garrick wrote on his return to Jean-Baptiste Sauvé, an actor and dramatist who was a member of the Comédie-Française. (Letters, 107.)

Answers; so that we have thought it wisest and best (knowing that we can Make freer with You than greater folks) to defer our Expedition into Staffordshire . . . . . We are at Chiswick at present & Expect Every Moment an Order for Yorkshire, which tho a little too late in ye Year for my affairs, must be comply'd with—[6]

He travelled to Londesburgh early in August. As always he poured out a stream of gossipy letters to his friends—in one he told Lady Hartington that he had written three dozen in the space of a fortnight.* When he wrote to Somerset Draper, the gossip was laced with weightier matters:

I am working and studying here like a horse.—I intend playing *Coriolanus* and the *Rehearsal*, alternately—*All's Well*, &c and *Merope*, in the same manner: and then I shall present you with *Don John* and *So[s]ia*, into the bargain; besides new plays without number. But *mum*! do not even tell this to that deepest of all politicians, *James Lacy*, Esq.

His relations with Lacy were clearly scratchy, and he does not seem to have found it easy to deal with his co-manager with any great degree of directness. 'Have you seen the *Great Lacy* lately?' he had enquired of Draper earlier in the same letter:

I wish, when you have that pleasure, that you would hint your great surprise and dislike to *Maddox's* rope-dancing upon our stage. I cannot possibly agree to such a prostitution upon any account; and nothing but downright starving would induce me to bring such defilement and abomination into the *house of William Shakespeare*. What a mean, mistaken creature is this Par[tn]er of mine!

Has George told you that he has signed a memorandum with *Maddox* for double the sum he told us that he had engaged him for?—What can be the meaning of this?—Oh, I am *sick, sick, sick of him*!

Sick of him or not, Garrick was soon back in double harness. Drury Lane opened on 7 September with *The Beggar's Opera* and *The Lying Valet*, and Garrick himself made his first appearance of the season as Hamlet eleven days later. Not all the plans he had sketched to Draper in the summer came to immediate fruition. *Coriolanus* was not produced at Drury Lane until 1754, and Garrick did not in the event appear in it; it would also be three years before he first played Don John in the Duke of Buckingham's alteration of *The Chances*, by Beaumont and Fletcher. Dryden's *Amphitryon, or The Two Sosias*, had to wait even longer and, when it was finally revived towards the end of 1756, the part of Sosia went to Woodward.

---

* *Letters*, 111. Letter dated 25 August. He was remarkably well informed about all manner of things — the gossip was by no means confined to what was going on in Yorkshire. 'I had forgot to inform You in my last,' he told Lady Hartington in the same letter, 'that your Poet Laureat Mr Bronsdon was taken up for robbing ye Western Mail, & was in some Jail from Thursday to Saturday—' This suggests that the Burlingtons kept themselves supplied with the London papers. There was a news item about Bronsdon in the *London Daily Advertiser* of 16 August.

His fears about the house of Shakespeare being sullied by the antics of a slack-wire dancer were not realized; Anthony Maddox, who had won sudden popularity at Sadler's Wells earlier in the year, would not get his chance at one of the patent theatres until Rich took him on the following year. What was it exactly that Garrick was so high-mindedly determined to deny his Drury Lane patrons? One of Maddox's routines was the subject of an engraving in the *New Universal Magazine* in the spring of 1753; a central portrait was surrounded by twelve smaller, numbered figures:

At No. 1. He tosses 6 balls with such dexterity, that he catches them all alternately, without letting one of 'em drop to the ground, and that with surprising activity.

2. He ballanceth his hat upon his chin.

3. He ballanceth a sword with its point on the edge of a wine-glass.

4. He at the same time plays a violin.

5. He lies extended on his back up-on a small wire.

6. He ballanceth a coach-wheel upon his chin.

7. He standeth upon his head upon the wire.

8. He ballanceth a chair on his chin.

9. He ballanceth seven pipes, one in another: And

10. Blows a trumpet on the wire.

11. Ballanceth several wine-glasses full, on the wire.

12. Ballanceth two pipes across a hoop, on the wire.

13. Tosseth a straw from his foot to his nose.

Garrick had recruited some fresh blood for the new season—three young actors who had been making a name for themselves in Ireland. The first of them was thrown in at the deep end as Young Bevil in Steele's *The Conscious Lovers*, supported by Woodward, Mrs Pritchard and Kitty Clive, and he acquitted himself well: 'Person engaging; voice musical; countenance expressive; judgment correct in general, but he lacks a certain easiness of carriage and gracefulness of deportment.'[7] David Ross was a young man of twenty-three, and although he had served his apprenticeship at Smock Alley, he was the son of a Scottish lawyer and had been born in London and educated at Westminster. Tom Davies thought that his young fellow-countryman had raised the tone of the proceedings:

He was approved by a polite and distinguished audience, who seemed to congratulate themselves in seeing an actor whom they imagined capable of restoring to the stage the long-lost character of the real fine gentleman.*

---

* *Davies*, i, 195. The fact that Ross was still acting when Davies published his life of Garrick was something of an inhibition. 'Mr Ross is still living,' he wrote circumspectly, 'and it will look uncandid and invidious to take notice of his defects, which are evidently owing to his great love of ease, and his fondness for social pleasure.'

Cross's diary indicates that the following night, behind the scenes, the tone was less elevated: 'A Quarrel in yᵉ Green room between old Cibber & Mrs Clive occasioned by his saying, the stage wanted a handsome Woman, &c.'

Garrick's second new recruit, John Dexter, had been at Trinity College, Dublin, but had no stage experience. Allowing him to make his début in the title role of *Oroonoko* was clearly something of a gamble, particularly as his voice was rather weak and thin, but he was received with great enthusiasm: 'Mr Dexter has given us in the character of Oroonoko the greatest first essay that perhaps any stage has produced,' wrote the critic in the *Daily Advertiser*. He was also, for a novice, extraordinarily relaxed:

> This gentleman was so far master of himself, that he continued in conver-
> sation with his friends in the pit, on the first night of his performing, till
> the second music, which is generally played about half an hour before the
> curtain is drawn up, put him in mind that it was time to think of the stage
> apparatus.⁸

Dexter's early promise was not sustained, however. Garrick tried him in both comedy and tragedy, but after two seasons his contract was not renewed and he returned to Dublin.

The third of Garrick's débutants in the season of 1751–2 was Henry Mossop. The son of a clergyman, Mossop had been born in Dublin in 1729 and he too had originally been intended for the church. Garrick had turned him down on an earlier occasion, as had Rich, but Thomas Sheridan had taken him on at Smock Alley. He was thought by some to have modelled himself too closely on Quin, but he enjoyed some success during two Dublin seasons and for his Drury Lane début Garrick allowed him to attempt Richard III. 'He was receiv'd with great Applause but happening to crack towards the end a few hiss'd, but were overpower'd by the Claps,' noted the ever-watchful Cross.⁹ He was an awkward actor; Davies speaks of the 'untowardness of his deportment' and describes him as 'rather a powerful speaker rather than a pleasing actor'. Mossop was also totally without a sense of humour: in Carola Oman's happy phrase, 'he never pretended to be anything but a great tragic actor'. The audience did not always take him as seriously as he took himself. He often adopted a pose with one hand on his hip and the other arm extended, and he quickly became known as 'the teapot actor'.

The first new offering of the season was a well-received musical masque called *The Shepherd's Lottery*, with words by Moses Mendez and music by Boyce. This was presented as an afterpiece to *The Revenge* on 19 November. Ten days later came the most important and most ambitious event of the season—a revival of Ben Jonson's *Every Man in His Humour*.

Garrick had been working at it with his usual thoroughness over many months. His sense of what his audience would take told him that it would not be easy to gain acceptance for a comedy of humours in which the plot was of the sketchiest, the love interest nil and much of the wit distinctly earthy. There was some hissing on the first night, but there were fifteen further performances that season and the piece was quickly firmly re-established in the repertoire. Kitely, the jealous merchant, became one of Garrick's most popular roles. He only once gave it up to another actor, and between 1751 and his retirement twenty-four years later he performed it in all but three seasons.

Garrick cut the text substantially—his version is more than 700 lines shorter than Jonson's. He reduced the number of scenes from thirty-three to sixteen and extensively rewrote Act IV, largely to point up Kitely's jealousy. He removed puns that would no longer be intelligible 150 years after they were first perpetrated, and references to events of contemporary interest—an allusion to Drake's ship at Deptford, for example. He cleaned up the language slightly—the odd mention of dung disappears, as does a line about someone not being able to hold his water at the reading of a ballad—but on the whole he made few concessions to eighteenth-century susceptibilities.

Garrick devoted equally close attention to the casting of the piece, and Davies, in his *Dramatic Miscellanies*, gives an interesting insight into how he prepared the company for this particular production in the green-room:

> As no man more perfectly knew the various characters of the drama than himself, his reading a new or revived piece was a matter of instruction, as well as entertainment, to the players. He generally seasoned the dry part of the lecture with acute remarks, shrewd application to the company present, or some gay jokes . . . . . As he took infinite pains to inform, he expected an implicit submission to his instructions. A compliance, after all, which could not be expected from men of great professional abilities, such as Yates and Woodward. All that can be expected from genius is, to take the out-line and observe a few hints towards the colouring of a character; the heightening, or finishing, must be left to the performer.

Davies here seems to corroborate the traditional view of Garrick as something of a martinet in the green-room, but he continues with an anecdote which calls for that view to be modified:

> During the greatest part of the rehearsals of Every Man in his Humour, Woodward seemed very attentive to Garrick's idea of Bobadil. But, in his absence one morning, he indulged hiself in the exhibition of his own intended manner of representation. While the actors were laughing and applauding Woodward, Garrick entered the playhouse, and, unperceived, attended to the transaction of the scene. After waiting sometime, he stept on the stage, and cried, "Bravo, Harry! bravo! upon my soul, bravo!— Why, now this is—no, no, I can't say this is quite my idea of the thing— Yours is, after all—to be sure, rather—ha!"—Woodward perceiving the manager a little embarrassed, with much seeming modesty, said, "Sir, I will act the part, if you desire it, exactly according to your notion of it."— "No, no! by no means, Harry. D—n it, you have actually clenched the matter.—But why, my dear Harry, would you not communicate before."[10]

*

Over at Covent Garden, things went forward much less smoothly. Rich had the larger company this year, but it had been seriously weakened by the departure of Quin and Peg Woffington. Quin was now close to sixty. The death in the spring of his old patron the Prince of Wales had been a blow to him, and he had decided that the time had come to retire to Bath for good.* Woffington, for her part, seems simply to have had enough of Covent Garden and of London and to have set off impulsively for Dublin, although she had no offer of employment there.†

Rich leant increasingly heavily on Barry not only as chief player, but as his lieutenant in charge of tragedy. This was a mistake. Barry's gifts as an actor and his agreeable social qualities—he was a generous host and told an Irish story very engagingly—were not accompanied by any degree of administrative or technical aptitude for theatre matters. Rehearsals bored him. He professed, as lazy people often do, to be a firm believer in spontaneity and improvisation, and this often meant his productions were under-prepared and that things went wrong on the night.

Later in the season, Barry's insouciant ways got him even deeper into the mire. On Mrs Cibber's benefit night, in the middle of March, she had chosen to appear for the first time as Lady Macbeth. Barry was Macbeth, and Lacy Ryan appeared as Macduff. Barry was celebrated for his swashbuckling style of fencing, and many a female heart beat more quickly as he cavorted about the stage, lunging and parrying. Unlike Garrick, however, who would always meticulously choreograph every move in any sequence of swordplay, Barry was inclined to leave a good deal to the inspiration of the moment, and on the night of 17 March, the final confrontation between Macbeth and Macduff went horribly wrong:

> Those heroic full-bottomed perukes, whose bushy expanse is spread over the whole back of the wearer, have lately been exploded on the stage, and a more natural, I mean a less enormous covering for the head substituted in its stead. Unfortunately Mr Barry chose this night to appear in one of the most curiously frizzled out and of the fullest tragical flow I ever saw: When in the last act it was our heroes turn to be kill'd, honest Ryan being eager to dispatch him, just as he was to plump down upon the carpet, entangled his hand in the vast profusion of Macbeth's hair; and by jerking back his sword after the concluding stab, away came poor periwig along with it, while our hero was left expos'd, in the last agonies of death— bare headed. Ryan in the meanwhile with some confusion contemplated Full-Bottom, which he held dangling in his hand, but sadly tumbled out

---

* He returned twice to play Falstaff for his friend Ryan's benefit, but then he felt able to come no more. 'It seems the Loss of his Teeth has in some Measure disabled him,' reported the *Grays Inn Journal* on 23 February 1754. ' "By God (says he) I will not whistle *Falstaff* for any Body." '
† Thomas Sheridan soon signed her up at Smock Alley with a guarantee of £400 for the season and two clear benefits.

Woodward as Bobadil. Woodward was taught acting and dancing by John Rich and became one of the most versatile and accomplished comic actors of the century. 'In Woodward's gestures, speech, and face,' declared the London Evening Post *in 1752, 'Rare Ben's own Bobadil we trace.' (*Bell's British Theatre, Vol. 2, *1780)*

of curl; at length he good naturedly adjusted it on the bald pate of the tyrant, who was then enabled to make his dying speech with proper regularity and decorum.*

A week before Christmas, the bills for a performance of *The Revenge*, with *Lethe* as the afterpiece, carried a reminder that fortune was as fickle in the theatre as elsewhere. The evening was for the benefit of Norton Amber, the former banker who only seven years previously, with his partner Richard Green, had advanced money to Lacy for the purchase of the Drury Lane patent from Fleetwood. Soon afterwards he had fallen on hard times; the theatre of which he had once been part-owner now employed him as pit-doorkeeper. Receipts for the night came to £252; Amber cleared about £160, and inserted a note in the *General Advertiser* thanking his friends for 'their generous appearance'.

London had for some time been deprived of the stimulating company of Samuel Foote, who had been living in Paris. There was a rumour that he had been killed in a duel there; he was also reported to have died of drink or to have been hanged. These all proved to be exaggerated. He had bobbed up in London again in the autumn of 1751, and Garrick now put on a new farce by him, called *Taste*. 'It was relished by the boxes only,' wrote Murphy,[11] but it seems likely that some of those sitting there would have been distinctly unamused, because the piece ridiculed rich collectors who paid inflated prices for mutilated pieces of sculpture and old masters of doubtful authenticity and had some shrewd thrusts at the auctioneers and dealers who fed on their ignorance. Garrick wrote and performed an agreeably sly prologue:

> Before this Court I *Peter Puff* appear,
> A Briton born, and bred an Auctioneer . . . . .
> 'Tis said this night a certain wag intends
> To laugh at us, our calling, and our friends:
> If lords and ladies, and such dainty folks,
> Are cur'd of auction-hunting by his jokes;
> Should this odd doctrine spread throughout the land,
> *Before you buy, be sure to understand,*
> Oh think on us what various ills will flow,
> When great ones only purchase—what they know . . . . .
> 'Tis said Virtû to such a height is grown,
> All artists are encourag'd—but our own.
> Be not deceiv'd, I here declare on oath,
> I never yet sold goods of *foreign* growth:
> Ne'er sent commissions out to Greece or Rome;
> My best antiquities are made at home.

---

* *Have at you all; or, the Drury Lane Journal*, 19 March 1752. The fiasco was doubly galling for Mrs Cibber. It was not only her first attempt at one of Shakespeare's 'virago' roles. The afterpiece that evening was *The Oracle*, a pastoral allegory by St Foix which she had seen on a recent visit to Paris, and which she had herself translated and adapted.

> I've Romans, Greeks, Italians near at hand,
> True Britons all—and living in the Strand . . . . .*

Taste was not a great success, but for a few nights at least it made a modest contribution to the gaiety of the town.

It is possible that it was during this winter that Hogarth began work on the elegant double portrait of Garrick and his wife now in the royal collection— Garrick sits at his escritoire, and the half-completed page before him is the prologue of *Taste*. His wife stands behind his chair, reaching out over his head to take his quill, teasingly intent on disturbing him. Hogarth, as he so often did, agonized over the composition, and made many adjustments to it; the picture seems not to have been completed for several years. The extreme mobility of Garrick's features made him a difficult subject. According to George Steevens,† Garrick expressed dislike of the expression Hogarth had caught; or perhaps he simply did not like being portrayed with a double chin. Steevens said that Hogarth became offended, blacked out the face and took the picture away. Certainly, it was still in his studio when he died.‡

The last new play to be offered at Drury Lane in the 1751–2 season was a tragedy called *Eugenia*. This was the work of the Reverend Philip Francis, a son of the Dean of Lismore and a member of that sizeable band of stage-struck clergy who bombarded eighteenth-century theatre managers with their dramatic outpourings. His parishioners at Skeyton in Norfolk did not see a great deal of him. Nor did the pupils at the small private academy which he was notionally conducting in Surrey, where he had briefly in his charge there at that time a sickly, red-haired youth of fourteen called Edward Gibbon. 'The experience of a few weeks was sufficient to discover that Mr Francis's spirit was too lively for his profession,' he later recorded: 'and while he indulged himself in the pleasures of London, his pupils were left idle at Esher in the custody of a Dutch Usher, of low manners and contemptible learning. From such careless or unworthy hands I was indignantly rescued.'§

Eugenia was pretty poor stuff. It is not clear why Garrick decided to write a prologue for it and take the leading part of Mercour—there is no evidence that he was leant on, and in 1752 Francis does not seem to have enjoyed the protection of a patron.¶ Although it was presented as a tragedy, it was based on a French

---

* *Taste* was published later in the month. Foote dedicated it to Francis Delaval.

† Steevens (1736–1800) is best known for his Shakespearean commentaries (for which Garrick lent him many quarto editions from his library), but he also assembled at his house in Hampstead a fine collection of Hogarth engravings.

‡ Mrs Hogarth then made a present of it to Garrick. After Mrs Garrick's death in 1822, it was bought at Christie's for £75 11s by Edward Locker, the commissioner of Greenwich Hospital. It was subsequently acquired by George IV, and now forms part of the royal collection at Windsor.

§ Gibbon, Edward, *Memoirs of My Life*, ed. Georges A. Bonnard, London, 1966, pp. 40–41. Gibbon had previously been briefly at Westminster. After removing him from the Francis establishment his father entered him in April 1752 at Magdalen College, Oxford.

¶ He was, however, shortly afterwards recommended to Henry Fox, and became Lady Caroline's private chaplain. He taught Charles James Fox to read, and accompanied him when he went to Eton in 1757.

comedy called *Cenie*, the work of a lady author called Madame de Graffigny.*
There was a good deal of noise before the curtain went up on the first night;
some candles were thrown, and Garrick had to go on to restore order. Things
were no better the second night: 'Went off very dull,' noted Cross, '& great
hissing &c. when over.' The author got his benefit, but after six performances,
Eugenia sank without trace. Francis found a publisher for his text, and penned
some effusive words in his preface: 'Mr Garrick is intitled to my sincerest
Gratitude for his Performance as an Actor, and for his Punctuality as a Manager
. . . his strong good Sense, with that Spirit of Theatrical Criticism, which is his
peculiar natural Genius.'

Garrick could never have too much praise and flattery, but it so happened
that in those early months of 1752 he stood in need of as much as he could get
of both. Two days before *Eugenia* began its run, he had been subjected to an
extraordinary outpouring of bile from what must have been a totally unexpected
quarter. For the past two years, partly as a relief from his work on the *Dictionary*,
partly because he needed the money, Samuel Johnson had been writing a series
of twice-weekly periodical essays which he called *The Rambler*.

Number 200 in the series resembled an exchange between the agony aunt in a
modern newspaper and one of her disgruntled correspondents. The correspondent
was called Asper, and Johnson has him describe the miseries he has endured
during a recent morning visit to his friend Prospero—'a man lately raised to
wealth by a lucky project, and too much intoxicated by sudden elevation, or too
little polished by thought and conversation, to enjoy his present fortune with
elegance and decency.' It is a highly entertaining piece of writing, but a remarkably
bitter one, and most of Johnson's readers would have immediately understood
that Asper's friend lived in a rather fine house in Southampton Street:

> When I told my name at the door, the footman went to see if his master
> was at home, and, by the tardiness of his return, gave me reason to suspect
> that time was taken to deliberate. He then informed me, that Prospero
> desired my company, and shewed the staircase carefully secured by mats
> from the pollution of my feet. The best apartments were ostentatiously set
> open, that I might have a distant view of the magnificence which I was not
> permitted to approach; and my old friend receiving me with all the insolence
> of condescension at the top of the stairs, conducted me to a back room,
> where he told me he always breakfasted when he had not great company.

Prospero then orders his servant to draw back the cloth covering the carpet, so
that his visitor may admire the brightness of the colours and the elegance of the
texture: 'I did not gratify his folly with any outcries of admiration, but coldly
bade the footman let down the cloth.' But there is worse to come:

> Breakfast was at last set, and as I was not willing to indulge the peevishness
> that began to seize me, I commended the tea; Prospero then told me, that

---

* Françoise de Graffigny (1695–1758) was born at Nancy. She was a friend of Voltaire's.

another time I should taste his finest sort, but that he had only a very small quantity remaining, and reserved it for those whom he thought himself obliged to treat with particular respect.

While we were conversing upon such subjects as imagination happened to suggest, he frequently digressed into directions to the servant that waited, or made a slight inquiry after the jeweller or silversmith; and once, as I was pursuing an argument with some degree of earnestness, he started from his posture of attention, and ordered, that if lord Lofty called on him that morning, he should be shown into the best parlour.

This is all very funny, but it is also very painful. Prospero/Garrick now produces some pieces of fine Dresden china to be admired. Asper/Johnson resolves at first that he will pay no attention to them, but curiosity quickly gets the better of him:

When I had examined them a little, Prospero desired me to set them down, for they who were accustomed only to common dishes, seldom handled china with much care. You will, I hope, commend my philosophy, when I tell you that I did not dash his baubles to the ground . . . . .

The piece concludes with The Rambler, in his agony-aunt role, trying to smooth Asper's ruffled feathers and help him to set the matter in perspective:

Though I am not wholly insensible of the provocations which my correspondent has received, I cannot altogether commend the keenness of his resentment, nor encourage him to persist in his resolution of breaking off all commerce with his old acquaintance. One of the golden precepts of Pythagoras directs, that *a friend should not be hated for little faults* . . . . . Such improprieties often proceed rather from stupidity than malice.[12]

Less than two years after exerting himself so strenuously on Johnson's behalf over *Irene*, Garrick had some reason to feel himself ill-used.

He had more congenial company in Southampton Street in the early spring when his brother Peter and his unmarried sister, Lenny, came on a visit from Lichfield.* They brought him a cask of Lichfield ale: 'must I bottle off ye Ale when it is fine,' he asked Peter, 'or what must I do with it besides making myself & friends merry?'[13] Garrick remained very close to his family, concerned for their welfare, solicitous for their health. 'I am sorry to hear Sister Linney is so bad,' he wrote to Peter during the summer:

I have consulted many of my Physical friends about her; have told 'Em of ye Redness of her face, & that we believe her case to be scorbutic—they think Scarborough would do well—but they think Cheltenham as well, & in some Cases better—& they say Cheltenham Water is so little alter'd by Carriage that if she lik'd it she might drink it at home—[14]

* Garrick's younger sister, Merrial, was now married to Thomas Docksey, a Lichfield merchant twenty years her senior; his younger brother, William, was overseas with his regiment.

The Garricks were at Chiswick for a time with the Burlingtons in the summer of 1752, and then accompanied them to Yorkshire. A few letters to George survive, and it emerges from one of them that Garrick was beginning to look around for a house outside London. 'I could wish that You would take a ride to Ealing & inspect ye house & premises You mention,' he wrote; 'by y^r Description it must fit Me; I hope it wont be gone before I can see it wth my wife; pray send me ye particulars of it, has it any prospect?' It is also plain that his opinion of Lacy had not greatly improved, and that he still preferred when he could to deal with him through intermediaries: 'I hope by this You have fathom'd ye Dirty heart of my Partner,' he told George, and elsewhere in the same letter he refers to Lacy as *Timbertop*.[15]

He badgered George for news—'Is there any talk of Rich's Opening? when? & who has he got.' For reasons which are not clear he had become exasperated with some of his own Drury Lane dancers, and he expressed himself coarsely on the matter:

> Miss Auretti, Mon^r Pitro, Mad^me Janeton, ye Father, Mother & all their Generation may Kiss my A—se; I am so sick of their no meaning Messages & Compliments, that Every time I see her Name in a Letter, my Stomach falls a heaving as Yours would do, if You were to sit with Your Nose over a Pot with a Stale Turd in it, & that turd not y^r own—No more of y^e *Aurettis* I beg you—heugh—*

Garrick decided this year to return to London by road, and asked George to arrange for his coachman Robin to meet them 'with ye Charriot & four & a Postillion' at Winteringham on the south side of the Humber: 'Pray desire him not to hurry ye horses, & let nobody ride in the Charriot—remember to tell him this.' When he heard from his friend Clutterbuck, a week before his departure, that Lacy was 'almost dead with ye bloody Flux' he was decidedly unsympathetic:

> He ought to have a thorough Scouring before his inside will be tolerably clear from ye filth & Nastiness that he has been gathering from his Youth upwards till now—He desires me to *forgive* him; that I will do with all my heart, for I thank my God that I have no Malice in my Nature, but I can't *forget* him soon, nor will I be upon Brotherly terms wth him; there is a rank viciousness in his Disposition that can only be kept under by ye Whip & curb—†

In this not entirely Christian frame of mind, Garrick set out for London. He planned to stop for half a day at Welwyn in Hertfordshire. The poet Edward Young, who had achieved immediate popularity with his *Night Thoughts* ten

---

* *Letters*, 120. A passage in an earlier letter suggests that he thought Lacy had engaged too many dancers. When the season opened in September, the company was 88 strong, of whom 22 were dancers and 5 singers.

† *Letters*, 121. Flux was a rather vague word used to describe any excessive discharge from the bowels or other organs. Bloody flux was an early name for dysentery.

years previously, was the rector there. Now close to seventy, he had ambitions to revive a tragedy which he had written but set aside many years previously. If Garrick had known what trouble the unwordly old widower and his play were going to cause him, he might well have ordered Robin to whip up the horses and head straight on down the Great North Road.

15

Wire Dancers, the Jew Bill and a Place
in the Country

'Thirty days hath September......' Except that is, in the year 1752, when
for the subjects of King George II it was concertinaed to nineteen. A hundred
and seventy years after most of Catholic Europe, half a century after Sweden,
Denmark and the Protestant states of Germany, Great Britain finally adopted
the reform of the calendar decreed by Pope Gregory XIII in 1582. By that
time, the British were eleven days adrift from continental Europe.* The
difference between the Old Style and the New was removed by declaring the
day following the second of September to be the fourteenth of that month;
at the same time the beginning of the legal year was changed from 25 March
to 1 January.†

Not everybody was best pleased. Natural conservatism was strong, and so
was antipathy to the Pope. When Lord Chesterfield was steering the Calendar
(New Style) Bill through Parliament in 1750, the Duke of Newcastle urged his
peers not to meddle with 'new-fangled things' or 'stir matters that had long been
quiet'. There were those who believed that an immovable feast was an immovable
feast, and that to alter saints' days was an act of sacrilege. Chesterfield had the
assistance of James Bradley, the Astronomer Royal of the day, and of Lord
Macclesfield, like Bradley a distinguished mathematician and astronomer. A
decade after the change to the New Style, when Bradley was dying of an obscure
lingering disease, some said it was a judgement on him. In 1754, when Lord
Macclesfield's eldest son, Lord Parker, contested the Oxfordshire election as one
of the Whig candidates, the mob pursued him with cries of 'Give us back the
eleven days we have been robbed of.'

None of this was of great concern to the managers of Drury Lane, who opened
their season on 16 September (New Style) with a performance of Steele's *The
Conscious Lovers*. It was the beginning of a year of particularly strenuous
competition between the two houses. Garrick made his own first appearance at
the end of September as Archer in *The Stratagem* and by Christmas he had
performed more than a dozen of his established roles.

---

* Except for Russia, which retained the old Julian calendar until the Bolshevik revolution of
1917.
† In Scotland, 1 January had been adopted as New Year's Day in 1600.

During November, the rivalry between the two patent theatres erupted in a rather childish spat. Rich had brought in Maddox, the wire-dancer, together with some animals, to enliven one of his afterpieces. Garrick, abetted or prompted by Woodward, inserted into a performance of *Harlequin Ranger* what the *Gentleman's Magazine* described as 'a mock entertainment of the same kind', which involved 'a figure like Maddox upon ye Wire', a lion, a dog, a monkey and several ostriches.

This was a little too clever. There was a good deal of hissing, and a party was got up intent on damning the entertainment. As Woodward, playing Harlequin, was being carried across the stage in a sedan chair, someone in one of the side boxes aimed a couple of apples at him. The first shattered the glass of the chair; when the second hit him in the face, Woodward responded by doffing his cap, bowing ironically and saying 'Sir, I thank you.' The apples had been thrown by an idle young Irish man about town called Thaddeus Fitzpatrick, who spent a good deal of his time at the Bedford. He was prominent there in a body called the Shakespeare Club, whose members regarded themselves as the arbiters of all things concerning the stage. Fitzpatrick, the 'pale-faced orator' as he was nicknamed, insisted that Woodward had said, 'I have noticed you, and will see you another time.' This, he maintained, from a player to a gentleman, was both insulting and threatening.

The affair now spiralled into absurdity, with both sides swearing affidavits before magistrates about the actual words used. Garrick went on stage and lowered the temperature by announcing that the offending scene would be removed from *Harlequin Ranger* after that night's performance. 'But I hope,' he added, 'when the other House is merry with us, we may be merry with them.' Fitzpatrick insisted on carrying his complaint about Woodward's 'insolence' to the Lord Chamberlain, but his Lordship sensibly checked this out against Garrick's version of the story and gave him short shrift. Garrick had made a tiresome enemy, however, and some years later Fitzpatrick, with his effeminate macaroni ways, would bob up again and plague him rather more seriously.

Garrick had meanwhile put into rehearsal *The Gamester*, a new tragedy by his friend Edward Moore. Neither of Moore's earlier efforts, *The Foundling* and *Gil Blas*, had exactly been a smash hit, and Garrick exerted himself to improve the effectiveness of this latest offering, adding a scene in the fourth act and generally toning up the writing. Moore was convinced that *Gil Blas* had suffered unjustly, and that his enemies had formed a party against it. It was therefore initially put about on this occasion that *The Gamester* was the work of Joseph Spence, the friend of Pope and now Regius Professor of Modern History at Oxford.

Tom Davies describes it as 'an honest attack upon one of the most alluring and most pernicious vices to which mankind in general, and this nation in particular, are unhappily subject'.[1] Davies, as it happens, had a part in this first production of the play. He and his wife had recently joined the company from Covent Garden, and when Havard fell ill, Davies was drafted in at short notice to play the villain, Stukely. It was the first play to challenge the convention that a tragedy could only be written in blank verse, although Garrick stuck to rhyme in his prologue:

> Like famed La Mancha's knight, who, launce in hand,
> Mounted his steed to free th'enchanted land,
> Our Quixote bard sets forth a monster-taming,
> Arm'd at all points to fight that hydra—*gaming*.

Never slow to have a dig at the French, Garrick goes on to suggest that it is all the fault of his own degenerate forebears across the Channel:

> Ye slaves of passion, and ye dupes of France,
> Wake all your pow'rs from this destructive trance!
> Shake off the shackles of this tyrant vice:
> Hear other calls than those of cards and dice!*

Garrick, who played Beverly, was widely praised for his spirited performance, and was particularly admired in the last scene where he puts an end to it all by taking poison. Habitués of White's and other high-rollers were unmoved by this moral tale, however. On the first night, Arthur Murphy sat in a front box near a noted gambler of the day. 'The fellow from the very beginning is not worth a suskin,' he heard him growl. 'Who would play a single rubber with him?'†

Then it was Dr Young's turn with his tragedy *The Brothers*. Young was no stranger to Drury Lane. His *Busiris, King of Egypt* had been performed there more than thirty years previously (and had been ridiculed, along with other tragedies of the time, by Henry Fielding in his *Tom Thumb*). He was also the author of *The Revenge*, a variation on the theme of *Othello*, which offered splendid opportunities for rant. *The Brothers* had been written in the 1720s and put into rehearsal, but this coincided with Young's entry into holy orders and he withdrew it, having decided that play-writing was not a proper occupation for the clergy.

Now he had changed his mind. He also announced that he intended to donate the proceeds to the Society for the Propagation of the Gospel. Young had found his subject in Livy. The brothers in question are Perseus and Demetrius, the sons of Philip of Macedon. Garrick proposed to play Demetrius himself; Mossop, who had been a great success as Zanga in *The Revenge*, was to be cast as Perseus and Garrick intended that the part of his lover, the Thracian princess Erixene, should go to Mrs Pritchard.

He had reckoned without George Anne Bellamy, however. Bellamy, recently up and about after one of her frequent confinements,‡ had written a wheedling

---

* Expressions of Francophobia always went down well with the gallery. The Peace of Aix-la-Chapelle had never been much more than a truce; it was only a few months since the French had surrendered to Clive before Trichinopoly, and in North America both French and English were strengthening their defences on Lakes Champlain and Ontario.

† A suskin, or seskyn, was a small Dutch coin of negligible value.

‡ 'Miss Bellamy has lain in & is up,' Cross noted succinctly in his diary on 1 February. This was by way of being an annual habit of hers; it was particularly tiresome for the management

letter to Young to ask whether she might see the manuscript in advance of rehearsals—she wanted to have as long as possible to study the part intended for her, as she had been told it was very long . . . Garrick was quickly on his highest horse: 'The liberty you have taken in asking to peruse Doctor Young's piece, is unwarrantable,' he told her. 'And I will convince you that I *alone* am the person to be addressed in whatever concerns the theatre.' But he knew there was little he could do. The authors of new plays were traditionally allowed a generous say in the distribution of parts, and if Young wanted Bellamy to play Erixene, play Erixene she would.

When she entered the green-room for the first reading of the piece, Garrick was reduced to bluster: 'Ah, ah, ah, madam, you are come at last. It was unfortunate for us that the doctor insisted upon your being his heroine.' If this makes it sound as if Bellamy had the better of these exchanges, that is only partly because hers is the only account we have of them. She was undoubtedly very quick on her feet, and had a highly developed tactical sense. The minute she was challenged in this way by Garrick, she made a brilliantly impertinent show of conceding. 'I have such a natural dislike of hautiness,' she told him, 'that it is with difficulty I can assume it;' she was sure that the manager's favourite, Mrs Pritchard, would carry it off much better. This had precisely the effect she intended—'No! no!' cried Dr Young.

Tucking Garrick's scalp into her cleavage, Bellamy now began to make suggestions to the author for the improvement of his text, proposing specifically the removal from Erixene's part of the line 'I will speak to you in thunder.' It was a line to which Young was particularly attached, and he strode around the room in some agitation; then, to the general astonishment, he took up his pen and struck it out. He rounded off this morning of high drama by inviting himself home to dine with his heroine.

Garrick was always very good at collaborating with the inevitable. He managed to have inserted in the *Public Advertiser* a puff for the play in the form of a letter from the Shades from the great Barton Booth, dead these good twenty years. The letter is addressed to Young, and in it Booth forgives him for withdrawing the play from rehearsal all those years ago and thus denying him the chance of playing Demetrius. Even by Garrick's standards, it was a pretty brazen piece of self-congratulation:

And I the more readily pardon you, as you have not disgraced me by giving the part to any of my successors, till this Garrick appeared, whose reputation, I can assure you, is by no means confined to your world, and who, I am told, hath more than supply'd my place, hath rendered the loss even of Betterton himself very supportable.*

---

because it usually happened after she had been cast and advertised in such un-maternal roles as Juliet or Cordelia. There began to be suggestions that even though she had not acquired a husband, it would now be appropriate that she should be known as 'Mrs' Bellamy.
* This appeared on 10 March, a week after the first night.

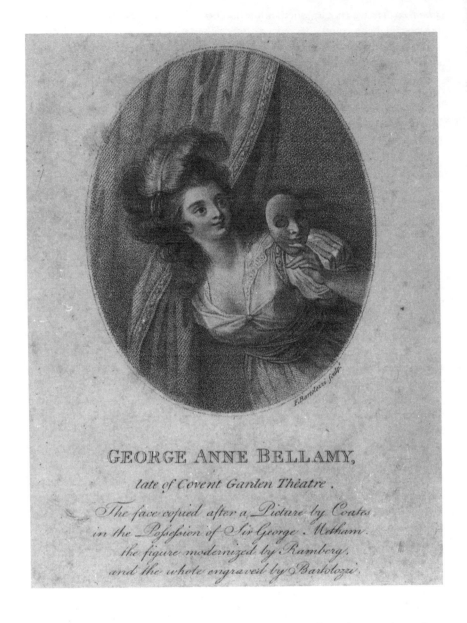

GEORGE ANNE BELLAMY,

late of Covent Garden Theatre.

*The face copied after a Picture by Coates
in the Possession of Sir George Metham.
the figure modernized by Ramberg,
and the whole engraved by Bartolozzi.*

'Enchanting Bellamy' was the illegitimate daughter of Lord Tyrawley, whom
Garrick had met during his first Dublin season. She was Garrick's Juliet during
the 'War of the Romeos' with Barry and Mrs Cibber in 1750. She had a highly
complicated private life, and her frequent pregnancies constituted an occupational
hazard for theatre managers. Her six-volume autobiography is an entertaining
blend of fact and fiction. (Mander & Mitchenson)

The Brothers was not an outstanding success. There was an excellent house for the first night (receipts totalled £220), but the author, sitting in Garrick's box, was startled to hear an epilogue which was not only distinctly coarse, but appeared to hold up his charitable intentions to ridicule:

> The man must be a widgeon;
> Drury may propagate,—but not religion.

It was the work of David Mallet and it was delivered with gusto by Mrs Clive. Garrick's intention, in commissioning it, was almost certainly malicious; for the remainder of the run, Young was allowed to substitute some inoffensive verses of his own. His hopes of raising £1,000 for the Society of the Propagation of the Gospel were disappointed, but he generously made up the sum out of his own pocket.

The season was notable for the extremely good houses achieved during the benefit season in March and April. On the same night that Quin appeared for Ryan, Mrs Pritchard's benefit at Drury Lane—a performance of *Merope* in which Garrick appeared as Dorilas—brought in £250. The following night it was Woodward's benefit, and he did even better. He had chosen to appear for the first time as Face in *The Alchymist*, and with Garrick as Abel Drugger and Mrs Pritchard as Dol Common, receipts totalled £330. Two nights later it was Mrs Clive's turn, and she appeared as Zara in *The Mourning Bride*—'first time and "by Desire",' announced the playbills. Garrick played against her as Osmyn, and she gave her public their money's worth by also appearing as Mrs Hazard in her own *Bayes in Petticoats*.

As always, towards the end of a season, one or two players became convinced that the grass was greener elsewhere. Rich succeeded in luring Ned Shuter away to Covent Garden, and this was quite a blow to Garrick—'Perhaps Nature never bestowed on any Body a greater Fund of Drollery,' the anonymous author of *The Present State of the Stage in Great-Britain and Ireland* wrote that year, 'and I think he bids fair for being as great in low comedy, as it is possible for Man to conceive.' He and Garrick appeared together for the last time in a performance of *The Rehearsal* on 21 May. 'You are a good Actor,' said Garrick, '& I am sorry you have left me,' and there was a round of applause.

The Garricks followed their now familiar summer routine, spending some time with the Burlingtons at Chiswick before joining them for several weeks in Yorkshire. Garrick was still on the look-out for a country property, and at the beginning of July, shortly before setting out for the north, he wrote urgently to his brother Peter about a place he had heard about in Derbyshire:

> I wish you would make some Enquiry about it, & let me know ye particulars as soon as You can—pray inform Me if there is ye River Dove near ye house, & what kind of a house, what Wood, what prospect &c &c?—I should be glad to purchase a Good thing in Derbyshire, that I might serve ye Devonshire family upon Occasions. I could be glad that you would get ye best information you can, but not mention my Name Yet, for fear they

should rise upon it . . . . . I own I love a good Situation prodigiously, & I think the four great Requisites to make one are, Wood, Water, Extent, & inequality of Ground—[2]

His brother George had also been enlisted in the search, and he had been looking at something in Hertfordshire; Garrick wrote to him from Booth Ferry in Lincolnshire as they made their way north:

> Our Objection to Great Amwell is, that there is not house at all to Lye in—I don't insist upon a good house, but a Hut to sleep in will be necessary, till we can rebuild or look about us a little; so You are mistaken if You think I am Nice about a Mansion.[3]

A general election was now in prospect. During his stay at Londesburgh Garrick visited York and took a keen interest in the preparations for the contest there. The Earl of Holderness was working for the return of his kinsman, the 69-year-old Sir Conyers D'Arcy; the Marquess of Rockingham, on the other hand, supported Sir George Savile, who was only twenty-nine. Garrick became so caught up that on the way back to London he scribbled some verses on the contest, and enclosed them in a letter to Lady Hartington:

> . . . . . Quoth *Darcy*, my Lord, that I'm Old is a truth;
> But Old as I am, I can yet cope with Youth;
> Shall Age & Experience be counted demerit,
> Tho Time has not blited the Flesh or ye Spirit?
> To Prove that my Powers can support ye Old Member
> Let us try if Your *May* can outdo my December;
> While thus My Lord Marquis I'm hearty and strong,
> 'Tis better so *Old*, than be always too Young.

'Y^r Ladyship may dispose of 'Em as You think proper,' he wrote, 'but I must not be known for many Reasons to be the Author of 'Em.'[4]

Curiously enough, there is no reference in Garrick's surviving correspondence to a major political controversy which caused bitter divisions in the country during the summer of 1753—the attempt by the administration of his friend Henry Pelham to legalize the naturalization of Jews. The Jew Bill, as it was called, was partly a measure of tolerance, partly an acknowledgement of the important services performed by such men as Sampson Gideon.*

England had been the last country in Western Europe to be penetrated by Jews and the first to drive them out. The earliest Jewish settlers had crossed from the continent in the wake of the Norman Conquest. Racial and religious prejudice quickly took root in the popular mind. It was put about that it was a Jewish custom to crucify a Christian boy on Good Friday and, after the doctrine

---

* Sampson Gideon (1699–1762), a Jewish financier of Portuguese extraction, was frequently consulted by Pelham and Walpole on matters of financial policy. He had raised £1,700,000 for the government in 1745; he later advised on the consolidation of the National Debt and raised a number of government loans during the Seven Years War.

1. 'A horse, a horse, my Kingdom for a horse!' Garrick as Richard III – the role which propelled him to instant celebrity in October 1741. Henry Morland's picture, in the collection of the Garrick Club, is the best of many copies of the original by Nathaniel Dance.

2. Peg Woffington has been almost as poorly served by painters as by her biographers. This portrait may be of her – and then again it may not. The artist was Philip Mercier, like Garrick of Huguenot descent, and an important figure in the introduction of French taste into England.

3. *James Quin, by Hogarth: 'His utterance is a continual singsong, like the chanting of vespers; and his action resembles that of heaving ballast in the hold of a ship.' (Tobias Smollet, Peregrine Pickle.)*

4. *Charles Macklin (hatless) as Shylock, a canvas by the itinerant Irish portrait painter Herbert Stoppelaer. Macklin overturned the traditional view of Shylock as a comic figure, but his interpretation was controversial – one critic said he had 'the looks of a Judas, and the howl of a Hyena'. His views about naturalism in the theatre were an important early influence on Garrick.*

5. Kitty Clive, painted by Willem Verelst in 1740, when she was twenty-nine. 'Clive, sir,' Johnson told Boswell, 'is a good thing to sit by; she always understands what you say.'

6. Colley Cibber. Grisoni's picture shows Cibber – actor, manager, playwright, Poet Laureate – as Lord Foppington in The Relapse. When he published An Apology for the Life of Mr Colley Cibber, Comedian in 1740, a wag said that he had lived his life only so that he might apologize for it, but for all its oddities of style and grammar it remains one of the most important books ever written about the theatre.

7. *Mrs Garrick, by Jean-Etienne Liotard. 'His likenesses,' wrote Sir Ellis Waterhouse, 'were sometimes embarrassingly accurate.' The picture therefore probably gives a good impression of how Mrs Garrick looked as a young married woman in the early 1750s.*

8. *The dagger scene in* Macbeth. *Garrick is seen here with Mrs Pritchard; Zoffany's canvas was possibly intended to mark her retirement after a partnership of twenty years. What is thought to be the original canvas is now in the Baroda Museum in India.*

9. *'Oh! Mercy!' Mrs Cibber and Garrick in Otway's* Venice Preserved. *'She was the greatest female plague belonging to my house,' said Garrick after her death. 'I could easily parry the artless thrusts and despise the coarse language of some of my other heroines; but whatever was Cibber's object, a new part or a new dress, she was always sure to carry her point by the acuteness of her invective and the steadiness of her perseverance.'*

10. The Provok'd Wife, *by Vanbrugh – Garrick as Sir John Brute in the lady-in-disguise scene. The painting is by Zoffany.*

11. *A portrait of Samuel Foote, painted in Reynolds's studio some time in the late 1760s.*

12. 'Garrick at the Breakfast Table.' Pencil drawing by Nathaniel Dance. Garrick thought it the best likeness ever made of him.

of transubstantiation was recognized at the beginning of the thirteenth century, stories circulated about the desecration of the Host. Hostility persisted long after their expulsion by Edward I in 1290; a hundred years later, in *The Prioress's Tale*, Chaucer retold the legend of a widow's child murdered by Jews because he sang the Marian hymn 'O alma redemptoris mater' when passing through the ghetto in Lincoln on his way to school.

Although Cromwell had winked at their return, the Jews were not formally authorized to re-establish themselves in England till after the Restoration—no synagogue was built in London before 1662. The wealth they brought to the country and the importance of their commercial activity, especially in the colonial trade, were quickly recognized in the City; Sir Josiah Child, the despotic governor of the East India Company, argued the case for their naturalization as early as 1668.

The measure had an easy passage through Parliament and received the royal assent, but the ministry, which normally had its ear close to the ground, was quite unprepared for the uproar which it provoked in the country. There were elements in the parliamentary opposition, not averse to a quick, pre-electoral roll in the gutter, who were happy to foster agitation by the mob. The Jew Bill was depicted as an abandonment of Christianity, and there were predictions that it would draw down on the nation those curses which Providence from time immemorial had heaped on the Jews themselves. The Act was denounced by the landed classes, by commercial interests and by the clergy. Bishops who had voted for it in the Lords were insulted in the streets; Pelham's brother, the Duke of Newcastle, visiting Cambridge in his capacity as chancellor of the university, was mockingly hailed as 'King of the Jews'.

When Drury Lane opened its doors for the new season on 8 September with a production of *The Beggar's Opera*, there was an attempt to carry the controversy into the theatre. 'Ye Naturalizing Bill having made some Noise against the Jews,' Cross noted in his diary, 'some people called out for ye Merch[an]t of Venice, & a Letter was thrown upon ye Stage desiring that play instead of the Opera, but we took no notice of it, some little hissing but it died away.'

On the larger political stage, Newcastle became convinced that the hissing would not die away so easily. By the autumn, he had persuaded Pelham that if the Bill remained on the statute book, the outcome of the general election could be in jeopardy. Ignominiously, when Parliament resumed in November, he introduced a motion for repeal in the Lords. 'There is no page in the history of the eighteenth century,' wrote Lecky, 'that shows more decisively how low was the intellectual and political condition of English public opinion.'[5]

Garrick and Lacy had signed up the largest company since the beginning of their joint management. For the season of 1753–4, in a theatre newly re-painted and gilded, they could draw on the talents of 63 players, 24 dancers and 7 singers. Rich's company was smaller. He employed the same number of actors and actresses, but only 17 dancers and singers. For Garrick, the most important thing was that he had won back Mrs Cibber from Covent Garden. Somerset Draper had been wooing her insistently on his behalf. The first sign that there might be a *rapprochement* in the making had come the previous February when Garrick had written an epilogue for her to perform after the première of *The Earl of Essex**—an unusual gesture from the manager of one of the Theatres Royal to a production by the rival house. A few weeks later, he had taken her masque *The Oracle* into the Drury Lane repertory and given it an even more lavish production than Rich had done.

Mrs Cibber made her first appearance at Drury Lane in October as Monimia in *The Orphan* to Garrick's Chamont, and before the month was out they had appeared together in *Romeo and Juliet*, *Hamlet* and *The Fair Penitent*. There was no return to the tender relationship of other days, but Garrick treated her with elaborate courtesy and went to great pains to ensure that she stayed with him for the rest of her career.†

Rich had also lost Macklin, who after more than thirty-five years on the stage, felt it was time to try something new. He had been talking for years of founding a school of oratory, and he had also nursed the ambition to establish a superior coffee-house for actors and authors. In September 1753, for an annual rent of £45, he took a 21-year lease on chambers under the Great Piazza of Covent Garden. (His landlord was the Duke of Bedford.) He hired a builder called John Tinkler to refurbish the apartments as 'a Magnificent Coffee-Room & a School of Oratory'. In December, for old times' sake, Garrick gave him a benefit—cynics said it was to make sure he really did retire. Macklin spoke a farewell prologue (essentially an advertisement for his new venture) and three months later, in March 1754, he presided over the grand opening of his coffee-house—'the temple of luxury under the Piazza', as Fielding called it.

Everything was done with great decorum. On the stroke of four, a bell was rung. Ten minutes later the outer doors were shut and patrons were invited to be seated. Macklin, formally attired, brought in the first dish himself, placed it on the table, made a deep bow and withdrew to the sideboard. The waiters were forbidden to speak unless spoken to. Macklin directed them by a series of signals, copied, he said, from those devised for use in the fleet by the Duke of York.

For a time this all went very well. Getting the other half of the scheme off the ground proved more difficult, however. In addition to his initial outlay of £1,200, Macklin had to find another £700 before the space above the dining room could accommodate what he called his 'British Inquisition'. He had long been active in several debating societies and forensic coffee-houses. He now issued a rather grandiose advertisement for this new enterprise. 'This Institution is upon the plan of the ancient Greek, Roman, and Modern French and Italian Societies of liberal investigation,' he announced:

---

* A tragedy by Henry Jones (1721–70). He began life as a bricklayer in Ireland, was patronized by Chesterfield and followed him to London. He subsequently took to drink, was run over by a wagon in St Martin's Lane and died in the parish workhouse.

† Bellamy, against the advice of her friends, yielded to overtures from Rich and returned to Covent Garden, a move she came to regret.

TheatreRoyal in *Drury-Lane*,

This present *Saturday*, being the 14th of *February*,
Will be presented the T R A G E D Y, of

H A M L E T.

(Written by S H A K E S P E A R.)

Hamlet by Mr. G A R R I C K,
The *King* by Mr. D A V I E S,
The *Ghost* by Mr. B E R R Y,
Horatio by Mr. H A V A R D,
Polonius by Mr. T A S W E L L,
Laertes by Mr. B L A K E S,
Ostrick by Mr. W O O D W A R D,

Rosencrans Mr. *Simson*,	*Marcellus* Mr. *Bransby*,
Guildenstern Mr. *Usher*,	Player *King* Mr. *Burton*,
Bernardo Mr. *Marr*,	Player *Queen* Mrs. *Bennet*,

The *Gravediggers* by Mr. Y A T E S and Mr. *Vaughan*,
Ophelia by Mrs. C I B B E R,
Queen by Mrs. P R I T C H A R D.
With a N E W *Comic* D A N C E.
To which will be added a Dramatic *Satire*, call'd

L E T H E.

The *Fine Gentleman* by Mr. W O O D W A R D,
Old Man by Mr. B L A K E S,
Drunken Man by Mr. Y A T E S,
Æsop by Mr. B R A N S B Y,
Mercury by Mr. B E A R D,
Mrs. *Tattoo* by Miss M I N O R S,
The *Fine Lady* by Mrs. C L I V E.

Boxes 5s. Pit 3s. First Gallery 2s. Upper Gallery 1s.
PLACES for the Boxes to be had of Mr. V A R N E Y, at the Stage-
door of the *Theatre*.
❧ No Persons to be admitted behind the Scenes, nor any Money to be returned
after the Curtain is drawn up. Vivat R E X.

On *Monday* (*By Desire*) The S U S P I C I O U S H U S B A N D.

Garrick made his début as Hamlet in Dublin in 1742 and went on playing the part until his retirement 34 years later. It was his most frequently performed tragic role. (Mander & Mitchenson)

..... particularly Mr Macklin intends to lecture upon the Comedy of the Ancients, the use of their masks and flutes, their mimes and pantomimes, and the use and abuse of the Stage ..... and he purposes to lecture also upon each of Shakespeare's Plays; to consider the original stories from whence they are taken; the artificial or inartificial use, according to the laws of the drama, that Shakespeare has made of them; his fable, moral character, passions, manners will likewise be criticized, and how his capital characters have been acted heretofore, are acted, and ought to be acted.

Unwisely, Macklin gradually began to range more widely, and was soon pontificating on such themes as the depraved taste of the age (he instanced bear-baiting and pantomine), the arguments for Protestantism and the 'ingenious nation of the Pygmies'. He even offered his views on such topical matters as the alleged kidnapping of the maidservant Elizabeth Canning, which was dividing public opinion at the time and was the subject of a brisk pamphleteering war.*

Inevitably, Samuel Foote was a constant and unwelcome member of the audience. One night, as Macklin was about to begin, he could hear Foote rattling away at the lower end of the room. 'Pray, young gentleman,' he called out sarcastically, 'do you know what I am going to say?'—'No, Sir,' came the reply; '*do you?*'

The following winter, at the Haymarket, Foote embarked on a series of comic lectures. 'A Writ of Enquiry Will be Executed on the Inquisitor General', announced the playbills, and over a couple of weeks Macklin was mercilessly lampooned. At the other end of the Piazza from his establishment there was a well-known brothel. Foote published An Epistle from Tully in the Shades to Orator MA****N in which 'Tully' proposed as a motion for debate 'whether an academy for Moral Lectures carried on in one End of a House, is more likely to make Converts, more than one for Fornication in the other'.

Although Macklin was hot-tempered, and foolishly hit back in a pamphlet of his own, his years in the theatre had given him a thick enough skin to take all this. What he lacked was a purse long enough to cope with rapidly dwindling custom. Early in 1755 he was declared bankrupt, and was obliged to fall back on the earnings of his wife and daughter.†

Garrick also had been having dealings with Foote, but this time of an entirely amicable nature. He had engaged him for a number of nights the previous autumn, and in October he allowed him to play Buck in a production of *The Englishman in Paris* and wrote a lively prologue for him:

---

* Elizabeth Canning was a sawyer's daughter who claimed she had been held prisoner by a procuress for most of January 1753. She was examined before Henry Fielding in his capacity as a Bow Street magistrate, and the people she accused were convicted. The following year she was found guilty of perjury and transported to New England.

† Macklin's daughter Maria had joined the Drury Lane company in the autumn of 1753.

> . . ."Paper! boy." "Here, Sir, I am." "What news today?"
> "Foote, Sir, is advertised." "What! run away?"
> "No, Sir; this week he acts at Drury Lane."
> "How's that?" (cries feeble Grub). "Foote come again!
> I thought that fool had done his devil's dance;
> Was he not hanged some months ago in France?"

Garrick had taken some flak the previous week for mounting a performance of *Harlequin Ranger* so early in the season. 'It is surprising that Mr Garrick should be the first to introduce Pantomime Entertainments,' wrote the *Gray's Inn Journal*, 'especially as his own universal talents are seconded by a good company of performers. We suppose he does it to gratify the taste of the town; but such *Smithfield* exhibitions should certainly be banish'd from all regular theatres.'

The *Gray's Inn Journal* was being published, and largely written, at that time by Garrick's future biographer, Arthur Murphy, a young Irishman in his mid-twenties who had only recently abandoned commerce for literature.* *Boadicia*, Garrick's first new tragedy of the season, was much more to his liking:

> The music and scenery were both suited to the piece, and the acting of it, were there no other inducement, should be sufficient to draw numerous audiences . . . I cannot but remark that the applause it met with, was scarcely warm enough for such fine writing . . . I am convinced that this Tragedy will prove an elegant Closet-companion to every reader of taste.[6]

Someone with more experience of the stage than Murphy had at this time would have realized that this was a somewhat back-handed compliment—a piece that reads well in the closet is not at all the same as one that plays well in the theatre. The author was Richard Glover, whose epic poem *Leonidas*, regarded as a political manifesto for Walpole's opponents, had been so widely admired when it was published in 1737. This, and his appearance before the Commons to complain of the inedaquate protection of British commerce, had won him a high reputation for patriotism; when the Duchess of Marlborough died in 1744, she left him £500 in her will if he would undertake to write the life of the Duke.† Garrick had been greatly flattered to be praised by him early in his career, and his acceptance of *Boadicia* was not based solely on an appreciation of its dramatic merits.‡

---

* Murphy, born in Roscommon in 1727, had been educated by English Jesuits in France where he distinguished himself in the study of the classics. He had subsequently worked as a clerk to a merchant in Cork and in the London banking house of Ironside and Belchier in Lombard Street.

† He declined.

‡ He frankly admitted as much many years later in a letter to John Cleland, the author of *Fanny Hill*: 'Why do You raise the Ghosts of Boadicia and Barbarossa to haunt me? If I had not perform'd the first, I should have been a very Shallow Politician . . .' (Letter dated 24 May 1772, *Letters*, 689.)

Thomas Davies, who had a part in the production, left an account of some of the problems it posed for Garrick:

> The amiable author read his Boadicea to the actors. But surely his manner of conveying the meaning of his poem was very unhappy; his voice was harsh, and his elocution disagreeable. Mr Garrick was vexed to see him mangle his own work, and politely offered to relieve him by reading an act or two; but the author imagining that he was the only person fit to unfold his intention to the players, persisted to read the play to the end, to the great mortification of the actors, who would have been better pleased with the fine melody of their master, who excelled all men in giving proportional weight to the various characters of a dramatic piece.[7]

The manager did what he could. He cast Mrs Pritchard as Boadicia, Mrs Cibber played the 'innocent and sentimental' Venusia, he himself was Dumnorix, chief of the Trinobantians. New music was commissioned from Boyce to be played between the acts. There was a good house on the first two nights, but it was uphill work. 'There is no plot in the play,' complained one critic. 'Never was Author more oblig'd to Performers, they acted to the full amount of his meaning; the Matter often fail'd Mr Garrick's continued and vigorous exertion.'*

Garrick's search for a place in the country had still not borne fruit. His old friend from Lichfield days, the Reverend Joseph Smith, who was the rector of Stanmore in Middlesex, had alerted him to the fact that there was an estate on the market near Watford, just across the county boundary in Hertfordshire, but Garrick appears to have encountered some unpleasantness in the course of viewing it. 'I met with such a kind of treatment at *Grove* that I have conceiv'd Resentment & dislike against the place,' he told Smith:

> We are told that some Persons of Family & Fortune are about it, I shall therefore not contend with my betters, Especially as yᵉ Bone in Question does not absolutely hit my Tooth—To have been near you, would have been my principal Enducement; but as that must be had upon very unreasonable & some disagreeable terms I shall content Myself with yᵉ Bank of yᵉ Thames—I have a place in my Eye that I think will Suit us . . .[8]

The place on the bank of the Thames—the Middlesex bank—was a property at Hampton known as the Fuller House. In January 1754 Garrick agreed to rent it, gardens, drying-ground and stable-yard included, for £60 a year; the following August he contracted to buy it. Thirteen miles from Hyde Park Corner and built of yellow brick, the house faced south over the river, its six acres intersected by the main road from London to Hampton Court. Here Garrick would now spend every hour he could snatch from the theatre, surrounded by his books and pictures, entertaining in some style. 'Ah, David,' Samuel Johnson would say, 'it is the leaving of such a place that makes a death-bed terrible.'

---

* The Irish writer Paul Hiffernan, writing in *The Tuner*, a vehicle for dramatic and literary criticism which he founded in 1754 and which sold for 1s. It survived for only a few numbers.

At the end of February, Garrick put on *Virginia*, a tragedy by Samuel Crisp. Like *Boadicia* earlier in the season, the piece did not make its way into the schedule entirely on merit. Murphy, who once he turned playwright did not always find it easy to sell his wares to Garrick, gives a nicely malicious account of how Crisp succeeded in having his drama accepted:

He was related to, or patronized by, Lord Coventry. His Countess, the celebrated beauty of that day, as Garrick often related, drove to his house, and sent in word, that she had a moment's business. He went to the side of her carriage, "There, Mr Garrick," said Lady Coventry, "I put into your hands a play, which the best judges tell me will do honour to you and the author." It was not necesary for her to say more: "*Those eyes that tell us what the sun is made of*," as Dr. Young says in one of his tragedies, had all the power of persuasion, and even of command; Garrick obeyed, as if she had been a *tenth muse*, and prepared the play with the utmost dispatch.[9]

This 'tenth muse' was Maria, the elder of the two famously beautiful Gunning sisters. The *Dictionary of National Biography* describes them as 'lacking in sense and in knowledge of the world', but that would scarcely be surprising; when they had turned up in London three years previously, poor as church mice, from County Roscommon, they were still only seventeen and eighteen. At all events, Maria's lack of sense did nothing to impair her marriage prospects, because within a year she was the wife of Mrs Garrick's one-time admirer, the Earl of Coventry;* while her tactics in pressing Crisp's tragedy on Garrick suggest that she was not entirely ignorant of the ways of the world.†

Garrick did his best for the piece, although he allowed some of his irritation with the author to show in the prologue he wrote for it:

Prologues, like compliments, are loss of time,
'Tis penning bows, and making legs in rhime;
'Tis cringing at the door with simple grin,
When we should shew the company within—
So thinks our bard, who stiff in classic knowledge,
Preserves too much the buckram of the college—
Lord, sir, said I, an audience must be woo'd,
And, lady-like, with flattery pursu'd . . .

Garrick went on to beg the indulgence of the house for a new performer:

If novelties can please, tonight we've two—
Tho' English both, yet spare 'em as they're new.
To one at least your usual favour shew—
A female asks it—can a man say no?—

---

* Maria's sister Elizabeth did even better for herself. She was married first to James, sixth Duke of Hamilton, and after his death to the Marquess of Lorne, later the first Duke of Argyll.
† George II, on the other hand, is said to have been greatly amused at court one day when she told him she longed to see a coronation.

This was a young actress from Birmingham called Mary Anne Graham. Later she would marry Richard Yates as his second wife, eclipsing him in performance and becoming one of the most celebrated tragediennes of the century. She was billed on this occasion as 'a Gentlewoman (1st time on any stage)', which was not strictly true, because Sheridan had put her on in Dublin the previous year, but she was well received as Marcia. The first-night audience was in a lively mood; Cross noted that 'Mr Carey had his fiddle broke by an apple playing the first Music'. Mrs Cibber played Virginia, and Garrick himself took the part of Virginius. He may have felt rather sourly about the production, but he did not allow that to affect his performance. 'The great stroke which crowned it with success, (which will appear almost incredible) was Garrick's manner of uttering two words,' wrote Murphy:

> *Claudius*, the iniquitous tool of the Decemvir, claims *Virginia*, as a slave born in his house. He pleads his cause before *Appius* on his tribunal. During that time, Garrick, representing *Virginius*, stood on the opposite side of the scene, next to the stage-door, with his arms folded across his breast, his eyes rivetted to the ground, like a mute and lifeless statue. Being told at length that the tyrant is willing to hear him, he continued for some time in the same attitude, his countenance expressing a variety of passions, and the spectators fixed in ardent gaze. By slow degrees he raised his head; he paused; he turned round in the slowest manner, till his eyes fixed on *Claudius*; he still remained silent, and after looking eagerly at the impostor, he uttered in a low tone of voice, that spoke the fullness of a broken heart, "*Thou traitor!*" The whole audience was electrified; they felt the impression, and a thunder of applause testified their delight. Pliny the elder, speaking of certain minerals, says, nature is never more fully displayed than in the minutest objects. This remark may be applied to the nice touches of such an actor as Garrick.[10]

Garrick had spent some time during the winter tinkering extensively with another of Shakespeare's plays, and for Mrs Pritchard's benefit on 18 March he provided her with a new three-act farce called *Catherine and Petruchio*.* There had been at least four earlier adaptations of *The Taming of the Shrew*, most recently in 1735 when Richard Worsdale had brought out *A Cure for a Scold*. As in his earlier reworkings of Shakespeare, Garrick was concerned to clean up the language, to abbreviate in the interest of pace and to devise opportunities for more stage business. He loses nine of Shakespeare's twenty-five characters, expands some of the briefer roles and introduces 175 new lines of his own.

The audience liked it, and went on liking it almost until the end of the next century; it fell out of the repertory only when *The Taming of the Shrew* was revived by Augustin Daly in 1886, but over the years Garrick's rewriting of the text has sharply divided critical opinion. 'The most contemptible piece of work

---

* It was presented as the afterpiece. For the mainpiece Mrs Pritchard had chosen to play the title role in Rowe's *Jane Shore*, with Garrick as Hastings. The evening brought in a healthy £298.

Garrick has accomplished,' wrote Joseph Knight snappishly,[11] and Frank Hedgcock grumbled that 'Shakespeare's joyous farce finishes on a grave note suitable for a homily on the whole duty of women'.[12] George Winchester Stone came to Garrick's defence in the 1930s, absolving him of any 'improving' intentions: 'Surely there is more unadulterated Shakespeare here than in any of the other versions . . . seen after the Restoration.'[13] More recently the critical pendulum has again swung the other way. Michael Dobson, writing in the early 1990s, saw the Garrick text as both adulterated and sentimentalized. The result is a much less brutal play than the original; Garrick's main concern, Dobson believes, was to palliate what he describes as 'Shakespeare's embarrassingly frank presentation of power relations between the sexes'.[14]

Garrick had lost two good friends in recent months. Lord Burlington had died in December, during the run of *Boadicia*. He was only in his late fifties, but had been in indifferent health for some time. Then in March, Henry Pelham was carried off by an attack of erysipelas—St Anthony's Fire, as it used to be called. Horace Walpole, who disliked Pelham, although they were neighbours in Arlington Street, put it about that it had been brought on by immoderate eating and a lack of exercise, but in the eighteenth century, before the advent of anti-bacterial chemotherapy, streptococcal infections of this nature were extremely dangerous.

Garrick, who had formed the view that appropriate tributes were scandalously slow to appear, composed an ode, which ran through four editions in less than six weeks. 'No bounty past provokes my praise,' he wrote, 'No future prospect prompt my lays.' For some tastes, it might have seemed that in the course of his eighteen stanzas he dwelt unduly on his own disinterestedness in singing the praises of the dead statesman:

> What! mute ye bards?—no mournful verse,
> No chaplets to adorn his hearse,
> To crown the good and just?
> Your flow'rs in warmer regions bloom,
> You seek no pension from the tomb,
> No laurels from the dust.
>
> When pow'r departed with his breath,
> The sons of flatt'ry fled from death:
> Such insects swarm at *noon*.
> Not for herself my muse is griev'd,
> She never ask'd, nor e'er receiv'd,
> One ministerial boon.

Pelham was, in fact, widely mourned. 'Now I shall have no more peace,' said George II; it would certainly not be easy for him to replace a minister who had been so successful in securing acceptance of his leadership by such ambitious and powerful personalities as Pitt and Henry Fox.

The Garricks visited William Windham during the summer of 1754 and spent a week with a family called Young in Wiltshire,* but they were mainly preoccupied with work on the house at Hampton. Somewhat curiously, Garrick relied for the recruitment of domestic staff on Peter in Lichfield. He was particularly eager that the gardener his brother had found for him should get down to work as soon as possible. 'I sh^d be glad to see him Settled here, before I repair to London to begin ye Acting Season,' he wrote to Peter at the beginning of September:

> I hope he has a good Character in his Neighbourhood, for he will be left in trust of Every thing, house, Garden Workmen &c &c—you must likewise be so good to say what Expences I am to be at for his Journey, tho as I agree to his wages wch are high I think that he might have bore his own Expences to Town—however that I leave to you—We shall have no occasion for a Laundry Maid, so we shall spare you that trouble, for my Wife has alter'd that scheme, at least for a time—but if you sh^d know of two Maids between this & next Spring, one for Laundry & ye other for a Dairy & the Chickens wch are prime in their Way, we sh^d be greatly oblig'd to You . . .

It was a good time to be thinking of refurbishing a newly acquired villa. A few minutes' walk from Old Drury, a Yorkshireman of about Garrick's age had recently moved his furniture and upholstery business into new premises in St Martin's Lane. In 1754 he published *The Gentleman and Cabinet Maker's Director*, a handsome folio volume with 160 engraved plates. It was quite the most important collection of furniture designs to appear in England up to that time—cabinets and escritoires, mirrors in the Chinese taste, four-poster beds, small tables with fretwork galleries for the display of china. Above all a great variety of chairs—chairs with claw and ball feet, chairs with cabriole legs, chairs with elegant ribbon backs. The list of subscribers indicated that Thomas Chippendale already had a large and distinguished body of customers. David Garrick Esq. would shortly be added to their number.

---

* William Young, their host, was later made a baronet and appointed Lieutenant-Governor of Dominica. His estate, near Dowton, was called Standlynch Park, and he is said to have ruined himself in doing it up — he engaged Cipriani to paint one of the rooms in fresco. The house had an interesting later history. After the death of Nelson in 1805, his clergyman brother, William, was created an earl and granted the sum of £90,000 for the purchase of a mansion and estates. In 1814 this was laid out in the purchase of Standlynch and its name was changed to Trafalgar House.

View of the Seat of the late DAVID GARRICK Esq.r at HAMPTON, with the Temple of Shakespeare.

Garrick's place on the Thames at Hampton. 'Ah, David!' Johnson said to him. 'It is the leaving of such a place that makes a death-bed terrible.' (Mander & Mitchenson)

16

Signor Shakespearelli

Peg Woffington's stay in Dublin had been both profitable and eventful. She and Sheridan drew large audiences, and the Irish capital opened its heart to her. Towards the end of 1752, her old admirer Owen Swiney, now in his seventies and not in the best of health, told her that he had left her most of his estate in his will. His property in County Wexford was to be left in trust for her. (He had appointed as trustees the Duke of Dorset, then the Lord Lieutenant, and a lawyer and Fellow of Trinity College called Francis Andrews.) His household goods, his books and his considerable collection of pictures were also to be sold for her benefit.

There was one small problem. Woffington might be the toast of the town and the darling of the Protestant establishment, but she had been born a Roman Catholic. The penal laws that were directed at five-sixths of the Irish population might (except at times of Jacobite scares) be laxly administered, but it was none the less legally impossible for Roman Catholics to inherit property. Accordingly, in the last days of 1752, Woffington had travelled to Sheridan's dilapidated estate at Quilca. Here, in County Cavan, a Protestant clergyman prepared her for recantation, and a month later the Bishop of Kilmore's seal on a document made it official:

> We do hereby certify that Margaret Woffington now an inhabitant of the City of Dublin hath Renounced the Errors of the church of Rome and that she was by our order Received into the Communion of the Church on Sunday the thirty-first day of December last, and that the said Margaret Woffington is a protestant and doth conform to the Church of Ireland as by Law Established.

By the early months of 1754 Woffington's popularity with the Dublin audience was in decline. Whether her apostasy for the sake of an inheritance became public knowledge is not known; what is certain is that her close identification with Sheridan and the Lord Lieutenant were no longer to her advantage.

The closing years of the reign of George II saw a rapid growth of Protestant nationalism directed against the English control of Ireland; this had been fuelled during 1753 by the government's renewed insistence that it was entitled to appropriate the healthy surpluses generated by the Irish exchequer. Early in 1754, in the very week that the prorogation of the Dublin parliament was announced, Sheridan mounted James Miller's tragedy *Mahomet*. The audience quickly detected a parallel between the theme of the play and current discontents, and when one of the characters spoke of bringing to account 'those vipers' who sold their public trust to the enemy, there was rapturous applause and calls for an encore.

Sheridan's political antennae were seriously stunted. When he put the play on again a month later, having previously lectured the cast on the impropriety of responding to calls for an encore,* the result was a full-blown riot which lasted from eight in the evening until two o'clock the following morning. Benches were torn up, scenery was destroyed and the curtain set on fire. Only the bravery of the house servants prevented the theatre from being burnt to the ground. Sheridan lost thousands of pounds in the wreckage.† He withdrew briefly to Quilca. By June he had completed negotiations to sub-let the theatre for two years.‡ By the early autumn he was in London and had engaged for the season with Rich at Covent Garden.

Rich had also signed up Woffington. She had soldiered on in Dublin until the season ended in May, but had failed to persuade the new management at Smock Alley to renew her contract for another year at £800. Benjamin Victor thought it excessive, and hinted that her appeal was not what it had been: 'Novelty,' he told her, somewhat pompously, 'is the very spirit and life of all public entertainment.' On her return to London, Rich had offered her what she asked without a murmur, but then Rich was not well placed to argue, because he had just lost Barry.

Barry—it is thought his first wife had died some years earlier—was living with a nineteen-year-old actress called Maria Nossiter, who had become his Juliet the previous year after Susannah Cibber's return to Drury Lane. She had had a hugely successful first season, but when her lover decided that he would also act as her agent, his demands struck Rich as exorbitant. Barry accordingly took her off to Dublin where, with some reluctance, Victor agreed to his terms— £500 for Miss Nossiter, and for himself, the £800 that had been refused to Woffington.

For Garrick, these alarums and excursions changed the complexion of the competition he must face in the new season. He met it with a company more modest in size than the previous year's, and he also had to contend with an apparent change of tack on Rich's part. For the last few seasons the two companies had produced roughly the same number of new plays; this year, however, when Garrick would offer four, Rich would choose to produce none, preferring instead

---

* It seems, however, that in dressing down the company, Sheridan was fatally indecisive. When West Digges, the actor in question, asked for specific instructions about how he should respond, Sheridan replied, 'I leave you to act in that manner you think proper.'
† He also lost a child; his wife had gone into premature labour in the week of the riot and the infant died of convulsions two months later.
‡ The new joint managers were the theatre's treasurer, Benjamin Victor, and the actor John Sowdon.

to revive no fewer than twenty-one older plays—among them Addison's *Cato*, which dated from 1713, Colley Cibber's *The Non-Juror* (1717) and Milton's *Comus* (1634).

Sheridan as a performer did not pose a major threat. Rich gave him a number of the roles Garrick had made his own—Hamlet, Richard III, Macbeth, Romeo—but he was not received with great enthusiasm. Woffington, however, was still very much to be reckoned with. Rich allowed her to range freely through many of her favourite parts, and she added to them Zara in *The Mourning Bride* and Jocasta in a revival of Dryden's *Oedipus, King of Thebes*. She was still arrestingly beautiful, and her figure still allowed her to play Sir Harry Wildair, which she would do to great applause in the last performance of the season.

Early in November, Garrick appeared as Don John in a revival of Fletcher's *The Chances*. It was a triumph, and became one of the dozen or so comedy roles in which he appeared most frequently.* Davies says that Garrick's interest in the play was roused by a chance remark of George II's:

> The King happened to recollect that Wilks and Oldfield had greatly diverted him in that comedy, and he asked one of his courtiers why it was never played. Mr Garrick, as soon as he learned the King's inclination to see the Chances, immediately set about reforming the play, so as to render it less exceptionable in language and action.[1]

Fitzgerald, writing a century later, put the matter more crudely. 'Garrick,' he wrote, 'whose eyes always turned fondly to Court, and whose loyalty verged on obsequiousness, had it put in rehearsal at once.'[2] As we have seen, however, Garrick had been at work on the play as early as the summer of 1751; and if the story about the King's interest is more than a piece of tittle-tattle, the most that can be reasonably surmised is that it jogged Garrick's memory about something he had laid aside in the press of other business. We also now have evidence that the King's interest was at best fleeting. A matter of hours before the curtain went up on the first night, Garrick dashed off a letter to the Marquis of Hartington. His purpose in writing was to apologize for not being able to call on him that evening, but he added a paragraph on what he called 'a distress of my own':

> Six days ago, his Majesty sent for a List of Plays—I sent one ye Next Morning, with y^e *Chances* at ye head of it—I went to Court on Sunday, saw Lord Northumberland, but no Orders had been given—but Yesterday Morning it was known, that ye King goes certainly to Covent Garden, wch indeed Surpriz'd Me; for No Care has been wanting on my Part to make ye Reception & Entertainment for his Majesty, as well as I possibly could—I have new dress'd ye Play, put Every Performer I could of Merit in it—nay hir'd Mrs Macklin on purpose for one of ye Characters . . . †

---

* He played it on 31 occasions.
† *Letters*, 144. Hugh Percy (1715–86), second Earl of Northumberland, later the first Duke, had been appointed a Lord of the Bedchamber the previous year.

Fletcher had based his plot on one of Cervantes' *Novelas ejemplares*; the 'chances' are the coincidences by which Constantia and the Duke of Ferrara, with whom she is about to elope, become embroiled in all manner of complications. The play had been altered by George Villiers, second Duke of Buckingham, and his version, which was a good deal more indecent than the original, had held the stage at Drury Lane until the late 1730s.

Davies gives an amusing account of the problems the play posed for Garrick in dealing with his various leading ladies:

> The manager's great difficulty was, how to cast the part of the second Constantia, in such a manner, as that she might bear some resemblance to the first. Mrs Pritchard was the only actress in the company who had, in a superior degree, much vivacity, variety of humour, and engaging action; but this lady was become so bulky in her person, that she could not be mistaken for Miss Macklin, whose figure was elegant, and who acted the first Constantia. But could Mr Garrick have surmounted this difficulty, Mrs Cibber, by a clause in her articles, claimed a right to choose any character she pleased to act in a new or revived play. This actress, whose tones of voice were so expressive of all the tender passions, and was by nature formed for tragic representation, was unaccountably desirous of acting characters of gaiety and humour, to which she was an absolute stranger; she had no idea of comedy, but such as implied a representation of childish simplicity.
>
> Mr Garrick knew that it was impossible to divert her from the resolution to play Constantia; and therefore determined to give way to her humour, till the want of applause should admonish her to resign the part . . .*

A week before Christmas, Garrick unveiled a new tragedy called *Barbarossa*, the first work for the theatre of a somewhat unstable clergyman called John Brown.† It was a turgid affair, but Garrick cast himself as Achmet, Mossop as Barbarossa and Mrs Cibber as Zaphira. (According to Murphy, she 'spoke daggers in every sentence'.)[3] Garrick also wrote a slightly bizarre prologue which he delivered in the character of a country boy who was the playwright's servant:

> Measter! Measter!
> Is not my measter here among ye, pray?
> Nay, speak; my measter wrote this fine new play.
> The actor-folks are making such a clatter!
> They want the pro-log. I know nought o' th' matter!
> He must be there among you; look about;
> A weezen, pale-fac'd man; do find him out . . .

---

* *Davies*, i, 223–4. Mrs Cibber quickly tired of the part and it was taken over for a time by a young actress called Miss Haughton. Later Mrs Abington made it very much her own.
† In 1766, prevented by ill-health from advancing a grandiose scheme he had proposed to Catherine the Great for the civilization of Russia, Brown became depressed and cut his throat.

How gratified the author was to be described in this way is not known, but he took grave offence at a passage in the epilogue, also by Garrick, but spoken by Woodward 'in the character of a Fine Gentleman':

> How could you suffer that same country booby,
> That pro-logue speaking savage, that great looby,
> To talk his nonsense?—give me leave to say,
> 'Twas low, Damn'd low!—but save the fellow's play:
> Let the poor devil eat; allow him that . . .

The audience did, and handsomely, apparently unconcerned by 'two improprieties' Samuel Johnson claimed to have detected in the last act.* *Barbarossa* attracted good houses for eleven nights and held its place in the repertory for the rest of the century.

For all his attachment to Shakespeare and the 'old comedies' and his professed contempt for rope-dancers and the like, Garrick knew very well that the public's taste for music and colour and movement was not something the manager of Drury Lane could legislate out of existence; indeed, in the mid-1750s all the signs were that the appetite for pantomime, opera and any form of spectacle was growing. Early in February 1755 he responded to that by presenting *The Fairies*, an opera based on *A Midsummer Night's Dream*.

Horace Walpole, writing to his friend Richard Bentley, drew his skirt fastidiously aside:

> Garrick has produced a detestable English opera, which is crowded by all true lovers of their country . . . it is Shakespeare's *Midsummer Night's Dream*, which is forty times more nonsensical than the worst translation of any Italian opera-books—But such sense and such harmony are irresistible![4]

The first-night audience certainly thought so. Receipts came to £200 and Cross recorded 'Very great applause'. The music was by John Christopher Smith, who was one of Handel's pupils. The songs were taken not only from Shakespeare, but from Milton, Waller, Hammond and Dryden. Modern critics have not marked the word setting very highly. Roger Fiske, for instance, allows 'You spotted snakes' to be 'mildly charming' and concedes that Theseus has a 'big rumbustious hunting song,' but his general conclusion is that the music is 'in rather tepid good taste'.[5]

Garrick denied—somewhat feebly, it must be said—his authorship of *The*

---

* He was referring to the tolling of a bell for the execution of the character Selim: 'In the first place, the use of a bell is unknown to the Mahometans; and secondly Otway had tolled a bell before Dr Brown, and we are not to be made April fools twice by the same trick.' (A bell tolls for the execution of Pierre in Otway's *Venice Preserv'd*. Fitzgerald speculates that in *Barbarossa* the idea was Garrick's: during his 'war of the Romeos' with Rich he had bought, at great expense, a bell for the funeral procession, and was eager to see it put to further use.)

Fairies, but the rather coy prologue he wrote for the piece offers convincing proof that the book was his:

> An Op'ra too—play'd by an English band,
> Wrote in a language which you understand—
> I dare not say, WHO wrote it—I could tell ye,
> To soften matters—Signor *Shakespearelli* . . .*

Of Signor Shakespearelli's original text, Garrick made use only of the fairy scenes and the story of the crossed lovers. Bottom and his fellow Athenian rustics have gone, and with them the play of *Pyramus and Thisbe*. Of Shakespeare's 2,000-odd lines, Garrick cut more than 1,600.

Garrick had some unruly audience behaviour to contend with that winter. Early in February *The Tuner* noted that Guards were stationed on the stage,[6] and later in the month, a notice was inserted in the press:

> Whereas several complaints, by letter and otherwise, have been lately made to the Managers of Drury Lane Theatre, of the ill Behavior of some persons in the Upper Gallery, who throw down Apples, Potatoes, and other things into the Pit: This is therefore to assure the Ladies and Gentlemen that the Managers will take all imaginable care to discover and prosecute any person or persons, who shall disturb, or insult them for the future. If any person will discover who it was that flung a hard piece of cheese, of near half a Pound Weight, from one of the Galleries last Tuesday Night and greatly hurt a young Lady in the Pit, shall receive Ten Guineas from Mr Pritchard, the Treasurer of the Theatre.[7]

Perhaps the person who threw the cheese was merely expressing the national mood, which was increasingly truculent. America had re-emerged as a focus of ministerial concern early in 1755 and the prospect of war with France again loomed large. The truculence was laced with a certain sullen despondency; there was a feeling abroad that at a time of great danger the leadership offered by the Newcastle ministry was limp and indecisive.†

In North America, the French and British had both been strengthening their defences on Lakes Ontario and Champlain, and the French were pushing ahead with the construction of a chain of forts along the Ohio and the Mississippi to

---

* The denial of authorship occurs in a letter dated 7 December 1756 to James Murphy French, elder brother of Arthur Murphy: '—for if you mean that *I* was the person who altered the *Midsummer's Night Dream*, and the *Tempest*, into operas, you are much mistaken.—However, as old Cibber said in his last epilogue,

  'But right or wrong, or true or false—'tis pleasant.—' (*Letters*, 178.)

† 'There was no particular complaint,' one well-placed observer wrote in his diary, 'and yet the nation was sinking by degrees, and there was a general indisposition proceeding from the weakness and worthlessness of the minister who would embrace everything, and was fit for nothing.' (Dodington, George Bubb, *Diary*, London, 1784, edited by J. Cadwell and L. H. Dralle, Oxford, 1965.)

block any British expansion west of the Alleghenies.* Talks begun in London in January 1755 came to nothing. The French insisted there could be no true negotiation before there was an armistice; the British feared that an armistice would allow the French to despatch reinforcements and that this would tip the military balance. Newcastle's diplomatic initiatives also included the despatch to St Petersburg as ambassador of Woffington's old admirer, Sir Charles Hanbury Williams.† If war broke out and Prussia attacked Britain or Hanover, it would be important to have plenty of Russian troops massed on Prussia's eastern frontier. The Tsar was amenable; or, as one of Newcastle's American biographers puts it, 'Hanbury Williams used cunning and an appreciation of the venal nature of Russian politics to secure a treaty.'[8]

Talks were not allowed to interrupt Britain's efforts to bring the navy up to strength. Bounties were offered to volunteers and the press gangs were out in force. In March the French fleet set sail with reinforcements for Canada; a British squadron was sent out in pursuit, but without clear instructions about how to proceed if they intercepted it before war was declared. The French ambassador was scathing. The government, he wrote in a despatch, was giving way to public caprice: '*Le duc de Newcastle, par impuissance, timidité, et légèreté, suit le torrent comme les autres.*'[9]

Garrick's contribution to the war effort was to mount *Britannia*, a masque with words by Mallet and music by Arne. He scored an enormous success with the prologue, a collaborative effort between Mallet and himself, and which he performed in the character of a drunken sailor:‡

> Well, if thou art, my boy, a little mellow?
> A sailer, half seas o'er—'s a pretty fellow!
> What cheer ho? (*to the pit*) Zounds, I carry too much sail—
> No—tight and trim—I scud before the gale.
> (*He staggers forward, then stops.*)
> But softly, tho'—the vessel seems to heel:
> Steady, steady, boy!—must not shew her keel . . .

Having steadied himself, he hesitates briefly between staying at home 'with Sall and Sue' and going to sea again to 'bang *Mounseer*'. There isn't really a choice:

---

* The first skirmish had occurred the previous May on the borders of Virginia. British troops led by Colonel George Washington, the 22-year-old son of a tobacco planter, overpowered a French detachment advancing from Fort Duquesne on the Ohio, but were subsequently attacked by a superior force and obliged to surrender.

† Williams was no great admirer of the First Minister. When Newcastle succeeded Pelham at the Treasury the previous year, Williams wrote to Henry Fox: 'To whom are the Members of the House of Commons to address themselves? To the D. of Newcastle? Alas! he wont know their names in two years, and will forget them in two days.' (*Letters to Henry Fox, Lord Holland*, ed. the Earl of Ilchester, London, 1915, p. 60.)

‡ The prologue was so popular that it was quite often called for on nights when *Britannia* was not being performed and Garrick had to hold himself in readiness to stagger on.

> What! shall we sons of beef and freedom stoop,
> Or lower our flag to slavery and soup?
> What! shall these *parly-vous* make such a racket,
> And shall not we, my boys, well trim their jacket?
> What! shall Old England be a Frenchman's butt?
> When'er he shuffles, we should always cut . . .

Before he lurches off, a final thought detains him;

> I wish you landmen, ho, would leave your tricks,
> Your factions, parties, and damn'd politics:
> And like us, honest tars drink, fight, and sing!
> True to *yourselves*, your *country*, and your *king*!

There is no record of a command performance of *Britannia*. The King, indeed, was not in town. Concerned at the threat which Franco-British hostilities would pose to his German interests, George II had rejected the advice of his ministers and set off in the spring to attend to arrangements for the defence of Hanover.

A month before his drunken sailor routine Garrick had produced a piece of writing with a somewhat different purpose, although it too, as it happened, made much of the presumed inferiority of the French. 15 April 1755 had seen the publication of Johnson's *Dictionary*. In that melancholy, haunting monument of English prose which is his *Preface*, Johnson, now in his forty-sixth year, reminded his readers of how the work had been accomplished:

> The English Dictionary was written with little assistance of the learned, and without any patronage of the great; not in the soft obscurities of retirement, or under the shelter of academick bowers, but amidst inconvenience and distraction, in sickness and in sorrow . . . I have protracted my work till most of those, whom I wished to please, have sunk into the grave, and success and miscarriage are empty sounds: I, therefore, dismiss it with frigid tranquillity, having little to fear or hope from censure or from praise.

Garrick was moved to salute the achievement of his old friend, and his verses received wide distribution:[10]

> In the deep mines of science tho' Frenchmen may toil,
> Can their strength be compar'd to Locke, Newton, and Boyle?
> Let them rally their heroes, send forth all their pow'rs,
> Their verse-men, and prose-men; then match them with ours!
> First Shakespeare and Milton, like gods in the fight,
> Have put their whole drama and epic to flight;
> In satires, epistles, and odes would they cope,
> Their numbers retreat before Dryden and Pope;
> And Johnson, well arm'd, like a hero of yore,
> Has beat forty French, and will beat forty more.

The forty Frenchmen in question were the members of the Académie-Française, who had taken fifty-five years to do what Johnson and his handful of amanuenses had achieved in seven.* Garrick's tribute did not exactly force its way into the anthologies, but from someone whom only three years previously Johnson had sourly traduced as Prospero it represented a generous turning of the other cheek.

Since the death of the Earl eighteen months previously, Garrick's relationship with the Burlington family had undergone a change. Lady Burlington had been deeply affected by the loss of her husband. It is more than probable that there were financial problems—the Earl's passion for building had certainly got him into serious difficulties some years before his death, and he had been obliged to dispose of portions of his Irish estates. Lady Burlington had also fallen out with her son-in-law, Lord Hartington—it seems likely that there was some disagreement over the terms of Lord Burlington's will, under which Lismore Castle and the substantial properties still remaining in Ireland had passed to his daughter Charlotte, Hartington's wife.

Garrick, whose status in the family had previously been somewhat indeterminate, now found himself promoted to the position of Lady Burlington's confidant. Whenever the Garricks visited her she poured out her feelings of loneliness, her worries about household matters and her grievances, real or imagined, against Hartington. She was tearful, suspicious and confused. 'She vows a most prodigious, unalterable regard & Love for You,' Garrick wrote to Hartington in October 1754, '& has perceiv'd with much affliction & distress, Y^r Coolness & Gloom for this Month past . . . She is affraid there is some Snake in ye Grass, who has set You against her.'[11]

Over the next twelve months Garrick fired off to Hartington a whole stream of letters largely devoted to Burlington family affairs. They read like a running commentary on some obscure game of emotional snakes and ladders enlivened by sudden changes to the rules. In November he reports on a 'critical Tete a tete' he had had the day before with 'her almost unintelligible Ladyship'.[12] By May he is able to announce an improvement: 'My wife is there constantly Every day— We are in most prodigious favor, & all ye Old Affections are returning again.'[13] In July, however, he himself has the father and mother of all rows with Lady Burlington, and he sends Hartington a copy of a letter of high-flown remonstrance he has sent to her. It is very long, and it is intensely theatrical. It is also richly comic:

> . . . . . The Arrows that fly by Night, have been abroad for Some time, but I secretly despis'd them, imagining that Your Lad$^{p's}$ Good Sense & former Good Will to Me & my Wife would have been my Shield & defence; but when I find, that my once best Friend (in y^r Lady$^{p's}$ Breast), has deserted Me; it is high time to gird on my Sword & rely on y^e Strength of my own

---

* The Academy, founded in 1635, began work on its dictionary four years later. The first edition appeared in 1694.

Arm. I have hitherto curb'd my resentments in deference to Your Ladyship, but as my passiveness is only a stronger incitement to Malice & Slander, I am resolv'd (to speak in ye Scripture Phrase again) *that ye Mischief of their Lips shall fall upon their own heads* . . . . .*

No question here, clearly, of some trifling misdemeanour. The eye leaps ahead to see what terrible felony he stands accused of. In an age when stealing linen from a bleaching ground or breaking down a fish-pond were still capital offences, there were many possibilities. Coining money? Sodomy? Attempting to kill a privy councillor? Had somebody put it about, as they did of his friend William Murray, now the Attorney-General, that he was a closet Jacobite? Well, not exactly:

The Accusation against Me . . . was, that I had spirited away one of Your servants, that I had promis'd to provide for him, & as an Encouragement for joining Me in this Plot, I had brib'd him with the sum of two Shillings & Sixpence! was this Madam (after what has pass'd) a proper subject for my Smiles? this vile mean Falsehood? The mere malice & wickedness of it, I could have laugh'd at and despis'd; but when y^r Lady^P contrary to y^r usual greatness & strength of Mind, & let me add Affection too, seem'd to credit this of Me; I was no longer Myself—I was torn to pieces—[14]

Just how much Hartington appreciated these frequent and lengthy communiqués of Garrick's about the physical and mental state of his mother-in-law is open to question; the poor man had a great many other things on his mind. At the end of 1754, after little more than six years of marriage, he had lost his wife; four months later, leaving his small children to be cared for in the Burlington household, he had gone off to take up residence in Dublin Castle: like his father before him, he had been appointed Lord Lieutenant.

The Garricks, as childless couples often do, took a warm interest in other people's offspring, and Hartington was kept posted of how his brood were faring in his absence. 'I said so much & in such a hurry, in my last, that I forgot to mention the Sweet-ones, whom I had seen ye Day before, & with whom I play'd a long time Yesterday,' Garrick wrote at the end of June:

L^d C[avendish] rides like a Man, & in Every thing will answer & fulfill all y^r Lordship's Wishes—He grows greatly & tho not without his merriment his disposition seems to be reserv's & Sedate: *Master Rich^d* is most surprizingly alter'd . . . he turns out ye liveliest drollest most Engaging Child, that Ever was seen—He is in high favor indeed!

As is also sometimes the case with childless couples, the Garricks were doting pet-owners, and assumed that others would share their enthusiasm. In the middle of May Garrick thought Hartington would like to know that 'this day a Marriage

---

* Garrick's second 'Scripture Phrase' is from Psalm 140. The 'Arrows that fly by Night' are from Psalm 91.

was consummated between *Biddy* and Mrs Chandler's *Sweet-lips*'.[15] (Biddy was Mrs Garrick's lap-dog, a miniature black-and-white King Charles spaniel.) The Lord Lieutenant, grappling with the thankless task of conciliating the official English party and the first organized opposition in the Irish Parliament, cannot have regarded this as a major piece of intelligence, but *noblesse oblige*, and the Cavendish manners remained impeccable. 'My best respects to Mrs Garrick,' he replied. 'I congratulate her upon Mrs Biddy's happy nuptials, and hope that Sweet-lips has performed his part to her satisfaction.'*

Garrick felt that he knew Hartington well enough by now to solicit a sinecure for his brother Peter:

> Your Lordship loves plain Dealing & therefore this is ye plain truth—
> Peter has a small business at Lichfield wch barely Answers his Gentlemanlike
> Notions of things; wch Notions indeed are very, very Moderate—could
> he have y^e least Assistance, he w^d be as happy, as he is honest; & I sh^d
> then have no other care in y^e World, but that of expressing and Shewing
> my Gratitude. If any small Matter in y^e irish revenue sh^d lye upon Y^r
> Lord$^{p's}$ hands, (which is impossible) & that y^r Excellency has no other
> calls upon You, (which is impossible too) I could then wish that one Peter
> Garrick Brother to y^r most faithfull Servt might feel with y^e rest of his
> Family y^r Goodness & favor . . . . .[16]

Peter seems to have pressed him—there are indications that his business was not going well—and in a letter from Hampton in July, Garrick read his brother a mild lecture on how the best tacticians approach such matters in the great world:

> You may be assur'd that I shall loose no proper time to bring about w^t I
> before hinted to You; but as I am so well acquainted wth his Lordship, my
> own obligations to him, & human Nature, there is a proper Manner &
> delicacy to be Us'd wch shall be exerted, when the hour arrives, with y^e
> greatest Zeal in Y^r Service—Some Places you know are to be taken by
> Sap, & Some by Storm, & if in this Case I work *Slow*, it is to make my
> Way *Sure* . . .†

Sapper Garrick's efforts came to naught. Hartington replied promptly, but discouragingly. If it lay in his power, he wrote, nothing would give him more

---

* *Boaden*, i, 60–61. Biddy subsequently went into extended labour, and an anxious Garrick was moved to verse. The Folger Library has an autograph copy of the resulting 'Ode to the Goddess Hygeia Upon Biddy's Illness':

> Goddess Hygeia, hear our prayer,
> Descend, our little Bid to save!
> Comfort her with a loving pair.
> Biddy's the only child we have.

The Goddess of Health obliged, and Biddy was to prove notably fertile.

† *Letters*, 151. The suggestion that he was keeping his powder dry and waiting to choose his moment is disingenuous. It is clear from his correspondence that he had already broached the matter, and on more than one occasion.

pleasure than to be of service: 'but at the same time I must inform you that I have very few things to give away.'[17] Garrick brought what had plainly become an embarrassing exchange to an end with a distinctly servile expression of gratitude:

> I cannot help taking ye first opportunity to thank y^r Excellency, for your most kind intentions & Goodwill towards Me & My Family—if I have not offended by my impertinent Request, I am as Equally Oblig'd by y^r gracious Manner of receiving it, as if it had been granted—all I have now to desire is, that, should Y^r Lordship's delicacy have been hurt by my forwardness, I may appeal to Your heart only (which so warmly feels ye Tyes of Brotherhood) for my full pardon.[18]

Troilus and Cressida is one of the few Shakespearean plays that seems never to have excited Garrick's interest. Perhaps its mistrust of the heroic and the cruel light it shines on the frailty of human nature were too strong meat. But he might have recognized in one of the speeches of Ulysses a strikingly prophetic description of the age and society in which he himself lived:

> The heavens themselves, the planets, and this centre
> Observe degree, priority, and place,
> Infixture, course, proportion, season, form,
> Office and custom, all in line of order . . .[19]

As in King Priam's Troy, so in the England of the Hanoverian Georges. Very important to know your place—even if you were the manager of Drury Lane.

For much of that summer of 1755 the house at Hampton was full of workmen. 'We are here at present over head & Ears in dirt & Mortar,' Garrick wrote to Peter in early July.[20] Not far away, at Twickenham, was Strawberry Hill, Horace Walpole's 'little Gothic castle', and the two men began to see something of each other. 'I have contracted a sort of intimacy with Garrick,' Walpole wrote to Richard Bentley:

> He affects to study my taste: I lay it all upon you—he admires you. He is building a grateful temple to Shakespeare . . . . . The truth is, I make the most of this acquaintance to protect my poor neighbour at *Clivden*—you understand the conundrum, *Clive's den*.[21]

Walpole's 'poor neighbour' was Kitty Clive, to whom some time previously he had offered rent-free tenure of a villa close to his house. Mrs Clive's relations with Garrick, as with most other people, could be explosive, but she was well able to look after herself and there is no convincing evidence that she was in any need of protection. Garrick was in no doubt about her value to the company, and she, in spite of their occasional clashes, ungrudgingly acknowledged his pre-eminence.

The 'grateful temple to Shakespeare' which Walpole mentions had been designed by Robert Adam, then still in his twenties and relatively unknown.

Over the next twenty years or so Adam would advise Garrick on the substantial alterations and enlargements he made to the house, including a handsome orangerie to the rear. An octagonal structure built of brick, the temple when completed would have a dome and a portico supported by Ionic pillars. Here in a few years' time Garrick would place the life-sized statue of Shakespeare which he commissioned from Roubillac,* and which would set him back £500; it would also house his ever-growing collection of Shakespeare memorabilia, some of them more beautiful and more authentic than others.

Another letter from Walpole to Bentley indicates that by the summer of 1755 Garrick was already entertaining in some style at Hampton and that his guests were by no means only country neighbours:

> I dined today at Garrick's: there were the Duke of Grafton, Lord and Lady Rochford, Lady Holderness, the crooked Mostyn, and Dabreu the Spanish minister; two regents, one of whom is Lord Chamberlain, the other Groom of the Stole; and the wife of a Secretary of State. This is being sur un assez bon ton for a player! Don't you want to ask me how I like him? Do want, and I will tell you—I like her exceedingly; her behaviour is all sense, and all sweetness too. I don't know how, but he does not improve so fast upon me: there is a great deal of parts and vivacity and variety, but there is a great deal too of mimicry and burlesque. I am very ungrateful, for he flatters me abundantly; but unluckily I know it. I was accustomed to it enough when my father was First Minister: on his fall I lost it all at once.†

There were no broad acres to pay for Garrick's life as a country gentleman. It all had to be financed by his success as a player and as joint manager of Drury Lane. He returned there in the early autumn bubbling with enthusiasm for an exciting scheme designed to catch Rich bathing and run away with his clothes. Since the summer of 1754 he had been negotiating to bring over from Paris a phenomenally successful ballet called *Les Fêtes Chinoises*. Confident of a long run, he had almost tripled the number of dancers in his own company.

It was as well that he was denied the gift of second sight. As he drove up to town from Hampton, Garrick was heading for the most disastrous and humiliating episode of his managerial career.

---

* Louis François Roubillac (1695–1762) was born in Lyons. He had settled in England in the 1730s and gained the patronage of Horace Walpole's brother Edward. On a visit to Italy in 1752 he had been profoundly impressed by the work of Bernini. On his return he told Reynolds that all his own earlier work now seemed 'meagre and starved, as if made of nothing but tobacco pipes'. Garrick bequeathed the Shakespeare statue (for which he himself posed) to the British Museum.

† *Walpole*, xxxv, 244. Letter dated 15 August 1755 to Richard Bentley. Lady Holderness's husband, the 4th Earl, was Secretary of State for the Southern Department. Vice-Admiral Savage Mostyn had been MP for Weobley, in Herefordshire, since 1747, and was a former Comptroller of the Navy. Walpole is presumably alluding to an incident ten years earlier when as the captain of a ship of the line he had been severely criticized for failing to engage with the French fleet. He requested a court-martial, and was acquitted.

17

The Chinese Festival

Chinoiserie is not a word that French contemporaries of David Garrick's would have understood—it entered the language only in the nineteenth century. And yet the appeal to the European mind of the faraway and the exotic was age-old. Marco Polo's account of the court of the Grand Khan of Tartary was second in popularity only to 'The Voiage of Sir John Maundevile' which originally appeared in Anglo-Norman French in the middle of the fourteenth century and established itself in many languages as the model of the fabulous travel book.

By the middle years of the eighteenth century, Great Britain, like the rest of Europe, had embarked on its second serious flirtation with things Chinese. The first, more than a hundred years earlier, had been stimulated largely by the enormous quantities of blue and white porcelain imported by the Dutch. This passion for the exotic was reinforced by imports from elsewhere in the Far East. The English East India Company was already trading directly with Japan at the beginning of the seventeenth century; in September 1614, the *Clove* returned from a maiden voyage to Japan with a cargo of chests, desks, screens and bowls, all finished in an excellent varnish.

The eighteenth-century vogue of *chinoiserie* had a broader and more powerful impact. In France, Chinese influence was apparent in the paintings of Watteau and of François Boucher, the favourite artist of Madame de Pompadour. European intellectual interest in China had originally been stimulated by the Jesuits and by other western travellers; to many of the thinkers of the Enlightenment, Confucius would become almost a patron saint; the Chinese, Voltaire wrote in his 'Essai sur les Moeurs', 'have perfected moral science and that is the first of the sciences'.

In England, unsurprisingly, interest centred on more material things, most importantly on the decorative and industrial arts. William Halfpenny's *New Designs for Chinese Temples* had appeared in 1750, and Chippendale's *Director*, although influenced by the French rococo, also clearly drew inspiration from the art of China.

Imports of Chinese porcelain, wallpapers and silks all had their effect on European taste, and designs such as the 'willow-pattern', derived from the famous gardens of Soochow, conjured a beguiling mental picture of the Chinese landscape. Someone who had actually seen Chinese gardens for himself was a young architect called William Chambers, whose first employment had been as a supercargo with the Swedish East India Company. In 1757 he would publish his enormously influential *Designs of Chinese Buildings, Furniture, Dresses, Machines and Utensiles, from the Originals Drawn in China*. Commissioned by the Dowager Princess of Wales to adorn the gardens of her villa at Kew, the buildings he constructed there between 1757 and 1762 included the famous pagoda.*

None of this is to say that the aesthetic influence of China in the eighteenth century was particularly profound, important as it was in the development of the rococo style. A modern sinologist resuméd the matter well in *The Legacy of China*:

> The inspiration of rococo was neither the glory of God, nor the heroism of warriors, nor the grandeur of princes and statesmen, but the life of aristocratic leisure in its more relaxed, playful, and sentimental moods, and this outlook as it prevailed in Western Europe in the last epoch of the *ancien régime* had much in common with the spirit of Chinese scholar-gentry in Hangchow or Soochow about the same time.[1]

Such was the breaker on which Garrick confidently expected that he would surf to profitable acclaim in the autumn of 1755. *Les Fêtes Chinoises* was the work of a young dancer and choreographer called Jean Georges Noverre who, like Garrick, had come a long way in a short time. He had been born in Paris in 1727, the son of a native of Lausanne who was a member of the Swiss Guard at the French court. He had made his début at the Opéra-Comique at the age of sixteen when Garrick's friend Monnet was manager there. He danced for a time at the court in Berlin, where he amused Frederick the Great by his imitations of the leading *danseuses* and entertained Voltaire with his talent for wicked stories.† After a spell as ballet master at Marseilles he moved on to Lyons and to Strasbourg; when Monnet returned to the Opéra-Comique after his disastrous London foray, Noverre accepted an invitation to rejoin him and quickly made his mark. Even Charles Collé, no lover of the ballet, was impressed:

> This ballet has been designed by a certain Noverre, a young man of 27 or 28 years. He seems to have a wide and agreeable imagination for his profession. He is novel and prolific, varied and a painter. It is not by the *pas* and the *entrées* that he pleased, it is by the variegated and novel tableaux that he achieved this prodigious success. If there is anyone who can drag us out of the childhood in which we are still in the matter of ballets, it must be a man such as this Noverre.[2]

When news of the success of *Les Fêtes Chinoises* reached London Garrick moved

---

* The 'Chinese—English garden' would enjoy an even greater vogue in Germany and France than in England. Chambers (1726—96) later became court architect, and designed Somerset House. He was a founder-member and the first Treasurer of the Royal Academy. Garrick, Johnson, Goldsmith, Reynolds and Burney all became close friends.
† The *prima ballerina* at the time was La Barbarina, who had performed at Smock Alley with Garrick and Woffington in the summer of 1742.

quickly and asked Charles Selwyn, an English lawyer in Paris, to make an offer to Noverre to bring the ballet to Drury Lane. Selwyn opened the negotiations by naming a figure of £200, but this came nowhere near Noverre's view of what he was worth in the market place, and he sent a distinctly imperious letter to Garrick saying that the proposals put to him by 'Monsieur Silvain' were unacceptable. 'I earn in Paris in five months two hundred and fifty golden louis without taking into account my students,' he wrote (a louis was worth a guinea): his terms for appearing in London were three hundred guineas and a benefit, without the deduction of any expenses. 'This is my last word,' he told Garrick, indicating at the same time that he was not short of offers: 'Please be so good as to make up your mind because I do not wish to answer the proposals of the Bavarian Court before I know your latest intentions.' And there was a postscript: 'I have my sister, who is a pretty dancer, for whom I ask one hundred guineas.'[3]

That letter was written in September 1754. The negotiations were still in train in January, although they seem to have been a little one-sided: 'Since the proposals I put to you seem to me to be fair,' Noverre wrote to Garrick, 'I cannot reduce them in anyway.' But he was prepared to be magnanimous:

> I will, however, sacrifice my interest by paying the expenses of the benefit mentioned in your letter, not so much to fall in with the customs of your theatre as to give you a proof of my desire to work with you.

The agreement to which both men put their signature early in February gave Noverre all that he asked for. His sister was to have her hundred guineas, and he was to be compensated for meeting the expenses of his benefit by an increase in his fee to 350 guineas. He had even persuaded Garrick that he should be indemnified against the possible effects of some injury that he had apparently suffered: 'If my accident should prevent my dancing this will in no way alter my engagement and I will be paid my salary in full for the composition of the ballets alone.'

Noverre now suggested that he should travel to London after Easter to familiarize himself with Drury Lane. He had also been invited to go to Lyons for two months, however, which would earn him very much more than the twenty-five louis that Selwyn had been authorized to offer him for travelling expenses. 'The pleasure I shall have in forwarding our acquaintance and in cementing it,' he wrote to Garrick, 'will make me shut my eyes to the sacrifice I am making you of my time . . .'

Garrick paid up, but the meter on this bandwaggon was still ticking merrily away. Noverre saw no reason why his friends and relations should not sample the apparently endless supply of golden eggs he had stumbled on in London. He recommended to Garrick his good friend the dancer de Laître:

> He still pleases in Paris and I think he will greatly please in London. I judge by his anxiety to see that Town that he would come down somewhat on his interests. As I find myself entrusted with this negotiation I ask you to finalise it by a prompt decision on your side, so that I do not find myself in a position where I have to reproach myself . . .

And then there was his friend Louis-René Boquet. Boquet, now in his late thirties, had been a costume designer at the Opéra and was responsible for the costumes and scenery when there were fêtes at the French court. His drawings were widely admired, but he did not, of course, come cheap. Noverre, writing to Garrick early in May, outlined his requirements:

> The Sieur Boquet wishes to undertake to go to London, to have executed his four décors and have made before his eyes all the costumes necessary to my ballets, have your theatre arranged without a chandelier and, finally, make it the most agreeable in London. He asks for this, for the journey and for his efforts and the supply of his drawings, one hundred and fifty louis, on the condition that you will supply him with workmen because his time is precious and he could only remain in London for six weeks.

Noverre also reported that he had engaged three supernumeraries; he was confident that they would not 'dishonour our nation'. He was on the lookout for three more, but it was not the easiest of tasks: 'It is impossible to find supernumeraries for 40 louis; you know that woman is an expensive, if common, merchandise, and so I await your orders on this subject.'

All this activity resulted in what a later age would describe as a cash-flow problem. 'I need some for my own account,' Noverre told Garrick, 'and I would be greatly obliged to you if you would give instructions accordingly, for I am in difficulty with my affairs.'* Then, almost as an afterthought:

> I could not live in London without my wife, see if she can be of use to you for your pantomimes; she would dance in my ballets. What is the salary you could pay her?
>
> Answer me, Sir, under all these headings, and give me news of your health and that of Mrs Garrick. I have been greatly grieved since my return. I lost two rings of sixty golden louis, which my wife had put on my watch chain without fastening the clasp, and I lost them on the way to M. Silvain's. I had the drum beaten and sent out notes and had posters put up, but in vain. However, one must console onself and accept philosophically the accidents which befall us. . .[4]

Was Noverre hinting that Garrick should compensate him for his wife's carelessness? He was undoubtedly brassy enough to do just that; all allowance made for the letter-writing conventions of the day, the fulsome tone of his reply indicates that he had got most of what he had asked for. 'I have received the charming letter which you have done me the favour of writing me,' he wrote. 'I have a lively sentiment of your proofs of esteem . . . You are a heavenly man, and all

---

* His 'affairs' were not confined to the theatre; he also had an unsuccessful sideline as a distiller. Garrick corresponded at this time with a young French lawyer called Claude-Pierre Patu, who had been introduced to him in London the previous year by John Cleland, the author of *Fanny Hill*. In a letter from Geneva dated 1 November 1755 Patu retailed some gossip about Noverre's business interests: 'His great reputation has not caused his liqueurs to be bought (who the devil would imagine that a dancing fellow would at the same time be a distiller!)'

the artists and *savants* of this country would be glad to have the happiness of knowing you.'[5]

What was Garrick hoping to get for the substantial sums of money he was laying out? The mature Noverre retained no great fondness for his early work and did not preserve a scenario of *Les Fêtes Chinoises*, but a contemporary account of the ballet, published in 1755 in the *Nouveau Calendrier des Spectacles de Paris* does survive:

> ... The scene represents at first an avenue ending in terraces and in a flight of steps leading to a palace situated on a height. This first set changes, and shows a public square, decorated for a festival; at the back is an amphitheatre, on which sixteen Chinamen are seated. By a quick change of scene, thirty-two Chinamen appear instead of sixteen, and go through a pantomimic performance on the steps. As they descend, sixteen other Chinamen, mandarins and slaves, come out of their houses and take their places on the steps. All these persons form eight ranks of dancers, who, by bending down and rising up in succession, give a fair imitation of the waves of a stormy sea. . . . When this procession is finished the ballet begins, and leaves nothing to be desired, neither for the variety nor for the neatness of the figures. It ends by a round-dance, in which there are thirty-two persons; their movements form a prodigious quantity of new and perfectly planned figures, which are linked and unlinked with the greatest ease. At the end of this round dance the Chinamen take up their places anew on the amphitheatre, which changes into a porcelain shop. Thirty-two vases rise up, and hide from the audience the thirty-two Chinese . . .[6]

That makes it sound all rather formal and static, a procession or pageant rather than a ballet, but Garrick clearly felt that it marked an advance on previous productions of the kind. He may also have been looking beyond the one season specified in Noverre's contract, hoping that he might persuade him to stay in London and become in effect Drury Lane's *maître de ballet*, although he must have realized that his fellow-manager would need a lot of persuading. Lacy may have wanted to engage rope-dancers, but he looked on this French extravaganza with no enthusiasm whatever, particularly as they had laid out a good deal during the summer in having the theatre painted and regilded.

The season started quietly enough in mid-September. Garrick, to his regret, had lost Mossop, who had gone off to Dublin. 'There was a little Misunderstanding between Us,' he wrote to Hartington, 'but upon an Eclaircissement, We were both most Sorry that other engagements had hinder'd Us from being together.'[*]
A new recruit to the company was the 22-year-old Charles Holland. Handsome

---

* *Letters*, 156. Victor and Sowdon at Smock Alley had offered Mossop an engagement which included a share of the profits, and in spite of illness the season brought him more than £800. He returned to Drury Lane the following year.

THE HUMOURS OF A BENEFIT NIGHT,
OR THE BOXES IN AN UPROAR.

'The Boxes in an Uproar.' The generally decorous behaviour of modern theatre-goers would have astonished their eighteenth-century forebears, who regarded themselves as the masters and expected their servants the players to gratify their every whim. Their response in the case of non-compliance could swiftly progress from the robust to the riotous. (The Lennox-Boyd Collection)

and athletic, Holland was the son of a baker in Chiswick. He had served an apprenticeship with a turpentine merchant and had distinguished himself in private theatricals. Garrick gave him his chance early in the season as Oroonoko, with Mrs Cibber as Imoinda. 'He perform'd very well, & had great Applause,' Cross wrote in his diary, although he noted that things had gone slightly awry towards the end: 'In stabbing the Governor in the last Scene, he struck him on the Cheek, & upon hearing him cry, O God! was so shock'd that he did not die so well as was expected.'*

Garrick himself drew good houses in the first two months of the season with a selection of his most popular roles. Early in November, he was Hastings in *Jane Shore*, and Cross made an ominous entry in his diary:

> When Mr Garrick ended the 3ᵈ Act with "Die wᵗʰ pleasure for my Country's good"—a person in the Gall: cried no french Dancers then—wᶜʰ seems to say much resentment will be shewn when the 24 we have engag'd appear.

They were due to appear in precisely two days' time. Very late in the day, Garrick inserted a defensive and not altogether accurate advertisement in the *Public Advertiser*:

> Mr Noverre, whose entertainments of Dancing have been celebrated in almost all the courts of Europe, exhibits this evening his Chinese Festival at the Theatre Royal in Drury Lane, in pursuance of a contract made above a year ago with the managers of the said theatre: The Insinuation that at this time, an extraordinary number of French dancers are engaged, is groundless, there being at Drury Lane at present as few of that nation, as any other theatre now has, or perhaps ever had. Mr Noverre and his brothers are Swiss, of a protestant family in the Canton of Berne, his wife and her sisters Germans; there are above sixty performers concerned in the entertainment; more than forty of which are English, assisted only by a few French (five men and four women) to complete the Ballet as usual . . .

It is remarkable that Garrick, whose sensibilities were normally so finely attuned to the public mood, seems to have taken so little account of the rising tide of anti-French feeling. He had many friends in court and ministerial circles, and he was far from being totally absorbed in the affairs of the theatre. His correspondence abounds in comment on the political events of the day. 'The news from America has damp'd our spirits a little' he had written to Hartington three months previously, for instance—a reference to the death of General Braddock and the rout of his force by a smaller body of French and Indians at Fort Duquesne. Equally it is plain that he kept himself well informed about the detail

---

* Holland was inclined to be accident-prone. Later in the season, for his benefit, he chose to play Hamlet. While he was speaking his first lines to the Ghost his hat fell off — a traditional piece of business at that time. 'An Ignorant man took up his hat & clapt it upon his head,' reported Cross. 'Holland unconcern'd play'd with it so, & went off with it, (great Prudence).' (*Cross Diary*, 20 April 1756.)

of what Hartington himself was trying to achieve in Ireland as Lord Lieutenant.

Although the Newcastle ministry was still not finally committed to war with France, no one doubted that the outbreak of hostilities was only a matter of time. By the end of 1755 some 300 French merchant ships and upwards of 7,000 French seamen had been brought into English ports, a proceeding which the French not unnaturally stigmatized as piracy. The English press did little to dampen war fever: 'We are assured,' the *London Evening Post* informed its readers, 'that the French are gathering together a great number of small craft at Boulogne, Calais and other Northern ports of France for a descent on England.'

Sections of the press also did their best to foment a descent on Drury Lane. Arthur Murphy had joined the company there as an actor that season and witnessed the developing battle over *The Chinese Festival* from the ringside:

> The scriblers, the small wits, and the whole tribe of disappointed authors, declared war against the manager. In newspapers, essays, and paragraphs, they railed at an undertaking, calculated, as they said, to maintain a gang of Frenchmen. The spirit of the inferior class was rouzed, and spread like wildfire through London and Westminster.*

It occurred to Garrick that there would be less likelihood of trouble if the first night were a Command Performance, and that was arranged through the Lord Chamberlain. To no great effect. 'The presence of a crowned head,' wrote Davies, 'was not sufficient to curb that ill-placed zeal against Papists and Frenchmen, which had seized many well-meaning people.'[7] The mainpiece was quietly received, but when the ballet began there was a good deal of hissing, and some cries of 'No French dancers.' Reports of what the old King made of it all vary. A French account of the occasion says that he was received 'with as much joy as indecency'. Davies maintains that when the cause of the uproar was explained to him, he 'seemed to enjoy the folly of the hour, and laughed very heartily'; Cross, however, has it that 'the King did turn his back to the Audience', which suggests that the behaviour of his loyal subjects was not entirely to his liking.

Lacy was all for cutting their losses and abandoning the project, but Garrick persisted in the view that the audience could be won round. At the second performance four nights later, things got much rougher. The theatre was crowded by three o'clock in the afternoon. Cross noted that a good many army officers were in evidence—they had taken the hissing in the presence of the King on the first night as an affront and were determined to level the score.

The Chinese Festival was a gift to Grub Street and the pamphleteers were soon furiously at work. One of them, describing himself as 'Grub-street Literatus'

---

* *Murphy*, i, 278. Murphy's evidence must, for all that, be treated with some caution. He authenticates an anecdote about the first night of *The Festival* by saying that he happened to be in the green-room at the time. The anecdote turns on the ballet's having been preceded by *Richard III*, but the mainpiece that night was *The Fair Quaker of Deal*. He may have been following Davies, who makes the same mistake, although Davies was also a member of the company that year (as was his wife).

rushed out 'The Dancers Damn'd; Or The Devil to Pay at the Old House', ostensibly an eye-witness account of the proceedings, although the author had plainly had the benefit of a comprehensive briefing from the Drury Lane management:*

> When the Chinese scene was expos'd, the leader of the Loyal party advanced to the front of the Gallery and thus bespake the House: 'O Britons! O my Countrymen! Ye will certainly not suffer these foreign dogs to amuse us. Our destruction is at hand. These sixty dancers are come over with a design to undermine our constitution. This Navarre is Marshall Lewendahl,† and the least among them is an ensign, disguised, in order to perpetrate our ruin!'

This speech is answered by Reason, newly descended from the clouds:

> I came hither by the persuasion of Truth and Justice to tell you that among all this number of dancers that now stand ready to entertain you there are no more than Four French men and about the same number of females; that their Chief is a Swiss Protestant, who, had not his merit protected him would have been hiss'd off the stage at Paris, for being a Swiss Protestant. And will you damn him for the same reason? Will you pay less regard to Genius than a French Audience?

This was greeted by cat-calls, and a cry of 'Swiss! What the devil do we know of Swiss! a Swiss is a foreigner, and all foreigners are Frenchmen; and so damn you all!' Grub-street Literatus's account ends with one of the rioters being thrown from the gallery into the pit:

> His head pitched upon that of one of his own wise party, and both were dashed to pieces. A skilful anatomist who stood not far from the place where they fell, expressed great desire to examine the texture of their brains, which he said must certainly be very extraordinary; but notwithstanding he was assisted in his search, by the whole pit, it was not in the power of any one to find aught in either of their strange heads that bore the least resemblance to brains.

A month later in Paris, the December edition of the Journal Etranger published what reads like an account by someone who was actually on stage—perhaps a member of the corps de ballet, possibly Noverre himself. Whoever he was, he had a different conspiracy theory to advance, asserting that the demonstration was fomented partly by disgruntled English actors and dancers and partly by the

---

* In one passage he describes those opposed to the Festival as 'a blind, ignorant and tasteless mob, deaf to the voice of reason and determined on the riots they raised, rather for the sake of rioting than from a laudable principle of public spirit or generous resentment against the enemies of this country'.

† Count Löwendahl was a Dane in the French service who had distinguished himself by the capture of the almost impregnable fortress of Bergen-op-Zoom in 1747. An even more imaginative story that went the rounds was that Noverre was Bonnie Prince Charlie in disguise.

management and staff of other theatres. He also gave his French readers a spirited blow-by-blow description of the action:

> First a man was thrown into the Pit and another into the Stalls. All the My Lords leaped into the Pit, some with staves others sword in hand, and descended upon a group of demonstrators whom they covered with blows. The English Ladies, far from being affrighted by the horrible scuffle, gave a hand to the gallants that they might leap into the pit and pointed out to them the people to be knocked out. A number of innocent people paid for the guilty. The outraged Nobility struck right and left regardless, breaking arms and heads, and blood was running everywhere; the ballet ceased until finally the Nobility turned out the mutilated rioters. The ballet began once more; all the spectators flourished their hats on high crying 'Huzza,' a term of applause corresponding to the Italian 'Bravo'; the clapping was general and there were no more catcallers, they were all round at the surgeons . . . .

At this stage Garrick seemed to be slightly ahead on points. It was part of his strategy—in a later age he would have made a mean television scheduler—to present strongly cast, popular mainpieces before the ballet: Woodward and Mrs Clive appeared in *The Inconstant* on the second night, he himself played opposite Mrs Cibber in *The Provok'd Wife* on the third. On the fourth night, the honours went to the pit and the gallery. There was no violence, but Parliament had reassembled that day, which meant that attendance in the boxes was thin. The ballet was performed, but against such a cacophony of noise that it was impossible to hear the music.

For the fifth performance Garrick and Mrs Pritchard were billed in *Much Ado About Nothing*, always a sure-fire crowd-puller. Unfortunately there was a counter-attraction—'Our friends were at the Opera,' Cross noted in his diary, '& the common people had leisure to do Mischief.' Garrick's appearance as Benedick was greeted with a shout of 'Monsieur' and there was a great deal of hissing. The correspondent of the *Journal Etranger* recorded the triumph of the 'blagards', as he called them: 'They tore up the benches and threw them into the Pit on the opposing party; they broke all the mirrors, the chandeliers, &c., and tried to climb onto the stage to massacre everybody.' But he was greatly impressed by the cool efficiency with which the management responded. 'There is a magnificent organization in this theatre,' he wrote:

> In three minutes all the décor had been removed, all the traps were ready to come into play to swallow up those who might venture up, all the wings were filled with men armed with sticks, swords, halberds, etc. and, behind the scenes, the great reservoir was ready to be opened to drown those who might fall on the stage itself. All the public called for Garrick who had very good reason for not showing himself . . . . .

The rioting went on until midnight, and the mob dispersed only when Lacy went on to announce that *The Chinese Festival* would not be performed again.

That was not the end of the story, however. Drury Lane was closed on Sunday, but the taverns and coffee-houses were not. 'A number of tragic scenes were enacted between the two parties,' reported the *Journal Etranger*, 'which, far from healing the trouble, envenomed it more and more.' Both factions were out in force the next night to see Garrick as Chamont in *The Orphan*. At the beginning of the fifth act the occupants of the boxes, many of whom had turned up in uniform, disrupted the performance with cries for *The Chinese Festival* to be announced for the next night.

Garrick was in an impossible position. He must try to please his aristocratic patrons on the one hand while not offending the pit and gallery on the other. An extended dialogue with the audience came to an abrupt end when several of those in the boxes drew their swords and vaulted down into the pit. Seizing one of those they identified as a ringleader, they held him suspended in the air and seemed about to strangle him; the man may well have owed his life to Garrick, who jumped into the pit with the improbable cry, 'Gentlemen, do not hurt him, he is a friend of mine.' Cross's understanding was that the evening ended with an agreement that *The Chinese Festival* should be performed three nights a week to please the boxes and that there should be some other entertainment on other nights to satisfy the pit. The *Journal Etranger* version was that the boxes insisted on a vote, and carried the day by intimidation.

The last act of this eighteenth-century version of *High Noon* was played out on 18 November. By three o'clock the theatre was already packed. The 'blagards' had turned the servants of the nobility and gentry out of the first row of boxes and remained in occupation until about five, when the quality began to arrive in large numbers, the men armed with swords and loaded sticks. Bawdy choruses were sung, there were calls for the orchestra to play 'The Roast Beef of Old England' and there was a great deal of farmyard noise.

The play—it was *The Earl of Essex*—was heard quietly, but the overture for the ballet was the signal for a chorus of boos and the ringing of handbells. Several gentlemen of rank jumped from the boxes on to the stage, but found that it had been liberally sprinkled with iron tacks. One of them was struck in the face by an apple, and from that moment the touch-paper was well and truly alight: 'Broken arms, legs and heads, people half crushed under the benches, the Chinese dancers hiding in corners.' The pit was cleared, but reinforcements from the gallery won it back:

> The ballet begins, the stage is covered with several bushels of peas mixed with tacks. The *milords* sweep the stage with their hats, fresh peas are thrown; the *milords* jumps once more into the Pit, the doors of which are forced open by a troup of butchers,* who declare themselves for the Nobility, hitting right and left at the demonstrators . . .

Accompanied by constables and a detachment of troops, two magistrates appeared. One of them was Sir John Fielding, who had succeeded his half-brother

---

* The butchers of Clare Market were enthusiastic patrons of the theatre.

Henry as Justice of the Peace for Westminster on the latter's death the previous year. Sir John, blind since birth, was said to know more than 3,000 thieves by their voices, an accomplishment of no great use to him on this occasion. He and his colleague stood around on the stage for a time, but for some reason failed to read the Riot Act.* Later it was reported to them that some of the rioters had made their way to Garrick's house and smashed his windows and some of the troops were despatched to Southampton Street to prevent worse mischief.

There is conflicting evidence on how much damage was done to the theatre. Murphy talks of the necessary repairs taking five or six days, but Lacy and Garrick managed to open for business the night after the riot. The company played to a thin house, with takings of only £100. 'Some people had assembled in the Passages, to what intent we knew not,' wrote Cross, 'Justice Welch and Fielding came in case of a Riot but all was quiet.'[8]

Garrick himself appeared as Archer two nights later. A good house gave him a mixed reception:

> Soon as Mr Garrick appear'd, a great Clap, with some hissing upon wch he said—Gentlemen it is impossible to go on with these hisses, I don't know what offence I am guilty of—they clap'd greatly—& he proceeded— Let one Gentleman speak for the rest & I'll give an Answer—there was a moments pause & then a general cry of—Go on with the Play &c., all ceased—& all continu'd quiet.†

The management was out of pocket to the tune of £4,000. Susannah Cibber, who had appeared with Garrick in *The Earl of Essex* on the worst night of the rioting, fell ill and was unable to appear again until the middle of December. Noverre and his family went to ground; during the riot his younger brother Augustin, who had been a member of the cast, had run a man through with his sword.‡

One of the nastier pieces of writing prompted by *The Chinese Festival* was 'A Epistle from Theophilus Cibber to David Garrick'. Theophilus, now in his early

---

* The Riot Act of 1714 made it the duty of a justice to proceed to any place where twelve or more persons were 'unlawfully, riotously and tumultuously assembled' and read a proclamation requiring them to disperse. The penalty for non-compliance was penal servitude for life.

† *Cross Diary*, 21 November 1755. In his *Memoirs*, Tate Wilkinson, who was a boy of sixteen at the time, gives a more dramatic version of what Garrick said: 'He acknowledged all favours received, but unless he was that night permitted to perform his duty to the best of his abilities, he was above want, superior to insult, and would never, *never*, appear on the stage again.' According to Wilkinson the audience responded to this 'like true-hearted Britons', and for several minutes their applause 'shook the fabric of Old Drury' (*Wilkinson*, iv, 215–16). Neither Davies nor Murphy mention this, although both were members of the company that season, while Mrs Davies was actually on stage with Garrick that evening in the part of Dorinda.

‡ The man recovered. Augustin later returned to Drury Lane and danced there on and off until the early 1770s. He ultimately settled in Norwich, where several generations of his descendants gave dancing lessons. Although he tried to take on local colouring by larding his speech with the occasional 'goddem' his English was never good, and he was known — affectionately — as 'Dancing Froggy'. He died in 1805 at the age of seventy-six.

fifties, had been having a thin time of it, and was struggling in his efforts to secure public appearances. He saw in the fracas over the French dancers an opportunity both to lay his 'case' once more before the town and to do an injury to Garrick:

> Is it not possible, some People may think it a little hard, that an *Englishman*, the Son of an *Englishman*, (whose Birth entitled him to a better Fortune than a Playhouse Promised) and who, in his Theatrical Capacity, as Author, and Actor, has been judged one of the greatest Ornaments of the *English* Stage)—is it not hard, that His Son, after having spent many Years, with Approbation, in the Service of the Public, should be obstructed in his honest Views, of getting his Bread still in their Service?—and really, by whom obstructed? may one not reply, by the Son of a *Frenchman*, who not content with having amassed a princely Fortune, is still jealous a Shilling should be added to a poor Man's Purse, lest his Coffers should not sufficiently run over? . . . . .

A couple of pages later, he creeps up on the presumed xenophobia of his readers from a different direction:

> In how much a happier Situation are the *French* Players, tho' in a Country of hateful arbitrary Power?—Tho' Superstition, and Priestcraft, deny them Christian Burial, yet humanity denies them not a comfortable Livelihood. . . . . But you, Sir, may probably know more of this, as your Father, a Native of *France*, was capable of acquainting you more fully therewith.

There is a threatening hint of action against Mrs Cibber: 'Let me remind you, Sir, I have not made Use of that incontestible Power the Law has given me, to deprive you of a potent Assistant, in your Theatrical Business.' Then one last thrust at Garrick's French antecedents:

> For my own Part, I have but simple English Honesty to proceed upon;— whether that will be of as much Service to me as *French* Jesuitical Policy, Time must determine.

The ill wind which blew away all that Garrick had hoped for from *The Chinese Festival* was not entirely without profit. Jean Georges Noverre carried away important lessons from the shambles of his first London engagement. The new approach to dance which he would set out in his *Lettres sur la danse* in 1760 owed a great deal to his encounter with Garrick. Until then, his ballets had essentially been spectacles for the eye alone; now he would increasingly break with traditional forms and evolve a choreographic style able to tell a story and express human passions. When he urged the need to do away with the masks traditionally worn by dancers and trust to the natural play of their features, Noverre, not normally lavish with his praise of others, freely acknowledged the source of his inspiration:

> Mr Garrick, the celebrated English actor, is the model I propose. A finer
> one does not exist ... He was so natural, his expression had so much
> truth, his gestures, his physiognomy, and his looks were so eloquent and
> so persuasive that they acquainted even those who did not understand
> English with what was going on on the stage.*

Garrick returned the compliment by calling Noverre 'the Shakespeare of the
dance'—although he also, in a more unbuttoned moment, referred to him as
'that most fantastick toe'.⁹ There may also have surfaced in that lively and
well-stocked mind what the father of Shakespeare's Juliet says to his companion
as the masquers and musicians make their way into the hall of his palazzo in
Verona:

> Nay, sit, nay, sit, good cousin Capulet,
> For you and I are past our dancing days.

The rest of the season passed quietly and profitably enough. Murphy's first play,
a farce called *The Apprentice*, which poked fun at the spouting clubs, was well
received in January; it ran for sixteen nights, and Murphy claimed to have cleared
'within a trifle of £800' at his benefits. Garrick, who had initially turned the piece
down, wrote the prologue, and permitted himself a wry look back at the events
of November:

> No mangled, pilfer'd scenes from France we shew,
> 'Tis English—English, sirs, from top to toe.

Later in the month, he offered his public a Shakespearean double-bill—a version
of *The Winter's Tale* to go with *Catherine and Petruchio*, the alteration of *The
Taming of the Shrew* which he had provided for Mrs Pritchard's benefit two
seasons previously. *The Winter's Tale* had last been seen at Covent Garden in
1741. Garrick now pruned it severely, telescoping the action into three acts,
cutting some six hundred of Shakespeare's lines and adding four hundred or so
of his own. He clearly anticipated some criticism. 'A vintner once acquir'd both
praise and gain,/ And sold much Perry for the best Champaign,' he wrote in a
long prologue, in which he compared Drury Lane to a tavern:

> In this night's various and enchanted cup,
> Some little Perry's mixt for filling up.
> The five long acts, from which our three are taken,
> Stretch'd out to sixteen years, lay by, forsaken.
> Lest then this precious liquor run to waste,
> 'Tis now confin'd and bottled for your taste.

Theophilus Cibber was predictably quick to put the boot in: '*The Winter's Tale*,
of Shakespear, thus lop'd, hack'd, and dock'd, appears without Head or

---

* It was a change long resisted by the management of the Paris Opera, many of whose rich
and noble patrons liked to don masks and mingle with the dancers.

Tail.'* Murphy, on the other hand, noting that Shakespeare had played fast and loose with the unities of time and place, had nothing but praise for the alterations: 'Garrick saw that the public would be little obliged to him for a revival of the entire play, and therefore, with great judgement, extracted from the chaos before him a clear and regular fable.'[10] Davies also approved: 'Mutilated as Mr Garrick's revived play was, it had considerable merit as well as success.' He thought Garrick masterly as Leontes, and had high praise for the rest of the cast: 'Mrs Cibber's Perdita, Mrs Pritchard's Hermione, Woodward's Clown, Berry's Old Shepherd, John Beard's Peasant, and, above all, Yates's Autolicus, were such portraits of nature as we must almost despair of seeing again in one piece.'† (Modesty forbade him to mention that on the first night he himself had created the part of Camillo.)

In some quarters, there was a feeling that Garrick's championing of the bard was a shade too proprietary and during the run of The Winter's Tale one C. Marsh went reprovingly into print on the subject:

> Think'st thou, the Swan of Avon spreads her wings,
> Her brooding wings, for thee alone, to plume
> And nestle there, O Garrick? Thou deserv'st
> Indeed much cherishing; thy Melody
> Charms every ear. But sure it ill beseems
> One Cygnet thus to stretch its little pinions,
> Ambitiously intent, to fill that nest,
> Whose roomy limits well may shelter numbers . . .'[11]

The audience, however, had no reservations. Within a year, thirteen performances of Florizel and Perdita, as it was later known, put £2,260 into Drury Lane's depleted coffers.

Garrick's next venture in adapting Shakespeare to the taste of his own age fared less well. He now tried his hand at an operatic version of The Tempest. An earlier version, a collaborative effort between Davenant and Dryden, had enjoyed great popularity on the Restoration stage (Pepys saw it eight times in less than eighteen months). Garrick, indeed, had put it on—with no great success—in the first year of his Drury Lane managership.

As in The Fairies, the music for this new adaptation was written by Handel's pupil John Christopher Smith. Of the opera's thirty-two songs only four (including 'Come Unto These Yellow Sands' and 'Full Fathom Five') were from

---

* Dissertations on Theatrical Subjects, London, 1756, First Dissertation, pp. 33–8. Cibber fancied himself as a phrase-maker. Garrick is variously described as 'this sly Prince', 'this pilfering Pedlar in poetry' and 'this merciless Procrustes of the stage'.

† Davies, i, 314. Woodward had a busy evening, because he also appeared as Petruchio in the afterpiece, playing opposite Kitty Clive as Catherine. Cross noted a piece of unrehearsed stage business: 'Mrs Clive fell down in ye Farce, and accused Woodward wth doing it on purpose.' Davies adds that when Petruchio and his bride were at supper, Woodward stuck a fork in Mrs Clive's finger. (Ibid., i, 312.)

Shakespeare's play. Garrick's prologue, aimed, as so often, at disarming criticism before it was expressed, took the form of a prose dialogue between Heartly, an actor, and Wormwood, a critic:

WORMWOOD: . . . I say that this frittering and sol-fa-ing our best poets is a damn'd thing. I have yet heard no reason to justify it, and I have no patience when I think of it.

HEARTLY: I see you have not—

WORMWOOD: What! Are we to be quivered and quavered out of our senses? Give me Shakespeare, in all his force, rigor, and spirit! What! would you make an eunuch of him?

Heartly, having got Wormwood to concede that he hates music ('Damn-ably, and dancing too') eventually wins him over by playing the patriotic card:

HEARTLY: Let us suppose an invasion!

WORMWOOD: Ha, ha, ha! An invasion! Music and an invasion! They are well coupled, truly!

HEARTLY: Patience, sir, I say, let us suppose ten thousand French landed.

WORMWOOD: I had rather suppose 'em at the bottom of the sea.

HEARTLY: So had I, but that ten thousand are upon the coast.

WORMWOOD: The devil they are! What then?

HEARTLY: Why, then I say, let but *Britons strike home* or *God save the King* be sounded in the ears of five thousand brave Englishmen with a protestant prince at the head of 'em, and they'll drive every monsieur into the sea and make 'em food for sprats and mackerel.

WORMWOOD: Huzza! and so they will!—'Egad, you're right; I'll say no more. *Britons strike home!* You have warm'd me and pleas'd me; nay, you have converted me. I'll get a place in the house, and be as hearty as the best of 'em for the musick of old England! Sprats and mackarel! ha, ha, ha! that's good! excellent! I thank you for it; musick for ever! *Britons strike home! God save the King!*

This did not go down well on the first night—'much hiss'd & dislik'd,' noted Cross—although on the second night it was called for and got some applause. By the fourth performance, receipts had dropped to £90. A command performance by the Prince of Wales did little to improve matters, and after six nights Garrick sensibly took it off.

The energy and stamina of the man were prodigious. He had bounced back from *The Chinese Festival* fiasco with impressive ease. He continued to combine his duties as manager with a punishing performance schedule. His social life was as busy as ever and he was an untiring and entertaining correspondent. He made time not only to work on his ambitious adaptations of Shakespeare but to scribble away on his own account—not just the prologues and epilogues routinely produced for the theatre, but the occasional poem or song.

One such, which had wide circulation in the course of 1756, was the rousingly jingoistic 'The Lilies of France':

> The lilies of *France*, and the fair *English* rose,
> Cou'd never agree, as old history shows . . .

The drift to war had gathered pace. The perceived threat of a French invasion induced a mood of near panic in the ministry about the state of the country's defences. A bill to establish a national militia got through the Commons but was thrown out by the Lords. Newcastle, nervously aware of the looming shadow of Pitt, was obliged to attend to the nation's security by ignominiously buying in mercenary effort from Hesse and Hanover. War was not declared until news came of the French landing in Minorca in May; the squadron of ten ships sent out to relieve the garrison there had gone about its business in a manner judged to be unduly dilatory, and nine months later the wretched Admiral Byng was shot on the quarter-deck of the *Monarque* in Portsmouth Harbour—*pour encourager les autres*.*

'The Lilies of France' served two functions. It struck an appropriately defiant note in the gloomy early days of what the history books would describe as the Seven Years War. It was also a neatly oblique way of reiterating that anyone who had entertained doubts about Garrick's patriotism during *The Chinese Festival* had been scandalously deceived:

> Beat drums, trumpets sound, and huzza for our king,
> Then welcome, *Belleisle*, with what troops thou can'st bring.
> Huzza for *Old England*, whose strong-pointed lance
> Shall humble the pride and the glory of *France*.†

Garrick also found time that year to introduce a new character into his farce *Lethe*. Lord Chalkestone became one of his most celebrated characterizations. The gouty old peer is the only member of the cast who has no wish to drink the waters of Lethe—and forms a poor opinion of Aesop's talents as a landscape gardener:

LORD CHALKESTONE: None of your Waters for me; damn 'em all; I never
    drink any but at Bath—I came merely for a little Conversation with you,
    and to see your *Elysian* Fields here—(*Looking about thro' his Glass.*)
    which, by the bye, Mr Aesop, are laid out most detestably—No Taste, no
    Fancy in the whole World!—Your River here—what d'ye call—
AESOP: *Styx*—
LORD CHALKESTONE: Ay, *Styx*—why 'tis as straight as *Fleet-ditch*—You

---

* If Byng was negligent, Britain's intelligence services were not notably less so; they failed to pick up that the French troop movements on the Channel coast which prompted the fears of invasion were a diversionary tactic to mask preparations at Toulon for the attack on Minorca.
† Charles Louis Auguste Fouquet (1684–1761), duc de Belle-Isle and Marshal of France, was presumed to be in charge of the invasion preparations. He was appointed Minister of War the following year.

should have given it a Serpentine Sweep, and slope the Banks of it.—The Place, indeed, has very fine *Capabilities*; but you should clear the Wood to the Left, and clump the Trees upon the Right: In short, the whole wants Variety, Extent, Contrast, and Inequality—

Chalkestone was the only part in which Garrick ever appeared on stage the worse for drink. On a night when he was not billed to appear in the main piece, he made the mistake of lingering over dinner at 'a very great table'. He told the story years later to his young friend Joseph Cradock:

> When he came upon the stage, he appeared all spirits, laughed as he attempted to act, but could not articulate. Many in the house did not perceive what was the matter; for his friends endeavoured to stifle or cover this trespass with loud applause; but next day Mr Garrick was horribly vexed at what had passed, and said: "I do not wish to disguise the truth; I am fully aware of all that happened; I was absolutely tipsy; and shall only take care that the like shall never occur again;" and he strictly kept his word.*

In the last week of February 1756, Garrick mounted a second tragedy by John Brown, the author of *Barbarossa*. *Athelstan*, a plodding affair set in the reign of Ethelred the Unready, concerned the defection of the Duke of Mercia to the invading Danes and the various distresses this brought upon him. (These included his accidental murder, in a dark grove, of his daughter Thyra, a part allocated, inevitably, to Mrs Cibber.)

Garrick cast himself in the title role—it was the theatre's first new main piece of the season—but the part proved unexpectedly demanding, and after three performances it was announced that the fourth night would be deferred, 'as the principal Character is too fatiguing to be acted ten nights together'.† As things turned out, it ran for only seven. Murphy detected in Browne's prologue 'an excellent warning to every insurgent, who, at any time, shall be so mad and wicked as to think of aiding a French invasion', but he was a lone voice;‡ the

---

* Cradock, Joseph, *Literary and Miscellaneous Memoirs*, 4 vols., London 1828, iv, 248. Cited henceforth as *Cradock*. Cradock (1742–1826) is said to have borne a strong resemblance to Garrick, both physically and mentally. He acquired an early taste for London society and for the stage, and left Cambridge without taking his degree. Later he organized private theatricals at his mansion in Leicestershire, where Garrick offered to play the Ghost to his Hamlet. He was a man of extremely temperate habits, never drinking wine, and living chiefly on small quantities of turnips, roasted apples and coffee.

† There may have been an undeclared reason. The deferred fourth performance turned out to be a Command Performance, attended by the Prince of Wales and his mother and several other members of the royal family.

‡ In Smollett's *Critical Review* for March 1756 a more discerning critic dealt severely with the play but generously with Garrick: 'We often see this inimitable actor, labouring through five tedious acts, to support a lifeless piece, with a mixture of pity and indignation; and cannot help wishing there were in this age good poets, to write for one who so well deserves them.' The reviewer was the Reverend Thomas Francklin, himself a playwright, at that time Professor of Poetry at Cambridge — and the man who had officiated at Garrick's wedding.

treacherous Athelstan (Alfric in real life) returned to the dustbin of history and moulders there to this day.

It is conceivable that *Athelstan* was hastened on its way by what was on offer at the other house, because its short run coincided with a highly successful revival at Covent Garden of *King Lear*. It had not been played there for ten years, and the title role was being attempted for the first time by Barry. His Irish foray with Miss Nossiter had been brief. Since his return he had been highly praised for his performance in Nathaniel Lee's *The Rival Queens*—'He charmed every audience,' wrote Davies, 'and gave new life to a play which had not been seen since the death of Delane.'

The playbills had promised an evening of spectacle—'the Triumphal Entry of Alexander into Babylon'—but the Covent Garden punters also enjoyed a bonus which did not figure in Rich's plans. The play's sub-title is *The Death of Alexander the Great*, and the queens in question are Statira, his second wife, and Roxana, her predecessor, with whom Alexander has once again become besotted in the course of his campaigns. These parts were allotted to Bellamy and Woffington—an inspired piece of casting but a certain recipe for trouble.

Bellamy, determined to upstage her rival, had commissioned a certain Madame Montête, the wife of a fashionable hairdresser of the day, to bring back from Paris 'two tragedy dresses, the most elegant she could purchase'. One must always aim off substantially in following Bellamy's accounts of such matters, but there is no reason to doubt that Madame Montête did her proud, enabling her to make a triumphant entry resplendent in a yellow gown under a robe of regal purple. This made Woffington's outfit (Rich had bought her a cast-off dress belonging to the Dowager Princess of Wales) look distinctly dowdy—the colour of delicate straw by day, candlelight reduced it to a dirty white.

On the first night this occasioned no more than an acid exchange in the green-room. For the second performance, however, Bellamy appeared in her second Paris creation, which was even more gorgeous than the first. Woffington became apoplectic with rage, and the scene in which Roxana stabs Statira looked as if it might turn into a real-life drama. The confrontation simmered on in the green-room. Rich was called for, but sensibly did not come. Woffington remarked loudly that it was well for Bellamy that she had a Minister to keep her in jewels and the like (the reference was to Henry Fox, who had been appointed Secretary of State two months previously); Bellamy (a touch of *esprit de l'escalier* here, perhaps?) riposted that she was sorry that *even half the town* did not seem able to do the same for Mrs Woffington. All this and the prospect of Barry's Lear still to come. The town hugged itself with joy.

By attempting the mad king, Barry was of course once again inviting direct comparison with Garrick. There was no repetition of the 'War of the Romeos', however. Garrick, who had played Lear several times earlier in the season, was content to let his rival show what he could do and leave the pit to deliver its verdict. One or two epigrams appeared:

> The town has found out different ways
> To praise the different Lears;
> To Barry they give loud huzzas,
> To Garrick—only tears.

This was generally attributed to Garrick's friend Richard Berenger (although Theo Cibber maintained it was by Garrick himself).* The general view seems to have been that the figure and voice which served Barry so well as Romeo did little for him as Lear. One critic felt that his reading sprang from 'a hundred different critical opinions jumbled'; in the mad scenes, in particular, he appears to have been totally outclassed.

At the end of March it was Garrick's turn to create a new role. For Woodward's benefit night he agreed to appear as Leon in Fletcher's *Rule a Wife and Have a Wife*, which had not been acted since the early 1740s. The takings for the night came to a gratifying £250. Garrick scored an instant success and Leon would become one of his ten most frequently performed comedy roles. There was another good house two nights later for Kitty Clive's benefit. The afterpiece was *Lethe*. Garrick appeared as Chalkestone for her, and she herself performed 'a New Mimic Italian Song'—parodies of the Opera at the Haymarket were always good for a laugh.

By early June Garrick managed to escape to Hampton, but that did not mean an escape from the cares of management. Arthur Murphy was being difficult and making heavy weather of the renewal of his contract as a player. Garrick had given him plenty of encouragement during the past year. Murphy, however, with aborted careers in banking and Grub Street already behind him, was a young man in a hurry, and Garrick had to devote precious time to answering a succession of increasingly tedious letters in which Murphy expressed doubts about the managers' good faith in their negotiations, grumbled about the prospect of Mossop's return to the company and yet infuriatingly declined repeated invitations to state what sort of terms would be agreeable to him. He was not re-engaged for the following season, and for the time being drifted back into journalism, publishing a weekly paper called *The Test*, in support of Henry Fox.†

Before going off to Lichfield on a family visit Garrick also had a difficult letter to write to the Earl of Bute. High in favour with the Dowager Princess of Wales and deeply involved in the education of her son, the heir-apparent, Bute was not a man one could ignore. A play that came to the manager of Drury Lane with his recommendation had to be considered with extreme care. Garrick had done

---

* Berenger, later Gentleman of the Horse to George III, was famous for his charm. Hannah More described him as 'all chivalry, and blank verse, and anecdote'. He would later be indebted to Garrick for a notable act of friendship and generosity.
† This proved useful when he was later refused entry to the Middle Temple on the grounds that he had been an actor. Fox induced Lord Mansfield to secure his admission to Lincoln's Inn, and he was called to the bar in June 1762.

ARTHUR MURPHY ESQ.ᵣ

Arthur Murphy, one of Garrick's early biographers, was the son of a Dublin merchant. Educated by the Jesuits in France, he tried his hand at commerce before turning to journalism and the theatre. Later, the desire for security and respectability drew him to the law, but he continued to write plays (and to quarrel frequently with Garrick) until the late 1770s. (Mander & Mitchenson)

just that and his conclusion was that the play in question was very bad indeed; but to find the right words to convey that to his Lordship required him to chew his quill most thoughtfully.

Bute's protégé was a 34-year-old Scottish clergyman called John Home, minister of Athelstaneford in East Lothian. Garrick had turned down an earlier tragedy of his in 1747. He was quite clear that he must do the same with his latest effort (it was called *Douglas*) and he had taken the precaution of having his opinion confirmed by his (and Johnson's) friend John Hawkesworth, one of the proprietors of the *Gentleman's Magazine*.

Getting started is always the difficult bit. 'My Lord,' he wrote. 'It is with ye Greatest Uneasiness that I trouble Your Lordship with my Sentiments of Mr Hume's Tragedy.' His uneasiness soon evaporated, however, and once he was launched he did not wrap up what he had to say:

> Nobody knows as well as You do, that all ye Endeavors of a Patron & the Skill of a Manager, will avail Nothing, if the dramatic Requisites & Tragic Force are Wanting—I am so strongly convinc'd that this is the case of ye Tragedy in Question, that I durst not upon any Acc^t venture it upon ye Stage of Drury Lane, & I would stake all my credit, that the author would sorely repent it, if ever it should be Exhibited upon any Theatre.

The day would come when Garrick would change his mind about Home's abilities as a playwright. For the moment he could put affairs of the theatre briefly aside. It was already late July. At five o'clock on a Sunday morning he and his wife left Hampton and headed with relief for Staffordshire.

18

Memento Mori

The summer months of 1756 brought no relief to Newcastle's beleaguered administration. In August, in North America, Montcalm captured the important fort of Oswego, and some 1,600 men and 120 cannon fell into French hands. Nor was France the only enemy. Two months earlier, in Bengal, the ferocious new Nawab, Siraj-ud-Daula, had mounted an assault on the English factory at Kasimbazar; a fortnight later he was master of Calcutta. The detention cell at Fort William was a semi-basement measuring about eighteen feet by fifteen, with a raised sleeping area and barred windows on one side. Exactly how many British prisoners were consigned to it for the night on 20 June is not known; what is certain is that by morning many of them had perished, either from dehydration or suffocation, and that only twenty-three survivors emerged from the so-called Black Hole to tell their terrible story.

Garrick had never been short of friends in high places, and before the year was out one of them was briefly to occupy one of the highest places in the land. His friend Hartington had succeeded his father as Duke of Devonshire the previous year; now, after much convoluted negotiation, he succeeded Newcastle. 'He is made first Lord of yᵉ Treasury, much against his will, but intreated to it by his Majesty,' Garrick wrote excitedly to his brother. He had breakfasted with Devonshire that very morning,* and he was eager to let his brother know that the conversation had not been solely about politics: 'He told me among other Things of his intention to Serve You, & You may depend upon it, that He will keep his Word.' It seemed to Garrick that a sinecure might well mean a move to London for Peter, and he urged him to give his mind to the winding up of his affairs in Lichfield:

> Estimate Yʳ Property, & if an Opportunity, a good one, offers, to You, for yᵉ Disposal of it—lay hold upon it . . . Nothing will give me more pleasure than to contribute to your Ease & independence, & to draw You out of that Melancholly, disagreeable Situation, You are at present in—

---

* Garrick's letter was written on 6 November, ten days before Devonshire was actually sworn in as First Lord.

indeed, it is unworthy of You, & I hope my Noble Friend, will give You his Finger, to take You out of those cursed Vaults—*

Peter eventually got his sinecure, but he did not uproot himself. He was made collector of customs at Whitehaven, in Cumberland, arranged for his duties to be performed by a deputy and continued in his 'cursed vaults', happily and prosperously enough, for the rest of his days.

The new season at Drury Lane was to prove blessedly less eventful than the last.† Gratifyingly, it was also more profitable, with income increased by £1,612 over the previous year. It was again a large company, and strengthened by the return from Ireland of Mossop. The playbills show that he topped the bill even more frequently than Garrick himself. His first appearance after his return was as Richard III; in the first three months of the season his parts included Wolsey in *Henry VIII*, Macbeth, Zanga in *The Revenge* and Maskwell in *The Double Dealer*.‡

Garrick got off the mark with a performance of Ranger five days into the season, and by Christmas he had cantered through ten or so of his most popular roles. When he played Romeo early in October his Juliet was Mrs Pritchard's youngest daughter, Hannah, making her début at the age of seventeen. 'Her fond parents,' declared the *Theatrical Review*, had kept her off the stage 'till she was of age to make that choice, without danger of being dazzled with the tinsel of the profession.' She was a strikingly beautiful young woman, and the previous year Garrick had arranged for her to spend some time in Paris under Noverre's wing.

To usher her daughter through the ordeal of her first night, Mrs Pritchard 'stooped to play Lady Capulet', as Davies rather oddly put it:

> The daughter's timidity was contrasted by the mother's apprehensions, which were strongly painted in their looks, and these were incessantly interchanged by stolen glances at each other. This scene of mutual sensibility was so affecting, that many of the audience burst into involuntary tears.[1]

---

* *Letters*, 173. Peter's business would obviously be damaged by the war, which had put an end to trade with France. Portuguese wines would still be obtainable, but shipping was likely to be harried by French privateers.

† Apart from a nasty accident on 13 November which almost deprived the company of one of its leading lights. Cross made a matter-of-fact note in his diary: 'The ballance Weight of the Candles of the Branches fell from ye top of the house upon ye Stage, & broke a great piece in the Stage, the Weight was 200lb. Mr Woodward had just mov'd from the Spot where it fell.'

‡ Cross recorded in his deadpan way that on the second night of *The Double Dealer* there was a further skirmish in the running battle between Woodward and Kitty Clive. 'This Night when Brisk (Mr Woodward) was reading the Verses with Lady Froth (Mrs Clive) instead of observing, with the Author, that her Ladyship's Coachman, John, had a red Face, said *because Y^r ladyship has a red face*, & as Mrs Clive is of that Complexion the Audience burst into a loud roar, to her no small Mortification; but she behav'd well & took no Notice of it.'

Mrs Pritchard was greatly loved, and the town was indulgent. Cross recorded that Hannah's performance 'met with uncommon Applause, tho' so frightened the first Act, we scarce cou'd hear her'.*

Garrick had again been busy with his pen. By far the most interesting—certainly the most unusual—of the five new afterpieces he put on in 1756–7 was his own *Lilliput*, performed before the Prince of Wales and other members of the royal family at a command performance in early December. It was based on Swift's *Gulliver's Travels*, and with the exception of Gulliver himself, who was played by an actor called Astley Bransby,† it was performed by a horde of children—according to Murphy, 'the parents of not less than a hundred were most liberally rewarded'.[2]

Although it played seventeen times during the season, the piece met with a hostile reception from the critics. '*Lilliput* is, I think, the most petit, trifling, indecent, immoral, stupid parcel of rubbish I ever met with,' wrote the reviewer in the *Theatrical Examiner*; he accused Garrick of 'debauching the minds of infants'.

What Garrick had done was to take that part of Swift's story which concerns Lady Flimnap and her 'violent affection' for Gulliver and use it to satirize the contemporary laxity of morals, particularly as regards marriage. The tone is set by the soliloquy of Lord Flimnap with which the play opens:

This marriage is the devil. I have sold my liberty, ease, and pleasure, and in exchange have got a wife, a very wife! Ambition began my misery and matrimony has completed it.

Garrick also, as in *Lethe*, has the *beau monde* in his sights—his spokesman here is Bolgolam, Lord High Admiral of the Lilliputian navy and a stout upholder of honour and virtue. '*He* advise you?' he exclaims when Flimnap talks of seeking counsel from his brother Fripperel:

What can he advise you about? He was bred to nothing but to pick his teeth and dangle after a court. So, unless you have a coat to lace, a feather to choose, or a monkey to buy, Fripperel can't assist you . . . Time was when we had as little vice here in Lilliput as anywhere; but since we imported politeness and fashions from Blefuscu, we have thought of nothing but being fine gentlemen.

It was as sophisticated a comedy of manners as Garrick had yet attempted. He brings it to an end with Gulliver's escape to the land of the Blefuscadians and a short, suggestive epilogue spoken by the child who played Lady Flimnap:

* It was a packed house. Receipts amounted to £226. Later in the season Miss Pritchard was allowed to play Beatrice to Garrick's Benedick. She also, by command, danced a minuet for the King.
† Bransby, appropriately enough, was a very tall man. Gulliver appears to have been the nearest he got to playing a leading role in the course of his thirty-three years on the London stage. He is thought to have been represented as Kent in Benjamin Wilson's 1760 painting, now lost, but known to us through engravings, of Garrick as Lear in the storm.

> Well now! Could you who are of larger size
> Bid to a bolder heighth your passions rise?
> Was it not great? A lady of my span
> To undertake this monstrous Mountain Man?

Not the sort of lines that modern parents would expect to hear in the mouths of their offspring at the annual prep school play, perhaps, but this was the eighteenth century, not the twentieth. Garrick himself, after all, had produced and appeared in *The Recruiting Officer* all those years ago in Lichfield before he was into his teens.

Mrs Cibber's health was causing problems once again. She had appeared only thirteen times during the previous season, and as the end of 1756 approached things looked even worse. A performance of *Comus* had to be postponed because of her indisposition in early December, and a week before Christmas, Lacy and Garrick both put their signatures to a firmly worded letter:

> . . . We did not in the least hesitate the last Season at paying your whole Sallery tho You were not capable of going thro' the business of it; And in Order to recover your health, We permitted You to leave the Company a considerable time before the finishing of it—This Winter You came to Us very late; and your Illness is now unfortunately return'd, two thirds of *our* Season are now Expired, and Mrs Cibber has play'd but *four* times.*

Mrs Cibber had been receiving £700 a year together with the proceeds of her benefit; her articles also provided that all her requirements in the way of costume should be found by the managers, apart from 'yᵉ mere garniture of her head'. She did not at first prove at all amenable, and appeared unwilling to accept arbitration: 'Yʳ terms of accommodation are in our Opinion so partial & unreasonable that we cannot comply with them,' the managers told her stiffly early in the New Year, and it was made clear to her that if she did not accept arbitration she could not expect to remain with the company.[3] She eventually settled for £300.

Garrick was now regularly presenting at least twice as many new pieces as the rival house at Covent Garden—eight against two the previous year, and in the current season six against Rich's one. Early in 1757 a farce by Smollett called *The Reprisal, or The Tars of Old England* had a successful run. Smollett had come to regret the bitterness of his attacks on Garrick over the rejection of *The Regicide* ten years previously, and had cut them out of the second edition of *Peregrine Pickle*.† Later in the year, it was discovered that Smollett had not been paid as much as he was entitled to for his author's benefit, and Garrick, always scrupulous in such matters, wrote him a gracious letter enclosing a draft

---

* *Letters*, 179. The reference to the season being two-thirds expired is explained by the fact that after the annual round of benefits began, usually towards the end of February, all the profits, apart from the basic expenses of the theatre, went to the actors.
† Similarly disobliging references to Cibber, Rich, Akenside and Fielding were also removed.

on Clutterbuck for the difference.[4] The warm friendship which now grew up
between the two men lasted until Smollett's death in 1771. In his *History of
England*, writing with what Davies calls 'all the warm colouring of laboured
panegyric', he made handsome amends to the man he had once savaged as
Marmozet:

> The exhibitions of the stage were improved to the most exquisite entertain-
> ment by the talents and management of Garrick, who greatly surpassed
> all his predecessors of this, and, perhaps, every other nation, in his genius
> for acting, in the sweetness and variety of his tones, the irresistible magic
> of his eye, the fire and vivacity of his action, the elegance of his attitude,
> and the whole pathos of expression.

Garrick was not, however, to be allowed to forget his rejection of *Douglas*. After
he had been rebuffed in London, Home had succeeded in having the play put
into rehearsal at the theatre in the Canongate in Edinburgh. It would be nice to
think that a jubilant son of Caledonia really did leap to his feet on the first night
and cry out 'Whaur's your Wullie Shakespeare noo?' Home's friend 'Jupiter'
Carlyle was certainly present. 'The play had unbounded success,' he wrote, 'and
was attended by all of the literati and most of the judges, who, except one or
two, had not been in use to attend the theatre.* The town in general was in an
uproar of exultation that a Scotchman had written a tragedy of the first rate,
and that its merit was first submitted to their judgment.'

The orthodox party in the church—the so-called 'high-flyers'—were outraged.
They regarded the theatre as 'the Temple of the Father of Lies' and were
scandalized that a minister should write any play, however virtuous its tendency.
The Presbytery of Edinburgh suspended all clergymen who had gone to see
Douglas;† Carlyle was prosecuted by his own Presbytery of Dalkeith; Home
himself was cited to appear before the Presbytery of Haddington, but he delayed
obeying the summons and in February quietly took himself off to London.

Rich, presented with an irresistible opportunity to tweak Garrick's tail, rushed
Douglas into production at Covent Garden in the middle of March with Barry
as Young Norval and Woffington as Lady Randolph. The *Public Advertiser*
printed a lengthy extract from a letter of extravagant praise written to the author
by David Hume. He detected in the play 'incontestable proofs' that Home possessed
'the true Theatric Genius of Shakespear and Otway, refined from the unhappy
Barbarism of the one, and Licentiousness of the other'. Samuel Johnson, however,
never the slave of fashionable opinion, declared that there were not 'ten good
lines in the whole play'.[5] Perhaps his old pupil had been right in the first place.

---

* The theatre was unlicensed — plays were generally performed 'free' in the interval of a
concert.
† One of them, Thomas Whyte, the minister of Liberton, had his six weeks' suspension mitigated
— although he had been present in the theatre he had made efforts to conceal himself behind
a pillar.

Hostilities had no discernible effect on theatre attendance, although there was the occasional reminder that the times were not entirely normal. One Friday in February, for example, the theatres remained dark—'Fast Day on account of War with France,' announced the bills. In May the Drury Lane management did its bit for the war effort by arranging a benefit performance for the Marine Society. Garrick and Mrs Pritchard appeared in *The Suspicious Husband*, and this was followed by *Britannia*, with Garrick speaking the prologue and doing his ever-popular turn as a drunken sailor. Receipts were earmarked for 'clothing Friendless Boys and Men for the Sea'.

As the season drew to a close, there was a moment of real-life drama at Covent Garden. Peg Woffington had been appearing in *As You Like It*. She had complained of feeling unwell during the fifth act, but had soldiered on, as she always did. She launched into the short epilogue which Rosalind speaks after the final dance and got almost to the end of it: 'If I were a woman I would kiss as many of you as had beards that pleased me . . .' One of those watching her from the wings was young Tate Wilkinson:

> Her voice broke, she faultered, endeavoured to go on, but could not proceed—then in a voice of tremor screamed, O God! O God! tottered to the stage door speechless, where she was caught. The audience of course applauded till she was out of sight, and then sunk into awful looks of astonishment, both young and old, before and behind the curtain, to see one of the most handsome women of the age, a favourite principal actress . . . struck so suddenly by the hand of death in such a situation of time and place, and in her prime of life, being then about forty-four.[6]

She had suffered a paralytic seizure. Her life was despaired of that night, and for some days, but she made a partial recovery, and lived on for several years, though she never acted again. She was cared for by one of her admirers, a Colonel Caesar of the Guards; the gossip was that they had married. One day in late November Horace Walpole sat at his writing desk. 'I shall wind up this letter,' he told his friend Mann, 'with an admirable bon mot', although he might equally well have congratulated himself on his impeccable bad taste:

> Somebody asked me at the play t'other night what was become of Mrs Woffington; I replied she is taken off by Colonel Caesar—Lord Tyrawley said, I suppose she is reduced to *aut Caesar aut nullus.**

But then she was only a player.

Shortly after Woffington's collapse at Covent Garden, Wilkinson, having been told by Rich that he would never make an actor, presented himself at Garrick's door. He was equipped with a letter of introduction from Lord Mansfield, who

---

* *Walpole*, xxi, 157. Letter dated 20 November 1757. Not a great deal is known about the Colonel. He was promoted Major-General in 1759 and died three years later.

was a family friend, but he was intensely nervous, and marched several times up and down Southampton Street before daring to knock.

Garrick, it seems, had by then developed the highly idiosyncratic way of speech which was so much remarked—and imitated—by his contemporaries: "Well, Sir—Hey!—what, now you are a stage candidate? Well, Sir, let me have a taste of your quality." The audition did not begin well, Wilkinson being, as he put it, 'distilled almost to jelly with my fear', but when he felt more composed, he asked if he might attempt some imitations:

> "Nay—now," says Garrick, "Sir, you must take care of this, for I used to call myself the first at this business."—I luckily began with an imitation of Foote. It is difficult here to determine whether Garrick hated or feared Foote the most; sometimes one, sometimes the other was predominant; but from the attention of a few minutes, his looks brightened—the glow of his countenance transfused to mine, and he eagerly desired a repetition of the same speech. I was animated—forgot Garrick was present, and spoke at perfect ease.—"How—really this—this—is—(with his usual hesitation and repetition of words)—Why—well—well—Do call on me again on Monday at eleven, and you may depend upon every assistance in my power."

Wilkinson returned two days later to be told he would be put on the books at Drury Lane at thirty shillings a week. Garrick was pressed for time, as he was due at Hampton for dinner, but he asked Wilkinson to repeat his imitation of Foote:

> I readily complied, and executed it with spirit.—From the imitation of Foote I proceeded with great alacrity to several others; and when I came to those of Mr. Barry and Mrs. Woffington, as Macbeth and Lady Macbeth, I was obliged to stop, he seemed so truly entertained. I thought it very comical, and that the joke might not be lost, I laughed too; but on the merriment ceasing, I perceived a concealed third laughter—the Lady Teazle behind the screen, which greatly puzzled me; when on a sudden, a green cloth double door flew open, which I found led to a little breakfast parlour, and discovered a most elegant lady—no less a personage than Mrs. Garrick, who had it seems been purposely posted there for her secret opinion. . .[7]

It had been clear from the start that the Devonshire administration was no more than a *pis-aller*, and in the event it lasted not quite five months. For eleven weeks, the country was without a ministry. Then, at the end of June, Newcastle returned to the Treasury, accepting however that Pitt should have the lead in the Commons and the supreme direction of the war and foreign affairs as Secretary of State for the Southern Department. Devonshire became Lord Chamberlain—from the point of view of the manager of Drury Lane a most satisfactory arrangement.

A letter Garrick wrote to Devonshire that autumn shows how close their friendship had become and provides touching evidence of how the lonely widower turned to Garrick and his wife for help and guidance on quite minor matters. It was the custom each year for all members of the royal household to attend the King on his birthday, which fell in November, and to mark the importance of the occasion by turning up in elegant new clothes. Devonshire regularly looked to the Garricks not just for advice on what he should wear, but for help in the choice of materials and in how they should be tailored and decorated.

The Drury Lane season opened that year on 10 September. One might have thought that Garrick the manager had plenty to occupy him on that day, but he still found time to dash off a long letter in his capacity as Garrick the costumier:

> Mrs Garrick & I are very happy that You are pleas'd to Express such confidence of our Taste, but our great desire & Endeavour to do Nothing that shall displease Y^r Grace has induc'd Us to send the Enclos'd—which I must beg to have return'd to Me by ye next Post, that the Embroiderer may finish his Work in Time. We think that ye two pieces of Velvet y^t are pin'd togeather will make a most agreeable Mixture; the figur'd Velvet for ye Sleeves & Wastecoat, & ye plain one, for ye Coat; but then to be compleat it must be Embroider'd with Silver, for we fear that Gold will be too heavy—the Single pattern of figur'd Velvet would likewise make waistcoat & Sleeves with ye Plain one, tho not so Gay; or a whole Suit of it Embroider'd with Silver or Gold, would look well—We shall wait for Your Grace's Determination & immediatly go to work—[8]

Garrick would never be free of the attentions of a sizeable battalion of critics, hacks and assorted scribblers. The previous year's offerings had ranged from 'A Visionary Interview at the Shrine of Shakespear, Inscribed to Mr. Garrick' to *The Juvenile Adventures of David Ranger*, a picaresque novel in which an actor called Ranger becomes a manager and is married in the house of a noble family to a lady by the name of Tulip. In 1757, however, there appeared a 26-page pamphlet that was refreshingly different. *A Letter of Abuse to D—d G—k, Esq.* was written with some style:

> ... This arbitrary Power, lodged in the manager, of refusing what is absolutely unfit for the Stage, is such an encroachment upon the Liberties of a free People, that, it is to be hoped, the Legislature, under the present happy Settlement of the Ministry, will take the unspeakable Hardships we lie under into Consideration ...

There is a passing swipe at Theophilus Cibber:

> To the elaborate Researches of this indefatigable Enquirer, we are obliged for a very singular Discovery, namely, that your father was a *Frenchman*, which anecdote will, in some Measure, tend to elucidate the Motives of your Conduct last *Winter*, in introducing an Army of *Frenchmen*, under the Disguise of Dancers into this Kingdom. What might have been the Event of so deep-laid a Design, if the good People of *England* had not immediately taken the Alarm, every sincere Friend to our happy Establishment in Church and State must shudder to think on. . . .

Finally, the author puts his cards on the table:

> . . . And now Sir, having discharged my duty, by traducing you, according
> to the Dictates of my Conscience, that I may not deviate from modern
> Forms, I shall conclude with requesting a Favour. You must know, Mr.
> G——k, that I have had by me, for some Years, a Dramatic Piece of two
> Acts, which I should be extremely glad if you would exhibit at your House.
> It is a Composition of infinite Wit and Humour, and if you consent to
> produce it, will in some Measure retrieve your Reputation among the
> choice Spirits of the Age . . . . .*

The author of this entertaining squib was a diminutive 25-year-old called George
Colman, the son of a diplomat and the nephew of the Earl of Bath. His contemporaries at Westminster had included William Cowper and Edward Gibbon, and
while still an undergraduate at Christ Church he had contributed to *The Connoisseur*, one of the best of the essay periodicals of the mid-century. He had been
called to the bar in 1757 and joined the Oxford circuit, but he described himself
in a largely autobiographical sketch written in the same year as already 'Deep
in the drama, shallow in the Law'.

A Letter attracted a good deal of attention, not all of it friendly. It should be
read backwards, 'like a witch's prayer,' the *Critical Review* commented sourly:
'It seems to have been written by some dirty menial of the theatre, with a view
of showing his loyalty, and recommending himself to the favour of the sovereign
of Drury-Lane.' Which was, of course, precisely what Colman had in mind. It
was the beginning of a long and close friendship and of an important professional
collaboration.

The theatre had once again been redecorated during the summer of 1757 and
Drury Lane opened its door four days ahead of Covent Garden. *The Beggar's
Opera* was always a safe bet to get the season off to a good start, and within the
first week Garrick also offered his public Mossop as Richard III and himself as
Ranger and as Romeo.

It was a time-honoured practice each 5 November to revive Rowe's
Whig tragedy, *Tamerlane*, to mark the anniversary of the landing of William
of Orange in 1688.† Garrick was at the theatre that night, although he was not
acting, and once the mainpiece was under way, he withdrew to his dressing
room.

---

* The play is called *The Conspiracy*, and its characters include Shylock, 'An unfortunate Hero,
of an enterprizing Disposition, but unhappily out of Employment, on Account of his seditious
Principles'; and Bronze, 'a Gentleman of uncommon great Qualities, superior to those Evils
which depress the vulgar Class of Mortals, particularly the disgrace of Cuckolddom'. These
are obviously Macklin and T. Cibber. There is also a doctor called Liffey and an amanuensis
called Reptile.
† Drury Lane and Covent Garden had both put on *Tamerlane* the previous evening, but on
the night of the anniversary Rich got a much better house than Garrick with *Henry V*, which
had been commanded by the Prince of Wales — 'with the Conquest of the French at Agincourt'.

My dear Sir,

I sit down to write you in the midst of drums, trumpets, and, above all, the roarings of the mighty Bajazet; we are celebrating the glorious and immortal memory as loudly as we can, but I have stole away to say a word to you upon *Agis*.

It was not only the success of *Douglas* that had made him look again at Home's earlier tragedy. The last few months had changed the course of Home's life. He had returned to Scotland after the success of *Douglas* at Covent Garden, but when his presbytery resumed proceedings against him he quietly resigned his living. Soon afterwards Bute appointed him to be his private secretary and he was also made tutor to the Prince of Wales. Circumstances alter cases, and Garrick, in a letter to Home, now discerned qualities in *Agis* which had previously eluded him:

The subject itself is of the least dramatic kind, (viz. political and sentimental,) not but there are some affecting scenes in these three acts; and if your two last are gloriously poetical, I will insure you both fame and profit.

He then submits the text to detailed scrutiny, and gives Home the benefit of his unrivalled sense of stagecraft. 'Is there not too little matter in the second act?' 'Lysander comes too suddenly upon the stage, for Agis has but just quitted it.' 'I cannot as yet see what use we can make of *Sandane*; she is very insignificant hitherto, and unless she has something to do in the last two acts, she will appear to have no business in the tragedy.' Suddenly, more pressing matters intervene: 'I am called away, and can only say, that the more I read of Agis, the more I like it; and if the pathos rises to a proper height in the two last acts, *l'affaire est faite*.'[9]

As indeed it was—'Went off wth. great Applause' wrote Cross when it had its first night in February. Garrick had commissioned music from Boyce, and he himself took the part of Lysander, with Mrs Pritchard as Agesistrata and Mrs Cibber as Euanthe. The Prince of Wales came on the third night to see what his tutor got up to in his spare time; he clearly liked what he saw, because he honoured him, quite exceptionally, with two Command Performances in the course of the following week.*

Earlier, Garrick had put on another piece of his own, although his authorship was not immediately disclosed. It had been performed once during the previous season under the title *The Modern Fine Gentleman*. Now this miniature comedy of manners was brought out as *The Male-Coquette* and enjoyed considerable success. 'The following Scenes,' Garrick wrote in his introductory notice, 'were written with no other View than to serve Mr. *Woodward* last year at his Benefit; and to expose a Set of People, (the Daffodils) whom the Author thinks more prejudicial to the Community, than the various Characters of Bucks, Bloods,

---

* Not everyone was impressed, however. 'I cry to think that it should be by the author of *Douglas*,' the poet Gray wrote to a friend. 'Why, it is all modern Greek; the story is an Antique Statue, painted white and red, frizzed and dressed in a negligee made by a Yorkshire mantua-maker.'

Flashes, and Fribbles, which have by Turns infected the Town, and have been justly ridicul'd upon the Stage. He expects no mercy from the Critics . . .'

Garrick took his characters straight from the comic tradition of the Restoration. Daffodil is cast in the same mould as the rake Horner in Wycherley's *The Country Wife*. His valet, Ruffle, finds his master's antics incomprehensible:

RUFFLE: I don't understand it. What do you intend to do with 'em all? Ruin 'em?

DAFFODIL: Not I, faith.

RUFFLE: But you'll ruin their reputations.

DAFFODIL: That's their business not mine.

RUFFLE: Will you marry any one of 'em?

DAFFODIL: Oh, no. That would be finishing the game at once. If I preferred one, the rest would take it ill; so, because I won't be particular, I give 'em all hopes without going a step further.

RUFFLE: Widows can't live upon such slender diet.

DAFFODIL: A true sportsman has no pleasure but in the chase. The game is always given to those who have less taste and better stomachs.

Garrick's second target is the rage for wagering, and he has a lively scene set in a London club where the betting book has such entries as 'Lord Racket has betted 70 pounds to 50 with the Honourable George Daffodil that the latter does not walk from Buckingham-Gate to the Bun-house at Chelsea, eat a bun there, run back to the turnpike, and from thence hop upon one leg, with the other tied to the cue of his wig, to Buckingham-Gate again, in an hour and half.'

One of the members present is Dizzy, Daffodil's sickly cousin, from whom he stands to inherit a sizeable estate; shortly after his exit a club servant enters to announce that he has dropped down at the foot of the stairs:

LORD RACKET: I'll bet fifty pound that he don't live till morning.

SIR WILLIAM: I'll lay six to four he don't live a week.

DAFFODIL: I'll take your fifty pound.

SPINNER: I'll take your lordship again.

LORD RACKET: Done, with you both.

SIR TAN-TIVY: I'll take it again.

LORD RACKET: Done, done, done. But I bar all assistance to him. Not a physician or surgeon sent for, or I am off.

DAFFODIL: No, no; we are upon honour. There shall be none, else it would be a bubble bet. There shall be none.

Dizzy, however, unsportingly spoils their fun. The club servant reappears to announce that he is quite recovered. 'He is in the Phoenix with two ladies and has ordered a boiled chicken and jellies.'*

It was the sort of piece that would have suited Colley Cibber marvellously well before the years had taken their toll, but Cibber was now an old man of eighty-six, and indeed a few days after *The Male-Coquette* began its run, he died

---

* Garrick, in a nice touch, has the club servants wagering on the bets laid by the members.

quietly in his bed at his elegant house in Berkeley Square.* His passing excited curiously little attention—rather less certainly than another death that occurred shortly afterwards. Caroline Elizabeth, the King's third daughter, had lived for some years in seclusion, absorbed in religious exercises, secretly dispensing charity and seeing only members of her own family. Grief at her mother's death twenty years before, and a hopeless passion for Lord Hervey—Pope's 'Lord Fanny'—had plunged her into melancholy and undermined her health and on 28 December she died at her apartments in St James's Palace. She was forty-four—only four years older than Garrick. By eight the next morning, the order had gone out from the Lord Chamberlain that the theatres should not play till further notice. The bills for that night were torn down, and both patent houses remained dark until Twelfth Night.

Garrick, always casting about for challenging new roles for himself, substantially rewrote two plays which had successful revivals that winter. Southerne's lurid tragi-comedy *The Fatal Marriage; or, The Innocent Adultery* had first been performed in 1694,† and Garrick had played the part of Biron once or twice in the 1740s and early 1750s. He now stripped the play of its comic sub-plot (he describes it in the advertisement to the printed version as 'not only indelicate but immoral') and reduced the number of speaking roles from sixteen to ten. He also introduced a number of elaborate musical episodes, including an epithalamium set by Arne.

Critical opinion was divided, but Garrick undoubtedly gave new life to the piece.‡ Eager as he always was to demonstrate how good he was at expiring on stage, he cobbled together a speech for Biron as he is mortally wounded and added to the dying speech that Southerne had already provided. Earlier in the last act he also provided himself with a characteristic piece of fustian:

> Horrors come fast around me;
> My Mind is overcast—the gath'ring clouds
> Darken the prospect—I approach the brink,
> And soon must leap the precipice! O, heav'n!
> While yet my senses are my own, thus kneeling
> Let me implore thy mercies on my wife . . .

Garrick's search for a major new comedy role for himself that season proved less successful. *The Gamesters*, adapted from a coarse comedy by James Shirley

---

* Colley had been convinced his hour had come some years previously. 'Tho Death has been cooling his heels at my door these Three weeks,' he wrote to Samuel Richardson on Christmas Day 1750, 'I have not had time to see him.' (Barbaud, Anna, (ed.), *Correspondence of Samuel Richardson*, 6 vols., London, 1804, ii, 174–5.)

† It was based on an equally lurid novel of Aphra Behn's called *The Nun, or the Perjur'd Beauty.*

‡ Later in the century Isabella became one of Mrs Siddons's favourite roles. It was the first part she played on her return to Drury Lane in 1782. Many in the audience wept. 'Literally the greater part of the spectators were too ill to use their hands in her applause,' wrote Boaden.

first acted in 1633, never really got off the ground, in spite of good supporting performances from Woodward and Mrs Cibber; on the first night there was some hissing, and after six performances it was dropped.

Garrick, for once, seems to have misread his audience. Shirley had found his plot in Marguerite of Navarre's *Heptameron*. The main character, Wilding, has ambitions to seduce his ward Penelope, and crudely conveys his intention to his wife (who, to make matters worse, happens to be distantly related to the girl). Wilding is a gambler as well as a lecher, however, and as a way of settling a debt to his crony Hazard, sends him in his place to the assignation—unaware that Penelope's place has been taken by Mrs Wilding. Humiliated, he tries to persuade Hazard to marry Penelope. But then he discovers that the assignation never really took place—the gamester has cheated himself twice over.

Ostensibly, Garrick was merely setting himself the same task that he had successfully undertaken in altering *The Chances* and *Rule a Wife and Have a Wife*—to retain the robust spirit which so appealed to him in the original 'old comedy' in a way that would not offend the susceptibilities of his audience. As before, he set about it by discarding the sub-plot, drastically reducing the number of characters (he retained only fifteen of the original twenty-four) and cutting or softening some of the more indelicate passages.

His friend William Warburton, then Dean of Gloucester, to whom he often turned for advice, did not share his surprise at the failure of the piece, and sent him a soothing explanation:

> The Miscarriage of the first nights, from the cause you mention, was very natural. It was not the virtue of the audience which took offence at a supposed adultery; it was not their vice which was disappointed when they saw none committed; it was their vanity which was shocked, in finding themselves outwitted by the poet. They had sat long enough in their suspense to be secure in their sagacity, that Wilding had been really cuckolded; and to find themselves mistaken at last, was enough to put them out of humour.[10]

Garrick had taken Foote back on to the books as a performer the previous season, although to no great effect. When he had appeared as Sir Paul Plyant in *The Double Dealer* and Buck in his own *The Englishman in Paris*, receipts were a meagre £80. 'Mr Foote brings sad houses,' wrote Cross. He did much better business for the house as an author, although his new farce, *The Author*, was the cause of a sizeable managerial headache.

On the day of the opening, Foote had inserted a notice in the *Public Advertiser* giving an assurance that all the characters in the play were 'fictitious and general', but that was a characteristic piece of Foote impertinence—the part of Cadwallader, which he himself played, was an unmistakable caricature of a man called Apreece, an uncle of his friend Francis Delaval and someone he knew extremely well. 'His peculiarities were of so singular a nature, as to render him a very easy prey to the English Aristophanes,' wrote Davies:

In his person he approached to the larger size, but seemed to be incumbered more by his deportment than his corpulence; with a broad unmeaning stare, and awkward step, he seemed to look and walk absurdity. His voice was loud, his manner of speaking boisterous, and his words were uttered rapidly and indistinctly; his head was constantly moving to his left shoulder with his mouth open, as if to recall what he had inadvertently spoken.[11]

The victim, who was a kindly and good-natured man, seems initially to have enjoyed the joke as well as the next man. The farce ran for a respectable seventeen nights that season, and it had been performed a dozen times in 1757–8 before Apreece decided that he had had enough of being pointed out and giggled at in public places. Appealing to Foote was a waste of time—'When gain was in view,' as Davies economically put it, 'humanity was out of the question.' Apreece eventually marched into Drury Lane one morning while Garrick was conducting a rehearsal. 'A long and high Argument ensu'd,' wrote Cross:

> Nor was it settled, but a farther meeting appointed at eight that Night at the Rose, where Foote join'd 'em—a great deal of abuse between him & Aprice; I don't know ye particulars, but it was order'd to remain at the bottom for Tuesday, but, as I hear, it is to be done no more.[12]

Cross was right. The piece was not seen again, although if Davies's account of how matters were arranged is correct, Garrick does not emerge particularly well from the affair:

> The gentleman was at first so warm, that he declared, if the farce was not suppressed, that he should demand satisfaction of the manager. Mr Garrick smiled at Mr A——'s heat, and told him, that, upon an honourable occasion, he should not decline a gentleman's invitation; but begged him to consider the disadvantages under which he laboured; that he was much more advanced in years than himself, and was grown somewhat corpulent and unwieldy. However, as he really felt for Mr A——, he advised him to apply to the Lord Chamberlain, a nobleman who, he was sure, had too much humanity to suffer any gentleman to be hurt by personal representation; as for himself, he was only a sharer in the author with Mr Lacy and Mr Foote . . .[13]

That reads like a fairly craven abdication of managerial function, but Apreece accepted the advice that was offered. When the farce—'with Alterations'—was advertised once more later in the year, he applied to Devonshire and obtained an order to stop it.

In the early spring of 1758 the Garrick family suffered a bereavement. 'On March 21,' announced the *Public Advertiser*, 'died of a Consumption, at Somerset House, Mrs George Garrick, wife of Mr George Garrick, a Lady in whom was united every amiable quality.' In six short years of marriage she had borne five children, and Garrick and his wife were to take an increasingly close and generous interest in their welfare—George was not the most provident of men.

Death was also to revisit the Cibber family in 1758. William Sloper had sent his little natural son, Charles, to Westminster as a boarder, and in April he died there, not quite nine years old, the third of Susannah's four children to die.* It was the height of the benefit season, and Cross recorded the event with a spurt of uncharacteristic venom: 'Mrs Cibber's son dy'd two Days ago & she never came to play for Holland, Mrs Yates or me, ye olde Game at this Season.'

Theophilus, meanwhile, was still struggling. There had been thin pickings for him in the death of his father; out of his considerable estate, Colley had left him precisely £50. All that had come his way since then was a licence to present ten performances at the Haymarket between 1 January and 7 February. Characteristically, he tested the tolerance of the Lord Chamberlain by running on into March and presenting Aaron Hill's *The Insolvent; or Filial Piety*, which he prefaced by a maudlin prologue on the death of Colley. Nothing further was heard of him until July, when he somehow contrived to have Covent Garden opened for one night for a performance of *Madrigal and Truletta*. It was described as a mock tragedy, and the bills give a flavour of the evening:

> Characters by Mr Cibber & Co., with a *Prologue* and *Epilogue*, an Ode, a Dirge, a Funeral and Procession. Parts: Madrigal, Buckramo, Straspada, Lyric, Acrostic, Fustiano, Epigram, Goosino, Bodkinda, Presboardalia, Yardwandelli, Buttonelli, Thimbletorio, Truletta, Sculliona, Scourella, Ghosts of Cabbagino and Truletta, Poets, Taylors, Drums, Trumpets . . .

As autumn came on, it looked as if things might be looking up for Theophilus. Benjamin Victor invited him to Dublin for the season, and in mid-October he set off for Chester. His travelling companions included a Mrs Pockrich,† with whom he had formed a liaison some years previously, and Maddox, the celebrated wire-dancer from Sadler's Wells. The *Dublin Trader* weighed anchor at noon on 27 October. Once out in the Irish Sea it was driven north before a violent gale. Two weeks later, on the Scottish coast near the Mull of Galloway, the sea washed up several trunks filled with stage costumes and a fiddle case 'directed to Mr Cibber in Dublin'.

Theophilus was taken no more seriously in death than he had been in life. Oliver Goldsmith wrote a mock elegy called 'Serious Reflections on the Life and Death of the late Mr T— C—, by the Ordinary of New Gate Prison'. The author prayed that Theo's sad death by drowning might be a lesson to those smug persons who had long believed 'that a man so bad was born to be hanged'.[14]

For Susannah Cibber, it was the end of an extended nightmare. For the first time in twenty years, she need no longer fear for her property.

---

* He appeared in the school register as 'Master Cibber'.
† Mrs Pockrich's husband, Richard (1690?–1759), a native of County Monaghan, was the inventor of the musical glasses. He had gone through a large fortune in what the *DNB* describes as 'the pursuit of visionary projects'. These included supplying men-of-war with unsinkable tin boats and the planting of vineyards in Irish bogs.

19

Slings and Arrows

Benjamin Victor's invitation to Theophilus to go to Ireland had been prompted by the prospect of competition from a new theatre that was about to open there. When Spranger Barry had been in Dublin two years previously he had taken a lease on the old Music Hall in Crow Street. He subsequently bought up four adjacent lots, had the Music Hall demolished and set about building a new theatre that was to be 'as ample and magnificent as that of Drury-lane'.*

Barry had initially offered a partnership to Macklin. When that fell through, he made a proposition to Woodward, whom he knew to be ambitious to manage a company and who over the years had put by a considerable sum. Woodward, a cautious man, was flattered, although his wife was against the idea; he therefore went to Garrick and offered to stay at Drury Lane if he were guaranteed, then and in the future, as large a salary as any other player. He met with a refusal. Garrick pointed out that he was already paid more than any other comic actor and enjoyed a second benefit each year as Harlequin; to tie the managers to such articles would make it impossible for them to reward any outstanding new talent that might unexpectedly emerge. Garrick was persuasive, but Barry was even more so—Rich said that he had a tongue 'that could wheedle a bird from a tree, and squeeze it to death in his hand'. Woodward went off to Dublin, and his departure gave Garrick a busy summer. 'I wish that my Affairs would permit my flying to Standlich to See You' he wrote to his friend William Young at the beginning of August, '—but indeed I have so much to do, since ye Desertion of some of my troops, that I have not a Moment to spare for writing or jaunting.'†

Desertions notwithstanding, he still found time for some entertaining. 'Jupiter' Carlyle had come to London that summer, and one day found himself included in an invitation to John Home and others to dine. A party of six bowled off down to Hampton in a landau. Garrick had urged them to take their golf clubs: 'Immediatly after we arriv'd we cross'd the River to the Golphing Ground which

---

* The approach to Theophilus was suggested by Garrick, to whom Victor had written for suggestions. (Victor, Benjamin, *Original Letters, Dramatic Pieces and Poems*, 3 vols., London, 1776, i, 288.)

† *Letters*, 208. Young was planning a private production of *Julius Caesar*, and had asked Garrick if he might borrow some costumes from Drury Lane.

was very Good. None of the Company could play but J. Home and myself and Parson Black from Aberdeen,' Carlyle noted:

> We Return'd and Din'd sumptuously, and Mrs Garrick the only Lady, now Grown Fat, tho' still very lively, being a Woman of uncommon Good Sense, and now Mistress of English, was in all respects most agreable Company. She did not Seem at all to Recognise me, which was no wonder, at the end of 12 years, Having Thrown away my Bag-Wig and Sword and appearing in my own Grisly Hairs, and in Parsons clothes.

Carlyle had seen quite a lot of Garrick during his stay in London, both socially and at Drury Lane. A shrewd judge of human nature, he was in no doubt about what had swayed him to accept Home's *Agis*:

> I am affraid it was not his own more mature Judgment that brought him Round, but his Idolatry to the Rising Sun, For he had Observ'd what a Hold Home had Got of Lord Bute, and by his Means of the Prince of Wales. As Garricks Vanity and Interestedness had made him Digest the Mortification, of Seeing Douglas already become the most Popular play on the Stage, so John Homes Facility, and the Hopes of Getting him to play in his Future Tragedies, made him forgive Garricks former want of Taste and Judgment, and they were now become the Greatest Friends in the World.*

The canny parish minister observed his host closely during their day together beside the Thames:

> Garrick tho' not of an understanding of the First, nor of the highest Cultivated Mind, had Great Vivacity and Quickness and was very Entertaining Company. Tho' Vanity was his Prominent Feature, and a Troublesome and Watchfull Jealousy the Constant Visible Guard of his Reputation to a Ridiculous Degree; Yet his Desire to Oblige, his Want of Arrogance, and the Delicacy of his Mimickry, made him very agreable.[1]

Garrick was still laying out substantial sums on the property at Hampton and in the autumn of 1758 he wrote to Devonshire to ask a favour:

> Your Grace was once pleas'd to make Me an offer of a Draught upon Y^r Banker; The Stocks are at present fall'n so low that I must sell out to great disadvantage, & I have at present occasion for about four or five hundred

---

* Carlyle offers interesting proof of this: 'If anything had been wanting to Compleat Garricks Conquest of Home, it was making Choice of him, as his 2nd in a Quarrel he had with Calcraft (for John was very Heroick) which never came to a Duel, as well as Several other Quarrels of the same Kind, and with the same issue, in which John was chosen Second.' John Calcraft (1726–72) was thought by some to be the illegitimate son of Henry Fox, who made him the agent for several regiments. He amassed a large fortune as an army contractor, and later became an MP. He was for some years the protector of Mrs Bellamy. The cause of his quarrel with Garrick is not known. They were later good friends.

pounds to compleat my folly at Hampton; I sh^d therefore be greatly oblig'd to y^r Grace's favor for such an Assistance at this time.[2]

Devonshire, who was at Chatsworth, sent him a draft for £500 within the week. Garrick, in his letter of thanks, had disturbing news to convey about the Duke's mother-in-law, Lady Burlington:

> My Wife was quite in ye vapors at her return from Chiswick last Night, & still thinks she cannot possibly hold long as She is—She goes again to day & is resolv'd, if she can, to persuade her to be remov'd from the filth, she is at present in—It is Exactly, by her Account, Dean Swift's Description of the Yahoos—her looks are dreadful & her Shrieks more so—all is not right within![3]

The old lady died ten days later. She was not universally mourned. 'Lady Burlington is dead,' Messenger Monsey wrote to his friend Mrs Montagu, 'the Queen of the Bluestockings'. 'Mrs G— gets nothing but rid of her, and that's a great deal, I think.'[4]

If news-cutting agencies had existed in the eighteenth century, there would have been fierce competition to have Garrick as a client. By the late 1750s he was at the receiving end of a constant stream of praise, blame and abuse, much of it anonymous. One of the more disagreeable effusions to appear in 1758 was an 8-page poem called *A Bone for the Chroniclers to pick; or A Take-Off Scene from behind the Curtain*. This took the form of a dialogue in verse between 'David' and an assistant called Jemmy to whom Garrick confesses that he is guilty of hypocrisy, avarice and vanity. Jemmy hastens to reassure him:

> Nay, there are who have thought, that, instead of a Farce,
> Should you print your Intention to shew 'em your A—e,
> The Design all Reward would of Novelty reap,
> For they'd hurry, and cluster, and pay for a Peep . . .[5]

Printers, then as now, could not afford to be choosy about the work they accepted. From the same press as that sort of rubbish there came the entirely unexceptionable 'Letter to Mr G——k on Opening of the Theatre, With Observations on Managers, Actors, Authors, and their Audiences and Particularly New Performers'. This asked Garrick to appear more frequently himself, particularly, now that Woodward had gone, in lighter parts, and urged that promising young actors should be trained up gradually and not cast so quickly in parts that were beyond their capacity.

Garrick needed no urging to seek out new blood. The departure of Woodward did not in itself constitute a major haemorrhage, but it had deprived Drury Lane of a major talent, and he had not gone alone. Cross noted in his prompter's diary that 'he has taken from us Mr Walker & Wife (Miss Minors that was) Mr Vernon, Mr Jefferson & Wife—from Mr Rich, Mr Arthur, Mr White, Mr Chambers, Mr Finny (his Scene-man) & others'.[6] A month into the new season,

Garrick began a letter to John Home by apologizing for being such a poor correspondent: 'I have been so hurried & busied with my two new Pupils *Fleetewod* & *Obrien*, who have lately appear'd with Success upon the Stage, that I have scarce had time to see a Single Friend, or write a Single Letter—'[7]

Charles Fleetwood was the son of the former Drury Lane patentee and made his début as Romeo at the end of September, when he was 'receiv'd with great and deserv'd Applause'.* He had a good season, and by the time his benefit came round in April, he was given the opportunity to play Hamlet to Mrs Cibber's Ophelia. William O'Brien, the son of a fencing master, also acquitted himself well when he made his début as Brazen in *The Recruiting Officer*. He was a quick study, and in the course of that first season learned a further fourteen parts. Like Fleetwood, he was allowed a solo benefit—a rare concession for one so new to the profession—and he appeared as Foppington in *The Careless Husband*.

Garrick found it more difficult to find appropriate outlets for the talents of Tate Wilkinson, who had also now joined the company. Wilkinson claims in his memoirs that at the beginning of the season he was assigned the part of Volscius in *The Rehearsal*, but that Garrick subsequently humiliated him by telling Cross in front of the other players that he must have 'some steady person to depend on' for the part:

> Volscius was of course taken from me, and I retired amidst the sneers and laughter of His Majesty's company of comedians, with Garrick saying to them all, 'Did you ever now see such a d—d exotic? he would have destroyed my whole play of the Rehearsal and be d—d to him.'

There was rather more to the story than that, however, and if one looks at the chronology of the early months of the season Garrick's decision does not seem at all capricious. *The Rehearsal* was played for the first time on 16 November, but a month previously Foote, freelancing once again at Drury Lane, had been allowed to put on a new version of his *Diversions of the Morning*. The number of those exposed to ridicule was greatly increased and the new part of Bounce had been given to Wilkinson. The audience loved it, but it naturally went down less well with those at the receiving end. One of Wilkinson's victims was Luke Sparks, the popular Irish actor who was currently playing a number of leading roles at Covent Garden, and on the night it had been given out for its second performance, Cross's diary indicates that Garrick found himself between the devil and the deep blue sea:

> As Mr Sparks & others complain'd of Mr Wilkinson for taking them off, it [Diversions of yᵉ Morning] was intended to be omitted this Night, But

---

* Cross recorded an anxious moment for the novice during his third appearance in the role two weeks later: 'Mr Fleetwood in yᵉ fight with Paris in yᵉ last Act, having a Sword by his Side instead of a Foil, run Mr Austin (Paris) into the belly, he lay some time but at last call'd to be taken off — a Surgeon was sent for—No harm, a Small Wound, & he is recover'd.' (*Cross Diary*, 13 October 1758.)

the Audience call'd so violently for it, that we were oblig'd to let him Do it—he took off Foote & Sheridan, & wou'd have left out Sparks but yᵉ Audience wou'd not be satisfied without it.[8]

Wilkinson's brashness had also exposed Garrick to fire from another quarter, and this he may well have felt more keenly. Wilkinson had had a successful summer engagement in Portsmouth—his benefit there in July had been attended by the Duke of York and a number of other army officers, who were then fitting out for the Cherbourg expedition.* His roles had included Richard III, Hamlet and Lear, and he had also done some impersonations, including one of the stricken Peg Woffington. It was his bad luck that Colonel Caesar had been in the audience one night; the Colonel now waited on Garrick and told him that if he permitted a repetition of this in his theatre, he must expect 'to be seriously called upon as a gentleman to answer it'.

Wilkinson's efforts eventually earned him a second dressing down in front of the company:

> Now, hey, d—n it, Wilkinson!—now, why will you take a liberty with these gentlemen the players, and without my consent? you never consulted or told me you were *to take off* as you call it; hey, why now, I never take such liberties.—Indeed I once did it, but I gave up such d—d impudence. Hey now, that is I say—but you and Foote, and Foote and you, think you are managers of this theatre.—But to convince you of the contrary, and be d—d to ye, I here order you, before these gentlemen, to desist from taking any liberty with any one of Covent Garden theatre . . .

To add to Wilkinson's mortification, he was now attacked by Kitty Clive, who expressed herself shocked at the impudence of a young tyro's attempts to raise a laugh at the expense of his fellow-players:

> "Now," added she, "I can and do myself *take off*, but it is only the Mingottii,† and a set of Italian squalling devils who come over to England to get our bread from us; and I say curse them all for a parcel of Italian bitches;"—and so Madam Clive made her exit, and with the approbation of all the stage lords and ladies in waiting, whilst I stood like a puppy dog in a dancing-school . . .‡

Garrick's decree that Wilkinson should take no further liberties with Covent Garden players was not at all well received by the audience, who clamoured

---

* This was one of the more successful attacks which Pitt mounted on the French coast in the course of 1758. The town was occupied, its docks destroyed and numbers of ships burnt.

† The singer Regina Mingotti (1722–1808), wife of the impresario Pietro Mingotti, had made her London début in 1754. Horace Walpole described her as 'a noble figure, a great mistress of music, and a most incomparable actress'.

‡ Mossop, 'his gills all swelling,' breathing hard and hand on sword, also weighed in: 'If you were to take such a liberty with me, *Sir*, I would draw my sword, *Sir*, and run you through the body. *You should not live, Sir!*'

insistently for more. Nor could the manager prevent Foote from explaining silkily to the audience that so far as he himself was concerned, he had naturally not the slightest objection to being taken off ... Garrick's position was quickly undermined, and in very short order he found himself manoeuvred into agreeing, no doubt through gritted teeth, that he too was fair game. Whereupon Wilkinson treated the house to impressions of his employer as Lear, Hamlet and Biron:

> From that whimsical night Mr. Garrick was so hurt and offended with my representation of his likeness, that almost during the remainder of the season, he never deigned to let his eye grace me with its observance, and of course not a single word to comfort me from his royal lips; all conveyed whenever I met him austerity, anger, and dislike.

Foote and Garrick quite often coincided at the noon rehearsal at Drury Lane at this time. A good deal of sparring went on between them, some of it quite sharp and edgy, and Wilkinson thought that Garrick generally came off second best. Foote's instinct to bite the hand that fed him was highly developed, and he could be breathtakingly insolent. 'He took every occasion to have a stroke at Garrick's parsimony,' wrote his first biographer, William Cooke:

> After rehearsals he would sometimes say, "Bless me! here we have been laughing away our time, and 'tis now past four o'clock, without ever thinking of dinner. Garrick, have you enough for a *third*, without infringing on your servants' generosity—as I know they are all upon board wages?"
>
> Garrick, rather embarrassed, would sometimes say: "Why, hey, now, Sam; if, if you are really serious, and not engaged, and would finish our laugh in Southampton-street, I dare say Mrs Garrick would find a chair for you."
>
> "Oh! don't let me break in upon her generosity. If the kitchen fire should *be* out, or if this is cold-meat day, or one of her fast days, I can pop into a coffee-house; though, I must confess, the want of Mrs Garrick's company must make every place a desert." Garrick generally forced a laugh upon these occasions, but was always glad to conclude a truce at the expense of a dinner.[9]

Wilkinson's account of how Foote responded to an invitation to perform in Edinburgh that winter is of some interest. 'Well,' says he, 'this Scotch experiment must be tried, but where's the means? Damn it, I must sollicit that hound Garrick!' The hound Garrick immediately agreed to lend him £100, and Foote was in high good humour:

> On the evening he received the cash, he not only feasted with Mr. Garrick's money, but by way of returning thanks, told more ludicrous stories of him than at any other time I ever recollect. He ridiculed him much as a poet, and said, "David's verses were so bad, (and Garrick so fond of writing) that if he died first, he dreaded the thought of his composing his epitaph."[10]

Foote's London colleagues thought he was mad to go. 'It was judged impossible,' wrote Wilkinson, 'for a London theatrical sunflower to survive the chillness of such a barbarous northern clime.' Foote proved them wrong. He arrived there in the middle of March 1759, and was back in London five weeks later with a full purse. On his return, a lady asked him whether it was true that there were no trees in Scotland. 'A very malicious report indeed, my lady,' he replied; 'for, just as I was crossing Fortpatrick to Dannaghdee, I saw two black birds perched on *as fine a thistle* as ever I saw in my life.'[11]

Foote and Wilkinson were not the only people who got up Garrick's nose that winter. In accepting for production a farce called *The Rout*, he also found himself embroiled with the notorious Dr John Hill, a figure who, even by the standards of the eighteenth century, must be rated as outstandingly bizarre.* Hill was much the same age as Garrick; originally apprenticed to an apothecary, he later studied botany and was employed by the Duke of Richmond and others to lay out their gardens and collect rare plants. For a time he had been an actor of sorts, and then he had gravitated to Grub Street, where he wrote with great facility about everything under the sun. Having somehow acquired a diploma in medicine from St Andrews, he aspired to be elected to the Royal Society; when he failed to secure sufficient support, he attacked it in a number of scurrilous pamphlets.

A recklessly extravagant man—'in a chariot one month, in jail the next for debt'[12]—Hill had also published two treatises on the theatre. The first, which had appeared in 1750 as *The Actor: a Treatise on the Art of Playing*, he had simply lifted from an earlier French work,† but the expanded version of it which he brought out five years later was a much more substantial affair, with a number of pertinent observations both on acting theory and on the performance of the leading players of the day. 'Playing is a science,' he asserted, 'and is to be studied as a science', and 'A perfection in the player is the hiding himself in his character.' Managers, he observed, had an inclination to judge a part by its size rather than its quality, so that smaller roles such as Montano in *Othello* usually went to a person 'somewhat above the degree of a scene-shifter'. He contended that as much skill should be deployed in the portrayal of a soldier as of a monarch—a view, as it happened, which Garrick shared.

Hill's talents as a dramatic writer were altogether more slender. Garrick offered him detailed suggestions for the improvement of *The Rout*, and these Hill accepted. The piece was put on for the benefit of the General Lying-In Hospital, and as the mainpiece that night was Aaron Hill's *Zara*, with Garrick

* Hill later took to styling himself Sir John Hill—this on the strength of the award of the Order of Vasa by the King of Sweden. This was in recognition of his work *The Vegetable System*, which he had started publishing in 1759, at the instance of Bute. It eventually ran to 26 folio volumes, with 1,600 copper-plate engravings, and lost him a great deal of money. Meanwhile, however, he had branched out as a quack doctor, and did extremely well out of a range of herbal preparations with names like essence of waterdock and tincture of bardana.
† *Le Comédien*, by Pierre Rémond de Sainte-Albine, was published in Paris in 1747.

as Lusignan and Mrs Cibber in the title role, a good house was guaranteed.*
The farce was poor stuff, however, and on the second night it was hissed into
oblivion.† Hill responded by feeding the press with disobliging paragraphs about
the Drury Lane management, but Garrick had the better of him with a nicely
turned couplet which he produced extempore at a dinner with friends:

> For Physick & Farces, his Equal there scarce is,
> His Farces are Physick, his Physick a Farce is.[13]

The paper war between the two men continued for the best part of two months,
before Garrick, somewhat belatedly, declined to continue the correspondence. 'Could you have imagin'd that there could Exist such a Being as Hill?' he
wrote in exasperation to Hawkesworth. 'He wants to make a printed Quarrel
of it—but I'll write no more Except with my Crabstick upon his back &
Shoulders.'[14]

Hill was not easily silenced, however. A month later he opened up a new
front with a pamphlet called *The Petition of I. In behalf of herself and her
Sisters.*[15] This was quite a witty attack on Garrick for the way he pronounced
certain vowels:

> ... Your Petitioner does, and must conceive, the original and natural
> Pronunciation of the good Word FIRM, to be at least as elegant, and as
> expressive of the Sense, as the coarse boggy FURM, (Walk I on Land?
> FURM Land? Winter's Tale) which you have introduced into its place,
> and which your many Excellencies, fixing the Stamp of Judgement upon
> Folly, have forced into the Throats of others.
>
> She requests, nay she demands, if the Supreme public owns the justice
> of her title, that she be reinstated in that Epithet: And from her natural
> Love to Things neglected, she prays most earnestly to be no longer banished
> from the sacred name of VIRTUE; (Calls VURTUE Hypocrite. Hamlet).
>
> Entering your Borders I beheld a Temple sacred to HURCULES.
> Merope. Turn back dull URTH. Romeo) who since she is doomed to
> lose her Being in the present Age, should be allowed to keep her Name
> immaculate.
>
> .... That the indelicate and indeterminate Sound *u* having taken the
> Place of most of the Vowels and diphthongs; it will be easy to introduce
> it for the rest; and after this to place it for the Consonants.
>
> Your petitioner foresees, in one Year more, the English may be written
> with Points; having no more need of Vowels than the HEBREW...

Garrick laid aside his crabstick and made a good-natured response in
verse:

---

* Receipts for the evening amounted to £320, an outstanding figure.
† The play was given out for a third night, which was normally the author's benefit, but the
management resorted then, and on one further occasion, to the fiction that it had been deferred
'on account of the indisposition of a principal performer'.

> If 'tis true, as you say, that I've injur'd a letter,
> I'll change my note soon, and I hope for the better;
> May the right use of letters, as well as of men,
> Hereafter be fix'd by the tongue and the pen;
> Most devoutly I wish that they both have their due,
> And that *I* may be never mistaken for *U*.

Hill refused to be mollified and, some time in March, he took his grievances to the Lord Chamberlain—not a promising line of attack, because the close friendship between Devonshire and Garrick must have been common knowledge, but not one, for all that, which Garrick felt he could ignore: 'I have prov'd Every assertion in his Petition to be Lyes from his own Letters,' he wrote to Hawkesworth. 'I am almost kill'd with my fatigues—dead! dead . . .'[16]

The controversy spluttered on until the late spring. Hill published one more anonymous pamphlet* in which he called for theatrical affairs to be made the responsibility of the government and proposed that 'a person of judgment and integrity [be] appointed by the name of comptroller, or conductor of the stage, who *alone* shall determine what old plays shall be acted, and what new ones received'. Nobody paid the least attention, and Hill returned to his botanical studies.†

Garrick drove himself very hard that autumn and winter, no doubt partly to make up for the loss of Woodward. At the end of October he had been taken ill while playing Lear, although he insisted on going through with it. There were several other occasions during the season when he was unwell, one of them, in early December, on the night when he appeared as Marplot in *The Busy Body*. He had never attempted the role before—perhaps there was an element of bravado in his decision to do so now, because it was one of the most popular and successful in Woodward's repertory. Murphy, for one, thought it was an attempt to outshine the renegade, and that it failed:

> The deserter to Dublin could put on such a vacant innocent countenance, that all the mischief he did by being busy in other people's affairs, appeared to be the effect of accident; whereas Garrick had so much meaning, such strong intelligence in his countenance, that he seemed to do every thing by design.‡

Murphy, as it happens, proved a sizeable thorn in the flesh to Garrick that season.

---

* *Observations on the importance and use of theatres; their present regulation, and possible improvements.*
† The following year, on the accession of George III, he was once again the beneficiary of the patronage of Bute and was given charge of the gardens of Kensington Palace — a sinecure, according to Horace Walpole, worth £2,000 a year. (*Walpole*, xvi, 42. Letter to Henry Zouch dated 3 January 1761.)
‡ *Murphy*, i, 327. Rather ungenerously, Garrick was later to claim the credit for Woodward's success in the part, telling Percival Stockdale that it had been 'all beaten into him'. (*Stockdale*, ii, 160.)

Some years previously he had begun work on a tragedy called *The Orphan of China*—an adaptation of Voltaire's play of the same name which had been put on in Paris in 1755. Garrick initially turned the idea down—he had already suggested that Hawkesworth should try his hand at a version of the same piece. Later, when Hawkesworth failed to deliver, he agreed to look at Murphy's text, but formed the view that as it stood it would not do.

Murphy reacted with characteristic intemperance. The lengthy account of their quarrel which he gives in his *Life of Garrick* is hardly a model of objectivity; happily, many of the extraordinarily acrimonious letters which passed between them have survived, and they make it possible to piece together a more reliable impression of the two years of wrangling that preceded the eventual production of *The Orphan of China*.

At one point Murphy withdrew the play and offered it instead to Covent Garden. Garrick was quick to seize the opportunity to harden his position:

> How is it possible, with the least Shadow of Reason, or without yᵉ greatest
> Inconveniences to me, both as a Man & a Manager, to receive a performance
> . that was taken so abruptly out of my hands, & so unaccountably put into
> those of other people? I wou'd desire you to reflect a little upon my
> Situation . . .[17]

Murphy had a shrewd appreciation of Garrick's weaknesses. 'Anxiety for his fame was the manager's reigning foible,' he wrote in the *Life*; 'on the slightest attack, he was *tremblingly alive all o'er*.' If his account is to be believed, he somehow induced Henry Fox and Horace Walpole to read the play. Fox told Murphy that Garrick was to dine at Holland House shortly, and invited him to call there the following morning:

> At that meeting, the first word from Mr Fox was, 'Have you heard from
> Garrick?'—'No, Sir.'—'You will hear from him,' said Mr Fox: 'After
> dinner yesterday, Mr Walpole and I repeated, at different times, some lines
> that had struck us; Garrick stared with an air of surprise, and at last said,
> 'I perceive that you two gentlemen have been reading what I have read.'
> 'Yes, Mr Garrick,' replied Mr Fox, 'We have been reading, and admiring,
> what, we are sure you admire.' Not a word more passed on the occasion,
> but in a day or two after, Garrick, by letter, desired to see the *Orphan of
> China* once more, as, in his hurry, he might have passed an erroneous
> judgement.*

Garrick may have found it politic to bend before the breeze, but his evening at Holland House had done nothing to cloud his professional judgement about the piece. He confirmed to Murphy in the early summer of 1758 that it had been

---

* *Murphy*, i, 332–3. Although there is nothing inherently implausible about this part of the story, it is more than a little surprising that Horace Walpole makes no mention of it to any of his correspondents. He disliked Garrick and was never slow to retail any gossip that reflected ill on him.

pencilled into the schedule for the following season—'alway reserving to Myself,' he added, 'yᵉ right of Judging of It's fitness for appearing upon yᵉ Stage.' And he was clearly beginning to find Murphy extremely tiresome to deal with:

> People in general do their own Business best, but as we have been somewhat unfortunate, I must desire that our theatrical Concerns for yᵉ future may be adjusted by Letter or by Mediation of a Common Friend—[18]

A meeting was arranged at the house of Vaillant, the bookseller—Murphy went alone, but Garrick was accompanied both by Lacy and by his friend Berenger. Garrick was still unpersuaded that *The Orphan* was 'fit for representation', but after much altercation he and Lacy agreed—generously, it might be thought— that the question should be settled by an arbiter of Murphy's choosing. He settled on Whitehead, Colley Cibber's successor as Poet Laureate, who was then at Bath, and the hapless *Orphan* was bundled off there for his adjudication.

Before Whitehead could deliver his verdict, Murphy succeeded in enraging Garrick and muddying the waters by accusing the Drury Lane management of condoning 'literary piracy'. *The Rout*, he wrote, which was about to appear, was a 'little project' of his, and the idea had been stolen from him: 'I will not silently sink under acts of oppression; I think I have a right to expect of the managers of Drury-lane, that, if they will do me no good, they will at least refrain from doing me any harm.'[19] Garrick was seldom a good tactician in paper wars, and Murphy caught him at a bad moment—exhausted after the first night of *The Busy Body* and far from well. He fired off a furious reply, and wound himself up to a pitch of exasperation: 'As I have really no time, health or inclination to continue these illiberal Wringlings I hope you'll Excuse me if I am silent hence- forth: I can do no more . . .'[20]

'I have always declar'd that my private Resentments shall never interfere with yᵉ Public Entertainments,' Garrick had told Murphy in an earlier letter.[21] It says much for his professionalism and magnanimity that when Whitehead pronounced in favour of the play he thrust his reservations aside and did everything in his power to make a success of it. Even so, there were further squalls before the first night. Garrick, with a thousand other things on his mind,* felt he could not do justice to the leading part, Zamti, unless the opening, originally fixed for 25 February, were postponed. Here was a fresh grievance about which Murphy could wax rhetorical—'You had an opportunity, by acting genteelly on this occasion, of making me blush for some things that have happened; *but revenge perhaps is more agreeable.*'[22] But Garrick had not received the script in its final form until 23 January. The play was still being altered and cut on 18 February. Halfway through rehearsals Mrs Cibber, who was to play Mandane, became ill and had to withdraw; her place was taken by Mrs Yates—whom Murphy,

---

* Within a matter of days at the turn of the year, there had been three deaths in the company— John Oram, one of Garrick's scene-painters, Macklin's wife, Ann, and James Taswell, a well-regarded repertory stalwart whose roles included Polonius and Dogberry, and whose Lord Mayor in *Richard III* had so greatly pleased George II.

unknown to Garrick, had been secretly rehearsing in the part for several weeks past.

On the day, a friend arranged a celebratory dinner for Murphy at the Rose Tavern. Sir Francis Delaval and Berenger were present, and so were Hogarth and Foote. As they sat at table, a letter was brought to Murphy from Mrs Cibber, regretting that her name was not on the playbill and telling him that she would offer up her prayers for his success. Foote read the letter aloud to the company, and raised a hearty laugh by observing gravely that Mrs Cibber was a Catholic, and that Catholics always prayed for the dead.

As it happened, the first night passed off well. Garrick had pulled out all the stops. 'Scenes, Habits, and Decorations entirely New,' noted Cross—it is possible that a use may have been found for what had been salvaged from the fiasco of *The Chinese Festival*. Garrick himself played brilliantly, and Mrs Yates's performance established her as a firm favourite with the public.

The season was not without its lesser irritations. Early in November, Garrick had played Hastings in *Jane Shore*, with Mrs Cibber as Alicia and the ever-dependable Mrs Pritchard in the title role. It had not gone unnoticed that Mrs Pritchard—she was coming up to fifty—had recently put on a lot of weight, something to which Oliver Goldsmith paid ungallant attention in his publication *The Bee*. It was, he wrote, distressing to see 'an actress that might act the Wapping Landlady without a bolster, pining in the character of Jane Shore, and while unwieldy with fat endeavouring to convince the audience that she is dying with hunger'.[23] The part passed to Mrs Yates, and Mrs Pritchard only ever played it once more, for her daughter's benefit night eight years later.

During December Garrick had also found himself at odds with the writer and bookseller Robert Dodsley. Some time previously he had turned down Dodsley's tragedy *Cleone*, describing it as 'cruel, bloody and unnatural'.* When it was accepted by Covent Garden and advertised, he placed his own début in *The Busy Body* against it, and there were those—they included Davies—who regarded this as an unworthy spoiling tactic.† 'David and Doddy have had a new quarrel,' Johnson wrote to Langton, who was in Lincolnshire, 'and, I think, cannot conveniently quarrel any more. I went to the first night, and supported it as well as I might; for Doddy, you know, is my patron, and I would not desert him.'‡

When Garrick wrote Dodsley a note of congratulation, it was frostily received:

I thank you for your Compliments on the success of Cleone, and could have wished you had thought proper to have put it in my power to have

---

* Johnson, who was on terms of close friendship with Dodsley, had formed a similar view when the play was read to him by his young friend Bennet Langton. 'Come,' he said at the end of an act, 'let's go into the slaughter-house again, Lanky. But I am afraid there is more blood than brains.' (*Life*, iv, 20.)

† 'It must be confessed by those who esteemed Mr Garrick most,' wrote Davies, 'that his conduct in the whole dispute was unjustifiable, and that he treated a worthy man and an old acquaintance with severity and unkindness.' (*Davies*, i, 252.)

‡ *Life*, i, 326. Dodsley had not only suggested the scheme of the *Dictionary* to Johnson, but had also published his *Vanity of Human Wishes* and would shortly bring out *Rasselas*.

thank'd you for contributing towards it: but I think it is not now in your own to redress the injury you have done me. You know full well that *profit* was but my second motive for bringing this piece on the Stage, and you have taken effectual care to nip its *Reputation* in the bud, by preventing ye Town, as far as lay in your power, from attending to it.*

Dodsley need not have worried. The play did extremely well, running for sixteen nights, largely due to the performance of Mrs Bellamy in the title role.† It was published almost at once and 2,000 copies were sold in a matter of weeks.

The two months on either side of Christmas 1758 illustrate both the relentless pressure to which Garrick was subjected at this time and the quite remarkable resilience with which he withstood it. A punishing performance schedule and his seemingly never-ending disputes with writers do not seem to have interfered with either his correspondence or his reading. William Robertson, who had been one of the golfing party at Hampton in the summer, sent him his newly published *History of Scotland*, and Garrick responded enthusiastically: 'Upon my word, I was never more entertained in all my life; and though I read it aloud to a friend and Mrs Garrick, I finished the first three books at two sittings.'‡

Garrick had also found time (this over a period of some months) to work on the text of *Antony and Cleopatra* and early in January he put on the first recorded performance of the play since Shakespeare's own day.§ It was a sumptuous affair—'New Habits, Scenes, and Decorations,' said the playbill—and yet it was indifferently received: 'Did not seem to give ye Audience any plasure,' wrote Cross, 'or draw any Applause.' Garrick took it off after six performances, and never played it again.

The eighteenth-century audience may well not have appreciated the ease and rapidity of the action. Garrick cut several hundred lines, but attempted little in

---

* *Boaden*, i, 79f. Letter dated 5 December. Garrick might have been wise to let the matter rest there; instead he made matters worse with a further note in which he described Dodsley's letter as 'peevish'. (*Letters*, 219.)

† Mrs Bellamy in her *Life* (iii, 109), says that on the evening before the piece opened, Garrick 'had anticipated the damnation of it' at the Bedford Coffee-house, 'where he had declared that it could not pass muster, as it was the very worst piece ever exhibited'.

‡ *Letters*, 220. Robertson's covering letter makes it clear that like so many others, he found Mrs Garrick enchanting: 'I beg leave to offer my most respectful compliments to Mrs Garrick, with whom, as I am a parson, and a married man, and at four hundred miles distance, I may acknowledge, even to you, that I am much in love. . . . (*Boaden*, i, 95, letter dated 9 January 1759.)

§ Garrick was helped, in his work on the text, by his friend Edward Capell (1713–81), deputy-inspector of plays in the Lord Chamberlain's office since 1737, who was then at work on his own edition of Shakespeare. They later became estranged, possibly because it came to Garrick's ears that Capell said he 'spoke many speeches in Shakespeare without understanding them.' (Nichols, John, *Illustrations of the Literary History of the Eighteenth Century*, 8 vols., London, 1817–58, i, 474f.).

the way of revision or 'improvement'.* A number of minor characters were removed; the general effect of the cuts is to reduce the political and historical elements in the plot while leaving the love interest unaffected. The famous opening scene of Act IV, in which Caesar rages at Antony's calling him a boy, disappears, and so does scene ii, the powerful 'last supper' scene, in which Antony reduces his followers to tears and even Enobarbus becomes 'onion-eyed'.

Davies, who played Eros, suggests that Mrs Yates was still not ready for Cleopatra and that for once Garrick's acting failed to fire the audience: 'It must be confessed, that, in Antony, he wanted one necessary accomplishment: his person was not sufficiently important and commanding to represent the part.'[24] It was also the case that Garrick was quite simply not well: 'I was so ill & Weak with a kind of bilious Colick, when I play'd Anthony,' he wrote to the painter Benjamin Wilson, 'that I was not in a condition the next Morn^g to do half my Business, that I sh^d have done.'[25]

Years later, when he was close to retirement, he would look back on the production with a touch of wistfulness: 'An^y & Cleopatra I reviv'd Some Years ago, When I & Mrs Yates were Younger,' he wrote to George Steevens—'it gain'd ground Every time it was play'd, but I grew tir'd, & gave it up.'[26] Steevens sent him a reassuring and perceptive reply:

> . . . Your Antony and Cleopatra was a splendid performance; but you were out of love with it because it afforded you few opportunities of showing those sharp turns, and that coachmanship in which you excel all others.†

The Princess Royal died towards the end of January, and the theatres were closed for a week of mourning. Shortly after the reopening, Drury Lane staged an unusual benefit—'For the Benefit of Mr Cris^r Smart,' Cross noted in his diary, 'an Ingenious young Man in poetry, but now confin'd in a Mad house.' Smart, by then in his late thirties, had distinguished himself as a classical scholar at Cambridge, but in the *DNB*'s delicate phase, 'he combined with small means some extravagant habits and a predilection for tavern parlours.' Garrick had been one of the subscribers to his first collection of verse, *Poems on Several Occasions*, published in 1752; it was some anonymous abuse of this volume from the pen of John Hill that prompted Smart, with some help from Murphy, to produce *The Hilliad*. He had been confined to Bedlam once previously, his derangement taking the form of a compulsion to fall on his knees and say his prayers in the street.‡

* Although Enobarbus's famous description of Cleopatra ('The barge she sat in, like a burnished throne/ Burned on the water . . .') is brought forward from Act II to the very first scene in the play and given to Thyreus.

† *Boaden*, ii, 122. Steevens (1736–1800), 'the Puck of Commentators' as William Gifford called him, was best known for his annotated editions of Shakespeare. He also assisted Johnson with *Lives of the Poets*.

‡ Johnson visited him during a later period of confinement and told Dr Burney he ought never to have been shut up. 'His infirmities were not noxious to society. He insisted on people praying with him; and I'd as lief pray with Kit Smart as any one else. Another charge was, that he did not love clean linen; and I have no passion for it.' (*Life*, i, 397.)

Receipts for the benefit totalled £285. The mainpiece was Aaron Hill's *Meropé*, and this was followed by a new two-act comedy called *The Guardian*, in which the main parts were played by Garrick, Mrs Clive and Miss Pritchard. The following week, when the Prince of Wales brought a family party to a Command Performance, the Prince's brother, Edward, Duke of York, enquired about the authorship of the farce, which had not been made public. This was not something Garrick was keen to disclose, and he wrote to Bute in some embarrassment to explain why:

> I was in great Confusion at ye Question, because I happen'd to be the Guilty person Myself, But I have so many Enemies among the Writers on Account of my refusing so many of their Performances Every Year, that I am oblig'd to conceal Myself in order to avoid the Torrent of abuse that their Malice would pour upon Me—I thought it proper (and I hope Your Lordship will Excuse Me) to discover this; lest his Royal Highness should be angry at my not answering his Question directly, as I ought to have done—[27]

Garrick, as he announced in the advertisement to the first edition of the play, had once more gone to a French source: 'The *Pupille* of Monsieur *Fagan* is mentioned by Voltaire, and other French writers, as the most complete *Petite-Piece* upon their stage.'* So far as the text was concerned, he did little more than move the scene to London and speed up the action by the judicious introduction of stage business. But he heightened the sentimental tone of the play considerably; the excessive delicacy of his heroine, Harriet, and of her guardian, Heartly, invites ridicule rather than sympathy; what Fagan intended to be edifying, Garrick makes comical. 'I take care that my eyes don't tell too much, and he has too much delicacy to interpret looks to his advantage,' Harriet tells Lucy, her maid, played by Kitty Clive:

Besides, he would certainly disapprove my passion; and if I should ever make
   the declaration and meet with a denial, I should absolutely die with shame.
LUCY. I'll insure your life for a silver thimble. But what can possibly hinder
   your coming together?
MISS HARRIET. His excess of merit.
LUCY. His excess of a fiddlestick.[28]

Garrick, without straying any great distance from Fagan's miniature *comédie larmoyante*, deftly transmutes it into an elegant attack on the genre itself. The 'universal applause' recorded by Cross was well merited, and *The Guardian* retained a place in the repertory into the nineteenth century.

---

* *Fagan* was Barthélemi-Christophe Fagan, 1702–55. *La Pupille*, clearly derivative of Molière's *L'Ecole des Femmes*, had appeared in 1734.

20

Heart of Oak

My dear Friend.   March 20th 1759
I shall send the boy tomorrow by yᵉ Bromley Stage consigned to you, & I
must desire you to give him safe into yᵉ hands of his Master. He is a very
pretty Lad but my great fatigues & *Strangeness of Temper* (as Dʳ Hill is
pleas'd to call it) make me incapable of attending to his Education as I
ought to do—he has fine parts & good Nature but being too much fondled
by yᵉ Ladies, he is a little spoil'd . . .[1]

Garrick was writing to his friend Dr John Hawkesworth, who in addition to his
literary pursuits took a hand in the running of a small school kept by his wife
at Bromley in Kent.* The boy in question was a child actor called Samuel
Cautherley, and he was persistently rumoured to be Garrick's illegitimate
son.

Who the ladies were who had spoiled him with over-much fondling we do
not know—most likely the actresses among whom he seems to have spent a
good deal of his early life. His first appearance was as Jasper in a performance
of *Miss in Her Teens* played entirely by children. That was at Drury Lane in
April 1755.† In the autumn he was seen as the young Duke of York in *Richard
III*, a role traditionally given to promising youngsters, and the following year he
was Lord Flimnap in Garrick's *Lilliput*.

Garrick was in general intensely reticent about private matters and his correspondence offers few clues to the nature of his relationship with—or to—the
boy. Stage people quite often led disorderly lives, and casual sexual liaisons were
commonplace. Laetitia-Matilda Hawkins recalls in her memoirs that at one time
there were rumours that Garrick and his wife were about to separate because of

---

* The Hawkesworths' school was for girls. Garrick had asked his friend to arrange for the boy
to be admitted to some other establishment in Bromley and to keep an eye on him.
† The name Cautherley does however make one isolated earlier appearance — in the roster of
Rich's company at Covent Garden for the season 1749–50. Although he is not listed on any of
the playbills, the theatre records show that he had tickets for one of the lowlier benefit nights
which five members of the company shared towards the end of the season on 7 May 1750.
(*London Stage*, Part 4, i, 197.) It seems unlikely that this was Samuel. Possibly the child had
been fostered by someone of that name who was briefly connected with the company.

his infidelity. 'He came to my father in complete dejection,' she wrote (the Hawkinses had a house at Twickenham, not far from Hampton):

> With an expression of contrition, he confessed that the early part of his life had been productive of much irregularity; but he declared that from the hour of his marriage, his affection had never for a moment swerved from Mrs Garrick.*

There were, inevitably, those who maintained that Peg Woffington was Cautherley's mother. Others favoured the actress Jane Hippisley, daughter of the well-known comedian John Hippisley. She was two years younger than Garrick, and he had known her since the earliest days of his career. She had been a member of Giffard's troupe and had been in Ipswich when he played there in the summer of 1741. They were together again at Goodman's Fields the following season— when Garrick made his début in *Richard III*, she played the part of Prince Edward. In 1747 he had recruited her to the 70-strong company he assembled for his first season as manager at Drury Lane, and in that same year, two years before Garrick himself married, she became the wife of the actor Henry Green, by whom she would have three sons.

Somewhat curiously, the gossip about Jane Green and Garrick began to find its way into print only in the 1770s, towards the end of both their careers.† The 1772 edition of *Theatrical Biography* was slyly explicit:

> The very great care and attention this skilful director took in the culti-vation of her talents, might very well account for her progress; nor is it to be wondered at, when it is said that there were still stronger reasons for attentions than mere managerical regard . . . . The lady *could* not be . . . cruel; sensible of the mischiefs she had done to Garrick's heart, she repaired them by good nature—a chopping boy bore witness to their loves—‡

Whether Garrick was the father of a 'chopping boy' by Jane Hippisley or by Peg Woffington or by anyone else, and whether that child was Samuel Cautherley, cannot now be determined. What is not in doubt is that over an extremely long period Garrick lavished on Cautherley a degree of loving care which can only properly be described as paternal—and that he did so with the full-hearted consent of his wife.

For many years Cautherley was a member of the Garrick household. In a

---

* Hawkins, Laetitia-Matilda, *Anecdotes, Biographical Sketches and Memoirs*, London, 1822, 26–7. Miss Hawkins was the daughter of the lawyer and author Sir John Hawkins, whose *Life and Works of Samuel Johnson* appeared in 11 volumes in 1787–89. He and Boswell, wrote Leslie Stephen, were 'comically jealous of each other'.

† Mrs Green created the role of Mrs Hardcastle in Goldsmith's *She Stoops to Conquer* in 1773 and was the original Mrs Malaprop in Sheridan's *The Rivals* two years later. She retired in 1780.

‡ *Theatrical Biography: or, Memoirs of the Principal Performers of the Three Theatres Royal*, London, 1772. 'Chopping' is an old word meaning strapping or vigorous.

busy, gossipy letter to his friend Richard Berenger, written from Bath in 1766, Garrick asked him to pass on a number of messages to his brother George. 'Moreover,' he added, 'Tell him from my wife, that Cautherly's bed must be washt as soon as possible, & to put it up again wth yᵉ window-curtains.'² A letter survives which Cautherley wrote to Mrs Garrick long after her husband's death: 'The Gratitude I shall ever feel for the many kindnesses confer'd on me, while under your Hospitable Roof (for almost Twenty years) can never be effaced.'

Garrick would not only see to his schooling, but would try all he knew to launch Cautherley on an adult career as an actor. When this proved uphill work, he sent him off to Paris for eighteen months and laid out on him during that time the considerable sum of 22,982 *livres*. A document preserved in the Victoria and Albert Museum lists a large number of payments made on Garrick's behalf between June 1763 and November 1764. Garrick's agent in these trans-actions was his Paris banker, Selwyn, and the entries are made in eighteenth-century *franglais*: '18 June, 1st quarter a l'academe pour Mr Cautherley Livres 724, plus 240 livres to J. Convert for same: total 964.' Convert was possibly a tutor.

All that—and the eventual breach between Garrick and his protégé—lay in the future. For the moment, in the summer of 1759, Garrick was concerned only with getting the basics drummed into the boy: 'He is very deficient in his Reading, & repeats his Catechism very imperfectly,' he wrote to Hawkesworth. 'I shall try him at that school another Quarter & then shall determine about him. therefore pray be so kind to Speak to Mʳ Booth in behalf of yᵉ Lad for I fear he is Idle—'³

Theatre business was never laid aside, even during Garrick's precious summers. Mrs Cibber's health had once again been playing havoc with his schedules. She was in the habit, when she found herself at odds with the management, of turning to some third party to make her case for her, and in the summer of 1759 she had enlisted the aid of Dr Edward Barry, the Dublin physician whom she and Garrick had both known since the season they had played there. Garrick, in his reply, was barely able to conceal his exasperation:

> Mʳˢ Cibber herself Acknowledges that She *greatly disappointed* us the last winter, & had our Success wholly depended upon her, We must have been Bankrupt . . . I am Surprised a little, that She Should Urge an attendance upon Rehearsals as a Sufficient plea for her Sallary; the Managers Must support their large property not by Rehearsals but by her Appearance in public . . .*

The manager was well aware that the rest of the company believed Mrs Cibber received special treatment. 'You gave Mrs Cibber £600 for playing 60 nights,' a

* *Letters*, 237. Barry (1696–1776) had sat in the Irish House of Commons for several years and was Physician-General to the forces in Ireland. He was created a baronet in 1775.

furious Kitty Clive wrote to him on one occasion, 'and £300 to me for playing I80.'[4]

Garrick managed a brief excursion to Hampshire during July and visited John Hoadly at Winchester, but all too soon it was back to the strictures of the pamphleteers and the whining of disaffected authors. There had been a complaint from Dodsley that he had been denied admittance to the theatre and that this had been done on Garrick's instructions. It was a misunderstanding—he usually sat in the pit, and when he had presented himself at the entrance to the boxes, an old house servant had failed to recognize him. Garrick was incensed. 'I must desire You to retract the Wrong You have done Me in censuring Me too hastily,' he wrote:

> Since I have been Manager, Every Author, from y[e] highest to y[e] lowest, who has wrote for our Stage, has had, & Shall have, the Liberty of the house—It is their Right & not to be taken away at y[e] Caprice of a Manager: therefore You may Enjoy it freely without being Oblig'd to Me; a Circumstance w[ch] will give You no little pleasure, as You have lately boasted wth some Warmth that you never *was* oblig'd to me—[5]

One of the more fatuous efforts on the pamphleteering front was by a man called Edward Purdon—*A Letter to David Garrick Esq; on Opening the Theatre. In which, With Great Freedom He is Told How He Ought to Behave.* 'You have acquired such a degree of importance,' Purdon informed Garrick, 'that Nero was scarce more despotic in his theatre than you in yours.' He did not do enough to encourage new writers. Plays for the repertory should be chosen by allowing a committee of the whole audience to view everything that was submitted: 'It is better no doubt that twenty indifferent pieces should be represented than one good one be suppressed.' No doubt.*

Compared with the surge and press of events on the national stage, it was all rather tawdry and petty. Although in Choiseul, the new minister in France, Pitt now faced a formidable adversary, 1759 had been for him an *annus mirabilis*; Horace Walpole complained that the church bells had been worn threadbare with ringing for victory. In May there had been the capture of Guadeloupe, a haven for French privateers; in August, Ferdinand of Brunswick won a decisive victory at Minden;† a month later the fate of Canada was settled when Wolfe's men scaled the Heights of Abraham at Quebec; in November, Hawke swooped on Conflans' fleet of twenty-six ships as it sailed out of Brest and drove it to destruction in Quiberon Bay.

---

* This was followed a week or so later by *Reasons why David Garrick should not appear on the Stage.* Couched in the form of a letter to John Rich, it is full of extravagant praise for Garrick: 'I am so blinded either by prejudice or admiration that I can see nobody else.' The catalogue in the British Library suggests that this may have been by Garrick himself.

† No thanks to Lord George Sackville, the commander of the British contingent, who disregarded an order for his cavalry to advance. He was court-martialled, and it was directed that his sentence be recorded in the order-book of every regiment, so that all might be convinced 'that neither high birth nor great employments can shelter offences of such a nature'.

Garrick, like Noël Coward in a later war, laid a sure finger on the national pulse:

> Come cheer up, my lads, 'tis to glory we steer,
> To add something new to this wonderful year,
> 'Tis to honour we call you, not press you like slaves,
> For who are so free as the Sons of the Waves?

He wrote 'Heart of Oak'* for *Harlequin's Invasion*, that year's traditional Christmas entertainment at Drury Lane, and it was an immediate success.† Woodward's departure three years previously had made it that much more difficult to compete with Rich's spectacular pantomimes. Garrick now boldly decided to challenge 'Lun' with a Harlequin of his own, but it was a Harlequin with a difference—this one, in a break with age-long convention, *spoke*. After Rich's death, Garrick wrote a new prologue to the piece, which explained his reasons:

> When Lun appear'd, with matchless art and whim,
> He gave the power of speech to ev'ry limb;
> Tho' mask'd and mute, convey'd his quick intent,
> And told in frolic gesture all he meant
> But now the motley coat, and sword of wood,
> Requires a tongue to make them understood.

It was a gracious tribute to his dead rival. Garrick, always the realist, knew that he no longer had anyone able to excel in the art of pantomime, and wisely chose to write to his company's strengths.

Years before, a stage-struck young wine merchant, he had been thrust on at Goodman's Fields to do two or three scenes as Harlequin when Yates had been taken ill, and it was on that piece that he now drew for one strand in his plot.‡ Harlequin threatens to invade the realm of King Shakespeare—or is it the realm of King George that is under threat from the fleet of ships and flat-bottomed boats that Choiseul's admirals were known to have been assembling in Dunkirk

---

* The music was by Boyce, although the original tune differed somewhat from the Victorianized version with which we are familiar today.

† Rich was slower to respond. Only towards the end of the season, in May, would he mount *The Siege of Quebec; or, Harlequin Engineer*; Pantaloon and Colombine rubbed shoulders with Britannia, 'The Genius of England', and the performance concluded with 'an Emblematical Representation of General Wolfe's Monument'.

‡ *Harlequin Student*, presented in March 1741, had been put on to exploit the erection of Shakespeare's statue in Westminster Abbey, and was subtitled *The Fall of Pantomime, with the Restoration of the Drama*. It was for the most part an entirely orthodox harlequinade, veering only at the end into an extravagant panegyric to the bard. 'Banish Foreign songsters hence,' Minerva urges the audience:

> Doat on *Shakespear's* manly Sense.
> Send th'Invading Triflers home,
> To lull the Fools of *France* and *Rome*!

and Le Havre? The decree which Mercury reads out from Apollo leaves the matter artfully unclear:

> Whereas it is feared French trick may be played ye,
> Be it known Monsieur Harlequin means to invade ye.
> And hither transporting his legions, he floats
> On an ocean of canvas in flat bottom boats.

The comic sub-plot has Dolly, the daughter of Snip the tailor, fall in love with Harlequin. She dreams of her life as a lady of quality, giving Garrick an opportunity to glance slyly both at the hairstyles of the day and the idiosyncrasies of certain sections of his audience:

> O Law, if I should be Lady Doll Snip . . . I won't be stuffed up twice or thrice a year at holiday time at the top of the playhouse among folk that laugh and cry, just as they feel. Then I'll carry my head as high and have as high a head as the best of 'em, and it shall be all set out with curls. It shall be too high to go in at any door without stooping, and so broad that I must always go in sideways. Then I shall keep a chair with a cupola o'top to hold my featherhead in, and I shall be carried in it by day and by night, dingle-dangle, bobbing and nodding, all the way I go. Then I shall sit in the side boxes among my equals, laugh, talk aloud, mind nothing, stare at the low people in the galleries without ever looking at them. . . .[6]

Harlequin's Invasion is notable as the first production in which Garrick made use of scenic transparencies and coloured silk screens. He was indebted for the idea to Domenico Angelo, the Italian fencing-master who had been swept up in Peg Woffington's train in Paris and accompanied her to England. Angelo had lived for some years in Venice, and had there got to know Canaletto, who had originally, like his father before him, been a scene-painter. Welcomed behind the scenes of the Venetian theatres, and being of a mechanical turn of mind, Angelo had become quite knowledgeable about stage machinery.

Sitting over the wine one night after dining with Angelo, Garrick described some of the situations in which the characters in his 'speaking' pantomime would find themselves—how Snip, for instance, must pursue Harlequin through an enchanted wood. Angelo came up with some suggestions, and one of the Drury Lane scene-painters produced 'a very fine composition, which was painted with masterly execution'. The slips or screens were painted in the usual opaque manner, but the back scene was a transparency, 'behind which visionary figures were seen flitting across, upon the plan of the *Tableau mouvant*' (the description occurs in the memoirs of Angelo's son, Henry):

> That which rendered this scene apparently the work of enchantment, however, was a contrivance, which originated in the inventive faculties of my father. He caused screens to be placed diagonally, which were covered with scarlet, crimson, and bright blue moreen, which, having a powerful

light before them, by turning them towards the scenes, reflected these varous colours alternately, with a success that astonished and delighted the audience. Indeed, the whole stage appeared on fire.*

New lighting arrangements like these would have an important effect on both directing and acting technique. The players might now move further towards the back of the stage without being swallowed up in shadow; the audience could now catch nuances of expression or gesture that would previously have gone unnoticed other than on the apron.

Garrick was fortunate in being able to cast Tom King as Harlequin. Nine years in Ireland had refined his comic gifts and won him a devoted following. His return to the fold came at a good moment, because the traffic between London and Dublin continued to be two-way. Mossop had just taken his vanity and ill-temper off to try his luck with Barry and Woodward at Crow Street† and after a disagreement of some sort early in the season Garrick also lost one of his most promising young actresses to Dublin. Frances Abington had been at Drury Lane for only three years, and was still only twenty-two. She quickly had the Irish capital at her feet, both professionally and socially. The cap she wore as Kitty in *High Life Below Stairs* became all the rage, and was to be seen in milliners' windows identified in large letters by the one word ABINGTON.

A much more serious blow was the departure to Covent Garden of John Beard, easily the most celebrated singer of the mid-century. Beard, who had been at Drury Lane for more than ten years, seems to have made his move for personal rather than professional reasons—he had recently, in his middle forties, remarried, and his bride was Charlotte, one of John Rich's four daughters.‡ Before the season was a month old, Rich had his new son-in-law singing Macheath in *The Beggar's Opera*. Polly was sung by a pupil—some suspected the mistress— of Thomas Arne, a young woman called Charlotte Brent who had a voice of great range and colour but was totally devoid of physical charms.§

A good deal of nonsense has found its way into print over the years both

---

* *Angelo*, i, 10–15. Moreen is a woollen material, or a mixture of wool and cotton, used for making curtains and the like.

† Mossop listened too readily to those who said that Garrick undervalued him. He had also been roughly handled in the pamphlet *A Letter to David Garrick*, which contended that he failed to bring individuality to the characters he played — 'He is the same unmeaning bellower in them all.'

‡ His first marriage, twenty years previously, to a daughter of the Earl Waldegrave, had been the first regular union in England between an actor and a member of the aristocracy, and had occasioned much cruel gossip. 'This week the Lady Henrietta Powis married Birde the singing man,' the Earl of Egmont wrote in his diary. 'Her brother, an Ensign in the Guards, told her that her lover had the pox, and that she would be disappointed of the only thing she married him for, which was her lust ... But there is no prudence below the girdle.' The marriage, imprudent or no, was a happy one. Lady Henrietta died in 1753.

§ She also suffered from halitosis. When someone asked Foote what he thought of her rendering of a new song, he replied that he found the words pretty, but that he could hardly 'relish the air'. (*Cooke, op. cit.*, ii, 80.)

about Miss Brent and about this particular run of *The Beggar's Opera*. Most of it is traceable to Tom Davies, who asserted that Garrick declined an offer of her services from Arne, to whom at this stage she was still formally articled. 'A taste for music, or even a tolerable ear for a song,' he wrote, 'was not among Mr Garrick's endowments'[7]—an eccentric verdict on someone who had just written 'Heart of Oak' and who for the past decade had had the discrimination and good sense to have John Beard on his books. Miss Brent, what's more, had also been a member of the Drury Lane company between 1756 and 1758. Why she went over to Covent Garden at the beginning of the 1758–9 season is not known, but she made the change two years before Arne himself did.*

'The people were allured this year by nothing but the power of sound and sing-song,' writes Davies; 'Shakespeare and Garrick were obliged to quit the field to Beard and Brent',[8] and he has been followed in this by a number of modern biographers—Mary Nash, for instance, in her life of Susannah Cibber, declares that 'Garrick's temple to Shakespeare was deserted, while London ran to hear the young woman he had discarded'.† The account books of the two theatres tell a rather different story.

The Covent Garden production had certainly run for thirty-nine nights by the beginning of December, and had attracted respectable, although not remarkable, houses—average takings were of the order of £130 a night. There is a note in the Winston MS which says, 'Rich has cleared £5,000 besides his expenses by the run of *The Beggar's Opera*',[9] but on examination that turns out to be the total of the theatre's *receipts* for those performances, which is a different matter. The accounts of Drury Lane, what's more, show that for thirty-six of those nights (there was one night when Cross failed to make an entry, and on two others the house was dark), the takings were *greater* than those of Covent Garden—a total of £5,220, giving average receipts of £145 a night. Garrick's temple to Shakespeare clearly did not do so disastrously after all.

Part of the reason was that Garrick exerted himself prodigiously. A performance by the manager could always guarantee a good house at Drury Lane, and in the period in which Davies would have us believe that he 'quit the field to Beard and Brent' Garrick appeared no fewer than eighteen times in a range of his established roles—Macbeth, Richard, Romeo, Benedick, twice as Bayes and Biron, three times as Lear.

The creation of a new role by Garrick was always a red letter day in the theatrical calendar, and on 1 December he appeared for the first time as Oroonoko, with Mrs Cibber playing Imoinda. Hawkesworth had slimmed Southerne's tragedy down from five acts to three, getting rid of most of the low comedy in the process. 'Oroonoko and Imoinda are no longer surrounded by an idle crowd,' wrote

---

* Arne and Garrick had never got on, but although he had been writing more for Covent Garden and less for Drury Lane since his return from Ireland in 1756, Arne did not transfer his talents to the other house until 1760.

† *Nash, op. cit.*, 305. Nash says that Mrs Cibber (who was Arne's sister) was one of those who tried to persuade Garrick of Miss Brent's merits.

Murphy; 'they proceed without impertinent interruptions, and display their characters.'[10] A somewhat lukewarm notice of the piece by Johnson appeared in the *Critical Review*. It did well enough at the box-office—receipts over the eight-night run averaged more than £170—but Garrick did not appear in it again.

Two weeks later, the Drury Lane audience was offered something infinitely more entertaining—a double bill in which Macklin played the lead in both the mainpiece and the farce which followed it. The old trooper—he was now sixty—had not been finding it easy to get work, and had turned his attention once more to writing. The result was *Love à-la-Mode*, and in spite of all that had passed between them in years gone by, he had persuaded Garrick to put it on.

Garrick was taking no chances. The agreement signed with Macklin two weeks before the first night has survived; he plainly felt that if he was to sup even briefly with his one-time mentor, he would be prudent to equip himself with a fairly long spoon. Macklin was to have a fifth of the profits of the first five nights and a benefit on the sixth, after the deduction of £63 each night for house charges. The managers, however, reserved the right to take the play off after six nights if their other engagements required it, or if the receipts on any one night fell short of £100, and this was buttressed by a catch-all clause which gave them discretion to take it off 'if the said Farce shall meet with the disapprobation of the Publick'.[11]

As things turned out, it met with the disapprobation only of a few prickly Scots, who did not altogether appreciate the character of Sir Archy Macsarcasm.* On the opening night Cross noted in his diary that the farce 'went off very greatly', adding, almost as an afterthought, 'He play'd Shylock too.'†

There were not to be many more of these laconic entries in Cross's neat, stylish hand. He died the following February, and was buried at the actors' church, St Paul's, Covent Garden. He had been a hugely versatile man—an actor and dancer before taking on the prompter's job in 1741, he was frequently called on to fill in for other players. 'No Man understands better the Business of the Stage,' an anonymous pamphleteer had written some years previously:

> From a long Acquaintance with all the Pieces that have been play'd for some Years past, he is perfect in a Number of Characters, and can, at an Hour's Warning, fill up a Chasm caused by the sudden Sickness, or any other unexpected Accident befalling a Performer.[12]

---

* Macklin had struck a rich vein. Five years later he would create, in his *True-Born Scotsman*, that stock figure the Scottish careerist. 'I ha' acquired a noble fortune,' boasts Sir Pertinax Macsycophant. 'I raised it by boowing; by boowing, sir; I naver in my life could stond straight i' the presence of a great mon . . . Sir, I boowed, and watched, and attended, and dangled upo' the then great mon, till I got intill the very bowells of his confidence.'

† George II, who was now quite elderly and had largely given up going to the theatre, sent for the script of Macklin's play and got one of his old Hanoverian courtiers to read it to him. 'This person spent eleven weeks in misrepresenting the author's meaning,' wrote Davies. 'He was totally void of humour, and unacquainted with the English language. — The King, however, was much pleased with the Irishman's getting the better of his rivals, and gaining the lady.' (*Davies*, i, 326.)

Peg Woffington was also now close to death. Since her paralytic seizure three years previously she had lingered on at her home in the country at Teddington. In her final weeks she was brought to her house in Queen's Square, Westminster. She died there on 28 March 1760, and the most famously dissonant voice of the eighteenth-century theatre was stilled.

Murphy, who when he came to write his *Life*, had the impudence to say that Garrick and he had only ever quarrelled over *The Orphan of China*, was being tiresome again:

> Mr Garrick's Comp^{ts} to Mr Murphy—He owns himself much Surpriz'd at ye Note, that he has receiv'd from him—he was in hopes that Mr Murphy would never again have cause to Suspect his Willingness to promote the Interest of him or his Works—[13]

Garrick had accepted two more pieces from him—a dramatic poem, *The Desert Island*, which Murphy had taken from Metastasio's *L'Isola Disabitata* and a comedy called *The Way to Keep Him*, whose message was that a wife should take as great pains to keep a husband as she had taken to get him in the first place.* When Garrick told him he did not feel able to play a capital part in either piece, Murphy threatened to take them off to Dublin. Garrick called his bluff on this, but he was once again beset with casting problems caused by the increasingly frequent indispositions of Mrs Cibber:

> I beg to know how you find Yourself to day . . . the Comedy will require four or five regular Rehearsals at least, and tho *You* may be able to appear with two, Yet I am afraid the rest of the Dramatis Personae will be perplex'd and disjointed if they have not the advantage of your Character to Rehearse with them—[14]

The part went to Mrs Yates. Garrick himself played Lovemore, and also wrote a prologue for *The Desert Island*, delivered 'in character of a Drunken Poet'. How much his generosity in doing so was appreciated is open to doubt. Fitzgerald has a story about the poet Samuel Rogers quizzing Murphy after Garrick's death about their friendship:

> 'Mr Murphy, sir, you knew Mr Garrick?' 'Yes, sir, I did; and no man better.' 'Well, sir, what did you think of his acting?' After a pause—'Well, sir, *off* the stage, he was a mean, sneaking little fellow. But *on* the stage'— throwing up his eyes and hands—'Oh, my great God!'[15]

February saw another of Home's leaden tragedies—"one of the eternal Greek or Roman plays", as Fitzgerald wearily describes it—" 'Sieges' of this town, or 'Fall' of that." This one was *The Siege of Aquileia*, in which Mrs Cibber played Cornelia and Garrick was the Roman consul Aemilius. It survived for nine nights,

---

* The comedy was also derivative. Murphy had based it on Moissy's *La Nouvelle Ecole des Femmes*, which had been produced a couple of years previously at the Théâtre Italien in Paris.

benefiting from two performances commanded by the Prince of Wales. 'With its merits and defects alike,' Joseph Knight observes crisply, 'subsequent times have declined to concern themselves.'[16]

Garrick's final appearance before the summer was on 31 May, when he played Richard III in a Command Performance for the Prince of Wales. It was the last time he would do so. Before the new season was more than a few weeks old, George II was dead—carried off early one morning by a stroke in his water closet.* The theatres were dark for nineteen playing days while the nation mourned. The Covent Garden Account Book shows that Rich attempted to minimize his losses by docking the annual salaries of twenty-three members of the company by about 10 per cent.[17] Whether Lacy and Garrick found it necessary to prefigure Thomas Gradgrind in this way is not known.

---

* This embarrassing detail was not deemed to invalidate a quaint perquisite which came the way of Garrick's friend Lord Rochford on the King's death. As groom of the stole, he was entitled to the furniture of the room in which the monarch died. A bed-quilt which he acquired in this way did service for many years as an altar-cloth in St Osyth's church.

21

A Pleasant and Reasonable Retaliation

George III was twenty-two when he succeeded his grandfather, and made a favourable impression—even on Horace Walpole, who was present at the first levee. 'I was surprised to find the levee room had lost so entirely the air of the lion's den,' he wrote to Montagu:

> This young man don't stand in one spot, with his eyes fixed royally on the ground, and dropping bits of German news. He walks about and speaks to everybody.[1]

His first speech to Parliament went down well, too: 'Born and educated in this country, I glory in the name of Briton,' he told the assembled Lords and Commons. Old Quin, down in Bath, was suitably gratified: 'I knew he would speak well,' he growled, 'for I taught the boy.'

A week after his accession, George III had issued a royal proclamation 'For the encouragement of piety and virtue, and for preventing and punishing of vice, profaneness, and immorality.' What he had in mind, however, was the cleansing of political life; he was not thinking of the whores who plied their trade in the galleries of Covent Garden and Drury Lane. And so far as attendance at the theatre was concerned, the young 'Patriot King' was to prove a rather more assiduous patron than his grandfather had been. The first command performance of the reign came only four days after the theatres reopened—*Richard III* with Garrick in the title role.* As the king entered the whole audience rose and sang 'God Save the King'.

During the summer, Garrick had indulged in something of a night of the long knives. Sixteen actors and actresses did not have their articles renewed, and there were eighteen new faces among the sixty-three players with whom he opened the new season. He sprang a big surprise by taking on Sheridan. The competition from Barry at Crow Street had been too much for 'King Tom'. In debt to the

---

* Command performances had normally fallen on a Friday, but early in the new reign this was changed. In an undated note to Joshua Reynolds, regretting his inability to accept an invitation to dinner, Garrick wrote that he was 'oblig'd to disengage himself Every Thursday to wait ye Commands of ye King'. (*Letters*, 278.)

tune of £7,000 he had decided to abandon the struggle. 'He wakes as from a dream,' he wrote in a letter of farewell to his Dublin public, 'and finds that the best and most vigorous of his years have been employed to no purpose.'* For the past two years he had been in London, scraping a livelihood by giving lectures on elocution and the English language and trying to drum up support for the establishment of an academy where he could develop his educational ideas.

After much negotiation, he had reached an agreement with Lacy and Garrick 'to be together on shares on those nights he performs', a new arrangement at Drury Lane at that time; for each night he appeared he was to receive a quarter-share of the receipts after the deduction of £80 to cover house charges. Sheridan was seen for the first time on 9 October, when he played Richard III, and he subsequently appeared in a number of other principal roles normally played by Garrick—he was Hamlet to Mrs Pritchard's Gertrude, Macbeth, and Pierre in *Venice Preserv'd*. On some evenings they shared the spotlight—Sheridan was Horatio in *The Fair Penitent* to Garrick's Lothario, for instance.

Davies, although he was by now once again devoting some of his energies to bookselling, was still a member of the company, his ear as close to the ground as ever. By his account things initially went entirely smoothly between the two men:

> The manager himself owned that, except Barry, he had never found so able an assistant; for the best of them, he said, could scarcely draw together an hundred pounds audience. But Garrick's ruling passion was the love of fame; and his uneasiness, arising from the success of Sheridan, began every day to be more and more visible. However, he seemed for a time to suspend his jealousy, and promote every scheme proposed by Sheridan for their mutual profit.[2]

A week before Christmas, however, Sheridan had a resounding success as King John, which he had not acted in London before. It was performed again by royal command the following week, and the gossip was that Garrick, who took the role of Philip the Bastard, was not exactly overjoyed when it was reported to him that the King had been 'uncommonly pleased' with Sheridan's performance:

> Upon his asking whether His Majesty approved his playing the Bastard, he was told, without the least compliment paid to his action, it was imagined that the King thought the character was rather too bold in the drawing, and that the colouring was overcharged and glaring.[3]

Davies goes on to assert that the royal opinion of *King John* made it impossible for Garrick and Sheridan to continue performing together in the same theatre: 'these heroes of the stage resembled the two great chiefs of Rome; one could not bear an equal, nor the other a superior.'[4] Davies was exaggerating—Sheridan acted on to the end of the season and the two men appeared together in *King*

---

* He was, in fact, not yet forty.

John as late as April. Even so, when Sheridan returned to London after a summer spent lecturing in Edinburgh, it was to act Hamlet at Covent Garden.*

On the night that the old king died, Drury Lane had been due to put on *The Minor*, Foote's satire on George Whitefield and the Methodists, which had run for 35 nights at the Haymarket during the summer and caused a considerable uproar, with a flurry of pamphlets accusing Foote of blasphemy and worse. Foote himself played three parts, including that of the bawd, Mother Cole, who was modelled on a well-known London procuress called Mother Jennie Douglas. Mother Cole attributes her conversion to Methodism to a character called Mr Squintum (Whitefield had a cast in one eye) who does not appear in the play, but whom Foote mimicked in the epilogue. A characteristic Foote stroke was to have Mother Cole mouth Methodist pieties as she tries to sell the young hero one of her girls.

The Minor eventually opened at Drury Lane on 22 November, but not before there had been intense pressure to have it suppressed. Lady Huntingdon,† who had appointed Whitefield her chaplain in 1747, intervened, and so did the Archbishop of Canterbury,‡ who approached the Lord Chamberlain. 'For once the Duke of Devonshire was firm,' Horace Walpole told Montagu, 'and would only let him correct some passages, & even of those the Duke has restored some.' One that the Prelate effaced was 'You snub-nosed son of a bitch.'[5] In the event the Archbishop, who knew something of the ways of the world, had the good sense to draw back; he had no wish to see the play in the bookshops with the endorsement 'as corrected and prepared for the press by his Grace the Archbishop of Canterbury'.

Wilkinson, meantime, now back at Covent Garden, had offered to mount a pirated version of the piece. Foote, getting wind of this, stormed in on Rich, an occasion which Wilkinson described with relish in his memoirs:

> Damn it, you old hound! if you dare let Wilkinson, that pug nosed son of a b—h, take any liberty with me as to mimicry, I will bring you yourself, Rich, on the stage! If you want to engage that pug, black his face, and let him hand the tea-kettle in a pantomime; for damn the fellow he is as ignorant as a whore's maid! And if he dares to appear in my characters, in the Minor, I will instantly produce your old stupid ridiculous self, with your three cats, and your hound of a mimic altogether, next week at Drury-Lane, for the general diversion of the pit, boxes and galleries; and that will be paying you, you squinting old Hecate, too great a compliment![6]

---

* Those who attended his elocution lessons in Edinburgh hoping to slough off their Scots accent included James Boswell.

† Selina Hastings, Countess of Huntingdon (1707–91), was an early convert to Methodism, and had been instrumental in introducing the 'new light' into aristocratic circles.

‡ Thomas Secker (1693–1768) had been appointed to Canterbury two years previously. Although he was the son of a Nottinghamshire dissenter, and had originally been destined for the dissenting ministry, he had developed a typical eighteenth-century horror of 'enthusiasm' and deprecated the advance of Methodism.

Rich was deterred neither by Foote's threats nor Mrs Rich's Methodism, and *The Minor* went ahead at Covent Garden. Wilkinson, for his part, decided on a reckless improvement on Foote's performance at the rival house:

> As to Mr Garrick I made no scruple, though I had him before me, as his curiosity had led him to see me, not expecting that I would take him off, or he would not have been so publicly surrounded, but have carefully avoided such a queer situation . . . Nor was I a little pleased, when repeating from Macbeth, "Who can be wise, amazed, &c." I heard the audience echo from one to the other, "O Garrick! Garrick!"—O thought I, my master, this is my day of triumph!—and from that night he never forgave or forgot his being so surrounded in the front box, nor did he ever speak to me again to the day of his death.*

During the spring or early summer of 1760, George Colman, who had successfully ingratiated himself with Garrick three years previously with his *Letter of Abuse*, had submitted a draft of his first play. Garrick's response had been cordial but frank:

> I have much to say to You upon the Play—& I fear that You'll find more to do than You at first imagin'd—the Characters are in general good, but the Conduct of them & of the Plot is (I think) very deficient—I am persuaded too when You come to reconsider it, that You'll find the Dialogue in many parts too hastily written—[7]

Polly Honeycombe was a short afterpiece that satirized the vogue for novel-reading. It is clear that Garrick offered Colman a good deal of assistance in improving it and that he proved much more amenable to advice than the general run of authors. By the time the piece was ready to be staged, a warm friendship had sprung up between the two men.

On the first night, things did not go too well. Garrick had written both a prologue and an epilogue, but it sounds as if the piece was seriously under-rehearsed. 'Indifferently received,' noted Hopkins, Cross's successor as prompter, 'partly oweing to the Fright and Confusion of the performers, who omitted some speeches on which the plot depended.'† By the time the author's benefit night arrived at the end of December, however, things had obviously been tightened up. Garrick, who always had pen and paper to hand, scribbled an excited note to Colman from the theatre (he was waiting to go on as Kitely in *Every Man in his Humour*):

---

* *Wilkinson*, iii, 27. Methodists, with their opposition to the theatre, were understandably not much liked by the acting fraternity. An interesting exception to the rule was the drunken and unruly comedian Ned Shuter, who was a devout follower of Whitefield's and donated substantial sums to his cause.

† William Hopkins had previously been an actor, mainly in the provinces. His wife also joined the company when he was taken on as prompter, and acted at Drury Lane for the next thirty-four years.

My dear Sir

I have this moment took a peep at the house for the Author of *Polley Hon*. The Pit & Galleries are cramed—the Boxes full to yᵉ last Rows, & Every thing as You & I could Wish for our Friend—I am most happy about it & could not help communicating it to one, I so much Love and Esteem—pray let me see you at yʳ arrival—the Second Music—& time for me to put on my Fools' Coat—

Yrs Ever & most affecty
D: Garrick*

For his 1760 Christmas offering, Garrick had written *The Enchanter*, a two-act miniature opera very much in the Italian style. For the music he turned once again, as he had done for *The Tempest* and *The Fairies*, to John Christopher Smith. The characters were all conventional enough: Moroc, an evil enchanter, is in love with the beautiful Zaida, and has spirited her away from her lover Zoreb—to whom, needless to say, she is determined to remain faithful. Moroc, an eighteenth-century forerunner of Inspector Clouseau, clumsily drops his magic wand at quite the wrong moment; it is snatched up by his downtrodden attendant spirit, Kaliel, who sees to it that virtue and constancy triumph. Benjamin Victor says that the piece 'was written to shew to Advantage the fine Voice of *Lione*, a Jew Boy'.† It was exactly the sort of undemanding fare that appeals to Christmas audiences. Its music and spectacle entertained the town for seventeen nights.

Garrick made use of what little free time he could snatch from the theatre over the holiday period to keep his friendships in repair. On Christmas Day his dinner guests at Hampton included both Samuel Johnson and Edmund Burke, whose literary successes were now bringing him increasingly into society and who for some time past had been working as a kind of private secretary to 'Single-speech' Hamilton.‡

Burke had been keenly interested in the theatre since his student days in Dublin. He knew Sheridan at that time, and may have seen Garrick act there in 1745–6. One of his earliest acquaintances after he came to London to read for the bar in 1750 was Arthur Murphy, and it could well have been Murphy who introduced him to Garrick. They certainly knew each other well enough for Burke to have been a Christmas guest two years previously, in 1758. Murphy was also present, and remembered it as the first time he had known Johnson to

---

* *Letters*, 261. Garrick refers playfully to Colman as 'our Friend' because he was not at first identified as the author of the piece. Some believed it was by Garrick himself.

† *History of the Theatres of London*, iii, 11–12. James de Castro, in his *Memoirs*, says that Michael Leoni, who sang Kaliel, was born Myer Leon in Frankfurt. 'The moment the German Jews [in London] heard of his reading and warbling they immediately sent to his native spot and brought him to England, where, by his great powers, he astonished all the members of the synagogue in Duke's Place.' Garrick is thought to have met him through the Earl of Sandwich and to have sought the permission of the Elders of the synagogue for the boy to appear on the stage.

‡ William Gerard Hamilton (1729–96) owed his nickname to the fact that his brilliant maiden speech in the Commons in 1755 had been followed by several years of unbroken silence. When he was appointed Chief Secretary for Ireland in 1761 Burke accompanied him to Dublin.

allow himself to be contradicted in conversation—the subject had been the affairs of Bengal, one of many on which Burke was prodigiously well informed.

Some weeks before Christmas—and therefore before the town had pronounced its verdict on *Polly Honeycombe*—Colman had already put a much more ambitious piece into Garrick's hands. *The Jealous Wife* was loosely based on Fielding's *Tom Jones*. Garrick was very taken with it, but had to tell Colman that he found himself in a difficulty over the part of Oakly: 'I have consider'd it thoroughly & I find that it will be impossible for me to get it so soon into my head as I imagin'd.' He could see a possible solution, but it was one which would call for some diplomacy:

> If Mr Home will defer his performance to ye next Year to which purpose
> I shall write immediately to him, I can Master Oakly very well by ye time—
> but he is so connected with Ld Bute & a much greater personnage, that I
> must be a little delicate in that Business—[8]

That 'much greater personnage' was showing a very gratifying interest in the theatre in those early months of his reign, as it happened, but Garrick had reason to be circumspect. It was very convenient for the manager of Drury Lane to have a friend at court in the person of the Duke of Devonshire as Lord Chamberlain, but it quickly became plain that the young king had less inclination than his grandfather to be governed by the great Whig families.* There was also a strong rumour that winter that a bid was afoot to establish a third patent theatre, and that two well-known performers had already invested in the project and were recruiting a company.

In the event, Garrick succeeded in squaring his scheduling circle. *Agis* was performed—by royal command—on 23 January. *The Jealous Wife* had its first night three weeks later. Garrick played the lead in both, and Hopkins noted in his diary that Colman's comedy 'met with greater applause than anything since the *Suspicious Husband*'. It entered the standard repertory, and was played for many years.

Garrick and Colman were soon also to be associated in a non-theatrical venture. Together with Colman's Westminster and Oxford friend Bonnell Thornton,† they launched the *St James's Chronicle*, a paper that came out three times a week and was devoted chiefly to gossip, letters, puffs, and the occasional essay. Thornton was the titular manager and he, Colman and Garrick held most of the stock. It appeared for the first time in April 1761. Garrick would find it a useful channel for the promotion of his interests over the years, and much of his occasional verse would appear there, as would many of his songs and prologues.

Colman contributed a series of extremely popular 'Genius' papers to the *Chronicle*, some of them under the signature 'Rhapsodista'. The second of them, published in June 1761, was devoted to a 'Portrait of the Author, and Description

---

* Devonshire was dismissed in 1762.
† Colman and Thornton had previously collaborated to bring out *The Connoisseur*, which ran to 140 weekly numbers between 1754 and 1756.

of his Person'. Colman was an extremely small man, and like Garrick, rather touchy about it:

> The whole truth is, that I am of a remarkably low stature; a sort of diminutive plaything of Madam Nature, that seems to have been made, like a girl's doll, to divert the good lady in her infancy . . . a minim of nature, a mannikin, not to say minnikin; and indeed rather an abstract or brief chronicle of man's fair proportions than a man at large. . . . In a word, it is my irreparable misfortune to be, without my shoes, little more than five feet in height.

Despite the playful tone, there was plainly an exposed nerve there; and a later passage suggests that his new friend Garrick sometimes had a way of making it jangle:

> There is no circumstance moves my spleen more forcibly than the insolence of those, whose stature very little exceeds my own, and who seem to look down on such urchins as myself with a consciousness of their happy superiority. One of these always affects to call me *the little man*; and another small gentleman (a great actor I mean, who in some future *histrio-mastix*, some *nescio quid majus Rosciade*, I may possibly take a peg or two lower) is fond of sidling up to me in all publick places, as second-rate beauties commonly contrive to take a dowdy abroad with them for a foil.

Nescio quid majus Rosciade? None of Colman's readers in the summer of 1761 would have needed any help with the allusion, even if they had not a word of Latin. *The Rosciad* had burst on London in March. There had been nothing like it since Pope's *The Dunciad* more than thirty years previously, and there would be nothing like it again until Byron let fly with *English Bards and Scotch Reviewers* in 1809.

The plan of the poem is simple. The author, convinced that since the first century BC nobody had arisen to fill the void created by the death of the great Roman actor, Roscius, resolves on a contest to determine who should be crowned as his modern successor. Jonson and Shakespeare are appointed the judges, and pass in review such talent as the mid eighteenth century had to offer.

'The author soon found that he had no occasion to advertise his poem in the public prints,' wrote Davies:

> The players spread its fame all over the town; they ran about like so many stricken deer; they strove to extract the arrow from the wound by communicating the knowledge of it to their friends. The public, so far from being aggrieved, enjoyed the distress of the players; they thought The Rosciad a pleasant and reasonable retaliation for the mirth which the stage had continually excited at their expense.[9]

Like *The Dunciad*, *The Rosciad* was initially published anonymously—Smollett, then editing the *Critical Review*, thought it was a joint effort by Colman and Thornton and their friend Robert Lloyd. It quickly became known that it was none of these, although the author, as it happened, had been a contemporary of theirs at Westminster.* Charles Churchill was a disreputable clergyman, bankrupt and separated from his wife (he had gone through a Fleet marriage at the age of seventeen).† He haunted the theatre, a bulky, lumbering man dressed in black and wearing a black scratch wig. He was to be seen almost nightly in the front row of the pit, just behind the spikes that separated it from the orchestra. 'In this place,' wrote Davies, 'he thought he could best discern the real workings of the passions in the actors, or what they substituted in the place of them.'

Several of the leading actresses of the day—Kitty Clive, for instance—were warmly eulogized:

> Original in spirit and in ease,
> She pleas'd by hiding all attempts to please.
> No comic actress ever yet could raise
> On Humour's base, more merit or more praise.

With the actors it was otherwise. Davies exaggerates when he says that nobody escaped Churchill's lash—he praised Charles Blakes, for example, who excelled in the portrayal of Frenchmen,‡ and had kind words for John Moody, who specialized in Irish character roles,§ but they were lucky exceptions to the rule. Most of the theatrical luminaries of the day, whether they currently graced the London or the Dublin stage, were comprehensively mauled:

> Macklin, who largely deals in half-formed sounds,
> Who wantonly transgresses Nature's bounds,
> Whose acting's hard, affected and constrain'd,
> Whose features, as each other they disdain'd,
> At variance set, inflexible and coarse,
> Ne'er knew the workings of united force . . .

Barry was scornfully dismissed as a none-too-intelligent ham:

> Some dozen lines before the ghost is there
> Behold him for the solemn scene prepare:
> See how he frames his eyes, poises each limb,
> Puts the whole body into proper trim:—
> From whence we learn, with no great stretch of art,
> Five lines hence comes a ghost, and, ha! a start.

---

* Eton, said the wits of the day, was the House of Commons, Westminster the House of Lords. Churchill's contemporaries there also included Warren Hastings and the poet Cowper.
† Although on his father's death three years previously he had succeeded him as curate at St John's, Westminster, Churchill found it necessary to supplement his income by teaching at a boarding school run by a Mrs Dennis. The pupils there in 1761 included Fanny Burney.
‡ When he performed his memorable Monsieur le Médecin in Ravenscroft's *The Anatomist*, it was usually announced that 'at the end Blakes will speak the Epilogue, Riding on an Ass, in the character of M Le Médecin'.
§ Moody had created the part of Sir Callaghan O'Brallagan in Macklin's *Love à-la-Mode* two years previously.

Mossop, sometimes labelled 'the Distiller of Syllable', was ridiculed for his idiosyncratic ideas about where emphasis should be placed:

> With studied impropriety of speech,
> He soars beyond the hacknied critic's reach.
> To epithets allots emphatic state,
> Whilst principals, ungraced, like lackeys wait . . .

Retirement from the stage offered no protection, and the fact that Churchill had not seen a particular actor in his prime did not operate as any sort of inhibition:

> In fancy'd scenes, as in life's real plan,
> He could not for a moment sink the man.
> In whate'er cast his character was laid,
> Self still, like oil, upon the surface play'd.
> Nature, in spite of all his skills crept in,
> Horatio, Dorax, Falstaff—still was Quin.

Foote offered an irresistibly broad target:

> By turns transformed into all kinds of shapes,
> Constant to none, Foote laughs, cries, struts and scrapes:
> Now in the centre, now in van or rear,
> The Proteus shifts, bawd, parson, auctioneer.
> His strokes of humour, and his bursts of sport
> Are all contain'd in this one word *Distort*.

Churchill took aim at writers as well as players, and peppered Murphy with both barrels:

> Still in extremes, he knows no happy mean,
> Or raving mad, or stupidly serene.
> In cold-wrought scenes the lifeless actor flags;
> In passion tears the passion into rags.
> Can none remember? Yes—I know all must—
> When in the Moor he ground his teeth to dust,
> When o'er the stage he Folly's standard bore,
> Whilst Common Sense stood trembling at the door.

Having herded the greater part of the profession into the shambles, Churchill calls on Shakespeare to deliver his and Jonson's verdict and to award the palm:

> If manly sense; if Nature link'd with art;
> If thorough knowledge of the human heart;
> If powers of acting vast and unconfined;
> If fewest faults with greatest beauties join'd;
> If strong expression, and strange powers which lie
> Within the magic circle of his eye;

> If feelings which few hearts, like his, can know,
> And which no face as well as his can show,
> Deserve the preference;—Garrick! take the chair,
> Nor quit it—till thou place an equal there.

'Churchill,' wrote Davies, 'had raised a magnificent colossus to him on the broken statues of his contemporaries' (one of them Davies's own—Churchill had smashed such reputation as he had as an actor with one savage line—'He mouths a sentence as curs mouth a bone'). All very gratifying, no doubt, to a man as hungry for praise as Garrick, but awkward, too. Many of the strictures on his fellow-actors were manifestly unjust; even if they had not been, it was part of his business as manager to cosset his players, to jolly them along, to reassure them that they were nothing like as bad as Churchill had painted them. And it was very possibly in the course of doing just that that he made a costly mistake—Churchill, he was reported as saying, was no doubt hoping by his flattery to gain free admission to Drury Lane.

When this got back to Churchill he was enraged. He rushed out *The Apology*, in effect a sequel to *The Rosciad* but, if anything, even more brutal in tone. And this time, although Garrick was not mentioned by name, the bludgeon swished unmistakably close to his head:

> But if kind fortune, who sometimes we know
> Can take a hero from a puppet-show,
> In mood propitious should her favourite call
> On royal stage in royal pomp to bawl,
> Forgetful of himself he rears the head,
> And scorns the dung-hill, where he first was bred.
> Conversing now with well dress'd kings and queens,
> With gods and goddesses behind the scenes,
> He sweats beneath the terror-nodding plume,
> Taught by mock honours, real pride t'assume.
> On the great stage, the world, no monarch e'er
> Was half so haughty as a monarch player . . .

Garrick's first instinct was to write to Churchill—at this stage the two had not met. Happily he was talked out of it, and wrote a much better letter to their mutual friend Robert Lloyd, knowing that it would quickly reach its true address. It was a skilful and good-humoured piece of damage limitation, and it showed Garrick at his best:

> I see and read so much of Mr Churchill's spirit, without having the pleasure of his acquaintance, that I am persuaded that his genius disdains any direction, and that resolutions once taken by him will withstand the warmest importunity of his friends.
>
> At the first reading of his 'Apology,' I was so charmed and raised with the power of his writing, that I really forgot that I was delighted when I ought to have been alarmed. This puts me in mind of the Highland officer,

who was so warmed and elevated by the heat of the battle, that he forgot till he was reminded by the smarting, that he had received no less than eleven wounds in different parts of his body.

All I have to say, or will say, upon the occasion is this:—if Mr Churchill has attacked his pasteboard majesty of Drury-lane from resentment, I should be sorry for it, though I am conscious it is ill-founded. If he has attacked me merely because I am the Punch of the puppet-show, I shall not turn my back upon him, and salute him in Punch's fashion, but make myself easy with this thought—that my situation made the attack necessary, and that it would have been a pity that so much strong, high-coloured poetry should have been thrown away, either in justice or in friendship, to so insignificant a person as myself.

In his Rosciad he raised me too high; in his 'Apology' he may have sunk me too low: he had done as his Israelites did, made an idol of a calf, and now—'The idol dwindles to a calf again!' He has thought fit, a few weeks ago, to declare me the best actor of my time (which, by the by, is no great compliment, if there is as much truth as wit in his 'Apology'); and I will show the superiority I have over my brethren on this occasion, by seeming at least that I am not dissatisfied, and appear, as I once saw a poor soldier on the parade, who was acting a pleasantry of countenance, while his back was most woefully striped with the cat-o'nine-tails . . .*

It may be that it was the success of *The Rosciad*† which now betrayed Garrick into a further mistake that was to prove even more expensive. He had long been plagued by the antics of Thaddeus Fitzpatrick. Fitzpatrick had matured not at all since throwing an apple at Woodward several years previously. Egged on by his companions, he would stand up in the pit and whinny with laughter during one of the more harrowing scenes in *Lear*. He also fancied himself as a writer of letters to the press. Signing themselves X.Y.Z., Theatricus, Philo-Tragicus, and the like, he and his cronies had taken to attacking Garrick in *The Craftsman* and other weekly papers, and a selection of these letters had subsequently been published in the form of a pamphlet entitled *An Enquiry into the Real Merit of a Certain Popular Performer.*

A too-indulgent public, Garrick was told, 'has enabled you to acquire a large stock of fame, upon the credit of theatrical science, which you never possessed'. His performance as Pierre in *Venice Preserv'd* was unfavourably compared with that of Quin and Mossop. One letter took the form of an 'Edict' from Garrick to his 'trusty and well-beloved ADULATORS':

Whereas we have determined to close the theatrical season this day, with the tragedy of KING RICHARD, and it being of the utmost importance to us, that the said performance should go off with singular eclat, we

---

* *Letters*, 267. 'The idol dwindles to a calf again' echoes a line in the poem.
† Churchill's biographer, Wallace Cable Brown, says that it went through eight editions in his lifetime and earned him £3,500 in two years.

hereby enjoin you, our trusty and well-beloved adulators, to attend at your several stations in Drury-lane, between the hours of five and six in the evening. And we farther require you most carefully and attentively to applaud us, with observable emotions of admiration and astonishment, at the several CLAP-CUES which our most faithul servant T—— P——s shall deliver out respectively to each and every one of you. And we do moreover strictly command you, at the peril of our deepest displeasure, that you become remarkably clamorous and vociferous at every passage, requiring even common exertion of voice, in the said tragedy, that the unavoidable huskiness of our tones, and the unhappy decline of our powers, which have been too universally taken notice of this winter, may (if possible) be concealed from the audience . . .

We moreover absolutely order you, upon the immediate conclusion of the play, to take the round of the several coffee-houses, within the theatrical district, and attest, with proper confidence, *that we never played the character so well, that our powers were more clear and forcible than they have been for many years—and that our elocution was regulated by the most refined taste and accurate precision.*

It was all pretty feeble stuff. It was now, what's more, the best part of a year since the pamphlet had been published, and Garrick might have been wise to regard it as so much water under the bridge. What seems likely is that his judgement was warped by Churchill's success, and that he came to believe that he could wreak similar carnage with his own pen on the Fitzpatrick *galère*.

Fifteen years previously, in *Miss in her Teens*, he had created the effeminate macaroni Fribble. Now he brought out *The Fribbleriad*, in which the main character, Fitzgig, was instantly recognizable:

> Say, *Garrick*, does he write for bread,
> This friend of yours, This X,Y, Z?
> For pleasure sure, not bread—'twere vain,
> To write for that he ne'er could gain:
> No calls of nature to excuse him,
> He deals in rancour to amuse him;
> A *Man* it seems—'tis hard to say—
> A *Woman* then?—a moment pray—
> Unknown as yet by sex or feature,
> Suppose we try to guess the creature;
> Whether a *wit*, or a *pretender*?
> Of *masculine* or *female* gender?
>
> . . . What! Of that wriggling, fribbling race,
> The curse of nature, and disgrace?
> That mixture base, which fiends send forth
> To taint and vilify all worth—

> Whose rancour knows nor bounds nor measure,
> Feels every passion, tastes no pleasure;
> The want of power, all peace destroying,
> For ever wishing, ne'er enjoying—
> So smiling, smirking, soft in feature,
> You'd swear it was the gentlest creature—

Whether, as some thought at the time, Churchill had a hand in it cannot now be known; there is certainly a good deal more edge and bite than is usual in Garrick's occasional verse. But although it sold well and made the town laugh, the Fribble tribe would have its revenge. Garrick might have been wise to leave Fitzpatrick and his quibbling coterie to the scalpel of Laurence Sterne, who in that same year published the third volume of *Tristram Shandy*:

> And how did Garrick speak the soliloquy last night? 'Oh against all rule, My Lord. Most ungrammatically! Betwixt the substantive and the adjective, which should agree together in number, case, and gender, he made a breech thus—, stopping as if the point wanted settling; and betwixt the nominative case, which your Lordship knows must govern the verb, he suspended his voice in the Epilogue a dozen times, three seconds and three fifths by a stop-watch, my Lord, each time!'—'Admirable grammarian! But in suspending his voice was the sense suspended likewise? Did no expression of attitude, or countenance fill up the chasm? Was the eye silent? Did you narrowly look?' 'I looked only at the stop-watch, My Lord.'—Excellent observer!

The season drew to an uneventful close, and Garrick was able to get down to Hampton, although he continued from there to conduct his usual mixed bag of theatre business. Murphy had taken a mistress, a young prostitute called Ann Elliot, and had asked the manager to give her an audition. Garrick did not beat about the bush:

> She does not appear to Me to have a Genius for ye Stage—She may be made decent, but will never, I doubt, arrive at any Excellence. Her Powers are weak, Her Voice is indifferent, Her pronunciation Erroneous, & her Face more formed to create Passion, than to Express it.

The letter is interesting as an illustration of the extraordinary lengths to which Garrick was prepared to go to be obliging, even to such a difficult customer as Murphy. 'Our Company is so Overloaded, that unless one of great Merit should arise, Every addition to us will be an Incumbrance,' he wrote:

> However, Sir, if her Heart is fixd upon it, We will give her a Tryal, & a very fair one—but it will be impossible for Us to give ye Lady any Sallary for what little she may do the approaching Season, & we must be quite at Liberty to Engage her, or Not, for the Winter afterwards—[10]

The offer was not taken up. It so happened that Murphy had entered into an improbable partnership with Foote for the summer months. They had originally hoped to lease the Haymarket, but somebody had got in before them. They then approached Garrick, who generously agreed to let them have Drury Lane at a rental of one-fifth of their profits. When Murphy's new play *The Citizen* had its première there on 1 July, Miss Elliot was given the part of Maria.

Later in the month she played Columbine in a new pantomime called *The Wishes*, an occasion when Foote and Murphy almost had a riot on their hands. In the last act Harlequin is shown toying on a couch with his mistress, Isabella, who has the power of possessing whatever she wishes for. In a moment of displeasure with Harlequin, she announces that she wishes him hanged—whereupon a gibbet rises from behind the couch and draws him up by the neck. Davies has a nice description of how this was received by the audience: 'The taste of the English not being refined enough to relish this admirable piece of Italian pleasantry, the comedy shared the fate of its hero.'* Which is to say that there was prolonged hissing, and that for a time things looked decidedly nasty for the management.

The epilogue to *The Wishes* concluded with some satirical abuse of Garrick on his own stage. Foote had once more demonstrated how accomplished he was at biting the hand that fed him.

* *Davies*, i, 379. Miss Elliot later acted in Dublin and at Covent Garden. After a few years Murphy lost his place in her affections to the Duke of Cumberland. She died in 1769 at the age of twenty-six.

22

Scratching Fanny and the
Riotous Fribbles

My Lord   April 9th 1761
It is with the greatest apprehension of being impertinent that I address
Myself to Your Lordship; But as I was permitted once before to request
Your favor for my Friend, whose Character in private Life, & whose merit
in his Profession are well known, I hope Your Lordship will Excuse My
giving You this Second, & last trouble about him.

The Public Papers Speak with great Confidence of an additional Happiness to this Kingdom, & that in Consequence, a New Establishment will
take place in yᵉ Household; Should this be the case, and Mʳ Gataker should
find Your Lordship's Goodness continu'd to Him, You would make one
of the most deserving men a Happy one. . . .[1]

Garrick was writing to Lord Bute. He didn't really think he was being impertinent,
but if you were asking a favour of a great man you naturally observed the
conventions. The 'additional Happiness' of which the public prints were speaking
was the marriage of the King. His consort would clearly deserve the best medical
advice and attention. Who better to supply it than Garrick's friend Thomas
Gataker, a surgeon at the Charing Cross Hospital? He had drawn him to
Bute's attention three years previously, and that had secured his appointment as
Surgeon-Extraordinary to the King's mother, the Dowager Princess of Wales.*
Ask and have. Five months later Bute procured Gataker's appointment as surgeon
to the new Queen.

There had been talk of a royal marriage almost from the moment of the young
King's accession. 'Animal passion and the unique sense of public duty in the
need for an heir,' wrote J. H. Plumb, 'combined to make the matter one of almost
neurotic, compulsive frenzy for George III.'[2]

Two years previously, when he was still Prince of Wales, he had wished to
marry Lady Sarah Lennox, the fifteen-year-old daughter of the Duke of Richmond,
and had floated the idea in an extraordinary and pathetic letter to Bute:

---

* One good turn deserved another. In November 1757, Gataker had mediated between Garrick
and Robert Dodsley when the latter was being tiresome over the rejection of his tragedy *Cleone*.
He had also acted as a go-between during Garrick's running battle with Hill in 1759.

I submit my happiness to you, who are the best of friends, whose friendship I value if possible above my love for the most charming of her sex; if you can give me no hopes how to be happy, I surrender my fortune into your hands, and will keep my thoughts even from the dear object of my love, grieve in silence, and never trouble you more with this unhappy tale; for if I must either lose my friend or my love, I will give up the latter, for I esteme your friendship above every earthly joy.[3]

His mentor said no, and George bowed to his judgement, although why marriage to Lady Sarah would have ended his friendship with Bute is obscure. 'He turned away from his natural inclinations,' wrote Plumb, 'and began to search the *Almanach de Gotha* for a suitable German Protestant princess.'[4]

The choice fell on Charlotte Sophia of Mecklenburg-Strelitz. She landed at Harwich on 7 September. There had been strong winds, and the voyage from Cuxhaven had taken ten days; she had passed the time by practising English tunes on her harpsichord. She saw her bridegroom for the first time the next day, and they were married late the same evening in the chapel at St James's. A fortnight later George was crowned, he and his seventeen-year-old bride travelling to the Abbey in separate sedan chairs. As he returned to Westminster Hall, the great diamond fell out of the King's crown, a mishap which the supersitious later declared to be an omen, although of what they were not clear.*

Since the time of James I, a coronation had traditionally been the cue for both playhouses to mount a lavish spectacle. When George II was crowned, in 1727, it had been incorporated at Drury Lane in a production of Shakespeare's *Henry VIII*, and the managers of the day, Cibber, Wilks and Booth, had done very well out of it. Garrick decided to repeat the formula, and it was announced for the first time on 30 September. 'In the Play will be introduc'd A CORONATION,' said the bills, 'and the Ceremony of the Champion in Westminster Hall.' At Covent Garden, Rich held off until November, and would choose to associate his pageant with a production of *Henry V*.

Garrick decided against new costumes, and made do with those which had been used at the last coronation thirty-four years previously. Davies, who played the part of Surrey, was unimpressed: 'The exhibition was the meanest, and the most unworthy of a theatre, I ever saw,' he wrote:

The stage indeed was opened into Drury Lane; and a new and unexpected sight surprised the audience, of a real bonfire, and the populace huzzaing, and drinking porter to the health of Queen Anne Bullen. The stage in the mean time, amidst the parading of dukes, dutchesses, archbishops, peeresses, heralds, &c. was covered with a thick fog from the smoke of

---

* Charlotte was no beauty. 'Pale and very thin,' Horace Walpole wrote to Mann, although he conceded that she looked 'genteel' and sensible. 'Her hair is darkish and fine; her forehead low, her nose very well, except the nostrils spreading too wide. The mouth has the same fault, but her teeth are good. She talks a great deal, and French tolerably.' (*Walpole*, xxi, 529. Letter dated 10 September 1761.)

the fire, which served to hide the tawdry dresses of the processionalists. During this idle piece of mockery, the actors, being exposed to the suffocation of smoke, and the raw air from the open street, were seized with colds, rheumatisms, and swelled faces. At length the indignation of the audience delivered the comedians from this wretched badge of nightly slavery, which gained nothing to the managers but disgrace and empty benches.[5]

It was no doubt very disagreeable for Davies and the rest of the cast to get smoke in their eyes and find that their faces swelled up in the cold night air, but it is difficult to believe that Garrick and Lacy would have kept the show going into early December if the response was as poor as Davies suggests.*

Equally, however, there can be no doubt that Rich, with his flair for the spectacular, did very much better, partly because he was prepared to splash out on costumes.† A note in the Winston Theatrical Record for 19 November mentions a bill for £107 16s for 'Crimson Duchess Velvet & White Sattin used in *Coronation*' and also shows that Rich laid out £138 10s on velvet and white satin to decorate the Royal Boxes. The total cost of the production is thought to have been in the region of £3,000. It was money well spent. Receipts for the first six performances averaged £225, and the show ran for 67 nights.

Rich himself had planned to walk in the procession as the Queen's chamberlain. Not all the players shared his enthusiasm for pure spectacle, and he felt his presence might make it more difficult for anyone to refuse to appear. At the final rehearsal, however, he was taken ill and two weeks later, at the age of sixty-nine, he was dead. The managership at Covent Garden passed to his son-in-law, Beard. Rich was undoubtedly an outstanding harlequin and had a splendid talent for mimicry—it is said that he once ruined a horn player's concert by sitting opposite him and imitating a man eating a lemon. As a manager, his treatment of actors and playwrights and his celebrated eccentricities had combined to give Garrick and Lacy an easier ride than they might have expected from more conventional competition.

Garrick now once again turned his mind to Shakespeare. He had long been fascinated by the role of Posthumus in *Cymbeline*. This late tragi-comedy of Shakespeare's, with its beautiful verse and its flower-strewn corpses, is by turns grotesque and implausible. It had most recently been seen at Covent Garden three years previously in a version by William Hawkins, the former professor of poetry at Oxford, who had tailored Shakespeare's account of the war between Rome and ancient Britain to meet the requirements of eighteenth-century classical tragedy. The unities of time and place were restored by telescoping the action and confining it to Britain. Hawkins also changed the ending. Shakespeare has

---

* Davies's was not a lone voice, however. The *Court Magazine* criticized Garrick for 'ill-timed parsimony'.

† Historical accuracy was not a consideration. In the course of the season the procession was incorporated in productions of *Henry IV Part 2*, *Richard III* and *King John*.

Cymbeline, the British king, submitting to Rome and agreeing once again to pay 'our wonted tribute' to Caesar; Hawkins—his version was presented in the Year of Victories, it should be remembered—transforms this into a total triumph for Britain over the Romans.

Garrick's version is much more faithful to the original and was shaped, as his alterations always were, by essentially practical requirements. He changed the division of the acts, transposed a number of scenes and cut some 600 of Shakespeare's lines, mostly in Act V.* Posthumus was to become one of Garrick's most popular roles. For the first night, on 28 November, he had ordered new costumes and scenery. Imogen's splendid bedchamber, in Act II, was particularly admired—it was executed, wrote the *Court Magazine*, 'in a taste that does no little honour to the abilities of the artist, and the judgment of the manager'.†

Johnson, when he eventually got round to completing his *Preface to Shakespeare* some years later, clearly believed that Garrick could have spared himself the effort:

> To remark the folly of the fiction, the absurdity of the conduct, the confusion of the names, and manners of different times, and the impossibility of the events in any system of life, were to waste criticism upon unresisting imbecility, upon faults too evident for detection, and too gross for aggravation.

Garrick was looking more and more to Colman to keep him supplied with suitable material for the lighter end of the repertory, and Colman was proving obligingly prolific. His latest offering was a new afterpiece called *The Musical Lady*, and Garrick was enthusiastic: 'I have read y^r last, & think it a fine Plan a little too hastily finish'd,' he wrote; 'I want more laugh & pleasantry.' He was also taking Colman increasingly into his confidence about the affairs of Drury Lane, and could be quite indiscreet. 'Our new Tragedy creeps on,' he told him (he was writing shortly after the first night of a dreary piece called *Hecuba*, by Dr John Delap,‡ which borrowed heavily from Euripides):

> We might steal it on to Six Nights with much loss, but, I hope, that the Author will be reasonable, & satisfy'd with what We have already done, without insist[ing] upon our losing more to *force* a Reputation—this Entre Nous—[6]

He could also afford to be frank with his brother Peter, to whom he still dashed

---

* At the close, Garrick's *Cymbeline* strikes the same note of pacific benevolence as Shakespeare's. Garrick does, however, follow Hawkins's nationalistic line in deciding that the British king shall no longer pay tribute to Rome.

† 1 (December 1761), 172. This may of course have been Garrick patting himself on the back. 'My husband always wrote his own criticisms,' Mrs Garrick told Edmund Kean after his death.

‡ Delap was a parson, and bombarded Garrick over many years with his indifferent tragedies. He used to visit the Thrales, where he came under Johnson's lash for dwelling unduly on his internal complaints. Like many hypochondriacs, he lived to be very old, dying in 1812 at the age of eighty-seven.

off chatty, disjointed letters from time to time, as often as not to kill time at the
theatre while he waited for the prompter's call:

> I am now Writing, during the first Act of a New Comedy, call'd the School
> for Lovers—I have Spoke the Prologue, & don't appear in ye Play till the
> beginning of the 2d when Sr John Dorilant (that's ye Name) makes his
> Entrance—and a fine, polite, Sentimental, *Windling* son of a Bitch it is—
> a great favourite of ye Ladies, & much admir'd by the Clergy, & the
> Aldermen & Common Council of the City of London—Humbug for Nine
> Nights—

Garrick was clearly feeling jaded. The King and Queen had been at the theatre
the night before, and he had also had visitors from Lichfield who came to supper
and stayed till two in the morning. 'I was in some allarm all ye Night on Account
of a few Symptomatic Creepings about my Kidneys,' he told Peter:

> We were very cheerfull, tho not roaring—I have undergone a terrible hour
> & a half three Weeks ago, & now am taking Soap by ye Pound, & Lime
> water by ye Gallon by way of prevention.*

The School for Lovers was by William Whitehead, the Poet Laureate—very
different from such earlier offerings as *The Roman Father* and *Creusa*. His work
tended to be roughly handled by the critics—Churchill had recently called him
'Dulness and Method's darling Son'—but it must be assumed that once Garrick's
kidneys were in better shape he took a kindlier view of the laureate's first attempt
at comedy; the following year, at any rate, he took him on at Drury Lane as a
reader of plays.

At the end of January 1762, Covent Garden and Drury Lane both put on revivals
of Addison's *The Drummer; or, The Haunted House.* They did so to exploit the
fever of public interest in the affair of the Cock Lane Ghost. Witchcraft still had
a powerful hold on the popular mind. Word had got about that at a small house
in Cock Lane, near Smithfield, mysterious knockings and scratchings were to be
heard, supposedly made by the ghost of one Fanny Lynes, buried two years
before at the nearby church of St Sepulchre.

The message which 'Scratching Fanny' was trying to convey to the world was
that she had been poisoned by her widowed brother-in-law William Kent, whose
mistress she had been. The medium was a twelve-year-old girl, the daughter of
one William Parsons, a clerk at the church. As the child lay in bed in a trance,
she would put questions to Fanny and receive answers, one knock signifying yes,
two no.

The local ale-houses did a roaring trade, but it was not only the lower orders
who flocked to Smithfield to witness these strange happenings. 'We set out from

---

* *Letters*, 284. Garrick's supper guests also included Colman and the Reverend John Douglas,
a sociable Scots-born cleric who had been at Balliol with Adam Smith and was later Bishop of
Salisbury.

the opera,' Horace Walpole wrote to George Montagu, 'changed our clothes at Northumberland House, the Duke of York, Lady Northumberland, Lady Mary Coke, Lord Hertford, and I, all in one hackney coach, and drove to the spot; it rained torrents; yet the lane was full of mob, and the house so full we could not get in.'[7] When they did, they found the heat and the stench intolerable—and heard nothing, although they stayed till half-past one in the morning.

Eventually, a neighbouring clergyman invited a number of public figures to investigate the matter; they included Samuel Johnson, the magistrate Sir John Fielding and Garrick's friend John Douglas. The theatre managers had cashed in just in time. When Johnson wrote up his colleagues' findings in the *Gentleman's Magazine* for February, he declared that 'the child has some art of making or counterfeiting a particular noise, and . . . there is no agency of any higher cause'. The deception had been got up by the girl's father, who bore some sort of grudge; he and several others passed by way of the King's Bench to the pillory and prison; and William Hogarth worked a representation of the wretched Fanny into his 'Credulity, Superstition, and Fanaticism', along with the celebrated Mary Tofts, of Godalming, in Surrey, who was widely believed to have given birth to rabbits.

Hogarth, who was an avid theatre-goer, was also moved to pick up his pencil by a short interlude which Garrick wrote for Mrs Pritchard's benefit in March. 'The Farmer's Return from London' was only ninety-four lines long, but in that short compass Garrick deftly flighted a number of satirical darts. The farmer describes to his wife and children the wonders he had seen in London at the time of the 'Crownation'. He had been to the theatre:

> Above 'twas like Bedlam, all roaring and rattling!
> Below, the fine folk were all curts'ying and prattling!
> Strange jumble together—Turks, Christians, and Jews!
> At the Temple of Folly, all crowd to the pews.

The play he had seen was *The School for Lovers*, which the 'cratticks' had not liked. 'Pray, what are your *cratticks*?' asks his wife, and this allows Garrick to settle a score or two:

> Like watchmen in town,
> Lame, feeble, half-blind, yet they knock poets down.
> Like old Justice Wormwood—a crattick's a man,
> That can't sin himself, and he heates those that can.

The farmer had also, naturally, joined the pilgrimage to Smithfield to make the acquaintance of Fanny:

With her nails, and her knuckles, she answer'd so noice.
   For *Yes* she knock'd *Once*, and for *No* she knocked *Twoice*.
   I asked her *one* thing—
WIFE: What thing?
FARMER: If yo', Dame, was true?
WIFE: And the poor soul knocked *one*.

FARMER: By the zounds, it was *two*!
WIFE: I'll not be abused, Jahn. (*Cries*)
FARMER: Come, prithee, no croying.
    The ghoast, among friends, was much giv'n to loying.

Hogarth's drawing was used as the frontispiece when the Interlude was published and Garrick dedicated the piece to him—'a faint testimony of the sincere esteem which the writer bears him, both as a man and an artist'.

    'The Farmer's Return from London' is also the subject of a painting by Johann Zoffany. Zoffany had come to London in 1758 and Garrick had met him in the studio of Benjamin Wilson, where he was employed as a drapery painter and assistant.* The painting was exhibited in May of that year at the Society of Arts. This was also the occasion on which Joshua Reynolds exhibited his first picture of Garrick. 'Garrick between Tragedy and Comedy' was immediately bought by the second Earl of Halifax for £300, and today forms part of the Rothschild family collection. Before the advent of the camera, no English actor was the subject of as many portraits as Garrick. In his own century he would be painted more frequently even than George III, and in the catalogue of British portraits published by the British Museum only Queen Victoria commands more entries.†

    Garrick gave further expression to his esteem for Hogarth later in 1762 when he bought for 200 guineas the four paintings of his *Election* series, it is said to spare Hogarth the embarrassment of raffling them.[8] In the autumn, Garrick also found himself caught up in an acrimonious dispute between Hogarth and Charles Churchill. Early in September, Hogarth published a satirical print called 'The Times, No. 1', a defence of the Bute administration's attempts to make peace with France. The print depicts the city ablaze and Bute exerting himself to damp down the flames; Churchill and John Wilkes are shown spraying water on Bute rather than helping to put out the fire.

    Churchill and Wilkes had become thick as thieves, and were constantly in each other's company in the taverns and coffee-houses.[9] When Wilkes started the *North Briton* that summer, he had persuaded Churchill to join him as a sort of unofficial associate editor. He had been instrumental in enrolling him in the Society of Beefsteaks and took him as a guest to the Hellfire Club, to which he had recently been elected. Although the blasphemies and obscenities of the club did not greatly appeal to him—Sir Francis Dashwood and his fellow-'monks' at Medmenham amused themselves by importing London prostitutes dressed as nuns and administering the sacraments to a baboon‡—Churchill grew increasingly

---

* Zoffany's first London employer had been the clock-maker Stephen Rimbault, who ornamented his clock-faces with landscapes and moving figures.
† O'Donoghue, Freeman, *Catalogue of Engraved British Portraits Preserved in the Department of Prints and Drawings in the British Museum*, 2 vols., London, 1908–25. In *The Catalogue of Engraved Dramatic Portraits in the Harvard Theatre Collection* more than twice as many portraits of Garrick are listed than of any other performer.
‡ Dashwood had founded 'The Knights of St Francis of Wycombe' in the 1740s. The membership included at various times Frederick, Prince of Wales, the Duke of Queensberry and the Earls of Bute and Sandwich. The brotherhood was dissolved in 1763.

reckless and dissolute. He conducted numerous love affairs and contracted syphilis—'what I imagined to be St Anthony's fire turns out to be St Cytherea's,' he wrote to Wilkes.* The considerable sums he earned from *The Rosciad* ran through his fingers like water. He had been fastidious about not accepting the freedom of the house at Drury Lane, but borrowing money from the manager was a different matter, and at the time Hogarth's print had appeared he had written to Garrick asking for the loan of forty or fifty pounds.†

Garrick replied that he could not immediately oblige him, but would be able to do so by the end of the following week. He went on to urge Churchill not to retaliate immediately against Hogarth: 'I must intreat of You by yᵉ Regard You profess to Me, that You don't tilt at my Friend Hogarth before You See Me,' he pleaded:

> He is a great & original Genius, I love him as a Man & reverence him as an Artist—I would not for all yᵉ Politicks and Politicians in yᵉ Universe that You two should have the least Cause of Illwill to Each other. I am sure You will not publish against him if You think twice—‡

Although Garrick was also on friendly terms with Wilkes, his plea went unheeded. The next issue of the *North Briton* contained a savage attack on Hogarth, and it was this which the following year would prompt his famous caricature of Wilkes—'that brilliant cartoon,' as Linda Colley has memorably described it, 'in which the patriot's slim elegance and journalistic pretensions are utterly offset by his cynical leer, obvious squint and a bogus cap of liberty suspended over his fashionably bewigged head like an inverted chamber-pot.'[10]

Hogarth could be prickly, and early in 1763 he seems to have grumbled to Benjamin Wilson that Garrick was neglecting him. Garrick instantly sent him a charming letter which cannot have left Hogarth in any doubt about the depth of the affection in which he was held:

> Montaigne, who was a good Judge of Human Nature, takes Notice, that when Friends grow Exact, & Ceremonious, it is a certain Sign of Coolness, for the true Spirit of Friendship keeps no Account of Triffles—We are, I hope, a Strong Exception to this Rule—
>
> . . . Could I follow my inclinations I would see You Every day in yᵉ week, without caring whether it was in Leicester Fields or Southampton Street, but what with an indifferent State of health, and yᵉ Care of a large

---

* Undated note, BM Add MSS. 30,878. f.57. St Anthony's Fire was erysipelas. The Greek island of Cythera was one of the oldest seats of worship of Aphrodite, the goddess of love.

† It was not the only begging letter Garrick received from Churchill. An undated note, shorter and more desperate, survives; 'My dear Mr. Garrick, Half drunk—half mad—and quite stripped of all my money, I should be much obliged if you would enclose and send by the bearer five pieces, by way of adding to the favours already received by Yours sincerely Charles Churchill.' (*Boaden*, ii, 338.)

‡ *Letters*, 296. Garrick also reproved Churchill for his recent attack on Whitehead: 'I was in hopes your Ghost was laid, or at least Your Acrimony against the Laureat, for still I cannot get it in to my Mind that Your Attack upon him, is a justifiable One.'

family, in which there are many froward Children, I have scarce half-an hour to myself—However since You are grown a Polite Devil, & have a Mind to play at Lords & Ladies, have at You,—I will certainly call upon You soon & if you should not be at home, I will leave my Card

I am Yours Dear Hogy Most Sincerely

D: Garrick[11]

Garrick's reference to his health and to the many 'froward Children' in his large theatrical family suggests a certain weariness. A letter which he had written to Peter some weeks earlier strikes a similar note and also conveys for the first time an impression of underlying frustration and irritability. 'I am very glad that You are all so merry at Lichfield with your Balls, Players, &c' he wrote:

> For my part I detest Balls, & the name of Players makes me Sick—I have a goodly parcel of 'Em Myself, & a pretty choice set of Devils they are; however they are less damnable with Me, than Any body Else; but Woe to ye Manager who is not the first Actor in his Company. I don't know how it is, but the Strollers are a hundred years behind hand—We in Town are Endeavouring to bring the Sock & Buskin down to Nature, but *they* still keep to their Strutting, bouncing and mouthing, that with Whiskers on, they put me in mind of ye late Czar of Russia, who was both an Ideot & a Madman—*

Having got his feelings about his players off his chest, it occurred to Garrick that there was something rather more upbeat that he could tell his brother: 'Our theatre is most amazingly improved, & I really think it is the first Playhouse in Europe. You will say so, whenever You can rouze from y^r Lichfield Lethargy, & make us a Visit—'

During the summer, Drury Lane had been swarming with workmen. A press report on 2 August had given details of the alterations:

> The stage has been greatly lengthened, and the Pit and Boxes considerably enlarged, having taken in one of the lobbies for that purpose; the two galleries are also entirely rebuilt, and rendered much larger and more commodious, and the slips on each side are formed into green boxes. It is computed from the several alterations made that the house will contain £90 more than heretofore.[12]

It was fifteen years since Garrick and Lacy had first announced their intention of not allowing members of the audience behind the scenes, but the rule had not always been observed. On benefit nights, in particular, it was a dead letter, and the actors' friends (and actresses' admirers) still swarmed into the green-room, stood about in the wings, and, worst of all, sat in a specially constructed

---

* *Letters*, 297. Peter III had been deposed in July 1762 after a reign of only a few months and murdered a few days later. He was succeeded by his wife, Catherine, who had led the palace revolution against him. Catherine the Great remained on the throne until her death in 1796.

amphitheatre on the stage itself. Simply to do away with this would not be acceptable to the players, who might find the value of their benefit reduced by a hundred pounds or more, but the enlargement of the auditorium would remove all reasonable objections on that score.

A glance back at the playbills for the previous season suggests that Garrick was already then preparing the ground; once the benefit season got under way it is noticeable that they quite often state 'No Building on the Stage'. It is also possible that there was some collusion with Beard, because the Covent Garden playbills frequently carried a similar wording. Now, with the enlarged capacity provided by Lacy's alterations, Garrick could afford to be more explicit. But he was also quite cunning, because the form of words he devised suggested that the reform had been triggered by the public-spirited concern of the players for the audience:

> As frequenters of the theatre have often complained of the interruptions in the performance, occasioned by the crowded stage at the Benefits—the Performers will have no building on the stage, nor take any money behind the scenes, being willing to forego that advantage, for the sake of rendering the Representation more agreeable to the Public.*

From that time on, the privilege of going into the orchestra or behind the scenes was extended only to members of the Royal Family.

Apart from an extended altercation between Garrick and Thomas Arne, the first three months of the 1762–3 season passed quietly enough. Drury Lane put on a new afterpiece in October, a pastoral called *The Spring*, and there was some hissing of a young singer called Norris. It got back to Arne that Garrick thought he was responsible, something he vehemently denied, and this led to some ill-tempered exchanges. 'I did not charge you with hissing Master Norris,' Garrick wrote, 'but when Mrs Cibber spoke to me about that Affair, I told her the truth, that You was charg'd with being in the Company of Hissers, & tho' You might not hiss, the person averr'd that You were pleas'd, and Laugh'd at the Malecontents about You.'[13]

Although he struck a lofty note to Arne—'I have too much to do, to trouble my Self about these Matters'—Garrick thought it necessary after the second performance to insert a lengthy and rather laboured puff in the *Public Advertiser*. This explained, a shade lamely, that the piece had not originally been designed for the theatre, but 'had been several times performed at Salisbury, and greatly admired by many of the first Rank'.

Salisbury was where the author of the piece lived—in a rather grand house in the cathedral Close. James Harris was a well-connected scholar of independent means whose interests were mainly philosophical. Since 1761 he had been the Member of Parliament for Christchurch, and shortly, in January 1763, he would

---

* The announcement appeared on the front page of the *Public Advertiser* on 21 February 1763, well ahead of the start of the benefit season, and was occasionally repeated.

become a Lord of the Admiralty. Those 'of the first Rank' who had so greatly admired the pastoral may have included members of the Ashley Cooper family— he was a nephew of the third Earl of Shaftesbury.

There must be a strong supposition that Garrick had been leant on to produce the piece and that privately he had no very high opinion of it. 'Words set to the music of eminent masters' the playbills announced, but that was just a grand way of saying that much of the music had been filched from Handel—Arne and his neighbours in the pit would not have been deceived. Garrick kept it going until the author's night—the sixth performance—and then dropped it from the repertoire.

He had rather more success with the only other new afterpiece he mounted before Christmas, which was a pantomime called *The Witches, or, Harlequin Cherokee.* (In June the 'King' of the Cherokee Indians had arrived in London with two of his chiefs to pay his respects to George III, and in August they had been paraded at Marylebone Gardens—price of admission to see them 6d.) This extravaganza was written by the actor James Love, who had joined the company that summer after several years as an actor and manager in Edinburgh.* Garrick splashed out on new costumes and scenery and it proved popular, running on through the Christmas season.

It faced formidable competition, however, from a new comic opera called *Love in a Village* which Beard mounted at Covent Garden. This was the work of a young Irishman called Isaac Bickerstaffe. He made skilful use of music by an eclectic range of composers, including not only Handel, Boyce and Arne but also Geminiani, Giardini and Paradies. Beard himself sang the leading part of Hawthorn and Shuter was Justice Woodcock; a scene between them, with John Dunstall as Hodge, is the subject of a painting by Zoffany which is now at the Royal National Theatre.† *Love in a Village* ran and ran, although not without incident; at a command performance on 30 December a dancer called Miss Poitier behaved in a manner which the tabloid tendency felt it would be improper to keep from their readers:

> Would any person suppose she could have the confidence to appear with her bosom so scandalously bare, that to use the expression of a public writer, who took some moderate notice of the circumstance, the breast hung flabbing over a pair of stays cut remarkably low, like a couple of empty bladders in an oil shop. One thing the author of that letter has omitted, which, if possible is still more gross; and that is, in the course of Miss Poitier's hornpipe, one of her shoes happening to slipt down at the heel, she lifted up her leg, and danced upon the other till she had drawn it up. This had she worn drawers, would have been the more excusable;

---

* Love's real name was Dance. His father was the architect George Dance, who designed the Mansion House. He was a brother of Nathaniel Dance the portrait painter, and of George Dance the younger, who designed the second Newgate and the front of Guildhall.
† Another version of this painting realized £345,000 at Christie's in 1985 and was acquired by the Yale Centre for British Art.

but unhappily, there was little occasion for standing in the pit to see that she was not provided with so much as a fig-leaf. The Court turned instantly from the stage—The Pit was Astonished! and scarcely any thing, but a disapproving murmur, was heard, from the most unthinking spectator in the twelvepenny gallery.*

Garrick was to see something in the course of 1763 of a plump, swarthy young Scotsman who was every bit as stage-struck as he himself had been in his early twenties: 'I used to walk down the Cannongate and think of Players with a mixture of narrow-minded horror, and lively-minded pleasure; and used to wonder at painted equipages and powdered Ladies.'[14]

James Boswell had contrived an introduction to Garrick three years previously when he had fled briefly from his studies in civil law in Glasgow and, for three heady months, lived it up in London. On that occasion his tutor in the ways of the town had been a failed actor and literary man called Samuel Derrick.† Now, after a running battle of wills with his father, he was back, hoping somehow to procure a commission in the Guards—an open sesame, as he thought, to a life of gilded leisure and dissipation at the heart of things.

It was not the best of times for a young Scot to embark on the conquest of the capital. Lord Bute's reputation for favouring his compatriots in the distribution of patronage was the source of powerful resentments. Soon after his arrival in London, Boswell had gone to Covent Garden to see *Love in a Village*. Just before the overture, two Highlanders came in, officers in Lord John Murray's Regiment, and recently home from service in Havana. They were hissed and pelted with apples. 'No Scots! No Scots!' roared the upper gallery. 'Out with them!' Boswell took his life in his hands:

> My Scotch blood boiled with indignation. I jumped up on the benches, roared out, 'Damn you, you rascals!,' hissed and was in the greatest rage. I am very sure at that time I should have been the most distinguished of heroes. I hated the English; I wished from my soul that the Union was broke and that we might give them another battle of Bannockburn.[15]

London was in the grip of a severe frost in the early weeks of 1763. Boswell, standing on top of London Bridge, 'viewed with a pleasing horror the rude and terrible appearance of the river, partly froze up, partly covered with enormous shoals of floating ice which often crashed against each other'.

The *Gentleman's Magazine* for 20 January reported that two soldiers had frozen to death on sentry duty. It was a day that did not begin well for Boswell,

---

* *Theatrical Review*, 1 January 1763. Miss Poitier's career did not suffer. In his *Thespis*, a feeble imitation of *The Rosciad* published in 1766, Hugh Kelly described her as 'the liveliest baggage on the modern stage'.

† Derrick (1724–69) was a native of Dublin. His literary talents were slender. Johnson, asked whether he or Smart was the better poet, said there was 'no settling the point of precedency between a louse and a flea'. He later succeeded Beau Nash as master of the ceremonies at Bath.

although his low spirits had nothing to do with the cold weather. 'I rose very disconsolate,' he recorded in his journal:

> Can she who professed delicacy of sentiment and sincere regard for me, use me so very basely and so very cruelly? No, it is impossible, I have just got a gleet by irritating the parts too much with excessive venery. And yet these damned twinges, that scalding heat, and that deep-tinged loathsome matter are the strongest proofs of an infection . . .[16]

He toyed briefly with the idea of going to a quack, but when he eventually left his Downing Street lodgings he directed his steps to Pall Mall and took breakfast with his surgeon friend, Andrew Douglas. There, after Mrs Douglas had withdrawn, his suspicions were confirmed. Louisa, his enchanting young Covent Garden actress, was not what she had seemed; his 'intrigue' with her, from which he had expected 'at least a winter's safe copulation', was at an end:

> It is indeed very hard. I cannot say, like young fellows who get themselves clapped in a bawdy house, that I will take better care again. For I really did take care. However, since I am fairly trapped, let me make the best of it. I have not got it from imprudence. It is merely the chance of war.[17]

In this philosophical frame of mind, he went off to call on Garrick at Drury Lane. He was warmly received, and the gloom of the morning was quickly dispelled:

> I was quite in raptures with Garrick's kindness—the man whom from a boy I used to adore and look upon as a heathen god—to find him paying me so much respect! How amiable he is in comparison with Sheridan!*

Garrick might well have been less amiable if he had known how Boswell had spent the previous evening. Together with two friends he had gone to Drury Lane to see the first night of *Elvira*, a new tragedy, in which Garrick had created the role of Don Alonzo. The author was David Mallet, a fellow Scot, but the fact that he had changed his name to that from David Malloch had persuaded Boswell that he was 'an arrant puppy' and that his play deserved to be damned.†
They had accordingly planted themselves in the middle of the pit, 'and with oaken cudgels in our hands and shrill-sounding catcalls in our pockets, sat

---

* *London Journal*, p. 161. Boswell had got to know Sheridan two years previously in Edinburgh, when he was exploiting the ingenious idea of offering the Scots a course of elocution lessons to improve their English pronunciation. Boswell quickly succumbed to a bout of hero-worship: 'My Mentor! My Socrates!' he wrote, 'direct my heedless steps!' The older man responded by lending him money to settle his gambling debts and arranging for him to be admitted to the Inner Temple. Two days before calling on Garrick, however, Boswell had learned that the prologue he had been invited to write for a new comedy by Mrs Sheridan did not meet with her husband's approval. Only then had his eyes had been opened to Sheridan's general stupidity, insolence and lack of taste.
† The fact that he was the son of a tenant farmer may also have had something to do with it. Boswell was a tremendous snob. He also undoubtedly envied Mallet's success in so completely shedding his Scottish accent.

ready prepared, with a generous resentment in our breasts against dullness and impudence, to be the swift ministers of vengeance'.*

Unaware that he was nursing a viper in his bosom, Garrick assured Boswell that he would one day be 'a very great man' and pressed him to fix a day to drink tea at Southampton Street. Boswell's capacity to soak up flattery was not less than Garrick's own, but he also knew how to dispense it, and seized his host by the hand:

> 'Thou greatest of men,' said I, 'I cannot express how happy you make me.'
> This, upon my soul, was no flattery. He saw it was not. And the dear great
> man was truly pleased with it. The scene gave me a charming flutter of
> spirits . . .†

Boswell saw Garrick perform several times that season—as Scrub in *The Beaux' Stratagem*, and as the King in *Henry IV Part 2*. Then, towards the end of the season, he saw him as Lear:

> So very high is his reputation, even after playing so long, that the pit was
> full in ten minutes after four, although the play did not begin till half an
> hour after six. I kept myself at a distance from all acquaintants, and got
> into a proper frame. Mr. Garrick gave me the most perfect satisfaction. I
> was fully moved, and I shed abundance of tears.[18]

That was on 12 May. Four days later, when he was drinking tea with Davies and his wife in the back-parlour of their bookshop in Russell Street, he was thrown into agitation by the appearance of Samuel Johnson. Davies introduced them, and there followed the celebrated exchange about Boswell's origins: 'Mr Johnson,' said I, 'I do indeed come from Scotland, but I cannot help it.' 'That, Sir, I find, is what a very great many of your countrymen cannot help.' This stroke, Boswell recorded, 'stunned me a good deal' and he waited apprehensively for what might come next:

> He then addressed himself to Davies: "What do you think of Garrick? He
> has refused me an order for the play for Miss Williams, because he knows
> the house will be full, and that an order would be worth three shillings."
> Eager to take any opening to get into conversation with him, I ventured to

---

* Boswell was not the only member of the audience to write up the events of that night in his journal. Young Edward Gibbon was also present at the première of *Elvira*:

> My father and I went to the Rose, in the Passage of the Playhouse, where we found
> Mallet, with about thirty friends. We dined together, and went from thence into the
> Pitt, where we took our places in a body, ready to silence all opposition. However, we
> had no occasion to exert ourselves . . . we heard nothing but applause.

(*Gibbon's Journal to January 28th 1763*, ed. D.M. Low, London, 1929. pp. 202–4.)
† *London Journal*, p. 161. Gratified as he was by Garrick's attentions, Boswell, when he came to write up his journal for that day, received them as no more than his due: 'What he meant by my being a great man I can understand. For really, to speak seriously, I think there is a blossom about me of something more distinguished than the generality of mankind.'

say, "O, Sir, I cannot think Mr Garrick would grudge such a trifle to you."— "Sir," said he, with a stern look, "I have known David Garrick longer than you have done: and I know no right you have to talk to me on the subject."

It is the greatest of pities that Boswell's encounter with the fair Louisa earlier in the year resulted in his being confined to his lodgings for several weeks, because it means that we have no account from him of the serious riots that occurred at both Drury Lane and Covent Garden in January and February.

Moving on from the rearrangement of seating in the auditorium, Lacy and Garrick had turned their attention to what seemed an increasingly glaring anomaly in their admissions policy. It had long been the custom to charge only half-price to patrons admitted after the end of the third act of the mainpiece. Over the years, however, production costs had risen sharply, and the concession now appeared to the managers to be eating into their profits to an unacceptable degree.*

They decided to grasp the nettle with a new production of Shakespeare's *Two Gentlemen of Verona*. Benjamin Victor† had prepared a new version for the occasion, and the bills for his benefit on 25 January carried the words 'Nothing under Full Price will be taken'. On the day, a handbill was distributed in the taverns and coffee houses in the neighbourhood of the theatre:

> ... Will you acquiesce, gentlemen, in this insolent extortion, without any other pretence, than new dressing the characters of an old play in Linsey-woolsey; or in reviving a spurious comedy, under the reputable name of Shakespeare?

The writer signed himself *An Enemy to Imposition*, and he added a footnote:

> N.B. The reason of my addressing the town in this manner is, that all communication with the public, by the channel of the news-papers, is cut off, through the influence of one of the theatrical managers; who has found means to lay that restraint upon the liberty of the press, which no minister of state has hitherto been able to effect in this country ...

That night a cry went up from the pit and boxes: 'Garrick! Garrick!' An actor came on to announce that a messenger had gone to fetch him, and when Garrick appeared, a familiar figure arose in the pit:

> But touch its pride, the Lady-fellow,
> From sickly pale, turns deadly yellow—
> Male, female, vanish,—fiends appear—
> And all is malice, rage and fear—

---

* From a figure of £34 at the beginning of the century, costs had risen by the 1760s to more than £90.

† Victor had returned from Dublin in 1759 and been appointed treasurer of Drury Lane, a position he was to hold until his death in 1778. His *History of the Theatres of London and Dublin* had come out in 1761.

Fitzpatrick had had two years to nurse his rage at the treatment meted out to him in *The Fribbleriad*, and now it came spilling out. 'I call on you in the name of the public to answer for your rascally impositions,' he cried, but when Garrick tried to do so he was denied a hearing. When he could finally make himself heard, he said that he must consult his partner, 'who was then at a great distance', but Fitzpatrick, in his role of tribune of the people, would have none of this: 'Will you, or will you not, admit the public at half prices to all entertainments, except the first winter of a new pantomime?' Garrick replied once again that he must consult Lacy; this enraged the town still further and, after several more minutes of hissing and catcalls, Garrick made a bow and withdrew.

There were some calls for the play to begin, and the actors appeared several times on stage. The uproar continued until eight o'clock, at which point the rioters called on the ladies to retire so that they might set fire to the house. Benches were torn up, sconces and chandeliers smashed. Two of the players, John Moody and Ellis Ackman, had gone out into the auditorium to see what was afoot, and Moody, by his courage and presence of mind, may well have averted a disaster:

> He saw a gentleman strike the glass lustre, and down fell the candle alight, which another slyly shoved with his foot against the wainscot. This candle Mr Moody put out and kept his eye upon the person. When the magistrate with the guard appeared, he pointed him out to be apprehended, but his brethren either bribed or shouldered the soldiers that the person escaped.[19]

Garrick had a notice inserted in the next day's *Public Advertiser* asserting that the management was not conscious of having broken with precedent and reiterating his promise that a full answer to the charges made would be published in a few days. The carpenters worked through the day. By early evening Drury Lane was packed to the rafters and Garrick and the rest of the cast stood ready to go on in *Elvira*, the tragedy which Boswell and Gibbon had seen the previous week—its sixth performance, and therefore once again an author's benefit night.

Holland came on to speak the prologue and was hissed. Garrick, too, was once again given a rough ride. What the rioters did not know was that after consultation with Lacy he had come on to announce that the management would submit to their demands: 'They would not hear him speak. He stood sweating upon the stage near twenty minutes before he was permitted to say YES.'[20]

The capitulation of the management was not enough for the rioters, however. Some of the lesser fry must also be humiliated. Who better than the two players who had shown some spirit on the first night of the disturbances? Ackman proved easy game. When he appeared on stage two nights later in the next performance of *Elvira* and was called forward by the bravos in the pit he quickly advanced and did what was expected of him. He was, he said, extremely sorry he had done anything to give offence to the gentlemen; that had been far from his intention and he humbly begged their pardon.

Moody had no part in *Elvira* and was not in the house. 'Send for him,' bellowed the bully boys. 'We will have him, send for him,' and the play was not allowed to proceed before someone was despatched to find him. His appearance at the end of the act was greeted with a great roar. When it died down, Moody, adopting the accents of one of the low-bred Irish characters in which he specialized, said that he was very sorry if he had displeased them by saving their lives in putting out the fire. At this the house erupted, and there was a chant of 'Knees, knees! Down on your knees!' but Moody, by now every bit as incensed as the rioters, shouted 'I will not, by God!' and strode off.

'When he came off the stage,' wrote Davies, 'Mr Garrick was so pleased with his behaviour, that he received him with open arms, and assured him, that whilst he was master of a guinea, he should be paid his income.'[21] But things looked so nasty out front that there was nothing for it but to go out and offer Moody up to the rioters: 'Mr Garrick promised he should not appear on the stage again during the time he was under their displeasure.'[22]

It is not at all clear how this sorry tale ended. Moody was faced with a choice between staying in London as Garrick's pensioner or reverting to the precarious life of a strolling player. Davies says that he found neither prospect appealing; regarding Fitzpatrick as the cause of all the mischief, he decided to seek redress by confronting him.

The long, circumstantial account which Davies gives of what passed between them can only have come from Moody himself—of how he bearded Fitzpatrick at his chambers in the Temple, and after much stubborn argument prevailed upon him to write to Garrick 'in a strain very condescending, and to a proud man sufficiently humiliating'. It is an account, however, which cannot be squared with a notice which appeared ten days later in the *Public Advertiser*:

> Mr Moody begs leave to inform the Public that the impropriety of his behaviour at the theatre was intirely owing to the confusion of mind he was then under; which unhappily for him was misconstrued into disrespect; tho' nothing could at that, or at any other time, be farther from his thoughts. He therefore earnestly hopes and entreats that he may be permitted to appear before them again; as he hereby most humbly asks their pardon for whatever he inadvertently said or did to incur their displeasure.[23]

Meanwhile Fitzpatrick, Garrick's scalp dangling from his belt, turned his gaze on Covent Garden. He saw his opportunity at the end of February, when Arne's *Artaxerxes* was announced. 'Opera not perform'd this season,' proclaimed the bills. 'Nothing under FULL PRICE can be taken.' Before the curtain rose Fitzpatrick jumped to his feet and harangued the house much as he had done at Drury Lane. Beard, who was due to sing in the opera, came forward and attempted a reasoned defence of the management's decision—nightly charges had increased prodigiously, and no expense had been spared on scenery and costumes.

He could have saved his breath. 'Fitzgig' and his friends set about wrecking the theatre, and made an even more thorough job of it than they had done at Drury Lane:

The mischief done was the greatest ever known on any occasion of the like kind; all the benches of the boxes and Pit being entirely tore up, the glasses and chandeliers broken, and the linings of the Boxes cut to pieces. The rashness of the rioters was so great, that they cut away the wooden pillars between the Boxes, so that if the inside of them had not been iron, they would have brought down the Galleries upon their heads.[24]

An eighteenth-century forerunner of *Reader's Digest* entertained its readers with an eyewitness account of the riot couched in terms of a naval encounter: 'As to my 5s., why the owners are welcome to it towards repair, for you stripped plank, timbers, and scantlings,—you gutted her; she looked like a French prize, after a yard-arm engagement.'[25]

The damage amounted to more than £2,000, and the theatre remained closed for a week. Beard, however, was made of sterner stuff than Lacy and Garrick— or so, for a time, it seemed. He secured a Chief Justice's warrant, and had four of the rioters, including Fitzpatrick, brought before Lord Mansfield at his house in Bloomsbury Square. Mansfield told them that if a life had been lost, they would have faced trial for murder; in return for assurances of future good conduct, Beard agreed not to press charges.

At which moment, their point apparently won, the Covent Garden management unaccountably decided to throw in the towel. Just why they felt it necessary to do so is unclear—the most likely explantion is that his fellow-proprietors had weaker nerves than Beard and feared that as Drury Lane had already sold the pass on the half-price issue, their own position must sooner or later become untenable. At all events, on 1 March a long letter from Beard appeared in the *Public Advertiser*. It makes sorry reading—there is about it a whiff of the confessional tone heard at show trials in the Soviet Union two centuries later. He apologized for not acquiescing with more alacrity on the nights the rioters had made their demands. He was, he explained, merely the manager for other proprietors. Then, after a full column of none-too-convincing explanation, this grovelling conclusion:

Nevertheless, in gratitude for the many favours and indulgencies received from *the* Publick, and from an earnest desire to promote that order and decorum so essential in all Public Assemblies, the Proprietors have now jointly authorized Mr Beard to declare that they shall think themselves equally bound with the managers of the *other* Theatre to an observance of those limitations which *they* have agreed to.

With the white flag fluttering bravely over both theatres, Covent Garden and Drury Lane moved into the benefit season. Mrs Cibber was, as usual, accorded pride of place, and chose to appear as Calista in *The Fair Penitent*. Garrick ceded the role of Lotario to O'Brien and for the first time took the part of Sciolto.*

---

* In April, for Palmer's benefit, Garrick ceded the part of Hamlet to Holland and appeared himself as the Ghost.

Some weeks later, when it was the turn of two members of the company further down the pecking order and Mrs Cibber was playing Ophelia, her behaviour provoked one reviewer to remonstrate with Garrick:

> I hope you will not let so flagrant an outrage to the decorum of the stage as the following pass unnoticed. As [Mrs Cibber] sat upon the stage, with Hamlet at her feet, in the third act, she rose up three several times, and made as many courtsies, and those very low ones, to some ladies in the boxes. Pray, good Sir, ask her in what part of the play it is said that the Danish Ophelia is acquainted with so many British Ladies?[26]

The unhappiest season of Garrick's managership drew to a close. He did not know it, but a chapter in his life had ended, too; when he appeared as Sir Anthony Branville in *The Discovery*, shortly after the rioting, it was the last time that he would create a new role.*

At the end of May he hastened down to Hampton, burdened as always with a mass of paper. To one of his correspondents, the young engraver John Hall, who had written to recommend the work of a friend, he replied in a manner that was both uncharacteristic and mysterious:

> I should with great pleasure reconsider the tragedy of Jugurtha . . . were I not so particularly circumstanc'd, that I cannot with propriety read it at present, nor tell You my reasons till I have settled an affair of some Consequence to me:
>
> The Moment I am at liberty to explain Myself, I most certainly will, & in the mean time I must beg of You to let Ev'n this riddle be a Secret till I shall expound it to You.†

Meanwhile, hugging his secret to himself, Garrick went off to the races at Ascot with the Duke of Devonshire. Later in the summer, he was bidden to Chatsworth. Hearing that Quin was to be a fellow-guest, he wrote a playful, affectionate letter to express his pleasure; the old rivalry and wariness had mellowed into warm friendship:

> I s'd have had ten times the satisfaction in this News, had not my wife taken more pleasure in hearing of it, than is quite agreable to the Temper of a prudent Husband . . . but my good Frien[d] as you are stout be mercifull; I have been very Ailing of late, & am order'd by the Faculty to keep my Mind Quiet, and my Body Cool, Therefor[e] spare me & mine I beseech you.‡

---

* The author was Frances Sheridan, wife of Thomas, who was cast as Lord Medway.

† *Letters*, 305. Hall (1739–97) engraved several portraits of Garrick after the paintings by Dance, Zoffany and de Loutherbourg. He was later appointed historical engraver to George III.

‡ *Ibid.*, 306. 'The Faculty' was a common generic term for doctors. Lawyers were known as 'The Profession' and booksellers as 'The Trade'.

Chatsworth was just what the Faculty ordered. 'Were you near us,' Garrick wrote to Colman, 'you would be happy to be with Us—all Mirth, Bagatelle, Liberty, & a little drinking at times.'[27]

He returned to Hampton, and to an acrimonious correspondence with Tom Davies. Relations between Garrick and his future biographer had been deteriorating for some time. Davies had made his last appearance at Drury Lane in May of the previous year. He told friends that he was leaving the stage to concentrate on his bookshop, but he now confirmed to Garrick what he had told Johnson some time previously—'I should not have quitted the theatre when I did, if your warmth of temper had not provoked me to it.'[28]

Garrick replied sarcastically, taunting Davies by reminding him of a frequently repeated rumour—'that the Stage became disagreeable to you from ye first publication of ye Rosciad, & that you were resolved to quit it, as you were always *confus'd & unhappy* whenever you saw Mr Churchill before You.' Then, smarting under what had been said about temper, he brutally called into question Davies's professional competence as an actor:

> If you mean by the warmth of temper (You have accus'd me of to Mr Johnson) a certain anxiety for ye business of the Stage, your accusation was well founded; for I must confess I have been often too much agitated by yr want of that care & readiness in your parts which I thought I had a right to resent, & which made your leaving us of such little Consequence: this warmth of temper is certainly my Weakness, but I could never find that any Actors have left us upon that account . . .[29]

Davies was also deeply wounded by what he saw as a reflection on his personal integrity. Garrick's share in the *St James's Chronicle* had apparently been held in trust for him by Davies, but Garrick had recently requested Colman to terminate the arrangement. 'What is this,' wrote Davies, 'but to brand me as a fellow not fit to be trusted?'[30]

There were further recriminations over the financial arrangements for the purchase of Davies's house and shop in Russell Street. Garrick had lent him £50 when he needed to put down a deposit on the property; when it got back to him through his brother George that Davies now claimed he had refused to help him, he was understandably indignant. He none the less agreed to abide by an earlier agreement to accept some books in partial repayment of the debt, although he did so with a sneer:

> I am very ready to perform the conditional promise I have made you about the Musaeum Florentinum, tho from your Behaviour You have no claim to it: and I congratulate Your prudence which does not forget your interest in the midst of your passion.[31]

The hurt felt by Davies clearly went very deep. Stubbornly, in a final letter, he returned to the treatment he had received at the manager's hands:

> Be pleased, Sir, to hear a short history of your own conduct to me, which

brought on these exquisite feelings you are so merry with. . . If I met Mr Garrick behind the scenes, or in the street, or elsewhere, he would not speak, scarce return his hat when bowed to. At rehearsals he took all imaginable pains to make me unhappy—some jest or galling speech, which he seems to be excessively ready at, was sure to be at my service; the gentlest expression of his resentment was a laugh, not indeed of the most good-natured kind. He would not condescend to settle the business of a scene without some mark of cool disgust and displeasure. This behaviour my exquisite feelings submitted to bear for above two months. At last, seeing no end of it, I told your brother that I perceived I was become extremely disagreeable to you, that all my submissions were to no purpose, and that such a life was extremely irksome to me, and that I would much rather quit any man's roof, than live under it with his continual frown. . .[32]

Exchanges like this were not calculated to prolong the tonic effects of Garrick's stay in Derbyshire. Happily, a more extended remedy was to hand. On 9 August, his secret was out. 'We are assured that David Garrick Esqre, Patentee of Drury Lane Theatre, will set out for Italy the beginning of next month,' announced the *St James's Chronicle.* Realizing that his friends might have preferred to hear such news direct, he was at pains to explain. 'I had no right to avow it, till I had Met with ye Lord Chamberlain's Approbation,' he wrote to Mrs Cibber:

I have had it, & Now I proclaim ye Certainty of it to my friends—I have been advis'd by several Physicians at ye head of which I reckon Dr Bary to give Myself a Winter's respite; I have dearly Earn'd it, & shall take it in hopes of being better able to undergo my great fatigues of acting & Management, if You or Mr Sloper have any Commands to France or Italy I shall Obey them with pleasure . . .*

Mrs Cibber was mollified—just:

I was last night favoured with yours, and greatly surprised with the news in it, for though I had read a paragraph in the papers that you intended going abroad, I gave no credit to it. However sorry I am for my own sake, I think you do right, and wish to God I could do the same: my best wishes and compliments wait on you and Mrs Garrick . . . Health and pleasure attend you both![33]

They set out on 15 September, two days before the opening of the new season. The editor of the *London Chronicle* felt that the occasion called for something more than straight reporting:

Yesterday departed this kingdom, to the inexpressible grief of Drury-Lane Theatre, David Garrick, Esq; Poet, Painter, and Philosopher; Musician, Manager, and Mimic; Critic, Censor and Composer, and Professor of Tragedy, Comedy, and Farce . . . His chariot was attended out of town by

---

* *Letters,* 315. As patentee of Drury Lane, Garrick was technically a servant of the Crown.

innumerable Sons of the Buskin, and a prodigious train of Danglers on the Sock.—Mr Holland in the character of Tragedy, was drest in a deep suit of mourning, and poor Mrs Cibber had her hair all dishevel'd, representing a picture of the greatest distress.—A universal silence for a long time reigned thro' the cavalcade, which Mrs Clive at last broke by an exclamation of G—d's b—d! and a rivulet of tears.[34]

23

Away from It All

At forty-six, Garrick was in the prime of middle life. Twenty-two years had passed since the callow young wine-merchant from Staffordshire, masquerading as 'A Gentleman who never appear'd on any Stage', had taken the town by storm as Richard III. There had been the golden summer when Dublin playgoers elbowed their way into Smock Alley and succumbed to 'Garrick fever'. He had survived, wiser and warier, both his stormy entanglement with Woffington and the wreck of his friendship with Macklin. When he took on Quin, it had seemed to the young Richard Cumberland 'as if a whole century had been stept over in the transition of a single scene'.

It was sixteen years since he had taken over as joint patentee at Drury Lane. He had not delivered on all the promises held out in Johnson's resounding prologue, but then 'chasing the new-blown bubbles of the day' had always been a chancy business, and manifestos are not generally written under oath. He had banished the beaux and the danglers from behind the scenes, for all that; and he had been the victor in the battle of the Romeos, both on and off the stage—his marriage to Violette, 'the paragon, the marvellous she', had been of the happiest, even if he did still tease her about her Austrian accent.

He was famous, and he was rich—the house in Southampton Street, his property on the river at Hampton, the fine coach in which he was even now jolting his way towards Dover, all testified to that. The patronage of the Burlingtons had given him an entrée to fashionable society to which few 'mere players' could aspire (and of which not a few were jealously resentful), but he also enjoyed the friendship of Hogarth and Johnson, of the wealthy bluestocking Mrs Montagu, of Joshua Reynolds and of Edmund Burke.

It had not all been plain sailing. There had been the costly fiasco of *The Chinese Festival*; he had lost, at the time of George III's coronation, the final round in his long-running battle of spectacle with Rich; he had been forced to capitulate to the odious Fitzpatrick after the half-price riots. But his position at the head of his profession was unassailable, for all the sniping of the critics and the pamphleteers. His unrivalled versatility as a performer had won him the ascendancy in both tragedy and comedy. His skills as director and manager had brought new order to the affairs of Drury Lane, and the theatre had twice been refurbished and enlarged.

He had already made a significant contribution to the revival of interest in Shakespeare. If the claim on the playbills that his 1744 production of *Macbeth* was 'as Shakespeare wrote it' had not been entirely true, the text was a good deal closer to the original than the entrenched Davenant version, and he had gone on since then to alter or adapt nine more of the plays in the canon. He had also brought to the stage new versions of the work of eleven other playwrights— Jonson, Fletcher, Wycherley, Vanbrugh—and there had been productions of nine pieces from his own pen.

Twelve years previously, when the Garricks had last crossed to the Continent, they had had as their travelling companion Charles Denis. This time, Mrs Garrick had decided that her King Charles spaniel, Biddy, must accompany them, but Garrick's dog, Phill, had been boarded out with the Burneys.

Garrick had determined to keep a journal, and for a time his resolution held:

> I had a much better opinion of the Country of France this time than the last . . . I scarce saw an acre of land that was not cultivated, tho' very little of it Enclos'd—the appearance of Poverty among ye lower sort was very great, & the Carriers upon ye road, with whom I often enter'd into conversation, complain'd sorely of taxes &c—My barber at Calais told me that the Officers of ye army had no Money & were so much reduc'd by ye Peace that he knew of *ten* of them who kept one sev^t Girl among them.
>
> We met with no Accidents, & were Entr'ing Paris in high Spirits when we were stop'd by ye Custom house Officers & tho our trunk was *plombée* at *Calais*, & we were searched afterwards at *Peronne*, yet having mislaid our *permitt* from Calais we were oblig'd to be taken to ye Custom house & have our Trunk open'd.[1]

Garrick was well aware that his fame had gone before him. Noverre had written highly flattering things about him in his *Lettres sur la Danse* which had appeared three years previously and Laurence Sterne, writing more recently from Paris, had told him that he was much talked of—'and much expected, as soon as the peace will let you,' he added. 'These last two days you have happened to engross the whole conversation of two great houses where I was at dinner.'* Even so, it was particularly gratifying, on his arrival, to be waited on by the controller of the 'French Company of Comedians' and presented with a gold snuff box containing the freedom of their house—'not excepting the King's Box when unengaged by ye royal family,' he noted proudly.†

Although the Peace of Paris had been signed only a matter of months earlier, the French capital was in the grip of a mild bout of anglomania, and Garrick

---

* Curtis, L.P. (ed.), *The Letters of Laurence Sterne*, Oxford, 1935, p. 162. It was thanks to Garrick that Sterne had been able to set out on his travels. 'Dear Garrick,' he had written on Christmas Eve, 1761, 'Upon reviewing my finances this morning, . . . I find I should set out with twenty pounds less than a prudent man ought. Will you lend me twenty pounds?' *Ibid.*, p. 146.
† The pass, signed by the members of the company, was dated 18 July 1763. Garrick's visit was clearly not entirely unprepared.

was, if anything, received with even greater enthusiasm by the French than he was by the English colony:

> You can't imagine, my dear Colman, what honours I have receiv'd from all kind of People here—the Nobles & the Litterati have made so much of Me that I am quite asham'd of opening my heart Ev'n to You.

Colman was minding the shop, and had sent Garrick a copy of a flattering prologue he had written for Beaumont and Fletcher's *Philaster*, which was to be one of his first productions:

> Genius is rare; and while our great comptroller,
> No more a manager, turns *arrant stroller*,
> Let new adventurers your care engage,
> And nurse the infant saplings of the stage.

Garrick was pleased—and cheerfully resigned to the fact that when the cat was away the critical mice would play:

> If they love to hear me abus'd, they will have great Pleasure this winter, for I am told they have begun already, but I am happy & in Spirits, & shall not read any Newspapers on this Side the Alps.

He hated loose ends, and was anxious that Colman and George should tidy up behind him:

> I believe I forgot to pay a little bill for yᵉ Gazeteers, owing to one Owen, yᵉ bill lay in my Study window, will you discharge it for me, & pay for a pair of Spectacles I bought & forgot at yᵉ optician's (I forgot his name) at Charing Cross: it is on yᵉ left side going down to Whitehall—I hate to be in debt & if you or George will clear me there I shall thank you most sincerely—²

There was an early invitation to the British Embassy, where he was entertained to dinner by Richard Neville, the minister-plenipotentiary.* Neville had conducted an energetic trawl of the capital's literary and theatrical personalities. D'Alembert was present ('& sings my praises to all yᵉ authors of the *Encyclopedie*,' Garrick told Colman). Another guest was the fashionable but essentially mediocre author Marmontel, who afterwards wrote 'yᵉ most flattering Letter'—Garrick promised he would send it to Colman by the first person he found going to England.† The great Clairon was there, of course—she was d'Alembert's mistress at the time—and knew what was expected of her:

---

* Neville had been one of the young men who engaged in amateur theatricals with Garrick's friend William Windham at Geneva twenty years previously.

† Garrick had good reason to be flattered. 'Le sommeil n'a point effacé, Monsieur, l'impression que vous m'avez faite,' wrote Marmontel. 'J'espère même qu'elle ne s'effacera jamais; et l'image de Macbeth sans cesse présente à mon esprit, sera pour moi le modèle intellectuel de la déclamation théâtrale à son plus haut point d'énergie et de vérité . . .' And much else in the same vein. (*Boaden*, ii, 427.)

She got up to set me a going & spoke something in Racine's Athalie most charmingly—upon which I gave them the Dagger Scene in Macbeth, ye Curse in Lear, & the falling asleep in Sr John Brute, the consequence of which is, that I am now star'd at ye Playhouse, & talk'd of by Gentle & Simple as ye most wonderfull Wonder of Wonders—[3]

When the Wonder of Wonders went to the playhouse he did not—privately—think that what he saw was all that wonderful. On 20 September he was at the Comédie-Française:

It looked so dark & dirty that I was hurt at my first Entrance—I saw Mad^l[l]e *Duminile* in ye Gouvernante—She has certainly expression in her face, & some other requisites, but she is made up of trick; looks too much upon ye ground & makes use of little startings and twitchings which are visibly artificial & the mere mimickry of the free, simple noble workings of ye Passions.*

France's leading comic actor also failed meet his expectations:

The first time I saw Preville I thought he was a great Comedian & he certainly has comic Powers—but the 2^d & 3^d time I did not see ye variety I expected—He has ye same looks in Ev'ry part I saw him Act and throws a kind of drunken folly into his Eyes wch in some parts would have a fine Effect, but to be us'd continually is a proof of confin'd talents.[4]

On 28 September the Garricks' coach rumbled out of Paris and headed south. Garrick recorded his satisfaction at covering almost 400 miles in four days:

We met with a most polite reception from Every body, but the impositions on ye English have reached *Lyons*, & a french Woman told me, that whenever English Travellers pass through their Gates they laugh & wink at Each other, as much as to say *there goes our prey.*

Always quick to absorb what went on around him, he mused on the puzzling differences between French and English ways of doing things:

A criminal was broke upon ye Wheel three Days before our Arrival & he was upon ye rack for twelve hours before he dy'd & all his Crime was robbing a Smith of 7 Livres—the French can't bear Murder upon ye Stage but rack Criminals for Small thefts, we can bear any Butchery upon ye Stage & hang only for ye greatest Thefts & Murder.

The approach to the Alps he found enchanting: 'All ye part of Savoy that I have yet seen is admirable,' he wrote in his journal, 'and looks like one great Garden & indeed Nature has done more without the least art, than all ye Expence that

---

* *La Gouvernante* was a one-act comedy by La Chaussée. It had seventeen performances that year.

I ever saw bestow'd on any place in England.' From Montmélian, he wrote to George. He and Mrs Garrick were both in better health than they had been for some time, 'and when We have pass'd *Mont Cenis*, we shall be quite at our Ease'. He was eager for news from home:

> My friend Colman & You may take it by turns & then I shall have a Succession—I long to hear of Y^r Success & indeed I flatter Myself that You will have a good Season with few altercations—if you should hear of any persons you can trust coming to *Florence* or *Rome*, pray send me Churchill's Ghost or any thing will divert Me—remember Me kindly to him, & tell him that I have had a most warm invitation from *Voltaire*, whom I shall take in my return; tho I am rather angry with him for saying in his last thing, that tho Shakespear is surprising, there is more *Barbarism* than *Genius* in his Works—O the damn'd fellow!*

A week later, the travellers were in Turin, and it was Colman's turn to receive the latest communiqué on their progress:

> We got to this pretty City (for it is no better) last Fryday Night, & are oblig'd much against our wills to stay here till next Saturday, for the Perch of our carriage was broke upon the top of Mount Cenis, by the carlessness of our Voiturier, who instead of carrying it upon ye backs of Mules (as he ought) had it drag'd up that wonderfule Mountain by 12 Men, & it is a great Miracle that it was not dash'd into ten thousand pieces . . .^{5}

He had caught up with some of the gossip from home. Somebody had shown him a couple of London newspapers 'in which they have abus'd Me most clumsily'. There had, in fact, been more than one caustic article on his departure for the continent. One of them speculated on the likelihood of his being created an Irish peer—'a circumstance very far from improbable, as so many comical people are daily rais'd to coronets in that kingdom.' Garrick affected an Olympian indifference: 'I read their Malignity with as much sang froid as Plato himself would have done,' he told Colman.

Turin had little to offer in the way of entertainment:

> We have nothing here in our way, but a miserable Bouffi Opera, & ye worst dancing I Ever saw—the People in ye Pitt & Boxes talk all ye while as in a Coffee house, & ye Performers are Even with 'Em, for they are very little attentive, laugh & talk to one another, pick their Noses, & while they are unEngag'd in singing, they walk up to ye Stage Boxes (in which the other Actors & dancers sit dress'd in sight of ye audience) turn their backs, & join in ye laugh & Conversation of their brethren, without y^e

---

* *Letters*, 318. The fourth and last book of Churchill's *The Ghost* appeared in November 1763. Voltaire's strictures on Shakespeare were not all that recent. They occur in his *Essai sur les moeurs, et l'esprit des nations*, which had appeared between 1753 and 1758. Presumably Garrick had caught up with it in the translation of his works, by Smollett and others, which had begun to appear two years previously.

least decency or regard to ye Audience; I never was more astonish'd in my life—[6]

Milan on the whole was a disappointment, though he admired the cathedral. And he was greatly flattered to be received so warmly by the Governor of Lombardy, Count von Firmian: 'You would think, as You Us'd to say to me, that all my Geese were Swans,' he wrote to the Duke of Devonshire. 'I had no Letter of recommendation to him, but his Servants were Enquiring after Me long before I came, & when I was there, there was no Civility that I did not receive from him.'[7]

From Genoa they sailed to Leghorn in a felucca. The voyage lasted two days and a night, and Mrs Garrick (and Biddy) were 'very much disordered'. Then on to Florence. The Garricks had a magnificent apartment overlooking the Arno, and there they entertained members of the English colony: 'There is one Mr Kaye among them,' Garrick told Devonshire, 'who is known to y^r Grace, & is beat constantly by Mrs Garrick at Chess.'* Garrick also had introductions to the celebrated polymath Francesco Algarotti, Voltaire's *cher cygne de Padoue*. Frederick the Great had been so taken with him that he made him his court chamberlain and created him a count. Finding him in poor health, Garrick suggested he try tar-water, a fashionable panacea of the day in England, but Algarotti died in Pisa the following year before they could meet again.†

Garrick was so excited at the prospect of seeing Rome that on the night before their arrival he hardly slept, but as they entered the Porta del Populo his spirits sank—'I fell at once from my Airy vision & Utopian Ideas into a very dirty ill looking *place*.' Then in the afternoon he was taken to see the Pantheon. 'My God, w^t was my Pleasure & Surprize!' he told Colman:

> I never felt so much in my life as when I entered that glorious Structure: I gap'd, but could not speak for 5 Minutes—It is so very noble, that it has not been in ye Power of Modern Frippery, or Popery (for it is a Church you know) to extinguish Its grandeur & Elegance . . . I have such a thirst to return to Rome, as cannot possibly be slak'd till I have drunk up half ye Tiber, which in it's present state, is but a scurvy draught neither. it is very strange that so much good poetry sh^d be thrown away upon such a pitiful River . . .[8]

He was writing this from Naples—'our Journey's End', he called it. The journey from Rome had been a nightmare. Impatient to arrive before nightfall, Garrick

---

* *Letters*, 320. A family called Kaye lived at Fulford Waters in the East Riding of Yorkshire, not far from Londesburgh.
† More than twenty-five years previously, when Algarotti had first visited London, Lady Mary Wortley Montagu had fallen hopelessly in love with him—this despite his flagrant bisexuality and the fact that she was old enough to be his mother. Lord Hervey had also been hugely taken with him. See *Lady Mary Wortley Montagu, Comet of the Enlightenment*, by Isobel Grundy, Oxford, 1999.

had abandoned his coach in favour of a chaise put at his disposal by Lord Exeter, but this had broken down during a violent thunderstorm. 'As the Servant was gone before to prepare post horses, I was oblig'd to send my wife in a Calash four Miles with a Strange Man to send me help from ye next town, while I sat cooling my heels in ye Road, & taking Care of the nimble-finger'd Neapolitans.'* Now, however, they basked in warm sunshine: 'Tho it is Xmas, we have green peas every day, & dine with our Windows open.' And he was to have the honour of seeing the King's troop of actors perform at the palace:

> They perform Extempore, & ye Nobleman, who stands in ye place of ye Lord Chamberlain, has sent me word, that if I will write down any dramatic Fable & give ye Argument only of ye Scenes, in 24 hours after, they shall play it before Me as ye greatest Comp^t they can pay Me . . . I was last Night at their great Theatre, which is a most Magnificent one indeed; I was really astonish'd at first coming into it—it was quite full, & well lighted up—but it is too great, & the singers were Scarcely heard—[9]

Garrick spent three months in Naples, and was determined to make the most of it. 'Now I am out of y^r Clutches I must make a Meal, & a good one, in Italy,' he wrote to George:

> I shall never return to it again, & therefore I will make Good Use of my time—We have been very happy here & have receiv'd Every mark of favour from all sorts of People—I eat and drink too much, & laugh from Morning to Night. . . . We are continually with Lady Orford, Lady Spencer, Lord Exeter Lord Palmerstn & the Nobility of ye Country, who have descended from their great pride and Magnificence to honour Us with their Smiles—in short we are in great fashion & I have forgot England & all my trumpery at Drury Lane . . .†

Garrick struck a similar note in one of his letters to Devonshire. 'My health and Spirits have been so much improv'd by this recess, that I am almost tempted to repent of my Follies, & be a Merry Andrew no longer—I have lost all relish for the stage both as Manager and Actor.'[10]

Well, perhaps. The idea of wiping off the grease-paint and getting away from it all may occasionally have flitted through Garrick's mind as he toiled up Vesuvius or explored the streets of Herculaneum with the Spencers. Home

---

* *Letters*, 326. Garrick was writing three months after the event to Devonshire. He was by this time back in Rome and able to view their adventures on the road to Naples more philosophically.
† *Ibid.*, 323. Not everyone had thought the Italian nobility would be so welcoming. 'I shall be expecting Mr Garrick and his wife,' Mann had written to Horace Walpole, 'but shall be much embarrassed to know what to do with them in regard to the Italians. Sanosino, after having been courted for twenty years by the first nobility in England, was not permitted to sit down in the presence of a Siena Countess.' (Senesino was the stage name of the *castrato* Francesco Bernardi, who had been idolized by the London opera-going public in the 1720s and 1730s and was reputed to have returned to his native Siena with a fortune of £15,000.) *Walpole*, xxii, 170, letter dated 1 October 1763.

thoughts from abroad often assume a tinge of Horatian fantasy. But they must be set beside the barrage of questions about theatrical affairs to which he subjected friends and relatives in London. 'I want much to know how You have gone on wth my good Partner,' he wrote George from Naples, '& don't forget to desire *Burton* to keep an exact list of ye Plays for me wth ye forces, & all occurences as [may] happen in ye Course of ye Season.'* Colman, too, was badgered for news: 'What is become of y^e *Invasion*, y^e *Dupe*, & y^e *new Entertainment*; I hope I shall have some account of 'Em, & a good one, in your next.'† That does not sound remotely like a man looking forward only to cultivating his garden at Hampton.

Garrick had promised his friend Charles Burney that he would keep his eyes and ears open on his behalf while he was in Italy, and from Naples he sent him an interim report on the music of that country. It was 'all execution, without Simplicity or Pathos', he wrote:

> I have heard the famous Gabrielli, who has indeed astonishing powers, great compass of voice and great flexibility, but she is always ye same, and though you are highly transported at first with her, yet wanting that nice feeling of ye passions (without which everything in ye dramatic way will cease to entertain) she cannot give that variety and that peculiar Pleasure which alone can support the tediousness of an Opera—[11]

Caterina Gabrielli, then in her early thirties, was regarded by many as one of the outstanding coloratura sopranos of the eighteenth century. Burney had the opportunity of forming his own judgement when Gabrielli came to London in the mid-1770s, although he had by then already published his *Present State of Music in France and Italy*. Given that Garrick was sometimes said to have a tin ear it is interesting to note that the young Mozart later echoed his view of Gabrielli. She was 'adept only in runs and roulades', he wrote to his father. 'She was not capable of sustaining a breve properly, and as she had no *messa di voce*, she could not dwell on her notes; in short, she sang with skill, but without understanding.'[12]

Garrick also gave Burney an account of a magnificent ceremony he had attended at which the daughter of a duke took her vows as a nun. 'The church was richly ornamented, and there were two large bands of Music of all kinds,' he wrote:

> The consecration was performed with great solemnity, and I was very much affected; and to crown the whole the principal part was sung by the famous *Caffarelli*, who, though old, has pleased me more than all the

---

* *Ibid.*, 322. Burton was presumably a house-servant at Drury Lane.
† *Ibid.*, 321. *Harlequin's Invasion* was not, in the event, produced that season. Mrs Sheridan's comedy *The Dupe* was, but lasted for only three nights. The 'new Entertainment' was a pantomime by James Love called *The Rites of Hecate; or, Harlequin from the Moon*, and it enjoyed considerable success.

singers I have heard. He *touched* me; and it was the first time I have been touched since I came to Italy.*

He saw the English papers regularly, but evidence that he was not forgotten at home could be a source of irritation rather than pleasure. Writing in the *St James's Chronicle* just before Christmas, one 'Bettsey Schemewell' had proposed a grand fete in celebration of the peace, and proposed that a number of prominent personages should dance together: 'Lord B—te is to begin, with the Duke of New—tle, to the tune of *Cause I was a Boney Lad*; then follows . . . . Mr. Ga—ck with the Duke of D—n—shire.' Garrick was not amused. 'Pray tell Colman that I think Baldwin us'd me like a Scoundrel to print such a heap of Stuff,' he instructed George.[13]

Garrick had dutifully kept Devonshire informed of their progress. 'I have had an opportunity to consider the Characters of the People of Naples in different lights,' he wrote towards the end of March:

> I have seen them, happy & very Miserable in ye space of three Months— the Scarcity of Corn produc'd such dreadfull sights, which I would not but have seen for ye world, & yet my heart sinks at ye very remembrance on them—†

Garrick was eager to offer his services to the Duke:

> I cannot flatter myself that Your Grace will send me any Commissions to buy Pictures or Statues, for I fear that You will not think my Taste in these Matters (which you always underrated) so improv'd by my travels to place any confidence in it . . .

If the Duke thought Garrick was being unduly modest, he was far too well-bred to say so. 'I am much obliged to you for your offer of purchasing pictures and statues,' he replied, 'but I have no money. I should, however, be obliged to you if you would get me all the prints that Bartolozzi has engraved: as you are such a connoisseur, you must know him.' Devonshire also twitted his friend mildly about his protestations that he was tired of the theatre:

> As you have lost your relish for the stage, and *virtù* has taken its place, we shall have you come over a perfect Dilettante, and I trust we shall have some battles upon the subject.[14]

The Garricks had originally intended to return to Rome, visit Bologna and Venice

---

* Caffarelli was the stage name of Gaetano Maiorano, one of the most celebrated *castrato* singers of his time, and Farinelli's greatest rival. He was notorious for his bad manners and feline brawling; on one occasion his behaviour on stage towards a female singer was described as 'bordering on lasciviousness'. He was, in fact, only fifty-three when Garrick heard him sing; he lived for another twenty years and purchased a dukedom and two *palazzi*.

† With good reason. Italy, and in particular Naples and the papal states, had been visited by severe famine in the early months of 1764. In the kingdom of Naples alone, over a six-month period, the number of deaths was estimated at half a million.

and then return home through Germany. 'This is our intended Route,' he told George, 'which I will dispatch wth all convenient speed, but am affraid that I shall not see Your fat face, or kiss ye brawn of it, till ye middle of June.'

These plans were disrupted, however. Soon after arriving in Naples, Mrs Garrick had suffered an attack of rheumatism in her hip and was obliged to stay in bed for a fortnight. 'She has been blister'd &c &c,' Garrick told George, '& tho she is better, yet still continues lame & Weak. however she hopes to be at A Carnaval Masquerade (which begins next Tuesday) in ye dress of a lame old Woman I have scolded & phyz'd about it, but if she can wag, she goes—'[15]

She had still not fully recovered by the time they returned to Rome three months later. 'This has been a great drawback upon our Pleasures,' Garrick wrote to Devonshire, 'for tho some Husbands would have rejoic'd to have their Wives tyd by ye leg; yet I must confess that I have been fool Enough to wish her Ev'n at ye top of Vesuvius with Me.'

Garrick, for his part, felt less well on their return to Rome than he had done at Naples. 'I have had some disagreeable nervous flutterings that made me as grave as an Owl for a few days,' he told Colman. This did not interfere with his pursuit of *virtù*, however. 'You must know that I am antiquity-hunting from Morning to Night & my poor wife drags her lame leg after me.' He loved his wife dearly, but he retained a tendency to view her religion a shade satirically:

> His Holyness the Pope is trying by prayers tears & intercessions to avert the Famine which his State is threaten'd with—He has crept up the holy stairs (santa Scala) wch were brought from Jerusalem, he has order'd processions & what not—

In the intervals of his antiquity-hunting, Garrick found time to sit to Pompeo Batoni and to Nathaniel Dance. One day in the street he recognized the unmistakable features of Joseph Nollekens—his nose, it was said, 'resembled the rudder of an Antwerp packet boat'. Nollekens, now twenty-seven, had come to Rome four years previously and was supplementing the precarious living he made from his sculpture by restoring and trafficking in antiques.* Garrick invited him to breakfast and commissioned a marble bust. It was Nollekens's first attempt at portraiture and it earned him twelve golden guineas.†

Hazards began to loom over the next stage of the Garricks' tour. There was plague at Venice, and it had spread as far as Trieste, leading to talk of quarantine in the neighbouring states. 'If so, we shall run ye gauntlet terribly,' he told Colman, 'but we are not dismay'd, & must go thro' with it—' And so they did, making a detour on the way to Parma. The Duke of York, then on his travels, happened to be in the town, and invited Garrick to dine in a party that included the Duke of Parma, his First Minister and Lord Spencer. The Duke was a

---

* He is said to have bought great quantities of fragments, supplied them with missing limbs and heads, stained them with tobacco-water and sold them for imposing sums.

† The bust is now in Earl Spencer's collection at Althorp. The Batoni portrait is in the Ashmolean Museum, Oxford (the Garrick Club owns a copy).

cultivated man who spoke good English and knew his Shakespeare. Garrick did not need too much persuading to perform the dagger scene from *Macbeth*, and the Duke showed his appreciation the following morning by the gift of a finely enamelled gold box. 'He likewise ordered apartments for me,' Garrick wrote, 'and sent me from his court more conceited by half than I came to it.'*

Venice made a powerful impression. 'It glares upon you at first, & inchants you,' he told Colman, 'but living a Month here (like yᵉ honey moon) brings you to a temperate consideration of things, & you long for yʳ terra firma liberty again!'[16] With the assistance of his guide, Giuseppe Baretti, Garrick busied himself buying a great many books. George Winchester Stone, noting that only a handful of the 180 or so volumes listed in Garrick's journal appeared in the catalogue when his library was sold long after his death, speculates that this book-buying spree might have been in the nature of a business venture. It is possible he was acting for his friend Topham Beauclerk, who was a considerable bibliomane: at one time his library contained 30,000 volumes—housed, as Horace Walpole put it, in a building 'that reaches half-way to Highgate'.

Garrick also witnessed a magnificent regatta which the Venetians put on to celebrate George III's birthday on 4 June—one of the events organized on the occasion of the Duke of York's visit to 'the Queen of the Adriatic'. 'I shall be a Week in telling you all I saw & felt that Day,' he wrote to Colman:

> Such Elegant luxury! which plainly shew'd, that the Contrivers were as little formidable in war & Politicks, as they were superiour to all ye World as Managers of a Puppet-Shew.†

Intensely curious as always, he had not confined his attention to the theatre and to the 'Visions of the Arabian Night' that he had seen on the water:

> But then their Courts of Justice! & their Lawyers! If there is any thing more particularly ridiculous than another, it is one of their Pleadings—It was some Minutes before I recover'd my Senses, & when I found I was really awake & in a Court of Justice, I was ready to burst wᵗʰ laughter— it is inconceivably strange, & more whimsical & outrée than the Italian theatre—& yet all sober People agree that their decrees are generally just & impartial.[17]

'I am grown fat, and sleep half the day in a Gondola,' he had told George, but the allure of foreign places was beginning to fade, and there were continuing anxieties about his wife's health. 'I shall leave this Place to morrow & return to Padua in order to be near the famous Mud of Abano, which the Physicians here

---

* *Letters*, 335. It is not known to whom Garrick addressed this letter. It appeared in the *London Magazine* in August 1764. There is a story that after his return he was showing the box and other mementos of his travels to Charles Holland, who had played many of his roles in his absence. 'And so you went about the Continent mouthing for snuff-boxes!' said Holland.
† *Ibid.*, 332. 'It is said that this visit of his Royal Highness has cost the state & yᵉ four Noble deputed Venetians, more than a hundred & twenty thousand Sequins,' Garrick wrote in a later letter to the Duke of Devonshire. (*Ibid.*, 334.)

tell us, will certainly restore Mrs Garrick,' he wrote to Colman in the middle of June:

> She is not worse, but she continues lame & the Continuance is very allarming—I fret to be at home, I dread the Italian Suns, & I am affraid that my presence is necessary to make a Plan for ye next Winter—If I can be at home a Month before ye opening of ye house, I shall think that I have done wonders—[18]

He might long to be home, but home meant Southampton Street and Hampton, not Drury Lane. 'I have no Joy now in thinking on ye Stage,' he told Colman in the same letter, '& shall return (if I must) like a Bear to the Stake—and this baiting, my good friend, is no joke after forty—'

They were lent a pleasant Palladian villa at Abano, and while Mrs Garrick endured her treatment at the hot springs and the mud-baths, her husband continued his pursuit of books and paintings. 'I am at this moment in treaty for no less than two Pictures by Tempesto, two Bassans, a Vandyke, a Rubens, a Paul Veronese &c.' he told Devonshire. 'I have a little money to throw away,' he added, '& I don't see why I should not be a little ridiculous as well as My betters.'[19]

Garrick's plan at this stage was to travel by way of Augsburg, Strasburg and Nancy and reach home in the second week in August, but by 5 August they had got no further than 'Munick, the Capital of Bavaria', as he called it in his letters. Mrs Garrick was still very lame, in spite of the 'fiery tryal' she had gone through for five weeks at Abano, and they were obliged to rest up for a few days. He seems by this time to have abandoned his original schedule, and to have floated the idea of meeting up with George at the fashionable watering resort of Spa, though without any great expectation that it would be adopted: 'I don't Expect that You will venture y^r Carcass on this Side the Water,' he wrote, 'tho' I think ye little voyage from Dover to Calais, & back again, would clear Your bowels for You.'

He was pleased to have made the return journey through Germany: 'ye Prospects of the Tyrol are Superiour to any thing I have Ever yet seen.' Food, drink and beds had all been better than those encountered in Italy, '& their neatness is equal to ye Inns (almost) in England'. And he asked George to pass on a message to his clergyman friend James Townley, whose *High Life Below Stairs* had been such a success in 1759 and whose interests apparently extended to the scatological:

> Pray tell *Townley* (with my Love to him), that I never, since I left England, till now, have regal'd Myself with a *good house of Office*, or as he calls it, a *Conveniency*—the holes in Germany are generaly too large, & too round, chiefly owing I believe to the broader bottoms of the Germans, for they are *swingers* indeed all thro' Bavaria—We have a little English Gentleman with us, who Slipt up to ye Middle in one of ye holes, & we were some Minutes before we could disEngage him—in short You may

assure Townley, (Who loves to hear of the state of these Matters) that in Italy the People *do their Needs*, in Germany they *disEmbogue*, but in England (& in England only) they *Ease* themselves—[20]

Garrick's plans were now thrown into further disarray because he himself was laid low by what was described as 'violent bilious fever'. Conceivably it was typhoid. By great good fortune his friend Turton had been travelling with them, and refused to continue his journey before Garrick was out of danger. He was confined to bed for more than a month. No sooner had the fever left him, however, than he was seized with 'a fit of the Gravel & Stone', which delayed his recovery by a further week:

I am most truly ye Knight of ye Woefull Countenance & have lost legs arms belly cheeks &c & have scarce any thing left but bones & a pair of dark lack-lustre Eyes that are retir'd an inch or two more in their Sockets & wonderfully set off ye yellow Parchment that covers ye cheek bones—[*]

Although it was now out of the question that he should be home in time for the new season, his mind ran insistently and fussily on the affairs of the theatre: 'I have hir'd no dancers, I am in treaty for a pair for next Year, if you had written yr Wants sooner, I could have got a very active Girl at Padua' (this in a letter to George towards the end of August):

I shall certainly follow Your & My Friends Advice about not acting, yr Judgment coincides so much wth my own, that it is resolv'd . . . I am a little at a loss what You will do for a Woman Tragedian to stare & tremble wth yr Heroes, if *Yates* should bitch You—but she must come. . . . *Clive* I suppose more Fussocky than Ever, & *Pritchard* often ailing—*Pope* I hope flourishes—Pray let me know if You think of ye Invasion next Year—or do you keep it till I can oversee it Myself—[21]

Garrick realized that he had become somewhat absorbed in his illness ('Invalids will prate of their Ailments,' he had written apologetically to Arden), but he remained solicitous of the well-being of friends at home. 'Dear Clut,' he wrote at the end of October, 'I forgot in my last letter to You to Send You a Receipt which I got at Strasburgh, & which I procured with the pleasing hopes of It's being of service to You.' James Clutterbuck, it seems, was a martyr to haemorrhoids. One of Garrick's attendants during his illness had been a bright young physician called François Renaudin, and he had shown himself to be something of a miracle-worker in that department:

The Manager of the Theatre at Strasburgh was so affected with the piles, that he could do no business for several weeks, & he was oblig'd to creep upon his hands & knees on a carpet & the Easiest posture he could find was leaning upon his Elbows, for he could not bear to lye upon his Side—

---

[*] *Letters*, 338. Garrick was writing to the Reverend William Arden, Lord Spencer's tutor, whom he had met earlier at Naples and Venice.

The poor man had tried everything, from leeches to some unspecified procedure with a lancet. Then Renaudin came on the scene, and 'gave him Ease in two hours, & cur'd him without return'. Garrick enclosed the recipe:

> Six grains of Opium.
> Forty grains of white lead in fine powder with a piece of very fresh butter, as large as a Nutmeg, they must be well mix'd togeather & spread upon a piece of linnen that will cover the part affected & remember to put it on cold or at most just & barely warm.

'I am persuaded of yᵉ Efficacy of this Simple thing,' he told Clutterbuck, '& hope You'll try it when you are very bad—'[22]

The Garricks were now moving by easy stages towards Paris. Sometime during the summer news reached them of a family bereavement. One of his letters to George carries a brief postscript: 'I have wrote about poor Linney several times.' It is the only reference that survives to the death of his unmarried sister Magdalen. Two years older than Garrick, she had lived all her life in Lichfield and was buried there in May.

From Nancy he felt obliged to write to Voltaire at Ferney: regretfully, his weakened state of health would not allow him to pay his respects:

> You were pleas'd to tell a Gentleman that You had a theatre ready to receive me; I should with great pleasure have exerted what little talents I have, & could I have been the means of bringing our Shakespeare into some favour with Mr Voltaire, I should have been happy indeed!
> No enthusiastick Missionary who had converted the Emperor of China to his religion would have been prouder than I, could I have reconcil'd the first Genius of Europe to our Dramatic faith.[23]

Garrick was still in a much reduced state when they reached Paris towards the end of October. He had been so changed, he told Colman, that people did not know him till he spoke. Now he was filling out, and 'I can pass for a tolerable looking French Man'. His condition had not been improved by a devastating piece of news which his wife had for some time kept from him. 'My Nerves, Sr: my Nerves,' he wrote:

> They are agitated at times; & the Duke of Devonshire's death had very near crackt them—they kept his Death from Me by the managᵗ of the best of Women & Wives, till I was better able to struggle with such a Heart breaking loss . . . I must not dwell upon this subject, it shakes me from head to foot—I can't forget him—

Devonshire's health had been in decline for some time. He had died at Spa on 3 October, at forty-four Garrick's junior by three years. From Colman he had also learned of the death of Hogarth and of another close friend called Hubert, and this affected him keenly. He was able in return to send Colman melancholy news of another of their friends:

Churchill I hear, is at yᵉ point of death at Boulogn, This may be report only—he is certainly very ill—what a lust of publishing has possess'd him for sometime past—the greatest Genius no more than the greatest Beauty, can withstand such continu'd prostitution—I am sorry, very sorry for him—[24]

Two days later, when he had confirmation of Churchill's death, Garrick, always prompt in the despatch of business, dashed off a hasty note to George. With it he sent the key to the table which stood in his study window:

I thought it might be necessary to send you that, to look for *Hubert's* Bond, & a Note of hand of *Churchill*, who You know is dead; Mr Wilkes tells me there is money Enough for all his debts & money besides for his *Wife*, Miss *Carr*, whom he liv'd wᵗʰ &c &c—You'll do with both what is proper, but put in yʳ Claim . . .

Churchill You'll see paid me 40 pᵈˢ (I Think) of the Note—wᶜʰ is Either in yᵉ iron chest wᵗʰ yᵉ rest or in yᵉ table itself in yᵉ Study—*

Wilkes, who had slipped through the government's net and escaped to France the previous year, had been with Churchill when he died. He was living in high style in the Hôtel de Malthe, and it is clear from a note written towards the end of November that Garrick had been seeing something of him—and that he found his company strenuous:

Dear Sir

I was taken last Night in the Playhouse with a Shivering Fit, wᶜʰ was follow'd by a hot one.

I got home by yᵉ help of Madˡᵉ Clairon, and was much alarm'd wᵗʰ the disagreable Symptoms that Attack'd Me in the Stomick—these were succeeded by a Sickness & tho I had some Physick wᵗʰ Me, I took a puke & find myself much better this Morning [but not we]ll enough to meet You at Mr Huet's [?] I must be quiet for a day, or two or I shall suffer my Spirits are too much for me & particularly in Your Company. . .[25]

Their association throws interesting light on the fluidity of social relationships, and on how easily they could override political enmities. For some time past, after all, between Wilkes and Churchill on the one hand and Hogarth on the other, it had been war to the knife; Wilkes, expelled from the Commons earlier that year, had a matter of weeks previously been outlawed—this in consequence of his failure to appear at the Court of the King's Bench on charges of printing *Number 45* of the *North Briton* and publishing the obscene *Essay on Woman*;†

---

* *Letters*, 342. Garrick told George that he was sending the letter 'by my Friend Mr Burnett a most sensible Man, & a great Scotch lawyer'. James Burnett, later Lord Monboddo, was in Paris on legal business for the Duke of Queensberry.

† This parody of Pope's *Essay on Man* was read to the House of Lords by the Earl of Sandwich on 15 November 1763. One noble lord demanded that the reading cease, but others cried, 'Go on! Go on!'

Garrick was a close friend of William Murray, Lord Mansfield, the presiding judge who, in Wilkes's absence, had found him guilty on those charges. When Wilkes departed on a tour of Italy on Christmas Day the Garricks would take over his rather grand lodgings, close to the Opera and with a garden gate that opened directly on to the Tuileries.

It may well have been Wilkes who introduced Garrick to the salon of the baron d'Holbach. 'We had a fine laugh at Baron D'Albach's about the *Wicked Comp*^y I keep,' he wrote to Colman; 'I am always with that Set.'[26] Holbach was of German origin—he had been born at Heidelsheim in the Palatinate in 1723 and had studied at Leyden. Every Thursday and Sunday he entertained his fellow-*encyclopédistes* and a stream of foreign visitors at his elegant house in the rue Royale—the 'Café de l'Europe' as it came to be called. His contributions to the *Encyclopédie* consisted largely of articles on mineralogy and chemistry, chiefly from German sources. He would become best known for his *Christianisme dévoilé*, published in 1767 and *Le Système de la Nature*, which appeared three years later. He is supposed to be have been the model for Wolmar, the virtuous atheist in Rousseau's *La Nouvelle Héloïse*. Garrick always remembered him with affection. 'Let my most dear and worthy Baron d'Holback know that his kindnesses and attentions to us, when at Paris, are never out of our hearts and minds,' he wrote many years later.*

Garrick had returned to the French capital at an exciting moment. In 1765 that sprawling work-in-progress which was the *Encyclopédie* was at last nearing completion. Diderot, its inspired energizer and chief artificer, had written the prospectus for it fifteen years previously and had got out the first volume within months. By the time seven volumes had appeared, however, authority had become seriously alarmed at the speculative freedom he permitted his contributors; D'Alembert, his chief collaborator, lost heart and withdrew from the project and in 1759 the work had been formally suppressed and driven underground. Only recently, with the discreet support of such powerful figures as Madame de Pompadour and Choiseul, had it become possible to start supplying the 4,000 or so subscribers with the remaining ten volumes.

It was variously described as the gospel of Satan, a work of disorder and destruction and the Tower of Babel (Voltaire, this; he also said it was built half of marble, half of wood). It was, inevitably, very uneven, because although Voltaire himself, and Montesquieu, and Turgot, and Helvétius all contributed, so too did a host of unknowns—doctors, engineers, economists and lawyers, some of whom were more talented than others. The style is sometimes loose and discursive; not all of those who wrote for it were free of the dogmatism they deplored in others; editorial supervision was not all it might have been—there were occasional cross-references to articles which did not exist. D'Alembert compared it to a harlequin's coat, in which there was some good stuff but too

---

* *Letters*, 989. Letter dated 7 March 1776. Garrick was writing to Jean-Baptiste-Antoine Suard, a journalist who was one of d'Holbach's closest friends.

many rags. When it was too late Diderot, to his rage, discovered that after he had passed the proofs, the printer had mutilated many of the articles by cutting out anything which seemed likely to give offence.

Diderot's closest friend was Friedrich Melchior Grimm—'a kind of German Frenchman (no bad Mixture),' as Garrick later described him: 'he is lively, clever, & honourable—belov'd by his friends, & has no Enemies.'* Grimm was the son of a German pastor, and had come to Paris in 1748 after studying at Leipzig. Between the 1750s and the 1770s, unknown to almost all his contemporaries, he carried on an extensive correspondence with a number of crowned heads— Catherine the Great, Stanislas Poniatowski, King of Poland, and a number of German princelings. What began as a mainly literary correspondence developed into what was essentially a twice-monthly newsletter on the whole range of subjects which engaged the interest of the *encyclopédistes*—not only philosophy and politics, but the theatre and much else besides.

It is to Grimm that we owe the fullest account we have of the impact Garrick made in Paris with his 'salon' acting. 'The great art of David Garrick consists in the facility with which he abandons his own personality,' he wrote:

> He never oversteps truth, and he knows that other inconceivable secret of making his appearance increase in beauty by no other aid than that of passion. . . . Garrick is of middle stature, small rather than big. His face is agreeable, and wears a witty expression; his eyes are wonderfully animated. His vivacity is extreme. He has much wit, and his intelligence is keen and precise. He is a perfect monkey, (*il est naturellement singe*) imitating everything he sees; yet he always remains graceful. He has perfected his great talents by a profound study of nature and by researches full of shrewdness and of broadness of thought. For that purpose he is ever mingling with the crowd, and it is there that he comes on nature in all its native originality.

Garrick even seems to have won Grimm and his friends over to the view he had formed of the French classical theatre:

> He maintains that Racine, so beautiful and enchanting to read, cannot be acted, because he says everything, and leaves the actor nothing to do, and that, moreover, the harmony of Racine's verse necessitates a sort of sing-song far removed from true declamation. We soon agreed with Roscius-Garrick on all these points, we who form here a little flock of faithful believers, acknowledging Homer, Aeschylus and Sophocles for the law and the prophets, intoxicating ourselves with genius wherever it is to be found, without distinction of language or nation. The English Roscius was of the religion and church of our little flock.[27]

---

* *Letters*, 652. Garrick was writing, in 1771, to Mrs Montagu, 'Queen of the Blue-Stockings'. It is not strictly true that Grimm had no enemies. Rousseau certainly became one after Grimm succeeded him in the affections of Madame d'Epinay, and handled his old friend very roughly in the *Confessions*.

There was a price to be paid for this celebrity, and before Garrick had been a month in Paris he was obliged to write to George for assistance:

> I am so plagu'd here for my Prints or rather Prints of Me—that I must desire You to send me by ye first opportunity *six* prints from Reynolds's picture, You may apply to ye Engraver he lives in Leicester fields, & his name is Fisher, he will give you good ones, if he knows they are for Me— You must likewise send me a *King Lear* by *Wilson*, *Hamlet* d^o *Jaffier* & Belv[idera] by *Zoffani*, speak to him for two or 3, & what Else he may have done of Me—*

Garrick sat during this stay in Paris to the artist and playwright Louis Carrogis, who called himself Carmontelle. The portrait, a wash-drawing, was commissioned by the duc d'Orléans, and shows the tragic Garrick, dressed in blue, stepping towards a door from which emerges the comic Garrick, clad in red.†

Many of the people Garrick met at the Holbachs were also regular guests of Helvétius and his wife at their splendid mansion in the rue St Anne. He got on particularly well with the abbé Morellet, a notably unclerical cleric with a sharp wit and caustic tongue—Voltaire called him 'L'Abbé Mord-les' (i.e. 'Bite them').‡ Garrick was fascinated by his style of argument—his vehemence and the natural freedom of his gestures. Morellet wrote in his memoirs that when Garrick saw him locked in argument with Diderot or Marmontel he would sit with his arms crossed and look at them like an artist studying a face that he wished to draw.§

Garrick was also welcome at Madame Geoffrin's in the rue St Honoré. The widow of a rich manufacturer (her husband had made mirrors and been an officer in the National Guard), her walls were hung with pictures by Boucher, Vernet and Quentin de la Tour. On Monday, she entertained artists—here Garrick met the engraver Henri Gravelot and the sculptor Lemoine, to whom he sat for a bust that was exhibited at that year's *Salon*. Every Wednesday, Madame Geoffrin received her friends the *philosophes* and other men of letters. Unlike many of them, she continued to observe the forms of religion, and anyone who was openly disgraced incurred her displeasure. When Marmontel published his romance *Bélisaire* in 1767, and a chapter on religious toleration was censured by the Archbishop of Paris and the Sorbonne, he quickly fell from favour.

Although relatively few letters written by Garrick during these months in

---

* *Letters*, 343. The Reynolds picture was 'Garrick Between Tragedy and Comedy', exhibited at the Society of Artists three years previously. A pirated copy later went on sale in Paris under the title 'L'homme entre le vice et la vertu'.

† The same artist had already painted Sterne for the Duke's collection.

‡ André Morellet (1727–1819) was educated by the Jesuits in Lyons, his native town, and at the Sorbonne before taking holy orders. He was an economist, but wrote on a wide range of subjects.

§ 'Lorsqu'il me voyait aux prises avec Diderot ou Marmontel, il s'asseyait les bras croisés et nous regardait comme un dessinateur observant une figure qu'il veut saisir.' (Lemontey, P.E. (ed.), *Mémoires de l'Abbé Morellet*, Paris, 1822, i, 205.)

Paris have survived, we know something of the friendships he formed then from his later correspondence. One was with the dashing Chevalier de Chastellux, who had fought through the Seven Years War and was the author of a pamphlet on smallpox in which he supported Jenner's views on vaccination. He then turned his attention to music and literature, though his admiration for Garrick led him seriously to overreach himself with an appalling translation of *Romeo and Juliet.**

Garrick was also much in the company of a young journalist called Jean-Baptiste Suard, whom Madame Geoffrin and Marmontel had taken under their wing some years previously, and of the somewhat older Antoine de Laplace, a translator and miscellaneous writer for whom Madame de Pompadour had procured the post of director of *Le Mercure de France*. (He did not make a great success of it. By 1768 the number of subscribers had fallen by half, and he was persuaded to accept a pension and retire.)†

Garrick's most determined correspondent in later years, however, was to be the formidable Marie-Jeanne Riccoboni. Riccoboni had escaped from a miserable childhood into an early and equally miserable marriage to an Italian actor. Her father-in-law was the director of the Comédie-Italienne,‡ and for twenty-seven years she had been a member of the company, cast for the most part in comedy roles which she did not find congenial. She had retired from the stage only three or four years before her first meeting with Garrick; her pension of a thousand crowns made a welcome addition to what she earned from her writing, because she continued to support not only her 'graceless' mother but also her useless husband.§

For the past decade she had shared an apartment in the rue Poissonnière with an actress called Marie Thérèse Biancolelli. Her first book, *Lettres de mistress Fanny Butler*, had appeared in 1757, when she was forty-three, and by 1765 she had added four more. Marivaux was the most obvious French influence—in English translation they read like novels of sensibility in the style of Richardson or Henry Mackenzie.¶ Garrick would never meet her again, but he preserved thirty-eight of her letters, in which she kept him abreast of developments in literature, the kaleidoscopic shifts of French politics and the gossip and intrigues of the theatre and the salons. Garrick in return exerted himself to find translators for her novels, to promote their publication in England and to procure favourable reviews.

---

* Mlle de Lespinasse demolished it succinctly: 'Cela n'est pas mauvais, cela n'est pas médiocre, cela n'est pas même ennuyeux; cela est monstrueux, cela est à faire fuire.' (*Correspondance*, ii, 115.)

† De la Place had been educated at the English Jesuit College at Saint-Omer, where he was said to have learned English so well there that he forgot how to speak French; malicious tongues said that he never learned it again.

‡ Luigi Riccoboni was also a noted historian of continental drama. Garrick would eventually have half a dozen of his books in his library.

§ Her mother lived until 1769 and her husband until 1772.

¶ Three of her novels have English characters and purport to be translations from the English.

To Garrick she was 'Thou Dear, Wild, Agreeable Devil!' his 'Sweet, witty Barbarian', his 'dear, and very dear Riccoboni'. To her, he was 'the dearling of my heart', *'mon très-cher ami'*, 'my dear, my sweet friend' and 'the little acting manager'. She switched from French to English, often in mid-sentence, and occasionally lapsed into Italian. She sometimes addressed both Garrick and his wife in the same letter; happily, even Riccoboni at her most torrid appears not to have disturbed Mrs Garrick's habitual serenity.*

Garrick did not spend all his waking hours in Paris chattering to the *encyclopédistes*. He saw much of his old friend Monnet, now in easy circumstances. 'He is the gayest man at Paris,' Garrick told Colman. 'He has got Enough by his Operas to live happily, and has honorably paid all his debts that his unfortunate expedition to London brought upon him.'[28] Monnet was to become a sort of general factotum for Garrick. Over the years he would hire dancers for him, send him books and engravings, look after members of the Drury Lane company who came to Paris. For Mrs Garrick he would procure embroidered cuffs and silk petticoats; he also sent her the French original of *Forty-five Ways of Dressing the Hair*, an aid to fashion that was to remain in vogue almost until the end of the century.†

Garrick also renewed his acquaintance with many of the leading French players of the day—with La Clairon and Dumesnil, with Préville and Le Kain. With Préville he struck up a particularly close friendship—not something he had ever done with a fellow-actor in England. A decade or so later he wrote a letter of introduction to Préville for Domenico Angelo's son Henry, who had been sent to Paris to learn French and polish up his fencing. His letter began with a question: *'Ne m'avez vous pas oublié mon cher Compagnon en ivresse?'* There may well have been occasions when they had cracked a bottle or two together: Garrick, however, was referring not to their convivial moments but to a particular incident. The story had gone the rounds in Paris, and Grimm had felt it deserved a place in his *Correspondance*:

> *Un jour, en revenant avec Préville, à cheval, du bois de Boulogne,* [Garrick] *lui dit: 'Je m'en vais faire l'homme ivre; faites-en autant.' Ils traversèrent ainsi le village de Passy, sans dire un mot, et, en un clin d'oeil, tout le village fut assemblé pour les voir passer. Les jeunes gens se moquèrent d'eux, les femmes crièrent de peur de les voir tomber de cheval, les vieillards haussèrent les épaules et en eurent pitié, ou, suivant leur humeur, poufferent de rire. En sortant du village, Préville dit à Garrick: 'Ai-je bien fait, mon*

---

* *Boaden*, ii, 435. Letter dated 15 May 1765. 'O quelle longue lettre!' Riccoboni wrote shortly after Garrick had returned to England. 'Patience; je finis. Vous me donnerez bien le tems de vous embrasser, peut-être? . . . Voulez-vous me baiser,—si, o, no? Addio amico mio diletissimo; baccio, no i mani de vostra Signoria, ma bene gli vostri occhi malitiosi . . .' Garrick sent a suitably roguish reply: 'How could a Lady of Y^r wit & delicacy, make so good a Creature as Mrs Garrick (whom you pretend to love, & admire too) so jealous by writing such a flattering Love-Letter to her husband? . . .'
† Monnet, in a letter dated 20 November 1767, described it as *'un livre fait par un perruquier nommé Le Gros, qui indique 45 façons de se coiffer'*.

maître?'—*'Bien, fort bien, en vérité,' lui dit Garrick; 'mais vous n'étiez pas ivre des jambes.'**

Garrick, for his part, developed a high regard for his friend's versatility, and dwelt on it admiringly in a sketch of Préville which Suard had asked him to write for the *Gazette littéraire*:

> He performs no less than five different parts in a comedy (not a good one) called the *Mercure galant*. In the first, he is a miserable, half-starved, sneaking compound of flattery and absurdity; in the second, he represents a shrewd, sly, suspicious, obstinate *campagnard*—both which, though whimsical, are made natural by his manner of playing them; in the third, he is a Swiss soldier, most importantly drunk without grimace; in the fourth, he swells his figure and features into the full-blown pride, pomp, and passionate arrogance of a serjeant-at-law, and then in a moment changes himself totally, and enters with all the soft, smirking, self-conceited, familiar insignificance of a scribbling Abbé. His performance of this last character, perhaps, equals anything that was ever seen upon any stage; no humour or comic passion escapes him. . .†

Garrick held back from expressing himself with complete frankness. 'I have not said all that might be said upon Preville,' he told Suard. 'I have given the bright side without the shades.' And he added, characteristically, 'I had rather be thought a good friend, than a fine painter.'‡

Garrick also left unsaid some of what he thought about La Clairon. To her face, he uttered the eighteenth-century equivalent of 'Dahling, you were mahvellous', but behind the façade there was a penetrating critical intelligence at work; some years later, to a German correspondent, he disclosed his reservations:

> She has every thing that Art and a good understanding, with great Natural Spirit can give her—But then I fear (and I only tell you my fears, and open

---

* *Grimm, op. cit.*, vi, 320: 'One day, returning with Préville on horseback from the Bois de Boulogne, Garrick said to him: 'I'm going to pretend to be drunk; you do the same.' They passed through the village of Passy, without saying a word, and in an instant the whole village turned out to see them go by. The young folk jeered at them, the women screamed for fear of seeing them fall from their horses, the old men either shrugged pityingly or roared with laughter. As they left the village, Préville said to Garrick: 'Did I do all right, Master?' 'Oh yes, very well indeed,' said Garrick—'except that your legs weren't drunk.'

Noverre has a similar story. Garrick, pretending to be drunk on his return from an outing on horseback, makes an attempt at clearing a wall and falls to the ground. Préville, completely taken in, rushes to his aid, whereupon Garrick, his eyes half-closed, murmurs, 'Is that a glass of rum you've brought me?' and then bursts into roars of laughter. (*Lettres sur les arts imitateurs*, ii, 191.)

† At Colman's urging, Garrick offered his pen-portrait of Préville to the *St James's Chronicle*, and it appeared there in the issue of 22–4 June 1765.

‡ *Letters*, 362. When Préville published his memoirs, he awarded the palm to his friend without reservation: 'Garrick n'eut de rival dans aucun pays, et le titre qu'il mérita [i.e. Roscius] est encore vacant.' (*Mémoires de Préville*, Paris, 1823.)

my Soul to You) the Heart has none of those instantaneous feelings, that Life blood, that keen Sensibility, that bursts at once from Genius, and like Electrical fire shoots thro' the Veins, Marrow, Bones and all, of every Spectator.—Madm *Clairon* is so conscious and certain of what she can do, that she never (I believe) had the feelings of the instant come upon her unexpectedly.—but I pronounce that the greatest strokes of Genius, have been unknown to the Actor himself, 'till Circumstances, and the warmth of the Scene has sprung the Mine as it were, as much to his own Surprize, as that of the Audience—Thus I make a great difference between a great Genius, and a good Actor.*

'I have with great Freedom communicated my Ideas of acting,' Garrick wrote, 'but you must not betray me my good Friend; The Clairon wou'd never forgive me, tho' I call'd her an excellent Actress, if I did not swear by all the Gods, that she was the greatest Genius too.'

Garrick had now been abroad for some fifteen months. It was a longer absence than he had planned, but the ambivalence with which he contemplated his return to London is clear from one of his letters to Colman:

You wish me in Southampton Street—& so do I wish myself there, but not for Acting or Managing, but to see you, my Dr Colman, & other Friends—ye Doctors all have forbid me thinking of Business—I have at present lost all taste for ye Stage—it was once my greatest Passion, & I labor'd for many years like a true Lover—but I am grown cold—should my desires return, I am the Town's humble Servant again—tho she is a great Coquette, & want Youth, vigorous Youth, to bear up against her occasional Capriciousness—[29]

In his absence from Drury Lane that 'vigorous Youth' had been supplied to some extent by Charles Holland. Sixteen years younger than Garrick, he had been a member of the company since 1755. A handsome bachelor with a reputation as something of a gallant, he had been criticized for modelling himself too closely on Garrick,† but in the master's absence he acquitted himself creditably in such capital roles as Hamlet, Romeo and Richard.

Holland, however, was speedily eclipsed by a theatrical unknown. Horace Walpole, in a letter to Mann in Florence barely a month after Garrick's departure

---

* *Ibid.*, 528. Garrick was writing, early in 1769, to Helfrich Peter Sturz, a keen student of the theatre, who, though born and educated in Germany, had held several appointments in the Danish court, and would accompany Christian VII on his tour of England and France in 1768–9.

† Churchill, in *The Rosciad*, had been particularly savage:

> Next Holland came—with truly tragic stalk,
> He creeps, he flies—a hero should not walk . . .
> The actor who would hold a solid fame,
> Must imitation's servile arts disclaim:
> Act from himself, on his own bottom stand;
> I hate e'en Garrick thus at second-hand.

from England, had scarcely been able to contain his feline excitement: 'Have you got Mr Garrick yet? If you have, you may keep him,' he wrote:

> —there is come forth within these ten days a young actor, who has turned the heads of the whole town. The first night of his appearance the audience, not content with clapping, stood up and shouted. His name is Powel; he was clerk to Sir Robert Ladbroke, and so clever in business, that his master would have taken him in partner, but he had an impulse for the stage— was a *heaven-born hero*, as Mr Pitt called my Lord Clive. His figure is fine, and voice most sonorous—as they say, for I wait for the rebound of his fame, and till I can get in, for at present all the boxes are taken for a month.[30]

William Powell was twenty-three at the time, and had made the acquaintance of Holland in the various spouting clubs they had both frequented as teenagers. It was Holland who had introduced him to Garrick, and the young man made such an impression that he was offered an immediate engagement; indeed, Garrick had invited him down to Hampton before leaving for France and coached him in several parts. These included the title role in Beaumont and Fletcher's *Philaster*, and it was in this that he had made his triumphant début, in spite of a severe attack of nerves—'he was so very much frightened, he could not speak for some time,' Hopkins noted in his diary, 'and, when he did, the tears ran fast down his cheeks,—but he soon recovered himself, and went through the part with a great deal of nature and feeling,—Continued claps and huzza of bravo! &c. &c.'*

He played the part thirteen times before the end of the month, one evening before the King and Queen. Hopkins reported that the King seemed 'vastly pleased' and that after the play 'he sent Lord Huntington to return Mr Powell thanks in his name for the entertainment he gave them, and his good wishes for his success'.[31]

For the rest of the season the town was at his feet. His second role was Jaffier in *Venice Preserv'd* and he followed this with Posthumus in *Cymbeline*; he was greatly applauded in both (though Hopkins thought that in the latter he was 'very Wild and Stampt too much with his foot').† Early in the new year he again challenged comparison with Garrick when he apeared as Lusignan in *Zara*, and his first season continued with Lord Townly in *The Provok'd Husband*, Alexander in *The Rival Queens* and the title role in *Oroonoko*. For his benefit he played

---

* Davies confirms the brilliance of his success. 'Foote was in the boxes,' he adds, 'and was the only snarler in the house; he endeavoured to laugh those who sat near him out of there feelings, but the power of nature was too strong for the efforts of wit.' (*Davies*, ii, 69).

† Davies also had reservations: 'Amongst his worst failings we may reckon an inclination sometimes to rant and bluster, and sometimes a propensity to whine and blubber. There is no part of acting so difficult as that sort of feeling which is expressed by loud sorrow; the tragic tear, if too wantonly shed, becomes ridiculous.' (*Davies*, ii, 91–2.) Davies also says that Powell was round-shouldered; Murphy, on the other hand, writes that 'the habit of projecting his head forward, gave him the appearance of being high-shouldered'; he ought, he suggests, 'to have frequented a school for grown gentlemen to dance.' (*Murphy*, ii, 7.)

Othello, and made a profit of more than £200: 'This Night there was the greatest over flow ever known,' Hopkins recorded. The crush was so great that after the play had begun it was necessary to lower the curtain for fifteen minutes so that the ladies might push their way to their seats. By the end of the season, he had appeared in seventeen different roles. There were two opportunities to try Garrick's crown for size which he was wise enough to forgo; in *Richard III* he opted to play Henry VI, and in *Hamlet* he contented himself with the part of the Ghost.

Barry apart, no player had enjoyed such instant success since Garrick himself first burst upon the scene. Lacy told Davies that the season had been as profitable as any he had known and took a certain amount of pleasure in assuring Garrick that 'he need not abandon any pleasure or amusement which he enjoyed abroad, from any anxiety which he might possibly feel on account of the theatre at home'.*

There is no evidence to support the suggestion that Garrick was made jealous and uneasy by the success of his young protégé. 'I hope that Pow[e]l will continue to please,' he wrote to George from Munich, although he added, 'He must have a [M]aster to watch his English wch I suppose Coley will do.'[32] A letter which Garrick received from Powell some months after his début left no doubt that the young man deeply appreciated what Garrick had done for him:

> . . . I am confident I can never cease to think that all the gratitude which can possess the heart of man, is due to *you* from *me*; for you, Sir, laid the foundation of all, by your kind care of me during the course of last summer . . .[33]

Garrick did not get round to replying until his return to Paris, but from there in December 1764 he wrote a long and cordial letter: 'If you will give an older Soldier leave to hint a little advice to You; I will answer for its being sincere at least, which from a Brother Actor is no Small Merit.' He impressed on Powell the importance of preparation, urging him to spend in study 'those Hours which Young Men too generally give to their Friends & fflatterers':

> The common excuse is, that they frequent Clubs for the Sake of their Benefit; but nothing can be more absurd or contemptible.—Your Benefits will only encrease with your fame, & Should that Ever sink by your Idleness, those friends who have made you idle, will be the first to forsake You—When the publick has mark'd you for a favourite (& their favor must be purchas'd wth Sweat & labour) You may chuse what Company you please, and none but the best can be of service to you. . . . Study hard, my friend for Seven Years, & you may play the rest of your life . . . But above all, never let your Shakespear be out of your hands, or your Pocket— Keep him about you, as a Charm—[34]

---

* *Davies*, ii, 72–3. It also came to Garrick's ears that Lacy had pronounced Powell to be the better actor. (*Letters*, 351.)

The lease of the apartments which the Garricks were renting was due to expire on 1 April, and he counted on being in England by the middle of that month. Before the end of January, however, he was already preoccupied with preparing the ground for his return. 'Suppose there was an Extract of a Letter from Paris?' he suggested to Colman—'in wch many things may be mentioned & y^r friend among ye rest, that it take off all suspicion from me: I should be glad that you would add, diminish, correct, & blow a little pepper into ye tail of ye following Nonsense.'* Just how much pepper Colman felt Garrick's draft needed is not known, but a paragraph duly appeared in the *St James's Chronicle* little more than a week later:

> Now I am up on Theatricals, & cannot omit mentioning Garrick, whom you have enquired after: I have met him often in the Bois de Boulogne. He looked miserable indeed when he first came here, and so much brought down by a Fever he caught in Germany, that he seemed fitter to go through a Hoop at Sadler's-Wells, than to play Tragedy or Comedy at Drury Lane. Within this fortnight or three weeks he looks much better and will be well again soon, if the Wits and other wicked Company that he keeps do not kill him with kindness. If I am rightly informed, you are in woeful want of him in London, both as Actor and Manager.[35]

When Garrick saw it in print, he had second thoughts. 'My dear Colman you frighten'd me with ye Extract of a Lett^r from Paris,' he wrote:

> I am very sorry that you mentioned y^e *woeful want of me as Manag^r & Act^r*—they will suspect it came from me, & I have no right to say so much. . . I beg that you will do all you can to make them not think ye paragraph mine, if I am suspected—I never in my life prais'd myself knowingly except a little matter in y^e *Fribbleriad*, wch always pinch'd me—perhaps I am too sensible about this delicacy . . . I desir'd you to say something *against* me, & you stuck y^r Pen in y^r heart, & wrote as you felt—I wish from my Soul that you had not . . .†

He was already busy with a much more ambitious piece of self-promotion, however, and early in March he warned Colman to expect 'a little parcel'. It was, he said, 'a Fable I have written, *ye Sick Monkey*, to be publish'd at my

---

* *Letters*, 347. 'I write in confusion,' Garrick told Colman at the end of this letter, 'for ye Ambassador's Private Secretary has promis'd to send this for me in his packet & the man waits for it.' The Private Secretary who was extending the courtesy of the diplomatic bag to Garrick was David Hume, who had come to Paris two years previously with Lord Hertford; in spite of his lumbering gait and lack of small talk, *le bon David* was received in the salons with quite as much honour as Garrick.

† *Ibid.*, 350. Years later Colman's son, who did not entertain particularly warm feelings towards Garrick, commented acidly on this exercise in self-advertisement: 'Oh, Garrick, Garrick! that a man, of true talent, (whether fully aware of his established fame or not,) should forget the dignity of genius, and descend to this!!!' (Colman, George, the Younger, *Random Records*, 2 vols., London, 1830, i. 271.)

return—Severe upon myself.' He had gone to very considerable pains, and commissioned Gravelot to engrave a print for it. 'For Heaven's sake take care to be Secret,' he adjured Colman—'when Becket gives it to be publish'd, he must swear the Printer to Secresy for fear of offending Me.'[36]

He was still plagued by doubts about how he would be received, and two days later he shot off another long letter to Colman. 'I must intreat you to be very sincere with me,' he wrote:

> Do the Town in general really wish to see me on ye Stage? or are they (which I rather think ye truth) as cool about it as their humble Servant?— I have no maw for it at all, & yet something must be done to restore our credit: that I may be able to play, & as well as Ever, I will not deny, but that I am able to do so as I have done, wear & tear, I neither must or can, or will . . .

Apart from his professed lack of stomach for a return to the fray, there remained a question mark over his health. The fever had gone, but he still suffered from headaches and indigestion:

> The Physicians here, Dr Gem among the rest, advise me, to a man, against appearing again—I had a little nervous attack last week, & the D^r croakt more hoarse than usual against my thinking to do as formerly. Tranquillity & retirem^t from business (he says) are the only means to make me Myself again.*

Garrick set out for home shortly after Easter. He left the French capital with regret: 'I don't know a more agreeable Company, & where wit & true Social liberty reign so triumphantly,' he wrote.[37]

He would never return, but France and many of the friends he made there remained important to him for the rest of his life—more than half of the 2,700 books in his library at the time of his death were in French. He was to have some influence on literature in France, and his name and reputation were to prove remarkably enduring there. Diderot, for instance, would invite his comments on his essay *Le Paradoxe sur le Comédien* before it was published, and when Beaumarchais was in England in 1774 as an agent for the French government he read the manuscript of his *Barbier de Séville* to Garrick and gratefully accepted a suggestion for improving a scene in the second act.† In revolutionary France, when critics wrote about the celebrated tragedian François-Joseph Talma,‡ it

---

* *Letters*, 353. Richard Gem, a man of roughly Garrick's own age, was physician to the British Embassy. He knew most of the *encyclopédistes* and met many prominent English visitors socially.

† Garrick suggested giving opium to Bartolo's valet L'Eveillé and showing him still drowsy on the stage.

‡ Talma (1763–1826) practised briefly as a dentist before making his début at the Comédie-Française in 1787 in Voltaire's *Mahomet*. He became a friend of Napoleon's, and was for a time the lover of Pauline Bonaparte. He was the first French actor to play Roman parts in a

was Garrick with whom he was most frequently compared; his name also crops up in the work of nineteenth-century writers on English literature such as Sainte-Beuve and Taine.

When Frank Hedgcock was preparing his thesis on Garrick for presentation to the Sorbonne in the early years of this century, he was told a curious tale by a French academic. As a child, his mother used to say that if he was not good, 'Garrigues the Englishman' would come and get him—'the threat was accompanied with a grimace that perpetuated the actor's reputation as a pantomimist'.*

An ogre. A bogeyman. Not merely famous, but the stuff of legend in the land of his forebears. That would have tickled Garrick's vanity most deliciously.

---

toga instead of contemporary dress and worked to suppress the exaggerations of the declamatory style.

* Hedgcock's informant was Mario Roques, a professor at the Ecole des Langues Orientales.

24

The Sick Monkey Restored

> Return'd from travel to your native shore,
>   Again to make us laugh or cry,
> To turn your back, we hope, no more,
>   Nor from your colours fly.
>
> Whether you fled for health, or quiet,
> Harrass'd with rule, or sick with riot,
> Or whether you have kept us lean,
>   As slander says,
>   With lenten plays,
> To make our appetites more keen;
> Whether it be this or that,
>   No matter what,
> For we before the curtain see but blindly . . .

The Sick Monkey, 'a Fable addressed to Mr Garrick, upon his Arrival', appeared a week after his return home. He himself is the monkey, and the other creatures—the hog, the ass, the toad, the viper—are the enemies whose malice had driven him abroad. Prosy old Tom Davies did not see in the least blindly: 'He was resolved to put in practice his usual method of preventing censure, and blunting the edge of ridicule, by anticipation.'[1] It is quite the silliest thing Garrick ever wrote, and his description of it as a fable must have had Aesop and La Fontaine turning indignantly in the grave. Luckily for him, its publication passed largely unnoticed. 'It died almost still-born,' wrote Davies. 'In short, he missed his aim; for having no enemies to fight with, his shafts spent themselves idly in the air.'*

Garrick was clearly gratified by the warmth of the welcome he received on

---

* *Davies*, ii, 96. Garrick managed to convince himself that things were otherwise. 'The *Sick Monkey* is publish'd, & makes a noise,' he wrote to Suard. 'It was thought at first to be a terrible satire, & none of the papers (so much were their Authors & publishers my friends) would advertise it—but at present they begin to find out the joke & the Sale will be a great one. it is a most profound Secret who is the Author, and I beg that you will keep it so—' (*Letters*, 358. Letter dated 7 May 1765.)

his return.* In one letter he talks of 'a multiplicity of business and friendly congratulations since I have been at home'[2] and a fortnight after his return he told Suard that he had met with a most gracious reception at court, but that he had not yet answered 'the general question from all sorts of people— *Whether I shall act again?*' The London stage, he wrote, 'is at present in a declining state, and must have some assistance from me either as actor, manager, or both'.[3] By the time he wrote to Le Kain a couple of months later, however, he sounded like a man who had decided to devote himself to the cultivation of his garden:

> *Mes résolutions sont prises, et nonobstant que j'ai été reçu de mes compat-riotes d'une manière la plus honorable pour moi, je suis presque déterminé de quitter le théâtre comme comédien, tout de suite, et aussitôt que je le pourrais, comme directeur. Je suis très-heureux avec ma femme, ma famille et ma fortune, et il n'est pas dans le pouvoir du premier homme, dans le royaume, de me faire le moindre tort . . .†*

For the moment he plunged back into the familiar social round. He dined with Charles Townshend, who had just become Paymaster-General on the dismissal of Fox, he sat in the gallery of the Commons while the Regency Bill was debated‡ and he and Mrs Garrick went down to Mistley Hall in Essex to stay with Richard Rigby, who had recently been appointed Vice-Treasurer of Ireland.§

Another friend who had recently secured advancement was Edmund Burke, who had become private secretary to the Marquess of Rockingham, the new First Lord of the Treasury. He had also recently acquired an estate, Gregories, near Beaconsfield, where he was enjoying living beyond his means in the guise of a country gentleman. 'We have now got a little settled in our New habitation,' he wrote. 'When will you and Mrs Garrick come and make it complete to us by your Company for a day or two?'[4] Garrick was never easy to pin down. On another occasion Burke tried to tempt him down to Buckinghamshire by present-ing Gregories as a place where he might 'repose your person and understand-ing on early hours, boiled Mutton, drowsy conversation, and a little Clabber Milk'.[5]

Quin came up from Bath during the summer and spent some convivial days

---

* His dog Phill, however, was so miserable to be back in Southampton Street that Garrick returned him for good to the care of the Burney children. His place in the Garrick household was taken by an English mastiff called Dragon. This enormous beast was generally kept at Hampton, though he did on one occasion come up to town to appear on stage at Drury Lane.

† *Letters*, 368. 'My mind is made up, and although I have been received with great honour by my countrymen, I have all but decided to give up as an actor straight away and as soon as I can as manager. I am very happy with my wife, my family and my fortune, and not even the first man in the kingdom can do me the least harm.'

‡ George III had been ill for three months earlier in the year and wished to make provision for a regency. The measure had already been passed by the Lords.

§ Rigby, who already held the Mastership of the Rolls in Ireland, received a salary of £3,500 as Vice-Treasurer. His real ambition was the immensely lucrative Paymaster-Generalship, and this he would achieve three years later.

at Hampton—'an excursion,' his biographer wrote, 'productive of the most agreeable sallies of wit and merriment.'[6] Garrick also went to stay with Mrs Cibber at West Woodhay. They had corresponded since his return, and she had taken it very ill to hear that he was contemplating retirement:

> I have friendship enough for you to wish to know particulars with regard to your health, which you were lazy enough never to mention, yet could cruelly knock me down with hinting all our amours were at an end, and if I had any thought of playing the fool again it should be by myself. This is so unpleasing a situation that I believe, like yourself, I shall take care of number one, and leave them a clear stage and all the favour they can get.[7]

Garrick had an ulterior motive in going to see her in Berkshire. If he did decide to return to the stage, he badly wanted Mrs Cibber's support. It was plain from her letters, however, that no amount of flattery delivered at long-range would win him that; his only hope was to go down to the country and woo her in person. The visit meant a great deal to her, and she wrote to thank him with all the skittish lightness of heart of earlier days:

> You cannot imagine how much we are obliged to you and sweet Mrs Garrick, for your kind intentions of looking upon us at Woodhay . . . Our common way of passing our time is in lively jokes, smart repartees, etc. . . . My very parrot is the wonder of the time!; equally excellent in the sock or buskin, and when you come, shall cut a joke and tip you a tragedy stiffle that will make your very foretop stand on end. As I hoped to be saved! I have taught him to speak tragedy . . .[8]

Garrick came away with her promise that she would appear with him as soon as she felt strong enough. We do not know what impression he formed of her state of health, because no mention of the visit survives in his correspondence, but another visitor to West Woodhay that summer saw very clearly that she was dying. Charles Burney went to see her with the score of his new comic opera, *The Cunning Man.* She was eager to appear in the part of Phoebe that winter and they rehearsed it together every day for a week, but Burney did not believe that she would sing again on any stage—'her voice,' he wrote, 'however sweet and touching, was too much in decay, as well as her constitution.'[9]

Garrick had not been home very long before he discovered that one of his oldest friendships was not in very good repair. For several years past Johnson had been hovering on the verge of a breakdown. 'I would suffer a limb to be amputated to recover my spirits,' he had said one day to his friend Dr Adams. He had written virtually nothing since 1760 and fallen into a distressing state of helplessness; there are entries in his journal which show that he was frequently in the grip of anxiety and sometimes of despair. Early in 1765, however, he had met the Thrales, an event which was to prove of immense importance for his life and happiness. The very next day he entered in his diary the words 'Corrected a sheet'—the first reference for several years to his edition of Shakespeare.

It was nine years since Johnson had issued his proposals and solicited subscriptions, and he had promised publication then by Christmas 1757. Churchill's famous gibe dates from 1762: *He for subscribers baits his hook,/ And takes their cash—but where's the Book?* Now, when he had finally pulled himself together and publication seemed likely within a few months, George came running to tell his brother that Johnson believed that he was not among the subscribers. Garrick immediately put pen to paper:

> Dear Sir,
>
>   My brother greatly astonished me this morning by asking me, "if I was a subscriber to your Shakespeare?" I told him yes, that I was one of the first, and as soon as I had heard of your intention. . . . I hope that you will recollect it, and not think me capable of neglecting to make you so trifling a compliment, which was doubly due from me, not only on account of the respect I have always had for your abilities, but from the sincere regard I shall ever pay to your friendship.[10]

We do not know how Johnson responded to this rather stilted note, but when the eight volumes appeared in October, there was a passage in the preface which was widely taken to be aimed at Garrick: 'I collated such copies as I could procure, and wished for more, but have not found the collectors of these rarities very communicative.' Johnson was, of course, notoriously careless with books, and word had got about how he had treated volumes that had been lent to him for the *Dictionary*. Garrick, however, made no secret of the fact that he felt aggrieved at being lumped together with these unnamed reluctant lenders, and Boswell took the matter up with Johnson:

> I told him that Garrick had complained to me of it, and had vindicated himself by assuring me that Johnson was made welcome to the full use of his collection, and that he left the key of it with a servant with orders to have a fire and every convenience for him. I found Johnson's notion was that Garrick wanted to be courted for them, and that, on the contrary, Garrick should have courted him, and sent him the plays of his own accord.*

Garrick had a second reason for feeling disgruntled with his old friend at this time. During the winter of 1763–4, sitting one evening at Johnson's fireside, Joshua Reynolds had proposed that they should form a dining club. Johnson was enthusiastic. The plan was that a small group of friends should meet weekly at the Turk's Head in Gerrard Street. The other founding members were John Hawkins, Goldsmith, Burke and his father-in-law, the physician Christopher Nugent, Bennet Langton and Topham Beauclerk, and Anthony Chamier, who

---

* *Life*, ii, 192. Mrs Thrale suggests that Garrick had another reason for being offended: 'Mr Johnson being told that Garrick took umbrage at not being mentioned in His edition of Shakespear: why what is it to me says he as Editor of Shakespear, that Mr Garrick can mouthe a Tragedy,—or skip a Comedy?—' Thrale, Hester, *Thraliana: The Diary of Mrs Hester Lynch Thrale (Later Mrs. Piozzi) 1776–1809*, edited by Katharine C. Balderston, 2 vols., Oxford, 1942, i, 176–7.

had been a stockbroker and later went into politics.* The club met for the first time in February 1764. Hearing about it from Reynolds on his return from abroad, Garrick, by Boswell's account, said 'I like it much, I think I shall be of you.' Johnson, however, took a different view: 'How does he know we will permit him? the first duke in England has no right to hold such language.' Mrs Thrale's version of how Johnson reacted (jealously denied by Boswell) is somewhat racier: 'If Garrick does apply, I'll blackball him.—Surely, one ought to sit in a society like ours,

> "Unelbow'd by a gamester, pimp, or player".'

Hawkins, in his *Life*, claims that he himself favoured Garrick's admission, but that Johnson opposed it, saying, 'He will disturb us by his buffoonery.' This too Boswell dismisses as inaccurate, but he is silent on why it was that Garrick was not finally admitted until 1773—eight years after Bishop Percy and Robert Chambers and five years after George Colman.†

When Drury Lane opened in September 1765 Garrick was still being coy about his intentions. Most of the leading parts which would formerly have been his— Romeo, Macbeth, Lothario, Lear—were again assigned to Holland and Powell. There is, however, a clue to what he was angling for in the letter from Mrs Cibber quoted above—a letter, it should be remembered, written before the start of the season:

> And now, Sir, let me tell you, I should be excessively shocked at your intention of quitting the stage, if I did not hope that the judgment, taste, and authority of that great Personage you hint at, would put it out of your power to keep such a barbarous resolution!

Garrick had easy access to the entourage of that 'great Personage', and a letter which survives to his friend Richard Berenger, Gentleman of the Horse to the King, shows how the little game was played. 'I am Sorry that I was not at home, when you call'd upon me,' Garrick wrote:

> Mrs Garrick tells me, that You desire to know in writing, what are my intentions with regard to the Stage—You know that I had some time ago labour'd so much, that I was oblig'd to retire from the fatigues of the Theatre, (By the order of Doctor Barry & others) to recruit my Self abroad; I was unluckily seiz'd with a Malignant Fever in Germany that fell upon my Spirits, and tho' I am now much better than I was, yet I fear the double business of Manager, & Actor, would be too violent for me, & therefore I had determin'd from Necessity to give up Acting; as the pursuing

---

* Chamier (1725–80) was of Huguenot descent. In the 1770s he would serve as deputy Secretary at War and Under-Secretary of State, and he was briefly MP for Tamworth. He had a country house at Streatham, near the Thrales, and Johnson was a frequent visitor there.
† Boswell himself was also elected in 1773. Personalities apart, Johnson took the view that if the membership rose above nine, general discussion would become impossible.

both might have disagreeable Consequences—this Sir was my Resolution, which can be only broke thro' by a Command; which my duty, my Pride, my inclination, & my Gratitude, will always make me obey. . . .[11]

Garrick, who was an orderly correspondent, kept a copy of his letter and filed it away with an endorsement—'Copy of a Letter to Berenger with Mr Ramus's Answer'. Nicholas Ramus, a Senior Page of the Backstairs, was the courtier who had charge of the King's entertainments. Garrick announced the success of the ploy in a note to George:

> Dear Brother,   November 9, 1765
> His Majesty has desir'd me to appear again to Oblige him & the Queen.
> I shall Obey their Commands, but only for a few Nights; my resolution is
> to draw my Neck as well as I can out of ye Collar, & sit quietly with my
> wife & books by my fire-side—

The command performance—the play chosen was *Much Ado About Nothing*—took place five nights later. Garrick had composed a suitably arch prologue for the occasion:

> With doubt—joy—apprehension almost dumb,
> Once more to face this awful court I come . . .
> I'm told (what flattery to my heart!) that you
> Have wish'd to see me, nay have press'd it too . . .

(a respectful bow at this point in the direction of the royal box). He reminded his audience that it was now twenty-four years since he had first appeared before them:

> A very nine-pin, I, my stage-life through,
> Knock'd down by wits, set up again by you.

He was only forty-eight, but poetic licence allowed him, in conclusion, to compare himself with a resident of the Royal Hospital:

> The Chelsea pensioner, who, rich in scars,
> Fights o'er in prattle all his former wars;
> Tho' past the service, may the young ones teach,
> To march—present—to fire—to mount the breach.
> Should the drum beat to arms, at first he'll grieve
> For wooden leg, lost eye—and armless sleeve;
> Then cocks his hat, looks fierce, and swells his chest;
> 'Tis for my King, and zounds, I'll do my best!

The evening was a triumph. 'The joy of the audience,' wrote Davies, 'was expressed, not in the usual methods of clapping of hands and clattering of sticks, but in loud shouts and huzzas.'* The sick monkey's convalescence was at an end.

---

* *Davies*, ii, 97. There was in fact, a disturbance at Drury Lane that evening, but it had nothing to do with Garrick's reappearance. The theatres had just been closed for ten days because of the death of the Duke of Cumberland, and those members of the audience who were not dressed

From Woodhay, Mrs Cibber wrote that on the day of the performance, he had been 'the subject of my thoughts and discourse the whole day'. She was full of admiration for his prologue. 'I have taken it into my head that you have planned it upon Horace's First Epistle to Maecenas,' she told him, 'as it is so strikingly applicable and fine for your purpose.'[12]

She usually referred to her illness as 'nerves'. 'This cold, damp weather plays the vengeance with my delicacy,' she wrote. 'I wish with Lady Townshend that my nerves were made of cart ropes.'* But she left West Woodhay at the end of November, and agreed on her arrival in London that she would play opposite Garrick in *Venice Preserved*. Garrick immediately saw to it that a short puff appeared in the press: 'Mrs Cibber is come to town and so well recovered as to be able to appear in Belvidera the latter end of the week.'

A message from the palace led to a change of plan. The King and Queen wished to honour Mrs Cibber and Garrick by their presence the following Thusday, but expressed the wish to see a comedy. There was nothing for it but to substitute *The Provok'd Wife*; majesty was entertained by Garrick and Mrs Cibber in the parts of Sir John and Lady Brute.

Benjamin Victor, the theatre's treasurer, was watching from the wings. He had known Susannah since she was a young singer in her teens. Tonight, he sadly observed her tremor and strained to hear her barely audible voice: 'It was the last, and I am sorry to say, the worst performance of her life.'[13] After the curtain came down, she was helped to her house in Scotland Yard. She died there at the end of January at the age of fifty-one. Garrick decreed that Drury Lane should remain dark that night and Beard followed suit at Covent Garden. The gesture was without precedent—normally the theatres closed only on the death of royalty or at the passing of some national hero. She was buried a week later in the North Cloister of Westminster Abbey.

Tradition has it that when the news of her death was brought to Garrick he exclaimed theatrically, 'Then half of Tragedy is dead!' Later, he spoke less gallantly but much more interestingly about her:

> She was the greatest female plague belonging to my house. I could easily parry the artless thrusts and despise the coarse language of some of my other heroines; but whatever was Cibber's object, a new part or a new dress, she was always sure to carry her point by the acuteness of her invective and the steadiness of her perseverance.[14]

A week before Mrs Cibber's death Garrick had again performed by royal command, appearing on this occasion both as Lusignan in *Zara* and as Lord Chalkstone in his own *Lethe*. Hopkins was full of praise: 'It is almost

---

in black were abused and in some cases assaulted by those who were. 'One young gentleman from Bond Street had a sword run into his eye.' (*Winston MS* 9.)

* *Boaden*, i, 208. Lady Townshend was the wife of Charles, third Viscount Townshend. During the 1750s and 60s she showed great stoicism in the face of a whole chapter of family vicissitudes— the death of several children, the elopement of a daughter and the prolonged absence of several sons in foreign wars. (See Sherson, Errol, *The Lively Lady Townshend*, London, 1926.)

Aaron Hill's Zara – Mrs Yates in the title role and Garrick as Lusignan. It was
during a performance of Zara in 1766 that Mrs Garrick had to hold on to
Rousseau's coat-tails to prevent him tumbling out of her box into the pit – this
because he was more interested in displaying himself to the audience than in the
action on the stage. (Bell's British Theatre, Vol. 1, 1780)

impossible to express how finely he played both characters.' *Lethe* was not the only comedy played out that evening, however. Ten days previously, Jean-Jacques Rousseau had arrived in England to take up David Hume's generous offer to find him asylum. On the evening of the command performance, Hume had persuaded him to go to the theatre; he set the scene in a letter to the marquise de Barbentane:

> Mrs. Garrick gave him her box, which is much concealed from the audience, but opposite to that of the King and Queen; and their Majesties were privately informed that they might there expect to see Monsieur Rousseau. When the hour came, he told me that he had changed his resolution, and would not go: for—'What shall I do with Sultan?' That is the name of his dog. 'You must leave him behind,' said I. 'But the first person,' replied he, 'who opens the door, Sultan will run into the street in search of me, and will be lost.' 'You must then,' said I, 'lock him up in your room, and put the key in your pocket.' This was accordingly done; but as we went downstairs, the dog howled and made a noise; his master turned back and said he had not resolution to leave him in that condition; but I caught him in my arms and told him that Mrs. Garrick had dismissed another company in order to make room for him; that the King and Queen were expecting to see him; and without a better reason than Sultan's impatience, it would be ridiculous to disappoint them. Partly by these reasons and partly by force, I engaged him to proceed. The King and Queen looked more at him than at the players.[15]

Mrs Garrick, for her part, declared that she had never passed a more uncomfortable evening in her life, 'for the recluse philosopher was so very anxious to display himself, and hung so forward over the front of the box, that she was obliged to hold him by the skirt of his coat, that he might not fall over into the pit'. After the performance, Rousseau paid Garrick what he presumably intended to be a compliment: 'I have cried all through your Tragedy, and laughed all through your Comedy, without being at all able to understand the language.'[16]

The death of Susannah Cibber early in 1766 (and of James Quin—she had outlived her old champion and protector by only sixteen days) is a good moment to pause and consider the state of the London stage two-thirds of the way through the eighteenth century. Garrick, as he had reminded the audience in his prologue to *Much Ado*, had now been its dominant force for almost a quarter of a century, and yet in one of the first letters written after his return from the continent, he had announced to his friend Suard that 'our stage is at present in a declining state'. Were there objective reasons why he should believe this, or was he merely, after his two-year absence, indulging in a mildly boastful rhetorical flourish?

It was not apparent that the affairs of Drury Lane had suffered unduly while he had been away. The triumvirate of Lacy, Colman and Brother George had kept the show on the road and rubbed along reasonably well, even if Colman had occasion to report to Garrick that his fellow-manager had spoken disobligingly about him.* We do not have financial records for the two seasons in question, but there had been good houses, particularly in 1763–4, when Powell had first burst on the town. Colman, in that first year, had put on a new comedy by Frances Sheridan (*The Dupe*) and *The Royal Shepherd*, a new English opera by Richard Rolt. Over at Covent Garden, Beard's revival of *Harlequin Sorcerer* had enjoyed a run of twenty-seven performances; he had produced a new comedy and a new afterpiece by Arthur Murphy, Kane O'Hara's burletta *Midas* and, as afterpieces, a couple of new farces and a pastoral.

In the following year, both houses had placed stronger emphasis on musical productions, and this had been less successful. At Drury Lane, an English adaptation of Lucchini's opera *Pharnaces* died after six performances, and Richard Rolt's *Almena* enjoyed only modest success. Beard's fortunes were also mixed. *The Spanish Lady*, a musical interlude by Thomas Hull, was withdrawn after one performance, and Thomas Arne's comic opera *The Guardian Outwitted* was lucky to make six nights. Isaac Bickerstaff's *The Maid of the Mill*, on the other hand, adapted from Richardson's *Pamela*, did very good business, and achieved twenty-nine performances.† Covent Garden and Drury Lane both exerted themselves to 'dress characters in the habits of the time', and the results of this drive to achieve greater historical accuracy in costuming were seen in productions of *Richard III, Jane Shore, Rule a Wife* and both parts of *Henry IV*.

Finding and nurturing new talent had always been a prime concern of Garrick's, and there is evidence from his correspondence during his travels in Europe that this preoccupied him increasingly. 'Pray tell me truly,' he wrote to James Love from Paris in January 1765, 'if there is no hopefull Young Man springing up that I could make Use of in Obrien's room—' (O'Brien had recently eloped with the elder daughter of the Earl of Ilchester and gone off with her to New York). Later in the same letter, he reverted to the subject:

> Give me an Acc^t I beseech you (an impartial one) of any Youngsters of Either Sex, who promise something—I have my reasons for this desire, so pray be particular and distinguish their Merits, if you can perceive any— I have many Schemes, & a hint from You will be of Service—[17]

Love sent him a favourable account of a provincial actor he had seen and Garrick responded eagerly: 'Pray Enquire, & let me know more about that *Dodd*—We

---

* *Letters*, 353. Letter dated 10 March 1765. 'I can very readily believe what You tell me of my Brother Consul,' Garrick had written to Colman from Paris. 'He will never forgive my being the means of his making a figure in the world—but this between Ourselves.'

† Beard, with his strong interest in mounting musical productions, did not command the respect of all his players. A letter survives from one of them, Ross, in which he opened his heart to Colman: 'My present situation is most irksome to me and must be to any gentleman or man of merit in his profession to have such an ignorant and now ill-bred fellow as B[eard] presume to conduct the business of a theatre Royal, of which he is totally ignorant.' Beard, he went on, 'despises every degree of merit that is not compris'd in *sol fa* and wishes the theatre only to substitute as an opera house'. (Harvard Theatre Collection, A.L.S.)

want a second Obrien most dreadfully.' James Dodd and his wife were playing at Bath at the time, and Garrick enlisted the help of his friend John Hoadly, whom he frequently relied on as a talent-spotter: 'Ten thousand thanks for y^r information about Dodd,' he wrote. 'I must intreat you to see them again and again, & let me know their qualities a little more minutely.'*

There was by now a larger pool of talent in which the London managers might go fishing; they were no longer so dependent on the strolling players whom Garrick so despised. The Orchard Street playhouse had opened in Bath in 1750 and the cheekily named Drury Lane Theatre in Liverpool dated form the same period. In Plymouth, two older buildings had been knocked together in 1758 to make the Frankfort Gate Theatre; in the same year the *Norwich Gazette* claimed that the 'Grand and Magnificent Theatre' newly opened there 'is allow'd by all Connoisseurs and Judges to be the most perfect and compleat structure of the kind in this Kingdom'. A playhouse had been under construction in Bristol since 1764 (designed, like Norwich, on the plan of Drury Lane) and one of the first things Garrick had been asked to do on his return from abroad was write a prologue for the opening of the new theatre on Richmond Green.†

During his time in France and Italy, it had been borne in on Garrick that there was much to be achieved at Drury Lane by the introduction of new and more flexible lighting techniques. Although his first impression of the Comédie-Française had been that the house seemed 'dark and dirty', he quickly came to see that it benefited enormously from the absence of the unshielded overhead lighting fixtures, and he went home determined to make changes. Within weeks there was a letter from the invaluable Monnet. 'I have carried out your two commissions,' he wrote:

> I will send you a reflector and two different samples of the lamp you want for the footlights at your theatre. There are two kinds of reflectors: those that are placed in a niche in the wall, and which have one wick; and those which are hung up like a chandelier, and which have five . . . As to the lamps for lighting your stage, they are of two kinds: some are of earthenware, and in biscuit form; they have six or eight wicks, and you put oil in them; the others are of tin, in the shape of a candle, with a spring, and you put candles in them. The first are less costly, and give more light. But for them not to smell, you must use the best oil and keep the lamps very clean.[18]

Garrick—and presumably Lacy—moved quickly. By the time the new season opened in September, the chandeliers had gone, the footlights had been improved and a system of side-wing lights on the French model had been introduced. 'The Drury Lane Managers have absolutely created an Artificial Day, or to vary my

---

* *Letters*, 357. Hoadly's report was not entirely favourable—'more the stalk and *menage* of a dancing master, than the ease of a gentleman,' he wrote. 'I fear there must be a dash of the *coxcomb* in every part in which you would see him in perfection.' Hoadly was perceptive: Dodd was to become the finest stage fop and coxcomb since the death of Colley Cibber.

† No theatre outside London was yet known as a Theatre Royal. The first was Bath in 1768.

expression and sentiment they have given us a perfect meridian of wax,' announced the *Public Advertiser*. 'They seem to have brought down the Milky Way to the Bottom of the Stage.'[19] The new lights in the wings consisted of batteries of lamps mounted perpendicularly. Masked from view by the wings, they could be turned away from the stage to dim the light. For the first time in an English theatre it became possible to achieve the effect of dawn or twilight.

These innovations had important consequences for both actors and directors. Now that the audience had a clear view of the whole stage, players could increasingly move back from the platform, occupying a much larger acting area and no longer making their exits and entrances exclusively through the stage-doors. There would also, as we shall see, be new opportunities for scenic designers, who would acquire a control over the instruments of their craft beyond the dreams of their predecessors.

There was a price to be paid for these improvements. Annual lighting costs at Drury Lane in the early days of Garrick's managership, for instance, had come to a little over £400; by the 1766–7 season that figure would increase to £1,240. This may well not have pleased Lacy, either because he regarded it as an extravagance, or because he saw it as an intrusion into matters that were properly his concern. Possibly he had been resentful that Garrick had delegated his duties to someone so relatively young and inexperienced as Colman. Garrick, for his part, seems to have taken the view on his return that Lacy had been poaching on his preserves. Whatever the precise reasons, relations between the two men now declined sharply—so much so that Garrick asked his friend James Clutterbuck to look into the mechanics of dissolving the partnership.

Clutterbuck told him that the value of his share was of the order of £27,500, but that was a price he would not advise his worst enemy to give: 'Your peculiar infelicity,' he wrote shrewdly, 'is, that unless you sell *yourself* too, the moiety is not worth so much as your partner's in any market whatever.' Garrick's chances of disentangling himself from the partnership seemed to him to be slim. 'Avoid disputes with him as much as possible, for your healths sake; be cool and firm,' he advised:

> Nothing is more certain than that "it was his agreement not to meddle in the management;" and that agreement was contended for by poor Draper to be inserted in the articles, but was omitted by your delicacy in favour of the gentleman's vanity. With regard to his ridiculous charge against me, and his subsequent behaviour, banish the whole from your thoughts, and owe him no resentment on that score; he measures other people's minds by his own, the crookedness of which makes it his inclination and interest to suppose every body's else is so too, and therefore I look upon him with an eye of pity instead of indignation, and pray for his cure.[20]

John Paterson, the lawyer who had advised Garrick when the agreement was drawn up, was now called in to act the honest broker. He failed to get Lacy to subscribe to a memorandum that would formalize what had been agreed verbally all those years before, but he had found him eager to reach an accommodation:

He declares ye most sincere desire of continuing with you in Partnership as well as friendship and says that in the 20 years you have been together he does not recollect his having interrupted you in the Management of the Stage more than twice & as to the last time seems to think himself to blame for ye manner of doing it & I really believe is sorry for it. He says he desires you may go on upon the old footing & has given me his word of honour that in such case he will never object to your management but in a private & friendly manner and in case you two cannot agree he will Leave it to my determination as the Common friend of both tho originally yours.

Paterson urged Garrick to meet Lacy half-way and 'disappoint the little arts of those who endeavour to make a total breach between you'.[21] Garrick responded immediately, and it is clear from the relieved tone of his reply that he was every bit as eager to be reconciled as Lacy was:

As I am most willing to put an end to Your trouble, & my own anxiety— I shall certainly submit to Your Opinion—If Mr Lacy, as you have told me, is sorry for our late quarrel, & sincere in his desire of continuing in partnership with Me—I shall at Once come in to Your determination—I should have quitted Drury Lane Theatre with reluctance, & nothing but being convinced that Mr Lacy had chose to part with me, should have drove me to ye Step, that I was oblig'd to take—therefore I fully subscribe to Your proposals in y^r letter & am ready to meet Mr Lacy as my Partner & friend without having the least remembrance that we Ever disagreed—*

Garrick had also fallen out quite seriously with Colman towards the end of 1765. The two friends had been cheerfully collaborating for some years in the writing of a comedy called *The Clandestine Marriage*. Garrick's letters to Colman during the time he was on the Continent frequently refer to it. 'Speed y^r Plow my d^r friend,' he wrote from Rome in the summer of 1764, 'have you thought of the *Clandestine M?* I am at it—';[22] and from Paris, five months later, 'I have consider'd our 3 Acts, & with some little alterations they will do—I'll ensure them.'[23]

The play was complete by the late autumn of 1765. The quarrel arose over Garrick's refusal to take the part of Lord Ogleby, and was aggravated by controversy over who had written which parts of the play. Clutterbuck made an attempt to keep the peace:

Colman and you are men of most quick sensations, and are apt sometimes to catch at words instead of things, and those very words may probably receive great alteration by the medium through which they pass. I know

---

* *Letters*, 390. Garrick's professions of friendship for Lacy are somewhat belied by a tetchy reference to him in a letter to George only three days later: 'What ye Devil has he in his maggot-breeding pericranium?' But perhaps allowance must be made from the fact that Garrick was writing from an inn in Marlborough—he had been suffering from gout and was on his way to Bath to take the waters. (*Letters*, 391.)

you love one another, and a third person might call up such explanations
as would satisfy ye both; I myself should not doubt being able to do it
were we assembled together.[24]

That did not happen, however. By early December, Colman had caught at all
too many words, a good number of them very greatly altered not only by the
medium through which they had passed but also by malice. He wrote a lengthy
letter to Garrick, full of angry reproach:

> Since my return from Bath I have been told, but I can hardly believe it,
> that, in speaking of 'The Clandestine Marriage,' you have gone so far as
> to say, 'Colman lays a great stress on his having written this character on
> purpose for me, suppose it should come out that *I wrote it!*'

Colman was outraged. 'I cannot help being hurt at your betraying so earnest a
desire to winnow your wheat from my chaff,' he wrote: 'I understood it was to
be a joint work, in the fullest sense of the word; and never imagined that either
of us was to lay his finger on a particular scene, and cry, "this is mine!"' He
was also both baffled and exasperated by Garrick's refusal to play the role that
from the very start had been written expressly for him:

> In all our conversations concerning your return to the stage, for you always
> allowed a possibility, did you ever tell me, that if you *did* return, you
> would never play in a new piece? never play in 'The Clandestine Marriage?'
> Did you not often regret the want of a performer for this character? and
> did not I often express my hopes that you might still perform it?[25]

He reminded Garrick of their agreement that on the publication of the play,
their names were to appear together on the title-page. 'For both our sakes,' he
concluded, 'the secret of our partnership, I think, ought to be made known.'

Garrick received Colman's letter on 5 December—the day, although he could
not know it, on which he was to play opposite Mrs Cibber for the last time. A
wiser man would have laid it aside, but Garrick's 'quick sensations' would not
allow that and he instantly seized his pen:

> Tho I am to obey His Majesty's Commands this Evening, and my head is
> full of the Character I am to play, Yet I will answer your long letter,
> however hastily, or inaccurately.

He too was indignant. He rebuked Colman for not disclosing his source—'let
me know what indifferent person told you, & I will answer both him and you,'
he wrote:

> I hope I shall always know what is due to myself and an old friend; and
> by having that best of feelings, I was astonish'd & unhappy to hear that
> you had complained of me (peevishly indeed) for not acting the character
> you had written on Purpose for me; & if you did not add, that *there was
> an end of our friendship*, I was misinformed . . . You say that you never
> knew of my resolution not to act in a new *Piece* till after the Season had

commenc'd—I am greatly deceiv'd, If I cannot mention some persons, among which is one of your own friends; who can attest the Contrary.

It is a long, disorderly letter, the words tumbling over each other, the plain prose sense not always clear. He signs himself 'Your old friend', but then launches into a rambling postscript. A string of accusing rhetorical questions is followed by a concession that there may have been faults on both sides:

I have ever thought you & loved you as a faithfull & affectionate friend, but surely y^r leaving London so abruptly & leaving complaints of me behind You was not among the many instances of y^r Kindness & moderation to me: & if I betrayed any Warmth in consequence of y^r Conduct, such warmth was at least more natural & excusable than Your own.[26]

By the end of the month, the dark clouds had lifted and the two men were once more on the most cordial of terms.* 'Dr Coley,' Garrick wrote on Christmas Day. 'God forgive Me—I wrote the nonsense on ye other side, or rather compos'd it, while our Parson was preaching this morning—it is a kind of Rondeau which the french, & our fools that imitated y^m were once very fond of.'

To George Colman

May Xmas give thee all her cheer,
And lead thee to a happy Year!
Tho Wicked Gout has come by stealth,
And threats Encroachments on my health;
Tho still my foes indulge their spite,
And, what their malice prompts, will write;
Tho now to Me the Stage is hatefull,
And He, who owes me most, ungratefull;
Yet think not, George, my hours are sad,
O No—my heart is more than glad;
That Moment all my cares were gone,
When You & I again were One . . .

The Clandestine Marriage opened on 20 February, and was an instant success, with an initial run of thirteen nights. Lord Ogleby, the part Colman had so badly wanted Garrick to play, fell to Thomas King, and his performance was widely praised. Joseph Cradock records that years later, after Garrick's retirement, the conversation turned one day on King's interpretation, which still held the stage.

---

* A note from Garrick in the middle of the month suggests that it was the younger man who took the first step. 'My dear Colman. Becket has been wth Me, and tells me of Y^r friendly intentions towards me—I should have been before hand with You had I not been ill wth ye beef-steaks & arrack punch last Saturday, & oblig'd to leave ye Playhouse.' Garrick signed himself 'Ever Yours Old & New friend'. He had possibly over-indulged at a meeting of the Sublime Society of Beef Steaks, where he was an occasional guest. (*Letters*, 379.)

'But it is not *my* Lord Ogleby,' protested Garrick, 'and it is the only character in which I should now wish to appear.'

His wistfulness is understandable. Ogleby has clear affinities with three or four of the characters for which Garrick was most famous—the gouty and amorous old rake Lord Chalkstone in *Lethe*, the coxcomb Bayes in *The Rehearsal*, the Simple Simon figure of Abel Drugger in *The Alchymist*, even the sottish Sir John Brute in *The Provok'd Wife*. It is plain that as they wrote, the two dramatists had firmly in mind the specific comic strengths of the best players in the Drury Lane company—they were not fleshing out variants on traditional stock characters but working with the grain of the talent available to them. The earliest surviving draft of the play, now at the Garrick Club in London—its title at that stage was *The Sisters*—specifies, for instance, that Garrick is to play 'an Old Beau, vain, &c'; later, it indicates that the audience 'must learn that *Mrs Clive* yᵉ aunt has two nieces Coheiresses & one of them is to be married to *O'Brien* the Son of *Garrick* & Nephew to Yates'. Mrs Clive was indeed a triumphant Mrs Heidelberg; the part of Brush fitted John Palmer like a glove (Charles Lamb described him as 'a *gentleman* with a slight infusion of the *footman*'); O'Brien's elopement had by then made him unavailable, however, and the part of Lovewell went to Powell.

When the text of the play was published, the following form of words appeared in the 'Advertisement': 'Some friends, and some enemies, have endeavoured to allot distinct portions of this play to each of the authors. Each, however, considers himself as responsible for the whole.' That did nothing to dampen what became one of the more celebrated—and partisan—debates of the eighteenth century. Only in comparatively recent times has it been possible to abandon conjecture. The Garrick Club's manuscript sketch for *The Sisters* and the manuscript working copy of the play preserved at the Folger Library convincingly establish that the piece is by Garrick and Colman rather than the other way round.*

The Clandestine Marriage stands out as one of the few comedies of real quality written in the middle years of the eighteenth century. Nothing comparable appeared between Fielding's day in the earlier years of the century and that of Goldsmith and Sheridan. It reads today like a mildly sanitized version of a Restoration comedy of manners, all but untouched by the sentimentalism of the day—laughter, not tears, was the object of the exercise.† It was translated into French and German, and forms the basis of Cimarosa's opera *Il Matrimonio Segreto*. It became very popular in the United States—George Washington was present at a performance in New York in the summer of 1789. It was seen regularly throughout the nineteenth century, and when it was revived at the

---

* The most authoritative accounts of the play's genesis are to be found in Elizabeth Stein's *David Garrick, Dramatist*, and in the commentary to volume 1 of *The Plays of David Garrick*, edited by Harry William Pedicord and Frederick Louis Bergmann, 7 vols., Carbondale, Ill., 1980–82.

† Drury Lane was never a no-go area for sentimental comedy, but Garrick did not neglect opportunities to make known his feelings about the genre. When, for instance, he put on Kelly's hugely successful *False Delicacy* in 1768, he included in his prologue the lines, 'Write moral plays—the blockhead!—why, good people,/ You'll soon expect this house to wear a steeple!'

Haymarket Theatre in London in 1903, *The Times* discovered in Lord Ogleby 'the supreme merit of sometimes talking like Lord Chesterfield'. And so he does. 'Beauty,' he announces to Fanny in Act II, 'is a religion in which I was born and bred a bigot and would die a martyr.' Colman's disappointment at not hearing such lines spoken by the man who wrote them is understandable.

Garrick had set off for Bath before the end of the play's successful first run, and stayed there until early in May—an absence of almost two months. He kept up a steady stream of letters to his friends and to George—the usual jumble of gossip, business and small commissions. 'I must beg of You to keep a Watch upon our house in Southampton Street,' he wrote to his brother:

> If I suspect any Mortal to be more particularly bebitch'd than any other, it is our house maid, *Molly*—She has all kind of People follow^g her, & I have great fears about her. I wish you w^d take her by Surprize, & if You find her bad, turn her out, directly—she is a great peeper into papers. . . as for Cautherly *Mansquibbing* her (wch he certainly does) I don't mind— but I suspect she has all kinds of fellows in our Absence & I don't know w^t may be ye Consequence—[27]

Mansquibbing is an activity unknown both to the editors of the *Oxford English Dictionary* and to Eric Partridge; possibly Cautherley was showing Molly his etchings. In working hours, he was being kept pretty busy; whether he owed this to the manager's determination to bring on young players or simply to his partiality is difficult to determine. He had played Barnwell in *The London Merchant* earlier that season, his first appearance in a man's role, and Highfill suggests that the puff printed in the *Universal Museum* of September 1765 ('The moment he appeared, his interesting figure, so admirably adapted to the Character, spoke for him') may have been planted by Garrick.

Two months later, when Garrick altered *Mahomet* for its first performance in twenty years, he coached Cautherley in the part of Zaphna, which had originally been his own. Davies, judging Cautherley's 'natural requisites' for tragedy to be weak, was unimpressed: 'Mr Garrick had an affection for him,' he wrote, 'and often pushed his abilities beyond their reach.'[28] Using Hopkins as an intermediary, Garrick also suggested to James Love, who was running the new summer theatre at Richmond, that Cautherley should be offered some work there, and he was invited to play both Romeo and Hamlet.

Relations with Colman were now entirely restored; from Bath Garrick wrote urging him to join him there, and sending cheerful bulletins about his health: 'I am as well as can be expected, the riding from London all ye Morning, has been of great Service to me, & I repeat the same prescription constantly after breakfast.'[29]

He also wrote to Foote, who had suffered a dreadful accident, and was badly in need of cheering up. Earlier in the year he had gone to stay with his friends Lord and Lady Mexborough. He was not above boasting about his skill as a horseman, and the company egged him on to show what he could do on a horse belonging to the Duke of York, who was a fellow-guest. The beast was a good deal more spirited than Foote realized. He was thrown, and sustained a double fracture of the leg. The eminent surgeon William Bromfield was called in, but the leg had to be amputated.* There were complications from a burst artery, and for a week it was not certain that he would pull through.

Garrick had written to him at the time in characteristically generous vein: 'All I shall say at present is, that should you be prevented from persuing any plan for yʳ Theatre, I am wholly at yʳ Service, & will labour in yʳ vineyard for you, in any Capacity, till you are able to do it, so much better, for yourself.'† Now, from Bath, he told him how much his wit and courage in adversity had been admired: 'You have had a trying time, my dear Foote, & I hope for yʳ life to come, that with one leg, You will be an overmatch for Your Enemies, & out run the foul Fiend—'[30] Foote soon bounced back. He acquired two artificial legs, one for every day use, the other 'equipped with silk stockings and a polished shoe with a gold buckle'. He was also able to exploit the Duke of York's bad conscience; thanks to his influence he secured a patent to open the Haymarket Theatre between May and September each year when the two winter houses were dark.

The disorders which had taken Garrick to Bath were proving stubborn, and by late April he was still not entirely well. A letter to Richard Berenger spared his friend few of the details:

> The Bile, which is my chief Complaint, is so very uncertain in Its motions that it comes upon me like a Thief in yᵉ Night. I went to Bed very well the Night before last, but was rous'd with such an overcoming Sickness that I was half dead for near 3 hours—the waters have made me better, but left a kind of hoarseness, & weakness in my Bowels, which our Friend Dr. Schomberg combats most wisely with Rhubarb, Magnesia &c. I am now much better, but I fret myself a little to think I cannot possibly venture upon Macbeth; which is a treble mortification to me, as I fear his Majesty has a desire to see it—[31]

By early May he was back at Hampton, busy as always in the pursuit of preferment for his friends and their relations. His doctor, Isaac Schomberg, had a younger brother, Alexander, who was a naval captain. He had served at the capture of Quebec and at the siege of Belle-Isle, but was now once again on half pay and in reduced circumstances. He desperately wanted to be appointed the Governor of a fort in North America and Charles Townshend, as Paymaster-General to the Forces, exercised patronage in such matters. Garrick agreed to petition him; when a first appeal went unanswered, he decided to try again—this time in verse:

---

* Bromfield (1712–92) was Surgeon to the Queen's Household and the Duke of York's personal physician.
† *Letters*, 388. Garrick also wrote some verses, published in the *London Chronicle* of 18–20 February 1766, to counter the unsympathetic and tasteless comment that had greeted Foote's misfortunes. Typical of these was some doggerel that had appeared in the previous issue of the same paper, ending with the lines, 'A Foot too little now you are;/ Before a Foote too much.'

If true that as the Wit is great,
The Mem'ry's in proportion small;
Ask him, or Her, the first You meet,
They'll swear that YOU have none at all.

Garrick told one of his French correspondents that Schomberg had spent so long in America that he had 'almost forgot European Manners'.* He hoped Townshend would see this as a recommendation:

Send Him where oft, he fought, & bled,
Again to cross th'Atlantic Sea;
To Tomahawk, and Wampum bred,
He's more than half a Cherokee!†

Garrick had visited Bristol during his stay in Bath and had seen the new theatre nearing completion there. It was to be run by a partnership that included Powell and John Palmer, and when it opened at the end of May he supplied both a prologue and an epilogue. Another of the partners was John Arthur, with whom Garrick had collaborated many years previously in the curious invention which he referred to as 'our Catapult Project'. Arthur was going to speak the epilogue, and in sending it to him, Garrick took time to offer him some instruction on how to speak it:

Mr. Garrick's compliments to Mr. Arthur—he desires him not to give a Copy of it upon any account—that is yᵉ first condition—the next is that he take pains to give the full Effect of it in yᵉ speaking—Mr G. has vary'd yᵉ Matter on Purpose—Mr. A must mimic the *Prude* drawing up herself & speaking affectedly—and he must pronounce yᵉ french *Madame* not like our *Madam*—but broad & Long *Mawdawme*—³²

During the 1750s, Arthur had been involved with William Pritchard in a scheme to make provision for players who had fallen on hard times. He had got as far as drawing up plans for a large building, complete with chapel, on the model of Dulwich College, but the undertaking proved over-ambitious and came to nothing. The managements of both patent houses had tended to be leery of such projects; players were players, after all, and must not be allowed to get above themselves; distress could always be alleviated by acts of charity or the allocation of a share in a benefit.

While Garrick was abroad, however, a popular Covent Garden actor called Thomas Hull had taken the initiative to establish a fund. An initial appeal raised

---

* *Letters*, 401. Letter dated 3 May 1766. Garrick was writing to the duc de Nivernois, whom he had met in Paris the previous year. He was so pleased with his verses to Townshend that he sent the Duke a copy of them. He told the Duke that there had been plans to publish his 'dramatick & poetical triffles' that spring, but that they had been delayed. *The Dramatic Works of David Garrick, Esq.* eventually appeared in 3 volumes in 1768.
† Schomberg did not, in the event, secure further employment until 1770. He later commanded the yacht attached to the Lord-Lieutenant of Ireland, and was knighted in 1777.

more than £100 in a matter of days; contributions were set at sixpence in the pound from the weekly income of those who chose to join; in order to build up a substantial sum, it was agreed that there should be no call on the fund for the first five years. Beard and Mrs Rich gave liberal support to the scheme and agreed that it should have the profits of an annual benefit.

According to Davies, Garrick was not best pleased to discover that such a fund had been set up without reference to him: 'he was, he said, universally acknowledged to be at the head of his profession, besides being a patentee and manager of the oldest company of the King's servants'.[33] The players might reasonably have retorted that what happened at Covent Garden was no concern of his; they might further have pointed out that their colleagues at Garrick's own theatre had more than once made application to the management for such a theatrical fund to be set up, but without success.

That was all water under the bridge. Garrick and Lacy now acted swiftly to follow Covent Garden's lead. Both made generous financial contributions and at the end of the season Garrick made further amends for his tardiness by appearing for the benefit of the fund as Kitely in *Every Man in His Humour*.* Both funds were subsequently incorporated by Act of Parliament. Garrick assumed the expense associated with the Drury Lane legislation; he acted as steward of the fund, responsible to a committee elected by the company; he also made a gift of a house in Drury Lane where the business of the fund might be transacted. 'It is computed,' wrote Davies, 'that, by the product of his labours in acting annually capital parts, and by donations of one kind or other, he gained for this beneficial institution a capital of near 4,500*l*.'[34]

During the summer of 1766 the Garricks again spent time in Essex as Rigby's guests at Mistley. It was also that summer that Garrick formed an important new friendship. Charles Pratt was a prominent lawyer and politician. He had been a contemporary of Pitt's at Eton, and the two men were life-long friends. When Pitt came to power in 1757 Pratt was appointed Attorney-General. His decision in the case of Wilkes that general warrants were illegal had made him almost as much of a popular hero as Wilkes himself; he was made a freeman of the City of London, and the mayor and corporation commissioned Reynolds to paint his portrait. He had been raised to the peerage as Baron Camden in 1765, and when Chatham formed his second administration in July 1766 he became Lord Chancellor. Small and handsome, Camden was an agreeably indolent man, fond of music and the theatre, a great reader of romances and an engaging conversationalist. He was also a stylish and charming letter-writer. 'Dear Garrick,' he wrote on one occasion, 'It is such a long time since we met, that I begin to feel that kind of desire to see you and Mrs Garrick that makes a Swiss sick when he has [been] absent any considerable time from his own country.'[35]

---

* On 22 June. Covent Garden had mounted its benefit on 13 May with a performance of *The Albion Queens; or, The Death of Mary Queen of Scots*. Queen Mary was played by Mrs Bellamy, and the epilogue was spoken by Woodward and Shuter.

The Garricks also kept a friendly eye on Colman's three-year-old son Georgie during the summer months—Colman and his common-law wife had gone off to Paris, leaving the boy behind at Richmond in the care of servants. Garrick took his unofficial guardianship seriously. 'I have made him two visits since y^r departure, which he has taken most kindly,' he wrote to Colman:

> We have work'd very hard in the Garden togeather, & have play'd at Ninepins till I was oblig'd to declare off . . . We are to have a day at Hampton, & he is to make love to my niece Kitty, & a plumb-pudding— he seems very fond of ye Party, & we will endeavour to make him forget his loving parents—once more my dear friend, Let not a single thought about y^r Boy disquiet You—*

Garrick would have been more than a little mortified to know how young Georgie looked back on those childhood days in later life:

> I always, on arriving at Garrick's, ran about his gardens, where he taught me the game of trap ball, which superseded our former nine-pins.— He practiced, too, a thousand monkey tricks upon me;—he was Punch, Harlequin, a Cat in a Gutter—then King Lear, with a mad touch, at times, that almost terrified me;—and he had a peculiar mode of flashing the lightning of his eye, by darting it into the astonish'd mind of a child, (as a serpent is said to fascinate a bird,) which was an attribute belonging only to this theatrical Jupiter.
>
> All this was very kind and condescending,—but it wanted the *bonhomie* of Goldsmith, who play'd to please the boy; whereas Garrick always seem'd playing to please himself,—as he did in a theatre, where, doubtless, he tickled his *amour propre*, while he charmed the spectators;—he diverted and dazzled me, but never made me love him; and I had always this feeling for him, though I was too young to define it.[36]

Garrick kept up a frequent correspondence with Suard in Paris, and in one of his letters that summer he passed on the latest gossip about Rousseau:

> I suppose it will be no small amusement to You & the rest of my friends, to hear, that Monsr Rousseau has behav'd to Mr David Hume as he formerly did to his other friends—Mr Hume has procur'd him a pension from our King's private purse of one hundred Guineas a Year, for which he has written ye most abusive letter to him, calling him *Noir* & *Coquin* . . .[37]

There is evidence that during the summer of 1766 Garrick made another of his periodic attempts to secure patronage for George: 'Tho I hate to give trouble or be impertinent, I am afraid that I am going to do both.'[38] He appears to have been writing to Lord John Cavendish, who at the time was briefly serving as one of the Commissioners of the Treasury. Garrick told him that he had had a promise of something from George Grenville, who had been First Lord of the

---

* *Letters*, 413. Kitty was George's youngest daughter Catherine, at that time a girl of eleven.

Treasury until the previous year, but that nothing had come of it because of the abruptness of Grenville's departure from office. He also tried to enlist the help of John Paterson, at that time the MP for Wiltshire, but his efforts were unavailing.

A later age would have described George as Garrick's gofer. At the court of King David he was a glorified groom of the chamber—confidant, errand boy, personnel officer, bouncer, understrapper-in-chief. He was far too useful for Garrick to wish to be rid of his services at Drury Lane, although with his five children he was a steady drain on resources. It was also the case that Garrick was very fond of his brother, and quick to defend him from the inevitable sniping he attracted from high and low as his unofficial deputy. At the end of August 1766, George was enjoying a break in Lichfield. Although the new season loomed, Garrick generously urged him to extend his stay:

> Dear George.
>
> If You find such benefit by Lichfield Air, or rather have such Pleasure in Staffordshire Society in the Name of health & Joy, why don't You take another Week's run in the Moggs, Dimble, & Bessy Bonk's Grave—We shall not open till ye 20th, & if You are with Us before that time it is sufficient—*

Somebody signing himself 'Amor Virtutis' had sent Garrick a letter about George, and he wanted his brother to see it. 'The Enclos'd piece of Rascality came to my hand Yesterday Morning—by the Spelling, Grammar & Ignorance, I guess the Writer to be of ye very vulgar kind,' he wrote. Poisonous, too:

> Sir,
>
> Spending the evening very often near where your brother George lives, he is very often the subject of the conversation—that he who has such a family of fine children, should have such a crew of women about his house, besides his Dancer etc. out of doors. . . . Such a sett is enough to ruin any man, besides making him the laughing stock of all that knows him. It has often been told to him, to no purpose, and had I not seen the title of a pamphlet 'The History of the little Groom in the Green near Somerset House with his surprising Seraglio,' I should not have taken this means of acquainting you . . .[39]

George had been a widower since 1758. 'His Dancer' sounds like a reference to Elizabeth Tetley, then a member of the Drury Lane company, who was to become his second wife in 1771. Garrick hit on a form of words which combined worldly wisdom with delicacy:

> You perhaps may guess whence it comes—however there is an old latin adage, which says—*fas Est et ab Hoste doceri*, that it is right to be

---

* Garrick is calling up Lichfield place names remembered from his childhood. Bessy Bonk's Grave was a supposedly haunted spot north of the town; Dimble was the name of the dry ditch on the east and north sides of the Close; Moggs was the marshy ground at the edge of Munster Pool below the Garricks' garden.

instructed by an Enemy, if you are conscious that he has hit upon any thing, that had better be Otherwise, You will profit by it—if not, bid ye Writer kiss Your Arse, & throw the epistle into the fire—I hate, & detest Anonymous Correspondents, & if it gives You one Moment's pain You are sillier than I take You to be—[40]

In the same letter there is an interesting indication that Garrick occasionally toyed with the idea of entering Parliament. 'The Seat at Lichfield is too costly a one for Me,' he told George:

Lord G. has too much interest, & tho' I may have half a Dozen Loving friends for Me, yet I shd be oblig'd to sneak, with my tail between my Legs, out of ye Town Hall, up Bow-Street, & pass by the Free School as Miserable, as I once was Merry. I have a Place in my Eye, where I am told I shall be chose for ye Sum of—if my Inclination lies that way, & I have a kind of a propensity; My Money must purchase My Ambition without much Care or trouble—*

It seems unlikely that thoughts of strutting his stuff on the political stage were more than a passing fancy. For the moment, he must return to the common round he knew best. He had assembled a company of 81 performers. He had ten new productions in preparation, no less than four of them pieces of his own.† The new season opened on 20 September with a performance of *The Busy Body*, but if anyone in the Drury Lane audience had hoped to see the manager in the part of Marplot, they were disappointed.‡

---

* *Letters*, 426. Lord G. was the well-connected and immensely wealthy Lord Gower, a former MP for Lichfield and brother-in-law of the Duke of Bedford, through whose influence he had been appointed Lord Privy Seal in 1755. He later served as President of the Council, and in 1786 was created Marquess of Stafford.

† At Covent Garden Beard would mount only four new productions, although he had assembled a company of 108 performers.

‡ The part was allotted to Dodd, who had given a good account of himself in his first season the previous year.

25

Assorted Theatrical Trash

Although Garrick stuck to his resolve to appear less frequently, there was general agreement that his acting had acquired a new dimension since his return from abroad. 'It was remarked by the most discerning judges, that our Roscius had, by visiting foreign theatres, greatly profited in his mode of representation,' wrote Davies:

> They observed, that his action, though always spirited and proper, was become easy and unrestrained; that his deportment was more graceful, and his manner more elegant; that he did not now appear so solicitous for applause, as to disturb his own feelings, and lessen the pleasure of the audience; that he had entirely dropped that anxious exertion at the close of a speech, both in look and behaviour, which is called by the comedians a clap-trap.[1]

Whether these improvements can be ascribed entirely to Garrick's visits to the theatre during his travels is doubtful. It is possible that some of the refinements noticed by Davies represented a reaction against the bombastic excesses Garrick had witnessed at the Comédie-Française. What is more likely, however, is that his foreign travels and, in particular, his stay in Paris, had bolstered Garrick's self-esteem, and that this was reflected in the greater ease and confidence with which he performed on his return.

In spite of his immense celebrity, his material success, his easy entrée into the houses of the great, there was a part of Garrick which remained uneasily aware that he was only a player, and that he could never entirely escape from the traditionally low regard in which those of his trade were held. Shortly before his arrival in Florence two years previously, Horace Walpole had written about him to his friend Sir Horace Mann, the British envoy: 'We are sending you another couple, the famous Garrick, and his once famous wife. He will make you laugh as a mimic, and as he knows we are great friends, will affect great partiality to me; but be a little upon your guard, remember he is an *actor*.'[2]

The writers and philosophers in whose company Garrick spent so much time in France were in no danger of forgetting that, but in their friendship there was no element of condescension. For them acting was a branch of the fine arts; when they discussed the theatre, they did so with the same philosophical seriousness that they brought to the consideration of literature or painting. They turned to Garrick not just for his expertise in dramatic technique but for his views on the literary quality of the plays he saw performed. And—the evidence of *The Sick Monkey* notwithstanding—they had sent him back to England more relaxed, more self-confident, less inclined to believe that he was only as good as his last performance.

His decision to act less afforded him more leisure to write. Early in the season he put on *The Country Girl*, which he had adapted from Wycherley's *The Country Wife*. It was designed principally as a vehicle for an actress called Ann Reynolds, a newcomer to the company. Although she had danced at Drury Lane, the role of Peggy was her first acting part. Garrick coached her intensively, though with no more than moderate success: 'Miss Reynolds,' wrote Davies, 'though not deficient in merit, neither in age, person, or look, could pretend to be the innocent and simple lass of sixteen.'* Devoted as he was to the 'old comedy' Garrick knew well enough that Wycherley was strong meat for the audience of his own day. 'The alterer claims no merit but his endeavour to clear one of our most celebrated comedies from immorality and obscenity,' he wrote in the Advertisement (i.e. the preface) to the published text:

> He thought himself bound to preserve as much of the original as could be presented to an audience of these times without offence; and if this wanton of Charles's days is now so reclaimed as to become innocent without being insipid, the present editor will not think his time ill employed . . .

The piece was not well received by the critics. Some felt that by cutting most of the indecencies in the first act, Garrick had stripped the comedy of most of its wit. A writer in *The Theatrical Monitor* alleged that the 'overbearing manager' had kept it going in the face of public disapproval only by playing 'to houses filled with *orders*' (i.e. by papering the house), but this is not borne out by the Drury Lane Treasurer's Book, which shows that it had fourteen performances that season and took in some £1,500. Garrick kept it in the repertory for three more seasons.†

A few weeks after *The Country Girl*, Garrick put on his own new afterpiece *Neck or Nothing*, although it did not originally have his name attached to it—a ploy he often adopted to protect himself from retaliation by playwrights whose work he had rejected. He acknowledged that he was once again indebted to a French original—the piece is an anglicized version of a farce by Le Sage called *Crispin, rival de son maître* which had appeared in 1707—and Garrick toned it up with some agreeable nonsense of his own. When, for instance, Sir Harry Harlowe decides to withdraw his consent to the marriage of his son to the

---

* *Davies*, ii, 122. Miss Reynolds did not last long at Drury Lane. She was popular with the audience, but according to Tate Wilkinson, Garrick found her 'careless and dissipated' and she was dismissed. She went off to Dublin and Edinburgh, was twice married and died an alcoholic.
† It was revived in 1785, however, and over the next fifteen years the celebrated Mrs Jordan played the part of Peggy on ninety-seven occasions.

daughter of his old friends the Stockwells, the valet, Slip, fires him up with a cock-and-bull story about how the disappointed parents had set about him:

SLIP: . . . On a sudden—for I pushed the argument pretty home—she caught hold of my throat, thus, sir, and knocked me down with the butt end of her fan.

SIR HARRY: Did she? But what did her husband say to this? Let us hear that.

SLIP: Oh, sir, I found him pretty reasonable. He only showed me the door and kicked me down stairs.

SIR HARRY: If he's for that work, we can kick too.

SLIP: Dear sir, consider your gout.

SIR HARRY: No, sir; when my blood is up I never feel the gout . . .[3]

Lively and entertaining as it was, the play achieved no great popularity with the Drury Lane audience. In a letter he wrote years later to an old Lichfield school friend who had sent him a comedy, Garrick identified a weakness in the plot by referring back to his own play: 'To convince you how over delicate the Publick may be at times—I will relate to you a passage in a Farce call'd *Neck or Nothing*.' His conclusion, after rehearsing the story line, was that an audience 'will not Suffer the dupe to be cheated too extravagantly even in a Farcical piece'.*

Garrick enjoyed much greater success with the so-called 'dramatic romance' which was his holiday offering to Drury Lane patrons that year. *Cymon*, as Garrick made clear in his prologue, was aimed unashamedly at the upper gallery:

> You are our patrons now:
> If you but grin, the critics won't bow wow.
> As for the plot, wit, humour, language—I
> Beg you such trifles kindly to pass by;
> The most essential part, which something means,
> As dresses, dances, sinkings, flyings, scenes—
> They'll make you stare—

Feats of magic, music,† extravagant spectacle—the audience loved it, and not just those who sat in the cheaper seats. The scene is Arcadia. Magnificent gardens are conjured at the wave of a wand, and an old castle vanishes by the same agency. Demons arise and 'perform their rites' and Merlin is carried away by his dragons and chariot. One of the more ambitious effects required that a tower be enveloped in flames before sinking into the ground.

Garrick had based his piece on Dryden's poem *Cymon and Iphigenia* which in turn was derived from Boccaccio's *Decameron*. Horace Walpole's disparaging description of it as 'Garrick's ginger-bread, double-gilt' has been much quoted,

---

* *Letters*, 817. Letter dated 10 January 1774. Garrick was writing to Herbert Lawrence, who had combined a career as an apothecary and surgeon with that of a miscellaneous writer.
† The music was by Michael Arne, Thomas Arne's son and therefore the nephew of Susannah Cibber. He was to receive 'one third part of the Profits of the first three Nights which the author shall take for his own benefits' (i.e. the third, sixth and ninth performances), which brought him the sum of £119 17s 10d. Garrick himself, as the author, took slightly more than £240.

but Walpole was writing to the Countess of Upper Ossory about a *revival* of the piece in 1792—the audience, that is to say, had retained its taste for this particular piece of gingerbread for more than twenty-five years.

By that time the staging had become even more elaborate than in Garrick's day, and the procession in the last act had swollen to more than a hundred—Ancient British, Anglo-Saxon and Norman knights, Indians, Turks, Scythians, Romans, a dwarf, a giant, piping fauns, bands of cupids and a troop of Arcadian shepherds.[4] There was also a tournament, in which the combatants fought with lances, swords and battle-axes. 'The Prince of Wales' Highlander made one of the procession, and entered the lists as a champion, fighting with an enormous club; against him a small female warrior was opposed, by whom he was subdued.'[*]

Garrick himself never claimed any great literary or dramatic merit for the piece—indeed, when he sent the printed text to Wilkes in Paris he described it as 'Some theatrical Trash, which I have Exhibited to yᵉ Public this winter'.[5] Very profitable trash, for all that. *Cymon* was still drawing the crowds as late as 1850.

Cautherley continued to enjoy Garrick's support and patronage. He had been allowed to try his hand at *Hamlet* and *Romeo* early in the season, and shortly before Christmas he was assigned another of Garrick's old parts when he appeared as Felix in *The Wonder*. He was also extensively puffed. A long review in the *Public Advertiser* described him as 'a pupil of the greatest master of the art of acting that ever graced the English stage (if not European)'. He had demonstrated, the writer continued, that he was 'susceptible of the most refined instructions of his great patron and tutor'.[6]

His great patron and tutor certainly kept a close eye on his interests. His benefit had been set for the end of April, and Garrick was anxious that it should be a success. 'I have seen a *paragraph* for *Cautherley* but not an *Advertisement*,' he wrote to George from Bath at the beginning of the month. 'I hope yᵉ Lad will get Something.'[7] Writing again on the day before the benefit, he expressed some concern: 'Notwithstanding Cautherly has many tickets out, I tremble for his benefit. I hope he will not lose by it.'[8]

In the earlier part of the season Garrick himself had acted only occasionally, and then only in parts in which he felt utterly secure—Sir John Brute, Lusignan, Chalkstone, Benedick, Drugger.[†] When he heard in February that there had been a request from the palace for him to appear in *The Jealous Wife*, he made uncharacteristically heavy weather of it. 'I am very much *flabbergasted* that my good King will see me in Oakly,' he wrote to George, '& the deuce is in You, for not sending Me the Prompter's Book—how could You Mistake it so—'

He was writing from the comfort of Hampton on a winter's Sunday evening.

* Oulton, Walley Chamberlain, *The History of the Theatres of London*, London, 1796, ii, 215. The Drury Lane Account Book records that three horses were hired from Hughes's Royal Circus for the sum of £16 19s 6d and an animal trainer called Gough was paid £5 19s 6d for the use of his greyhounds.
† Mrs Cibber's place as Lady Brute was taken by Mrs Palmer, and as Zara she was succeeded by Mrs Yates.

He had not played Oakly since his return from Europe (Holland had taken it on in his absence) but it emerges later in the letter that getting up a part in which he felt rusty was by no means the only thing that was eating him. It also seems distinctly possible that he was writing with a bottle at his elbow:

> This damn'd Oakly is a Crust for Me indeed, I wish it don't prove too hard for my teeth, & rub my Gums . . . I must be a[t] London (which I'm sorry for) on Tuesday to run over my Scenes on *Wednesday Morning*—I have not played Oakly these three Years—Sick—Sick—Sick—& Mrs P[ritchar]d will make me Sicker—great Bubbies, Noddling head, & no teeth—O Sick—Sick—Spew—

Mrs Pritchard (who would play Mrs Oakly, and who was now within a season of retirement) was not the only colleague on whom he vented his spleen in this extraordinary and highly uncharacteristic way. It is plain that Powell's popularity with the Drury Lane audience (he had appeared the previous evening as King John) was something that Garrick was beginning to find irksome:

> Could I hope that Mr Ramus would get yᵉ Jealous Wife put off—but that's impossible I must do it, I'd give 5 Guineas to have the Prompter's Book now—but that can't be—Sick—Sick—King John beshit—bouncing, strutting, Striding, straddling, thumping, grinning, Swaggering, Staggering all be shit—No Matter—the more turd, yᵉ More Stink, I hold my Nose, You Leave in a Morning; I lick My Paper, & am clean as a Whistle—
> Yours, Dear George Sick, or Well clean or beshit . . .'

Garrick had not in fact been entirely well that winter. 'My cough began to alarm Me—a nervous One & took away my Senses,' he told Colman. 'I am like yᵉ Weather—breaking a little.'[10] By the middle of February—he was writing two days before his fiftieth birthday—he was able to report that a stay at Hampton had had 'a prodigious Effect' upon him; 'my Cough & hoarseness are 50 p cent better for yᵉ Change of air—instead of coughing all night, I have been disturb'd but twice & thrice & that not rudely.'[11] A month later, however, he decided that he must take the waters and he and his wife set off for Bath.

He was soon in better shape. 'I am grown as fat as a Hog' he was able to tell George by early April, '& You may measure with Me at my return to London, without tucking in Your Guts, till Your face is as red, as bull-beef.' As always, between visits to the pump-room, he conducted an enormous volume of business by correspondence. Noverre had written from Paris to offer his services—was Lacy still opposed to the idea? George must send him a full account of 'the New hodge podge of Linco'—this was an interlude called *Linco's Travels* which he had dashed off to capitalize on King's success in the part of Linco in *Cymon*, and which was performed for King's benefit night.*

---

* *Letters*, 450. It had been rather successful. Garrick employed the formula that had served him well in *The Farmer's Return from London* six years previously. After briefly satirizing various foreigners, he homes in on a favourite target—the Englishman who returns from the Grand Tour practically disabled by affectation.

He also wrote to congratulate one Joseph Reed on the success of his tragedy *Dido*, although the piece had been withdrawn after only three performances. The production had gone forward much against Garrick's better judgement. Reed, a rope-maker with literary ambitions and a friend of Lacy's, had been pestering Garrick since the late 1750s and *Dido* had been the subject of protracted bickering. A writer in the *St James's Chronicle* had dismissed it as 'the greatest insult on the Taste and Judgment of the Town, of any Performance that was ever publickly exhibited'. It was a view very close to Garrick's own. 'And does *Dido* please?' he wrote to George. 'Good God! 'tis time to leave ye Stage, if such a performance can Stand upon It's legs.'*

Garrick's relations with Colman had once again deteriorated. Colman had arrived in Bath in the company of Philip Changuion, a diplomat who was the secretary to the British Embassy in Naples and Sicily. 'We pull'd off our hats, but did not smile,' Garrick told George. 'Our Friends here will stir heaven & Earth to bring Us togeather—make ye best of it, it will be but a darn.'[12]

There had been some coolness during the winter over the arrangements for Colman's play *The English Merchant*, which had been given its first performance in February.† Garrick had come to believe that the practice of dispensing with an afterpiece during the initial run of a new play was not in the interest either of author or management. Judging that Colman's latest offering would appeal more to the boxes and the pit than to other parts of the house, he argued that it would benefit from the support of a farce or a light comedy. The management also took the view that the recent enlargement of the house justified an increase in the charge made to authors on their benefit night.‡ Colman did not take kindly to either proposal, and Garrick deferred to his friend's wishes. The play did not, however, as Murphy put it, 'make a good trading voyage' and Colman realized—too late—that he would have done better to accept the managers' suggestions.

More seriously, it had now come to Garrick's ears that Colman was negotiating to buy into the management of Covent Garden. There had been rumours since the previous summer that Beard, increasingly afflicted by deafness, was contemplating premature retirement. Garrick, indeed, in an excited note to Colman during the latter's stay in Paris, had been the first to give him news of it:

Beard & co. are going (*positively*) to sell their Patent &c for 60000—'tis true—but Mum—we have not yet discover'd ye Purchasers—When I know you shall know—there will be ye Devil to do—[13]

---

* *Letters*, 450. A farce by Reed called *The Register Office* had been performed at Drury Lane six years previously. It had fallen foul of the Licenser, who took exception to its profanities and *double entendres* and ordered the excision of two of the characters, Lady Wrinkle and Mrs Snarewell. In the text the latter is warm in her praise of the comfort she has received from Mr Watchlight, twice called from his bed to pray and 'so earnest in his ejaculations'.
† Colman adapted it from an unperformed play of Voltaire's called *L'Ecossaise*.
‡ The capacity of the house had been increased from £220 to £337. It was proposed to raise the charge to authors from sixty to seventy guineas.

When Colman mentioned a letter he had received from a certain 'person of fashion' Garrick, whose ear was always very close to the ground, made a shrewd guess that his friend was being invited to join in the purchase of the rival house. Now, nine months later, when they were thrown together almost daily in Bath, Colman still maintained an embarrassed silence, although Garrick, with his incomparable network of contacts, was quietly piecing the jigsaw together. 'Now to the *grand* affair,' he wrote to George at the end of April:

> Pray return my best respects to my partner, and tell him, if you think proper, that the news of the sale of the other house gives me not the least uneasiness. . . . What a strange affair! We shall know all in time. I am satisfied, be the news true or false. I shall most certainly keep the secret. I think Forest would not deceive you.[14]

If George had been briefed by Theodosius Forrest it is unlikely that there was much which Garrick did not know. Forrest was a prosperous lawyer. Passionately interested in the arts, he was also a talented painter—he exhibited for many years at the Royal Academy. He was a close friend of both Colman's and Garrick's; he was also, crucially, the solicitor to Covent Garden, and therefore undoubtedly privy to the smallest detail relating to the negotiations for the sale of the patent.

Colman had still not come clean by the end of April. 'Colman has told me that he has an affair to open to Me,' Garrick wrote to George, 'but we have always been interrupted by Somebody, or another, so I have not yet had ye Whole, & which he has some qualms in bringing out.'[15] Colman's qualms were understandable. His passion for the theatre tugged him one way, but there was strong family pressure for him to move in another. The death of the Earl of Bath three years previously had brought him an income of 900 guineas, but the bulk of the Bath estates had passed to the Earl's brother, General Pulteney. The General had made it plain that any further expectations Colman entertained would be fulfilled only if he totally abandoned his theatrical connections—and that that included his connection with Miss Ford, the mother of little Georgy.

That was a higher price than Colman was willing to pay. His mind finally made up, he sought Garrick out on 2 May and told him the whole story. 'I rec'd ye News very calmly, & I believe Surpriz'd him,' Garrick told George—'You shall know all when I see You.'[16] Colman had originally been approached by William Powell, who had secured the backing of a wine merchant called Rutherford and a soap manufacturer called Harris. Between them they had found the £60,000 which was the asking price for the patent.

Although Garrick regretted the ending of his association with Colman, there was no reason to take formal exception to what had happened. Powell was a different matter. 'I have told Colman that I cannot forgive Powell's behaviour to me, and breach of articles,' he wrote to George. Powell, he declared, was a scoundrel. Lacy concurred, and they agreed that they would exact their pound of flesh—Powell's articles with Drury Lane were for three years, and carried a penalty bond of £1,000.

Garrick returned to London at the beginning of May. He appeared as Chalk-stone by royal command on the seventh of the month, and two nights later, when the mainpiece was *Othello*, the diarist Sylas Neville* spotted him in the audience:

> End of ye play Baddeley spoke a composition of his own, called "Search after Scrubs," to hear which Garrick came into ye orchestra. He looks healthy and strong, and should oftener entertain ye Public to which he owes so much.[17]

He also owed it to the public to make his dispositions for meeting the sharpened competition which must now be expected from Colman. Richard Yates and his wife had decided to follow Powell to Covent Garden. Yates was one of Garrick's oldest friends in the theatre; he had less time for his wife, although professionally she was the greater loss to the company. The death of Mrs Cibber and the indifferent health of Mrs Pritchard meant that she now had no real rival for the main tragic parts. She and her husband overplayed their hand, however, and Garrick and Lacy refused to come up with the sort of salary increase they had asked for.†

King, recently recovered from a riding accident in which he had broken his thigh, had been propositioned by the new management at Covent Garden, but had decided to stay put—a relief to Garrick, because he was now established as Drury Lane's chief comedian and, after Garrick himself, its chief attraction. Kitty Clive was now well into her fifties. She had been an inimitable Mrs Heidelberg in *The Clandestine Marriage*, but she had created no new parts in the most recent season; possibly beginning to feel her age, she had subscribed two guineas to the new Drury Lane retirement fund.

There was new talent filling in behind, however. Jane Pope, very much a *protégée* of Clive's, was now in her mid-twenties and had come on impressively since her adult début in 1759. She too had done well in *The Clandestine Marriage*, where she was Miss Sterling, and she had created the role of Lucy in *The Country Girl*. Garrick could also look for strong performances to Miss Abington, who had rejoined the company two years previously after six hugely successful seasons in Dublin. She was temperamental, certainly, but the day when an exasperated manager would call her 'the worst of bad women' still lay some way ahead. There would obviously now be a shift in emphasis at Covent Garden from the musical to the theatrical, but all in all, the managers of Drury Lane could contemplate the challenge from Colman's new enterprise with relative equanimity.

---

* Neville, Sylas, *The Diary of Sylas Neville, 1767–1788*, ed. Basil Cozens-Hardy, London, 1950. The passage quoted occurs in a typescript of unpublished portions of the *Diary*, of which there is a microfilm in the Folger Library.

† The Yateses' salary negotiations came to public notice, and Mrs Yates felt obliged to write to the press denying that she had asked for sixteen hundred pounds for herself and her husband for the season. Their joint demand, she asserted, was 'scarcely more than Mrs Cibber had for her own single services'. (The *Gazetteer*, 5 October 1767.)

There has sometimes been a tendency, in probing the character and temperament of David Garrick, to lay undue emphasis on how cautious and orderly a man he was. He was certainly both those things, and they were qualities which would have commanded the grave approval of his Huguenot grandfather. Two other salient characteristics should not be overlooked, however. They are traits common to successful men in all ages, whether they have made their mark as admirals or impresarios or captains of industry—the capacity to surprise, and a readiness to take risks.

By deciding to offer terms for the new season to his old rival Spranger Barry, Garrick was risking a great deal.

26

All Hurry and Bustle

Barry had not appeared at Drury Lane for ten years. His affairs in Ireland had ceased to prosper, and for the past two summers he had returned to London, performing at the King's Theatre and the Haymarket.

Like Garrick, he was now into his fifties. Sylas Neville, who saw him in *The Beggar's Opera* that summer, thought he was a good Macheath, but noted that 'most persons who have seen him when young observe that he has not ye activity and fire he then had'. Garrick made it his business to satisfy himself about such matters; Neville sat near him in the pit at the Haymarket one night when Barry was appearing as Hastings in *Jane Shore*.*

Barry had not returned to London alone. Mrs Ann Dancer was the daughter of a Bath apothecary and the widow of another actor. She had been on the stage since she was seventeen and was now in her early thirties. She had taken up openly with Barry shortly after her husband's death eight years previously, and under his tuition her acting had greatly improved.

Whether in other circumstances Garrick would have recruited Ann Dancer on her individual merits is not certain; the *London Magazine* in July of that year expressed the view that 'her passion very frequently rises into turbulence'. She was part of the package, however, and an expensive package it was. Garrick and Lacy initially agreed to a combined salary of £1,300, and this was later raised to £1,500.

Battle was joined between the two houses in the second week of September. Garrick chose to open the season with *The Clandestine Marriage*, and Colman opted for *The Rehearsal*. Powell spoke a prologue which harked back to the beginning of Garrick's tenure at Drury Lane and seemed to suggest that he had not delivered all that he had promised:

> Like Brother Monarchs, who, to coax the nation
> Began their reign, with some fair proclamation,

---

* Disappointingly, Neville records no reaction. We do know, however, what Garrick thought of Ned Shuter's performance in the afterpiece, which was his own *Lethe*: he 'laughed at his understanding y^e character of Lord Chalkstone so little, as to say—"She married for money, and I for a title." ' Shuter may have been drunk, which he frequently was. He should have said the opposite: 'I married for a fortune; she for a title.'

Spranger Barry, the son of a wealthy Dublin silversmith, was an almost exact contemporary of Garrick's, and for some years a serious rival. Later he and his wife became increasingly temperamental and difficult and gave Garrick a good many managerial headaches. They are shown here as Jaffier and Belvidera in Otway's Venice Preserved. *(Bell's British Theatre, Vol. 1, 1780)*

We too should talk at least—of reformation . . .

It then went on, as manifestos do in any walk of life, to pledge that there would be something for everybody. There was, for instance, an ever-so-slightly barbed promise of classical fare for *'those deep sages of the judging pit/ Whose taste is too refined for modern wit.'* For the gallery there would, naturally, be pantomime, although that assurance, accompanied as it was by a ritual obeisance to the memory of 'good King Rich', was qualified by a hint that Colman intended to move slightly up market:

> Yet 'midst the pomp and magic of machines,
> Some plot may mark the meaning of our scenes.

There was also a delicate indication that under the new order, musical offerings would be scrutinized with a beadier eye than had recently been the case:

> Gay Opera shall all its charms dispense,
> Yet boast no tuneful triumph over sense;
> The nobler Bard shall still assert his right,
> Nor Handel rob a Shakespeare of his night . . .

Before the season was three days old, an entry in Hopkins's diary indicated that the Drury Lane prompter felt the other house was being unsporting: 'This evening Covent Garden played against us unexpected, on which account both houses performed every night.' It was clearly going to be war to the knife.

Colman made a start on beefing up the repertoire by attacking the long-standing discrepancy between the number of new productions put on at the two houses. In the previous season Garrick had presented eleven new pieces to Beard's four; this year the ratio was narrowed and came out at seven to five. It was a modest beginning, but it signalled that Colman intended to bring managerial—and editorial—muscle to bear.

Significantly, one of the new mainpieces presented at Covent Garden had earlier been rejected by Drury Lane. Garrick had never got on with Oliver Goldsmith; he may also still have harboured some resentment at the disobliging references Goldsmith had made to him in his *Enquiry into the Present State of Polite Learning* eight years previously.* He endorsed one of the author's letters about an early draft of the play in question 'Goldsmith's parlaver', and although he found honeyed words to excuse his lack of enthusiasm for the piece—'it has been ye business & ambition of my Life to live upon ye best terms wth Men of Genius'[1]—that ambition did not translate into accepting *The Good-natur'd Man* for production.

When Colman picked it up and placed it in the Covent Garden schedule for

---

* When Goldsmith sought Garrick's support in a bid for the vacant secretaryship of the Society of Arts two years later, he was met with a sour refusal: 'Mr Goldsmith having taken pains to deprive himself of his assistance by an unprovoked attack upon his management of the theatre in his 'Present State of Learning,' it was impossible he could lay claim to any recommendation from him.'

January, Garrick decided on a spoiling tactic; six nights before Goldsmith's piece was due to open, he put on the sentimental comedy *False Delicacy* by Hugh Kelly. That he was able to do so said a good deal for his powers of persuasion. Kelly had been born in Killarney, the son of a tavern keeper, and was originally apprenticed to a staymaker. Deciding that there must be more to life than corsets, he had come to London some years previously to try his hand at literature. Davies says that by frequenting a public house close to Drury Lane he picked up, 'from the lowest retainers of the stage', all manner of gossip about the characters and private lives of the players; he wrote about them with such severity in the public prints that he had to take to wearing a sword.[2]

In 1766 he had brought out a poem called *Thespis*, a sort of poor man's *Rosciad*. It was sub-titled *A Critical Examination into the Merits of all the Principal Performers Belonging to Drury-Lane Theatre*, and although he was lavish in his praise of what Davies called 'the lowest of the comedians', he was extremely abusive about some of the more prominent members of the company, writing of Kitty Clive's 'weak head and execrable heart' and describing Mrs Dancer as 'a moon-eyed ideot'. As he was busy with his comedy at the time, it seemed politic to praise the manager. The audience he averred, was insufficiently appreciative of Garrick's genius; the only criticism he had of him was that at a crucial moment in *Lear* he turned his back on the audience, thus robbing them of the sight of his facial expressions.

Garrick thought well enough of the play's potential to touch it up for Kelly, but when it came to the distribution of parts, he faced a wall of hostility. 'To Mrs Clive, I fancy,' Davies writes, 'he had not the courage to make any application.'[3] Moody, still one of the company's comic mainstays and the man to whom Garrick was indebted for his stout behaviour during the Fitzpatrick riots, refused point-blank to be cast; Garrick did, however, succeed in mollifying Mrs Dancer, and she took the part of the widow, Mrs Harley.

Johnson pronounced the play to be 'totally void of character'. The critics attacked what they saw as its dull sentimentality. Garrick, in his cleverly pre-emptive prologue, conceded that the piece was 'quite a *Sermon*—only preached in *Acts*', but once again, his incomparable nose for what would work paid handsome dividends. Davies has a nice passage describing Kelly's delight at his sudden emergence 'from obscurity into sunshine':

> When he went to the playhouse treasury to receive the profits of his first third night, which amounted to 150*l*. not having ever seen so much money of his own before, he was all astonishment; he put the money into his pocket as fast as he could, and ran home to his wife in a rapture to communicate to her the pleasure he had enjoyed.[4]

The theatres and public gardens had been closed for a week early in the season by order of the Lord Chamberlain—the king's brother, the Duke of York, had died in Monaco. Edward Augustus was known mainly for his dissipation and his fondness for amateur theatricals—he had a private theatre in James Street off the Haymarket, and Garrick had been in the audience for his production of

The Fair Penitent there the previous April.* The Duke was not universally mourned. Sylas Neville, who harboured strongly republican sentiments, wrote in his diary, 'Glad to hear that the Lothario of that Company, the infamous York, is called to that Tribunal where there is no respect of persons.'

Covent Garden had naturally relied heavily on Powell in the early weeks of the new season, and before September was out he had been seen as Jaffier in *Venice Preserv'd* and as King John and Romeo. Garrick for some reason held his fire with Barry and Mrs Dancer. Her first appearance was in the middle of October, and they played together a week later in *Lear*. Garrick responded to the sharpened competition from Colman by acting rather more frequently himself than he had the previous year, appearing during September and October as Brute, Kitely, Ranger and Benedick. For his performance in *Much Ado*, Sylas Neville managed—just—to find a place in the pit. 'Was so squeezed I could scarcely use my glass,' he wrote in his diary. 'How well and with what Agility Garrick dances.'

Garrick also notched up a further success as a playwright. *A Peep Behind the Curtain* had its first performance on 23 October, and was in no need of the fulsome puff which appeared in that day's *Theatrical Observer*.† With brilliant performances from Tom King as Glib, the author, and from Kitty Clive as the absurd Lady Fuz, it played for twenty-five nights in its first season and went into three editions before the end of the year.

This two-act playlet was the first of a number of burlesque-rehearsal pieces which Garrick would write. The device of a play-within-a-play had a long history. Peele had employed it in *The Old Wives' Tale* in 1595, as had Shakespeare in *A Midsummer Night's Dream* and *Hamlet*, while nearer to Garrick's own day there had been Buckingham's *The Rehearsal*. Garrick departed from the traditional pattern by making his play-within-a-play a burletta.‡ The music was by François Hippolyte Barthélemon, a French violinist who at the time was leader of the band at the King's Theatre and had had an opera, *Pelopida*, produced there in 1766. Garrick, impressed, had sought him out to enquire whether he could set English words to music, and on being told that he could, sat down there and then to write out the words of a song he wished to use in *The Country Girl*. The story goes that as Garrick scribbled, the Frenchman looked over his shoulder and scribbled every bit as quickly. 'There, sir, is my song,' said

---

* He commented on the performance in a letter to Sir John Hussey Delaval: 'There was one passage in Lothario, which I thought at the time, his Royal Highness might have spoken with more levity, and a kind of profligate insensibility to yᵉ distresses of Calista.' He praised the playing of Calista; the part had been taken by Lady Stanhope, who was Delaval's sister and the Duke's current mistress. (*Letters*, 448.)
† The piece has the finger prints of the Drury Lane management all over it—'very extensive fund of humour' . . . 'the entertainment it affords is exquisite' . . . 'Mrs Clive is extremely capital' . . . 'one of the most pleasing productions, in its kind, which the stage has ever exhibited'.
‡ A burletta was technically any piece of three acts which contained at least five songs. Enterprising managers at some of the minor theatres occasionally used it as a ploy to get round the terms of the Licensing Act.

Garrick as he laid down his pen. 'And there, sir,' countered Barthélemon, 'is my music.'*

Slight as it is, *A Peep Behind the Curtain* represents an intriguing snapshot of how Garrick viewed the theatrical landscape of the day. As the curtain rises on Scene II to discover two women sweeping the stage at Drury Lane, he glances at the rivalry between the two houses:

FIRST WOMAN. Come, Betty, dust away, dust away, girl, the managers will
   be here presently. Here's no lying in bed for them now. We are up early
   and late, all hurry and bustle from morning to night. I wonder what the
   deuce they have got into their heads?
SECOND WOMAN. Why to get money, Mrs. Besom, to be sure. The folks say
   about us, that the other house will make them stir their stumps and they'll
   make us stir ours. If they are in motion we must not stand still, Mrs.
   Besom.

In a sequence between the prompter and the manager, he mocks the pretensions and bickerings of the players:

PROMPTER. The young fellow from Edinburgh won't accept of the second
   Lord; he desires to have the first.
PATENT (The Manager). I don't doubt it—Well, well, if the author can make
   him speak English, I have no objection.
PROMPTER. Mr. Rantly is indisposed and can't play tomorrow.
PATENT. Well, well, let his lungs rest a little. They want it, I'm sure. What a
   campaign we shall make of it. All our subalterns will be general officers
   and our generals will only fight when they please.

Sir Macaroni Virtu ('he's too polite to be punctual') is the fashionable fop who turns up late at the theatre and pretty well everywhere else. Interestingly, it is into his mouth that Garrick puts his own view of sentimental comedy: 'My ingenious countrymen have no taste now for the high-seasoned comedies, and I am sure I have none for the pap and loplolly of our present writers.'

In the burletta, Garrick first takes aim at Italian opera. Patent, the manager, warns the author against emptying the boxes. 'Take care, Mr. Glib, not to make it so much above proof that the boxes can't taste it,' he cautions:

GLIB. Empty boxes! I'll engage that my Cerberus alone shall fill the boxes for
   a month.
PATENT. Cerberus?
GLIB. Be quiet a little. You know, I suppose, that Cerberus is a dog and has
   three heads?

---

* Barthélemon (1741–1808) was a native of Bordeaux. He had come to London in 1764 and made his first public appearance on 5 June that year at the Spring Garden in St James's Park. The same concert saw another notable London début; the bills announced that it was for the benefit of 'Miss Mozart of eleven, and Master Mozart of seven Years of age, Prodigies of Nature'.

PATENT. I have heard as much.

GLIB. Then you shall see some sport. He shall be a comical dog, too, I warrant you. Ha, ha, ha!

PATENT. What, is Cerberus a character in your performance?

GLIB. Capital, capital! I have thrown all my fancy and invention into his mouth, or rather mouths. There are three of 'em, you know.

PATENT. Most certainly, if there are three heads.

GLIB. Poh, that's nothing to what I have *in petto* for you. Observe me now. When Orpheus comes to the gates of hell, Cerberus stops him. But how, how? Now for it—guess—

PATENT. Upon my soul, I can't guess.

GLIB. I make his three heads sing a trio.

PATENT. A trio?

GLIB. A trio! I knew I should hit you. A trio, treble, tenor and bass, and what shall they sing? Nothing in the world but 'Bow, wow, wow!' . . .

PATENT. Very ingenious and very new. I hope the critics will understand it.

Having revenged himself thus sweetly on the regiment of inane dramatists he has had to humour over the years, Garrick decides that although he has already winged the writers of sentimental comedy, they are still worth his second barrel. He represents Orpheus as a man of fashion who 'upon a qualm of conscience quits his mistress and sets out for hell with a resolution to fetch his wife'—a nice thrust at the sentimental convention that the rake becomes a reformed character at the eleventh hour:

PATENT. Is that, too, like a man of fashion, Mr. Glib?

GLIB. No, that's the *moral* part of him. He's a mixed character. But as he approaches and gets into the infernal regions, his principles melt away by degrees, as it were by the heat of the climate. And finding that his wife Eurydice is kept by Pluto, he immediately makes up to Proserpine and is kept by her. Then they all four agree matters amicably, change partners, as one may say, make a general *partie quarrée*, and finish the whole with a song and a chorus. And a stinger it is. The subject of the song is the old proverb, 'Exchange is no robbery' . . .

It is plain from his correspondence that autumn that Garrick was far from having recovered his former zest for the theatre—was indeed still actively considering retirement from it. Early in October he wrote to his 'dear, charming, scolding Friend' Madame Riccoboni:

I have now a nearer prospect, than I have had for Years, of getting rid of all my Cares at once—I need not tell You, who know Something of theatres, that I mean to break my theatrical Chains, & be a Gentleman at large—when that happy Day is arriv'd my first thoughts will fly to My dear Friends in Paris, & do You, above all Madam Riccoboni, prepare Yourself for being tormented from Morning to Night—I'll haunt You more than Ghosts ever did a guilty Conscience, or to come little nearer the truth, more than Ever Lover did a Mistress—I will so torment You, that our Names shall be eccho'd all over Paris, & we will make a figure in ye Chronique Scandaleuse.[5]

He was also now finding it easier to fend off the importunities of the great when they pressed him for favours. 'I shall always be happy to obey Your Grace's Commands,' he wrote to the Duchess of Portland, 'but our Company at present is so full and all the Parts dispos'd of, that I could not without great injustice to those Actors I have already Engag'd, employ the person you recommend.' He assured the Duchess that he had given her protégé, a Mr Collins, what advice he could, but he was not inclined, as he might have been some years earlier, to leave it at that:

If your Grace will permit me to speak my Mind, I think he has the most unpromising Aspect for an Actor I ever saw—a small pair of unmeaning Eyes stuck in a round unthinking face are not the most desirable requisites for a Hero, or a fine Gentleman—[6]

Garrick responded amiably during the autumn to an offer from Isaac Bickerstaffe to attempt a reconciliation with Murphy (the most recent of their many misunderstandings had been over The Country Girl a year previously—Murphy had accused Garrick of putting it on to 'hurt' the actress Ann Elliot, who was his mistress, and for whom he had written his own version of The Country Wife). 'You are a good Christian,' Garrick wrote to Bickerstaffe. 'As I am almost upon my Theatrical death-bed, I wish to die in Charity & Good Will with all Men of Merit & wth None more so (as He wishes it too) than with Mr Murphy.'[7]

Relations were restored and a few weeks later we find Murphy writing a friendly letter about a performance of Macbeth. One of the most impressive—and attractive—things about Garrick was the way in which throughout his life he remained open to criticism: 'I was indeed not quite Master of my feelings till I got to clutching the air-drawn dagger,' he conceded in his reply. It was a mark of his intense professionalism that he was always ready to discuss any aspect of his art—the state of mind of a character, the delivery of a particular line, the emphasis to be given to a single word. That Murphy had many times shown himself to be both tiresome and treacherous mattered not at all. 'You have flatter'd me much by Your very Obliging letter,' Garrick told him:

I shall profit by y^r Criticisms this evening, if I should happen to be in Order—I am an Old Hunter, touch'd a little in Wind, & somewhat founder'd, but stroke me, & clap me on the back, as You have kindly done, and I can make a Shift to gallop over the Course.[8]

This cleared the way for the production of Murphy's Zenobia, which became Drury Lane's main tragic offering of the season. The plot was based on the story of Rhadamistus, which Murphy knew from Tacitus, and which Crébillon had used in his Rhadamiste et Zénobie, a farrago of love, jealousy, incest and parricide which was the best the French theatre had been able to do in the early years of the century to fill the void left by Racine and Corneille.* 'All that this writer will say of himself,' Murphy wrote modestly, 'is that he did not choose to be a mere copyist, but had the ambition to aim at originality.'⁹

Garrick pulled out all the stops. The play was in rehearsal for the best part of a month, he took great pains over the scenery ('magnificent and new,' a *Court Miscellany* writer thought) and Barry and Mrs Dancer took the main parts.† The run was interrupted, however, by a display of thespian temperament. After the sixth performance, Mrs Dancer (she was by now married to Barry) announced that she was not well enough to play Zenobia again two nights later. When *False Delicacy* was substituted, and the ailing Mrs Dancer appeared in it as Mrs Harley, Murphy was understandably put out, although his description of the incident as 'without precedent in the annals of the theatre' was something of an exaggeration.

Zenobia had one more outing on 19 March, but after that the other half of the Barry ménage fell genuinely ill, and it was played no more that season.‡ Murphy did rather well out of it—his share of the profits came to just over £467—and when the play was published he included in the preface a fulsome tribute to Garrick: 'His politeness from the moment he saw the play, his assiduity in preparing it for representation, the taste in which he decorated it, and the warmth of his zeal for the honour of the piece, are circumstances that call upon me for the strongest acknowledgements.' They would not quarrel again for five years.

No Drury Lane season would be complete without Kitty Clive making a fuss about her benefit. 'I am Surpriz'd that You have not thank'd the Managers for their kindness instead of writing so peevish a Letter,' Garrick told her in the middle of February. 'If you will not Advertise & fix your play, Your folly be upon your own head.' The fiery Kitty did not yield easily, and Garrick had to try again the next day: 'Dear Clive, How can you be so ridiculous & still so cross to Mistake every word of my letter?' he wrote:

> You will find in your present humour objections to any day, but we really meant you *kindly* in giving You your own day, that You might avoid Opera Nights, & have nobody to come immediately before or After you— This I did not do out of *Charity*, but out of that respect, which I ever pay to Genius; And it is not my fault that Mrs Clive will not be as rational off the Stage as She is Meritorious on it.§

---

* First produced in 1711, it had remained in the repertory of the Comédie-Française. Joseph Knight suggests that Garrick may have seen it there and recommended it to Murphy's attention.
† The casting of Barry as Rhadamistus while a much younger actor, Aickin, played his father, Pharasmanes, was condemned by one critic as a solecism: 'In old plays, where the parts are already cast, this may be allowable, where the actors have been long in possession of a character,' he wrote, 'but in new plays nothing is so sensibly felt as this inversion of scenical propriety.' (*Court Miscellany* IV, 40, March 1768.)
‡ Barry's illness was followed in April by the death of his son, Thomas, in Dublin. Garrick wrote a letter of condolence and agreed to the postponement of his benefit.
§ *Letters*, 488. A performance of opera at the Haymarket could have an effect on attendances at Drury Lane.

Peace was restored, and the date of 17 March was agreed, although it turned out that Mrs Yates had chosen the same night for her benefit at the other house. The Drury Lane audience got their money's worth. Mrs Clive acted Lady Wishfort in *The Way of the World* and Lady Fuz in *A Peep Behind the Curtain*, and for that night only Mrs Pritchard paid her the compliment of appearing as Millamant in the mainpiece.

A month later, after thirty-six years on the stage, Mrs Pritchard made her final appearance. Her farewell performances that season had included Gertrude, Mrs Oakly, Queen Elizabeth in *Richard III* and Dol Common. Now, for the last time, she appeared as Lady Macbeth, and Garrick, who played opposite her, provided her with a suitably tear-jerking epilogue:

> The Curtain dropt—my Mimic life is past;
> That Scene of Sleep & terror was my last . . .
> I now appear Myself—distress'd, dismay'd,
> More than in All the Characters I've play'd—

She spoke the epilogue 'with many sobs and tears,' wrote Davies, 'which were increased by the generous feelings of a numerous and splendid audience.'[10] She retired to Bath, but enjoyed only the shortest of retirements, dying there on 20 August—Garrick heard the news in a letter from Thomas Gainsborough.*

Rather unsportingly, Covent Garden had chosen the night of Mrs Pritchard's last appearance to mount Powell's début as Hamlet. Colman was having a bumpy ride during his first season as manager. He had quickly won the loyalty of most of the players, and the company was by no means short of talent. In addition to Powell, he could, after all, rely on the varied experience of Mrs Bellamy and Mrs Yates and of Harry Woodward, Ned Shuter and 'Gentleman' Smith. Colman's troubles lay elsewhere. It soon emerged that the terms of the contract with his partners were both vague and ambiguous; the limits of his authority were unclear, and his actions appeared to be subject to the veto of Harris and Rutherford. What also emerged was that these two worthies had come on board for reasons very different from Colman's. A principal interest, naturally, was to make money, but they were also eager, in Highfill's delicate euphemism, 'to enlarge their scope for gallantry'.

Before the season was a month old the new manager was faced with demands for private dressing rooms from Jane Lessingham, who had become Harris's mistress and from la Bellamy, who had taken shelter under Rutherford's wing. This was followed by interference over a production of *Cymbeline*. Colman had cast Miss Ward as Imogen, but came under pressure from Harris to give it instead to Miss Lessingham. Colman, his streak of native stubbornness privately reinforced by advice from Garrick, responded by taking the part from Miss Ward

---

* Davies describes the cause of death as 'a mortification in her foot'—presumably some form of gangrene. The strength of the company had also been depleted, three months previously, by the death of Mrs Pritchard's son-in-law, 'Gentleman' John Palmer. He was only forty, and had been with Garrick since the 1748–9 season.

and giving it instead to Mrs Yates, who had owned it at Drury Lane, and this provoked Harris and Rutherford to intemperate retaliation. They arbitrarily fired the prompter, took over the account book from the treasurer and accused Colman of defrauding them of £65 over an alteration that he proposed to *King Lear*.

By early March, private strife had become public warfare, and both sides went into print. At the end of the season, Harris and Rutherford tried to commandeer the premises, whereupon Colman ordered the doors and windows to be barricaded. On 17 June his partners forced their way in with a band of bully boys, and for three weeks Colman was locked out of the theatre, regaining entry only by virtue of a warrant issued by the high sheriffs of London and Middlesex.

That Colman managed in such circumstances to keep the show on the road is remarkable enough. That he actually contrived to make a success of the season both artistically and financially is astonishing. Gross receipts came to £31,105. The theatre mounted 79 different plays and afterpieces. Colman's five new productions included, as well as Goldsmith's *Good-Natur'd Man*, his own *The Oxonian in Town*. This ran for twenty-two nights, although for some of that time Colman lived dangerously. Handbills were distributed at the theatre on the third night to pacify the London Irish, who were threatening to riot on the ground that the play slandered their compatriots.*

By comparison with these continuing dramas of Colman's, Garrick's managerial problems appeared no more than little local difficulties, although his relations with Lacy were once again not of the most cordial. 'I am sick of his *mean, ungratefull, wretched behaviour*' he wrote to George in July (Lacy had shown some resistance to the idea that George's salary should be increased).[11] Later in the summer, in a letter to Paterson, he spoke of 'some disagreeable circumstances which have lately happen'd between my Partner and me' and declared that he had resolved to 'close our theatrical Connection' as soon as possible:

> Mr Lacy thinks & speaks very injuriously and unjustly of my Brother, has very ill requited my Services and has lately done some things which I think shews a spirit contrary to that of our Articles, and the terms of our reconciliation settled before you therefore I will immediatly prepare for my Brother's retreat, & will most assuredly follow him.[12]

Whatever these disagreeable circumstances were, they were not allowed to interfere with Garrick's customary round of summer pleasures. He had committed himself to so much that he was having difficulty fitting in a visit to the Burkes at Gregories: 'I endeavour'd to get Clear of Mistley this Year,' he explained,

---

* The play was also attacked as immoral, because several of the characters were whores, sharpers or pickpockets. Sylas Neville, who was in the pit that night, gave it his qualified approval: 'If vice must not be exposed to hatred and contempt, the usefulness of our theatres is at an end. Only I think the Covent Garden pleasures are represented in too favourable a light.'

apologetically but not entirely convincingly, in the middle of June. Rigby had recently got his heart's desire and been appointed Paymaster. It is true that in his letter of congratulation Garrick had referred to the press of business in his new office, but Rigby was very clear about his priorities. He might be one of the most venal men in public life, but in private considerations of friendship were paramount. Garrick was so flattered with the proof of this that he enclosed Rigby's letter for Burke to see:

> Do you imagine, my David, that any paltry consideration of office or business shall deprive me of the pleasure of our Mistley party? I should be worth but half the Pay-Office, indeed, if I could sacrifice the rites of Mistley to any earthly consideration. No; they begin the 25th, at dinner, and you and your *Cara Sposa* are expected by her, and your, faithful humble servant.*

Several weeks later, still somewhat fragile from the Paymaster's hospitality, Garrick was obliged to send renewed excuses to Burke: 'Had I not kept my room ever since I left his honour's Claret at Mistley, You should have heard from Me, seen me before this—' Further obstacles now had to be explained. He must make good a promise he had broken the previous year to visit Lord De La Warr at his seat in the New Forest;† he must entertain Lord Camden and his wife to dinner at Hampton; he must rush up to town 'to prepare some thing, as I am told for his Majesty of Denmark'.

Christian VII, a youth of nineteen, had ascended the Danish throne in 1766, and had been married in the same year to the Princess Caroline-Matilda, George III's fifteen-year-old sister. The Lord Chamberlain's command to Garrick was that he should entertain the Danish monarch by performing six of his principal characters. John Hawkins, who lived at Twickenham, remembered Garrick calling on him with the news: 'I could plainly discern in his looks the joy that transported him; but he affected to be vexed at the shortness of the notice.'[13]

It was a tall order, for all that. The two patent theatres were closed for the summer. Many of the players were on holiday or engaged in the provinces. Garrick took stock of who was in town and persuaded Mrs Bellamy and Woodward to come over from Covent Garden to help him out. They both appeared with him in *The Suspicious Husband* on 18 August. One of those present was Mrs Delany. 'Such a crowd as was in the pit I never heard of. They were so close and so *hot*, that every man pulled off his coat and sat in his waistcoat,' she wrote:

> When the King of Denmark came in the clapping and noise was prodigious; the poor boy looked almost frightened, but bowed on all sides over and over. When Garrick came in the house redoubled; his little majesty took it all to himself and redoubled his bows . . .[14]

---

* Rigby's letter is printed in *Boaden*, i, 304. Garrick was anxious that the disorderly Burke should not lose or mislay it: 'Return it to me in the note You'll send by Saturday's post,' he wrote. (*Letters*, 511.)
† De La Warr was at the time Vice-Chamberlain and Master of the Horse to Queen Charlotte.

Three weeks later Mrs Bellamy was Lady Fanciful when Garrick appeared as Sir John Brute in *The Provok'd Wife*.* Horace Walpole was highly diverted by the royal visitor's behaviour: 'He clapped whenever there was a sentence against matrimony; a very civil proceeding, when his wife is an English Princess!'† A few days after this the Danish king and his suite paid a visit to Hampton. 'You would think me vain should I tell you what he said,' Garrick wrote to Madame Riccoboni, '& I hope you will think me sincere, when I tell you that I had rather see You & yʳ friend there than all the Kings & Princes of Europe.'‡

There were further command performances for Christian after the start of the new season. It was said that Garrick had resolved that with Mrs Pritchard gone he would never again appear as Macbeth, but now he bowed to the royal wish and played it one last time. He was concerned that he should not be suspected of discourtesy, but he also wanted to make a point, and on the day of the performance sent a note to the Danish ambassador:

> Mʳ Garrick presents his respects to Baron Diede, & begs leave to inform Him, that it will be impossible after performing so violent a Character as Macbeth to attend his duty in lighting out the King of Denmark, He thought proper to acquaint the Baron Diede with this circumstance that Mʳ Garrick might not be thought wanting in Duty where he is so happy, & proud to pay it—§

He also, by the king's particular desire, appeared as Richard III, a performance which aroused enormous public interest. One of those who succeeded in fighting his way into the pit was Sylas Neville:

> Hearing about 7 o'clock that Garrick did Rich. III, one of his very capital characters which he has not done these 7 or 8 years, resolved (if I could get in to see him) to bear the abhorred sight of that woman-like painted puppy, the King of Denmark. After one unsuccessful attempt got into the Pit with the greatest difficulty after the 3rd Act. Garrick is inimitably great in Richard & very different from the other Richards I have seen; his expression of the dying agony of that wretch is beyond description. Some

---

* Lady Brute was played by an actress called Mrs Stephens, making her first appearance at Drury Lane after a dozen years in relatively minor parts at Covent Garden.

† *Walpole*, xxiii, 57. Letter to Mann dated 22 September 1768. Very little of what went on in the royal box passed unobserved. A few weeks previously, at the opera, Lady Mary Coke had spied the Danish King picking his nose.

‡ *Letters*, 519. Garrick had suggested the visit in a note to Lord Weymouth, at that time Secretary of State for the Southern Department, and a favourite of the King's: 'If the King of Denmark is pleas'd to see a farce, after Seeing Hampton Court, my little place will answer the purpose extremely well.' (*Letters*, 518.)

§ Garrick need not have worried, as a paragraph some weeks later in the *Gazeteer and New Daily Advertiser* made plain: 'We hear that Mr Garrick had the honour of being with the King of Denmark on Wednesday morning last; when talking with him for near half an hour upon the state of the stage in England and France, the King gave him a very elegant gold box, studded with diamonds, desiring him to receive it as a small mark of the great regard he had for his extraordinary talents.'

actors speak with as strong & loud a voice in that scene as if they had received no wound & were not dying. . . .[15]

Neville's virulently anti-monarchical sentiments made it difficult for him to give his undivided attention to what was happening on the stage:

During the Dance (for there was no Farce) I was within a yard of the Danish tyrant. O Heaven! what an instance of the corruption of mankind that a great nation should submit to the will—nay, the absolute will—of a puny vicious boy, unfit to govern himself & made for the distaff (like Sardanapalus) not for the rod of power.*

Christian had not, in fact, shown himself to be especially tyrannical in the first two years of his reign; when the German historian Niebuhr later compared him to Caligula he had in mind more the vices and excesses of the private man. It was noted in 1768 that his young queen did not accompany him on his European tour, but he was preceded by his unsavoury reputation. Self-indulgent and of feeble character, he had been poorly educated and comprehensively debauched by corrupt courtiers, chief among them the royal favourite Count Holck, who at twenty-three was Marshal of the Court. One of Holck's functions was to keep the king supplied with mistresses: 'a complete jackanapes,' Horace Walpole wrote to Montagu, 'who will be tumbled down long before he is prepared for it.'[16]

So he was, and so were several others of those who had strolled on Garrick's lawns at Hampton that summer. The preposterous Gothic saga that would unfold at the Danish court over the next few years—treason, adultery, imbecility, judicial beheadings and disembowellings—contained more horrors than Arthur Murphy would have dared to include in one of his tragedies.†

By the time the Danish king and his entourage moved on to Paris in search of further amusements, the new season was well under way. Garrick had an early success with *The Padlock*, a comic opera by Isaac Bickerstaffe presented as an afterpiece at the beginning of October. Hopkins thought it 'a very compleat, pretty piece', and so did the audience—over the next nine seasons it would be seen more than 140 times.

It was mounted with new scenery and costumes and Garrick worked very hard on it with the cast. He had struck up a friendship with a member of the Danish king's suite called Sturz, who was a keen student of the theatre, and allowed him to sit in on rehearsals. Sturz later wrote of how he marvelled that

---

* Neville's editor, concerned that modern readers might not understand the allusion, adds a note: 'The last king of the Assyrian empire of Nineveh, noted for his licentiousness and effeminacy.'

† The Danish King also patronized Covent Garden. According to Genest he fell asleep during a performance of *Jane Shore*: 'Annoyed, Mrs Yates, playing Alicia, drew near his Box and with violent exertion of voice cried out in her part "O Thou False Lord!" The King aroused declared he would not be married to a woman with such a voice for the world.' (*Genest*, v, 237.) Mrs Bellamy, however, in her memoirs, claims the starring role in this anecdote for herself.

The PIT DOOR.   La PORTE du PARTERRE.

Queuing for admission formed no part of the theatre-going culture of Garrick's day. The throwing open of the pit door was a signal for elbows and sticks to be brought into vigorous play. 'Went to Drury Lane, but could not get in,' the diarist Sylas Neville recorded in May 1767. 'Stayed from ‰ past 4, sometime at one Pit door and sometime at the other, till past 6 and got in at the right hand side just as the play began, and was dreadfully squeezed, but rewarded by seeing Mr. Garrick play Hamlet.' (The Lennox-Boyd Collection)

Garrick's none too robust health could stand the constant strain as he turned from one actor and character to another, 'attempting to kindle a fire where often no spark existed'.* Garrick offered the players very detailed guidance about how they should interpret their roles, often acting out whole scenes for their benefit in the green-room. He once compared his task as director with that of a teacher 'required to transform parrots into scholars and orators'.†

A new tragedy called *Zingis* fared less well. It was the work of a Scot called Alexander Dow, home on leave from the Bengal Infantry. 'He brought with him to England,' wrote Murphy, 'an imagination replete and warm with the works of the Persic writers.' That had helped him to publish a well-received *History of Hindoostan* the previous year, but Murphy dismissed his play with Johnsonian disdain: 'It abounded with absurdity, and a strange jargon of names and words, that were dissonant to the English ear.' It survived for the regulation nine nights, but 'the spectators were constantly asking each other, *What is it about?* To enquire now about the unintelligible, were a waste of time.'[17]

Garrick yielded this season for the second time to the importunities of Mrs Elizabeth Griffith, who had been stalking him relentlessly for some years. A native of Glamorganshire, married to an Irishman of good family but no fortune, she had been briefly on the stage in the 1750s before deciding to try her hand at novels and plays. Her *Platonic Wife* had been performed at Drury Lane without much success in 1765. A year later she had taken her second comedy, *The Double Mistake*, to Covent Garden, where it had an encouraging run of twelve nights, and before long she was pestering Garrick again, deploying a range of weaponry: 'Dear Sir,' she wrote in June 1766, 'I have been ill these ten days, and I really think it is you who have made me so, by unkindly refusing me an indulgence which I have set my heart upon—that of dedicating my play to you; but I am not so easily said nay to as you may imagine . . .'[18]

If she could be coy, Mrs Griffith could also be pin-headed:

> My dear Sir, how shall I tell you? You will hang me! . . . I have by some unfortunate accident lost the paper of memorandums, which I made in consequence of our last conversation: this has fretted me considerably, and almost addled my poor brains. I am afraid to proceed, and yet unwilling to stop. I remember your plan for the fourth and fifth acts, but the second and third have quite escaped me. May I hope you will be so good as to recollect your own observations, and enclose them to me as soon as it is convenient?[19]

By the autumn of 1768 Garrick, *de guerre lasse*, had accepted a new comedy from her. *The School for Rakes* was adapted from Beaumarchais' *Eugénie*, which

---

* Sturz, Helfrich Peter, *Vermischte Schriften*, Starnberg am See, 1946, p. 61. Sturz (1736–79) had been born and educated in Germany. He appears to have conducted an extensive correspondence with Garrick after his visit to England, although only six of his letters and one of Garrick's survive.

† 'David Garrick at Rehearsal. Written by himself. From an Original Letter in the Possession of the Publisher.' This appeared in a nineteenth-century pamphlet called *Behind the Curtain*. It is bound into an extra-illustrated *Life of Garrick* now at the Folger Library.

had been given two years earlier at the Comédie-Française, and it was Garrick who had drawn it to her attention. When Mrs Griffith began trying to dictate the casting of the play, however, he felt that the time had come to be clear about a number of things: 'Madam,' he wrote tetchily, 'You must depend upon my settling the parts to the best of my Judgment for your Sake as well as my own.' He was clearly at a pitch of exasperation, and went on to demand from her a rather curious assurance:

> You have Madam in most of Your Letters to me acknowledg'd your obligations to me in furnishing you with a Subject for your play, and often repeating what advantages it has receiv'd by my advice, Alterations, Additions, &c in the Plot, Scenes, Language &c. . . . Now Madam all I desire in return for this, is to [h]ave under Your, & Mr Griffiths's hand, that You [r]eally beleive that what I have done to the [P]lay has been to its advantage; or if you [d]o not think so, that you or *He* will be so good to [l]et me know what I may have alter'd for the worse . . .[20]

Mrs Griffith and her husband, who often collaborated in her writing, gave the desired assurance. The play was carefully rehearsed, Garrick wrote a prologue for King to deliver and the production had the benefit of new scenery and costumes. It ran for nine nights, and was the only one of the season's three new mainpieces to have an occasional revival.

Garrick pushed the boat out again shortly afterwards for *The Fatal Discovery*, John Home's latest tragic offering. *Town and Country Magazine* thought the scenes and dresses 'remarkably striking', although the editors of *Biographica Dramatica* found it absurd that the monarch of a rock off the coast of Scotland should inhabit a Grecian palace. Home was a firm believer in the authenticity of the writings of Macpherson, and it was on *Ossian* that his new piece was based. Although it was six years since Bute's fall from power there was still a good deal of hostility to him in London. Garrick feared that Home's association with the former Prime Minister might damage the play's prospects and persuaded him to conceal his authorship. It was arranged for an Oxford undergraduate to attend rehearsals and it was put about that the work was his; Home, however, was unable to hold his tongue, and the secret was a secret no more. Murphy, whose view of such matters was a touch proprietary, liked it no better than *Zingis*: 'That both were endured nine nights, is a disgrace to the audiences of that day,' he pronounced:

> The names of the persons of the piece are grating to an English ear. *Kastreel*, *Dunton*, *Connon*, and the like, are exotics beneath the dignity of tragedy. The play might as well be written in Erse; it has neither poetry nor sentiment, nor a single scene or incident to alarm the passions. It was not fit to be represented any where on this side of Johnny Grots, at the remotest part of Scotland.[21]

By the standards of the day, Garrick ran a pretty tight ship at Drury Lane, but it was inevitable that the occasional disciplinary problem should arise. 'Mrs W.

Barry very bad in Almeria,' Hopkins noted of a performance of *The Mourning Bride* in the second week of the season—'imagine she was in Liquor.'* In December he recorded a similar lapse during a performance of *Zenobia*: 'Mrs Hippisley dr——k, and could not speak.' More seriously, the airs and graces of the Barrys were beginning to cause friction. We know from Davies that Garrick had leant over backwards to make life agreeable for Barry, offering him his choice of parts 'and never calling upon him to do any thing which would either degrade or displease him'. Gradually, however, it had begun to appear that both he and his wife could be 'degraded or displeased' by very little.

During their first appearance of the season (it did not take place until 21 October—they were the principals in *The Countess of Salisbury*) tempers flared for some reason behind the scenes: 'A quarrel in the Green Room between Mrs Barry and Mr Aickin,' Hopkins recorded in his diary. Then, in February, there is a revealing passage in a letter from Garrick to the Reverend Thomas Francklin. Francklin, the man who had conducted the Garricks' Anglican wedding twenty years previously, had written a cantankerous letter complaining among other things that the standard of acting at Drury Lane fell below what was required for a new tragedy he was at work on. 'I must speak my Mind freely to you,' Garrick told him in reply:

> Mr & Mrs Barry are not yet engag'd with us for another Season, & by their last Answer, I rather think, they will not: and if so, how can I therefore promise that they shall perform in your play: nay, if they were Engag'd, how can I say whether they will approve of the parts You would wish 'Em to Act: They did not like those in *Zingis*, or *The School for Rakes*; and you know that it is not in the power of a Manager to force such Performers against their will.—†

Garrick was not at all well that winter. He was confined to bed for a time at the turn of the year, and a letter to his friend Clutterbuck in March indicates that he had been quite seriously ill:

> Tho I can scarce hold my pen in my hand, yet I must tell You, that I am just rising from ye Bed of Death by ye help of Our Friend Schomberg—
> I have had a very sad bout indeed with Stone, Gout, fever & Jaundice—
> I must away for Bath directly . . . the Waters have ye Devil & all to wash away, however we must try, as I shall see You, my dear Clut, & that will be ye best cordial I can have for my present low Spirits—[22]

He was badly reduced. His hand shook so violently that when he tried to write the result was barely legible. For a time, indeed, he was forbidden pen and paper, although when the Earl of Halifax sent some game round to the invalid, he felt that Schomberg's orders must be defied:

---

* This was Barry's sister-in-law, the wife of his younger brother Thomas. She had joined the company in 1766.
† *Letters*, 531. Garrick was mistaken. The Barrys stayed with him until 1774.

When our old friend Quin was once ill, and had received a present, (I believe, from the same bounteous hand that has sent me mine,) his doctor told him that he would not be fit to touch such a thing for fortnight. "Sha'n't I?" says Quin; "then by G—it shall travel with me till I am fit!" I am in the same predicament with Quin, and shall most certainly take the wild turkey with me to Bath on Tuesday morning.[23]

By the middle of April he was almost restored. 'I hear of nothing from Bath but the wonderful progress you have made,' Murphy wrote to him. 'The Saffron tinge is quite gone, and Every Body talks of your roses and Lilies.'[24]

It was important that he should be back in London. Kitty Clive had decided to retire. Her last performance and benefit had been fixed for 24 April, and Garrick had offered to appear with her in *The Wonder*. She was grateful, and she was touched. ' How charming you can be when you are good,' she wrote to him:

I shall certainly make use of the favour you offer me; it gives me a double pleasure—the entertainment my friends will receive from your performance, and the being convinced that you have a sort of sneaking kindness for your Pivy. I suppose I shall have you tapping me on the shoulder, (as you do to Violante), when I bid you farewell, and desiring one tender look before we part, though perhaps you may recollect and toss the pancake into the cinders. You see I never forget any of your good things. . . .[25]

Her pleasure would have been even greater if she had known what Garrick scrawled on her letter before filing it away: 'A love-letter—the first I ever had from that truly great comedian, Mrs. Clive.'

He had in truth been more than a little afraid of her. 'Whenever he had a difference with Mrs Clive,' wrote Davies, 'he was happy to make a drawn battle of it.'[26] Johnson, in the days when he ventured into the green-room, had formed the highest opinion of her: 'Clive, Sir,' he told Boswell, 'is a good thing to sit by; she always understands what you say.'[27] He was also a perceptive judge of her strengths in comedy: 'What Clive did best,' he observed years later to Mrs Siddons, 'she did better than Garrick; but she could not do half so many things well; she was a better romp than any I ever saw in nature.'[28]

Garrick in future must look elsewhere for his romps and his hoydens, his chambermaids and his country girls, his viragos and his dowdies, his Lady Fancifuls and his Mrs Heidelbergs. It was more than forty years since Colley Cibber had put the seventeen-year-old Kitty down in the list of performers at twenty shillings a week. Now Dame Clive had gone off to the country to garden and cook, to play at loo and quadrille and to laugh and gossip with her friend and neighbour at Twickenham, Horace Walpole.

27

Rain Stops Play

Some time in 1767, the Mayor and Corporation of Stratford-on-Avon decided to demolish the old Town Hall in the High Street and build a new one. It was to be a modest affair in the classical style, built of Cotswold stone. The front elevation was embellished only by a large shield on the gable; on the north face, however, the design provided for a large ornamental niche, looking down on Sheep Street—just the place for a statue of the town's most famous son.

Stratford was then a small market town with some 3,000 inhabitants. The wordy agreement with the contractors demonstrated that the Council had no intention of squandering the townspeople's money. Wherever possible salvaged materials were to be used: 'Good Doors for the two Water Closets to be made out of the old Doors.' A price of £678 was initially agreed, but the Council decided that its own contribution should be limited to £200. The task of raising the balance fell to the town clerk, William Hunt.

It proved uphill work. The odd ten guineas was subscribed, but by the end of the year contributions had slowed to a trickle. There was a distinct possibility that work would have to be halted; and if there were insufficient funds to complete the building, there would certainly not be enough to decorate its bare inner walls—or fill that niche on the north face.

Then a man called Francis Wheler had an idea of brilliant simplicity. Wheler was a lawyer, who for the past dozen years had served as the Steward of the Stratford Court of Records. He was also a shrewd observer of human nature, and early in December, having cleared the idea with the Corporation, he addressed a letter to Garrick. He began with a brief description of the new building; then, with an elegance that would have excited the admiration of Izaac Walton, Wheler sent his fly hissing over the water:

> It would be a Reflection on the Town of Stratford to have any publick Building erected Here without some Ornamental Memorial of their immortal Townsman, And the Corporation would be happy in receiving from your hands some Statue Bust or Picture of him to be placed within this Building, they woud be equally pleased to have some Picture of yourself that the Memory of both may be perpetuated together in that place wch gave him birth & where he still lives in the mind of every Inhabitant—

If that had been strictly true, the inhabitants might have prodded the Corporation to celebrate the bi-centenary of the birth of their immortal Townsman three years previously. No matter; Wheler reeled in his line and cast a second time:

> The Corporation of Stratford ever desirous of Expressing their Gratitude to all who do Honour & Justice to the Memory of Shakespeare, & highly sensible that no person in any Age hath Excelled you therein woud think themselves much honoured if you woud become one of their Body . . . And to render the Freedom of such a place the more acceptable to you the Corporation propose to send it in a Box made of that very Mulberry tree planted by Shakespears own hand . . .*

Hook, line and sinker, naturally. The Corporation commissioned a casket, and Garrick approached Thomas Gainsborough to paint a portrait of Shakespeare, suggesting that he might use as a model the familiar Martin Droeshout engraving with the high forehead from the first Folio.

Gainsborough expressed his coolness to the idea with characteristic forthrightness:

> Shakespeare shall come forth forthwith, as the lawyer says. Damn the original picture of him, *with your leave*; for I think a stupider face I never beheld . . .
>
> I intend, with your approbation, my dear friend, to take the form from his pictures and statues, just enough to preserve his likeness *past the doubt of all blockheads* at first sight, and supply a *soul* from his works: it is impossible that such a mind and ray of heaven could shine with such a face and pair of eyes as the picture has . . .[1]

Garrick then suggested he should inspect the bust over his tomb in Stratford, but this proved equally unfruitful: 'God damn it,' Gainsborough replied, 'Shakespeare's bust is a silly smiling thing, and I have not sense enough to make him more sensible in the picture, and so I tell ye, you shall not see it.'[2] And no more he did, because Garrick settled instead for an unremarkable painting by Benjamin Wilson.

'Some Statue Bust or Picture.' Stratford was plainly soliciting a piece of sculpture or a painting—one or the other. But what if Garrick were to offer them both? There was no question of parting with the Roubillac he had commissioned for his Temple to Shakespeare at Hampton a decade previously—

---

* Shakespeare is supposed to have planted the tree in his garden in 1609, at a time when King James was eager to develop a silk industry. In 1753 the house passed into the hands of a Cheshire clergyman called Gastrell; he thought the mulberry made his house damp and dark, and had it chopped down, an act which so incensed the good people of Stratford that they ran him out of town. (He later compounded his offence by having the house demolished.) Most of the wood from the tree was bought by an enterprising local man called Thomas Sharp, a clock-maker and woodcarver, who used it to turn out a seemingly unlimited supply of Shakespeare mementos. Garrick had bought four logs from the tree in 1762, and Hogarth made them into a somewhat heavy carved chair, which is now on display at the Folger Library.

nor, for that matter of laying out a similar sum (he had paid Roubillac £315) on a new commission. Thriftily, he turned instead to the sculptor John Cheere, the partner of his better-known brother Sir Henry. Henry, a pupil of Scheemaker, had done the statue of Shakespeare erected in Westminster Abbey in 1741 and a later version of it for Lord Pembroke at Wilton. The Cheeres had a flourishing practice in funeral monuments; more to the point, their work yard at Hyde Park Corner churned out copies of well-known statues in lead, and it was the Wilton Shakespeare which served as the model for Garrick's gift to Stratford.*

Having responded thus generously to the Corporation's overtures, Garrick felt justified in suggesting that the expense of his own portrait might reasonably be borne by Stratford. The City Fathers—with what degree of enthusiasm is not known—agreed that this would be an appropriate way of honouring their first Freeman. Garrick thereupon returned to Gainsborough and asked him to rework a portrait he had done two years previously, and which had been shown at the annual exhibition of the Incorporated Society of Artists. Garrick looks pretty pleased with himself—possibly because like so many of Gainsborough's subjects, he had been flatteringly elongated. Hat in hand, he leans nonchalantly against a bust of Shakespeare, rather like a drunk propping up a lamp-post. One arm is draped in a casually proprietary way round the top of the plinth; the bard might *just* be saying something to him out of the corner of his mouth.

Gainsborough had originally entitled it simply *A Gentleman Whole Length*, but it was immediately recognized as Garrick and attracted some adverse criticism in the press. The Stratford Borough Chamberlain's accounts show that Gainsborough was paid a fee of 60 guineas. Mrs Garrick thought it the best likeness of her husband that was ever painted.†

Exactly when the idea of some sort of Shakespearean celebration at Stratford first occurred to Garrick is not clear. Henry Angelo records in his memoirs that he had often heard his father say that Garrick 'had long contemplated some public act of devotion as it were, to his favourite saint'. His thoughts certainly crystallized rapidly during the negotiations about the freedom of the town: when he filed Wheler's first letter away, he endorsed it 'The Steward of Stratford's letter to me which produc'd yᵉ Jubilee'.

Garrick had to wait for his freeman's casket. The commission had gone to a well-known Birmingham wood-carver called Thomas Davies and took 'four months constant application'. The box was an elaborate affair, supported by silver dragons, the front devoted to Shakespeare and the back to a carving of Garrick as Lear, modelled on the picture Benjamin Wilson had painted in 1762.‡ By the time it was handed over to Garrick at Southampton Street on 8 May he had clearly already been in touch with the Corporation and agreed some outline

---

* Ironically, Henry Cheere had numbered Roubillac among his pupils.
† During the Second World War the picture was removed for safety to Ilmington Manor. In December 1946, not long after it had been returned, there was a fire in the Town Hall and the picture was destroyed, together with that by Benjamin Wilson.
‡ The box is now in the British Museum.

proposals with them, because the *St James's Chronicle* for 6–9 May did not limit itself to reporting the presentation of the Freedom:

> In consequence of the above, a jubile in honour and to the memory of Shakespeare will be appointed at Stratford the beginning of September next, to be kept up every seventh year. Mr. Garrick, at the particular request of the Corporation and gentlemen of the neighbourhood, has accepted the stewardship. At the first jubile, a large handsome edifice, lately erected in Stratford by subscription, will be named Shakespeare's Hall, and dedicated to his memory.

This has Garrick's fingerprints all over it. Press releases have never had the status of sworn affidavits, but the suggestion that the Stratford Corporation and local gentry had to twist his arm to get him to take on the stewardship is deliciously improbable.

In the last week of the season Drury Lane mounted a performance of *The Beaux' Stratagem* for the benefit of the Theatrical Fund. Garrick played Archer, and also spoke an occasional prologue. He took leave of the audience until the following season in the conventional way, but he added a coda:

> My Eyes, till then, no Sight like this shall see,
> Unless we meet at Shakespeare's Jubilee!
> On Avon's Banks, where flow'rs eternal blow,
> Like It's full Stream, our Gratitude should flow!
> There let Us revel, shew our fond regard,
> On that lov'd Spot first breath'd our Matchless *Bard*!

In the middle of June, accompanied by his wife, George and an architect called Latimore, Garrick set out for Stratford. The new burgess was greeted by the ringing of church bells, and entertained at the White Lion. After dinner, he addressed the company and outlined his ideas 'with much perspicuity, to the perfect approval of the meeting'.

Garrick's way with words disguised the fact that those ideas were still extremely sketchy, but once Hunt had walked him round the town his fertile mind was soon racing. A site must be found for what he thought of as 'the Great Booth', a structure to serve as the main venue for formal dinners and indoor entertainments. There were souvenir ribbons to be sewn and a commemorative medal to be struck.* Where could a display of fireworks be mounted to best advantage? What could be made of the River Avon? What sort of financial backing would be needed for all this—and where would it come from?

On some fronts, things moved forward with remarkable speed. Garrick had marked down a meadow, on the far side of the river, as a promising site for the

---

* Garrick, as Steward, must naturally have something a little bigger and better than the run of the mill commercial product. Mr Davies, who had made his freeman's casket, produced a large oval medallion—of mulberry wood, naturally—with a portrait of the Bard and set in an ornamental gold frame.

fireworks. The view from the town, however, would be obstructed by trees, and Garrick asked Hunt to see if they could be felled. The land belonged to the Duke of Dorset, then High Steward of Stratford; on 14 July a gang of workmen appeared, and by nightfall Banstead Mead had been cleared of well over a hundred willow trees.*

The opening of this vista towards the river was welcomed by local house-holders, who could now enjoy a view of the bridge, with its fourteen arches. It also cleared the way for Garrick's 'Great Booth'—it was now being referred to as the Rotunda—to be built there, although he noted in one of the many memoranda which he fired off to Hunt and George at this time that 'there must surely be a sort of fence or Pallisade at a certain distance, to keep off yᵉ Mob'.

Back in London Garrick gave his mind to the Jubilee to the exclusion of all else. 'I shᵈ have call'd upon you often had not yᵉ Stratford matters in honor of our immortal Friend engross'd me wholly,' he told Richard Berenger towards the end of July:

> Have you nothing to say about him? no Song—Epigram—Frisk, fun or flibbertygibbet upon the Occasion? . . . In yᵉ mean time pray think of some good Inscription to be put upon a blank part of yᵉ Pedestal of his Statue . . .[3]

He had already polished off the words of the dedication ode which he proposed to declaim to music: 'Dʳ Arne works like a dragon at it—he is all fire, & flame about it,' he told Hunt. And he added: 'You must know, for I tell you all my Secrets, that I have brought in a Compᵗ (delicately) to yᵉ Duke of Dorset, for his great Generosity and Kindness about yᵉ Trees.'[4]

As summer wore on, however, reports reached Garrick that not everyone in Stratford was as well-disposed as his Grace of Dorset, and he quizzed Hunt about them:

> I heard Yesterday to my Surprize, that the Country People did not seem to relish our *Jubilee*, that they looked upon it to be *popish* & that we shd raise yᵉ Devil, & wᵗ not—I suppose this may be a joke,—but after all my trouble, pains labour & Expence for their Service, & yᵉ honor of yᵉ County, I shall think it very hard, if I am not to be receiv'd kindly by them—

He also pressed Hunt into service to find extras. 'We shall want 8, 10, or a dozen of yᵉ handsomest children in yʳ Town, by way of Fairies & Cupids for our Pageant,' Garrick wrote. 'Will you be so obliging to cast an Eye upon yʳ Schools for this Purpose?—We must likewise collect as many seemly, Clean-made fellows as we can get to assist in yᵉ Pageant.'[5]

Garrick's enthusiasm for a grand Shakespearean pageant was not shared by

---

* Only in the 1960s did it become known how the trees had been disposed of. Christian Deelman, in the course of his research for his book on the Jubilee, established that they had been acquired by a local carpenter and auctioneer called Thomas Taylor. Some years later, he disposed of the matured wood to Thomas Sharp, the carver and dealer who had made the famous mulberry tree go such a long way. (*The Great Shakespeare Jubilee*, London, 1964, 127.)

Lacy, who objected to his intended use of the Drury Lane wardrobe. Samuel Foote claimed to have had a conversation with him on the subject. 'Why,' said Lacy, 'if the day should turn out, as you say, wet and windy, Garrick and his mummers may parade it as much as they please, but *none of the clothes shall walk*.'[6]

Foote was prominent among those beginning to show a keen interest in the Jubilee, by no means all of it friendly. He was playing in *The Devil upon Two Sticks* at the Haymarket that summer, and regularly inserted satirical allusions to the Jubilee—one of them compared the enthusiasm for it to that generated by Whitefield and the Methodists. He also caused a teasing paragraph to be inserted in a provincial paper—interest in what was going on in Stratford extended far beyond the capital:

> It is said our English Aristophanes has declared his Intention of going to Stratford, at the Time of the Jubilee, in order to collect Incidents for a humorous Piece, which he will lay before the Public, for their Amusement next Winter, under a very odd Title.

The English Aristophanes intended no such thing of course, but giving Garrick a *mauvais quart d'heure* was one of Foote's major pleasures in life, and he knew how to do it better than most. The proposed title was *Drugger's Jubilee*.[7] Garrick sweated in silence, turned the other cheek and scribbled yet another memorandum to himself: 'To secure Some good Lodgings for my Friends—a good Bed for Mr Foote—'

Quite a few of these memoranda which he was constantly firing off to Hunt or to George have survived, and they give an entertaining insight into how conscientiously the Steward took his duties and how all-embracing he conceived them to be:

> To know precisely what boats there are upon ye River Avon, that may be made use of, if thought necessary—& if any Gentleman there or near Stratford have any pleasure boats—

George was not able to promise a great deal on the nautical front: 'May have 3 Barges & Fishing Boat,' he reported.

> to know if Shrewsbury Races are upon ye same Days with ye Jub^{ee} for It is said Ld Grosvenor intends to desire Mr G to put it off till ye 8th or 9th that they may not clash.

Lord Grosvenor was the greatest breeder of racing stock of the day. There was no clash. He turned up at the Jubilee resplendent in a Turkish costume.

> to Enquire if there seems to be any Spirit among the People for Erecting Booths, or if ye town's-people seem to intend to decorate their houses at ye Jubilee.[8]

'They do,' George noted laconically, but Garrick was not proposing to rely solely on the aesthetic taste of the good people of Stratford, and had taken on his friend

Benjamin Wilson as a sort of general artistic consultant to the Jubilee. A series of large transparent paintings was being prepared, to be hung over windows throughout the town and illuminated from behind. The work on these and on the many other props Garrick had ordered was going forward in the vaulted hall of a large historic building called the College. It had been built in the fourteenth century to house the priests attached to the great church but now stood conveniently empty. John French, the scene painter from Drury Lane who had collaborated so successfully with Domenico Angelo in producing the settings for *Harlequin's Invasion*, directed the efforts of a team of workmen shipped in for the purpose. French would also be responsible for the painting and decoration of the Rotunda.

By the middle of August Garrick was exhausted. 'I have really half kill'd Myself wth this business,' he told Hunt, '& if I Escape Madness, or fevers I shall be very happy.' On a more cheerful note, he had another secret to impart: 'I will whisper a word in y^r Ear,' he wrote. 'I am told that his Majesty wishes to hear the Ode, & I shall tomorrow make an Offer of performing it before him, at his Palace privately —' The offer was graciously accepted, and Garrick's next letter to Hunt announced that the reading had met with 'much approbation'; he had been with the King and Queen for three and a quarter hours.

Garrick had also been busy churning out a range of ballads, glees and roundelays to be performed at the Jubilee, but getting these set to music was not easy. He had a particularly difficult time with Charles Dibdin, the young singer and composer who had written the score for *The Padlock*. Dibdin, who was only twenty-four at the time, was convinced that Garrick had no ear for music. More than thirty years later, in his memoirs, he relived the exasperation he had felt during the Jubilee preparations:

> I was a slave to it for months, I set and reset songs to it till my patience was exhausted, which were received or rejected just as ignorance or caprice prevailed . . . One thing galled him very much. He really had not an idea of how to write for music, and I frequently ventured at hinting alterations, as to measure, for the advantage of what he wrote . . . Matters went on in this train, till at last I was so palpably insulted that I declared I would not go to Stratford.[9]

Slowly—very slowly—the Rotunda began to take shape.* It was loosely modelled on the structure Lacy had erected in Ranelagh Gardens twenty-seven years previously. Octagonal in shape, it was made entirely of wood; it was designed to hold an audience of a thousand and covered an area of 500 square yards. George did not shine as a progress-chaser,† and when Garrick's friend Cradock

---

* It stood almost exactly where the Memorial Theatre is today.

† His own natural indolence apart, he had problems with French. Many years later Wheler spoke to an old man who in his youth had seen something of what went on at the College: 'It was with difficulty that Mr. George Garrick could induce him to proceed, as French frequently made it necessary that drink should be sent to the painting rooms to secure his attendance there.' (Wheler, R.B., *Collections on the Stratford Jubilee*, Birthplace MSS, No. 14, f. 88v.)

rode over to Stratford at the end of August he was appalled. The workmen were short of tools, and some of the building materials had still not been delivered. 'Take care,' said the acquaintance who showed him round, 'that you do not cut your shoes from the broken lamps, which have just arrived; they were intended for the illumination of this building; but, if they ever left Drury-lane in safety, you see they are all here shivered to pieces.'[10] What had been shivered to pieces on the journey by cart from London was a huge chandelier of 800 lights.

Garrick became worried as the Jubilee approached by reports of profiteering by the Stratford townspeople, and he wrote to Hunt in some agitation:

> The exorbitant price that some of ye People ask, will Effect the whole Jubilee, and rise up a mortal Sin against us—such imposition may serve ye Ends of a few selfish people, but the Town will suffer for it hereafter, & we for the present—I was in hopes that you & ye other Gentlemen of the Corporation might have prevented this. Again, if your Innkeepers intend to raise their victuals & liquor, it will be abominable, & perhaps occasion riot & disorder. . . .[11]

The press was having a field day. No need in 1769, with Stratford to write about, for the silly season to be brought forward. Garrick was reported to have despatched Robert Baddeley, celebrated for his portrayal of the Lord Mayor in *Richard III*, to give the Mayor of Stratford lessons in etiquette; a fat landlady in the town was reported to have been injured falling from a hay-loft while practising the balcony scene from *Romeo and Juliet*.

Garrick himself had to put up with the efforts of numbers of hacks who fancied themselves as satirists or parodists. More wounding were the attacks of someone who was under considerable obligation to him. 'When I was busied about that foolish hobby-horse of mine the Jubilee,' he later wrote, 'my good friend Master Steevens was busying himself every other day in abusing me and the design.'[12] Garrick's generosity in lending him material when he was editing the Shakespeare Quartos some years previously did not weigh with Steevens; he denied it at the time, but later boasted that he had been the author of between thirty or forty of the attacks on Garrick or the Jubilee which appeared in the press in the course of the summer. He was a clever man—sometimes too clever by half. One of his efforts took the form of a bogus letter to the press announcing that as well as the Ode, Garrick intended to deliver 'an Eulogium, in the Manner of Monsieur Fontenelle':

> . . . These Observations the great Artist will exemplify by reading several passages, in which Occasion will offer of pointing out, but with great good Nature, the Errors of some modern Performers, in Respect to Accent, Emphasis and Rest. Much delightful Instruction, it is expected, will be derived from this part of the intellectual Feast. Afterwards he will exhibit a Specimen of the projected Edition of the Stratford Swan, which a Retreat from the Stage may perhaps some Time or other (O! may that Time

be far distant!) enable him to accomplish. Hence will be introduced an Elucidation of several Passages hitherto totally misunderstood, which will convince Envy herself of the profound Erudition and extensive classical Attainment of Mr. Garrick . . .

This extended sneer at Garrick's pretensions to Shakespearean scholarship—it appeared first in the *Public Advertiser* on 29 August—no doubt raised the intended snigger among some of Steevens's fellow-literati.[13] With some modern scholars it has succeeded too well, prompting earnest academic enquiry into the Jubilee Oration that never was and was never even projected.[14]

The Garricks left London for Stratford early on 1 September. They dined that evening at the Star Inn in Oxford with the Angelos; young Harry remembered that 'a very handsome display of fruit appeared in the dessert, which Mrs. Garrick had brought from their garden at Hampton.'[15] Two days later, at the unchristian hour of four o'clock on Sunday morning, the 'Gentlemen of the Band of Music' and those who were to walk in the pageant assembled at the establishment of a Mr Pritchard on the Oxford Road. They set out, reported *Lloyd's Evening Post*, 'in grand Cavalcade'—ten coaches and four, six post-chaises and a great number of saddle-horses.

Stratford had been filling up for a week past. The correspondent of the *London Chronicle* established that there were upward of forty carriages at the White Lion, and 'they were obliged to turn several great families away'. It was not just the quality who were flooding in, however. 'The number of Cooks in town is incredible,' he reported, although they were not the only trades and professions offering their services:

Hairdressers?—a world; though when one sees what numbers of bushel-heads there are in town every day, it is not to be wondered where they find employment . . . Wenches! never was any paradise so plentifully and beautifully inhabited as here at this time . . .[16]

By the time Joseph Cradock and his party arrived on the Monday evening, they found 'that there were so many loose horses, that the ladies could not safely alight'.[17] The town was well supplied with sedan chairs, however—there had been a mass descent on the town by the chairmen of Bath, a body of men sensitively attuned to market forces.

Stratford-mania spilled from the editorial columns into the advertisements:

For the STRATFORD JUBILEE

To those who would appear really elegant there, or elsewhere, the Albion Dentifrice is recommended, as without a sweet Breath and clean Mouth (which no cloying Odours of perfumed Essence will give) there can be no communicative Satisfaction . . .

Someone who was beginning to be thoughtful about communicative satisfaction—more precisely the lack of it—was Charles Dibdin. He had made his gesture. He had flounced out, and, rather spitefully, he had taken with him the still unset words of 'Let Beauty with the Sun Arise', the dawn serenade with which Garrick had hoped to start the first day's proceedings. Now the young composer was having second thoughts, and the desire to hear his music publicly performed grew by the hour. 'I, therefore, changed my mind,' he wrote, 'and set the words, as everybody knows, for guitars and flutes.'

He then rushed off to Stratford, scoured the taverns and lodging houses for musicians and rehearsed them through the night. Soon after five the next morning, wearing masks and got up in rags and tatters as grimy-faced yokels, they made their way to Hunt's house, where the Garricks were lodged:

> Let beauty with the sun arise,
> To SHAKESPEARE tribute pay,
> With heavenly smiles and speaking eyes,
> Give grace and lustre to the day . . .

It was the very thing which Garrick 'had set his heart upon, but which he had given up as lost,' wrote Dibdin. 'His reception of me was the warmest that can be conceived. He said he took shame to himself, that he should never forget my generosity.' It is true that, much later, and rather ungenerously, Dibdin added 'I knew what credit to give to his protestation', but for the moment all was sweetness and light.

Most of the town was in fact already wide wake; Dibdin's masqueraders provided only part of the mass reveille to which Stratford was subjected that morning. At first light, on the river bank, there had been a triple discharge of seventeen cannon and twelve mortars. This was followed by the ringing of church bells—the Corporation had laid out three guineas and retained a small army of ringers. A musical detachment from the Warwickshire Militia was also on duty, parading through the streets to the fife and drum.

Garrick arrived at the Town Hall shortly after eight to check the preparations for breakfast. Mrs Garrick accompanied him in a tight-waisted gown of white corded silk, patterned with silver stars and roses and edged around its flowing hem with silver lace. Garrick himself was attired in his velvet Jubilee suit. Trimmed with gold and lined with taffeta, the colour shifted in the light from mole to amber; he wore a long waistcoat with thirteen gold buttons and a rather special pair of white gloves—they had been presented to him by the actor John Ward, and were said to be the very ones worn on the stage by Shakespeare himself.

The proceedings were formally opened by Hunt, who invested Garrick with the insignia of his office—the medallion, and a long thin wand made (who would have thought it?) of mulberry. A couple of dukes, half a dozen earls—Garrick's grand friends and the quality more generally had turned out in force. Dorset, Manchester, Beauchamp and Grosvenor; Archer, Denbigh, Northampton and Hertford; Plymouth, Shrewsbury, Pembroke, Spencer and Craven—the roll call of the nobility stretched out like Banquo's posterity.

Charles Fox was there, and so was Admiral Rodney; Kitty Clive had come (but not Horace Walpole—he was in Paris);* Murphy and Colman were present, casting a cold professional eye over the proceedings, and so were Foote and Macklin. They had both been found lodgings at the Bear Inn in Bridgetown, directly over a large store of gunpowder brought in for the fireworks—clearly a devilish plot by Garrick, declared Foote, to send his enemies economically to kingdom come. Foote was in good form, and was soon busy inventing or embroidering many of the more outrageous Jubilee stories. He had, he would say, paid nine guineas for six hours sleep; when he had asked a local for the time, the man demanded two shillings; when Foote agreed, the yokel disclosed only the hour—there would be an extra charge for the minutes.

Breakfast was followed by Thomas Arne's oratorio *Judith*, conducted in the great collegiate church by the composer himself. One visitor arrived too late to hear the performance, but contrived to make a gratifyingly arresting entry just as the elegant audience was beginning to leave the church:

> I was exceedingly dirty; my hair hung wet about my ears; my black suit and the postillion's grey duffle above it, several inches too short every way, made a very strange appearance. I could observe people getting together and whispering about me, for the church was full of well-dressed people. At last Mr. Garrick observed me. We first made an attitude to each other and then cordially shook hands. I gave him a line I had written to let him know I was incognito, as I wished to appear in the Corsican dress for the first time they should know me. Many of those who had stared, seeing that I was intimate with the steward of the Jubilee, came up and asked who I was. He answered, 'A clergyman in disguise.'[18]

James Boswell had arrived in town. Accident-prone as ever, he had reached Stratford only after a complicated journey in the course of which he had been parted for a time from his watch, purse and pocket book. Since his last meeting with Garrick he had achieved some celebrity. His account of his adventures in Corsica, and his friendship with the rebel general Paoli, now in exile in England, had sold 7,000 copies and was already in a third edition.

He had not originally intended to come to Stratford. Having recently won a promise of marriage from his cousin, Margaret Montgomerie, he had travelled to London for medical treatment of his old venereal complaint; once in the capital, however, he found himself 'within the whirlpool of curiosity, which could not fail to carry me down'. It was also a splendid opportunity to publicize himself and his book. The Corsican patriot's uniform acquired on his travels was unfortunately in Edinburgh, but in the course of three days in London he had assembled a reasonable replica, complete with pistol, stiletto, long musket

---

* From where he none the less kept a close eye on what was going on at Stratford: 'I have blushed at Paris,' he wrote sourly to George Montagu, 'when the papers came over crammed with ribaldry, or with Garrick's insufferable nonsense about Shakespeare. As that man's writings will be preserved by his name, who will believe that he was a tolerable actor?' (*Walpole*, x, 298, letter dated 16 October 1769.)

Boswell in his Corsican finery. 'Empty your head of Corsica,' Johnson had advised him, but Boswell's admiring Account of the island sold like hotcakes and, within a year of publication, was translated into French, Dutch, German and Italian. (The London Magazine, September 1769)

and a black grenadier's cap embroidered in letters of gold with *Viva la Libertà*. The connection with Shakespeare was not immediately obvious, but that did not bother 'Corsican' Boswell.

There were a great many processions during the Jubilee—it was a good way of filling the gap between one set-piece performance and the next, and Garrick was often to be seen marshalling the visitors and joining enthusiastically in the singing as they marched to the Birthplace or made their way to the Rotunda. The undoubted hit of the festival was the ballad 'Warwickshire Lads'. Dibdin had written the music, to words by Garrick—seven stanzas of pretty average doggerel:

> . . . Our SHAKESPEARE compar'd is to no man,
> Nor *Frenchman*, nor *Grecian*, nor *Roman*,
> Their swans are all geese, to the *Avon's* sweet swan,
> And the man of all men, was *a Warwickshire* man,
>   *Warwickshire* man,
>   *Avon's* swan.
> And the man of all men was a *Warwickshire man*.

This was too tempting a target for Grub Street, and before long it was the subject of one of the less dreadful of the hundreds of parodies spawned by the Jubilee:

> . . . Your Priors, your Otways, your Drydens outbraved,
> Apollo has giv'n all their laurels to David;
> Nay I vow, and I swear, without any abuse,
> That the Mantuan swan to Garrick's a goose,
> Without any abuse,
> Garrick's a goose,
> And the goose of all geese is a Warwickshire goose.[19]

Dibdin's tune was to carry all before it, however. Soon it conquered London, and was heard at Vauxhall and Ranelagh. Later it became the regimental quick march of the Royal Warwickshire Regiment.

Seven hundred guests sat down to dinner at the Rotunda that afternoon. According to Wheler the fare included 'all the rarities the season could afford'. Service was slow, but the wine was good; Lord Grosvenor proposed a full bumper to the Steward's health 'for his Care and Attention', and Garrick responded with a toast to the Bard of Avon. One of the highlights of the singing which followed was a rendering of Garrick's lyric 'Sweet Willy O'. This had an unsettling effect on Boswell: 'I rose and went near the orchestra,' he wrote, 'and looked steadfastly at that beautiful, insinuating creature Mrs Baddley of Drury Lane.'*

A small army of stage-hands and assistants had little more than two hours to

---

* Sophia Baddeley, then in her middle twenties, was the daughter of George II's serjeant-trumpeter. She had eloped at the age of eighteen with the actor Robert Baddeley, from whom she was now estranged. She was equally celebrated for her exceptional beauty and the looseness of her morals.

turn the Rotunda round for that evening's Assembly Ball—minuets until midnight, and then cotillions and country dances until three. The correspondent of
the *Gentleman's Magazine* found the ball 'remarkable chiefly for the most elegant
minuet I ever saw or ever shall see'. Since their marriage Garrick had frowned
on his wife's dancing, but tonight he relented, and Eva-Maria moved elegantly
around the floor partnered by Joseph Cradock.

Three short hours after the last dance, the cannon boomed out again and the
church bells rang. Dibdin and his serenaders had a damper time of it this second
morning, however. There had been occasional drizzle the day before, but now
the English autumn declared itself in earnest; the cobbled streets were awash and
the Avon, already high after a wet summer, was rising ominously.

Local wiseacres had theories. Some pointed to the effect of the early morning
cannonades on swollen rain clouds. Others put it down to the comet which had
been observed for some nights past: 'of a livid blue Colour, situate to the Right
of the Pleiades, a little below Taurus,' reported *Jackson's Oxford Journal*. 'As
there is none expected at the Time, it gives Rise to various Conjectures'—that
it could bring about rain and storms by 'a flick of its tail', for example.* Darker
reasons were also adduced—it was a sign of divine displeasure at the town's
lapse into pagan idolatry. Out and about in the streets, young Henry Angelo
encountered an elderly dowager who sounds like a character from one of
Garrick's afterpieces: 'What an *absurd* climate!' she exclaimed.

The morning handbills announced a crowded programme:

> The STEWARD of the JUBILEE informs the
> Company that at nine o'clock will be a
> PUBLIC BREAKFAST
> at the TOWN HALL
> At Eleven o'Clock, a PAGEANT
> (if the Weather will permit) to proceed
> from the college to the Amphitheatre
> Where an ODE
> (upon the dedicating a BUILDING and erecting
> a STATUE to the Memory of SHAKE-
> SPEARE) will be performed after which
> the PAGEANT will return to the College.
> At FOUR an ORDINARY for Ladies and Gentlemen.
> At EIGHT, the Fireworks.
> And at ELEVEN o'Clock
> The MASQUERADE.

Garrick's day began badly. He had developed a cold, and his voice was affected,
but there was worse:

---

* The comet attracted keen interest all over Europe until the end of September; books were
published on it in Hamburg and St Petersburg.

The man who was to shave him, perhaps not quite sober, absolutely cut him from the corner of his mouth to his chin . . . the ladies were engaged in applying constant stiptics to stop the bleeding.[20]

Then Boswell was announced. The blood-stained Steward's feelings have not come down to us. He appears to have received his visitor with his usual courtesy, and the irrepressible Boswell chattered away:

I pleased myself with a variety of ideas with regard to the Jubilee, peculiar to my own mind. I was like a Frenchman at an ordinary, who takes out a box of pepper and other spices, and seasons a dish in his own way.[21]

Once the stiptics had done their work, Garrick set out to see what could be salvaged of the day's events. He was deeply reluctant to abandon the pageant—two hundred and seventeen walkers stood ready to march, most of them dressed as Shakespearean characters, the rest got up in mythical attire. Apart from the fireworks, it was the element in the festival best calculated to appeal to the sceptical townsfolk—no tickets were required. Colman, who had lent some costumes from the Covent Garden wardrobe, seems not to have offered much of an opinion one way or the other, but Lacy, hostile to the scheme from the start, was adamant:

See—who the devil, Davy, would venture upon the procession under such a lowering aspect? Sir, all the ostrich feathers will be spoiled, and the property will be damnified five thousand pounds.

The procession was abandoned. Garrick scrawled a few lines on a scrap of paper and sent an urgent order to the printer for 500 quarto handbills—the Ode would be performed in the amphitheatre at noon.*

The audience that assembled there was not in the best of moods. Many of them were cold and wet. The roof of the hastily completed Rotunda was beginning to leak. When the cannons outside boomed at twelve o'clock and Garrick took his place in front of Arne and the hundred-strong orchestra and chorus, it seemed to the correspondent of *Lloyd's Evening Post* that he looked 'a little confused or intimidated'. Not for long, however. There was a brief overture. Garrick made a respectful bow to the company, and received in return 'a very respectful Clap of unanimous Applause'. Then, quietly, he launched into the first recitative:

> To what blest genius of the isle,
> Shall Gratitude her tribute pay,
> Decree the festive day,
> Erect the statue, and devote the pile? . . .
> 'Tis he! 'tis he!
> 'The god of our idolatry!'

---

* Garrick's note is preserved in the Harvard Theatre Collection. The Pageant, he wrote, 'is oblig'd to be deferr'd'.

He took his audience by surprise. To most of them recitative meant 'that which is in general the most languid and neglected Part of a musical Performance'. Here the words were *spoken*, and they were spoken by the most famous and most brilliantly controlled voice in England. As he sat down, the low ostinato over which he had been heard swelled suddenly to a great chord, and the choir made its first entry:

> ... With trumpet-tongues proclaim,
> The lov'd, rever'd, immortal name!
> Shakespeare! Shakespeare! Shakespeare!

For the rest of the performance Garrick held the audience in the palm of his hand. The Ode does not withstand particularly rigorous scrutiny as poetry—it is, in truth, something of a hodge-podge, echoes of Shakespeare, Milton and the oratorios of Handel cheek by jowl with commonplace phrases like 'tuneful numbers' and 'our humble strains'. The performance was all. It was frequently interrupted by 'turbulent applause'. Garrick had composed a score for the incomparable instrument which was his own voice. Even Charles Dibdin, who found little good to say of the rest of the Jubilee, praised it without reserve, declaring 'that there was never enthusiasm so ardently conveyed, nor so worthily felt; that it was magic; that it was fairyland'.

The Ode was not without its lighter moments. At one point Garrick imagines the birth of Falstaff. In a passage which later occasioned some tut-tutting on grounds of indelicacy, Fancy, Wit and Humour hover round the head of the Bard and impregnate his mind:

> Which teeming soon, as soon brought forth,
> Not a tiny spurious birth,
> But out a mountain came.
> A Mountain of delight!

It was a part Garrick's form and stature had never allowed him to play, but he clearly enraptured the Stratford audience that day with a lightning master class in the role. 'His comic Powers rushed upon the Character of Falstaff,' a correspondent wrote in the *Public Advertiser*, and the amphitheatre was filled with 'incessant Bursts of Laughter'.[22]

Towards the end, there was a sequence in which Garrick sang the praises of the Avon, setting it higher than the Thames, the Cam and the Isis. This was followed by the sixth air. The words are the most appalling rubbish, but the ravishing Mrs Baddeley sang them so enchantingly that an encore was called for:

> ... Flow on, silver Avon; in song ever flow,
> Be the swans on thy bosom still whiter than snow,
> Ever full be thy stream, like his fame may it spread,
> And the turf ever hallow'd which pillow'd his head.

At this point Garrick permitted himself an audacious *coup de théâtre*. The great doors in the side of the Rotunda were thrown open. Little of the ever-hallowed turf was to be seen; the meadow had been churned into mud, and the silver Avon—rather a dirty brown by now—was swirling alarmingly close to where the audience sat. Nobody giggled. The spell was unbroken. At that moment the magic of the Steward's wand was every bit as powerful as Prospero's.

It was a triumph. As Garrick made his final bow, there was a rush of admirers to the orchestra rail, many of them 'illustrious for rank and literary talent'. The cheering crowd included Lord Grosvenor, apparently in a state of high emotion. He told Garrick, wrote Boswell, 'that he had affected his whole Frame, shewing him his Veins and Nerves still quivering with Agitation'.[23] The enthusiasm of the audience was too much for the fabric of the Rotunda. A number of benches gave way under the strain, and people were thrown to the floor. In some places the walls buckled: 'had it not been for a peculiar Interposition of Providence, Lord Carlisle, who was very much hurt by the fall of a Door, must inevitably have been destroyed.'

When Garrick could make himself heard, he lamented the fact that none of the university poets, 'eminently more capable than himself', had undertaken to write the Ode. He feared that his zeal for the honour of Shakespeare 'had led him to expose the weakness of his own abilities'. (Gratifying cries of 'No! No!') He paid a compliment to Arne—'the first musical genius of this country'—and he declaimed Milton's well-known lines on Shakespeare, first printed in the second folio in 1632:

> What needs my *Shakespear* for his honour'd Bones,
> The labour of an age in piled Stones,
> Or that his hallow'd reliques should be hid
> Under a Star-ypointing *Pyramid*?

Then, always a chancy proceeding, Garrick set about painting the lily. Benjamin Victor, who was present, made a careful note of what was said. 'Your attendance here upon this Occasion is a Proof that you have felt, powerfully felt, his Genius,' Garrick declared. 'The only remaining honour to him now (and it is the greatest Honour you can do him) is to speak for him.' There was some laughter, but it was the laughter of embarrassment—what did the Steward actually mean? 'Perhaps my Proposition comes a little too abruptly upon you?' he continued. 'With your Permission, we will desire the Gentlemen to give you time, by a Piece of Music, to recollect and adjust your thoughts.' Then, when the band had done what was required of them: 'Now Ladies and Gentlemen, will you be pleased to say any thing *for* or *against* SHAKESPEARE.'[24]

At this point a man came forward and positioned himself in front of the orchestra. When he removed his greatcoat he was seen to be wearing a fashionable suit of blue, embellished with silver frogs. Those in the audience who were London theatre-goers recognized Thomas King—and recognized the suit as the one he had worn in such roles as Lord Ogleby in *The Clandestine Marriage*. What the uninitiated saw and heard was a foppish, Frenchified figure with a drawling high-pitched lisp. 'This person tried the force of his ingenuity to decry and ridicule Shakespeare and his writings,' wrote Tom Davies:

The Macaroni's chief objection to Shakespeare arose from his being a vulgar author, who excites those common emotions of laughing and crying, which were entirely indecent and unbecoming in polite assemblies; that the criterion of a fine gentleman was to be moved at nothing—to feel nothing—to admire nothing—He wished to civilize the barbarous manners of the country; and the first step to it was, never to suffer such an execrable fellow as Shakespeare, with his things called comedies and tragedies, to debauch their minds and understanding, and to disturb that *ennui* which was the sole pleasure of a gentleman. He concluded with a string of sarcasms against the Jubilee, the Steward, the corporation and the whole company.[25]

The whole routine had, of course, been carefully rehearsed. Garrick rounded it off, none too soon, with a roguish appeal to the Fair Sex: 'O Ladies! It is You and You alone who can put a Stop to this terrible progress and irruption of the anti-Goths . . .'

Many of those who realized what Garrick was up to had quickly found it tedious; the less sophisticated were either confused or indignant. Boswell, *plus royaliste que le roi*, thought it undignified:

We were enthusiastic Admirers of Shakespeare. We had not Time to think of his cavilling Critics. We were wrapped into Wonder and Admiration of our Immortal Bard; and the Levity of the fine Gentleman disturbed the Tone of our Minds. . . . I was angry to find any Notice taken of the venomous Insects, who have shot their stings in the News-Papers against the Jubilee, and particularly against Mr. Garrick. It had the Appearance of a Soreness unworthy of our Lord-High-Steward.[26]

The performance had overrun. With dinner to serve at four, the cooks and the waiters were becoming impatient. When the guests were re-admitted, they feasted on a huge turtle. When alive, it had weighed 327 pounds—'which with a number of other Dainties, and rich Wines,' wrote Victor, 'was only a proper Entertainment for the splendid Company assembled there.'[27] Not everyone agreed. 'We, indeed, had something which was called turtle,' wrote one correspondent, 'and something which went under the denomination of claret; but if it had not been for the dignity of the appellations, we might as well have been regaled upon neck of beef, and Southampton port.'

But the band played, and there were glees and ballads and catches. More ambitiously, a cantata called *Queen Mab* was performed, a collaboration between Dibdin and Bickerstaffe. There was also another of Garrick's offerings, a comic serenata called *The Country Girl*:

> All this for a Poet—o no—
> Who liv'd lord knows how long ago!

Outside, on the far bank of the river, Domenico Angelo was contemplating the collapse of his dreams. He had volunteered to look after the firework display for

Garrick; his son Harry never forgot how wholeheartedly he had thrown himself
into the preparations:

> I think I yet see my father, looking another *Marlborough*—great as that
> hero, ordering the lines and circumvallations before Lisle or Tournay, as
> he stood, directing his engineers, in the fabricating of *rockets, crackers,*
> *catherine-wheels*, and *squibs* . . .[28]

In the meadow, a huge transparent screen had been erected. The design on the
great central arch (French had worked 'from the fine ideas of Sir Joshua Reynolds')
showed Shakespeare being led by Time to Immortality, flanked by Tragedy and
Comedy. On the parapet of the bridge three turrets had been built and on the
wires strung between them blazing 'serpents' were to run. The townspeople had
braved the rain in large numbers, and lined the river bank beside the Rotunda.
The leaflets handed out to them promised all manner of pyrotechnic marvels—
Diamond Pieces of Stars and Fountains, Porcupine's Quills, Tourbillons, Pyra-
mids of Chinese Fires.

Still the rain fell. 'The fireworks were in dudgeon with the waterworks. The
rockets would not ascend for fear of catching cold, and the surly crackers went
out at a single pop.' Henry Angelo managed to make it sound amusing years
later in his memoirs, but his father was not amused on the night. The touch-papers
were sodden, fuses fell into the mud, matches fizzled out the moment they were
struck. After half an hour, little more than half way through the programme,
Angelo conceded defeat.

One last item remained on the day's programme—the Masquerade. The
Rotunda was now surrounded not just by mud but by great expanses of water.
'The floods threated to carry the mighty fabric clean off,' wrote Henry Angelo:

> As it was, the horses had to wade through the meadow, knee-deep to reach
> it; and planks were stretched from the entrance to the floors of the carriages,
> for the company to alight. Such a flood had not been witnessed there in
> the memory of man.

Anything resembling a party spirit was slow to develop. An over-long speech of
welcome by Garrick went down like a lead balloon. 'I must observe that a
Masquerade is an entertainment, which does not seem to be much suited to the
Genius of the British Nation,' Boswell informed readers of the *Public Advertiser*.
'The Reserve and Taciturnity which is observable among us, makes us appear
awkward and embarrassed in feigned Characters.'

William Kenrick, who was said to resemble the Bard, appeared as Shakespeare's Ghost. Lady Pembroke and two other celebrated beauties ran about
cackling hideously as the witches from *Macbeth*; when, to great applause, they
unmasked, 'the contrast between the Deformity of the feigned, and the Beauty
of the real Appearance was universally admired'. There were Shepherdesses,
Pierrots, Chinese Mandarins, Foxhunters and Highlanders. Some were more
imaginative:

One gentleman had no other disguise than a pair of horns, publickly owning himself for a cuckold . . . and wearing the badges of his dignity erect. Some indeed said, this character ought not to be admitted, lest it should be deemed a reflection on the worthy corporation.

At one point a fight broke out between one of the several Devils present and a parson called Cook from Worcestershire who had come as a chimney-sweep—both wished to dance with the same lady. Later in the evening, Cook was accosted by the lively and extremely pretty Lady Craven, already at nineteen well-known in London society for her forward ways. 'Well, Mr Sweep,' she demanded, 'why don't you come and sweep my Chimney?' To which Cook, with some presence of mind, replied, 'Why, an' please your Ladyship, the last time I swept it I burnt my Brush.'*

The *Public Advertiser*'s account of the evening says that 'one of the most remarkable masks upon this occasion was James Boswell Esq., in the dress of an armed Corsican Chief'. When he entered at midnight, he was equally distinguished by 'the novelty of the Corsican dress, its becoming appearance, and the character of that brave nation'. All of which was no doubt true, even though the author of the report was the Corsican Chief himself. Dibdin marvelled at his irrepressible good humour, 'for I saw him at the masquerade dancing with the water over his shoes'.[29]

They danced till dawn. 'All zealous friends endeavoured to keep up the spirit of it as long as they could,' wrote Cradock, 'till they were at last informed that the Avon was rising so very fast, that no delay could be admitted.'[30] Descriptions of the scenes that followed suggest a painting by Breughel. Planks were once again laid to the footsteps of coaches. Some of the revellers decided that the only thing for it was to wade through the flood, and an unfortunate few found themselves wallowing in ditches concealed by the rising water. Several gallants—they included the Devil who had done battle with Parson Cook—offered to carry ladies to safety on their backs. One helpless female hoisted on to the Devil's back was not what she seemed, however. Halfway to firm ground, 'the Rudeness of the Wind occasion'd the Discovery of a Pair of Buck-skin Breeches underneath her outer Garments'. The impostor was promptly dumped, and the Devil waded on alone, holding his tail clear of the water.

The Jubilee was now clearly holed below the water-line. On the third morning Garrick grimly took stock, cancelled the pageant for the second time and also quietly shelved a projected repeat of the Ode. This posed no problem for those with private carriages, but it was quickly borne in on those who had not arrived in Stratford under their own steam that they might be stranded for days. The influx had extended over a week or more. Now all the available post-chaises and coaches were bespoke several times over.

---

* The Countess of Craven (1750–1828), wife of the Sixth Earl, later left her husband (by whom she had had six children) and travelled extensively abroad. She lived with, and subsequently married, the Margrave of Anspach. She published an account of her travels, and several of her plays were performed on the London stage.

In spite of the state of the course at Shottery, it was decided that the race for the Jubilee Cup should go ahead. All five entries ran, if that is what horses do when they are knee-deep in water—the race, Lady Archer was heard to say, 'should have been between Pegasuses'. Lord Grosvenor's highly-bred colt, Scholes, didn't have a chance; the race was won by a groom called Pratt on a brown colt called Whirligig. He received a silver cup worth £50 engraved with Shakespeare's arms. Afterwards, he declared that he was resolved never to part with it, though 'he knew very little about *Plays*, or Master S H A K E S P E A R E'.*

Boswell paid a final call on Garrick before leaving, partly to present him with some verses, partly to touch him for a loan:

> I asked him to let me have five guineas. He told me his brother George had taken almost all he had from him. "Come, come," said I, "that won't do. Five guineas I must have, and you must find them for me." I saw very well that he was not making any serious difficulty.[31]

Garrick found such impertinence unanswerable. An appeal was made to Mrs Garrick and Boswell was restored to solvency.

The rain finally stopped, and that evening Angelo was able to salve his pride by letting off the handful of serviceable fireworks that remained. The Rotunda was unusable, but at eleven o'clock, at the request of a number of determined ladies, a small company assembled for the last time at the Town Hall. 'Mrs Garrick danced a Minuet beyond description gracefully, and joined in the Country Dances, which ended at Four, and put an end to the Jubilee.'[32]

An end to the Jubilee, but the beginning of a national and international cult. This curious festival—at which not a single work of Shakespeare's was performed—marked the birth of Bardolatry, even though more than a hundred and thirty years would pass before George Bernard Shaw coined the actual word.† The Rotunda was the first location of that flourishing multinational concern which we know today as the Shakespeare industry. Nowadays it has plant on both sides of the Atlantic—from London's Barbican to the festival theatres at Stratford, Ontario, from the splendid Folger Shakespeare Library in Washington D C to the mock-tudor Mcdonald's on Waterside.

The man who started it all got back to his house at Hampton on 11 September. He was dispirited, angry and exhausted. The new season at Drury Lane was due to begin in five days' time.

---

* *Victor*, iii, 229. In old age Pratt, then living in Newmarket, fell on hard times and his resolution faltered. He fell in with a suggestion by his son for a subscription race for the cup, which was retained by the winner.
† Shaw first used the word in the preface to his *Plays for Puritans* in 1901.

28

A Devilish Lucky Hit

Garrick had every reason to be dispirited. Even before the bills started coming in, he knew that the unsporting behaviour of the weather gods meant severe financial loss. He had left his brother behind in Stratford to sweep up what he could of the mess. The best George could manage in the way of bright ideas was a conducted tour of the Rotunda at a shilling a time, but a week later an advertisement in the *Warwickshire Journal* announced that the materials used in the building of the amphitheatre were to be sold off in lots.

When Hunt conveyed the Corporation's formal expression of thanks, he wrote in a covering letter, 'I expect you'll burn every Letter with a Stratford post mark, without opening it, after your Brother has left yᵉ place.'[1] George soon began to complain of being ill-used, and by early October Garrick's tone to Hunt was both pained and prickly:

> I will not suffer yᵉ least dirt to be thrown upon me, or my Conduct, in an Affair which I undertook for yᵉ good of Stratford, & which has Employ'd both my Mind, Body, & purse.[2]

The only part of the Jubilee on which he could look back with unalloyed satisfaction was the success of his Ode. During September it was published in almost every newspaper and magazine in the land and Garrick himself sent it to a great many people—to the Warton brothers, to Macklin, to his friend Suard in Paris, even to Voltaire—'Sir, I have taken the liberty of offering my small poetical tribute to the first Genius in the World . . .' Careless drafting, or calculated ambiguity?[3]

Although most of the recipients made conventionally flattering acknowledgements, some of them were less polite behind his back. In a letter to Richard Hurd, his Archdeacon, Warburton, now Bishop of Gloucester, was particularly waspish:

> Garrick's *portentous* ode, as you truly call it, had but one line of *truth* in it, which is where he calls Shakespeare the *God of our Idolatry*: for *sense* I will not allow it . . . The ode itself is below any of Cibber's. Cibber's nonsense was something like sense; but this man's sense, whenever he deviates into it, is much more like nonsense.[4]

Macklin, true to type, took the poem extensively apart, and there was scarcely a line with which he did not find fault. Garrick, equally characteristically, found it necessary to send an interminable reply, tediously rebutting Macklin's criticisms seriatim. He asked to have his letter back, and before filing the correspondence away, he wrote a wry endorsement: 'I might have spent my time better than supporting a foolish business against a very foolish Man.'*

Stratford continued to provide grist to the mill of Grub Street. The *London Chronicle* floated the idea of an Ossian Jubilee, to be held 'near Crief, in Perthshire', where the non-existent poet was said to be buried. It would, readers were assured, be every bit as expensive and uncomfortable as the Stratford prototype. Supporters of John Wilkes proposed a Patriot Jubilee to celebrate his forty-fifth birthday in October, and though their hero was still paying his debt to society for publishing No. 45 of the *North Briton*, a celebration did indeed take place inside the King's Bench Prison, complete with catches, glees and a 300-pound turtle.†

The flood of pamphlets which appeared in September was followed over the next few months by an unremitting flow of plays, pantomimes, prologues and masques, few of them of any literary or dramatic merit.‡ The author of *Garrick's Vagary: or England Run Mad* took the precaution of announcing that it was not intended for performance, which was just as well, as it lacked anything that might be described as a plot. 'Sad stuff indeed!' pronounced *Biographica Dramatica*.§

Foote, naturally, was not slow to get in on the act, and introduced into *The Devil upon Two Sticks* at the Haymarket what became known as the Devil's Definition, offered by Foote in response to a question from one of the other characters—'What exactly is a Jubilee?'

A Jubilee, as it hath lately appeared, is a public invitation urged by puffing, to go post without horses, to an obscure borough without representatives, governed by a mayor and aldermen who are no magistrates, to celebrate a great poet whose own works have made him immortal by an ode without

---

* *Letters*, 565. Thomas Sheridan was also highly critical, but then he would be. In a series of articles in the *Public Ledger* he put the language and imagery of the Ode through the analytical mangle, pronouncing them to be bombastic, false, illogical and ungrammatical. (*Public Ledger*, 30 October, 1, 2 and 6 November.) Somebody thought Sheridan worth answering, and published anonymously a 35-page pamphet entitled *Anti-Midas: A Jubilee Preservative from Unclassical, Ignorant, False, and Invidious Criticism*.

† It would have been a matter of indifference to scribblers in London, but the Jubilee was to have an influence on the pre-Romantic *Sturm und Drang* movement in Germany in the following decade. Wieland's translation of more than twenty of Shakespeare's plays had been available since the middle 1760s; Goethe, Schiller and Herder were all profoundly influenced, and two Jubilees were held in Germany in imitation of Garrick's.

‡ The Jubilee did not go unnoticed in Paris. Under the title 'Fête de Shakespear', the December issue of the *Mercure de France* carried a glowing account of it, very possibly supplied by Garrick to one of his French friends.

§ The anonymous author did, however, have one amusing idea—Hemlock, an unsuccessful playwright, looks into the law against strolling players and concludes that as Garrick has no legal settlement in Stratford, he is liable to prosecution as a rogue and vagabond.

M.ʳ Garrick reciting the Ode, in honor of Shakespeare, at the Jubilee at Stratford: with the Musical Performers &c.

Garrick delivering his Ode to Shakespeare *at Stratford. The Jubilee was ruined by rain, but although his detractors had a deal of fun at his expense, Garrick had the last laugh – transferred to Drury Lane the spectacle played on 90 occasions, and helped him to recoup his losses. His ode to 'the God of his Idolatry' was published in almost every newspaper in the land. (*The Town & Country Magazine, *September 1769)*

poetry, music without harmony, dinners without victuals and lodging without beds, a masquerade where half the people appear bare-faced, a horse-race up to the knees in water, fireworks extinguished as soon as they were lighted, and a gingerbread amphitheatre which, like a house of cards, tumbled to pieces as soon as it was finished.[5]

Garrick kept his head down. Stratford had taken a lot out of him,* but he was hard at work on something that had been suggested by Benjamin Wilson as they travelled home together—why not perform the Ode and adapt the pageant for Drury Lane? The Ode was easy and it was performed for the first time on 30 September. Garrick had his Roubillac statue brought up from Hampton for the occasion, and enjoyed a great success: 'Mr G. speaking in this performance is equal to anything he ever did,' noted Hopkins, 'and met with as much applause as his heart could desire.'

So far as the Jubilee was concerned, however, he faced competition—'Mr Colman Enters ye lists with Us, much to my Surprize,' he wrote to Cradock on 2 October, and sure enough, five days later, Colman was first out of the trap with a three-act comedy called *Man and Wife; or, The Shakespeare Jubilee*. It is not clear why Garrick should have been surprised. It was a competitive and light-fingered age, and running away with the other house's clothes was not considered in the least reprehensible.

Colman had dusted down an old comedy of intrigue by Destouches called *La Fausse Agnès* and set it in Stratford.† He introduced the pageant of Shakespearean characters at the end of the second act, without any attempt to link it to the action—it is possible that he had been asked to walk in the procession that never was at Stratford and had a sight of the proposed order of Garrick's pageant. It got a good press, on the whole—even from the *St James's Chronicle*, of which Garrick was the part-owner, although the writer contrived to make his praise of Colman sound a shade back-handed:

> Necessity they say is the Mother of Invention, and perhaps the heavy Loss sustained by this Author, in the Death of the late Mr. Powell, induced him to turn his Thoughts forward to this Undertaking, in which we think he acquitted himself very happily, though very hastily.‡

The fulsome praise of Garrick included in the Prelude to the comedy suggested to some that Colman had something of a conscience. 'The Manager,' wrote one

---

* 'I have been much out of order,' he wrote to Peter Fountain on 19 September, and in a letter to Joseph Warton two days later he speaks of being 'confused and unsettled'. (*Letters*, 558, 559.)

† Philippe Destouches—his real name was Néricault—was born in Tours in 1680 and died in 1754. He served in the French embassies in Switzerland and London and married a Lancashire woman called Dorothea Johnston.

‡ The *St James's Chronicle*, 7–10 October 1769. The loss of Powell, still only in his early thirties, was indeed a blow to Colman. He had died at Bristol in July. He had stripped and thrown himself down on damp grass after a game of cricket. He developed a violent cold and fever and died a month later of pneumonia.

critic, 'offers incense to the Drury-Lane Chief, till every nostril is offended.' Foote, as always, put it more colourfully—it put him in mind, he said, 'of a *Ludgate-hill Prostitute* tickling Mr G— with one hand, and picking his pocket with the other'.[6]

Mr G— responded a week later and effectively blew Colman out of the water. *The Jubilee*, presented on the first night at Drury Lane as an afterpiece to *The School for Rakes*, was to create the record run for any piece in the whole of the eighteenth century. It played to packed houses for ninety-one nights in that first season alone. One enthusiastic German visitor went to see it twenty-eight times. Garrick recouped his Stratford losses fourfold. 'Sirs,' Lacy was heard to say, 'this was a devilish lucky hit.'[7]

Garrick's prologue, spoken by King in the character of Bustling Tom, a waiter, glanced artlessly at the rivalry with Colman:

> 'Twixt Hounslow and Colnbrooke—two houses of fame,
> Well known on that road—the two Magpies by name;
> The one of long standing, the other a new one,
> That boasts he's the old one, and this he's the true one . . .
> A race we have had, for your pastime and laughter,—
> Young Mag started first, with Old Mag hopping after:
> 'Tis said the *old* House hath possess'd a receipt
> To make a choice mixture of sour, strong, and sweet;
> A Jubilee punch—which, right skilfully made,
> Insur'd the Old Magpye a good running trade . . .
> Each Magpye, your honours, will peck at his brother,
> And their natures were always to crib from each other;
> Young landlords, and old ones, are taught by their calling,
> To laugh at engrossing, but practice forestalling:
> Our landlords are game-cocks . . . and fair play but grant 'em,
> I'll warrant you pastime for each little bantum . . .

In the play itself Garrick cleverly and good-naturedly turns the disasters of Stratford to comic advantage. 'I wrote ye petite piece upon one Single Idea, which struck me at ye time,' he told his friend Evan Lloyd:

> I suppose an Irishman (excellently perform'd by Moody) to come from Dublin to See ye Pageant—he is oblig'd to lye in a post Chaise all Night—undergoes all kind of fatigue & inconvenience to see ye Pageant, but unluckily goes to Sleep as ye Pageant passes by; & returns to Ireland without knowing any thing of ye Matter—*

Garrick told Lloyd that he wrote the piece in a day and a half when word of what Colman was up to was brought to him at Hampton. We know that was

---

* *Letters*, 576. Lloyd (1734–76), a Welshman, had a curacy at Rotherhithe and wrote satirical poetry. In one poem, *The Methodist*, he was held to have libelled a Welsh neighbour, and spent two weeks in the King's Bench Prison, where he struck up a friendship with Wilkes.

not the case, but Garrick was writing as *The Jubilee* approached its fortieth performance, and the little bantam had every reason to crow. Years before, when he was under attack from Churchill in *The Apology*, he had defined his strategy of response as 'acting a pleasantry of countenance while his back was most woefully striped with the cat-o'-nine tails'. The stripes inflicted on him during those nightmarish days in Stratford were now transmuted into sprightly comic dialogue.

In the first scene he mocks the clay-brained townsfolk of Stratford. 'There's some plot afoot with this Jubillo,' says one. 'Why, there are a hundred tailors in town. And all from London. 'Tis certainly a plot of the Jews and Papishes.' In the second, when the Irishman is wakened by the serenaders and asks 'What is this same Jubilee that I am come so far to see?' Garrick elegantly evens the score with Foote by having the musicians reply with a paraphrase of his Devil's Definition:

> Odes, Sir, without poetry
> Music without melody
> Singing without harmony . . .
> Blankets without sheeting, Sir,
> Dinners without eating, Sir,
> Not without much cheating, Sir . . .

As a final twist of the knife, he has the Irishman suggest that Foote purloined his definition from an old piece of doggerel about Kilkenny.

The scene in the yard of the White Lion which follows is pure Feydeau.* A note scrawled by Garrick on the copy of the manuscript in the Huntington Library reads, 'N.B. this is perhaps a Scene of the most regular confusion that was Ever exhibited.' It could well be.

—*Enter a Gentleman in slippers:* 'Why, Bootcatcher, you, Sirrah! Where are my boots?' 'I wish I could tell you, sir,' *comes the reply.* 'The boots are all thrown together in a heap yonder, and first come, first sarv'd.'
—*Enter a Fat Cook, pursuing two gentlemen who, tired of waiting, had raided the kitchen to help themselves:* 'Here you with the three ribs of beef! Don't touch 'em! They are for my Lord's servants, and they must be served first. See, see, hunger has no manners. They are at it already . . .'
—*Enter a Fellow selling toothpick cases, punch ladles, tobacco stoppers and nutmeg graters, all made out of the famous Mulberry Tree:*
FIRST GENTLEMAN. Here you, Mulberry Tree. Let me have some of the true dandy to carry back to my wife and relations in Ireland.
Enter Second Man with ware
SECOND MAN. Don't buy of that fellow, your honor, he never had an inch of the Mulberry Tree in his life. His goods are made out of old chairs and

---

* To Pedicord and Bergmann the vitality of the scene anticipated the opening of the second part of the American musical *Hello, Dolly.*

stools coloured to cheat gentlefolks with. It was I, your honour, bought
all the true Mulberry Tree. Here's my affidavit of it.

FIRST MAN. Yes, you villain, but you sold it all two years ago, and you have
purchased since more mulberry trees than would serve to hang your whole
generation upon . . .

Garrick must have found all this marvellously cathartic. Then, 'with Bells ringing,
fifes play^g, drums beating, & Cannon firing', he was able to launch into the
grand pageant which the rain had denied him at Stratford. At Covent Garden
Colman's characters had simply trooped past, and the characters had not always
been recognized. Garrick had a much better idea—a note in his hand on the
manuscript reads, 'In the procession, Every Scene in ye different Plays represents
some capital part of it in Action.' In *The Merchant of Venice*, it was the casket
scene and Shylock's plea for justice that were played out in dumb show; in *Much
Ado*, Garrick himself danced across the stage in masquerade as Benedick; in
Henry V, Fluellen makes Pistol eat the leek.

The Tempest was spectacular. First came Ariel, with a wand, 'raising a
tempest'. Then a great 'ship in distress' came sailing down the stage. Prospero
and Miranda were followed by Caliban, played by the Irish comedian Sparks;
he carried a wooden bottle and went through a slapstick routine with two
drunken sailors. *Antony and Cleopatra*, with a cast of more than fifty, must have
looked like a trailer for a Cecil B. de Mille film—Persian guards and eunuchs,
two black boys to fan the lovers with peacock feathers and two more to hold
up Cleopatra's train. The Demon of Revenge carried a burning torch, and the
Tragic Muse was drawn in a chariot by six Furies and attended by Fame, Grief,
Pity, Despair and Madness.

The procession was met with constant bursts of applause. 'It is the most
Superb that ever was Exhibited or I believe ever will,' wrote Hopkins. 'There
never was an entertainment produc'd that gave so much pleasure to all Degrees
Boxes pit and Gallery.'

Or so much pleasure to the man who devised it. *The Jubilee* served not only
as a vehicle for the pageant but as a lively satire on the entire Stratford venture.
Characteristically, Garrick did not laugh only at the good people of Stratford;
he also contrived a little self-mockery—seasoned with a judicious pinch of
self-congratulation:

FIRST OLD WOMAN. Have you seen, Ralph, the mon that is the ring leader of
the Jubillo, who is to fly about the town by conjuration?

RALPH. Yes, I ha' seen him. Not much to be seen, though, I did not care to
come too near him. He's not so big as I, but a good deal plumper. He's
auld enough to be wiser, too. But he knows what he's about, I warrant
'en.

Apart from his appearances in *The Jubilee*, Garrick acted infrequently this
season. This was partly because he was not in the best of health, but also because
managerial problems crowded in on him. The Barrys were proving increasingly

difficult. Hopkins's diary for the autumn of 1769 catalogues a suspiciously large number of occasions on which they were unable to appear, sometimes because they claimed to be ill, sometimes for reasons which sound more specious. 'Wrote to Mr Barry to know when they could play,' Hopkins noted in his Memorandum Book on 21 September. 'Receiv'd a letter from him on Monday, desiring they might be excus'd playing till Saturday sennight, as they were both ill.' On 10 October, a rehearsal was called for the following night's performance of *The Fair Penitent*. 'About nine o'clock in the morning,' wrote Hopkins, 'Mr Barry sent for & told me he was so ill that it would be impossible for him to play for sometime & that he would give up his salary till he was able to play.' Two days later, Hopkins made yet another tight-lipped entry:

> A rehearsal of *As You Like It* was call'd by Mrs Barry's desire at Ten. She sent word to have the Rehearsal put off for half an hour. The Performers staid for her till past Eleven, but she not coming they went away.

The long-suffering Hopkins was at the receiving end of a further display of temperament the following week. 'Waited on Mrs Barry to know if she would be agreeable to play lady Townly with Mr Reddish. She said she had no cloaths fit for it.' It is plain that both husband and wife thought they were far too grand to appear in *The Pageant* and that although Garrick and Lacy were prepared to go to some lengths to keep them sweet they did not relish the prospect of a confrontation. On 21 October Hopkins was once again the go-between:

> I waited on her by the manager's orders & told her they would excuse her playing on Monday if she would come out & do her part in the Pageant; & as it was a thing of great consequence to them, they desir'd and expected as she had begun it [she was cast as the Tragic Muse] that she would continue it as long as she was able. Her answer was, that as they seem'd to think it of such consequence she would come out & do it tonight & Monday night, but after that desir'd to be excused from doing it. On Tuesday Morning Mr Barry sent a note that Mrs Barry was ill in her Bed & could not come out till she was better. *Tancred & Sigismund* was call'd, and I did not receive the note till the rehearsal was begun. I also on Saturday deliver'd a message to Mrs Barry from Mr Garrick that he would never ask her to play in anything in which he was particularly interested. Her answer was that was in his Rage. But if his mind should alter, she was ready and willing to do anything he would desire her to do.

James Boswell was making the most of his short time in London that autumn. He exerted himself to see as much as he could of Johnson, and one evening at the Mitre, descanting on 'the superior happiness of savage life', provoked one of his hero's more crushing retorts. Boswell: 'Sometimes I have been in the humour of retiring to a desart.' Johnson: 'Sir, you have desart enough in Scotland.'

A couple of weeks later the unsnubbable Jamie gave a dinner at his lodgings in Old Bond Street, and was hugely pleased at his ability to assemble such a distinguished company. Johnson, Reynolds, Garrick and Goldsmith all came, and Murphy, Bickerstaffe and Tom Davies were also present. Boswell had been upset that Johnson had preferred to stay at Brighton with the Thrales during the Stratford festivities—'I particularly lamented that he had not that warmth of friendship for his brilliant pupil, which we may suppose would have had a benignant effect on both.' This evening, to his delight, both men appeared to take pleasure in each other's company:

> Garrick played round him with a fond vivacity, taking hold of the breasts of his coat, and looking up in his face with a lively archness, complimented him on the good health which he seemed then to enjoy; while the Sage, shaking his head, beheld him with a gentle complacency.[8]

When Boswell again passed the evening with Johnson later the same week he took it upon himself to complain that he had not mentioned Garrick in his *Preface to Shakespeare*, and asked if he did not admire him. Johnson was not disposed to measure out more than faint praise: "Yes, as 'a poor player, who frets and struts his hour upon the stage';—as a shadow." Boswell persisted: 'But has he not brought Shakespeare into notice?' Johnson: 'Sir, to allow that, would be to lampoon the age. Many of Shakespeare's plays are the worse for being acted: *Macbeth*, for instance.' At which point Boswell wisely changed the subject, and turned the conversation to the execution of several convicts which he had recently witnessed at Tyburn.[9]

The very next day, as it happens, Johnson and Garrick were among those who helped to lift the shadow of Tyburn from one of their own circle. Giuseppe Baretti, a native of Turin, had come to London in the early 1750s and was the author of a highly regarded *Italian and English Dictionary*. Baretti had been accosted in the Haymarket one night by a prostitute who grasped him painfully by the genitals. Startled, the short-sighted Baretti struck out at her, and when the woman screamed he was set upon by three ruffians. Baretti took to his heels, but when his attackers caught up with him, he pulled out a knife and one of the men was fatally wounded.

The 'constellation of genius' which turned out to speak in his defence also included Reynolds, Burke and Goldsmith; William Fitzherbert, the Member of Parliament for Derby and Dr Samuel Hallifax, Professor of Arabic in the University of Cambridge and later Bishop of Gloucester. Johnson described Baretti as 'a man that I never knew to be otherwise than peaceable'. Garrick testified that he himself, when travelling abroad, had carried the sort of fruit knife that Baretti had drawn—in foreign inns, he informed the jury, only forks were provided. Baretti was acquitted.*

Many of the tragic roles which Garrick had made his own had increasingly been assumed by Charles Holland. He had begun this season by playing Hamlet, and

---

* While waiting trial, Baretti had been visited in Newgate not only by his friends in the Johnson circle but by a rival Italian teacher. This tactful soul intimated that after Baretti's execution, he would like to take over his pupils, and asked the prisoner to write him a letter of recommendation.

had also appeared in *Tancred and Sigismunda*, as Richard III and in a prodigious number of other parts, comic as well as tragic. Suddenly, at the end of November, he was taken ill with smallpox. Stricken with blindness, he was attended by a number of eminent physicians called in by Garrick, but within days he was dead, at the age of thirty-six. He was buried in his family vault at St Nicholas, Chiswick, in the same churchyard where Hogarth lies buried. Garrick was suffering from a severe attack of the stone—'I am too bad to attend the doleful Ceremony,' he wrote to Evan Lloyd.* Holland made a number of bequests to his friends, 'as a Mark of My affection and Great Regard'. To Garrick he left his 'Best Diamond Ring' and to Foote his 'gold headed cane'. In his will, made the day before he died, he also asked Garrick 'to make an Inscription of a few decent lines upon my Tomb Stone as the last token of his regard for me.'

Holland died unmarried. He had been engaged for a time to Jane Pope, but after she discovered him in a boat on the river at Richmond with another actress, she never spoke to him again, except on the stage. The actress in the boat was 'that seductive piece of mischief' Sophia Baddeley, and before the season was out she was to be the cause of further mischief at Drury Lane. After Holland's death, his place in her affections was quickly taken by his physician, Dr Hayes. Her husband, Robert, seems to have accepted all this with complaisance—he himself, it was said, 'loved as great variety in his amours as in his clothes'—but Garrick, concerned to maintain a degree of good order and discipline in the company, insisted that she stop living with Hayes. This, somewhat surprisingly, she agreed to, on condition that her salary be paid directly to her rather than through her husband; Baddeley also agreed to the proposed arrangement, provided his wife paid some of his debts.

At this point George Garrick made an improbable entry into the affair, and comedy quickly degenerated into farce. George appears to have taken exception to what he regarded as Baddeley's cavalier treatment of his wife. Angry words were exchanged, a challenge was issued and early on the morning of 17 March the two men repaired to Hyde Park to give each other satisfaction, Baddeley taking with him as his second a Mr Mendez, one of his wife's many discarded lovers.

Baddeley fired first, and missed. At this point Mrs Baddeley leapt out of a hackney coach, and implored George to spare her husband's life. George sportingly fired in the air, and the combatants shook hands. Their antics were immediately lampooned in the *Westminster Magazine*, which published 'A Short History of DUELLING, illustrated by a wooden picturesque Representation of a late Theatrical Engagement'. The woodcut shows Mrs Baddeley on her knees while each duellist presents his pistol with his left hand: 'The SINISTER (or Left-Handed) THEATRICAL DUEL', reads the caption.

It was the sort of publicity Garrick could well do without, and it followed

---

* Foote was not, however, and was able to tell his friends that he had seen Holland 'shoved into the family oven'—Holland's father had been a baker and the family mausoleum did indeed bear some resemblance to an oven.

hard on the heels of a disagreeable episode at Drury Lane itself. The occasion was a new comedy called a *Word to the Wise* by Hugh Kelly. After his success with *False Delicacy* two years previously, Kelly had found lucrative employment as a hack for the ministry,* and on the first night of this new piece a party was made to damn it by supporters of Wilkes.† There was uproar as soon as the curtain went up. Garrick was called for, but did not come on: 'At last the play was got thro' with much hissing and Groaning,' Hopkins noted.

Bills for the piece were posted again the next night. There was once again a storm of hissing as soon as the curtain rose, and this time Garrick did come out and face the music—indeed he seems to have appeared some half a dozen times in the course of the evening, although it was often several minutes before he could make himself heard. At one stage he announced that the author was willing to withdraw the play, but that turned out to be unacceptable to Kelly's supporters. Garrick also offered to appear himself in some other piece, but that too was rejected. King eventually came on and attempted to speak the prologue, but his voice was lost in the hubbub and he was pelted with oranges. After several hours of this the audience began to leave, and were given their money back.

Garrick was pursued once more in the spring of 1770 by Mrs Griffith, who sent him a copy of Marivaux's farce *Les Fausses Confidences* and urged him to consider it for Drury Lane: 'I well know, that with *your assistance*,' she wrote, 'it might be improved into a comedy.' Garrick was unimpressed:

> Notwithstanding his Wit & great reputation he is of all ye french Play-wrights of Credit, the least to my taste. He is too refin'd—& particular in his dialogue, & drawing his Characters, He wants that fine Simple unaffected forcible flow of Stile & humour, which in my opinion marks yᵉ true dramatic Genius.

That apart, he told her, he was simply too busy to help her as he had done in the past: 'I have an affair of Consequence upon my hands, & for Which I have given up the pleasures of yᵉ Dauphin's Marriage which Mʳˢ Garrick & I had resolv'd to partake of—' (The Dauphin had been married to Marie Antoinette at Vienna two days previously.) What the 'affair of Consequence' was to which Garrick refers is not known. It may simply have been an excuse. He was, however, due to play Lear in a few days' time—his first appearance in the role for seven years.‡

---

* Forster, in his *Life of Goldsmith*, says that he was eventually rewarded by Lord North with a pension of £200.

† Parson Horne—John Horne Tooke as he later called himself—at the time one of Wilkes's most rabid supporters, was seen in the theatre that night, and was generally supposed to have had a major hand in the disturbance.

‡ Garrick may also have been preoccupied with the unusually large number of command performances called for at Drury Lane that year, the tenth anniversary of the King's accession—there were no fewer than ten during March and April. The King asked mainly for oratorios; *Messiah* was given three times, *Alexander's Feast* twice, on each occasion with the Coronation Anthems, and there were also performances of *Samson*, *Gideon* and *Judas Maccabeus*.

He did not let the rough handling he had received from Foote over the Jubilee stand in the way of civilized social relations. Foote had put it about that when he opened at the Haymarket in May he would offer the town a play called *The Drugger's Jubilee*, but all he got round to in the end was a prologue. Garrick addressed him in verse:

> The Remonstrance
> of D: G: of Drury-Lane
> to
> his Brother Manager S: Foote Esqr of the Haymarket.
>
> I've call'd, and call'd, and call'd again,
> To gossip with You, but in vain:
> What tho in Prologue You will lick me,
>   Why of your Conversation trick me?
> Shall all Enjoy Your Wit but Me,
> Who more than all delight in Thee?
> Tho wth the Manager You War,
> Let not, my Friend, our heart-strings jar . . .[10]

Another letter, written at about the same time to the Reverend Charles Jenner, a parson in the Midlands who had just made Garrick a present of his latest novel, throws interesting light on how Garrick viewed the direction in which stage comedy was moving:

> I could wish that You would think of giving a Comedy of Character to ye S[tage]—One calculated more to make an audience Laugh, than cry—the Comedie Larmoyante is getting too Much ground upon Us, & if those who can write the better Species of ye Comic drama don't make a Stand for ye Genuine Comedy & vis comic[a] the stage in a few Years, will be (as Hamlet says) like Niobe all tears—*

Although he was ill again early in May, Garrick was able to appear in the benefit for the Theatrical Fund towards the end of the month, and played Kitely in *Every Man in his Humour*. The season came to a triumphant end on 5 June with the 91st performance of *The Jubilee*, and the Garricks embarked on one of their most strenuous rounds of summer visits for several years.

Early July saw them rattling through Hertfordshire, Buckinghamshire and Essex. Towards the end of the month they were in Hampshire, and after the briefest of stops at Hampton they were again on the move. At Stamford, their host at Burghley House was Lord Exeter; from Lincolnshire they moved on to Cambridgeshire and Suffolk. By the time he returned to Hampton in the middle

---

* *Letters*, 583. Jenner (1736–74), ordained three years previously, held livings in Leicestershire and Northamptonshire. In his reply, he agreed that the stage 'may be getting too much into the handkerchief strain'. (*Boaden*, i, 384.) His novel, *The Placid Man*, enjoyed some success, but his efforts for the stage came to nothing.

of August, Garrick was once again in need of medical attention: 'Tho' our theatre opens the 19th of next month, I must go to Bath,' he wrote to Suard. 'I have a sort of flying gout, which I must keep under by the Bath waters.'

There was something else he wanted Suard to know:

> I will tell you a secret which is known only to my wife and a few select friends; at the end of the next theatrical campaign, I shall write up over my door *caestus artemque repono*.[11]

'I lay down the glove and my art.' Garrick still remembered some of his Virgil.* And Suard may have remembered that he had heard something of the sort before.

---

* The line occurs in the *Aeneid*, V, 484. *Caestus* was a glove made of leather thongs used by boxers.

29

'Nothing Till Lately Could Subdue My Spirits'

Garrick set off for Bath only two days after the start of the new season. 'I shall leave my Army to take the field without It's General' he wrote to Suard. 'I hope to God that we are to have no real War,' he added, 'tho the Clouds seem to look rather dark & Stormy.'[1]

The threat of war—with Spain, not France—had arisen over the desolate Falkland Islands, far away in the south Atlantic. The French explorer de Bougainville had taken possession of them in 1764 and established a colony at Port Louis on Berkeley Sound; the following year Commodore John Byron (the grandfather of the poet) was instructed to assert a claim on the ground of prior discovery— a Captain Strong had sailed between the two principal islands in 1690 and named the passage Falkland Sound.

In 1766, the French handed over their settlement to the Spanish: three years later Britain and Spain each invited the other to leave. Early in 1770, a powerful Spanish expedition overwhelmed the small British garrison and detained a British frigate for twenty days. Throughout the summer war seemed increasingly likely; the poor state of the Navy, which made the prospect of a successful campaign unlikely, gave the opposition a convenient stick with which to beat the new administration of Lord North. Garrick would have been well-informed on these matters through his friendship with Lord Rochford, whose guest he had been at St Osyth during the summer. Rochford, who had been ambassador to Spain from 1763 to 1768, was now one of the Secretaries of State; the following year it was he who conducted the negotiations with Spain which consigned the dispute to limbo.

Garrick's gout kept him in Bath for several weeks, and he did not act until November. It was to be a busy season, if an unremarkable one. Garrick brought out three new mainpieces, as against Colman's one, and the critical honours, such as they were, went to Drury Lane. When Covent Garden mounted *Clementina*, a new tragedy by Hugh Kelly, Colman prudently withheld the author's name for fear of political repercussions, but anonymity afforded little protection. 'The performance of Mrs Yates alone could have counteracted, for nine nights, its natural tendency towards damnation,' wrote the reviewer in *Biographica Dramatica*:

A gentleman, being asked, after one of the representations of this play, if he did not hiss it, replied, 'How could I? A Man can't hiss and yawn at the same time.'

The gratifying success of *The Jubilee* encouraged Garrick to think of further ways of satisfying the audience's obvious appetite for spectacle, and in the middle of December he brought forward a revision of Dryden's *King Arthur; or The British Worthy*. This dramatic opera, with music by Purcell, had first been seen in 1691 with Betterton and Mrs Bracegirdle in the leading roles. The story was drawn partly from Geoffrey of Monmouth's twelfth-century *Historia Regum Britanniae* and partly from Torquato Tasso's epic *Jerusalem Delivered*, written more than four hundred years later, and there was more than one view about how successful a marriage had been achieved between Italian romance and British legend.

Garrick called his alteration a masque. He changed very little of Dryden's text, and although he commissioned some additional music from Arne he retained the best of the songs, including the lovely 'Fairest Isle, all Isles Excelling'. His main interest was clearly in heightening the element of the spectacular, and he was able to do that by the use of machinery and effects unknown to Restoration stagecraft.

Hopkins—with one reservation—thought it succeeded brilliantly: 'This Masque was got up in a Superb manner the Scenery exquisitely fine & greatly applauded—. Miss Hayward play'd Emmeline very bad.'[2] Horace Walpole, who saw it a few days before Christmas, was altogether sniffier: 'I went to *King Arthur* on Saturday, and was tired to death, both of the nonsense of the piece and the execrable performance, the singers being still worse than the actors,' he wrote to his cousin Henry Seymour Conway:

> The scenes are little better (though Garrick boasts of rivalling the French opera), except a pretty bridge, and a Gothic church with windows of painted glass. This scene, which should be a barbarous temple of Woden, is a perfect cathedral, and the devil officiates at a kind of high mass! I never saw greater absurdities.[3]

The Drury Lane audience as a whole was easier to please. The King and Queen came to see it early in the New Year, and by the end of the season there had been twenty-six performances.

In January Garrick brought out a tragedy called *Almida*. This was an alteration of Voltaire's *Tancrède*, and was the work of Dorothea Celesia, the daughter of David Mallet* and the wife of Pietro Paolo Celesia, who had been the Genoese ambassador in London in the 1750s. Like Bickerstaffe's piece, *Almida* had the benefit of new scenes and costumes. The Barrys took the leading parts, and Mrs Barry spoke one of Garrick's less distinguished epilogues:

---

* Mallet had died in 1765. Garrick had been been the guest of the Celesias during his travels in Italy.

> A Female Bard, far from her native land,
> A female should protect—lo! here I stand,
> To claim of chivalry the ancient rites,
> And throw my gauntlet, at all critick Knights!
> Not only for our Auth'ress am I come;
> I rise a champion for the sex at home! . . .

The piece was enthusiastically received on the first night, but was the subject of a lengthy and hostile review in the February edition of the *Gentleman's Magazine*, although the writer gallantly excluded Mrs Barry from his strictures: 'In performing the part allotted to her in this piece, she rises like perfection out of chaos.'

The outstanding success of the season at Drury Lane was a new comedy by Cumberland called *The West Indian*. Cumberland had brought nothing to Garrick since the rejection of a piece of juvenilia ten years previously. In 1769, however, Colman had put on his comedy *The Brothers*, and it had done rather well. Garrick had been in the house for the first night, and had therefore heard Mrs Yates speak Cumberland's epilogue, which began with a reference to Reynolds's celebrated picture 'Garrick between Tragedy and Comedy':

> Who but hath seen the celebrated strife,
> Where Reynold call the canvass into life,
> And 'twixt the tragic and the comic muse,
> Courted of both, and dubious where to chuse,
> Th' immortal actor stands—?

Cumberland, who could see Garrick from where he sat, was able to observe his reaction, and shortly afterwards his friend William Fitzherbert,* who had been in Garrick's box, came across to say that 'the *immortal actor* had been taken by surprise, but was not displeased with the unexpected compliment from an author, with whom he had supposed he did not stand upon the best terms'.[4] By Cumberland's account, Garrick now took pains to cultivate his acquaintance, and he became a frequent visitor both at Southampton Street and at Hampton. He acknowledged that he had profited greatly from Garrick's advice in polishing up the manuscript of *The West Indian* for the stage:

> I punctually remember the very instant when he said to me in his chariot on our way to Hampton—"I want something more to be announced of your West Indian before you bring him on the stage to give eclat to his entrance, and rouse the curiosity of the audience; that they may say—Aye, here he comes with all his colours flying—." When I asked how this was to be done, and who was to do it, he considered awhile and then replied—"Why that is your look out, my friend, not mine; but if neither your

---

* Fitzherbert was the MP for Derby and a Commissioner of the Board of Trade. In 1772, believing that he was in severe financial difficulties, he hanged himself with a bridle in his stable.

Merchant nor his clerk can do it, why, why send in the servants, and let them talk about him. Never let me see a hero step upon the stage without his trumpeters of some sort or other."[5]

Cumberland records that before the play opened, when his expectations for it did not run very high, he made Garrick an offer: he would exchange his author's profits for a painting of the Holy Family—a copy of an Andrea del Sarto, he believed—which hung over Garrick's chimney-piece in Southampton Street. 'He would have closed with me upon the bargain,' Cumberland wrote in his memoirs, 'but that the picture had been a present to him from Lord Baltimore.'* As things turned out, Cumberland did rather well out of his author's profits. The play ran for twenty-nine nights in that first season, and was regularly revived over the next thirty years. It also sold 12,000 copies.

For all their intimacy at this time, Garrick found Cumberland rather heavy going. 'Damn his dish-clout face,' he said one day to Reynolds; 'his plays would never do if I did not cook them up and make prologues and epilogues for him, so that they go down with the public.'† Just occasionally the temptation to take a rise out of such a dull dog proved irresistible:

One morning when I called upon Mr. Garrick I found him with the St. James's evening paper in his hand, which he began to read with a voice and action of surprise, most admirably counterfeited, as if he had discovered a mine under my feet, and a train to blow me up to destruction—"Here, here," he cried, "if your skin is less thick than a rhinoceros's hide, egad, here is that will cut you to the bone. This is a terrible fellow; I wonder who it can be." He began to sing out his libel in a high declamatory tone, with a most comic countenance, and pausing at the end of the first sentence, which seemed to favour his contrivance for a little ingenious tormenting, when he found he had hooked me, he laid down the paper, and began to comment upon the cruelty of newspapers, and moan over me with a great deal of malicious fun and good humour—"Confound these fellows, they spare nobody. I daresay this is Bickerstaff again; but you don't mind him; a little galled, but not much hurt: you may stop his mouth with a golden gag, but we'll see how he goes on." He then resumed his reading, cheering me all the way as it began to soften, till winding up in the most profest panegyric, of which he was himself the writer, I found my friend had had his joke, and I had enjoyed his praise. . .[6]

---

* Further evidence that Garrick's enormous circle of acquaintance constituted a very mixed bag. Frederick Calvert (1731–71) the sixth Baron Baltimore, lived much of his life abroad. The German archaeologist Winckelmann, who encountered him in Italy, described him as 'one of those worn-out beings, a hipped [i.e. morbidly depressed] Englishman, who had lost all moral and physical taste'. A notorious rake, Baltimore had been acquitted at Kingston in 1768 on a charge of rape. He died in Naples in September 1771.
† The remark was overheard by Reynolds's pupil James Northcote, who included it in his Life. (The Life of Sir Joshua Reynolds, 2 vols., 2nd ed. 1819, i, 234.)

Cumberland tried to interest Garrick in the work of his friend George Romney and persuaded him to visit the painter's studio in Great Newport Street. Romney, the son of a Lancashire builder and cabinet-maker, had come to London nine years previously after an apprenticeship to an itinerant portrait painter, but was establishing himself only slowly—he was then charging only eight guineas for a three-quarters figure. Cumberland's efforts to interest Garrick in his favour did not get off to a good start:

> A large family piece unluckily arrested his attention; a gentleman in a close-buckled bob wig and a scarlet waistcoat laced with gold, with his wife and children, (some sitting, some standing) had taken possession of some yards of canvass very much, as it appeared, to their own satisfaction, for they were perfectly amused in a contented abstinence from all thought or action. Upon this unfortunate group when Garrick had fixed his lynx's eye, he began to put himself into the attitude of the gentleman, and turning to Mr. Romney—"Upon my word, Sir, said he, this is a very regular well-ordered family, and that is a very bright well-rubbed mahogany table, at which that motherly good lady is sitting, and this worthy gentleman in the scarlet waistcoat is doubtless a very excellent subject to the state I mean, (if all these are his children) but not for your art, Mr. Romney, if you mean to pursue it with that success, which I hope will attend you—."

Not for nothing had Garrick been the friend of Hogarth—a portrait that did not depict action or tell a story was not a portrait at all. 'The modest artist took the hint, as it was meant, in good part,' wrote Cumberland, 'and turned his family with their faces to the wall.'

A portrait described as of Garrick by Romney was sold at Christie's in June 1859, but the attribution seems doubtful, even though several years after his visit to Great Newport Street, Garrick did agree to sit. Romney was by then extremely fashionable, and had installed himself in a large house and studio in Cavendish Square; an attempt to study Garrick in his last appearance in Drury Lane ended in a soaking and a fever from which he almost died; Cumberland's hopes of seeing Garrick immortalized by his 'second Correggio' almost certainly died on that same June night in 1776.*

Although Cumberland's memoirs are loosely written and not free of inaccuracies, he is good evidence on the Pied Piper effect which Garrick exercised on children. Cumberland had two girls and four boys. Garrick he wrote, 'could charm a circle of them about him while he acted the turkey-cocks, and peacocks and water-wagtails to their infinite and undescribable amusement.'[7]

---

* The comparison with Correggio is recorded by Northcote: " 'He hates you, Sir Joshua, because you do not admire the painter whom he considers as a second Corregio. 'Who is that?' replied Sir Joshua. 'Why, his Corregio,' answered Garrick, 'is Romney the painter!' " (*Northcote, op. cit*, i, 234.)

Garrick and his wife regarded George's five children* very much as their own, and provided generously for all of them. It was Garrick who would arrange for his two nieces, Arabella and Catherine, to spend time at a carefully selected *pension* in Paris and their three brothers had all been sent to Eton, which made a sizeable dent in George's notional income.

Perhaps because of his affection for the children, Garrick displayed considerable indulgence towards his brother's chronic Micawberism. There were frequent requests for loans: 'It is with the greatest reluctance that I make this application to you, for nothing gives me so much uneasiness as to think that I am the least troublesome,' George had written in the summer of 1767, and he then went on to detail just where the shoe pinched:

My allowance from the theatre is 200*l*. out of which I pay for stamps, engrossments, &c. upwards of 50*l*. So that there remains clear 150*l*. which with your kind allowance makes 250*l*. My boys' bare schooling costs me upwards of 120*l*. So that there remains 130*l*. clear, out of which I pay for the boys more than 40*l*. for clothes, shirts, &c. &c. which reduces the above to 90*l*. This is what remains to maintain myself and the rest of my family, and to find us in clothes and every other necessary. I mention these particulars by way of apology, and that you may in some measure account for this application, and at a time when every thing is so very dear with regard to housekeeping. If you will therefore be so good as to lend me two hundred pounds, I will give you an order upon Mr. Pritchard to receive my salary at the house in the winter, and I hope before next winter to be in such a situation as to repay without any inconvenience . . .⁸

George had got his £200 then (although his brother endorsed the letter 'Ill Management') and Garrick had accommodated him on many other similar occasions. Then at the end of January 1771 George received a letter from his easy-going and generous brother which made it plain that he had broken the camel's back: 'Dear Brother,' Garrick wrote, 'I sit down at this time to do a most disagreeable thing to me, which is to tax you with Neglect, unkindness, & I will not add injustice to me.' George had seemed of late to be uneasy in his presence, full of excuses of pressing business to get away as soon as possible. Garrick had now discovered the reason, and he was hurt, indignant and angry in roughly equal proportions:

Did I Ever keep any Concern of any kind from you, have I not always open'd my heart, & designs to You, have You not had permission to open my letters, & know Every thing about me, & my affairs?—have you returned this kindness?—have you not been possess'd sometime of a Country house of horses, Chariot &c without so much as in yᵉ least hinting it to Me?—had you been possess'd of yᵉ fortune of Lord Clive† such a

* A sixth, George, was born to his second wife, Elizabeth Tetley, in 1775.
† Clive, broken in health, had returned from the Governship of Bengal five years previously, his fortune much multiplied by the popular imagination.

Brother (as I think I have been to You) should have been in common
civility at least acquainted with it—

Where George had found the money to set up an apparently opulent establishment
in the country remains a mystery. What mortified Garrick most in all this was
that George's deceit had made him look foolish:

I have never heard of it but from y^r Neighbors, to whom I have always
express'd my ignorance—an old Clergyman attack'd me at Court on y^e
Birthday [i.e the Queen's birthday] as Your Neighbor in ye Country—
What is this Mistery?—

George had also been dilatory in settling the estate of their cousin Peter Fermignac,
who had died the year before and under whose will they were beneficiaries.
Garrick had intended to use this legacy to pay the debts of those who had been
associated with him in the Jubilee at Stratford, and he now reproached George
with making him appear in an unfavourable light:

It sh^d not have been drag'd on to this time, to make what would have
been a piece of Generosity quickly done, a flat tame Action so laggingly
perform'd—I must intreat You to lay ye account before Me, that I may
Act accordingly—I can have no pleasure in knowing more of your Secrets,
than what immediatly concern Me, But these I have a right to, & my
affairs demand that I be instructed immediatly—[9]

Although Garrick was affronted by George's deviousness, it did not cause him
any degree of financial embarrassment. He was able without difficulty at this
time to raise £3,000 for the purchase of a property in Essex. He described it in
a letter at the time as a farm,[10] but it was in fact a small estate of 192 acres about
five miles from Colchester.

He suffered another bad attack of gout early in 1771—'attack'd in both legs,
& one knee,' he told Mrs Montagu towards the end of February, 'without rest
in ye Night, or Spirits in ye Day.'[11] He was still far from well two weeks later
when he wrote from Hampton to the new Mayor of Stratford, William Eaves:

I have been very low with my late illness, & scarce able to write 3 lines
togeather—the Air of this Place has tun'd my Spirits again, & restor'd my
Appetite, tho my legs will not yet permit me to dance an Allemande—

Eaves had sought Garrick's advice about how Stratford should continue to
celebrate 'the memory of our Immortal Bard'. There had been some talk of this
happening annually. Garrick suggested that it should take place on Shakespeare's
birthday, but did not respond to the hint that he should have some part in it:
'The Manner how—must be left to ye Gentlemen who feel the honour of being
Shakespear's Townsmen, & who have a proper Zeal for the first Genius of y^e
World—'

Garrick also offered the City Fathers some candid advice about how to ensure
that their infant tourist industry flourished:

... But my good Friend, w^d the Gentlmen do real honour, & Shew their Love to Shakespeare—Let 'Em decorate Y^e Town, (y^e *happiest* & Why not y^e *handsomest*, in England) let your Streets be well pav'd, & kept clean, do Something wth ye delightful Meadow, allure Every body to Visit y^e *holy Land*; let it be well lighted, & clean under foot, and let it not be said for Y^r honour, & I hope for Y^r Interest, that the Town, which gave Birth to the first Genius since ye Creation, is the most dirty, unseemly, ill-pav'd, wretched-looking Town in all Britain—*

Garrick was constantly solicited for seats at Drury Lane, particularly on the increasingly rare occasions when he himself was performing, and he exerted himself to meet such requests, especially when they were made on behalf of the great and the good. An undated note survives from Grey Cooper, a Secretary of the Treasury with whom Garrick was on friendly terms, expressing appreciation of one such occasion:

I give you my most cordial thanks for the delight I received last night; and Lord North commands me to express his obligation to you in the strongest manner . . . I beg my best compliments to Mrs Garrick. I saw her stooping from her cloud, and gazing at you; I thought the spirit of Shakspeare was probably doing the same, and with equal pleasure.†

Goodwill was a bankable commodity, and now, a year or so later, Garrick was able to draw on his account:

... As I hope you believe me not very unworthy of Ministerial Indulgence, perhaps Lord North with your mediation will have no objection to granting my Suit—I have had a long friendship with Mr Richard Burke, in his last letter to me, he complains much of his ill state of health, & has desir'd my assistance to get him leave for a twelvemonth's Absense—

Richard Burke was Edmund's younger brother, and had been Collector of the Port of Grenada in the West Indies for several years.‡ Cooper undertook to approach the Prime Minister. 'Lord North is the best-natured man in the world,' he told Garrick—'and I know,' he added delicately, 'he will as readily do a favour, or grant a reasonable indulgence, to the brother of Mr E Burke, as to any of those who stand in the ranks of his political friends . . .'§

Sir Edward Hawke, the hero of Quiberon Bay, now First Lord of the Admiralty,

---

* *Letters*, 624. A celebration did take place that year, but then not again till 1827, when the newly formed Shakespearean Club organized a three-day festival on the lines of Garrick's Jubilee.

† *Boaden*, i, 376. The occasion could well have been the night in February 1770 when Garrick played Lear for the first time in seven years.

‡ 'Remember me to Brother Pepper,' says a footnote in one of Garrick's letters to Burke. (*Letters*, 372.)

§ *Boaden*, i, 417. And so it was arranged. Cooper wrote again to Garrick four days later to say that he had obtained North's permission to order a warrant granting Burke a year's leave of absence. (*Boaden*, i, 418.)

proved equally obliging. Garrick had petitioned him on behalf of a young naval officer of his acquaintance, a member of the Colman—Churchill circle who had literary aspirations. 'I received your letter in favour of Captain Thompson, and shall be very glad to oblige you, when it shall be in my power,' the Admiral replied, although to someone sensitive to nuance, the letter may have conveyed the mildest suggestion of a rebuke:

> I cannot take upon me to make a promotion of officers myself; but when his Majesty shall please to order a promotion to be made, you may be assured I shall not be unmindful of your friend.*

If the answer to such requests was no, the refusal was invariably elegantly phrased. Lady Spencer, writing at the end of December 1770, had shown an easy mastery of the form:

> I sincerely wish it was in my power to find expressions that would convince you beyond the possibility of a doubt, that what I am going to say is not a mere excuse, but a reality that gives both Lord Spencer and myself pain, as it prevents his complying with a request of yours. It is very true that there is a strong connexion, as far as friendship goes, between Lord Spencer and the Bishop of St. Asaph; but, from an idea that the Bishop owed his promotion to Lord Spencer, which is entirely without foundation, he has been so pressed to make applications to him for small livings and prebends in his gift, that he cannot with any degree of delicacy request any thing farther of him. . . .[12]

The bout of illness which Garrick suffered early in 1771 proved so severe and prolonged that his thoughts began once again to turn towards retirement. 'Nothing till lately could subdue my Spirits, but I begin to discover that I am growing Old,' he wrote to Boswell in the middle of April, 'that it is time for me to get into port, and drop my Anchor.' He was writing to congratulate Boswell on his marriage—'I have been so happy in that State, that I pity all those miserable Mortals who live out of yᵉ Pale of my Faith, & lie alone.' At the end of the letter, recollecting that Boswell was not always the soul of discretion, he thought it prudent to add a postscript: 'I must intreat you not to mention wᵗ I have said about yᵉ theatre—'

His plans for the following season were complicated by the fact that the Barrys were becoming increasingly difficult, lazy and unreliable. At the beginning of May he decided that he must take the bull by the horns. The management had resolved, he told Barry, 'not to go on in the same manner, nor upon the same Terms, we have done this last Season; Many great inconveniences & losses,

---

* *Boaden*, i, 402. Thompson's promotion eventually came through in 1772. Four years previously, Garrick had written a somewhat swaggering letter to him about his influence with Hawke: 'As Sʳ Edᵈ has ask'd *Me* some favours in *My* Way, for we are in great vogue I assure you, I shall surround him wᵗʰ applications.' (*Letters*, 489.) The Admiral had presumably asked for places at the theatre. Garrick may also have been trading on the fact that Hawke, with a house at Sunbury, was a close neighbour.

with frequent disappointments to the Publick, make such a Resolution necessary.'

He reminded Barry that he had received '*a great Sum of Money for performing a very small number of Nights*'. In fact Barry had appeared on only nineteen occasions since the beginning of the season. He had played only one new part, and had not been seen in a revival for two years. George had been very lenient in the matter of making deductions for non-appearance, but even if forfeits had been 'exacted in their utmost rigour,' Garrick wrote, '*they wou'd not have been an adequate satisfaction for the disappointments of Business*'.

It was an ultimatum. Unless Barry agreed to a realistic revision of the forfeits formula, and unless he undertook to perform more frequently, the management would not wish to renew his engagement. Garrick set out their conditions:

First. A reasonable Number of times shall be ascertain'd for your performing, your Sallary be divided into the same Number of parts, & so many parts forfeited as You fall short of your performance, (when call'd upon by us) as Shall be Stipulated in the Agreement.

Secondly. You must revive certain Characters which we will mutually settle upon closing our Agreement; and take your Share of the New ones.

Thirdly—You must make no Objection to perform without Mrs Barry, the ill consequences of which Objection, have been Severely felt.

Fourthly. Mrs Barry must likewise agree to play without you if the Business requires it.

Fifthly. Upon these terms, we make no Objection to your Salary and we have no New Conditions to propose to Mrs Barry.[13]

The letter carried the signatures of both Lacy and Garrick. Barry replied the following day, accepting their terms.

A letter to his old friend John Hoadly shows just how much the approach of summer had lifted Garrick's spirits:

I have been really blighted with ye Spring, & till the Warm Weather came to make me bud a little with ye trees, I was resolv'd to send no cold-blooded prosing to Thee my Merry Wag of ten thousand! I am tight in my Limbs, better in my head, & my belly is as big as Ever—I cannot quit *Peck & Booze*—What's Life without Sack & Sugar! my lips were made to be lick'd, & if the Devil appears to me in the Shape of Turbot & Claret, my Crutches are forgot, & I laugh & Eat till my Navel rosebud is as full blown as a Sun flower—[14]

It was a point of honour that he should perform in the annual benefit for the Theatrical Fund at the end of May, and he duly appeared in *Much Ado*. A fortnight later he rounded off the season by playing Leon in Fletcher's *Rule a Wife and Have a Wife* and he was free to retreat briefly to Hampton before embarking on another taxing round of summer visits.

First into Berkshire, to stay at Park Place with Henry Seymour Conway, favourite cousin and lifelong correspondent of Horace Walpole. Conway had been the MP for various pocket boroughs, had fought at Dettingen, Fontenoy and Culloden and had served as ADC both to Marshal Wade and to the Duke of Cumberland; he had also been secretary to Garrick's old friend Hartington when he was Lord Lieutenant of Ireland. For three years in the middle 1760s he had been a Secretary of State and Leader of the Commons and he was currently Lieutenant-General of the Ordnance; his wife, Caroline, was the widow of the Earl of Ailesbury.

Garrick was a relentless name-dropper, and grand names like these came in extremely useful when he returned to Hampton to find an invitation which he was obliged to decline:

> My Lord
> We have been with Lady Ailesbury & General Conway at park place or I should have return'd my Acknowledgments to Your Lordship sooner for ye honour You have done Us—a long settled Journey into ye West to our Friends Lord & Lady Edgecumbe, & from thence to return With Lord Lyttelton to Hagley will take up all ye time We can spare this Summer. . . .

This was addressed to Lord Hardwicke, at that time High Steward of the University of Cambridge and Lord Lieutenant of the county. He had country seats at Wimpole Hall near Cambridge and at Wrest Park in Bedfordshire, and was the elder brother of Garrick's friend Charles Yorke, who had died the previous year three days after being appointed Lord Chancellor. Garrick also had to disappoint someone else who was eager to enjoy his company; the mail awaiting him on his return from Park Place had included a less conventional communication:

> At the Court of Apollo, it was resolved—
> That a pilgrimage be made to Hampton, on Monday next, by Messrs. Wilkes and Loyd, to pay their Devoirs to the *Prophet Shakspeare and his Priest.*
> N.B. Miss Wilkes will pay her compliments to Mrs. Garrick at the same time.

The irrepressible Wilkes was once again riding high in popular favour. The liberality of his supporters on both sides of the Atlantic had ensured that when he was discharged from the King's Bench prison the previous year he had emerged with his finances repaired. He had taken a villa at Fulham, and was once again living high on the hog; his portrait was to be seen in shop windows and dangling from the signs of ale houses; he had just been nominated for the office of Sheriff of London and Middlesex.

Not even emissaries from the court of Apollo could hope to see the priest of the prophet Shakespeare at that sort of notice, however:

> Dear Sir
> After wishing You Joy, of Y^r late Success, Mrs Garrick and I are very sorry that We have been Engag'd for some time to Meet Lord and Lady Camden tomorrow at Egham . . . When we return from Mount Edgecumbe &

Hagley, where we are going with all convenient Speed, We Shall be happy to see You & Miss Wilkes at Hampton . . .[15]

If Garrick had had to invent an excuse for putting off Wilkes and his daughter, he could not have improved on a prior engagement with Lord Camden. Eight years previously it was he, as Chief Justice of the Court of Common Pleas, who had deemed the general warrant issued for the arrest of Wilkes to be illegal, and granted a writ of habeas corpus; when Wilkes was subsequently committed to the Tower it was Camden—Sir Charles Pratt as he still was at the time—who had ordered his release on the ground of parliamentary privilege. From 1766 to 1770 he had been Lord Chancellor. Since his dismissal from the Woolsack, he had resumed his role as a vigilant guardian of the constitution; he had supported Chatham's bill for restoring Wilkes to the House of Commons and his subsequent resolution declaring eligibility for Parliament to be an inherent right of the subject.

It is evident from a number of charming and elegant letters of Camden's which survive that he valued his friendship with Garrick highly. We also know from Boswell that this irked Johnson not a little: 'Nor could he patiently endure to hear that such respect as he thought due only to higher intellectual qualities, should be bestowed on men of slighter, though perhaps more amusing talents,' he writes in the *Life*:

I told him, that one morning, when I went to breakfast with Garrick, who was very vain of his intimacy with Lord Camden, he accosted me thus:— 'Pray now, did you—did you meet a little lawyer turning the corner, eh?'— 'No, Sir, (said I.) Pray what do you mean by the question?'—'Why, (replied Garrick, with an affected indifference, yet as if standing on tip-toe,) Lord Camden has this moment left me. We have had a long walk together.' JOHNSON. 'Well, Sir, Garrick talked very properly. Lord Camden *was* a *little lawyer* to be associating so familiarly with a player.'[16]

Mount-Edgcumbe was in Devon, a long journey from Hampton on eighteenth-century roads, but in a later age the estate would undoubtedly have earned Michelin's three-star *vaut le voyage*. Garrick, writing to William Burke just before setting off, called it 'the Iliad of Situations'.[17] Ten years later, when its owner was advanced to a viscountcy, it was said to be in compensation for the damage caused to the woods of Mount-Edgcumbe in strengthening the fortifications of Plymouth.

The Garricks' host was a sailor and his wife was the daughter of the Archbishop of York. He had been Commander-in-Chief, Plymouth, from 1766 to 1770, and was now a Vice-Admiral and Lord Lieutenant of Cornwall. His father was said to have been popular with George II because he was even shorter than the King himself; his bachelor brother, whom he had succeeded in the title, had been a close friend of Horace Walpole's and among the first to recognize the genius of Joshua Reynolds.

Garrick's old friend Lord Lyttelton was a fellow-guest at Mount-Edgcumbe, and they travelled back together in the middle of August to his estate at Hagley in Worcestershire, ten miles or so from the growing sprawl of Birmingham. Amiable and absent-minded, tall and scrawny (he is Smollett's Gosling Scragg in *Peregrine Pickle*), George Lyttelton was now in his early sixties; the friend of Pope and former 'chief favourite' of Frederick, Prince of Wales had entered the twilight of his twin careers as politician and author. Hagley had been in the family for more than two centuries. Lyttelton had laid out enormous sums on restoring and remodelling it, and it boasted every fashionable feature of the day—a grotto, a hermitage, a ruined castle, a cascade, a Greek temple. In the midst of these splendours, the talented, unworldly man who had created them cut a melancholy figure. His second wife had left him. His heir, Thomas, a notorious libertine, was a constant cause of concern: 'I can tell you nothing about my son, but have reason to fear he will take up money by selling reversions of the best part of my estate,' he confided in Garrick later in the year. 'Resignation and patience are my only remedies for these evils.'[18]

The large house party at Hagley included Mrs Montagu and Mrs Vesey, another bluestocking famous for the informality of her London parties (Horace Walpole called them 'Babels').* The Garricks always earned their keep as house-guests. 'We are preparing for another expedition,' Lyttelton wrote when their week's stay was over, 'but all parties of pleasure without Garrick and Pid-Pad appear dull and insipid.'[19] ('Pid-Pad' was his affectionate nickname for Mrs Garrick, who never quite got the hang of how to pronounce the English letter t.)

The measure of Lyttelton's affection for Garrick may be gauged from another letter from Hagley later in the year when he had heard from Mrs Montagu that Garrick had once again been quite ill. 'I cannot be easy about you, without an assurance under your own hand of your continuing well,' he wrote:

> I think I love you more than one of my age ought to do; for at a certain time of life the heart should lose something of its sensibility: but you have called back all mine, and I feel for you as I did for the dearest of my friends in the first warmth of my youth . . .[20]

There were muddy-minded souls in whom these summer peregrinations from one stately home to another excited both envy and malice. Joseph Cradock records that sometimes on arrival Garrick would find 'little dirty letters' addressed to 'Mr David Garrick, Player'. 'He once expressed himself excessively annoyed by this,' Cradock wrote, 'but he knew all the parties concerned.'[21]

Boswell tried to make mischief with Johnson in this area one day, but totally failed to trigger the sort of response he hoped to elicit:

> I then slily introduced Mr Garrick's fame, and his assuming the airs of a great man. JOHNSON: "Sir, it is wonderful how *little* Garrick assumes . . .

---

* She was the daughter of the Bishop of Ossory. Agmondesham Vesey, her second husband, was Accountant-General of Ireland and a close friend of Burke's. Her husband was elected to The Club in 1773; its members then used to come to her after dining every other Tuesday. Towards the end of her life she lapsed into depression and was eventually 'bereft of her faculties'.

Consider, Sir; celebrated men, such as you have mentioned, have had their applause at a distance; but Garrick had it dashed in his face, sounded in his ears, and went home every night with the plaudits of a thousand in his *cranium*. Then, Sir, Garrick did not *find*, but *made* his way to the tables, the *levées*, and almost the bed-chambers of the great . . . If all this had happened to me, I should have had a couple of fellows with long poles walking before me, to knock down everybody that stood in the way. Consider, if all this had happened to Cibber or Quin, they'd have jumped over the moon.—Yet Garrick speaks to *us*" (smiling).[22]

By the end of August, Garrick was back in London—not entirely well, but completely caught up in preparations for the new season. 'I have had a small fit of yᵉ Gravel,' he wrote to Cradock, 'but am better, & working like a Horse.' His immediate concern was with an ambitious new spectacle which he was to present as an afterpiece at the end of October, *The Institution of the Garter; or, Arthur's Roundtable Restored*. 'We have all hands at work,' he told Cradock, '& shall make as good a Puppet Shew of it, as it really is—I have a thought beyond yᵉ mere Exhibition of Procession & feasting, & if I please myself in it, You shall know it, but *Mum* I beseech you.'

During the summer there had been great public interest in the installation of nine new Knights of the Garter at Windsor, the most to be created for a number of years. They included the Hereditary Prince of Brunswick Lunenburg, the King's younger brother the Duke of Cumberland and two of his sons—the nine-year-old Prince of Wales (the future George IV) and his younger brother Frederick. Frederick, although still only eight years old, was no stranger to honours, his father's influence as Elector of Hanover having procured his election to the lucrative bishopric of Osnaburg at the age of six months.

Several members of the aristocracy were also honoured—the Dukes of Albemarle, Marlborough and Grafton, the Earl of Halifax and the second Earl Gower. Gower was of particular interest to Garrick. He had represented Lichfield briefly in the Commons before succeeding to the title, was a former Lord Chamberlain and since 1767 had served as Lord President of the Council.

Garrick prepared the masque with characteristic thoroughness. He consulted John Seldon's *Titles of Honor*, published in 1614 and *The History of the Order of the Garter*, by Elias Ashmole, which had appeared in 1672. He also turned to a more recent work, a dramatic poem called *The Institution of the Order of the Garter* by Gilbert West, published in 1742. He explained in his Advertisement that it had not been possible to stage this in its original form because 'though rich in machinery, it was little more than a poem in dialogue without action'.

Garrick attended to the difficulty of transferring this 'great solemnity' to the stage by adding some comic scenes, getting Dibdin to write some music and spending lavishly on 'New Scenes, Machines, Habits, and Decorations'. It was met with great applause on the first night, although Hopkins, unusually, had reservations: "This Entertainment is got up at Vast Expence both in Scenery &

Dresses,' he wrote, 'But I wish it may answer the expence.' The following evening he was still not persuaded: 'The Serious part of the Entertainment Dull & heavy.'

The theatrical grapevine saw to it that the managers of the two houses were kept well-informed about each other's battle plans. Wind of Garrick's intentions had sent Colman scurrying to Ben Jonson's *Masque of Oberon* and he was able, only a fortnight later than Drury Lane, to come up with a rival attraction which he called *The Fairy Prince, with Installation of Knights of the Garter*. Garrick, in turn, had had early intelligence of what was afoot at Covent Garden, but was unruffled by it. 'I rejoice my little Antagonist is so Cocksure,' he told Edward Thompson twelve days before his own first night:

> I have heard from all quarters that he triumphs, before he has struck one Stroke, that he proclaims loudly that his piece is ye most classical, pure, divine & what not,—piece, that was Ever Exhibited; & that We Shall get ye Start, but that he will distance Us, before ye race is finish'd—I hear his trumpet, & fart at it—[23]

That, roughly speaking, was how some critics responded to both trumpets— 'too contemptible to meet with countenance from any but the sons of riot,' sniffed the *Theatrical Review*. Both pieces did well, however, Garrick's extravaganza running for thirty-three nights and Colman's for thirty-six.

It is not clear why Garrick, in the one and only contemporary printing of the work, did not publish the scenes of rustic comedy with which he sought to please the upper gallery; the Advertisement, quite unconvincingly, says simply that 'they would lose much of their effect by being separated from the action of the performer', which is an argument against the printing of practically every play in the canon.[24] The character of Sir Dingle, the king's fool, proved an ideal vehicle for the comic gifts of Tom King. When a woman at the castle gate at Windsor complains that he had promised to let her in, he waves her airily aside:

> I live in the land of promises, and I'll give you a hundred more. We give nothing else here. Besides, I am a wit and have a very short memory, and yesterday is an age. Do you think I am so vulgar, or so little a courtier, to remember what I promised yesterday? Fie, for shame. Come along, Signior.

In Garrick's first draft, 'Signior'—or 'Signior of the Neuter Gender' as Dingle also calls him—was Signior Catterwawlins, a role which once again allowed him to take a swipe at the Italian opera. During rehearsals, however, he had second thoughts and the Signior underwent a change of sex; by the first night the character's name had become Squallini, and the role was sung by Mary Ann Wrighten, who had made her Drury Lane début the previous season.*

During this frenzy of activity in the early part of the season, Garrick had once again been battling with ill-health. Writing to Lyttelton in the middle of October he made no attempt to conceal the fact that he had been seriously unwell. He

---

* Mrs Wrighten's first appearance had been as Diana in *The School for Fathers*. 'A very fine Voice,' noted Hopkins—'Awkward & Clumsy figure—Well faced.' (8 February 1770.)

was no hypochondriac, but eighteenth-century Englishmen, like some modern Americans, believed that no detail of their medical history was too insignificant to be of interest to their friends:

> Since I revell'd in delight upon the hills at Hagley, I have had a drawback with some attacks of my old disorder to make me sensible of my mortal condition, I am now, as I may say, well again, and I have put my philosophy to the trial—I drink no wine, eat but one thing, and don't so much as smell at supper. This regulation with a spoonful of Castor oyl every night and a moderate use of honey and barley-water, will I am persuaded, make me whole again. I have produced no less than two or three small stones with very little pain for many days. The Faculty have given me spirits by assuring me that I shall get rid of small ones . . .[25]

He was well enough to play Benedick on 17 October—his first appearance of the season—but shortly afterwards he was once more laid low, again by an attack of the stone. He had been posted to play Kitely in *Every Man in his Humour* on 1 November, but at noon that day the theatre was obliged to rush out fresh bills. He insisted on appearing the following week, which was certainly sooner than he should have done—*The Institution of the Garter* was less than two weeks into its run and he was no doubt eager to maintain its momentum and buttress it against the forthcoming challenge from Colman with as strong a sequence of mainpieces as possible.

It was while he was in this reduced state in the middle of November that there was delivered to him a brief communication that bristled with menace:

> I am very exactly informed of your *practices*, and of the information you so busily send to Richmond, and with what triumph and exultation it was received. I knew every particular of it the *next day*.—Now, mark me, vagabond! Keep to your pantomimes, or be assured you shall hear of it. Meddle no more, thou busy informer!—it is in *my* power to make you curse the hour in which you dared to interfere with
>
> JUNIUS.

30

The House Shows the Owner

The question of what malign intelligence lurked behind the pseudonym of Junius had exercised political and court circles for almost three years. The letters had begun to appear in the *Public Advertiser* early in 1769 and were principally aimed at discrediting the Grafton administration and urging the return of Chatham. Personal abuse was no novelty in English political controversy, but the unbridled savagery with which Junius laid about him was unequalled.

Grafton was 'a black and cowardly tyrant'—but Junius also lingered over the infidelity of his wife; the Duke of Bedford, distraught at the death of his only son, was described as destitute of all natural affection and accused of selling his country for money to France. When the Princess Dowager lay dying of cancer, Junius gloated over her condition and the revolting treatment she was subjected to by her doctors: 'The lady herself is now preparing for a different situation. Nothing keeps her alive but the horrible suction of toads. Such an instance of divine justice would convert an atheist.'

In December 1769, when Junius turned his attention from the ministers of the crown to the sovereign himself, the Attorney-General had prosecuted Wood-fall, the printer and part-proprietor of the *Public Advertiser*, but secured no more than a verdict of 'guilty of printing and publishing only'. Parliament and the courts were equally discredited; no matter how gross and scurrilous the libels, the instinct of the London juries of the day was to shrug, even to snigger at them. The drip-drip from the tap of venom was not without effect, and sizeable numbers of people were prepared to believe that the Grafton ministry constituted some sort of threat to English liberties.

Garrick's offence had been to pass on a piece of news which he knew would be received with pleasure and relief. He held a share in the *Advertiser*, and Woodfall had let drop to him that Junius would be writing no more letters for publication. Garrick in turn had told Ramus, with whom he was in frequent touch at Court. This had somehow got back to Junius, and he may have believed that Garrick either knew or suspected his identity and might betray him.*

---

* The matter has never been conclusively resolved, but Junius is generally believed to have been Sir Philip Francis (1740–1818), who had been at St Paul's with Woodfall. He acted for a year as amanuensis to Pitt and from 1762 to 1772 was first clerk at the War Office. He later made a large fortune in India, fought a duel with Warren Hastings, became a Member of Parliament and was close to the Prince Regent.

Garrick's reply—necessarily—took the form of a letter to Woodfall. He got off to a somewhat otiose start by expressing surprise that 'such talents could have descended to such Scurrility'. As was often the case he wrote at excessive length, and although he huffs and puffs a little ('I will make Use of no foul language—my Vindication wants neither violence or abuse to support it') the general impression created by the letter is one of spinelessness:

> I beg you will assure Junius that I have as proper an abhorrence of an Informer, as he can have, that I have been honour'd with ye Confidence of men, of all Parties, & I defy my greatest Enemy to produce a Single instance of any one repenting of such Confidence—I have always declar'd that were I by any Accident to discover Junius, no consideration should prevail upon me to reveal a Secret productive of so much mischief . . .

His courage revived slightly as he reached his conclusion—'I am with great regard for Junius's Talents,' he subscribed himself to Woodfall, 'but without the least for his threatnings.'[1] The exchange petered out, and indeed after January 1772 Junius, at least under that name, wrote no more.

In the six weeks or so leading up to Christmas, the Drury Lane audience was treated to a flurry of performances by Garrick. They saw him as Kitely in *Every Man in His Humour*, as Leon in *Rule a Wife and Have a Wife* and as Lusignan in *Zara*; he also appeared as Sir John Brute, as Ranger and as Archer, as Abel Drugger in *The Alchymist* and as Hamlet. By way of holiday entertainment he offered a revival of James Love's *The Witches; or a Trip to Naples*. The audience liked it well enough—there was a view of Vesuvius, reflected in the waters of the Bay of Naples, and another of the volcano erupting, with lava cascading down like liquid fire—but the *Theatrical Review* pursed its lips at 'this what-shall-we-call-it—one of those Mummeries, in which the carpenters, painters and taylors belonging to the theatre are the principal projectors; who torture dull brains to furnish out most contemptible pieces of entertainment . . .'

The season was notable for the extraordinarily free rein which Garrick gave to Cumberland to display his distinctly uneven talents as a dramatist.* Early in December, he staged Cumberland's reworking of *Timon of Athens*. Barry appeared in the demanding title role, and the production was elaborately staged, with 'New Scenes, Decorations, &c.' Davies thought it 'a miserable alteration of one of Shakespeare's noblest productions', although Hopkins noted that the first night's performance was generally well received. The critic of the *Theatrical Review* thought very ill of the player who took the part of Alcibiades and who was announced as making his first appearance on the stage:

> . . . His deportment is aukward and void of grace to an extreme; and he labours under the disdvantage of having a face destitute of expression. His gestures are extremely ungraceful, and the whole of his execution is

---

* Not without exciting a degree of envy. Murphy, when he came to write his *Life* of Garrick thirty years later, achieved a splendidly barbed description of his rival: 'A gentleman who had been for some time hovering about the skirts of Parnassus, without entering far enough to taste the Pierian spring, and without gaining a sprig of laurel.' (*Murphy*, ii, 87.)

glaringly untutored, and misconceived. His person is very ill formed, and therefore it makes greatly against him . . . .*

Who had discovered this paragon? How did it come about that a complete tiro, and one apparently so slenderly endowed, had been cast in the important role of Alcibiades in the first place? And how had he retained it through the two months of rehearsal which Garrick had given to the piece?

Henry Croft or Crofts was the stage-struck son of a clergyman and had served his time as a stationer in the Temple. He had been badgering Garrick since the end of 1770, and had finally been invited down to Hampton to show what he could do. Only someone heavily carapaced with self-conceit would not have been deterred by the letter which Garrick wrote to him from Mount-Edgcumbe the following summer:

> . . . I must frankly open my heart to you, & declare as a Man of honour, that I most Sincerely think that you have not talents for the Stage, & that You may repent making your Tryal there—I was certainly right in my *first* judgment, but seeing Y^r mind so absolutely bent upon making Y^r appearance upon the Stage, I gave way to y^r Solicitations, in hopes of your disclosing some Powers, which might be kept down from diffidence, or want of Exercise—I am not yet satisfyd—[2]

Instead of indicating that the matter was closed, however, Garrick foolishly concluded by divulging his movements for the next few weeks. This earned him a three-page letter to Hagley in which Croft insisted that he had been promised a chance—whereupon, well-nigh unbelievably, the manager of Drury Lane capitulated:

> . . . I shall be ready, (now I have open'd my mind to You) to assist You with great pleasure—I thank you for your very friendly, sensible polite Letter—You must not be frighten'd for ye future when You rehearse, but Shew Me all y^r Powers, & I will do my best for You—I have a character in my mind for You.[3]

There is no evidence that Croft enjoyed the patronage of powerful friends. It can only be assumed that his 'friendly, sensible polite Letter' was in such agreeable contrast to the general run of Garrick's thespian correspondence that he was flattered into a temporary suspension of his critical faculties.†

Hard on the heels of *Timon* came another offering by Cumberland, a musical afterpiece called *Amelia*. This too had a very mixed reception, although it is

---

* Hopkins, watching from the prompter's corner, formed a similar judgement but put it more succinctly: 'Bad figure bad voice & Play'd bad.'

† Croft got one more chance. He was cast as Chamont in *The Orphan* two months later. 'If necessity has obliged Mr. Croft to tread the Actor's walk,' wrote the *Theatrical Review*, 'he is truly an object of pity, but this will not justify Mr. *Garrick's* neglect of that duty he owes to the Public.' Croft was allowed a benefit early in May and played Posthumus in *Cymbeline*. After that he was seen no more.

difficult at a distance of more than two centuries to distinguish between lack of enthusiasm for the piece and dislike of the author.* His prolificacy was offence enough; that he should also be touchy and something of a prig guaranteed him a good deal of unfriendly attention. 'Mr Cumberland is unquestionably a man of very considerable abilities,' wrote Davies:

> It is his misfortune to rate them greatly above their value, and to suppose that he has no equal. . . . Mr Cumberland should consider too, that an author, by too much indulging the fluency of his fancy and the rapidity of his pen, may possibly write below himself. Let his Pegasus go to grass for a reasonable time, and he will return to the race with renewed vigour.[4]

Cumberland's Pegasus was not left out at grass for more than a few weeks. Before the end of January, Garrick put on his new comedy *The Fashionable Lover*, once more with the benefit of 'New Scenes and Dresses'. Hopkins recorded that it was warmly applauded on the first night, but predicted 'it will not be so successful as the West Indian was'. He was proved right, although there were strong performances by the Barrys, King and Reddish and by the end of the season it had achieved a respectable seventeen performances.† 'The plot is intricate, and the catastrophe of the weeping sort,' wrote Davies. 'Mr Cumberland's comic muse seems to be always in mourning.'

Early in 1772, Garrick seems briefly to have considered breaking his resolution no longer to play new parts. Relations with Murphy were in one of their phases of sweetness and light, and Garrick wrote to him from Hampton to express his delight with his new tragedy: 'I brought The Grecian Daughter with me here, have examined her well, and am wonderfully pleased with the Lady. Mrs Garrick was more affected than ever I knew her to be with any play.'[5] That was important. Garrick always paid great attention to his wife's views; she was quite often present when he read a play through and frequently attended rehearsals.

It was the leading role of Evander which Garrick told Murphy he was tempted to play. In the normal course of events, the part would have gone to Barry; Murphy says that when he heard what was going through Garrick's mind, he said: 'Let him play it; it will come to me at last, and I shall be able to act it better after seeing him.' Garrick, however, decided that it would be too much for him, and it was Barry who created the role when *The Grecian Daughter* opened on 26 February—'the finest feeble venerable old man that imagination can figure to itself,' Murphy thought.[6]

Garrick had entered the new year in excellent spirits and with his health much improved. 'By advice, & much Philosophy, I took to ye great remedy for ye stone ye Lixivium, or soap-lye,' he wrote to his Welsh clerical friend Evan Lloyd:

---

* The reviewer of the *Theatrical Review* was once again in the van: 'We confess we pitied the situation of the performers, who all exerted their utmost efforts to support it in the representation; but it is not the eminent abilities of a Vernon, a Parsons, a Hunt, or a Fitzgerald, that can render a piece worthy of notice, which has nothing in it, and is absolutely devoid of merit.'
† Its run was interrupted early in February when the theatres were closed for a week by the death of the Dowager Princess of Wales.

I have got health, voice Spirits & Strength, & lost my belly—in short I
have play'd with some credit, & the people are really mad after Me as if
I were a new face—I tell not this in vanity, but in ye spirit of truth—I will
venture to say that by abstaining from Wine, which, tho no Drunkard, I
really lov'd, (at first for ye sake of Society & at last for It's own) that I
have shewn as much philosophy as any of y^e *Ancients* ever practis'd, &
more than some *Moderns* (friends of Mine) Ever Will—*

It was just as well, because the early months of 1772 were a particularly busy
time for Garrick, domestically as well as professionally. After more than twenty
years in Southampton Street, he had decided to move. Four years previously the
Adam brothers had acquired from the Duke of St Albans a lease of Durham
Yard—the same Durham Yard where thirty years previously the Garrick brothers
had established their wine vaults. There, on a series of huge causeway arches,
they planned to build a handsome terrace—a Thames-side echo of the Palace of
Diocletian at Spalato on the Adriatic, which Robert Adam had studied during
his visit to Italy in 1754.†

'In a spirit of Scotch nationality,' says Fitzgerald, 'they had brought all their
masons and bricklayers from Scotland, and the work was stimulated by the
monotonous drone of the bagpipe.' There was to be provision for wharfage and
storage on the banks of the river; in order to complete the project, it became
necessary to reclaim land from the Thames, and in 1771 the brothers obtained
a parliamentary bill for that purpose—an application opposed by the Corporation
of London, who claimed a right to the soil and bed of the river. Bute was no
longer a power behind the throne, and a generation had passed since the '45, but
anti-Scottish (and anti-Jacobite) sentiment was not dead in the capital; under
the title 'On Some Encroachments on the River', the 1771 edition of *The Foundling
Hospital for Wits* published some lines by 'Londinensis Liberty':

> . . . Ye friends of George, and friends of James,
> Envy us not our river Thames.
> The Pr—ss, fond of raw-bon'd faces,
> May give you all our posts and places;
> Take all—to gratify your pride,
> But dip your oatmeal in the Clyde.‡

Garrick and the Adam brothers were old friends—they had done quite a lot
of work for him at Hampton over the years. A note which survives from

---

* *Letters*, 670. Soap-lye was water impregnated with alkaline salts extracted by a process of
lixiviation from wood ash. It was also used as manure.
† Spalato, the modern Split, was then in Venetian Dalmatia. Ten years later Adam published
a folio volume with numerous engravings of the palace, explaining that his prime interest lay
in the residential character of the ruin. The work was used by Gibbon.
‡ 'Ye friends of George' refers to the fact that until his resignation in 1768 on being elected
MP for Kinrossshire, Robert Adam had for six years been architect to the King and Queen.
'The Pr-ss' was the Dowager Princess of Wales, widely maligned as the supposed mistress of
Bute.

13. 'Garrick with the Bust of Shakespeare.' Commissioned to paint Garrick
for the Jubilee of 1769, Gainsborough reworked a picture he had exhibited
in London three years earlier. It was destroyed in a fire at the Stratford Town
Hall in 1946. Mrs Garrick thought no one had ever caught a better likeness
of her 'dear Davy'.

14. 'A Stage Box in London.' John Nixon's caricature shows George III and Queen Charlotte in the Royal Box. One of the pieces mentioned on the playbills draped over the edge is The Two Misers – presumably an allusion to the King and Queen's alleged meanness.

15. Henry Woodward (1714-77), the son of a Southwark tallow chandler, was a stalwart of the London stage for almost half a century. He is seen here as Razor in Arthur Murphy's The Upholsterer, first performed at Drury Lane in 1758.

16. George Colman the Elder, painted by Gainsborough in 1778.

17. Garrick as Lear, the tragic role he played more often than any other. When he performed it for the last time, in 1776, Sir Joshua Reynolds found the experience so overwhelming that it took him three days to recover.

18. *This portrait of Johnson by Sir Joshua Reynolds was exhibited at the Royal Academy in 1770, when it made a pair with one of Goldsmith.*

19. *Oliver Goldsmith, by Reynolds. 'Here lies Nolly Goldsmith, for shortness call'd Noll/ Who wrote like an angel but talk'd like poor Poll.' Goldsmith was only slightly amused by Garrick's mock epitaph, and struck back to deadly effect with his 'Retaliation': 'On the stage he was natural, simple, affecting;/ 'Twas only that when he was off he was acting.'*

20. *Zoffany's picture, dating from the 1760s, shows the Garricks looking out over the Thames from the steps of his Temple to Shakespeare at Hampton. The huge dog taking his ease in the foreground is Garrick's English mastiff, Dragon, who made occasional stage appearances at Drury Lane.*

21. *Garrick as Steward of the Shakespeare Jubilee at Stratford in* 1769. *Benjamin Van der Gucht's portrait shows him gazing fondly at his badge of office - a medallion depicting the head of the Bard.*

22. No one painted Garrick more frequently than Zoffany. In this portrait, from the Garrick Club collection, only the head is finished.

23. Hannah More – the daughter the Garricks never had. 'And must those refulgent Eyes be ever clos'd in Night?' she wrote rapturously to her sister after seeing him for the first time as Lear. 'Must those exquisite Powers be suspended, & that Silver Tongue be Stopp'd? His Talents are capacious beyond human credibility.'

24. Reynolds's portrait of Mrs Abington as Miss Prue, the wanton ingénue in Congreve's Love for Love. Although she drove Garrick to distraction, there were others in his circle who were more susceptible: 'Mrs Abington's jelly, my dear lady, was better than yours,' Johnson told Mrs Thrale.

25. Richard Brinsley Sheridan. His habit, after he assumed the managership, of dipping his hand into the Drury Lane treasury to finance his extravagant style of living was in sharp contrast to Garrick's careful husbandry.

26. *Thomas King as Touchstone. King was one of Garrick's most trusted lieutenants at Drury Lane, and one of the few theatrical colleagues he admitted to close friendship. After his retirement he sent King his stage sword – 'Accept a small token of our long & constant attachment to Each other.'*

early December 1771 gives a flavour of the easy, unbuttoned nature of their relations:

> Mr Garrick will be always ready to Obey the Commands of those unprincipled Gentlemen, & vile Architects the Adams. Mrs Garrick send her detestation to d^o.[7]

Preparations for the move must already by then have been well-advanced; the first entry in the accounts of Chippendale, Haig and Company for furnishing the Adelphi house dates from the previous January.* Over the next year, many small items—chairs, firescreens, small picture frames—went from Southampton Street to Chippendale's premises in St Martin's Lane for repair, and some furniture was brought up from Hampton. The firm was also retained to decorate the house; they supplied soft furnishings, stuffed mattresses and pillows, hung wallpaper— imported from China by the East India Company. On 5 March 1772, a team of Chippendale labourers hauled thirty horse-loads of 'Sundry Goods' from Southampton Street to the Adelphi—the cost was entered at one shilling per load. The following week, the beds were removed; Garrick, writing to his friend Bennet Langton, announced that 'Mrs Garrick is almost kill'd wth ye fatigue of removing to ye Adelphi, where we shall be fix'd in ye next Week; Mr Beauclerk is to be our Neighbour—'[8]

The Garricks were moving up in the world. Topham Beauclerk, who was to occupy No. 3, was the grandson of Charles II and Nell Gwynne. Dr John Turton, who attended Garrick in Munich, would be at No. 7—he had recently been appointed physician to the Queen's Household. Another neighbour was Henry Hoare, nephew and heir of the head of the banking house. Robert Adam himself had decided to live at No. 4.

There were twenty-four rooms at No. 5 Adelphi Terrace, and Chippendale's accounts show that between January 1771 and April 1772 Garrick ran up bills totalling £931 9s 3$^{1/2}$d. The grandeur of his new surroundings dictated that he should live in considerable style, and the clarity and precision of Chippendale's bookkeeping makes it possible to form a detailed picture of how the house was furnished.[9] For the drawing-room on the first floor, for instance, with its marble chimney-piece and Zucchi† ceiling (Venus adorned by the Graces, in a cloudscape of pink and blue), Chippendale supplied two Pembroke tables, three commodes, two large armchairs with a matching sofa and twelve 'Carbreole' armchairs; the fringed curtains were of green silk damask, and there were three large green Venetian sunblinds. For the dining room, all of mahogony, he made a sideboard,

---

* The Adams had employed Chippendale to furnish many of the houses restored or built by them. These included Nostell Priory, Yorkshire (1766–70) and Lord Mansfield's house at Kenwood in Highgate (1769). They would also later work at Harewood House.
† The Venetian painter Antonio Zucchi (1726–95) had accompanied Robert Adam to Italy. Adam invited him to England in 1766 and employed him on the interior decoration of many of the grand houses he designed or altered, including Syon House, Osterley and Kenwood. He was assisted in much of this work by Angelica Kauffmann, who had painted Garrick in Naples, and whose second husband he later became.

two pedestals (one to contain bottles, the other fitted as a plate-warmer), a table and twelve parlour chairs with red morocco seats.

The pillared hall was austerely furnished—a clock in a japanned case, six mahogany chairs and a huge brass-mounted hanging lantern. Also in evidence there—a very necessary precaution in eighteenth-century London—were sixteen fire-bags, made of Russia-duck.* Adam's plans had provided for the dining room to be the front room on the ground floor, with the library at the rear, but Garrick decided to transpose this arrangement. This allowed him to look out at the unceasing bustle of the river (he kept a reflecting telescope there), although on bright days the blinds had to be lowered to protect his paintings and fine bindings.

The move extended Garrick financially. An undated draft of a letter survives which he wrote about this time to his sister Merrial. She had obviously asked him for a loan, but he pleaded the expense of the Adelphi for not being able to oblige: 'I have built a New house & furnish'd it from top to bottom,' he told her, 'all my ready Money is Exhausted.' The draft continues, 'I have some upon Mortgage, too,' but those words are struck out.[10]

Not all of Garrick's friends approved of the acquisition of No. 5. Cradock thought its situation bleak, and 'ill-contrasted with his own warm and sheltered apartments in Southampton-street'.† Another friend, the eccentric elderly physician Sir William Browne,‡ had tried to dissuade him in verse, hinting at social climbing and suggesting that proximity to the Thames could lead to his early death:

> In the *Adelphi*, Garrick sinks his *Art*:
> By hoping There, to act a proper *Part*.
> He There, has ventur'd on a wat'ry *Stage*,
> That points an *Exit*, long before Old-Age.§

There were others, however, who were charmed. 'We were so happy as to be let in at Mr Garrick's, and saw his new House, in the Adelphi Buildings, a sweet situation'—thus young Fanny Burney, writing up her journal at the end of April. 'The House is large, & most elegantly fitted up. Mrs Garrick received us with a politeness & sweetness of manners, inseperable from her.'[11]

---

* Russia-duck was a strong jean-like material made of coarse linen. It was also used for trousering.

† *Cradock*, i, 97. Cradock was perhaps not entirely disinterested; he had for some time lived opposite Garrick in Southampton Street.

‡ Browne (1692–1774) had made his fortune as a doctor in Norfolk before moving to London in his late fifties. He was a past President of the College of Physicians. Foote caricatured him in *The Devil on Two Sticks*.

§ Garrick made a good-natured response in kind:

> In vain wise Sr William with horror You'll fill me,
> And foretell if I move to th' Adelphi t'will kill me:
> Some friends somewhat Foolish have rung in my Ears
> The same Silly doubts, and possess'd me with fears,
> But Now I'll pack up & away in a trice,
> For there can be no doubt, when *You* give advice.

Miss Burney was now twenty. Her father had known Garrick for more than a quarter of a century. Initially backward as a child, she had been scribbling farces, tragedies and epic poems since she was ten. Success with her first novel, *Evelina*, still lay in the future, but she was an assiduous diarist; a month before going with her father and sister to inspect the Adelphi, she had seen Garrick as Bayes in *The Rehearsal*. It was the first time he had appeared in the role for four years:

> O he was great beyond measure! ... I was almost in convulsions with excessive laughter—which he kept me in from the moment he entered, to the End of the Play—never in my life did I see any thing so Entertaining, so ridiculous—so humourous,—so absurd—! Sue & I have talked of Nothing else—& we have laughed almost as much at the recollection, as at the representation.[12]

At the end of May she saw him again, this time in *Richard III*. His performance struck her as 'sublimely horrible'. At fifty-five his hold over the audience was clearly as strong as it had ever been:

> ... How he made me shudder when he appeared! it is inconceivable, how terribly great he is in this Character. I will never see him so disfigured again—he seemed so truly the monster he performed, that I felt myself glow with indignation every time I saw him. The Applause he met with exceeds all belief of the Absent. I thought, at the End, they would have torn the House down: our seats shook under us.[13]

Not everyone was so enthusiastic. The season was notable for the sharp tone of much critical commentary. December had seen the publication of *The Theatres*, an 80-page satirical survey of the acting styles of some seventy performers. It appeared under the name 'Sir Nicholas Nipclose', a pseudonym adopted by the feckless and treacherous Francis Gentleman. Gentleman, now in his mid-forties, had been at school in Dublin with Mossop and had spent some years in the army. He had drifted about the country as an actor, and was a playwright of sorts. The most substantial thing ever to come from his pen was *The Dramatic Censor*, which had appeared in 1770.[14] The first volume, offering extended critical commentary on both plays and performers, was dedicated to Garrick, whom Gentleman had been flattering on and off for twenty years or so.

Now, however, he had changed his tune. The fact that Garrick had more than once lent him money over the years, had written a letter of recommendation to John Home when he went to try his luck in Edinburgh in the 1750s, counted for nothing. Gentleman had become convinced (a belief for which there was no foundation) that Garrick had stolen various ideas of his, and in *The Theatres*— a pale imitation of Churchill's *Rosciad*, to which he gave the subtitle 'a Poetical Dissection'—he launched a furious attack. Garrick was accused in the preface of venality and artistic insensitivity; he was snobbish, jealous and his powers were in decline.

'Nipclose' dedicated this tirade to Mrs Abington—'a cordial tribute of respect,

View of the ADELPHI (late Durham Yard) June 1771.

When Garrick moved to the Adelphi in the early 1770s, he was returning to old haunts. The Adam brothers built their grand terrace on the site of Durham Yard, where Garrick had briefly and unenthusiastically plied his trade as a wine merchant thirty years previously. (The Town & Country Magazine, *June 1771*)

for such singular merit, highly conspicuous, tho' injured by want of proper support'. It was six years since Garrick had encouraged Fanny Abington to return to Drury Lane, and he regretted it more with each day that passed. She was important to the box-office, but her temperamental behaviour and ever-swelling sense of her own importance—she was convinced in particular that the manager unfairly favoured Jane Pope—were a sore trial to him. After his death, a scrap of verse was found among his papers:

> Tell me, Dame Abington, how much you gave
> To that same dirty, dedicating knave?
> Alas! that you should think to gather fame,
> From one that's only Gentleman by name!*

A little later in the season Garrick came in for further abuse in *A Letter to David Garrick Esq. on His Conduct and Talents as Manager and Performer*. This was the work of a dissenting minister called David Williams, a Welshman in his middle thirties who had the charge of a congregation in Highgate. Garrick, he wrote, spoke through his nose and had lost the power of pronouncing many English words. He accused him of buying out newspapers to silence criticism and of miscasting other players so that he himself would shine. 'Why is Barry thrust into parts wholly unsuited to him? Is it to exhibit him to contempt as the ruins of a great actor? *Why was Mossop excluded?*'

Mossop, broken in health, had only recently returned from Ireland. On the eve of his departure from Dublin he had been arrested for debt. When he was declared bankrupt in London in January 1772, it emerged that his main creditor, to whom he owed £200, was Garrick. Williams was much in Mossop's company, and that was plainly where he acquired most of the ammunition for his pamphlet, although it is also possible that he had submitted a play to Garrick and bore a grudge because it had been rejected. Several letters written by Williams shortly after his pamphlet was published make it plain that he was intent on blackmailing Garrick; a curiously convoluted reply which Garrick drafted but thought the better of sending indicates that he did not immediately reject the idea of buying him off.[15] He bundled together several of Williams's letters and wrote on the wrapper, 'Curious letters written against Me by one *Williams* a Presbyterian Parson a great friend of Mossop's and a Great—'

Boswell was being tiresome again. He had taken it upon himself to promote a fellow-Scot called William Julius Mickle. Before devoting himself exclusively to literary pursuits Mickle, a son of the manse, had made a none too successful fist of running a brewery in Edinburgh. He was now working in Oxford as a corrector to the Clarendon Press, and Boswell, describing him as 'a true poetical Genius', tried to engage Garrick's interest in a historical tragedy he had written

---

* Garrick was by no means Gentleman's only target; he insulted Colman ('tiny George') and lashed out at numbers of his fellow-actors. Others at whom his critical blunderbuss was directed included Hugh Kelly, Cumberland, Bickerstaffe, Goldsmith and Johnson. Even George III was savaged.

called *Chateaubriant*. 'I would hope that Mr. Mickle who has waited long in the Antichamber, will soon be introduced,' he wrote, 'and not be shoved back by others who are more bustling and forward.'[16]

Garrick was unimpressed. 'Mr Mickle Whom you so warmly recommend is a most ingenious Man; but I fear from what I have seen, that his talents will not shine in the Drama,' he told Boswell:

> His Play before ye alteration, was not in ye least calculated for representation—there were good passages; but Speeches & mere poetry will no more make a Play, than planks and timbers in ye dock-Yard can be call'd a Ship—It is Fable, passion & Action which constitute a Tragedy, & without them, we might as well exhibit one of Tillotsons Sermons—*

Mickle did not accept rejection gracefully, declaring that he did not intend to 'submit to the infallibility of Mr Garrick and starve'. He wrote abusively of Garrick in the preface to the version of the play prepared for publication (it was now called *The Siege of Marseilles*) and also threatened—idly, as it turned out—that he would pillory him in a new *Dunciad*. In the end, his retaliation amounted to very little; when he published his translation of the *Lusiads* in 1776 there was a slighting reference to Garrick tucked away in a footnote.† As Garrick had taken out twenty subscriptions to the translation at twelve shillings a time, he was understandably nettled, and let off steam in a letter to Boswell. 'You, I am sure,' he wrote with some asperity, 'will no more recommend Your Poetasters to my civility & Good Offices.'[17]

Garrick knew exactly how to handle his bouncy young Scottish admirer, however, and there is a deliciously ironical passage in one letter expressing the pleasure it gave Boswell's London friends to hear that he was so happy in his recent marriage:

> It is an old observation, & may be a true one, that Rakes make ye best husbands, however between You & Me, I think there is some risque in ye Experiment, & I most sincerely wish Your Lady joy of her Success in ye Tryal.[18]

Their difference over Mickle did nothing to cloud their friendship when Boswell was next in London in the spring of 1772. In April he had to appear for a client in an appeal from the Court of Session in Edinburgh to the House of Lords. Garrick, a keen student of performance on any stage, turned up to listen. He had done very well, he told him, 'only might have been a little more animated'.[19]

---

* *Letters*, 677. John Tillotson had been Archbishop of Canterbury towards the end of the previous century. He was a notable preacher.

† Mickle's translation of Camoëns's epic poem was extremely well received, and when he visited Lisbon in 1779 he was made a member of the Royal Academy of Portugal. Nor did he starve. He returned home as purser on a man o' war, and in London was appointed joint agent for the disposal of the prizes taken by the squadron. This assured him a handsome competence for life.

A few weeks later, announcing himself as 'Rantum Scantum', Garrick appeared at Boswell's lodgings one morning before he was out of bed.* They walked through St James's Park together, Garrick entertaining his companion by impersonating Johnson: 'Davy has some convivial pleasantry about him, but 'tis a futile fellow.' Later they made their way down to the Thames, and on the bank of the river an enraptured Boswell was treated to the 'Cans't thou not minister to a mind diseas'd?' soliloquy from *Macbeth*.†

One of Garrick's more eccentric correspondents at this time was the writer John Cleland, who had achieved notoriety more than twenty years previously with the novel *Fanny Hill; or, The Memoirs of a Woman of Pleasure*, for which he had been hauled before the Privy Council and charged with indecency. Although the book had netted his publisher some £10,000, Cleland had been paid only 20 guineas. Now, in his sixties, he principally immersed himself in philology and eked out a living with hack-work. Hearing that Garrick was ill, and that he was treating himself with lixivium, he had written warning him of the deleterious effects of 'this poisonous, infernal caustic' and drawing attention to 'its uncontrollable power of collateral damage to your tenderest internals, to your unguarded vitals'. There were, on the other hand, no such horrors to dread 'from warm sippings, parsley, testaceous, or other fish, stock-fish especially, and above all from the ginseng'.

Garrick brushed aside Cleland's concern for his disorder in one brief sentence—'had you ever felt its pangs you would not be surpriz'd at my risquing any thing to get clear of them.' There was another passage in Cleland's letter, however, which irritated him intensely. 'Balancing between a visit and a note, I at length preferred this last,' Cleland had written:

> —And why?—you are continually beset with attendants on indispensable business. This is nothing more than in course. But you are besides so infested with Lords, Counts, Marquises, Dukes, &c. that I most readily acquiesce in my *no-title* to admission among them, and less yet, preferably to them.[20]

Cleland had touched a tender spot, and Garrick flared up. 'Your Observation upon my Marquisses, Counts &c, and my *indispensable* business, appears to carry an Edge with it,' he wrote testily:

> If you suspect me of being fond of worthless Titles, you wrong me—I wou'd no more avoid the Company of a Man because he was a Marquis, than I wou'd keep him Company if he was a fool or a Scoundrel; I readily beleive that you might have kept what Company you please, & in return

---

* A variant on harum-scarum. But Garrick may also have had in mind a line from Davenant and Dryden's version of *The Tempest*, Act IV, Scene iii: 'I found her . . . singing Tory Rory, and Rantum Scantum, with her own natural brother.'
† Boswell wrote to Garrick from Edinburgh the following spring reminding of the occasion and begging him to play Macbeth when he was next in London. (*Correspondence*, 53, 29 March 1773.)

I expect that you will believe Me as little inclin'd to lose my time, or prostitute my Understanding, as Mr Cleland.[21]

Having got that off his chest, Garrick turned to his arrangements for the holiday months. These included visits to the Duke of Richmond at Goodwood and to Knighton on the Isle of Wight, country seat of his young friend Thomas Fitz-maurice, the brother of the Earl of Shelburne. The summer, however, would be clouded for him by an attempt at character assassination which even by the standards of Grub Street was exceptionally squalid.

31

Clipping the Wings of Calumny

On 30 April, a curious advertisement had appeared in the *Daily Advertiser*:

> Whereas on Tuesday Night last, between the hours of Eight and Ten, A Gentleman left with a Centinel belonging to Whitehall Guard, a Guinea and a half, and a Metal Watch with two Seals, the one a Cypher, the other a Coat of Arms, a Locket, and a Pistol Hook. The Owner may have it again by applying to the Adjutant of the first Battalion of the first Regiment of Foot-Guards at the Savoy Barracks, and paying for this Advertisement.

The editors of the *St James's Chronicle* and *Lloyd's Evening Post* did rather better for their readers, and were able to flesh the story out:

> ... The History of this Watch, &c. is this: A Gentleman grew enamoured, the other Night at Whitehall, with one of the Centinels, and made Love to him; the Soldier being of that rough cast, who would rather act in the Character of Mars than a Venus, not only rejected the Lover's Suit, but seizing him, threatened to take him immediately to the Guard-Room. The affrighted Enamorato, to avoid the consequences of Exposure, with the greatest Precipitation gave the Soldier his Watch, Rings, and other Valuables, for his Liberty. The Centinel, rejoicing at his good Fortune, soon after tells the Corporal, the Corporal the Serjeant, the Serjeant the Adjutant, and he to the whole Corps of Officers. The Articles of Ransom were examined; one was a Mourning Ring of a Lady who died at Gibraltar; and the Watch had its Maker's Name; he was applied to, and he instantly declared to whom he had sold it, about two months since, a Man of some Fame in the Literary World. Here at present the Incident rests; and there is no Doubt but the honest Soldier will become entitled to the Whole, as it is presumed the owner will scarcely apply for a return of them.

A reasonably safe presumption. Sodomy was still a capital offence. Early in May the 'Man of some Fame in the Literary World' fled to France, and it was soon widely known that he was Isaac Bickerstaffe. 'On Eagle's Wings immortal Scandals fly!' Garrick wrote to Robert Jephson in Dublin on 19 May:

> He is gone, & has written to Mr Griffin the Bookseller a letter, which

shock'd Me beyond imagination—all his friends hang their heads & grieve sincerely at his Misfortune—My Wife & I have long thought him to be out of his Mind—he has hurry'd away in the midst of Conversation, without any apparent reason for it—the Story they tell, if true, is a most unaccountable one; but the Watch, Seal & ring are in the Soldier's hands & B— would not claim them but absconded—this business has hurt me greatly, as well as my Wife . . .[1]

Before the summer was out, it would hurt them a great deal more. On 18 June, the *Public Ledger* published a poem entitled 'Leap-Frog':

> As Dapper *Davy* & his favourite Bick
> Gambol'd from sport to sport from trick to trick
> Davy in glee his Sooty Bick ajog.
> They play'd at length that hateful game *leap-frog.*
> Poor Bicky fear'd discovery & shame,
> But Davy sooth'd him, & *play'd out the game.*
> "No eye, tho' e'er so peircing now can *bore* us"
> Says the Theatric Caesar to his *Sporus*
> "These pleasures licenc'd for the Rich, I prove,
> Illicit rapture, & forbidden Love. . ."

Within a few days the suggestion of a homosexual relationship between Bicker-staffe and Garrick was given much wider currency with the circulation of a lampoon from the pen of the drunken, malevolent, attention-seeking William Kenrick, a thorn in the flesh of Garrick and many others—Fielding, Johnson, Goldsmith—for long years past. It was entitled *Love in the Suds; A Town Eclogue. Being the Lamentations of Roscius for the Loss of his Nyky.** It ran to 340 lines. By turns vicious, coarse and suggestive, it makes singularly vile reading:

> For me, alas! who well composed the song
> When lovely PEGGY liv'd, and I was young;
> By age impair'd, my piping days are done,
> My memory fails, and ev'n my voice is gone . . .
>
> Whom fliest thou, frantic youth, and whence thy fear?
> Blest had there never been a grenadier!
> Unhappy NYKY, by what frenzy seiz'd,
> Couldst thou with such a monstrous thing be pleas'd?
> What, tho' thyself a loving horse-marine,†
> A common foot-soldier's a thing obscene . . .

---

* 'In the suds' was an expression meaning 'in trouble', 'in a difficulty'.

† Kenrick's occasional mock-scholarly footnotes are as poisonous as his text: 'Nyky is a half-pay officer of marines. A horse-marine is a kind of *meretricious* HOBBY-HORSE, *modo vir modo foemina.*' 'Hobby-horse' was an old term for a prostitute.

And yet, ah why should NYKY thus be blam'd?
Of manly love ah! why are men asham'd?
A new red coat, fierce cock and killing air
Will captivate the most obdurate fair . . .

Yet slight the cause of NYKY's late mishap;
NYK but mistook the colour of the cap:
A common errour, frequent in the Park,
Where love is apt to stumble in the dark.
Why rais'd the haughty female head so high,
With the tall caps of grenadiers to vie? . . .

Ah! therefore why in these enlighten'd times
Should rigid Nature call such errours crimes?
Must not the taste of Attic wits be nice?
Can antient virtue be a modern vice? . . .

Nor need my NYKY fear a London jury
Will e'er be influenc'd with a female fury.
Can they who let a prov'd assassin 'scape
Hang up poor NYKY for a friendly rape?
If in the dark to stab, be thought no crime,
What may'nt be hop'd from jurymen in time?
Soon Southern modes, no doubt, they'll reconcile
With the plain manners of our Northern isle;
And e'en new-married citizens be brought
To reckon S——y a venial fault.

Kenrick would subsequently claim that only a small number of copies of his 'eclogue' had originally been printed, and that these were for distribution among his acquaintance, 'many of whom knew in what manner I had been ill-treated both by Roscius and Nyky'. Malevolence is seldom that finely focussed, however. Apart from the desire to bespatter Bickerstaffe, it is plain that he also hoped to blackmail Garrick into accepting for early production a piece called *The Duellist* which he had submitted to Drury Lane.

Garrick found it difficult to decide how best to respond. Some would have followed Johnson's example and treated Kenrick with silent contempt;* others would instantly have sought legal redress. Garrick did not immediately do either. He wrote several letters to Kenrick, although not all of them were sent; the varying tone of these notes suggests that he may have been receiving conflicting advice. (But from whom? He numbered among his friends some of the most eminent lawyers in the land.) 'My brother greatly surprised me by your refusal

---

* Johnson had refused to answer Kenrick's attack on his edition of Shakespeare, saying 'a man whose business it is to be talked of, is much helped by being attacked'.

to meet me with or without a friend,' he wrote on 14 June. 'Be that as it may, as I have something of consequence to both of us to communicate to you, I must again desire to see you.' And he added a surprisingly accommodating postscript: 'Though I am engaged to go to the installation of the Knights of the Bath, I shall put it off, upon your notice, to attend upon you.'[2]

Matters then took a melodramatic turn. Kenrick agreed to a meeting, but suddenly changed his mind, claiming that he had been warned by his publisher that Garrick and two friends intended to waylay and thrash him. 'Though I am ever ready to meet a gentleman on a gentleman's footing,' he wrote, 'I may not always be aware of the bludgeon of a ruffian or the knife of an assassin.'

Garrick dashed off (but did not send) an instant retort—'a poor tale from ye beginning to ye End,' he wrote scornfully:

> Do You imagine that I would have risk'd my reputation to have acted unlike a Man Even to Him who has been ungratefully vilifying Me in Every Manner that his falshood & Malignity could invent?—No, Sir, I would have honour'd You by giving the Satisfaction of a Gentleman, if *you could* (as Shakespeare says) *have skrewd y^r Courage to the Sticking place*, to have taken it—*

This clearly suggests that Garrick had called out his tormentor, but that the challenge had been declined. Kenrick's version was that he had been entirely happy to offer Garrick satisfaction, subject to one breathtakingly impertinent condition—as he was a married man and a father, he had required that in the event of his death, Garrick should settle half his fortune on his widow and her orphan brood.

In the middle of these absurd exchanges, Garrick received a pathetic letter from the man who was the cause of all the trouble. Bickerstaffe had gone to ground in St Malo, and from there, on 24 June, he addressed himself to his former patron, choosing to do so in his somewhat rickety French—possibly as a precaution in the case of interception:

> . . . *Penetrer avec une chagrin le plus amer que peut blesser le coeur, soyez persuadé Monsieur que je ne rien de demander de votre bonté que la seul licence de vous ecrire plus au large; si vous n'etes pas dans le sentiment de me permetre, imaginez que cette lettre vien d'un mort, au vivant, jettez la dans le feu, et n'en pensez plus. Je ne pas la moindre doute Mon^r que mon chagrin me portera au tombeau, mais par une chemin peutetre, plus long que Je ne le souheterai, et cette pensée et une grand augmentation de mes peines car ayant perdu mes amis, mes esperances; tombé, exilé, et livré au*

---

* *Letters*, 694. Stone and Kahrl place an intriguing question mark over Garrick's 'poor tale' by quoting from a letter, now lost, which he wrote from the Adelphi on 20 June to his friend Edward Thompson: he had, he said, been going to beat Dr Kenrick for his infamy, but the latter 'smok'd ye crab tree', and wrote a most cowardly letter. Bickerstaffe's biographer, however, believes that it was Foote who was going to beat Kenrick. (Tasch, Peter A., *The Dramatic Cobbler. The Life and Works of Isaac Bickerstaff*, Lewisburg, Pa., 1971, 297, n.12.)

desespoir comme je suis, la vie et un fardeau presque insupportable: j'etois loin de soup'zonner, que le dernier fois que J'entré dans votre Librairie, sera Le dernier fois que j'y entrerai de ma vie, et que je ne reverai plus le maitre! . . .*

Garrick endorsed the letter, 'From that poor wretch Bickerstaff. I could not answer it.' No more, however, could he allow the paper war which was now unleashed to continue indefinitely. His influence with those newspapers in which he held an interest and his friendly relations with a number of editors and booksellers could not do a great deal to stem the flood of fables, eclogues, verse epistles and assorted doggerel with which the pages of the public prints were now awash. Between 19 June and 15 August the *Morning Chronicle* alone published some 130 items in verse and prose; the fact that a majority of them favoured Garrick was not in itself particularly helpful. There is evidence that at one point he was tempted to retaliate with some verses of his own; the Harvard Theatre Collection has a photocopy of two pages in Garrick's hand in which Kenrick ('Brandy Billy') is portrayed as a shiftless drunk moving from one lodging house to another, churning out plays which are seldom acted and never read and generally making a profession of spreading ill-will and dissension:

> While good folks wish & Strive for peace
> I would my Country's feuds Encrease,
>   A Carrion Crow for blood,
> What Genius does I would undo,
> And cry with Judas, & his Crew,
>   *Evil be Thou my good.*†

It was not one of his happier efforts, and it was as well it did not see the light of day. Only in July, however, did Garrick's solicitors, Messrs Wallis and Parkes, belatedly initiate proceedings for libel. Affidavits were presented from three witnesses. The most detailed, by a man called William Parker, declared that having perused the poem, he apprehended that by the word Roscius on the title page the author meant David Garrick Esquire and by the word Nyky one Isaac Bickerstaff, 'a person heretofore occasionally Employed by David Garrick in writing or correcting of writings and productions'—

---

* '. . . Pierced by the bitterest sorrow that can wound the heart, please accept, Sir, that I have nothing to ask of your goodness except your permission to write to you at greater length; if you do not feel inclined to allow me this, then look on this as a letter to the living from the dead, throw it on the fire and do not give it a further thought. I have not the slightest doubt, Sir, that my sorrow will carry me to the grave, although perhaps by a longer road than I would wish, and this adds greatly to my trouble, because having lost my friends and my hopes; fallen, exiled and given over to despair as I am, life is an almost unbearable burden: little did I suspect, the last time I entered your library, that I should never in my life set foot in it again or see its owner! . . .' The original of the letter is in the Forster Collection.

† The pages were auctioned at Sotheby's on 17 December 1935. The verses are numbered 6–9. The whereabouts of the original, and of the first five verses, are unknown.

And this Deponent saith that by common report he hath heard that the said Isaac Bickerstaff hath been lately accused of having made an attempt to commit an unnatural crime with a Grenadier or Soldier in Saint James's Park and hath since on account thereof left this kingdom and gone abroad beyond seas.

Parker further understood from the poem that it was Kenrick's intention 'to raise and propagate a scandalous insinuation against the character of the said David Garrick and if possible to induce the Publick to consider the said David Garrick as a person concerned in sodomitical practices with the said Isaac Bickerstaff'.

The hearing was in the Court of the King's Bench on 7 July, and the case was set down for the first week of the following term—a delay of several months, because the Michaelmas term did not begin until well into the autumn. Kenrick did not regard the prospect of a charge of libel as any sort of constraint. On 9 July, *Love in the Suds* was advertised as being prepared for a second edition, and by the middle of August it would go through three more.

During those summer months Bickerstaffe was variously reported to have hanged himself, drowned himself and died of natural causes in Sussex. The story was edged out of the papers for a time by an even juicier scandal—on 20 July a Captain Robert Jones was sentenced to death for 'committing a detestable crime upon Francis Henry Hay, a boy of 13 years of age'.* Interest revived early in August when Kenrick published a 34-page pamphlet called *A Letter to David Garrick, Esq.* and the *Morning Chronicle* published long extracts from it on four successive days. Kenrick brazenly asserted that he had never actually accused Garrick of Bickerstaffe's crime, merely of condoning it by not shunning him; Garrick, what's more, deserved to be attacked for having rejected Kenrick's *Falstaff's Wedding* twenty years previously.

Garrick was bouyed up by various messages of support during the holiday season. Fitzmaurice, from the Isle of Wight, wrote that he hoped that on his return to London he would find himself shielded 'from further attacks of the shocking fiend who plagued you, and us, here'. The faithful and good-hearted Moody, writing to George on theatre business from Bath, expressed himself more forcefully:

It wounds me to the heart to think that that execrable fiend K— should have power to disturb the tranquillity of my most honoured friend . . . I hope the law will have sufficient power to punish him as he really deserves, and make him an example for the tribe of scoundrels of his stamp. I hope to God he does not suffer this injury a place in his mind, but lets it go to hell from whence it came. May God almighty give him health and peace of mind! Amen.[3]

---

* Captain Jones's fellow-officers rallied round and got up a petition to the Crown, which eventually secured him a royal pardon.

Equally, however, Garrick came under pressure not to proceed with his libel action—pressure which he initially resisted. 'What, shall it be said my dear Friend that I turn my back upon my Antagonist now, who have fought face to face,' he wrote to Richard Berenger. 'No no—we shall clip the wings of Calumny & make defamation peep through timber, as ye blackguards call it.'*

Another who urged him more than once to seek some sort of accommodation and avoid the renewed publicity that a trial would bring was his lawyer friend Peter Fountain, but to him too, Garrick indicated that he had every intention of standing firm:

> As to my Law-Matters I never think of 'Em, & therefore never write or talk about 'Em. I have submitted my Cause to ye Laws of my Country, & shall abide by their Determination—I am told the Papers mention my having drop'd my prosecution—I cannot help what they say, it is not so, nor can it be so—⁴

Garrick's refusal to compromise was uncharacteristic. He seems to have believed that Kenrick was plotting further mischief and had come to see himself not merely as engaged on his own account but as the champion of others:

> Mr G. is resolv'd for ye Peace of Mankind in General, his own credit, and, he hopes, to the Confusion of ye most abandon'd Profligate, to have the business thoroughly canvass'd in a Court of Law—Mr G. defies the Malice of ye Devil & ye Dr in Conjunction—⁵

If a report in the *London Evening Post* for 12 November was to be believed, Kenrick was equally determined not to budge: 'Mr Garrick's information against Mr Kenrick for *backbiting*, it is thought, will come on the latter end of this week in the Court of King's Bench, where the latter gentleman intends pleading his own cause *in propria persona*.' On that same day, however, a paragraph appeared in another newspaper which radically altered matters. Francis Newbery, the publisher of the *Public Ledger*—the paper where the 'Leap-Frog' poem had appeared almost five months previously—belatedly saw the error of his ways and published an abject apology:

> A Copy of Verses, containing the basest and most malignant Reflections upon Mr GARRICK, having appeared in the Public Ledger on the 18th of June last, the Publisher of that Paper, after solemnly declaring that he has not the least Knowledge of the Author, thinks it his Duty as a Man who wishes to do every Act of Justice in his Power, to express his Concern that he was any Way accessory to so vile and groundless a Calumny. He is most sincerely sorry that the Lines were inserted without his Privity, and takes this public Method of begging Mr Garrick's Pardon.

Newbery was a young man in his late twenties who had inherited the *Public Ledger* from his father five years previously. Devoted to music and poetry, he

---

* *Letters*, 697. 'Peep through timber'—i.e. lie in the stocks.

had been totally out of his depth in the Kenrick affair. Garrick, who had known Newbery senior, treated him generously: 'I shall not suffer Mr Newberry to pay my Costs,' he told Fountain the day after the apology was published.[6]

Newbery's retraction seriously undermined Kenrick's position. The lawyers put their heads together, and the following week Garrick accepted a second apology:

> The author of a Pamphlet entitled LOVE in the SUDS, is much concerned to find it has been conceived that he meant to convey a Charge of a scandalous and detestable Nature against DAVID GARRICK, Esq; . . . He thinks it incumbent on him therefore, as well in Justice to himself as to Mr Garrick, thus publicly to declare, that he had no Intention whatever to convey or insinuate any such Charge against him; being well convinced there is no ground for casting an Imputation, or even harbouring a Suspicion of the Kind against his Character. He thinks it also further incumbent on him to apologize to Mr Garrick, as a Gentleman, for the Uneasiness he may have unintentionally given him on this Occasion; at the same Time assuring him he will suppress the Sale of the Pamphlet and reprint it no more.[7]

As apologies go, it is remarkable for its tone of barely concealed impertinence. Garrick either did not notice or was too relieved to care. 'Kenrick has made a publick recantation which has blacken'd him more,' he wrote to the Dublin publisher George Faulkner—'He has done what we wanted, & I am content.'[8]

Curiously enough, the unspeakable Kenrick seems to have got what he wanted, too. 'I did not believe him guilty,' he said airily to the bookseller Thomas Evans, 'but did it to plague the fellow.'[9]

32

Doing Away with the Gravediggers

Disagreeable and stressful as the Kenrick affair had been to Garrick the man, it did nothing to blunt the effectiveness of Garrick the manager. Drury Lane had reopened on 19 September, and his plans for the season included three new mainpieces and three new afterpieces. The first to see the light of day was his own farce *The Irish Widow*, although his authorship was not immediately disclosed. He had written it as a vehicle for Mrs Barry—in less than a week, he told a friend; there were some reviewers who thought he might profitably have spent a little longer on it. The *Westminster Magazine* was particularly severe:

> This piece was full of those uncouth ramblings after novelty which men destitute of Genius and Taste may be supposed to produce. Short as it was, it proved that the Author was possessed of neither; and every Scene seemed to be a literary Monster which teemed with Errors against Nature.

The audience took a different view, and the piece achieved twenty performances in its first season. Writing to George Faulkner a week after the first night, Garrick was distinctly bullish: 'If you see at y[r] return to Dublin any handsome actress who can perform the part of the *Irish Widow* well, pray run away with her, & by that time you will be thoroughly sick of her, I will take her off y[r] hands & make her Fortune reviving the Widow.'*

Garrick had once again found the elements of his plot, such as it was, in Molière, borrowing partly from *L'Avare* and partly from *Le Mariage forcé*—Old Whittle, an otherwise sensible old buffer, becomes the rival in love of a young relative and makes a fool of himself in the traditional manner. 'You never saw such an altered man in your born days,' declares Thomas, his servant:

> He frisks and prances and runs about as if he had a new pair of legs. He has left off his brown camlet surtout, which he wore all summer, and now with his hat under his arm he goes open breasted, and he dresses and powders and smirks so, that you would take him for the mad Frenchman in Bedlam, something wrong in his upper story.[1]

---

* *Letters*, 720. Mrs Barry, whose performance as Widow Brady had come in for some criticism, had become reluctant to continue in what was both a breeches and a dialect part.

Days before the first night of *The Irish Widow*, Garrick suffered the loss of an old friend to whom he owed much. Henry Giffard, virtually ruined by the 1737 Licensing Act, had been retired from the theatre for a quarter of a century. He died 'in a very advanced Age, and much regretted by all', said the press notices. They recalled that it was he who had introduced Garrick to the London stage, and praised his judgement and his encouragement of young actors. Ironically, his death coincided with a period when Garrick's own efforts in that direction were going through a barren patch. Hopkins's diary for the late months of 1772 is a catalogue of promise unfulfilled:

> Two young Gentlewomen appeared in the characters of Polly and Lucy . . . Miss Weller's figure was very well for Polly; but she is a piece of still life, sings out of tune and will never make an actress.—Mrs Bradley,—very tall, and appears to have blackguard requisites enough for Lucy, but will not do for anything else.[2]

A month later, in a performance of *Alexander the Great*, 'A Young Gentleman' was given his chance in the title role, but made a poor fist of it: 'Mr Clinch made his first appearance in the part of Alexander tolerable figure & Voice a Little too much upon the Brogue, he is very wild and Aukward.'*

No theatrical season was complete, at Drury Lane or any other theatre, without a domestic quarrel or two, but Garrick was dismayed in November to find himself at odds with Tom King: 'I rec'd last Wed^y a long letter from you charg'd with much matter, had you fir'd a long Gun at me it could not have been wth more astonishment on my part & I will say with less justice on Yours.'

King had come up with a whole raft of grievances—that his wife, who danced for the company, was undervalued, that he himself was underpaid and—much worse—taken for granted:

> I, without a murmur, begin at the opening of the theatre, if required, and never repine at playing, if called on, six nights in the week, till every door-keeper is served and the theatre shut up; while those who are better, much better, allow me to say shamefully better paid, never enter the lists till the theatre has been opened some time, are periodically sick, or impertinent about the month of April, and in the very heat of the season are never expected to play two nights running. Some evasion is also found out by them when called on to play on a night immediately subsequent to your performing, their Majesties coming to the theatre, or in short any thing that attracts the public notice, so as to strengthen one night and weaken another. I am, on most occasions of this sort, thrust into the gap. . . .

He complained specifically about being paid less than the Barrys; looking across

---

* Lawrence Clinch improved with time. In 1775 he stepped into the revised role of Sir Lucius O'Trigger on the third night of *The Rivals* at Covent Garden. Sheridan was so grateful to him for saving the play from ruin that he wrote the afterpiece *St Patrick's Day* for him.

at the rival house, he pointed out that he also earned less than Woodward: 'If you say Mr Woodward is a Harlequin, I reply, he never appears as such but in the first run of some new piece of his own.'

Garrick could obfuscate an issue with the best of them and responded with a masterly display of sorrowful disbelief: 'These are ye allegations of my friend Mr King in ye midst of our Friendship & when He was possess'd of my utmost Confidence . . . If I have been guilty in thought word or deed of all or any of ye above sins against You and Mrs King, I will most willingly declare that Dr Kenrick is no Libeller.' But then came a shift of key, and with it, a gleam of the stiletto:

—Have not you Mr King been conscious of some breaches of Friendship to me, & are producing these allegations, as excuses for your own behaviour?—have not you instead of an open manly declaration of Y^r thoughts to y^r Friends, Whisper'd about in hints & ambiguities your uneasiness, all wch by circulation have partly crept into the News papers . . .

There were further emotionally charged exchanges, but a week was enough for both of them to get it out of their system:

Dear Sir—My very dear Mr Garrick, . . . I have been under many obligations to you, and you have continued to behave to me as if you had never conferred one. . . . I will henceforth rather come to you with twenty farthing complaints a week, than wear a frown at the playhouse. . .[3]

Dear Tom
You shall have Y^r Terms, or I won't be a Manager . . . I go to Hampton to Morrow Morning to open my throat, & I hope to see you directly upon my return—We must Scheme some business togeather, I have a Whim— but that When I see You—God bless You—good Night—
—never again
may come mischance betwixt us twain.
Quite hoarse but truly Y^{rs}
D Garrick*

This was Garrick's only serious difference with King. A season without an altercation with Mrs Abington, on the other hand, would have gone against nature. Her complaint this autumn was that a part in a new comedy which she imagined Murphy had promised to her had been assigned instead to Mrs Barry.†
'I am always happy to see the performers of Merit, who belong to us, happy & Satisfy'd,' Garrick told her. 'After I have said this, let me be permitted to Say

* *Letters*, 716. Garrick's quotation is from *Hamlet*, Act III, scene ii. King had agreed to sign on for three years, the first two at £15 a week, the third at £500 for the year, with an option to extend for a further two-year period.
† The part in question was that of Lady Bell in *Know Your Own Mind*. Murphy eventually withdrew it; it was subsequently produced in 1777 at Covent Garden.

farther, that I never yet Saw M*rs Abington* theatrically happy for a Week together.'

He reminded her that throughout his management, he had observed the convention that an author was at liberty to distribute parts 'as he thinks will be of most Service to his Interest'; he had only ever interfered if something was proposed which seemed to him 'contrary to common Sense'. Once launched, however, the temptation to rub Mrs Abington's nose in it was overpowering:

> You Sometimes pay me the Compliment to say, that You would do any thing I should advise—I flatter my Self if You had done So, You would not have repented of your Politeness.—I never advis'd You to play Ophelia, tho' that has been unjustly laid to my Charge—[4]

Garrick was reminding her, none too kindly, of how she had been received when she had played opposite him the previous December, an occasion which remained in the mind of one member of the audience when he wrote his memoirs sixty years later: 'Like many of her profession, she thought herself capable of characters not within the scope of her powers. I once saw her play Ophelia to Mr. Garrick's Hamlet; and to use a simile of my old friend Dr. Monsey, she appeared "like mackerel on a gravel walk." '[5]

Hamlet, as it happened, had been much in Garrick's mind. On 18 December he appeared in his own greatly altered version, and he was still full of it when he wrote to his French friend the Abbé Morellet in the New Year:

> I have play'd the Devil this Winter, I have dar'd to alter Hamlet, I have thrown away the gravediggers, & all y*e* 5th Act, & notwithstanding the Galleries were so fond of them, I have met with more applause than I did at five & twenty—this is a great revolution in our theatrical history, & for w*ch* 20 years ago instead of Shouts of approbation, I should have had y*e* benches thrown at my head—*

The first-night audience certainly liked what it saw. 'Mr Garrick playd divinely & Merited the great applause he receivd,' noted Hopkins. Garrick had been mulling over this new version, and in particular the cutting of what he called 'the rubbish of the 5th act'† ever since returning from his second visit to France, and contemporary reviewers were enthusiastic. 'The tedious interruptions of this beautiful tale no longer disgrace it,' wrote the *Westminster Magazine*; 'its absurd digressions are no longer disgusting.'

Garrick did not simply eliminate the greater part of Shakespeare's Act V. He

---

* *Letters*, 730. He also wrote about the production to his friend de Laplace, who in reply praised him for his courage in making the changes. He told Garrick that he had written a detailed account of the changes for *l'Observateur françois à Londres*, and that this would undoubtedly be picked up by the other papers 'comme chose vraiment intéressante et digne de faire Epoque'. (*Boaden*, ii, 601.)

† *Letters*, 733. Letter dated 10 January 1773. 'It was the most imprudent thing I ever did in all my life,' he wrote to Sir William Young, 'but I had sworn I would not leave the Stage till I had rescued that noble play from all the rubbish of the 5th Act'.

also restored more than six hundred lines from the earlier acts which had not been heard for more than fifty years and which presented his eighteenth-century audience with a new interpretation of almost every character in the play. Later critical opinion was much more hostile. Boaden, for instance, writing in the nineteenth century, declared that the 1772 alteration was written 'in a mean and trashy common-place manner, and in a word, sullied the page of Shakespeare and disgraced the taste and judgment of Mr Garrick'.[6] In Garrick's own day, scarcely any other play brought in higher receipts at the box-office.* He played it a dozen times himself before surrendering the role to others. It was seen another twenty-two times in his lifetime.†

The three other new productions brought forward in December fared less well. Hopkins thought *The Rose*, a new musical effort of Arne's, 'a very dull insipid piece'. He also noted, however, that 'Mr G. protested against its being perform'd', so quite how it had found its way on to the boards at Drury Lane is something of a puzzle. It was loudly hissed, and its first performance was also its last.

There was more hissing a week later for a new mainpiece called *The Duel*. This was the work of William O'Brien, now returned from his American exile and living the life of a country gentleman near Dorchester.‡ He had brought off a remarkable theatrical coup—a farce premièred at Covent Garden on a Saturday evening, a comedy at Drury Lane the following Tuesday. The farce, *Cross Purposes*, did well.§ Three nights later at the rival house, however, his hopes were dashed. Garrick had thought well of the piece, also an adaptation from the French—'an interesting Story & very pathetick,' he had written to Boswell while it was in rehearsal—but that counted for nothing.¶ A party had been got up to damn the piece: 'It was very much hiss'd from the 2d Act,' wrote Hopkins, '& with the greatest difficulty we got thro' the Play amidst Groans, hisses &c.' O'Brien and his wife looked down on these farmyard scenes from Mrs Garrick's box. Garrick and King both went on to reason with the pit, but the case was hopeless. With the author's consent the comedy was withdrawn. O'Brien wrote no more.

Garrick's Christmas offering was a new pantomime called *The Pigmy Revels; or, Harlequin Foundling*. It was pretty standard holiday fare—the *Westminster Magazine* thought well of the scenery and liked Dibdin's music, but their reviewer

---

* An average full house at that time brought in about £160. For the first three performances of Garrick's altered version, takings averaged over £270.

† Garrick's text was never published in his lifetime. His preparation copy, with cuts and emendations in his own hand, was lost for many years but rediscovered in the Folger Library in 1934 by George Winchester Stone Jr. The full text appears in Pedicord and Bergmann.

‡ Lord Ilchester had gradually got over his daughter's elopement. O'Brien had been made Secretary and Provost-Master-General of Bermuda in 1768, and on his return to England his father-in-law had procured for him the Receiver-Generalship of Dorset.

§ It was taken from a French piece by La Font called *Les trois frères rivaux* and it would keep its place in the repertory until well into the nineteenth century.

¶ *Letters*, 717. It was an adaptation of *Le philosophe sans le savoir*, by Sedaine, which had been produced in Paris in 1765.

continued on a less seasonable note: 'The Stage now seems buried in universal darkness,' he wrote dyspeptically. 'The Publick for several weeks, has been fed with the lean carcass of two villainous pantomimes.'*

Elsewhere in the same issue, there was more generalized gloom and doom:

> We are of opinion, that the English Theatre is now in its decline . . . We have seen the Morning star of Wit—the Noon too is past; we have now arriv'd at its evening . . . There is in Arts, as in Empires, a progress which leads to Refinement; and this Refinement leads to Ruin.

Curiously enough the publication of this Gibbonian jeremiad coincided almost exactly with the beginning of a period in which one particular aspect of the art of the theatre took an exciting leap forward. Indeed it is possible that *The Pigmy Revels* was the first production at Drury Lane with which the celebrated painter and scene designer de Loutherbourg was associated, although the theatre account books do not record any payments to him before March 1773.

Philippe Jacques de Loutherbourg had been born in 1740 in Strasbourg, where his father was painter to the court of Darmstadt. The family was Polish in origin; de Loutherbourg's immediate forebears were recusants who had fled to Switzerland to escape persecution. He studied in Paris with Carle Van Loo and later entered the studio of François Joseph Casanova, who led a quieter life than his notorious elder brother and specialized in painting battles and landscapes. De Loutherbourg exhibited at the Salon, and was elected a member of the Académie Royale three years before reaching the normal minimum age of thirty. Garrick had first heard of him from Monnet, who described him as 'un de nos plus grands peintres, et garçon fort aimable'. He had first come to London in 1771, in search of painting commissions. He lodged initially with Domenico Angelo in Titchfield Street, and there he soon met Garrick, who invited him to elaborate his ideas on stage design and lighting.

De Loutherbourg responded with a comprehensive set of proposals for coordinating the whole range of scenic effect—not just lighting and scenery, but also the theatre's mechanical systems and even the design of costumes for both actors and dancers. He offered to provide drawings and models for the painters and machinists and to undertake some of the scene painting himself. Garrick liked the sound of all this, and paid him £300 for three months work in the spring and summer of 1773. De Loutherbourg was subsequently retained on a full-time basis at an annual salary of £500 and was to stay at Drury Lane for the next eight years.

Over the years he has been both undervalued and overpraised. When, for instance, the Irish dramatist John O'Keeffe declared in his rambling *Recollections* in 1826 that de Loutherbourg had invented transparent scenery—'moonshine, sunshine, fire, volcanoes &c'—he was overlooking the fact that Garrick had used scenic transparencies and coloured sidelights in a production of *Harlequin's*

---

* 1 January 1773. Covent Garden was staging a revival of *Harlequin Sorcerer*, 'not acted these 8 years'.

Invasion as early as 1759.* De Loutherbourg was no cultural revolutionary. Things were not suddenly and dramatically different after his arrival at Drury Lane. He was less an innovator than someone who brought refinement and sophistication to what had already been essayed by others. And he was by any standard a graceful and accomplished artist, as the many surviving examples of his work show—his battle piece 'Earl Howe's Victory on 1 June 1794' at the Greenwich Hospital in London, for instance, or 'Summer Afternoon with a Methodist Preacher' in the National Gallery of Canada in Ottawa. It is clear that under his direction the treatment of stage space evolved in a manner at once more romantic and more realistic than it had been before. He would come to be acknowledged as the most influential designer in the English theatre since Inigo Jones.

Garrick's increasing interest in spectacle, and the experiments in sound and lighting which it led him to, did not command universal approval. An interesting letter from Thomas Gainsborough survives—it was written sometime in 1772, and therefore before de Loutherbourg's influence had begun to make itself felt— and in his forthright way he fires a friendly shot across Garrick's bows:

> When the streets are paved with brilliants and the skies made of rainbows, I suppose you'll be contented and satisfied with red, blue and yellow. It appears to me that fashion, let it consist of false or true taste, will have its run like a runaway horse. For when eyes and ears are thoroughly debauched by glare and noise, the returning to modest truth will seem very gloomy for a time. And I know you are cursedly puzzled how to make this retreat without putting out your lights and losing the advantage of all our new discoveries of transparent painting, etc. How to satisfy your tawdry friends whilst you steal back into the mild evening gleam and quiet middle term.
>
> Now I'll tell you, my sprightly genius, how this is to be done: maintain all your light, but spare the abused colours till the eye rests and recovers. Keep up your music by supplying the place of *noise* by more sound, more harmony and more tune, and split that cursed fife and drum . . .[7]

Relations with Murphy, mended only twelve months previously by the success of *The Grecian Daughter*, deteriorated again this winter, and he ended up by withdrawing his tragedy *Alzuma* from Drury Lane and offering it instead to the rival house. Murphy was at his most paranoid: 'I am very much hurt to hear that He has rip'd up old Sores,' Garrick wrote resignedly to Barry, who had offered to act as a mediator:

> When we came before to a reconciliation at his request, I resolv'd, nay I thought it my duty, to forget what I thought former injuries—has he still retain'd them in his Mind for Occasional Use?—I do not Envy him that particular quality—[8]

---

* Vol. ii, p. 114. O'Keeffe, who was born in 1747, did not come to London until the early 1780s, towards the end of de Loutherbourg's time at Drury Lane.

Garrick was mellowing with the years. If he had chosen to, he might have mentioned a more recent injury—Murphy had been foolish enough within the past month to circulate a satirical piece called *Hamlet with Alterations*, a parody of Garrick's revised version. It was not intended for publication, but there was very little that did not come to the ears of the manager of Drury Lane. He wisely chose to ignore it, and drew the tedious correspondence with Murphy to a close with a terse note:

> Sir
> I am too much indispos'd to write long Letters, & too old, & too happy to love Altercation . . . I really have no more to say upon the Occasion, & am sorry that You have renew'd your old Way of making War, when I thought we had concluded a lasting Peace.[9]

One reason for his happiness was that this winter, at last, he had been elected to The Club. He had also once again begun to contemplate retirement—he had mentioned it in passing when he had written to the Abbé Morellet to tell him about *Hamlet*, and he did the same in a letter to another French friend, Pierre-Antoine de Laplace.[10]

His health had been particularly troublesome in the past few months. 'An aching head, sore throat & wretched pen must be my excuse for this Scrawl,' he had written to Tom King in November.[11] Early in January he told a friend that his 'old complaint'—the stone—had sent him into the country: 'I was Yesterday very apprehensive of an inflammation at ye Neck of my bladder but, thank God, it is abated.'[12] This kept him away from the theatre every evening except one until the middle of the month, and there was a recurrence a few weeks later after a convivial day at Hampton with the Adam brothers:

> Whether I had exerted my Spirits too much, or gave too great a loose to my love of drinking with those I like, I know not, but I was attack'd terribly with a fit of ye Stone, & had it all yesterday Morning till I was deliver'd of twins—to ye great Joy of my Wife & family—I was 4 hours upon ye rack & now as free from pain as Ever I was, I am weak wth my delivery, but I could Eat Turtle & laugh with You again to day as if Nothing had ail'd me—'Tis a curs'd Disorder . . .*

A week later he had to decline an invitation from Thomas Fitzmaurice: 'My sore throat is better, but not so well to risk it wth a beefstake party.'[13] In March, he was visited by another old friend—'a Sad Scrawl but I write with pain,' he told de Laplace,[14] and there was a similar postscript to a letter to Morellet four weeks later: 'I write this scrawl with the gout in my thumb and forefinger.'[15]

In February there was a disagreeable reminder of the Kenrick affair on the first night of a new comic opera called *The Wedding Ring*. Word had gone round that it was by Bickerstaffe; word had also gone round that there would be a riot. The piece was, in fact, by Dibdin, who had largely purloined it from Goldoni's

---

* *Letters*, 744. Garrick addressed the brothers as 'My dear Adelphi'.

Il Filosofo di Campagna, but for some reason he had not wished to be identified as the author. Maria Macklin, who had heard that trouble was brewing, had gone with a party into the gallery, and wrote an account of the evening to her father: 'Never did I see an audience more inflamed.' The management's assurances that the piece was not by Bickerstaffe failed to satisfy them. 'After some time the house being nothing but confusion,' Miss Macklin wrote, 'Dibdin was push'd upon the stage ready to drop with fright, and declared that he was the author himself.'

Garrick still paid more attention than good sense decreed to the endless tales and tittle-tattle that were constantly brought to him. There is a revealing—and amusing—instance of this in an exchange of letters that winter with Mrs Montagu. It had come to Garrick's ears that Lord Lyttelton's ne'er-do-well son had spoken ill of him at a dinner-party ('Garrick is so mean'). That would have been a matter of indifference to him—'I have no concern for what a young, crack'd-brain profligate may say of Me,' he wrote. What had agitated him very considerably, however, was to hear that young Lyttelton had attributed the same opinion to his father, and it was to probe this delicate matter that he addressed himself to the Queen of the Blues:

> My Sensibility perhaps may go too far, & therefore I have not hinted the least word of this business, Ev'n to my wife; nor will I—my Lord too shall not know a Sillable of the matter, for if he bears me ye good will, which I have long flatter'd myself, he does, his delicate Mind will suffer for it: all I would wish to know, is, whether it may not be possible from some Action or behaviour of mine, or for my not writing to his Lord^p upon his Son's marriage (Which I certainly did not, & upon principles, as I believe I told you) that his Opinion of me may be alter'd, & so have given a little ground for Malice & falsehood to build upon?*

Garrick had written from Hampton on a Friday. When he got back to the Adelphi on Sunday evening, the reassurance he so badly wanted was waiting for him:

> A thousand thanks, my dear Madam, for your very balsamic Letter. I am this moment arriv'd & can not Ev'n take my Lixivium till I have shewn my gratitide.
>
> I am much better in my health since I went out of Town, & quite recover'd in Mind since I rec'd Y^r Wise, feeling, charming friendly ten-thousand-Epithet-Epistle—I must shew it Madam that is poz . . .
>
> I believe if my blood sh^d freeze in my heart this very cold weather, that it would liquify, like St Januarius's at ye Sight of y^r hand Writing—indeed my good Lady, You have made me quite Easy—I love Lord Lyttelton, & would not lose him for Millions—[16]

It so happened that the dinner table at which young Lyttelton had expressed

---

* *Letters*, 723. Thomas Lyttelton had been married the previous June to Mrs Apphia Peach, the wealthy widow of the Governor of Calcutta.

himself so disobligingly was Samuel Foote's, and in his first letter to Mrs Montagu Garrick had written 'you must know, (to my credit be spoken), that Foote hates me'. He was always apprehensive about Foote, and in the early months of 1773 he had particular reason to be—the town, as Maria Macklin wote to her father, was 'big with Expectation of Foote's Puppet Shew' and it was generally expected that Roscius would come in for rough handling. 'Pray, sir,' a lady of fashion was said to have asked Foote, 'are your puppets to be as large as life?'—'Oh dear, Madam, no,' came the sweet reply: 'not much above the size of Garrick!'[17]

In the event, *The Handsome Housemaid; or, Piety in Pattens*, as it was called, was to come in for a good deal of praise in the press as an antidote to the 'crying comedies' of Cumberland and Kelly: 'The leading business of this Puppet Drama,' wrote the *St James's Chronicle*, 'is to ridicule those dull sentimental Comedies which now set our Audiences fast asleep at both the theatres.'[18] Foote was cleverly suggesting that the plots of such plays were no better than those in puppet shows, and the acting so stiff that wooden figures might be used to better advantage than flesh and blood actors.

Garrick escaped with a few good-natured thrusts. Horace Walpole had got wind of some sort of deal between the two rivals, and there is an intriguing passage in a letter he wrote to the Countess of Upper Ossory only days before the opening at the Haymarket: 'Garrick, by the negotiation of a secretary of state has made peace with Foote, and by the secret article of the treaty is to be left out of the puppet-show.'[19] The editor of Walpole's letters speculates that the Secretary of State in question was Garrick's friend Lord Rochford, at that time Secretary of State for the Southern Department. What sort of ransom Garrick paid if he did buy immunity from ridicule is not known, but he was certainly in a very relaxed mood on the day *The Handsome Housemaid* opened. 'I hope you will be Entertain'd to Night with Aristophanes,' he wrote to Peter Fountain:

> He is a Genius, & ought to be encourag'd, He means Me no harm I am sure; & I hope & trust y^t you & your friends go to Support the Cause, the Cause of Wit, humor, & Genius,—You can't have a better—I Wish him Success from my Soul.*

Sentimental comedy received another broadside a month later with the first performance of Oliver Goldsmith's *She Stoops to Conquer*. Percy Fitzgerald, writing a century later with all the iron certainty of hindsight, could still feel indignant that what he saw as one of the great comedies of the eighteenth century should have seen the light of day at Covent Garden:

> While Garrick could thus accept pieces from clergymen, and Indian colonels, 'staymakers,' and 'rope-makers,' it is to be lamented that he

---

* *Letters*, 745. Aristophanes was one of Foote's nicknames. Success hung in the balance on the first night. The entertainment was both too short and too subtle for the upper gallery, who expressed their displeasure by tearing up some benches. Foote made some revisions, and the piece had a respectable run.

should have done nothing for a real genius of his time, a single scene of whose plays was worth whole trunkfuls of such work. The names of Garrick and Goldsmith should have been associated in the history of the stage, and his two admirable comedies have belonged to Drury Lane.[20]

Colman, as it happens, was initially as lukewarm about this second comedy of Goldsmith's as Garrick had been about his first. He sat on the manuscript for many months after accepting it, and by January 1773, Goldsmith was so desperate that he actually withdrew it and sent it to Garrick. At this point Johnson intervened, persuading Goldsmith to return the play to Covent Garden and Colman to honour his engagement. He did, but reluctantly; Johnson later said that he was 'prevailed on at last by much solicitation, nay, a kind of force, to bring it on'.*

Colman's lack of enthusiasm for the piece had communicated itself to the players. 'Gentleman' Smith declined to play Young Marlow; Woodward turned down the role of Tony Lumpkin and Mrs Abington refused to appear as Miss Hardcastle. Some of Goldsmith's friends urged him to accept a postponement, but he was obdurate. 'No,' he said, 'I'd rather my play were damned by bad players than merely saved by good acting.'

On the night, Johnson presided over dinner at a tavern for Goldsmith's friends; the party included Reynolds and Burke.† Goldsmith himself was so miserable that he could scarcely swallow a mouthful, and did not accompany the others to the theatre; later in the evening a friend found him walking to and fro in St James's Park and coaxed him to Covent Garden only in time for the fifth act. He could safely have come sooner. Garrick had written a prologue, which was admirably spoken by Woodward. Johnson, positioned in the front row of a side box, operated as a powerful one-man claque. Cumberland recorded that all eyes were on him, 'and when he laughed, everybody thought himself warranted to roar'.[21] By the end of the second act the success of the piece was no longer in doubt. It played to packed houses and at the beginning of May the King and Queen came to see it. The battle against 'that monster called Sentimental Comedy', as the *London Magazine* put it, had been joined in earnest.

The only new tragedy at Drury Lane that season was John Home's *Alonzo*. Murphy, for one, did not find it difficult to restrain his enthusiasm for this bloody and improbable tale: 'The poetry, if it may be so called, is a mixture of cold prosaic language and sudden eruptions of the false sublime.'‡ There was plenty for Mrs Barry to get her teeth into in the role of Ormisinda, for all that, and

* The remark, recorded by Boswell, was made at dinner at Joshua Reynolds's house. (*Life*, iii, 320–1.)

† George Steevens, calling to pick Johnson up, found him smartly but colourfully dressed, and had to remind him that as court mourning was being observed for the late King of Sardinia, everyone else would be in black. Johnson was grateful, and changed at once, saying that he would not 'for ten pounds have seemed so retrograde to any general observance'. (*Ibid.*, iv, 325.)

‡ *Murphy*, ii, 102. The *Westminster Magazine* was equally unimpressed, concluding that Home's genius 'lies not in the tragic way'.

there was general agreement that she enjoyed a great success in it—at one point, horrified at the prospect of her son meeting her husband in single combat, she offers to submit to trial by ordeal, and walk bare-foot over burning plough-shares. She finally kills herself, but reappeared after the curtain had fallen to speak one of Garrick's more excruciating epilogues:

> Though lately dead, a princess, and of Spain,
> I am no ghost, but flesh and blood again!
> No time to change this dress; it is expedient
> I pass for British, and your most obedient.
> How happy ladies, for us all—That we
> Born in this isle, by Magna Charta free,
> Are not like Spanish wives, kept under lock and key?. . .

There was a degree of panic behind the scenes on the seventh night. 'Mr Reddish who was to perform the part of Alonzo was not come to begin the 3d Act, which put us in great Confusion,' wrote Hopkins. The only remedy which suggested itself was a drastic one—Aickin was prevailed upon to go on and read the part, and his own role as the King of Asturia was simply eliminated. The situation was explained to the audience, and the play continued after a fashion. Before the evening was over, however, Reddish, who was noted for his eccentricities, showed up:

> When the Play was over Mr King & Mr Reddish went on the Stage Mr King apologis'd the Audience in behalf of Mr Reddish & told them that Mr R. was ready to make oath that he had entirely forgot it was a play Night, & that it was by meer chance he came to the House at all—his looks were so truely pitiable, the Audience had Compassion & excus'd him.*

Garrick's thoughts still turned frequently and fondly to his friends in France. 'When you see the divine Clairon give her an affectionate salute for me, with a gentle squeeze, for I love and honour her'—this in a long letter at the beginning of April to the Abbé Morellet:

> Pray let the Baron d'Holbach and Madame le Baronne know they are always in the minds and hearts of the Garricks. Need I desire you to remember me to the choice spirits I us'd to converse with in the most affectionate manner? The Diderots, Grims, Marmontels, &c. &c. and especially to M. and Madame Suard, the last of whom I was wise enough to be in love with before he was.[22]

---

* *Hopkins Diary*, 9 March 1773. Eccentricity later gave way to insanity. 'Mr Reddish being a little out of his senses he could not Play,' Hopkins noted in March 1775. By 1 April, things had got worse: '*Matilda* was advertis'd for this Night, but Mr Reddish came Yesterday as Mad as a March Hare, Said he had all the Terrors of the Damn's upon him . . . behav'd like a Man in Despair.'

There was no longer talk of a return visit to Paris, however. He almost certainly realized by now that his health was no longer equal to the rigours of continental travel; his letters to French friends, like the rest of his correspondence, are dotted with references to gout in his hand ('a Sad Scrawl but I write with pain') or to recurrent attacks of the stone or the gravel.

He was flattered in the late spring by a request from the Queen that he should revive and alter Fletcher's comedy *The Chances*, which had been popular after the Restoration in an adaptation by Buckingham. Apart from one performance the previous year, when Cautherley had attempted the role of Don John for his benefit,* the play had not been seen at Drury Lane since the late 1750s, when Garrick had appeared in it with Kitty Clive. The revival was a great success: 'The play went off vastly well,' wrote Hopkins in one of his matter-of-fact, punctuation-free diary entries. 'Mr G. Play'd with great Spirit & much Applauded the Alterations are vastly lik'd it will now be a living Play.'[23]

Garrick had written into one of his speeches in the last act a compliment to the Queen: 'Ay, but when things are at the worst, they'll mend—example does every thing, . . . and the fair sex will certainly grow better, whenever the greatest is the best woman in the kingdom.' Goldsmith, dining some days later at the house of General Oglethorpe, the soldier and philanthropist who had colonized Georgia, described this as 'mean and gross flattery'; Johnson, who was also present, came to the defence of his old pupil, though whether Garrick would have appreciated the terms in which he did so is uncertain:

> How is it mean in a player,—a showman,—a fellow who exhibits himself for a shilling, to flatter his Queen? The attempt, indeed, was dangerous; for if it had missed, what became of Garrick, and what became of the Queen? . . . . . Sir, it is right, at a time when the Royal family is not generally liked, to let it be seen that the people like at least one of them.†

There were signs as the end of the season approached that Garrick's temper was becoming ragged, and he fell out for a time over nothing of any great importance with his old friend John Hawkesworth. Two years previously, on Garrick's recommendation, Lord Sandwich had commissioned Hawkesworth to prepare for publication accounts of the recent voyages to the South Seas by Wallis, Carteret, Byron and Cook. Garrick had suggested his friend Becket as a printer, and Hawkesworth's decision to give the work instead to William Strahan earned him a stiff note of rebuke:

> Mr Garrick presents his Comp^{ts} to Dr Hawkesworth, and as he has the Misfortune to differ totally with him in opinion upon the subject of his letter—He will not give ye Doctor the trouble, or himself again to enter into any further discussion of this very disagreeable business.[24]

---

* Rashly, it seems—'Don John Mr Cautherly—la, la!' Hopkins wrote in his diary (22 April 1772).
† *Life*, ii, 234. Reynolds, Thrale and Langton were also present.

Hawkesworth replied the same day in an attempt to mend matters, although he could not conceal that he was hurt by what he called the 'cold expressions' in Garrick's note. He acknowledged that he had failed 'in what I trust you will look upon more as a matter of form than as an instance of want of affection or a sense of your friendship, the strength of which is such as makes me digest, though with difficulty, the terms of what I flatter myself was a hasty billet'.[25]

Garrick plainly realized he was making heavy weather of it, but there was something in his temperament which would not allow him to let the matter rest. Instead of suggesting to Hawkesworth that they should drink a glass of wine together, he picked up his pen and drew a vivid and revealing character sketch of himself:

> It may be the fault of my temper but I am so form'd, that when my Mind receives a Wound particularly from the hand of a friend, I cannot get it heal'd, so readily, as I could wish—as I have always been thought, & by yourself too, very sincere, Zealous & Active in my Friendships, I hope my being agitated (for any real or suppos'd Neglect of a Friend) in proportion to that Zeal & Activity may meet with indulgence—the moment I am at peace with myself, I will answer your letter in the Spirit in which it is written . . .[26]

Garrick kept a draft of the letter among his papers and endorsed it 'A very disagreeable mistake between us.' So it was. Happily, summer was drawing on. He made one last appearance as Lear in aid of a relief fund benefit. Then he was free to come and go as he chose between the Adelphi and Hampton and to prepare for the customary round of holiday excursions.

33

Lawful Game in the Winter

Garrick carried Drury Lane business with him everywhere like a hump on his back. 'I am here with my family spending my time as innocently & as thoughtlessly as the Theatre & my slanderers will permit me,' he wrote to Richard Berenger from Hampton:

> I look upon myself as lawfull Game in the winter, when I am justly hunted & shot at from all quarters; but surely a manager ought to have the same priviledges with hares & Partridges, & not be disturb'd till such a Day, as should be settled by Parliament.[1]

It was sometimes his own fault, because he had a tendency to resume responsibility for business which he had previously delegated to others. Precious hours were squandered in early June that summer, for instance, on correspondence with 'Gentleman' Smith, who, not for the first time, had fallen out with Colman over terms and opened secret negotiations about changing houses.* George Garrick had been authorized to offer him £12 a week, but Smith, who had been getting 12 guineas at Covent Garden, asked for £13 'by way of *rank*'. When this was refused, he announced that he would apply instead to Richard and Mary Ann Yates, who were seeking (unsuccessfully as it turned out) a licence to act with a company at the King's Theatre. Garrick, although he could have made good use of him, called his bluff, and after much to-ing and fro-ing Smith apologized and admitted that 'the golden hopes of a field-marshal's staff misled my judgment'. In the autumn, his tail between his legs, he returned to Covent Garden.

Garrick's holiday correspondence was not uniformly tedious. Earlier in the year he had received an unusual request from Richard Penn, then serving, in the absence of his brother John, as Deputy-Governor of Pennsylvania. 'Your Fame is extended even to the most distant woods of North America, where you are often made the topic of our conversation,' he wrote:

> Your age not long since was brought on the carpet, upon which I have betted a very large sum of money; whether I win or not I shall be particularly

---

* Smith, tall and good-looking, owed his nickname, of which he was not a little proud, to his genteel stage manners. The son of a tea importer and wholesale grocer in the City, he had been educated at Eton, drifting into the theatre after his father fell on hard times.

obliged to you if you will send me over a certificate of it, properly authenticated.

Before Garrick could reply, an account of the wager had appeared in the *London Chronicle*. He learned there not only that Penn's bet was for 500 guineas, but that a party of gentlemen had already visited Hereford to consult the All Saints register. The reply he now sent to Penn from his Hampton retreat was in his most relaxed and sparkling vein:

> . . . You have too much good Sense to expect that I should be Sorry for the loss of your Wager, indeed Sir, I had rather that you had lost Thousands for Hundreds, than that I should have been, what you have endeavour'd to make me, four Years Older than I am. Your Excellency knows that Persons upon the Stage, like Ladies upon the Town, must endeavour by dress, paint, & Candle-light to set themselves off for what they are not, & that a Publication of Registers, would ruin the Practice of half the Antonys, & Cleopatra's in London. . .[2]

There also survives from that summer a charming, affectionate letter from Garrick to his two nieces. George's daughters, Arabella and Catherine, were now twenty and seventeen.* Garrick and his wife regarded them almost as their own children, and he had arranged through Monnet that they should spend some time at an exclusive boarding school in the Faubourg St. Honoré run by a Mme Descombes:

> Your safe Arrival in Paris has given Us the utmost Satisfaction, tho I have not yet got over Your being four hours in ye Ship tossing & puking within Sight of Shore, & no boat to take you from the Ship:—I hope your liking to Paris continues, & that by beginning to taste ye language, your relish for Every thing will Encrease. . . the Moment You think you can understand & Enjoy a tragedy, I hope Mad^e De Combes will let You see Mad^lle Raucour, who makes such a noise in Paris . . .†

In June the Garricks were the guests of Earl Temple at Stowe, in Buckinghamshire, and early in July they were at Mistley, enjoying the celebrated hospitality of the Paymaster to the Forces—Garrick once suggested that Rigby had fixed his abode in a swamp in order that he might have an excuse for using brandy as the rest of the world used small-beer.

---

* Fanny Burney had met the sisters two years previously and described the occasion in her diary: 'But after Tea, we were *cheered* indeed, for Rap, Tap, Tap—& enter M^r and Mrs Garrick, with their two nieces . . . The Miss Garricks resemble, the Eldest her Aunt, the youngest her Uncle, in a striking manner. Softness, modesty, reserve and silence characterise Miss Garrick, while Kitty is all animation, spirit and openness. They are both very fine Girls, but the youngest is most handsome, her face is the most expressive I almost ever saw of liveliness and sweetness.' (*The Early Letters and Journals of Fanny Burney*, vol. 1, 1768–1773, ed. Lars E. Troide, Oxford, 1988, pp. 148–50.)

† *Letters*, 777. Raucourt was the stage name of Françoise Marie Antoinette Saucerotte, who had made her début at the Comédie-Française the previous September at the age of sixteen.

The Garricks also travelled to Northamptonshire that summer and were the guests of the Spencers at Althorp. On their way back to London they encountered the ubiquitous Cradock:

> I met with them resting their horses at Dunstable, and by a little exchange of servants, accompanied them in their coach to Saint Alban's, where we all took tea together, and from my persuasion, for the first time, they visited the old Abbey Church, and were greatly struck with the beauty of the interior. The Clerk entreated us to examine the vault, where the remains of Duke Humphrey were deposited, after he had been murdered by Cardinal Beaufort; and the recollection of the exquisite scene in Shakespeare, so animated the great Actor, that he violated, I fear, the rules of decorum, till Mrs Garrick was obliged to remind him of the sacred precints that he was about to profane.[3]

Of all Garrick's grand friends none emerges more attractively and engagingly from his correspondence than Lord Camden. There runs through his letters a thread of good-natured complaint at how difficult the Garricks were to pin down. 'Now I despair for the rest of the summer,' he wrote after they had visited him, as he thought all too briefly, at Chislehurst in August:

> You and Mrs Garrick are two restless people, whose minds are always upon the stretch for conversation at home and abroad, and are strangers to the pleasure of one day's solitude. The only time you allot for thought or reflection is eight to ten in the morning during the winter, and even these hours are generally interrupted by posts and boxkeepers.

He had hit on a solution:

> I once had the pleasure of meeting Mrs Garrick upon Honslow-heath. Suppose she would condescend to give me an assignation in the middle of that waste. It would be something in our passage to get a glimpse of you both, though but for half an hour. We have females enough to make a scene of witches, and you and I might personate Macbeth and Banquo.[4]

When Garrick returned to Hampton from Camden Place he settled down to read a manuscript he had received from John Home. It was Home's first attempt at a comedy; Garrick, profoundly unimpressed, did not beat about the bush:

> I must tell you with that frankness, Friendship & Sincerity, which I have always profess'd, that I never was more disappointed in my life:—indeed, my Worthy friend, if I have the least Judgment in these matter, Your Comedy is not in the least calculated for the Stage . . .[5]

Home was taken aback: 'If Shakspeare's statue at Hampton had pulled off one of his marble slippers, and hit me a slap in the face, I could not have been more astonished,' he wrote:

You say that you intend to read it a second time: *if you entertain* more favourable sentiments then, I shall be very glad to hear from you; *if you do not*, spare me the mortification of reading a second invective . . . I prefer friendship to authorship.[6]

Garrick did write again, quoting La Bruyère ('A true friend will speak with freedom to his friend, but will suffer Nobody Else to speak with freedom of him')[7] and Home was suitably mollified:

I received your letter, and am touched with the kind and affectionate concern you express from the apprehension of having given me uneasiness. I am still of the same mind to show the play to nobody but you . . . We need no mediators. If any, there is but one whom I would allow, I mean Mrs. Garrick, to whom I will submit; for in her infallibility I believe.[8]

Mrs Garrick's infallibility does not appear to have been tested. The friendship survived, although the play was never performed.*

Tireless, if not always entirely discriminating, in promoting the interests of his friends and acquaintances, Garrick was successful that summer in soliciting a naval chaplaincy for Percival Stockdale, a conceited miscellaneous writer and half-hearted clergyman then in his late thirties.† Several men-of-war had just been put in commission, and Garrick's approach to Lord Sandwich, then the First Lord of the Admiralty, resulted in Stockdale's appointment to the *Resolution*, a guard-ship lying at Spithead. Garrick's letter of thanks to Sandwich throws interesting light on how the clergy of the day were regarded:

My L^d
You have bestow'd a great favour upon a Man of letters & Talents when he most wanted it—tho ye Sons of ye Church in general are not remarkable for their Gratitude, I trust, as Mr Stockdale has Nothing of ye Hypocritical part of his profession, that he has more of ye Moral—[9]

All too soon it was time to ring up the curtain on a new season. Garrick chose to do so with a production of *The Beggar's Opera*—a decision, oddly enough, which was controversial. Sir John Fielding and his fellow-magistrates had written requesting that he suppress it, 'as they were of opinion it had done a great deal of mischief among the low class of people'. Garrick was praised in the *Morning Chronicle* for refusing to comply with the Justices' wishes, and a young man called William Augustus Miles came to his defence in a forty-four page *Letter*

---

* It seems likely that it was a piece called *The Surprise; or, Who Would Have Thought It?* which Henry Mackenzie found in manuscript among Home's papers after his death. (Mackenzie, Henry, *An Account of the Life and Writings of John Home, Esq.*, Edinburgh, 1822, p. 120.)
† Stockdale (1736–1811) had been introduced to Garrick by his friend Captain Thompson. A vicar's son, he had served for a time in the army before being ordained deacon at the age of twenty-three; it was another twenty-three years before he took priest's orders. Earlier in 1773 he had presented Garrick with a volume of three sermons he had just published: *Three Discourses*: two against Luxury and Dissipation, one on Universal Benevolence.

to Sir John Fielding, in which he countered the magistrate's moral objections to the play and offered his support to Garrick in resisting censorship.*

Before the season was a month old the manager felt obliged to crack the whip over two of the younger members of the company. Dibdin was making difficulties about setting a song for a new production of *Alfred*, and Garrick's patience snapped:

> . . . When I send for you I expect both from good manners & Duty, that you will come to me & know what I have to Say, before you will presume to answer it.—You are *our Composer*, & are not to do what *you* please; but what the *Managers* please . . . I am oblig'd to You for your opinion of what will be of Service or not, but as I have not yet given up the Management, You must excuse me for not following your opinion . . .[10]

Samuel Cautherley was also getting big for his boots. He had been married two years previously to a daughter of the card-maker to George III. She had brought with her a fortune of several thousand pounds, and Cautherley's weekly £4 from Drury Lane was no longer as important to him as it had been before. When he turned up his nose at the part of Lelio in a planned revival of the comedy *Albumazar*, he got the rough edge of his patron's tongue:

> Sir,
> Some peculiaritys in Your behaviour of late, demand my Notice, which I shall communicate to you now, & from this time all Correspondence shall cease between us . . . You say, that if I desire You to do this, or that, You will condesend—Sir, I will receive no favours from *You*, I cannot, but I will desire you to do your business or to leave it—one or the other you *must*, & *shall* do.—You talk'd to my Brother of being *Just to your self*, a foolish conceited phrase—You had better take care to be Just to other people, & to your Duty; The rank, & Importance you have assum'd, I have given you, & for which I have been frequently abus'd publickly & privately.—[11]

This brought Cautherley momentarily to heel. He wrote an abject reply to his 'Benefactor and best friend whose favor shall ever be thought of with Gratitude'. He was a reformed character—for a year or two.

Arne's *Alfred*, the cause of Garrick's spat with Dibdin, had not been performed since the 1750s. 'This Masque is very well got up with New Scenes & Decorations,' wrote Hopkins, 'particularly a Representation of the Grand Naval Review design'd by Mons de Loutherberg & vastly well Executed.' There had, he noted, been 'great Applause', though he added, in his even-handed way, 'the piece is very dull'.

Garrick, greatly pleased with the effect that had been achieved, saw an occasion to introduce the review again a month later at the end of Shadwell's

---

* Garrick responded by approaching Lord Sandwich on Miles's behalf and securing for him a civil appointment in the navy.

The Fair Quaker, which had been altered by his friend Captain Thompson.*
This went down well on the night, but it earned Garrick a critical letter from
John Hoadly:

> . . . *The Fair Quaker* we agreed to be skimmed milk, (nay, hogwash)
> whipped up into syllabub, and swallowed by a foolish audience as if
> substantial as roast beef. You think you may do what you please with Mr.
> Town, so you give him but a raree-show; but take a little care he does not
> revolt against absolute nonsense, however decorated.†

Garrick himself was seen more frequently in the early part of the season than
for some years, although he confined himself to the familiar routines of his
favourite comedy roles. Seeing in the newspapers that he was to perform Abel
Drugger, Fanny Burney prevailed on her father to write a note begging for two
places. 'My dear Dr.,' came the reply, 'I would rather have your family in my
box, than all the Lords and Commons.'[12]

Miss Burney was overwhelmed. 'He is really too good,' she wrote in her
journal. 'It is so difficult to get places when he acts, that I am almost ashamed
of his good nature.' That night, she recorded her impressions of his performance:

> Never could I have imagined such a metamorphose as I saw! The extreme
> meanness—the vulgarity—the low wit—the vacancy of Countenance—
> the appearance of *unlicked Nature* in all his motions.—
>
> In short, never was Character so well entered into, yet so opposite to
> his own.[13]

Shortly after this Fanny's father and Garrick fell out for a time—the reasons are
not clear, but seem in some way to have concerned Burney's nephew, Charles
Rousseau Burney, who was a harpsichordist and violinist and was married to
Fanny's elder sister Esther.‡ The rift was distressing to Fanny. Garrick 'by no
means acted as he ought', she wrote in her journal:

> With all my partiality for Mr Garrick, I cannot help noticing, that he has
> by no means the virtue of *Steadiness* in his attachment, &, indeed, is almost
> perpetually giving offence to some of his friends. Dr. Johnson told my
> Father that he attributes almost all the ill errors of Mr. Garrick's Life, to
> the *fire* & hastiness of his temper, which is continually misleading him.[14]

Garrick had once again been busy with his pen, and on 19 October presented a

---

* The alternative title of the piece was *Humours of the Navy*.
† *Boaden*, i, 583. Letter dated 16 November 1773. Horace Walpole, in a letter to his friend
Mason, struck a characteristically sour and mean note: 'Mr Garrick has been wondrously
jealous of the King's going twice to Covent garden, and to lure him back, has crammed the
town's maw with shows of the Portsmouth review and interlarded every play with the most
fulsome loyalties. He has new-written The Fair Quaker of Deal, and made it ten times worse
than it was originally, and all to the tune of Portsmouth and George forever . . .' *Walpole*,
xxviii, 110. Letter to Mason dated 19 November 1773.
‡ Charles Burney figures in the Drury Lane playbills for the 1766–7 season, but not thereafter.

much altered version of Thomas Tomkis's old comedy *Albumazar*, which had not been acted for 26 years. It had been Garrick's first 'new' production after his assumption of the managership; it seems likely that in reviving it now, he had been casting around for a non-sentimental comedy which might draw to Drury Lane some of the crowds who had flocked to Covent Garden to laugh at *She Stoops to Conquer* earlier in the year. 'Some smiles from Tony Lumpkin, if you spare,' he wrote in the prologue, 'Let Trincalo of Totnam have his share.' The prologue, indeed, is eloquent testimony to how ready Garrick was to trim his sails to catch the shifting breeze of popular taste:

> Since your old taste for laughing is come back,
> And you have dropp'd the melancholy pack
> Of tragi-comic-sentimental matter,
> Resolving to laugh more, and be the fatter,
> We bring a piece drawn from our ancient store,
> Which made old English sides with laughing sore . . .
> Each sister muse a sep'rate shop should keep,
> Comedy to laugh, Tragedy to weep,
> And sentimental laudanum to make you sleep . . .

If 'laughing comedy' was what they wanted, then that was what they should have.

Garrick's revision played much more briskly than the old text—in all he shed close to 800 lines.* There was a lot about astrology in the original. That was cut, along with references to the finer points of Jacobean duelling and the lore of herbs. Garrick also cleaned the text up a bit. Flavia's remark that her father smells 'Of putrifaction' was taken out, and so was one of Armelina's franker characterizations of Trincalo: ''Tis a tough Clowne and lusty: he works day & night.'

During the run of *Albumazar* Charles Macklin, now in his seventies, made a controversial return to the boards at Covent Garden. He had been haggling over terms with Colman for the best part of a year, and he now appeared in a new production of *Macbeth*. He had prepared himself for the role with the same thoroughness as for Shylock more than thirty years previously. The part was usually played in a suit of scarlet and gold, with a tail wig, very much like an eighteenth-century army officer—that was certainly how Garrick had always appeared.† Macklin, wrote his biographer, Cooke, 'saw the absurdity of exhibiting a Scotch character, existing many years before the Norman Conquest,

---

* In 1747 it had run without an afterpiece; that would not have gone down well with the audiences of the 1770s, and Garrick would have had that in mind in cutting as extensively as he did.

† During the brief run of Macklin's *Macbeth*, an anonymous letter was published in the *St James's Chronicle* which gave a satirical description of Garrick's appearance in the cave scene in Act IV: '[He] looked like a Beau who had unfortunately slipped his Foot, and tumbled into a Night Cellar, where a Parcel of old Women were boiling Tripe for their Supper' (*St James's Chronicle*, 28–30 October 1773.)

in this manner, and therefore very properly abandoned it for the old Caledonian habit'.

No very clear picture emerges from contemporary sources of just how Macklin looked. An engraving entitled 'Shylock Turnd Macbeth' shows him in tartan stockings, a voluminous and loosely belted tunic with tartan cuffs to the sleeves, a plaid and a large and floppy feathered bonnet; he is wearing a basket-hilted sword and brandishing what could be a *sgian dubh*.*

That he should be hissed at his first entry on the night was perhaps predictable. A few days previously, one of the papers had carried a report of how he had conducted himself at rehearsal:

> Sir! Sir! Do you know what you are about? None of your hackneyed turns and practises with me! Throw Garrick to the dogs! I'll have none of him. He is for Nature and Shakespeare; I am for Shakespeare and Nature! Hark you, ye witches! Manage your broomsticks with dignity and be damned to you! Ride through the air like gentlewomen, and as if mounted on so many Pegasuses![15]

Mrs Macklin, seated in the gallery with a friend, was convinced that the hissing had been started by Samuel Reddish, and by the young son of the actor Luke Sparks. Macklin took her word for it and published the charge in the newspapers. Rumours circulated that they had been put up to it by 'King David'; Reddish, carpeted by Garrick, denied the allegations against him; returning to Covent Garden for the second performance, he disrupted the proceedings for a time by a speech asserting his innocence.

Macklin's Macbeth got mixed reviews. The *Morning Chronicle* thought he did well in the first and last acts, but gave way to stage rant and 'vehemence of energetic expression' in between; it also noted that he forgot some of his lines. The *London Evening Post* put the boot in without ceremony: 'In Act II, Sc. i, Shakespeare has made Macbeth murder Duncan; now Mr Macklin, being determined to copy from no man, reversed this incident, and in the very first act, scene the second, murdered *Macbeth*.'

There was more trouble to come, this time from Covent Garden sources. Colman had offered Macklin Richard III as well as Macbeth; these were both 'Gentleman' Smith's roles, and he had accepted a proposal that he and Macklin should alternate in them with extreme reluctance. On the fourth night, without great success, some of his friends tried to engineer a riot. The following week, however, when Macklin was billed to appear in *The Merchant of Venice*, they managed to assemble a party of idle tailors who, suitably primed with drink, succeeded in halting the performance. Calls for Macklin to come on stage and kneel in submission were disregarded, as might be expected; equally predictably, the tailors then caused a good deal of damage to the fabric of the playhouse.

---

* Published by M. Darly, 5 November 1773. The engraver is unknown; it bears the legend 'Old Envy sculp., after Young Envy invt.' Strictly speaking, of course, the kilt and the tartan are just as much an anachronism for *Macbeth* as the scarlet coat of an eighteenth-century officer.

The night was a total loss to the theatre; the Account Book does not even record it as a night of performance. Colman bowed to the inevitable, and Macklin was dismissed.

He was not the man to leave matters there, however. He busied himself in his obsessional way seeking indictments and collecting affidavits. Five men were eventually brought to trial on charges of 'riotous conspiracy to deprive Mr Macklin of his livelihood'; a lifelong subscriber to conspiracy theory, Macklin was convinced that the manager of Drury Lane Theatre should have stood in the dock beside them.* The prosecutions succeeded, and the accused went before Lord Mansfield in the Court of the King's Bench to be sentenced. Macklin rose to deny that he sought either money or revenge; he would be satisfied if the defendants paid his costs, took tickets worth £100 for his daughter's and his benefit and indemnified the theatre management for their losses by the same amount. Mansfield praised his magnanimity and the 'honourable complexion and singular moderation' of what he proposed. 'You have met with great applause today,' he told him. 'You never acted better.'

Drury Lane audiences were still saying the same of Garrick during the 1773–4 season. 'Mr G. Play'd most divinely,' noted Hopkins in his diary when he appeared as Don John in *The Chances* in the middle of November. The prompter had also been full of praise for his performance as Hastings in *Jane Shore* earlier in the month, although he had his reservations about Mrs Canning, a good-looking young widow who played the title role — 'a Small mean figure very little power (very So, So.)' Billed only as 'A Gentlewoman', it was her first appearance on any stage—possibly Garrick gave her her chance for sentimental reasons, because her husband had been a boon companion of Colman's and Churchill's and a strong supporter of Wilkes. It seems likely that she had turned to the stage under the influence of Reddish, with whom she had gone to live soon after the death of her husband two years previously. She never rose above mediocrity as an actress, but her son George Canning would one day achieve fame on a wider stage.

There was a good reception in December for a comedy by Hugh Kelly called *The School for Wives*, although because of Kelly's employment as a newspaper hack by the ministry, it was given out under the name of a friend called William Addington†—the last thing manager and author wanted was a repetition of the disturbances that had marred the performances of Kelly's *A Word to the Wise* three years previously.‡ On the day, the Garricks dined at Beauclerk's house, along with Goldsmith, the Edgecumbes and Horace Walpole, who described the occasion in a letter to Lady Ossory. 'I was most thoroughly tired as I

---

* When *Macbeth* had been disrupted, he had publicly charged Smith with complicity. Smith issued a challenge to a duel, which Macklin accepted, but bloodshed was averted.

† Addington (1728–1811), formerly a major in Burgoyne's regiment, was at the time an official at Bow Street under Sir John Fielding, but had ambitions to be a playwright.

‡ Kelly had taken similar precautions at the other house. When a blank-verse tragedy of his called *Clementina* was put on at Covent Garden in 1771 it had been billed as the first production of 'a young American clergyman not yet arrived in England'.

knew I should be, I, who hate the playing off a butt,' he wrote in his prissy way:

> Goldsmith is a fool the more wearing for having some sense. It was the night of a new comedy called the *School for Wives*, which was exceedingly applauded and which Charles Fox says is execrable. Garrick has at least the chief hand in it. I never saw anybody in a greater fidget, nor more vain when he returned, for he went to the playhouse at half an hour after five and we sat waiting for him till ten, when he was to act a speech in *Cato* with Goldsmith. That is, the latter sat in t'other's lap, covered with a cloak, and while Goldsmith spoke, Garrick's arms that embraced him, made foolish actions. How could one laugh when one had expected this for four hours?*

Although they were happy enough to perform the occasional party piece together, relations between Garrick and Goldsmith were to retain a certain edginess to the end. Goldsmith's oddities of speech and manner did not grow less with the years—he was now forty-five—and his friends and acquaintances still quite often made him the butt of their wit. At a meeting of The Club that winter at which Goldsmith was not present, it was proposed that he be made the subject of a number of mock epitaphs, and Garrick, with his celebrated facility in such matters, came up more or less extempore with a notably hurtful couplet:

> Here lies Nolly Goldsmith, for shortness call'd Noll,
> Who wrote like an angel but talked like poor Poll.

Goldsmith, when he heard it, was sufficiently provoked to produce in reply one of the most sharply observed characterizations of Garrick that has come down to us from any of his contemporaries:

> Here lies David Garrick, describe me who can,
> An abridgment of all that was pleasant in man;
> As an actor, confest without rival to shine;
> As a wit, if not first, in the very first line;
> Yet, with talents like these, and an excellent heart,
> The man had his failings, a dupe to his art.
> Like an ill-judging beauty, his colours he spread,
> And beplaster'd with rouge his own natural red.
> On the stage he was natural, simple, affecting;
> 'Twas only that when he was off he was acting . . .

---

* *Walpole*, xxxii, 170–1. Letter dated 14 December 1773. Joshua Reynolds's niece, Mrs Gwatkin, saw the pair go through the same routine on another occasion with the roles reversed: 'Garrick sat on Goldsmith's knee; a table-cloth was pinned under Garrick's chin, and brought behind Goldsmith, hiding both their figures. Garrick then spoke in his finest style, Hamlet's speech to his father's ghost. Goldsmith put out his hands on each side of the cloth, and made burlesque action, tapping his heart, and putting his hands to Garrick's head and nose, all at the wrong time.' The painter Benjamin Haydon tells the story in his unpublished journal.

He cast off his friends as a huntsman his pack,
For he knew when he pleased he could whistle them back.
Of praise a mere glutton, he swallowed what came,
And the puff of a dunce he mistook it for fame,
Till, his relish grown callous, almost to disease,
Who pepper'd the highest was surest to please . . .

Goldsmith did not stop at Garrick. He went on working at *Retaliation*, as the poem came to be called, throughout the winter, and completed epitaphs on several of his friends; his affectionate lines on Reynolds were still unfinished when he was carried off by a fever at the beginning of April.*

As Drury Lane's offering for the festive season that year, Garrick had written *A Christmas Tale*, an extravaganza of love and magic with a score by Dibdin ('the worst he ever Compos'd,' wrote Hopkins in his diary).† 'My food is meant for honest, hearty grinners!' Garrick told the audience in his prologue, with a gesture to the upper gallery. It was not over-demanding fare. Hopkins says Garrick wrote it in a hurry; he based it on a fairy play by Favart called *La Fée Urgèle* which had been performed in Paris eight years previously. Once again, he gave de Loutherbourg his head, and the effects he achieved were sensational. Horace Walpole, not an easy man to please, wrote that the production was 'adorned with the most beautiful scenes next to those in the opera at Paradise'.‡ The *Westminster Magazine* took a sterner view:

> We were sorry to see the genius and abilities of Mr Loutherbourg so misemployed. The scenes and machines were all admirable; and we could not help wishing that the talents of this man, instead of being used to save paltry things from damnation, were united to those of a Shakespeare, to astonish or to enchant us into virtue.

The audience thought differently, as Garrick had shrewdly calculated they would.

---

* Burke burst into tears when he heard the news. Forster, in his life of Goldsmith, says that Reynolds was in his studio when the messenger came to him; 'At once he laid his pencil aside, which in times of great family distress he had not been known to do; left his painting-room; and did not re-enter it that day.' (*Forster, op. cit.*, ii, 422.)

† Dibdin, in his memoirs, left a characteristically bilious account of how he was called upon to make his contribution. 'I was summoned to HAMPTON, to take instructions for the *Christmas-tale*,' he wrote, 'His muse was very often in want of obstetrick assistance as to songs and chorusses, however easily she might bring forth prologues and epilogues, so was I either obliged to set up after the family, or get up before them, to lend musical aid to bits and scraps of which nobody could guess either the drift or meaning, and all this music was to be extracted from an old virginal, with half the strings broke; a prodigious fine antique, which graced Mrs GARRICK'S beautiful drawing room, with much about the elegance and embellishment as a spot of rust upon a polished register-stove. I used to tell him, I hoped he would bequeath it to the Antiquarian-Society.' (*Dibdin*, i, 102.)

‡ Walpole was writing to Lady Ossory. He was much less polite about the text, however, the authorship of which was not immediately made public: 'It is believed to be Garrick's own, and a new proof that it is possible to be the best actor and worst author in the world, as Shakespeare was just the contrary.' (*Walpole*, xxxii, 177. Letter dated 30 December 1773.)

The piece provided just the sort of glittering spectacle the holiday audience wanted; the King came to see the third performance and it ran for seventeen profitable nights.

The speculation of the Adams brothers at the Adelphi had not gone as well as they had hoped, and they had petitioned Parliament to allow them to conduct a lottery to raise the funds necessary to complete the project. Tickets went on sale in December, and at the end of the month Garrick wrote to Wilkes, who was Sheriff of London at the time, to enlist his assistance: 'My Friends & Neighbors yᵉ Adams have solicited me to desire Yʳ Interest with yᵉ Lord Mayor, that they may be permitted to draw their Lottery in Guild-hall.'[16] The Lord Mayor agreed, and lots were drawn in the Guildhall, as well as in 'the great room in Exchange Alley, Cornhill', on 1 March 1774.

Garrick was unwell again. 'Had my Cold & Sore permitted me to leave home, I should have ask'd this favour in Person,' he had told Wilkes. He had still not recovered a week later. 'I have been very ill wᵗʰ a Cold & hoarseness,' he wrote to Cradock, '& am oblig'd to go tomorrow into ye Country to try if the Air will be of Service to Me.'[17] Cradock had written to him from Cassiobury, near Watford in Hertfordshire, pressing him to attend some amateur theatricals that the Earl of Essex and his wife were getting up at their country seat there. Garrick, however, was aggrieved as well as indisposed. It was at the urging of Lord and Lady Essex that he had played in *Jane Shore* before Christmas, and he told Cradock sharply why he was not inclined to bestow further favours in that quarter:

> This filthy cold I partly got, by Exhibiting my person in the gallant Hastings, as the best Compliment I could Pay to the Noble Host & Hostess where You are—but indeed my Pride was very much mortify'd, when I found the Family did not come to their box till in yᵉ middle of the third Act—it will not be long in my Power to pay many such Compᵗˢ.[18]

That sounds very much like a hint that he was once again contemplating retirement, and the wheel of the rumour mill was soon turning: 'If you really are to make your *exit* this winter,' George Steevens wrote to him, 'I shall strive to see you in your principal characters from the pit, that I may acquire the last knowledge of Shakespeare that I can ever expect to receive from the stage.'[19]

For the moment, however, colds, hoarseness and gouty fingers notwithstanding, he was too busy to do more than play with the idea. Particularly when he received letters from the likes of Kitty Clive which began with the salutation 'Wonderful Sir' and continued in equally flattering vein:

> who have been for these thirty years contradicting an old established proverb—you cannot make bricks without straw; but you have done what is infinitely more difficult, for you have made actors and actresses without genius; that is, you have made them pass for such, which has answered your end, though it has given you infinite trouble . . .[20]

He was even more flattered, returning to the Adelphi after a weekend at Hampton, to learn that his friend Grey Cooper had called in his absence, and that he had brought with him Lord North, the Prime Minister. This was heady news, and the letter which Garrick immediately dispatched to Grey shows him at his sprightly and exuberant best:

I beg & beseech You, my good friend, not to make me too vain, but if there are any commands to Either of yᵉ Indies, if it is thought proper that I shᵈ be Commander in Chief instead of General Clavering, (whose nomination I & my friends intended to support next thursday) or if I should be fix'd to make yᵉ Bostonians drink their tea as they ought, or send them after yᵉ tea into yᵉ atlantic, pray let me know directly that I may seize the Kingdoms of England, & Scotland, (in yᵉ Persons of Richd yᵉ 3d & Macbeth) & prepare to go anywhere or Every where, as that Noble Lord shall be pleas'd to command Me.*

'The wit and pleasantry of your letter have delighted us all,' Cooper wrote in his elegantly turned reply:

Lord North cannot afford, either on the account of his taste or his popularity, to send the favourite of the nation to such barbarous places as Bengal or Boston. He hopes, however, that you will soon prove, that you have neither abdicated nor deserted the kingdoms of Scotland or England.[21]

Thoughts of retirement were also pushed to the back of Garrick's mind for a time by the death of his partner Lacy. As well as a house in Berners Street, Marylebone, he had owned a fine estate, called Turk's House, on the Thames at Isleworth, only a few miles from Hampton, and it was there that he died on 21 January at the age of seventy-eight. His wife had died some years previously, and he left almost everything to his only son Willoughby—his books, his diamond ring ('weight about fourteen grains'), some property in Oxfordshire and the estate at Isleworth. Most importantly, he also left him his 'moiety of Drury Lane Theatre Patents Leases Cloathes Scenes and whatever else appertains to my partnership with David Garrick Esqr'.

Willoughby Lacy was a brash young man of twenty-five. Under the terms of their agreement, Garrick, on James Lacy's death, had the option to buy his half of Drury Lane, a share valued in 1774 at £32,000. He would come to regret his decision not to do so; he was to have more trouble with the son in a few short years than he had experienced in more than a quarter of a century with the father. 'You must excuse all my hurry & interlineations,' he scribbled in an ominous postscript to a letter on 1 February, 'for I am with three Lawyers & my Partner's Son.'[22]

Within days of the proving of his father's will, young Lacy wrote to Garrick

* *Letters*, 820. The purpose of North's call is not known. Lieutenant-General John Clavering (1722–77), the hero of the capture of Guadeloupe in 1759, was a candidate for nomination as Commander-in-Chief of the East India Company's forces in India. Garrick had bought 5,000 shares in the company in 1768, and would therefore have a vote in the election, which was due to take place in a week's time—and at which Clavering was duly elected. The Boston Tea Party had taken place six weeks previously, on 16 December.

saying that his counsel, having studied the original articles of agreement, 'was clearly of opinion that I have an equal Right with you in the Management of every Branch of the Business, relative to the Theatre'.[23] Garrick sent a restrained reply, registering surprise that Lacy had consulted counsel 'in a less amicable Way than I proposed—'

> You do me Justice in supposing y^t I have no wish to deprive you of any R^t you are entitled to—I commend Your prudence, And before I give you a final answer I shall follow you Example and be properly advised.[24]

Possibly on the advice of his lawyers, Lacy's tone now became less abrasive. For a time his mind was on other things; on 22 March he was married to Maria Ann, the seventeen-year-old daughter of one Daniel Orpen, described as 'an eminent hatter'. Whether the 'prodigious concourse of people' who attended the ceremony at St Marylebone Church included the Garricks is not known. Lacy settled into the estate at Isleworth and a new town house in Great Queen Street and began spending his way through his inheritance.

Garrick had been trying for some time to entice Noverre back to London, but was philosophical about his failure to do so. 'That most fantastick toe, & great Genius & I have been in treaty for some time,' he told Richard Cox:

> I left the business to be settled by his Brother, & I imagined that he, & his dancing crew, would have *caper'd* Tragedy at Drury Lane, as we are not at present in the highest repute to *Act* it. If he has preferr'd Milan to London, We must be contented, the distance between us & the Brother's inexperience of Treaty-making may have Occasion'd some blunder.*

It is not altogether clear what Garrick meant by not being in the 'highest repute' to act tragedy, although it was certainly no longer as strong a suit at Drury Lane as it had been a few years previously. This was partly because he himself was appearing much less frequently than formerly in tragic roles; Barry's increasing infirmities meant that he too was seen less often. There were also those who maintained that once Garrick ceased to see a new play as a vehicle for himself he became less discriminating. That was certainly Murphy's opinion (although he, of course, was an interested party), and he was one of those who took a poor view of *Sethona*, a second tragedy by Alexander Dow, who had previously written *Zingis*.

The play had its première on 19 February. The settings were once again by de Loutherbourg, and the main parts were taken by the Barrys. The two-column account of it which appeared in the *Public Advertiser* reads more like a puff than a critique, and suggests that the manager of Drury Lane may have been standing at the writer's elbow. The tragedy had been met with 'universal Applause' by 'a crowded and brilliant Audience,' he warbled:

---

* *Ibid.*, 821. Noverre had gone from a two-year contract in Vienna to the Teatro Reggio Ducal in Milan.

The Dresses, Decorations and Scenery of this Play are much superior to those of any modern Tragedy; they do ample Justice to the Author, and likewise do Honour to the Taste and Spirit of the Manager, who seems to have spared no Expence to furnish a splendid and rational Entertainment.

Murphy, writing his life of Garrick more than thirty years later, remembered what he called 'this wild production' somewhat differently:

The scene lies at Memphis in Egypt, but we look in vain for a single trace of oriental poetry. It is rather a tragedy in the Erse language. The fable is a chaos of absurdities, without one interesting situation. . . . The author was then in India, where he did not survive long enough to enjoy his fame. A party in his favour was formed by his countrymen and his friends in Leadenhall-street. By their influence, *Sethona* drawled through nine nights, without yielding any profits to the manager, or a sprig of bays to the poet.[25]

Biographica Dramatica took a similar view: 'This play may be properly styled a faggot of utter improbabilities, connected by a band of the strongest Northern fustian.' It was also asserted that although Drury Lane was '*apparently* full' several times during the nine nights' run of the play, it brought little into Garrick's treasury: 'It expired on his premises, but hardly left enough behind it to defray expenses of its funeral.'

On that point both Murphy and the authors of *Biographica Dramatica* were either malicious or ill informed—possibly both. The Drury Lane Treasurer's Book shows that receipts for the run were entirely healthy, averaging £220 a night. Dow, however, made no further attempts to scale Parnassus. He had, in fact, travelled home to see *Sethona* performed, but he now returned to India and died at Bhagalpur five years later.

Tension remained high over the situation in the American colonies, and Garrick maintained a keen interest in the course of events. In the House of Commons, on 7 March, Lord North read a message from the King on the 'Information of the unwarrantable Practices which have been lately concerted and carried on in *North America* and particularly of the violent and outrageous Proceedings of the Town and Port of Boston in the Province of *Massachusetts Bay*, resulting from the tax on tea.' Garrick listened from the gallery, and suffered for it—'I caught cold in yᵉ house of Commons Yesterday,' he wrote to George Steevens from Hampton. 'I came here this Morning almost dying with a headach attended wᵗʰ a small fever, & some Symptoms of the Stone.'[26]

He was obliged in the spring to look to his defences for the following season, and in April he wrote to Mary Ann Yates, who had not been a member of his company since she went off to Covent Garden in the summer of 1767. He did not beat about the bush. 'Madam. In all dealings the plain and simple truth is the best policy,' he wrote:

As Mrs Barry is in treaty with another Theatre, it is natural for Me to Wish a treaty with another Lady; & it is as natural that my inclinations look towards You: If You have no objections to Enter into a treaty with

Me, be pleas'd to name Your time & place and I shall be as punctual as I ought to be to so fine a Woman, & so good an Actress.[27]

Garrick was clear by this time that his constant disagreements with the Barrys made a breach inevitable and even desirable. He must have been equally clear, however, that in courting Mrs Yates he was running a certain risk, and not merely because of her imperious ways. She had most recently been appearing in Edinburgh, and she and her husband had also joined with a couple called Brookes in the management of the King's Theatre. It was common knowledge that she had taken to drinking heavily; Dibdin, in his *Annals of the Edinburgh Stage*, says that she often appeared on stage 'more than half seas over' and the tone of her reply to Garrick could certainly pass for that of a rather tipsy *grande dame*:

> On considering every circumstance of my situation here, and my novelty, to say nothing of my *beauty*, I think I cannot in conscience take less than 700*l.* a year for my salary; for my clothes, as I love to be well dressed, and the characters I appear in require it, I expect 200*l.*; as to benefit, you shall settle that yourself, but as I have an infinity of *Scotch pride*, had rather not take one, though I am sure of losing by it. Dickey, who considers only the main chance, is of a different opinion; but I am clear the worst advice a woman can possibly follow is that of her husband, and I had much rather you should determine that point for me than he. . . . .[28]

At the beginning of May, Garrick's negotiations with Mrs Yates were suddenly interrupted: 'My Brother's dangerous situation has made me unfit for business,' he wrote to her.[29] The nature of the illness is not known, but it was serious—'My Brother George has been dying these three weeks,' Garrick wrote to Fountain in the middle of the month.[30] It wasn't quite as bad as that; George was packed off to the country and began slowly to recover, but his absence meant much extra work for Garrick, who was himself once again far from well: 'when you called last Night my foot was flanell'd up wth ye Gout,' he said in a letter to Mrs Montagu:

> A sight of you, and ten words from You, would have been a Charm for ye foul Fiend—but I was order'd to see Nobody, & did not know it was my cure till it was gone—[31]

He was well enough a few days later, however, to perform an important piece of theatrical business. Since setting up the Theatrical Fund eight years previously he had served as its chief executive officer, responsible to an elected committee of thirteen.* The records of the fund, now in the Folger Library, contain a grateful minute dated 18 May 1774 noting the end of his stewardship:

> Dav Gar Esq the father founder & Proct^r of this Inst this day convened the male members of the theater in the green R & then like a good and faithful Steward del into their hands the foll^g possession & securities.

---

* It was later incorporated by Parliament as 'The Society Established for the Relief of Indigent Persons belonging to His Majesty's Company of Comedians'.

He had served the Fund well. He handed over assets that amounted to £2,918 11s 9d.

The previous evening he had, as was his custom, played for the benefit of the Fund and had appeared as Lear. Sitting in the audience with two of her sisters was a young woman called Hannah More. The daughters of a West Country schoolmaster, they were paying only their second visit to London. The previous week they had seen Garrick as Lusignan in *Zara*. 'Yes I have seen Him!' Miss More wrote excitedly to a neighbour at home:

> I have heard Him!—& the Music of his Voice, & the Lightening of his Eyes still act so forcibly on my Imagination, that I see, & hear Him still. . . . No Rant, no Pomp, for He never outsteps the Modesty of Nature. What an enchanting Simplicity! What an eternally varying Cadence, yet without one Stop, one Inequality!

Fresh from the provinces, she was indignant at the manners of the *blasé* London theatre-goers:

> I could have murder'd half the audience with great Composure for the inneffable *Non-chalence*, with which some of them behav'd. They took the Liberty to breathe, to look at the other Actors, nay even to blow their Noses, & fan themselves, with many other like Impertinences; nor was *He* clapped more, than that insipid Vegetable, the unpungent *Reddish*, unless indeed on his first Entrance . . .*

When she came to describe Garrick as Lear, mere excitement gave way to something approaching religious ecstasy:

> Surely he is above Mortality.—Is it possible He can be subject to Pain, Disease, & Death, like *other* Men?—And must those refulgent Eyes be ever clos'd in Night? Must those exquisite Powers be suspended, & that Silver Tongue be Stopp'd? His Talents are capacious beyond human credibility. I felt myself annihilated before Him, & every Faculty of my Soul was swallowed up in Attention. . . . I thought I should have been suffocated with Grief: it was not like the superficial Sorrow one feels at a well-acted Play, but the deep, substantial Grief of real Trouble . . . In the Midst of the Play I whisperd my Sister Patty—"I could never be angry with Him, if he refusd ten of my Tragedies."—In short I am quite ridiculous about Him.—Whether I eat, stand still, or walk—Still I can nothing but of *Garrick* talk. . . .
> Yet *my Heart ach'd* for the Depredations Time is beginning to make in his Face, which was not visible, till He appear'd in his own Form in the Epilogue; & of which He affectingly reminded us in these Words "I was *young* Hamlet once."[32]

---

* Reddish played the part of Osman.

Intelligent and widely read, Hannah More had for some years helped her four sisters in the running of a school they had founded in Bristol. After a lengthy engagement she had been jilted by a local squire who, overcome with conscience, provided her with an annuity of £200; this made her financially independent and allowed her to devote herself to literature. She had written a number of *Sacred Dramas* for the school, acquired something of a reputation locally as a composer of epitaphs and tried her hand at a tragedy—which the friend to whom she was now pouring out her London impressions had sent to Garrick the year before.*

That friend was Dr James Stonhouse, an elderly doctor turned clergyman. He had some acquaintance with Garrick—he quite often preached in Bath†—and he now wrote to tell him of Hannah's presence in London and to express the hope that he would see her; she was, he declared, 'a young Woman of an amazing Genius, & remarkable Humility'. He must have known his man, because he also transcribed for Garrick's benefit her rapturous account of her visits to Drury Lane.

It worked like a charm. Four days later a note was delivered to the house in Southampton Street where the Misses More had their lodgings.‡ Garrick presented his best compliments:

> He must desire them to give Mrs Garrick & him the Pleasure of their Company on Fryday—the Coach will be with them between Nine & ten—what can Mr Garrick say for the most flattering Compliment which he *Ever* receiv'd—? he must be Silent.[33]

It was the beginning of an unusually close and warm relationship. Over the next few years, the Garricks would come to regard Hannah More very much as they regarded 'the girls'—George's daughters. Indeed 'Madam Hannah'—Horace Walpole's affectionate name for her—is a chief authority for Garrick's home life in the brief years of his retirement. She was also admitted into a wider circle that included Reynolds, Johnson, Baretti, Burke and many of the bluestocking ladies. 'Her introduction to the great and the greatly-endowed,' as an early biographer rather quaintly put it, 'was sudden and general.'[34]

Meanwhile, there were changes afoot at the other house. Colman's health had never been robust, and he had lost much of his old sparkle. Seven years of management had taken their toll; most recently, after the Macbeth fiasco, Macklin had begun an action against him for 1,000 guineas.§ He now, in May 1774, sold

---

* It was called *The Inflexible Captive; or Regulus*. Garrick had turned it down on the ground that Havard had written a play on the same subject.

† William Prideaux Courtney, in his *DNB* article on Stonhouse, says that Garrick once reproved him 'for his faults of manner while ministering in church'. 'His egotism and love of flattery were excessive,' wrote Courtney.

‡ They had made a less happy choice on their first visit during the winter, when they had taken rooms in Henrietta Street, a thoroughfare which was home to a number of well-known brothels.

§ It dragged on for ten years. Lord Mansfield finally brokered a settlement under which Macklin agreed to accept £500.

his share of the patent and properties for £20,000 to the actor Thomas Hull and took himself off with evident relief to Bath.

Garrick was not yet prepared to follow his example. He had finally secured Mrs Yates for the new season, but before he could go off for the summer there were one or two other inflated egos that required his attention. According to Dibdin, Garrick aimed always to have an actress in reserve—what he called a 'bisque'—someone good enough to remind his more temperamental stars that they were not indispensable. That had been Elizabeth Younge's role when he recruited her shortly after Mrs Pritchard's retirement—to stop Mrs Barry from overstepping the mark too frequently. Now, six years on, she had extended the range of her accomplishments, and could try Garrick's patience in salary negotiations or the assignment of parts with the best of them. 'It gives me much concern that we are not yet agreed,' he wrote to her in the middle of May, '& indeed if you will not give up part of y^r demand, I fear, we shall still remain in a Situation disagreeable & very inconvenient to all parties.'

His differences with Miss Younge were resolved, and she stayed at Drury Lane for the remaining years of his managership. Frances Abington gave him an altogether harder time. Although she had agreed new terms at the beginning of May—a three-year contract, twelve pounds a week, with £60 for clothes and a benefit—she sent him a few short weeks later a catalogue of highly exaggerated grievances:

> Except for the very charming part which you Made for me in the Chances,
> I have not been permitted to speak one comic line in any new Piece these
> six years past—and Indeed Miss Pope is in possession of all the comic
> characters in every class without Exception, while my Rolle has been
> confined to Melancholy walking gentlewomen only.[35]

'What still complaining, my dear Mad^m, of my Injustice?' Garrick replied wearily (he had just succeeded in escaping to Hampton):

> For Heaven's sake let ye poor Manager have some respite from his many
> labours, & enjoy a few unmurmuring Weeks in the Summer; the Month
> of September will be soon here, & then it will be as Natural for you to
> find fault with him, as for Him to find fault with You . . . Every thing has
> it's time & season, & as the poor Devil has been ill lately, & very ill, let
> him rest from his torments till ye 17th of Sepr next . . .[36]

There was much to detain Garrick at Hampton in the summer of 1774, and he travelled about the shires much less than had been his recent custom. Pleased with what had been achieved at the Adelphi, he now commissioned Robert Adam to design a classical façade for his villa, and there, in late August, he offered a splendid entertainment.

It was partly a belated celebration of his twenty-fifth wedding anniversary, which had fallen in June. The *London Chronicle* reported the presence of 'a great number of Nobility and Gentry'. There was a concert of music and the Temple of Shakespeare and the gardens were illuminated by 6,000 lamps. There was also 'a most brilliant fire-work.' This was the work of the eminent Italian pyrotechnist Morel Torré,* who offered Garrick's guests his *pièce de résistance*, 'The Forge of Vulcan'. Vulcan is discovered at his forge behind Mount Etna with the Cyclops. As the fire blazes, Venus enters with Cupid, and begs them to make arrows for her son; they agree to do so, and there is a spectacular eruption of the volcano.

Over-indulgence at his *fête champêtre* laid Garrick low for a few days with an attack of what he called 'the nasty bile'. Someone who had not attended the festivities was his near-neighbour Kitty Clive. They had recently fallen out—the reason is not known—but as soon as he was well again, Garrick was anxious to mend his fences:

> If your heart (somewhat combustible like my own) has play'd off all the Squibs, & Rockets which lately occasion'd a little cracking & bouncing about me, & can receive again, the more gentle & pleasing firework of Love & friendship, I will be with you at Six this evening, to revive by the help of those Spirits in your tea Kettle lamp that flame, which was almost blown out by the flouncing of your petticoat, when my name was mention'd.

It is a captivating letter—when Garrick set out to charm and persuade, he was as thorough as in anything else he set his hand to. 'Can my Pivy know so little of me, to think that I prefer the Clack of Lords & Ladies to the enjoyment of humour & Genius?' he asked:

> Your Misconception about that fatal Champetre (the Devil take the Word) has made me so cross about every thing that belongs to it, that I curse all Squibs, Crackers, Rockets, Air-Ballons, Mines, serpents and Catherine Wheels, and can think of nothing & Wish for nothing, but laugh, Jig, humour, fun, pun, conundrum carriwitchet & Catherine Clive!—†

Lord Camden had been ill with jaundice and had not been 'fit for convivial riot', as he put it. 'Will you and your wife come and see us out of charity, and sacrifice wit for a few days to friendship?' he enquired. 'I do very much, dear Garrick, wish for a quiet day with you, when you are not interrupted every minute with authors and actors.'[38] There was time for a quick visit to Camden Place, but by early September, Garrick was once more immobilized although, to judge by the tone of his correspondence, in the best of spirits:

---

* Torré had supervised the fireworks for the marriage of Marie Antionette to the Dauphin four years previously. When he fell foul of a monopoly arrangement introduced into the pleasure-garden business in Paris in 1771, Monnet recommended him to Garrick, who effected introductions to the managers of Ranelagh and Marylebone. Torré was a versatile man of wide interests. He devised a licopodium torch for use on the stage at Drury Lane; the Forster Collection at the Victoria and Albert Museum contains a number of letters from him in which he offers to reveal to Garrick the secret of the cabbala and to give instructions 'for harvesting the Celestial Manna'.

† *Letters*, 855. A carriwitchet was a conundrum or puzzle.

Mr Garrick from his Bed, (confin'd there by the Gout) presents his respects
to Lord Ossory, & thanks him for as fine a haunch of Venison, as Ever
Quin roll'd an Amorous Eye at—*

'Dreadfull work,' he wrote to another correspondent, 'a Lame General & so
strong an Alliance in ye field!' and when 17 September arrived, the first day of
the new season, the *London Chronicle* announced that he was still at Hampton,
'much indisposed with the gout'. The curtain went up on time, for all that. And
rose, what's more, on a sprightly new piece of Garrick's own—the nineteenth
to come from his pen since he had first tried his hand at writing for the stage
with *Lethe* thirty-four years previously.

* *Letters*, 858. The venison had come from the Ossory estate at Ampthill in Bedfordshire.

34

The Monstrous Regiment of Actresses

The bonne-bouche with which Garrick chose to open the season was called *The Meeting of the Company*, a brief prelude which took the place of the customary 'occasional prologue'. He cast it in the form of a burlesque-rehearsal, a formula he had employed in 1767 in *A Peep Behind the Curtain*.

The curtain rises on Drury Lane at the start of a season, with players returning from their summer engagements in the provinces and singers and dancers milling about on the stage, getting under the feet of the painters and technicians who are battling to prepare the house for the opening. As Molière did in *L'Impromptu de Versailles*, Garrick offers the audience a candid peep behind the scenes and for the most part allows his actors to play themselves.

'We shall never be ready if you don't give up the stage to us,' grumbles Phill the carpenter:

> Lower the clouds there, Rag, and bid Jack Trundle sweep out the thunder-truck. We had very slovenly storms last season . . . What with coronations, installations, Portsmouth Reviews, masquerades, Jubilees, Fetes Champetres and the devil, we have no rest at all. Master's head is always at work, and we are never idle. If you want the perpetual motion, let 'em come to our theatre.

There is no plot to speak of. The central character, a pompous dramatist, treats the company to a fatuous lecture on the art of acting:

> Shakespeare has said—a silly, empty, creature!
> 'Never o'erstep the modesty of nature.'
> I say you *must*. . .

Garrick has some fun at the expense of his less-talented fellow-tragedians by making Weston, a member of the company celebrated for his low comedy roles, boast that he can play tragedy with the best of them:

TRAGEDY ACTOR. Don't imagine, Sir, because you can make an audience laugh in Jerry Sneak, Dr. Last, etc.,* that you can speak heroic verse and touch the passions. (*Struts about.*)

---

* Sneak and Last were both characters in plays by Foote.

WESTON. Why not? I can set my arms so, take two strides, roar as well as the best of you, and look like an owl.

TRAGEDY ACTOR. (*with contempt*) Is there nothing else requisite to form a tragedian?

WESTON. O, yes, the perriwig maker to make me a bush, a tailor a hoop petticoat, a carpenter a truncheon, a shoemaker high heels and cork soles. And as for strange faces and strange noises I can make them myself.

Garrick is even-handed in his satire, however, and comedians must also sit in the stocks:

> Observe in comedy to frisk about.
> Never stand still. Jerk, work; fly in, fly out,
> Your faults conceal in flutter and in hurry,
> And with snip, snap, the poet's meaning worry,
> Like bullies hide your wants in bounce and vapor.
> If mem'ry fails, take snuff, laugh, curse and caper.
> Hey, Jack! what!—damn it! ha, ha! Cloud, dull, sad,
> Cuss it! Hell devil! Woman, wine, drunk, mad!

Garrick also gets in a dig at the likes of Mrs Abington, with her tendency to last-minute indisposition—a thrust cleverly combined with an allusion to his own all too frequent illnesses:

WESTON. There's a pleasure in being ill which none but actors know.

PARSONS. I don't understand you.

WESTON. It vexes a manager and pays him in kind.

The players finally tire of the dramatist's stupidities. Left alone on a deserted stage he struggles briefly, but unsuccessfully, to control his resentment: 'It won't do. The devil has got the better, and I must leave my curses behind me.' Now it is the audience's turn to look in the mirror that Garrick holds up to them:

> May this house be always as empty as it is now. Or if it must fill, let it be with fine ladies to disturb the actors, fine gentlemen to admire themselves, and fat citizens to snore in the boxes. May the pit be filled with nothing but crabbed critics, unemployed actors, and managers' orders. May places be kept in the green boxes without being paid for, and may the galleries never bring good humor or horse laughs with them again . . .

The Meeting of the Company runs to little more than 430 lines, but it was a well-judged start to what would inevitably be a testing season. 'An Excellent Lesson to all perfomers,' opined Hopkins. Garrick knew that Hull would be straining every nerve to prove himself as Colman's successor at Covent Garden, and that the Barrys, for all their advancing years and tiresome ways, represented an accession of strength to the rival company. But Phill the carpenter was right: 'Master's head is always at work, and we are never idle.' In the course of the season, although often far from well and still handicapped by the absence of his brother, Garrick would offer the Drury Lane audience an assortment of eleven new pieces, whereas Hull at Covent Garden came up with only six.

Managerial input from Garrick's new partner was slight. Willoughby Lacy rather fancied himself as an actor, and had made his début at the new Theatre Royal, Birmingham, at the beginning of September, playing the lead in Nathaniel Lee's *Alexander the Great; or, The Rival Queens*, opposite Mrs Yates. Garrick seems to have thought he showed some promise: 'I wish You would go there & see him,' he wrote to his brother Peter, 'I think you will be pleased.'[1] Peter's verdict, if he returned one, has not survived, but the *London Chronicle* reported that 'Mr Lacy, like all young performers the first night, seemed a good deal confused.'*

A month later he appeared at Drury Lane in the same part. The bills described him as 'a Young Gentleman, first appearance on this stage'. The convention that players making their début should enjoy the protection of anonymity was a venerable one, but to resort to it on this occasion was singularly pointless—there cannot have been a soul in the theatre who was ignorant of his identity. Garrick wrote an occasional prologue to introduce him, which was spoken by King:

> Twice our young hero, who for glory tow'rs,
> In fields less dang'rous try'd his unknown pow'rs;
> Like a young swimmer, whom his fears command,
> In shallow streams first ventur'd from the land;
> 'Till bolder grown, the rougher wave he stems,
> Plunges from giddy heights into the Thames . . .

'This image is certainly an apt one,' commented the *Westminster Magazine*, 'though, it is no great compliment to the audiences of Norwich and Birmingham.' Lacy himself was judged less impressive:

> His figure is at present lank, awkward, and unengaging; his voice distinctly powerful, but inharmonious; his action *outre*, vulgar and forced: his attitudes unnatural, affected and disgustful; and his delivery a continued rant, without proper change, a pleasing variety, or a just discrimination of the necessary difference of tone demanded by the different passions.†

Mrs Yates chose to make her return to the Drury Lane stage in *Electra*, which Dr Francklin had adapted from Voltaire's *Orestes*. Garrick gave it the full treatment. De Loutherbourg's designs included a perspective of Argos, the palace of Aegisthus and the tomb of Agamemnon—'warm and spirited,' enthused the *Westminster Magazine*. The reception for Mrs Yates was only lukewarm, however, and the play limped through no more than three nights:

---

* *London Chronicle*, 13–15 September 1774. Shortly afterwards he acted a second time at Norwich.
† *Westminster Magazine*, October 1774. Hopkins was less severe: 'He is very Tall, & Thin, a good Voice but His Fright took away from it's power.'

From its want of business, it is a very heavy, tedious performance. Most of the scenes are mere declamations; and a certain air of coldness and apathy, which is the peculiar characteristic of French drama, runs thro the whole, which must ever render it unpleasing as well as uninteresting to an English Audience.[2]

The frequency of Garrick's own performances had declined drastically over the years. In his prime, before he had gone off to France and Italy in 1763, he had averaged over 90 appearances in a season. Since then he had never played on more than 35 occasions, and in 1774–5 the pressure of his managerial duties was such he would appear only 22 times, generally in parts such as Benedick or Abel Drugger which he could have performed in his sleep.*

He still took great pains to seek out and bring on new talent, though he did not always pick winners. When a revival of *The Country Girl* was announced in the autumn, the *Middlesex Journal, and Evening Advertiser* told its readers, with the assurance of someone who has had it from the horse's mouth, that this was to serve as a vehicle for a star in the making:

> This lively lass, of eighteen, having been under the tuition of the great *theatrical school-master*, who has been indefatigable in his endeavours to introduce a pupil on the stage, who shall be an honor to himself, and an acquisition to the dramatic world, is expected to burst upon us with unparalleled *eclat* . . . .

The young lady in question was called Robins, and in a diary note on the night of her début, Hopkins confirmed that Garrick had devoted a lot of time to her. 'An agreeable figure as a Woman & also in Breeches,' he added—'she has a particular Cuddenish way with her wch is not amiss in this Character, but I am afraid it will be a disadvantage to her in any other.' As cudden meant a dolt or a fool, that did not sound promising. Later in the season, when she played Leonora in *The Padlock*, Hopkins noted 'Miss Robins very bad sung out of Tune. Some hisses.' She had a minor role as a Country Lass in *May Day* a year later, and thereafter dropped out of theatrical history.

Quite the most ambitious of Garrick's offerings that autumn was a piece called *The Maid of the Oaks*. The *Westminster Magazine* was severe:

> Had it not appeared obvious that the whole was intended as a mere vehicle for the *splendid spectacle*, we do not suppose, in spite of the managers Orders and Puffs, that the author's labors would have been tolerated. The very excellent scenery, however, of the ingenious Mr Loutherbourg preserved this piece from that damnation, which as a dramatic production, it justly merited.[3]

The author in question was General John Burgoyne, who was then in his early

---

* He did, however, on 2 December and 12 December, reclaim Hamlet for two nights from 'Gentleman' Smith, who had assumed a great many of his roles.

fifties. A member of the best clubs, a friend of Reynolds and a reckless gambler, his life had been colourful. A cornet of light dragoons at eighteen, he eloped with the daughter of the Earl of Derby at twenty-three and was obliged to live for some years in France to escape his creditors. He had distinguished himself in action against the Spaniards in Portugal in the 1760s and had been elected to Parliament. He had argued for a degree of governmental control over the affairs of the East India Company, and the previous year he had launched a violent attack in the Commons on Lord Clive.

Burgoyne was also, like so many of his class, devoted to amateur theatricals, and he had originally written *The Maid of the Oaks* as an entertainment for the wedding of his wife's nephew, Lord Stanley. The marriage had been celebrated in June by an elaborate *fête champêtre* which went on for several days at the Burgoynes' estate, The Oaks, near Epsom;* Garrick, who would normally run a mile rather than become involved in private theatricals, seems to have been roped in to help with the preparations.† It is not clear whose idea it was to extend Burgoyne's original two-act masque to the five-act extravaganza that eventually saw the light of day at Drury Lane. It is possible that Garrick was leant on while he was at The Oaks—Murphy has a feline passage implying something of the sort.‡ It may equally be the case, however, that he recognized the scope which an enlarged piece would offer to the talents of de Loutherbourg, encouraged Burgoyne to work it up and put the finishing touches to it himself.§ As was so often the case, his judgement of what would play well was sound. Aided by de Loutherbourg's representation of a celestial garden with a prospect of the Temple of Love, *The Maid of the Oaks* ran for twenty-four nights and did excellent business for the house treasury.¶

During the summer, Henry Woodfall had been tried before Lord Mansfield and convicted of publishing a letter in the *Public Advertiser* containing 'scandalous, traiterous, and seditious libel' on the Glorious Revolution of 1688. (His brother William, who had published the same letter in the *Morning Chronicle*), was also convicted.) Now, in November, they were both fined and sentenced to serve three months in the King's Bench Prison. Garrick, intensely loyal in his friendships, was quick to express his concern, but managed to do so in a tone of encouraging chirpiness:

* Stanley, who became the twelfth Earl of Derby in succession to his father two years later, would subsequently establish Epsom's two best-known horse races, the Derby and the Oaks.
† There is a reference in his correspondence to having met someone at Lord Stanley's in May. (*Letters*, 863.)
‡ 'The General was known to be a polite scholar. To his taste for literature he added a pleasing elegance of manners. Garrick was glad of an opportunity to shew his respect for a writer of that class.' (*Murphy*, ii, 106.)
§ That was certainly Murphy's view. The passage quoted above continues: 'He attended to the conduct of the plot, and, by the touches of his pen, gave new life and spirit to the dialogue.'
¶ The next chapter in Burgoyne's life proved less successful. Sent out to serve in North America and Canada, he was obliged in October 1777 to surrender to General Gates at Saratoga, and returned home to a storm of critical abuse.

... Can I be of the least Service to You, or Y^r Brother Culprit? tho full of business, if you have ye least desire to see Me, I will go to You directly—

I never see You while You are hopping between London & Islington, but now they have Shorten'd your tether, & you are got into a Cage, one may take a peep at You.*

Garrick also kept his French friendships in good repair. Early in December he wrote to congratulate Suard on his election to the Academy and on his acceptance speech: 'Votre discours me plait infinem^t,' he wrote:

It is so closely *Weav'd* & *wrought*, & the *piece* (if you'll allow me to pun) altogeather is so well *work'd up*, that You may be assur'd that no Moths, bugs or any litterary Vermin can eat into it, or befoul it—[4]

George was still in the hands of the doctors in Bath, although showing signs of improvement. 'I was much rejoic'd at your letter,' Garrick told him in the middle of December, '& I hope your friend Dr Faulkener will land you safe again amongst Us.'† He was writing at the theatre: 'I have this moment finish'd ye long part of Hamlet, & my hand trembles while I am writing wth ye worst Pen in ye world.' Out front, as he wrote, a new piece by Dibdin, described as a ballad farce, was having a rough ride. It was called *The Cobler; or, a Wife of Ten Thousand.* It had been roundly hissed when it opened three nights previously and Garrick clearly had no great opinion of it: 'There is a good ballad or two, ye rest Washy & Slop Dawdry.'‡

Two days later, William Hopkins also wrote to George. 'If you have any regard for your health, don't come home till it is perfectly restored,' he told him; 'for the fatigue of the Theatre will soon make a Relapse.' Some of George's duties had been assumed in his absence by Tom King, an arrangement which Hopkins did not think was working well:

I believe Mr King is not charm'd with his situation of deputy manager.—
The Theatre seems quite Melancholy without you, and I assure you I find a great want of you . . .

Hopkins's letter also makes plain that Garrick's temper had not improved in George's absence:

Your Brother is very well but has not forgot to Scold I have enough of that . . . so much that my Spirits are not able to bear it, good god what an

---

* *Letters*, 871. Woodfall lived at Canonbury, then very much in the country.
† William Falconer (1744–1824) was a highly regarded young doctor who had studied at Edinburgh and Leyden and established himself in practice in Bath four years previously. He later became physician to the Bath General Hospital. A Fellow of the Royal Society at twenty-nine, he wrote and published extensively, not only on medical topics but also on geography, religion and gardening.
‡ *Letters*, 873. In the event 'Dibdin's Nonsense', as Garrick described it to George, hobbled on for nine nights.

angel He would be if he would do his business with good temper but that's impossible!—[5]

A new comedy, *The Choleric Man*, was to have its première the following week. 'I have my fears about its success,' Hopkins told George. 'I can't say I am charm'd with it.' Murphy was predictably offensive: 'Mr Cumberland appears again! His prolific muse was delivered of another bantling.'* Garrick did his best for it, and his epilogue, spoken by Mrs Abington, was much applauded. The *Westminster Magazine*, as it so often was, was sniffy, finding the plot 'ill-conducted', but the device of presenting the piece in harness with the season's Christmas panto-mime—'the Choleric Man with Harlequin's Jacket wrapt about him,' as Hopkins put it—secured quite tolerable houses.

Hopkins wrote again to George in the middle of January with a further instalment of Drury Lane gossip; his letter suggests that Garrick's brother was rather more than the plodding dogsbody he has sometimes been made out to be, and that his skill in oiling the wheels was quite important to the functioning of the company:

> I assure you we want your Company much in the Theatre; Mr K— is getting the illwill of many of the Company daily; & many prayers & hearty wishes for your health & Safe return are often given in the Green Room; your good Natur'd offices in reconciling the little differences &c that often happen are much wanted. . . . Miss Younge has been in her airs for this Week or Ten days past & has given us a good deal of trouble—but 'tis what we must Expect from that Lady—[6]

On the last day of 1774 Garrick appeared as Lusignan in *Zara*. He was in good form. 'My dearest Sir,' wrote George Steevens, 'I think you never played Lusignan so happily as on Saturday night; at least you never affected me in it so much before.' He was violently critical of the rest of the cast, however:

> Are there words to be found that can convey any adequate idea of their incomparable badness? Had I been a cannibal, I think I could scarce have ventured to sup upon them, so surely should I have been sick with gorging such cat's-meat and dog's-meat. Have you no better stuff behind the scenes? Or can you be so mistaken as to suppose you need these wretched foils to show you off to advantage? . . . To say the truth, I never saw such a miserable pack of strollers in quiet possession of a Theatre Royal.[7]

Covent Garden, meanwhile, was serving up a brand of holiday fare calcu-lated to raise the blood pressure of purists quite sharply. On 6 January they spatchcocked into their afterpiece the first London appearance of Signor Rossignol. The bills promised that he would perform 'his celebrated IMITATIONS of BIRDS with his throat only, AND afterwards, in the Character of a Country

---

* According to the *OED*, probably a corruption of the German *bänkling* meaning bastard—'a child begotten on a bench, and not in the marriage-bed'.

Fiddler will lead the orchestra in a Concerto on *A Violin Without Strings*'.

Critical opinion was divided. 'For heaven's sake recommend them to banish that Italian whistler from their stage,' a Mr No-Whistler wrote stuffily to the *Morning Post*. 'I have often been tormented by such nonsense in the Chop-House, but never before on the British Theatre.' Another correspondent, on the other hand, was eager to advertise what he and his brother could do in the same line:

> Tho'f I am only a country barbur, I hav grate taluns for the stage; I can squeake like a pig, grunt lyk a saw, and nay like a horce. I can do sum burds tow, and will do the owle and the cookow with the Itallyun man at Common Garden, for any munny. . . . I hav a bruther who is a very gud actor, and can braey lyk an ass, which, we heard will grately recummend him to the managers of Common Garden, and can play upon a Jews trump without his hands, Your Humble Servant, John BUM.[8]

Drury Lane was slower than Mr Bum to appreciate how broad a target was being offered to it; only on 1 February did Garrick get round to putting Tom Weston up to deliver a satirical epilogue.*

Garrick had been distressed and embarrassed, in the early days of the New Year, by the circumstances surrounding the death of Henry Mossop. After his bankruptcy in 1772, with Garrick listed as his chief creditor, Mossop had settled for a time in the south of France. The warmer climate did little for him, and returning home, he had died two days after Christmas. 'A most disagreeable affair has happen'd,' Garrick wrote to Colman, who was in Bath:

> Mossop on his death-bed sends me his play, begging that I would Ease his Mind in his last moments, by taking his play, and doing all in my power with it for ye service of his Creditors—he is dead, & I have ye Comedy— I have not yet read a speech—a Friend has, & says it is like the *Patron*, wth out ye humour—What a scrape—†

Garrick offered to pay the funeral expenses, but an uncle of Mossop's, a bencher at the Inner Temple, to whom 'out of delicacy' he first wrote, declined the proposition. A week later, there came a letter from the Reverend David Williams, the Welsh dissenting minister and friend of Mossop's who three years previously had savaged Garrick in a singularly abusive pamphlet. In writing now to tell him about a conversation with Mossop on the night he died, his tone was very different:

---

* Weston was accompanied by Garrick's English mastiff, Dragon. The *Westminster Magazine* noted that as it was his first appearance on the stage, 'he, like all young performers of true feeling, seemed a good deal frightened'. He quickly recovered himself, however, and 'performed his part very *chastely*'. This presumably means that the dog did not lift its leg.

† *Letters*, 875. *The Patron* was a three-act comedy of Foote's, first performed at the Haymarket in 1764.

... He often cried out, "Oh, my dear friend, how mean and little does Mr. Garrick's present behaviour make me appear in your eyes, to whom I have given so different an idea of him! Great God forgive me! Witness, my dear Williams, that I die, not only in charity with him, but that I honour him as a virtuous and great man. God Almighty bless and prosper him for ever!"[9]

Garrick replied by return. 'Your Account of poor Mossop's death distress'd me greatly,' he wrote:

> With regard to his returning to us, it was his own peculiar resolution of not letting us know his terms, that prevented his engagement at our Theatre, had I known his distress I Shoud most certainly have reliev'd it—he was too great a Credit to our Profession, not to have done all in our Power to have made him *easy*, at least, if not *happy*—[10]

The ladies of the company continued to test the manager's patience. The King and Queen had commanded a performance of *Twelfth Night*, and Miss Younge was making difficulties about appearing. 'If you are able to play Viola, I suppose you will,' Garrick wrote acidly, 'as his Majesty of England, not the copper one of Drury-lane, commands it.'[11] Miss Younge agreed to appear, but felt herself badly done by, telling Garrick that she could not think herself 'humanely treated, when I complain and feel the bad effects of playing with a cough, that you should send me this haughty style of letter'.[12] Garrick, exasperated beyond measure, blew his top:

> I am very warm & sincere in my Attachments, but if I find any Actor, or Actress distressing me or ye Business unjustly or fantastically I will with draw my Attachment ye Moment, that they shew Me they have none. the Theatre is quite destroy'd by a New fashion among Us—I was long ye Slave of the Stage, I play'd for Everybody's Benefit, & Even reviv'd parts for them, & sometimes Acted new ones—this was at a time When by Myself I could fill a house—that favour luckily for Me the Publick still continues, or We might play to Empty benches—[13]

January saw the première of one of the handful of eighteenth-century plays that have survived to the present day.* It saw the light of day not at Drury Lane but at Covent Garden, and on the first night it flopped resoundingly. 'This comedy was acted so imperfectly,' wrote that month's *Westminster Magazine*, 'either from the timidity of the actors on a first night's performance, or from an improper distribution of the parts, that it was generally disapproved.'

Richard Brinsley Sheridan was the son of old Tom Sheridan. At Harrow he had been taunted as 'a poor player's son'. He was now twenty-three. Three years previously he had eloped with the beautiful young singer Elizabeth Linley, whose

---

* The only others to have lasted are *Douglas* and *She Stoops to Conquer*, both first seen at Covent Garden, and *The Jealous Wife*, *The Clandestine Marriage* and *The West Indian*, all first produced at Drury Lane.

earlier betrothal to a wealthy bachelor worth £10,000 a year had given Sam
Foote the raw materials for his comedy *The Maid of Bath*. Sheridan had subsequently fought two duels with another of her many admirers and very nearly
died from wounds to his neck and chest.

The Rivals was his first play. It had been in rehearsal since mid-November.
'Sheridan's Comedy has raised great Expectations in yᵉ Publick,' Garrick wrote
to George Steevens in the middle of January,[14] and yet on the night Edward
Shuter as Sir Anthony Absolute seemed scarcely to know his lines, and John Lee,
as Sir Lucius O'Trigger, appeared disastrously miscast. The *Morning Chronicle*
wrote that his interpretation 'scarce equals the picture of a respectable Hottentot;
gabbling in an uncouth dialect neither Welch, English nor Irish'. When he was
struck by an apple from the pit, he stepped out of character and angrily challenged
his tormentors. 'By the powers,' he shouted, 'is it personal; is it me or the matter?'
It was the only time during the evening, remarked Sheridan, that his Irish brogue
was perfect.

After two nights, the piece was withdrawn. Sheridan did some extensive
rewriting, and John Lee was replaced by Lawrence Clinch. When it re-opened
ten days later Sir Lucius seemed several degrees more respectable, Sir Anthony
several degrees less lascivious and the text had been pruned of some of its more
salacious *double entendres*. 'I see this play will creep,' Garrick is supposed to
have said early in the performance; but when the curtain came down he said 'I
see this play will run.'

So it did—helped by a little judicious puffing. Sheridan had been quick to
learn the tricks of the trade. 'Aristarchus', in the *Morning Chronicle*, conceded
that the play 'from some levities and want of experience was near being crushed
the first night'. It would now, however, 'certainly stand foremost in the list of
modern comedies'. *Ipse dixit*. Aristarchus was Sheridan himself. He had found
the materials for his comedy largely in his own history; he had cheerfully
appropriated many of the theatrical clichés of the day; he had created that joyous
figure of linguistic anarchy Mrs Malaprop; and he had injected into the essentially
static repertoire of the two patent theatres a robust new strain of comic life.

Garrick, meanwhile, was once again caught up in tedious exchanges with one
of his leading ladies:

> Mrs. Abington has kept her room with a fever for some days past, or she
> would have complained to Mr. Garrick of a letter she has received from
> Mr. Hopkins, dictated in the spirit of incivility and misrepresentation. . . .
> She apprehends that for some time past she has had enemies about Mr.
> Garrick; and it is to them she supposes herself indebted for the very great
> change in Mr. Garrick's behaviour, after all the fatigue she has undergone,
> and the disappointments she has experienced in respect to the business
> that was by agreement to be done for her this winter . . .[15]

The lengthy reply which Garrick drafted must have made serious inroads into
his weekend leisure at Hampton. He began quietly enough with a literary

Fanny Abington – 'the worst of bad women' as Garrick eventually came to regard her. Her box-office appeal was undeniable, but she became increasingly temperamental and manipulative, and in the closing years of his management they quarrelled with increasing frequency. She is seen here as Estifania in Fletcher's Rule a Wife and Have a Wife. *(Bell's British Theatre, Vol. 4, 1780)*

allusion—'The famous french Writer Fontenelle takes notice that nothing is so difficult to a Man of Sensibility, as writing to a Lady even with just grounds of Complaint'—but suavity was soon swept aside by a mixture of indignation and scorn:

Whenever You are really ill, I feel both for You & myself; but ye Servant said last Wedy that you were Well, & had a great deal of Company:
    You mention *your great fatigue*: What is the stage come to, if I must continually hear of your *hard labour*, when from the beginning of the season to this time, you have not play'd more than *twice* a Week? Mrs Oldfield perform'd Lady Townly for 29 Nights successively . . .*

He was now well launched:

Let us now examine how just & genteel Your complaint is against me: I promis'd You, that I would procure a Character of consequence to be written on purpose for You, and that it should be Your own fault, if you were not on the highest pinnacle of Yr profession—I have been at great pains, & you know it, to be as good as my word—

Garrick is almost certainly referring to *The Maid of the Oaks*, in which Mrs Abington had been given the part of Lady Bab Lardoon:

I directed & assisted the Author to make a small character, a very considerable one for You, I spar'd no Expence in dresses, Musick, scenes & decorations for the piece, and now the *fatigue of Acting* this Character, is very unjustly, as well as unkindly brought against me: had you play'd this part 40 times, instead of 20, my gains would be less than by any other Succesful play, I have produc'd in my Management—

Having got all this off his chest, Garrick decided for some reason not to send the letter. Before many weeks had passed, however, Mrs Abington succeeded in provoking him to an even greater pitch of fury. The trouble began when Reddish, being as Hopkins put it, 'a little out of his Senses', was unable to play the part of Morcar in *Matilda*. Fresh bills were hastily put up at two in the afternoon announcing a change to *The West Indian*, but Mrs Abington sent word to say that she could not play her part of Miss Rusport at such short notice, and the management was obliged to borrow an actress from Covent Garden to fill the gap.
    Garrick, who had been suffering from an attack of the stone, was in a great rage, and brushed her excuses aside contemptuously:

You want a day's notice to perform a character you play'd originally & which you have appeared in several times this season; you knew our distress yesterday almost as soon as I did, & did not plead the want of a day's

* Anne Oldfield had indeed played in *The Provok'd Husband*, although she did so in 1728, when Garrick was a schoolboy of eleven in Lichfield. He had probably read about it in Colley Cibber's *Apology*, published in 1740.

notice, cloaths, hair dresser &c, but you refus'd on account of your health, tho' you were in spirits & rehearsing a new farce. . . . It was happy for us that we found a lady tho' not of our company, who had a feeling for our distress, & reliev'd us from it, without requiring 2 days notice, or wanting any thing but an opportunity to shew her politeness—these are serious truths Madam, & are not to be described like the lesser peccadillos of a fine Lady—*

In the course of defending herself, Mrs Abington, somewhat rashly, put her head on the block: 'If Mr. Garrick really thinks Mrs. Abington so bad a subject as he is pleased to describe her in all the companies he goes into,' she wrote, 'she thinks his remedy is very easy, and is willing on her part to release him from so great an inconvenience as he pleases.'[16] The temptation to pocket the proffered resignation must have been strong, but Garrick resisted it. In responding, however, he may in the heat of the moment have let slip more than he intended about his own plans:

> As to your wishes of delivering me from the inconvenience of your engage-ment, that, I hope, will soon be another's concern; my greatest comfort is, that I shall soon be deliver'd from the capriciousness, inconsistency, injus-tice, & unkindness of those, to whom I always intended the greatest good in my power.

He added an angry footnote: 'Your refusing to play this evening has obliged me, tho' but just recover'd from a dreadful disorder to risk a relapse.'†

A few days previously, while Garrick was still confined to his room with the stone, it was Mrs Yates's turn to be in hot water. She had had a great success a few weeks previously in Robert Jephson's new tragedy *Braganza*, but on 4 March there was uproar at the theatre when it was discovered that she had left before speaking the epilogue. 'The House was clamorous and would not give up their right,' wrote Hopkins. Vernon went on to explain that Mrs Yates had been overcome by hoarseness, but he was shouted down, and so, a little later, was her husband: 'They told him bluntly they did not want to see him, but to hear his wife, whose obstinacy and pride had betrayed her into the present insult.' The clamour continued for an hour and a half before the farce could begin.

Garrick had invested a lot of time and effort in *Braganza* and de Loutherbourg had again been called upon to provide new scenes and dresses. Conditions for rehearsal were not ideal. Since the late 1760s, Jephson had served as Master of

---

* The actress who saved Garrick's bacon was Jane Barsanti, who had created the role of Lydia Languish in *The Rivals* two months previously. She was also a singer, and had been a favourite pupil of Dr Burney's. Highfill records, oddly enough, that she modelled her social behaviour on Mrs Abington's—'or on that part of Mrs Abington's behaviour which suited her strict moral canons'.

† *Letters*, 893. Garrick played Lusignan in *Zara* that evening, though there is no indication from the playbills that this was a late change. Her health and spirits were so much hurt by his 'unprovoked incivility,' Mrs Abington had told him, 'that she is not able to say *what* or when she can play'.

the Horse to successive Lords-Lieutenant of Ireland, and revisions to the text arrived in dribs and drabs by the Dublin packet.

On the first night, Hopkins had his reservations: 'the four first Acts are heavy & want incident & Plot'. Horace Walpole, on the other hand, was for once in raptures: '*Braganza* was acted with prodigious success,' he wrote to Mason:

> The audience, the most impartial I ever saw, sat mute for two acts, and seemed determined to judge for themselves, and not to be the dupes of the encomiums that had been so lavishly trumpeted . . . but at the catastrophe in the fifth they were transported. They clapped, shouted, hussaed, cried bravo, and thundered out applause.

Walpole was particularly warm in his praise of Mrs Yates; but then he was the author of the epilogue.

For his benefit in March, Tom King chose to appear in a somewhat unusual double bill. He took the part of Lucio, the 'fantastic' in Shakespeare's *Measure for Measure*, which had not been seen at Drury Lane for sixteen years, and he was also Sir John Trotley in a miniature comedy called *Bon Ton* which Garrick had written many years previously but which had never been staged. When it was published later in the year, Garrick wrote that he had offered it to King 'as a token of regard for one, who, during a long engagement, was never known, unless confined by real illness, to disappoint the Public, or distress the Managers', economically combining a compliment to King with a rebuke to certain temperamental ladies of the company who effortlessly caused disappointment and distress several times in a season.

The evening made King a handsome profit of £224, and although Hopkins recorded that there were good performances and 'the highest Applause', he also noted that 'the Play was very Imperfect'. Garrick, who for some reason was not present at the first night, seems to have agreed. A note survives which he sent shortly afterwards to Colman, who had written a stylish and witty prologue:

> The author of Bon Ton presents his best Comp^{ts} & thanks to Mr Colman for his excellent Prologue, & would wish to add to ye obligation by desiring him to look over the Farce & draw his pencil thro' the parts his judgment would omit in ye next representation—*

Garrick did not immediately disclose his authorship. Word got about that the piece was the work of John Burgoyne, who had written *The Maid of the Oaks*; it appeared, wrote the *Westminster Magazine*, 'to be a cut from the same cloth, ornamented with a little of Mr Garrick's fringe'.[17] The audience thought much better of it than the critics. March was late for a new piece, and it was seen only eight times before the summer closure, but it got eighteen outings in the course of the following season and quickly established itself as a highly popular afterpiece; it

---

* *Letters*, 898. The prologue, spoken by King, was extremely well received, and there were frequent calls for it during the rest of the season.

held its place in the repertoire well into the nineteenth century, on both sides of the Atlantic.

Garrick must have written it in the middle 1750s, at about the time he wrote *Lilliput* and *The Male Coquette*. All three demonstrate his admiration for the astringencies of Restoration comedy. The satire in *Bon Ton; or High Life above Stairs*, is directed at the extravagance with which fashionable families embraced the manners—and morals—they had encountered abroad. 'What a great revolution in this family, in the space of fifteen months!' exclaims Miss Lucretia Tittup, who is conducting an affair with her cousin's husband Lord Minikin:

> We went out of England a very awkward, regular, good English family! but half a year in France, and a winter passed in the warmer climate of Italy, have ripen'd our minds to every refinement of ease, dissipation, and pleasure.

Honest Sir John Trotley, Miss Tittup's uncle, up for a visit from the country, is unimpressed:

> My niece Lucretia is so be-fashioned and be-devil'd, that nothing I fear, can save her; however, to ease my conscience, I must try; but what can be expected from young women of these times, but sallow looks, wild schemes, saucy words, and loose morals!—they lie a-bed all day, sit up all night; if they are silent, they are gaming, and if they talk, 'tis either scandal or infidelity; and that they may look what they are, their heads are all feather, and round their necks are twisted, rattle-snake tippets—*O Tempora, O Mores!*

Miss Tittup was played by Mrs Abington, and she chose to appear in the part when her own benefit came round some days later; as a mainpiece she decided on Bickerstaffe's *The Hypocrite*, in which she was Charlotte. Sir Joshua Reynolds, who was a fervent admirer, and who painted her several times,* took forty places in the front boxes. His guests included Johnson and Boswell. 'Johnson sat on the seat directly behind me,' Boswell wrote, 'and as he could neither see not hear at such a distance from the stage, he was wrapped up in grave abstraction, and seemed quite a cloud, amidst all the sunshine and glitter and gaiety.'†

Boswell went on to supper at Topham Beauclerk's, and there encountered Garrick, who subjected him to some gentle ribbing about the clannishness, or, as he put it, the 'nationality' of the Scots:

> Why now, the Adams are as liberal-minded men as any in the world: but, I don't know how it is, all their workmen are Scotch. You are, to be sure,

---

* Notably in 'Mrs Abington as the Comic Muse', a pendant to his 'Mrs Siddons as the Tragic Muse'. The picture is now at Waddesdon Manor.

† Boswell records, however, that Reynolds himself did not make it to the theatre: 'Sir Joshua himself dined with so many sea-officers, Mediterranean friends as he called them; and I suppose they had drank like fishes, for he did not appear at the play, when he should have been at our head.' (Ryskamp, Charles, and Pottle, Frederick A., *Boswell: The Ominous Years*, London, 1963, 102.)

wonderfully free from that nationality: but so it happens, that you employ the only Scotch shoeblack in London.[18]

Garrick's indifferent health in those early months of 1775 had little effect on his incurable sociability. Hannah More and her sisters were once again in London. 'Yesterday Mr Garrick called upon us,' Sarah wrote in a letter home:

> A volume of Pope lay upon the table; we asked him to read; and he went through the latter part of the 'Essay on Man.' He was exceedingly good-humoured, and expressed himself quite delighted with our eager desire for information; and when he had satisfied one interrogatory, said, 'Now, madam, what next!' . . . He sat with us from half-past twelve till three, reading and criticising.[19]

He was frequently up with the lark, and quite often out and about at a most unchristian hour. 'Early in the morning, this most entertaining of mortals came,' Fanny Burney wrote in her journal one Sunday in March:

> He marched up stairs immediately into the study where my Father was having his Hair Dressed . . . He then began to look very gravely at the Hair Dresser; he was Himself in a most odious scratch wig, which Nobody but himself could dare be seen in: He put on a look, in the Abel Drugger style, of *envy* & sadness as he examined the Hair Dresser's progress;—& when he had done, he turned to him with a dejected Face, & said '—pray Sir,—could you touch up *This* a little? taking hold of his frightful scratch. The man only Grinned, & left the Room. . . .
> My Father asked him to Breakfast; but he said he was Engaged at Home with Mr Boswell and Mr Twiss. He then took the latter off, as he did also Dr Arne, very comically; & afterwards Dr Johnson, in a little Conversation concerning his borrowing a Book of him;—'David—will you lend me Petraca?' 'Yes, Sir.' 'David,—you sigh?'—'Sir, you shall have it!' Accordingly, the Book—finely bound!—was sent; but scarse had he received it, when uttering a Latin Ejaculation, (which Mr G. repeated) in a fit of Enthusiasm—over his Head goes poor Petraca,—Russian Leather and all! . . .[20]

At the end of March, plagued once more by the stone, Garrick took himself off to Bath. He found the company less than inspiring. 'I despair of seeing you here,' he wrote to Colman, 'so that I must beat ye parade with the folks here, whose conversation lies as heavy upon my mind as the hot cakes & devilments at breakfast upon my Stomach.'

While there he was able to form a view about the progress of a young actor called John Henderson. Garrick had auditioned him some years previously, but had turned him down—'he had in his mouth too much wool or worsted,' he said, 'which he must absolutely get rid of before he would be fit for Drury-lane stage.' He did, however, indicate to John Palmer, the proprietor of the Theatre Royal at Bath, that Henderson was not without promise, and he had been engaged for three years at a guinea a week, rising to two.

A face-lift for Old Drury. The imposing new front designed for Drury Lane in 1775 by Robert Adam. (Robert Adam, The Works in Architecture, *Volume 2, 1779)*

He had quickly made his mark, making his début as Hamlet and going on, despite a clumsy figure, to win golden opinions for his Richard, his Benedick, his Macbeth and his Lear. By the end of his first season, with some twenty major roles under his belt, he was being referred to as the 'Bath Roscius'. Early in 1773, Garrick had written to congratulate him on his success. It was very much the sort of letter he had written to Powell nine years previously from Paris: 'As the older soldier, I will venture to point out some rocks, which former young Men of Merit have split upon,' he wrote:

They have generally Neglected study, to Keep indifferent Company; by which behaviour their little Stock of Merit has been soon exhausted, and in exchange they have got the habit of idling & drinking, contenting themselves in publick with barely getting the words of their parts into their heads, and in private with the poor, unedifying common-place gabble of every ignorant pretender (who to the disgrace of it) belongs to a Theatre—

He also urged Henderson not to confine his reading to books about the theatre:

The Majority of Actors content themselves (like Parrots) with delivering words they get from others, repeat them again & again without the least alteration and confine their notions, talking and acquirements to ye Theatre only, as the parrot to his Cage.[21]

If Henderson was encouraged by this to think that there might be an opening for him at Drury Lane, he would be disappointed, although he did not lack friends to plead his cause. A persistent champion was Cumberland, who told Garrick that he had 'great sensibility, just elocution, a perfect ear, good sense, and the most marking pauses (next to your own) I ever heard; in the latter respect he stands next to you, very near you'.

Any suggestion that Garrick remained unresponsive to such promptings because he feared comparisons with a rising new star is unconvincing. There had been lukewarm reports from George, who during his convalescence in Bath had seen Henderson in action, and even Cumberland's praise was not unqualified: 'Nature has not been beneficent to him in figure or in face,' he conceded; 'a prominent forehead, corpulent habit, inactive features, and not a quick eye.'[22] Garrick had, none the less, in the autumn of 1774, made an offer of a trial engagement, but Henderson, in distinctly lordly fashion, had pronounced the terms unacceptable, and had re-engaged with Palmer for a further three years.

That was how matters stood when Garrick arrived in Bath in April 1775. He was now able to form his own opinion of the Bath Roscius, and he lost no time in communicating it to Colman. 'I have seen ye great Henderson, who has something, & is Nothing,' he wrote:

He might be made to figure among the puppets of these times—his Don John is a Comic Cato, & his Hamlet a mixture of Tragedy Comedy pastoral farce & nonsense—however, tho' my Wife is outrageous, I am in ye Secret, & see sparks of fire which might be blown to warm even a London Audience at Xmas—he is a dramatic Phoenomenon, & his Friends, but more particularly Cumberland has ruin'd him—he has a manner of raving, when he w^d be Emphatical that is ridiculous, & must be chang'd, or he would not be suffer'd at ye Bedford Coffeehouse—[23]

During their stay the Garricks visited Hannah More in Bristol. Garrick also took a hand in the first production at the Theatre Royal of her tragedy—that same *Inflexible Captive* which he had previously turned down. He made some alterations and supplied an epilogue, which was a spirited defence of women writers. The piece was well received, although Garrick didn't think much of Henderson as Regulus—'You would have wish'd him bung'd up with his nails before ye End of ye 3d act,' he wrote to Colman (Regulus meets a grisly end by being placed in a nail-studded barrel, which is then rolled down a hill).

His letters to Colman from Bath are unfailingly lively and amusing, and he was clearly much the better for his stay: 'I have gain'd two inches in the Waist,' he wrote, '& the Girls at Night call me Fatty!' It is clear, however, from a letter to Hannah More, written early in May, that his thoughts were once more turning to the bustle and stresses of London:

> We begin to think of leaving this land of Circé, where, I do this, & do that, & do Nothing, & I go here & go there & go nowhere—Such is ye life of Bath & such the Effects of this place upon me—I forget my Cares, & my large family in London . . .[24]

By the middle of May he was back at the Adelphi. He appeared as Don Felix in *The Wonder* for the benefit of the Theatrical Fund but otherwise did not act again that season: 'Much better, Dear Sir,' he wrote to a friend a few days after his return, 'but still Weak & ruffled.'[25] He had talked many times about retirement, but now it had become a settled intention. One of his more persistent lady authors, Elizabeth Griffith, had written asking him for 'a hint of any subject . . . suited to the Theatre'. Garrick apologized for having been slow to reply:

> Indeed, my dear Madam, it will not be in my power to follow my inclination and oblige you: the business at the Theatre is grown too mighty for me, & I shall retreat from it with all good speed.[26]

35

A Face-Lift for the Old Lady

Garrick was always quick to respond to requests for help, even from complete strangers and no matter how improbable the quarter from which they came. Some months previously, the *London Chronicle* had reported one such act of generosity:

> The Officers of the Companies troops, and the Gentlemen of the factory at *Calcutta*, in BENGAL, having erected a most elegant theatre for their amusement, applied to Mr GARRICK, through their friends in England, for his assistance and advice, respecting the conduct of it: In consequence of which, he sent them over the best dramatic works in our language, together with complete setts of scenery, under the care of an ingenious young Mechanist from Drury-lane, whom he recommended to superintend that department . . .[1]

The gentlemen in Calcutta had shown their appreciation by sending Garrick some madeira, together with a quantity of chintz for Mrs Garrick. Pleased at the thought of a re-upholstered bed and some new curtains for Hampton, she had sent the fabric to Chippendale's, only to learn that it had been seized by customs officers. Material from India, her servant was told, was 'so very Strongly prohibited that if the King Was to Send his Signmanul down they could not deliver it'.[2]

Garrick decided to see what his friends in high places could do, and appealed in mock distress to Sir Grey Cooper, Lord North's joint Secretary of the Treasury: 'Not Rachel weeping for her Children could show more sorrow than Mrs Garrick,' he wrote. 'If you have ye least pity for a distressed Female . . . You may put yr thum & finger to ye business, & take ye thorn out of poor Rachel's side.'[3]

Standing as he did at the Prime Minister's right hand, Cooper was not exactly short of business to put his thumb and finger to in that summer of 1775. In April, shots had been fired at Lexington, and there would shortly be more serious bloodshed at Bunker's Hill. The new Continental Congress was in session at Philadelphia and the measures on which it agreed would include the establishment of an American post office under Benjamin Franklin and the appointment of a modest and taciturn Virginian planter called George Washington as commander in chief of the colonial armies.

Cooper nevertheless replied to Garrick the same day, saying he had sent 'a Supplication' to the Secretary to the Commissioners of the Customs, Edward Stanley. 'The Linnen drapers and Cotton Printers & all that Cursed Bourgeoisie, I fear will be as powerfull as they are merciless,' he wrote. 'But let Mrs Garrick be assured that all that the Secular arm can do shall be done.'⁴ Garrick apparently knew Stanley, and thought it worth sending him what he called 'a few doggrl Verses':

> O Stanley give ear to a Husband's Petition,
> Whose Wife well deserves her distressful condition,
> Regardless of his, & the Law's prohibition.
> If You knew what I suffer, since she has been caught,
> (On the Husband's poor head ever falls the Wife's fault)
> You would lend a kind hand to the Contraband Jade,
> And screen her for once in her illicit trade . . .⁵

Eager as always for his verse to have a wide circulation, he sent a copy to Cooper. 'If amidst the Truths and Lies that are daily arizing about American affairs, my Nonsense can steal You a few minutes from y^r Cares,' he wrote, 'I shall have my desire.' Whether the Commissioners of the Customs bent the rules for Mrs Garrick's chintz is not known.

Of rather more serious concern to Garrick and his wife was news from Paris concerning their niece Arabella, who had formed an attachment to a junior officer in the recently formed Légion de Corse. This enterprising dragoon—his name was de Molière—had hit on the idea of taking a room in the same house in the rue Verte where Madame Descombes had her *pension*. This made possible chance meetings on the stairs and the passing of letters—one of which, inevitably, was intercepted by Madame. Garrick, alerted to what was going on, ordered Bell and her sister back to London, and they arrived there, accompanied by Madame Descombes, towards the end of June.

An agitated letter from Bell to Garrick is extant. 'Mrs Descombes is this instant returned and had made me very unhappy indeed by repeating to me some part of this morning's conversation at the Adelphi,' she wrote (there had been a misunderstanding—Garrick had expected to see both nieces as well as Madame):

> The idea you have of my still corresponding with M. de Molière is indeed very unjust . . . Dear sir, shut me up for ever rather than abandon me; and cease for Heaven's sake to load me with your curses. I have many more ills than I can bear; ease me of one which outweighs all the rest, that of your hatred . . .⁶

This tearful appeal was delivered to Garrick as he was about to leave London to visit Rigby at Mistley. When he replied from there two days later he had calmed down somewhat:

> Your letter is so properly written, with such a feeling of y^r Situation, a true compunction for the cause of it, & a resolution to take Warning for ye future, that I will forgive You, never upbraid you again with the distress

you have brought upon us, & y^{r}self, provided that You will Shew Your gratitude, by telling Every circumstance of this unhappy affair, that I may be ye better able to deliver you from ye villain . . .

The tone is stern. Garrick promised to treat her 'with fatherly kindness' but he was still plainly disturbed by what he had heard from Mme Descombes, and even more by what he had read in the intercepted letter:

> He says you are violently in Love with him, that you will be unhappy without him—is this true—is not he near fifty & very plain? *good God!* have you not met him Somewhere unknown to Mrs Descombes? . . .[7]

Bell was a clear-headed young woman. She was one of five sisters and brothers. Her father, George, had re-married four years previously, and her stepmother had recently borne him a son. Her celebrated, wealthy and childless uncle must now at all costs be propitiated and she composed a long letter to that end. She admitted their correspondence, although she maintained that after Mme Descombes had intercepted the fatal letter it had ceased, except for one final exchange in which he had asked permission to follow her to England, a request she had refused. She then proceeded to rat comprehensively on her French admirer:

> His behaviour ever since has been inconsistent with reason, or honour; since I find he has not only put what really did pass between us, in the most favourable disposition (that is) for himself; but has added to it the grossest falsehoods . . . I am not suprized to find that he says I am violently in love with him, and can't live without him; judge of the truth of it, when I tell you, that after the untruths and shamefull reports he has rais'd about me; were he everything that is aimiable, had a scepter to offer me, and to crown all had your *encouragement*, I would not accept of him.[8]

Garrick, in the meantime, had asked his old friend Monnet to call on de Molière's colonel, the marquis d'Arcambal, and try to retrieve Bell's letters. This the amiable Monnet agreed to do, although he clearly thought his friend was making a mountain out of a molehill—'Put all that under your feet,' he advised him, 'and forget all about it.'

Garrick apparently accepted Monnet's advice. Whether he would have done so if he had seen a letter de Molière wrote to Bell at the end of July is open to doubt. He had had great trouble in discovering her address, he told her. He also told her that his colonel had been quizzed about him, and had 'done him justice'. He in turn had some questions for Bell:

> I should be glad to know if you are still of the same mind, and beg you to inform me, if you think it appropriate that I should write to your father, whether he would look favourably on my application. It is some time since I requested this favour, and you are now well placed to tell him how greatly I desire to be united with you. Let me know the state of your health, which is a matter of great concern to me, and tell me to whom I must write to

obtain your hand; give me their proper style and title, so that they should not be unfavourably disposed to me.[9]

Perhaps de Molière was not such a villain after all. It is not known whether he received a reply to his eminently proper and well-turned questions. What we do know is that three years later, his faithless Arabella married Captain Frederick Schaw; Garrick met the wedding expenses and in his will directed his executors to hold in trust for her the sum of £6,000.

As always, in the summer months, Garrick and his wife were showered with invitations. 'How did you escape the temptatations at Mistley?' enquired Camden in early July. 'Can you condescend, after the voluptuous feasting with Rigby, to fast with a forgotten Chancellor? I am abstinence itself.'[10] In August the Garricks received the Duke of Newcastle at Hampton and the following day they dined at his country seat, Oatlands, which lay on the Surrey side of the Thames, just above Hampton Court. Towards the end of the summer they travelled north to Derbyshire. The previous year the Fifth Duke of Devonshire, the son of Garrick's old friend, had been married to Earl Spencer's seventeen-year-old daughter, Georgiana, and Chatsworth had a chatelaine again for the first time in twenty years. Garrick was quite bowled over:

> Her Grace of Devonshire is a most inchanting Exquisite, beautiful Young Creature—were I five & twenty I could go mad about her, as I am past five and fifty, I would only suffer Martyrdom for her—[11]

He was writing to a young friend called Henry Bate. Although he was in holy orders Bate devoted most of his considerable energies to journalism, and was currently editor of the *Morning Post*, founded three years previously; he had also written a comic opera called *The Rival Candidates* which had been well received as an afterpiece during the winter. He was a colourful character, hot-tempered and famously quick with his fists. The vigour with which he expressed himself in his articles frequently got him into scrapes, and he was known as the 'Fighting Parson'. The previous year Garrick had recommended him to the Vicar of Hendon as his curate, and more recently he had solicited the Duke of Northumberland, the Lord-Lieutenant of Middlesex, for some office for him in the county.*

Garrick occasionally made use of Bate on theatre business, and a couple of months previously, knowing he had been invited to Hagley by Richard Rigby, had asked him to act as a talent-scout:

> If you pass by Cheltenham in Your Way to Worcester, I wish you would see an Actress there, a Mrs *Siddon's*, She has a desire I hear to try her Fortune with Us; if she seems in Your Eyes worthy of being trans-planted, pray desire to know upon what conditions She would make ye Tryal . . .[12]

---

* Unsuccessfully, as it turned out. The Duke had promised a commissionership of the peace, but had then for some reason, found himself unable to deliver.

Garrick was, in fact, seeking a second opinion, because he had already sent King down to Cheltenham to cast an eye over the young actress.* Sarah Kemble had been born twenty years previously at the Shoulder of Mutton Inn in Brecon, the first of twelve children of the provincial manager Roger Kemble. Her first known role was Ariel in *The Tempest* when she was eleven. At fifteen she was sent off into service for two years to dampen her affection for William Siddons, an actor eleven years her senior, but her parents eventually relented and the couple had married in Coventry in 1773.

Bate saw Mrs Siddons in *As You Like It*, and sent Garrick a comprehensive report:

> After combatting the various difficulties of one of the cussedest cross-roads in this kingdom, we arrived safe at Cheltenham on Thursday last, and saw the theatrical heroine of that place in the character of *Rosalind*: : tho' I beheld her from the side wings of the stage (a barn about three yards over and consequently under almost every disadvantage) I own she made so strong an impression upon me that I think she cannot fail to be a valuable acquisition to Drury Lane. Her figure must be remarkably fine, when she is happily delivered of a big belly, which entirely mars for the present her whole shape.—Her face (if I could judge from where I saw it) is one of the most strikingly beautiful for stage effect that ever I beheld: but I shall surprize you more, when I assure you that these are nothing to her action, and general stage deportment which are remarkably pleasing and characteristic . . . . It is necessary after this panegyric to inform you that her voice struck me at first as rather dissonant; and I fancy from the private conversation I had with her that in unimpassioned scenes it must be somewhat grating. . . . . . She is as you have been informed a very good breeches figure, and plays the Widow Brady I am informed admirably: I should not wonder from her ease, figure and manner if she made the proudest she of either house tremble in genteel comedy:—nay beware yourself *Great Little* Man, for she plays Hamlet to the satisfaction of the Worcestershire Critics.†

Bate quickly registered that he was not the only talent-spotter who had descended on Cheltenham, and took it upon himself to move quickly on Garrick's behalf:

> The moment the play was over I wrote a note to her husband (who is a damned rascally player tho' seemingly a very civil fellow) requesting an interview with him and his wife intimating at the same time the nature of my business. You will not blame me for making this forced march in

---

* Her acting there as Belvidera in *Venice Preserv'd* had been much admired by Henrietta Boyle, the rich and fashionable stepdaughter of Lord Bruce, and it was Bruce, on his return to London, who had enthused about her to Garrick.

† It seems that Bate was not simply twitting Garrick. When she played Hamlet two years later in Birmingham, she was billed as making her second appearance in the role.

your favour, as I learnt that some of the Covent Garden Mohawks were entrench'd near the place I intended carrying her by surprize. . . . . .[13]

Garrick replied by return, asking Bate to sign her up. His report on her voice seems to have concerned him not at all, although there was one passage in his letter which did: 'Your account of the big belly alarms me!—when shall we be in shapes again?'* He also plainly saw Mrs Siddons not simply as a promising addition to the company but as a secret weapon to be deployed the next time one of his leading ladies stepped out of line:

> If she has merit (and I am sure by your letter she must have) and will be wholly governed by me, I will make her theatrical fortune; if any lady begins to play at tricks, I will immediately play off my masked battery of Siddons against her.[14]

The awkward squad had, as Garrick saw it, recently acquired a surprising new recruit in the person of Jane Pope, who had made her adult début at Drury Lane in 1759 and had been warmly praised by Churchill in *The Rosciad* two years later:

> Not without art, and yet to nature true,
> She charms the town with humour ever new.
> Cheer'd by her promise, we the less deplore,
> The fatal time when Clive shall be no more.

That time had come and gone, and Miss Pope, a little bulkier than she had once been, had indeed inherited most of the parts that had belonged to Kitty Clive, who had taken her under her wing in the early days and was still a close friend. As she moved into her thirties, however, 'Popie' began to feel that she was undervalued. She was being paid £8 a week, and thought it should be increased to £10—'the sum usually paid to actresses in her walk'; when this was refused she announced that although she would leave Drury Lane with 'infinite regret', she had decided 'to shake all affection off, and like the Swiss to perform only with those that pay best'.[15]

Garrick declined to budge: 'The Patentees, with their best wishes to Miss Pope, feel as much regret in losing her, as she can possibly do in quitting them.' Quite unnecessarily, however, and none too graciously, he was determined to have the last word:

> At the same time, they beg leave to Observe, that if Mr Garrick would have agreed to let Mrs Barry perform Beatrice & Clarinda, and Mr Barry to have had for his Benefit, the day which he gave last year to Miss Pope they should not have lost those capital performers—Mr Garrick takes no merit to himself in having done this, but that of shewing a little more than *Swiss attachment* to Miss Pope—[16]

---

* Bate established that the child was due in December, and suggested that until she was able to appear, Garrick should support her and her family somewhere in the country (Mrs Siddons and her husband already had one child).

That was well below the belt.* Miss Pope had shown herself to be an excellent trooper over the years. She was never difficult, and, unlike several of the divas in the company who so regularly drove the manager to distraction, little scandal attached to her private life.† After a few weeks reflection her resolve crumbled; full of contrition, she tried to retrieve the situation:

> You will have the goodness to remember that this is the first disagreement we ever had in the course of fourteen years, and you will the readier pardon it, when you consider that a little vanity is almost inseparable from our profession, and that I unfortunately listened to its dictates, and have made myself unhappy. . . .
> As I know no excuse to palliate my wrong conduct, I must rely upon your generosity *to forgive* and *still to be my friend*.[17]

Garrick, however, was not in a forgiving mood. ''Entre nous:' he wrote unfeelingly to Colman, 'Pope has squeaked & sent her penitentials, but I cannot receive 'Em.'[18] Her parts had already gone to others, and there was nothing for it but to try her luck in Ireland. Kitty Clive tried to smooth her path by letters to some of her acquaintance there. 'She comes to Dublin by my advice Mr Garrick and she having had a dispute about sallary,' she wrote to one lady, adding drily: 'She wanted to be a little *Richer*, and he being *Poor* could not afford to let her.'[19]

Garrick's relations with the touchy and quarrelsome Thomas Arne had never been close, and when he received a rambling, grumbling letter from him that August, he sent a sharp reply which not only contained a number of home truths but also corrected Arne's English:

> How can you imagine that I have an irrisistable *Apathy* to you? I suppose you mean *Antipathy* my dear Doctor . . . You ask me why I won't make use of your Pupils—shall I tell you fairly, because I have not the opinion of them which you have?—I try'd Mrs Bradford, Miss Weller and I have now Mr Faucet: the two first (As I in a most friendly manner foretold) did no credit to you or myself by appearing in a Piece which you obstinately insisted upon bringing out, tho you knew it would be the means of making a coolness between us—[20]

Garrick's temper had not been improved by a further sharp attack of the stone. 'Since you left me, I have been upon ye rack, & almost despair'd of fighting a battle or committing a Murder again,' he told Colman three weeks before the start of the new season:

> —but a fortnight ago my good Genius led me to ye Duke of Newcastle's where I met an old Naples friend, & he recommended a remedy which

---

* It was also, given the history of his constant disagreements with the Barrys, highly specious.
† She never married, and lived together for sixty years with her sister Susanna. She had been engaged at one time to Charles Holland, but that came to an end after she discovered him in a boat on the river at Richmond with the seductive Sophia Baddeley. Another engagement, to a stockbroker, had foundered on his insistence that she should abandon the stage.

has work'd Wonders—It has taken away half the Evil of my life, & at this moment I can piss well, and have ambition enough to think of something more—but Lord help Us, we little Men make nothing of swelling ourselves to a *Hercules* or a *Robinson Crusoe*! —to be serious—You will be pleas'd to see me, as I am—my spirits are return'd, and redeant Saturnia regna—[21]

Colman was at this time travelling around in the wilds of Yorkshire: 'Pray come away, & see my Sword drawn,' Garrick wrote at the end of his letter—'ye Theatre is noble!—' He had decided that for his last season Drury Lane must have a face-lift. He had once again turned to the Adam brothers, and the place had been swarming with workmen through the summer months. There are no entries in the theatre account books for that year relating to the cost of the work, but an unidentified contemporary press cutting in the Folger Library estimates it at close to 4,000 guineas, a figure equivalent to a quarter of a million at present-day prices, and approximating to a year's profit. Garrick was greatly pleased with the result. 'Drury Lane Theatre will delight y^r Eyes, when you cast them upon the Old Lady,' he wrote to Moody, who was acting in Liverpool for the summer.

Externally, the theatre had acquired an imposing new entrance in Bridge Street, doing away with the insignificant alley-way which had previously run alongside the Rose Tavern and led to the doors of the pit and the boxes. Inside, the architect had removed the old heavy pilasters; *Town and Country Magazine* described the graceful new pillars which replaced them as '*leste* and brilliant, being inlaid with plate glass on a crimson and green ground'. The ceiling had been raised by twelve feet, which improved the acoustics. More spacious side boxes had been created, lined with crimson spotted paper, and there were new gilt chandeliers.

'Some hypercritics were of opinion,' reported *Town and Country Magazine*, 'that such a blaze of ornament, in the audience part of the theatre, would diminish the effect of the stage decorations.' Colman seems to have tended to that view, but he was very much in a minority. Most agreed with the *Oxford Magazine*, which asserted, a shade sweepingly, that the Adam brothers had converted the building from 'an old barn into the most splendid and complete theatre in Europe'.

That was certainly the view of those who crowded in on the first night of the new season, and there was a burst of applause from the audience even before the curtain rose:

Upon the curtain drawing up (which by the bye is judiciously constructed without a slit) a clap of thunder precedes the entrance of Mercury, who compares the new painting of the theatre to the arts of a *fille de joye*, who tickles her face afresh to tickle your fancy.[22]

Garrick's last season of attempting to tickle the fancy of his public had begun.

36

Enter Garrick's Venus

Enter MERCURY

> I, GOD of wits and thieves—birds of a feather,
> (For wit and thieving often go together)
> Am sent to see this house's transformation,
> Ask if the critics give their approbation,
> Or as in other cases—'yawn at alteration'. . .

The Theatrical Candidates, the musical playlet which Garrick had dashed off to salute the elegant new Adam interior of his theatre (the score was by William Bates) was a flimsy enough affair. Comedy and Tragedy—'these rival petticoats'—canvass the votes of the audience and abuse each other like a pair of fishwives:

> Think you, your strutting, straddling, puffy pride,
> Your rolling eyes, arms kimbo'd, tragic stride
> Can frighten me?—Britons, 'tis yours to choose,
> That murd'ring lady or this laughing muse.
> Now make your choice. With smiles I'll strive to win ye.
> If you choose her, she'll stick a dagger in ye!

Enter Harlequin. He is there to make the case for Pantomime, and he pitches strongly, if excruciatingly, for the vote of the gallery:

> Each friend I have above, whose voice so loud is,
> Will never give me up for two such dowdies.

The case is referred for judgement to Apollo, and an out-of-breath Mercury returns with it from Parnassus:

> You, Tragedy, must weep and love and rage,
> And keep your turn, but not engross the stage.
> And you, gay madam, gay to give delight,
> Must not, turned prude, encroach upon her right.
> Each sep'rate charm: you grave, you light as feather,
> Unless that Shakespeare bring you both together . . .

'Though it neither teemed with the wit of a Chesterfield, nor the polished style of a Lyttelton,' wrote the *Westminster Magazine* in its ponderous way, 'it had a sufficient share of merit to recommend itself to the audience.' The public agreed; there was a command performance early in October, and the piece was given sixteen times during the season.

The season was only a few days old when Garrick was laid low by his old enemy the stone. It was a severe attack, and he was unable to attend to any business for several days. One of his first actions on recovering was to enquire after Mrs Siddons, then at Gloucester, who was now seven months pregnant. 'I beg that she will not make herself uneasy about coming, till she will run no risk by the journey,' he wrote to her husband ('My hand shakes with weakness,' he told him, 'but I hope You will understand this Scrawl'):

> All I desire is that I may have the earliest information that can be had with any certainty, for I shall settle some business by that direction, which may be of immediate Service to Mrs Siddons & the Manager—if in the mean time You find it convenient to have any pecuniary Assistance from Me, I shall give it You with great pleasure—*

Mrs Siddons was not Garrick's only new recruit that season. He had also taken on a Mrs King, who had most recently been Tate Wilkinson's 'tragedy queen' in York. She made her first appearance in the middle of October as Rosalind in *As You Like It*. 'She is very Tall,' noted Hopkins, 'and would look well enough if she did not paint her face so much with white and Red. She has a course Voice—and does not speak very Naturally.' She appeared again as Rosalind a few days later. Hopkins had no comment to offer on her appearance on this occasion, but he was startled by the way she was presented:

> Mrs King was put in the Bills in the following manner: Rosalind By Command by Mrs King. A Circumstance I never knew before, nor do I know by what accident it happened. I'm Sure it's a particular Honour, which her acting cannot deserve.

Theatre gossip, however, held that it was no accident. Years later, when John Philip Kemble copied Hopkins's comment on to his copy of the playbill, he added an explanatory note: 'This circumstance was a contrivance of Mr Garrick's in order to mortify Mrs Yates, Mrs Abington, and Miss Younge.'† Tate Wilkinson tells much the same story: 'In order to mortify Miss Young,' he wrote in *The Wandering Patentee*, 'Garrick had interest at Court sufficient for his Majesty to have that play ordered.'[1]

It sounds entirely probable. Garrick could not expect to get far into a season without a show of temperament from one or other of his 'great Ladies', as he

---

* *Letters*, 944. The offer was accepted. Garrick, in a further letter twelve days later, wrote 'Whenever You please to draw upon Me for the fifteen pounds I shall pay it immediately.' (*Ibid.*, 947.)

† Kemble, Mrs Siddons's younger brother, took over the management of Drury Lane in 1788.

wearily called them. At the end of October he composed a long, angry letter to Richard Yates, who managed his wife's affairs:

> You left word with Mr Hopkins *that we are to think no more of Mrs Yates, 'till She will let us know her pleasure*, or words to that Effect. Do You, & Mrs Yates imagine that the Proprietors will submit to this manner of going on, or that they will pay such a large Sum of Money for having their Business so destroy'd as it was in great part of the last Season and has been wholly this, by waiting for Mrs Yates's pleasure to perform? . . . It was observ'd by many of the audience last Night that she never perform'd better, and therefore She gives Notice that She must not be advertis'd till *She* pleases. As I was at the Theatre, & heard with my own Ears that her Voice was never clearer, I shall not Submit to this very unaccountable & unreasonable Behaviour—*

It was not only his 'Capital performers' who raised his blood pressure. Some days into the season he had received a letter from Cautherley:

> My Situation in the Theatre for these four Years past has been worse and worse & the impossibility I find of living on my Salary without involving myself in difficulties obliges me (tho' with the greatest reluctance) to take my leave of Drury Lane . . .[2]

This put Garrick into a cold rage. Cautherley's letter 'will be ever memorable, in the annals of a Theatre', he told him:

> Has this Young Man a proper sense of right & wrong? for taking Mr Garrick out of ye Question, should not he, have given Notice before the beginning of the Season to any indifferent Manager of his intentions of quitting the Theatre?—to begin the season was misleading the Manager, & not to go on, is not only contrary to the Establish'd rules of a Theatre, but unjust, illegal, & dishonourable—what would the publick & Mr Cautherly's friends have said, had Mr G: discharged Mr C: during the Acting Season?—[3]

With chilling, third-person formality, Garrick brought their relations to an end. Many believed that his seeming blindness over the year to the young man's inadequacies could be ascribed only to paternal indulgence or a sense of obligation. Whether they were father and son cannot now be known. Cautherley, who lived on until 1805, does not figure in either of the two wills written by Garrick. In the will of his wife Susanna, however, who outlived him by fifteen years, there is a reference to an Indenture of Settlement that had been drawn up on the day before their marriage in 1771. This provided for a substantial amount of property and securities to pass to Cautherley, and, on his death, to his widow—Bank of England stock, South Sea annuities, a number of leasehold properties, and securities 'granted by Commissioners for paving the City of Westminster'. One

---

* *Letters*, 949. Gout in his right hand obliged Garrick to dictate the letter to Hopkins.

of the parties to that settlement was George Garrick, who had always done his brother's bidding in so many different ways.

At the end of October Garrick brought out the last piece he would ever write for the stage. It was called *May-Day; or, The Little Gipsy*, and he had devised it as a vehicle for a promising young singer. 'This Musical Farce of one Act,' wrote Hopkins, 'was wrote by Mr G on purpose to introduce Miss Abrams (a Jew) about 17 years old. She is very small, a Swarthy Complexion, has a very sweet Voice and a fine Shake, but not quite power enough yet.'

Harriet Abrams was only fifteen, as it happens. She was also a pupil of Thomas Arne's, who had written the music, which suggests that for a time at least his relations with Garrick had become less frosty. Garrick made no great claims for his libretto. 'The piece was produced at an early part of the season,' he wrote when it was published, 'when better writers are not willing to come forth.' It went into three editions, for all that, and Arne's music, which is full of charm, helped it to a run of sixteen performances.

Garrick made his own first appearance of the season as Lusignan in *Zara*, and a few days later he was seen in *The Provok'd Wife*. His appearance as Brute was the talk of the town. 'Mr G.—never play'd better,' enthused Hopkins, 'and when he was in Woman's Cloaths he had a head drest with Feathers, Fruit etc. as extravagant as possible to Burlesque the present Mode of dressing—it had a Monstrous Effect.' It had been the fashion for some time to wear the hair piled high on the head, but Georgiana, the young Duchess of Devonshire, had pushed matters to extremes by creating a fashion for the three-foot hair tower. This was embellished with anything from waxed fruit or stuffed birds to a ship in full sail; it provided several hours work for at least two hairdressers and imposed severe restrictions on mobility—ladies wishing to ride in a carriage were obliged to sit on the floor.*

There was an epidemic of some sort in London in the early winter of 1775. The proprietors of Covent Garden referred to it in a note as a 'time of dearth & Sickness' and proposed cutting back to five performances a week, but Garrick turned them down. It would 'Subject Us to very injurious suspicions,' he wrote, and would also 'bring on great distresses upon the lower part of our Companies'.[4] It did, however, cause him to revise his own plans for appearing, and the *Gazetteer and New Daily Advertiser* for 7 November carried what reads like a singularly brazen puff:

> The desertion of the theatres in consequence of the disease with which so many are afflicted, has been productive of one agreeable effect, that of bringing Mr Garrick forward in Benedict much earlier than was expected.

---

* An incident at Covent Garden demonstrated that the fashion had its practical uses. 'A fellow who sat on the sixth row of the Upper Gallery,' reported *Lloyd's Evening Post* on 29 February 1776, 'threw a Keg (which he had brought full of liquor into the House) over the Gallery front. It fell upon a lady's head, who sat in that part of the Pit which was railed into the Boxes, but the Lady's hair being dress'd in high *ton*, the artificial mountain luckily prevented the mischief that otherwise might have been occasioned.'

Garrick as Sir John Brute. Betterton, Quin and Cibber had all played the lead in the piece that established Vanbrugh's reputation, and of all seventeenth-century plays The Provok'd Wife *was the vehicle best suited to Garrick's comic genius. He attempted the role for the first time opposite Peg Woffington in 1744 and chose it for one of his farewell appearances more than three decades later. (Bell's British Theatre, Vol. 2, 1780)*

It cannot be a matter of surprise that Roscius should have escaped the infection and his spirits and constitution seem proof against the attacks of age itself; after above 30 campaigns, his ardour and execution appear rather to increase . . .*

It wasn't entirely true, as it happens, and Garrick had admitted as much to a friend the day before the performance: 'I have been very ill,' he wrote to Peter Fountain, '—am not Well, & don't know when I shall be—'5 Well or ill, the night after playing Benedick he was to be found at Almack's (Topham Beauclerk had put him up for membership in 1773),† and from there he wrote a cheerful, gossipy letter to George, who was still in Bath but who once again appeared to be on the mend. 'We rejoice at your visible alteration of health & Spirits,' Garrick told him:

> I likewise must insist that you never think of leaving that fountain of *Your* health, till you can shew us a pair of rosy Cheeks, spirited eyes, and a Belly out of the perpendicular—the little Gypsy goes on Hummingly, & rises nightly in repute—there was a little odd talk of some party against us, but to this Minute there has not been one Single disapprobation—Weston is dying, & with him goes a good Actor, & a very bad man—Mrs King is useful, but not excellent—she stops gaps but will not allure.6

That Mrs King's eagerness to oblige by stepping in at short notice sometimes outran her preparedness had been demonstrated only a few nights previously, when both houses, as was traditional on 4 November, had put on *Tamerlane*. The part of Arpasia belonged at Drury Lane to Miss Younge, but she had been ill. Hopkins recorded cryptically that poor Mrs King's efforts in her place were not appreciated: '*Very bad*, much hiss'd.'

As for drunken, quarrelsome Tom Weston, son of an undercook in the royal kitchens, he was indeed close to his end, although he was not yet forty, and would die two months later. Although he had latterly been drawing £7 a week, he was perpetually in debt, not only to tradesmen, but also to the theatre, from which he frequently borrowed. In 1772, the management had decided that the amount he owed was unacceptable and impounded his benefit receipts. Word came from Weston that he had been arrested for debt and confined in a sponging house; he requested the management not to resort to the formula usually employed on such occasions, which was that his absence was due to 'sudden illness'. His wishes were disregarded—whereupon Weston bobbed up from a seat in the upper gallery, denounced the managers as liars and made a determined attempt to win the sympathy of the audience for his predicament. After a protracted wrangle, he came down and played his part on stage.7

---

* He appeared in the part again three nights later. 'At the Play Mr Garrick acted,' Cumberland wrote to a friend, 'and the house was so full you could not have thrust your little finger in, not withstanding the plague sweeps us away by dozens.'

† Almack's, famous for its high play, had been founded in Pall Mall in 1764. It was taken over in 1778 by one Brooks, and established as Brooks's Club in St James's Street.

Supremely tiresome as he was, his death was a severe blow to the company; Ned Shuter apart, he had no equal as a low comedian. Garrick, playing Archer to his Scrub, frequently had difficulty in keeping his face straight, and he acknowledged that Weston's Abel Drugger was one of the finest comic performances he had ever seen.

Meanwhile, there was cheering news from Gloucester. William Siddons had written to say that his wife had been unexpectedly been taken ill on stage, 'And early the next morning produced me a fine girl.' Garrick was delighted:

> The Sooner I see You here, wth convenience to Mrs Siddons, will be of more consequence to her & to me—she may have something to do, if I see her soon, which may not be in my power to give her if she comes later ... let me desire You to give me the earliest Notice when you & Mrs Siddons can be here, & what part or parts she Would rather chuse for her Onset, that I may prepare Accordingly—[8]

He was once again at a pitch of exasperation with Mrs Yates, who had decided that she no longer wished to play the lead in *The Mourning Bride*. 'You wish to be quit of the part of *Almeria*, because you say it is *unfit* for You,' he wrote:

> But why is it *unfit*, if it is the Capital part of the Play, and always perform'd by the first Actresses?—But there is still a stronger Reason for urging the Necessity of your appearing in that Character.—At the time of the Benefits last year, hearing how much the Plays suffer by the Performers taking part for one Night only, I put up an order in the Green Room, that the Manager should expect every Performer to do for the House what they should do for the Benefits, and for this good reason; why is not the Publick at large to be as well entertain'd, as the Friends of any Single Actor?[*]

Between late November and Christmas, Garrick appeared no fewer than nine times, performing six of his major roles. There was a particular reason for driving himself so hard, as he explained to a young university friend—'The Devil of a Duenna has laid hold upon the Town, & nothing but your old friend can get her a little out of her clutches—'[†]

Sheridan's comic opera *The Duenna* had had its first night at Covent Garden on 21 November, and was playing to packed houses—it would be seen more than seventy times in the course of the season.[‡] There had been a command performance on 29 November, which Garrick had attempted to counter by going

---

[*] *Letters*, 957. On this occasion Garrick prevailed, although Mrs Yates did not play the part in the following season, after his departure. In 1779 she returned to Covent Garden—and took Almeria back into her repertoire.

[†] *Ibid.*, 960. Garrick was writing to the son of an old friend called Thomas Rackett, an army tailor. The son, also Thomas, had attended the Shakespeare Jubilee as a boy of twelve and delighted Garrick by reciting the *Ode*. He was now an Oxford undergraduate. He later became a parson, and was one of the executors of Mrs Garrick's estate.

[‡] It might well have done even better, but Michael Leoni, who played Carlos, was Jewish, and would therefore not act on Friday nights.

on as Hamlet. He told young Rackett that this had drawn 'ye most crowded house we ever had', a claim supported by the Drury Lane Treasurer's book, which shows receipts for the night of £286 14s 6d.*

A second performance of *Hamlet* ten days later did almost as well, and there were also packed houses for his appearances as Drugger and Archer and Leon and Kitely. These triumphant evenings of Garrick's did not, however, pass entirely without incident. During *Every Man in His Humour*, at a moment when the house was very silent and Garrick as Kitely 'very fine' there came a shout of 'Speak louder!' from someone in the gallery. 'It disconcerted Mr G very much,' noted Hopkins. A couple of weeks earlier when he was Archer in *The Stratagem*, the young actress playing Cherry had stumbled and fallen. 'Miss Jaratt being in certain condition,' reported Hopkins, 'Mr G could not very easily raise her.' It is not clear whether she was drunk or pregnant.

Garrick was hugely gratified, just before Christmas, to receive a volume of poetry which Hannah More had just published and which she had dedicated to him.† He acknowledged it in his most flowery vein ('What can I possibly say to You, that can in the best manner declare the feelings of my heart, for the great honour you have done Me . . .'). He sent her in return a copy of *May Day* and *The Theatrical Candidates* which had been published together: 'I have two little performances for You,' he wrote, 'which are not worth Your Acceptance—I am oblig'd to write for us because other people will not.' He urged her to advance the date of her proposed visit to London:

> It gives me great joy that you will be wth us after Xmas—but why not *soon* after? if you cannot come till March, I dread my being oblig'd to go to Bath—besides if Your flattery has any foundation, & that my Fool's Coat draws You this way, why not draw You *Sooner?*[9]

Garrick revived *The Jubilee* to draw the crowds over the holiday season. On 29 December it was preceded by *The Merchant of Venice*. King was cast as Shylock, and the bills announced that Portia would be played by 'A Young Lady, first appearance'. Only Bate's *Morning Post* had anything good to say about her performance. The *Middlesex Journal* was particularly scathing:

> . . . There is not room to expect anything beyond mediocrity. Her figure and face, although agreeable, have nothing striking, her voice (that requisite of all public speakers) is far from being favourable to her progress as an actress. It is feared she possess a monotone not to be got rid of; there is also vulgarity in her tones . . .[10]

Sarah Siddons had made her London début.

---

* Garrick always made it his business to know at first hand what the other house was up to. 'You were not at Cov^t Garden,' he wrote to George Colman, 'I like the Duenna much with some few objections—It will do their business—' (*Letters*, 963.)
† The volume contained her *Sir Eldred of the Bower* and *The Bleeding Rock*.

37

To Strut and Fret No More

Garrick's mind had been on other things on the day that his new protégée flopped so resoundingly. Partly on his health. 'My disorder increases & distresses me much,' he wrote to Colman; 'my friend Pott is to search for yᵉ cause next Week.' That was not the main burden of his letter, however:

> As I promis'd to let You know before I parted with my theatrical Property that You might be the purchaser if You pleas'd—I must now seriously acquaint You that I shall most certainly part with it—I Saw a Gentleman Yesterday of great property, & who has no Objection to the price Viz: 35000 pounds for my Part ... I beg you will write to me directly & be explicit, for I must determine or perhaps lose My Market ...*

Garrick had in fact been in negotiation for the sale of his half-share in Drury Lane for some two months past, initially with Sheridan's father-in-law, Thomas Linley, but now with a consortium in which Linley had been joined by Sheridan himself, an elderly relative of the Sheridans called Simon Ewart, who was a prosperous brandy merchant, and a wealthy medical man called James Ford, a fashionable West End obstetrician who was Physician Extraordinary to Queen Charlotte.† Linley had assured Garrick that Sheridan was 'more than ever sure' of making good his share of the money, although he added, 'How this is possible, I no more know than I do how Subsidies are raised in Saturn.'[1] Garrick might have wondered, too—it was only a few weeks since the penniless, 25-year-old Sheridan had borrowed £200 from him.‡ Now, to secure his share in the proposed transaction, he would have to raise £10,000.§

Colman did not take long to decline Garrick's offer; the idea of acquiring only his share of the property did not interest him:

---

* *Letters*, 971. Percival Pott (1714–88) had been surgeon to St Bartholomew's Hospital since 1749. His pupils included the celebrated John Hunter.

† Ewart was to withdraw almost immediately.

‡ The promissory note came up for sale at Maggs in 1952; see their Catalogue no. 809, item 259.

§ He did so mainly by borrowing £7,700 from Dr Ford, with his portion of the patent as security. He raised a further £1,000 in mortgages, and scraped the rest together from the profits that were beginning to come in from the success of *The Duenna*.

I would not for worlds again sit on the throne of Brentford* with any assessor, except it were yourself. And you may remember I told you so at the time above-mentioned, assigning as my reason, that you were the only man in the kingdom I would suffer to govern me, and I did not know a man in the kingdom who would suffer me to govern him—therefore I can have no other partner. If you are enabled to treat *for the whole*, or to reserve your own half, we must talk further. But if the gentleman you speak of is ready and willing to buy your part only, and there is no more upon sale, let who will buy for me, and I wish the purchaser a merry Christmas.†

The sale contract was not completed until 18 January, but a good two weeks before that Garrick was writing to friends as if it were already signed and sealed:

I shall take my leave of the Stage, & bid Farewell to the plumed troops & the big Wars, & welcome content & the tranquil Mind—in Short—I will not stay to be Sixty with my Cap & bells—Active as I am, & full of Spirit, with the drawback of a *gravel-complaint* . . .‡

With an old and trusted friend like Hoadly he was frank about his reasons:

Mrs Garrick & I are happy wth the thoughts of my *Strutting & fretting no more upon ye Stage*, & leaving to Younger Spirits the present race of Theatrical Heroines with all their Airs, indispositions, tricks & importances which have reduc'd the Stage to be a dependant upon the Wills of our insolent, vain, & let me add insignificant female trumpery—there must be a revolution, or my Successors will Suffer much, I had a resource in my own Acting, that counteracted all the Evil designs of these Gentry—Linley will be of great Service—Sing Song is much the Fashion, & his knowledge of Musick & preparing fit Subjects for the Stage, will be a Strength, that the Proprietors may depend upon, when the Heroines are prankish—[2]

The news was quickly all over the town. On the day the contract was signed, Garrick was appearing in *The Alchymist*, and when Face asked Drugger whether

---

* 'Like the two kings of Brentford smelling at one nosegay' was an expression used of persons who were once rivals but have become reconciled. The allusion is to Buckingham's *The Rehearsal*, where a stage direction in Act II, scene ii, reads 'The two kings of Brentford enter hand in hand.' To heighten the absurdity, the two actors used to make their entrance 'smelling at one nosegay'.

† *Boaden*, ii, 118. Letter dated 30 December 1775. Colman also expressed his concern about his friend's disorder: 'Believe me, my dear Garrick, I love and honour you, and have never, in my most petulant moments, gone beyond the *amantium irae*. Take care of yourself; your dear good woman will, I know, take care of you.'

‡ Garrick, not entirely appropriately, is making free with the speech in which Othello contemplates Desdemona's unfaithfulness: 'I had been happy if the general camp,/ Pioneers and all, had tasted her sweet body,/ So I had nothing known. O, now for ever/ Farewell the tranquil mind, farewell content,/ Farewell the plumèd troops and the big wars/ That makes ambition virtue!' (*Othello*, Act III, scene iii.)

he had any interest with the players, Garrick ad-libbed a topical reply: 'I believe I had once, but don't know if I have now or not.'*

He had a flood of letters. James Clutterbuck, who had done so much business for him over the years, was now old and infirm, but could still take pleasure in an old friend's ship coming home so well laden: 'Joy! much joy! to my dear Garrick for having wound up his bottom so wisely. You have made a retreat as glorious as that of Xenophon.'† Richard Rigby, writing from Mistley, was surprisingly ponderous:

> . . . I do not know, nor you neither, till you have tried it, how you will relish an idle life, who have been always used to a most active one: if your quitting the stage will contribute to your health, that is the first consideration; amusement is the next, and that people do not always find as they grow older, especially those who have been used to much business . . .³

At Little Strawberry Hill in Twickenham, Kitty Clive found the detail of the sale highly entertaining: 'What a strange jumble of people they have put in the papers as the purchasers of the patent!' she wrote. 'I thought I should have died with laughing when I saw a man-midwife amongst them: I suppose they have taken him in to prevent *miscarriages*!' She also had more serious things to say, however:

> . . . In the height of the public admiration for you, when you were never mentioned with any other appellation but the Garrick, the charming man, the fine fellow, the delightful creature, both by men and ladies; when they were admiring every thing you did, and every thing you scribbled,—at this very time, *I the Pivy*, was a living witness that they did not know, nor could they be sensible, of half your perfections. I have seen you, with your magical hammer in your hand, *endeavouring* to beat your ideas into the heads of creatures who had none of their own—I have seen you, with lamb-like patience, endeavouring to make them comprehend you; and I have seen you, when that could not be done—I have seen your lamb turned into a lion: by this your great labour and pains the public was entertained; *they* thought they all acted very fine,—they did not see you pull the wires.
>
> There are people *now* on the stage to whom you gave their consequence; they think themselves very great; now let them go on in their new parts without your leading-strings, and they will soon convince the world what their genius is; I have always said this to every body, even when your horses and mine were in their highest prancing. While I was under your control, I did not say half the fine things I thought of you, because it looked like flattery; and you know your Pivy was always proud: besides, I thought you did not like me then; but *now* I am sure you do, which makes me send you this letter.⁴

<hr/>

* Not everyone was persuaded that he meant to go. Wagers were entered in the betting books at White's Club that he would act again.

† *Boaden*, ii, 127. Letter dated 23 January 1776. Clutterbuck died the following December.

Of all the tributes Garrick received, none was more affecting and, before filing it away, he endorsed it: 'My Pivy, excellent!'

There were some loose ends that required his attention. The Theatrical Fund now stood close to £5,000, and Garrick wrote to enlist Grey Cooper's help in guaranteeing its future:

> If we could procure an Act of Parliament to incorporate Us, & many of the grave & Younger part of the house seem desirous of doing it, I should finish my theatrical Life, as I would Wish, by presenting the Actors with this necessary & honourable Security for their Money—[5]

Garrick also wrote to Burke ('I flatter Myself, that You will not oppose it, if it seems proper & to the purpose').[6] A petition for a bill to secure the Theatrical Fund against 'any Misapplication or Embezzlement' was introduced in the House of Commons on 7 February. It was referred to a committee headed by Cooper and Burke, and received the Royal Assent on 25 March.*

Garrick was less successful in an application he made on his brother's behalf to Rigby. George had now returned from Bath, in much better shape than for some time, but Garrick's departure would obviously place a question-mark over his future at Drury Lane. 'It would make both him & Me Extremely happy, if he could deserve Your Notice in any way,' Garrick had written to Rigby. 'He is honest & faithful & would (as well as his Brother) be the most Grateful of Men, if he could at any time & in any manner be number'd among Your humble Servants.'† Rigby sent a gracious reply: 'If it should fall in my way to be of service to Him, I shall have great pleasure in publickly marking the regard I privately profess to have for you.' Poor George was out of luck, however. By the end of the year nothing had turned up. Back in Bath, and clearly feeling the pinch, he wrote apologetically to Garrick asking for £50: 'I was in hopes that before this time, our friend Mr Rigby wou'd have procur'd me some Employment, which wou'd have prevented my giving you so much trouble.'[7]

His own performances apart, Garrick had not been able to come up with anything to counter the phenomenal success of *The Duenna* at Covent Garden. Sheridan's triumph—there had not been anything like it since *The Beggar's Opera* fifty years previously—was the subject of a popular street ballad:

> In the days of Gay, they sing and say,
> The town was full of folly:
> For all day long, its sole sing-sing
> Was pretty, pretty Polly.
> So now-a-days, as it was in Gay's,
> The world's run mad again-a

---

* *Journals of the House of Commons*, 1776, XXXV, 517, 554, 633, 651, 679. A bill enclosed in a letter in the Forster Collection shows that the legal expenses involved, amounting to £116 9s 10d, were met by Garrick.

† *Letters*, 977. Garrick seems to have felt some embarrassment in writing. He signed himself as Rigby's 'Very much asham'd but Most truly attached hu^le Ser^t.'

> From morn to night its whole delight
> To cry up the Duenna. . .

In January Garrick mounted a lavish new production of Ben Jonson's *Epicoene; or, The Silent Woman*, which had not been seen for more than twenty years. The piece had been extensively altered by Colman and Garrick once again courted criticism, as he had done in the earlier revival, by casting an actress in the title role, a part clearly designed for a man. On that occasion, the piece had been unenthusiastically received, and had been dropped after five performances, even though Epicoene had been played by Mrs Pritchard. This time the part went to Mrs Siddons, but the play was no more liked than it had been in 1752: 'It don't seem to hit the present Taste,' Hopkins noted in his diary, and Hoadly gave it as his opinion that the role should definitely be played by 'a young smooth-face' man.[8] After three nights, Garrick backed down. 'As many admirers of Ben Jonson have expressed a Desire to see the Silent Woman performed as the author originally intended it,' said a notice in the *Public Advertiser*, 'Mr Le Mash will perform the part of Epicoene on Monday next.'

Philip Lamash, the son of a French tutor to the Duke of Gloucester's children, was a handsome but not particularly gifted young man whom Garrick had taken on the previous season. The *Public Advertiser* reported that the substitution of an actor for an actress 'was received with particular Marks of Approbation'. Box office receipts told another story, however, and the play once again lost its place in the repertory.

Two of the reviews which the piece received demonstrate the extreme difficulty of deciding what weight to give to eighteenth-century theatre criticism. The *Westminster Magazine* recognized the 'fine manner' in which it was got up and acknowledged the expense incurred by the managers 'in habiting the whole *dramatis personae* in splendid and characterisitic Old English dresses'. Apart from King and Parsons, however, the performances were judged to be abysmal:

> Bensley is the worst Old Man we ever saw. He presents the countenance
> of a sickly old woman; and the uniform goggle of his eye, by which he
> means to express infirmity and distress is the look of a man in anguish
> from the colic. Mr Palmer, Mr Brereton, and Mr Davis have a bloated
> vulgarity about them, which should ever deter the manager from assigning
> them the parts of cavaliers or men of fashion. Baddeley, as usual, overdid
> his part, and Mr Yates, as usual, was not very perfect in his.[9]

Had the reviewer for the *Morning Post and Daily Advertiser* seen the same play?

> Mr Bensley's *Morose* was capital; now and then he forgot the surly old
> man, and sunk into the superannuated driveller . . . Mr Yates' *Otter* and
> Mr Baddeley's *Cutbeard* were all we could expect.—Mr Palmer was a
> admirable in the long unprofitable part of *True-Wit*, and discovered great
> spirit and comic vivacity through every scene . . .[10]

The *Morning Post* piece was written by its editor, Garrick's friend Henry Bate.

Bate, an intelligent and perceptive man, was not one of nature's under-arm bowlers. He did, on the other hand, have a comic opera of his own coming on at Drury Lane in two weeks; possibly the Fighting Parson thought it would be ungentlemanly to bite the hand which he hoped would shortly be feeding him.

As things turned out, *The Blackamoor Wash'd White*, as it was called, did not provide particularly rich pickings, although it was a livelier and more original piece than many of the offerings of the day. Sir Oliver Oddfish, mistrustful of his servants, proposes to replace them with blacks, allowing his daughter's lover, disguised as a blackamoor, to effect an elopement. The first act, critical of Londoners, ends with the line, 'O that I should ever live to see the day when white Englishmen must give place to foreign blacks.' Bate had many enemies, however. He guessed—correctly—that a party was likely to be got up to damn his farce and took the precaution of planting a number of ruffians in the audience. This got him through the first night, although when the play was given out for the next night there was a great deal of hissing, and shouts of 'No more! No more!'

Things got rougher on the second night, and on the third threatened to get out of hand completely. Henry Angelo was sitting in a corner box next to the gallery with a party of Bate's friends, doing their best for the piece, but they were eventually driven out by a shower of missiles from the gallery.[11] Things were made worse during the second act when a Captain Roper, of the 30th Regiment of Foot, appeared in one of the stage boxes.* He and his friends were extremely drunk. Their noisy and truculent support for the piece provoked a response from the pit as well as the gallery and they were pelted with apples and oranges; at one point a member of the Roper party jumped on to the stage, and fighting broke out—'I thought they would have pull'd the House down,' wrote Hopkins.

The piece was billed again two nights later along with *The Maid of the Oaks*, but as Mrs Abington was ill, Garrick decided to substitute *The Provok'd Wife* and see whether his own appearance as Brute would take some of the heat out of the proceedings. The anti-Bate faction had scented blood, however, and the players were unable to make themselves heard. King went on several times to ask the audience's pleasure but could not get a hearing. Nor at first could Garrick, although Hopkins reported that he stood his ground and announced he was prepared to stay there all night:

> As soon as they were quiet Mr G. told them that his Theatrical Life would be very Short and he should be glad to end it in peace—A Man in the Pit said if you have a mind to die in Peace don't let this Farce be play'd again ... At Length Mr King told them that the author had taken the Copy from the Prompter and was gone away with it.—Soon after this they withdrew.

The *Blackamoor* saga led to some sharp exchanges between Garrick and his friend William Woodfall, of the *Morning Chronicle*. Garrick felt that the paper

---

* Roper was the only brother of Charles Trevor Roper (1745–94), later Lord Dacre.

had not given the piece—or him—a fair crack of the whip. Woodfall was indignant—partly, perhaps, because Garrick had not voiced his complaint to him directly—and felt that his professional integrity was being impugned: 'You cannot, Mr Garrick, but know that, as the printer of the Morning Chronicle, I am the servant of the public—their message carrier—their mouth-piece.' He also had the advantage of having himself been present at the first three performances, and was therefore well placed to apportion blame for the disturbances:

> The first day after its appearance, I stood aloof, as my friends tell me, to a fault; the second day, I was under the necessity of coming nearer the point, and even then I spoke an unwilling language, although I was forced either to lose my character for impartiality, or to confess it was obvious the piece was recited before a packed jury. On the Saturday evening, the party of the author did not content themselves with ill-language and hard words, but fell to hard blows. I myself narrowly escaped being murdered . . .
> You are, without doubt, a man of great genius and ability; but, like all other triumphant heroes, you are surrounded with interested flatterers, and serious truth so rarely meets your ear, that it comes with an unwelcome sound.[12]

The part of Julia, Sir Oliver's daughter in *The Blackamoor*, had been played by Mrs Siddons. She was not having an easy time in her first Drury Lane season. 'The fulsome adulation that courted him in the Theatre cannot be imagined,' she wrote of Garrick in later life, 'and whosoever was the luckless wight who should be honord by his distinguished and envied smiles of course became an object of spite and malevolence.' She became convinced that Garrick's main aim in 'the exaltation of poor me' was 'the mortification and irritation' of Mrs Yates and Miss Younge. He would, she recalled, hand her from her own place in the green-room to the seat next to his, and whenever he appeared in any of his great roles would see to it that she was found a place in the boxes.* She maintained, however, that he was reluctant to let her appear in any very prominent character— these ladies, he said, 'would poison her if she did'.

One part which he did assign to her was that of Venus in his revival of *The Jubilee*:

> This gained me the malicious appellation of *Garrick's Venus* and the ladies who so kindly bestowed it on me, so determinedly rushed before me in the last scene, that had he not broken through them all, and brought us forward with him with his own hand, my little Cupid and myself, whose appointed situations were in the very front of the stage, might have as well been in the Island of Paphos at that moment.[13]

Mrs Siddons did not mention Mrs Abington, but there is nothing to suggest that she had become a reformed character in Garrick's last season at Drury Lane. An

---

* '—Oh!' she added in her memoirs, 'It was enough to turn an older and wiser head, cruel cruel treatment!'

imperious note of hers to Hopkins at the end of January indicated that she had lost none of her zest for waging guerrilla warfare against the management:

> You will be pleased to let the manager know that I am ill, (though I thank God I have not lost the use of my limbs as he has been pleased to tell the public); but I am too ill too attempt to perform tomorrow night . . .[14]

Later in the season, Mrs Abington engineered her last anti-Garrick coup. It was as brilliant as it was brazen. The manager, to his considerable astonishment, received a letter announcing her 'fixed determination' to leave the stage. Would he oblige her by playing for her benefit? Garrick, while urging her to reconsider her decision very carefully, had no alternative but to agree: 'If you are still absolutely resolv'd to quit the Stage for Ever, I will certainly in May, do for Mrs Abington, what I have done for others who have made the Same resolution.'[15]

The play she chose was, appropriately enough, *The Beaux' Stratagem*. She was Mrs Sullen, and Garrick was Archer—his last appearance in the role. She gave it out that she would now, at the ripe old age of thirty-nine, retire to a life of seclusion in Wales. A likely story. When Sheridan took over from Garrick the following autumn she signed new articles which kept her pay at £12 a week, gave her £200 in lieu of a benefit and doubled her clothing allowance to £120. Garrick, orderly in all things, filed her deceitful letter away, endorsing it with an indignant plea to some Court of Theatrical Justice Above the Sky: 'The above is a true Copy of the letter examin'd Word by Word of that worst of bad Women Mrs Abington to ask my Playing for her Benefit & Why—'*

By late winter, there were signs that the rigours and stresses of this last season were beginning to tell on his health. In February he had another attack of the stone, and he told a correspondent that he might be obliged to go abroad for some time.[16] He was in good spirits, for all that, and clearly not for a moment disposed to regret his decision to 'slip his theatrical shell' as he put it. An amusing letter to a friend in Ireland shows no great desire to remain at the tiller:

> My successors, (who are Young & Spirited Adventurers) have no Notion of Danger, laugh at the rocks and quicksands, & tho they lower their flag now & then to ye Old Admiral, yet they intend to Shew him I believe, that his manner (of) Sailing will do well enough for a dung barge, but *not* for a first rate the Royal George—bon voyage to the Young Gentlemen—†

As spring came on, his excitement at the prospect of release mounted. 'I shall shake off my Chains, & no Culprit at a Jail delivery will be happier—I really feel ye Joy, I us'd to do, when I was a boy at a breaking up,' he wrote to Peter. He was also bursting to tell his brother of his latest distinction: 'I receive Every honour that a Man can do from all Sorts of people, & I was yesterday enroll'd a member among the first & greatest people in this Kingdom—'

---

* The 'worst of bad Women' was the first Lady Teazle in Sheridan's *The School for Scandal* the following year. She did not make her last appearance on the stage until 1799.
† *Letters*, 987. He was writing to the Irish Member of Parliament Edward Tighe.

A dukedom? The Garter? Not quite:

> We have a New house built in the best Taste in yᵉ middle of St James's Street, & it is furnished like a palace—Each Member pays 12 Guineas at Entrance—It is yᵉ first Society for titles & property in the known world—14 Dukes at the head of us . . .¹⁷

Garrick had joined the Savoir Vivre, a club founded by a General Joseph Smith who had been kicked out of Almack's. On the opening night, the management informed members at the gaming tables that they might have credit up to £40,000. Happily, there was little time for the fourteen dukes to lead Garrick astray. Two months later Smith was jailed for bribery, and the club closed its doors.

Boswell had come south on his annual pilgrimage. He and Johnson were to travel to Oxford together, and met at the Somerset Coffee-House in the Strand to board the coach:

> I observed that Garrick, who was about to quit the stage, would soon have an easier life. Johnson. 'I doubt that, Sir,' Boswell. 'Why, Sir, he will be an Atlas with the burthen off his back.' Johnson. 'But I know not, Sir, if he will be so steady without his load. However, he should never play any more, but be entirely the gentleman, and not partly the player: he should no longer subject himself to be hissed by a mob, or to be insolently treated by performers, whom he used to rule with a high hand, and who would gladly retaliate.' Boswell. 'I think he should play once a year for the benefit of decayed actors, as it has been said he means to do.' Johnson. 'Alas, Sir! he will soon be a decayed actor himself.'¹⁸

Not before he had put himself through a punishing range of final performances, however. He was Lusignan in *Zara* for the last time in early March, and during April he dispatched Kitely and Abel Drugger. 'I thought yᵉ Audience were Mad,' he wrote to George after playing in *The Alchymist*, '& they almost turn'd my brain.'* In May he made his last appearance as Benedick and embarked on a sequence of farewell performances as Lear. On 13 May there were crowds at the door of the theatre by two in the afternoon. 'The eagerness of the people to see Garrick is beyond anything you can have an idea of,' Hannah More wrote to her friend Mrs Gwatkin in Bristol:

> You will see half-a-dozen duchesses and countesses of a night, in the upper boxes: for the fear of not seeing him at all, has humbled those who used to go, not for the purpose of seeing, but of being seen; and they now courtsy to the ground for the worst places in the house.

These final performances as Lear seem to have been particularly powerful, and to have roused the audience to an exceptional pitch of emotion. 'The Applause was beyond description,' noted Hopkins, '3 or 4 loud Claps Succeeding one

---

* *Ibid.*, 1005. George had once again retreated to Bath.

another at all his exits and many Cry'd out Garrick for Ever &c., &c.' Hannah More was deeply affected: 'It is literally true that my spirits have not yet recovered from the shock they sustained,' she told Mrs Gwatkin, and she added: 'I called today in Leicester Fields, and Sir Joshua declared it was full three days before he got the better of it.'

A week later Garrick fulfilled a long-standing ambition and brought the play out with new scenery and historical costumes. 'The play received considerable improvement last night from the characters being judiciously habited in Old English Dresses,' reported the *London Chronicle*. 'Human Nature cannot arrive at greater Excellence in Acting than Mr Garrick was possess'd of this Night,' wrote Hopkins, while his wife, who played Regan, and Miss Sherry, as Goneril, were both observed, wildly out of character, to be weeping on stage.*

Amid the general euphoria, an occasional dissenting voice was to be heard— that of Horace Walpole, for instance, whose regard for Garrick had always stopped some way short of idolatry:

> I saw *Lear* the last time Garrick played it, and as I told him I was more shocked at the rest of the company than pleased with him, which I believe was not just what he desired; but to give a greater brilliance to his own setting, he had selected the very worst performers of his troop; just as Voltaire would wish there were no better poets than Thompson and Akenside.[19]

It was five years since Garrick had appeared in *Richard III*, but he knew there was no escaping a farewell appearance in the role that had brought him instant celebrity 35 years previously. 'I can play Richard,' he had told Cradock in the spring, 'but I dread the fight and the fall. I am afterwards in agonies.'[20] But play it he did, with Mrs Siddons cast for the first time as Lady Anne. Years later, the actor John Taylor repeated to her a remark of Sheridan's—Garrick's Richard, he said, had been very fine, but he did not think it terrible enough:

> 'God bless me!' said she, 'what could be more terrible?' She then informed me, that when she was rehearsing the part of Lady Anne to his Richard, he desired her, as he drew her from the couch, to follow him step by step, for otherwise he should be obliged to turn his face from the audience, and he acted much with his features. Mrs. Siddons promised to attend to his desire, but assured me there was such an expression in his acting, that it entirely overcame her, and she was obliged to pause, when he gave her such a look of reprehension as she never could recollect without terror.[21]

A second performance of *Richard* was given out for 3 June and billed as Garrick's last appearance in the role, but then there came a royal command and Garrick, now close to exhaustion, had to draw heavily on his physical and emotional reserves. 'It will absolutely kill me,' he told Hannah More. 'What a Trial of

---

* Katherine Sherry, then thirty-one, was a relative newcomer to the Drury Lane company. Her début, four years previously, had been as Lady Macbeth.

breast, lungs, ribs & What not.'* When the curtain went up there was uproar in the pit, and the players had to leave the stage for a time—so many people had crowded in that it was impossible to sit down, and there was a cry for the doors to be opened to relieve the crush. It was after seven before the play could resume. 'During this time,' reads the entry in Hopkins's diary, 'the King Sent Two Messages to Mr G. to desire that he would not let this Noise disconcert him and his Majesty would take care that all should be quiet before the play began.'

Garrick's fatigue was such that further performances were now abandoned until 8 June. To the stress of performance was added the strain of an exhausting social round. Hannah More, who in the past few months had been living *en famille* with the Garricks, had maintained a stream of excited communiqués from Hampton and the Adelphi to her sisters in the West Country:

> . . . . On Wednesday, we had a very large party to dinner, consisting chiefly of French persons of distinction and talents who are come over to take a last look at the beams of the great dramatic sun, before he sets. We had beaux esprit, femmes sçavantes, academicians, &c. and no English person except Mr. Gibbon, the Garricks and myself. We had not one English sentence the whole day.[22]

One of those who had come from Paris to see Garrick act before he retired was Madame Necker, whose husband would later that year become Louis XVI's finance minister.† His friends Suard and the Chevalier de Chastellux also made the journey. The barrage of requests for seats and boxes from such visitors— they came from Ireland and Scotland as well as from France—was something of a nightmare for Garrick. '*Je viens vous persécuter encore pour Madame la baronne de Diede*,' wrote Suard in a note from his lodgings in Suffolk Street. 'We accept the very kind offer of the row,' wrote Sir Grey Cooper, 'but if I remember right, you promised me some particular attention for moving your Fund Bill at the beginning of the Session. I have heard that a certain Monsr. Necker, & a certain Dean of Derry, have boxes every night you Play . . .'‡

Garrick was offended: 'Your Letter this morning has hurt me greatly.—When have I been inattentive to your and Lady Cooper's demands?' he demanded:

What you tell me about the Dean of Derry was quite a secret to me—by

---

* *Letters*, 1022. He also passed on, with evident *Schadenfreude*, a titbit about the previous night's performance: 'My Partner Lacy would play Richm^d with me last Night & was hiss'd— Mum.'

† Madame du Deffand told Horace Walpole that the Neckers had also been drawn to London by the other great tourist attraction the capital had to offer in the spring of 1776, which was the trial for bigamy of the Duchess of Kingston. (*Walpole*, vi, 293, letter dated 31 March 1776.) Garrick had had a ticket for this spectacle, which had taken place in Westminster Hall, which he gave to Hannah More.

‡ *Boaden*, ii, 152. The Dean of Derry was Thomas Barnard (1728–1806). He had been a close friend of Goldsmith's, and the previous year had been elected a member of The Club, along with Adam Smith. He was later Bishop of Killaloe, and then of Limerick.

my honour he never yet got a single place thro me:—if Bribery and Corruption have crept behind the Scenes, I am sorry for it. . .

P.S. I plead guilty to Madame Necker: I rec^d many favours from her in France: she came over on purpose to see me act, and I thought myself bound in duty and gratitude to be attentive to her.—[23]

Garrick appeared for the last time on 10 June. He chose to do so in comedy, and played Don Felix in *The Wonder*. He had decided to donate the profits to the Theatrical Fund, and had composed an appropriate prologue:

> A Veteran see! whose last act on the stage
> Intreats your smiles for sickness and for age;
> Their cause I plead—plead it in heart and mind;
> A fellow-feeling makes one wond'rous kind . . .

When the play ended, Garrick came forward slowly on an empty stage and bowed. The speech he made was brief, and he was able to begin only after what Davies described as 'a short struggle of nature':

> Ladies and Gentlemen,
> It has been customary with persons under my circumstances to address you in a farewell epilogue. I had the same intention, and turned my thoughts that way; but indeed I found myself then as incapable of writing such an epilogue, as I should be now of speaking it.
> The jingle of rhime, and the language of fiction, would but ill suit my present feelings. This is to me a very awful moment; it is no less than parting for ever with those from whom I have received the greatest kindness and favours, and upon the spot where that kindness and those favours were enjoyed.

'Here his voice failed him,' said a newspaper report the following day; 'he paused, till a gush of tears relieved him.'

> Whatever may be the changes of my future life, the deepest impression of your kindness will always remain here [*putting his hand on his breast*], fixed and unaltered.
> I will very readily agree to my successors having more skill and ability for their station than I have; but I defy them all to take more sincere, and more uninterrupted pains for your favour, or to be more truly sensible of it, than is your humble servant.

There were sobs and tears when he had finished, and shouts of 'Farewell'. There was to have been an afterpiece—Dibdin's ballad opera *The Waterman* had been billed—but the audience would have none of it; the players in any case were in no state to perform.

There was one surprising absentee from this night of high drama. Hannah More had for some reason gone back to Bristol the previous week, and was unaware that the command performance and Garrick's near-exhaustion had extended his schedule of final appearances:

I have devoured the newspapers for the last week with the appetite of a famished politician, to learn if my general had yet laid down arms; but I find you go on with a true American spirit, destroying thousands of his Majesty's liege subjects, breaking the limbs of many, and the hearts of all.[24]

News of Garrick's retirement that summer had to compete for space with accounts of a drama being played out on a larger stage. Three weeks later, in Philadelphia, President John Hancock and Secretary Charles Thomson put their signatures to 'A Declaration by the Representatives of the United States in General Congress Assembled'. Post riders carried printed copies to each state. On the night it was read out in New York, a lead equestrian statue of King George III was dragged from its plinth, and a local literary gentleman compared the fallen monarch to Lucifer.

The close of King David's reign at Drury Lane thus coincided very neatly with the ending of royal authority in the New World. Independence celebrations in America laid emphasis on what the former colonists were escaping from, and when Garrick next wrote to Miss More he did the same:

I never pass'd two days with more real pleasure than I did Yesterday & today at Hampton, reliev'd from the Slavery of Government: such a Night as Monday last was never Seen!—Such clapping, sighing, crying, roaring &c &c &c—it is not to be describ'd!—in short—it was as we could Wish, et finis coronat Opus—yᵉ Bell rings—Exit Nonsense—*

* *Letters*, 1024. Finis coronat Opus—'The end crowns the work.' Little and Kahrl suggest that Garrick may have had lines from *All's Well That Ends Well* in mind: 'All's well that ends well. Still the fine's the crown./ Whate'er the course, the end is the renown.'

38

Frail Tenement

One of the luckiest young men in London on the night of Garrick's farewell was Harry Angelo, who was a guest with his parents in the manager's own box:

> Mrs. Garrick and my mother continued their sobbing after they quitted the theatre, which induced my father to observe, "One should suppose you ladies had been following my honoured friend to the grave; whereas, it is his labours which are buried this night, that he may live the longer and the happier."*

Garrick would enjoy a happy retirement, as it happened, although not a long one. He now had more time for his friends, for his books and his correspondence, and for what he called his 'jaunts' or 'rambles'. For a brief period after his release, however, he was content to relax and bask in an agreeable afterglow of adulation. 'Another man has his dram and is satisfied,' Colman once said to Boswell, 'but Garrick must have a sip every quarter of an hour.' In the days and weeks that followed his final performances he could sip to his heart's content. 'Whatever reputation the world may ascribe to you,' wrote Hannah More, 'I, who have had the happy privilege of knowing you intimately, shall always think you derived your greatest glory from the temperance with which you enjoyed it, and the true greatness of mind with which you laid it down.'[1] Mrs Garrick, who was every bit as fond of Hannah as her husband, decided that she must have a memento of him: 'I have sav'd his Buckles for you, which he wore in that last moment, and which was the only thing that They could not take from him'†— a generous gift, because they were buckles which she herself had given to Garrick.

Another tribute which gave him inordinate pleasure came from Madame Necker:

> *Je pourrai donc dire à mes amis: je l'ai vu cet homme unique; cet homme, l'admiration de toute l'Europe et les délices de ses amis . . . Je ne ferai plus de voyage; j'ai observé les moeurs de tous les hommes dans le jeu de*

---

* *Angelo*, I, 37. Lady Spencer, Mrs Vesey and Mrs Montagu were also in the Garricks' box and went on to supper afterwards at the Adelphi.

† This was written for her, in Garrick's hand, in the course of a lengthy postscript to his letter (1024) of 12 June 1776.

Monsieur Garrick et j'ai plus fait de découvertes sur le coeur humain que si j'avais parcouru l'Europe entière . . .*

Garrick replied that her praise had added a cubit to his stature: 'I defy the whole French Academy to give such power to words as you have done.' And it is clear that he still had it in mind to revisit France: 'If my multiplicity of business would permit, I should be at your feet almost as soon as this reaches your hands.'[2]

Although he no longer had any formal connection with Drury Lane, some of the 'multiplicity of business' of which Garrick spoke to Madame Necker related to the ownership of the theatre—he held mortgages from the new partners and also from Willoughby Lacy, who had inherited an obligation of £22,000 from his father. Lacy was fingering the idea of selling out part of his share—not simply as a commercial transaction to the highest bidder, but to someone he could regard as an ally, and who would help him to maintain a balance of power in the management. At the end of June, Garrick cautioned him against what he saw as 'a destructive measure':

> How will you be assur'd that by selling part of your property to this or that person, that you will at the same time purchase a friend?—on the other hand, why are you to distrust your present partners? I have had indeed no knowledge of them, but by our late transaction & in that I find them Men of their Words, & punctual in their dealings—they have ventur'd their all in this undertaking, & may be undone shou'd it fail of Success. What better security my good friend can you have for their zeal & attachment to their interest, which is the well doing of the theatre, than that your mutual all of fortune & happiness is embark'd on the same bottom, & that you will prosper by pulling together, or be sunk by a contrary behaviour—[3]

Lacy disregarded Garrick's advice, a decision which would occasion a good deal of disruption before Sheridan's first season as manager was more than a few weeks old.

Garrick transacted a simpler and more agreeable piece of business in a note to his old friend Tom King:

> Accept a Small token of our long & constant attachment to Each other— I flatter Myself that this Sword, as it is a theatrical one, will not cut Love between us, and that it will not be less valuable to You for having dangled at my side part of the last Winter—†

---

* 'So I can say to my friends that I saw this unique man; this man who is the admiration of Europe and the delight of his friends . . . I will travel no more; I have seen in the acting of Monsieur Garrick the manners of all mankind, and I have made more discoveries about the human heart than if I had journeyed over the whole of Europe.'

† *Letters*, 1028. King thanked him in an elegantly turned reply: 'Your retiring from the Stage being justly consider'd as a severe stroke to every Performer on it, and regretted by every admirer of the Drama, how must I feel, who not only suffer in each of those capacities, but lament at the same time the absence of a worthy Patron and most affectionate Friend?' (*Boaden*, ii, 163.)

By July he was launched on the first of his summer excursions, which took him to Barton Hall, in Suffolk. This was the home of his young friend Henry Bunbury, well-known in his day for his drawings and caricatures in pencil and chalk—Horace Walpole, a shade enthusiastically, compared him with Hogarth. Genial and unmalicious, Bunbury seems to have been a determined amateur in all he set his hand to—a later age might have called him 'laid-back'. Some verses survive in which Garrick saluted his host's agreeably uncompetitive talents:

> Shall *I* so long, old *Hayman* said, and swore,
>   Of Painting till the barren soil,
> While this young *Bunbury* not twenty four,
>   Gets Fame, for which in vain I toil:
>
> Yet he's so whimsical, perverse, & idle,
>   Tho Phoebus self should bid him stay,
> He'll quit the magic Pencil for the Bridle
>   And gallop Fame, and life away . . .[4]

From Suffolk it was a short journey to Mistley, in Essex. Garrick, in a letter from there, wrote that he had been obliged to 'take a jaunt into different parts of the Kingdom to recruit my health'.[5] This was not something one would normally expect to do at Mistley, where Rigby, still faring richly on the fruits of office, continued to entertain his guests as lavishly as he did at his notorious parties at the Pay Office in London. Advancing years and increasingly poor health had no effect on Garrick's unfailing sociability, however, even if, as when he wrote to Peter that summer, he sometimes contrived to give the impression that his arm had been twisted:

> The Duke of Devonshire meeting me 3 Weeks ago at Lord Spencer's at Wimbleton, desir'd me, in so affectionate Manner to go to Chatsworth that I could not resist him—Lady Spencer, the first of Women, hearing what was passing, insisted as affect^y that we should be there at ye Same time with them—*

Very occasionally, he said no. Towards the end of his last season there had been a string of pressing invitations from Sir James Caldwell, who lived in County Fermanagh, but Garrick had temporized:

> It has long been my wish to visit a Kingdom, where I was honoured with every Mark of regard & kindness—as I have not left Mrs Garrick one day since we were Married, Near 28 years, I cannot now leave her, and She is

---

* *Ibid.*, 1041. There was always a speedy reminder when Garrick allowed his conviviality too free a rein. 'Two Glasses of Champaign wch I drank Yesterday with Earl Spencer at Wimbledon are now tickling the ball of my great toe,' he wrote to his Adelphi neighbour Henry Hoare in July (*Letters*, 1035).

so Sick & distress'd by the sea, that I have Not had the resolution to follow my inclinations on account of her fears.*

The English seaside was another matter, however, and in August, after paying their respects to Lord Pembroke in Wiltshire, they bowled down to what was then still called Brighthelmstone, abandoning an earlier plan to go to Bath and to call on Hannah More in Bristol: 'We sincerely hope & believe, my dear Nine,' Garrick wrote to her just before setting off for Brighton, 'that you were Woefully disappointed at our not peeping in at You at Bristol.'

She was 'Nine' because Garrick, with his fondness for nicknames, had decreed that she was the embodiment of all the Muses. She was also sometimes 'Sunday'— this because of her evangelical sabbatarianism: for Miss More, the Sabbath was a day when those who feared their creditors went abroad, and those who feared God remained at home. Although some twelve months were to pass before they met again after Garrick's final season, his friendship with Hannah was clearly of great importance to him in those last years of his life, and we know more from her of the Garricks in their domestic setting in that period than from any other source.

Her original admiration for him bordered on hero-worship, and she may well, like many less level-headed young women, have been more than a little in love with him. 'Let the Muses shed tears,' she had written elegiacally to her sisters when his retirement was announced:

He retires with all his blushing honours thick about him, his laurels as green as in their early spring. Who shall supply his loss to the stage? Who shall now hold the master-key of the human heart? Who direct the passions with more than magic power? Who purify the stage?

She had also, however, a less high-minded and more personal concern: 'Who, in short,' she concluded, 'shall direct and nurse my dramatic muse?'[6] She need not have worried. She saw to it that the first two acts of her tragedy *Percy* were in his hands before he embarked on his summer rambles, and he had scribbled a hasty acknowledgement before setting out for Suffolk: 'I cannot criticise as I ought, because I am in a hurry, but they will do, & do well with a few Omissions,' he wrote. 'Keep up ye fire, & We shall do Wonders!'[7] From his next letter, Miss More learned that her play was going through more than one critical mill:

Mrs Garrick is studying your two acts . . . and she will criticise you to the bone. A German commentator (Montaigne says) will suck an author dry. She is resolved to dry you up to a slender shape, and has all her wits at work upon you.[8]

---

* *Ibid.*, 1014. Boswell, breakfasting with Garrick four years previously, had failed to persuade him to travel to Edinburgh: 'I pressed Mr. Garrick to come to Scotland, and said we had a right to a visit from him; that he had favoured Ireland with his presence, and why not Scotland? Sir, said he, when I went to Ireland, I went to get money. It was harvest time then with me. But when the barn's full (stretching himself in his chair) one grows lazy.' (*Boswell for the Defence*, 124.)

By the middle of August, Garrick had had the sight of two more acts:

> May I take the Liberty to say, that I don't think You were in y^r most Acute
> & best feeling when You wrote ye 3d Act—I am not satisfy'd with it, it is
> the Weakest of the four, & raises such Expectation from the Circumstances,
> that a great deal more must be done . . .'

He undertook to give his mind more fully to the deficiencies of the third act after
returning from Brighton, but in the course of his peregrinations he mislaid parts
of the manuscript, and *Percy* does not figure again in their correspondence until
he found them again towards the end of the year.

In early September Garrick and his wife drove north to Derbyshire and spent
some days with the Devonshires at Chatsworth. A year earlier, when he had
written in such glowing terms to his friend Bate about the Duchess, he had said
something which must have caused the eyebrows of that worldly parson to rise
in disbelief—'She is no Gamester my friend, nor was there Ever any Gaming at
Chatsworth.' It is one of the most puzzling sentences in the whole of Garrick's
correspondence. In the summer of 1776 the whole of London knew that the
young Duchess was up to her ears in debt. Two months previously, her creditors
had threatened to apply directly to the Duke. When she eventually got round to
confessing—initially to her mother, Lady Spencer, herself no stranger to the
gaming tables—that her gambling debts were not less than £3,000 (say £170,000
at present-day prices) her parents immediately settled them for her, but insisted
that she should tell all to her husband.*

How Garrick could be ignorant of all this remains an intriguing minor mystery.
He knew everybody, and he normally knew everything. He was a member of
Almack's, the capital's rialto for gambling gossip. His visit to Chatsworth in
that first week of September 1776, what's more, coincided with the appearance
of the following paragraph in the *Morning Post*—of which Bate was the editor:

> Gaming among the females at Chatsworth has been carried to such a pitch
> that the phlegmatic Duke has been provoked to express at it and he has
> spoken to the duchess in the severest terms against a conduct which has
> driven many from the house who could not afford to partake of amusements
> carried on at the expense of £500 or £1000 a night.[10]

That year, for the first time in almost three decades, there was no obligation to
hurry back to town for what Garrick often called the 'new campaign'. But he
was in London on 21 September when Drury Lane re-opened, and it seems
inconceivable that he was not drawn back—it had been agreed with the new
management that he should retain his old box. Sheridan had also persuaded him
to write a prologue for the piece that opened the season—described as a Prelude,
it had been written by Colman, there was incidental music by Linley and it was
cheekily, if a little obviously, entitled *New Brooms*!

---

* For a good account of the addictive gambling habits of the Devonshire House circle see
Foreman, Amanda, *Georgiana, Duchess of Devonshire*, London, 1998.

A sketch of Garrick in later life by de Loutherbourg. (Mrs Clement Parsons, Garrick and his Circle, *London, 1906)*

Comparing the theatre to a stage coach, Garrick managed to introduce a coy personal reference:

> Your late old coachman, tho' oft splash'd by dirt,
> And out in many a storm, retires unhurt;
> Enjoys your kind reward for all his pains,
> And now to other hands resigns the reins . . .*

There were eight hands now instead of four, and it soon became apparent that they were not equipped to handle the reins with anything like the requisite skill. Within weeks, Sheridan was having serious difficulties with Lacy, who, ignoring Garrick's advice, had arranged to sell half his share. He had hit on an improbable pair of allies. One was a man called Abraham Langford, the son of a well-known auctioneer of the same name. The other, Edward Thompson, now a naval captain, had in earlier days been a member of the Colman-Churchill circle; Garrick had helped him to secure promotion and lent him money. His play *The Hobby-Horse*, which Garrick had put on ten years previously, had not been a success; more recently, in March 1776, his masque, *The Syrens*, had survived for only three nights at Covent Garden, and he had savaged Garrick in the press, accusing him of conspiracy to damn the piece.

Lacy's determination to sell was prompted partly by pressure from Garrick, to whom he had fallen behind in his mortgage interest payments. Deviously, he concealed his intentions from his fellow-managers. It was Hopkins who first got wind of what was afoot, and when Sheridan was told he informed Lacy that if he persisted, he would withdraw from the management. This threw the affairs of the theatre into confusion. Mrs Abington announced that as she had made her agreement with Sheridan, she would play under no other manager. Three days later, disaffection had spread. 'The Provoked Husband and Rival Candidates was given out for Tuesday,' noted Hopkins:

> On Sunday Morning Mrs Yates sent word she was ill and could not play—
> sent to Miss Younge, and she sent word she was ill in bed—King sent
> word he had a sore Throat, and could not play . . . On Monday the
> Managers met, but nothing was settled. At twelve o'clock Mrs Baddeley
> sent word she had a sore Throat . . .

Sheridan was still new enough in the job to regard this as an enjoyable game, and sent Garrick, who was visiting the Spencers at Althorp, an entertaining account of these tiresome developments:

> Indeed there never was known such an uncommonly epidemic Disorder
> as has raged among our unfortunate Company—it differs from the Plague
> by attacking the better sort first—the manner too in which they are seiz'd
> I am told is very extraordinary; many who were in perfect Health at one

---

* The main offering of the evening was *Twelfth Night*, which suggests a further puzzling question: why did Garrick, that incomparable player of stage drunks, never attempt Sir Toby Belch? Or, for that matter, Malvolio?

moment, on receiving a Billet from the Prompter to summon them to their Business, are seiz'd with sudden Qualms—and before they can get thro' the contents, are absolutely unfit to leave their Rooms; so that Hopkins's Notes seem to operate like what we hear of Italian poisoned Letters, which strike with Sickness those to whom they are addressed . . . .[11]

Sheridan and his other two colleagues contended that the original agreement between Garrick and Lacy's father was still in force; this had stipulated that if either wished to sell his share, he must offer first refusal to the other, and that this might be done only during the summer closure. By selling to Langford and Thompson, therefore, Lacy would in their view be acting illegally—they had not been offered first refusal, and the sale was being negotiated at a time when the theatre was open. Lacy disputed this, but eventually yielded to pressure;* in a statement in the *Public Advertiser* on 17 October he reiterated his view that he was not bound by the original agreement, but announced that in the interests of the theatre he had persuaded the would-be purchasers to withdraw their claim to partnership.

Garrick, a pampered guest at Althorp, viewed all this with some detachment. He and his wife had posted down to Northamptonshire in easy stages. Lady Spencer had put Holywell House in St Albans at their disposal for an overnight stay ('You must allow me to add that our servants are not allowed to take anything,' she had written).† She had also sent her coach as far as Newport Pagnell, in Buckinghamshire, to meet them. Garrick found himself 'in the Midst of Joy & the best Society', he wrote to a friend:

> Three of the most beautiful Young Women in Europe are at this instant trying their Skill to prevent my writing this . . . I was never in Such Spirits; no School boy is half so Wild & ridiculous, & I never was in a place Where all my follies are so much indulg'd & forgiven—Lady Spencer is a divine Woman!‡

There was a meeting of the local hunt during his stay. The stone and the gout meant that Garrick could no longer always sit a horse with comfort, but his hostess was determined that he should not miss the sport. An entry in a surviving 'Chace Book' at Althorp records that 'Lady Spencer and Mr Garrick were out in the cabriolet and viewed the fox several times over Holdenby Grounds.'

---

* Walter Sichel, whose *Sheridan* appeared in 1909, believed that Sheridan in effect orchestrated a strike by the actors to make it impossible for Lacy to carry on the business of the theatre alone.

† *Letters of David Garrick and Georgiana Countess Spencer, 1759–1779*, edited by Earl Spencer and Christopher Dobson, Cambridge, 1960 (hereafter referred to as *Althorp Letters*), Letter 14. There were hidden costs involved in the social round. As often as not departing guests would find the servants of the house lined up at the door expecting 'vails' as tips were then called. At a large party these might come to anything between 10s and two guineas.

‡ *Letters*, 1052. The three beautiful young women were presumably Lady Spencer herself and her two daughers, the Duchess of Devonshire and her sister Harriet, then a girl of fifteen. Later Lady Duncannon and the Countess of Bessborough, she was for a time Sheridan's mistress.

Back in London at the end of October, Garrick dispensed some hospitality on his own account. He was an unreconstructed name-dropper, even in letters of invitation:

Dear Murphy,

I have a noble turtle to-morrow, the gift of the Right honourable Richard Rigby—if you have no objection to drinking his health, and meeting some of your friends, be to-morrow at my house at four . . .[12]

He had returned to find that Colman had bought the Little Theatre in the Haymarket from Foote,* and that Foote's former coachman had charged him with an attempted homosexual assault. As so often, Foote was the main author of his own troubles. He had written a play, originally called *A Trip to Calais*, which through its main character, Lady Crocodile, was an unmistakable attack on the Duchess of Kingston.† When the Lord Chamberlain refused the piece a licence, Foote threatened to publish the text. When he rejected the offer of a bribe from the Duchess, she charged him with extortion; much more seriously, a man called William Jackson, who was the publisher of the *Public Ledger* and had championed her cause, put it about that Foote was homosexual.‡

Garrick did not find writing easy that autumn ('I have this nasty Gout still nibbling at me,' he told Colman), but he kept up an extensive correspondence. He had found waiting for him a letter from Madame Necker which had pleased him hugely: she had been defending him—and Shakespeare—from the assaults of Voltaire and other 'beaux ésprits François'.[13] He thanked her for 'the most flattering, charming, bewitching letter that ever came to my hand', but he had a confession to make. It had arrived when he was in company with 'our learned friend & excellent writer' Mr Gibbon:

I could not resist the temptation of shewing it to him—he read—Star'd at me—was silent—then gave it me, with these Emphatical words, Emphatically Spoken—*This is the very best letter that Ever was written*: Upon Which, a la mode d'Angleterre, The writer was remember'd with true devotion, & in full libations . . .§

Garrick also wrote frequently to Lady Spencer. He liked to pass on snippets of political gossip picked up from his friends in the administration: 'There is a

---

* Colman got a good bargain. The arrangement was that he should pay Foote a guaranteed annuity of £1,600, to be paid twice yearly. Foote died in October 1777, having received only one payment of £800.

† The Duchess had retreated to Calais when the charge of bigamy was first brought against her.

‡ It also seems likely that it was Jackson who encouraged John Sangster, the former coachman, to make his allegations of assault.

§ *Letters*, 1061. Gibbon, who had published the first volume of his *Decline and Fall* earlier that year, was, of course, prejudiced. Madame Necker was the same Suzanne Curchod, the belle of Lausanne, who had captivated him during his stay there almost twenty years previously and whom he had hoped to marry.

whispering, & from the best whispering place at St James's, that something like a treaty between general Howe and the Americans is on foot,' he told her early in November (Howe had taken New York two months previously):

> On the other hand, I am assured from the best Authority (Ministerial) that a great cargo of Ammunition is sent openly by the French to America, & that an Officer, of rank & consequence, with several others, & Engineers are gone over to assist the Provincials—in short, my best of Ladies, the clouds are gathering on all sides, & I fear cannot be dispers'd, without much thunder and lightning.[14]

A letter he wrote six days later makes less agreeable reading, because he chose to retail to his 'best of Ladies' an abusive mock epitaph on Johnson that was going the rounds. It was the work of Soame Jenyns, an elderly miscellaneous writer who was also the MP for Cambridge:

> Here lies poor Johnson: reader, have a care;
> Tread lightly, lest you rouse a sleeping bear.
> Religious, moral, generous and humane
> He was; but self-sufficient, rude and vain;
> Ill-bred and overbearing in dispute;
> A scholar and a Christian, and a brute.
> Would you know all his wisdom and his folly,
> His actions, sayings, mirth and melancholy,
> Boswell and Thrale, retailers of his wit,
> Will tell you how he wrote and talked, and coughed and spit![15]

Jenyns, a good-natured man who was not normally malicious, was settling new and old scores. Almost twenty years had passed since Johnson had demolished his *Free Enquiry into the Nature and Origins of Evil*. He had been in equally deadly form when Jenyns's *View of the Internal Evidence of the Christian Religion* had appeared earlier in 1776. 'A pretty book,' he had conceded, but there was a casually devastating rider—'there seems to be an affectation of ease and carelessness, as if it were not suitable to his character to be very serious about the matter.' Jenyns's resentment did not, however, make him bold enough to publish his squib in Johnson's lifetime.*

Early in 1777, Garrick had another bout of illness—there is mention in one of his letters of Mrs Garrick 'nursing and sitting up with a sick Husband for near three Weeks'.† By early February, however, he was busy at his desk: 'I have written within these two days 3 Scenes & 2 fables,' he told William Woodfall— 'if you behave well & don't abuse Managers—perhaps you may have a Slice,

---

* When it did finally appear—Jenyns was by then in his eighties—Boswell retaliated with a venomous 'Epitaph, *prepared for a creature* not quite dead *yet*'.
† *Letters*, 1077. He was writing to Mrs Thrale, the wife of the wealthy Southwark brewer Henry Thrale and friend of Samuel Johnson. She had first known Garrick when she was a child, and the acquaintance had recently been renewed.

before they are tasted by Royalty.'[16] He had been summoned to read from his own works before the Royal Family at Windsor—or, if Horace Walpole is to be believed, he had 'solicited king George to solicit him to read a play'.

'The piece was quite new,' Walpole wrote in his feline way, '*Lethe*, which their Majesties have not seen above ten times every year for the last ten years.'[17] Garrick had composed a rather embarrassing prologue, in which he depicts himself as an ageing, greying blackbird, called out of retirement by the royal Eagle:

> . . . He never felt before such pride;
> Though crippled, old, and cracked his note,
> The royal smile each want supplied,
> Gave him a new melodious throat,
> And youth, and health, and fame;
> Gave spirit, voice, and art,
> Gave rapture to his loyal heart,
> Years to his life, and honour to his name.

Garrick performed before the King and Queen, the Princess Royal and several ladies of the court, and word soon went about that he had been mortified by his reception: 'All went off perfectly ill,' sniggered Walpole, 'with no exclamations of applause and two or three formal compliments at the end. Bayes is dying of chagrin, and swears he will read no more.'

The matter was still being discussed in Mrs Thrale's drawing room a month later. Fanny Burney was present, and that night she made a lengthy entry in her journal:

> 'He has been so long accustomed,' said Mr. Seward, 'to the Thundering approbation of the Theatre, that a mere *very well*, must necessarily & naturally disappoint him.'
>
> 'Sir', said Dr. Johnson, 'he should not, in a Royal apartment, expect the hallowing & clamour of the one shilling gallery. The King, I doubt not, gave him as much applause as was rationally his due . . .'

Johnson was enjoying himself and warmed to his theme:

> Yet, Mr. Garrick will complain to his Friends, and his Friends will lament the King's want of feeling & taste;—and then, Mr. Garrick will *excuse* the King! he will say that he might be thinking of something else;—that the affairs of America might occur to him,—or some subject of more importance than Lethe;—but though he will say this himself, he will not forgive his Friends, if they do not contradict him.*

---

* Burney, *op. cit.*, ii, 227, 27–8 March 1777. Years later, when she had served as Second Keeper of the Queen's Robes, Miss Burney recalled Garrick's 'disappointment and mortification', but having herself read Colman's *Polly Honeycombe* to the Queen, she understood that a profound silence was 'the settled etiquette'. (Dobson, Austin (ed.), *Diary and Letters of Madame d'Arblay (1778–1840)*, 6 vols., 1904–5, iv, 360–61.)

In later years, when she had recovered from her unpromising start at Drury Lane, Sarah Siddons was frequently invited to both Buckingham House and Windsor to read to the royals. Her experience was happier than Garrick's:

> The King was a most judicious and tasteful critick both in acting and Dramatick composition. He told me he had endeavourd vainly to detect me in a false emphasis, and very humourously repeated many of M^r. Smith's, who was then the principal Actor. He graciously commended the propriety of my action particularly my total repose in certain situations. 'This is,' he said, 'a quality in which Garrick faild. He never could stand still; he was a great fidget.'[18]

If Garrick was disappointed by the seeming coldness of the royal family, there was consolation in the warmth of Lady Spencer's concern for him. 'I heard the other day that you had not been quite well,' she wrote at the end of March, 'pray send me word how you do, but pray be very particular in your account of yourself as I cannot possibly allow you to be sick or sad.'[19] He and Mrs Garrick had both been unwell, in fact. He wrote back cheerfully enough but was, as usual, generous with the medical details:

> What with my vertigo, & madam's Rash, & sore throat, our Easter rather continu'd the week of Sackcloth & Ashes, but we have got our heads, bodies, & throats tolerably clear at present and we snap out fingers at future calamities. . . .

London was abuzz that spring with the misfortunes of Dr William Dodd, a fashionable preacher celebrated in particular for his sermons at Magdalen House, a charity for reformed prostitutes; these were often attended by the nobility and his hearers wailed and sobbed as he spoke. He was known as 'the macaroni parson'—he preached in a perfumed silk robe and wore a large diamond ring. The paintings on the walls of his country house included work by Rubens, Titian and Rembrandt.

All this had to be paid for. Dodd had been struck off the list of chaplains to the King three years previously for improperly soliciting preferment from the Lord Chancellor; now, rather more seriously, he had been convicted of forging a bond for £4,200 in the name of Lord Chesterfield, whose tutor he had been.* Many pamphlets had been written about the case, and numerous petitions to have him pardoned—one signed by 23,000 people—had been circulated; Johnson, although they had met only once, composed several papers for him. Garrick had also been approached, but viewed the fate of the wretched doctor (sentence had not yet been passed, but forgery was a capital offence) with a colder eye:

---

* Not the famous Earl, who had died without issue four years previously, but his twenty-two-year-old cousin.

> Dr Dodd is stirring heav'n (which he never did before) & Earth, & all that
> therein is, to save his poor, worthless life.* I have been apply'd to by him,
> as having more interest with the King & Lord Mansfield than anybody—
> by being created a Baronet. The Newspapers have brought all this trouble
> upon me.

There had indeed been rumours in the press that Garrick was to be honoured
by the King. It is unlikely that he would have declined a distinction never before
conferred on an actor, but he knew the reports were without foundation; for
Lady Spencer's benefit, at least, he managed to put on a reasonably convincing
display of indifference and even to combine it with a piece of gross flattery:

> I am so satisfy'd with the troubles I have undergone already, & the Honour
> I have of being smil'd upon by a certain lady Huntress, that I would not,
> if I could, accept of honours which I don't deserve, & which cannot add
> a mite to my happiness, or keep my ancles from swelling . . .†

He was still sought after as a writer of occasional pieces. Murphy persuaded him
to write an epilogue for his new comedy *Know Your Own Mind* which came
on at Covent Garden in February, and he supplied a prologue for Isaac Jackman's
farce *All The World's A Stage* at Drury Lane in April. He also responded to a
more challenging request. Barry had died in January, and his widow asked if he
would compose an address to the public for her to deliver on her first stage
appearance after his death. It was not an easy commission, because he and Barry
had never really got on, but he turned out a couple of dozen lines in a suitably
tear-jerking mode:

> . . . The tree cut down to which she clung and grew,
> Behold the propless Woodbine bends to you;
> Your fost'ring pow'r will spread protection round,
> And tho' she droops, may raise her from the ground.‡

On several occasions in the last few years of Garrick's life the Drury Lane
Company expressed their appreciation of his creation of the Theatrical Fund.
Before his retirement the Committee had voted that he should be styled 'Father,
Founder and Protector'. In March 1777 an elaborately decorated 'Testimony of
Duty and Affection' was drawn up; shortly afterwards he was designated 'Master

---

* Dodd mounted the scaffold on 27 June, a faint smile on his lips. The Prussian traveller
Archenhholtz was impressed: 'The English know how to die!' he said to his companion.

† *Althorp Letters*, Letter 38. The rumour was also current in Paris. The blue-stocking Mrs Pye,
whose play *The Capricious Lady* had been given its first and only performance at Drury Lane
in 1771, was now living there with her soldier husband. 'I do most sincerely rejoice,' she wrote,
'to find that you are not sunk into Sir David; for, as I said before, titles can add nothing to
fame like yours . . .' (*Boaden*, ii, 219, letter dated 15 April 1777.) The theatre had to wait some
time before it was honoured in this way; Queen Victoria knighted Henry Irving in 1895.

‡ Later in the year, Mrs Barry made a further call on him: 'She has desir'd me to write an
Epitaph for *Barry*,' he told his friend Becket the bookseller. 'I can't refuse her, & yet I don't
like yᵉ office.' (*Letters*, 1138.) Barry's tomb in Westminster Abbey bears no epitaph, however.

of the Corporation' and a delegation from the theatre presented him with a medal designed by Reynolds. He was conscientious in soliciting subscriptions from his friends. When Mrs Montagu generously stumped up 5 guineas instead of the £1 she had been asked for, Garrick let her into what he called 'a little Secret history of this Charity':

> A Nobleman in your Street whom I visit & who looks like benevolence itself—had a Ticket from Me at ye same time, that I was impertinent enough to send one to You—Your two Names like A fat & lean rabbit in a poulterer's Shop—stand thus together—
>
> | | |
> |---|---|
> | Mrs Montagu | 5: 5: 0—no ticket |
> | Rt. Honble Lord: W. de B— | 0: 5: 0—one ticket.* |

Although, in the uninhibited manner of the day, Garrick talked and wrote a good deal about his health, he had always been the sturdy philosopher and generally made light of his various ailments. It was plain, however, that the attacks of gout and the stone, the bouts of hoarseness and fever, were now coming on more frequently and proving more difficult to shake off. A passage in one of his letters to Lady Spencer in those spring days of 1777 is arrestingly different in tone from anything he had written before:

> . . . . My head is much clearer than it has been for some time past, but a certain tumult in my heart at times, has whisper'd me very kindly, that I am Mortal. I never was conscious till lately, that my tenement was frail, & a tolerable blast would overset me.[20]

The frailty of that tenement, as Garrick entered his sixties, was greater than he knew.

---

* *Letters*, 1092. The tight-fisted peer was Lord Willoughby de Broke, at that time Lord of the King's Bedchamber.

39

Retired Leisure

A School for Scandal! tell me, I beseech you,
Needs there a School—this modish art to teach you?
No need of lessons now,—the knowing think—
We might as well be taught to eat and drink . . .

Garrick wrote the prologue for Sheridan's masterpiece, and it was one of his best; his successor had also welcomed his advice while the piece was in rehearsal. May 8 was exceptionally late in the season for a new play, but it had an immediate and overwhelming success. Even Horace Walpole approved: 'To my great astonishment there were more parts performed admirably in *The School for Scandal* than I almost ever saw in any play,' he wrote. 'It seemed a marvellous resurrection of the stage.'[1] Lady Teazle was played by Mrs Abington, and Tom King was Sir Peter. The part of Maria, his ward, went to Hopkins's daughter, Priscilla; it had been intended for a young actress called Mrs Robinson, but by the time the play went into rehearsal her second pregnancy was far advanced and she was judged too 'unshaped' for the role.

Mary Robinson was the daughter of a once prosperous Bristol sea-captain* and had for a time been a pupil at the school run by Hannah More's sisters. She had come to Garrick's attention during his last season as manager, but his notion of bringing her on as Cordelia (she reminded him of Mrs Cibber) had been frustrated by her first pregnancy. Sheridan was equally impressed by her, and accepted his predecessor's suggestion that she be allowed to attempt Juliet. Garrick coached her intensively, walked with her through rehearsals in the role of Romeo and on the night sat in his old place in the orchestra to boost her confidence. 'A genteel Figure,' noted the judicious Hopkins. 'A very tolerable first appearance and may do in time.'[2]

As indeed for a time she did, although not in tragedy. Two years later, still only twenty-two and at the height of her beauty, she played Perdita in a revival of Garrick's alteration of *The Tempest*. At a command performance she suffered some embarrassment, owing, she wrote, 'to the fixed attention with which the

---

* He lost his money in a hare-brained scheme to establish a whale fishery on the coast of Labrador.

prince of Wales honoured me'. Soon the eighteen-year-old Prince's go-between was bringing her notes signed 'Florizel'; then a portrait in miniature, with a small paper heart inscribed 'Je ne change qu'en mourant' on one side and 'Unalterable to my Perdita through life' on the other. The liaison lasted eighteen months. When it ended, another of Perdita's admirers, Charles James Fox, negotiated on her behalf an annuity of £500, 'the moiety of which was to descend to her daughter after her decease'.*

One of the best known of many stories about *The School for Scandal* was told in his memoirs by the prolific dramatist Frederic Reynolds, who in 1777 was a twelve-year-old schoolboy at Westminster. One evening he happened to be walking down the narrow passage between Vinegar Yard and Bridge Street. Suddenly there was a terrifying noise; convinced that Drury Lane Theatre, which formed one side of the passage, was collapsing, he covered his head with his hands and ran for his life. Only next morning did he discover his mistake— 'The noise did not arise from the falling of the house, but from the falling of the screen in the fourth act; so violent and tumultuous were the applause and laughter.'†

With a simple piece of stage business, Sheridan had devised one of the most electrifying moments in the history of English stage comedy. The throwing down of the screen discloses the cowering figure of Lady Teazle, and her duplicitous relations with the reptilian Joseph Surface are simultaneously revealed to her husband and to the audience.

Garrick was genuinely delighted with Sheridan's success; a note he sent him a few days into the run demonstrated that retirement had done nothing to blunt his sense of theatrical effect:

> A Gentleman who is as mad as myself about yᵉ *School* remark'd that the characters upon the Stage at yᵉ falling of yᵉ Screen Stand too long before they speak—I thought so too yᵉ first Night—he said it was yᵉ Same on yᵉ 2ᵈ & was remark'd by others—tho they should be astonish'd & a little petrify'd, yet it may be carry'd to too great a length—[3]

As summer came on, Garrick was in good spirits: 'No school Boy at a breaking up for yᵉ Holidays, had Ever Such rantipole Spirits,' he told Boswell—'however there is no good without some concomitant Evil, I grow fat, & Short-winded—'[4]

---

* The Prince's finances being what they were, payments continued for only a few years. Mrs Robinson's acting career did not prosper. She found consolation for a time with Colonel Banastre Tarleton, a dashing cavalryman who distinguished himself in the American campaigns, resisted improper proposals from the Duke of Orleans and became friendly with Marie-Antoinette. She also wrote poetry and novels and had a farce hissed off the stage at Drury Lane. She died in 1800 at the age of forty-two and was buried, by her own wish, in the churchyard at Old Windsor.
† Reynolds, Frederic, *The Life and Times of Frederic Reynolds*, London, 1826, vol. 1, p. 110. Sheridan, hugely excited by his success, went on the razzle. Years later he told Byron that he was 'knocked down and put into the watch-house for making a row in the street, and being found intoxicated by the watchmen'.

Early in July there came a melancholy letter from Camden complaining how difficult he was to get hold of:

> I am so retired form the world, that now, in the close of my life, I avoid company, being grown too nice to be satisfied with such trash as I meet with among the nobility; whereas you have the happiness of being courted by them, and so yield yourself to every invitation, by which means I have lost you. . . .[5]

Sure enough, the Garricks were soon on their way to Mistley and the end of the month found them at Farnborough Place as the guests of the Wilmots. They were accompanied there by Hannah More, who described to her sisters the opulence of her surroundings and Garrick's delicate concern for her religious susceptibilities:

> . . . . You will judge of the size of the house, when I tell you there are eleven visitors, and all perfectly well accommodated. The Wilmots live in the greatest magnificence; but what is a much better thing, they live also rationally and sensibly. On Sunday evening, however, I was a little alarmed; they were preparing for music (sacred music was the *ostensible* thing), but before I had time to feel uneasy, Garrick turned round and said, 'Nine, you are a *Sunday woman*; retire to your room—I will recal you when the music is over.'[6]

In the interval of these excursions, there was the summer season at the Haymarket to be sampled. Henderson had at last achieved his ambition of appearing in the capital. Colman had taken him on, and he made his début as Shylock on 11 June—not without trepidation, because Macklin, although now approaching eighty, was still firmly entrenched in the part. The reviews were mixed, but generally encouraging. 'His voice,' reported the *Gazetteer*, 'whether from nature or imitation, is exceedingly like Mr Garrick's in many of his tones, but without his power.' A fortnight later Henderson appeared as Hamlet, and he followed this with Leon in *Rule a Wife and Have a Wife*, Falstaff in *Henry IV Part 1*, Richard III, and Don John in *The Chances*. For his benefit he again invited comparison with Garrick by choosing to appear as Bayes in *The Rehearsal*; he rounded off the season as Falstaff in *The Merry Wives of Windsor*. Colman had every reason to be pleased with the houses,* although he was not amused when Henderson had the impertinence to imitate him to his face.

Pressed for a view about Henderson's performance as Shylock, Garrick is said to have replied, 'Oh, sir, I am no judge.' Horace Walpole, inevitably, was convinced that he was wildly jealous:

> . . . . . Garrick is dying of the yellow jaundice on the success of Henderson, a young actor from Bath—*Enfin donc desormais* there must never be a

---

* He had also engaged John Edwin, a rising young comedian who had played with Henderson in Bath, and Elizabeth Farren, the future Countess of Derby, who had been a child actor in the provinces for some years and was still only fifteen.

good player again. As Voltaire and Garrick are the god and goddess of Envy, the latter would put a stop to procreation, as the former would annihilate the traces of all antiquity, if there were no other gods but they.[7]

Not for the first time Walpole was retailing malicious nonsense. One of Garrick's letters to Lady Spencer preserved at Althorp makes it plain that he regarded Henderson's rise to popularity with equanimity:

> . . . . . The Haymarket Theatre is at present the Fashion. Mr Henderson the Bath Roscius, and whom Lord Camden calls the Birmingham Garrick, carried the People in crowds to that Theatre. The papers tells me, that notwithstanding I was Somebody, some time ago, that I shall soon be forgot in the more dazzling splendor of Mr Henderson's Genius. I am content, with lady Pentweazle, that I have *had my day*, & so give place to my betters.[*]

It is not clear, in the flurry of these multifarious retirement activities, how Garrick found time for reading, but he continued to add to his considerable library. His friend Benjamin Van der Gucht, the painter and picture dealer, was travelling on the continent that summer and had just reached Paris. 'You are luckily arriv'd in France to correct ye blunders which Noverre Junr has made in buying half a dozen books for Me,' Garrick told him cheerfully, and sent a varied if not altogether precise shopping list:

> Les trois Teatres de Paris—par Monsr Desessarts—is an Acc^t of ye Laws &c of the Theatres of Paris—L'Almanach litteraire—1776. There is likewise a book which I want the title of which I have forgot—it is I believe in *4 volumes* an Account of all kind of authors Greek, roman, & french with their Characters and a Small critique of their Works—Noverre brought me *les trois Sciecles de la litterature Françoise* for it—but this book is an Acc^t of Classick Authors as well as others—it is a late book, & I would have it more particularly as it treats of ye Classicks Greek & Roman . . . I give You such trouble but I am most truly Your friend & hearty well wisher . . .[8]

Edward Gibbon was also in Paris, and from him there came an elegantly turned letter full of the sweet music of flattery:

> . . . Foreign nations are a kind of posterity, and among them you already reap the full harvest of your fame. I can assure you that in every polite circle there is not any name so frequently repeated as the name of Garrick. The persons who have been in England before the fatal month of June, 1776, describe with transport what they have seen and what they have felt; and those who propose to undertake the same journey, express their regret that the principal object of their curiosity no longer subsists. . . . Your friends, and they are many, who have enjoyed your social qualities, are

---

[*] *Althorp Letters*, Letter 45. Lady Pentweazle was a character in Foote's play *Taste*.

sincere and earnest in their wishes that you would execute your promise of visiting this country; and I sometimes hear them exclaim,
with the good-natured vanity which constitutes no unamiable part of
the French character: "Ce Monsieur Garrick étoit fait pour vivre parmi
nous."*

The weather was very hot that summer, and when Colman asked him for an
epilogue (he was preparing an adaptation of Beaumarchais's *Barber of Seville*
for his season at the Haymarket) Garrick groaned. 'I would give You an Epilogue
wth as much readiness as I would a pinch of snuff, being both of Equal value,'
he wrote:

> But indeed, my dear Friend, I have such a listlessness about Me, that I
> have not Spirit to scribble a distich—I sh^d be most sorry to refuse You
> any thing, but I am really Sick of prologue & Epilogue writing—

Before the end of the letter, however, he relented, and undertook to 'squeeze his
brains' for his old friend—'tho upon my Soul, I expect Nothing but foul Water
from the Operation.'[9] *The Spanish Barber* opened on 30 August, and the epilogue
was entrusted to Miss Farren, who had played the part of Rosina.

Something of a mystery now arises. Garrick did not attend the first night,
although he received a report about it the next morning in a note from his friend
Caleb Whitefoord, who said that his 'excellent Epilogue' had been 'very prettily
spoken'. Why then, writing later that same day to Hannah More, should Garrick
complain that 'Miss Farren spoke it so ill, & so unintelligibly, that it of Course
had no Effect.'? It is possible that he had heard a different account of Miss
Farren's performance from another source; or it may be that Miss Farren simply
caught the fall-out from his displeasure with Colman: 'He Us'd me very unkindly
about ye Epilogue,' he told Miss More: 'I Sat up half ye Night to cook one
for him in his distress, but beg'd my Name might be conceal'd—but on ye Contrary—'[10]

The next day he decided to judge for himself, and travelled up from Hampton
to see the second performance. He was greatly impressed, and he wrote to
Colman to tell him so:

> I went from this Place Yesterday on purpose to see Your Nonsense, upon
> the information of our Friend Whitefoord, who wrote me a Line of
> Intelligence on Saturday night, tho Somebody Else would not—*I like Your
> Piece, & that other most promising Piece, Miss Farren*—'tis a Shame that
> she is not fix'd in London—I will venture my Life that I could teach her
> a capital part in Comedy, ay & tragedy too, that should drive half our
> Actresses mad—she is much too fine Stuff to be worn & Soil'd at Man-
> chester & Liverpool—[11]

---

* *Boaden*, ii, 255–6. 'May I beg to be remembered to Mrs. Garrick?' Gibbon added. 'By this
time she has probably discovered the philosopher's stone: she has long possessed a much more
valuable secret,—that of gaining the hearts of all who have the happiness of knowing her.'

'Tho Somebody Else would not'—the reproach was oblique, but unmistakable.

Mid-September found the Garricks preparing to set out for Denbighshire, in North Wales—one of their longest journeys since they had travelled on the continent. Setting the scene for Lady Spencer, Garrick was at his entertaining best:

> . . . . . Tomorrow Madame Garrick, her deaf German Neice, & her almost dumb Husband, by bawling to the said Neice, set out for the Land of Pippins & Cheese. Sir Watkin Williams Wynn, to whom I last year hastily gave a promise, will not suffer me to put off visiting the mountain Goats till the year 1778—but the Harps, & the old Bards are prepar'd to receive us at Wynstay, & go we must. Only think of me, my good Lady, to be stuff'd in a Coach, for 5 or 6 Days, with a score of Bandboxes, half a dozen hat-cases, bottles, boxes, & bags—two german females ringing bob majors upon B's and P's—& a tall, slim Staffordshire Abigail, with two large black dying eyes, rolling about without meaning, & not less than two Inches diameter; & with these three agreeable companions, Stuff'd into the corner of a coach this broiling weather, unable to stir, till half the moveables of the coach are lugg'd into an Inn, & I creep to a great chair with both my legs asleep, every avenue of my Head & face full of dust, & my shirt, like that of Hercules, sticking like a Blister to my body. . . . . .[12]

Garrick, endlessly curious about people and places, greatly enjoyed the journey, for all that. 'These Welch scenes are quite New to us, & very well worth anybody's Curiosity,' he wrote to Peter. He was also gratified to discover that his celebrity had gone before him:

> At Shrewsbury the Town was in an Alarm at my Coming, & the Raven-Inn besieg'd—I little expected so much honour from Salopian Swains, & Welch Mountaineers—their Observations upon my Person, age &c you shall have at Birmingham on Sunday ye 5th Octr if Nothing prevents your making Us happy—*

The Garricks' host in Denbighshire, a young man of twenty-eight, was the MP for the county and the biggest landowner in the Principality.† He was a member of the Society of Dilettanti, a club of connoisseurs which, in John Brewer's succinct definition, 'combined an interest in classical antiquities with an enthusiasm

---

* *Letters*, 1133. The 'deaf German niece' was Elisabeth ('Liserl') Fürst, then a girl of eleven, who was the daughter of Mrs Garrick's sister. She had come from Vienna to live with the Garricks in June 1777. The 'Staffordshire Abigail' was presumably Mrs Garrick's maid, named in other letters as Fosbrooke. The Garricks quite often asked Peter to find them domestic staff from Lichfield.

† His father, the third baronet, had been a leading supporter of the House of Stuart, although in 1745 the Young Pretender had come to believe that the Welsh Jacobites, like the English, were offering him all help short of actual assistance. 'I shall do for the Welsh Jacobites what they did for me,' the Prince later remarked: 'I shall drink their health.'

for erotica.'* He was also, like so many of his class, devoted to amateur theatricals, and had a private theatre at Wynnstay—originally a kitchen, it consisted, according to George Colman the Younger, 'merely, of a commodious Pit'.[13] Garrick had been roped in to supervise a production of Henry Carey's burlesque *Chrononhotonthologos*, which was performed there on 2 October. Sir Watkin also offered his guests musical entertainment. 'I am writing in yᵉ Dark,' says a postscript to one of Garrick's letters from Wynnstay, '& Mʳ Parry yᵉ famous Harper is playing like an Angel.'†

While Garrick was being lionized in north Wales, his histrionic talents were being more rigorously assessed in Derbyshire. Boswell had been invited to join Johnson at Ashbourne, where he was visiting his old school and Oxford friend John Taylor, and on the evening of Sunday, 21 September, the talk turned to actors and acting:

> BOSWELL: You will not allow merit to a player.
> JOHNSON: "Merit, Sir! What merit? Do you respect a rope-dancer or a ballad-singer?
> BOSWELL: "No, Sir. But we respect a great player as a man who can conceive noble sentiments, and can express them gracefully."
> JOHNSON: "What, Sir, a fellow who claps a hump on his back and a lump on his leg, and cries, 'I am Richard the Third'? Nay, Sir, a ballad-singer is higher, for he does two things: he both repeats and sings; there is both recitation and music. The player only recites."
> BOSWELL: "My dear Sir! You may turn anything into ridicule. I allow that a player of farce is not entitled to respect. He does a little thing. But he who can represent exalted characters, and touch the noblest passions, has very respectable powers; and mankind have agreed in admiring great talents for the stage. We must consider too that a great player does what very few are capable to do. His art is a very rare faculty. *Who* can repeat Hamlet's soliloquy, 'To be or not to be,' as Garrick does it?"
> JOHNSON: "Anybody may. Jemmy there. (Mr. Fieldhouse's son, a boy about eight years old) "will do it as well in a week."[14]

Garrick returned to Hampton in the middle of October, and was almost at once laid low:

> I have been very ill today & so Weaken'd with a purging that I can scarce walk about—it is not Stop'd yet, nor do I chuse it Should, as I

---

* Brewer, John, *The Pleasures of the Imagination: English Culture in the Eighteenth Century*, London, 1997, p. 43. 'The nominal qualification for membership is having been in Italy,' sneered Horace Walpole, 'and the real one, being drunk.' Established in 1734 as a dining club—one of the founders was Sir Francis Dashwood—the membership included an assortment of diplomats, Whig aristocrats and serious collectors.

† Garrick was writing to Peter, asking him to arrange accommodation in Birmingham on their way to Lichfield. He travelled in some style on these extended jaunts: 'I have Six horses for which I must have a good Stable,' he told his brother, 'and four Men Servants.' (*Letters*, 1134.)

believe Nature is throwing off some bad Matter, perhaps not less than a Fever—[15]

He was writing to Becket, the bookseller, and was eager for the latest theatrical gossip—'Was Falstaff follow'd this Evening, or did Mrs Barry bear ye prize away in *Zenobia*?' Sheridan had signed up Henderson at Drury Lane and he had been making his second appearance as the fat Knight in the first part of *Henry IV*. Henderson did not have the physique of a Quin or a Barry, and at his début in the role the previous week the audience had not always laughed in the right places: 'No joke ever raised such loud and repeated mirth, in the galleries, as Sir John's labour in getting the body of Hotspur on his back,' Davies wrote in his *Dramatic Miscellanies*:

> At length this upper-gallery merriment was done away by the difficulties which Henderson encountered in getting Smith on his shoulders. So much time was consumed in this pick-a-back business that the spectators grew tired, or rather, disgusted. It was thought best, for the future, that some of Falstaff's ragamuffins should bear off the dead body.[16]

George's father-in-law died that October, and Garrick was indignant at the provision made in his will for his grandchildren:

> Old Carrington has behav'd just as I thought he would—with wicked partiality to Nathan & with cruelty & injustice to ye others—He was a good for Nothing, ignorant old —— You may fill up ye blank as you please—*

A second death occurred in Garrick's circle within a few days of his return from North Wales. Samuel Foote had been acquitted of the charges brought against him,† but his health had been fatally undermined. He had been on his way to winter in the south of France. Early reports said that he had died at Calais, but he had not got that far; 'Captain Timbertoe', as he sometimes called himself, paid his debt to nature in Brighton, at the Ship Inn, on the afternoon of 21 October.

Garrick had frequently lent him money and performed many other kindnesses over the years, but that never won him protection from Foote's tongue. When Johnson heard that Foote intended to take him off, he announced that he would beat him with an oak stick: 'I would have saved him the trouble of cutting off a leg,' he told Boswell: 'I would not have left him a leg to cut off.' Garrick's temperament did not allow him to be so robust. He knew that he would always be vulnerable to the baiting of 'Beau Nasty', and that knowledge was corrosive

---

* *Letters*, 1138. Nathan, the youngest grandson, had been made Carrington's residuary legatee, and received £1,000 and an estate of £900 a year. Arabella and Catherine each received £1,500 and Carrington and David £1,000. To his son-in-law, George, 'Old Carrington' left 10 guineas, 'for Mourning'.

† The case had been heard the previous December before Lord Mansfield. Arthur Murphy was one of his lawyers, and Tom Davies one of those who testified to his absence from London on the day of the alleged assault.

of any real affection. Johnson was able to be generous: 'He was a fine fellow in his way,' he wrote to Mrs Thrale, 'and the world is really impoverished by his sinking glories.' Garrick conveyed the news of his death to Lady Spencer with a notable lack of emotion: 'He had much wit, no feeling, sacrific'd friends & foes to a joke, & so has dy'd very little regretted even by his nearest acquaintance.'[17]

Hannah More's tragedy *Percy* had been accepted at Covent Garden, and in November she returned to London, initially to lodgings in Gerrard Street in Soho. 'It is impossible to tell you of all the kindness and friendship of the Garricks,' she wrote to her sister:

> He thinks of nothing, talks of nothing, writes of nothing but Percy. He is too sanguine; it will have a fall, and so I tell him. When Garrick had finished his prologue and epilogue, (which are excellent) he desired I would pay him. Dryden, he said, used to have five guineas a piece, but as he was a richer man he would be content if I would treat him with a handsome supper and a bottle of claret. We haggled sadly about the price, I insisting that I could only afford to give him a beef steak and a pot of porter; and at about twelve we sat down to some toast and honey, with which the temperate bard contented himself.[18]

'Cordial applause—not a dry eye in the house.' Garrick took some pleasure in reporting a successful first night for *Percy* to Lady Spencer because she had not been particularly taken with some of Miss More's essays. Garrick also amused himself, as he quite often did, in making fun of his wife's ineradicable German accent:

> Mrs Garrick bresentz her pest respects to tearest Laty Sbencer—she is mutch petter, & dinks herself most barticularly honour'd py her gread gootness to her last Night.
>
> Mrs Garrick pelieves her Baleness was owing to the bretty little pape they sboke apout.[19]

The Garricks were invited to spend Christmas at Althorp, and drove north to Northamptonshire in the middle of December, having farmed Mrs Garrick's niece out to their friends the Racketts. They stayed longer than they had expected:

> Yesterday Morning Lady Spencer in full convocation assembled at Break-fast, declar'd her resolution and vow'd very seriously, that she would not suffer Us to Stir till 8 or 10 days after the Holidays.[20]

Garrick did not put up a great deal of resistance. Wilkinson was unkind when he said that there was nothing he liked better than 'to loll with a lord', but he certainly did not find the company at Althorp uncongenial. The Devonshires were there, and so were the Duke and Duchess of Marlborough. Another guest was the Earl of Jersey, a former Extra Lord of the Bedchamber and a future Master of the Buckhounds. He was renowned for his courtly manners; Mrs Montagu called him 'the Prince of Maccaronies'. His lovely young countess, eighteen years his junior and the daughter of a bishop, was thought to have been

Samuel Foote as Fondlewife in Congreve's The Old Bachelor. *Short and flabby, buffoon and mountebank, outstanding mimic and heartless wit — 'Beau Nasty' was not many people's cup of tea. Garrick's relations with him were always uneasy, and he shed no tears at the news of his death. 'He sacrific'd friends & foes to a joke,' he wrote to Lady Spencer, '& so has dy'd very little regretted even by his nearest acquaintance.' (Bell's British Theatre, Vol. 2, 1780)*

one of Sheridan's models for Lady Sneerwell in *The School for Scandal*. As unprincipled as she was beautiful, and an accomplished wrecker of the marriages of her friends, she would later have an affair with Devonshire and become the mistress of the Prince of Wales.

The Spencers had also invited a sprinkling of MPs. Samuel Egerton, a great-grandson of the second Earl of Bridgewater, sat for Cheshire. Robert Stewart was an Irish Member who was married to Camden's daughter; he would later become Viscount Castlereagh, and his son would be Prime Minister. The odd man out in this festive company was a cultivated, eccentric bachelor in his late fifties called Hans Stanley. Slow of speech and awkward of manner, Stanley had been both diplomat and politician. Currently the Member for Southampton, he was also Governor of the Isle of Wight and Cofferer of the Household. Three years later, when he was once again a Christmas guest at Althorp, he would go out into the woods and cut his throat with a penknife.

The Garricks' extended stay with the Spencers meant missing most of the run of *Percy* (although one evening he entertained the company at Althorp by reading it to them). Shortly after their return to town Hannah More fell ill, but could not be persuaded to move in with them at the Adelphi. 'Mrs Garrick came to me this morning,' she told her sister:

> She would have gone herself to fetch me a physician, and insisted upon sending me my dinner, which I refused: but at six this evening, when Garrick came to the Turk's head to dine, there accompanied him, in the coach, a minced chicken in a stew-pan, hot, a canister of her fine tea, and a pot of cream. Were there ever such people! Tell it not in Epic, or in Lyric, that the great Roscius rode with a stew-pan of minced meat with him in the coach for my dinner. . . .[21]

Garrick also kept a friendly eye on the business side of things for her. The author's nights and the sale of copyright had brought in almost £600, she told her friend Mrs Gwatkin: 'Mr. Garrick has been so good as to lay it out for me on the best security, and at five per cent, it makes a decent little addition to my small income.'[22]

Mrs Abington had lost none of her ability to get under his skin. In the first half of 1778, two newspapers published a series of articles called 'Modern Characters from Shakespeare'—selected quotations from the plays were applied to contemporary figures. Garrick, hearing that they were being attributed to him, sent the presumed culprit the feeblest of remonstrances:

> I sincerely agree with Montaigne that the smallest token of sorrow from a Lady ought to melt the hardest heart . . . If Mrs Abington has inadvertently mentioned me as the author of the Characters in question, I trust in her justice that she will not suffer any false impression of me to remain among her friends.[23]

To the Honourable Albinia Hobart, however, whom he clearly believed could help him in his enquiries, he wrote in very different terms:

A friend of mine assur'd me that You were lately in Campany with Mrs
Abington, who declar'd that I was the Author of the application of the
Words of Shakespear to Modern Characters in yᵉ Mᵍ Post—tho I shall no
longer appear before yᵉ Publick yet it is incumbent upon Me to shew, that
I am not altogether unworthy of their favour which I certainly shᵈ be,
were I guilty of what that Mischief Making Lady is pleas'd to accuse Me—
I flatter Myself that those who know that Lady & Me, will not give the
least Credit to so false & malignant a Suggestion—*

Whether Mrs Hobart added to the undoubted satisfaction of the 'Mischief
Making Lady' by letting her see this unwise letter is not known.

To at least one of his admirers, Garrick's relentless busyness, his inability or
unwillingness to ease up, signalled that he was not enjoying his retirement quite
as much as he professed to be. Wise old Kitty Clive, content to watch the world
go by from her retreat at Little Strawberry Hill, reflected on his restlessness to
Jane Pope:

What shall we say for the dear Garrick whose soul is never at rest, who
has the sweetest place in the World and is hardly ever there who instead
of admiring the beauties of the Country from his Temple of Shakespeare
is freting to see how the last Scene goes off in a new pantomime or trudging
in a Morning with a Tragedy Packet under his arm to Rehearse his new
play, to teach the actress, and order the scenes and dresses then come home
tired to death and swears he will never undertake such a thing again poor
Man he does not know why, but he certainly is not happy . . .[24]

The School for Scandal was still doing excellent business for Sheridan, which
was just as well, because the account books for the 1777–8 season would show
that receipts exceeded expenditure by a mere £10.† His style of management was
already being compared unfavourably with that of his predecessor. Cumberland,
whose new tragedy *The Battle of Hastings* had its première towards the end of
January, was unimpressed. 'I read the tragedy in the ears of the performers on
Friday morning,' he wrote to Garrick:

I was highly flattered by my audience, but your successor in management
is not a representative of your polite attention to authors on such occasions,
for he came in yawning at the fifth act, with no other apology than having
sate up two nights running. It gave me not the least offence, as I put it all
to habit of dissipation and indolence; but I fear his office will suffer for
want of due attention, and the present drop upon the theatre justifies my
apprehensions.[25]

---

* *Letters*, 1156. Mrs Hobart was the wife of George Hobart, who had become manager of the
King's Theatre at the beginning of the 1769–70 opera season and got into hot water by preferring
his then mistress, the Zamperina, to the sister of the great Guadagni. He later succeeded his
brother as the Earl of Buckinghamshire.
† Expenditure £34,027 17s 1d, receipts £34,037 19s 7d.

Rumblings against the new manager had also reached Kitty Clive. 'Everybody is raving against Mr. Sheridan for his supineness,' she wrote. 'There never was in nature such a contrast as Garrick and Sheridan: what, have you given him up that he creeps so?'[26]

Garrick had certainly not given him up socially—Sheridan and his wife were welcome guests at Hampton—but business relations with the new patentees were less than smooth. James Lacy's indebtedness to Garrick at the time of his death had stood at £4,500. When his son found himself unable to keep up the payments on the mortgage, Garrick had agreed to increase the loan to £22,500. The price he had exacted was that it should be secured on the shares of all four partners, and that they should face a penalty of £44,000 if they failed to discharge their liabilities on demand—''Tis a thumper!' he had written on the bond. The Drury Lane Account Books, now in the Folger Library, show that during the 1776–7 season, Garrick was paid interest at the rate of £6 each acting day, but as the theatre was open for only 180 nights or so each year, that would take care of barely half the sum due annually, which was £2,200. Lacy now told Garrick that as his share of the profits for the previous year had been only £500, further payments were for the moment beyond him. A string of increasingly heated meetings in the spring of 1778 resolved nothing; finally, on 6 May, Garrick received a letter signed by Benjamin Victor, the theatre's Treasurer:

> I am directed by the Proprietors to inform you, that it will not be in their power for the future, to pay the Interest of Mr Lacy's Mortgage until the Debts & Expenses of the Theatre, are discharged.[27]

Garrick's patience was now wearing thin:

> Gentlemen.
> I am rather surpris'd at the Letter I receiv'd from you yesterday, and as it is impossible for me to know when yr debts and Expences will be discharg'd, & as I imagine that my Mortgage is as just a debt as any upon the Theatre, & that it is as reasonable for Me to Expect my interest should be paid as punctually as any other Expence of the Theatre, I cannot defer a Moment giving You Notice Gentlemen, that I expect the Mortgage to be paid off at the time mention'd in the deeds . . .[28]

He softened this notice of foreclosure by sending a reassuring message to Lacy,* but before it could be delivered, Lacy had come to an agreement with Sheridan to sell his share of the patent. Sheridan paid him £31,500 and provided life annuities of £500 each for Mrs Lacy and for Langford, to whom Lacy was substantially in debt.† It was an outcome no less satisfactory to Garrick than it was to Sheridan, and there may well have been a degree of collusion between them to bring it about.

---

* George was sent to tell him he might depend on Garrick's 'not distressing him'. (*Boaden*, ii, 304.)
† Seven years later Lacy also signed over to Langford the Eynsham Hall estate in Oxfordshire which he had inherited from his father.

There was a notable instance in the spring of 1778 of Garrick's generosity to his friends. Richard Berenger, Gentleman of the Horse to George III, had lived for many years beyond his means. He was by this time so deeply in debt that he generally chose not to stir from his official residence in the King's Mews, then a privileged place which kept him out of the clutches of the bailiffs. His friends decided to come to his aid, and raised between them the £2,600 needed to satisfy his creditors. Garrick wrote him a friendly note:

> I did not hear till last Night—, and I heard it with the greatest pleasure, that Your Friends have generously contributed to your, & their own happiness—No one can more rejoice at this circumstance than I do, and as I hope We shall have a Bonfire upon the Occasion, I beg that You will light it with the inclos'd—

What he enclosed was Berenger's bond for £280 10s, bearing the date 1762. He also sent a bank note for £300, and arranged a grand dinner to celebrate his friend's liquidation. The promised bonfire took place before they sat down to table. Garrick threw all the notes and bonds which had been purchased from Berenger's creditors into the grate and claimed the honour of setting the pile alight.*

He was as assiduous as ever in seeking advancement for relatives and friends. 'As you are well known to smile upon Me,' he wrote to Lord Rochford in April, 'I am address'd on all quarters to befriend some petition or Other.' On this occasion he was pleading the case of a young doctor called Glover, who had for a time abandoned medicine for acting, but who now had ambitions to be a surgeon in the West Essex Militia, of which Rochford was Colonel. 'He is a most Skillful, worthy Man, & has always been a Steady friend to Government,' Garrick wrote:

> Ye worst thing I Ever heard of him, was, that by his Skill in his profession, he recover'd a Thief after he had hung half an hour, & which Thief before he had quite heal'd ye Circle ye Rope had Made, pick'd his Friend Glover's pocket, by Way of Gratitude . . .[29]

Rochford was unable to oblige immediately, but sent a gracious and witty reply:

> The case is as follows: the surgeon to the regiment I command, has been surgeon to it and Lieutenant in it for some years; he is a good surgeon, and liked by the *corps*; I cannot therefore get rid of him. He eats more than Dr. Gough, and should he by chance be choked when he over-gorges, your friend, Mr. Glover, shall superintend my ragamuffins, and as Falstaff says, "I will lead them where they shall be peppered," and find him work enough . . .†

---

* Berenger's debts grew in the telling. Lord Pembroke told Boswell at dinner that he had owed Garrick £500. (*Boswell in Extremes, op. cit.*, 305.)
† *Boaden*, ii, 301. Glover secured an appointment as surgeon in the East Essex Militia the following year.

Garrick was also much taken up with the affairs of his nephews and nieces in the spring of 1778. Arabella was married at the end of April,* and her brother was not far behind her: 'My Nephew David will soon be married to Miss Hart,' Garrick told Hannah More, '& I am to pay the Piper.'[30] He did so very handsomely, settling on his namesake the estate in Essex which he had bought some years previously. His intentions in this direction were known well beyond the family circle some time before the wedding, and earned him an approving pat on the back from Kitty Clive:

> I must now mention the noblest action of your life, your generosity to nephew David; all the world is repeating your praises; those people who always envied you, and wished to detract from you, always declaring you loved money too much ever to part from it, now they will feel *foolish* and look contemptible; all that I can say is, I *wish that Heaven had made me such an uncle.*†

Boswell was in town again. Irritated by something Johnson had said about his being more a favourite with Mrs Garrick than her husband, he tried the next evening to manoeuvre the great man into criticizing his old friend by saying something about Garrick's 'assuming the great man'. Johnson, however, was at his most benevolent. 'Nay, it is wonderful how little Garrick assumes,' he replied:

> Consider, Sir, Pitt and such men had their applause at a distance. But Garrick had it dashed in his face, sounded in his ear, went home every night with the applause of a thousand in his cranium. Then, Sir, did not find but made his way to the tables, the levees, and almost the bedchambers of the great. Then, Sir, he had under him a numerous body of people who from fear of his power, hopes of his favour, and admiration of his talents were very submissive. And here is a man who has advanced the dignity of his profession. Garrick has made a player a higher character. . . . And all this supported by great wealth of his own acquiring. Sir, if all this had happened to me, I should have had a couple of fellows with poles walking before me to knock down everybody that stood in the way. Consider if all this had happened to Cibber or Quin; they had have jumped over the moon. Yet Garrick speaks to us (smiling).[31]

Garrick was a keen observer of the political drama that was being played out in the American colonies. In February France and the colonists had signed an offensive and defensive alliance and a commercial treaty, and this had led to a British declaration of war on the French. In April, British commissioners had been appointed to negotiate with the Congress, and Chatham had delivered

---

* The groom was a widower, Captain Frederick Schaw, who had retired three years previously after twelve years' service in the 66th Regiment of Foot.

† *Boaden*, ii, 295. Letter dated 22 March 1778. Garrick also approached Rochford on his nephew's behalf. David Jr's health was much improved and he now regretted having sold out his cornetcy in Lord Pembroke's Regiment. (*Letters*, 1169.)

his last speech against continuing hostilities.* Garrick occasionally attended proceedings in the Commons. He happened to be present one day in the spring of 1778 when the debate became heated, and the Member for Shropshire, one Charles Baldwin, moved that the gallery should be cleared. Davies has an account of the occasion:

> Mr Burke rose, and appealed to the honourable Assembly, whether it could possibly be consistent with the rules of decency and liberality, to exclude from the hearing of their debates, a man to whom they were all obliged; one who was the great master of eloquence; in whose school they had all imbibed the art of speaking, and been taught the elements of rhetoric. For his part, he owned that he had been greatly indebted to his instructions. . . . The House almost unanimously concurred in exempting Mr Garrick from the general order of quitting the gallery.[32]

Garrick was enormously pleased by all this, and described the scene to his 'dearest of Hannahs':

> Burke & Mr Townshend behav'd nobly upon ye Occasion ye whole house groan'd at poor Baldwin, who is reckon'd, par excellence, ye dullest man in it—& a Question was going to be put to give me an Exclusive priviledge to go in whenever I pleas'd—in short I am a much greater Man than I thought—

He was writing from Lawford, a small town in Essex not far from Mistley where he and his wife were once again enjoying Rigby's hospitality. 'My theatrical curiosity diminishes daily & my Vanity as an Author is quite extinct,' he assured Miss More—not entirely true, because he enclosed a copy of some verses he had composed about his encounter with Squire Baldwin. He also brought her up to date with the latest gossip to reach him from London:

> To our very great Surprize a great friend of ours came from London & to his greater surprize found us drinking tea & laughing like ten Christ'nings under our Walnut tree—he took me aside & told Me, it was all over the Town from Hyde Park Corner to White Chappel dunghill that I had parted with Mrs Garrick . . . but to comfort y^r heart, be assur'd that we are still as much united as Ever & are both so well, that there is a prospect of dragging on our Clogs for some Years to come—[33]

That prospect was quickly to become ominously clouded.

---

* He died on 11 May.

40

'Farewell! Remember Me!'

For some years past Garrick had relied strongly for medical advice on William Cadogan, Physician to the Foundling Hospital and the author of a widely-read book on gout. Cadogan had a house just off Hanover Square and a villa at Fulham. He was six years older than Garrick, and they had become close friends—this despite Cadogan's low opinion of Shakespeare, something which had become the subject of an extended running joke between the two men. A widower since 1772, Cadogan had a daughter who attended to his social correspondence. Garrick was almost as fond of Frances Cadogan as he was of Hannah More. She wrote him delightful letters about her home life and her reading, and his affectionate, teasing replies show him at his relaxed best. 'My Dearly Beloved,' he had written to her shortly after his retirement, 'We shall be most happy to see you & your Anti-Shakespeare Father on Sunday next—tho he has manifold Sins & much wickedness, they shall all be forgiven on Your Account.'[1]

It was to Frances, on 21 July, that Mrs Garrick despatched an urgent note:

> I know you will excuse me to the Dr, for the liberty I take in sending for him so far as Hampton; but my poor Husd is so ill, that I can have no peaceful mind till he has seen him. I have wrote to the Dr this morning knowing that he is in Town on a Tuesday to tell him that the coach will wait for him till he can conveniently set out again for Hampton.[2]

Garrick had been seriously affected by the great heat of early July and plagued by what he described as 'a disagreeable fix'd pain in my head'.[3] Now it was his old enemy that was stalking him once more, and after two days of torment he had voided a number of stones. He was remarkably resilient, for all that, and as soon as he could hold a pen, Frances Cadogan was the first to hear from him. 'Mrs Garrick's impudence of sending for Dr Cadogan was unknown to me,' he protested, '& Nothing but her great fears to see me in such Agonies could have excus'd her.' Then he regaled her with a chirpily graphic account of his latest ordeal:

> I have got rid of two or three possessing Devils & the great Devil of 'Em all who has left me I hope Sulphur Brimstone & Sin but has taken the flesh & Spirit along with him too—I shall be well Enough to see you in a day

or two or three & Expect Banquo's Ghost to appear in his pale-brown terrors before you—[4]

He continued unwell through the summer, suffering first a violent bilious attack and then a severe chill, and was unable to oblige Sheridan with the 'little Triffle' he had promised him for the opening of the new season. He was not above dramatizing his condition—'I am, like a State Prisoner, debarr'd the use of Pen, Ink & paper,' he wrote unconvincingly to Cradock in September—but it was plain that he was much reduced: 'I am grown unfit for any thing, but sitting in a great chair, or walking, or rather at present, creeping about my Garden.'[5]

As his doctors had ordered 'Abstinence from all theatrical Matters', he amused himself by dipping into Fielding's *Tom Jones*. 'I intend to take a peep into all his Works,' he wrote to Lady Spencer, 'for as Tragedies & Comedies are now too much for the Old Gentleman, he must be gently & gradually set down at rest, with Novels, Tales, Fables, & lighter food of the mind.' But the banter and theatrical exaggeration could not mask a new seriousness:

> In short, if I live, for I am not yet quite safe on Shore, the poor remains of my foolish Life shall be devoted to your Ladyship's Commands. . . . Stone, Bile & gout are so fond of living with me & making my little tenement their house of revelling, that when they please to dance about me, my tongue is useless, & the rest of my faculties are watching their motions. . . . However I shall turn over a new leaf immediately, & hope to arrive at Althorp so brighten'd up with the Faculty's Regimen, that my Sweet duchess (I have her leave to call her so) shall so smile upon me, that I shall be the envy of all the younger Maccaronies.[6]

That was for later in the year. The immediate plan was to seek a change of air in Hampshire, and then possibly to go on to Bath. They travelled first to Lord Palmerston's seat at Broadlands, on the Test, its grounds laid out by 'Capability' Brown. 'We are very happy here—a good host a Sweet place & warm Wellcome,' he wrote to Frances Cadogan.[7] He was still subject to a strict convalescent regime, however: 'I am not suffered to write or read; therefore I am now pleasing myself by stealth,' he wrote to Hannah More. He had not been in touch with her since his most recent bout of illness, and he was obliged to keep to his bed again at Broadlands: 'I have been half-dead, and thought I should never see you more,' he told her. 'I took care of your property, and have shown my love to you by a trifling legacy.'[8]

The reference to her 'property' suggests that he had reinvested the proceeds of *Percy*, which he had placed in securities for her earlier in the year. What the 'trifling legacy' was is not known. It does not appear in his will—it was presumably made through an informal understanding with Mrs Garrick—but the mention of it suggests that Garrick's mind was running increasingly on his own mortality. It was, indeed, at Broadlands that he signed and sealed his second will, which replaced an earlier and longer one drawn up in 1767.*

---

* It was witnessed by his host, Lord Palmerston, and by two other members of the house-party.

Winchester was *en fête* at the end of September for a royal visit—the King was to pass his troops in grand review on the Downs to the north-east of the town, and the parade was to include militia detachments from Gloucestershire, Wiltshire, West Kent, Staffordshire, Lancashire and Yorkshire. The King was also to visit Winchester College, and Garrick and his wife were invited to dine there with his old friend Joseph Warton, who for the past twelve years had been headmaster.* Garrick attended the review the next morning on horseback, but at one point he dismounted, and the horse escaped from his grasp and ran off. James Northcote heard the story from Joshua Reynolds and retold it in his biography of the painter:

> Throwing himself immediately into his professional attitude he cried out, as if on Bosworth field, "A horse! a horse! my kingdom for a horse!"
>
> This exclamation, and the accompanying attitude, excited great amazement amongst the surrounding spectators, who knew him not; but it could not escape his Majesty's quick apprehension, for it being within his hearing, he immediately said, "Those must be the tones of Garrick! see if he is not on the ground." The theatrical and dismounted monarch was immediately brought to his Majesty, who not only condoled with him most good humouredly on his misfortune, but flatteringly added, "that his delivery of Shakespeare could never pass undiscovered."[9]

From Broadlands Garrick and his wife moved on the short distance to Hans Stanley's country seat, Paultons, and there he again fell quite seriously ill:

> I had no sooner got rid of the Stone, but I was attack'd at Mr Stanley's with the Bile, & underwent the torment of Martyrs. I am now a Yellow beauty & the Stream of Pactolus which they say is got into my Pocket, has now mounted into my face . . . ye great Cadogan thinks he can mend my Complexion by that royal beautifying Fluid the Thames; & here I am Swallowing pills every 4 hours by the River side—†

Although he made light of his condition, Garrick, now back at Hampton, was still heavily jaundiced. He was writing to Richard Cox, whom he had promised to visit at Quarley Manor, near Andover. He was sorely tempted to make the journey, but good sense prevailed:

> My heart and Soul cry Hey to Quarley; but a little nasty creeping ungenerous, fever pulls me back & cries—stay at home, & take y^r Physick quietly, & don't make an Hospital of Your Friend's House—

---

* Warton was an amiable and good-natured man, but not one of the great Wykehamist headmasters. 'He was neither an exact scholar nor a disciplinarian,' wrote his *DNB* biographer. 'Thrice in his headmastership the boys openly mutinied against him, and inflicted on him ludicrous humiliations. The third insurrection took place in the summer of 1793, and, after ingloriously suppressing it, Warton prudently resigned his post.'

† *Letters*, 1202. Pactolus was the river in which Midas was ordered to bathe by the gods and where the sands turned to gold.

With an old friend like Cox he could be frank; when he had been at Paultons, he told him, 'I never thought myself so near Kingdom come.'[10] Curiously, Garrick did not tell his wife that he had decided to stay at home; there survives in the Harvard Theatre Collection a letter which she wrote to Cox on the same day:

> I am very much alarmed, for fear he should fall ill again, and as I know that nothing will hinder him from fulfiling his promise but your absolute Comand to the contrary, I Beg you will put him off to an other season. I saw him write to you to day but do not know the contents.

In London, the new season was by now more than a month old. The decline in his 'theatrical curiosity' of which Garrick had written to Hannah More in the summer had been arrested, and the authorial vanity which he had pronounced extinct was giving every sign of having come vigorously alive again. 'You must oblige Me wth the sight of Fielding's Play or it will be impossible for me to write an Epilogue,' he wrote to Sheridan at the end of October, and he added an enthusiastic note about a play of Murphy's which he had seen that evening for the first time at Covent Garden—'It is well acted & very entertaining—I was likewise glad to see a good house.'*

He was also still generous with his time when it came to nurturing new talent. The last young hopeful to be taken under Garrick's wing during his retirement was John Bannister, whose father, Charles, had been singing and acting at Drury Lane since the 1760s.† Young Bannister had a talent for drawing and had originally enrolled at the Royal Academy as a pupil of de Loutherbourg,‡ but before long he was knocking at Garrick's door. He had some of his father's gift for mimicry, and for many years afterwards he dined out on his description of that first interview:

> One morning I was shown into his dressing-room, where he was before the glass, preparing to shave; a white night-cap covered his forehead; his chin and cheeks were enveloped in soap-suds; a razor-cloth was placed upon his left shoulder; and he turned and smoothed his shining blade upon the strop with as much dexterity as if he had been bred a barber at the Horse-Guards, and shaved for a penny: and I longed for a beard that I might imitate his incomparable method of handling the razor.
>
> 'Eh! well—what! young man—so, eh?' (this was to me) 'So you are

---

* *Letters*, 1204. The play in question was *The Fathers*. Fielding had written it some years before his death, but it had only recently come to light. Garrick composed an epilogue as well as a prologue, and even brought himself to write a civil note to Miss Younge, who was to speak it—'I will do my best Endeavors to produce Something that shall neither discredit You or Your humble Servt.' (*Ibid.*, 1206.) Murphy's play was the comedy *Three Weeks after Marriage*.

† Bannister Senior was an excellent mimic. It was said that Garrick had once brought the composer Giardini round to listen to his imitations of the bass singer Champness and the *castrato* Tenducci. Giardini declared that the imitations were well enough, but that the voices projected by Bannister were better than the originals.

‡ One of his contemporaries at the Academy was Rowlandson.

still for the stage? Well, how—what character do you—should you like to—eh?'

'I should like to attempt Hamlet, sir.'

'Eh! what? Hamlet the Dane! Zounds! that's bold—have you studied the part? Well, don't mind my shaving—speak the speech—the speech to the ghost—I can hear you—never mind my shaving.'

After a few hums and haws, and a disposing of my hair so that it might stand on end,

Like quills upon the fretful porcupine,

I supposed my father's ghost before me, armed cap-a-pie; and off I started.

Angels and ministers of grace, defend us!
(he wiped the razor)
Be thou a spirit of health, or goblin damn'd
(he stropped the razor)
Bring with thee airs from heaven, or blasts from hell
(he shaved on)
That com'st in such a questionable shape
That I will speak to thee.
(he took himself by the nose)
I'll call thee Hamlet,
King, father, royal Dane. O, answer me!
Let me not burst in ignorance.

He lathered on. I concluded, but still continued my attitude, expecting prodigious praise; when, to my eternal mortification, he turned quick upon me, brandishing the razor, and, thrusting his half-shaved face close to mine, he made such horrible mouths at me that I thought he was seized with insanity, and I was more frightened at him than my father's ghost. He exclaimed in a tone of ridicule,

Angels, and ministers of grace, defend us!

'Yaw, waw, waw, waw!' The abashed Prince Hamlet became sheepish, and looked more like a clown than the gravedigger. He finished shaving, put on his wig, and with a smile of good nature took me by the hand, and said, 'Come, young gentleman, eh! let's see now what we can do.' He spoke the speech; and how he spoke it, those who have heard him never can forget.[11]

Garrick had been sufficiently impressed by the performance of the seventeen-year-old to take him in hand, and when Bannister was offered the chance to appear in his father's benefit at the Haymarket in August, Garrick had given him some coaching. The play was Murphy's farce *The Apprentice*, and Bannister made a successful début as Dick, which had been one of Henry Woodward's most celebrated parts.* Bannister was then taken on at Drury Lane, and once more

---

* Woodward had died the previous year.

had the benefit of detailed instruction from Garrick when he appeared as Zaphna in *Mahomet*.*

This stirred up old jealousies, however. Sheridan had just brought his father in at Drury Lane and invested him with what one newspaper described as 'the management behind the curtain'.† 'Old Surly Boots', as he was now known behind his back,‡ resented the presence of his old rival in the green-room and sent him an offensive message. Garrick was philosophical. 'Pray assure Your Father, that I meant not to interfere in his department,' he told Sheridan:

> I imagin'd (foolishly indeed) that my attending Bannister's rehearsal of the part I once play'd, & wch y^r Father never saw, might have assisted ye Cause, without giving ye least offence—I love my Ease too well, to be thought an Interloper, & I should not have been impertinent enough to have attended any Rehearsal, had not *You* Sir in a very particular manner desir'd me—
>
> however upon no Consideration will I Ever interfere again in this business, nor be liable to receive such another Message as was brought to me this Evening by Young Bannister.
>
> You must not imagine that I write this in a pet, let me assure You upon my honour that I am in perfect peace with You all, & wish You from my heart, all that Yours can wish.§

More agreeable matters were in prospect. Christmas was approaching, and Lady Spencer was pressing him to travel to Althorp with them in good time for the holiday:

> Pray, Mr Garrick, where are you now? what are you about? and how do you do?—these are three questions I must have answered. We shall be in town for the meeting of the Parliament, and hope you will be ready to return with us here as soon as that sets us at liberty. Give my best compliments to Madame, and tell her, if her winter habiliments are not bought, there is a certain scarlet and white silk to be had at Mr. King's, the mercer's, which we have fixed upon as a sort of uniform for the ladies of the Althorp party. I would not have her make it up till I see her in town; but if she is so gracious as to intend to have one, she had better send Mr. King notice, lest there should be scarcity of the silk.[12]

* The part of Palmira on this occasion was played by Mrs Robinson.
† *Morning Chronicle*, 25 September 1778. The paper welcomed the appointment of Sheridan senior: 'In every sense of the words, he is a man of business, and God knows such a man was much wanted at Old Drury. Since Mr Garrick left the direction, the performers have been like ships without a pilot.'
‡ An earlier nickname, from his Dublin days, was 'Bubble-and-Squeak'.
§ *Letters*, 1204. Relaxed though the tone of Garrick's letter is, he could not resist one sharp side-swipe at Sheridan senior. The phrase '& wch y^r Father never saw' was a sly reminder that it was the riots occasioned by the revival of *Mahomet* in Dublin in 1754 that had forced Thomas Sheridan out of his management there.

The answer to Lady Spencer's questions was that he was housebound at the Adelphi and once again the subject of anxious discussion between his doctors: 'Yesterday some of the Faculty met to consider of what it were best for me to do,' he told her:

> Three very great men, were of three different opinions, and propos'd three different ways for me to go to that undiscover'd Country, from whose bourne No Traveller returns. However, good Spirits, and my wife's care of me at Hampton, with my usual Prudence in Eating and drinking may make me take the other Road.[13]

Meanwhile, he was caught up in reading the first three acts of Hannah More's new play, *Fatal Falsehood*. His sense of what would work in the theatre, of how dialogue would come off the page, was as acute as ever:

> . . . I think ye Scene, wch sh^d be capital between *Rivers* & Orlando in ye 3d Act not yet warm enough—the last should enquire whether some Intelligence about his Family, or some female Connection may not lie heavy upon his Mind—Why sh^d he doubt of his Father's Consent for his union w^th *Emiline*? If that had been mark'd or known before it would have done; & perhaps the Father's Objecting to marry his Daughter to a stranger &c might be an addition to the Fable—however do not alter till I have consider'd ye whole—You have good time before you, & we will turn it about in our Minds with Advantage—[14]

By mid-December it was plain that Garrick was not well enough to travel to Althorp, and his wife wrote to Lady Spencer to make their excuses:

> Mr. Garrick has been naughty last week and dined out three times without his nurse, for which he forfited that little health he gained at Hampton the week before: and instead, got every night swelled legs, and other symptoms of gout. They are therefore oblig'd to defer the Honour of waiting upon Lord and Lady Spencer at Althrop till after Christmas, hoping with a little regular way of living to prevent any great mischief. . . .[15]

Garrick's love of company meant that mischief was never far away, and an outing to the theatre to which he was tempted by Rigby did not help matters. But by Boxing Day the lure of Althorp had become overpowering. 'I am myself upon a tolerable footing—the Gout is not quite departed from my Ankles, but I am in travelling Order,' he wrote to Lady Spencer. He was in determinedly good spirits, and chattered on about a new manservant:

> Thomas is too bad to attend me, in whose place I shall bring a New Servant to us, tho' an old one to the late Lady Westmoreland's. His age is about 30, but he has the advantage of looking 60. I asked him if he could comb a Wig, he told me he gave two guineas to learn, to be able to dress Captain Webber, an East India Captain. 'Well, James, and how did the Captain like it?' 'O very well, Sir, but his friends thought that the Captain never

look'd worse.' This he spoke with such naiveté that I burst out laughing, and dismiss'd him as a Valet de Chambre, however tho' I think it is of great Consequence to me, surrounded with such beauty as I shall be at Althorp, to look a little spruce, yet rather than not come at all I will have my head Curry-comb'd by James, & that he can do well, for I have learnt he was formerly a Jockey.*

The Garricks left the Adelphi after breakfast, stopped to dine in St Albans and drove through the gates of Althorp in the small hours. The weather on New Year's Eve was wild—'the greatest high wind that was ever felt,' Mrs Garrick noted in her diary. Garrick had withstood the journey well, and was in good spirits, but within days of their arrival it became necessary to send to Northampton for the Spencers' local doctor, William Kerr. Garrick did not need to be told that his gout had flared up, but shingles was also diagnosed. He suffered in addition great pain in the region of his kidneys, and was able to make only the briefest of appearances downstairs.

A letter that came to him at Althorp brought further confirmation that things were going from bad to worse at Drury Lane. 'I have been silent thus long,' wrote Hopkins, 'in hopes to have sent you an account of the new pantomime which is again obliged (on account of the scenery's not being ready) to be deferred till Friday.' The delay had resulted in very bad houses—'having nothing ready to perform but the common hacknied plays,' Hopkins reported:

> We played last night "Much Ado about Nothing," and had an apology to make for the change of three principal parts. About twelve o'clock Mr. Henderson sent word he was not able to play. We got Mr. Lewis from Covent Garden, who supplied the part of Benedick. Soon after Mr. Parsons sent word he could not play. Mr. Moody supplied the part of Dogberry; and about four in the afternoon Mr. Vernon sent word he could not play. Mr. Mattocks supplied his part of Balthazar. I thought myself very happy in getting these wide gaps so well stopped. In the middle of the first act, a message was brought to me that Mr. La Mash (who was to play the part of Borachio) was not come to the House. I had nobody there that could go on for it, so I was obliged to cut his scenes in the first and second acts entirely out, and got Mr. Wrighten to go on for the remainder of the part. At length we got the play over without the audience finding it out. . . . . .[16]

Garrick in retirement had been no less the subject of incessant gossip than at the height of his celebrity. As he lay on his sick-bed at Althorp in those early days of 1779 several of his friends and acquaintances amused themselves by dissecting him in Mrs Thrale's drawing room, many miles to the south in Streatham. Fanny Burney was one of those present, and on 11 January she wrote an account of the evening to her sister Susannah.

---

* *Althorp Letters*, Letter 68, dated 26 December 1778. Mrs Garrick later told Hannah More that he had been 'reluctantly dragged' to Althorp, but it is not clear who could have done the dragging.

A prologue which Garrick had written for Colman's revival of *Bonduca* at the Haymarket the previous summer had come up. Johnson pronounced it 'a miserable performance', and the company agreed it was the worst he had ever written. 'I don't know what is the matter with David,' Johnson said. 'I am afraid he is grown superannuated, for his Prologues and Epilogues used to be incomparable.' His hostess was ready with an explanation:

> 'Nothing is so fatiguing,' said Mrs. Thrale, 'as the Life of a Wit: he & Wilks are the 2 oldest men of their ages I know, for they have both worn themselves out by being eternally on the rack to give entertainment to other.'
>
> 'David, Madam,' said the Doctor, '*looks* much older than he *is*; for his Face has had double the Business of any other mans,—it is never at rest,— when he speaks one minute, he has quite a different Countenance to what he assumes the next; I don't believe he ever kept the same look for half an Hour to gether in the whole course of his Life; & such an eternal, restless, fatiguing play of the muscles, must certainly wear out a man's Face much before it's real time . . . .'[17]

Johnson could not know it, but his old pupil was afflicted by something rather more serious than the 'fatiguing play of the muscles' and was anxious to regain the shelter of his own roof. The high winds had been followed by a hard frost and fog, and it was 14 January before the Garricks were able to set out for home. There had been a slight thaw, and the Northamptonshire countryside lay under snow. This time they travelled more slowly. They stayed the night at Dunstable, and Garrick scrawled a note to Lady Spencer:

> I am alive, my good Lady, but such a journey from Northampton to Dunstable I never went before, and hope never to go again. . . . I took the laudanum & had a deaf apothecary who was sensible and did well. I am out of pain now . . .
>
> My head is confused—my Pen Ink & paper bad & I can really scarce see to write—but you commanded & I have obeyed. . . .[18]

They reached the Adelphi the following afternoon to find Cadogan reading in the library. Garrick fired off another bulletin to Althorp:

> He says, I have had a pretty tolerable bout of it—that the Eruptions upon my once clear Spotless body, are much very much in my favour, that my blood has long been too highly charg'd with inflammable matter, but that he will put out the fire with all convenient speed, and then I may set fire to it again as soon as I please, at Wimbleton, or Mistley. . . . Mrs Garrick is very happy to have got me once again in her *Glutches*—she calls here and there, tings the bell, like Mrs Oakly, while I sit wrapt up in a suit of flannels, and look the very figure of Peter Grievous. . . . My pain is still lingering, as loth to quit so desirable a Mansion, but Dr Cadogan has rais'd the College Militia against the foe, and the battle has began already.[19]

The apothecary Herbert Lawrence, an old friend from Lichfield days, called the next morning and found him up and shaving, but was alarmed to discover that he had stopped passing water, and it quickly became apparent that the 'college militia' was fighting a losing battle. 'The distemper was incessantly gaining ground,' wrote Davies; 'the fluids not passing in their natural course brought on a kind of stupor, which increased gradually to the time of his death.' Cadogan, in his direct way, told Garrick that he should settle his worldly affairs. 'Mr Garrick assured him,' wrote Davies, 'that nothing of that sort lay on his mind; and that he was not afraid to die.'[20]

The Spencers had followed the Garricks to town, and Lady Spencer came daily to enquire after him. Another visitor was Thomas Rackett, and as he sat talking to Mrs Garrick, Garrick came into the room:

> But oh, how changed from that vivacity and sprightliness which used to accompany every thing he said, and every thing he did! His countenance was sallow and wan, his movement slow and solemn. He was wrapped in a rich night-gown, like that which he always wore in Lusignan, the venerable old king of Jerusalem; he presented himself to the imagination of his friend as if he was just ready to act that character. He sat down; and during the space of an hour, the time he remained in the room, he did not utter a word. He rose and withdrew to his chamber.[21]

There were still moments of lucidity and coherence. 'Well, Tom,' he said to his man when he brought him a draught one day, 'I shall do very well yet, and make you amends for all this trouble.' And even moments of wit. There had been a procession of distinguished medical men to his bedside—William Heberden the elder, Percivall Pott, Richard Warren, physician to George III and his old friend Schomberg among them. On the day before his death, seeing several figures in the room, he asked Lawrence who they were. When he heard they were all physicians, anxious to be of service to him, he shook his head and dug out of the recesses of his mind lines of Horatio's from Rowe's *The Fair Penitent*:

> Another, and another, still succeeds;
> And the last fool is welcome as the former.

He also told Lawrence that he did not regret his childlessness, 'for he knew the quickness of his feelings was so great that, in case it had been his misfortune to have had disobedient children, he could not have supported such an affliction.'

The end came on 20 January. 'At a quarter before eight,' Mrs Garrick wrote in her diary, 'my Husband sighed, and Died without one uneasy moment, the Lord be Praised.'

Faithful William Hopkins also recorded the event—not in his diary, but, appropriately enough, in a handwritten note on a Drury Lane playbill:

> This morning about Eight o'clock Died my most worthy Friend & Patron

David Garrick Esq. upon which melancholy Occasion Fresh Bills were put up that there would be no play this Evening. . . . He was the best performer that Ever Existed the World Over.[22]

Epilogue

Samuel Johnson had not believed—had not wished to believe—that Garrick was mortally ill. 'No arguments, or recitals of such facts as I had heard,' wrote Mrs Thrale, 'would persuade Mr Johnson of his danger.' After the body was opened, it seemed remarkable only that he had survived for so long.

Murphy had the details from a well-known physician called Fearon who happened to be a neighbour of Garrick's at the Adelphi and had quite often attended him in the last year of his life. In his view the symptoms had all pointed to a stone in the bladder;* but Garrick had 'an unconquerable aversion' to any instrument being passed into the urethra, and declared that he would rather die than be examined in that way. The post-mortem, however, disclosed something quite unsuspected:

> The viscera of the thorax and abdomen were perfectly free from the least appearance of disease. No stone was found in the bladder; but on moving the peritoneum covering the kidneys, the coats of the left only remained, as a cyst full of pus; and not a vestige of the right could be found.†

Garrick, that is to say, had been born with only one kidney, which had been either congenitally cystic or destroyed by infection. A modern death certificate would say that he died of uraemia.‡

* 'The first symptom with which he was attacked was a sickness at his stomach, attended with repeated vomitings, and acute pain in the region of the loins, which was encreased on bending the body forwards, and extending down his thighs, with a frequent propensity to discharge his urine, in the passing of which he suffered considerable pain. His water stopped suddenly, and the most uneasy sensations continued for some time. He had likewise a discharge of mucus from the urethra, accompanied with straining and considerable torture. His pulse was low and quick, about 95, as is the case in hectic fevers; his tongue white; he was sometimes costive, and occasionally subject to a diarrhoea, which lasted for some days.' (*Murphy*, Appendix XX.)

† *Ibid*. There is some conflict of evidence, however. Hannah More, who presumably heard it from Mrs Garrick, wrote to her sister that 'a stone was found that measured five inches and a half round one way, and four and a half the other'. (*Roberts, op. cit.*, i, 148.)

‡ A somewhat different account of the autopsy appeared in the *Public Advertiser* on 26 January: 'Mr. Garrick's Disorder was, (as Mr Pott predicted previous to the Opening of the Body), the Palsy in the Kidnies, which mouldered away on being handled. The ducts leading from the Kidnies to the Bladder were so stopped, that a Probe would not pass through them. In the Bladder was a Stone the Size of a Pullet's Egg; but with that he might have lived many Years.

The funeral was set for 1 February, a Monday, and Mrs Garrick was taken in by the Angelos while the undertakers made their preparations. Hannah More came up from Bristol to be with her. 'I paid a melancholy visit to his coffin yesterday,' she wrote to her sister:

> His new house is not so pleasant as Hampton, nor so splendid as the Adelphi, but it is commodious enough for all the wants of its inhabitant; and besides, it is so quiet, that he never will be disturbed till the eternal morning; and never till then will a sweeter voice than his own be heard.

She did not approve of the arrangements that had been put in hand:

> They are preparing to hang the house with black, for he is to lie in state till Monday. I dislike this pageantry, and cannot help thinking that the disembodied spirit must look with contempt upon the farce that is played over its miserable relics.

The 'disembodied spirit' might also have been reminded of nights of riot at Drury Lane. The lying-in-state was arranged for the weekend immediately before the funeral—from eleven o'clock till five on the Saturday, and till six on the Sunday. 'All genteel persons will be permitted to see the state during these hours, by applying to Mr. Ireland the undertaker, in Bow-street, for tickets of admission,' said a press notice. On Monday, the *Morning Post* reported that on Sunday alone, the numbers had been estimated at close to 50,000.* Curiosity was not confined to the genteel, however:

> A prodigious concourse of the lower class of the people likewise assembled before the house the whole day, and finding they could not gain admittance, became so troublesome, that an officer's guard was obliged to be sent from the Savoy, which with great difficulty prevented their committing some acts of outrage.

Henry Angelo, escorting his sisters, had the greatest difficulty approaching the house and had to wait for an hour before being admitted. Jostled in the crush, he was pushed violently against one of the funeral mutes on duty at the door and suddenly found himself surrounded by a crowd shouting 'A ring! A ring!' The Queensberry Rules still lay some way in the future:

> I had no alternative but to fall to—a few blows had passed when I got my sable gentleman's head in chancery (as they call it); whilst keeping my fist employed, a lusty woman bounded upon me, and with her nails scratched one side of my face, when the mute disengaging his head from under my

---

Twelve Months since Mr. Pott searched the Bladder, and no Stone was there; so that it must have accumulated within that time; the Heart, Liver, and Lungs were sound, the Intestines adhered to the Sides; and Mr. Pott declared he never saw a Subject so *internally* fat.'

* This seems an extraordinarily large figure. When Louis Armstrong died in 1971 and lay in state at the New York National Guard Armory, the number of people who went to pay their respects totalled 25,000.

arm, fell on receiving a *coup-de-grâce* on his *bread-basket*—the crowd then closing, thus ended the fight. I saw no more of my antagonist, who left me the *champ de bataille*, with a black eye, and four streaks down one side of my face, as if I had been seared by a hot gridiron; probably inflicted by his wife, who had taken her husband's part. I soon found my sisters, who were taken into a house during my pugnastics . . .[1]

Hannah More's word 'pageantry' was not ill-chosen. The funeral—the arrangements were made by Sheridan—was as richly magnificent a spectacle as any Garrick and de Loutherbourg between them had ever devised at Drury Lane. Several years later, Boswell was present at Johnson's when the occasion was talked of as 'prodigiously expensive':

Johnson, from his violent antipathy to exaggeration, lowered it, I thought, too much. "Were there not six horses in each coach?" said Mrs Burney. Johnson. "Madam, there were no more six horses than six phoenixes."[2]

Not so, however. The mourning coaches—there were thirty-three of them— had indeed each been drawn by six horses, and Johnson himself had travelled in one of five allotted to members of the Club.

Mourners were bidden to be at the Adelphi at eleven o'clock. Crowds began to assemble on the Terrace and the surrounding streets well before then, and by the time the cortège moved off, shortly after one, the throng was packed so tightly in front of the house that there was nearly a disaster:

The humanity of the Officers of the Guards, and activity of the detachment of men under their command, in all probability, saved the lives of some hundreds, who pressed so violently against the Adelphi rails over the Thames, that it cracked in several places; and had the populace not been immediately cleared away by force, the whole balustrade might have given way, and the most tragical consequences have ensued.

The order of procession appeared in full in the next day's papers:

Four Men in Mourning, with Staffs covered with
black silk and scarves, on horseback, as Porters.
Six ditto with mourning Cloaks, &c.
A Man in Mourning to bear the Pennon with
Scarf, &c.
Two Supporters.
Six Men in Cloaks as before.
Surcoat of Arms.
Helmet, with Crest, Wreath, and Mantle.
State Lid of black Ostrich Feathers, surrounded by
Escutchions.
Hearse full drest, with
The BODY
A Page—State-Coach empty—A Page . . .

Invitation to Garrick's funeral. It was an occasion of great pomp, but Garrick's executors were dilatory, and three years later the funeral expenses remained unpaid. 'The undertaker is broken,' Johnson told Mrs Thrale. Little wonder. At present-day prices, the hapless Mr Ireland of Bow Street was owed some £85,000. (The Fotomas Index)

The account rolled majestically on through seemingly endless column inches.

The coffin was draped in crimson velvet with silver gilt nails and plate; this bore Garrick's arms, and the motto 'Resurgam'. Four clergy rode in the second coach and then followed five coaches in which the pall-bearers sat in pairs—the Duke of Devonshire and Lord Camden, Lord Spencer and Lord Ossory, Lord Palmerston and Richard Rigby, Sir Watkin Williams Wynne and Hans Stanley, Albany Wallis and John Paterson. Sheridan, as Chief Mourner, rode alone.* Family mourners came next—Garrick's three nephews and Arabella's husband; George was too ill to attend, and Peter did not make the journey from Lichfield. In the tenth coach, Cadogan and Lawrence; they were accompanied by Philip Butler, the Drury Lane master carpenter and Thomas Fosbrook, the bookkeeper, two servants of the theatre whom Garrick had held in particular regard.

The two patent theatres were each represented by twelve actors and the Club by nineteen of its members. Burke had come posting up from Portsmouth, where he had been supporting Admiral Keppel at his court-martial;† Gibbon and Colman sat with Joseph Banks, and in the coach behind were Reynolds and Fox. Other friends in the procession included Sir Grey Cooper and Berenger and Robert Adam. Bate and Cumberland were there, and so were Linley and Burney, Domenico Angelo, de Loutherbourg and Noverre. To read the list of mourners is to review the whole of Garrick's life in cavalcade.

The mourning coaches were followed by as many empty family carriages. The windows and rooftops of the Strand and the rest of the route had been crowded with spectators since noon; it took the procession the best part of an hour to reach the Abbey and another hour passed before the carriages had discharged their passengers. Lady Spencer watched the cortège pass from a window in the Pay Office. Knowing her affection for Garrick, Rigby had offered her the use of a warm room 'where a fire is constantly kept and the window is to the Street'.

Hannah More and Frances Cadogan had made their way to a vantage point at Charing Cross: 'The bells of St Martin's and the Abbey gave a sound that smote upon my very soul,' Hannah told her sister. Only when they were there did a ticket of admittance reach them from the Dean,‡ and they hurried to the Abbey in a hackney coach, fearing to be late.

In their agitation they initially gave up their ticket at the wrong door, and spent a panicky half-hour locked in a dark tower with a winding staircase. Eventually they were rescued and placed in a small gallery directly over the grave—'we could see and hear everything as distinctly as if the Abbey had been a parlour'. From where she sat, Hannah had a sight of Handel's monument, and the scroll in his hand which read "I know that my Redeemer liveth." There was

---

* Thomas Sheridan, however, did not attend the funeral.

† Keppel, Commander-in-Chief of the Grand Fleet, was closely associated with opponents of the government. He stood accused of a number of capital charges in connection with operations off Brest, including going into the fight in an unofficer-like manner, scandalous haste in quitting it and not pursuing the flying enemy. The charges were dismissed as 'malicious and ill-founded'.

‡ Dr John Thomas (1712–93) was also Bishop of Rochester and Chaplain to the King.

music by Purcell and Handel, and the Dean read the funeral service in a low voice. 'Hardly a dry eye,' Hannah told her sister—'the very players, bred to the trade of counterfeiting, shed genuine tears.' They were not alone. Johnson's face was also bathed in tears, and Burke sobbed openly.* The coffin was lowered beneath the pavement in Poets' Corner, near the door leading to Saint Faith's Chapel—just below the base of Kent's Monument to Shakespeare.†

Hannah More was indignant that the life of the capital resumed its normal course as swiftly and as heedlessly as it did: 'The very night he was buried,' she wrote to her sister, 'the playhouses were as full, and the Pantheon was as crowded, as if no such thing had happened.'³ A carefully worded notice that appeared in the press two days later suggests that this was a point of some sensitivity with the theatre managements:

> The motive that influenced the Managers in not permitting the Theatres to be shut, according to the general expectation, on the evening when Nature took the only mortal part of our stage phaenomenon to herself, was certainly some compensation for the apparent disrespect. There are nearly five hundred inferior dependents upon these two theatres, whose situations entitle them but to very scanty allowances, and the deprivation of one night's pay would be to them a material disadvantage. In charitable consideration of this consequence, this last theatrical indication of respect was suspended: how far the cause palliates the effect, let our impartial readers determine.⁴

Privately, there were those who thought that Sheridan had overdone things; unsurprisingly, Horace Walpole was of their number. 'Yes, Madam, I do think the pomp of Garrick's funeral perfectly ridiculous,' he wrote on the day to Lady Ossory. 'It is confounding the immense space between pleasing talents and national services. What distinctions remain for a patriot hero, when the most solemn have been showered on a player?'‡ By the time he came to write his posthumously published *Journal of the Reign of George III*, a more malicious angle had occurred to him: 'The Court was delighted to see a more noble and splendid appearance at the interment of a comedian than had waited on the remains of the great Earl of Chatham.'§

---

* Burke was easily moved to tears. He had wept when told of the death of Goldsmith five years previously; after Joshua Reynolds's funeral in 1792, when he was deputed to thank the assembled Academicians on behalf of the family and executors, he managed only a few words before breaking down and leaving the room.

† Later, the bones of Samuel Johnson and the ashes of Henry Irving would also be buried close by.

‡ *Walpole*, xxxiii, 86–8. One of his French correspondents agreed with him. 'Je trouve les honneurs rendu a Garrick parfaitement ridicules,' Mme du Deffand wrote a week later. 'Ils sont le pendant de ceux qu'on rend ici à Voltaire, avec cette différence que ce ne sont que les beaux esprits et ceux qui prétendent à l'être qui en font les frais.' (*Ibid.*, vii, 111. Letter dated 7 February 1779.)

§ ii, 333. George Garrick, already dangerously ill, had been seriously affected by his loss. 'Some Person having very inadvertently told him of his Brother's Death,' said a press report, 'he was thrown into Fits, and now lies in a very doubtful and precarious Situation.' Two days after the

The many cards left at the Adelphi in the days following Garrick's funeral included one from Johnson: 'Dr Johnson presents respectful condolences to Mrs Garrick, and wishes that any endeavour of his could enable her to support a loss, which the world cannot repair.' If this was a hint that he stood ready to edit Garrick's works and write his life, Mrs Garrick did not take it. Possibly she feared the critical rigour of her husband's old mentor; the task, at all events, passed to Davies, and his two volumes appeared the following year.

For weeks and months after Garrick's death the press was inundated with tributes to him in prose and verse. The best known was the monody written by Sheridan and spoken at Drury Lane by Mrs Yates. Sheridan compared the enduring achievement of the painter, the sculptor or the poet with the ephemeral nature of the actor's art:

> The actor, only, shrinks from Time's award;
> Feeble tradition is his memory's guard;
> By whose faint breath his merits must abide,
> Unvouch'd by proof—to substance unallied!

He passed in review the 'pure and liquid tone' of Garrick's speech, his use of gesture and silence, his grace of action, and challenged the audience to keep the memory of them alive:

> Where then—while sunk in cold decay he lies,
> And pale eclipse for ever veils those eyes—
> Where is the blest memorial that ensures
> Our Garrick's fame?—whose is the trust?—'Tis yours.

Linley provided vocal and instrumental music, and de Loutherbourg designed a new scene for the occasion. The performers were requested to appear in black clothes. The monody was called for many times, and continued to be given until 1783. Although the Revolutionary War was still being fought, it was printed in December 1779 on the front page of the *Independent Chronicle* in Boston (Sheridan was closely involved in the Foxite campaigns against the war). 'We Americans have no quarrel with the Arts and Sciences,' wrote the contributor who submitted it:

> We only lament that a nation in which they have so long flourished, a nation from whose eyes Garrick has so often drawn floods of tears . . . should have carried on a war against America in so relentless and so barbarous a manner.

In its published form the monody carried a dedication to Lady Spencer—'whose

---

pomp at the Abbey, he too died, prompting a wag in the green-room to observe that 'David wanted him.' He was buried, rather less elaborately than Garrick had been, at Hendon; the relations and friends who attended were accommodated in six mourning coaches.

approbation and esteem was justly considered by Mr Garrick as the highest panegyric his talents or conduct could acquire.'*

Throughout the spring and summer, the *Gentleman's Magazine* published a notably accurate and balanced series under the title *Biographical Anecdotes of the Late Mr Garrick*. Amid the flood of eulogies, rhapsodies and elegies, however, a less admiring note was occasionally struck and there was a predictable amount of sheer nastiness. *The Apotheosis of Punch* was an attack on Sheridan's *Monody*. Dr Plunder (Sheridan) admits to hating Punch in his life but to jumping on the bandwagon to praise him in death. *Town and Country Magazine* published something a good deal uglier called 'A Dialogue in the Shades between Garrick and Kenrick', in which Garrick admits to being a usurer and Kenrick owns up to having written *Love in the Suds* merely to make money.

Camden, whom Garrick had named as an executor, for some reason declined to serve. The three who did—Rigby, John Paterson and Albany Wallis—did not have an easy time, partly because of the extreme dilatoriness of the Drury Lane management; Sheridan was already beginning to use the theatre treasury to subsidize the extravagant style of living to which he aspired. Kitty Clive, writing to Jane Pope in December 1779, asserted that Mrs Garrick had not received one shilling of the interest due to her from Sheridan's debt to her husband, and that the executors were considering a foreclosure. Four months later, her syntax and spelling as idiosyncratic as ever, Mrs Clive wrote to Mrs Garrick herself, expressing concern that she had not heard from her, and speculating about the reason:

> Not I hope from your having been ill, that woud be the worst I can conceive or next to that, perhaps the vexation you have had, from that uncertain, disipated wretch Mr Sheridan; who instead of minding the business of the theatre where he is throwing a way other people's Property; he is going about with Charl Fox to settle the afairs of the nation; which if he had the power he woud add to the confusion they are in at present . . .[5]

A year later, little had changed. 'Garrick's legatees at this place are very angry that they receive nothing,' Johnson wrote to Mrs Thrale from Lichfield in October 1781, and in another letter, six months later, he had further scandalous snippets to retail: 'They pay for the playhouse neither principal nor interest; and poor Garrick's funeral expences are yet unpaid, though the Undertaker is broken.' Small wonder. The cost of the funeral had been £1,500.

Under the terms of Garrick's will, his sister Merrial and his brother Peter were each to receive £3,000; George, if he had lived, would have received £10,000. There were generous bequests to George's children. Arabella and Catherine were

---

* Years later, however, in company with Byron one day, Sheridan picked up a copy of his monody and glanced at the dedication. 'On seeing it he flew into a rage—exclaimed 'that it must be a forgery—that he had never dedicated anything of his to such a damned canting bitch etc etc' and so went on for half an hour abusing his own dedication or at least the object of it.' (Marchand, Leslie A. (ed.), *Byron's Letters and Journals*, 12 vols., London, 1973–82, ix, 15.)

each left £6,000 in trust; Carrington also got £6,000, while David was to have £5,000 in addition to what he had received on his marriage. Mrs Garrick's niece was also remembered—she was to have £1,000.

The arrangements Garrick made for his widow have occasioned some adverse comment. The houses at Hampton and the Adelphi, together with their contents, were to be held in trust for Mrs Garrick 'for and during the Term of her natural life for her own Residence She keeping the House and Premises in Good repair and paying all the Quit Rent Taxes and other Rents and outgoings for the same'. She was also to have £1,000 immediately after his death, £5,000 after the passage of a year and an annuity of fifteen hundred pounds. These provisions were to be in lieu of any dividends and interest due to her from the £10,000 settled on her at the time of their marriage.

Nothing very unusual in any of that, although there was a stipulation that the annuity was to be 'for her Sole and seperate Use without being subject to the Debts Controul or intermeddling of any Husband she shall or may Marry'. There was, however, a condition, and the consequences of not meeting it were spelt out with as much clarity as the language of lawyers allows:

> It is my request and desire that my Wife shall continue in England and make Hampton and the Adelphi her chief places of Residence, but if she shall leave England and reside beyond Sea or in Scotland or Ireland, in such Case which I hope will not happen But in that Case I revoke and make void all the Devises and Bequests to her or for her use herein before mentioned . . . and instead thereof I give her only a clear annuity of One thousand pounds of Lawful Money of Great Britain . . .

It was further a condition that Mrs Garrick must within three months give her written consent to those provisions; otherwise they would become null and void. If that were to happen, or after her death, most of the property was to be sold. The statue of Shakespeare and his collection of old English plays Garrick bequeathed to the British Museum; his nephew Carrington was to get most of the rest of his library, and the use of the houses in Drury Lane which Garrick had bought from the Theatrical Fund; thereafter they were to revert to the Fund.

Mrs Garrick seems to have found difficulty only with the thought of parting with her husband's books; she offered to buy them from Carrington, and the offer was accepted. Carrington, as things turned out, would not have had long to enjoy them. He was, as was euphemistically said, 'too careless of his constitution'. The money laid out on his education at Eton and St John's College, Cambridge, had not been one of Garrick's better investments. The Reverend Carrington Garrick died only eight years after his uncle at the age of thirty-six, 'a martyr', as Cradock put it, to 'a too free use of the bottle'.

For the best part of two years after Garrick's death, his widow went into almost total seclusion. On the first anniversary of 'the fatal 20th' Hannah More travelled up from Bristol to be with her. 'Poor Mrs. Garrick is a greater recluse than ever, and has quite a horror at the thought of mixing in the world again,' she told her sister:

We never see a human face but each other's. Though in such deep retirement,
I am never dull, because I am not reduced to the fatigue of entertaining
dunces, or being obliged to listen to *them*. We dress like a couple of
Scaramouches, dispute like a couple of Jesuits, eat like a couple of aldermen,
walk like a couple of porters, and read as much as any two doctors at
either university.[6]

Little had changed by the time of her next visit the following winter: 'As to poor
Mrs. Garrick, she keeps herself as secret as a piece of smuggled goods, and
neither stirs out herself, or lets any body in.'[7] They passed the time reading over
Garrick's hoard of letters. 'The employment, though sad, is not without its
amusement,' Miss More wrote:

It embraces the friendly correspondence of all the men who have made a
figure in the annals of business or of literature for the last forty years; for
I think I hardly miss a name of any eminence in Great Britain, and not
many in France: it includes also all his answers: some of the first wits in
the country, confessing their obligations over and over again to his bounty;
money given to some, and lent to such numbers as would be incredible, if
one did not read it in their own letters . . .[8]

Gradually, as the spring of 1781 came on, going out into the world again no
longer seemed quite so terrible a thing to Mrs Garrick. Hannah More accompanied
her to a dinner party at Dr Shipley's, the Bishop of St Asaph. The Spencers were
there, and so were Reynolds and Johnson and Gibbon. Boswell was also present,
and blotted his copy-book; when he reappeared at the tea-table after dinner, he
was 'disordered with wine', and addressed Miss More in a manner which drew
from her a sharp rebuke.

Some weeks later, Mrs Garrick invited several of the same company to dine.
Her guests also included Mrs Carter and Mrs Boscawen, and on this occasion,
in the presence of two such formidable blue-stockings, Boswell minded his
manners, even though Mrs Garrick regaled them liberally with Lichfield ale. 'We
found ourselves very elegantly entertained,' he recorded:

She looked well, talked of her husband with complacency, and, while she
cast her eyes on his portrait which hung over the chimney-piece, said, that
death was now the most agreeable object to her.' The very semblance of
David Garrick was cheering.

At the end of the evening, Johnson and Boswell walked away together:

We stopped a little while by the rails of the Adelphi, looking on the Thames,
and I said to him with some emotion, that I was now thinking of two friends
we had lost, who once lived in the building behind us, Beauclerk and Garrick.
"Ay, Sir," said he, tenderly, "and two such friends as cannot be supplied."*

---

* *Life*, iv, 96–9. Beauclerk had died a year previously at the age of forty-one. The sale at auction
of his splendid library of 30,000 volumes, which began that April, was not completed until June.

The following winter, Johnson fell seriously ill. A cold had turned into bronchitis, which lasted for several months; he also now suffered from emphysema and from a congestive heart condition, and this left him weak and breathless. Hannah More, up for her annual visit, heard for the first time of something which moved her deeply. 'The following little touch of tenderness which I heard of him last night from one of the Turk's Head Club, endears him to me exceedingly,' she wrote to her sister:

> There are always a great many candidates ready, when any vacancy happens in that club, and it requires no small interest and reputation to get elected; but upon Garrick's death, when numberless applications were made to succeed him, Johnson was deaf to them all; he said, No, there never could be found any successor worthy of such a man; and he insisted upon it there should be a year's widowhood in the club, before they thought of a new election.*

In the spring of 1782, Mrs Garrick received a proposal of marriage. 'Does your ladyship know that Lord Monboddo has twice proposed to Mrs Garrick?' Horace Walpole wrote to Lady Ossory. 'She refused him; I don't know whether because he says in his book that men were born with tails, or because they have lost them.'⁹

The Scottish judge James Burnett, Lord Monboddo, was widely regarded as eccentric both in his views and his personal habits. Garrick had met him briefly in Paris in 1764. Now a widower in his late sixties, it was his habit during the court's spring vacation to travel to London on horseback, peering short-sightedly at his pocket Homer, his negro servant, Gory, leading an extra horse a short distance behind.

Monboddo had firm ideas about health and exercise. He rose at six and took a cold bath, if possible out of doors. During the day he ate little. After supper, while he dictated to his clerk or had a servant read to him, he took what he called his air bath, exercising naked before an open window; before he retired, he was massaged with a lotion of olive oil, rose water, aromatic spirit, saline and Venetian soap. Eager that others should share his vigour of body and mind, he urged this bracing regime on Henry Dundas and William Pitt; it would, he pointed out, not only improve their own health but be of benefit to the nation.

Monboddo's intellectual interests ranged widely. He shared with many eighteenth-century Scots an interest in the origin and development of language (as a law student in Holland he had written an essay on Chinese); he evolved an elaborate theory about the natural history of man, wrote about metaphysics and had a belief in second sight. Although his oddities caused some amusement, he was, on the whole, regarded more seriously in England than in Scotland, and he

---

* *Roberts, op. cit.,* i, 249. The records of the club confirm this. After the admission of Joseph Banks, William Windham, Sir William Scott and Earl Spencer in 1778, the next election was Dr Shipley's in 1780.

CONTEMPLATION.

James Burnett, Lord Monboddo, the eccentric Scottish judge whose offer of marriage Mrs Garrick felt unable to accept. He evolved an elaborate theory about the natural history of man, wrote about metaphysics and had a belief in second sight. He was also a keep-fit enthusiast, exercising naked before an open window before retiring. (The Scottish National Portrait Gallery)

was taken up in particular by the blues. Elizabeth Carter described a near-encounter with him to Mrs Montagu:

> The most fashionable object in all polite circles at present is Lord Monboddo, who you know has writ to prove, that human creatures, in their natural state, have tails like a cat. I have been in a room with him, but have not heard him speak, though our dear Mrs Vesey did all she could to procure me that honour . . .[10]

Monboddo was Mrs Garrick's guest on several occasions, and presented her and Hannah More with the second volume of his *Antient Metaphysics*. He did not come to London the following year, but it is possible that he renewed his suit by post; writing to a friend in June 1783, Mary Hamilton described an evening spent at Hampton:

> After we left the gentlemen, we went upstairs and drank coffee. Mrs Garrick gave us high entertainment by showing us Lord Monboddo's letter with an offer of his hand; ye stile and proposals I cannot well forget—we joined the gentlemen at tea in Shakespeare's Temple.*

Another story which went the rounds was that Monboddo, strolling in the gardens at Hampton, had also proposed to Hannah More, thirty-one years his junior. When he returned to the drawing room, he spoke to Mrs Garrick of his regret that she had turned him down: 'I am very sorry for this refusal: I should have so much liked to teach that nice girl Greek.'[11]

As the years passed, 'that nice girl' came less often to Hampton and the Adelphi. *The Fatal Falsehood* had been staged at Covent Garden a few months after Garrick's death, but with no great success. She gradually came to believe that playwriting and play-going were sinful. She surrendered the copyright of *Percy*, and when the piece was revived in 1787, with Mrs Siddons as the heroine, she refused to attend the performance. In 1782 she published her *Sacred Dramas*, intended for young people; thereafter her writing increasingly took the form of religious and moral reflections, and her books were among the most widely read of the day.

Mrs Garrick was to outlive almost all her husband's close relations. Peter died in 1795 and his sister Merrial four years later. None of George's children lived to a great age. Nathan, like Carrington, died in his thirties, and David lived only to be forty-one. Arabella survived into the next century, dying in 1819 at the age of sixty-six.†

There had been a residual clause in Garrick's will stipulating that after all bequests had been met, any surplus should be divided among the next of kin. In 1807 Mrs Garrick accepted the advice of her legal advisers that she should

---

* Anson, Elizabeth and Florence, *Mary Hamilton*, London, 1925, p. 137. Mrs Garrick may, of course, have still been showing round a letter she had received a year before.
† George's younger daughter, Catherine, born in 1756, married someone called Payne. The date of her death is unknown. George's son by his second marriage, also George, was born in 1775 and died in 1819.

institute proceedings in Chancery, claiming to be included in that category and suing for an equal portion. This was thought by some to be grasping; in the event the Chancellor refused the application, ruling that under such a construction, the testator would have defeated his own intentions. As can be the case with elderly ladies, Mrs Garrick was sometimes uncertain about whether she had enough for her needs, but the charge of parsimony does not bear serious scrutiny. By 1815, she had put aside some £12,000 since her husband's death, and this she distributed among her German relatives; Garrick had clearly had his reasons when he instructed Albany Wallis to insert in his will a condition of forfeiture.

When health and weather permitted, Mrs Garrick was faithful in her religious observance, attending mass in Golden Square when in London and at the chapel in Isleworth when in the country. Good Catholic that she was, she had none the less long been attracted to a range of less conventional beliefs. Even while Garrick was alive, she had corresponded with de Loutherbourg about his interest in alchemy, mesmerism and mysticism. She did not, fortunately, follow the great designer and his wife in their experiments in faith-healing. In 1789, a woman called Mary Pratt had published *A List of a few Cures performed by Mr. and Mrs De Loutherbourg of Hammersmith Terrace without Medicine, by a Lover of the Lamb of God*. Some of their cures were apparently more efficacious than others, and after his house had been attacked by a mob, the *Morning Chronicle* reported that 'Loutherbourg has entirely given up the practice of working miracles and taken to his pencil again'.[12]

Throughout her long widowhood Mrs Garrick retained her interest in the theatre. The Folger Library has a manuscript inventory of Drury Lane dating from August 1819 which details the sumptuous appointments of 'Mrs Garrick's Anti Room' and 'Mrs Garrick's Box'. They appear under the same names in a later inventory made four years after her death.

A new theatrical star had arisen, and a press report indicated that Mrs Garrick was prepared to allow it a degree of brilliance:

> The venerable Mrs. Garrick, relict of the celebrated actor, has constantly witnessed the performances of Mr Kean; and she was heard to declare that since the days of her husband she had never seen an actor who, throughout the part, so strongly impressed her with the recollection of his performance of Richard.[13]

Although she presented him with a malacca cane that had belonged to Garrick, she admired him less in one of her husband's favourite comedy roles: 'Dear Sir,' she wrote, 'You cannot act Abel Drugger.—Yours, M. Garrick.' 'Madam,' came the answer, 'I know it.—Yours, E. Kean.'

It is said that Queen Charlotte came to call one day at Hampton, and found Mrs Garrick peeling onions. A second knife and apron were produced, and the two chattered away in the kitchen like a pair of German *hausfraus*. She lived on into the reign of Charlotte's son; George IV and the brother who was to succeed him both came to pay their respects at Hampton. One of the privileges she enjoyed was a plaque giving her carriage admittance to the royal parks.

In January 1819, just before her ninety-fifth birthday, she decided it was time to make her will. Unlike Garrick, she remembered a great many old friends, and her numerous charitable bequests included one of £300, that sum to be invested and the interest to go to the purchase of coals for the poor of the parish of Hampton. Although Sarah Siddons had retired from the stage seven years previously, Mrs Garrick felt that she was the appropriate guardian of a theatrical relic to which her husband had been particularly attached:

> I give to Mrs Siddons a pair of Gloves which were Shakespeares and were presented by one of his ffamily to my late dear husband during the Jubilee at Stratford upon Avon.

Cruikshank's well-known drawing of Mrs Garrick, wearing a huge black bonnet and carrying an even larger muff, dates from 1820. Dean Stanley quoted a description of her in those last years as 'a little bowed-down old woman, who went about leaning on a gold-headed cane, dressed in deep widow's mourning, and always talking of her dear Davy'.[14] But she was happy to gossip about other things, too—about old days in the theatre, about her early life and about her age—'My coachman,' she informed one visitor, 'insists upon it that I am above a hundred.'[15]

She was now becoming very frail, although her appetite remained good and she continued to take an airing in her carriage every day before dinner. In the evening she liked to be read to by her footman, or by Clara, her maid; when she called on her friend Frederick Beltz at the College of Heralds one day in October 1822 she asked him to suggest some light reading, and he sent her a copy of *Waverley*.*

She had come up from Hampton intending to view some alterations at Drury Lane. She asked for two or three of her gowns to be laid out in the Adelphi drawing room so that she might consider which to wear as she took tea in her arm-chair. But when one of the maids handed her a cup, she felt the edge of her mistress's tongue: 'Put it down, you hussey, do you think I cannot help myself?' Moments later, she died.

One of those who came to the house to enquire about the funeral arrangements was John Thomas Smith, Keeper of Prints and Drawings at the British Museum. Mrs Garrick had called on him the previous year to examine the collection of playbills and engravings about her husband which Dr Burney had left to the Museum. He was invited to view the body:

> Upon entering the back room on the first-floor, in which Mr. Garrick died, I found the deceased's two female servants standing by her remains. I made a drawing of her, and intended to have etched it. "Pray, do tell me," looking at one of the maids, "why is the coffin covered with sheets?"

---

* George Frederick Beltz (1777–1841), was Portcullis Poursuivant from 1817 to 1822 and thereafter Lancaster Herald. He was one of Mrs Garrick's executors, and contributed a memoir of her to the *Gentleman's Magazine* for November 1822.

MRS GARRICK.
(taken Sept. 1820. Etat 97.)

Mrs Garrick in old age. 'A little bowed-down old woman, who went about leaning on a gold-headed cane, dressed in deep widow's mourning, and always talking of her dear Davy.' (The Fotomas Index)

"They are their wedding sheets, in which both Mr. and Mrs. Garrick wished to have died."[16]

So much for 'intermeddling Husbands', those improbable phantoms of Garrick's imagining whom he had licensed in his last will and testament to carry cardboard spears across the stage. Now, forty-three years after his death, his wife was laid beside him in Poets' Corner.

Monboddo had clearly never had a chance.

Bibliography

The A to Z of Georgian London, Introductory Notes by Ralph Hyde, London, 1982.

Adolphus, J., *Memoirs of John Bannister*, 2 vols., London, 1839.

Anderson, J.W., *The Manner Pointed Out, in which the Common Prayer was Read in Private by the late Mr Garrick, for the Instruction of a Young Clergyman: from whose manuscript notes this pamphlet is composed*, London, 1797.

Angelo, Henry, *Reminiscences, with Memoirs of his late Father and Friends*, 2 vols., London, vol. 1, 1828; vol. 2, 1830.

Anon, *An Essay upon the Present State of the Theatre in France, England and Italy*, London, 1760.

Anon, *Brief Remarks on the Original and Present State of the Drama: to which is added Hecate's Prophecy, being a Characteristic Dialogue betwixt Future Managers, and their Dependents*, London, 1758.

Anon, *An Historical and Succinct Account of the Late Riots at the Theatres Royal of Drury Lane and Covent Garden*, London, 1763.

Anon, *A Clear Stage, and no Favour: or, Tragedy and Comedy at War. Occasion'd by the Emulation of the two Theatric Heroes, David and Goliah. Left to the Impartial Decision of the Town*, London, 1746.

Anon, *A Letter to Mr. Garrick on the Opening of the Theatre, with Observations on the conduct of Managers, to Actors, Authors, and Audiences: And particularly to New-Performers*, London, 1758.

Anon, *An Appeal to the Public In Behalf of the Manager*, London, 1763.

Anon, *The Life of James Quin, Comedian*, London, 1766.

Anon, *Memoirs of the celebrated Mrs. W*ff**gt*n. Interspersed with several theatrical anecdotes; the amours of many persons of the first rank . . . drawn from real life*, London, 1760.

Anon, *The Dancers Damn'd; or, The Devil to Pay at the Old House*, London, 1755.

Anon, *A Treatise on the Passions, So Far as They Regard the Stage; With a critical Enquiry into the Theatrical Merit of Mr. G–k, Mr. Q–n, and Mr. B–y. The first considered in the part of Lear, the two last opposed in Othello*. London, 1747.

Appleton, William W., *Charles Macklin, An Actor's Life*, Cambridge, Mass., 1961.

Ashton, Geoffrey, Burnim, Kalman A. and Wilton, Andrew, *Pictures in the Garrick Club*, London, 1997.

Askham, Francis (J.E.C. Greenwood), *The Gay Delavals*, London, 1955.

Bellamy, George Anne, *An Apology for the Life of George Anne Bellamy, late of Covent Garden Theatre, Written by herself*, 6 vols., London, 1785.

Berkowitz, Gerald M., *David Garrick, a reference guide*, Boston, Mass., 1980.

Bernard, John, *Retrospections of the Stage*, 2 vols., London, 1830.

Bernbaum, Ernest, *The Drama of Sensibility*, Cambridge, Mass., 1915.

Bertelsen, Lance, 'David Garrick and English Painting', in *Eighteenth-Century Studies*, 11, No. 3, Spring 1978, pp. 308–24.

Besant, Sir Walter, *London in the Eighteenth Century*, London, 1902.

Bevis, Richard W., *The Laughing Tradition: Stage Comedy in Garrick's Day*, Athens, Ga. and London, 1980.

Boaden, James, *Memoirs of the Life of John Philip Kemble, Esq.*, 2 vols., London, 1825.

— (ed.), *The Private Correspondence of David Garrick with the most Celebrated Persons of his Time*, 2 vols., London, 1831.

Boswell, James, *Life of Johnson*, edited by George Birkbeck Hill, revised and enlarged by L.F. Powell, 6 vols., Oxford, 1934–50.

— *Boswell's London Journal, 1762–1763*, edited by Frederick A. Pottle, London, 1950.

— *Boswell on the Grand Tour: Germany and Switzerland 1764*, edited by Frederick A. Pottle, London, 1953.

— *Boswell on the Grand Tour: Italy, Corsica, and France 1765–1766*, edited by Frank Brady and Frederick A. Pottle, London, 1955.

— *Boswell in Search of a Wife 1766–1769*, edited by Frank Brady and Frederick A. Pottle, London, 1957.

— *Boswell for the Defence 1769–1774*, edited by William K. Wimsatt Jr and Frederick A. Pottle, London, 1960.

— *Boswell's Journal of a Tour to the Hebrides with Samuel Johnson, LL.D. 1773*, edited by Frederick A. Pottle and Charles H. Bennett, London, 1963.

— *Boswell: The Ominous Years 1774–1776*, edited by Charles Ryscamp and Frederick A. Pottle, London, 1963.

— *The Correspondence of James Boswell and John Johnston of Grange, Volume 1*, edited by Ralph S. Walker, New York, 1966.

— *Boswell in Extremes 1776–1778*, edited by Charles McC. Weiss and Frederick A. Pottle, New York, 1970.

— *Boswell Laird of Auchinleck 1778–1782*, edited by Joseph W. Reed and Frederick A. Pottle, New York, 1977.

— *Boswell: The Applause of the Jury 1782–1785*, edited by Irma S. Lustig and Frederick A. Pottle, New York, 1981.

— *The Correspondence of James Boswell*, vol. 4 of the Yale Editions of The Private Papers of James Boswell (Research Edition), London, 1986.

— *James Boswell's Life of Johnson, An Edition of the Original Manuscript in Four Volumes. Vol. 1: 1709–1765*, edited by Marshall Waingrow, Edinburgh, New Haven and London, 1994.

Brereton, Austin, *The Literary History of the Adelphi and its Neighbourhood*, London, 1907.

Brewer, John, *The Pleasures of the Imagination: English Culture in the Eighteenth Century*, London, 1997.

Brown, Wallace Cable, *Charles Churchill, Poet, Rake, and Rebel*, Lawrence, Kan., 1953.

Browning, Reed, *The Duke of Newcastle*, New Haven and London, 1975.

Bryant, Donald Cross, *Edmund Burke and his Literary Friends*, Washington University Studies – New Series, Language and Literature – No. 9, St. Louis, 1939.

Burney, Fanny, *The Early Diary of Frances Burney, 1768–78*, edited by Annie R. Ellis, 2 vols., London, 1907.

— *The Early Journals and Letters of Fanny Burney*, vol. I, 1768–1773, edited by Lars E. Troide, Oxford, 1988.

— *The Early Journals and Letters of Fanny Burney*, vol. III, Part I, 1778–9, edited by Lars E. Troide and Stewart J. Cooke, Oxford, 1994.

Burnim, Kalman A., *David Garrick, Director*, Pittsburgh, 1961.

Butt, John, *The Mid-Eighteenth Century*, edited and completed by Geoffrey Carnall (vol. 8 of *The Oxford History of English Literature*), Oxford, 1979.

Campbell, Thomas, *Life of Mrs. Siddons*, 2 vols., London, 1834.

Candid Observer of Men and Things, A, *A Bone for the Chroniclers to pick; or A Take-Off Scene from behind the Curtain. A Poem*, London, 1758.

Carlyle, Alexander, *Anecdotes and Characters of the Times*, edited by James Kinsley, London, 1973.

Chetwood, William Rufus, *A General History of the Stage*, London and Dublin, 1749.

Choiseul, duc Etienne-François de, *Mémoires du duc de Choiseul 1719–1785*, edited by Fernand Calmettes, Paris, 1904.

Cibber, Colley, *An Apology for the Life of Mr. Colley Cibber, Comedian, Written by Himself*, London, 1740.

Cibber, Theophilus, *An Epistle from Mr. Theophilus Cibber, to David Garrick, Esq.*, London, 1755.

Clifford, James L., *Young Samuel Johnson*, London, 1955.

Climenson, Emily J. (ed.), *Elizabeth Montagu, The Queen of the Blue-Stockings, Her Correspondence from 1720 to 1761, by her great-great-niece Emily J. Climenson*, 2 vols., London, 1906.

Collé, Charles, *Journal et Mémoires*, 3 vols., Paris, 1868.

A Collection of Cuttings relating to London Theatres, 1704–1779, British Library, Th. Cts. 1–6.

A Collection of the Dresses of Different Nations, Antient and Modern. Particularly Old English Dresses . . . . . . To which are added The Habits of the Principal Characters on the English Stage, 4 vols., London, 1773.

Colley, Linda, *Britons; Forging the Nation 1707–1837*, New Haven and London, 1992.

Colman, George, the Younger, *Random Records*, 2 vols., London, 1830.

[Colman, George], *A Letter of Abuse, to David Garrick, Esq.*, London, 1757.

Conolly, L.W., *The Censorship of English Drama 1737–1824*, San Marino, 1976.

Cooke, William, *Memoirs of Samuel Foote, Esq. with a Collection of his Genuine Bon-Mots, Anecdotes, Opinions, &c. Mostly Original*, 3 vols., London, 1805.

Copeland, Thomas W. (ed.), *The Correspondence of Edmund Burke, Volume 1, April 1744–June 1768*, Cambridge, 1958.

Cradock, Joseph, *Literary and Miscellaneous Memoirs*, 4 vols., London, 1828.

Cross, Richard and Hopkins, William, *Diaries, 1747–76*. Folger Shakespeare Library MSS. Also fully transcribed in *The London Stage, 1660–1800*, part 4.

Cumberland, Richard, *Memoirs of Richard Cumberland, Written by Himself*, 2 vols., London, 1807.

Davies, Thomas, *Dramatic Miscellanies*, 3 vols., London, 1784.

— *Memoirs of the Life of David Garrick, Esq.* (4th edition), 2 vols., London, 1808.

Deelman, Christian, *The Great Shakespeare Jubilee*, London, 1964.

Delany, Mary Granville, *Autobiography and Correspondence of Mary Granville, Mrs. Delany*, edited by Lady Llanover, 2nd series, 3 vols., London, 1862.

Dibdin, Charles, the Elder, *The Professional Life of Mr Dibdin*, 4 vols., London, 1803.

Dictionary of National Biography.

Dircks, Phyllis T., *David Garrick*, Boston, Mass., 1985.

Dobson, Michael, *The Making of the National Poet. Shakespeare, Adaptation and Authorship, 1660–1769*, Oxford, 1992.

Doddington, George Bubb, *Diary*, London, 1874 (modern edition by J. Carswell and L.A. Dralle, Oxford, 1965).

Donohue, Joseph W. Jr, *Dramatic Character in the English Romantic Age*, Princeton, New Jersey, 1970.

Doran, John, *Annals of the English Stage*, edited by R.H. Stoddard, 2 vols., London, 1890.

Downer, Alan S., 'Nature to Advantage Dressed: Eighteenth-Century Acting', *PMLA*, 58 (1943), 1002–37. Reprinted in *Restoration Drama, Modern Esssays in Criticism*, edited by John Loftus, New York, 1966.

Dunbar, Howard H., *The Dramatic Career of Arthur Murphy*, London, 1946.

F., E., *Mr Garrick's Conduct, as Manager of the Theatre-Royal in Drury-Lane, Considered. In a Letter. Addressed to Him*, London, 1747.

Fiske, Roger, *English Theatre Music in the Eighteenth Century*, London, 1973.

Fitzgerald, Percy, *The Life of Mrs Catherine Clive*, London, 1888.

— *The Life of David Garrick*, new and revised edition, London, 1899.

[Fitzpatrick, Thaddeus] *An Enquiry into the Real Merit of a Certain Popular Performer, in a Series of Letters, First published in the Craftsman or Gray's-Inn Journal; With an Introduction to D—d G—k, Esq.*, London, 1760.

Foote, Samuel, *A Treatise on the Passions so far as they regard the Stage; with a Critical Enquiry into the Theatrical merit of Mr. G—k, Mr. Q—n, and Mr. B—y*, London, 1747.

Forster, John, *The Life and Adventures of Oliver Goldsmith*, London, 1848.

Garrick, David, 'The Garrick Manuscripts', Forster Collection, Victoria and Albert Museum, London (41 volumes of original correspondence).

— *The Letters of David Garrick*, edited by David M. Little and George M. Kahrl, 3 vols., London, 1963.

— *Letters of David Garrick and Georgiana Countess Spencer, 1759–1779*, edited by Earl Spencer and Christopher Dobson, Cambridge, 1960.

— *David Garrick Scrapbook Collection*, 3 vols. in the Folger Library.

— *The Diary of David Garrick; being a record of his memorable trip to Paris in 1751*, edited by Ryllis Clair Alexander, London and New York, 1928.

— *The Journal of David Garrick, Describing his visit to France and Italy in 1763*, edited by George Winchester Stone Jr, New York, 1939.

— *The Plays of David Garrick. A Complete Collection of the Social Satires, French Adaptations, Pantomimes, Christmas and Musical Plays, Preludes, Interludes, and Burlesques, to which are added the Alterations and Adaptations of the Plays of Shakespeare and Other Dramatists from the Sixteenth to the Eighteenth Centuries*, edited with Commentary and Notes by Harry William Pedicord and Frederick Louis Bergmann, 7 vols., Carbondale, Ill., 1980–82.

— *Garrick and his Contemporaries*. A Scrapbook assembled by George Daniel. In the collection of the Folger Library, Washington, D.C.

— *An Essay on Acting: In which will be considered The Mimical behaviour of a Certain fashonable faulty Actor, and the Laudableness of such unmannerly, as well as inhumane Proceedings. To which will be added, A short Criticism on his acting Macbeth*, London, 1744.

Genest, John, *Some Account of the English Stage from the Restoration in 1660 to 1830*, 10 vols., Bath, 1832.

Gentleman, Francis, *The Dramatic Censor; or, Critical Companion*, 2 vols., London, 1770.

George, M. Dorothy, *London Life in the Eighteenth Century*, London, 1925.

Gibbon, Edward, *Memoirs of My Life*, edited by Georges A. Bonnard, London, 1966.

Goldman, Michael, *The Actor's Freedom. Towards a Theory of Drama*, New York, 1975.

Gray, Charles Harold, *Theatrical Criticism in London to 1795*, New York, 1931.

Grimm, Frédéric-Melchior, baron de, *Correspondance littéraire, philosophique et critique par Grimm, Diderot, Raynal, Meister etc. . . .* , edited by M. Tourneaux, 16 vols., Paris, 1877–92.

Hartmann, Cyril Hughes, *Enchanting Bellamy*, London, 1956.

Harwood, Thomas, *The History and Antiquities of the Church and City of Lichfield*, Gloucester, 1806.

Hawkins, Sir John, *The Life of Samuel Johnson, LL.D.*, London, 1787.

Hawkins, Laetitia-Mathilda, *Anecdotes, Biographical Sketches and Memoirs*, London, 1822.

Hedgcock, Frank A., *David Garrick and his French Friends*, London, 1911.

Henderson, John, *Letters and Poems by the late Mr John Henderson*, edited by John Ireland, London, 1786.

Hervey, John, Lord Hervey, *Some Materials towards Memoirs of the Reign of George II*, edited by Romney Sedgwick, 3 vols., London, 1931.

Highfill, Philip Jr., Burnim, Kalman A. and Langhans, Edward (eds.), *A Biographical Dictionary of Actors, Actresses, Musicians, Dancers, Managers and other stage personnel in London, 1660–1800*, 16 vols., Carbondale, Ill., 1973–93.

Hill, John, *The Actor, a Treatise on the Art of Playing. Interspersed with Theatrical Anecdotes, Critical Remarks on Plays, and Occasional Observations on Audiences*, London, 1750.

[Hill, John], *To David Garrick, Esq., The Petition of I. In behalf of herself and her Sisters*, London, 1759.

Hilles, Frederick W., *Portraits by Sir Joshua Reynolds*, London, 1952.

Hogan, C.B., *Shakespeare in the Theatre, 1701–1800*, 2 vols., Oxford, 1952–7.

Hughes, Leo, *A Century of English Farce*, Princeton, New Jersey, 1956.

— *The Drama's Patrons: A Study of the Eighteenth-Century London Audience*, Austin, Texas, 1970.

Hume, Robert D. (ed.), *The London Theatre World, 1660–1800*, Carbondale, Ill., 1980.

— *Henry Fielding and the London Theatre 1728–1737*, Oxford, 1988.

— *The Development of English Drama in the Late Seventeenth Century*, Oxford, 1976.

Hunter, J. Paul, *Occasional Form: Henry Fielding and the Chains of Circumstance*, Baltimore and London, 1975.

Irving, Henry, *David Garrick. A Memorial Illustrative of his Life*, The Garrick Club, London, n.d.

Jarrett, Derek, *England in the Age of Hogarth*, London, 1974.

Johnson, Samuel, *Works*, edited by Revd Robert Lynam, 6 vols., London, 1825.

— *The Letters of Samuel Johnson*, edited by Bruce Redford, 5 vols., Princeton, New Jersey, 1992–4.

Kelly, John A., *German Visitors to English Theaters in the Eighteenth Century*, Princeton, New Jersey, 1936.

Kerslake, J.F. (ed.), *Catalogue of Theatrical Portraits in London Public Collections*, London, 1961.

Ketton-Cremer, Robert Wyndham, *The Early Life and Diaries of William Windham*, London, 1930.

Kirkman, James Thomas, *Memoirs of the Life of Charles Macklin Esq.*, 2 vols., London, 1799.

Knapp, Lewis M., 'Smollett and Garrick', in *Elizabethan and Other Essays in Honor of George F. Reynolds*, University of Colorado Press, 1945.

Knapp, Mary E., 'Garrick's Last Command Performance', in *The Age of Johnson, Essays presented to Chauncey Brewster Tinker*, New Haven, 1949.
— *A Checklist of Verse by David Garrick*, Charlottesville, Va., 1955.
Koenig, B., 'Where was Garrick's Prompter?', *Theatre Notebook*, 37 (1983), 9–14.
Krutch, Joseph Wood, *Comedy and Conscience after the Restoration*, New York, 1924, revised edition 1949.
Laver, James, *Drama, Its Costume and Decor*, London, 1951.
Lecky, W.E.H., *A History of England in the Eighteenth Century*, 8 vols., London, 1877, Cabinet edition, 7 vols., 1891.
Lennox-Boyd, Christopher, Shaw, Guy and Halliwell, Sarah, *Theatre: the Age of Garrick. English mezzotints from the collection of the Hon. Christopher Lennox-Boyd*, London, 1994.
Lewes, Charles Lee, *Memoirs of Charles Lee Lewes, containing Anecdotes, Historical and Biographical, of the English and Scottish Stages, during a Period of Forty Years*, 4 vols., London, 1805.
Lewis, Wilmarth S. (ed.), the Yale Edition of *Horace Walpole's Correspondence*, 48 vols., New Haven & London, 1937–83.
Lichtenberg's Visits to England, as described in his Letters and Diaries, translated and annotated by Margaret L. Mare and W.H. Quarrell, Oxford, 1938.
Liesenfeld, V.J., *The Licensing Act of 1737*, Madison, Wis., 1984.
The London Stage 1660–1800, A Calendar of Plays, Entertainments & Afterpieces Together with Casts, Box-Receipts and Contemporary Comment compiled from the Playbills, Newspapers and Theatrical Diaries of the Period, edited in five parts by Emmett L. Avery, Arthur H. Scouten, George Winchester Stone, Jr and Charles Beecher Hogan, 11 vols., Carbondale, Ill., 1960–68.
Lynch, James J., *Box, Pit and Gallery, Stage and Society in Johnson's London*, Berkeley and Los Angeles, 1953.
Lynham, Deryck, *The Chevalier Noverre: A Biography*, New York and London, 1959.
Mack, Maynard, *Alexander Pope, A Life*, New Haven and London, 1985.
Mackenzie, Henry, *An Account of the Life and Writings of John Home, Esq.*, Edinburgh, 1822.
Mackintosh, Iain and Ashton, Geoffrey, *The Georgian Playhouse – Actors, Artists, Audiences and Architecture*, London, 1975.
MacMillan, Dougald, *Drury Lane Calendar, 1747–1776*, Oxford, 1938.
Manvell, Roger, *Sarah Siddons, Portrait of an Actress*, London, 1970.
Memoirs of Doctor Burney, arranged from his Own Manuscripts, from Family Papers, and from Personal Recollections, by his daughter, Madame d'Arblay, 3 vols., London, 1832.
Mitchell, Charles (ed.), *Hogarth's Peregrination*, Oxford, 1952.
Monnet, Jean, *Supplément au Roman Comique; ou, Mémoires pour servir à la vie de Jean Monnet*, 2 vols., Paris and London, 1772.
Morellet, André (Lemontey, P.E. [ed.]), *Mémoires de l'Abbé Morellet*, Paris, 1822.
Mullin, Donald C., 'Lamps for Garrick's Footlights', *Theatre Notebook*, 26 (1971–2), 92–4.
Murphy, Arthur, *The Life of David Garrick, Esq.*, 2 vols., London, 1801.
Nash, Mary, *The Provoked Wife. The Life and Times of Susannah Cibber*, London, 1977.
— 'Lighting on the Eighteenth-Century London Stage: A Reconsideration', *Theatre Notebook*, 34 (1980), 73–85.
Neville, Sylas, *The Diary of Sylas Neville, 1767–1788*, edited by Basil Cozens-Hardy, London, 1950.

Nicholls, James C. (ed.), *Mme Riccoboni's Letters to David Hume, David Garrick and Sir Robert Liston*, Oxford, 1976.

Nichols, John, *Illustrations of the Literary History of the Eighteenth Century*, 8 vols., London, 1817–58.

— *Literary Anecdotes of the Eighteenth Century*, 9 vols., London, 1812–16.

Nicoll, Allardyce, *A History of English Drama, 1660–1900*, Cambridge, 1959.

— *The Garrick Stage*, University Press, Manchester, 1980.

Northcote, James, *Memoirs of Sir Joshua Reynolds*, 2nd edition, 2 vols., London, 1819.

Noverre, Jean Georges, *Lettres sur La Danse, et sur Les Ballets*, Lyon, 1760. Translated as *Letters on Dancing and Ballet*, by Cyril Beaumont, London, 1930.

Noyes, Robert Gale, *The Neglected Muse: Restoration and Eighteenth-Century Tragedy in the Novel (1740–1780)*, Providence, Rhode Island, 1958.

— *The Thespian Mirror: Shakespeare in the Eighteenth-Century Novel*, Providence, Rhode Island, 1953.

Odell, George C.D., *Shakespeare from Betterton to Irving*, 2 vols., New York, 1920.

O'Donoghue, Freeman, *Catalogue of Engraved British Portraits Preserved in the Department of Prints and Drawings in the British Museum*, 2 vols., London, 1908–25.

O'Keeffe, John, *Recollections of the Life of John O'Keeffe, Written by Himself*, 2 vols., London, 1826.

Oman, Carola, *David Garrick*, London, 1958.

Oulton, Walley Chamberlain, *The History of the Theatres of London*, 2 vols., London, 1796.

Page, Eugene R., *George Colman the Elder, Essayist, Dramatist, and Theatrical Manager, 1732–1794*, New York, 1935.

Parsons, Mrs Clement, *Garrick and his Circle*, London, 1906.

Paulson, Ronald, *Hogarth: His Life, Art and Times*, 2 vols., New Haven and London, 1971.

— *Hogarth, Volume 1, The "Modern Moral Subject" 1697–1732*, Cambridge, 1992.

— *Hogarth, Volume 2, High Art and Low, 1732–1750*, Cambridge, 1992.

Pedicord, Harry William, *The Theatrical Public in the Time of Garrick*, New York, 1954.

Pennington, Montagu (ed.), *Elizabeth Carter, Memoirs of the Life of Mrs Elizabeth Carter*, London, 1808.

Pentzell, Raymond J., 'Garrick's Costuming', *Theatre Survey, The American Journal of Theatre History*, vol. 10, Number 1, May 1969.

Perrin, Michel, *David Garrick, Homme de Théâtre*, thesis submitted to the University of Paris III, 27 November 1976, 2 vols., Lille, 1978.

Pickering, Roger, *Reflections upon Theatrical Expression in Tragedy*, London, 1755.

Piozzi, Hester, *Piozziana, or Recollections of the late Mrs Piozzi*, edited by N. Mangin, London, 1833.

Pittard, Joseph, *Observations on Mr. Garrick's Acting; in a letter to the Right Hon. the Earl of Chesterfield*, London, 1758.

Plumb, J.H., *The First Four Georges*, London, 1956.

— *Sir Robert Walpole: The King's Minister*, London, 1960.

The Poetical Works of David Garrick, Esq. now first collected into Two Volumes. With Explanatory Notes, London, 1785.

[Pratt, Samuel Jackson], *Garrick's Looking-Glass: or, the Art of Rising on the Stage*, London, Dublin, Edinburgh, 1776.

Price, Cecil, *Theatre in the Age of Garrick*, Oxford, 1973.

[Purdon, Edward], *A Letter to David Garrick, Esq; on opening the Theatre. In which, with great Freedom, he is told how he ought to behave*, London, 1759.

Quintana, Ricardo, *Oliver Goldsmith, a Georgian Study*, London, 1967.

Rambler, Harry [pseud.], *Bays in Council: or, A Picture of a Green-Room. A Dramatic Poem, Containing The Speeches of Mr. G—RR—CK, [etc] . . . a few Days before Drury-Lane Theatre was open'd, on Account of the Strong Company that were engaged at the other House*, Dublin, 1751.

Reynolds, Frederic, *The Life and Times of Frederic Reynolds, written by himself*, 2 vols., London, 1826.

Richards, Kenneth, 'The French Actors in London, 1661–2', *Restoration and Eighteenth-Century Theatre Research*, 14, no. 2 (Nov 1975), 48–52.

Roberts, William, *Memoirs of the Life and Correspondence of Mrs. Hannah More*, 3rd edition, 4 vols., London, 1835.

Rogal, Samuel J., 'David Garrick at the Adelphi', *The Journal of the Rutgers University Library*, 37, Number 2, June 1974.

Rosenfeld, Sybil, *Strolling Players and Drama in the Provinces, 1660–1765*, 1939.

— *Georgian Scene Painters and Scene Painting*, 1981.

Scouten, A.H., 'The Increase in Popularity of Shakespeare's Plays in the Eighteenth Century', *Shakespeare Quarterly*, 7 (spring 1956), 189–202.

Sedgwick, R.R., *Letters of George III to Lord Bute, 1756–66*, London, 1939.

Sheppard, F.H.W. (ed.), *Survey of London*, vols. 20, 29, 30 and 35, London, 1960 and 1970.

Siddons, Sarah, *The Reminiscences of Mrs Sarah Siddons, 1773–1785*, edited by William Van Lennep, Cambridge, Mass., 1942.

Smith, John Thomas, *A Book for a Rainy Day, or Recollections of the Events of the Years 1766–1833*, London, 1845, 3rd edition, edited, with an introduction and notes, by Wilfred Whitten, 1905.

Sprague, Arthur Colby, *Shakespeare and the Actors. The Stage Business in his Plays (1660–1905)*, Cambridge, Mass., 1945.

Stanhope, Philip Dormer, Earl of Chesterfield, *Miscellaneous Works*, edited by M. Maty, 2nd edition, London, 1779.

Stein, Elizabeth P., *David Garrick, Dramatist*, New York, 1938.

Stockdale, Percival, *The Memoirs of the Life, and Writings of Percival Stockdale*, London, 1809.

Stockholm, Johanne M., *Garrick's Folly*, London, 1941.

Stone, George Winchester Jr, 'Garrick's Handling of Shakespeare's Plays and His Influence upon the Changed Attitudes of Shakespearean Criticism during the Eighteenth Century', Harvard dissertation, 2 vols., 1938.

— 'Garrick's Long-Lost Alteration of Hamlet', *PMLA*, 49 (September 1934), 890–921.

— 'The God of His Idolatry', in *Joseph Quincy Adams, Memorial Studies*, edited by James G. McManaway, Giles E. Dawson and Edwin E. Willoughby, Washington, D.C., 1948.

Stone, George Winchester Jr. and Kahrl, George M., *David Garrick, a Critical Biography*, Carbondale, Ill., 1979.

Sturz, Helferich Peter, *Vermischte Schriften*, Starber am See, 1946.

Summerson, John, *Georgian London*, London, 1948.

Tasch, Peter A., *The Dramatic Cobbler. The Life and Works of Isaac Bickerstaff*, Lewisburg, Pa., 1971.

Taylor, John, *Records of My Life*, 2 vols., London, 1832.

The Theatrical Review or Annals of the Drama, S. Williams *et al.*, London, 1763. Reprinted in James Agate, *The English dramatic critics – an anthology*, n.d.

Thomas, David, and Hare, Arnold, *Theatre in Europe: a documentary history. Restoration and Georgian England, 1660–1788*, Cambridge, 1989.

Thrale, Hester, *Thraliana: The Diary of Mrs Hester Lynch Thrale (Later Mrs. Piozzi) 1776–1809*, edited by Katharine C. Balderston, 2 vols., Oxford, 1942.

Trefman, Simon, *Sam. Foote, Comedian, 1720–1777*, New York, 1971.

Victor, Benjamin, *The History of the Theatres of London and Dublin from the year 1730 to the Present Time*, 3 vols., London, vols. 1 and 2, 1761; vol. 3, 1771.

— *Original Letters, Dramatic Pieces, and Poems*, 3 vols., London, 1776.

Visser, Colin, 'Garrick's Palace of Armida: A Neglected Document', *Theatre Notebook*, 34 (1980), 104–12.

Waddington, Richard, *Louis XV et le renversement des alliances: Préliminaires de la guerre de sept ans, 1754–1756*, Paris, 1896.

Whitty, J.C, 'The Half-Price Riots of 1763', *Theatre Notebook*, 24 (1969–70), 25–32.

Wilkinson, Tate, *Memoirs of his Own Life*, 4 vols., York, 1790.

— *The Wandering Patentee: or, a History of the Yorkshire Theatres from 1770 to the Present Time*, 4 vols., York, 1795.

Wilson, John Harold, 'Rant, Cant, and Tone on the Restoration Stage', *Studies in Philology*, vol. 52 (October 1955), pp. 592–8.

Woods, Leigh, *Garrick Claims the Stage: Acting as Social Emblem in Eighteenth-Century England*, Westport, Conn., 1984.

The Works of Arthur Murphy, Esq., London, 1786.

Wright, James, *Historia Histrionica: An Historical Account of the English Stage, Shewing the ancient Use, Improvement, and Perfection, of Dramatick Representations, in this Nation*, London, 1699.

Notes

Prologue

1. Kirkman, J.T., *Memoirs of the Life of Charles Macklin Esq.*, 2 vols., London, 1799, i, 244–5.
2. Grimm, *Correspondance littéraire*, 1er juillet 1765.
3. *The Monthly Mirror*, 1807, New series, i, 78.

1 Fat Central England

1. Lewis, Wilmarth S. (ed.), *Correspondence of Horace Walpole*, 48 vols., London and Newhaven, 1937–83, xl, 43. Cited henceforth as *Walpole*.
2. Harwood, Thomas, *The History and Antiquities of the Church and City of Lichfield*, Gloucester, 1806, p. 5.
3. Sedgwick, Romney, *The House of Commons, 1715–54*, 2 vols., London, 1970, i, 319.
4. Stafford Record Society, *Collections for a History of Staffordshire*, 1920 and 1922, Staffordshire Parliamentary History (1603–1780), 250 sqq; *ibid*, 4th Series vi, 115–35, The Struggle for the Lichfield Interest, 1747–68.)
5. Lichfield Joint Record Office, Lichfield City Council, records (additional) D. 77/4/6/1, f. 120; D. 77/4/6/1–2; D.77/4/7/1–2.)
6. *Ibid.*, D. 77/4/6/1.
7. *Ibid.*, D. 77/4/6/1, f. 172v; D. 77/4/7/1, f. 21.
8. Loveday, J.E.T. (ed.), *Diary of a Tour in 1732 made by John Loveday of Caversham*, Edinburgh, 1890, .p. 7.

9. Thomas Newton tells the story in his autobiography (*The Works of the Right Reverend Thomas Newton*, 2 vols., London, 1782, i, 22).

2 'To Save You from the Gallows'

1. Boswell, James, *The Life of Samuel Johnson, LL.D.*, edited by G.B. Hill, revised by L.F. Powell, 6 vols., Oxford, 1934–50, i, 44. Cited henceforth as *Life*.
2. *The Gentleman's Magazine*, 1750, p. 235.
3. *Memoirs of the Life of David Garrick, Esq, interspersed with Characters and Anecdotes of his Theatrical Contemporaries*, 2 vols., London, 1808, i, 4. I have relied on this in preference to the first edition published in 1780. Cited hereafter as *Davies*.
4. Murphy, Arthur, *The Life of David Garrick, Esq.*, 2 vols., London, 1801, i, 8. Cited hereafter as *Murphy*.
5. *Davies*, i, 6.
6. *Ibid.*, i, 3.
7. *Ibid.*, i, 4–5.
8. *The Letters of David Garrick*, edited by Little, David M. and Kahrl, George M., Phoebe de K. Wilson, Associate Editor, 3 vols., London, 1963, Letter 1, 23 January 1773. Cited henceforth as *Letters*.
9. *Ibid.*, 2.
10. *Ibid.*, 3.
11. *Ibid.*, 8.
12. *Ibid.*, 8.
13. *Davies*, i, 7.
14. *Letters*, 9.
15. *Ibid.*, 10.

16. Stockdale, Percival, *The Memoirs of the Life and Writings of Percival Stockdale*, 2 vols., London, 1808, ii, 137f. Cited henceforth as *Stockdale*.

17. *Life*, i, 98.

18. Boaden, James (ed.), *The Private Correspondence of David Garrick with the most Celebrated Persons of his Time*, 2 vols., London, 1831, i, 1–2. Cited henceforth as *Boaden*.

19. *Life*, i, 101, n.1.

3 The Stage-Struck Wine Merchant

1. Hervey, John, Lord Hervey, *Some Materials towards Memoirs of the Reign of George II* (ed. Romney Sedgwick), 3 vols., London, 1931, iii, 812–13.

2. *Ibid.*, ii, 565.

3. *Ibid.*, iii, 738.

4. *Journals of the House of Lords*, xxv, 151.

5. *Hervey, op. cit.*, iii, 751.

6. *The Usefulness of the Stage to Religion and to Government*, 2nd ed., London, 1738, p. 22.

7. Davies, Thomas, *Dramatic Miscellanies*, 3 vols., Dublin, 1784, i, 151–4.

8. *Lethe*, lines 296–303.

9. *Ibid.*, lines 318–330.

10. *Letters*, 13.

11. The story appears in James Northcote's *Memoirs of Sir Joshua Reynolds*, first published in 1813.

12. *Davies*, i, 40.

13. *Letters*, 17.

14. *Murphy*, i, 25–6.

15. *Stockdale*, ii, 153–4.

16. *Letters*, 19.

17. *Ibid.*, 20.

18. *Ibid.*, 21.

19. *Boaden*, i, 3. Letter dated 16 December 1741.

20. *Ibid.*, i, 5. Letter dated 18 January 1742.

21. *Dramatic Miscellanies, op. cit.*, iii, 304.

22. *Letters*, 22.

23. *The Works of Arthur Murphy, Esq.*, London, 1786, vi, 270.

24. *Murphy*, i, 28–30.

25. *Boaden*, i, 8. Letter dated Monday 26 April 1742.

26. *Letters*, 21.

27. *Ibid.*, 23.

4 Garrick Fever

1. Chetwood, William Rufus, *A General History of the Stage*, London and Dublin, 1749, p. 255.

2. *Fitzgerald*, 139.

3. Now at the Folger Library in Washington, W.a 94.

4. 19 November 1736.

5. *Faulkner's Journal*, 13 April 1742.

6. Lord Wentworth to Lord Strafford, 6 January 1739 in Cartwright, James J., [ed.], *The Wentworth Papers, 1705–1739*, London, 1883.

7. See Ball, F. Elrington, *The Correspondence of Jonathan Swift*, 6 vols., London, 1910–14, vi, 182, 184.

8. *Boaden*, i, 12–14.

9. Ketton-Cremer, Robert Wyndham, *The Early Life and Diaries of William Windham*, London, 1930, p. 77. Cited henceforth as *Ketton-Cremer*.

10. *Letters*, 25.

11. Quoted in *Highfill*, xvi, 204.

12. *Ketton-Cremer, op. cit.*, p. 79.

13. *Poetical Works, op. cit.*, ii, 487.

14. *The Life of Mr James Quin, Comedian, with the History of the Stage from his Commencing Actor to his Retreat to Bath*, London, 1766.

15. *Highfill*, xii, 240.

16. *Letters*, 20.

17. *Davies*, i, 46–7.

18. *Boaden*, i, 27.

19. *Gentleman's Magazine*, No. 13, May 1743 (reprinted from *The Champion*).

20. *Tom Jones*, Book 16, chapter 5.

21. *Walpole*, xviii, 180.

22. *Diary*, edited by Henry B. Wheatley, 9 vols., London, 1902–9, ii, 54.

23. *Davies*, i, 60–61.

24. *Ibid.*, 61.

25. *An Essay on Acting: In Which Will Be Consider'd The Mimical Behaviour of a*

Certain Fashionable Faulty Actor . . . . . ,
London, 1744, pp. 6–8.
26. *Murphy*, i, 35.
27. *Ketton-Cremer, op. cit.*, p. 80.
28. *Davies*, i, 70.

5 Pig in the Middle

1. *Murphy*, i, 61.
2. *London Daily Post*, 25 November 1743.
3. *Davies*, i, 92–3.
4. *Murphy*, i, 67–8.
5. *Kirkman, op. cit.*, i, 292.
6. *Davies*, i, 104–7.
7. *Kirkman, op. cit.*, i, 368–70.

6 Vaulting Ambition

1. *Dramatic Miscellanies, op. cit.*, ii, 166.
2. 1 September 1754.
3. *The Actor: A Treatise on the Art of Playing*, London, 1750.
4. *General Advertiser*, 14 March 1744.
5. *Ibid.*, 23 April 1744.
6. *Letters*, 28.
7. Victor, Benjamin, *The History of the Theatres of London and Dublin*, 2 vols., London, 1761, i, 44. Cited henceforth as *Victor*.
8. *General Advertiser*, 24 November 1744.
9. *Victor*, i, 62.
10. *Letters*, 29.
11. *Davies*, i, 131.
12. Dibdin, Charles, *The Professional Life of Mr Dibdin*, 4 vols., London, 1803. Cited henceforth as *Dibdin*.

7 Dear Charmers

1. *Cooke, 150–51.*
2. *London Chronicle*, 3–5 March 1757.
3. Mack, Maynard, *Alexander Pope, A Life*, New Haven and London, 1985, p. 777.
4. *Dramatic Miscellanies, op. cit.*, i, 37.
5. *Ibid.*
6. *Letters*, 29.
7. *Kirkman, op. cit.*, ii, 260.

8. *Walpole*, xix, 27.
9. *Daily Post*, 26 April 1745.
10. *Davies*, i, 116–17.
11. Peg's riposte is recorded in John Taylor's *Records of My Life*, 2 vols., London, 1832.
12. *Murphy*, i, 172.
13. *Ketton-Cremer, op. cit.*, 80–81.
14. *Cooke*, i, 120.
15. *The London Stage 1660–1800, A Calendar of Plays, Entertainments & Afterpieces Together with Casts, Box-Receipts and Contemporary Comment compiled from the Playbills, Newspapers and Theatrical Diaries of the Period*, edited in 5 parts by Emmett L. Avery, Arthur H. Scouten, George Winchester Stone, Jr and Charles Beecher Hogan, 11 vols., Carbondale, Ill., 1960–68. Cited henceforth as *London Stage*.
16. *Letters*, 32.
17. *Boaden*, i, 34–5. Letter dated 18 July 1745.
18. *Letters*, 37. Garrick is quoting from *The Orphan*, IV, i, 68.
19. *General Advertiser*, 28 September 1745.
20. *Letters*, 33.
21. *Ibid.*, 34.
22. Forster Collection, Victoria and Albert Museum, xxxv, 25.
23. *Letters*, 37.
24. *Ibid.*, 38.
25. *Boaden*, i, 38–9.
26. Nash, Mary, *The Provok'd Wife. The Life and Times of Susanah Cibber*, London, 1977.

8 Violette

1. *Davies*, i, 122.
2. *Letters*, 40.
3. *Ibid*, 41.
4. *London Gazette*, 21–4 December 1745, p. 7.
5. *Boaden*, i, 47–8.
6. *Letters*, 41.
7. *Ibid.*, 42.
8. *Ibid.*, 41.
9. Letter to Peter Garrick dated 24 May 1746. *Letters*, 44.
10. *Walpole*, ix, 28.

11. Carlyle, Alexander, *Anecdotes and Characters of the Times*, ed. James Kinsley, London, 1973, p. 95.

12. *Letters*, 47.

9 Enter the Manager

1. *Walpole*, xiii–xiv, 6–7.

2. *Davies*, i, 134–5.

3. The account books are in the British Library, where they are listed as Egerton 2268.

4. Cumberland, Richard, *Memoirs of Richard Cumberland, Written by himself*, 2 vols., London, 1807, i, 80–82. Cited henceforth as *Cumberland*.

5. Hedgcock, Frank, *David Garrick and His French Friends*, London, n.d. [1912], p. 38. Cited hereafter as *Hedgcock*.

6. Letter dated 3 November 1746. *Boaden*, i, 44.

7. *Walpole*, xix, 42.

8. *General Advertiser*, 16 January 1747.

9. *The Anatomist and News Regulator*, 31 January 1747.

10. *Murphy*, i, 117–18.

11. *Poetical Works*, i, 93–4.

12. The relevant documents are in the Folger Library and in the British Library, Add MSS 21508.

13. *Davies*, i, 142. By the time Covent Garden closed on 29 May, profits for the season were in excess of £8,000.

14. *Ibid.*, i, 130.

15. This document, a two-page unsigned manuscript, is now in the Harvard Theatre Collection (fMS Thr 12). It appears to have been either written or dictated by Lacy.

16. The contract is in the Forster Collection at the Victoria and Albert Museum, and is reproduced in *Boaden*, i, 50–53.

17. Wilkinson, Tate, *Memoirs of his Own Life* 4 vols, York, 1790, i, 24–5. Cited henceforth as *Wilkinson*.

18. *A Treatise on the Passions, So Far as They Regard the Stage; With a critical Enquiry into the Theatrical Merit of Mr. G–k, Mr. Q–n, and Mr. B–y. The first considered in the part of Lear, the two last opposed in Othello*, London, 1747.

19. T., J., *A Letter of Compliment to the Ingenious Author of A Treatise on the Passions*, London, 1747.

20. *Letters*, 51.

10 Rescued Nature and Reviving Sense

1. *The Life of Mr James Quin*, op. cit., 43.

2. F., E., *Mr Garrick's Conduct, as Manager of the Theatre-Royal in Drury-Lane, Considered. In a Letter. Addressed to Him*, London, 1747.

3. Letter of John Chamberlain to Sir Dudley Carlton at Turin, *Miscellaneous State Papers, 1501–1726*, i, 395.

4. Forster Collection, Garrick, XVII, 49. Letter dated 12 December 1747.

5. *Cross Diary*, 22 February 1748.

6. *Walpole*, xix, 469.

7. *Cross Diary*, 14 March 1748.

8. These figures are from the Clay MS *Drury Lane Actor's Account Book*. The authorship of this 80-page document, of which the Folger Library possesses a microfilm copy, is unknown. The figures agree broadly with those given by Cross in his *Diary* and by John Powel, the deputy treasurer at Drury Lane, in the MS entitled *Tit for Tat, &c* now in the Harvard Theatre Collection.

9. *Davies*, ii, 188–9.

10. *Ibid.*, ii, 346.

11. Angelo, Henry, *Reminiscences, with Memoirs of his late Father and Friends*, 2 vols, vol. 1, London, 1828, vol. 2, 1830, i, 3. Cited henceforth as *Angelo*.

12. Henderson, John, *Letters and Poems by the late Mr John Henderson*, ed. John Ireland, London, 1786, 122.

13. Smollett, Tobias, *The Adventures of Roderick Random*, chapters 62 and 63.

14. *Letters*, 56.

15. *Knight*, 115.

16. *Hedgcock*, chapter 4.

17. See Hogan, C.B., *Shakespeare in the Theatre, 1701–1800*, 2 vols., Oxford, 1952–7, i, 405.

18. *Davies*, i, 156.

19. *Life*, i, 199–200.

20. *Ibid.*, iv, 243.
21. *Ibid.*
22. *Ibid.*, iv, 7.

11 Fixing the Weathercock

1. Paulson, Ronald, *Hogarth: His Life, Art and Times*, 2 vols., New Haven and London, 1971, i, 85.
2. *Walpole*, xx, 74.
3. The letter, dated 18 July 1749, is now in the Folger Library.
4. *Letters*, 58.
5. *Letters*, 60.
6. Letter dated 8 August 1749, now in the Folger Library.
7. The two works were *Political, Moral and Miscellaneous Thoughts and Reflections* and *Character of King Charles II*. Both appeared the following year.
8. *Letters*, 69.
9. *Ibid.*, 70.
10. *Ibid.*, 71.
11. *Ibid.*, 70.
12. *Ibid.*, 57.
13. *Ibid.*, 74.
14. *Ibid.*, 71.
15. *Ibid.*, 73.

12 Britannia and the French Vagrants

1. *Murphy*, i, 173–4.
2. *Knight*, 128.
3. *Fitzgerald*, 129.
4. *Letters*, 74.
5. *Ibid.*, 77.
6. *Ibid.*, 81.
7. *Ibid.*, 81.
8. Monnet, Jean, *Supplément au Roman Comique; ou, Mémoires pour servir à la vie de Jean Monnet*, 2 vols., Paris and London, 1772.
9. *London Evening Post*, 21 December 1749.
10. *General Advertiser*, 21 May 1750.
11. Forster Collection.
12. *Letters*, 84.
13. Forster Collection.

14. Winston MS, Folger Library, Washington, D.C. VIII. Cited henceforth as *Winston MS*.
15. *Lives of the Poets*.
16. *Davies*, i, 159.
17. *Public Advertiser*, 20 November 1749.
18. *Letters*, 87.
19. *Ibid.*, 89.
20. *Ibid.*, 90.
21. *Ibid.*, 91.
22. *Ibid.*, 89.
23. *Ibid.*, 93.

13 The Battle of the Romeos

1. *Daily Advertiser*, 12 October 1750.
2. *Letters*, 95.
3. *Murphy*, i, 192.
4. Gentleman, Francis, *The Dramatic Censor; or, Critical Companion*, 2 vols., London, 1770, i, 189.
5. See Doran, John, *Annals of the English Stage*, ed. R.H. Stoddard, 2 vols., London, 1890, i, 366.
6. Holograph letter to a friend, dated 6 October, now in the Folger Library.
7. *Letters*, 96.
8. *Ibid.*, 97.
9. *Cross Diary*, 19 October 1750.
10. *Davies*, ii, 37–8.
11. *Cross Diary*, 23 February 1751.
12. *General Advertiser*, 25 February 1751.
13. *Walpole*, xx, 231, Letter dated 13 March 1751 OS.
14. *Letters*, 99.
15. *Ibid.*
16. *Walpole*, xx, 209, letter dated 19 December 1750 OS.

14 A Most Agreeable Jaunt

1. *Letters*, 103.
2. Garrick, David, *The Diary of David Garrick; being a record of his memorable trip to Paris in 1751*, Edited by Ryllis Clair Alexander, London and New York, 1928.
3. *Letters*, 105.

4. *Mémoires du duc de Choiseul 1719–1785*, ed. Fernand Calmettes, Paris, 1904.
5. Hedgcock found Bernage's letter in the Bibliothèque de l'Arsenal, *Archives de la Bastille*, (manuscrit 11743, fs. 357–83.) The translation is his. The French text appears as an appendix in *David Garrick and his French Friends*.
6. *Letters*, 106.
7. *Inspector No. 184*, in *Daily Advertiser and Literary Gazette*.
8. *Davies*, i, 194.
9. *Cross Diary*, 26 October 1751.
10. *Dramatic Miscellanies, op. cit. ii, 68*.
11. *Murphy*, i, 213.
12. *Rambler*, No. 200, Saturday, 15 February 1752.
13. *Letters*, 114.
14. *Ibid.*, 116.
15. *Ibid.*, 119.

15   Wire Dancers, the Jew Bill and a Place in the Country

1. *Davies*, i, 201.
2. *Letters*, 126.
3. *Ibid.*, 127.
4. *Ibid.*, 130. Garrick backed the right horse. Savile eventually withdrew, and D'Arcy was returned unopposed.
5. Lecky, W.E.H., *A History of England in the Eighteenth Century*, 8 vols., London, 1877, Cabinet edition, 7 vols., 1891, ii, 329.
6. *Gray's Inn Journal*, 8 December 1753.
7. *Davies*, i, 207–8.
8. *Letters*, 134.
9. *Murphy*, i, 247.
10. *Murphy*, i, 238–9.
11. *Knight*, 153.
12. *Hedgcock*, 62.
13. Stone, George Winchester, "Garrick's Handling of Shakespeare's Plays and His Influence upon the Changed Attitudes of Shakespearean Criticism during the Eighteenth Century," Harvard Dissertation, 2 vols., 1938, i, 226.
14. Dobson, Michael, *The Making of the National Poet. Shakespeare, Adaptation and Authorship, 1660–1769*, Oxford, 1992, 195.

16   Signor Shakespearelli

1. *Davies*, i, 222–3.
2. *Fitzgerald*, 154.
3. *Murphy*, i, 265.
4. *Walpole*, xxxv, 209–10, letter dated 23 February 1755.
5. *English Theatre Music in the Eighteenth Century*, Oxford, 1973, p. 244.
6. Letter No. 5.
7. *Public Advertiser*, 15 February 1755.
8. Browning, Reed, *The Duke of Newcastle*, New Haven and London, 1975, 220.
9. Quoted in Waddington, Richard, *Louis XV et le renversement des alliances: Préliminaires de la guerre de sept ans, 1754–1756*, Paris, 1896, p. 93.
10. It was published in the course of April 1755 in the *Public Advertiser*, the *Gentleman's Magazine*, the *London Magazine* and the *Scots Magazine*.
11. *Letters*, 141.
12. *Ibid.*, 143.
13. *Ibid.*, 146.
14. *Ibid.*, 152.
15. *Ibid.*, 146.
16. *Ibid.*, 149.
17. Forster Collection. Letter dated 6 August 1755.
18. *Letters*, 155.
19. Act I, scene iii, line 85.
20. *Letters*, 151.
21. *Walpole*, xxxv, 242. Letter dated 4 August 1755 to Richard Bentley.

17   The Chinese Festival

1. Hudson, G.F., 'China and the World', in *The Legacy of China*, ed. Raymond Dawson, Oxford, 1964, p. 352.
2. *Collé, op. cit.*, i, 248, July 1754.
3. Noverre's letters are printed in *Boaden*, vol. 2. The translations used here are Deryck Lynham's, from his *The Chevalier Noverre*, London, 1950.
4. *Boaden*, ii, 390, letter dated 9 May 1755.
5. *Ibid.*, ii, 391.
6. Quoted in *Hedgcock*, p. 128.

7. *Davies*, i, 215.
8. *Cross Diary*, 19 November 1755.
9. *Letters*, 821. Letter dated 1 February 1774 to Garrick's friend Richard Cox, the founder of Cox's Bank.
10. *Murphy*, i, 284–5.
11. Quoted in *London Stage*, Part 4, ii, 522.

18 Memento Mori

1. *Davies*, ii, 187.
2. *Murphy*, i, 298.
3. *Letters*, 181.
4. *Ibid.*, 197.
5. *Life*, v. 360.
6. *Wilkinson*, i, 118–19.
7. *Ibid.*, i, 125–30.
8. *Letters*, 191.
9. *Ibid.*, 196.
10. *Boaden*, i, 83. The letter of Garrick's to which this is a reply has not survived.
11. *Davies*, i, 230.
12. *Cross Diary*, 30 February 1758.
13. *Davies*, i, 232.
14. Friedman, Arthur (ed.), 'The Bee', *Collected Works of Oliver Goldsmith*, 5 vols., Oxford, 1966, iii, 267–8.

19 Slings and Arrows

1. *Carlyle, op. cit.*, pp. 173–5.
2. *Letters*, 210.
3. *Ibid.*, 211.
4. Climenson, Emily J. (ed.), *Elizabeth Montagu, The Queen of the Blue-Stockings, Her Correspondence from 1720 to 1761, by her great-great-niece Emily J. Climenson*, 2 vols., London, 1906, ii, 145.
5. Candid Observer of Men and Things, A, *A Bone for the Chroniclers to pick; or A Take-Off Scene from behind the Curtain. A Poem*, London, 1758.
6. *Cross Diary*, 16 September 1758.
7. *Letters*, 213.
8. *Cross Diary*, 27 October 1758.
9. *Memoirs of Samuel Foote*, 3 vols., London, 1805, ii, 163.
10. *Wilkinson*, ii, 75–6.
11. *Cooke, ii, 88.*
12. The phrase occurs in John Nichols's *Literary Anecdotes of the Eighteenth Century.*
13. *Letters*, 222. Garrick was writing to his friend Dr John Hawkesworth.
14. *Ibid.*, 226.
15. *To David Garrick, Esq., The Petition of I. In behalf of herself and her Sisters*, London, 1759.
16. *Letters*, 229.
17. *Ibid.*, 199.
18. *Ibid.*, 207.
19. *Boaden*, i, 90–91, letter dated 29 November 1758.
20. *Letters*, 218.
21. *Ibid.*, 175.
22. *Boaden*, i, 98.
23. *The Bee*, 1759, p. 14.
24. *Dramatic Miscellanies*, ii, 368.
25. *Letters*, 231.
26. *Ibid.*, 885.
27. *Ibid.*, 224.
28. Act I, scene i, lines 199–207.

20 Heart of Oak

1. *Letters*, 229.
2. *Ibid.*, 393.
3. *Ibid.*, 236.
4. *Boaden*, i, 204.
5. *Letters*, 243.
6. Act II, scene ii, lines 96–111.
7. *Davies*, ii, 62.
8. *Ibid.*, ii, 65.
9. *Winston MS 8.*
10. *Murphy*, i, 351.
11. The agreement, dated 28 November 1759, is preserved in the British Library (BM Add. MS 27925). It was signed by both Lacy and Garrick, and witnessed by Cross and Garrick's brother George.
12. *The Present State of the Stage in Great-Britain and Ireland. And the Theatrical Characters of the Principal Performers, in Both Kingdoms, Impartially Observed*, London, 1753.
13. *Letters*, 242.
14. *Ibid.*, 247.

15. *Fitzgerald*, 184n.
16. *Knight*, 178.
17. British Library Add. MS, Egerton 2271.

21   A Pleasant and Reasonable Retaliation

1. *Walpole*, ix, 321. Letter dated 13 November 1760.
2. *Davies*, i, 328.
3. *Ibid*, i, 336.
4. *Ibid.*, i, 337.
5. *Walpole*, ix, 326–7.
6. *Wilkinson*, iii, 20.
7. *Letters*, 252.
8. *Ibid.*, 262.
9. *Davies*, i, 349–50.
10. *Letters*, 270.

22   Scratching Fanny and the Riotous Fribbles

1. *Letters*, 265.
2. *The First Four Georges*, London, 1956, p. 95.
3. Sedgwick, Romney, *Letters of George III to Lord Bute, 1756–66*, London, 1939, pp. 38–9.
4. *Plumb, op. cit.*, p. 93.
5. *Davies*, i, 366–7.
6. *Letters*, 280. *Hecuba* came off after four nights.
7. *Walpole*, x, 6. Letter dated 2 February 1762.
8. *Hogarth: His Life, Art and Times, op cit.*, ii, 343–4.
9. Churchill's quarrel with Hogarth is said to have begun at the card tables of the Bedford (Timbs, John, *Club Life of London; with anecdotes of the Clubs, Coffee-Houses and Taverns of the Metropolis during the 17th, 18th, and 19th centuries*, 2 vols., London, 1866, ii, 80).
10. *Britons; Forging the Nation 1707–1837*, New Haven and London, 1992, p. 105.
11. *Letters*, 299.
12. *Theatrical Miscellanies*, Boston Public Library, Cuttings, G 60.23.4.

13. *Letters*, 298.
14. *London Journal*, p. 85 (14 December 1762).
15. *Ibid.*, p. 71.
16. *Ibid.*, p. 156.
17. *Ibid.*, p. 161.
18. *Ibid.*, p. 257.
19. *An Historical and Succinct Account of the Late Riots at the Theatres of Drury-Lane and Covent-Garden*, an anonymous pamphlet, broadly sympathetic to the managements, London, 1763.
20. *Ibid.*
21. *Davies*, ii, 6.
22. *Ibid.*, ii, 7.
23. *Public Advertiser*, 5 February 1763. Moody returned to the stage on 15 February, appearing without incident as Kingston in *High Life Below Stairs*, that night's afterpiece.
24. *Gentleman's Magazine*, February 1763.
25. *The Beauties of All Magazines Selected*, March 1763, p. 142, reprinted from the *Ledger*.
26. The *Theatrical Review; or, Annals of the Drama*, 1 May 1762, p. 212.
27. *Letters*, 310.
28. *Boaden*, i, 162–3. Letter dated 10 August 1763.
29. *Letters*, 313.
30. *Boaden*, i, 162. Letter dated 6 August 1763.
31. *Letters*, 313.
32. *Boaden*, i, 164–6. Letter dated 13 August 1763.
33. *Ibid.*, i, 167–8. Letter dated 8 September 1763.
34. *London Chronicle*, 15–17 September 1763.

23   Away from It All

1. Garrick, David, *The Journal of David Garrick, Describing his visit to France and Italy in 1763*. Edited by George Winchester Stone, Jr., New York, 1939, pp. 4–6.
2. *Letters*, 317.
3. *Ibid*.
4. *Diary*.

5. *Letters*, 319.
6. *Ibid.*
7. *Ibid.*, 320.
8. *Ibid.*, 321.
9. *Ibid.*
10. *Ibid.*, 326.
11. *Ibid.*, 324.
12. Letter dated 19 February 1778.
13. *Letters*, 323. Henry Baldwin was the paper's publisher. The offending item appeared in the issue of 22 December 1763.
14. *Boaden*, i, 170–71. Letter dated 17 April 1764.
15. *Letters*, 323.
16. *Ibid.*, 332.
17. *Ibid.*
18. *Ibid.*
19. *Ibid.*, 334.
20. *Ibid.*, 336. The *OED* defines 'swinger' as 'a vigorous performer, a powerful fellow'.
21. *Ibid.*, 337.
22. *Ibid.*, 339.
23. *Ibid.*, 340. Garrick's rough draft for this letter, full of corrections and erasures, survives in the Forster Collection.
24. *Ibid.*, 341.
25. *Ibid.*, 344.
26. *Ibid.*, 350.
27. *Correspondance littéraire, philosophique et critique par Grimm, Diderot, Raynal, Meister etc.* . . . ed. M. Tourneux, 16 vols., Paris, 1877–92, vi, 318. The translation is Hedgcock's.
28. *Letters*, 347.
29. *Ibid.*, 341.
30. *Walpole*, xxii, 176. Letter dated 17 October 1763.
31. *Hopkins Diary*, 20 October 1763.
32. *Letters*, 337.
33. *Boaden*, i, 169–70. Letter dated 30 March 1764.
34. *Letters*, 345.
35. *St James's Chronicle*, 5–7 February 1765. It also appeared in the *Public Advertiser* on 8 February.
36. *Letters*, 352.
37. *Ibid.*, 354. He was writing to his friend Charles Denis, who had been with him there in 1751.

24 The Sick Monkey Restored

1. *Davies*, ii, 95.
2. *Letters*, 362.
3. *Ibid.*, 358.
4. Copeland, Thomas W. (ed.), *The Correspondence of Edmund Burke, Volume 1, April 1744 – June 1768*, Cambridge, 1958, pp. 353–4. Letter dated 13 June 1765.
5. *Ibid.*, i, 356. Letter dated 7 June 1768.
6. *The Life of Mr James Quin, op. cit*, p. 60.
7. *Boaden*, i, 197.
8. *Ibid.*, i, 200–201.
9. Charles Burney Notebooks, Folder 4, Berg Collection, New York Public Library, New York City, quoted in Nash, *The Provok'd Wife*.
10. *Letters*, 360.
11. *Ibid.*, 373.
12. *Boaden*, i, 207–8.
13. *Victor*, iii, 84–5.
14. Quoted in *Highfill*, iii, 279.
15. Greig, J.Y.T. (ed.), *Letters of David Hume*, 2 vols., Oxford, 1932, ii, 14–15. Letter dated 16 February 1766.
16. *Cradock*, i, 205–6.
17. *Letters*, 348.
18. *Boaden*, ii, 441. Letter dated 15 June 1765. The translation is Hedgcock's.
19. 25 September 1765.
20. *Boaden*, i, 205–7. Letter dated 9 November 1765.
21. *Ibid.*, i, 223. Letter dated 4 March 1766.
22. *Letters*, 329.
23. *Ibid.*, 341.
24. *Boaden*, i, 205–7. Letter dated 9 November 1765.
25. *Ibid.*, i, 209–12. Letter dated 4 December 1765.
26. *Letters*, 378.
27. *Ibid.*, 391.
28. *Davies*, ii, 363.
29. *Letters*, 392.
30. *Ibid.*, 394.
31. *Ibid.*, 399.
32. *Ibid.*, 404.
33. *Davies*, ii, 337.
34. *Ibid.*, ii, 341.

35. *Boaden*, i, 649. Letter dated 5 August 1774.
36. *Colman, op. cit.*, i, 117–18.
37. *Letters*, 415.
38. *Ibid.*, 420.
39. Forster Collection, Garrick, XVII, 45.
40. *Letters*, 426. Garrick's Latin tag is from Ovid's *Metamorphoses*, book IV, 1. 428.

25 Assorted Theatrical Trash

1. *Davies*, ii, 99.
2. *Walpole*, xxii, 164. Letter dated 1 September 1763.
3. Act II, scene iii.
4. *Morning Post*, 3 January 1792.
5. *Letters*, 449.
6. *Public Advertiser*, 3 October 1766.
7. *Letters*, 450.
8. *Ibid.*, 455.
9. *Ibid.*, 445.
10. *Ibid.*, 443.
11. *Ibid.*, 447.
12. *Ibid*, 450.
13. *Ibid.*, 414.
14. *Ibid.*, 455.
15. *Ibid.*, 456.
16. *Ibid.*, 458.
17. Neville, Sylas, *The Diary of Sylas Neville, 1767–1788*, ed. Basil Cozens-Hardy, London, 1950. The passage quoted occurs in a typescript of unpublished portions of the *Diary*, of which there is a microfilm in the Folger Library.

26 All Hurry and Bustle

1. *Letters*, 470.
2. *Davies*, ii, 134–5.
3. *Ibid.*, ii, 136.
4. *Ibid.*, ii, 137–8.
5. *Letters*, 474.
6. *Ibid.*, 476.
7. *Ibid.*, 478.
8. *Ibid.*, 485.
9. *Murphy*, ii, 56.
10. *Davies*, ii, 190.
11. *Letters*, 512.

12. *Ibid.*, 515.
13. Hawkins, Sir John, *The Life of Samuel Johnson*, London, 1787, 427f.
14. *Autobiography and Correspondence of Mary Granville, Mrs. Delany*, ed. Lady Llanover, 2nd series, 3 vols., London, 1862, i, 155f.
15. *Neville, op. cit.*, 45.
16. *Walpole*, x, 264–5. Letter dated 13 August 1768.
17. *Murphy*, ii, 63.
18. *Boaden*, i, 226–7.
19. *Ibid.*, i, 309. Letter conjecturally dated August 1768.
20. *Letters*, 524.
21. *Murphy*, ii, 66.
22. *Letters*, 532.
23. *Ibid.*, 533.
24. *Boaden*, i, 339.
25. *Ibid.*, i, 320–21. Letter dated 27 November 1768.
26. *Davies*, ii, 196.
27. *Life*, iv, 7.
28. *Ibid.*, iv, 243.

27 Rain Stops Play

1. *Boaden*, i, 328–9.
2. *Ibid.*, i, 311–12.
3. *Letters*, 547.
4. *Ibid.*, 545.
5. *Ibid.*, 553.
6. *Cooke*, ii, 86.
7. *Jackson's Oxford Journal*, 2 September 1769.
8. The memoranda are in the Forster Collection at the Victoria and Albert Museum. They are reproduced as Appendix C to the *Letters*.
9. *Dibdin*, i, 78–9.
10. *Cradock*, i, 212.
11. *Letters*, 554.
12. *Ibid.*, 570. Garrick's correspondent has not been identified.
13. Steevens signed himself 'A Man of Letters' and dated his letter from the Smyrna Coffeehouse on 19 August. It was also printed in the August issue of the *Gentleman's Magazine*.

14. See, for example, *Garrick's Folly*, by Johanne M. Stockholm of Aarhus University in Denmark, London, 1964, 31–3.

15. *Angelo*, i, 43.

16. The *London Chronicle*, 5–7 September 1769.

17. *Cradock*, i, 215.

18. Boswell, James, *Boswell in Search of a Wife*, ed. Frank Brady and Frederick A. Pottle, London, 1957, 280–1.

19. The *Cambridge Magazine*, October 1769.

20. *Cradock*, i, 217.

21. *Boswell in Search of a Wife*, op. cit., 301.

22. The *Public Advertiser*, 16 September 1769.

23. Boswell was writing in the *Public Advertiser* for 16 September.

24. *Victor*, iii, 218–9.

25. *Davies*, ii, 229.

26. The *Public Advertiser*, 16 September 1769.

27. *Victor*, iii, 226.

28. *Angelo*, i, 41–2.

29. *Dibdin*, i, 78.

30. *Cradock*, i, 218.

31. *Boswell in Search of a Wife*, op. cit., 302–3.

32. The *St James's Chronicle*, 9–12 September 1769.

28 A Devilish Lucky Hit

1. *Hunt Correspondence*, Letter 1, Birthplace MSS.

2. *Letters*, 561.

3. *Ibid.*, 564.

4. [Warburton, William] *Letters from a Late Eminent Prelate to One of his Friends*, Kidderminster, 1808, p. 327.

5. The *Town and Country Magazine*, September 1769.

6. *Ibid.*, October 1769.

7. *Angelo*, i, 51.

8. *Life*, ii, 82–3.

9. *Ibid.*, ii, 92–3.

10. *Letters*, 581.

11. *Ibid.*, 602.

29 'Nothing Till Lately Could Subdue My Spirits'

1. *Letters*, 610.

2. *Hopkins Diary*, 13 December 1770.

3. *Walpole*, xxxix, 133–4, letter dated 25 December 1770.

4. *Cumberland*, i, 266.

5. *Ibid.*, i, 292–3.

6. *Ibid.*, i, 298–9.

7. *Northcote*, i, 333.

8. *Boaden*, i, 263–4 letter dated 5 July 1767.

9. *Letters*, 621.

10. *Ibid.*, 622. Letter dated 6 February 1771 to Peter Fountain.

11. *Ibid.*, 623.

12. *Boaden*, i, 407.

13. *Letters*, 630.

14. *Ibid.*, 632.

15. *Ibid.*, 638.

16. *Life*, iii, 311.

17. *Letters*, 640.

18. *Boaden*, i, 440, letter dated 12 October 1771.

19. *Ibid.*, i, 432, letter dated 29 August 1771.

20. *Ibid.*, i, 440. Letter dated 12 October 1771.

21. *Cradock*, iv, 251.

22. *Life*, iii, 263–4.

23. *Letters*, 657.

24. The full text, as it was submitted to the Lord Chamberlain, is now in the Huntington Library (Larpent MS 327). It was published for the first time by Pedicord and Bergmann in 1980.

25. *Letters*, 655.

30 The House Shows the Owner

1. *Letters*, 661.

2. *Ibid.*, 644.

3. *Ibid.*, 647.

4. *Davies*, ii, 301.

5. *Letters*, 672.

6. *Murphy*, ii, 92.

7. *Letters*, 664.

8. *Ibid.*, 680.

9. The accounts, now in the Victoria and

Albert Museum, were reproduced in Brackett, Oliver, *Thomas Chippendale. A Study of His Life, Work, and Influence*, London, 1925.

10. *Letters*, 683.

11. Burney, Fanny, *The Early Diary of Frances Burney, 1768–78*, ed. Annie R. Ellis, 2 vols., rev. edn, London 1907, i, 215, entry dated 30 April 1772.

12. *Ibid.*, i, 200, entry dated 31 March 1772.

13. *Ibid.*, i, 225, entry dated 31 May 1772.

14. *The Dramatic Censor; or, Critical Companion*, London and York, 1770. There was a second volume, which was dedicated to Foote.

15. *Letters*, 710.

16. *Correspondence*, 37–8, 18 September 1771.

17. *Letters*, 799.

18. *Ibid.*, 667.

19. *Journal*, 15 April 1772.

20. Boaden, i, 466–8. Letter dated 22 May 1772.

21. *Letters*, 689.

6. Boaden, James, *Memoirs of the Life of John Philip Kemble, Esq.*, 2 vols., London, 1825, i, 64–6.

7. Forster Collection, vol. 10.

8. *Letters*, 736.

9. *Ibid.*, 737.

10. *Ibid.*, 729.

11. *Ibid.*, 714.

12. *Ibid.*, 734.

13. *Ibid.*, 748.

14. *Ibid.*, 753.

15. *Ibid.*, 755.

16. *Ibid.*, 725.

17. *Cooke*, ii, 58

18. *St James's Chronicle*, 13–16 February 1773.

19. *Walpole*, xxxii, 97. Letter dated 11 February 1773.

20. *Fitzgerald*, 408.

21. *Cumberland*, i, 368.

22. *Letters*, 755.

23. *Hopkins Diary*, 21 April 1773.

24. *Letters*, 762.

25. *Boaden*, i, 536.

26. *Letters*, 763.

31 Clipping the Wings of Calumny

1. *Letters*, 688.

2. *Ibid.*, 692.

3. *Boaden*, i, 476–7. Letter dated 26 July 1772.

4. *Letters*, 711.

5. *Ibid.*, 712.

6. *Ibid.*, 715.

7. *London Evening Post*, 21 November 1772.

8. *Letters*, 720.

9. Forster, John, *The Life and Adventures of Oliver Goldsmith*, London, 1848, p. 491.

32 Doing Away with the Gravediggers

1. Act I, scene i.

2. *Hopkins Diary*, 22 September 1772.

3. *Boaden*, i, 496. Letter dated 13 November 1772.

4. *Letters*, 719.

5. *Taylor, op. cit.*, ii, 417.

33 Lawful Game in the Winter

1. *Letters*, 784.

2. *Ibid.*, 773.

3. *Cradock*, i, 198.

4. *Boaden*, i, 565–6. Letter dated 22 August 1773.

5. *Letters*, 795.

6. *Boaden*, i, 569. Letter dated 31 August 1773.

7. *Letters*, 797.

8. *Boaden*, i, 570. Letter dated 16 September 1773.

9. *Letters*, 798.

10. *Ibid.*, 802.

11. *Ibid.*, 803.

12. *Ibid.*, 804.

13. *Journal*, 313, 14 October 1773.

14. *Ibid.*, November 1773.

15. *St James's Chronicle*, 19–21 October 1773.

16. *Letters*, 812.

17. *Ibid.*, 816.

18. *Ibid.*
19. *Boaden*, i, 592. Letter dated 31 December 1773.
20. *Ibid.*, i, 610.
21. *Boaden*, i, 611. Letter dated 3 February 1774.
22. *Letters*, 821.
23. *Boaden*, i, 612. Letter dated 25 February 1774.
24. *Letters*, 822.
25. *Murphy*, ii, 105.
26. *Letters*, 823.
27. *Ibid.*, 830.
28. *Boaden*, i, 623. Letter dated 2 May 1774.
29. *Letters*, 831.
30. *Ibid.*, 835.
31. *Ibid.*, 833.
32. *Ibid.*, Appendix D.
33. *Ibid.*, 839.
34. Roberts, William, *Memoirs of the Life and Correspondence of Mrs. Hannah More*, 4 vols., 3rd edition, London, 1835, i, 47. Cited hereafter as *Roberts*.
35. Letter in the Harvard Theatre Collection.
36. *Letters*, 847.
37. *Boaden*, i, 655.

34 The Monstrous Regiment of Actresses

1. *Letters*, 857.
2. *Westminster Magazine*, October 1774.
3. *Ibid.*, November 1774.
4. *Letters*, 872.
5. *Ibid.*, Appendix F. Letter dated 14 December 1744.
6. *Ibid.*, Appendix F. Letter dated 14 January 1775.
7. *Boaden*, ii, 35. Letter dated 2 January 1775.
8. *Morning Post*, 13 January 1775.
9. *Boaden*, ii, 37. Letter dated 7 January 1775.
10. *Letters*, 882.
11. *Ibid.*, 883.
12. *Boaden*, ii, 65.
13. *Letters*, 884.
14. *Ibid.*, 888.
15. *Boaden*, ii, 27–8.
16. *Ibid.*, ii, 25. Letter dated 6 March 1775.
17. *Westminster Magazine*, March 1775.
18. *Life*, ii, 325–6.
19. *Roberts*, i, 54–5.
20. *Burney, op. cit.*, ii, 95–7.
21. *Letters*, 731.
22. *Highfill*, vii, 252.
23. *Letters*, 903.
24. *Ibid.*, 907.
25. *Ibid.*, 910. He was writing to Peter Fountain.
26. *Ibid.*, 913.

35 A Face-Lift for the Old Lady

1. *London Chronicle*, 10–13 December 1774.
2. Letter dated 17 April 1775 from Charles Hart to Mrs Garrick, now in the David M. Little Collection, Harvard College Library. A sign-manual was an autograph signature, especially that of the sovereign, serving to authenticate a document.
3. *Letters*, 912.
4. *European Magazine*, vol. xii, August 1787, p. 107.
5. *Letters*, 915.
6. Forster Collection.
7. *Letters*, 919. Garrick was mistaken about de Molière's age. He was in his mid-thirties.
8. Forster Collection.
9. The original of de Molière's letter, which is in the Forster Collection, reads as follows: 'Mademoiselle, Je n'ai pu jusqu' à ce moment m'informer si votre voyage a été heureux et si vous avez joui d'une bonne santé ainsi que Mlle votre soeur. J'ai été si embarrassé pour savoir votre adresse et je ne sais pas même si celle qu'on m'a donnée est bonne. Mon Colonel m'a dit que l'on avait fait des informations à mon sujet et qu'il m'avait rendu justice. Je désirerais savoir si vous êtes toujours dans les mêmes intentions et vous prie de me marquer si vous jugez à propos que j'écrive à M. votre père, s'il approuvera ma démarche. Il y a du temps que je vous ai demandé cette grâce, et vous êtes présentement à portée de le

prévenir combien je désire d'être uni avec vous. En me marquant l'état de votre santé, à laquelle je m'intéresse vivement, faites-moi connaître les personnes à qui je dois écrire pour obtenir votre main et donnez-moi leurs adresses et qualités afin que je ne les indispose pas plutôt que de me les rendre favorables.

En attendant l'honneur de votre réponse, j'ai celui d'être avec un profond respect, Mademoiselle,

Votre très humble et très obéissant serviteur, de MOLIÈRE, officier de dragons, légion de Corse.'

10. *Boaden*, ii, 67. Letter dated 9 July 1775.
11. *Letters*, 940.
12. *Ibid.*, 926.
13. British Library, ADD. MSS, No. 25, 383.
14. *Letters*, 932.
15. *Boaden*, ii, 57–9. Letter dated 10 June 1775.
16. *Letters*, 918.
17. *Boaden*, ii, 92.
18. *Letters*, 936.
19. *Highfill*, iii, 358. In a letter to Miss Pope she was less guarded, and wrote of 'Mr Garrick's avarice'.
20. *Letters*, 934. It was Mary Weller, making her début three years previously as Polly in *The Beggar's Opera*, whom Hopkins had described as 'a Piece of still Life'.
21. *Ibid.*, 936. He is quoting from Virgil's *Eclogues*: 'The reign of Saturn returns.' Garrick's language suggests that when his ailments permitted, he was still sexually active. 'He never was a husband to me, Mrs Garrick said in old age to a friend; 'during the thirty years of our marriage he was always my lover.' (*Elizabeth Montagu, The Queen of the Blue-Stockings, Her Correspondence from 1720 to 1761*, by her great-great-niece Emily J. Climenson, 2 vols., London, 1906, vol. 1, p. 366.)
22. *Town and Country Magazine*, September 1775.

36 Enter Garrick's Venus

1. i, 205.
2. Forster Collection.
3. *Letters*, 943.
4. *Ibid.*, 952.
5. *Ibid.*, 953.
6. *Ibid.*, 954.
7. *London Chronicle*, 25 April 1772. Quoted in *Highfill*, xvi, 7.
8. *Letters*, 956.
9. *Ibid.*, 967.
10. *Middlesex Journal*, 30 December 1775.

37 To Strut and Fret No More

1. Forster Collection, vol. 22, ff. 14–15.
2. *Letters*, 976.
3. *Boaden*, ii, 125. Letter dated 17 January 1776.
4. *Ibid.*, ii, 128–9. Letter dated 23 January 1766.
5. *Letters*, 979.
6. *Ibid.*, 981.
7. *Ibid.*, f2.
8. *Boaden*, ii, 123–4.
9. *Westminster Magazine*, January 1776.
10. *Morning Post and Daily Advertiser*, 15 January 1776.
11. *Angelo*, ii, 254.
12. *Boaden*, ii, 135–6.
13. *The Reminiscences of Mrs Sarah Siddons, 1773–1785*, edited by W. B. Van Lennep, Cambridge, Mass., 1942, pp. 4–6.
14. *Boaden*, ii, 133. Letter dated 30 January 1776.
15. *Letters*, 990.
16. *Ibid.*, 984, 986.
17. *Ibid.*, 995.
18. *Life*, ii, 438–9.
19. *Walpole*, xxviii, 277–8. Letter to Mason, dated 8 October 1776.
20. *Cradock*, iv, 251.
21. *Taylor, op. cit.*, i, 350.
22. *Roberts*, i, 84.
23. *Letters*, 1018.
24. *Roberts*, i, 94.

38 Frail Tenement

1. *Boaden*, ii, 159.
2. *Letters*, 1026.
3. *Ibid.*, 1029.
4. Bunbury, Sir Henry E. (ed.), *Correspondence of Sir Thomas Hanmer*, London, 1838, p. 377.
5. *Letters*, 1031.
6. *Roberts*, i, 63–4.
7. *Letters*, 1030.
8. *Ibid.*, 1036.
9. *Ibid.*, 1043.
10. *Morning Post and Daily Advertiser*, 4 September 1776.
11. *Boaden*, ii, 181–2. Letter dated 15 October 1776.
12. *Letters*, 1056.
13. *Boaden*, ii, 624.
14. *Althorp Letters*, Letter 21.
15. *Letters*, 1062.
16. *Ibid.*, 1079.
17. *Walpole*, xx, 285, Letter to Mason dated 27 February 1777.
18. *Van Lennep, op. cit.*, p. 13.
19. *Althorp Letters*, Letter 37.
20. *Ibid.*, Letter 39.

39 Retired Leisure

1. *Walpole*, x, 22. Letter dated 13 July 1777.
2. *Hopkins Diary*, 10 December 1776.
3. *Letters*, 1097.
4. *Ibid.*, 1107.
5. *Boaden*, ii, 230–1.
6. *Roberts*, i, 113
7. *Walpole*, xxviii, 36. Letter dated 4 August 1777 to William Mason.
8. *Letters*, 1116.
9. *Ibid.*, 1118.
10. *Ibid.*, 1127.
11. *Ibid.*, 1128.
12. *Althorp Letters*, Letter 46.
13. *Colman, op. cit.*, ii, 43.
14. Boswell, James, *Boswell in Extremes*, edited by Charles McC. Weiss and Frederick A. Pottle, New York, 1970. pp. 175–6.
15. *Letters*, 1138.

16. *Dramatic Miscellanies*, i, 273–5.
17. *Althorp Letters*, Letter 48.
18. *Roberts, i, 122.*
19. *Althorp Letters*, Letter 49.
20. *Letters*, 1149. Garrick was writing to Mrs Rackett.
21. *Roberts, i, 132–3.*
22. *Ibid.*, i, 138.
23. *Letters*, 1155.
24. Unpublished letter dated 10 January 1778, now in the Folger Library.
25. *Boaden*, ii, 285.
26. *Ibid.*, ii, 295.
27. *Ibid.*, ii, 303.
28. *Letters*, 1174.
29. *Ibid.*, 1171.
30. *Ibid.*, 1176.
31. *Boswell in Extremes, op. cit.*, p. 262.
32. *Davies*, ii, 358–9.
33. *Letters*, 1184.

40 'Farewell! Remember Me!'

1. *Letters*, 1040.
2. The letter is in an extra-illustrated edition of the Davies *Life* now in the Folger Library (W.b. 470).
3. *Letters*, 1185. He was writing from Lawford to Henry Bate.
4. *Ibid.*, 1188.
5. *Ibid.*, 1196.
6. *Althorp Letters*, Letter 59, dated 14 September 1778.
7. *Letters*, 1198.
8. *Ibid.*, 1199.
9. Northcote, James, *The Life of Sir Joshua Reynolds*, 2nd edn, 2 vols, London, 1819, ii, 80–88.
10. *Letters*, 1203.
11. Adolphus, J., *Memoirs of John Bannister, Comedian*, 2 vols., London, 1839, i, 21–4.
12. *Boaden*, ii, 317. Letter dated 13 November 1778.
13. *Althorp Letters*, Letter 61, dated 14 November 1778.
14. *Letters*, 1209.
15. *Althorp Letters*, Letter 66, dated 13 December 1778.

16. *Boaden*, ii, 328–9. Letter dated 6 January 1779.

17. Troide, Lars E. and Cooke, Stewart J. (eds.), *The Early Journals and Letters of Fanny Burney*, Vol. III, The Streatham Years, Part I, 1778–9, Oxford, 1994, 75.

18. *Althorp Letters*, Letter 70, dated 14 January 1779.

19. *Ibid.*, Letter 71, dated 15 January 1779. Mrs Oakly is a character in Colman's *The Jealous Wife*.

20. *Davies*, ii, 367.

21. *Ibid.*, ii, 369–70.

22. The playbill is preserved in the Huntington Public Library in the Augustin Daly Collection of Bills, No. 28751.

Epilogue

1. *Angelo*, ii, 64–5.

2. Boswell, James, *Boswell: The Applause of the Jury*, edited by Irma S. Lustig and Frederick A. Pottle, New York, 1981. pp. 104–5 (18 April 1783).

3. *Roberts*, i, 156. Letter dated 2 February 1779.

4. *Public Advertiser*, 3 February 1779.

5. Folger Library, MS ADD 969. Letter dated 13 April 1780.

6. *Roberts, i, 167.*

7. *Ibid.*, i, 197.

8. *Ibid.*, i, 193

9. *Walpole*, xxxiii, 363.

10. Pennington, Montagu (ed.), *Elizabeth Carter, Memoirs of the Life of Mrs Elizabeth Carter*, 2 vols., London, 1808, i, 472.

11. Harford, J.S., *Recollections of William Wilberforce, Esq.*, London, 1864, p. 274.

12. *Morning Chronicle*, 13 November 1789.

13. *Morning Post*, 1 March 1814.

14. *Historical Memorials of Westminster Abbey*, London, 1868, p. 287.

15. Smith, John Thomas, *A Book for a Rainy Day*, London, 1845, 3rd edition, ed. Wilfred Whitten, 1905, p. 238.

16. *Ibid.*, pp. 237–9.

Acknowledgements

Anyone who writes about the English theatre in the eighteenth century quickly runs up substantial debts to American academic scholarship. I have benefited in particular from the work of two institutions — the Southern Illinois University Press in Carbondale and the Folger Shakespeare Library in Washington, D.C.

The eleven volumes of *The London Stage, 1660-1800*, were the fruit of a cooperative scholarly enterprise that lasted for more than thirty years. Equally indispensable is Carbondale's *Biographical Dictionary*, a sort of theatrical *DNB* of the thousands of colourful figures who peopled the London stage from the Restoration to the Regency — not just actors and actresses, but dancers and musicians, scene painters and acrobats, managers and puppeteers. From the same publishing stable, twenty years ago, came the encyclopedic critical biography of Garrick by George Winchester Stone, Jr and George M. Karhl. Southern Illinois has also been responsible for a complete edition — the work of Harry William Pedicord and Frederick Louis Bergmann — of the Garrick canon: twenty-two plays which he wrote himself, twelve adaptations from Shakespeare, fifteen alterations by him of other English dramatists. I was also greatly helped by Ben Ross Schneider, Jr, Professor Emeritus at Lawrence University, Wisconsin, and the compiler of the index to *The London Stage*.

The Folger, in Washington, with its 79 copies of the First Folio, its thousand or so Shakespearean prompt-books and its collection of a quarter of a million playbills, is an unrivalled resource for students of the English stage. It provides a working environment as agreeable as it is efficient. I am grateful to its Librarian, Richard Kuhta, for according me the privilege of readership, and to all those members of his staff who made my time in their splendid building close to Capitol Hill so productive and so enjoyable.

On this side of the Atlantic I wish to pay tribute to the French scholar Michel Perrin. He submitted his *David Garrick, Homme de Théâtre*, as a thesis to the University of Paris III in 1976. As outstanding for its range as for its lucidity, it constitutes a major contribution to our understanding of English stage history.

In this country I drew on the riches of Cambridge University Library and the Victoria and Albert Museum. I also spent long and profitable days in the London Library; it is one of the capital's worst-kept secrets that Alan Bell's staff are not only supremely good at their job but also run the best club in London.

Enid Foster, the Librarian at the Garrick Club, gave me useful guidance at an early stage in my research. I am indebted to Felix Pryor, who drew my attention to the important sale of Garrick's papers which he catalogued for Phillips in 1992, and to Louise Neel, of the Bank of England Information Centre, who helped me in the matter of equivalent contemporary values of the pound.

My publisher, Stuart Proffitt, responded patiently to successive drafts of a long manuscript and nudged me towards important improvements in matters of shape and pace. I wish to thank Cecilia Mackay, whose flair and perseverance in picture research were outstanding and Jennifer Munka, who had to run something of a copy-editing marathon. I am grateful to the Penguin Press's Art Director, Pascale Hutton, and to Antonio Colaco for his arresting cover; the elegant text design of the book was the work of Andrew Barker. I am also indebted to Helen Eka, who handled production, Nikki Barrow, who looked after publicity, Penny Daniel, who coordinated proof-reading and Frederick Smyth, who created the index. Mark Handsley, Penguin Press's Managing Editor, remained calm but watchful during an occasionally eventful production process, and I am grateful to him, and to Andrew Rosenheim, Penguin Press's Managing Director, for seeing to it that everything was alright on the night.

During a decade or so as a BBC network Controller I worked closely with members of the Radio Drama Department. They taught me much about the theatre and the ways of theatre folk, and that has provided many valuable insights.

I have profited over very many years from the wisdom of John Wilders, an old and dear friend, a Shakespearean scholar of distinction but also someone who speaks with authority on the living theatre.

The idea that I should write the life of David Garrick came from my wife; but that is the least of many reasons why this book is dedicated to her.

Index

The name of David Garrick (which is hereunder, in most cases, abbreviated to DG) appears on all but a few pages of the text. To avoid an unnecessary overloading of the section under his name, many references to him have been placed under other headings. For instance, the numerous letters from him which are mentioned and usually quoted from are indexed under the names of their recipients.

Stage works, poems, pamphlets and books, when ascribed in the text, will be found under the names of their writers or, where relevant, composers. They are otherwise indexed under their titles. (Exceptions to this apply in the section on David Garrick himself, where the stage works in which he acted or for which he wrote prologues or epilogues are identified only by their titles.)

Bold figures (**234**) indicate the more important references; italic figures (*234*) denote illustrations or their captions; 'q.' stands for quoted; 'q.v.' for *quod vide* (which see); 'n' and 'nn' direct attention to one or more footnotes.

Abington, Frances, actress, 293, 391, *528*, 532n, 558, 572; roles, 225n, 524, 532, 559, 560n, 580; troublesome to DG, 469–71, 485–6, 493, 515, 527–30, 559–60, 590

Abrams, Harriet, singer, 548

Académie-Française, its dictionary, 230 and n

actors and actresses, the 18th-C. view, 1–2

Adam, Robert, architect, 233, 515, *534*, 611

Adam, Robert and James, architects, 466–7 and nn, 470, 490, 508, 544

Adams, Dr William, Johnson's friend, 363

Addington, William, Bow St official, 505 and n

Addison, Joseph, essayist, 89n; as playwright: *Cato* (1713), 224, 506; *The Drummer* (1715), 316

Adelphi, the, London, 466–7, 470, 508

Aickin, Francis, actor, 401n, 410, 494

Albion Queens, The, 380

Algarotti, Francesco, polymath, 339 and n

Almack's Club, London, 570

Amans Réunis, Les, 166

Amber, Norton, banker, 92–3, 109, 113, 198

Ambrose, Eleanor, of Dublin, 114 and n

Anatomist and News Regulator, The, q.129

Angelo, Domenico, fencing-master, 146 and n, 292; as stage designer, 292–3, 418, 420, 429–30, 488, 608, 611

Angelo, Henry, Domenico's son, 353, 414, 420, 425, q.430, 558, q.566; at DG's lying-in-state, 608–9

Apreece, Delaval's uncle, 269–70

ApShenkin, David and Winifred, *The Leek*, comic dance, 49n

Arden, Revd William, DG's acquaintance, 246 and n, 346

Arne (*née* Young), Cecilia, singer, wife of Thomas, 60 and n

Arne, Michael, composer, son of Thomas, 386n

Arne, Thomas, composer, 57, 60 and nn, 102, 268, 293–4, 447; relations with DG, 294n, 321–2, 543; letter from DG, q.543; music for the Stratford Jubilee, 426, 428, 461
   Alfred (1740), 60, 75n, 181, 190, 501
   Artaxerxes (1762), 328
   Britannia, 228–9
   Comus (1738), 60
   Don Severio (1750), 169
   Dirge for Juliet, 175
   God Save our Noble King, 106–7, 107n
   Guardian Outwitted, The, comic opera, 370
   Judith, oratorio (1761), 422
   May-Day (1775), 548
   Rose, The (1772), 487

Arthur, John, actor and stage machinery designer, 38 and n; DG's letter, q.379

Ashmole, Elias, antiquarian, 12 and n; *History of the Order of the Garter* (1672), 459

Ashmolean Museum, Oxford, 343n

Aston, Sir Thomas, 23 and n, 27n

Austin, Joseph, actor, 275n

Baddeley, Robert, actor, 391, 419, 424n, 442, 557

Baddeley, Sophia, actress and singer, 424 and n, 427, 442, 543n, 572

Baltimore, Frederick Calvert, 6th Lord, 449 and n

Banks, Joseph, botanist, 611, 617n

Bannister, Charles, singer and actor, 599 and n

Bannister, John, actor, son of Charles, 599–601

'Barbarina, La', prima ballerina, 236n

'bardolatry', the birth of, 432

Baretti, Joseph (Giuseppe), 344, 441 and n, 514

Barnard, Very Revd Thomas, Dean of Derry, 563 and n

Barrowby, Dr William, physician, 47 and n, 78

Barry (formerly Mrs Dancer), Ann, actress, wife of Spranger Barry (q.v.), 393, 515, 578 and n, 587; roles: (1768), 396–7,

401; (1771–4), 447–8, 465, 483 and n, 485 and n, 493–4, 510

Barry, Dr Edward, Dublin physician, 289 and n, 365

Barry, Spranger, actor: at Covent Garden, 105, 123, 128, 172–3, 184, 196, 519; at Drury Lane, 139, 145n, 165 and n, 170, 392–3; at Smock Alley, 223; at his new theatre in Dublin, 272, 293, 298; roles: (1746–51), 124, 141n, 146, 148, 151n, 196; (1756–68), 121n, 253–4, 261, 393, 397, 401 and n; (1771–4), 447, 463, 465, 510; DG's praise, 5, 114; compared with DG: as Romeo, 135–8; as Lear, 253–4; the Barrys troublesome to DG, 410 and n, 439–40, 454–5; Barry's Prologue at Covent Garden (1750), q.174–5; in Churchill's *Rosciad*, q.305; his illness (1768) and the death of his son, 401n; his death (1777), 578 and n

Barry, Mrs W., actress, Spranger Barry's sister-in-law, 409–10, 410n

Barsanti, Jane, actress and singer, 530 and n

Barthélemon, François Hippolyte, violinist and composer, 397–8, 398n; *Pelopida*, opera (1766), 397

Bartolozzi, Francesco, engraver, 342

Bate, Revd Henry, journalist and playwright, 540–42, 557–8, 570, 611
   Blackamoor Wash'd White, The (1776), 558–9
   Rival Candidates, The, comic opera (1775), 540

Bates, William, composer, 545

Bath, William Pulteney, 1st Earl of, 158 and n, 170, 390

Bath, Theatre Royal, 379, 533, 536

Batoni, Pompeo, painter, 343 and n

Beard, John, singer, 67, 106, 249, 293–4, 322, 328; manager at Covent Garden (1761), 314, 321–2, 328–9, 367, 370 and n, 380, 383n, 389

Beauclerk, Topham, 344, 364, 467, 505, 532, 550, 616 and n

Beaumarchais, Pierre Augustin Caron de, playwright: *Barbier de Séville, Le* (1775), 359 and n; *Eugénie* (1767), 408–9

Beaumont, Francis, playwright, 4
Beaumont, Francis and Fletcher, John
    Chances, The (1647), 192
    Philaster (1610–11), 131n, 336, 356
    Scornful Lady, The, 142
Becket, Thomas, printer and bookseller,
    359, 375n, 495, 578n, 587
Behn, Mrs Aphra, novelist (17th C.), *The
    Nun*, 268n
Bellamy, George Ann, actress, 45n, 60,
    114, 165, *208*, 273n, 406n; roles:
    (1744–52), 89 and n, 175, 177–8,
    206–7 and nn; (1756–68), 253, 284
    and n, 389n, 404n, 405; moves
    between theatres, 172–3, 173n, 212n,
    402
'Bellario', in the *Daily Post*, critic, q.100
Beltz, Frederick, Mrs Garrick's executor,
    621 and n
Bensley, Robert, actor, 557
Bentley, Richard, Walpole's
    correspondent, 226, 233, 234 and n
Berenger, Richard, DG's friend, 254 and
    n, 283, 611; letters from DG quoted,
    289, 365–6, 378, 416, 481, 497, 593;
    DG's generosity, 593 and n
Berry, Edward, actor, 151, 249
Berryer de Ranenoville, Nicolas-René, Lt-
    Gen of Police, Paris, 190 and n, 191
Betterton, Thomas, actor-manager, 4,
    73n, 95–6, 99, 126, 447, 549
Biancolelli, Marie Thérèse, actress, 352
Bickerstaffe, Isaac, playwright, 179n, 400,
    441, 471n, **475–80**, 490–91
    Hypocrite, The (1769), 532
    Love in a Village, comic opera (1762),
        322
    Maid of the Mill, The (1765?), 379
    Padlock, The, comic opera (1768), 406,
        418, 521
    Queen Mab, cantata (with Dibdin,
        1769), 429
Biographica Dramatica, 409, 434,
    q.446–7, q.511
Blakes, Charles, actor, 305
Boaden, James, q.268n, q.487
Boccaccio, Giovanni, *Decameron* (1358),
    386
Bonduca [Fletcher, early 17th C.], 604
Booth, Barton, actor, 2, 63 and n, 99, 207,
    313

Boscawen, Mrs, scholar, 616
Boswell, James, 71 and n, 101, 151, 300n,
    324 and n; comes to London, 323–6;
    marries (1771), 454; entertains
    friends, 179n, 440–41
    and Garrick, 25, 323, q.324, 471–3,
        q.532–3, q.569n, 581; letters from
        DG, q.454, q.472
    and Johnson, 19n, 150n, 152, 325, q.364
        and n, q.457; discussions with him
        quoted, 11, 12n, 78n, 458–9, 561,
        586, 616; other quotations, 411,
        440–41, 493n, 594, 609
    at and on the Stratford Jubilee, 422,
        423, q.426, q.428–32
Boyce, William, composer, 169, 175, 194,
    216, 266, 291n, 322
Bracegirdle, Anne, actress, 65 and n, 73n,
    96, 447
Bradley, Mrs, actress, 484
Bransby, Astley, actor, 259 and n
Brent, Charlotte, singer, 293–4
Brereton, William, actor, 557
Brewer, John, writer, q.585–6
Bridgwater, Roger, actor and dancer, 45,
    130 and n
Bromfield, William, surgeon, 377, 378n
Broughton, John, pugilist, 79 and n
Brown, Revd John, 225n; as a playwright,
    Athelstan (1756), 252–3
    Barbarossa (1754), 225–6
Brown, Wallace Cable, biographer, 308n
Browne, Sir William, 468 and nn
Buckingham, George Villiers, 2nd Duke
    of, as a playwright, 192, 225, 495
    The Rehearsal (1671), 2, 45n, 376, 397,
        554n; performances: (1742–3),
        45–6, 51, 61, 77; (1758–77), 275,
        393, 469, 582
Bunbury, Henry, caricaturist and writer,
    568
Burbage, Richard, actor-manager, 4
Burgoyne, General Sir John, 522 and n; as
    a playwright, *The Maid of the Oaks*
    (1774), 521–2, 529, 531
Burke, Edmund, statesman and
    philosopher, 302 and n, 303, 362,
    441, 453, 612n; and DG, 302, 334,
    403–4, 594, 611–12; and other
    friends, 364, 493, 507n, 514; and the
    Theatrical Fund, 556

Burke, Richard, Edmund's brother, 453 and n

Burlington, Richard Boyle, 3rd Earl of: and Violette, 129, 153, 155; his houses, 158 and n, 160n; letter from DG, q.161; DG's 1st wedding anniversary, 191; his death (1753), 219; his Will, 230

Burlington, Dorothy, Countess of: and Violette, 129, 133n, 153, 155–9; letters from DG quoted, 159–62, 164–6, 175–8; confides in and withdraws from DG, 230–31; her death (1758), 274

Burnett, James, lawyer (later Lord Monboddo, q.v.), 348n

Burney, Dr Charles, musicologist, 60n, 107, 236n, 285n, 469, 502 and n, 621; and Mrs Cibber, 363; letter from DG, q.341–2; at DG's funeral, 611; The Cunning Man, his comic opera (1765), 363

Burney, Fanny, novelist and diarist, 102, 130n, 305n, 469; on Garrick, quoted, 468–9, 498, 502, 538, 578 and n; Evelina (1778), 469

Burns, Robert, poet, q.106

Busy Body, The [Centlivre, 1709], 280, 282–3

Bute, John Stuart, 3rd Earl of, courtier and politician, 254, 278n, 318, 323, 466 and n; and the Prince of Wales, 312–13; and Home, 266, 273, 303, 409; letters from DG, quoted, 254–6, 286, 312

Butler, Philip, master carpenter, 519, 611

Butler, Samuel, satirist, 45n

Byron, George, 6th Lord, poet, English Bards and Scotch Reviewers (1809), 304

Cadogan, Frances: Mrs Garrick's letter, q.596; letters from DG, q.596–7; at DG's funeral, 611

Cadogan, Dr William, DG's physician, 596, 598, 604–5, 611

Cafarelli (Gaetano Maiorano), castrato, 341–2, 342n

Calcraft, John, army contractor and MP, 273n

Caldwell, Sir James, letter from DG, q.568–9

Camden, Charles Pratt, 1st Lord (1765), 1st Earl of (1786), 380, 457; DG's friend, 380, 404, 456, 611, 614; letters to DG, quoted, 380, 499, 516, 540, 582

Camoëns, Luis de, poet, The Lusiads (1572), 472n

Canning, Mrs, actress, 505

Capell, Edward, DG's friend, 284n

Carey, Henry, Chrononhotonthologos, burlesque (1734), 586

Carlisle, Frederick Howard, 5th Earl of, 428

Carlyle, Alexander, and Mrs Garrick, 117–18 and nn, 261, q.272–3, 273n

Carlyle, Thomas, historian, q.116, 153

Carmontelle (Louis Carrogis), artist and playwright, 351

Carrington, Nathan, King's Messenger, father-in-law to George Garrick, 183

Carter, Elizabeth, scholar and poet, 616, 619

Casanova, François Joseph, painter, 488

Cautherley, Samuel, 287–9; as an actor, 287, 377, 387, 495 and n, 501, 547–8; his letters from DG, quoted, 501, 547

Cave, Edward, founder of the Gentleman's Magazine, 36, 78, 170n

Cavendish, Lord John, 381

Celesia, Dorothea, playwright, Almida (1771), 447–8

Cervantes, Miguel de, novelist, Novelas Ejemplares (1613), 225

Chad, St, 10

Charles I, King, 10

Charlotte Sophia, Queen of England: marriage to George III, 313 and n; at the theatre, 356, 369, 418, 447, 493; visits Mrs Garrick, 620

Chastellux, Chevalier de, soldier and writer, 352 and n, 563

Cheere, Sir Henry, sculptor, 414 and n

Cheere, John, sculptor, 414

Chesterfield, Philip, 4th Earl of, 114–15 and nn, 121, 128, 138, 147, 204

Chetwood, William, former prompter at Drury Lane, 74–5; Queries to be Answer'd, q.75

Chippendale, Thomas, furniture-maker, 220, 467 and n; *The Gentleman and Cabinet Maker's Director* (1754), 220, 235

Christian VII, King of Denmark, 404–6, 406n

Churchill, Charles, satirist, 305 and nn, 318–19, 319nn, q.364, 505; letters from DG, q.319 and n; borrows money from DG, 319 and n; his death (1764), 348; *The Rosciad* (1761), q.63, q.96, 304–8, 308n, 331, q.355n, q.542; *The Apology* (1761), q.307, 438; *The Ghost* (1762–3), 338 and n

Cibber, Caius Gabriel, sculptor, 64 and n

Cibber, Charles, son of Mrs Cibber and William Sloper, 271

Cibber, Colley, actor, playwright and manager, 33n, 64–5, 70, 87n, 137, 178, 267; on DG, 83–4; DG on Cibber, 160–61; on players of Othello, 99, 124; an epilogue quoted, 227n; as Poet Laureate, 64, q.97; his malicious *Letter*, q.64n; his *An Apology for the Life of . . .* (1740), q.vi, 529n; his death (1757), 267–8, 268n, 271

Careless Husband, The (1704), 38, 49, 56, 61, 64, 165, 275

Double Gallant, The, 56

Love's Last Shift (1696), 64

Non-Juror, The (1717), 64, 107, 224

School Boy, The, 2, 49

his version of *Richard III*, 38

reconstructs *King John*, 97–8

completes Vanbrugh's *A Journey to London* as *The Provok'd Husband* (1728), 87

Cibber, Jane, daughter of Theophilus, actress, 178

Cibber, Molly, Susannah's daughter, 111

Cibber (*née* Arne), Susannah, singer and actress, 57–8 and nn, 60–61, 98–101, 109 and n, 113, 139, 172; at Covent Garden, 123, 128, 173 and n, 177, 184; entertains DG at her home, 121–2; Johnson's opinion, 152; health problems, 246, 260, 282–3,

289, 296; her letters to DG, quoted: (1744), 102, 105, 110, 113, 116 and n, 117; (1763–5), 332, 363, 365, 367; DG's letter to her, q.332; her translation of the masque, *The Oracle*, 198, 212; the death of her son, 271; her death (1766), 367

her roles: as singer, 57, 67, 104, 106; as actress: Dublin (1739), 58; Covent Garden: (1739), 61; (1746–51), 125, 175, 182, 196; Drury Lane: (1744), 98–101; (1747–54), 145, 148, 151n, 212, 216, 218, 225 and n; (1755–8), 241, 244, 249, 252, 266, 269, 275; (1759–65), 279, 294, 329–30, 367

Cibber, Theophilus, actor, 33n, 65, 69, 100, 254, 264, 265n; his mistreatment of his wife, 57–8, 105; his daughter, Jane, 178; his duel with Quin, 63; his 'Epistle' to Garrick, 246–7; other criticisms of DG, 147, 248–249, 249n; roles, 61, 74 and n, 109n, 124, 148 and n; his death (1758)

Cimarosa, Domenico, composer, *Il Matrimonio Segreto* (1792), 4, 376

Clairon (Claire de Latude), Mlle, actress, 5–6, 188 and n, 336–7, 348, 353, 354–5, q.494

Cleland, John, author of *Fanny Hill* (1748–9), 215n, 238n, 473–4

Clinch, Lawrence, actor, 484 and n, 527

Clive, Kitty, actress, 45n, 55n, 56, 58n, 67, 233, 333; at Drury Lane, 60–61, 76n, 123, 139, 145 and n, 164, 173; roles: (1741–50), 56, 61, 76, 165, 169, 174, 177–8; (1751–9), 193, 209, 244, 249n, 254, 258n, 286; (1766–9), 376, 391, 397, 402, 411; retires (1769), 411; at the Stratford Jubilee, 421; on DG, q.1; letters to DG, quoted, 411, 508, 555, 594; letters from DG, quoted, 401, 516; letter to Mrs Garrick, q.614; in Churchill's *Rosciad*, q.305; and Jane Pope, 542–3, q.591–2, 614; on Wilkinson, 276; comments on her: Davies, 181n; Johnson, 152, 411; Kelly, 396

as a playwright, *Bayes in Petticoats* (1750), 169–70, 209

Clough, Mrs, Garrick's grandmother, 21

Clutterbuck, James, DG's friend, 109 and n, 132, 171–2, 261, 372, 555n; letters from DG, quoted, 202, 346–7, 410–11; letters to DG, quoted, 373–4, 555

Coleridge, Samuel Taylor, poet, 67

Collé, Charles, dramatist and song-writer, his journal (1750), q.189, 189n, q.236

Colley, Linda, on 'Wilkes' by Hogarth, q.319

Collier, Revd Jeremy, ... the Immorality and Profaneness of the English Stage (1698), 96 and n

Colman, George (the elder), playwright and theatre manager, 316n, 354n, 365, 422, 426, q.566, 611; at Drury Lane, 369–70, 370n, 372, 377, 389; buys into Covent Garden, 389–90; at Covent Garden: (1767–8), 391, 393, 395, 402–3; (1770–73), 446, 471, 497, 503; retires to Bath, 514–15; buys Haymarket Theatre, 574 and n; at the Haymarket, 582 and n, 604

A Letter of Abuse to D—d G—k, pamphlet (1757), q.264–5, 301; his prologue to Bon Ton (Garrick, 1775), 531 and n; and the St James's Chronicle (1761), 303 and n, q.304, 331

letters to DG, quoted, 374, 554, 554n; letters from DG, quoted: (1760), 301–2; (1763–4), 331, 336, 338–9, 341, 343–5, 347–9; (1765–7), 353, 355, 358 and n, 359, 370n, 374–5, 381, 388; (1775–7), 525, 533, 535–6, 543, 552n, 553, 574, 584

Clandestine Marriage, The, (with Garrick, 1766), 4, 37, 373–7, 391, 526n

Conspiracy, The (1757), 265n

English Merchant, The (1767), 389

Fairy Prince, The (1771), 460

Jealous Wife, The (1761), 303, 387–8, 526n

Man and Wife; or, The Shakespeare Jubilee (1769), 436–7, 439

Musical Lady, The (1761), 315

New Brooms (1776), 570–72

Oxonian in Town, The (1768), 403 and n

Polly Honeycombe (1760), 301–2, 302n, 303, 576n

Colman, George (the younger), theatre manager, 381, 586; on DG, quoted, 137n, 338n, 381n

Colson, Revd John, mathematician and schoolmaster, 27–8, 29 and n

Congreve, William, playwright, 4, 45n
    Double Dealer, The (1694), 258 and n, 269
    Love for Love (1695), 65, 91
    Mourning Bride, The (1697), 178–9, 179nn, 209, 224, 410, 551
    Old Bachelor, The (1693), 2, 44
    Way of the World, The (1700), 44, 65, 402

Connoisseur, The (1754–6), q.1–2, 84, 265, 303n

Conway, Henry Seymour, MP, Walpole's cousin, 447, 455–6: his wife, Caroline, 456

Cooke, William, theatre critic and biographer, 47–8nn, 103–4, q.277, q.503–4

Cooper, Sir Grey, DG's friend, 453 and n, 508–9, 537–8, q.563, 611; his letters from DG, quoted, 509, 537, 556

Coquelin, Benoît-Constant, actor, 101 and n

Corneille, Pierre, dramatist: Horace (1640), 169; Rodogune (1644?), 188

Corneille, Thomas, dramatist, Ariane, 188

Countess of Salisbury, play, 410

Court Magazine, 314n, 315

Court Miscellany, 401

Courtney, William P., on Stonhouse, q.514n

Covent Garden Theatre, 34, 142–3, 205, 328–9; see also under the names of its managers (Rich and Beard) and of the many actors and actresses who performed there

Coventry (née Gunning), Maria, Countess of, 217

Cowley, Abraham, poet, 45n

Cox, Richard: letters from DG, quoted, 510, 598–9; letter from Mrs Garrick, quoted, 599

Cradock, Joseph, DG's friend, 252 and n, 375, q.458, 468 and n, q.499, 615; at the Stratford Jubilee, 418–20, 425, q.431; letters from DG, quoted, 436, 459, 508, 562, 597

Craftsman, The, weekly, 308

Craven, Countess of, 431 and n

Crébillon, Prosper Jolyot de, playwright, *Rhadamiste et Zénobie* (1711), 400–401, 401nn

Crisp, Samuel, playwright, *Virginia* (1754), 217

Critical Review, q.265, 295, 304

Croft (or Crofts), Henry, would-be actor, 463–4, 464n

Cross, Richard, actor, dancer and (from 1741) Drury Lane prompter, 295; his diary, quoted: (1747–51), 142, 148, 164, 169, 178, 181, 194; (1752–5), 97, 206n, 218, 226, 242, 244–6, 249n, 250; (1756–8), 258nn, 266, 269–71, 274, 275 and n; (1759), 283–6

Cumberland, HRH William Augustus, Duke of, 115–17, 182, 366n

Cumberland, Richard, later a playwright, 448–50, 463, q.493, 535–6, 611; his comment on DG, q.550n; his letter to DG, q.591

as a schoolboy, on a performance of *The Fair Penitent* (1746), q.125–6, 334

Amelia, musical afterpiece (1771), 464–5, 465n

Battle of Hastings, The (1778), 591

Brothers, The (1769), 448

Choleric Man, The (1774), 524

Fashionable Lover, The (1772), 465 and n

West Indian, The (1771), 448–9, 526n, 529

Daily Advertiser, 74–5, 80, 102, 135, 182, 194, 475

Daily Gazetteer, 108–9

Daily Post and General Advertiser, 39, 47, 55–6, 75, 100

D'Alembert, Jean le Rond, philosopher, 336, 349

Daly, John Augustin, theatre manager, 218

Dance, Nathaniel, portrait painter, 322n, 330n, 343

Dancer, Mrs Ann, *see* Barry, Mrs Ann

Dancourt, Florent Carton, playwright, *La Parisienne* (1691), 103n

Darnley, Edward, 2nd Earl of, 55, 88, 103

Dashwood, Sir Francis, member of the Dilettanti, 586n

Davenant, Sir William: his version (1664) of *Macbeth*, 82–3, 335; with Dryden, his operatic version of *The Tempest*, 249

Davies, Thomas, Garrick's first biographer, 5, 19 and n, 80, 441, 613; introduces Johnson to Boswell, 325–6; acrimony between Garrick and Davies, 331–2; as an actor, 205, 216, 242n, 246n, 299, 313–14

Dramatic Miscellanies (1784), q.195, q.587

Memoirs of the Life of David Garrick Esq. . . . (1780, 2nd ed., 1808), quoted *passim* throughout the text. Selected quotations: 98, 100–101, 216, 225, 384, 428–9, 595

Davies, Thomas, wood-carver, 414, 415n

Davis, William, actor, 557

de Bernage, Louis-Basile, provost of the Paris merchants, 190–91

de Castro, James, *Memoirs*, q.302n

Defoe, Daniel, writer, 10, 16, q.139n

Delane, Dennis, actor, 45–6, 59–60, 74, 91, 136, 139, 145

Delany, Mary, her letters, q.129, 129–30n, q.404

Delap, Dr John, playwright, *Hecuba* (1761), 315 and n

de Laplace, Antoine, translator, 352, 486n, 490

Delaval, Francis, 199n, 269, 283; his *Othello* at Drury Lane, 182 and n

Delaval, Sir John Hussey, 397n

De La Warr, 1st Earl, 404 and n

de Loutherbourg, Philippe Jacques, painter and scene-designer, 488–9, 501, 507, 510, 520–22, 530, 599, 613; his sketch of Garrick, 571; at Garrick's funeral, 611; his interests in mysticism, etc., 620

Denis, Charles, 186 and n, 187

Dennis, John, critic and playwright, *Liberty Asserted . . .* (c.1706), 116

Derrick, Samuel, and Boswell, 323 and n

Descombes, Mme, of Paris, 498, 538–9

Destouches, Philippe, playwright, *La Fausse Agnès*, 436

Dévisse, Monsieur, dancer, 190–91

Devonshire, William, 3rd Duke of and Catherine, Duchess of, 171

Devonshire, William, 4th Duke of
    (formerly Marquis of Hartington,
    q.v.), 257, 263, 270, 273–4, 280, 300,
    303 and n, 330; his letters from DG,
    quoted, 263–4, 273–4, 339, 340 and
    n, 342–3, 344n, 345; his letter to DG,
    q.342; his death (1764), 347
Devonshire, William, 5th Duke of, 510,
    568, 570, 588, 590, 611; Georgiana,
    Duchess of Devonshire, 540, 548, 570
    and n, 573n, 588
Dexter, John, actor, 194
Dibdin, Charles, singer and composer,
    418, 439, 487, 507 and n, 512; and
    the Stratford Jubilee, q.418, 420–21,
    424–5, 427, 431
    Cobler, The, ballad farce (1774), 523
        and n
    Waterman, The, ballad opera (1776),
        564
    Wedding Ring, The, comic opera
        (1773), 490–91
    'Warwickshire Lads', ballad, 424
Diderot, Denis, writer, 3, 174n, 249–50,
    351 and n, 359
Digges, West, actor, 223n
Dilettanti, Society of, 585–6, 586n
Dodd, James, actor, 270–71, 371n, 383n
Dodd, Revd Dr William, 577, 578n
Dodsley, Robert, writer and bookseller,
    152 and n, 283n, 290; Cleone (1757),
    283–4 and nn, 312
Doggett, Thomas, actor, 45n
Dorset, Lionel, 1st Duke of, 222
Dorset, Charles, 2nd Duke of, 416, 421
Douglas, Andrew, surgeon, 324
Douglas, Revd John, DG's friend, 316n,
    317
Dow, Alexander, soldier and playwright:
    Sethona (1774), 510–11; Zingis
    (1768), 408
Draper, Somerset, DG's friend, 90 and n,
    109n, 132, 191–2, 211–12: letters from
    DG, quoted, 90–91, 104–6, 108–10,
    112–13, 148n, 171–2, 186, 192
Droeshout, Martin, engraver, his
    Shakespeare portrait, 413
Drury Lane, Theatre Royal, 34, 140–41,
    205, 326–8, 371–2, 534, 544; see also
    under the names of its managers
    (Fleetwood, Lacy, Garrick, Sheridan)

    and those of the many actors and
    actresses who appeared there
'Drury Lane ague', 1
Dryden, John, poet, 226, 249
    'Absalom and Achitophel' (1681), 45n,
        48n
    Amphitryon (1690), 192
    Cymon and Iphigenia, 386
    King Arthur, opera (music by Purcell,
        1691), 447
    Oedipus, King of Thebes (1679), 224
Dublin: Aungier Street Theatre Royal, 52,
    58–9; Crow Street Theatre, 272, 293;
    Fishamble Hall, 57, 60n; Smock Alley
    Theatre, 51, 58–9, 74n, 110, 193–4,
    196, 236n, 239n
Duck, Stephen, 'peasant' poet, 136 and n
Dugdale, William, historian, 11
Dumesnil, Marie (Marie-Françoise
    Marchand), actress, 146, 188, 337,
    353
Dunstall, John, singer, 322

Eardley-Wilmot, Sir John, of the
    justiciary, 12, 18, 157–8
Earl, Thomas, writer, Common Sense
    (1739), q.87n
Eaves, William, Mayor of Stratford,
    DG's letter, q.452–3
Edgecumbe, George, Lord, and Lady
    Emma, 456–7, 505
Edinburgh, theatre in the Canongate, 261
Edward III, King, 10
Edwin, John, actor, 582n
Eliot, George (Mary Ann Evans), novelist,
    16
Elizabeth I, Queen, 10
Elliott, Ann, actress, 310–11, 311n
Encyclopédie, L' (Diderot, D'Alembert,
    et al., 1751–76), 349–50
Englishman in Paris, The, 214, 269
Essex, William, 4th Earl of, and Countess
    of, 508
Estienne, Henri, writer, Apologie pour
    Hérodote (1566), 6n
Eusden, Laurence, Poet Laureate
    (1718–30), 65n
Evans, Thomas, bookseller, 482

Fagan, Barthélemi-Christophe,
    playwright, La Pupille, 286

Fair Quaker of Deal, The, 242n
Falconer, Dr William, of Bath, 523 and n
False Delicacy, 401
Farquhar, George, playwright, 45n
  Beaux' Stratagem, The (1707), 56, 551;
    DG's appearances, 82, 101, 142,
    174, 204, 415, 463
  Constant Couple, The (1699), 38, 53,
    55, 124 and n
  Love and a Bottle (1699), 127n
  Recruiting Officer, The (1706), 53, 55,
    74, 275; DG's youthful
    production, 20, 260; his later
    appearances, 44, 59, 61
Farinelli (Carlo Broschi), castrato, 342n
Farren, Elizabeth, actress, 582n, 584
Faulkner, George, Dublin publisher, his
  letter from DG, q.482–3
Favart, Charles Simon, playwright, *La Fée*
  Urgèle (*c.*1765), 507
Fearon, Dr, physician, 607
Fermignac, Peter, DG's cousin, 41n, 452
Fielding, Henry, novelist, 212, 476; *Tom*
  Jones (1749), q.**65–6**, 303, 597; as
  magistrate, 214n, 246; attr. *Apology*
  for T . . . C . . ., q.63n;
  as playwright:
  Debauchees, The, 107
  Fathers, The (1778), 599 and n
  Miser, The, 76, 174
  Mock Doctor, The (1732), 36 and n
  Pasquin (1736), 33
  Tom Thumb, burlesque (1730), 206
  Wedding Day, The (1743), **66**
Fielding, Sir John, magistrate, 254–6, 317,
  500–501
Fiennes, Celia, writer, 9 and n
Fiske, Roger, critic, q.226
Fitzgerald, Percy, DG's 19th-C.
  biographer, 53, 56, 73, q.169, q.466;
  on DG, quoted, 164, 224, 226n, 296,
  492–3
Fitzherbert, William, MP, 441, 448
  and n
Fitzmaurice, Thomas, DG's friend, 474,
  480, 490
Fitzpatrick, Thaddeus, 'man about town',
  205, 305; and riots at Drury Lane
  and Covent Garden, 327–9, 334
Fleetwood, Charles (senior), manager,
  Drury Lane, 42, 51, 71–2, 104n, 133;

in management (1736–45), 56,
  60–61, 73–9, 82, 86, 90, **91–3**, 97
Fleetwood, Charles (junior), actor, 275
  and n
Fletcher, John, playwright, 4, 335 (*see*
  also Beaumont and Fletcher)
  Chances, The (1620), 224–5, 495, 505,
    515, 582
  Rule a Wife and Have a Wife (1624),
    254, 370, 455, 463, 582
Floyer, Sir John, physician, 15 and n
Foote, Samuel, playwright and actor, 57,
  198, 278, 311, 444, 589; roles, 94,
  214, 269; his plays at the Haymarket,
  135–7, 145 and n; in Churchill's
  Rosciad, q.306; and DG, 5, 29n, 120,
  277–8, 417, 422, 437; DG's letters,
  q.378, q.444 (in verse); and Macklin,
  214; other victims of his pen, q.123n,
  q.239n, 365n, 442 and n; his riding
  accident, 377–8, 378n; sells
  Haymarket Theatre, 574; is charged
  by former coachman, 574, 587 and n;
  his death (1777), 574n, 587–8
  Author, The (1758), **269–70**
  Devil Upon Two Sticks, The (1768),
    417, 434–6, 468n
  Diversions of the Morning, 275–7
  Handsome Housemaid, The (1773), 492
    and n
  Maid of Bath, The (1771), 527
  Minor, The (1760), 300–301
  Patron, The (1764), 525 and n
  Taste (1751), 198–9, 199n, 583n
  Trip to Calais, A (1776), 574
  Wishes, The, pantomime (1761), 311
Ford, Dr James, patentee (1776) of Drury
  Lane, 553 and n
Forrest, Theodosius, solicitor to Covent
  Garden, 390
Foster, Mrs Elizabeth, granddaughter of
  Milton, 170
Foster, John, *The Life . . . of Goldsmith*
  (1848), 443n, 507n
Foundling Hospital for Wits, The (1771
  ed.), q.466
Fountain, Peter, lawyer, 481–2; letters
  from DG, quoted, 436n, 481, 492,
  512, 550
Fox, Charles James, statesman, 199n, 421,
  581, 611, 614

Fox, Henry, 1st Lord Holland, 199n, 253, 254 and n, 273, 281

Fox, Stephen, friend of Hanbury-Williams, 88

Francis, Revd Philip, as playwright, *Eugenia* (1752), 199–200

Francis, Sir Philip, son of Revd Philip, civil servant, 462n

Francklin, Revd Dr Thomas, D G's friend, 156 and n, q.252n, 410; *Electra* (1774), 520–21

Franklin, Benjamin, American statesman, 537

French, James Murphy, his letter from D G, q.227n

French, John, scene-painter, 418 and n, 430

Fürst, Elisabeth, Mrs Garrick's niece, 585 and n, 615

Gabrielli, Caterina, singer, 341

Gainsborough, Thomas, painter, 402, 413–14, q.489

Garric, David, Garrick's grandfather, 7–8 and nn

Garrick (*née* Clough), Arabella, D G's mother, 8, 19–23; her death (1740), 37–8

Garrick, Arabella, George's daughter, 451, 498 and n, 614–15; and de Molière, 538–40, 587n; marries, 540, 594 and n; her death (1819), 619

Garrick, Revd Carrington, George's son, 587n, 615

Garrick (*née* Carrington), George's first wife, 183

Garrick, Catherine, George's daughter, 381 and n, 451, 498 and n, 587n, 614–15, 619n

GARRICK, DAVID

ancestry and birth (at Hereford, 19 February 1717), 7–8, 9; his brothers, sisters and other relatives, 17; his boyhood, development and education (at Lichfield), 17–27; his production (c.1727) of *The Recruiting Officer*, 20

goes to London (1737) and is enrolled at Lincoln's Inn, 27; becomes a wine-merchant, 29; produces and acts in *The Mock Doctor*, 36; his own first play (*Lethe*) produced at Drury Lane (1740), 36; becomes a professional actor (1741), **38**

THE ACTOR

at Ipswich (1741), 38; at Goodman's Fields (1741–2), 38–51; at Smock Alley, Dublin (1742), 51, **58–60**; at Drury Lane (1742–5), 60–111 *passim*; at Smock Alley (in joint management with Sheridan, 1745–6), **112–15**; at Covent Garden (1746–7), 116–17, 123–35 *passim* (*see also* Covent Garden Theatre)

THE ACTOR-MANAGER

buys a half interest in the Drury Lane patent (1747), **132–3**; begins joint management with James Lacy (1747), 137; disagreements with him, 168, 372–3; Willoughby Lacy inherits (1774), 509–10; Garrick sells his half-interest to R. B. Sheridan (1776), 553 and n (*see also* Drury Lane Theatre)

his retirement from the stage, **554–65**

HIS ROLES AND PERFORMANCES

Agis, 266, 303

Alchymist, The: (1743–66), **67–70**, 68, 209, 376, 387; (1771–6), 463, 521, 552, 554, 561

Antony and Cleopatra, 284–5

Athelstan, 252–3

Barbarossa, 225–6

Beaux' Strategem, The: (1743–52), 82, 101, 117n, 142, 174, 204; (1763–76), 325, 415, 463, 551, 552, 560

Boadicia, 215–16

Busy Body, The, 280, 282–3

Careless Husband, The, 38, 49

Chances, The, 224, 495, 505

Constant Couple, The, 38

Cymbeline, 146n, 315 and nn

Discovery, The, 127n, 330

Distressed Mother, The, 89

Elvira, 324

Eugenia, 199–200

Every Man in His Humour: (1751–68), **195**, 301, 380, 397; (1770–75), 444, 463, 552

Fair Penitent, The: (1741–6), 44, 51, 82, 110n, 125; (1753–63), 212, 299, 329
Fatal Message, The, 268
Gamester, The, 205–6
Gamesters, The, 268–9
Guardian, The, 286
Hamlet: (1741–6), 44, 59, 61, 82, 117n; (1748–53), 144, 169, 192, 212, 213; (1763–75), 329n, 463, 486, 521n, 552
Henry IV Part I, 128
Henry IV Part II, 325
Iphigenia, 38
Irene, 150–52
Jane Shore: (1743–55), 67, 144, 178, 218n, 241; (1758–73), 283, 505, 508
Jealous Wife, The, 303, 387–8
King John, 97, 299–300
King Lear: (1742–6), 47–8, 51, 61, 82, 115; (1747–58), 136–7, 145, 165, 280; (1763–76), 325, 443, 453n, 496, 513, 561–2
Lethe, 251–2, 254, 367, 376, 387, 391
Love Makes a Man, 41
Lying Valet, The, 43, 49n, 51, 67
Macbeth, 82–5, 115, 117n, 335, 402, 405
Mahomet the Impostor, 86–7
Meropé, 209, 286
Miss in Her Teens, 129–30, 133, 136
Mourning Bride, The, 178–9, 209
Much Ado About Nothing: (1748–65), 146–7, 164, 244, 259n, 366; (1766–76), 387, 397, 481, 521, 550 and n, 561
Old Bachelor, The, 44
Oroonoko, 38, 294–5
Orphan, The, 42–3, 61, 212, 245
Orphan of China, The, 283
Othello, 99, 117n
Pamela, 42
Provok'd Husband, The, 87
Provok'd Wife, The: (1743–66), 92, 95–7, 244, 367, 376, 387; (1768–76), 397, 405, 463, 548, 549, 558
Recruiting Officer, The, 44, 59, 61
Rehearsal, The, 45–6, 51, 61, 77, 376, 469

Richard III: (1741–3), 38–9, 40–41, 51, 61, 82; (1746–76), 117n, 124, 297–8, 405, 469, 562–3
Roman Father, The, 169 and n, 170
Rule a Wife and Have a Wife, 254, 455, 463
Romeo and Juliet, 175–8, 212, 258
School for Lovers, The, 316
Siege of Aquileia, The, 296–7
Suspicious Husband, The: (1749–56), 130–32, 135, 146, 258; (1757–71), 262, 265, 397, 404, 463
Tancred and Sigismunda, 100
Venice Preserv'd, 49, 144, 308
Virginia, 217–18
Way of the World, The, 44
Way to Keep Him, The, 296
Wedding Day, The, 66
Winter's Tale, The, 146n, 248–9
Wonder, The, 536, 564
Zara, 278–9, 367, 463, 513, 524, 548, 561

AS A WRITER
the breadth of his output, 4
plays:
Bon Ton, miniature comedy (1750s), 531–2
Catherine and Petruchio (1754), 218–19, 248
Guardian, The (1759), 286
Irish Widow, The (1772), 483–4
Jubilee, The (1769), 437–9, 444, 447, 552, 559
Lethe (1740), iv, 213, 376; revised, 251–2; productions, 36–7, 174, 198, 387, 393n
Lilliput (1756), 259nn, 259–60, 287
Lying Valet, The (1741), 2, 43, 49n, 51, 192
Male Coquette, The (1757), 266–7
May Day (1775), 521, 548
Miss in Her Teens (1747), 103 and n, 129–30, 287, 309
Meeting of the Company, The, burlesque-rehearsal (1774), 518–19
Neck or Nothing (1766), 385–6
Peep Behind the Curtain, A (1768), 397–9, 402, 518
Ragandjaw (1746), 119–21, 121n
Theatrical Candidates, The, musical playlet (1775), 545–6

Clandestine Marriage, The (1766) (with
    George Colman), 4–5, 37, 373–7,
    391, 393, 526n
adaptations:
Albumazar (1773), 502–3
Chances, The (1754), 224, 269
Country Girl, The (1766), 385 and n,
    391, 397–8, 521
Gamesters, The (1758), 268–9
Hamlet (1772), 486–7, 487n
Romeo and Juliet, 148–50
Rule a Wife and Have a Wife (1756),
    254, 269
operas:
Enchanter, The (1760), 302
Fairies, The (1755), 226–7
Tempest, The (1756), 249–50
other presentations:
Chinese Festival, The (1755), 241–8,
    283
Christmas Tale, A (1773), 507nn, 507–8
Country Girl, The, comic seranata
    (1769), 429
Cymon, dramatic romance (1766),
    386–7
Harlequin's Invasion (1759), 291–3, 341
    and n, 418, 488–9
Institution of the Garter, The (1771),
    459–61
Linco's Travels, interlude (1767), 388
Pigmy Revels, The (1772), 487–8
The Stratford Jubilee (1769), 4, 412–32
prologues and epilogues to the works
    of others:
Albumazar, q.503
All the World's A Stage, 578
Almida, q.448
Alonzo, q.494
Apprentice, The, q.248
Barbarossa, q.225–6
Beaux' Stratagem, The, q.415
Bonduca, 604
Britannia, 228n, 262
Choleric Man, The, 524
Desert Island, The, 296
Englishman in Paris, The, q.214–15
False Delicacy, q.276n
Fathers, The, 599 and n
Gamester, The, q.206
Inflexible Captive, The, 536
Know Your Own Mind, 578

Merchant of Venice, The, q.141–2,
    q.194
Much Ado About Nothing, q.366, 369
New Brooms, 570–72
Percy, 588
Polly Honeycombe, 301
Rival Queens, The, q.250
Romeo and Juliet, q.177–8
School for Rakes, The, 409
School for Scandal, The, q.580
She Stoops to Conquer, 493
Spanish Barber, The, 584
Taste, q.198–9
Tempest, The, q.250
Thespis, 396
Virginia, q.217
Winter's Tale, The, q.248
Wonder, The, q.564
other verse works, 250 and:
'Heart of Oak', q.291
'Lilies of France, The', q.251
ode on his dog's pregnancy, q.232n
ode on Pelham's death, q.219
'Ode to Shakespeare', 426–8, 433, 435
on Quin, q.62
Sick Monkey, The, a fable, 358, 361
    and n
'Sweet Willy O', 424
'The Farmer's Return from London',
    interlude, q.317–18
The Fribbleriad (1761), q.309–10
verses on Bunbury, q.568
verses on Johnson's Dictionary, 229–30
'Warwickshire Lads', q.424
An Essay on Acting (1744), 70, 84–5
RELATIONSHIPS, ACTUAL OR
    SUPPOSED
with Peg Woffington, 51, 56, 58–9,
    70–71, 103–4, 105; with Susannah
    Cibber, 110–11
COURTSHIP AND MARRIAGE
in love with Violette, 153; the wedding
    (22 June 1749), 156–7;
    contentment, 288, 334
HOMES
Merton (rented), 158–9
Southampton Street (purchased), 159
Hampton (purchased), 216, 221, 233–4
The Adelphi, 466–7
FRIENDS IN SOCIETY
see (among others) The Earl and

Countess of Burlington, the Earl of
Camden, the 4th Duke of
Devonshire, the Marquess and
Marchioness of Hartington,
Richard Rigby
OTHER FRIENDSHIPS (sometimes
mercurial)
see (among many too numerous to
index here), James Boswell,
Samuel Johnson, Hannah More
PROBLEM PEOPLE
among the many, see Abington, Arne,
Churchill, Colman, Foote,
Murphy, Macklin
UNPLEASANT INCIDENTS
the Cautherley rumours, 287–9; the
Bickerstaffe slur, 476–7, 478–82
TRAVELS TO EUROPE
to Paris (May–July, 1751), 186–9;
further afield: (1763–5), 335–59;
Paris, 335–7, 347–59; Turin, 338;
Milan, 339; Florence, 339; Rome,
339, 343; Naples, 339–43; Venice,
344; Abano, 344–5; Munich, 345–6
CHARACTERISTICS
a compulsive letter-writer, 5; generosity
to friends and colleagues, 5–6, 11,
595 (see also Theatrical Fund);
gregariousness, 4–5; self-
congratulation, 207; vanity, 5
GARRICK AS SEEN BY OTHERS
T. Cibber, 147, 246–7, 248–9, 249n;
Clive, 1, 508, 555; de Grimm, 3;
Gentleman's Magazine (1742),
61–2; John Hill, 279–80; Macklin,
2; Murphy, 218; Molly Porter, 50;
Swinfen, 39–40; 'the subject of
critics, hacks and scribblers', 264,
274, 290 and n, 307–9
DEPICTED BY ARTISTS
Batoni, 343 and n; Dance, 343; de
Loutherbourg, 571; Gainsborough,
414 and n; Hogarth, 118 and n,
199; Kauffmann, 467n; Lemoine,
351; Nollekens, 343; Reynolds, 6,
318, 351 and n; Romney (?), 450;
West, 414; Wilson, 351, 414n;
Zoffany, 127n, 351; engravings, iv,
549
THE 'FRAIL TENEMENT'
his major illnesses, 102, 346, 410–11,

460–61, 575, 579, 596–7; his final
illness and death (20 January 1779),
604–5, 605–6; his lying-in-state,
608–9; his funeral, 609–12, 610
Garrick, David, Garrick's uncle, 19, 29
Garrick, David, George's son, 587n,
594n, 611, 615, 619; married (1778),
594
Garrick (née Tetley), Elizabeth, George's
second wife, 451n
Garrick (née Veigel), Eva Maria, Garrick's
wife, 199 and n, 353, 465, 537–8
as the dancer, Violette, 117n, 117–18,
123 and n, 128–9, 133n, 153–6
marriage, 156–7; domesticity, 157–8,
162n; illnesses, 161, 185, 343, 345;
with Rousseau at Drury lane, 369;
described by: Fanny Burney, 468;
A. Carlyle, 273; Gibbon, 584n;
Robertson, 284n; at Stratford, 421,
425; her letter to a friend, q.177;
her letters to Lady Burlington,
q.158–60
nursing her husband, 158–9, 575, 596,
604; records his death, 605; his
bequests to her, 615; widowhood,
615–21; and Lord Monboddo, 617,
618, 619; Queen Charlotte calls,
620; and Edmund Kean, 620; as
seen by Cruikshank, 622; her will,
621; her death (1822), 621
Garrick, George, Garrick's brother, 17,
25, 28, 451–2, 587 and n; courtship
and marriage, 183; wife's death
(1759), 270; second marriage, 451n,
539; illness and convalescence, 512,
523–4, 535, 550, 561n; final illness
and death, 611, 612–13
DG seeks patronage for him, 132n,
381, 556; employed at Drury Lane,
168, 369, 382, 451, 455, 487; at the
Stratford Jubilee, 415–18, 433;
duel with Baddeley, 442
letters from DG, quoted: (1747–52),
137, 183, 202, 210; (1763–4, from
the Continent), 338, 340–46, 348
and n, 351, 357; (1765–7), 366,
373n, 377, 382–3, 387–90;
(1768–76), 403, 523, 561
Garrick, George, George's sixth child,
451n, 619n

Garrick, Jane, Garrick's sister, 17, 21, 23, 28, 112

Garrick, Magdalene, Garrick's sister, 17, 20, 23, 28, 201; her death (1764), 347

Garrick, Merrial, Garrick's sister, 17, 28, 201n, 468, 614; her death (1799), 619

Garrick, Nathan, George's son, 587n, 619

Garrick, Captain Peter, Garrick's father, 8–9, 16, 19, 20–24; his death (1737), 28

Garrick, Peter, Garrick's brother, 17, 20 and n, 26, 28, 69, 258 and n, 611; enters wine trade, 29 and n; letter from Swinfen, q.38–9; letter from Windham, q.143; bequest from DG, 614; his death (1795), 619
     letters from DG, quoted: (1740–42), 37–8, 40–43, 46, 50–51, 59, 64; (1746–54), 132, 159, 189, 191–2, 201, 209–10, 220; (1755–62), 232–3, 257–8, 316, 320; (1774–7), 520, 560–61, 568, 585, 586 and n

Garrick, William, Garrick's brother, 17, 28, 201n

Gastrell, mercer, 109n

Gastrell, Francis, Cheshire clergyman, 413n

Gataker, Thomas, surgeon, 312 and n

Gay, John, playwright, The Beggar's Opera (1728), 31–2, 192, 211, 265, 500–501; players, 56, 124, 174, 293–4

Gazette Littéraire, 354

Gazetteer and New Daily Advertiser, quoted, 405n, 548–50, 582

Gem, Richard, physician, 359 and n

Geminiani, Francesco, violinist and composer, 60 and n, 322

General Advertiser: (1744–7), q.86, 91n, q.92, q.107, q.124, q.129, q.135; (1748–51), q.150, 167, 170, 178, q.181, 198

Genest, John, writer, 406n

Gentleman, Francis, writer: The Dramatic Censor (1770), 176, 469; The Theatres (1772), 469–71, 471n

Gentleman's Magazine, 25, 165, 256, 323, q.425, 448; on DG, q.61–2, q.153; Johnson's contributions, 38, 78, 170n, q.317; Biographical Anecdotes of . . . Garrick (1779), 614; Memoir of Mrs Garrick (1822), 621n

Geoffrey of Monmouth, Historia Regium Brittaniae (12th C.), 447

Geoffrin, Marie-Thérèse, patron of literature, 351–2

George I, King, 20

George II, King, 12n, 22n, 31–3, 106n, 182, 219, 229; at Dettingen, 72; and Angelo, 146n; and Maria Gunning, 217; his first opinions on the theatre, etc., q.4; at the theatre, 37, 61, 130, 141n, 165, 224, 242, 295n; his death (1760), 287 and n

George III, King, 63n, 471n, 598; marriage, 312–13; and the theatre, 298–9, 303, 356, 369, 447, 493, 562–3; hears DG's 'Ode', privately, 418; see also Wales, George, Prince of

George IV, King, 199n, 620; see also Wales, George, Prince of

George Dandin (after Molière), 143

Giardini, Felice [de], violinist and composer, 322, 599n

Gibbon, Edward, historian, 199 and n, 325n, 466n, 563, 574 and n, 616; his letter to DG, q.583–4, 584n; at Garrick's funeral, 611

Giffard, Henry, actor-manager, 35, 38, 74, 288; at Lincoln's Inn Fields, 33, 61; at Goodman's Fields, 38 and n, 43n, 47, 49, 132; his death (1772), 484

Gifford, William, editor and critic, 285n

Glover, Richard, playwright: Boadicia (1753), 215–16; Leonidas (1737), 215

Gluck, Christoph Willibald, composer, Artamene, pasticcio, 117n

Goethe, Johann Wolfgang von, poet, 434n

Goldsmith, Oliver, playwright, poet and novelist, 4, 174n, 236n, 271, 381, 563n; dines with friends, 179n, 364, 440–41, 505; and DG, 395n, 395–6, 495, 506 and n; his publication, The Bee (1759); his death (1774), 507 and n
     Good-natur'd Man, The (1768), 395–6, 403
     She Stoops to Conquer, (1773), 288n, 492–3, 526n
     Retaliation, poem (1773–4), 506–7

Goldoni, Carlo, playwright, Il Filosofo di Campagna, 490–91

Goodman's Fields Theatre, 38, 43, 49–51, 61, 107, 116, 132
Grace, Ann, actress, *see* 'Macklin, Mrs'
Grafton, Charles, 2nd Duke of, Lord Chamberlain, 64, 132, 167, 234
Grafton, Augustus, 3rd Duke of, statesman, 462
Graham, Mary Ann, actress, *see* Yates, Mary Ann
Gravelot, Henri, engraver, 351, 359
Gray, Thomas, poet, q.124, q.266n
Gray's Inn Journal, q.215
Green, Henry, actor, 288
Green (*née* Hippisley), Jane, actress, 288 and n
Green, Richard, banker, 92–3, 109, 113, 198
Griffith, Mrs Elizabeth, playwright, 408–9, 443; letter from D G, q.536
    Double Mistake, The (1766), 408
    Platonic Wife, The (1765), 408
    School for Rakes, The (1768), 408–9, 437
Grimm, Friedrich Melchior, baron de, 350 and n; on D G, quoted, 2–3, 350, 353–4, 354n
Grosvenor, Richard, 1st Earl, 417, 421, 424, 428, 432
'Grub-street Literatus', *The Dancers Damn'd* (1755), q.243

Halifax, George Savile, 1st Marquess of, 160
Hall, John, engraver, 330 and n
Hallifax, Dr Samuel, and Baretti, 441
Hamilton, Mary, Mrs Garrick's guest, q.619
Handel, George Frederick, 87n, 102, 114, 226, 322
    Alexander's Feast (1736), 443n
    Coronation Anthems (1727), 443n
    Hercules (1745), 104
    Judas Maccabeus (1747), 116, 443n
    Messiah (1742), 57 and n, 443n
    Musick for the Royal Fireworks (1749), 154
    'Stand around, my brave boys', song, 108
    Te Deum (1743), 72
Hardwicke, Philip Yorke, 1st Earl of, D G's letter, q.456

Harlequin, A Captive in France, 116
Harlequin Ranger, an entertainment (1752), **205**, 215
Harlequin Sorcerer, 370, 488
Harlequin Student (1741), 291n
Harnage, Henry, D G's friend, 113
Harris, Thomas, and the Covent Garden patent, 390, 402–3
Harris, James, MP, his pastoral, *The Spring* (1762), 321–2
Harris' List of Covent Garden Ladies, 2
Hartington, William, Marquess of (later 4th Duke of Devonshire, q.v.), 155, 157n, 170–71, 230–33, 241–2; D G's letters to him, quoted, 171, 224, 231–3, 239
Hartington, Charlotte, Marchioness of, 230; D G's letters to her, quoted, 192 and n, 210; her death (1754), 231
Haughton, Miss, actress, 225n
Havard, William, actor, 77, 128, 139, 142, 205, 514n
Have at you all; or, the Drury Lane Journal (1752), q.**196–8**
Hawke, Admiral Sir Edward, 453–4, 454n
Hawkesworth, Dr John, 256, 281, 287 and n, 294, **495–6**; letters from D G, quoted, 279–80, 287, 289, 495–6
Hawkins, Sir John, writer, 288n, 364, 404; *Life and Works of Samuel Johnson* (1787–9), 288n, 365
Hawkins, Laetitia-Matilda, *Anecdotes . . . and Memoirs* (1827), 287–8, 288n
Hawkins, William, his version of *Cymbeline*, 314–15, 315n
Hayman, Francis, painter, 104 and n, 108, 120
Haymarket Theatre, 34, 73, 94, 148, 166, 393, 497; Foote's management, 135, 214, 378, 393, 417; Colman buys it, 574, 582 and n
Hayward, Clara, actress, 447
Heberden, William, physician, 605
Hedgcock, Frank, writer on Garrick (1911), q.127, 150, 190, q.219, 360 and n
Helvétius, Claude-Adrien, philosopher, 351
Henderson, John, actor, 146, 533, 536, 582–3, 587, 603; D G's letter to him, q.535

Henley, John ('Orator'), preacher, 135 and n

Herder, Johann Gottfried, philosopher and critic, 434n

Hertford, Francis, 1st Earl of, 358n, 421

Hertford, Lady Isabella, (later Countess of), q.66, 66n

Hervey, Henry, son of the Earl of Bristol, 23, 25, 27n, 32

Hesse, Prince of, 117

Hiffernan, Paul, critic, 216 and n

High Life Below Stairs [Townley], 293

Hill, Aaron, poet and playwright
    Insolvent, The (1758), 271
    Meropé (after Voltaire, 1749), 209, 286
    Prompter, The (1734-6), 126-7
    Zara (1735), 278-9, 356, 387, 463, 513, 524, 530n, 548

Hill, Dr John, 278 and n, 280n, 285; as a playwright, *The Rout* (1759), 278-9; his attacks on Garrick, 279-80; *The Actor: A Treatise . . .* (1750), q.62n, q.84, 278

Hippisley, Elizabeth, actress, 410

Hippisley, Jane, actress, *see* Green, Jane

Hippisley, John, actor, 123 and n, 288

Hoadly, Benjamin, royal physician and playwright, 118; with John Hoadly, *The Suspicious Husband* (1747), 130-32, 146, 262, 265, 397, 404, 469

Hoadly, Revd John, Benjamin's brother, 86n, 118-21, 119n, 290, 371 and n, q.502, 557; DG's letters to him, quoted, 92, 99, 102-3, 120-21, 189, 371, 445, 554

Hoare, Henry, banker, 467, 568n

Hobart, Hon. Albinia, 591n; letter to her from DG, q.590-91

Hobart, George, theatre manager, 591n

Hobart, Lord Henry, MP, 143

Hogarth, William, painter and engraver, 118 and n, 119-20, 156, 283, 317-20, 347-8, 413n, 442; 'A Harlot's Progress', 100; 'Garrick and His Wife', 199; 'Garrick as Richard III', 118 and n

Holbach, Paul Henri, baron d', encyclopedist, 349 and n, 351, 494

Holland, Charles, actor, 239, 241 and n, 333, 355-6, 543n; roles, 327, 329n,

344n, 365, 441-2; his death (1769), 442 and n

Home, Revd John, playwright, 256, 272-3, 275, 469, 499-500; letters to him from DG, quoted, 275, 499-500
    Agis (1747), 266, 273, 303
    Alonzo (1773), 493-4
    Douglas (1756), 256, 261, 273, 526n
    Fatal Discovery, The (1768), 409
    Siege of Aquileia, The, (1760), 296-7
    Surprise, The (1773), 499-500, 500n

Hopkins, Mrs, wife of William, actress, 301n, 562

Hopkins, Priscilla, daughter of William, actress, 580

Hopkins, William, prompter at Drury Lane, 301n, 377; letters to George Garrick, q.523-4; letter from Mrs Abington, q.560; letter to DG, q.603; reports Garrick's death on a playbill, q.605-6; his memorandum book, q.440

quotations from his diary, maintained from 1760 onwards, appear throughout the text from page 301 to page 580 but are far too numerous to be indexed

Horace (Quintus Horatius Flaccus), poet and satirist, q.133n

Huguenots, the, 6-7

Hull, Thomas, actor and patentee at Covent Garden, 379, 515, 519-20; *The Spanish Lady*, musical interlude, 370

Hume, David, philosopher and historian, 6, 77n, 152, 261, 358n, q.369, 381

Humours of the Army . . ., The (1713), 116

Hunt, William, town clerk, Stratford, 412, 415-19, 421, 433

Hunter, Revd John, Lichfield schoolmaster, 18, 24

Huntingdon, Selina Hastings, Countess of, convert to Methodism, 300 and n

Inconstant, The, 244

Independent Chronicle (Boston, Mass., 1779), q.613

Ireland, undertaker in Bow Street, 608, 610

Irving, Henry, actor, 3, 150, 578n

Jackman, Isaac, playwright, *All The World's A Stage* (1777), 578
Jackson, William, publisher, 574 and n
Jackson's Oxford Journal, q.425
James II, King, 10, 15n
Jaratt, Miss, actress, 552
Jenner, Revd Charles, his letter from D G, q.444 and n
Jenyns, Soame, 575 and n; his mock epitaph on Johnson, q.575
Jephson, Robert, playwright, 475–6, 530–31; *Braganza* (1775), 530–31
Jersey, George, 4th Earl of, 588
Jews, the naturalization of, 210–11
John, King, 10
Johnson, Mrs Elizabeth, wife of Samuel, 25–6, 150–51
Johnson, Nathaniel, Samuel's brother, 28
Johnson, Samuel: 26, 71n, 102, 302–3, 363, 440–41; on the Garrick family at Lichfield, 19; his school at Edial (Lichfield), 24–5; moves to London, 27; and *Gentleman's Magazine*, 36, 78, 170n, q.317; and 'Scratching Fanny', 317; meets Boswell, 325–6; meets the Thrales, 363; the Turk's Head dining club, 364–5; Garrick's death and funeral, 607, 609, 610, 612–13
Throughout the text, Johnson's words are quoted, often as recorded by Boswell (q.v.). Selected references: on D G, 200–201, 457–9, 576, 594, 604, 616–17; on D G's house at Hampton, 216, 221; on actors and acting, 411, 586; on stage works, 226 and n, 261, 295, 396, 493 and n
Dictionary (1755), 148n, 150, 152n, 200, 283, 364; preface, q.229; *Plan of a Dictionary . . .* (1747), 138
Irene (1736), 150–52, 201
Lives of the Poets, The (1779–81), q.19 and n, 42n, 178–9, 179n, 285n
Poetical Works (1785), 39n
prologue, *The Merchant of Venice* (1747), 138, q.139 and n
Rambler, The, periodical (1750–52), 200
Rasselas (1759), 283n
Shakespeare, his edition (1765), 4,

363–4, 364n, 477n; *Preface to Shakespeare*, q.315, 441
The Vanity of Human Wishes, poem (1749), 150 and n, 283n
Jones, Henry, playwright, *The Earl of Essex* (1753), 212, 245–6
Jonson, Ben, playwright, 4, 304, 335
Alchymist, The (1610), **67–70**, 209, 376, 402, 463, 521, 551, 561
Epicoene (1609), **557**
Every Man in His Humour (1589), 158n, **194–5**, 301, 380, 397, 463
The Masque of Oberon, 460
Jordan, Mrs Dorothy, actress, 385n
Journal Etranger, Le (Paris, 1755), q.244–5

Kahrl, George M., *see* Stone and Kahrl
Kauffmann, Angelica, painter, 467n
Kean, Edmund, actor, 315n, 620
Kelly, Hugh, playwright, 471n
Clementina (1771), 446, 505
False Delicacy (1768), 376n, 396, 443
School for Wives, The (1773), 505–6
Thespis (1766), 323n, 396, 505n
Word to the Wise, A (1770), 443, 505
Kemble, John Philip, actor-manager, 546 and n
Kemble, Roger, theatre manager, 541
Kenrick, Thomas, *The British Stage* (1822), 185n
Kenrick, William, miscellaneous writer, 430; his libellous lampoon (1772), q.476–7, **478–82**, 614; *A Letter to David Garrick* (1772), 480
Kent, William, painter, architect and landscape gardener, 155 and n
Kerr, William, the Spencers' doctor, 603
King, Gregory, of the College of Arms, 12
King, Thomas, actor, q.3, 494, 523–4; at the Stratford Jubilee, 428–9; differences with D G, **484–5**, 485n; letters from D G, quoted, 484–5, 490, 567; letters to D G, quoted, 484–5, 567n; roles: (1759–71), 293, 375, 388, 391, 397, 443, 460; (1772–5), 465, 487, 520, 531 and n
King, Mrs (wife of Thomas), actress, 546, 550
King's Theatre, 117, 397, 591n
Kirkman, James Thomas, Macklin's biographer (1799), q.80, 138n, q.176

Knight, Joseph, 52 and n; his 19th-C. biography of Garrick, quoted, 73, 84n, 149–50, 164, 219, 297, 401n

La Bruyère, Jean de, writer, q.500
La Chaussée, Pierre Claude de, playwright, *La Gouvernante*, 337 and n
La Condé, Louis, Garrick's uncle, 41, 104
Lacy, James, Drury Lane manager, 92–3, 134, 416; in management (selected references): (1743–7), 94–5, 97–8, 105–9, 113, 123, 137; (1755–64), 242, 357 and n; DG purchases half-interest, 132–3; problems between DG and Lacy, 108, 168, 202 and n, 372–3, 403; DG's letter to him (1750), q.172–3; and the Stratford Jubilee, 417, 426; his death (1774), 509, 592
Lacy, Willoughby, James's son, 509–10; as an actor, 520, 563n, 567, 572–3, 592 and n; DG's letter to him, q.567
La Fontaine, Jean de, poet, 166n
Lamash, Philip, actor, 557, 603
Lamb, Charles, essayist, 376
Langford, Abraham, and the Drury Lane patent, 572–3, 592 and n
Langton, Bennet, Johnson's friend, 18n, 283 and n, 364, 467, 495n
Latimore, architect, 415
Lauder, William, scholar and fraud, 170n
Lawrence, Herbert, surgeon and writer, 386n, 605, 611
le Breton, Noël-Jacques, *Le Souper mal apprêté*, verse-comedy (17th C.), 43
Lee, John, actor, 527
Lee, Nathaniel, playwright
  Massacre at Paris, 107n, 107–8
  Rival Queens, The (1677), 45, 253, 356, 520
  Theodosius, 121 and n
Le Kain (Henri-Louis Cain), actor, 353, 362 and n
Lemoine, sculptor, his bust of DG, 351
Leoni, Michael, singer, 302 and n, 551n
Lesage, Alain René, novelist: *Crispin, rival de son maître*, farce (1707); *Gil Blas* (1715–24), 100, 181
Lessingham, Jane, actress, 402
Leviez, Charles, ballet-master, 190–91

Lewes, Charles Lee, actor and writer, 52 and n, 155, 170n
Lichfield, 9–16, 17–27; cathedral, 10–11, 17
Lichfield, William de, poet and divine, 12
Lillo, George, playwright, *The London Merchant* (1731), 174 and n, 377
Lincoln's Inn Fields Theatre, 33, 61, 73n, 82
Linley, Elizabeth (Mrs R. B. Sheridan), singer, 526–7
Linley, Thomas, composer and (1776) patentee at Drury Lane, 553–4, 611, 613
Liotard, Jean-Etienne, painter, 188–9, 189n
Lloyd, Revd Evan, DG's letters to him, quoted, 437 and n, 441, 465–6
Lloyd, Robert, Colman's and DG's friend, 304; his letter from DG, q.307–8
Lloyd's Evening Post, 420, 426, q.475, q.548n
London Chronicle: (1749–69), q.166 and n, q.332–3, 378n, q.420, 434; (1773–6), 498, q.515–17, q.520, q.537, q.562
London Courant, 128–9
London Evening Post, quoted, 197, 242, 481, 504
London Magazine, quoted, 393, 493
London Morning Post, q.112
London Stage, The, q.54, 104, 168n
Louis XIV, King of France, 6–7
Lovat, Simon Fraser, 12th Lord, his execution (1747), 133 and nn
Love (Dance), James, actor, 322n, 370, 377; his pantomimes: *The Rites of Hecate* (1763), 341 and n; *The Witches* (1762), 322, 463
Love Makes a Man, at Drury Lane (1743), 74
Lowe, Thomas, actor and singer, 75 and n
Lucchini, *Pharnaces*, opera, 370
Lyttelton, George, 1st Lord, politician and writer, 100, 102, 456–8, 460–61, 491
Lyttelton, Thomas, Lord Lyttelton's son, 491 and n, 492

Mack, Maynard, Pope's biographer (1985), q.97

Mackenzie, Henry, Home's biographer (1822), 500n

Macklin, Charles, actor, 1, 63, 72, 85n, 127–8n, 272; as Shylock: (to 1747), 2, 37, 60–61, 84n, 94, 124, 138; (1759), 295; his prologue (1743), q.94; other roles (1743–50), 94, 98–9, 142, 174; leaves the stage (1753), 212; returns as Macbeth (1773), 503–5

the problems at Drury Lane (1743) and his break with Garrick, 73–81; his coffee-house and 'school of oratory', 212–14; in Churchill's *Rosciad*, q.305; at the Stratford Jubilee, 422; criticizes Garrick's Jubilee Ode, 434; other tensions between him and Garrick, 48n, 89, 108, 113, 138n

his biographers: Cooke, 47n; Kirkman, q.80, 138n, 176

his *Love-à-la-Mode* (1759), 295 and nn, 305n; *True-Born Scotsman* (1764?), 295n

'Macklin, Mrs' (Ann Grace), 70–71, 76, 224, 282n, 504

Macklin, Maria, daughter of Charles, 70, 214n, 225, q.491–2

Macpherson, James, his Ossianic poems (1763), 409

Maddox, Anthony, wire-dancer, 192–3, 205, 271

Madrigal and Truletta, 'mock tragedy' (1758), 271

Mallet, David, poet and playwright, 324–5nn, 447 and n
  Alfred, masque (with Thomson, 1740), 181
  Britannia, masque (1755), 228–9
  Elvira (1739), 35
  Mustapha (1739), 35

Mann, Sir Horace, Walpole's correspondent, *see* Walpole, Horace

Mansfield, William Murray, Lord, Chief Justice, 329, 349, 505, 514n, 522, 587

Marguerite, Queen of Navarre, *The Heptameron*, collection of tales, 269

Marivaux, Pierre Carlet de Chamblain de, playwright and novelist, 187, 352; *Les Fausses Confidences* (1737), 443

Marlborough, George, 4th Duke, and the Duchess of, 588

Marmontel, Jean François, author, 336 and n, 351–2; *Bélisaire* (1767), 351

Marsh, C., on Garrick and Shakespeare, q.249

Mason, Revd William, Walpole's correspondent, 502n, 531

Matilda, play (1775), 529

Mendez, Moses: *The Chaplet*, musical entertainment (1749), 169; *The Shepherd's Lottery* (1750), 194

Metastasio, Pietro, poet, *L'Isola Disabitata*, 296

Mickle, William Julius, poet, 471–2; his translation of *The Lusiads*, 472 and n

Middlesex, Lord, director of the *King's Theatre*, 123n

Middlesex Journal and Evening Advertiser, q.521, q.552

Midwife, The (1750), q.169

Miles, William Augustus, *Letter to Sir John Fielding* (1773), 500–501, 501n

Miller, James, his English version of Voltaire's *Mahomet*, 86 and n, 223, 601 and n

Mills, William, actor, 77, 102

Milton, John, poet, 170: on Shakespeare, q.428; *Comus* (1634), 170, 224, 260; *Paradise Lost*, 170 and n

Moissy, playwright, *La Nouvelle Ecole des Femmes* (1758), 296n

Molière (Jean-Bapiste Poquelin), 141n, 143
  Avare, L' (1668), 483
  Dépit Amoureux, Le (1658), 101n
  Ecole des Femmes, L' (1662), 167, 286n
  Ecole des Maris, L' (1661), 187
  Impromptu de Versailles, L' (1663), 518
  Mariage forcé, Le (1664), 483

Monboddo, James Burnett, Lord, Scottish judge, 348n, 617, 618, 619, 623

Monnet, Jean Louis, director of L'Opéra-Comique, 6, 236, 353 and n, q.371, 488, 498, 516n, 539; at Drury Lane, 166–8, 168n

Monsey, Messenger, physician, 18, 185, 274, 486

Montagu, John, 2nd Duke of, 154

Montagu, Mrs Elizabeth, D G's friend,
    334, 350n, 458, 491, 566n, 579, 588,
    619; her letters from D G, quoted,
    350 and n, 452, 491–2, 512, 579
Montagu, George, Walpole's friend,
    153–4, 298, 300, 317, 406, 422n
Montagu, Lady Mary Wortley, 339n
Montgomerie, Margaret, Boswell's cousin
    and his wife, 422
Moody, John, actor, 305 and n, 327–8,
    396, 437, q.480, 544, 603
Moore, Edward, playwright
    Foundling, The (1748), 143, q.155–6
    Gamester, The (1752), 205–6
    Gil Blas (1750), 181
More, Hannah, admirer of D G, 514, 563
    and n, 564–5, 569, 582, 590, 603n; on
    D G, quoted, 513, 536, 561–3, 565,
    569, 590; letter to D G, q.566; letters
    from D G, quoted, 536, 552, 562–3,
    565, 569–70, 584, 594–5, 597, 602;
    D G's death and funeral, q.607n,
    q.608, 611–12, q.617; visits to Mrs
    Garrick, q.615–16, 619; on Berenger,
    q.254n, q.593; her volume of poems
    (1775), 552 and n
    Fatal Falsehood (1779), 602, 619
    Inflexible Captive, The (1773), 514, 536
    Percy (1777), 569–70, 588, 590, 597, 619
    Sacred Dramas (1782), 619
More, Sarah, Hannah's sister, on D G,
    q.533
Morellet, Abbé André, economist, 351
    and n; his letters from D G, q.486,
    490, q.494
Morning Chronicle: (1757–74), 110,
    479–80, 500, 504, 522; (1775–89),
    q.527, 601n, q.620; D G and
    Woodfall, 558–9
Morning Post, q.525, 540, 552, q.557,
    q.570, q.608
Morris, Corbyn, polemicist, 77 and n
Mossop, Henry, actor, 194, 239 and n,
    254, 258, 276n, 293 and n, 308; roles,
    194, 206, 225, 258, 265; his
    bankruptcy, 471; his death (1774),
    525–6
Mozart, Wolfgang Amadeus, q.341, 398n
Mundy, Francis, poet, 10
Mure, Hutchinson, and Drury Lane, 93,
    113

Murphy, Arthur, actor, playwright and
    Garrick's biographer, 215 and n, 217,
    254 and n, 255, 310–11; as an actor,
    242, 254; as a playwright, 296;
    changeable relationships with
    Garrick, 280–83, 296, 400–401, 465,
    489–90; his letters from D G, quoted,
    296, 310, 490; and Burke, 302; and
    Foote, 311, 587n; his weekly paper,
    The Test, 254; in Churchill's
    Rosciad, q.306; on the causes of
    Garrick's death, 607 and n
    The Life of David Garrick, Esq. (1801),
        quoted passim throughout the
        text. Selected quotations: 45–6, 49,
        217, 218, 296, 510–11
    Alzuma (1773), 489
    Apprentice, The (1756), 248, 600
    Citizen, The (1761), 311
    Desert Island, The, dramatic poem, 296
    Grecian Daughter, The (1772), 465, 489
    Hamlet with Alterations, satire (1773),
        490
    Know Your Own Mind (1777), 485 and
        n, 578
    Orphan of China, The, 281–3, 296
    Three Weeks After Marriage (1764),
        599 and n
    Zenobia (1768), 400–401, 410

Nardi, Mlle, dancer, 123n
Nash, Mary, Mrs Cibber's biographer,
    111, 139–40, q.294 and n
Necker, Mme Suzanne, 563 and n, 564;
    her letter to D G, q.566–7, 567n, 574
    and n; her letter from D G, q.574
Neville, Richard, British Minister in Paris,
    336 and n
Neville, Sylas, diarist, quoted, 391, 393,
    397, 403n, 405–6, 407
New Universal Magazine (1753), 193
Newbery, Francis, publisher, 481–2
Newcastle, Thomas Pelham-Holles, 1st
    Duke of, Prime Minister, 251, 257,
    263
Newcastle, Henry Pelham, 2nd Duke of,
    540, 543
Newton, Revd Thomas, his letters to D G,
    q.44–5, q.47–8, 49, q.50, 170
Nollekens, Joseph, sculptor, 5, 343 and n
Norris, Thomas, singer, 321

North, Frederick, 8th Lord, Prime Minister
(1770), 453 and n, 509 and n, 511
Northcote, James, Reynolds's pupil,
449–50nn, q.598
Northumberland, Hugh Percy, 2nd Earl
and 1st Duke of (1766), 224 and n,
540 and n
Nossiter, Maria, actress, 223, 253
*Nouveau Calendrier des Spectacles de
Paris* (1755), q.239
Noverre, Augustin, dancer, 246 and n, 583
Noverre, Jean Georges, dancer and
choreographer, 258, 335, 354n, 388,
510 and n, 611; on DG's Macbeth,
83; *Lettres sur la danse* (1760), 247,
335; *Les Fêtes Chinoises*, ballet, 234,
239; negotiations with Garrick,
237–9; *The Chinese Festival* (at
Drury Lane, 1755), 241–8
Nugent, Christopher, physician, 364

O'Brien, William, actor and playwright,
275, 329, 370, 376, 487n; *Cross
Purposes* and *The Duel* (both 1772),
487
Offley, Lawrence, DG's schoolfellow,
25–6
O'Hara, Kane, *Midas*, burletta, 370
O'Keeffe, John, dramatist, his
Recollections (1826), q.488, 489n
Oldfield, Anne, actress, 95, 224, 529 and n
Orrery, John Boyle, 5th Earl of, writer,
41, 59 and n
Ossory [or Upper Ossory], Countess of,
Walpole's correspondent, 387, 492,
505–6, 507n, 612, 617
Ossory, Earl of, 611
Otway, Thomas, playwright, 4
History and Fall of Caius Marius, The
(1680), 148 and n
Orphan, The (1680), 42–3, 61, 165,
212, 245, 464n
Venice Preserv'd (1682), 49, 63, 226n,
308; productions, 58, 74, 299, 356,
397, 541n
Oulton, Walley Chamberlain, writer, 387n
Oxford Magazine (1775), q.544

Palmer (*née* Pritchard), Hannah Mary,
actress, 147 and n, 258–9, 259n, 387n
Palmer, John (1728–68), actor, 147n,

329n, 376; as proprietor, Royal
Theatre, Bath, 379
Palmer, John (1744–98), actor, 533, 535,
557
Palmerston, Viscount (*fl.*1778), 597 and n,
611
Paradies, Domenico, composer, 322
Paris, theatres
Comédie-Française, 187, 337, 401n,
409; players, 6, 101n, 188 and n,
191n, 359n, 498n; Garrick's
impressions, 337, 371, 384
Comédie-Italienne, 187, 188n, 352
Opéra-Comique, 166, 168n, 236
Théâtre Italien, 296n
Parma, Philip, Duke of, 343–4
Partridge, Eric, lexicographer, 37
Paterson, John, solicitor, DG's friend and
executor, 132 and n, 168, 372–3, 382,
611, 614; his letters from DG,
quoted, 373, 409
Patu, Claude-Pierre, lawyer, 238n
Peele, George, playwright, *The Old
Wives' Tale* (1595), 397
Pelham, Henry, Prime Minister, 210–11;
his death (1754), 219; Garrick's Ode,
q.219
Pembroke, Henry, 10th Earl of, 414, 421,
569, 593n
Pembroke, Elizabeth, Countess of, 430
Penn, Richard, Deputy-Governor of
Pennsylvania, his letter to DG and
DG's reply, q.497–8
Pepys, Samuel, diarist, 67, 148, 249
Percy, Bishop, 365
Philips, Ambrose, playwright, 89n; *The
Distressed Mother*, 62n, 89, 141n,
169n
Pitt, William (later the Earl of Chatham),
100, 102, 462 and n
Players' Scourge (anon, 1757), q.1
Pliny (Gaius Plinius Secundus), the elder,
Roman writer, q.218
Plumb, J. H., historian, q.312–13
Poitier, Jane, dancer, 322–3, 323n
Pope, Alexander, writer, 41, 59n, 63–4,
82n, 169n, 174n, 458; his edition of
Shakespeare, 4
Dunciad, The (1728), 48n, 97, 135n, 304
Essay on Man (1733–4), 348n
New Dunciad, The (1742), 64

Pope, Jane, actress, 391, 442, 471, 515, 542–3, 591, 614

Porter, Molly, actress, 50 and n

Portland, Duchess of, her letter from D G, q.400

Pott, Percival, surgeon, 553 and n, 605, 607–8n

Powell, William, actor, 356–7, 370, 379, 388, 390; roles, 365, 376, 393, 397, 402; his death (1769), 436 and n

Préville, Pierre-Louis, actor, 337, 353–4, 354nn

Pritchard, Mrs Hannah, actress, 84, 126, 145, 147n, 225, 283; roles: (1743–9), 97, 129, 131, 146, 151–2 and nn, 165; (1750–52), 169, 174, 178, 181, 193, 209, 557; (1753–8), 216, 218 and n, 244, 249, 258–9, 262, 266; (1759–68), 283, 286, 299, 317, 388, 402; her death (1768), 402 and n

Pritchard, Hannah Mary, see Palmer, Hannah Mary

Pritchard, William, treasurer at Drury Lane, 137n, 227, 379

Public Advertiser: D G's 'puffs', 207, 241, 321, 327; other subjects: (1757–66), 261, 269–70, 328, 372, 387; (1769–76), 419–20, 427, 430–31, 510–11, 522, 557, 573; on Garrick's autopsy (1779), 607–8n

Public Ledger, 434n, q.476, q.481, q.574

Purcell, Henry, composer: Dido and Aeneas (1689), 48; King Arthur (1691), 447

Purdon, Edward, A Letter to David Garrick . . . (1759), q.290

Pye, Mrs, and her play, The Capricious Lady (1771), 578n

Quin, James, actor, 1–2, 62–4, 63nn, 126, 181n, 298, q.411; versus Macklin, 37, 96; in Ireland, 58 and n; as Macbeth, 85; as Othello, 99; abroad, 109 and n; in retirement, 139–40, 172; in Churchill's Rosciad, q.306; letter from D G, q.330; visits the Garricks, 362–3; his death (1766), 369
    roles: (1719), 95; (1742–9), 61, 98, 124–5, 128, 130n, 133, 145 and n, 164

Racine, Jean, dramatist and poet, 350; Andromaque (1667), 89; Phèdre (1677), 188n

Rackett, Thomas (senior), D G's friend, 551n, 605

Rackett, Thomas, (junior), 551n, 551–2, 588

Raftor, James, actor, 145–6

Ramus, Nicholas, courtier, 366, 462

'Rancourt' (Françoise Marie Antoinette Saucerotte), actress, 498 and n

Ravenscroft, Edward, playwright: The Anatomist (1697), 305n; The Cuckolds (1681), 165–6, 166n

Reddish, Samuel, actor, 440, 465, 494 and n, 504–5, 513 and n, 529

Reed, Joseph, rope-maker and aspiring playwright: Dido (1767), 389; The Register Office (1761), 389n

Reinhold, Thomas, singer, 106

Renaudin, François, physician, 346–7

Reynolds, Ann, actress, 385 and n

Reynolds, Frederick, dramatist, The Life and Times of . . . (1826), 581 and n

Reynolds, Sir Joshua, painter, q.53, 507 and n, 532n, 579, 598; D G as a sitter, 127n; note from D G, q.298n; and the Turk's Head club, 364–5; at Garrick's funeral, 611
    his paintings: 'Garrick Between Tragedy and Comedy', 6, 318, 351 and n, 448; 'Mrs Abington as the Comic Muse', 532n; 'Mrs Siddons as the Tragic Muse', 532n

Riccoboni, Luigi, theatre director and historian, 352 and n

Riccoboni, Marie-Jeanne, actress, 352–3, 353n; her letters from D G, quoted, 399–400, 405; Lettres de mistress Fanny Butler (1757), 352

Rich, Christopher, lawyer and theatre manager, 53, 73n

Rich, John, actor and manager at Covent Garden, 54, 165n, 197, 293; in management (selected references), 51, 53, 55, 131–2, 140, 174–5, 313–14; Foote's diatribe, 300–301; his death (1761), 314

Rich, Mrs, John's widow, 380

Richard II, King, 10

Richardson, Samuel, novelist, 268n;

Clarissa (1748), 148 and n; *Pamela* (1749), stage adaptation, 42, 370

Richmond, Charles, 2nd Duke of, 154–5, 312

Richmond, Charles, 3rd Duke of, 474

Rigby, Richard, D G's friend, 88, 161n, 362n, 404; on D G, q.99; his letter to D G, q.555; letter from D G, q.556; the Garricks' visits to him, 89–90, 362, 380, 404, 498, 540, 578, 595; at Garrick's funeral, 611; his executor, 614

Robertson, Revd William, *History of Scotland . . .* (1759), 254 and n

Robins, Miss, actress, 521

Robinson, Mary, actress, 580–81, 581n, 601n

Rochford, Earl of, 90 and n, 234, 297n, 446, 492, 594n; letters to D G, q.108, q.593; letter from D G, q.593

Rockingham, Thomas, 1st Marquess of, 171 and n

Rockingham, Charles, 2nd Marquess of, 210, 362

Rogers, Samuel, poet, 296

Rolt, Richard, *Almena* and *The Royal Shepherd*, operas, 370

Romney, George, painter, 450 and n

Ross, David, actor, 193 and n, 370

'Rossignol, Signor', bird imitator, 524–5

Roubiliac, Louis François, sculptor, his statue of Shakespeare, 234 and n, 413–14, 436

Rousseau, Jean-Jacques, philosopher and writer, 189, *368*, 369, 381; *Confessions* (1782–9), 350n; *La Nouvelle Héloïse* (1761), 349

Rowe, Nicholas, playwright, 65n
Fair Penitent, The (1703), q.605; productions: (to 1746), 44, 51, 67n, 82, 102, 125; (1753–69), 212, 299, 329, 397 and n, 440
Jane Shore (1714), productions: (1743–55), 67 and n, 74, 144, 218n, 241; (1758–73), 283, 393, 406n, 505
Lady Jane Grey (1715), 108
Tamerlane (1702), 265 and n, 551

Rutherford, John, Covent Garden patentee, 390, 402–3

Ryan, Lacy, actor, 45, 123n, 123–4, 131, 136, 196 and n, 209

St Foix, *The Oracle*, pastoral allegory, 198n

St James's Chronicle (1761), 303, 331, 354n; quoted: (1761–4), 304, 332, 342, 358; (1767–73), 389, 415, 436, 475, 492, 503n

Salomon (Giuseppe Salomoni), dancer, 123 and n, 128

Sandwich, John Montagu, 4th Earl of, 495, 500, 501n

Sarrazin, Jeanne, Garrick's grandmother, 7 and n, 8

Sauvé, Jean-Baptiste, actor and dramatist, 191n

Scarron, Paul, French novelist, 166n

Schaw, Captain Frederick, Arabella Garrick's husband, 540, 594n, 611

Schiller, Johann Christian Friedrich von, dramatist and poet, 434n

Schomberg, Captain Alexander, R N, D G's petition for, 378–9, 379n

Schomberg, Isaac, D G's doctor, 378, 410, 605

School for Fathers, The (performed in 1770), 460n

Scott, [Sir] Walter, on Alexander Carlyle, q.117n

Scott, Sir William, of the Turk's Head club, 617n

'Scratching Fanny', 316–18

Secker, Thomas, Archbishop of Canterbury, 300 and n

Seddon, John, *Titles of Honor* (1614), 459

Selwyn, Charles, lawyer, 237, 287

Senesino (Francesco Bernardi), castrato, 340n

Servandoni, Giovanni Niccolò, stage designer, 153

Shadwell, Charles, playwright, *The Fair Quaker of Deal*, 52, 501–2, 502n

Shakespeare, William, his plays produced
Antony and Cleopatra, 284–5
As You Like It, 56, 61, 440, 541, 546
Coriolanus, 192
·*Cymbeline*, 121, 146n, 314–15, 356, 464n
Hamlet: (1741–54), 44, 61, 82, 124, 146, 212, 224; (1758–69), 275–6, 299–300, 357, 397, 402, 441; (1771–7), 463, **486–7**, 535, 541n, 582
Henry IV Part 1, 128, 370, 587
Henry IV Part 2, 314n, 370, 582

Shakespeare, William – *cont.*
  Henry V, 86, 265n, 313
  Henry VIII, 258, 313
  King John, 97–9, 299–300, 314n, 397
  King Lear: (1742–58), 47–9, 61, 82,
      145, 253–4, 276; (1768–76), 397,
      496, 513, 535, 561
  Macbeth: (1744–60), 82–5, 196, 224,
      258, 299, 335; (1768–75), 402,
      503–4, 535
  Measure for Measure, 531
  Merchant of Venice, The: (1740–47),
      37, 61, 85, 94, 124, 138; (1752–77),
      166, 174 and n, 504, 552, 582
  Merry Wives of Windsor, The, 582
  Midsummer Night's Dream, A, 397
  Much Ado About Nothing: (1748–68),
      146–7, 164, 244, 259n, 366, 397;
      (1771–9), 455, 535, 550 and n, 561,
      603
  Othello, 61, 94, **99–100**, 124, 146, 182,
      357
  Richard II, 35
  Richard III: (1741–6), 4, **38–41**, 51, 61,
      82, 123n, 124; (1749–59), 164, 194,
      224, 258, 265, 276, 287; (1760–73),
      297–9, 314n, 357, 402, 442, 469,
      504; (1775–7), 535, 562–3, 582
  Romeo and Juliet: (1748–56), **148–50**,
      175–8, 212, 224, 258; (1757–68),
      265, 275 and n, 397
  Taming of the Shrew, The, 218–19
  Tempest, The, 541, 580
  Timon of Athens, 463
  Troilus and Cressida, 263
  Twelfth Night, 165, 526, 572n
  Two Gentlemen of Verona, The, 148n,
      326
  Winter's Tale, The, 146n, **248–9**
Sharp, Samuel, surgeon, 132 and n
Sharp, Thomas, Stratford wood-carver,
    413n, 416n
Shaw, George Bernard, 432; *Plays for
    Puritans* (1901), 432n
Sheridan, Frances, playwright: *The
    Discovery* (1763), 127n, 330 and n;
    The Dupe (1763), 241 and n, 370
Sheridan, Richard Brinsley, playwright
    and manager, 3–4, 45n, 73, q.562; as
    patentee of Drury Lane, 553 and n,
    592; as manager, 560, 570, 572–3,
        580, 587, 591–2, 601 and n; misuses
        theatre funds, 614; letters from DG,
        quoted, 581, 589, 601
    arranges Garrick's funeral, 609,
        611–12; funeral expenses unpaid,
        610, 614; his monody on Garrick,
        613–14, 614n
    Duenna, The, comic opera (1775), 551
        and n, 552n, 556–7
    Rivals, The (1775), 37, 288n, 484n,
        526–7, 530n
    St Patrick's Day (1775), 484n
    School for Scandal, The (1777), 560n,
        580–81, 581n, 590–91
Sheridan, Thomas, actor-manager, 57,
    89n, 115n, 300n, 526, 611n; at Smock
    Alley: as an actor, 74 and n; in joint
    management with Garrick, 112, 114;
    as sole manager, 139n, 141, 194,
    196n, 222–3, 223n; at Drury Lane,
    105, 298–300; acting at Covent
    Garden, 223–4, 300; and Boswell,
    300n, 324 and n; his criticism of
    DG's Jubilee Ode, 434n; assists his
    son at Drury Lane, 601 and nn; his
    anecdotes of others, recorded by
    Windham, 59–60, 60n, 71
Sherry, Katherine, 562 and n
Shipley, Dr, Bishop of St Asaph, 616, 617n
Shirley, James, playwright, *The
    Gamesters* (1633), 268–9
Shirley, William, playwright, 169n;
    Edward, the Black Prince (1749), 169;
    The Parricide (1739?), 169
Shuter, Edward, actor and singer, 53n,
    173, 209, 301n, 402; roles, 322, 380n,
    393n, 527, 551
Sichel, Walter, biographer, *Sheridan*
    (1909), 573n
Siddons (*née* Kemble), Mrs Sarah, actress,
    67n, 268n, **540–42**, 542n, 546, 551,
    621; roles, 552, 557, 559, 562, 619;
    her *Reminiscences*, quoted, 559, 577
Siddons, William, actor, 541, 546, 551
Sloper, William, and Mrs Cibber, 58,
    109n, 111, 121, 172, 271, 332
Smart, Christopher, poet, 285 and n
Smith, Edmund, poet, 19–20n
Smith, 'Gentleman', actor, 402, 493, 497
    and n, 504, 505n, 521n
Smith, John Christopher, composer, of

operas by Garrick: *The Enchanter*
(1760), 302; *The Fairies* (1755), 226;
The Tempest (1756), 249
Smith, John Thomas, of the British
Museum, 621–3
Smith, Revd Joseph, rector of Stanmore,
216
Smollet, Tobias: editor, *Critical Review*
(1756), q.252, 304; his *History of
England* (1757), q.261
as novelist: *Peregrine Pickle* (1751), 42n,
63, 260n; *Roderick Random*
(1748), 53n, **147**
as playwright, *The Regicide* (1740), 121
and n, 147, 260; *The Reprisal*
(1757), 260
Southerne, Thomas, playwright, 45n;
Fatal Marriage, The (1694), 268;
Oroonoko (1695), 38, 194, 241,
294–5, 356
Sowdon, John, actor and manager, 223n,
239n
Sparks, Luke, actor, 145, 275–6, 504
Spencer, John, 1st Lord (1st Earl, 1765),
346n, 540, 605; and the Garricks,
340, 343, 421, 499, 568 and n, 572–3,
590; pall-bearer at Garrick's funeral,
611; elected to the Turk's Head club,
617n
Spencer, Margaret Georgiana, Lady
(Countess, 1765), 340, 566n, 570, 573
and nn, 605, 611; Sheridan's monody
dedicated to her, 613–14, 614n;
letters from DG, quoted: (1776–7),
574–5, 577–9, 583, 585, 588;
(1778–9), 597, 602–3, 604; letters to
DG, quoted, 454, 577, 601; letter
from Mrs Garrick, q.602
Stage Licensing Act (1737), 32–5, 38, 61
Stanley, Lord Edward (later 12th Earl of
Derby), 522 and nn
Stanley, Edward, of the Customs, 538
Stanley, Hans, DG's friend, 598, 611
Steele, Richard, playwright, 45n; *The
Conscious Lovers* (1722), 58, 74, 91,
193, 204
Steevens, George, Shakespeare
commentator, 199 and n, 285n,
419–20, 493n; letters to DG, quoted,
508, 524; letters from DG, quoted,
511, 527

Stephen, Sir Leslie, writer, 288n
Stephens, Mrs, actress, 405n
Sterne, Laurence, novelist, 6, 157, 335 and
n, 351n; *Tristram Shandy* (1760–67),
q.310
Stockdale, Percival, 500 and n; *Memoirs
. . .* (1809), 280n
Stone, George Winchester, writer, q.219,
344, 487n
Stone, George Winchester and George M.
Kahrl, Garrick's biographers (1979),
165 and n
Stonhouse, Revd Dr James, and Hannah
More, 514 and n
Stratford Jubilee, the (1769), 4, 412–32
Sturm und Drang, and the Stratford
Jubilee, 634n
Sturz, Helfrich Peter, of the Danish king's
suite, 344–5, 345n, 406–8, 408n
Suard, Jean-Baptiste-Antoine, journalist,
349n, 352, 354, 433, 494, 563; DG's
letters to him, quoted, 349, 361n,
362, 369, 381, 445–6, 523
Sullivan, Francis, Tom Sheridan's friend,
89 and n
Swift, Jonathan, poet and satirist, 6, 58
and n, 63, 130n; *Gulliver's Travels*
(1726), 259
Swiney, Owen Mac, former theatre
manager, 87 and n, 145–6, 222
Swinfen, John, on DG's stage début,
q.39–40

Talma, François-Joseph, actor, 359–60
and n
Tasso, Torquato, author, *Jerusalem
Delivered* (1581), 447
Taswell, James, actor, 4, 282n
Tate, Nahum, poet and dramatist, 48n;
his version of *King Lear*, 48–9,
49n
Taylor, Revd Dr, Johnson's friend, 151
Taylor, John, actor, 562
Taylor, Thomas, carpenter and
auctioneer, 416n
Temple, Richard Grenville, 1st Earl,
DG's friend, 498
Tetley, Elizabeth, actress, 382
theatre audiences, 141, 205, 227, 240, 242,
320–21, 326–7, 407
theatre legislation, 32–5

theatre lighting, 18th-C., 3, 140, 142, 143n, 371–2

theatre riots, 166–7, 243–6, 326–9, 443

theatre pay, back-stage, 75

theatre rivalries, Covent Garden and Drury Lane, 175–81, 184, 205, 260, 314

Theatrical Biography (1772 ed.), q.288

Theatrical Examiner, q.259

Theatrical Fund, initiated by Garrick, 379–80, 444, 512–13, 536, 564, 578–9, 615; Bill and Royal Assent, 556

Theatrical Monitor, The (1766), 385

Theatrical Observer (1768), q.397 and n

Theatrical Review, quoted, 258, 322–3, 460, 463, 464–5nn

'Theatrical Steelyards of 1750, The', cartoon, 179, *180*

Thomas, Dr John, Dean of Westminster, conducts Garrick's funeral service, 611 and n, 612

Thompson, Captain Edward, RN, 454 and n, 500n, 572–3; his letters from DG, 460, q.478n
    Fair Quaker, The, his alteration of Shadwell's play (1773), 502 and n
    Hobby-Horse, The (c.1776), 572
    Syrens, The, masque (1776), 572

Thomson, James, playwright:
    Agamemnon (1738), 35; *Tancred and Sigismunda* (1745), 100, 440, 442

Thomson, James and David Mallett, *Alfred*, a masque (1740), 181 (music by Arne, q.v.)

Thornton, Bonnell, and *St James's Chronicle*, 303 and n, 304

Thrale, Henry, 363n, 441, 495n, 575n

Thrale, Mrs Hester, writer and Johnson's friend, 5, 152n, 363, 441; she reports Johnson's comments on Garrick, 364n, 365, 576, 603–4, 607; Garrick's letter to her, 575 and n

Tighe, Edward, MP, his letter from DG, q.560 and n

Tomkis, Thomas, playwright, *Albumazar* (1615), 142–3, 501, 503

Torré, Morel, pyrotechnist, 516 and n

Town and Country Magazine, 409, q.544, 614

Townley, Revd James, 345–6; as

playwright, *High Life Below Stairs* (1759), 293, 345

Townshend, Charles, 3rd Viscount, 367n; his wife, 367 and n

Townshend, Charles (1725–67), statesman, 362, 378

Tuner, The (critical journal, 1754–5), 216, 227

Turk's Head, Gerrard Street, the club at the, 364–5, 365n, 490, 506, 609, 611, 617 and n

Turton, Dr John, DG's friend, 346, 467

Tyrawley, James O'Hara, 2nd Lord, 59–60, 89, 208, 262

Universal Museum, The (1765), q.377

Vaillant, Paul, bookseller, 282

Vanbrugh, [Sir] John, architect and playwright, 182, 335
    A Journey to London (completed by Colley Cibber as *The Provok'd Husband*, 1728), 87, 124, 356, 529n
    Provok'd Wife, The (1697), 95–6, 96n, 164n, 376, 549; productions: (1742–58), 56, 92, 95–7, 244; (1765–75), 367, 387, 397, 405, 463, 548
    Relapse, The (1696), 58, 74, 124

Van der Gucht, Benjamin, painter, his letter from DG, q.583

Van Loo, Carle, painter, 88n, 488

Van Loo, Jean-Baptiste, painter, 88 and n

Vaughan, Henry, actor, 139

Veigel, Eva Maria (Violette, dancer), *see* Garrick, Mrs Eva Maria

Veigel, Ferdinand Charles, dancer, 117

Veigel, Johan, Violette's (Mrs Garrick's) father, 155

Vernon, Joseph, actor, 530, 603

Vertue, George, engraver, 155 and n

Vesey, Mrs Elizabeth, literary hostess, 458 and n, 566n, 619

Victor, Benjamin, critic, quoted, 91, 99 and n, 302; as theatre manager, Dublin, 223 and n, 239n, 271, 272 and n; as treasurer at Drury Lane, 326 and n, 367, 428–9, 592

Violette (Eva Maria Veigel), *see* Garrick, Mrs Eva Maria

Voltaire, François Marie Arouet de, 6,

235–6, 286, 349, 351; DG buys his complete works, 189; DG on his comment on Shakespeare, 338 and n; his letter (1764) from DG, q.347; DG sends his Jubilee Ode to him, 433

Ecossaise, L' (unperformed), 389n

Essai sur les moeurs . . . (1753–8), 338n

Fanatisme, Le, ou Mahomet le Prophète (1741), 86, 359n, 377

Mérope (1743), 188

Orphelin de Chine, L' (*The Orphan of China*, 1755), 281

Wales, Frederick, Prince of, 63, 89, 118, 119n, 146n, 155n; and the masque, *Alfred*, 181; and Handel's *Judas Maccabeus*, 116; admires Violette, 117; at the theatre, 66, 85, 125, 129, 133, 145, 182; his death (1751) and funeral, 182–3

Wales, George, Prince of (b.1738), 183, 273; at the theatre, 250, 252n, 259, 266, 286, 297; from 1760, King George III, q.v.

Wales, George, Prince of (b.1762), 581 and n, 590; from 1820, King George IV, q.v.

Waller, Edmund, poet, 45n, 226

Wallis, Albany, Garrick's executor, 611, 614, 620

Wallis and Parkes, Garrick's solicitors, 479

Walmesley, Gilbert, of Lichfield, 19–20 and n, 21–2, 25–7, 27n, q.128

Walpole, Edward, Horace's brother, 234n

Walpole, Horace (later 4th Earl of Orford). There are numerous references in the text, the majority being quotations (usually brief) from his letters to Mann, Montagu and others. Those here selected include (*) Walpole's comments relating to Garrick: (1746–51), 51*, 128, 143–4, 153–5*, 157*, 182, 184; (1755–69), 226*, 233–4*, 298, 355–6*, 384, 386–7, 422 and n; (1771–6), 447, 492, 502n*, 505–6, 507n*, 531, 562*; (1777–9), 576*, 580, 582–3*, 612*

Walpole, Horatio or Horace, brother of Robert, 23 and n, 30n

Walpole, Sir Robert, statesman, 22n, 23 and n, 30nn, 30–33, 35, 37, 43, 135n

Warburton, William, scholar and theologian, 82 and n, q.269; as Bishop of Gloucester, q.433

Ward, John, actor, 421

Ward, Sarah, actress, 165, 402

Warren, Dr Richard, royal physician, 605

Warton, Joseph, 433, 436n, 598 and n

Washington, George, 376, 537

Weller, Mary, actress, 484

West, Gilbert, poet, *The Institution of the Order of the Garter* (1742), 459

Westminster Magazine, and the George Garrick–Baddeley duel, 442; its reviews quoted: (1772–4), 483, 486–8, 493n, 507, 520–21, 524; (1775–6), 525n, 526, 531, 546, 557

Weston, Tom, actor, 525 and n, 550–51

Whalley, Revd Peter, his letter to DG, 144

Wheler, Francis, of Stratford, 414, 418n, 424; his letter to DG, q.412–13

Whitefield, George, a founder of Methodism, 300, 417

Whitefoord, Caleb, DG's friend, 584

Whitehead, Paul, satirist and poet, 93

Whitehead, William, poet and playwright, 169n, 282, 319n
    Creusa (1754), 316
    Roman Father, The (1750), 169, 316
    School for Lovers, The (1762), 316–17

Wieland, Christoph Martin, poet, 434n

Wilkes, John, politician, 318, 348–9, 387, 434, 437n, 443 and n, 456–7, 505; and Churchill, 318–19, 348; as Sheriff of London, 508; *Essay on Women* (1763), 348 and n; *North Briton*, his weekly, 12, 318–19, 348, 434

Wilkes, Thomas, *A General View of the Stage* (1759), q.68

Wilkinson, Tate, theatre manager, his *Memoirs*: on Foote, 136, 300; on Garrick, 123n, 246n, 301; on Peg Woffington, 71, 262; on others, 46n, 53n, 176, 385n; as an aspiring actor, 262–3; causes trouble, 275–8; *The Wandering Patentee* (1795), q.546

Wilks, Robert, actor, 63 and n, 224, 614

Willes, Sir John, of the judiciary, 12

William III, King, 73n

Williams, Sir Charles Hanbury, 88, 88–9n, 228 and n

Williams, Revd David, 471, 525–6; *A Letter to David Garrick . . .* (1772), 471

Wilson, Benjamin, painter, 285, 318–19, 351, 413, 414, 418, 436

Windham, William, DG's friend, 79, 83n, 120–21, 121n, 336n, 617n; records Tom Sheridan anecdotes, 59–60, 71, 103; with DG, 90, 109; his letter from DG, q.115; his letter to Peter Garrick, q.143

Woffington, Hannah, Peg's mother, 60 and n

Woffington, Peg, actress, 53, 53n, 62n, 136, 184; and Garrick: in love, 51; in Dublin with him, 56, 58–9; living together in London, 70–71; other admirers, 87–9, final rift, 103–4, 105; roles: (1732–42), 52–6, 59, 61; (1743–4), 66, 74, 87, 91, 101; (1746–57), 124n, 142, 144, 164, 253, 261; becomes a Protestant (1753), 222; illness and retirement, 262; her death (1766), 296

Woffington, Polly, Peg's sister, 89, 101–2

Wonder, The (Centlivre, 1714), 387, 536, 564

Woodfall, Henry Simpson, printer and journalist, 462n, 462–3, 522–3, 523n

Woodfall, William, Henry's brother, 522–3, 558; his letter to DG, q.559; DG's letters to him, quoted, 463, 522–3, 575–6

Woodward, Henry, actor, 123 and n, 139n, 266, 272, 280 and n, 402, 600; his death (1777), 600n; roles: (1746–50), 124, 129–31, 148, 165, 174–5; (1751–2), 179, 181, 193, 195, 197, 205, 209; (1754–8), 192, 226, 244, 249 and n, 254, 258nn, 269;

(1766–73), 380n, 404, 493; his pantomime, *Queen Mab* (1750), 179, *180*, 181

Worsdale, Richard, playwright, *A Cure for a Scold* (1735), 218

Wren, Sir Christopher, architect, 64n, 140

Wrighten, Mary Ann, actress, 460 and n

Wycherley, William, playwright, *The Country Wife* (1675), 102, 267, 335, 385

Wyndham, Charles, actor, 150

Wynn, Sir Watkin Williams, Bt., 585 and n, 586, 611

Yates, Mary Ann, actress, 391 and n, 402, 497, 511–12, 515, 547; roles: (1754–68), 218, 282–3, 285, 296, 387n, 402, 406n; (1770–75), 446, 448, 520, 530–31, 551 and n; her letters from DG, q.511–12, q.551; speaks Sheridan's monody, 613

Yates, Richard, actor, 74, 218, 391, 497, 512; roles, 142, 174n, 249, 531, 557; his letter from DG, q.547

York, HRH Augustus Edward, Duke of, 276, 286, 317, 343–4, 377–8, 378n, 396–7

Yorke, Charles, DG's friend, 456

Young, Edward, poet and playwright, 217 *Brothers, The* (1720s), **206–9** *Busiris, King of Egypt* (1719), 206 *Night Thoughts*, poem (1742–5), 202–3 *Revenge, The* (1721), 194, 198, 206, 258

Young, [Sir] William, [Bt.], DG's friend, 220n, 272 and n, 486n

Younge, Elizabeth, actress, 515, 525, 546, 599n; roles, 526, 550

Zoffany, John (Johann), portrait painter, 84 and n, 127n, 318 and n, 322, 330n, 351

Zucchi, Antonio, painter, 476 and n